The World
of Psychology

Sixth Edition

The World *of* Psychology

Samuel E. Wood

Ellen Green Wood

Denise Boyd
Houston Community College System

PEARSON

Boston   New York   San Francisco
Mexico City   Montreal   Toronto   London   Madrid   Munich   Paris
Hong Kong   Singapore   Tokyo   Cape Town   Sydney

Editor-in-Chief: *Susan Hartman*

Senior Development Editors: *Sharon Geary; Julie Swasey*

Series Editorial Assistant: *Courtney Mullen*

Associate Editor: *Liz DiMenno*

Executive Marketing Manager, Psychology: *Karen Natale*

Production Editor: *Claudine Bellanton*

Editorial Production Service: *Nesbitt Graphics*

Composition Buyer: *Linda Cox*

Manufacturing Buyer: *JoAnne Sweeney*

Electronic Composition: *Nesbitt Graphics*

Interior Design: *Ellen Pettengell*

Photo Researcher: *Sarah Evertson*

Cover Administrator: *Linda Knowles*

For related titles and support materials, visit our online catalog at www.ablongman.com.

Between the time website information is gathered and then published, it is not unusual for some sites to have closed. Also, the transcription of URLs can result in typographical errors. The publisher would appreciate notification where these errors occur so that they may be corrected in subsequent editions.

Library of Congress Cataloging-in-Publication Data
Wood, Samuel E.
  The world of psychology / Samuel E. Wood, Ellen Green Wood, Denise Boyd.
— 6th ed.
    p. cm.
  Includes bibliographical references and index.
    ISBN 0-205-49941-4
    1. Psychology—Textbooks. I. Wood, Ellen R. Green. II. Boyd, Denise
Roberts. III. Title.
  BF121.W657 2007
  150—dc22   2006101656

0-205-49941-4 (casebound) — 0-205-53254-3 (paperback)

Printed in the United States of America

10 9 8 7 6 5 4 3 2 1   Q-WC-V   11 10 09 08 07

Photo and figure credits begin on page C-1 which constitutes a continuation of the copyright page.

Sam and Evie dedicate this book with love to their grandchildren:

Brittany, Danielle, Ashley, Hayley, Jesse, and Sarah.

Denise dedicates this book to the hundreds of introductory

psychology students she has taught over the past 17 years.

Their questions, comments, and concerns were the driving force

behind her contributions to The World of Psychology.

Brief Contents

Contents

Chapter 9   Adolescence and Adulthood   312

Chapter 10   Motivation and Emotion   348

Chapter 16 Social Psychology   552

Chapter 17 Psychology in the Workplace   584

Figures

The following is a complete list of numbered figures appearing in the Sixth Edition.

Using **mypsychlab** to Improve Your Grade

MyPsychLab is proven to help you improve your grades in this class! It is also fun and easy to use. The 7 easy steps below walk you through all of the features of MyPsychLab. To see data and satisfaction survey results from fellow psychology students, visit **www.mypsychlab.com.**

1. Login To register and login, go to **www.mypsychlab.com** and follow the on-screen instructions.

2. Choose Your Book The first time you log in to MyPsychLab, you will be asked to choose your book*. Please choose Wood/Wood/Boyd's *The World of Psychology*, 6th Edition.

***Note:** If your instructor has elected to use MyPsychLab CourseCompass version, you will be given a Course ID and you will not have to select your book.

3. Pre-Test and Study Plan MyPsychLab gives you multiple opportunities to test your knowledge within each chapter. Combined with your customized study plan, this helps you focus your efforts in the areas where you need the most review.

4. Using Your E-Book and the Multimedia Assets An E-Book matches the exact layout of the printed textbook. The E-Book contains multimedia icons in the margins that launch videos (with questions to help guide viewing), activities, simulations, and profiles of prominent psychologists.

5. Multimedia Library Each MyPsychLab course has a Multimedia Library, which lists all the media elements that appear within the E-Book. Searchable by chapter, topic, asset type, or a combination of the three, this Multimedia Library provides an easy, alternative way for you to find assets. The asset can be viewed by clicking directly on the title.

6. Research Navigator Pearson's **Research Navigator**™ is the easiest way for you to start a research assignment or research paper. Research Navigator offers extensive help on the research process and includes four exclusive databases of credible and reliable source material: EBSCO Academic Journal and Abstract Database, *New York Times* Search by Subject Archive, "Best of the Web" Link Library, and *Financial Times* Article Archive and Company Financials.

7. Post-Test After reading the chapter, you should take the Post-Test. Your test results will be reflected in the customized study plan, allowing you to compare your performance before reading the chapter versus after reading the chapter.

Preface

To the Student: How This Textbook Can Help You Study

As today's college students, you and your peers are vastly different from the students who filled classrooms just a few years ago. Indeed, you are now more diverse, more mobile, and more technologically astute than ever before. Many of you are balancing the demands of college with family, career, and other obligations outside of the classroom. This edition of *The World of Psychology* continues to evolve to meet the changing needs of all students. Extensive updates and new additions to content, research, pedagogy, and design combine with the accessible and engaging presentation for which the text is well known to make the study of psychology an enjoyable and meaningful experience for you.

The World of Psychology has a dedicated focus on learning and application. Like previous editions, the Sixth Edition provides superior pedagogical support while making the connection between the scientific principles of psychology and the everyday lives of today's diverse student audience. *The World of Psychology* introduces the field of psychology in an appealing way whether you are an accomplished student or a student developing your skills.

Our Commitment to Learning: SQ3R

The text's commitment to learning begins with the learning method called SQ3R. Made up of five steps—**Survey, Question, Read, Recite,** and **Review**—this method serves as the foundation for your success. Introduced in Chapter 1, the SQ3R method is integrated throughout the text to help you make the connection between psychology and life, while promoting a more efficient way to approach reading, studying, and test taking.

Among the key learning features that promote use of the SQ3R method are the following:

READ: As you read each chapter section, try to answer the learning objective questions and your own questions that come to mind. If you find particular areas of the section very long or complex, try breaking the section into smaller sections of reading.

1.4 What roles did Wundt and Titchener play in the founding of psychology?

Structuralism

Who were the "founders" of psychology? Historians acknowledge that three German scientists—Ernst Weber, Gustav Fechner, and Hermann von Helmholtz—were the first to systematically study behavior and mental processes. But it is Wilhelm Wundt (1832–1920) who is generally thought of as the "father" of psychology. Wundt's vision for the new discipline included studies of social and cultural influences on human thought (Benjafield, 1996).

Wundt established a psychological laboratory at the University of Leipzig, Germany in 1879, an event considered to mark the birth of psychology as a formal academic discipline. Using a method called *introspection*, Wundt and his associates studied the perception of a variety of visual, tactile, and auditory stimuli, including the rhythm patterns produced by metronomes set at different speeds. Introspection

Learning Objectives

New to this edition, every chapter is structured around specific learning objectives. We have added numbered learning objective questions in the margin of each section to help focus your attention on key information. These learning objectives also appear in the chapter outline and in the Summary and Review section. In addition, a complete list of all of the learning objectives appears as a foldout poster at the front of the text. It is designed to be torn out and used as a study aid. Some examples of the learning objectives are:

- 1.21 What kinds of factors introduce bias into experimental studies? (Chapter 1, "Introduction to Psychology")
- 2.9 What is the difference between the sympathetic and parasympathetic systems? (Chapter 2, "Biology and Behavior")

- 5.20 What has research shown regarding the influence of media violence on aggressive feelings and behavior? (Chapter 5, "Learning")
- 8.18 How do learning theory and the nativist position explain the acquisition of language? (Chapter 8, "Child Development")
- 10.20 How do facial expressions influence internal emotional states? (Chapter 10, "Motivation and Emotion")

Chapter-Opening Vignettes These stories, based on real-life events and people, offer an accessible and interesting introduction to the chapter material. Topics include the following:

- The cult of two: the "Beltway Snipers" John Allen Muhammad and Lee Boyd Malvo (Chapter 4, "States of Consciousness")
- Theories on why video games are more engaging than textbooks (Chapter 5, "Learning")
- Findings from the New England Centenarian Study (Chapter 9, "Adolescence and Adulthood")
- Using Maslow's Hierarchy of Needs to explain the motivations of Superman (Chapter 10, "Motivation and Emotion")
- A young woman with schizophrenia who has auditioned for *American Idol* (Chapter 14, "Psychological Disorders")

Remember It The Process of Sensation

1. The process through which the senses detect visual, auditory, and other sensory stimuli and transmit them to the brain is called _____.
2. The point at which you can barely sense a stimulus 50% of the time is called the _____ threshold.
3. _____ transmit sensory information from the sense organs to the brain.
4. The process by which a sensory stimulus is converted into a neural impulse is called _____.
5. Each day, when Jessica goes to work at a coffee house, she smells the strong odor of fresh-brewed coffee. After she is there for a few minutes, she is no longer aware of the smell. The phenomenon known as _____ accounts for Jessica's experience.

Answers: 1. sensation; 2. absolute; 3. Sensory receptors; 4. transduction; 5. sensory adaptation.

Remember It Appearing after all major text sections, these quick reviews reinforce comprehension by testing you on the section content. For the Sixth Edition, these questions have been rewritten to sharpen their focus on core concepts.

---

the dog to salivate. Pavlov found that after the tone and the food were paired times, usually 20 or more, the tone alone would elicit salivation (Pavlov, 1927/19 385). Pavlov called the tone the learned stimulus, or **conditioned stimulus (CS** salivation to the tone the learned response, or **conditioned response (CR)**.

Higher-Order Conditioning. Once a connection between a conditioned sti and a conditioned response has been learned, new stimuli can be introduced by ing them with the conditioned stimulus. This process creates a series of signals known as **higher-order conditioning.** The sequence of events that occurs whe go to a laboratory for a blood test provides a good example of higher-order cond ing. First, you sit in a chair next to a table on which are arranged materials such a dles, syringes, and such. Next, some kind of constricting device is tied around arm, and the nurse or technician pats on the surface of your skin until a vein be visible. Each step in the sequence tells you that the unavoidable "stick" of the n and the pain, which is largely the result of reflexive muscle tension, is coming stick itself is the unconditioned stimulus, to which you reflexively respond. But a steps that precede it are conditioned stimuli that cause you to anticipate the p

unconditioned stimulus (US) A stimulus that elicits a specific unconditioned response without prior learning.

conditioned stimulus (CS) A neutral stimulus that, after repeated pairing with an unconditioned stimulus, becomes associated with it and elicits a conditioned response.

Key Terms Bolded key terms are now highlighted in the text and defined in the margin on the page on which they first appear. A complete list of key terms, with page references, is supplied at the end of the chapter.

Review and Reflect Approaches to Decision Making

Approach	Description
systematic decision making	Consideration of all possible alternatives prior to making a decision.
elimination by aspects	Factors on which alternatives are ordered from most to least important; any alternatives that do not satisfy the most important factor are eliminated; elimination of alternatives then continues factor by factor until one choice remains.
availability heuristic	Information that comes easily to mind determines the decision that is made.
representativeness heuristic	The decision is based on how closely an object or situation resembles or matches an existing prototype.
recognition heuristic	A rapid decision based on recognition of one of the alternatives.
framing	Potential gains and losses associated with alternatives are emphasized and influence the decision.
intuition	Decisions are motivated by "gut feelings" that may be influenced by perceptions of gains.

Review and Reflect Tables These comprehensive summary tables help consolidate major concepts, their components, and their relationships to one another. The tables offer information in a visual form that provides a unique study tool.

Summary and Review Sections Organized around the marginal learning objectives, each end-of-chapter summary provides a comprehensive study tool as well as a quick reference to the chapter's key terms, listed alphabetically.

Summary and Review

Cognition p. 231

7.1 **What is the difference between deductive and inductive reasoning? p. 231**
Deductive reasoning involves reasoning from the general to the specific, or drawing particular conclusions from general principles. In inductive reasoning, general conclusions are drawn from particular facts or individual cases.

7.2 **How does imagery help us think? p. 232**
Imagery is helpful for learning new skills and for practicing those we already know. It can also help us store

7.3 **What kinds of concepts help us man tion? p. 233**
Concepts are categories that allow us to q hend information. Rules and definitions mal concepts, whereas natural concepts a everyday experiences. We also match info prototypes, or examples, that include mos features associated with the concepts they Exemplars are examples of concepts with have the most familiarity.

Learning through Application

The authors recognize that your success lies not only in a strong learning pedagogy, but also in the ability to relate key psychological principles to your life and career choices. The Sixth Edition provides a variety of opportunities for you to make hands-on use of your studies.

Try It This popular feature provides brief applied experiments, self-assessments, and hands-on activities, which help personalize psychology, making it simple for you to actively relate psychological principles to everyday life.

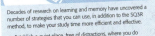

Try It Vision

To locate one of your blind spots, hold this book at arm's length. Close your right eye and look directly at the magician's eyes. Now slowly bring the book closer, keeping your eye fixed on the magi- cian. When the rabbit disappears, you have found the blind spot in your left eye.

The following Try Its appear in the text:

Apply It Best Practices for Effective Studying

Decades of research on learning and memory have uncovered a number of strategies that you can use, in addition to the SQ3R method, to make your study time more efficient and effective.

- Establish a quiet place, free of distractions, where you do nothing else but study. You can condition yourself to associate this environment with studying, so that entering the room or area will be your cue to begin work.
- Schedule your study time. Research on memory has proven that spaced learning is more effective than massed practice (cramming). Instead of studying for 5 hours straight, try five study sessions of 1 hour each.
- To be prepared for each class meeting, set specific goals for yourself each week and for individual study sessions. Your goals should be challenging but not overwhelming. If the task for an individual study session is manageable, it will be easier to sit down and face it. Completing the task you have set for yourself will give you a sense of accomplishment.

method is to use index cards as flash cards. Write a key term or study question on the front of each card. On the back, list pertinent information from the text and class lectures. Use these cards to help you prepare for tests.

- *Overlearning* means studying beyond the point at which you can just barely recite the information you are trying to memo- rize. Review the information again and again until it is firmly locked in memory. If you are subject to test anxiety, over- learning will help.
- Forgetting takes place most rapidly within the first 24 hours after you study. No matter how much you have studied for a test, always review shortly before you take it. Refreshing your memory will raise your grade.
- Sleeping immediately after you study will help you retain more of what you have learned. If you can't study before you go to sleep, at least review what you studied earlier in the day. This is also a good time to go through your index cards.

Apply It At the end of each chapter, an application box com- bines scientific research with practical advice to show you how to handle difficult or chal- lenging situations that may occur in your personal, academ- ic, or professional life. These boxes cover the following topics:

Thinking Critically about Psychology

1. Review the three basic approaches to decision making discussed in this chapter. Which approach do you think is most practical and efficient for making everyday decisions?
2. Based on what you have learned in this chapter, prepare arguments for and against raising a child in a bilingual environment and for and against requiring all school children in the United States to learn a second language.
3. Which of the theories of intelligence best fits your notion of intelligence? Why?

Thinking Critically About Psychology   New to this edition, each chapter ends with a feature that invites you to use your critical-thinking skills and your knowledge of psychology to answer three types of questions. One question invites you to use the information in the chapter to build pro and con cases for various issues; another question asks you to go beyond the information in the textbook; and the final question asks you to reflect on how the information in the chapter can be applied to your own everyday experience.

Appreciating and Reflecting Human Diversity

The authors have remained dedicated to the goal of promoting and expanding the understanding of human diversity throughout the evolution of this text. You and your fellow students come from diverse backgrounds, cultures, and regions and have unprecedented opportunities for travel, careers, and communications, both in the United States and internationally. In recognition of this reality, the Sixth Edition embraces a fully global perspective in presenting issues of diversity concerning gender, ethnicity, sexuality, and age. Some examples of issues addressed are as follows:

The Changing Face of Psychology (p. 11)
The Sociocultural Approach (p. 32)
Culture and Altered States of Consciousness (p. 140)
Memory and Culture (p. 209)
Learning a Second Language (p. 242)
Race and IQ (p. 259)
The Father-Child Relationship (p. 286)
Culture and Child Development (p. 305)
Cultural Differences in Care for the Elderly (p. 341)
Cultural Rules for Displaying Emotion (p. 372)
Gender Differences in Experiencing Emotion (p. 376)
Psychological Gender (p. 388)
Gender Differences in Cognitive Abilities (p. 397)
Gender Differences in Social Behavior and Personality (p. 400)
Gender and Cultural Differences (p. 402)
Social Attitudes toward Gays and Lesbians (p. 408)
Racism and Stress (p. 430)
Gender and Health (p. 442)
Culture and Personality Traits (p. 471)
Culture, Gender, and Depression (p. 500)
Suicide and Race, Gender, and Age (p. 502)
Culturally Sensitive and Gender-Sensitive Therapy (p. 547)
Prejudice and Discrimination (p. 577)
Gender Issues at Work (p. 600)
Human Diversity in the Workplace (p. 604)

To the Instructor: Changes to the Sixth Edition

As with each edition, we have closely examined and thoroughly updated all aspects of the text's content, organization, and pedagogy. Among the improvements made to the Sixth Edition are the following:

Learning Objectives   While we have always structured this text around specific learning objectives, we took special care to highlight them in the Sixth Edition. As noted above, every section of the text now has a corresponding, numbered learning objective. In addition, the Instructor's Manual and Test Bank are now organized by section, allowing you to design lectures, classroom activities, tests, and quizzes around specific learning objectives.

Artwork and Photos   We consider the artwork in this text to be an integral part of the learning process. As such, we have carefully examined each figure of the text to make sure that it is accurate and provides a clear explanation of the concept being illustrated. In addition, we wanted the figures to provide realistic representations of biological systems and their context in the human body. In the Sixth Edition, all of the art has been beautifully redrawn by Jay Alexander, in keeping with these goals. We have also added many new charts, tables, and figures to illustrate key concepts of the text.

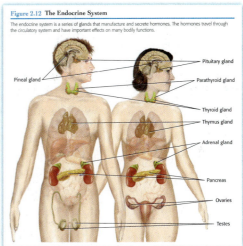

Figure 2.12 The Endocrine System
The endocrine system is a series of glands that manufacture and secrete hormones. The hormones travel through the circulatory system and have important effects on many bodily functions.

Pineal gland
Pituitary gland
Parathyroid gland
Thyroid gland
Thymus gland
Adrenal gland
Pancreas
Ovaries
Testes

Photos and their captions also serve a pedagogical purpose. In addition, they should be as diverse as the people and topics that they represent. We have examined all of the photos in the text with these goals in mind. All of the chapter-opening photos and many of the interior photos are new to the Sixth Edition.

Organizational Changes   A number of organizational changes have been made in the Sixth Edition to improve the clarity of the discussions and overall flow of material. Most notably, the book has been streamlined and shortened from 18 to 17 chapters. We achieved this by combining the last edition's Chapters 7 and 8 into a single chapter on cognition, intelligence, and language (new Chapter 7). The discussion of the history of psychology now precedes the discussion of research methods (Chapter 1, "Introduction"). Coverage of the structure of the nervous system has been reorganized, giving the reader a better sense of the components of the entire system (Chapter 2, "Biology and Behavior"). The discussion of memory now begins with an overview of the information-processing approach (Chapter 6, "Memory"). Cognition topics have been reorganized so that formal logic comes before less structured aspects of cognition (Chapter 7, "Cognition, Intelligence, and Language"). Theories of gender are now grouped in a single section that distinguishes between early and contemporary theories (Chapter 11, "Gender and Human Sexuality"). Social-cognitive theories are now discussed after trait theories so as to provide a counterpoint to them (Chapter 13, "Personality Theory and Assessment").

Updated Research   In this edition as in every other, the authors remain dedicated to citing current research and writing the most up-to-date text possible, while promoting an understanding of the foundation of psychology. To accomplish the goal of introducing the world of psychology accurately and clearly, the authors have gone back to original sources and have reread the basic works of the major figures in psychology and the classic studies in the field. The authors have also ensured that all presentations are reflective of current thinking about the science of psychology. Some examples of this include: the incorporation of systems theory into the discussion of the sociocultural approach (Chapter 1, "Introduction"); new research on delayed sleep phase syndrome and advanced sleep phase syndrome (Chapter 4, "States of Consciousness"); a new section on "Emerging Adulthood" that examines the neurological evidence for a development phase between adolescence and adulthood (Chapter 9, "Adolescence and Adulthood"); new research regarding the roles of the thalamus and hypothalamus in hunger, satiety, and obesity and new research on the neurological underpinnings of emotions (Chapter

10, "Motivation and Emotion"); the inclusion of Janet Hyde's theory of "gender similarities" and increased focus on the biological explanations of sexual orientation (Chapter 11, "Human Sexuality and Gender"); a revised and expanded discussion of the five factor model (Chapter 13, "Personality Theory and Assessment"); an extensively revised treatment of psychological disorders including an expanded discussion of schizophrenia and the disease's effects on the brain and a new section on childhood disorders that covers autism spectrum disorders and ADHD (Chapters 14, "Psychological Disorders"); and the addition of the APA's new healthy workplace award and the concept of work-life balance (Chapter 17, "Psychology in the Workplace").

Student Supplements

In addition to the SQ3R method and pedagogical learning features in the textbook, we have designed a number of supplemental materials to help you master the field of psychology.

Grade Aid Study Guide   This comprehensive and interactive study guide is filled with in-depth activities. Each chapter includes "Before You Read," presenting a brief chapter summary and chapter learning objectives; "As You Read," offering a collection of demonstrations, activities, and exercises; "After You Read," containing three short practice quizzes and one comprehensive practice test; "When You Have Finished," presenting Web links for further information and a crossword puzzle using key terms from the text. An appendix includes answers to all practice tests and crossword puzzles.

MyPsychLab   This online all-in-one study resource offers a dynamic, electronic version of *The World of Psychology* textbook with over 200 embedded video clips (2 to 4 minutes in length, close-captioned and with post-viewing activities) and over 100 embedded animations and simulations that dynamically illustrate chapter concepts. With over 100 text-specific practice test questions per chapter, MyPsychLab helps student master the concepts and prepare for exams. After a student completes a chapter pre-test, MyPsychLab generates a customized Study Plan for that student to help her focus her study effort where she needs it the most. MyPsychLab is available in both course management and website versions, and can be used as an instructor-driven assessment program and/or a student self-study learning program. Visit the site at *www.mypsychlab.com*.

Research Navigator Guide: Psychology, with access to Research Navigator™   Allyn & Bacon's new Research Navigator™ is the easiest way for students to start a research assignment or research paper. Complete with extensive help on the research process and four exclusive databases of credible and reliable source material including EBSCO Academic Journal and Abstract Database, *New York Times* Search by Subject Archive, "Best of the Web" Link Library, and *Financial Times* Article Archive and Company Financials. Research Navigator™ helps students quickly and efficiently make the most of their research time. The booklet contains a practical and to-the-point discussion of search engines; detailed information on evaluating online sources and citation guidelines for web resources; web links for Psychology; and a complete guide to Research Navigator.

Spanish Practice Tests   Practice tests and exercises from the Grade Aid Study Guide are available in Spanish.

Companion Website   A unique resource for connecting the Introductory Psychology course to the Internet. Each topic in the course table of contents includes updated and annotated web links for additional sources of information, Flash Card glossary terms, and online practice tests.

Instructor Supplements

We have designed a collection of instructor resources for the Sixth Edition that will help you prepare for class, enhance your course presentations, and assess your students' understanding of the material. These are only available to qualified instructors of the text. Please contact your Allyn & Bacon Sales Representative for more information.

MyPsychLab   This interactive and instructive multimedia resource can be used to supplement a traditional lecture course or to administer a course entirely online. It is an all-inclusive tool, a text-specific e-book plus multimedia tutorials, audio, video, simulations, animations, and controlled assessments to completely engage students and reinforce learning. Fully customizable and easy to use, MyPsychLab meets the individual teaching and learning needs of every instructor and every student. Visit the site at **www.mypsychlab.com.**

Instructor's Classroom Kit   Our unparalleled Classroom Kit includes every instructional aid an introductory psychology professor needs to manage the classroom. We have made our resources even easier to use by placing all of our print supplements in two convenient volumes. Organized by chapter, each volume contains an instructor's manual, test bank, and slides from *The World of Psychology* PowerPoint presentation. Fully revised for this edition, our new Classroom Kit model organizes all supplementary material by learning objective, integrating test questions, lecture launchers, MyPsychLab activities, and classroom demonstrations into one comprehensive resource.

> *Instructor's Classroom Kit CD-ROM*   This exciting new supplement for instructors brings together electronic copies of the Instructor's Manual, the Test Bank, the Grade Aid study guide, the PowerPoint Presentation, and images from the text for easy instructor access. Highly practical, the CD is organized by chapter and searchable by key terms.

> *Instructor's Manual*   Written by text author Denise Boyd, Houston Community College System, this wonderful tool can be used by first-time or experienced teachers. It includes numerous handouts, a sample syllabus, lecture materials, chapter outlines, suggested reading and video sources, teaching objectives, and more. Each chapter now contains a media resource grid and a unique activity integrating the boxed features available in the Sixth Edition.

> *Test Bank*   The fully reviewed Test Bank contains over 100 questions per chapter, including traditional multiple choice, true/false, short answer, and essay formats—and now new fill-in-the-blank, drag-and-drop, and flash demonstrations incorporating media into assessment. Each question has an answer justification, a page reference, a difficulty rating, and a type designation. In addition, the appendix includes a sample open-book quiz. This product is also available in Test Gen computerized version, for use in creating tests in the classroom.

> *PowerPoint Presentation*   The PowerPoint Presentation for *The World of Psychology*, authored by Stephen Tracy of Community College of Southern Nevada, pairs key points covered in the chapters with images from the textbook to encourage effective lectures and classroom discussions. The PowerPoint is included on the Instructor's Classroom Kit CD-ROM, and can also be downloaded from our Instructor Resource Center.

Allyn and Bacon Transparencies for Introductory Psychology   This set of approximately 200 revised, full-color acetates will enhance classroom lecture and discussion. It includes images from Allyn and Bacon's major introductory psychology texts.

Insights into Psychology, Volumes I, II, III, and IV   These video programs include 2-3 short clips per topic, covering such topics as animal research, parapsychology, health and stress, Alzheimer's, bilingual education, genetics and IQ, and much more. A Video Guide containing critical thinking questions accompanies each video. Also available on DVD.

Allyn and Bacon Digital Media Archive for Psychology   This comprehensive source includes still images, audio clips, web links, animation and video clips. Highlights include classic psychology experimental footage from Stanley Milgrim's Invitation to

Social Psychology, biology animations, and more–with coverage of such topics as eating disorders, aggression, therapy, intelligence, and sensation and perception.

CourseCompass   Powered by Blackboard, this course management system uses a powerful suite of tools that allow instructors to create an online presence for any course.

Acknowledgments

We are thankful for the support of several people at Allyn and Bacon who helped bring our plans for the Sixth Edition of *The World of Psychology* to fruition. On the editorial side, Susan Hartman monitored the progress of the book and ensured that the final product is an introductory text that achieves the goal of being thorough while also being timely and accessible. We are grateful for the assistance of developmental editors Sharon Geary and Julie Swasey, whose suggestions and encouragement helped immeasurably in the pursuit of this goal. Liz DiMenno, Associate Editor, helped us create new and improved ancillaries for both students and instructors. We would also like to acknowledge the fine work of Claudine Bellanton, Production Editor, and Michael Granger, Managing Editor, in overseeing the long and complex process of turning our manuscript into a book. Finally, copyeditor Kathy Smith provided suggestions that improved our writing and helped us produce a text that is clear, concise, and well organized. Finally, we thank our marketing team of Karen Natale and Pam Laskey for their work in promoting the text.

To Our Reviewers   Numerous reviewers were invaluable to the development of the Sixth Edition and prior editions of *The World of Psychology*, and we thank them for their input and time.

Reviewers of the Sixth Edition:

Elaine Adams, Houston Community College

James Brooks, Tarrant County College District

Wanda Clark, South Plains College

Curt Dunkel, Illinois Central College

Laura Duvall, Heartland Community College

Victor Gombos, University of California–Fullerton

Chuck Hallock, Pima Community College

Kim Kostere, Edison Community College

Bernard Levin, Blue Ridge Community College

Daniel Mayes, Seattle Community College

Carla Messenger, George Washington University

Mark O'Dekirk, Meredith College

Debra Schwiesow, Creighton University

Stacey Souther, Cuyahoga Community College

Monica Vines, Central Oregon Community College

Jeffrey B. Wagman, Illinois State University

Fred Whitford, Montana State University

Past Reviewers:

Mark D. Agars, California State University, San Bernadino

Patricia Alexander, Long Beach City College

Beth A. Barton, The University of North Carolina at Wilmington

Shirley A. Bass-Wright, St. Philip's College

Kenneth Benson, Hinds Community College

John Brennecke, Mt. San Antonio College

Cari Cannon, Santiago Canyon College

Jane Marie Cirillo, Houston Community College

Maria G. Cisneros-Solis, Austin Community College

Betty L. Clark, University of Mary Hardin-Baylor
Dennis Cogan, Texas Technical University
Betty S. Deckard, California State University, Long Beach
Kimberly J. Duff, Cerritos College
Laura Duvall, Heartland Community College
Joy Easton, DeVry University Orlando
Leticia Y. Flores, Southwest Texas State University
James Francis, San Jacinto College
Alexander B. Genov, Heartland Community College
Colleen Gift, Highland Community College
Paula Goolkasian, University of North Carolina at Charlotte
Allen Gottfried, California State University, Fullerton
Barbara J. Hart, Arizona State University–West
Brett Heintz, Delgado Community College
Debra Hollister, Valencia Community College
Steven Isorio, Golden West College
Victoria A. Kazmerski, Penn State Erie, The Behrend College
Norman E. Kinney, Southeast Missouri State University
Callista Lee, Fullerton College
Elizabeth Levin, Laurentian University
Barbara Lusk, Collin County Community College
Laura Madson, New Mexico State University
Barbara B. Marcel, Regis College
Catherine J. Massey, Slippery Rock University
Wendy Mills, San Jacinto College North
George Mount, Mountain View College
Peggy Norwood, Metropolitan State College of Denver
Fernando Ortiz, Santa Ana College
Ginger Osborne, Santa Ana College
Jack A. Palmer, University of Lousiana at Monroe
Debra Parish, Tomball College—NHMCC
Janet R. Pascal, DeVry University
Dan Perkins, Richland College
Michelle Pilati, Rio Hondo College
Vicki Ritts, St. Louis Community College–Meramec
Kevin S. Salisbury, Community College of Rhode Island
H. R. Schliffman, Rutgers University
Mark S. Schmidt, Columbus State University
Susan Siaw, California Polytechnic University, Pomona
Nancy Simpson, Trident Technical College
Lynn M. Skaggs, Central Texas College
Donette A. Steele, Cerritos College
Genevieve D. Stevens, Houston Community College System—Central College
Chuck Strong, Northwest Mississippi Community College
Inger Thompson, Glendale Community College
M. Lisa Valentino, Seminole Community College
Fred Whitford, Montana State University
Sandra Wilcox, California State University, Dominguez Hills
Diane E. Wille, Indiana University Southeast
Jeana Wolfe, Fullerton College

About the Authors

Samuel E. Wood received his doctorate from the University of Florida. He has taught at West Virginia University and the University of Missouri–St. Louis and was a member of the doctoral faculty at both universities. From 1984 to 1996, he served as president of the Higher Education Center, a consortium of 14 colleges and universities in the St. Louis area. He is a cofounder of the Higher Education Cable TV channel (HEC-TV) in St. Louis and served as its president and CEO from its founding in 1987 until 1996.

Ellen Green Wood received her doctorate in educational psychology from St. Louis University and was an adjunct professor of psychology at St. Louis Community College at Meramec. She has also taught in the clinical experiences program in education at Washington University and at the University of Missouri–St. Louis. In addition to her teaching, Dr. Wood has developed and taught seminars on critical thinking. She received the Telecourse Pioneer Award from 1982 through 1988 for her contributions to the field of distance learning.

Denise Boyd received her Ed.D. in educational psychology from the University of Houston and has been a psychology instructor in the Houston Community College System since 1988. From 1995 until 1998, she chaired the psychology, sociology, and anthropology department at Houston Community College–Central. She has coauthored three other Allyn and Bacon texts: with Helen Bee, *Lifespan Development* (Fourth Edition) and *The Developing Child* (Eleventh Edition); and with Genevieve Stevens, *Current Readings in Lifespan Development*. A licensed psychologist, she has presented a number of papers at professional meetings, reporting research in child, adolescent, and adult development. She has also presented workshops for teachers whose students range from preschool to college.

Together, Sam, Evie, and Denise have more than 45 years of experience teaching introductory psychology to thousands of students of all ages, backgrounds, and abilities. *The World of Psychology*, Sixth Edition is the direct result of their teaching experience.

Chapter 1

Introduction to Psychology

The SQ3R method will help you maximize your learning in 5 steps: SURVEY, QUESTION, READ, RECITE, and REVIEW. This chapter is annotated to show you where each step in the method occurs to help you visualize, practice, and master this learning system.

Continued

Descriptive Research Methods

1.13 How do psychological researchers use naturalistic and laboratory observation?

1.14 What are the advantages and disadvantages of the case study?

1.15 How do researchers ensure that survey results are useful?

1.16 What are the strengths and weaknesses of the correlational method?

The Experimental Method

1.17 Why do researchers use experiments to test hypotheses about cause-effect relationships?

1.18 How do independent and dependent variables differ?

1.19 Why are experimental and control groups necessary?

1.20 What kinds of factors introduce bias into experimental studies?

1.21 What are the limitations of the experimental method?

Participants in Psychological Research

1.22 In what ways can participants bias research results?

1.23 What ethical rules must researchers follow when humans are involved in studies?

1.24 Why are animals used in research?

Current Trends in Psychology

1.25 What is the main idea behind evolutionary psychology?

1.26 How is biological psychology changing the field of psychology?

1.27 What kinds of variables interest psychologists who take a sociocultural approach?

1.28 What are psychological perspectives, and how are they related to an eclectic position?

Psychologists at Work

1.29 What are some of the specialists working within psychology?

1.30 What kinds of employment opportunities are available for psychology majors?

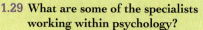

SURVEY: Begin with a scan of the chapter elements including chapter outline, headings, learning objective questions, illustrations, photos, tables, and end of chapter summary and study guide. This process gives you an overview of the chapter's main points. When approaching each section of the chapter, use the survey method for previewing that section's major coverage and features.

No **pain—no gain.** What comes to mind when you hear these words? Many people think about the link between exercise and physical fitness. One must exercise (the pain) in order to have a physically fit body (the gain). In fact, in 2005, an award-winning film about bodybuilding took this expression as its title. But did you know that the origin of this phrase is found in a publication that appeared more than 250 years ago, long before our modern era of fitness and bodybuilding?

In 1732, a Philadelphia editor and printer named Benjamin Franklin (1706–1790) began publishing a periodical called *Poor Richard's Almanack*. The publication contained calendars, weather predictions, and other kinds of practical information. What distinguished *Poor Richard's* from similar publications was Franklin's inclusion of brief expressions, usually a sentence or two, that captured abstract bits of wisdom in everyday language. He inserted several such phrases, called *maxims*, into every issue of *Poor Richard's Almanack*, and many continue to be used in American English today. For instance, he wrote, "A penny saved is a penny earned" and "Early to bed and early to rise, makes a man healthy, wealthy, and wise." One of Franklin's maxims, "Without pains, there are no gains," is shortened to the familiar phrase "no pain—no gain."

Finding verbally efficient ways to express abstract ideas appealed to Franklin because he was a proponent of a systematic approach to life that time-management guru Stephen Covey calls the *character ethic* (1989). Covey explains that most people believe in the *personality ethic*, the view that differences in success are expressions of an inborn characteristic that individuals possess in varying degrees. To put it simply, the personality ethic says that some people, the lucky ones, are born to be more successful than others. By contrast, the character ethic assumes that success results from effort. Specifically, Covey claims that people who want to be more successful can do so by developing a set of habits based on self-defined principles that are believed to be relevant to all domains of experience.

Covey cites Benjamin Franklin's *Autobiography* as the best source we can consult to learn how to use character ethic strategies to become more successful. One such strategy arose from Franklin's decision to pursue moral perfection. To facilitate a systematic approach to this goal, Franklin developed a list of 13 virtues and recorded them in a small notebook. These virtues were Temperance, Silence, Order, Resolution, Frugality, Industry, Sincerity, Justice, Moderation, Cleanliness, Tranquility, Chastity, and Humility. Franklin carried the notebook with him wherever he went and noted each time he violated a virtue with a check mark. When he could not find something because he had failed to put it in its proper place, he made a check mark beside "order." An angry outburst triggered a check by "Tranquility," and boasting about his accomplishments resulted in a mark by "Humility." At the end of each day, Franklin erased the check marks. He used the erasure ritual as an opportunity to reflect on his infractions and to think about how he might improve his performance the next day. He also noted whether the number of check marks increased or decreased over various periods of time—days, weeks, months, and so on.

After following this practice for several years, Franklin concluded that moral perfection was an unreachable goal. Still, he remained convinced that the degree of moral improvement he observed in himself as a result of his pursuit of moral perfection made it clear that his efforts were worth the trouble. In other words, the gain was worth the pain.

You may not be interested in committing yourself to the pursuit of moral perfection, but you can apply Franklin's self-observation strategies to achieve many other kinds of goals. One goal that is shared by many college students—that of developing effective study habits—fits well with Covey's character ethic approach to success, and it can be achieved through the kind of systematic techniques Franklin used in his quest for moral improvement. *The World of Psychology* includes many features that can help you do just that. The self-discipline you will acquire by using these features will increase the quantity and the quality of the information you learn from this text and those in your other courses. As a result, you will become both a more knowledgeable person and a more successful student. No doubt you will conclude that the gain is worth the pain, for, as Franklin put it, "An investment in knowledge pays the greatest dividends."

An Introduction to *The World of Psychology*

Many of Benjamin Franklin's maxims could be applied to the task of studying for a college course. However, Franklin is far from the only source of such pearls of wisdom. Students would do well, for instance, to reflect on the advice embodied in two African proverbs. One Ugandan expression says, "The hunter in pursuit of an elephant does not stop to throw stones at birds." In other words, to achieve any goal, including succeeding in a psychology course, one must remain focused and avoid distractions. Among the Mandinka, the saying, "Do a thing at its time and peace follows it" is often heard. This maxim addresses another common problem encountered by college students: procrastination. As you, like the Mandinka, probably know, procrastination leads to anxiety, so avoiding procrastination enhances your sense of well-being. Fortunately, the study strategies we have incorporated into *The World of Psychology* can help you stay focused on your goal of successfully completing your course in introductory psychology. If you remain focused, you are less likely to put off preparing for exams and other assignments. The next section discusses how the features of the text can help you.

QUESTION: As you begin each chapter section, look over its preview questions in the chapter outline and in the chapter margins to get a sense of the topics being covered. In addition, add any initial questions you may have about the content and key terms for this section. Keep these questions in mind to help focus your reading of each section.

▶ Sound advice for college students can be found in the maxims of many cultures. When you find yourself stressed out and trying to cram for a test that you know you should have studied for sooner, think about the Mandinka saying: "Do a thing at its time and peace follows it."

Studying Psychology: Some Tricks of the Trade

1.1 How can the SQ3R method help you study more effectively?

READ: As you read each chapter section, try to answer the learning objective questions and your own questions that come to mind. If you find particular areas of the section very long or complex, try breaking the section into smaller sections of reading.

The World of Psychology is organized to help you maximize your learning by using a series of five learning strategies developed and tested by a psychologist: *Survey, Question, Read, Recite,* and *Review.* Together, these steps are known as the **SQ3R method** (Robinson, 1970). You will learn and remember more if, instead of simply reading each chapter, you follow these steps. Here's how they work.

- *Survey.* First, scan the chapter. The chapter outline helps you preview the content and its organization. Read the section headings and the learning objective questions, which are designed to focus your attention on key information. Glance at the illustrations and tables, including the *Review and Reflect* tables, which organize, review, and summarize key concepts. Then read the *Summary and Review,* located at the end of each chapter. This survey process gives you an overview of the chapter.

- *Question.* You should approach each chapter by tackling one major section at a time. Before you actually read a section, reread its learning objective questions. But don't stop there; add a few questions of your own as you glance over the section's subheadings and key terms. For example, the first major section in this chapter is "An Introduction to *The World of Psychology.*" The first subheading is "Studying Psychology: Some Tricks of the Trade," and the associated question is "How can the SQ3R method help you study more effectively?" As you look over the section, you might add this question: "What is the difference between the explanation and prediction goals of psychology?" Asking such questions helps focus your reading.

- *Read.* Read the section. As you read, try to answer the learning objective questions and your own questions. After reading the section, stop. If the section is very long or if the material seems especially difficult or complex, you should pause after reading only one or two paragraphs.

- *Recite.* To better grasp each topic in a section, write a short summary of the material. If you have trouble summarizing a topic or answering any learning objective question, scan or read the section once more before trying again. Compare your summaries to the responses to the overview questions provided in the *Summary and Review* at the end of each chapter.

SQ3R method   A study method involving the following five steps: (1) survey, (2) question, (3) read, (4) recite, and (5) review.

- *Review.* Each major section in the book ends with a *Remember It* feature that consists of a few questions about the preceding topics. Answer these questions, and then check your responses against those provided. If you make errors, quickly review the preceding material until you know the answers. When you have finished a chapter, revisit each *Remember It* and then turn to the *Summary and Review.* Review the key terms. If you don't know the meaning of a term, turn to the page where that term is defined in the margin. The marginal definitions provide a ready reference for the important terms that appear in **boldface** print in the text. All of these terms and definitions also appear in the *Glossary* at the end of the book.

Now that you know how to study this text effectively, let's consider in more detail how the work of psychologists impacts our everyday lives. Before we begin, think about all of the ways in which psychology—and the language of psychology—play an integral role in our lives.

Psychology: Science or Common Sense?

You may not realize it, but when you incorporate into your daily routines self-discipline and study strategies such as those that make up the SQ3R approach, you are applying psychological principles to your life. Understanding this proposition, and everything else involved in the study of psychology, begins with a good definition of the field. Formally, **psychology** is defined as the scientific study of behavior and mental processes. If you are like most people, you have made many observations about both and perhaps have developed a few of your own theories to explain them. From television, radio, or the Internet, you probably also have had some exposure to "expert" opinions on behavior and mental processes. So, let's begin your exploration of psychology with an assessment of how much you already know, or think you know, about the topic. Answer the questions in *Try It*, and then check them against those given in the text that follows it.

> **1.2** What process do scientists use to answer questions about behavior and mental processes?

Try It   How Much Do You Know About Psychology?

Indicate whether each statement is true (T) or false (F).

1. Once damaged, brain cells never work again. F
2. All people dream during a night of normal sleep. T
3. As the number of bystanders at an emergency increases, the time it takes for the victim to get help decreases. T
4. Humans do not have a maternal instinct. F
5. It's impossible for human beings to hear a watch ticking 20 feet away. F

6. Eyewitness testimony is often unreliable. T
7. Chimpanzees have been taught to speak. F
8. Creativity and high intelligence do not necessarily go together. T
9. When it comes to close personal relationships, opposites attract. F
10. The majority of teenagers have good relationships with their parents. F

Can we make a valid claim that psychology is a science, or is it just common sense? In the *Try It*, common sense might have led you astray. All the odd-numbered items are false, and all the even-numbered items are true. So, common sense alone will not get you very far in your study of psychology.

Many people believe that a field is a science because of the nature of its body of knowledge. Few people question whether physics, for example, is a true science. But a science isn't a science because of its subject matter. A field of study qualifies as a science if it uses the scientific method to acquire knowledge. The **scientific method** consists of the orderly, systematic procedures that researchers follow as they identify a research problem, design a study to investigate the problem, collect and analyze data, draw conclusions, and communicate their findings (see **Figure 1.1**). The scientific method is the most objective method known for acquiring knowledge (Christensen, 2001). The knowledge gained is dependable because of the method used to obtain it.

psychology   The scientific study of behavior and mental processes.

scientific method   The orderly, systematic procedures that researchers follow as they identify a research problem, design a study to investigate the problem, collect and analyze data, draw conclusions, and communicate their findings.

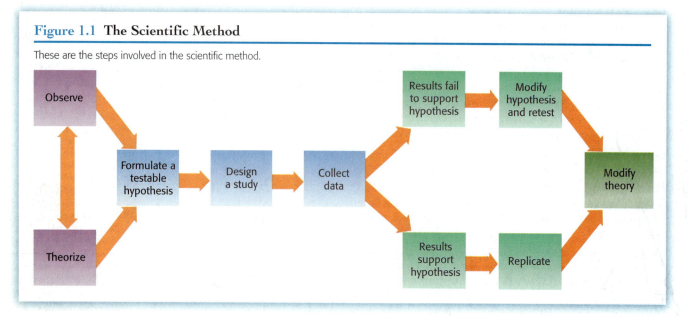

Figure 1.1 The Scientific Method

These are the steps involved in the scientific method.

Say, for example, that a researcher finds that men consistently score higher than women on a test of map reading. If the researcher claims that the gender difference in map-reading scores is attributable to the effects of male and female hormones on the brain, she has moved beyond the domain of facts and into that of theory. A **theory** is a general principle or set of principles proposed to explain how a number of separate facts are related. Other researchers may not agree with the explanation. Still, any alternative theory proposed to explain this researcher's findings must be able to account for the fact that men outscore women on tests of map reading. Other psychologists might propose that the difference exists because society encourages men to learn to read maps but discourages women from doing so. They can't simply say that there is no such thing as a gender difference in map reading, especially if the researcher's results have been *replicated* by other scientists. (**Replication** is the process of repeating a study with different participants and preferably a different investigator to verify research findings.)

You might be thinking: Why bother with theories? Why not just report the facts and let people draw their own conclusions? Well, theories enable scientists to fit many separate pieces of data into meaningful frameworks. For example, in the hormone theory of gender differences in map reading, two facts are connected: (1) Men and women have different hormones, and (2) men and women score differently on map-reading tests. Connecting these two facts results in a theory of gender differences from which researchers can make predictions that can be tested.

Theories also stimulate debates that lead to advances in knowledge. The psychologist who thinks gender differences in map reading are the result of learning may do a study in which male and female participants are trained in map reading. If the women read maps as well as the men do after training, then the researcher has support for her theory and has added a new fact to the knowledge base. Once the advocates of the hormone view modify their theory to include the new fact, they are likely to carry out new studies to test it. As a result of this back-and-forth process, knowledge about gender differences in map reading increases.

theory   A general principle or set of principles proposed to explain how a number of separate facts are related.

replication   The process of repeating a study with different participants and preferably a different investigator to verify research findings.

The Goals of Psychology

1.3 What are the goals of psychology?

What goals do psychological researchers pursue when they plan and conduct their studies? Briefly put, the goals of psychology are to describe, explain, predict, and influence behavior and mental processes. Let's look at each goal in a bit more detail.

Description is usually the first step in understanding any behavior or mental process and is therefore important in a very new area of research or in the early stages of research. To attain this goal, researchers describe the behavior or mental process of interest as accurately and completely as possible. A description tells *what* occurred.

The second goal, *explanation*, requires an understanding of the conditions under which a given behavior or mental process occurs. Such an understanding often enables researchers to state the causes of the behavior or mental process they are studying. But researchers do not reach the goal of explanation until their results have been tested, retested, and confirmed. The way researchers confirm an explanation is by eliminating or ruling out other explanations. An explanation tells *why* a given event or behavior occurred.

The goal of *prediction* is met when researchers can specify the conditions under which a behavior or event is likely to occur. Once researchers can identify all the antecedent (prior) conditions required for a behavior or event to occur, they can predict that behavior or event.

The goal of *influence* is accomplished when researchers know how to apply a principle or change a condition in order to prevent unwanted occurrences or bring about desired outcomes.

As an illustration of these goals, think back to the discussion of gender differences in map-reading skills. When a psychologist carries out a study in which male participants score higher than female participants on a map-reading test, she fulfills the description goal. Psychologists who theorize that the difference is due to the influences of male and female hormones on the brain are meeting the explanation goal. Formulating a hypothesis based on the hormone theory involves the prediction goal. Finally, researchers who devise and test training programs that help women learn to be better map readers are implementing the goal of influence.

Two types of research help psychologists accomplish the four goals just described: basic research and applied research. The purpose of **basic research** is to seek new knowledge and to explore and advance general scientific understanding. Basic research explores such topics as the nature of memory, brain function, motivation, and emotional expression. **Applied research** is conducted specifically for the purpose of solving practical problems and improving the quality of life. Applied research focuses on finding methods to improve memory or increase motivation, therapies to treat psychological disorders, ways to decrease stress, and so on. This type of research is primarily concerned with the fourth goal of psychology—influence—because it specifies ways and means of changing behavior.

◀ To achieve the goal of explaining road rage and the resulting violence—and perhaps eventually controlling it—psychological researchers might observe and describe the behavior of motorists under stressful conditions.

RECITE: After reading each section (or part of a section), try to answer the preview questions and your own questions—aloud or in writing or both. It can be helpful to write a brief summary of the material to help solidify your understanding of each topic. If you have trouble answering any of the preview questions or summarizing the material, take a few minutes to reread the section before trying again. Compare your responses or written summaries to those in the Summary and Review at the end of each chapter.

basic research Research conducted to seek new knowledge and to explore and advance general scientific understanding.

applied research Research conducted specifically to solve practical problems and improve the quality of life.

Remember It   An Introduction to *The World of Psychology*

1. The first step in the SQ3R study system is _____.

2. The _____ step in the SQ3R system helps you determine how well you understand and remember the text.

3. The orderly, systematic procedures scientists follow in acquiring a body of knowledge comprise the _____.

4. The four goals of psychology are _____, _____, _____, and _____.

Answers: 1. survey; 2. review; 3. scientific method; 4. description, explanation, prediction, influence

Exploring Psychology's Roots

If you were to trace the development of psychology from the beginning, you would need to start before the earliest pages of recorded history, beyond even the early Greek philosophers, such as Aristotle and Plato. However, it was not until experimental methods were applied to the study of psychological processes that psychology became recognized as a formal academic discipline.

Structuralism

Who were the "founders" of psychology? Historians acknowledge that three German scientists—Ernst Weber, Gustav Fechner, and Hermann von Helmholtz—were the first to systematically study behavior and mental processes. But it is Wilhelm Wundt (1832–1920) who is generally thought of as the "father" of psychology. Wundt's vision for the new discipline included studies of social and cultural influences on human thought (Benjafield, 1996).

Wundt established a psychological laboratory at the University of Leipzig in Germany in 1879, an event considered to mark the birth of psychology as a formal academic discipline. Using a method called *introspection*, Wundt and his associates studied the perception of a variety of visual, tactile, and auditory stimuli, including the rhythm patterns produced by metronomes set at different speeds. Introspection as a research method involves looking inward to examine one's own conscious experience and then reporting that experience.

Wundt's most famous student, Englishman Edward Bradford Titchener (1867–1927), took the new field to the United States, where he set up a psychological laboratory at Cornell University. He gave the name structuralism to this first formal school of thought in psychology, which endeavored to analyze the basic elements, or the structure, of conscious mental experience. Like Wundt before him, Titchener thought that consciousness could be reduced to its basic elements, just as water (H_2O) can be broken down into its constituent elements—hydrogen (H) and oxygen (O). For Wundt, pure sensations—such as sweetness, coldness, or redness—were the basic elements of consciousness. And these pure sensations, he believed, combined to form perceptions.

▲ Even though these children experience the same sensations (sweetness and coldness) as they enjoy eating their ice cream, their reported introspections of the experience would probably differ.

The work of both Wundt and Titchener was criticized for its primary method, introspection. Introspection is not objective, even though it involves observation, measurement, and experimentation. When different introspectionists were exposed to the same stimulus, such as the click of a metronome, they frequently reported different experiences. Therefore, structuralism was not in favor for long. Later schools of thought in psychology were established, partly as a reaction against structuralism, which did not survive after the death of its most ardent spokesperson, Titchener. Nevertheless, the structuralists were responsible for establishing psychology as a science through their insistence that psychological processes could be measured and studied using methods similar to those employed by scientists in other fields.

structuralism The first formal school of thought in psychology, which endeavored to analyze the basic elements, or structure, of conscious mental experience.

Functionalism

As structuralism was losing its influence in the United States in the early 20th century, a new school of psychology called functionalism was taking shape. Functionalism was concerned not with the structure of consciousness, but with how mental processes function—that is, how humans and animals use mental processes in adapting to their environment. The influential work of Charles Darwin (1809–1882), especially his ideas about evolution and the continuity of species, was largely responsible for an increasing use of animals in psychological experiments. Even though Darwin, who was British, contributed important seeds of thought that helped give birth to the new school of psychology, functionalism was primarily American in character and spirit.

functionalism An early school of psychology that was concerned with how humans and animals use mental processes in adapting to their environment.

The famous American psychologist William James (1842–1910) was an advocate of functionalism, even though he did much of his writing before this school of psychology emerged. James's best-known work is his highly regarded and frequently quoted textbook *Principles of Psychology*, published more than a century ago (1890). James taught that mental processes are fluid and have continuity, rather than the rigid, or fixed, structure that the structuralists suggested. James spoke of the "stream of consciousness," which, he said, functions to help humans adapt to their environment.

How did functionalism change psychology? Functionalism broadened the scope of psychology to include the study of behavior as well as mental processes. It also allowed the study of children, animals, and individuals with mental impairments, groups that could not be studied by the structuralists because they could not be trained to use introspection. Functionalism also focused on an applied, more practical use of psychology by encouraging the study of educational practices, individual differences, and adaptation in the workplace (industrial psychology).

▲ William James was the first American psychologist.

The Changing Face of Psychology

From its beginning until the mid–20th century, the field of psychology was shaped and dominated largely by White European and American males. For centuries, conventional thought had held that higher education was exclusively for White males, that women should rear children and be homemakers, and that minorities were best suited for manual labor. And, as Thomas Paine observed in his influential pamphlet *Common Sense* (1776), "A long habit of not thinking a thing wrong, gives it a superficial appearance of being right." However, beginning in the late 19th century, women and minorities overcame these prejudices to make notable achievements in and contributions to the study of psychology.

1.6 In what ways have women and minorities shaped the field of psychology, both in the past and today?

Pioneering Women. Christine Ladd-Franklin (1847–1930) completed the requirements for a Ph.D. at Johns Hopkins University in the mid-1880s but had to wait over 40 years before receiving her degree in 1926, when the university finally agreed to grant women doctoral degrees. Ladd-Franklin formulated a well-regarded, evolutionary theory of color vision.

In 1895, Mary Whiton Calkins (1863–1930) completed the requirements for a doctorate at Harvard. And even though William James described her as one of his most capable students, Harvard refused to grant the degree to a woman (Dewsbury, 2000). Undeterred, Calkins established a psychology laboratory at Wellesley College and developed the paired-associates test, an important research technique for the study of memory. She became the first female president of the American Psychological Association in 1905.

Margaret Floy Washburn (1871–1939) received her Ph.D. in psychology from Cornell University and later taught at Vassar College (Dewsbury, 2000). She wrote several books, among them *The Animal Mind* (1908), an influential book on animal behavior, and *Movement and Mental Imagery* (1916).

African Americans and Other Groups. Francis Cecil Sumner (1895–1954) was a self-taught scholar. In 1920, without benefit of a formal high school education, he became the first African American to earn a Ph.D. in psychology, from Clark University. This feat was accomplished "in spite of innumerable social and physical factors mitigating against such achievements by black people in America" (Guthrie, 1998, p. 177). Sumner translated more than 3,000 articles from German, French, and Spanish. He chaired the psychology department at Howard University and is known as the "father" of African American psychology.

▲ During the 1880s, Christine Ladd-Franklin beccame one of the first women to complete a doctoral degree in psychology, although Johns Hopkins University refused to officially grant her the degree until the mid 1920s.

Albert Sidney Beckham (1897–1964), another African American psychologist, conducted some impressive early studies on intelligence and showed how it is related to success in numerous occupational fields. Beckham also established the first psychological laboratory at an African American institution of higher learning—Howard University.

More recently, African American psychologist Kenneth Clark (1914–2005) achieved national recognition for his writings on the harmful effects of racial segregation. His work affected the Supreme Court ruling that declared racial segregation in U.S. schools to be unconstitutional (Benjamin & Crouse, 2002). His wife, Mamie Phipps Clark (1917–1983), also achieved recognition when the couple published their works on racial identification and self-esteem, which are regarded as classics in the field (Lal, 2002).

Hispanic American George Sánchez (1906–1972) conducted studies on bias in intelligence testing during the 1930s (Sánchez 1932, 1934). He pointed out that both cultural differences and language differences work against Hispanic students when they take IQ tests.

Native American and Asian American psychologists have made important contributions to psychological research as well. Moreover, they are the fastest growing minority groups in the field of psychology. The percentage of doctorates awarded to individuals in both groups more than doubled from the mid-1970s to the mid-1990s (National Science Foundation, 2000). One contemporary Native American psychologist, Marigold Linton, is known for her research examining autobiographical memory. In 1999, Richard Suinn, an eminent researcher in behavioral psychology, became the first Asian American president of the American Psychological Association.

Today, more women than men obtain degrees in psychology, and minority group representation is growing. However, there continues to be a gap between the proportion of minorities in the U.S. population and their representation among professional psychologists. Indeed, although the proportion of minorities in the U.S. population is about 28%, only 16% of students pursuing graduate degrees in psychology are of minority ethnicity (APA, 2000). Consequently, the APA and other organizations have established programs to encourage minority enrollment in graduate programs in psychology.

Kenneth (1914–2005) and Mamie (1917–1983) Clark's research examining self-esteem in African American children was cited in the 1954 U.S. Supreme Court decision *Brown v. Board of Education* that led to the desegregation of public schools in the United States.

Remember It   Exploring Psychology's Roots

1. Classify each of the following people and concepts as being associated with (a) Wundt, (b) structuralism, and/or (c) functionalism. (Hint: Some items apply to more than one.)
   ___ (1) James
   ___ (2) based on Darwin's theory of evolution
   ___ (3) stream of consciousness
   ___ (4) elements of experience
   ___ (5) Titchener
   ___ (6) introspection
   ___ (7) became known in the 19th century

2. Match each of the following individuals with his or her contribution to psychology.
   ___ (1) Francis Cecil Sumner
   ___ (2) Mary Whiton Calkins
   ___ (3) Kenneth Clark
   ___ (4) Christine Ladd-Franklin
   ___ (5) George Sánchez

   a. first female president of the APA
   b. conducted studies on cultural bias in intelligence testing
   c. first African American to earn a Ph.D. in psychology
   d. studied the harmful effects of racial segregation
   e. had to wait 40 years to receive a Ph.D. in psychology after completing all the requirements

Answers: 1. (1) c, (2) c, (3) c, (4) a, (5) b, (6) a, b, (7) a, b, c. 2. (1) c, (2) a, (3) d, (4) e, (5) b.

Schools of Thought in Psychology

Why don't we hear about structuralism and functionalism today? In the early 20th century, the debate between the two points of view sparked a veritable explosion of theoretical discussion and research examining psychological processes. The result was the appearance of new theories that were better able to explain behavior and mental processes. The foundations of the major schools of thought in the field were established during that period and continue to be influential today.

Behaviorism

Psychologist John B. Watson (1878–1958) looked at the study of psychology as defined by the structuralists and functionalists and disliked virtually everything he saw. In his article "Psychology as the Behaviorist Views It" (1913), Watson proposed a radically new approach to psychology, one that rejected the subjectivity of both structuralism and functionalism. This new school redefined psychology as the "science of behavior." Termed **behaviorism** by Watson, this school of psychology confines itself to the study of behavior because behavior is observable and measurable and, therefore, objective and scientific. Behaviorism also emphasizes that behavior is determined primarily by factors in the environment.

Behaviorism was the most influential school of thought in American psychology until the 1960s. It is still a major force in modern psychology, in large part because of the profound influence of B. F. Skinner (1904–1990). Skinner agreed with Watson that concepts such as mind, consciousness, and feelings are neither objective nor measurable and, therefore, not appropriate subject matter for psychology. Furthermore, Skinner argued that these concepts are not needed in order to explain behavior. One can explain behavior, he claimed, by analyzing the conditions that are present before a behavior occurs and then analyzing the consequences that follow the behavior.

Skinner's research on operant conditioning emphasized the importance of reinforcement in learning as well as in shaping and maintaining behavior. He maintained that any behavior that is reinforced (followed by pleasant or rewarding consequences) is more likely to be performed again. Skinner's work has had a powerful influence on modern psychology. You will read more about operant conditioning in Chapter 5.

1.7 How do behaviorists explain behavior and mental processes?

behaviorism The school of psychology founded by John B. Watson that views observable, measurable behavior as the appropriate subject matter for psychology and emphasizes the key role of environment as a determinant of behavior.

◄ Behaviorist B. F. Skinner claimed that any behavior is best understood by analyzing the conditions that are present before it occurs and by analyzing the consequences that follow the behavior. How would you apply this concept to the behavior of using an umbrella?

Psychoanalysis

Sigmund Freud (1856–1939), whose life and work you will study in Chapter 13, developed a theory of human behavior based largely on case studies of his patients. Freud's
theory, **psychoanalysis,** maintains that human mental life is like an iceberg. The smallest, visible part of the iceberg represents the conscious mental experience of the individual. But underwater, hidden from view, floats a vast store of unconscious impulses,
wishes, and desires. Freud insisted that individuals do not consciously control their
thoughts, feelings, and behavior; these are instead determined by unconscious forces.

Freud believed that the unconscious is the storehouse for material that threatens
the conscious life of the individual—disturbing sexual and aggressive impulses as
well as traumatic experiences that have been repressed, or pushed down to the unconscious. Once there, rather than resting quietly (out of sight, out of mind), the unconscious material festers and seethes.

The overriding importance that Freud placed on sexual and aggressive impulses
caused much controversy both inside and outside the field of psychology. The most
notable of Freud's famous students—Carl Jung, Alfred Adler, and Karen Horney—
broke away from their mentor and developed their own theories of personality. These
three and their followers are often collectively referred to as *neo-Freudians*.

The general public has heard of such concepts as the unconscious, repression, rationalization, and the Freudian slip. Such familiarity has made Sigmund Freud a
larger-than-life figure rather than an obscure Austrian doctor resting within the dusty
pages of history. Although Freud continues to influence popular culture, the volume
of research on psychoanalysis has continued to diminish steadily (Robins et al., 1999).
Still, the psychoanalytic approach continues to be influential, although in a form that
has been modified considerably over the past several decades by the neo-Freudians.

Humanistic Psychology

Humanistic psychologists reject with equal vigor (1) the behaviorist view that behavior is determined by factors in the environment and (2) the pessimistic view of the
psychoanalytic approach, that human behavior is determined primarily by unconscious forces. **Humanistic psychology** focuses on the uniqueness of human beings
and their capacity for choice, growth, and psychological health.

Abraham Maslow (1908–1970) and other early humanists, such as Carl Rogers
(1902–1987), pointed out that Freud based his theory primarily on data from his disturbed patients. By contrast, the humanists emphasize a much more positive view of
human nature. They maintain that people are innately good and that they possess free
will. The humanists believe that people are capable of making conscious, rational
choices, which can lead to personal growth and psychological health.

As you will learn in Chapter 13, Maslow proposed a theory of motivation that consists of a hierarchy of needs. He considered the need for self-actualization (developing
to one's fullest potential) to be the highest need on the hierarchy. Carl Rogers developed what he called *client-centered therapy,* an approach in which the client, or patient,
directs a discussion focused on his or her own view of a problem rather than on the
therapist's analysis. Rogers and other humanists also popularized group therapy as
part of the human potential movement. Thus, the humanistic perspective continues to
be important in research examining human motivation and in the practice of psychotherapy.

psychoanalysis (SY-ko-ah-NAL-
ih-sis) The term Freud used for both
his theory of personality and his
therapy for the treatment of psychological disorders; the unconscious is
the primary focus of psychoanalytic
theory.

humanistic psychology The
school of psychology that focuses on
the uniqueness of human beings and
their capacity for choice, growth, and
psychological health.

Cognitive Psychology

Cognitive psychology grew and developed partly in response to strict behaviorism,
especially in the United States (Robins et al., 1999). **Cognitive psychology** views humans not as passive recipients who are pushed and pulled by environmental forces, but
as active participants who seek out experiences, who alter and shape those experiences,

and who use mental processes to transform information in the course of their own cognitive development. It studies mental processes such as memory, problem solving, reasoning, decision making, perception, language, and other forms of cognition. Historically, modern cognitive psychology is derived from two streams of thought: one that began with a small group of German scientists studying human perception in the early 20th century and another that grew up alongside the emerging field of computer science in the second half of the century.

Gestalt Psychology. Gestalt psychology made its appearance in Germany in 1912. The Gestalt psychologists, notably Max Wertheimer, Kurt Koffka, and Wolfgang Köhler, emphasized that individuals perceive objects and patterns as whole units and that the perceived whole is more than the sum of its parts. The German word *Gestalt* roughly means "whole, form, or pattern."

▲ Is this person having a bad day? The perceptual processes described by the Gestalt psychologists are observable in everyday life. We often put frustrating events—such as getting up late and then having a flat tire—together to form a "whole" concept, such as "I'm having a bad day."

To support the Gestalt theory, Wertheimer, the leader of the Gestalt psychologists, performed his famous experiment demonstrating the *phi phenomenon*. In this experiment, two light bulbs are placed a short distance apart in a dark room. The first light is flashed on and then turned off just as the second light is flashed on. As this pattern of flashing the lights on and off continues, an observer sees what appears to be a single light moving back and forth from one position to another. Here, said the Gestaltists, is proof that people perceive wholes or patterns, rather than collections of separate sensations.

When the Nazis came to power in Germany in the 1930s, the Gestalt school disbanded, and its most prominent members emigrated to the United States. Today, the fundamental concept underlying Gestalt psychology—that the mind *interprets* experiences in predictable ways rather than simply reacts to them—is central to cognitive psychologists' ideas about learning, memory, problem solving, and even psychotherapy.

Information-Processing Theory. The advent of the computer provided cognitive psychologists with a new way to conceptualize mental structures and processes, known as **information-processing theory.** According to this view, the brain processes information in sequential steps, in much the same way as a computer does serial processing—that is, one step at a time. However, just as modern technology has changed computers and computer programs, cognitive psychologists also have changed their models. "Increasingly, parallel processing models [models in which several tasks are performed at once] are developed in addition to stage models of processing" (Haberlandt, 1997, p. 22).

A central idea of information-processing theory, which it shares with Gestalt psychology, is that the brain interprets information rather than just responding to it. For example, consider this statement: *The old woman was sweeping the steps.* If information-processing researchers ask people who have read the sentence to recall whether it includes the word *broom*, a majority will say that it does. According to information-processing theorists, rules for handling information lead us to find associations between new input, such as the statement about a woman sweeping, and previously acquired knowledge, such as our understanding that brooms are used for sweeping. As a result, most of us construct a memory of the sentence that leads us to incorrectly recall that it includes the word *broom*.

Designing computer programs that can process human language in the same way as the human brain is one of the goals of research on *artificial intelligence*. Today, such research represents one of the most important applications of information-processing theory.

cognitive psychology The school of psychology that views humans as active participants in their environment; studies mental processes such as memory, problem solving, decision making, perception, language, and other forms of cognition.

Gestalt psychology The school of psychology that emphasizes that individuals perceive objects and patterns as whole units and that the perceived whole is more than the sum of its parts.

information-processing theory An approach to the study of mental structures and processes that uses the computer as a model for human thinking.

Cognitive Psychology Today. Over the past 100 years or so, cognitive psychologists have carried out studies that have greatly increased our knowledge of the human memory system and the mental processes involved in problem solving. Moreover, the principles discovered in these experiments have been used to explain and study all kinds of psychological variables—from gender role development to individual differences in intelligence. As a result, cognitive psychology is currently recognized as one of the most prominent schools of psychological thought (Robins et al., 1999).

Remember It   Schools of Thought in Psychology

1. Match the school of psychology with its major emphasis:

____ (1) the scientific study of behavior

____ (2) the perception of whole units or patterns

____ (3) the study of the unconscious

____ (4) the use of the computer as a model for human cognition

____ (5) the uniqueness of human beings and their capacity for personal growth

____ (6) the study of mental processes

a. Gestalt psychology
b. humanistic psychology
c. cognitive psychology
d. behaviorism
e. information-processing theory
f. psychoanalysis

2. Match the major figure with the appropriate school of psychology. (Options may be used more than once.)

____ (1) Freud
____ (2) Skinner
____ (3) Maslow
____ (4) Wertheimer
____ (5) Watson
____ (6) Rogers

a. Gestalt psychology
b. humanistic psychology
c. behaviorism
d. psychoanalysis

Answers: 1. (1) d, (2) a, (3) f, (4) e, (5) b, (6) c; 2. (1) d, (2) c, (3) b, (4) a, (5) c, (6) b

Thinking about Theories and Research

Whenever we discuss theories, students want to know which are "true" and which are "false." However, psychologists and other scientists don't think about theories in this way. Instead, they evaluate theories in terms of their usefulness with regard to the scientific method. Remember, the scientific method involves a systematic approach to finding answers to important questions and is an integral part of our everyday thinking. Still, we can all benefit from practicing it to a greater extent than we ordinarily do. By practicing scientific thinking, we can develop a set of tools to use when we are confronted by sensational media reports about the results of a new study.

Evaluating Theories

1.11 How do psychologists evaluate theories?

Sometimes students wonder why we should bother with theories. Why not just report the facts, many ask. As you learned earlier in the chapter, theories provide us with explanations for facts, so they are indispensable to the scientific method. Clearly, though, some theories do a better job of explaining data than others. What makes one theory useful and another less so? There are several criteria for determining this.

The degree to which a theory leads to testable hypotheses is perhaps the most important criterion for judging its usefulness. When you use this standard to think about the theories we've discussed so far, those of behaviorists and cognitive psychologists appear more useful than those of psychoanalysts and humanists. B. F. Skinner's prediction that reinforcement increases behavior, for example, is far more testable than Maslow's claim that self-actualization is the highest of all human needs.

Useful theories also lead to the development of solutions to real-world problems. For instance, research based on the information-processing model has resulted in the development of practical strategies for improving memory. Similarly, even though psychoanalytic and humanistic theories have been criticized for lacking testability, they have produced a number of beneficial psychotherapies.

Hypotheses and practical applications are important, but a theory that possesses *heuristic value* is useful even if it falls short in these two areas. A theory that has heuristic value stimulates debate among psychologists and motivates both proponents and opponents of the theory to pursue research related to it. In other words, a theory that possesses heuristic value makes people think and spurs their curiosity and creativity.

All of the theories discussed so far earn high marks for their heuristic value. In fact, even if a theory has limited empirical support, professors who teach introductory psychology are justified in including it in the course if it has been of heuristic importance in the field. This is why we still teach about the structuralists and functionalists, and why we continue to rate Freud's theory as one of the most important in the field. Moreover, such theories usually affect students in the same way that they affect psychologists— that is, learning about them stimulates students' thinking about behavior and mental processes. Thus, introducing these theories helps professors achieve one of their most important instructional goals, that of motivating students to think critically.

Evaluating Research

Another important goal of most professors who teach introductory psychology is to equip students with the intellectual tools needed to evaluate claims based on psychological research. Living in the Information Age, we are bombarded with statistics and claims of all types every day. For instance, not long ago the news media carried a number of reports warning parents of young children that watching too much television in the early years of life might lead to attention deficit/hyperactivity disorder (ADHD) later in childhood (Clayton, 2004). These warnings were based, reporters said, on a scientific study that was published in the prestigious journal *Pediatrics*. How can a person who is not an expert on the subject in question evaluate claims such as these?

The thinking strategies used by psychologists and other scientists can help us sift through this kind of information. **Critical thinking,** the foundation of the scientific method, is the process of objectively evaluating claims, propositions, and conclusions to determine whether they follow logically from the evidence presented. When we engage in critical thinking, we exhibit these characteristics:

- *Independent thinking.* When thinking critically, we do not automatically accept and believe what we read or hear.
- *Suspension of judgment.* Critical thinking requires gathering relevant and up-to-date information on all sides of an issue before taking a position.
- *Willingness to modify or abandon prior judgments.* Critical thinking involves evaluating new evidence, even when it contradicts preexisting beliefs.

Applying the first of these three characteristics to the television-ADHD study requires recognizing that the validity of any study is not determined by the authority of its source. Prestigious journals—or psychology textbooks for that matter—shouldn't be regarded as sources of fixed, immutable truths. In fact, learning to question accepted "truths" is important to the scientific method itself. For example, as you will learn in Chapter 2, for many years scientists believed that the brain did not develop any new nerve cells after birth. However, once the technology became available to directly study neuronal development, researchers who were willing to challenge the status quo found that the brain produces new nerve cells throughout the life span (Gould et al., 1999).

1.12 How can critical thinking be used to interpret media reports of psychological research?

critical thinking The process of objectively evaluating claims, propositions, and conclusions to determine whether they follow logically from the evidence presented.

The second and third characteristics of critical thinking, suspension of judgment and willingness to change, may require abandoning some old habits. If you are like most people, you respond to media reports about research on the basis of your own personal experiences, a type of evidence scientists call *anecdotal evidence.* For instance, in response to the media report about television and ADHD, a person might say, "I agree with that study because my cousin has such severe ADHD that he had to drop out of high school, and he was always glued to the television when he was little." Another might counter, "I don't agree with that study because I watched a lot of television when I was a kid, and I don't have ADHD."

Suspension of judgment requires that you postpone either accepting or rejecting the study's findings until you have accumulated more evidence. It might involve determining what, if any, findings have been reported by other researchers regarding a possible link between television viewing and ADHD. Analysis of other relevant studies can help to create a comprehensive picture of what the entire body of research says about the issue. Ultimately, when enough evidence has been gathered, a critical thinker must be willing to abandon preconceived notions and prior beliefs that conflict with it.

The quality of the evidence is just as important as the quantity. Thus, a critical thinker would evaluate the findings of the television-ADHD study by considering the methods used to obtain them. After reading the next section, you should be better able to think critically about the methods used by researchers.

Remember It   Thinking about Theories and Research

1. A theory that generates debate among psychologists is said to have _____ value.

2. Useful theories provide researchers with _____.

3. Willingness to change one's prior beliefs is a component of critical thinking about research. (true/false)

4. Critical thinking about media reports of research requires some familiarity with _____.

Answers: 1. heuristic; 2. testable hypotheses; 3. true; 4. research methods

Descriptive Research Methods

What is the simplest kind of research? Research that involves direct observation is usually easy to perform and often provides the clearest results. **Descriptive research methods** yield descriptions of behavior and include naturalistic and laboratory observation, the case study, and the survey.

Naturalistic and Laboratory Observation

1.13 **How do psychological researchers use naturalistic and laboratory observation?**

descriptive research methods Research methods that yield descriptions of behavior.

naturalistic observation A descriptive research method in which researchers observe and record behavior in its natural setting, without attempting to influence or control it.

Have you ever sat in an airport or shopping mall and simply watched what people were doing? Such an activity is quite similar to **naturalistic observation,** a descriptive research method in which researchers observe and record behavior in its natural setting, without attempting to influence or control it. The major advantage of naturalistic observation is the opportunity to study behavior in normal settings, where it occurs more naturally and spontaneously than it does under artificial and contrived laboratory conditions. Sometimes, naturalistic observation is the only feasible way to study behavior. For example, there is no other way to study how people typically react during disasters such as earthquakes and fires.

Naturalistic observation has its limitations, however. Researchers must wait for events to occur; they cannot speed up or slow down the process. And because they have no control over the situation, researchers cannot reach conclusions about cause-effect relationships. Another potential problem with naturalistic observation is *observer bias*, which is a distortion in researchers' observations. Observer bias can result when researchers' expectations about a situation cause them to see what they expect to see or to make incorrect inferences about what they observe. Let's say, for example, that you're a psychologist studying aggression in preschool classrooms. You have decided to count every time a child hits or pushes another child as an aggressive act. Your decision to label this type of physical contact between children as "aggressive" may cause you to notice more such acts and label them as "aggressive" than you would if you were casually watching a group of children play. The effects of observer bias can be reduced substantially when two or more observers view the same behavior. So, if you and another observer independently count, say, 23 aggressive acts in an hour of free play, the findings are considered unbiased. If, on the other hand, you see 30 such acts and the other observer records only 15, there is some kind of bias at work. In such situations, observers usually clarify the criteria for classifying behavior and repeat the observations. Using videotapes can also help eliminate observer bias because behavior can be reviewed several times prior to making classification decisions.

Another method of studying behavior involves observation that takes place not in its natural setting, but in a laboratory. Researchers using **laboratory observation** can exert more control and use more precise equipment to measure responses. Much of what is known about sleep or the human sexual response, for example, has been learned through laboratory observation. However, like other research methods, laboratory observation has limitations. For one, laboratory behavior may not accurately reflect real-world behavior. For example, in sleep studies, some of the behavior people display while asleep in the laboratory may not occur in their homes. As a result, conclusions based on laboratory findings may not generalize beyond the walls of the laboratory itself. Another disadvantage is that building, staffing, equipping, and maintaining research laboratories can be expensive.

▲ A kind of naturalistic observation occurs on a large scale in England; about a million closed-circuit TV cameras like this one monitor activity in streets and shopping centers.

laboratory observation A descriptive research method in which behavior is studied in a laboratory setting, where researchers can exert more control and use more precise equipment to measure responses.

The Case Study

The **case study,** or case history, is another descriptive research method used by psychologists. In a case study, a single person or a small number of individuals are studied in great depth, usually over an extended period of time. A case study involves the use of observations, interviews, and sometimes psychological testing. Exploratory in nature, the case study's purpose is to provide a detailed description of some behavior or disorder. This method is particularly appropriate for studying people who have uncommon psychological or physiological disorders or brain injuries. Many case studies are written about patients being treated for such problems. In some instances, the results of detailed case studies have provided the foundation for psychological theories. In particular, the theory of Sigmund Freud was based primarily on case studies of his patients.

Although the case study has proven useful in advancing knowledge in several areas of psychology, it has certain limitations. Researchers cannot establish the cause of behavior observed in a case study, and observer bias is a potential problem. Moreover, because so few individuals are studied, researchers do not know how applicable, or generalizable, their findings may be to larger groups or to different cultures.

1.14 What are the advantages and disadvantages of the case study?

case study A descriptive research method in which a single person or a small number of individuals are studied in great depth, usually over an extended period of time.

survey A descriptive research method in which researchers use interviews and/or questionnaires to gather information about the attitudes, beliefs, experiences, or behaviors of a group of people.

Survey Research

Have you ever been questioned about your voting behavior or about the kind of toothpaste you prefer? If you have, chances are that you were a participant in another kind of research study. The **survey** is a descriptive research method in which researchers use interviews and/or questionnaires to gather information about the attitudes, beliefs, experiences, or behaviors of a group of people. The results of carefully conducted surveys have provided valuable information about drug use, sexual behavior, and the incidence of various mental disorders.

1.15 How do researchers ensure that survey results are useful?

Selecting a Sample. Researchers in psychology rarely conduct studies using all members of a group. For example, researchers interested in studying the sexual behavior of American women do not survey every woman in the United States. (Imagine trying to interview about 140 million people!) Instead of studying the whole **population** (the entire group of interest to researchers, to which they wish to apply their findings), researchers select a sample for study. A **sample** is a part of a population that is studied in order to reach conclusions about the entire population.

▲ Is the Hilton family *representative* of the general population of families in the United States? Why or why not?

Perhaps you have seen a carton of ice cream that contains three separate flavors—chocolate, strawberry, and vanilla—packed side by side. To properly sample the carton, you would need a small amount of ice cream containing all three flavors in the same proportions as in the whole carton—a representative sample. A **representative sample** mirrors the population of interest—that is, it includes important subgroups in the same proportions as they are found in that population. A *biased sample*, on the other hand, does not adequately reflect the larger population.

The best method for obtaining a representative sample is to select a *random sample* from a list of all members of the population of interest. Individuals are selected in such a way that every member of the larger population has an equal chance of being included in the sample. Using random samples, polling organizations can accurately represent the views of the American public with responses from as few as 1,000 people (O'Brien, 1996).

Interviews and Questionnaires. Survey results can be affected by the questions' wording and the context for the survey (Schwartz, 1999). Also, the truthfulness of the responses can be affected by characteristics of the interviewers, such as their gender, age, race, ethnicity, religion, social class, and accent. In general, people are most inhibited when they give personal information to interviewers who are of the same age but the opposite sex. Survey researchers, therefore, must select interviewers who have personal characteristics that are appropriate for the intended respondents.

▲ Internet surveys allow psychologists to gather lots of data from large numbers of respondents in a very short period of time. But how representative of the general population are people who respond to Internet surveys? How representative are they of Internet users in general? Questions such as these remain to be answered.

population   The entire group of interest to researchers, to which they wish to generalize their findings; the group from which a sample is selected.

sample   A part of a population that is studied in order to reach conclusions about the entire population.

representative sample   A sample that mirrors the population of interest; it includes important subgroups in the same proportions as they are found in that population.

Questionnaires can be completed more quickly and less expensively than interviews, especially when respondents can fill them out in their homes or online. The Internet offers psychologists a fast and inexpensive way of soliciting participants and collecting questionnaire data, and Internet surveys often generate large numbers of responses (Azar, 2000). For example, an Internet survey posted by researchers who wanted to collect data about suicidal feelings attracted more than 38,000 respondents from all over the world (Mathy, 2002). However, such surveys have problems, including technical glitches that sometimes prevent respondents from completing a questionnaire. Moreover, the sample is often biased in that it represents only the population of Internet users who choose to participate in online research, *not* the general population or even the population of Internet users. The critical point to remember is that surveys in which respondents *choose* whether or not to participate—rather than being selected through some kind of random process—are not scientific.

Advantages and Disadvantages of Survey Research. If conducted properly, surveys can provide highly accurate information. They can also track changes in attitudes or behavior over time. For example, Johnston and others (2001) have tracked drug use among high school students since 1975. However, large-scale surveys can be costly and time-consuming. Another important limitation of survey research is that respondents may provide inaccurate information. False information can result from a faulty memory or a desire to please the interviewer. Respondents may try to present themselves in a good light (a phenomenon called the *social desirability response*), or they may even deliberately mislead the interviewer. Finally, when respondents answer questions about sensitive subjects, such as sexual behavior, they are often less candid in face-to-face interviews than in self-administered or computerized questionnaires (Tourangeau et al., 1997).

The Correlational Method

Perhaps the most powerful descriptive method available to psychologists is the **correlational method,** a method used to establish the degree of relationship (correlation) between two characteristics, events, or behaviors. A group is selected for study, and the variables of interest are measured for each participant. For example, one researcher might examine the relationship between attainment of a college degree and subsequent income. Another might look for a correlation between the amount of time students devote to studying and their grade-point averages.

Correlations are not just important to scientists, they are also common in our everyday thinking. For example, what is the relationship between the price of a new car and the social status you gain from owning it? Isn't it true that as price goes up, status goes up as well? And isn't status one of the variables that many people take into account when buying a new car? As this example illustrates, correlations are part of our everyday lives, and we often use them in decision making.

When scientists study correlations, they apply a statistical formula to data representing two or more variables to obtain a *correlation coefficient*. A **correlation coefficient** is a numerical value that indicates the strength and direction of the relationship between two variables. A correlation coefficient ranges from +1.00 (a perfect positive correlation) to .00 (no relationship) to −1.00 (a perfect negative correlation). The number in a correlation coefficient indicates the relative strength of the relationship between two variables—the higher the number, the stronger the relationship. Therefore, a correlation of −.85 is stronger than a correlation of +.64.

The sign of a correlation coefficient (+ or −) indicates whether the two variables vary in the same or opposite directions. A positive correlation indicates that two variables vary in the same direction, like the price of a car and its associated social status. As another example, there is a positive though weak correlation between stress and illness. When stress increases, illness is likely to increase; when stress decreases, illness tends to decrease (see **Figure 1.2**).

1.16 What are the strengths and weaknesses of the correlational method?

correlational method A research method used to establish the degree of relationship (correlation) between two characteristics, events, or behaviors.

correlation coefficient A numerical value that indicates the strength and direction of the relationship between two variables; ranges from +1.00 (a perfect positive correlation) to −1.00 (a perfect negative correlation).

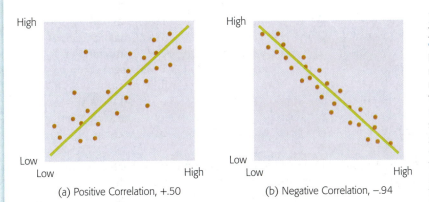

(a) Positive Correlation, +.50

(b) Negative Correlation, −.94

Figure 1.2 Positive and Negative Correlations

Here are two graphs showing positive and negative correlations. (a) When positively correlated scores on two variables are graphed, the points fall along a line that rises from left to right. This graph might represent two variables such as amount of time spent studying and grades on an exam. As study time goes up, exam grades go up as well. (b) When negatively correlated scores on two variables are graphed, the points follow a line that declines from left to right. This graph might represent two variables such as amount of time spent watching television and grades on an exam. As TV time goes up, grades go down.

Temperature is correlated with snow-cone sales. As temperature increases, so does the number of snow cones sold. Is this a positive or a negative correlation? What about the corresponding correlation between temperature and coffee sales? Is it positive or negative?

A negative correlation means that an increase in the value of one variable is associated with a decrease in the value of the other variable. For example, as mileage accumulates on a car's odometer, the less reliable it becomes. And there is a negative correlation between the number of cigarettes people smoke and the number of years they can expect to live. (For more information about correlation coefficients, see Appendix A.)

Does the fact that there is a correlation between two variables indicate that one variable causes the other? No. For instance, when two variables such as stress and illness are correlated, we cannot conclude that stress makes people sick. It might be that illness causes stress, or that a third factor such as poverty or poor general health causes people to be more susceptible to both illness and stress, as shown in **Figure 1.3**.

So, you might be thinking, if a researcher can't draw cause-effect conclusions, why do correlational studies? There are three reasons. One reason is that it is sometimes impossible, for ethical reasons, to study variables of interest using more direct methods. Scientists can't ethically ask pregnant women to drink alcohol just so they can find out whether it causes birth defects. The only option available in such cases is the correlational method. Researchers have to ask mothers about their drinking habits and note any association with birth defects in their babies. Knowing the correlation between prenatal alcohol consumption and the incidence of birth defects helps scientists make predictions about what may happen when pregnant women consume alcohol.

Another reason for using the correlational method is that many variables of interest to psychologists cannot be manipulated. Everyone wants to know whether biological sex (whether one is male or female) causes the differences we observe in men's and women's behavior. But we can't assign individuals to become male or female as we might ask them to take a drug or a placebo. Again, the only option is to study the correlations between biological sex and particular variables of interest, such as cognitive functioning and personality.

Finally, correlational studies can often be done fairly quickly. By contrast, as you will learn in the section that follows, *experiments* can be time-consuming and complex. Still, think back to Benjamin Franklin's pain—gain principle. The benefit of taking the time and trouble to carry out an experiment (the pain) is that the researcher can draw conclusions about cause-effect relationships between variables (the gain).

Figure 1.3 Correlation Does Not Prove Causation

A correlation between two variables does not prove that a cause-effect relationship exists between them. There is a correlation between stress and illness, but that does not mean that stress necessarily causes illness. Both stress and illness may result from another factor, such as poverty or poor general health.

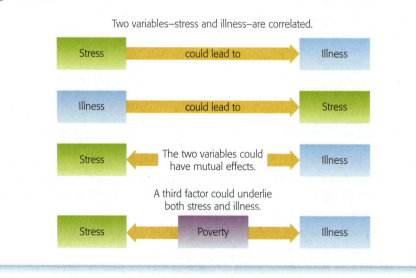

Remember It   Descriptive Research Methods

1. Which descriptive research method would be best for studying each of the following topics?

____ (1) attitudes toward racial profiling

____ (2) gender differences in how people position themselves and their belongings in the library

____ (3) physiological changes that occur during sleep

____ (4) the effects of oxygen deprivation during delivery on infant brain development

a. naturalistic observation
b. laboratory observation
c. case study
d. survey

2. One problem with the _____ is that it often does not generalize to individuals other than the subject of the study.

3. In order to be useful, a survey must be based on a _____ sample.

4. The _____ is a number describing the strength and direction of a relationship between two variables.

5. In positive correlations, two variables move in _____.

6. In negative correlations, two variables move in _____.

7. The closer a correlation coefficient is to +1.0 or −1.0, the _____ the relationship between two variables.

Answers: 1. (1) d, (2) a, (3) b, (4) c; 2. case study; 3. representative; 4. correlation coefficient; 5. the same direction; 6. opposite directions; 7. stronger

The Experimental Method

What comes to mind when you hear the word *experiment*? Many people use the word to refer to any kind of study. Among psychologists, though, the term *experiment* refers only to one kind of study, the kind in which researchers seek to determine the causes of behavior.

Experiments and Hypothesis Testing

The **experimental method** or the experiment, is the *only* research method that can be used to identify cause-effect relationships. An experiment is designed to test a **hypothesis**—a prediction about a cause-effect relationship between two or more variables. A *variable* is any condition or factor that can be manipulated, controlled, or measured. One variable of interest to you is the grade you will receive in this psychology course. Another variable that probably interests you is the amount of time you will spend studying for this course. Do you suppose there is a cause-effect relationship between the amount of time students spend studying and the grades they receive? Consider two other variables: alcohol consumption and aggression. Alcohol consumption and aggressive behavior are often observed occurring at the same time. But can we assume that alcohol consumption *causes* aggressive behavior?

Alan Lang and his colleagues (1975) conducted a classic experiment to determine if alcohol consumption itself increases aggression or if the beliefs or expectations about the effects of alcohol cause the aggressive behavior. The participants in the experiment were 96 male college students who were classified as heavy social drinkers. Half the students were given plain tonic to drink; the other half were given a vodka-and-tonic drink in amounts sufficient to raise their blood alcohol level to .10, which is higher than the .08 level that is the legal limit for intoxication in most states. Participants were assigned to four groups:

Group 1: Expected alcohol, received only tonic
Group 2: Expected alcohol, received alcohol mixed with tonic
Group 3: Expected tonic, received alcohol mixed with tonic
Group 4: Expected tonic, received only tonic

1.17 Why do researchers use experiments to test hypotheses about cause-effect relationships?

experimental method The only research method that can be used to identify cause-effect relationships between two or more conditions or variables.

hypothesis A prediction about a cause-effect relationship between two or more variables.

▲ Under what conditions might the happy, party mood of these young drinkers turn aggressive?

You might think that heavy social drinkers could detect the difference between plain tonic and a one-to-five mixture of vodka and tonic. But during a preliminary study, drinkers could distinguish between the two with no more than 50% accuracy (Marlatt & Rohsenow, 1981).

After the students had consumed the designated amount, the researchers had an accomplice, who posed as a participant, purposely provoke half the students by belittling their performance on a difficult task. All the students then participated in a learning experiment, in which the same accomplice posed as the learner. The subjects were told to administer an electric shock to the accomplice each time he made a mistake on a decoding task. Each participant was allowed to determine the intensity and duration of the "shock." (Although the students thought they were shocking the accomplice, no shocks were actually delivered.) The researchers measured the aggressiveness of the students in terms of the duration and the intensity of the shocks they chose to deliver.

What were the results of the experiment? As you might imagine, the students who had been provoked gave the accomplice stronger shocks than those who had not been provoked. But the students who drank the alcohol were not necessarily the most aggressive. Regardless of the actual content of their drinks, the participants who thought they were drinking alcohol gave significantly stronger shocks, whether provoked or not, than those who assumed they were drinking only tonic (see **Figure 1.4**). The researchers concluded that it was the *expectation* of drinking alcohol, not the alcohol itself, that caused the students to be more aggressive.

Independent and Dependent Variables

1.18 How do independent and dependent variables differ?

Recall that experiments test hypotheses about cause and effect. Examples of such hypotheses include "Studying causes good grades" and "Taking aspirin causes headaches to go away." Note that each hypothesis involves two variables: One is thought to be the cause (studying, taking aspirin), and the other is thought to be

Figure 1.4 The Mean Shock Intensity Chosen by Provoked and Unprovoked Participants

In the Lang experiment, participants who thought they were drinking alcohol chose to give significantly stronger shocks, whether provoked or not, than those who believed they were drinking only tonic.

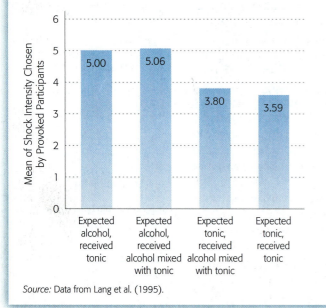
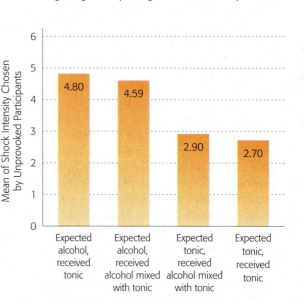

Source: Data from Lang et al. (1995).

affected by the cause. These two kinds of variables are found in all experiments. An experiment has at least one **independent variable**—a variable that the researcher believes causes a change in some other variable. The researcher deliberately manipulates the independent variable (hypothesized cause) in order to determine whether it causes any change in another behavior or condition. Sometimes the independent variable is referred to as the *treatment*. The Lang experiment had two independent variables: the alcoholic content of the drink and the expectation of drinking alcohol.

The second type of variable found in all experiments, the one that the hypothesis states is affected by the independent variable, is the **dependent variable.** It is measured at the end of the experiment and is presumed to vary (increase or decrease) as a result of the manipulations of the independent variable(s). Researchers must provide operational definitions of all variables in an experiment—that is, they must specify precisely how the variables will be observed and measured. In the Lang study, the dependent variable—aggression—was operationally defined as the intensity and duration of the "shocks" the participants chose to deliver to the accomplice.

Experimental and Control Groups

Most experiments are conducted using two or more groups of participants. There must always be at least one **experimental group**—a group of participants who are exposed to the independent variable, or the treatment. The Lang experiment used three experimental groups:

Group 1: Expected alcohol, received only tonic
Group 2: Expected alcohol, received alcohol mixed with tonic
Group 3: Expected tonic, received alcohol mixed with tonic

Most experiments also have a **control group**—a group that is similar to the experimental group and is also measured on the dependent variable at the end of the experiment, for purposes of comparison. The control group is exposed to the same experimental environment as the experimental group but is not given the treatment. The fourth group in the Lang study was exposed to neither of the two independent variables; that is, this group did not expect alcohol and did not receive alcohol. Because this group was similar to the experimental groups and was exposed to the same experimental environment, it served as a control group.

You may be wondering why a control group is necessary. Couldn't an experimenter just expose one group to the independent variable and see if there was a change? While this approach is sometimes used, it is usually preferable to have a control group because people and their behaviors often change without intervention. Having a control group reveals what kinds of changes happen "naturally" and provides a way of separating the effect of the independent variable from such changes. Say, for example, you want to find out if a certain medication relieves headaches. You could just find some people with headaches, give them the medication, and then find out how many still have headaches an hour later. But some headaches go away without treatment. So if the medication appears to work, it may only be because a number of headaches went away on their own. Having a control group allows you to know whether the medicine relieves headaches in addition to those that disappear without treatment.

Sources of Bias in Experimental Research

Can the researcher always assume that the independent variable is the cause of some change in the dependent variable? Not necessarily. Sometimes an experiment is affected by **confounding variables**—factors or conditions other than the independent variable that are not equivalent across groups and that could cause differences among the groups with respect to the dependent variable. By conducting their experiment in a laboratory, Lang and his colleagues were able to control environmental conditions such as extreme noise or heat, which could have acted as confounding variables by increasing aggressive responses. Three additional sources of confounding variables that must be controlled in all experiments are selection bias, the placebo effect, and experimenter bias.

1.19 Why are experimental and control groups necessary?

independent variable   In an experiment, a factor or condition that is deliberately manipulated in order to determine whether it causes any change in another behavior or condition.

dependent variable   The factor or condition that is measured at the end of an experiment and is presumed to vary as a result of the manipulations of the independent variable(s).

experimental group   In an experiment, the group that is exposed to an independent variable.

control group   In an experiment, a group similar to the experimental group that is exposed to the same experimental environment but is not given the treatment; used for purposes of comparison.

1.20 What kinds of factors introduce bias into experimental studies?

confounding variables Factors or conditions other than the independent variable(s) that are not equivalent across groups and could cause differences among the groups with respect to the dependent variable.

selection bias The assignment of participants to experimental or control groups in such a way that systematic differences among the groups are present at the beginning of the experiment.

random assignment The process of selecting participants for experimental and control groups by using a chance procedure to guarantee that each participant has an equal probability of being assigned to any of the groups; a control for selection bias.

placebo effect The phenomenon that occurs in an experiment when a participant's response to a treatment is due to his or her expectations about the treatment rather than to the treatment itself.

placebo (pluh-SEE-bo) An inert or harmless substance given to the control group in an experiment as a control for the placebo effect.

experimenter bias A phenomenon that occurs when a researcher's preconceived notions or expectations in some way influence participants' behavior and/or the researcher's interpretation of experimental results.

double-blind technique A procedure in which neither the participants nor the experimenter knows who is in the experimental and control groups until after the data have been gathered; a control for experimenter bias.

1.21 What are the limitations of the experimental method?

Selection Bias. Why can't researchers allow participants to choose to be in either the experimental or control group? Such a procedure would introduce *selection bias* into a study. **Selection bias** occurs when participants are assigned to experimental or control groups in such a way that systematic differences among the groups are present at the beginning of the experiment. If selection bias occurs, then differences at the end of the experiment may not reflect the change in the independent variable but may be due to pre-existing differences in the groups. To control for selection bias, researchers must use **random assignment.** This process consists of selecting participants by using a chance procedure (such as drawing the names of participants out of a hat) to guarantee that each participant has an equal probability of being assigned to any of the groups. Random assignment maximizes the likelihood that the groups will be as similar as possible at the beginning of the experiment. If there were pre-existing differences in students' levels of aggressiveness in the Lang experiment, random assignment would have spread those differences across all the groups.

The Placebo Effect. Can participants' expectations influence an experiment's results? Yes. The **placebo effect** occurs when a participant's response to a treatment is due to his or her expectations about the treatment rather than to the treatment itself. Suppose a drug is prescribed for a patient and the patient reports improvement. The improvement could be a direct result of the drug, or it could be a result of the patient's expectation that the drug will work. Studies have shown that sometimes patients' remarkable improvement can be attributed solely to the power of suggestion—the placebo effect.

In drug experiments, the control group is usually given a **placebo**—an inert or harmless substance such as a sugar pill or an injection of saline solution. To control for the placebo effect, researchers do not let participants know whether they are in the experimental group (receiving the treatment) or in the control group (receiving the placebo). If participants getting the real drug or treatment show a significantly greater improvement than those receiving the placebo, then the improvement can be attributed to the drug rather than to the participants' expectations about the drug's effects. In the Lang experiment, some students who expected alcohol mixed with tonic were given only tonic. The tonic without alcohol functioned as a placebo, allowing researchers to measure the effect of the expectations alone in producing aggression.

Experimenter Bias. What about the experimenter's expectations? **Experimenter bias** occurs when researchers' preconceived notions or expectations become a self-fulfilling prophecy and cause the researchers to find what they expect to find. A researcher's expectations can be communicated to participants, perhaps unintentionally, through tone of voice, gestures, or facial expressions. These communications can influence the participants' behavior. Expectations can also influence a researcher's interpretation of the experimental results, even if no influence occurred during the experiment. To control for experimenter bias, researchers must not know which participants are assigned to the experimental and control groups until after the research data are collected and recorded. (Obviously, someone assisting the researcher does know.) When neither the participants nor the researchers know which participants are getting the treatment and which are in the control group, the experiment is using the **double-blind technique.**

Limitations of the Experimental Method

You now know that experiments provide information about cause-effect relationships. But what are their limitations? For one thing, researchers who use the experimental method are able to exercise strict control over the setting, but the more control they exercise, the more unnatural and contrived the research setting becomes. And the more unnatural the setting becomes, the less generalizable findings may be to the real world. Another important limitation of the experimental method is that its use is either unethical or impossible for research in many areas of interest to psychologists. Some treatments cannot be given to human participants because their physical or psychological health would be endangered, or their constitutional rights violated.

What happens when we apply our knowledge about the problems associated with the experimental method to the results of Lang's study? Can we conclude that people in general tend to be more aggressive when they believe they are under the influence of alcohol? Before reaching such a conclusion, we must consider several factors: (1) All participants in this experiment were male college students. We cannot be sure that the same results would have occurred if females or males of other ages had been included. (2) The participants in this experiment were classified as heavy social drinkers. Would the same results have occurred if nondrinkers, moderate social drinkers, or alcoholics had been included? To apply this experiment's findings to other groups, researchers would have to replicate, or repeat, the experiment using different populations of subjects. (3) The amount of alcohol given to the students was just enough to bring their blood alcohol level to .10. We cannot be sure that the same results would have occurred if they had consumed more or less alcohol.

Review and Reflect summarizes the different types of research methods we've discussed in this chapter.

Review and Reflect — Research Methods in Psychology

Method	Description	Advantages	Limitations
Naturalistic and laboratory observation	Observation and recording of behavior in its natural setting or in a laboratory.	Behavior studied in everyday setting is more natural. A laboratory setting allows for precise measurement of variables. Can provide basis for hypotheses to be tested later.	Researchers' expectations can distort observations (observer bias). In a natural setting, the researcher has little or no control over conditions.
Case study	In-depth study of one or a few individuals using observation, interview, and/or psychological testing.	Source of information for rare or unusual conditions or events. Can provide a basis for hypotheses to be tested later.	May not be generalizable. Time-consuming. Subject to misinterpretation by the researcher.
Survey	Interviews and/or questionnaires used to gather information about attitudes, beliefs, experiences, or behaviors of a group of people.	Can provide accurate information about large numbers of people. Can track changes in attitudes and behavior over time.	Responses may be inaccurate. Sample may not be representative. Characteristics of the interviewer may influence responses.
Correlational method	Method used to determine the relationship (correlation) between two events, characteristics, or behaviors.	Can assess strength of the relationship between variables. Provides a basis for prediction.	Does not demonstrate cause and effect.
Experimental method	Random assignment of participants to groups. Manipulation of the independent variable(s) and measurement of the effect on the dependent variable.	Enables identification of cause-effect relationships.	Laboratory setting may inhibit natural behavior of participants. Findings may not be generalizable to the real world. In some cases, experiment is unethical or impossible.

Remember It — The Experimental Method

1. The _____ is the only research method that can be used to identify cause-effect relationships between variables.

2. In an experiment, the _____ is manipulated by the researcher, and its effects on the _____ are measured at the end of the study.

3. The _____ group sometimes receives a placebo.

4. Random assignment is used to control for _____ bias.

5. _____ bias is controlled for when researchers do not know which participants are in the experimental and control groups.

Answers: 1. experimental method; 2. independent variable, dependent variable; 3. control; 4. selection; 5. Experimenter

Participants in Psychological Research

You have learned about observer and experimenter bias in research, but were you aware that the findings of a study can be biased by the participants themselves? Furthermore, researchers are bound by ethical guidelines that specify how participants and animal subjects are supposed to be treated.

Participant-Related Bias in Psychological Research

1.22 In what ways can participants bias research results?

Do you remember reading earlier about the importance of representative samples in survey research? With other methods, representativeness becomes an issue when psychologists want to generalize the findings of studies to individuals other than the studies' participants. For example, projections by the U.S. Bureau of the Census (2000) indicate that the percentage of non-Hispanic Whites in the U.S. population is expected to decrease from 71.5% in the year 2000 to 53% in 2050. Yet, Whites are often overrepresented in psychological studies because the majority of studies with human participants in the last 30 years have drawn from the college student population (Graham, 1992), which has a lower proportion of minorities than the population in general. Moreover, college students, even those of minority ethnicity, are a relatively select group in terms of age, socioeconomic class, and educational level. Thus, they are not representative of the general population. This lack of representativeness in a research sample is a type of *participant-related bias*.

Gender bias is another type of participant-related bias. For example, Ader and Johnson (1994) found that, when conducting research in which all of the participants are of one sex, researchers typically specify the gender of the sample clearly when it is female, but not when the sample is exclusively male. Such a practice, according to Ader and Johnson, reveals a "tendency to consider male participants 'normative,' and results obtained from them generally applicable, whereas female participants are somehow 'different,' and results obtained from them are specific to female participants" (pp. 217–218). On a positive note, however, these researchers report that over the decades, gender bias in the sampling and selection of research subjects has been decreasing.

Another kind of bias happens when researchers, or consumers of research, overgeneralize the findings of a study to all members of a particular group. For example, Sandra Graham (1992) reported finding a methodological flaw—failure to include socioeconomic status—in much of the research literature comparing White Americans and African Americans. Graham pointed out that African Americans are overrepresented among the economically disadvantaged. She maintained that socioeconomic status should be incorporated into research designs "to disentangle race and social class effects" in studies that compare White and African Americans (p. 634).

Ageism is another continuing source of participant-related bias and is especially apparent in the language used in psychological research (Schaie, 1993). For example, the titles of research studies on aging often include words such as *loss, deterioration, decline,* and *dependency*. Moreover, researchers are likely to understate the great diversity among the older adults they study. According to Schaie, "most research on adulthood shows that differences between those in their 60s and those in their 80s are far greater than those between 20- and 60-year-olds" (p. 50). Researchers should guard against using descriptions or reaching conclu-

▲ College students are a convenient population from which many psychological researchers draw their participant samples. In so doing, the researchers must be careful to insure that these samples are as representative of the general population as possible. This means that their samples must include individuals from diverse racial, ethnic, cultural, and socioeconomic backgrounds.

sions that imply that all members of a given age group are defined by negative characteristics.

Protecting Research Participants' Rights

Researchers are ethically obligated to protect the rights of all study participants. In 2002, the American Psychological Association (APA) adopted a new set of ethical standards governing research with human participants so as to safeguard their rights while supporting the goals of scientific inquiry. Following are some of the main provisions of the code:

1.23 What ethical rules must researchers follow when humans are involved in studies?

- *Legality.* All research must conform to applicable federal, state, and local laws and regulations.
- *Institutional approval.* Researchers must obtain approval from all institutions involved in a study. For example, a researcher cannot conduct a study in a school without the school's approval.
- *Informed consent.* Participants must be informed of the purpose of the study and its potential for harming them. Researchers can deviate from this standard of informed consent only when they have a justifiable reason for doing so. Typically, an institutional committee examines whether there is justification for deceiving participants in a study. Most such committees find, for instance, that the use of placebos doesn't violate this standard because a placebo control group enables experimenters to more effectively measure the effects of a treatment by controlling for participants' expectations.
- *Deception.* Deception of participants is ethical when it is necessary. However, the code of ethics cautions researchers against using deception if another means can be found to test the study's hypothesis.
- *Debriefing.* Whenever a researcher deceives participants, including through the use of placebo treatments, he or she must tell participants about the deception as soon as the study is complete.
- *Clients, patients, students, and subordinates.* When participants are under another's authority (for example, a therapist's client, a patient in a hospital, a student in a psychology class, or an employee), researchers must take steps to ensure that participation in a study, and the information obtained during participation, will not damage the participants in any way. Professors, for example, cannot reduce students' grades if the students refuse to participate in a research study.
- *Payment for participation.* Participants can be paid, but the code of ethics requires that they be fully informed about what is expected in return for payment. In addition, researchers are to refrain from offering excessive payments that may bias the study's participants in some way.
- *Publication.* Psychological researchers must report their findings in an appropriate forum, such as a scientific journal, and they must make their data available to others who want to verify their findings. Even when a study produces no findings, its results must still be reported; in such cases, the appropriate forum is the institution that sponsored the research, the organization in which the research was conducted, or the agency or foundation that funded it. Results must also be made available to participants.

The Use of Animals in Research

The new APA code of ethics also includes guidelines for using animals in psychological research. Here are a few of the important provisions:

1.24 Why are animals used in research?

- *Legality.* Like research with human participants, animal research must follow all relevant federal, state, and local laws.
- *Supervision by experienced personnel.* The use of animals must be supervised by people who are trained in their care. These experienced personnel must teach all subordinates, such as research assistants, how to properly handle and feed the animals and to recognize signs of illness or distress.

- *Minimization of discomfort.* Researchers are ethically bound to minimize any discomfort to research animals. For example, it is unethical to perform surgery on research animals without appropriate anesthesia. And when researchers must terminate the lives of research animals, they must do so in a humane manner.

Even with these safeguards in place, the use of animals in research is controversial. Many animal rights advocates want all animal research stopped immediately. Books on animal rights devote an average of 63.3% of their content to the use of animals in research (Nicholl & Russell, 1990). Yet, of the approximately 6.3 million animals killed each year in the United States, only 0.3% are used in research and education, while 96.5% are used for food, 2.6% are killed by hunters, 0.4% are killed in animal shelters, and 0.2% are used for fur garments (Christensen, 1997).

In a survey of almost 4,000 randomly selected members of the APA, "80% of respondents expressed general support for psychological research on animals" (Plous, 1996, p. 1177). Among the general public, support for animal research is higher when the research is tied to human health and highest when the animals involved in such research are rats and mice rather than dogs, cats, or primates (Plous, 1996). Most agree that there are at least six reasons for using animals in research: (1) They provide a simpler model for studying processes that operate similarly in humans; (2) researchers can exercise far more control over animal subjects and thus be more certain of their conclusions; (3) a wider range of medical and other manipulations can be used with animals; (4) it is easier to study the entire life span and even multiple generations in some animal species; (5) animals are more economical to use as research subjects and are available at the researchers' convenience; and (6) some researchers simply want to learn more about the animals themselves.

▲ Most psychologists recognize that many scientific advances would not have been possible without animal research. Where do you stand on this issue?

Is animal research really necessary? Virtually all of the marvels of modern medicine are at least partially the result of experimentation using animals. Animal research has yielded much knowledge about the brain and the physiology of vision, hearing, and the other senses (Domjan & Purdy, 1995). It has also increased knowledge in the areas of learning, motivation, stress, memory, and the effects on the unborn of various drugs ingested during pregnancy. Similarly, animal research has helped psychopharmacologists better understand the side effects of drugs that are used to relieve the symptoms of serial mental illnesses such as schizophrenia (Ortega-Alvaro, Gilbert-Rahola, & Micó, 2006).

Overall, the animal rights controversy has had a positive effect on research ethics: It has served to increase concern for the treatment of animals as research subjects and to stimulate a search for alternative research methods that is reportedly resulting in a decrease in the numbers of animals needed (Mukerjee, 1997, p. 86).

Remember It — Participants in Psychological Research

1. Psychologists are required to debrief participants thoroughly after a study involving _____.

2. _____, _____, and _____ have been overrepresented in many kinds of psychological studies.

3. By using _____ in research, researchers have learned a great deal about topics such as the effects of drugs ingested during pregnancy.

Answers: 1. deception; 2. Whites, males, college students; 3. animals

Current Trends in Psychology

Do we know everything there is to know about psychology today? Absolutely not. Like the field of medicine, psychology is an evolving science in which new theories are being tested and more precise research is being conducted every day. Its ongoing advances will continue to illuminate our thinking and impact our behaviors. So, where is psychology headed today? In addition to the continuing influence of psychodynamic theory, behaviorism, humanistic psychology, and cognitive psychology, several other important trends in psychology have emerged in recent years.

Evolutionary Psychology

Why do you think all healthy babies form attachments to their primary caregivers? Why do you think most men prefer mates who are younger than they are? These are the kinds of questions that interest *evolutionary psychologists*. **Evolutionary psychology** focuses on how the human behaviors required for survival have adapted in the face of environmental pressures over the long course of evolution (Archer, 1996). As such, evolutionary psychology draws heavily upon Charles Darwin's theory of natural selection. Darwin's theory asserts that individual members of a given species who possess characteristics that help them survive are the most likely to pass on the genes underlying those characteristics to subsequent generations. As a result, traits that support individual survival become universal in the species, that is, every individual member of the species has them. For example, every human being possesses the capacity to acquire language. Natural selection would explain this universality as the result of the survival advantage conferred upon humans by having an efficient means of communicating information from one person to another.

Evolutionary psychology has been called, simply, a combination of evolutionary biology and cognitive psychology (Barker, 2006; Evans & Zarate, 2000). Two widely recognized proponents of evolutionary psychology, Leda Cosmides and John Tooby, hold that this perspective combines the forces of evolutionary biology, anthropology, cognitive psychology, and neuroscience. They explain that an evolutionary perspective can be applied to any topic within the field of psychology (Cosmides & Tooby, 2000). For example, one of the most influential evolutionary psychologists, David Buss, and his colleagues have conducted a number of fascinating studies examining men's and women's patterns of behavior in romantic relationships (1999, 2000a, 2000b, 2001, 2005). You'll read more about Buss's work and that of his critics in Chapter 11.

1.25 **What is the main idea behind evolutionary psychology?**

◀ According to evolutionary psychology, natural selection has provided infants and caregivers with a built-in genetic predisposition to form an emotional attachment to one another because such bonds help infants survive.

evolutionary psychology The school of psychology that studies how humans have adapted the behaviors required for survival in the face of environmental pressures over the long course of evolution.

biological psychology The school of psychology that looks for links between specific behaviors and equally specific biological processes that often help explain individual differences.

Biological (Physiological) Psychology

Sometimes students are confused about the difference between evolutionary psychology and **biological psychology** (also referred to as *physiological psychology*). After all, many think, isn't evolution "biological" in nature? Yes, it is, but evolutionary psychology provides explanations of how certain biologically based behaviors came to be

1.26 **How is biological psychology changing the field of psychology?**

common in an entire species. Consequently, it focuses on *universals*, traits that exist in every member of a species. For instance, language is a human universal.

By contrast, biological psychologists look for links between specific behaviors and particular biological factors that often help explain *individual differences*. They study the structures of the brain and central nervous system, the functioning of neurons, the delicate balance of neurotransmitters and hormones, and the effects of heredity to look for links between these biological factors and behavior. For example, the number of ear infections children have in the first year of life (a *biological* individual difference) is correlated with learning disabilities in the elementary school years (a *behavioral* individual difference) (Spreen et al., 1995). (Remember, this finding doesn't mean that ear infections *cause* learning disabilities; most likely, some other factor links the two.)

Many biological psychologists work under the umbrella of an interdisciplinary field known as **neuroscience.** Neuroscience combines the work of psychologists, biologists, biochemists, medical researchers, and others in the study of the structure and function of the nervous system. Important findings in psychology have resulted from this work. For example, researchers have learned that defects in nerve cell membranes interfere with the cells' ability to make use of brain chemicals that help us control body movement (Kurup & Kurup, 2002). These findings shed light on the physiological processes underlying serious neurological disorders such as Parkinson's disease and help pharmacological researchers in their efforts to create more effective medications for these disorders. And the recently completed map of the human genome promises to provide new explanations for many mental illnesses (Plomin et al., 2003).

The Sociocultural Approach

1.27 What kinds of variables interest psychologists who take a sociocultural approach?

How do your background and cultural experiences affect your behavior and mental processing? Just as important as the current trend toward biological explanations is the growing realization among psychologists that social and cultural forces may be as powerful as evolutionary and physiological factors. The **sociocultural approach** emphasizes social and cultural influences on human behavior and stresses the importance of understanding those influences when interpreting the behavior of others. For example, several psychologists (e.g., Tweed & Lehman, 2002) have researched philosophical differences between Asian and Western cultures that may help explain cross-national achievement differences. You will learn more about their findings in Chapter 7.

Social and cultural influences on behavior are often studied within the broader context of a *systems perspective*. The primary idea behind the systems approach is that multiple factors work together holistically; that is, their combined, interactive influences on behavior are greater than the sum of the individual factors that make up the system. A good example of the systems approach may be found in a theory proposed by psychologist Gerald Patterson and his colleagues that explains how variables interact to predispose some teenagers to antisocial behavior (Granic & Patterson, 2006). This systems approach argues that poverty (a sociocultural factor), for example, is predictive of juvenile delinquency, but, in and of itself, it is insufficient to produce the behavior. As a result, most teens from poor families do not engage in antisocial behavior. However, poverty may function as part of a system of influential variables that includes disengagement from school, association with peers who encourage antisocial behavior, lack of parental supervision, and a host of other variables to increase the risk of antisocial behavior for individual teenagers. At the same time, these variables interact to maintain themselves and, in some cases, to create a multigenerational cycle. For instance, disengagement from school increases the likelihood that teenagers will live in poverty when they reach adulthood. Poverty, in turn, increases the chances that they will have to work long hours, rendering them less able to supervise their own children's behavior, thus putting another generation at risk for antisocial behavior.

neuroscience An interdisciplinary field that combines the work of psychologists, biologists, biochemists, medical researchers, and others in the study of the structure and function of the nervous system.

sociocultural approach The view that social and cultural factors may be just as powerful as evolutionary and physiological factors in affecting behavior and mental processing and that these factors must be understood when interpreting the behavior of others.

Psychological Perspectives and Eclecticism

The views of modern psychologists are frequently difficult to categorize into traditional schools of thought. Thus, rather than discussing schools of thought, it is often
more useful to refer to **psychological perspectives**—general points of view used for
explaining people's behavior and thinking, whether normal or abnormal. So, for example, a psychologist may adopt a behavioral perspective without necessarily agree-
ing with all of Watson's or Skinner's ideas. What is important is that the psychologist
taking such a view will explain behavior in terms of environmental forces.

The major perspectives in psychology today and the kinds of variables each emphasizes in explaining behavior are as follows:

- *Behavioral perspective*—environmental factors
- *Psychoanalytic perspective*—emotions, unconscious motivations, early childhood ex-
  periences
- *Humanistic perspective*—subjective experiences, intrinsic motivation to achieve self-
  actualization
- *Cognitive perspective*—mental processes
- *Evolutionary perspective*—inherited traits that enhance adaptability
- *Biological perspective*—biological structures, processes, heredity
- *Sociocultural perspective*—social and cultural variables

Review and Reflect lists these perspectives along with an illustration of how each
might explain older adults' poor performance on researchers' memory tasks as compared to that of younger adults.

Psychologists need not limit themselves to only one perspective or approach. Many
take an *eclectic* (or integrative) *position*, choosing a combination of approaches to explain

1.28 What are psycho-
logical perspectives, and
how are they related to an
eclectic position?

psychological perspectives
General points of view used for
explaining people's behavior and
thinking, whether normal or
abnormal.

Review and Reflect   Major Perspectives in Psychology

Perspective	Emphasis	Explanation of Older Adults' Poor Performance on Researchers' Memory Tasks
Behavioral	The role of environment in shaping and controlling behavior	Older adults spend little or no time in environments such as school, where they would be reinforced for using their memories.
Psychoanalytic	The role of unconscious motivation and early childhood experiences in determining behavior and thought	Older adults' unconscious fear of impending death inter-feres with memory processes.
Humanistic	The importance of an individual's subjective experience as a key to understanding his or her behavior	Older adults are more concerned about finding meaning in their lives than about performing well on experimenters' memory tasks.
Cognitive	The role of mental processes—perception, thinking, and memory—that underlie behavior	Older adults fail to use effective memory strategies.
Evolutionary	The roles of inherited tendencies that have proven adap-tive in humans	Declines in cognitive and biological functions are pro-grammed into our genes so that younger, and presum-ably reproductively healthier, people will be more attrac-tive as potential mates.
Biological	The role of biological processes and structures, as well as heredity, in explaining behavior	As the brain ages, connections between neurons break down, causing a decline in intellectual functions such as memory.
Sociocultural	The roles of social and cultural influences on behavior	Older people have internalized the ageist expectations of society and, as a result, expect themselves to perform poorly on memory tasks.

▲ A sociocultural approach helps psychologists explain cross-cultural differences in behavior.

a particular behavior (Norcross, Karpiak, & Lister, 2005). For example, a psychologist may explain a behavior in terms of both environmental factors and mental processes. A child's unruly behavior in school may be seen as maintained by teacher attention (a behavioral explanation) but as initially caused by an emotional reaction to a family event such as divorce (a psychoanalytic explanation). By adopting multiple perspectives, psychologists are able to devise more complex theories and research studies, resulting in improved treatment strategies. In this way, their theories and studies can more closely mirror the behavior of real people in real situations.

Remember It   Current Trends in Psychology

1. A(n) _____ psychologist would be interested in whether attachment is a universal feature of infant-caregiver relations.

2. A(n) _____ psychologist would be interested in the relationship between hormones and aggressive behavior.

3. A(n) _____ psychologist would be interested in whether members of minority groups have lower self-esteem than those who belong to a dominant group.

4. Which of the following statements represent an eclectic position?

a. Individual differences in aggression are genetic, but parents and teachers can teach highly aggressive children to be less so.

b. Children who are highly aggressive have not received enough punishment for their inappropriate behavior.

c. Aggressive children are probably using aggression to release pent-up feelings of frustration.

d. Going through a trauma like parental divorce may lead to increased aggression in children because they are feeling anxious.

Answers: 1. evolutionary; 2. biological; 3. sociocultural; 4. a, d

Psychologists at Work

Psychology is a fascinating field. So fascinating, in fact, that many people choose careers that involve learning more about human behavior and mental processes or using psychological principles to improve people's lives. Most such careers require graduate degrees, but there are many job opportunities for undergraduate psychology majors, too.

Specialties in Psychology

1.29 What are some of the specialists working within psychology?

Wherever you find human activity, you are very likely to encounter psychologists. These professionals work in a number of specialties, most of which require a master's or a doctoral degree.

Clinical psychologists specialize in the diagnosis and treatment of mental and behavioral disorders, such as anxiety, phobias, and schizophrenia. Some also conduct research in these areas. Most clinical psychologists work in clinics, hospitals, or private practices, but many hold professorships at colleges and universities.

Counseling psychologists help people who have adjustment problems (marital, social, or behavioral) that are generally less severe than those handled by clinical psychologists. Counseling psychologists may also provide academic or vocational counseling. Counselors usually work in a nonmedical setting such as a school or university, or they may have a private practice. Approximately 53% of all psychologists in the United States may be classified as either clinical or counseling psychologists (APA, 2003).

Physiological psychologists, also called *biological psychologists* or *neuropsychologists*, study the relationship between physiological processes and behavior. They study the structure and function of the brain and central nervous system, the role of neurotransmitters and hormones, and other aspects of body chemistry to determine how physical and chemical processes affect behavior in both people and animals.

Experimental psychologists specialize in the use of experimental research methods. They conduct experiments in most areas of psychology—learning, memory, sensation, perception, motivation, emotion, and others. Some experimental psychologists study the brain and nervous system and how they affect behavior; their work overlaps with that of physiological psychologists. Experimental psychologists usually work in a laboratory, where they can exert precise control over the humans or animals being studied. Many experimental psychologists teach and conduct their research as faculty members at colleges or universities. In most of their psychology laboratories, however, the array of laboratory fixtures of the past, such as specimen jars, "have been replaced largely by a single instrument, the computer" (Benjamin, 2000, p. 321).

▲ Can you guess what type of psychologist is pictured here?

Developmental psychologists study how people grow, develop, and change throughout the life span. Some developmental psychologists specialize in a particular age group, such as infants, children (child psychologists), adolescents, or the elderly (gerontologists). Others may concentrate on a specific aspect of human development, such as physical, language, cognitive, or moral development.

Educational psychologists specialize in the study of teaching and learning. They may help train teachers and other educational professionals or conduct research in teaching and classroom behavior. Some help prepare school curricula, develop achievement tests, or conduct evaluations of teaching and learning.

Whereas most other psychologists are concerned with what makes the individual function, *social psychologists* investigate how the individual feels, thinks, and behaves in a social setting—in the presence of others.

Industry and business have found that expertise in psychology pays off in the workplace. *Industrial/organizational (I/O) psychologists* study the relationships between people and their work environments. You can read more about this subfield in Chapter 17.

Majoring in Psychology

Have you considered majoring in psychology? Many students do. In fact, the number of undergraduate degrees awarded in psychology is second only to the number awarded in business administration (APA, 1995; Horn & Zahn, 2001).

As mentioned earlier, professional psychologists have graduate degrees. The American Psychological Association reports that it takes about 5 years of study beyond the bachelor's degree to obtain a doctoral degree in psychology (APA, 2000). However, there are many jobs open to those with a bachelor's degree in psychology. **Figure 1.5** shows the variety of job settings in which individuals with undergraduate degrees in psychology are employed. And many men and women who intend to go on to postgraduate work in other fields—law, for example—major in psychology.

You may have wondered what kinds of courses are offered for psychology majors. One of the purposes of an introductory course in psychology is to survey the subfields

1.30 What kinds of employment opportunities are available for psychology majors?

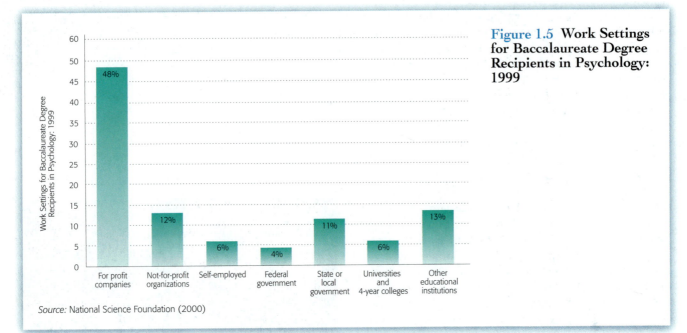

Figure 1.5 Work Settings for Baccalaureate Degree Recipients in Psychology: 1999

Source: National Science Foundation (2000)

in which more advanced courses are offered (Brewer et al., 1993). The contents of this textbook provide a good guide to the kinds of courses you would take if you majored in psychology. Table 1.1 provides an overview of the various components of a bachelor's degree program in psychology.

Table 1.1 Components of the Major in Psychology

Foundations Courses	Intermediate and Advanced Courses	Capstone Experiences
These courses are typically required of all students majoring in psychology. Many programs accept transfer courses from community colleges that fulfill these requirements. • Introduction to Psychology • Research Methods • Statistics	Students choose courses from broad domains such as those listed below. Some programs require at least one course in each of several such domains. In some programs, students may transfer intermediate (sophomore level) coursework from community colleges to satisfy some of these requirements. However, all bachelor's degree programs require a minimum number of junior- and senior-level courses regardless of how many credits a student transfers in. • Learning and Cognition • Individual Differences, Psychometrics, Personality, Social and Cultural Processes • Biological Bases of Behavior, Sensation, Perception, Animal Behavior, Motivation, Emotion • Developmental Changes across the Life Span	Some programs require a capstone experience in which seniors in the major are expected to integrate the knowledge and skills they have learned in prior courses. Other programs offer capstone experiences as options that may count toward advanced course requirements. Capstone experiences may include one or more of these: • History and Systems in Psychology (senior-level course) • Community Service • Senior Thesis • Research Practicum

Sources: Halonen et al., 2002; Brewer et al., 1993

Remember It   Psychologists at Work

1. The number of undergraduate degrees awarded in psychology is _____ only to those awarded in business administration.

2. There are _____ job opportunities for college graduates who major in psychology.

Answers: 1. second; 2. many

Apply It   Best Practices for Effective Studying

Decades of research on learning and memory have uncovered a number of strategies that you can use, in addition to the SQ3R method, to make your study time more efficient and effective.

- Establish a quiet place, free of distractions, where you do nothing else but study. You can condition yourself to associate this environment with studying, so that entering the room or area will be your cue to begin work.

- Schedule your study time. Research on memory has proven that spaced learning is more effective than massed practice (cramming). Instead of studying for 5 hours straight, try five study sessions of 1 hour each.

- To be prepared for each class meeting, set specific goals for yourself each week and for individual study sessions. Your goals should be challenging but not overwhelming. If the task for an individual study session is manageable, it will be easier to sit down and face it. Completing the task you have set for yourself will give you a sense of accomplishment.

- The more active a role you play in the learning process, the more you will remember. Spend some of your study time reciting rather than rereading the material. One effective method is to use index cards as flash cards. Write a key term or study question on the front of each card. On the back, list pertinent information from the text and class lectures. Use these cards to help you prepare for tests.

- *Overlearning* means studying beyond the point at which you can just barely recite the information you are trying to memorize. Review the information again and again until it is firmly locked in memory. If you are subject to test anxiety, overlearning will help.

- Forgetting takes place most rapidly within the first 24 hours after you study. No matter how much you have studied for a test, always review shortly before you take it. Refreshing your memory will raise your grade.

- Sleeping immediately after you study will help you retain more of what you have learned. If you can't study before you go to sleep, at least review what you studied earlier in the day. This is also a good time to go through your index cards.

Once you've mastered these study strategies, use them to improve your comprehension and success in all of your courses.

REVIEW: After you have read each section of the chapter and followed the previous steps, review the Summary and Review section at the end of the chapter. Review the list of key terms and turn back to the page where the term is defined and review that section if you find you cannot recite the term's meaning.

Summary and Review

An Introduction to *The World of Psychology* p. 5

1.1 How can the SQ3R method help you study more effectively? p. 6

The steps of the SQ3R method—survey, question, read, review, and recite—provide students with a systematic approach to studying the text. Using such an approach helps students manage their time more efficiently and gives them a sense of control over their learning and academic performance.

1.2 What process do scientists use to answer questions about behavior and mental processes? p. 7

The scientific method consists of the orderly, systematic procedures researchers follow as they identify a research problem, design a study to investigate the problem, collect and analyze data, draw conclusions, and communicate their findings.

1.3 What are the goals of psychology? p. 8

The four goals of psychology are the description, explanation, prediction, and influence of behavior and mental processes.

Exploring Psychology's Roots p. 9

1.4 What roles did Wundt and Titchener play in the founding of psychology? p. 10

Wundt, who is considered the "father" of psychology, established the first psychological laboratory in 1879 and launched the study of psychology as a formal academic discipline. One of his students, Titchener, founded the school of thought called structuralism.

1.5 Why is functionalism important in the history of psychology? p. 10

Functionalism, founded by William James, was the first American school of psychology and broadened the scope of the field to include examination of behavior as well as conscious mental processes.

1.6 In what ways have women and minorities shaped the field of psychology, both in the past and today? p. 11

Early female and minority psychologists had to overcome significant educational and professional barriers to work in the field. Still, many of these individuals made noteworthy contributions.

Schools of Thought in Psychology p. 13

1.7 How do behaviorists explain behavior and mental processes? p. 13

Behaviorists, adherents of the school of psychology founded by John B. Watson, view observable, measurable behavior as the only appropriate subject matter for psychology. Behaviorism also emphasizes the environment as the key determinant of behavior.

1.8 What do psychoanalytic psychologists believe about the role of the unconscious? p. 14

According to Freud's theory of psychoanalysis, an individual's thoughts, feelings, and behavior are determined primarily by the unconscious—the part of the mind that one cannot see and cannot control.

1.9 According to Maslow and Rogers, what motivates human behavior and mental processes? p. 14

The humanistic theories of Maslow and Rogers focus on the uniqueness of human beings and their capacity for choice, personal growth, and psychological health. Humans are motivated by the need for self-actualization.

1.10 What is the focus of cognitive psychology? p. 14

Cognitive psychology is an influential school that focuses on mental processes such as memory, problem solving, concept formation, reasoning and decision making, language, and perception.

Thinking About Theories and Research p. 16

1.11 How do psychologists evaluate theories? p. 16

Psychologists evaluate theories in terms of their usefulness. Useful theories generate testable hypotheses and practical solutions to problems. Theories possessing heuristic value are useful for stimulating debate and research.

1.12 How can critical thinking be used to interpret media reports of psychological research? p. 17

Critical thinkers are independent, able to suspend judgment, and willing to change prior beliefs. They also use knowledge of research methods to evaluate research findings reported in the news media.

Descriptive Research Methods p. 18

1.13 How do psychological researchers use naturalistic and laboratory observation? p. 18

In naturalistic observation, researchers observe and record the behavior of human participants or animal subjects in a natural setting without attempting to influence or control it. In laboratory observation, researchers exert more control and use more precise equipment to measure responses.

1.14 What are the advantages and disadvantages of the case study? p. 19

The case study is appropriate for studying people with rare psychological or physiological disorders or brain injuries. Disadvantages of this method include the time and expense involved and lack of generalizability.

1.15 How do researchers ensure that survey results are useful? p. 19

To be useful, surveys must involve a sample that is representative of the population to which the results will be applied.

1.16 What are the strengths and weaknesses of the correlational method? p. 21

When the correlation between two variables is known, information about one variable can be used to predict the other. However, a correlation cannot be used to support the conclusion that either variable causes the other.

The Experimental Method p. 23

1.17 Why do researchers use experiments to test hypotheses about cause-effect relationships? p. 23

The experimental method is the only research method that can identify cause-effect relationships.

1.18 How do independent and dependent variables differ? p. 24

In an experiment, an independent variable is a condition or factor manipulated by the researcher to determine its effect on the dependent variable.

1.19 Why are experimental and control groups necessary? p. 25

Comparing experimental and control groups allows researchers to judge the effects of the independent variable(s) compared to outcomes that occur naturally or in the presence of a placebo.

1.20 What kinds of factors introduce bias into experimental studies? p. 25

Environmental factors, such as heat or noise, can be a source of bias. Selection bias occurs when there are systematic differences among the groups before the experiment begins. The placebo effect occurs when a person's expectations influence the outcome of a treatment or experiment. Experimenter bias occurs when the researcher's expectations affect the outcome of the experiment.

1.21 What are the limitations of the experimental method? p. 26

Experiments are often conducted in unnatural settings, a factor that limits the generalizability of results. Also, this method may be unethical or impossible to use for some reseach.

Participants in Psychological Research p. 28

1.22 In what ways can participants bias research results? p. 28

Participant-related bias happens when researchers fail to include underrepresented groups in their samples.

1.23 What ethical rules must researchers follow when humans are involved in studies? p. 29

All research must conform to applicable laws and regulations. Researchers must obtain approval from all institutions involved in the study. Participants must give informed consent, may not be deceived unless necessary, and, if deceived, must be debriefed as soon as possible after they participate. Subordinates' participation in a study may not negatively affect them in any way. Participants may be paid after being fully informed about what is expected in return for payment. Researchers must report their findings in an appropriate forum, and results must be made available to participants.

1.24 Why are animals used in research? p. 29

Animals provide a simpler model for studying similar processes in humans; researchers can exercise more control over animals and use a wider range of medical and other manipulations.

Current Trends in Psychology p. 31

1.25 What is the main idea behind evolutionary psychology? p. 31

Evolutionary psychology focuses on how human behaviors necessary for survival have adapted in the face of environmental pressures over the course of evolution.

1.26 How is biological psychology changing the field of psychology? p. 31

Biological psychologists look for connections between specific behaviors (such as aggression) and particular biological factors (such as hormone levels) to help explain individual differences. Using modern technology, biological psychologists have discovered relationships between biological and behavioral variables that have resulted in more effective medications for certain disorders and new insight into the genetic base of many mental illnesses.

1.27 What kinds of variables interest psychologists who take a sociocultural approach? p. 32

The sociocultural approach focuses on how factors such as cultural values affect people's behavior.

1.28 What are psychological perspectives, and how are they related to an eclectic position? p. 33

Psychological perspectives are general points of view used for explaining people's behavior and thinking. In taking an eclectic position, psychologists use a combination of two or more perspectives to explain a particular behavior.

Psychologists at Work p. 34

1.29 What are some of the specialists working within psychology? p. 34

There are clinical and counseling psychologists, physiological psychologists, experimental psychologists, developmental psychologists, educational psychologists, social psychologists, and industrial/organizational (I/O) psychologists.

1.30 What kinds of employment opportunities are available for psychology majors? p. 35

Individuals with bachelor's degrees in psychology are employed in many different settings—colleges and universities, elementary and secondary schools, medical settings, public affairs, sales, and business management. Majoring in psychology is also good preparation for postgraduate study in other fields (for example, law).

Thinking Critically about Psychology

1. Consider three of the major forces in psychology: behaviorism, psychoanalysis, and humanistic psychology. Which appeals to you most, which least, and why?
2. Suppose you hear on the news that a researcher claims to have "proven" that day care is harmful to infants. How could you use what you've learned in this chapter to evaluate this statement?
3. If you become a psychologist, in which area (developmental, educational, clinical, counseling, social, etc.) would you specialize? Why?

Key Terms

Chapter 2

Biology and Behavior

The Neurons and the Neurotransmitters

The Human Nervous System

Discovering the Brain's Mysteries

A Closer Look at the Brain

Continued

Do you look forward to turning 60? Most of us dread getting older. For Nancy Wexler, though, her 60th birthday was the happiest of her adult life (Wexler, 2005). Why? Wexler's mother, Leonore Wexler, along with three uncles, her grandfather, and great-grandfather, had died from an inherited neurological disorder called *Huntington's disease (HD)*. The symptoms of this fatal disease include progressive deterioration of the sufferer's cognitive and motor functioning, including jerky movements and clumsiness sometimes called *chorea*. These symptoms result from a buildup of a toxic protein inside the cells of the brain and typically first appear between the ages of 40 and 60. Thus, when Nancy Wexler turned 60 without having exhibited any symptoms of the disease, she knew that it was unlikely she would be stricken by it.

Because of the Wexler family's personal experience with HD, the search for a cure has been a central feature of the lives of the entire family, including Nancy's father, Melvin Wexler, a clinical psychologist, and her sister, Alice Wexler, a historian who is affiliated with the Center for the Study of Women at the University of California at Los Angeles. In 1996, Alice Wexler told her family's story in a touching memoir, *Mapping Fate: A Memoir of Family, Risk, and Genetic Research*. Their story provides a compelling example of the way in which a personal tragedy sometimes inspires people to do great things. Here are a few highlights.

To increase his earning potential, Milton Wexler moved his psychotherapy practice from the Menninger Clinic in Kansas to the affluent neighborhood of west Los Angeles in the early 1960s. Extra money was needed in the Wexler household be-cause Leonore Wexler's three brothers suffered from HD, and Melvin had assumed financial responsibility for their treatment. Shortly after the family moved to California, though, Leonore began to show changes in personality. She had always been outgoing and optimistic, but suddenly, her moods turned melancholy. She insisted on divorcing Melvin and even attempted suicide. At the same time, her cognitive functioning began to deteriorate. The once-brilliant chemist had difficulty with simple daily tasks such as keeping track of money. Declines in Leonore's motor functions followed those in the emotional and cognitive domains. One morning, a police officer saw her staggering down a street in west Los Angeles and thought she might be intoxicated. This incident and others like it led Melvin, who had maintained a close relationship with his ex-wife, to urge Leonore to see a physician about her mounting problems. Ultimately, she was diagnosed with HD in 1968 and died of the disease 10 years later.

In response to his ex-wife's diagnosis, Melvin Wexler embarked on a quest to understand HD. Together with Nancy and Alice, he founded the Hereditary Disease Foundation in 1968. The primary goal of the foundation was to fund research aimed at understanding the genetic and biochemical nature of HD and finding effective treatments for it. To that end, Melvin enlisted the aid of the many wealthy celebrities, artists, writers, and film industry executives who had been clients in his private psychotherapy practice. With their financial help, he funded meetings of researchers, who brainstormed new approaches to the disease. As a result, scientific research on HD gained considerable momentum by the mid-1970s.

To find the gene that caused HD, however, researchers needed to find a large family with many living members who suffered from the disease. As a result of viewing a film shown at a medical conference in 1972, Nancy Wexler learned of a Venezuelan family that perfectly fit this description. By 1979, she had obtained funding for a comprehensive genetic study of the family and had made the first of many journeys in which she personally transported blood samples from Venezuela to the United States. In 1983, researchers identified a tiny bit of chromosomal material that could be used to distinguish individuals who carried the HD gene from their relatives who did not have this gene. Ten years later, researchers located the gene itself, which facilitated the development of an affordable test for the HD gene.

Thanks to the work of the Hereditary Disease Foundation, people whose relatives have had the disease no longer have to wait until symptoms appear to determine their own risk of developing it. Tests can detect the presence of the HD gene in a person's body at any age, even before birth. Having the HD gene means that an individual's risk of developing the disease is 100%.

Do you think you would get the test if you had a family member who suffered from HD? You might be surprised to learn that a minority of such individuals choose to be tested ("Way to delay . . . ," 1999). The reasons for their reluctance are not fully understood. However, it is likely that many of them have observed the effects of HD firsthand. As a result, they believe that the stress of knowing that they will develop the incurable, devastating disease will inhibit their ability to enjoy any remaining healthy years of their lives. Experts argue that, when a cure or effective treatment for the symptoms is found, many more people will opt to be tested.

Ironically, like the majority of individuals from HD-afflicted families, Nancy and Alice Wexler refused to be tested when the HD gene was discovered, even though they had devoted a significant portion of their adult lives to the research that ultimately produced the test. Melvin Wexler explained his agreement with his daughters' decision as resulting from the human need to maintain a sense of hope (Avins, 1999). That sense of hope, he argued, was vital both to their family's mental health and to their work with the Hereditary Disease Foundation. Although he is nearing 100 years of age, Melvin continues to serve as the foundation's chief executive officer. Nancy is the foundation's president, and Alice is a member of the governing board. Recent research sponsored by the foundation has encouraged the Wexlers and others interested in the disease to believe that effective treatments can and will be found in the very near future (see http://www.hdfoundation.org).

The effects of disorders such as Huntington's disease on the lives of those who suffer from them illustrate the vital link between biology and behavior. For this reason, students of psychology must have some familiarity with the biological components of psychological and behavioral processes to achieve any understanding of psychology. Therefore, this chapter introduces you to some of the most basic components: the nervous system, the endocrine system, and the mechanisms through which genetic traits are passed from one generation to the next.

The Neurons and the Neurotransmitters

Every thought you think, every emotion you feel, every sensation you experience, every decision you reach, every move you make—in short, all of human behavior—is rooted in a biological event. The story begins where the action begins, in the smallest functional unit of the brain—the nerve cell, or neuron.

The Structure of the Neuron

All our thoughts, feelings, and behavior can ultimately be traced to the activity of **neurons**—the specialized cells that conduct impulses through the nervous system. Neurons perform several important tasks: (1) *Afferent* (sensory) neurons relay messages from the sense organs and receptors—eyes, ears, nose, mouth, and skin—to the brain or spinal cord; (2) *efferent* (motor) neurons convey signals from the central nervous system to the glands and the muscles, enabling the body to move; and (3) *interneurons*, thousands of times more numerous than motor or sensory neurons, carry information between neurons in the brain and between neurons in the spinal cord.

Anatomy of a Neuron. Although no two neurons are exactly alike, nearly all are made up of three important parts: the cell body, the dendrites, and the axon. The **cell body,** or *soma,* contains the nucleus and carries out the metabolic, or life-sustaining, functions of a neuron. Branching out from the cell body are the **dendrites,** which look much like the leafless branches of a tree (*dendrite* comes from the Greek word for "tree"). The dendrites are the primary receivers of signals from other neurons, but the cell body can also receive signals directly.

The **axon** is the slender, tail-like extension of the neuron that sprouts into many branches, each ending in a bulbous axon terminal. Signals move from the axon terminals to the dendrites or cell bodies of other neurons and to muscles, glands, and other parts of the body. In humans, some axons are short—only thousandths of an inch long. Others can be as long as a meter (39.37 inches)—long enough to reach from the brain to the tip of the spinal cord, or from the spinal cord to remote parts of the body. **Figure 2.1** shows a neuron's structure.

Supporting the Neurons. **Glial cells** are specialized cells in the brain and spinal cord that hold the neurons together. They are smaller than neurons and make up more than one-half the volume of the human brain. Glial cells remove waste products, such as dead neurons, from the brain by engulfing and digesting them, and they handle other manufacturing, nourishing, and cleanup tasks. Glial cells in the spinal cord are also involved in the transmission of pain sensations from the various parts of the body to the brain (Spataro et al., 2004).

▲ This scanning electron micrograph shows numerous axon terminals (the orange, button-shaped structures) that could synapse with the cell body of the neuron (shown in green).

neuron   (NEW-ron) A specialized cell that conducts impulses through the nervous system and contains three major parts—a cell body, dendrites, and an axon.

cell body   The part of a neuron that contains the nucleus and carries out the metabolic functions of the neuron.

dendrites   (DEN-drytes) In a neuron, the branchlike extensions of the cell body that receive signals from other neurons.

Communication between Neurons

Remarkably, the billions of neurons that send and receive signals are not physically connected. The axon terminals are separated from the receiving neurons by tiny, fluid-filled gaps called *synaptic clefts*. The **synapse** is the junction where the axon terminal of a sending (presynaptic) neuron communicates with a receiving (postsynaptic) neuron across the synaptic cleft. There may be as many as 100 trillion synapses in the human nervous system (Swanson, 1995). And a single neuron may synapse with thousands of other neurons (Kelner, 1997). A technique that has recently been developed to monitor the action at the synapses may soon enable researchers to visualize the activity of all the synapses of a single neuron. If neurons aren't connected, how do they communicate with one another?

The Neural Impulse. Researchers have known for over 200 years that cells in the brain, the spinal cord, and the muscles generate electrical potentials. These tiny electric charges play a part in all bodily functions. Every time you move a muscle, experience a sensation, or have a thought or a feeling, a small but measurable electrical impulse is present.

How does this biological electricity work? Even though the impulse that travels down the axon is electrical, the axon does not transmit it the same way a wire conducts an electrical current. What actually changes is the permeability of the cell membrane (its capability of being penetrated or passed through). In other words, the membrane changes in a way that makes it easier for molecules to move through it and into the cell.

axon   (AK-sahn) The slender, tail-like extension of the neuron that transmits signals to the dendrites or cell body of other neurons and to muscles, glands, and other parts of the body.

glial cells   (GLEE-ul) Specialized cells in the brain and spinal cord that hold neurons together, remove waste products such as dead neurons, and perform other manufacturing, nourishing, and cleanup tasks.

synapse   (SIN-aps) The junction where the axon terminal of a sending neuron communicates with a receiving neuron across the synaptic cleft.

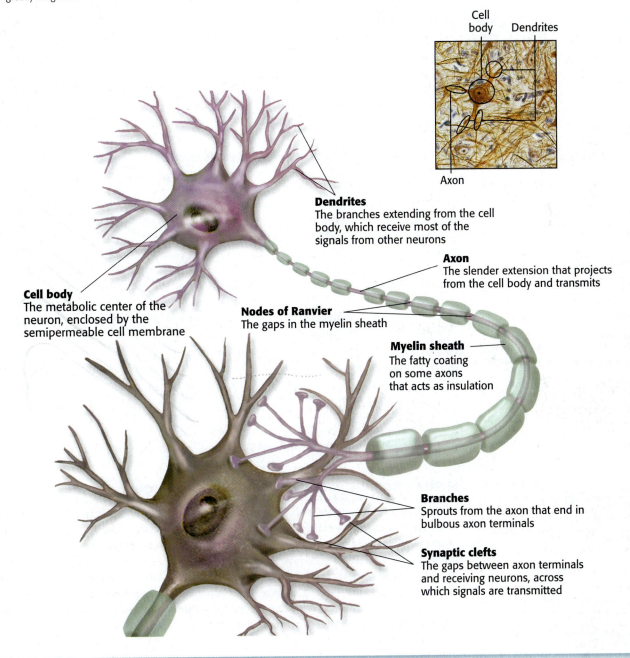

Figure 2.1 The Structure of a Typical Neuron

A typical neuron has three important parts: (1) a cell body, which carries out the metabolic functions of the neuron; (2) branched fibers called dendrites, which are the primary receivers of the impulses from other neurons; and (3) a slender, tail-like extension called an axon, the transmitting end of the neuron, which sprouts into many branches, each ending in an axon terminal. The photograph shows human neurons greatly magnified.

Cell body   Dendrites

Axon

Dendrites
The branches extending from the cell body, which receive most of the signals from other neurons

Axon
The slender extension that projects from the cell body and transmits

Cell body
The metabolic center of the neuron, enclosed by the semipermeable cell membrane

Nodes of Ranvier
The gaps in the myelin sheath

Myelin sheath
The fatty coating on some axons that acts as insulation

Branches
Sprouts from the axon that end in bulbous axon terminals

Synaptic clefts
The gaps between axon terminals and receiving neurons, across which signals are transmitted

This process allows ions (electrically charged atoms or molecules) to move into and out of the axon through ion channels in the membrane.

Body fluids contain ions, some with positive electrical charges and others with negative charges. Inside the axon, there are normally more negative than positive ions. When at rest (not firing), the axon membrane carries a negative electrical potential of about −70 millivolts (−70 thousandths of a volt) relative to the fluid outside the cell. This slight negative charge is referred to as the neuron's **resting potential.**

resting potential The slight negative electrical potential of the axon membrane of a neuron at rest, about −70 millivolts.

When a neuron receives an impulse, ion channels begin to open in the cell membrane of the axon at the point closest to the cell body, allowing positive ions to flow into the axon. This inflow of positive ions causes the membrane potential to change abruptly, to a positive value of about +50 millivolts (Pinel, 2000). This sudden reversal of the resting potential, which lasts for about 1 millisecond (1 thousandth of a second), is the **action potential.** Then, the ion channels admitting positive ions close, and other ion channels open, forcing some positive ions out of the axon. As a result, the original negative charge, or resting potential, is restored. The opening and closing of ion channels continues, segment by segment, down the length of the axon, causing the action potential to move along the axon (Cardoso et al., 2000). The action potential operates according to the "all or none" law—a neuron either fires completely or does not fire at all. Immediately after a neuron fires, it enters a *refractory period*, during which it cannot fire again for 1 to 2 milliseconds. But, even with these short resting periods, neurons can fire hundreds of times per second.

The Rate of Neural Firing and the Speed of the Impulse. If a neuron only fires or does not fire, how can we tell the difference between a very strong and a very weak stimulus? In other words, what is the neurological distinction between feeling anxious about being disciplined by your boss for being late to work and running for your life to avoid being the victim of a mugger? The answer lies in the number of neurons firing at the same time and their rate of firing. A weak stimulus may cause relatively few neurons to fire, while a strong stimulus may trigger thousands of neurons to fire at the same time. Also, a weak stimulus may be signaled by neurons firing very slowly; a stronger stimulus may incite neurons to fire hundreds of times per second.

Impulses travel at speeds from about 1 meter per second to approximately 100 meters per second (about 224 miles per hour). The most important factor in speeding the impulse on its way is the **myelin sheath**—a white, fatty coating wrapped around some axons that acts as insulation. If you look again at Figure 2.1, you will see that the coating has numerous gaps, called *nodes of Ranvier*. The electrical impulse is retriggered or regenerated at each node (or naked gap) on the axon. This regeneration makes the impulse up to 100 times faster than impulses in axons without myelin sheaths. Damage to the myelin sheath causes interruptions in the transmission of neural messages. In fact, the disease multiple sclerosis (MS) involves deterioration of the myelin sheath, resulting in loss of coordination, jerky movements, muscular weakness, and disturbances in speech.

Neurotransmitters: The Neuron's Messengers

Once a neuron fires, how does it get its message across the synaptic cleft and on to another neuron? Messages are transmitted between neurons by one or more of a large group of chemical substances known as **neurotransmitters.** Where are the neurotransmitters located? Inside the axon terminal are many small, sphere-shaped containers with thin membranes called *synaptic vesicles*, which hold the neurotransmitters. (*Vesicle* comes from a Latin word meaning "little bladder.") When an action potential arrives at the axon terminal, synaptic vesicles move toward the cell membrane, fuse with it, and release their neurotransmitter molecules. This process is shown in **Figure 2.2.**

The Receptor. Once released, neurotransmitters do not simply flow into the synaptic cleft and stimulate all the adjacent neurons. Each neurotransmitter has a distinctive molecular shape, as do **receptors,** which are protein molecules on the surfaces of dendrites and cell bodies. Neurotransmitters can affect only those neurons whose receptors are the right shape to receive them. In other words, each receptor is somewhat like a lock that only certain neurotransmitter keys can unlock (Cardoso et al., 2000; Restak, 1993). And as you'll learn in Chapter 4, many drugs affect the brain by mimicking the shapes of natural neurotransmitter molecules.

However, the binding of neurotransmitters with receptors is not as fixed and rigid a process as keys fitting locks or jigsaw puzzle pieces interlocking. Receptors on neurons are somewhat flexible; they can expand and contract their enclosed volumes.

action potential   The sudden reversal of the resting potential, which initiates the firing of a neuron.

myelin sheath   (MY-uh-lin) The white, fatty coating wrapped around some axons that acts as insulation and enables impulses to travel much faster.

2.3 **What are neurotransmitters, and what do they contribute to nervous system functioning?**

neurotransmitter   (NEW-ro-TRANS-mit-er) A chemical substance that is released into the synaptic cleft from the axon terminal of a sending neuron, crosses a synapse, and binds to appropriate receptor sites on the dendrites or cell body of a receiving neuron, influencing the cell either to fire or not to fire.

receptors   Protein molecules on the surfaces of dendrites and cell bodies that have distinctive shapes and will interact only with specific neurotransmitters.

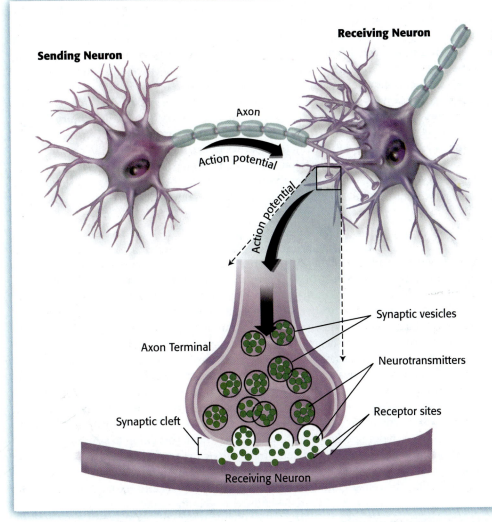

Sending Neuron

Receiving Neuron

Axon

Action potential

Action Potential

Axon Terminal

Synaptic vesicles

Neurotransmitters

Receptor sites

Synaptic cleft

Receiving Neuron

Figure 2.2 Synaptic Transmission

Sending neurons transmit their messages to receiving neurons by electrochemical action. When a neuron fires, the action potential arrives at the axon terminal and triggers the release of neurotransmitters from the synaptic vesicles. Neurotransmitters flow into the synaptic cleft and move toward the receiving neuron, which has numerous receptors. The receptors will bind only with neurotransmitters whose molecular shapes match their enclosed volumes. Neurotransmitters influence the receiving neuron to fire or not to fire.

And neurotransmitters of different types can have similar shapes. Thus, two different neurotransmitters may compete for the same receptor. The receptor will admit only one of the competing neurotransmitters—the one that fits it best. A receptor may sometimes receive a certain neurotransmitter, but then not receive it in the presence of a better-fitting neurotransmitter whose affinity with the receptor is even stronger.

The Action of Neurotransmitters. When neurotransmitters bind with receptors on the dendrites or cell bodies of receiving neurons, their action is either excitatory (influencing the neurons to fire) or inhibitory (influencing them not to fire). Because a single receiving neuron may synapse with thousands of other neurons at the same time, it will always be subject to both excitatory and inhibitory influences from incoming neurotransmitters. For the neuron to fire, the excitatory influences must exceed the inhibitory influences by a sufficient amount (the threshold).

You may wonder how the synaptic vesicles can continue to pour out neurotransmitters, yet have a ready supply so that the neuron can respond to continuing stimulation. First, the cell body of the neuron is always working to manufacture more of the neurotransmitter. Second, unused neurotransmitters in the synaptic cleft may be broken down into components and reclaimed by the axon terminal to be recycled and used again. Third, by an important process called **reuptake,** the neurotransmitter is taken back into the axon terminal, intact and ready for immediate use. This terminates the neurotransmitter's excitatory or inhibitory effect on the receiving neuron.

▲ The neurotransmitter acetylcholine helps you process new information by facilitating neural transmissions involved in learning.

reuptake The process by which neurotransmitters are taken from the synaptic cleft back into the axon terminal for later use, thus terminating their excitatory or inhibitory effect on the receiving neuron.

acetylcholine (ah-SEET-ul-KOH-leen) A neurotransmitter that plays a role in learning new information, causes the skeletal muscle fibers to contract, and keeps the heart from beating too rapidly.

dopamine (DOE-pah-meen) A neurotransmitter that plays a role in learning, attention, movement, and reinforcement; neurons in the brains of those with Parkinson's disease and schizophrenia are less sensitive to its effects.

norepinephrine (nor-EP-ih-NEF-rin) A neurotransmitter affecting eating, alertness, and sleep.

2.4 What are the functions of some of the major neurotransmitters?

epinephrine (EP-ih-NEF-rin) A neurotransmitter that affects the metabolism of glucose and nutrient energy stored in muscles to be released during strenuous exercise.

The nature of synaptic transmission—whether it is primarily chemical or electrical—was a subject of controversy during the first half of the 20th century. By the 1950s, it seemed clear that the means of communication between neurons was chemical. Yet, at some synapses, what was termed *gap junction,* or electrical transmission, occurred between the neurons. Recent research has shown that this electrical transmission may be more frequent than neuroscientists once believed (Bennett, 2000). One study found that gap junctions are involved in the spinal cord's transmission of "mirror image" pain sensations from one side of the body, the side on which an actual injury has occurred, to the other side (Spataro et al., 2004). Thus, current evidence suggests that synaptic transmission of information between neurons is primarily chemical, although some electrical transmission is known to occur. For example, electrical transmission takes place at synapses in the retina, the olfactory bulb (sense of smell), and the cerebral cortex, which we discuss further later in this chapter.

The Variety of Neurotransmitters

Researchers have identified 75 or more chemical substances that are manufactured in the brain, spinal cord, glands, and other parts of the body and may act as neurotransmitters (Greden, 1994). One of the most important is **acetylcholine** (Ach). This neurotransmitter exerts excitatory effects on the skeletal muscle fibers, causing them to contract so that the body can move. But it has an inhibitory effect on the muscle fibers in the heart, which keeps the heart from beating too rapidly. Thus, when you run to make it to class on time, acetylcholine helps your leg muscles contract quickly; at the same time, it prevents your heart muscle from pumping so rapidly that you pass out. The differing nature of the receptors on the receiving neurons in the two kinds of muscles causes these opposite effects. Acetylcholine also plays an excitatory role in stimulating the neurons involved in learning new information. So, as you are reading this text, acetylcholine is helping you understand and store the information in your memory.

Dopamine (DA), one of four neurotransmitters called *monoamines,* produces both excitatory and inhibitory effects and is involved in several functions, including learning, attention, movement, and reinforcement. Dopamine is also important to our ability to feel pleasure (Schultz, 2006).

The other three monoamines also serve important functions. **Norepinephrine** (NE) has an effect on eating habits (it stimulates the intake of carbohydrates) and plays a major role in alertness and wakefulness. **Epinephrine** complements norepinephrine by affecting the metabolism of glucose and causing the nutrient energy stored in muscles to be released during strenuous exercise. **Serotonin** plays an important role in regulating mood, sleep, impulsivity, aggression, and appetite. It has also been linked to depression and anxiety disorders (Leonardo & Hen, 2006).

Two amino acids that serve as neurotransmitters are more common than any other transmitter substances in the central nervous system. **Glutamate** is the primary excitatory neurotransmitter in the brain (Riedel, 1996). It may be released by about 40% of neurons and is active in areas of the brain involved in learning, thought, and emotions (Coyle & Draper, 1996). **GABA** (short for "*gamma-aminobutyric acid*") is the main inhibitory neurotransmitter in the brain (Miles, 1999). It is thought to facilitate the control of anxiety in humans. Tranquilizers, barbiturates, and alcohol appear to have a calming and relaxing effect because they bind with and stimulate one type of GABA receptor and thus increase GABA's anxiety-controlling effect. An abnormality in the neurons

▲ The "runner's high" is often attributed to the effects of endorphins.

that secrete GABA is believed to be one of the causes of epilepsy, a serious neurological disorder in which neural activity can become so heightened that seizures result.

More than 30 years ago, Candace Pert and her fellow researchers (1974) demonstrated that a localized region of the brain contains neurons with receptors that respond to the opiates—drugs such as opium, morphine, and heroin. Later, it was learned that the brain itself produces its own opiatelike substances, known as **endorphins.** (Endorphins provide relief from pain or the stress of vigorous exercise and produce feelings of pleasure and well-being. "Runner's high" is attributed to the release of endorphins.

Review and Reflect summarizes the various neurotransmitters.

serotonin (ser-oh-TOE-nin) A neurotransmitter that plays an important role in regulating mood, sleep, impulsivity, aggression, and appetite.

glutamate (GLOO-tah-mate) Primary excitatory neurotransmitter in the brain.

GABA Primary inhibitory neurotransmitter in the brain.

Review and Reflect — Major Neurotransmitters and Their Functions

Neurotransmitter	Functions
Acetylcholine (Ach)	Affects movement, learning, memory
Dopamine (DA)	Affects learning, attention, movement, reinforcement
Norepinephrine (NE)	Affects eating, alertness, wakefulness
Epinephrine	Affects metabolism of glucose, energy release during exercise
Serotonin	Affects mood, sleep, impulsivity, aggression, appetite
Glutamate	Active in areas of the brain involved in learning, thought, and emotion
GABA	Facilitates neural inhibition in the central nervous system
Endorphins	Provide relief from pain; produce feelings of pleasure and well-being

Remember It — The Neurons and the Neurotransmitters

1. The branchlike extensions of neurons that act as the *primary* receivers of signals from other neurons are the _____.
2. _____ support neurons, supplying them with nutrients and carrying away their waste products.
3. The _____ is the junction where the axon of a sending neuron communicates with a receiving neuron.
4. When a neuron fires, neurotransmitters are released from the synaptic vesicles in the _____ into the _____.
5. The _____ potential is the firing of a neuron; the _____ potential is the state in which the cell membrane is relatively impermeable.
6. Receptor sites on the receiving neuron receive only neurotransmitter molecules whose _____ is similar to theirs.
7. The neurotransmitter called _____ keeps the heart from beating too fast.
8. Individuals with schizophrenia may be less sensitive to the effects of _____.
9. _____ affects eating habits by stimulating the intake of carbohydrates.
10. _____ are neurotransmitters that act as natural pain killers.

Answers: 1. dendrites; 2. Glial cells; 3. synapse; 4. axon terminal, synaptic cleft; 5. action, resting; 6. shape; 7. acetylcholine; 8. dopamine; 9. Norepinephrine; 10. Endorphins

The Human Nervous System

Human functioning involves much more than the action of individual neurons. Collections of neurons, brain structures, and organ systems also play essential roles in the body. The nervous system is divided into two parts: (1) the **central nervous system (CNS),** which is composed of the brain and the spinal cord, and (2) the **peripheral nervous system,** which connects the central nervous system to all other parts of the body (see **Figure 2.3**).

endorphins (en-DOR-fins) Chemicals produced naturally by the brain that reduce pain and the stress of vigorous exercise and positively affect mood.

central nervous system (CNS) The part of the nervous system comprising the brain and the spinal cord.

peripheral nervous system (PNS) (peh-RIF-er-ul) The nerves connecting the central nervous system to the rest of the body.

Figure 2.3 The Human Nervous System

The nervous system is divided into two parts: the central nervous system and the peripheral nervous system. The diagram shows the relationships among the parts of the nervous system and provides a brief description of the functions of those parts.

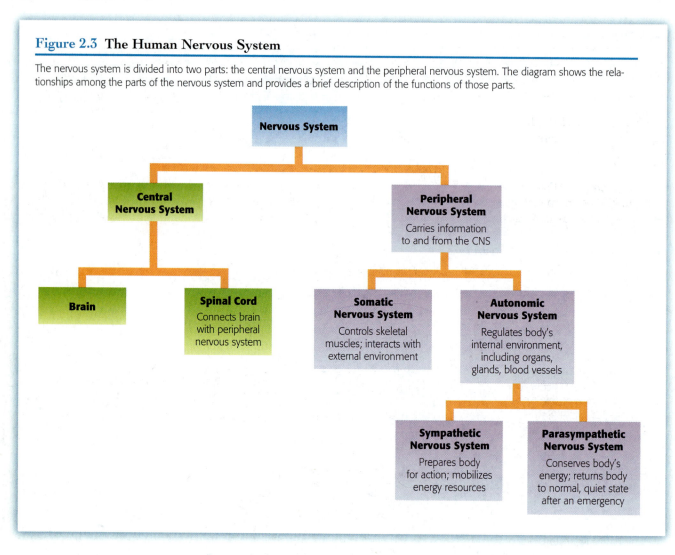

The Spinal Cord

The **spinal cord** (can best be thought of as an extension of the brain. A cylinder of neural tissue about the diameter of your little finger, the spinal cord reaches from the base of the brain, through the neck, and down the hollow center of the spinal column. The spinal cord is protected by bone and also by spinal fluid, which serves as a shock absorber. The spinal cord literally links the body with the brain. It transmits messages between the brain and the peripheral nervous system. Thus, sensory information can reach the brain, and messages from the brain can be sent to the muscles, the glands, and other parts of the body.

Although the spinal cord and the brain usually function together, the spinal cord can act without help from the brain to protect the body from injury. A simple withdrawal reflex triggered by a painful stimulus—touching a hot stove burner, for example—involves three types of neurons. Sensory neurons in your fingers detect the painful stimulus and relay this information to interneurons in the spinal cord. These interneurons activate motor neurons that control the muscles in your arm and cause you to jerk your hand away. All this happens within a fraction of a second, without any involvement of your brain. However, the brain quickly becomes aware and involved when the pain signal reaches it. At that point, you might plunge your hand into cold water to relieve the pain.

spinal cord An extension of the brain, from the base of the brain through the neck and spinal column, that transmits messages between the brain and the peripheral nervous system.

hindbrain A link between the spinal cord and the brain that contains structures that regulate physiological functions, including heart rate, respiration, and blood pressure.

The Hindbrain

Brain structures are often grouped into the *hindbrain*, the *midbrain*, and the *forebrain*, as shown in Figure 2.4. The structures of the **hindbrain** control heart rate, respiration, blood pressure, and many other vital functions.

The Brainstem and the Medulla. The part of the hindbrain known as the **brainstem** begins at the site where the spinal cord enlarges as it enters the skull. The brainstem handles functions that are so critical to physical survival that damage to it is life-threatening. The **medulla** is the part of the brainstem that controls heartbeat, breathing, blood pressure, coughing, and swallowing. Fortunately, the medulla handles these functions automatically, so you do not have to decide consciously to breathe or remember to keep your heart beating.

2.6 Which brain structures and functions are found in the hindbrain?

brainstem   The structure that begins at the point where the spinal cord enlarges as it enters the brain and handles functions critical to physical survival. It includes the medulla, the pons, and the reticular formation.

Figure 2.4 Major Structures of the Human Brain

This drawing shows some of the major structures of the brain with a brief description of the function of each. The brainstem contains the medulla, the reticular formation, and the pons.

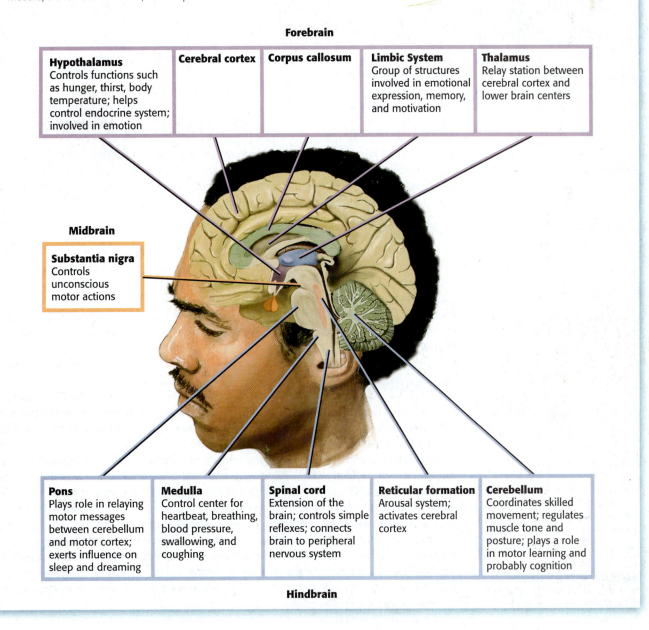

Forebrain

Hypothalamus
Controls functions such as hunger, thirst, body temperature; helps control endocrine system; involved in emotion

Cerebral cortex

Corpus callosum

Limbic System
Group of structures involved in emotional expression, memory, and motivation

Thalamus
Relay station between cerebral cortex and lower brain centers

Midbrain

Substantia nigra
Controls unconscious motor actions

Pons
Plays role in relaying motor messages between cerebellum and motor cortex; exerts influence on sleep and dreaming

Medulla
Control center for heartbeat, breathing, blood pressure, swallowing, and coughing

Spinal cord
Extension of the brain; controls simple reflexes; connects brain to peripheral nervous system

Reticular formation
Arousal system; activates cerebral cortex

Cerebellum
Coordinates skilled movement; regulates muscle tone and posture; plays a role in motor learning and probably cognition

Hindbrain

▲ Which area of the brain ensures that we can maintain our balance with little or no conscious effort?

medulla (muh-DUL-uh) The part of the brainstem that controls heartbeat, blood pressure, breathing, coughing, and swallowing.

reticular formation A structure in the brainstem that plays a crucial role in arousal and attention and that screens sensory messages entering the brain.

cerebellum (sehr-uh-BELL-um) The brain structure that helps the body execute smooth, skilled movements and regulates muscle tone and posture.

2.7 **What important structure is located in the midbrain?**

substantia nigra (sub-STAN-sha NI-gra) The structure in the midbrain that controls unconscious motor movements.

midbrain Area that contains structures linking the physiological functions of the hindbrain to the cognitive functions of the forebrain.

The Reticular Formation. Extending through the central core of the brainstem into the pons is another important structure, the **reticular formation,** sometimes called the *reticular activating system* (RAS) (refer to Figure 2.4). The reticular formation plays a crucial role in arousal and attention (Kinomura et al., 1996; Steriade, 1996). Every day, our sense organs are bombarded with stimuli, but we cannot possibly pay attention to everything we see or hear. The reticular formation blocks some messages and sends others on to structures in the midbrain and forebrain for processing. For example, a driver may be listening intently to a radio program when, suddenly, a car cuts in front of him. In response, the reticular formation blocks the sensory information coming from the radio and fixes the driver's attention on the potential danger posed by the other driver's action. Once the traffic pattern returns to normal, the reticular formation allows him to attend to the radio again, while continuing to monitor the traffic situation.

The reticular formation also determines how alert we are. When it slows down, we doze off or go to sleep. But, thanks to the reticular formation, important messages get through even when we are asleep. This is why parents may be able to sleep through a thunderstorm but will awaken to the slightest cry of their baby.

Above the medulla and at the top of the brainstem is a bridgelike structure called the *pons* that extends across the top front of the brainstem and connects to both halves of the cerebellum. The pons plays a role in body movement and even exerts an influence on sleep and dreaming.

The Cerebellum. The **cerebellum** makes up about 10% of the brain's volume and, with its two hemispheres, resembles the larger cerebrum that lies above it (Swanson, 1995) (refer to Figure 2.4). The cerebellum is critically important to the body's ability to execute smooth, skilled movements (Spencer et al., 2003). It also regulates muscle tone and posture. Furthermore, it has been found to play a role in motor learning and in retaining memories of motor activities (Nyberg et al., 2006). The cerebellum guides the graceful movements of the ballet dancer and the split-second timing of the skilled race car driver. But more typically, it coordinates the series of movements necessary to perform many simple activities—such as walking in a straight line or touching your finger to the tip of your nose—without conscious effort. For people who have damage to their cerebellum or who are temporarily impaired by too much alcohol, such simple acts may be difficult or impossible to perform.

Although some researchers remain skeptical, some studies suggest that the cerebellum is involved in cognitive and emotional functions as well as motor functions (Tumminga & Vogel, 2005). The cerebellum may help to heighten our ability to focus attention on incoming sensory stimuli and to shift attention efficiently when conditions require it (Allen et al., 1997). In addition, cerebellar dysfunction may be involved in the development of several psychiatric disorders (Konarski, McIntyre, Grupp, & Kennedy, 2005).

The Midbrain

As shown in Figure 2.4, the midbrain lies between the hindbrain and forebrain. The structures of this brain region act primarily as relay stations through which the basic physiological functions of the hindbrain are linked to the cognitive functions of the forebrain. For example, when you burn your finger, the physical feeling travels through the nerves of your hand and arm, eventually reaching the spinal cord. From there, nerve impulses are sent through the midbrain to the forebrain, where they are interpreted ("I'd better drop this hot pot because it hurts a lot and may result in serious injury!").

The **substantia nigra** is located in the **midbrain.** This structure is composed of darkly colored nuclei of nerve cells that control our unconscious motor actions. When you ride a bicycle or walk up stairs without giving your movements any conscious thought, the nuclei of the cells that allow you to do so are found in the substantia nigra. Research suggests that the loss of dopamine-producing neurons in the substantia nigra may explain the inability of people with Parkinson's disease to control their physical movements (Hauser et al., 2005).

The Forebrain

The largest part of the brain is the **forebrain.** This part of the brain controls most of the functions that come quickly to mind when we think about the brain and includes functions such as memory, logic, and self-awareness.

The Thalamus and Hypothalamus. Above the brainstem lie two extremely important structures (refer again to Figure 2.4). The **thalamus,** which has two egg-shaped parts, serves as the relay station for virtually all the information that flows into and out of the forebrain, including sensory information from all the senses except smell. (You'll learn more about the sense of smell in Chapter 3.)

   Animal studies suggest that the thalamus, or at least one small part of it, affects our ability to learn new verbal information (VanGreen Kadish, & Wyss, 2002). Another function of the thalamus is the regulation of sleep cycles (Sapar, Scammell, & Lu, 2005). The majority of people who have had acute brain injury and remain in an unresponsive "vegetative" state have suffered significant damage to the thalamus, to the neural tissue connecting it to parts of the forebrain, or to both (Adams et al., 2000).

   The **hypothalamus** lies directly below the thalamus and weighs only about 2 ounces. It regulates hunger, thirst, sexual behavior, and a wide variety of emotional behaviors. The hypothalamus also regulates internal body temperature, starting the process that causes you to perspire when you are too hot and to shiver to conserve body heat when you are too cold. It also houses the biological clock—the mechanism responsible for the timing of the sleep/wakefulness cycle and the daily fluctuation in more than 100 body functions (Sapar, Scammell, & Lu, 2005). Because of the biological clock, once your body gets used to waking up at a certain time, you tend to awaken at that time every day—even if you forget to set your alarm. The physiological changes in the body that accompany strong emotion—sweaty palms, a pounding heart, a hollow feeling in the pit of your stomach—are also initiated by neurons concentrated primarily in the hypothalamus.

The Limbic System. The **limbic system,** shown in **Figure 2.5**, is a group of structures in the forebrain, including the amygdala and the hippocampus, that are collectively involved in emotional expression, memory, and motivation. The **amygdala** plays an

2.8 Which brain structures and functions are found in the forebrain?

forebrain   The largest part of the brain, where cognitive functions as well as many of the motor functions of the brain are carried out.

thalamus   (THAL-uh-mus) The structure, located above the brainstem, that acts as a relay station for information flowing into or out of the forebrain.

hypothalamus   (HY-po-THAL-uh-mus) A small but influential brain structure that regulates hunger, thirst, sexual behavior, internal body temperature, other body functions, and a wide variety of emotional behaviors.

limbic system   A group of structures in the midbrain, including the amygdala and hippocampus, that are collectively involved in emotional expression, memory, and motivation.

amygdala   (ah-MIG-da-la) A structure in the limbic system that plays an important role in emotion, particularly in response to unpleasant or punishing stimuli.

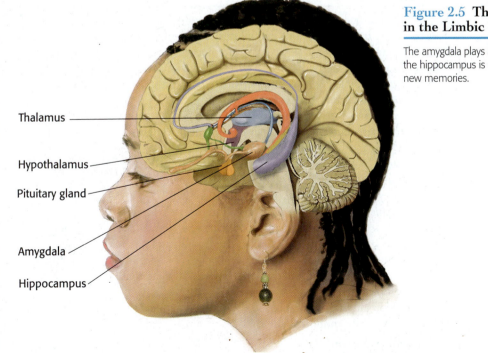

Thalamus
Hypothalamus
Pituitary gland
Amygdala
Hippocampus

Figure 2.5 The Principal Structures in the Limbic System

The amygdala plays an important role in emotion; the hippocampus is essential in the formation of new memories.

important role in emotion, particularly in response to unpleasant or punishing stimuli (Drevets et al., 2004; LeDoux, 1994, 2000). Heavily involved in the learning of fear responses, the amygdala helps form vivid memories of emotional events, which enable humans and other animals to avoid dangerous situations (Cahill et al., 1995; LeDoux, 1995). The mere sight of frightened faces causes neurons in the amygdala to fire (Morris et al., 1996). Damage to the amygdala can impair a person's ability to recognize facial expressions and tones of voice that are associated with fear and anger (LeDoux, 2000; Scott et al., 1997).

The **hippocampus** is an important brain structure of the limbic system located in the interior temporal lobes (see Figure 2.5). If your hippocampal region—the hippocampus and the underlying cortical areas—were destroyed, you would not be able to store or recall any new personal or cognitive information, such as that day's baseball score or the phone number of the person you met at dinner (Eichenbaum, 1997; Gluck & Myers, 1997; Varga-Khadem et al., 1997). However, memories already stored before the hippocampal region was destroyed would remain intact. Research indicates there is a possibility of cell regeneration in the hippocampus in human adults (Robertson & Murre, 1999). You will learn more about the central role of the hippocampal region in the formation of memories in Chapter 6.

Besides its critically important role in memory, researchers have discovered that the hippocampus is an essential part of a neurological network that detects and responds to unexpected or novel stimuli (Knight, 1996). For example, it's the hippocampus that directs your attention to a pop-up ad that suddenly appears on your computer screen. The hippocampus also plays a role in the brain's internal representation of space in the form of neural "maps" that help us learn our way about in new environments and remember where we have been (Wilson & McNaughton, 1993). An interesting study of taxi drivers in London revealed that their posterior (rear) hippocampus was significantly larger than that of participants in a control group who did not have extensive experience navigating the city's streets (Maguire et al., 2000). In fact, the more experience a taxi driver had, the larger that part of the hippocampus was. This study shows that the posterior hippocampus is important for navigational ability. More broadly, the study reveals that an important structure in the adult human brain has *plasticity*, the ability to respond to environmental demands (Maguire et al., 2000, 2003).

The Peripheral Nervous System

2.9 What is the difference between the sympathetic and parasympathetic nervous systems?

What makes your heart pound and palms sweat when you watch a scary movie? Such reactions result from the actions of the peripheral nervous system. The peripheral nervous system (PNS) is made up of all the nerves that connect the central nervous system to the rest of the body. It has two subdivisions: the somatic nervous system and the autonomic nervous system. Figure 2.3 on page 50 shows the subdivisions within the peripheral nervous system.

The *somatic nervous system* consists of (1) all the sensory nerves, which transmit information from the sense receptors—eyes, ears, nose, tongue, and skin—to the central nervous system, and (2) all the motor nerves, which relay messages from the central nervous system to all the skeletal muscles of the body. In short, the nerves of the somatic nervous system make it possible for you to sense your environment and to move, and they are primarily under conscious control.

The *autonomic nervous system* operates without any conscious control or awareness on your part. It transmits messages between the central nervous system and the glands, the cardiac (heart) muscle, and the smooth muscles (such as those in the large arteries and the gastrointestinal system), which are not normally under voluntary control. This system is further divided into two parts—the sympathetic and the parasympathetic nervous systems.

Any time you are under stress or faced with an emergency, the **sympathetic nervous system** automatically mobilizes the body's resources, preparing you for action. This physiological arousal produced by the sympathetic nervous system was named the *fight-or-flight response* by Walter Cannon (1929, 1935). If an ominous-looking stranger

hippocampus (hip-po-CAM-pus) A structure in the limbic system that plays a central role in the storing of new memories, the response to new or unexpected stimuli, and navigational ability.

sympathetic nervous system The division of the autonomic nervous system that mobilizes the body's resources during stress and emergencies, preparing the body for action.

started following you down a dark, deserted street, your sympathetic nervous system would automatically go to work. Your heart would begin to pound, your pulse rate would increase rapidly, your breathing would quicken, and your digestive system would nearly shut down. The blood flow to your skeletal muscles would be enhanced, and all of your bodily resources would be made ready to handle the emergency.

Once the emergency is over, the **parasympathetic nervous system** brings these heightened bodily functions back to normal. As a result of its action, your heart stops pounding and slows to normal, your pulse rate and breathing slow down, and your digestive system resumes its normal functioning. As shown in **Figure 2.6**, the sympathetic and parasympathetic branches act as opposing but complementary forces in the autonomic nervous system. Their balanced functioning is essential for health and survival.

parasympathetic nervous system
The division of the autonomic nervous system that brings the heightened bodily responses back to normal following an emergency.

Figure 2.6 The Autonomic Nervous System

The autonomic nervous system consists of (1) the sympathetic nervous system, which mobilizes the body's resources during emergencies or stress, and (2) the parasympathetic nervous system, which brings the heightened bodily responses back to normal afterward. This diagram shows the opposite effects of the sympathetic and parasympathetic nervous systems on various parts of the body.

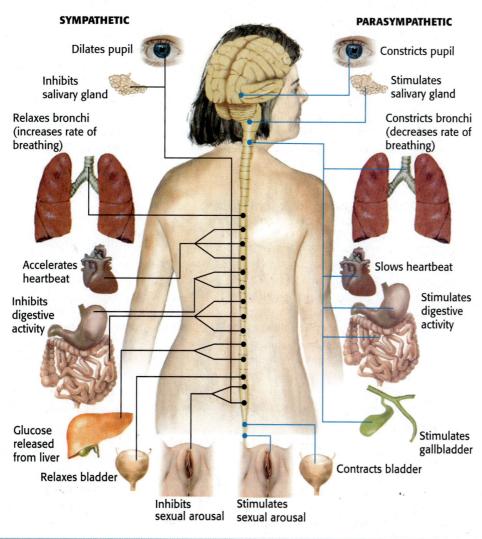

Remember It   The Human Nervous System

1. The _____ and _____ make up the central nervous system.
2. Internal body temperature is regulated by the _____.
3. The _____ is associated with emotions, and the _____ is involved in memory and learning.
4. The _____ serves as a relay station for most sensory information.
5. The _____ consists of the pons, medulla, and reticular formation.
6. Coordinated body movements are controlled by the _____.
7. The _____ nervous system connects the brain and spinal cord to the rest of the body.
8. The _____ nervous system mobilizes the body's resources during times of stress.
9. The _____ nervous system restores the body's functions to normal once a crisis has passed.

Answers: 1. brain, spinal cord; 2. hypothalamus; 3. amygdala, hippocampus; 4. thalamus; 5. brainstem; 6. cerebellum 7. peripheral; 8. sympathetic; 9. parasympathetic.

Discovering the Brain's Mysteries

As we have seen, the first attempts to discover the mysteries of the human brain were through autopsies and through clinical observations of the effects of brain injury and diseases. The next method of study was to insert electrical probes into live brains, as Fritsch and Hitzig did in 1870.

Modern researchers do not have to perform autopsies or wait for injuries to occur to learn more about the brain. Today, researchers are unlocking the mysteries of the human brain using the electroencephalograph (EEG), the microelectrode, and modern scanning techniques such as the CT scan, magnetic resonance imaging (MRI), the PET scan, functional MRI, and others (Andreasen et al., 1992).

electroencephalogram (EEG) (ee-lek-tro-en-SEFF-uh-lo-gram) A record of brain-wave activity made by a machine called the electroencephalograph.

The EEG and the Microelectrode

2.10 What does an electroencephalogram (EEG) reveal about the brain?

In 1924, Austrian psychiatrist Hans Berger invented the electroencephalograph, a machine that records the electrical activity occurring in the brain. This electrical activity, detected by electrodes placed at various points on the scalp and amplified greatly, provides the power to drive a pen across paper, producing a record of brain-wave activity called an **electroencephalogram (EEG)**. The **beta wave** is the brain-wave pattern associated with mental or physical activity. The **alpha wave** is associated with deep relaxation, and the **delta wave** with slow-wave (deep) sleep. (You will learn more about these brain-wave patterns in Chapter 4.)

A computerized EEG imaging technique shows the different levels of electrical activity occurring every millisecond on the surface of the brain (Gevins et al., 1995). It can show an epileptic seizure in progress and can be used to study neural activity in people with learning disabilities, schizophrenia, Alzheimer's disease, sleep disorders, and other neurological problems.

Although the EEG is able to detect electrical activity in different areas of the brain, it cannot reveal what is happening in individual neurons. However, the **microelectrode** can. A microelectrode is a wire so small that it can be inserted near or into a single neuron without damaging it. Microelectrodes can be used to monitor the electrical activity of a single neuron or to stimulate activity within it. Researchers have used microelectrodes to discover the exact functions of single cells within the primary visual cortex and the primary auditory cortex.

beta wave (BAY-tuh) The brain-wave pattern associated with mental or physical activity.

alpha wave The brain-wave pattern associated with deep relaxation.

delta wave The brain-wave pattern associated with slow-wave (deep) sleep.

microelectrode A small wire used to monitor the electrical activity of or stimulate activity within a single neuron.

The CT Scan and Magnetic Resonance Imaging

Since the early 1970s, a number of techniques that provide scientists and physicians with images of the brain's structures have become available. For example, a patient undergoing a **CT scan (computerized axial tomography)** of the brain is placed inside a large, doughnut-shaped structure where an X-ray tube encircles the entire head. The tube rotates in a complete circle and shoots X-rays through the brain as it does so. A series of computerized, cross-sectional images reveal the structures within the brain as well as abnormalities and injuries, including tumors and evidence of old or more recent strokes.

Another technique, **MRI (magnetic resonance imaging),** that became widely available in the 1980s produces clearer and more detailed images without exposing patients to potentially dangerous X-rays (Potts et al., 1993). MRI can be used to find abnormalities in the central nervous system and in other systems of the body. Although the CT scan and MRI do a remarkable job of showing what the brain looks like both inside and out, they cannot reveal what the brain is doing. But other technological marvels can.

The PET Scan, fMRI, and Other Imaging Techniques

As helpful as they are, CT and MRI images show only structures. By contrast, several techniques capture images of both brain structures and their functions. The oldest of these techniques, the **PET scan (positive-emission tomography)** has been used since the mid-1970s to identify malfunctions that cause physical and psychological disorders. It has also been used to study normal brain activity. A PET scan maps the patterns of blood flow, oxygen use, and glucose consumption (glucose is the food of the brain). It can also show the action of drugs and other biochemical substances in the brain and other bodily organs (Farde, 1996).

A technique that became available in the 1990s, **functional MRI (fMRI),** has several important advantages over PET: (1) It can provide images of both brain structure and brain activity; (2) it requires no injections (of radioactive or other material); (3) it can identify locations of activity more precisely than PET can; and (4) it can detect changes that take place in less than a second, compared with about a minute for PET ("Brain Imaging," 1997).

Still other imaging devices are now available. SQUID (superconducting quantum interference device) shows brain activity by measuring the magnetic changes produced

2.11 How are a CT scan and an MRI helpful in the study of brain structure?

CT scan (computerized axial tomography)   A brain-scanning technique that uses a rotating, computerized X-ray tube to produce cross-sectional images of the structures of the brain.

MRI (magnetic resonance imagery)   A diagnostic scanning technique that produces high-resolution images of the structures of the brain.

2.12 How are a PET scan and newer imaging techniques used to study the brain?

PET scan (positron-emission tomography)   A brain-imaging technique that reveals activity in various parts of the brain, based on patterns of blood flow, oxygen use, and glucose consumption.

functional MRI (fMRI)   A brain-imaging technique that reveals both brain structure and brain activity more precisely and rapidly than PET.

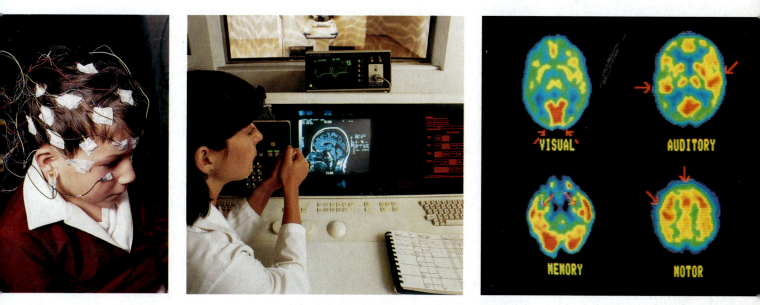

▲ The electroencephalograph, or EEG (left), uses electrodes placed on the scalp to amplify and record electrical activity in the brain. MRI (center) is a powerful tool for revealing what the brain looks like. Unlike PET, however, it cannot show what the brain is doing. PET scans (right) show activity in specific areas of the brain.

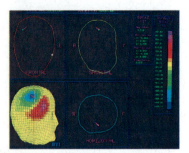

▲ SQUID is a relatively new brain-imaging tool that measures magnetic changes in the brain.

by the electric current that neurons discharge when they fire. Another imaging marvel, MEG (magnetoencephalography), also measures such magnetic changes and shows neural activity within the brain as rapidly as it occurs, much faster than PET or fMRI.

Brain-imaging techniques have helped neuroscientists develop an impressive store of knowledge about normal brain functions such as memory (Zhang et al., 2003). These imaging techniques have also been used to show abnormal brain patterns peculiar to certain psychiatric disorders and to reveal where and how various drugs affect the brain (Juengling et al., 2003; Tamminga & Conley, 1997). And some neuroscientists are experimenting with combining virtual reality with fMRI to study how the brain responds to situations and environments that would be impossible to observe using conventional imaging techniques (Travis, 1996).

Remember It   Discovering the Brain's Mysteries

1. The CT scan and MRI are used to produce images of the _____ of the brain.

2. The _____ reveals the electrical activity of the brain by producing a record of brain waves.

3. A _____ scan reveals brain activity and function, rather than the structure of the brain.

4. A newer imaging technique called _____ reveals both brain structure and brain activity.

5. Match the brain-wave pattern with the state associated with it.

_____ (1) slow-wave (deep) sleep   a. beta wave
_____ (2) deep relaxation   b. delta wave
_____ (3) physical or mental activity   c. alpha wave

Answers: 1. structures; 2. electroencephalograph; 3. PET; 4. fMRI; 5. (1) b, (2) c, (3) a

A Closer Look at the Brain

cerebrum (seh-REE-brum) The largest structure of the human brain, consisting of the two cerebral hemispheres connected by the corpus callosum and covered by the cerebral cortex.

cerebral hemispheres (seh-REE-brul) The right and left halves of the cerebrum, covered by the cerebral cortex and connected by the corpus callosum; they control movement and feeling on the opposing sides of the body.

Many important discoveries were made about the brain before scientists gained access to the marvelous techniques you have just finishing reading about. For one thing, researchers have known for more than a century that the majority of the functions that distinguish the human species from others, such as the use of language, reside in the part of the forebrain known as the *cerebrum*. Modern techniques, such as the EEG and the CT and MRI scans, have enabled researchers to localize many important functions, such as planning and logic, to specific parts of the cerebrum. They have also learned a great deal about the communication that goes on between the two sides of the cerebrum. A vast amount of knowledge regarding age and gender differences in brain structures and functions has also been accumulated.

Components of the Cerebrum

2.13 What are the components of the cerebrum?

corpus callosum (KOR-pus kah-LO-sum) The thick band of nerve fibers that connects the two cerebral hemispheres and makes possible the transfer of information and the synchronization of activity between the hemispheres.

If you could peer into your skull and look down on your brain, what you would see would resemble the inside of a huge walnut. Like a walnut, which has two matched halves connected to each other, the **cerebrum** is composed of two **cerebral hemispheres**— a left and a right hemisphere resting side by side (see **Figure 2.7**). The two hemispheres are physically connected at the bottom by a thick band of nerve fibers called the **corpus callosum.** This connection makes possible the transfer of information and the coordination of activity between the hemispheres. In general, the right cerebral hemisphere controls movement and feeling on the left side of the body; the left hemisphere controls the right side of the body.

The cerebral hemispheres have a thin outer covering about 1/8 inch thick called the **cerebral cortex,** which is primarily responsible for the higher mental processes of lan-

Figure 2.7 Two Views of the Cerebral Hemispheres

(a) The two hemispheres rest side by side like two matched halves, physically connected by the corpus callosum. (b) An inside view of the right hemisphere.

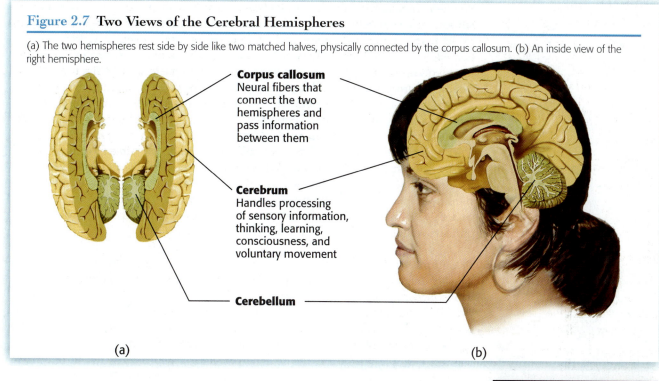

Corpus callosum
Neural fibers that connect the two hemispheres and pass information between them

Cerebrum
Handles processing of sensory information, thinking, learning, consciousness, and voluntary movement

Cerebellum

(a)   (b)

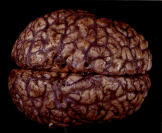

▲ The two cerebral hemispheres show up clearly in this view looking down on an actual brain.

guage, memory, and thinking. The presence of the cell bodies of billions of neurons in the cerebral cortex gives it a grayish appearance. Thus, the cortex is often referred to as *gray matter*. Immediately beneath the cortex are the white myelinated axons (referred to as *white matter*) that connect the neurons of the cortex with those of other brain regions. Research suggests that the amount of gray matter is positively correlated with intelligence in humans (Andreason et al., 1993, 2005).

In humans, the cerebral cortex is very large—if it were spread out flat, it would measure about 2 feet by 3 feet. Because the cortex is roughly three times the size of the cerebrum itself, it does not fit smoothly around the cerebrum. Rather, it is arranged in numerous folds or wrinkles, called *convolutions*. About two-thirds of the cortex is hidden from view in these folds. The cortex of less intelligent animals is much smaller in proportion to total brain size and, therefore, is much less convoluted. The cerebral cortex contains three types of areas: (1) sensory input areas, where vision, hearing, touch, pressure, and temperature register; (2) motor areas, which control voluntary movement; and (3) **association areas,** which house memories and are involved in thought, perception, and language. In each cerebral hemisphere, there are four lobes—the frontal lobe, the parietal lobe, the occipital lobe, and the temporal lobe.

cerebral cortex (seh-REE-brul KOR-tex) The gray, convoluted covering of the cerebral hemispheres that is responsible for the higher mental processes of language, memory, and thinking.

The Cerebral Hemispheres

You've probably heard about differences between "right-brained" and "left-brained" people. For instance, "right-brained" people are sometimes described as creative, while their "left-brained" counterparts are characterized as logical. These ideas emerged from the tendency of journalists to oversimplify and misinterpret research findings (Coren, 1993). Such a notion has no scientific basis, yet it has served to heighten public interest in hemispheric specialization and neuroscience in general (Hellige, 1993). In fact, despite their specialized functions, the right and left hemispheres are always in contact, thanks to the corpus callosum (shown in Figure 2.7). But research has shown that some **lateralization** of the hemispheres exists; that is, each hemisphere is specialized to handle certain functions. Let's look at the specific functions associated with the left and right hemispheres.

2.14 What are the specialized functions of the left and right cerebral hemispheres?

association areas Areas of the cerebral cortex that house memories and are involved in thought, perception, and language.

lateralization The specialization of one of the cerebral hemispheres to handle a particular function.

The Left Hemisphere. In 95% of right-handers and in about 62% of left-handers, the **left hemisphere** handles most of the language functions, including speaking, writing, reading, speech comprehension, and comprehension of the logic of written information (Hellige, 1990; Long & Baynes, 2002). But relating written information to its context involves both hemispheres. Likewise, American sign language (ASL), used by deaf persons, is processed by both hemispheres (Neville et al., 1998). The left hemisphere is also specialized for mathematical abilities, particularly calculation, and it processes information in an analytical and sequential, or step-by-step, manner (Corballis, 1989). Logic is primarily a left hemisphere activity.

The left hemisphere coordinates complex movements by directly controlling the right side of the body and by indirectly controlling the movements of the left side of the body. It accomplishes this by sending orders across the corpus callosum to the right hemisphere so that the proper movements will be coordinated and executed smoothly. (Remember that the cerebellum also plays an important role in helping coordinate complex movements.)

The Right Hemisphere. The **right hemisphere** is generally considered to be the hemisphere more adept at visual-spatial relations. And the auditory cortex in the right hemisphere appears to be far better able to process music than the left (Zatorre et al., 2002). When you arrange your bedroom furniture or notice that your favorite song is being played on the radio, you are relying primarily on your right hemisphere.

The right hemisphere also augments the left hemisphere's language-processing activities. For example, it produces the unusual verbal associations characteristic of creative thought and problem solving (Seger et al., 2000). As Van Lancker (1987) pointed out, "although the left hemisphere knows best what is being said, the right hemisphere figures out how it is meant and who is saying it" (p. 13). It is the right hemisphere that is able to understand familiar idiomatic expressions, such as "She let the cat out of the bag."

To experience an effect of the specialization of the cerebral hemispheres, try your hand at *Try It.*

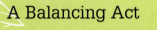

Try It   A Balancing Act

Get a meter stick or yardstick. Try balancing it vertically on the end of your left index finger, as shown in the drawing. Then try balancing it on your right index finger. Most people are better with their dominant hand—the right hand for right-handers, for example. Is this true for you?

Now try this: Begin reciting the ABCs out loud as fast as you can while balancing the stick with your left hand. Do you have less trouble this time? Why should that be? The right hemisphere controls the act of balancing with the left hand. However, your left hemisphere, though poor at controlling the left hand, still tries to coordinate your balancing efforts. When you distract the left hemisphere with a steady stream of talk, the right hemisphere can orchestrate more efficient balancing with your left hand without interference.

left hemisphere   The hemisphere that controls the right side of the body, coordinates complex movements, and, in most people, handles most of the language functions.

right hemisphere   The hemisphere that controls the left side of the body and, in most people, is specialized for visual-spatial perception.

Patients with right hemisphere damage may have difficulty understanding metaphors or orienting spatially, as in finding their way around, even in familiar surroundings. They may have attentional deficits and be unaware of objects in the left visual field, a condition called *unilateral neglect* (Deovell et al., 2000; Halligan & Marshall, 1994). Patients with this condition may eat only the food on the right side of a plate, read only the words on the right half of a page, groom only the right half of their body, or even deny that the arm on the side opposite the brain damage belongs to them (Bisiach, 1996; Chen-Sea, 2000; Posner, 1996; Tham et al., 2000). Researchers have found that a treatment combining visual training with forced movement of limbs on the neglected side helps some patients (Brunila et al., 2002).

The right hemisphere also responds to the emotional message conveyed by another's tone of voice (LeDoux, 2000). Reading and interpreting nonverbal behavior, such as gestures and facial expressions, is another right hemisphere task (Hauser, 1993; Kucharska-Pietura & Klimkowski, 2002). For example, the subtle clues that tell us someone is lying (such as excessive blinking or lack of eye contact) are processed in the right hemisphere (Etcoff et al., 2000).

The right hemisphere is involved in the expression of emotion through tone of voice and facial expressions. The left side of the face, controlled by the right hemisphere, usually conveys stronger emotion than the right side of the face. Lawrence Miller (1988) describes the facial expressions and the voice inflection of people with right hemisphere damage as "often strangely blank—almost robotic" (p. 39).

Evidence also continues to accumulate that brain mechanisms responsible for negative emotions are located in the right hemisphere, while those responsible for positive emotions are in the left hemisphere (Hellige, 1993). For instance, brain-imaging studies have shown that watching violent programs on television activates areas in the right hemisphere of children's brains that are not activated when they watch nonviolent programs (Murray et al., 2006). Research also shows that patients suffering from major depression experience decreased activity in the left prefrontal cortex, where positive emotions are produced (Drevets et al., 1997). Interestingly, too, patients with brain tumors in the right hemisphere perceive their situation more negatively than those with tumors on the left side of the brain (Salo et al., 2002). By contrast, doctors' ratings of patients' quality of life do not vary according to the hemisphere in which the tumor is located. **Figure 2.8** summarizes the functions associated with the left and right hemispheres.

Figure 2.8 Lateralized Functions of the Brain

Assigning functions to one hemisphere or the other allows the brain to function more efficiently.

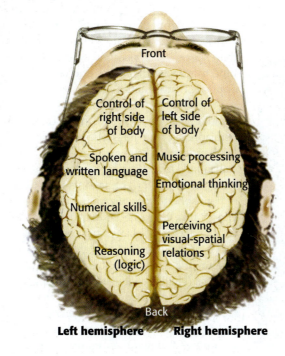

Left hemisphere   **Right hemisphere**

Source: Based on Gazzaniga (1983).

▲ Which side of the guitarist's brain is evaluating the quality of his playing?

split-brain operation A surgical procedure, performed to treat severe cases of epilepsy, in which the corpus callosum is cut, separating the cerebral hemispheres.

▲ Many creative people, such as actors Matthew Broderick and Sarah Jessica Parker, are left-handed.

The Split Brain. A great deal of knowledge about lateralization has been gained from studies involving individuals in whom the corpus callosum is absent or has been surgically modified. Many such individuals have had their corpus callosum severed in a drastic surgical procedure called the **split-brain operation.** Neurosurgeons Joseph Bogen and Philip Vogel (1963) found that patients with severe epilepsy, suffering frequent and uncontrollable grand mal seizures, could be helped by surgery that severed their corpus callosum, rendering communication between the two hemispheres impossible. The operation decreases the frequency of seizures in two-thirds of patients and causes minimal loss of cognitive functioning or change in personality (Washington University School of Medicine, 2003).

Research with split-brain patients by Roger Sperry (1964) and colleagues Michael Gazzaniga (1970, 1989) and Jerre Levy (1985) expanded knowledge of the unique capabilities of the individual hemispheres. Sperry (1968) found that when the brain was surgically divided, each hemisphere continued to have individual and private experiences, sensations, thoughts, and perceptions. However, most sensory experiences are shared almost simultaneously because each ear and eye has direct sensory connections to both hemispheres.

Sperry's research, for which he won a Nobel Prize in medicine in 1981, revealed some fascinating findings. In **Figure 2.9**, a split-brain patient sits in front of a screen that separates the right and left fields of vision. If an orange is flashed to the right field of vision, it will register in the left (verbal) hemisphere. If asked what he saw, the patient will readily reply, "I saw an orange." Suppose that, instead, an apple is flashed to the left visual field and is relayed to the right (nonverbal) hemisphere. The patient will reply, "I saw nothing."

Why could the patient report that he saw the orange but not the apple? Sperry (1964, 1968) maintains that in split-brain patients, only the verbal left hemisphere can report what it sees. In these experiments, the left hemisphere does not see what is flashed to the right hemisphere, and the right hemisphere is unable to report verbally what it has viewed. But did the right hemisphere actually see the apple that was flashed in the left visual field? Yes, because with his left hand (which is controlled by the right hemisphere), the patient can pick out from behind a screen the apple or any other object shown to the right hemisphere. The right hemisphere knows and remembers what it sees just as well as the left, but unlike the left hemisphere, the right cannot name what it has seen. (In these experiments, images must be flashed for no more than $1/10$ or $2/10$ of a second so that the subjects do not have time to refixate their eyes and send the information to the opposite hemisphere.)

Handedness. Since we've been discussing right and left hemispheres, you might be wondering whether right- and left-handedness have anything to do with hemispheric specialization. Investigators have identified differences in the brains of left- and right-handers that suggest that the process of hemispheric specialization and the development of handedness may be related. On average, the corpus callosum of left-handers is 11% larger and contains up to 2.5 million more nerve fibers than that of right-handers (Witelson, 1985). In general, the two sides of the brain are less specialized in left-handers (Hellige et al., 1994). There is also evidence that new learning is more easily transferred from one side of the brain to the other in left-handers (Schmidt et al., 2000).

In addition, left-handers tend to experience less language loss following an injury to either hemisphere. They are also more likely to recover, because the undamaged hemisphere can more easily take over the speech functions.

Figure 2.9 Testing a Split-Brain Person

Using special equipment, researchers are able to study the independent functioning of the hemispheres in split-brain patients. In this experiment, when a visual image (an orange) is flashed on the right side of the screen, it is transmitted to the left (talking) hemisphere. When asked what he sees, the split-brain patient replies, "I see an orange." When an image (an apple) is flashed on the left side of the screen, it is transmitted only to the right (nonverbal) hemisphere. Because the split-brain patient's left (language) hemisphere did not receive the image, he replies, "I see nothing." But he can pick out the apple by touch if he uses his left hand, proving that the right hemisphere "saw" the apple.

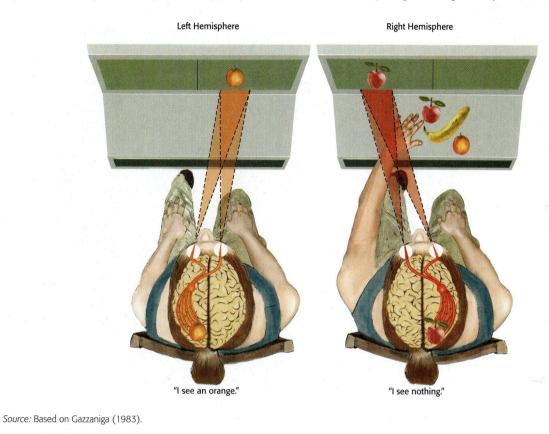

Source: Based on Gazzaniga (1983).

On the other hand, left-handers tend to have higher rates of learning disabilities and mental disorders than right-handers, perhaps because of differences in brain organization (Grouios et al., 1999; Hernandez et al., 1997; Tanner, 1990).

The Frontal Lobes

The largest of the brain's lobes, the **frontal lobes**, begin at the front of the brain and extend to the top center of the skull. They contain the motor cortex, Broca's area, and the frontal association areas.

The Motor Cortex. In 1870, two physicians, Gustav Fritsch and Eduard Hitzig, used a probe to apply a weak electrical current to the cortex of a dog. (The brain itself is insensitive to pain, so probing it causes no discomfort.) When they stimulated various points on the cortex along the rear of the frontal lobes, specific parts of the dog's body moved. Fritsch and Hitzig had discovered the **motor cortex**—the area that controls voluntary body movement (see **Figure 2.10**). The right motor cortex controls movement on the left side of the body, and the left motor cortex controls movement on the right side of the body.

2.15 Which psychological functions are associated with the frontal lobes?

frontal lobes The largest of the brain's lobes, which contain the motor cortex, Broca's area, and the frontal association areas.

Figure 2.10 The Cerebral Cortex of the Left Hemisphere

This illustration of the left cerebral hemisphere shows the four lobes: (1) the frontal lobe, including the motor cortex and Broca's area; (2) the parietal lobe, with the somatosensory cortex; (3) the occipital lobe, with the primary visual cortex; and (4) the temporal lobe, with the primary auditory cortex and Wernicke's area.

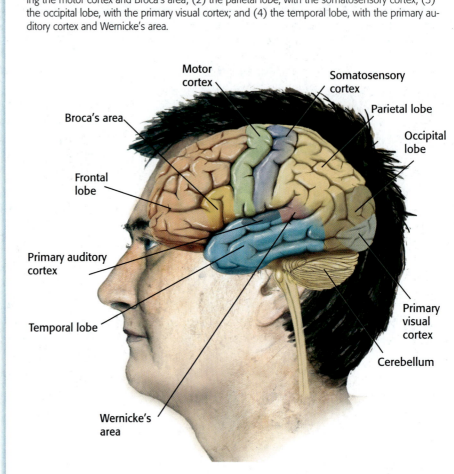

Later, in 1937, Canadian neurosurgeon Wilder Penfield applied electrical stimulation to the motor cortex of conscious human patients undergoing neurosurgery. He mapped the primary motor cortex in humans, as shown in **Figure 2.11**. Body parts are drawn in proportion to the amount of motor cortex involved in the movement of each. The parts of the body that are capable of the most finely coordinated movements, such as the fingers, lips, and tongue, have a larger share of the motor cortex. Movements in the lower parts of the body are controlled primarily by neurons at the top of the motor cortex, whereas movements in the upper body parts (face, lips, and tongue) are controlled mainly by neurons near the bottom of the motor cortex. For example, when you wiggle your right big toe, the movement is produced mainly by the firing of a cluster of brain cells at the top of the left motor cortex.

How accurately and completely does Penfield's map account for the control of body movement? Although it may be useful in a broad sense, more recent research has shown that there is not a precise one-to-one correspondence between specific points on the motor cortex and movement of particular body parts. Motor neurons that control the fingers, for example, play a role in the movement of more than a single finger. In fact, the control of movement of any single finger is handled by a network of neurons that are widely distributed over the entire hand area of the motor cortex (Sanes & Donoghue, 2000; Sanes et al., 1995; Schieber & Hibbard, 1993). Sometimes damage in

motor cortex The strip of tissue at the rear of the frontal lobes that controls voluntary body movement and participates in learning and cognitive events.

Figure 2.11 The Motor Cortex and the Somatosensory Cortex from the Left Hemisphere

The left motor cortex controls voluntary movement on the right side of the body. The left somatosensory cortex is the site where touch, pressure, temperature, and pain sensations from the right side of the body register. The more sensitive the body parts and the more capable they are of finely coordinated movements, the greater the areas of somatosensory cortex and motor cortex dedicated to those body parts.

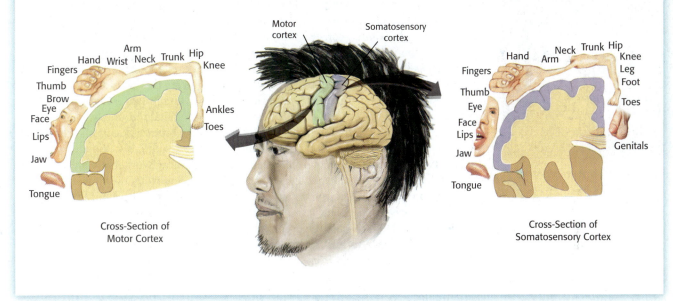

the motor cortex can cause the grand mal seizures of epilepsy. On the other hand, if an arm or leg is amputated, many of the neurons in the corresponding area of the motor cortex will eventually switch to another function (Murray, 1995).

Broca's Area. In 1861, physician Paul Broca performed autopsies on two patients—one who had been totally without speech, and another who could say only four words (Jenkins et al., 1975). Broca found that both individuals had damage in the left hemisphere, slightly in front of the part of the motor cortex that controls movements of the jaw, lips, and tongue. Broca was one of the first scientists to demonstrate the existence of localized functions in the cerebral cortex (Schiller, 1993). He concluded that the site of left hemisphere damage he identified through the autopsies was the part of the brain responsible for speech production, now called **Broca's area** (refer to Figure 2.10). Broca's area is involved in directing the pattern of muscle movement required to produce speech sounds.

If Broca's area is damaged as a result of head injury or stroke, **Broca's aphasia** may result. Aphasia is a general term for a loss or impairment of the ability to use or understand language, resulting from damage to the brain (Goodglass, 1993). Characteristically, patients with Broca's aphasia know what they want to say but can speak very little or not at all. If they are able to speak, their words are produced very slowly, with great effort, and are poorly articulated. Broca's aphasia, then, is a problem in *producing* language, not in understanding it (Maratsos & Matheny, 1994). Even patients who cannot speak are often able to sing songs they knew before suffering brain damage. Singing is normally controlled by the right hemisphere, and words to familiar songs are stored there (Albert & Helm-Estabrooks, 1988).

But Broca's area does more than just control the physical production of speech. One brain-imaging study (Embick et al., 2000) indicated that Broca's area buzzes with activity when a person makes grammatical errors, especially those involving word order. Some patients with damage to Broca's area are able to speak, but typically produce utterances in which words are out of order and grammatical features such as

Broca's area (BRO-kuz) The area in the frontal lobe, usually in the left hemisphere, that controls the production of speech sounds.

Broca's aphasia (BRO-kuz uh-FAY-zyah) An impairment in the physical ability to produce speech sounds or, in extreme cases, an inability to speak at all; caused by damage to Broca's area.

▲ This computer-generated image shows the likely path of the bar that tore through Phineas Gage's skull.

possessives are missing (Martin, 2006). These findings confirm the existence of distinct brain structures for language knowledge and provide direct evidence of a specialization for grammar in Broca's area.

Frontal Association Areas. Much of the frontal lobes consist of association areas involved in thinking, motivation, planning for the future, impulse control, and emotional responses (Stuss et al., 1992). One of the best known cases in medical history, that of the unfortunate railroad construction worker Phineas Gage, illustrated what can happen when the frontal association areas are damaged. On September 13, 1848, Gage, who was just 25 years old at the time, was using dynamite to blast rocks and dirt out of the pathway of the railroad tracks he was helping to lay that would connect the east and west coasts of the United States by rail. Suddenly, an unplanned explosion almost took Gage's head off, sending a 3½-foot-long, 13-point metal rod under his left cheekbone and out through the top of his skull. Much of the brain tissue in his frontal lobe was torn away, and he was rendered unconscious. Remarkably, though, Gage regained consciousness a few minutes later. When his fellow workers delivered him to his hotel in a cart, he was able to get out of the cart under his own power and was even able to walk up the front steps. A few weeks later, Gage appeared to be fully recovered. However, the other workers noticed changes in his personality. Prior to the accident, Gage had been an easygoing fellow. Afterward, he was rude and impulsive. His changed personality cost him his job, and he lived out the rest of his life as a circus sideshow exhibit (adapted from Harlow, 1848).

The Parietal Lobes

2.16 What important structure is found in the parietal lobes?

The **parietal lobes,** lie directly behind the frontal lobes, in the top middle portion of the brain (refer back to Figure 2.10). The parietal lobes are involved in the reception and processing of touch stimuli. The front strip of brain tissue in the parietal lobes is the **somatosensory cortex,** the site where touch, pressure, temperature, and pain register in the cerebral cortex (Stea & Apkarian, 1992). The somatosensory cortex also makes you aware of movement in your body and the positions of your body parts at any given moment.

The two halves of the somatosensory cortex, in the left and right parietal lobes, are wired to opposite sides of the body. Also, cells at the top of the somatosensory cortex govern feeling in the lower extremities of the body. Drop a brick on your right foot, and the topmost brain cells of the left somatosensory cortex will fire and register the pain sensation. (Note: This is *not* a *Try It!*) Notice in Figure 2.11 that large somatosensory areas are connected to sensitive body parts such as the tongue, lips, face, and hand, particularly the thumb and index finger. A person with damage to the somatosensory cortex of one hemisphere loses some sensitivity to touch on the opposite side of the body. If the damage is severe enough, the person might not be able to feel the difference between sandpaper and silk, or the affected part of the body might feel numb.

Experience can affect the somatosensory cortex (Juliano, 1998). For example, compared to nonmusicians, professional musicians who play stringed instruments have a significantly larger area of the somatosensory cortex dedicated to the fingers of their left hand. And the earlier the age at which they began to play, the larger this dedicated cortical area is (Elbert et al., 1995).

Other parts of the parietal lobes are responsible for spatial orientation and sense of direction—for example, helping you to retrace your path when you take a wrong turn. The hippocampus cooperates with these parts of the parietal lobes in performing such functions, as the study of London taxi drivers discussed on page 54 indicates (Maguire et al., 2000). Other research reveals a gender-related difference in human navigational thinking. Female and male participants had to find their way out of a complex, three-dimensional, computer-simulated maze. Brain imaging showed that male participants relied heavily on the left hippocampus while navigating through the maze, whereas

parietal lobes (puh-RY-uh-tul) The lobes that contain the somatosensory cortex (where touch, pressure, temperature, and pain register) and other areas that are responsible for body awareness and spatial orientation.

somatosensory cortex (so-MAT-oh-SENS-or-ee) The strip of tissue at the front of the parietal lobes where touch, pressure, temperature, and pain register in the cerebral cortex.

female participants consistently used both the right parietal cortex and the right frontal cortex (Gron et al., 2000).

Have you ever fumbled for your keys in a coat pocket, purse, or backpack? How did you distinguish between your keys and other objects without looking? There are association areas in the parietal lobes that house memories of how objects feel against the human skin, a fact that explains why we can identify objects by touch. People with damage to these areas could hold a computer mouse, a CD, or a baseball in their hand but not be able to identify the object by touch alone.

The Occipital Lobes

Behind the parietal lobes at the rear of the brain lie the **occipital lobes,** which are involved in the reception and interpretation of visual information (refer to Figure 2.10). At the very back of the occipital lobes is the **primary visual cortex,** the site where vision registers in the cortex.

Each eye is connected to the primary visual cortex in both the right and the left occipital lobes. Look straight ahead and draw an imaginary line down the middle of what you see. Everything to the left of the line is referred to as the left visual field and registers in the right visual cortex. Everything to the right of the line is the right visual field and registers in the left visual cortex. A person who sustains damage to one half of the primary visual cortex will still have partial vision in both eyes because each eye sends information to both the right and the left occipital lobes.

The association areas in the occipital lobes are involved in the interpretation of visual stimuli. The association areas hold memories of past visual experiences and enable us to recognize what is familiar among the things we see. That's why the face of a friend stands out in a crowd of unfamiliar people. When these areas are damaged, people can lose the ability to identify objects visually, although they will still be able to identify the same objects by touch or through some other sense.

The Temporal Lobes

The **temporal lobes,** located slightly above the ears, are involved in the reception and interpretation of auditory stimuli. The site in the cortex where hearing registers is known as the primary auditory cortex. The **primary auditory cortex,** in each temporal lobe receives sound inputs from both ears. Injury to one of these areas results in reduced hearing in both ears, and the destruction of both areas causes total deafness.

Wernicke's Area. Adjacent to the primary auditory cortex in the left temporal lobe is **Wernicke's area,** which is the language area involved in comprehending the spoken word and in formulating coherent written and spoken language (refer to Figure 2.10). In about 95% of people, Wernicke's area is in the left hemisphere. When you listen to someone speak, the sound registers first in the primary auditory cortex. The sound is then sent to Wernicke's area, where the speech sounds are unscrambled into meaningful patterns of words. The same areas that are active when you listen to someone speak are also active in deaf individuals when they watch a person using sign language (Söderfeldt et al., 1994). Wernicke's area is also involved when you select the words you want to use when speaking and writing (Nishimura et al., 1999).

Wernicke's aphasia is a type of aphasia resulting from damage to Wernicke's area. Although speech is fluent and words are clearly articulated, the actual message does not make sense to listeners (Maratsos & Matheney, 1994). The content may be vague or bizarre and may contain inappropriate words, parts of words, or a gibberish of nonexistent words. One Wernicke's patient, when asked how he was feeling, replied, "I think that there's an awful lot of mung, but I think I've a lot of net and tunged in a little wheat duhvayden" (Buckingham & Kertesz, 1974). People with Wernicke's aphasia are not aware that anything is wrong with their speech. Thus, this disorder is difficult to treat.

2.17 Why are the occipital lobes critical to vision?

occipital lobes (ahk-SIP-uh-tul) The lobes that are involved in the reception and interpretation of visual information; they contain the primary visual cortex.

primary visual cortex The area at the rear of the occipital lobes where vision registers in the cerebral cortex.

2.18 What are the major areas within the temporal lobes, and what are their functions?

temporal lobes The lobes that are involved in the reception and interpretation of auditory information; they contain the primary auditory cortex, Wernicke's area, and the temporal association areas.

primary auditory cortex The part of each temporal lobe where hearing registers in the cerebral cortex.

Wernicke's area (VUR-nih-keys) The language area in the left temporal lobe involved in comprehending the spoken word and in formulating coherent speech and written language.

Wernicke's aphasia Aphasia that results from damage to Wernicke's area and in which the person's speech is fluent and clearly articulated but does not make sense to listeners.

Another kind of aphasia is *auditory aphasia*, or word deafness. It can occur if there is damage to the nerves connecting the primary auditory cortex with Wernicke's area. The person is able to hear normally but may not understand spoken language—just as when you hear a foreign language spoken and perceive the sounds but have no idea what the speaker is saying.

The Temporal Association Areas. The remainder of the temporal lobes consists of the association areas that house memories and are involved in the interpretation of auditory stimuli. For example, the association area where your memories of various sounds are stored enables you to recognize the sounds of your favorite band, a computer booting up, your roommate snoring, and so on. There is also a special association area where familiar melodies are stored.

The Brain across the Life Span

2.19 In what ways does the brain change across a life span?

The principles of neurological functioning you've learned about—how action potentials occur and so on—work pretty much the same no matter what an individual's age. Still, there are some important age-related variations in brain structure and function that may contribute to psychological and behavioral age differences. You'll read about these variations in greater detail in Chapters 8 and 9; now let's discuss a few general principles of neurological development.

The Ever-Changing Brain. Do you consider your brain to be fully matured? When do you think the brain reaches full maturity? The answer to this question might surprise you. In fact, the brain grows in spurts from conception until well into adulthood (Fischer & Rose, 1994). In childhood and adolescence, many of these spurts are correlated with major advances in physical and intellectual skills, such as the acquisition of fluency in language that happens around age 4 for most children. Each growth spurt also seems to involve a different brain area. For example, the spurt that begins around age 17 and continues into the early 20s mainly affects the frontal lobes, where, you'll recall, the abilities to plan and to control one's emotions are located. Differences between teens and adults in these abilities may be the result of this growth spurt. Changes in brain function are influenced by several development processes.

pruning The process through which the developing brain eliminates unnecessary or redundant synapses.

Synaptogenesis. Synapses develop as a result of the growth of both dendrites and axons. This process, known as *synaptogenesis*, occurs in spurts throughout the life span. Each spurt is followed by a period of **pruning**, the process through which the developing brain eliminates unnecessary or redundant synapses. The activity of neurotransmitters within the synapses also varies with age. For example, acetylcholine is less plentiful in the brains of children than in teens and adults. This difference may help explain age differences in memory and other functions influenced by this excitatory neurotransmitter.

Myelination. The process of *myelination*, or the development of myelin sheaths around axons, begins prior to birth but continues well into adulthood. For example, the brain's association areas are not fully myelinated until age 12 or so (Tanner, 1990). And the reticular formation, which, as you'll recall, regulates attention, isn't fully myelinated until the mid-20s (Spreen et al., 1995). Thus, differences in myelination may account for differences between children and adults in processing speed, memory, and other functions.

▲ There are many differences between the brains of children and adults, which may help explain why children process information less efficiently than adults do.

Hemispheric Specialization. Some degree of hemispheric specialization is present very early in life. Language processing, for example, occurs primarily in the left hemisphere of the fetal and infant brain just as it does in the adult brain (Chilosi et al., 2001; de Lacoste et al., 1991). Other functions, such as spatial perception, aren't lateralized until age 8 or so. Consequently, children younger than 8 exhibit much poorer spatial skills than do those who are older (Roberts & Bell, 2000). For instance, children younger than 8 have difficulty using maps and distinguishing between statements such as *It's on your left* and *It's on my left*.

Plasticity. The ability of the brain to reorganize, to reshape itself in response to input from both internal (within the brain) and external (environmental) sources (Clifford, 2000), and to compensate for damage is termed plasticity. Plasticity is greatest in young children within whom the hemispheres are not yet completely lateralized. In one case study, researchers found that a prenatal hemorrhage that prevented the development of the left side of the cerebellum in one child was evidenced only by a slight tremor at age 3 (Mancini et al., 2001). As you might suspect, an adult who lost the left side of his or her cerebellum would probably experience much more functional impairment.

However, it is probably also true that the brain retains some degree of plasticity throughout life. For example, researchers have found that the correction of hearing defects in late-middle-aged adults results in changes in all the areas of the brain that are involved in sound perception (Giraud et al., 2001). Moreover, the brains of these individuals appear to develop responses to sounds in areas in which the brains of people with normal hearing do not.

Aging and the Brain. Does the brain ever stop changing? No, the brain both gains and loses synapses throughout life. At some point in adulthood, however, losses begin to exceed gains (Huttenlocher, 1994). Studies show that almost all areas of the brain lose volume across the early, middle, and late adult years (Raz et al., 2006). One brain-imaging study showed that gray matter, but not white matter, is lost with normal aging in both hemispheres of the cerebellum (Sullivan et al., 2000). Age-related deficits resulting from the loss of gray matter are common. For example, elderly people tend to experience problems with balance, they become less steady on their feet, and their gait is affected. However, as is true in childhood, intellectual and motor skill training can positively influence the brains of older adults.

Gender Differences in the Adult Brain

Throughout development, the brains of males and females differ to some degree. However, these differences and their possible links to behavior have been most thoroughly researched among adults. One such difference is that the brains of men have a higher proportion of white matter than do the brains of women (Gur et al., 1999). Moreover, men have a lower proportion of white matter in the left brain than in the right brain. In contrast, in women's brains, the proportions of gray matter and white matter in the two hemispheres are equivalent. Such findings have led some neuropsychologists to speculate that gender differences in the distribution of gray and white matter across the two hemispheres may explain men's superior performance on right-hemisphere tasks such as mental rotation of geometric figures. Likewise, women's superior abilities in the domain of emotional perception (more on this in Chapter 10) may be attributable to the fact that they have more gray matter than men do in the area of the brain that controls emotions (Gur et al., 2002).

Other research has revealed that some tasks stimulate different parts of the brain in men and women. For example, imaging studies have shown that men process navigational information, such as that needed to find the way out of a maze, in the left hippocampus. By contrast, women who are engaged in the same task use the right parietal cortex and the right frontal cortex (Gron et al., 2000). Similarly, studies show that men and women use different areas of the brain when searching for the location of a sound (Lewald, 2004).

2.20 How do the brains of men differ from those of women?

plasticity   The capacity of the brain to adapt to changes such as brain damage.

What is the meaning of these gender differences in the brain? The short answer is that scientists won't know for certain until a great deal more research is done. Moreover, studies that look for links between these brain differences and actual behavior are needed before any conclusions can be drawn regarding the possible neurological bases for gender differences in behavior.

Remember It | A Closer Look at the Brain

1. The band of fibers connecting the left and right cerebral hemispheres is the _____.

2. When you listen to a person talk, you most likely process her words in your _____ hemisphere.

3. You process facial expressions in your _____ hemisphere.

4. The split-brain operation is sometimes performed to cure _____.

5. _____ is to speech production as _____ is to speech understanding.

6. The primary auditory cortex is found in the _____ lobe, while the primary visual cortex is located in the _____ lobe.

7. A person with brain damage who has problems regulating emotion most likely has an injury to the _____ lobe.

8. The sense of touch is associated with the _____ lobe.

9. _____ is a gradual process during which connections between neurons develop.

10. The ability of the brain to adapt and change is known as _____.

11. Tasks that require _____ and _____ stimulate different parts of the brain in men and women.

Answers: 1. corpus callosum; 2. left; 3. right; 4. epilepsy; 5. Broca's area, Wernicke's area; 6. temporal, occipital; 7. frontal; 8. parietal 9. Synaptogenesis; 10. plasticity; 11. navigation, locating sounds

---

The Endocrine System

2.21 What functions are associated with the various glands of the endocrine system?

Most people think of the reproductive system when they hear the word *hormones*. Or they may associate hormones with particular physical changes, such as those of puberty, pregnancy, or menopause. However, these substances regulate many other physical and psychological functions. And their influence reaches far beyond the reproductive system.

The **endocrine system** is a series of ductless glands, located in various parts of the body, that manufacture and secrete the chemical substances known as **hormones,** which are manufactured and released in one part of the body but have an effect on other parts of the body. Hormones are released into the bloodstream and travel throughout the circulatory system, but each hormone performs its assigned job only when it connects with the body cells that have receptors for it. Some of the same chemical substances that are neurotransmitters act as hormones as well—norepinephrine and vasopressin, to name two. **Figure 2.12** shows the glands in the endocrine system and their locations in the body.

The **pituitary gland** rests in the brain just below the hypothalamus and is controlled by it (see Figure 2.12). The pituitary is considered to be the "master gland" of the body because it releases the hormones that activate, or turn on, the other glands in the endocrine system—a big job for a tiny structure about the size of a pea. The pituitary also produces the hormone that is responsible for body growth (Howard et al., 1996). Too little of this powerful substance will make a person a dwarf; too much will produce a giant.

The *thyroid gland* rests in the front, lower part of the neck just below the voice box (larynx). The thyroid produces the important hormone thyroxine, which regulates

endocrine system (EN-duh-krin) A system of ductless glands in various parts of the body that manufacture hormones and secrete them into the bloodstream, thus affecting cells in other parts of the body.

hormone A chemical substance that is manufactured and released in one part of the body and affects other parts of the body.

pituitary gland The endocrine gland located in the brain that releases hormones that activate other endocrine glands as well as growth hormone; often called the "master gland."

Figure 2.12   The Endocrine System

The endocrine system is a series of glands that manufacture and secrete hormones. The hormones travel through the circulatory system and have important effects on many bodily functions.

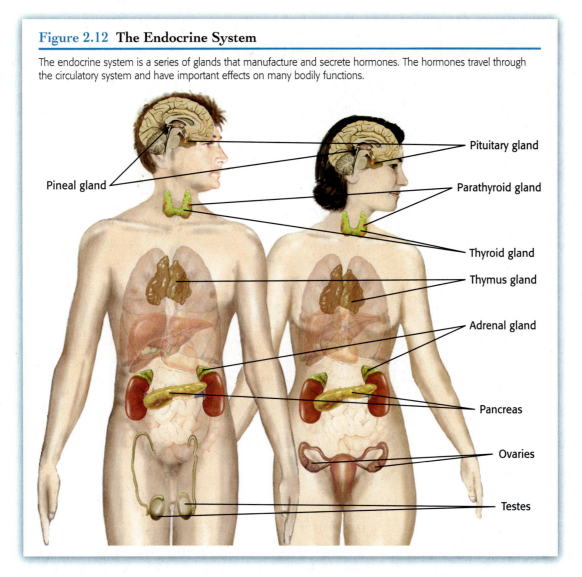

Pineal gland

Pituitary gland

Parathyroid gland

Thyroid gland

Thymus gland

Adrenal gland

Pancreas

Ovaries

Testes

the rate at which food is metabolized, or transformed into energy. The *pancreas* regulates the body's blood sugar levels by releasing the hormones insulin and glucagon into the bloodstream. In people with diabetes, too little insulin is produced. Without insulin to break down the sugars in food, blood-sugar levels can get dangerously high.

The two **adrenal glands,** which rest just above the kidneys (as shown in Figure 2.12), produce epinephrine and norepinephrine. By activating the sympathetic nervous system, these two hormones play an important role in the body's response to stress. The adrenal glands also release the corticoids, which control the important salt balance in the body, and small amounts of the sex hormones.

The *gonads* are the sex glands—the ovaries in females and the testes in males (refer to Figure 2.12). Activated by the pituitary gland, the gonads release the sex hormones that make reproduction possible and that are responsible for the secondary sex characteristics—pubic and underarm hair in both sexes, breasts in females, and facial hair and a deepened voice in males. Androgens, the male sex hormones, influence sexual motivation. Estrogen and progesterone, the female sex hormones, help regulate the menstrual cycle. Although both males and females have androgens and estrogens, males have considerably more androgens, and females have considerably more estrogens. (The sex hormones and their effects are discussed in more detail in Chapter 11.)

Review and Reflect summarizes the hormones you have just read about.

adrenal glands (ah-DREE-nal) A pair of endocrine glands that release hormones that prepare the body for emergencies and stressful situations and also release corticoids and small amounts of the sex hormones.

Review and Reflect   Glands, Hormones, and Their Functions

Gland(s)	Hormone(s)	Function
Pituitary	Growth hormone; many others	Controls growth rate; activates other endocrine glands
Thyroid	Thyroxine	Regulates metabolism
Pancreas	Insulin Glucagon	Regulates blood sugar
Adrenals	Epinephrine Norepinephrine Corticoids Sex hormones	Activate the sympathetic nervous system; control salt balance; play a role in puberty and sexual function
Gonads	Sex hormones	Regulate reproduction and sexual functions; are responsible for the secondary sex characteristics

Remember It   The Endocrine System

1. The endocrine glands secrete _____ directly into the _____.

2. The _____ gland acts as a "master gland" that activates the others.

3. Blood sugar levels are regulated by the _____ through the release of _____ and _____.

4. Sex hormones are produced by both the _____ and the _____.

5. The _____ is the gland responsible for maintaining balanced metabolism.

Answers: 1. hormones, bloodstream; 2. pituitary; 3. pancreas, insulin, glucagon; 4. gonads, adrenals; 5. thyroid

Genes and Behavioral Genetics

Perhaps you remember learning in your high school or college biology class about **genes,** segments of deoxyribonucleic acid (DNA), and the rod-like structures that carry them, called **chromosomes.** All of the physiological mechanisms you have learned about so far in this chapter owe the nature of their structures and functions to the 30,000 genes that constitute the human genetic code. Remarkably, after 13 years of work, the scientists associated with The Human Genome Project finished locating and identifying each of these genes in April 2003 (U.S. Department of Energy, 2006). They include the information needed for both the universal characteristics we all share and those that distinguish us from each other. In other words, the form of the human face is encoded in our genes, but so are the minute differences that make each face slightly different from every other.

Our individual genetic codes also include some genes that are not expressed. For example, some people carry the gene for a disease, but do not have the disorder associated with it. To help distinguish genetic traits that are expressed from those that are not expressed, scientists use the term **genotype** to refer to an individual's genetic make-up and

genes   The segments of DNA that are located on the chromosomes and are the basic units for the transmission of all hereditary traits.

chromosomes   Rod-shaped structures in the nuclei of body cells, which contain all the genes and carry all the genetic information necessary to make a human being.

genotype   An individual's genetic makeup.

phenotype to refer to his or her actual traits. Thus, if a person carries the gene for a disease but does not suffer from it, the disease is part of her genotype but not part of her phenotype. Scientists still do not fully understand all of the factors that govern the expression of genes. However, a few of the rules that determine which aspects of an individual's genotype are expressed in her phenotype have been well established by research.

The Mechanisms of Heredity

The nuclei of every cell in a person's body, other than sperm and egg cells, carry 23 pairs of chromosomes (46 in all). Each of the sperm and egg cells has 23 single chromosomes. At conception, the sperm adds its 23 chromosomes to the 23 of the egg. From this union, a single cell called a *zygote* is formed; it has the full complement of 46 chromosomes (23 pairs), which contain about 30,000 genes (Baltimore, 2000). These genes carry all the genetic information needed to make a human being. The researchers at The Human Genome Project are working to identify the functions of all the genes and their locations on the chromosomes.

Twenty-two of the 23 pairs of chromosomes are matching pairs, called *autosomes*, and each member of these pairs carries genes for particular physical and mental traits. The chromosomes in the 23rd pair are called *sex chromosomes* because they carry the genes that determine a person's sex. The sex chromosomes of females consist of two X chromosomes (XX); males have an X chromosome and a Y chromosome (XY). The egg cell always contains an X chromosome. Half of a man's sperm cells carry an X chromosome, and half carry a Y. Thus, the sex of an individual depends on which type of chromosome is carried by the sperm that fertilizes the egg. A single gene found only on the Y chromosome causes a fetus to become a male. This gene, which has been labeled *Sry*, orchestrates the development of the male sex organs (Capel, 2000).

Many traits are influenced by complementary gene pairs, one from the sperm and the other from the egg. In most cases, these gene pairs follow a set of inheritance rules known as the **dominant-recessive pattern.** The gene for curly hair, for example, is dominant over the gene for straight hair. Thus, a person having one gene for curly hair and one for straight hair will have curly hair, and people with straight hair have two recessive genes. A person who carries two copies of the same gene, whether both dominant or both recessive, is known as *homozygous*, while one who has two different genes is called *heterozygous*. **Figure 2.13** shows two of the possible hair types of offspring of a parent who has curly hair but is heterozygous for this trait and a parent who has straight hair. What are the others?

Several neurological and psychological disorders are associated with dominant or recessive genes. For instance, at the beginning of the chapter, you read about the Wexler family's struggle with Huntington's Disease, a degenerative disease of the nervous system caused by a dominant gene. Some kinds of schizophrenia also are linked to recessive genes. However, most of the traits of interest to psychologists follow more complex inheritance patterns.

In *polygenic inheritance*, many genes influence a particular characteristic. For example, skin color is determined by several genes. When one parent has dark skin and the other is fair-skinned, the child will have skin that is somewhere between the two. Many polygenic characteristics are subject to **multifactorial inheritance;** that is, they are influenced by both genes and environmental factors. For instance, a man's genes may allow him to reach a height of 6 feet, but if he suffers from malnutrition while still growing, his height may not reach its genetic potential. As you'll learn in later chapters, both intelligence (Chapter 7) and personality (Chapter 13) are believed to be polygenic and multifactorial in nature. In addition, many psychiatric diseases are multifactorial (Leonardo & Hen, 2006).

Sex-linked inheritance involves the genes on the X and Y chromosomes. In females, the two X chromosomes function pretty much like the autosomes: If one carries a harmful gene, the other usually has a gene that offsets its effects. In males, however, if the single X chromosome carries a harmful gene, there is no offsetting gene on the

2.22 What patterns of inheritance are evident in the transmission of genetic traits?

▲ This child's *phenotype* includes curly hair. What can you infer about her *genotype*? How likely is it that neither of her parents has curly hair? (Hint: Look at Figure 2.13.)

phenotype   An individual's actual characteristics.

dominant-recessive pattern   A set of inheritance rules in which the presence of a single dominant gene causes a trait to be expressed but two genes must be present for the expression of a recessive trait.

multifactorial inheritance   A pattern of inheritance in which a trait is influenced by both genes and environmental factors.

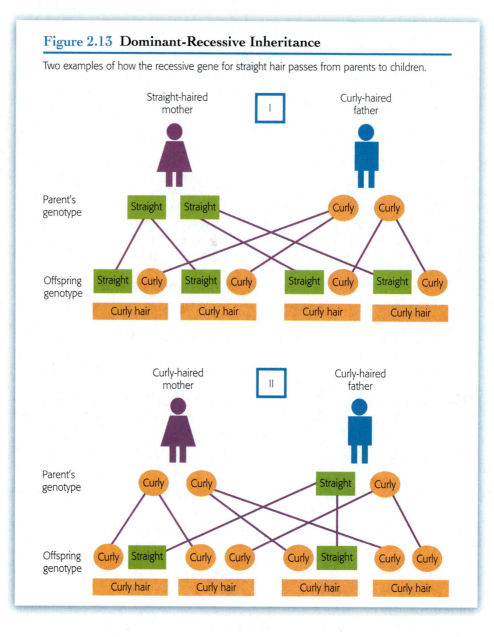

Figure 2.13 Dominant-Recessive Inheritance

Two examples of how the recessive gene for straight hair passes from parents to children.

Y chromosome because it is very small and carries only the genes needed to create the male body type. Consequently, disorders caused by genes on the X chromosome occur far more often in males than in females. For example, one fairly common sex-linked disorder you will read about in Chapter 3 is *red-green color blindness*. About 5% of men have the disorder, but less than 1% of women suffer from it (Neitz et al., 1996). About 1 in every 1,500 males and 1 in every 2,500 females have a far more serious sex-linked disorder called *fragile–X syndrome*, which can cause mental retardation (Adesman, 1996).

Behavioral Genetics

2.23 What kinds of studies are done by behavioral geneticists?

Behavioral genetics is a field of research that investigates the relative effects of heredity and environment—nature and nurture—on behavior (Plomin et al., 1997). In twin studies, behavioral geneticists study identical twins (monozygotic twins) and fraternal twins (dizygotic twins) to determine how much they resemble each other on a variety of characteristics. Identical twins have exactly the same genes because a single

Apply It   Why Consider Genetic Counseling?

Do you have relatives who suffer from genetic disorders? Surveys suggest that most relatives of individuals who suffer from such disorders or who have diseases that may have a genetic basis, such as breast cancer, are eager to know their own personal risk (Kinney et al., 2001). If you consult a genetic counselor, he or she will carry out a case study involving a detailed family history as well as genetic tests. The purpose of the study will be to estimate your risk of suffering from the same disorders and diseases as your relatives. The counselor will also estimate the likelihood that you will pass genetic defects on to your children.

The goal of genetic counseling is to help people make informed decisions about their own lives and those of their chil-

dren. This goal is important because most people, especially those whose relatives have genetic disorders, greatly overestimate their own chances of having a genetic defect (Quaid et al., 2001). Generally, genetic counseling leads to more realistic perceptions and feelings of relief (Tercyak et al., 2001). Moreover, parents of children who suffer from genetic diseases report that they feel less guilt about transmitting the disease to their children after receiving genetic counseling (Collins et al., 2001).

However, genetic counseling also has a downside. Once an individual's disease risk is known, especially for life-threatening illnesses such as breast cancer, it may be difficult for him or her to get health insurance (Geer et al., 2001). Although there is no evidence that insurance companies deny coverage based on the results of genetic testing, 28 states have enacted laws to prevent them from doing so in the future (Steinberg, 2000). Geneticists and genetic counselors believe that such legislation is needed because genetic testing is rapidly making prediction of future illness more accurate. Moreover, a growing number of people are seeking such testing. Experts point out that results from genetic testing do not differ much from the information on the family history that health insurers already use to accept or reject applicants (Steinberg, 2000). Thus, without legal protection in place, genetic testing could become a routine part of the application approval process for health insurance.

Another problem with genetic counseling is that many recipients report feeling overwhelmed by the amount of information provided by counselors and the sometimes difficult task of understanding the complex probability statements that often result from the case studies (Collins et al., 2001). Still, most people who seek genetic counseling say that, on balance, they are better off knowing the facts about potential genetic risks for themselves and their children (Collins et al., 2001).

sperm of the father fertilizes a single egg of the mother, forming a cell that then splits and forms two human beings—"carbon copies." In the case of fraternal twins, two separate sperm cells fertilize two separate eggs that happen to be released at the same time during ovulation. Fraternal twins are no more alike genetically than any two siblings born to the same parents.

Twins who are raised together, whether identical or fraternal, have similar environments. If identical twins raised together are found to be more alike on a certain trait than fraternal twins raised together, then that trait is assumed to be more influenced by heredity. But if the identical and fraternal twin pairs do not differ on the trait, then that trait is assumed to be influenced more by environment.

In adoption studies, behavioral geneticists study children adopted shortly after birth. Researchers compare the children's abilities and personality traits to those of their adoptive parents and those of their biological parents. This strategy allows researchers to disentangle the effects of heredity and environment (Plomin et al., 1988). As you will learn in later chapters, behavioral geneticists have found that genes clearly contribute to individual differences in both intelligence (Chapter 7) and personality (Chapter 14). However, their research has also demonstrated that environmental factors, such as poverty and culture, influence these characteristics as well.

behavioral genetics A field of research that uses twin studies and adoption studies to investigate the relative effects of heredity and environment on behavior.

Because heredity and environment work together to influence so many of the variables of interest to psychologists, you'll be reading a great deal more in later chapters about the debate concerning their relative influence.

Remember It — Genes and Behavioral Genetics

1. The X and Y chromosomes are known as the _____ chromosomes.
2. A _____ gene will not be expressed if the individual carries only one copy of it.
3. Characteristics that are affected by both genes and environment are said to be _____.
4. _____ is the field of research that investigates the relative effects of heredity and environment on behavior.
5. _____ twins develop from a single fertilized egg.
6. Researchers use _____ and _____ studies to disentangle the effects of heredity and environment.

Answers: 1. sex; 2. recessive; 3. multifactorial; 4. Behavioral genetics; 5. Identical; 6. twin, adoption

Summary and Review

The Neurons and the Neurotransmitters p. 43

2.1 What are the functions of the various parts of the neuron? p. 44

The cell body carries out metabolic functions. The dendrites receive messages from other neurons. The axon transmits messages to the dendrites of other neurons and to the muscles, glands, and other parts of the body.

2.2 How are messages transmitted through the nervous system? p. 44

The action potential, the primary means by which the brain and body communicate with one another via the nervous system, is the sudden reversal (from a negative to a positive value) of the resting potential on the cell membrane of a neuron; this reversal initiates the firing of a neuron. A strong stimulus will cause many more neurons to fire and to fire much more rapidly than a weak stimulus will.

2.3 What are neurotransmitters, and what do they contribute to nervous system functioning? p. 46

Neurotransmitters are chemicals released into the synaptic cleft from the axon terminal of the sending neuron. They cross the synaptic cleft and bind to receptors on the receiving neuron, influencing the cell to fire or not to fire. Neurotransmitters thus transmit messages between neurons.

2.4 What are the functions of some of the major neurotransmitters? p. 48

Some of the major neurotransmitters are acetylcholine, dopamine, norepinephrine, epinephrine, serotonin, glutamate, GABA, and endorphins. Acetylcholine (Ach) affects muscle fibers and is involved in learning. Dopamine affects learning, attention, movement, and reinforcement. Norepinephrine and epinephrine help regulate eating and energy release. Serotonin and GABA are inhibitory neurotransmitters that help us sleep, whereas glutamate, an excitatory neurotransmitter, helps us stay awake. Endorphins are natural pain-killers.

The Human Nervous System p. 49

2.5 Why is an intact spinal cord important to normal functioning? p. 50

The spinal cord must be intact so that sensory information can reach the brain and messages from the brain can reach muscles, glands, and other parts of the body.

2.6 Which brain structures and functions are found in the hindbrain? p. 51

The part of the hindbrain known as the brainstem contains both the medulla, which controls heartbeat, breathing, blood pressure, coughing, and swallowing, and the reticular formation, which plays a crucial role in arousal and attention. The cerebellum allows the body to execute smooth, skilled movements and regulates muscle tone and posture.

2.7 **What important structure is located in the midbrain? p. 52**

The substantia nigra, located in the midbrain, controls unconscious motor actions, such as riding a bicycle. Damage to this structure is believed to be one cause of Parkinson's disease.

2.8 **Which brain structures and functions are found in the forebrain? p. 53**

The thalamus acts as a relay station for virtually all the information flowing into and out of the forebrain. The hypothalamus regulates hunger, thirst, sexual behavior, internal body temperature, and a wide variety of emotional behaviors. The limbic system is a group of structures in the brain, including the amygdala and the hippocampus, that are collectively involved in emotional expression, memory, and motivation.

2.9 **What is the difference between the sympathetic and parasympathetic nervous systems? p. 54**

The sympathetic nervous system mobilizes the body's resources during emergencies or during stress, and the parasympathetic nervous system brings the heightened bodily responses back to normal after an emergency.

Discovering the Brain's Mysteries p. 56

2.10 **What does an electroencephalogram (EEG) reveal about the brain? p. 56**

An electroencephalogram (EEG) is a record of brain-wave activity. It can reveal an epileptic seizure and can show patterns of neural activity associated with learning disabilities, schizophrenia, Alzheimer's disease, sleep disorders, and other problems.

2.11 **How are a CT scan and an MRI helpful in the study of brain structure? p. 57**

Both the CT scan and MRI provide detailed images of brain structures. Functional MRI (fMRI) can also provide information about brain function.

2.12 **How are a PET scan and newer imaging techniques used to study the brain? p. 57**

The PET scan reveals patterns of blood flow, oxygen use, and glucose metabolism in the brain. It can also show the action of drugs in the brain and other organs. PET scan studies show that different brain areas are used to perform different tasks. Two more recently developed technologies, SQUID and MEG, measure magnetic changes to reveal neural activity within the brain as it occurs.

A Closer Look at the Brain p. 58

2.13 **What are the components of the cerebrum? p. 58**

The cerebral hemispheres are connected by the corpus callosum and covered by the cerebral cortex, which is primarily responsible for higher mental processes such as language, memory, and thinking.

2.14 **What are the specialized functions of the left and right cerebral hemispheres? p. 59**

The left hemisphere controls the right side of the body, coordinates complex movements, and handles most of the language functions, including speaking, writing, reading, and understanding the written and the spoken word. The right hemisphere controls the left side of the body. It is specialized for visual-spatial perception, the interpretation of nonverbal behavior, and the recognition and expression of emotion.

2.15 **Which psychological functions are associated with the frontal lobes? p. 63**

The frontal lobes contain (1) the motor cortex, which controls voluntary motor activity; (2) Broca's area, which functions in speech production; and (3) the frontal association areas, which are involved in thinking, motivation, planning for the future, impulse control, and emotional responses.

2.16 **What important structure is found in the parietal lobes? p. 66**

The somatosensory cortex is the front portion of the parietal lobes. It is the site where touch, pressure, temperature, and pain register in the cerebral cortex.

2.17 **Why are the occipital lobes critical to vision? p. 67**

The occipital lobes are involved in the reception and interpretation of visual information. They contain the primary visual cortex, where vision registers in the cerebral cortex.

2.18 **What are the major areas within the temporal lobes, and what are their functions? p. 67**

The temporal lobes contain (1) the primary auditory cortex, where hearing registers in the cortex; (2) Wernicke's area, which is involved in comprehending the spoken word and in formulating coherent speech and written language; and (3) the temporal association areas, where memories are stored and auditory stimuli are interpreted.

2.19 **In what ways does the brain change across a life span? p. 68**

The brain grows in spurts, each of which is followed by a period of pruning of unnecessary synapses. The activity of transmitters within the synapses also varies with age. Few neurons are myelinated at birth, but the process of myelination continues into the adult years. Language appears to be lateralized very early in life, but other functions, such as spatial perception, aren't fully lateralized until age 8 or so. Aging eventually leads to a reduction in the number of synapses.

2.20 **How do the brains of men differ from those of women? p. 69**

Men's brains have a higher proportion of white matter in the left brain; women have equal proportions of gray and white matter in the two hemispheres. Some tasks tap different areas in men's brains than they do in the brains of women.

The Endocrine System p. 70

2.21 What functions are associated with the various glands of the endocrine system? p. 70

The pituitary gland releases hormones that control other glands in the endocrine system and also releases a growth hormone. The thyroid gland produces thyroxine, which regulates metabolism. The pancreas produces insulin and glucagon and regulates blood sugar levels. The adrenal glands release epinephrine and norepinephrine, which prepare the body for emergencies and stressful situations; these glands also release corticoids and small amounts of the sex hormones. The gonads are the sex glands, which produce the sex hormones and make reproduction possible.

Genes and Behavioral Genetics p. 72

2.22 What patterns of inheritance are evident in the transmission of genetic traits? p. 73

Some genetic traits follow the dominant-recessive pattern, while others are polygenic and multifactorial. Both intelligence and personality are thought to be polygenic and multifactorial. Thus, they are influenced by many genes as well as factors in the environment.

2.23 What kinds of studies are done by behavioral geneticists? p. 74

Behavioral genetics is the study of the relative effects of heredity and environment on behavior. Researchers in this field use twin studies, which involve comparisons of identical and fraternal twins, and adoption studies, or studies of children adopted shortly after birth and their adoptive and biological parents. Such studies suggest that both intelligence and personality are influenced by heredity as well as by the environment.

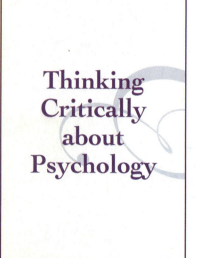

Thinking Critically about Psychology

1. Much of the brain research you have read about in this chapter was carried out using animals. In many studies, it is necessary to euthanize animals to study their brain tissues directly. Many people object to this practice, but others say it is justified because it advances knowledge about the brain. Prepare arguments to support both of the following positions: (a) The use of animals in brain research projects is ethical and justifiable because of the possible benefits to humankind. (b) The use of animals in brain research projects is not ethical or justifiable on the grounds of possible benefits to humankind.

2. How would your life change if you had a massive stroke affecting your left hemisphere? How would it change if the stroke damaged your right hemisphere? Which stroke would be more tragic for you, and why?

3. Imagine you heard someone make this statement: "All of the children conceived by one brown-eyed and one blue-eyed parent will have brown eyes because brown is dominant over blue." Is the statement accurate? Why or why not? How would you explain your argument in favor of or against the statement to someone who knows little about genetics?

Key Terms

acetylcholine, p. 48
action potential, p. 46
adrenal glands, p. 71
alpha wave, p. 56
amygdala, p. 53
association areas, p. 59
axon, p. 44
behavioral genetics, p. 75
beta wave, p. 56
brainstem, p. 51
Broca's aphasia, p. 65
Broca's area, p. 65
cell body, p. 44
central nervous system (CNS), p. 49
cerebellum, p. 52
cerebral cortex, p. 59
cerebral hemispheres, p. 58
cerebrum, p. 58
chromosomes, p. 72
corpus callosum, p. 58
CT scan (computerized axial tomography), p. 57
delta wave, p. 56
dendrites, p. 44
dominant-recessive pattern, p. 73
dopamine, p. 48
electroencephalogram (EEG), p. 56
endocrine system, p. 70

endorphins, p. 49
epinephrine, p. 48
forebrain, p. 53
functional MRI (fMRI), p. 57
frontal lobes, p. 63
GABA, p. 49
genes, p. 72
genotype, 72
glial cells, p. 44
glutamate, p. 49
hindbrain, 50
hippocampus, p. 54
hormone, p. 70
hypothalamus, p. 53
lateralization, p. 59
left hemisphere, p. 60
limbic system, p. 53
MRI (magnetic resonance imagery), p. 57
medulla, p. 52
microelectrode, p. 56
midbrain, 52
motor cortex, p. 64
multifactorial inheritance, p. 73
myelin sheath, p. 46
neuron, p. 44
neurotransmitter, p. 46
norepinephrine, p. 48
occipital lobes, p. 67

parasympathetic nervous system, p. 55
parietal lobes, p. 66
peripheral nervous system (PNS), p. 49
PET scan (positron-emission tomography), p. 57
phenotype, p. 72
pituitary gland, p. 70
plasticity, p. 69
primary auditory cortex, p. 67
primary visual cortex, p. 67
pruning, p. 68
receptors, p. 46
resting potential, p. 45
reticular formation, p. 52
reuptake, p. 47
right hemisphere, p. 60
serotonin, p. 49
somatosensory cortex, p. 66
spinal cord, p. 50
split-brain operation, p. 62
substantia nigra, p. 52
sympathetic nervous system, p. 54
synapse, p. 44
temporal lobes, p. 67
thalamus, p. 53
Wernicke's aphasia, p. 67
Wernicke's area, p. 67

Chapter 3

Sensation and Perception

Continued

Suppose you find out that your baby daughter has a profound hearing loss. Would you elect to have a device that might enable her to hear—called a *cochlear implant* (CI)—surgically implanted just above her ear? Your first reaction might be, "Of course, I would want my child to be able to hear." But how would you react to learning that getting the device to function properly might require months or even years of work with specially trained technicians? The doctors also inform you that there are many ordinary experiences, such as playing with balloons, that your child would have to avoid because they produce static electricity that might wipe out the programming on the device's microchip. You also learn that your child would never be able to undergo a magnetic resonance imaging exam (MRI) because of the magnet the device contains. Would you still pursue the surgery?

Most parents of children with serious hearing impairments consider the CI option because they hope that their children will be able to learn to speak and to engage in normal conversations with other people. However, if you asked the doctors to predict your child's speech development following CI surgery, they would tell you that they have no way of knowing. They only know that all children who receive CIs experience sound to a greater degree than they do without them. A better alternative for your child, some experts would argue, would be to learn sign language and to become a fully functioning member of the *deaf culture* (Delost & Lashley, 2000). As such, she would develop her self-concept and her sense of self-esteem in the context of a culture in which she would be accepted as normal. In contrast, a CI will require her to wear an external sound processor device that will identify her as different from her peers. In addition, she will have to undergo months or years of speech therapy and may never develop normal speech. Her poor articulation may cause her to be teased. Likewise, many children with CIs have to learn lip-reading because the device does not restore enough hearing for adequate oral speech perception.

As you can see, making a life-changing decision regarding the implantation of a CI in a child might be difficult. There are several relevant research findings that can help parents make this difficult decision. Understanding them begins with the concept that *sensation* and *perception* are distinct processes. **Sensation** is the process through which the senses pick up visual, auditory, and other sensory stimuli and transmit them to the brain. **Perception** is the process by which sensory information is actively organized and interpreted by the brain. In infants and young children who do not have hearing impairments, auditory sensation is present even before birth, but auditory perception develops gradually and requires sound input from the environment. Children who are born with hearing impairments have impaired sensation, but their capacity for developing perception is unaffected. You might expect that if hearing can be restored—the sensory part of the sensation–perception equation—then the brain ought to respond by developing the capacity for auditory perception. Is this what happens when a child receives a CI?

You should recall from Chapter 2 that sounds are processed and interpreted in the primary auditory cortex, found in the temporal lobes of the cerebral cortex. So, the question we are really asking about young children's responses to cochlear implantation concerns what happens in this area of the brain after a person receives a CI. Brain-imaging studies with adult CI patients show that within a few months of having their hearing restored, adult brains display cortical responses that are very similar to the cortical responses of hearing individuals, even if the patients have been without hearing for many years (Pantey, Dinnesen, Ross, Wolbrink, & Knief, 2006). Moreover, studies show that most adults who have CI surgery recover at least some of their speech perception and production abilities. These results mean that when the adult auditory cortex is deprived of sensation, it retains its capacity for perception.

How do these findings bear on our question about children's responses to CIs? You may recall from Chapter 2 that the brains of children possess greater *plasticity,* or capacity for change, than those of adults. Consequently, you might guess that their auditory cortices would respond to CIs similarly to those of adults. However, almost all adults in CI studies had normal hearing in childhood and developed perceptual neural networks in the auditory cortex in the same way as other children. Consequently, the positive results seen in studies with adults may be attributable to the brain's ability to preserve these networks during periods of hearing loss. But what happens in the auditory cortex when children who have never had normal hearing receive CIs?

Several studies have shown that, in general, the earlier a child receives a CI, the more likely she is to acquire normal speech perception and production abilities (Flipsen & Colvard, 2006). However, researchers have only recently begun using brain-imaging techniques to show that this age trend is explained by a change in the brain's capacity to respond to sound. These studies have identified age boundaries for what seems to be a sensitive period in human children for the development of perceptual neural networks in the auditory cortex. It appears that the neurological components of auditory perception will develop normally if a child has a CI prior to $3\frac{1}{2}$ years of age (Sharma, Dorman, & Kral, 2005; Sharma, Dorman, & Spahr, 2002). If children receive the device between $3\frac{1}{2}$ and 7 years of age, they develop some auditory cortical function, but it will not be fully normal. After age 7, the likelihood that a child's brain will develop the cortical capacity for speech perception diminishes considerably.

Returning to our original question about whether you would opt for CI for your own child, now that you have more information, what do you think your decision would be? It might help to know that even though they fully understand all of the risks and potential disappointments associated with CIs, most parents of children with serious hearing impairments respond affirmatively when they are informed that their child might benefit from implantation of the device. Furthermore, many years after the surgery, even parents whose children's results with the device proved to be somewhat disappointing say that they do not regret their decision (Sach & Whynes, 2005). Interviews with children who have CIs indicate that they, too, appreciate having sound as part of their worlds (Preisler, Tvingstedt, & Ahlström, 2005). However, children who learn sign language and who grow up in the deaf community are happy, too—particularly those who come from families in which deafness is common and all family members are fluent in sign language.

In this chapter, we will explore the world of sensation and perception. First, we'll consider the two dominant senses: vision and hearing. Then, we'll turn our attention to the other senses: smell, taste, touch, pain, and balance. You will learn how the senses detect sensory information and how this sensory information is actively organized and interpreted by the brain.

The Process of Sensation

Our senses serve as ports of entry for all information about our world. Yet it is amazing how little of the sensory world humans actually do sense, compared to animals. Some animals have a superior sense of hearing (bats and dolphins), others have extremely sharp vision (hawks), and still others have an amazingly keen sense of smell (bloodhounds). Nevertheless, humans have remarkable sensory and perceptual abilities.

sensation The process through which the senses pick up visual, auditory, and other sensory stimuli and transmit them to the brain.

perception The process by which sensory information is actively organized and interpreted by the brain.

The Absolute and Difference Thresholds

▲ What is the dimmest light this lifeguard could perceive in the darkness? Researchers in sensory psychology have performed many experiments over the years to answer such questions. Their research has established measures known as absolute thresholds. Just as the threshold of a doorway is the dividing point between being outside a room and being inside it, the absolute threshold of a sense marks the difference between not being able to perceive a stimulus and being just barely able to perceive it.

absolute threshold The minimum amount of sensory stimulation that can be detected 50% of the time.

difference threshold A measure of the smallest increase or decrease in a physical stimulus that is required to produce a difference in sensation that is noticeable 50% of the time.

just noticeable difference (JND) The smallest change in sensation that a person is able to detect 50% of the time.

Weber's law The law stating that the just noticeable difference (JND) for all the senses depends on a proportion or percentage of change in a stimulus rather than on a fixed amount of change.

What is the softest sound you can hear, the dimmest light you can see, the most diluted substance you can taste? Researchers in sensory psychology have performed many experiments over the years to answer these questions. Their research has established measures for the senses known as absolute thresholds. Just as the threshold of a doorway is the dividing point between being outside a room and inside, the **absolute threshold** of a sense marks the difference between not being able to perceive a stimulus and being just barely able to perceive it. Psychologists have arbitrarily defined this absolute threshold as the minimum amount of sensory stimulation that can be detected 50% of the time. The absolute thresholds for vision, hearing, taste, smell, and touch are illustrated in **Figure 3.1**.

If you are listening to music, the very fact that you can hear it means that the absolute threshold has been crossed. But how much must the volume be turned up or down for you to notice a difference? Or, if you are carrying some bags of groceries, how much weight must be added or taken away for you to be able to sense that your load is heavier or lighter? The **difference threshold** is a measure of the smallest increase or decrease in a physical stimulus that is required to produce the **just noticeable difference (JND).** The JND is the smallest change in sensation that a person is able to detect 50% of the time. If you were holding a 5-pound weight and 1 pound were added, you could easily notice the difference. But if you were holding 100 pounds and 1 additional pound were added, you could not sense the difference. Why not?

More than 150 years ago, researcher Ernst Weber (1795–1878) observed that the JND for all the senses depends on a proportion or percentage of change in a stimulus rather than on a fixed amount of change. This observation became known as **Weber's law.** A weight you are holding must increase or decrease by $\frac{1}{50}$, or 2%, for you to notice the difference; in contrast, if you were listening to music, you would notice a difference if a tone became slightly higher or lower in pitch by about only 0.33%. According to Weber's law, the greater the original stimulus, the more it must be increased or decreased for the difference to be noticeable.

As you might suspect, the difference threshold is not the same for all the senses. A very large ($\frac{1}{5}$, or 20%) difference is necessary for some changes in taste to be detected. Moreover, Weber's law best applies to people with average sensitivities and to sensory stimuli that are neither very strong (loud thunder) nor very weak (a faint whisper). For instance, expert wine tasters would know if a particular vintage was a little too sweet, even if its sweetness varied by only a fraction of the 20% necessary for changes in taste. Furthermore, people who have lost one sensory ability often gain greater sensitivity in others. One study found that children with early-onset blindness were more capable of correctly labeling 25 common odors than were sighted children, whereas another found that congenitally deaf students possessed motion-perception abilities superior to those of hearing students (Bavelier et al., 2000; Rosenbluth et al., 2000).

Transduction and Adaptation

Would you be surprised to learn that our eyes do not actually see and that our ears do not hear? The sense organs provide only the beginning of sensation, which must be completed by the brain. As you learned in Chapter 2, specific clusters of neurons in specialized parts of the brain must be stimulated for us to see, hear, taste, and so on. Yet the brain itself cannot respond directly to light, sound waves, odors, and tastes. How, then, does it get the message? The answer is through the sensory receptors.

The body's sense organs are equipped with highly specialized cells called **sensory receptors** which detect and respond to one type of sensory stimuli—light, sound waves, odors, and so on.

Figure 3.1   Absolute Thresholds

Absolute thresholds have been established for humans for vision, hearing, taste, smell, and touch.

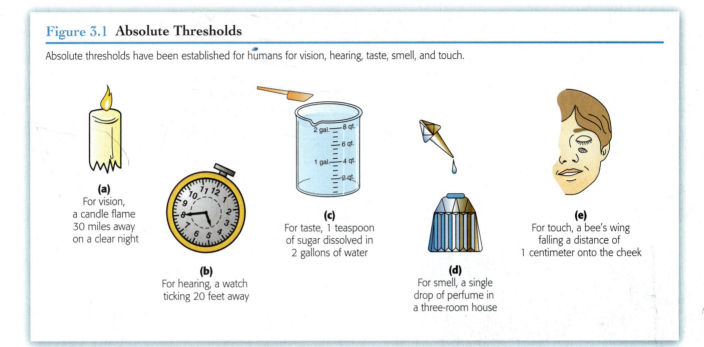

(a)
For vision,
a candle flame
30 miles away
on a clear night

(b)
For hearing, a watch
ticking 20 feet away

(c)
For taste, 1 teaspoon
of sugar dissolved in
2 gallons of water

(d)
For smell, a single
drop of perfume in
a three-room house

(e)
For touch, a bee's wing
falling a distance of
1 centimeter onto the cheek

Through a process known as **transduction,** the sensory receptors convert the sensory stimulation into neural impulses, the electrochemical language of the brain. The neural impulses are then transmitted to precise locations in the brain, such as the primary visual cortex for vision or the primary auditory cortex for hearing. We experience a sensation only when the appropriate part of the brain is stimulated. The sense receptors provide the essential link between the physical sensory world and the brain.

After a time, the sensory receptors grow accustomed to constant, unchanging levels of stimuli—sights, sounds, or smells—so we notice them less and less, or not at all. For example, smokers become accustomed to the smell of cigarette smoke in their homes and on their clothing. This process is known as **sensory adaptation.** Even though it reduces our sensory awareness, sensory adaptation enables us to shift our attention to what is most important at any given moment. However, sensory adaptation is not likely to occur in the presence of a very strong stimulus, such as the smell of ammonia, an ear-splitting sound, or the taste of rancid food.

▲ What role is played by sensory adaptation in the conversation in which these stock traders are engaged?

sensory receptors   Highly specialized cells in the sense organs that detect and respond to one type of sensory stimuli—light, sound, or odor, for example—and transduce (convert) the stimuli into neural impulses.

transduction   The process through which sensory receptors convert the sensory stimulation into neural impulses.

sensory adaptation   The process in which sensory receptors grow accustomed to constant, unchanging levels of stimuli over time.

Vision

Which of your senses do you regard as the most valuable? If you're like most people, you value vision more than any other sensory experience. So perhaps it is not surprising that vision is the most studied of all the senses. One thing vision researchers have known for a long time is that there is a great deal more information in the sensory environment than our eyes can take in. Our eyes can respond only to visible light waves, which form a small subgroup of *electromagnetic waves*, a band called the **visible spectrum** (see **Figure 3.2**). The shortest light waves we can see appear violet, while the longest visible waves appear red. But sight is much more than just response to light.

The Eye

3.3 How does each part of the eye function in vision?

The globe-shaped human eyeball, shown in **Figure 3.3**, measures about 1 inch in diameter. It is truly one of the marvels of nature.

The Cornea, Iris, and Pupil. Bulging from the eye's surface is the **cornea**—the tough, transparent, protective layer covering the front of the eye. The cornea performs the first step in vision by bending the light rays inward. It directs the light rays through the *pupil*, the small, dark opening in the center of the *iris*, or colored part of the eye. The iris dilates and contracts the pupil to regulate the amount of light entering the eye.

visible spectrum   The narrow band of electromagnetic waves that are visible to the human eye.

cornea   (KOR-nee-uh) The tough, transparent, protective layer that covers the front of the eye and bends light rays inward through the pupil.

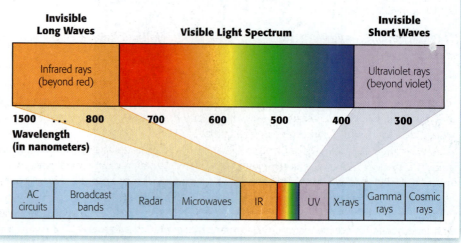

Figure 3.2 The Electromagnetic Spectrum

Human eyes can perceive only a very thin band of electromagnetic waves, known as the visible spectrum.

Figure 3.3 The Major Parts of the Human Eye

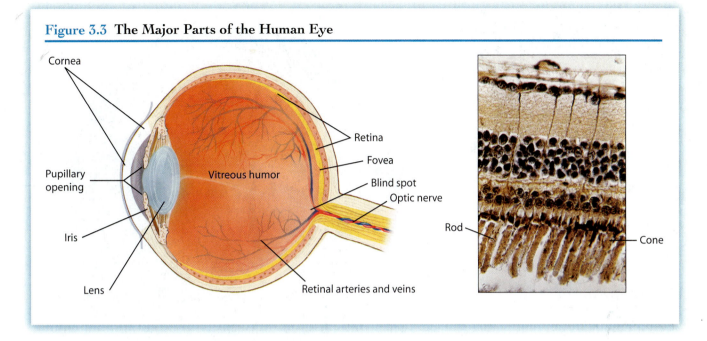

Suspended just behind the iris and the pupil, the **lens** is composed of many thin layers and looks like a transparent disc. The lens performs the task of focusing on viewed objects. It flattens as it focuses on objects at a distance and becomes more spherical, bulging in the center, as it focuses on close objects. This flattening and bulging action of the lens is known as **accommodation.** With age, the lens loses the ability to change its shape to accommodate for near vision, a condition called *presbyopia* ("old eyes"). This is why many people over age 40 must hold a book or newspaper at arm's length or use reading glasses to magnify the print.

From Lens to Retina. The lens focuses the incoming image onto the **retina**—a layer of tissue about the size of a small postage stamp and as thin as onion skin, located on the inner surface of the eyeball and containing the sensory receptors for vision. The image that is projected onto the retina is upside down and reversed left to right, as illustrated in **Figure 3.4**.

In some people, the distance through the eyeball (from the lens to the retina) is either too short or too long for proper focusing. Nearsightedness (*myopia*) occurs when the lens focuses images of distant objects in front of, rather than on, the retina. A person with this condition will be able to see near objects clearly, but distant images will be blurred. Farsightedness (*hyperopia*) occurs when the lens focuses images of close objects behind, rather than on, the retina. The individual is able to see far objects clearly, but close objects are blurred. Both conditions are correctable with eyeglasses or contact lenses, or by surgical procedures.

The Rods and Cones. At the back of the retina is a layer of light-sensitive receptor cells—the **rods** and the **cones.** Named for their shapes, the rods look like slender cylinders, and the cones appear shorter and more rounded. There are about 120 million rods and 6 million cones in each retina. The cones are the receptor cells that enable us to see color and fine detail in adequate light, but they do not function in very dim light. By contrast, the rods in the human eye are extremely sensitive, allowing the eye to respond to as few as five photons of light (Hecht et al., 1942).

A substance called *rhodopsin* present in the rods enables us to adapt to variations in light. Rhodopsin has two components: *opsin* and *retinal* (a chemical similar to Vitamin A). In bright light, opsin and retinal break apart, as the process of *light adaptation* takes place. During *dark adaptation*, opsin and retinal bond to one another, reforming rhodopsin. When you move from bright light to total darkness, as when you enter a darkened movie theater, you are momentarily blind until the opsin and

lens The transparent disc-shaped structure behind the iris and the pupil that changes shape as it focuses on objects at varying distances.

accommodation The flattening and bulging action of the lens as it focuses images of objects on the retina.

retina The layer of tissue that is located on the inner surface of the eyeball and contains the sensory receptors for vision.

rods The light-sensitive receptor cells in the retina that look like slender cylinders and allow the eye to respond to as few as five photons of light.

cones The light-sensitive, rounded receptor cells in the retina that enable humans to see color and fine detail in adequate light but do not function in very dim light.

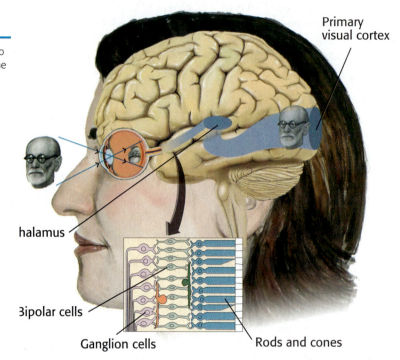

Figure 3.4 From Retinal Image to Meaningful Information

Because of the way the lens alters light rays in order to produce a clear image, images are upside down on the retina. The brain's visual processing system takes the upside-down retinal image and flips it so it is properly orientated.

Primary visual cortex

halamus

Bipolar cells

Ganglion cells

Rods and cones

retinal recombine. Similarly, when you leave the theater again, you become temporarily blind until the two substances break apart once again.

At the center of the retina is the **fovea,** a small area about the size of the period at the end of this sentence. When you look directly at an object, the image of the object is focused on the center of your fovea. The fovea contains no rods but has about 30,000 cones tightly packed together, providing the clearest and sharpest area of vision in the whole retina. The cones are most densely packed at the center of the fovea; their density decreases sharply just a few degrees beyond the fovea's center and then levels off more gradually to the periphery of the retina.

fovea (FO-vee-uh) A small area at the center of the retina that provides the clearest and sharpest vision because it has the largest concentration of cones.

Vision and the Brain

3.4 What path does visual information take from the retina to the primary visual cortex?

As you can see in Figure 3.4, the brain is responsible for converting the upside-down retinal images into meaningful visual information. But the first stages of neural processing actually take place in the retina itself.

From the Retina to the Brain. The rods and cones transduce, or change, light waves into neural impulses that are fed to the bipolar cells, which, in turn, pass the impulses along to the ganglion cells. The approximately 1 million axonlike extensions of the ganglion cells are bundled together in a pencil-sized cable that extends through the wall of the retina, leaving the eye and leading to the brain. There are no rods or cones where the cable runs through the retinal wall, and so this point is a **blind spot** in each eye (see *Try It*).

blind spot The point in each retina where there are no rods or cones because the cable of ganglion cells is extending through the retinal wall.

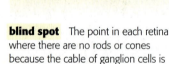

Try It   Vision

To locate one of your blind spots, hold this book at arm's length. Close your right eye and look directly at the magician's eyes. Now slowly bring the book closer, keeping your eye fixed on the magi- cian. When the rabbit disappears, you have found the blind spot in your left eye.

Beyond the retinal wall of each eye, the cable becomes the **optic nerve** (refer to Figure 3.3). The two optic nerves come together at the *optic chiasm*, a point where some of their nerve fibers cross to the opposite side of the brain. The nerve fibers from the right half of each retina go to the right hemisphere, and those from the left half of each retina go to the left hemisphere. This crossing over is important because it allows visual information from a single eye to be represented in the primary visual cortex of both hemispheres of the brain. Moreover, it plays an important part in depth perception. But if one eye is covered and deprived of vision during a critical period of visual development early in life, the visual cortex almost completely stops responding to signals sent by that eye (Fagiolini & Hensch, 2000).

From the optic chiasm, the optic nerve fibers extend to the thalamus, where they form synapses with neurons that transmit the impulses to the primary visual cortex. Approximately one-fourth of the primary visual cortex is dedicated exclusively to analyzing input from the fovea, which, as you'll recall, is a very small but extremely important part of the retina.

The Primary Visual Cortex. Thanks to researchers David Hubel and Torsten Wiesel (1959, 1979; Hubel, 1963, 1995), who won a Nobel Prize for their work in 1981, we know a great deal about how specialized the neurons of the **primary visual cortex** are. (Recall from Chapter 2 that the primary visual cortex is the part of the brain in which visual information is processed.) By inserting tiny microelectrodes into single cells in the visual cortexes of cats, Hubel and Wiesel (1959) were able to determine what was happening in individual cells when the cats were exposed to different kinds of visual stimuli. They discovered that each neuron responded only to specific patterns. Some neurons responded only to lines and angles, while others fired only when the cat saw a vertical or horizontal line. Still others were responsive to nothing but right angles or lines of specific lengths. Neurons of this type are known as **feature detectors,** and they are already coded at birth to make their unique responses. Yet we see whole images, not collections of isolated features, because visual perceptions are complete only when the primary visual cortex transmits the millions of pieces of visual information it receives to other areas in the brain, where they are combined and assembled into whole visual images (Self & Zeki, 2005).

The major structures of the visual system are summarized in *Review and Reflect.*

optic nerve   The nerve that carries visual information from each retina to both sides of the brain.

primary visual cortex   The part of the brain in which visual information is processed.

feature detectors   Neurons in the brain that respond only to specific visual patterns (for example, to lines or angles).

Review and Reflect   Major Structures of the Visual System

Structure	Function
Cornea	Translucent covering on the front of the eyeball that bends light rays entering the eye inward through the pupil
Iris	Colored part of the eye that adjusts to maintain a constant amount of light entering the eye through the pupil
Pupil	Opening in the center of the iris through which light rays enter the eye
Lens	Transparent disc-shaped structure behind the pupil that adjusts its shape to allow focusing on objects at varying distances
Retina	Layer of tissue on the inner surface of the eye that contains sensory receptors for vision
Rods	Specialized receptor cells in the retina that are sensitive to light changes
Cones	Specialized receptor cells in the retina that enable humans to see fine detail and color in adequate light
Fovea	Small area at the center of the retina, packed with cones, on which objects viewed directly are clearly and sharply focused
Optic nerve	Nerve that carries visual information from the retina to the brain
Blind spot	Area in each eye where the optic nerve joins the retinal wall and no vision is possible

Color Vision

Why does the skin of an apple appear to be red, while its flesh is perceived as an off-white color? Remember, what we actually see is reflected light. Some light waves striking an object are absorbed by it; others are reflected from it. So, why does an apple's skin look red? If you hold a red apple in bright light, light waves of all the different wavelengths strike the apple, but more of the longer red wavelengths of light are reflected from the apple's skin. The shorter wavelengths are absorbed, so you see only the reflected red. Bite into the apple, and it looks off-white. Why? You see the near-white color because, rather than being absorbed, almost all of the wavelengths of the visible spectrum are reflected from the inside part of the apple. The presence of all visible wavelengths gives the sensation of a near-white color. If an object does indeed reflect 100% of visible wavelengths, it appears to be pure white.

Our everyday visual experience goes far beyond the colors in the rainbow. We can detect thousands of subtle color shadings. What produces these fine color distinctions? Researchers have identified three dimensions of light that combine to provide the rich world of color we experience: (1) The chief dimension is **hue,** which refers to the specific color perceived—red, blue, or yellow, for example. (2) **Saturation** refers to the purity of a color; a color becomes less saturated, or less pure, as other wavelengths of light are mixed with it. (3) **Brightness** refers to the intensity of the light energy that is perceived as a color.

Theories of Color Vision

Scientists know that the cones are responsible for color vision, but exactly how do they work to produce color sensations? Two major theories have been offered to explain color vision, and both were formulated before the development of laboratory technology capable of testing them. The **trichromatic theory,** first proposed by Thomas Young in 1802, was modified by Hermann von Helmholtz about 50 years later. This theory states that there are three kinds of cones in the retina and that each kind makes a maximal chemical response to one of three colors—blue, green, or red. Research conducted in the 1950s and the 1960s by Nobel Prize winner George Wald (1964; Wald et al., 1954) supports the trichromatic theory. Wald discovered that even though all cones have basically the same structure, the retina does indeed contain three kinds of cones. Subsequent research demonstrated that each kind of cone is particularly sensitive to one of three colors—blue, green, or red (Roorda & Williams, 1999).

The other major attempt to explain color vision is the **opponent-process theory,** which was first proposed by physiologist Ewald Hering in 1878 and revised in 1957 by researchers Leon Hurvich and Dorthea Jamison. According to the opponent-process theory, three kinds of cells respond by increasing or decreasing their rate of firing when different colors are present. The red/green cells increase their firing rate when red is present and decrease it when green is present. The yellow/blue cells have an increased response to yellow and a decreased response to blue. A third kind of cells increase their response rate for white light and decrease it in the absence of light.

If you look long enough at one color in the opponent-process pair and then look at a white surface, your brain will give you the sensation of the opposite color—a negative **afterimage,** a visual sensation that remains after the stimulus is withdrawn. After you have stared at one color in an opponent-process pair (red/green, yellow/blue, white/black), the cell responding to that color tires and the opponent cell begins to fire, producing the afterimage. Demonstrate this for yourself in *Try It*.

But which theory of color vision is correct? It turns out that each theory explains a different phase of color processing. It is now generally accepted that the cones perform color processing in a way that is best explained by the trichromatic theory. The

hue   The dimension of light that refers to the specific color perceived.

saturation   The purity of a color, or the degree to which the light waves producing it are of the same wavelength.

brightness   The intensity of the light energy that is perceived as a color.

trichromatic theory   The theory of color vision suggesting that there are three types of cones in the retina that make a maximal chemical response to one of three colors—red, green, or blue.

opponent-process theory   The theory of color vision suggesting that three kinds of cells respond by increasing or decreasing their rate of firing when different colors are present.

afterimage   A visual sensation that remains after a stimulus is withdrawn.

Try It   A Negative Afterimage

Stare at the dot in the green, black, and yellow flag for approximately 1 minute. Then shift your gaze to the dot in the blank rectangle. You will see the American flag in its true colors—red, white, and blue, which are the opponent-process opposites of green, black, and yellow.

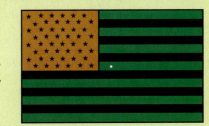

cones pass on information about wavelengths of light to the ganglion cells, the site of opponent processes. And color perception appears to involve more than just these two phases. Researchers think that color processing starts at the level of the retina, continues through the bipolar and ganglion cells, and is completed in the color detectors in the visual cortex (Masland, 1996; Sokolov, 2000). However, the trichromatic theory alone does not fully explain color perception because the cones are not distributed evenly across the surface of the retina. New theories that include motoric aspects of vision, such as the nearly invisible movements of the eyes called *saccades*, may turn out to provide researchers with a more comprehensive understanding of color vision (Bompas & O'Regan, 2006).

Color Blindness

You may have wondered what it means if someone is "color blind." Does that person see the world in black and white? No—the term **color blindness** refers to an inability to distinguish certain colors from one another. About 7% of males experience some kind of difficulty in distinguishing colors, most commonly red from green (Montgomery, 2003). By contrast, fewer than 1% of females suffer from color blindness. (Recall from Chapter 2 that this sex difference is explained by the fact that genes for color vision are carried on the X chromosome.)

Research has shown that color blindness can have degrees; it isn't simply a matter of either-you-have-it-or-you-don't. And why are some of us better able to make fine distinctions between colors, as we must do when sorting black and navy blue socks, for instance? These differences appear to be related to the number of color vision

3.7 Do individuals with color blindness see the world in black and white?

color blindness The inability to distinguish certain colors from one another.

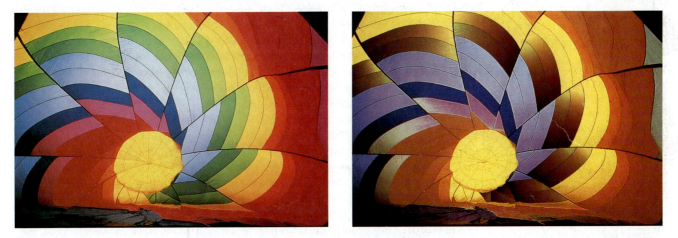

▲ On the left a hot air balloon is shown as it would appear to a person with normal color vision; on the right is the same balloon as it would appear to a person with red-green color blindness.

genes individuals have. Researchers have found that in people with normal color vision, the X chromosome may contain as few as two or as many as nine genes for color perception (Neitz & Neitz, 1995). Those who have more of such genes appear to be better able to make very fine distinctions between colors. These genetic differences lead to differences in the way that the various kinds of cones are distributed on an individual's retina (Hofer et al., 2005).

Remember It   Vision

1. Match each part of the eye with its description:
- _____ (1) the colored part of the eye
- _____ (2) the opening in the iris that dilates and constricts
- _____ (3) the transparent covering of the iris
- _____ (4) the transparent structure that focuses an inverted image on the retina
- _____ (5) the thin, light-sensitive membrane at the back of the eye on which the lens focuses an inverted image

a. retina
b. cornea
c. pupil
d. iris
e. lens

2. The _____ in the retina enable you to see in dim light.

3. The _____ in the retina enable you to see color and detail.

4. The optic nerve carries neural impulses from the retina to the _____, from which the impulses are passed on to the _____.

Answers: 1. (1) d, (2) c, (3) b, (4) e, (5) a; 2. rods; 3. cones; 4. thalamus, primary visual cortex

---

Hearing

Years ago, the frightening science fiction movie *Alien* was advertised this way: "In space, no one can hear you scream!" Although the movie was fiction, the statement is true. Light can travel through the vast nothingness of space, a vacuum, but sound cannot. In this section, you will learn why.

Sound

3.8 What determines the pitch and loudness of a sound, and how is each quality measured?

Sound requires a medium, such as air, water, or a solid object, through which to move. This fact was first demonstrated by Robert Boyle in 1660 when he suspended a ringing pocket watch by a thread inside a specially designed jar. When Boyle pumped all the air out of the jar, he could no longer hear the watch ring. But when he pumped the air back into the jar, he could again hear the watch ringing.

Frequency is determined by the number of cycles completed by a sound wave in one second. The unit used to measure a wave's frequency, or cycles per second, is known as the hertz (Hz). The *pitch*—how high or low the sound is—is chiefly determined by frequency—the higher the frequency (the more cycles per second), the higher the sound. The human ear can hear sound frequencies from low bass tones of around 20 Hz up to high-pitched sounds of about 20,000 Hz. The lowest tone on a piano sounds at a frequency of about 28 Hz, and the highest tone at about 4,214 Hz. Many mammals, such as dogs, cats, bats, and rats, can hear tones much higher in frequency than 20,000 Hz. Amazingly, dolphins can respond to frequencies up to 100,000 Hz.

The loudness of a sound is determined by a measure called **amplitude.** The force or pressure with which air molecules move chiefly determines loudness, which is measured using a unit called the *bel*, named for Alexander Graham Bell. Because the bel is a rather large unit, sound levels are expressed in tenths of a bel, or **decibels (dB).** The threshold of human hearing is set at 0 dB, which does not mean the absence of sound but rather the softest sound that can be heard in a very quiet set-

frequency The number of cycles completed by a sound wave in one second, determining the pitch of the sound; measured in the unit called the hertz.

amplitude The measure of the loudness of a sound; expressed in the unit called the decibel.

decibel (dB) (DES-ih-bel) A unit of measurement for the loudness of sounds.

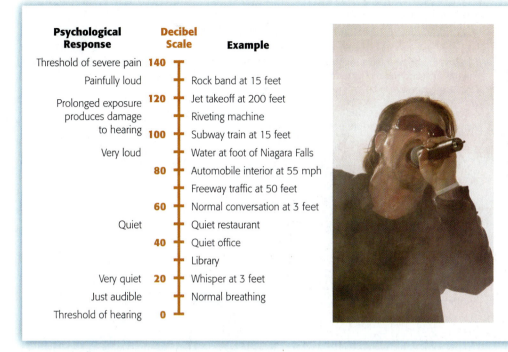

Psychological Response	Decibel Scale	Example
Threshold of severe pain	140	
Painfully loud		Rock band at 15 feet
Prolonged exposure produces damage to hearing	120	Jet takeoff at 200 feet
		Riveting machine
	100	Subway train at 15 feet
Very loud		Water at foot of Niagara Falls
	80	Automobile interior at 55 mph
		Freeway traffic at 50 feet
	60	Normal conversation at 3 feet
Quiet		Quiet restaurant
	40	Quiet office
		Library
Very quiet	20	Whisper at 3 feet
Just audible		Normal breathing
Threshold of hearing	0	

Figure 3.5 Decibel Levels of Various Sounds

The loudness of a sound (its amplitude) is measured in decibels. Each increase of 10 decibels makes a sound 10 times louder. A normal conversation at 3 feet measures about 60 decibels, which is 10,000 times louder than a soft whisper of 20 decibels. Any exposure to sounds of 130 decibels or higher puts a person at immediate risk for hearing damage.

ting. Each increase of 10 decibels makes a sound 10 times louder. **Figure 3.5** shows comparative decibel levels for a variety of sounds.

Another characteristic of sound is **timbre,** the distinctive quality of a sound that distinguishes it from other sounds of the same pitch and loudness. Have you ever thought about why a given musical note sounds different when played on a piano, a guitar, and a violin, even though all three instruments use vibrating strings to produce sounds? The characteristics of the strings, the technique used to initiate the vibrations, and the way the body of the instrument amplifies the vibrations work together to produce a unique "voice," or timbre, for each instrument. Human voices vary in timbre as well, providing us with a way of recognizing individuals when we can't see their faces. Timbres vary from one instrument to another, and from one voice to another, because most sounds consist of several different frequencies rather than a single pitch. The range of those frequencies gives each musical instrument, and each human voice, its unique sound.

timbre (TAM-burr) The distinctive quality of a sound that distinguishes it from other sounds of the same pitch and loudness.

audition The sensation and process of hearing.

The Ear

Would you still be able to hear if you lost your ears? In fact, the part of the human body called the ear plays only a minor role in **audition,** which is the sensation and process of hearing. So, even if the visible part of your ears were cut off, your hearing would suffer very little. Let's see how each part of the ear contributes to the ability to hear.

The oddly shaped, curved flap of cartilage and skin called the *pinna* is the visible part of the **outer ear** (see **Figure 3.6**). Inside the ear, the *auditory canal* is about 1 inch long, and its entrance is lined with hairs. At the end of the auditory canal is the *eardrum* (or *tympanic membrane*), a thin, flexible membrane about $\frac{1}{3}$ inch in diameter. The eardrum moves in response to the sound waves that travel through the auditory canal and strike it.

The **middle ear** is no larger than a shirt button. Inside its chamber are the *ossicles*, the three smallest bones in the human body. Named for their shapes, the ossicles—the hammer, the anvil, and the stirrup—are connected in that order, linking the eardrum to the oval window (see Figure 3.6). The ossicles amplify sound waves some 22 times (Békésy, 1957). The **inner ear** begins at the inner side of the oval window, at the **cochlea**—a fluid-filled, snail-shaped, bony chamber. When the stirrup pushes against the oval window, it sets up vibrations that move the fluid in the cochlea back and forth in waves. Inside the cochlea, attached to its thin basilar membrane are about 15,000 sensory

3.9 How do the outer ear, middle ear, and inner ear function in hearing?

outer ear The visible part of the ear, consisting of the pinna and the auditory canal.

middle ear The portion of the ear containing the ossicles, which connect the eardrum to the oval window and amplify sound waves.

inner ear The innermost portion of the ear, containing the cochlea, the vestibular sacs, and the semicircular canals.

Figure 3.6 The Anatomy of the Human Ear

Sound waves pass through the auditory canal to the eardrum, causing it to vibrate and set in motion the ossicles in the middle ear. When the stirrup pushes against the oval window, it sets up vibrations in the inner ear. This moves the fluid in the cochlea back and forth and sets in motion the hair cells, causing a message to be sent to the brain via the auditory nerve.

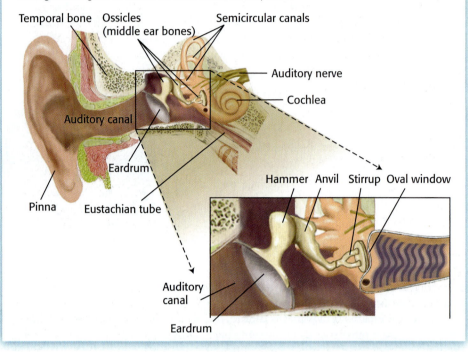

receptors called **hair cells,** each with a bundle of tiny hairs protruding from it. The tiny hair bundles are pushed and pulled by the motion of the fluid inside the cochlea. If the tip of a hair bundle is moved only as much as the width of an atom, an electrical impulse is generated, which is transmitted to the brain by way of the auditory nerve.

The ear isn't the only physical structure that contributes to hearing. We can hear some sounds through *bone conduction,* the vibrations of the bones in the face and skull. When you click your teeth or eat crunchy food, you hear these sounds mainly through bone conduction. And, if you have heard a recording of your voice, you may have thought it sounded odd. This is because recordings do not reproduce the sounds you hear through bone conduction when you speak, so you are hearing your voice as it sounds to others.

Having two ears, one on each side of the head, enables you to determine the direction from which sounds are coming (Konishi, 1993). Unless a sound is directly above, below, in front of, or behind you, it reaches one ear very shortly before it reaches the other (Spitzer & Semple, 1991). The brain detects differences as small as 0.0001 second and interprets them, revealing the direction of the sound (Rosenzweig, 1961). The source of a sound may also be determined by the difference in the intensity of the sound reaching each ear, as well as the position of the head when the sound is detected (Kopinska & Harris, 2003; Middlebrooks & Green, 1991).

cochlea   (KOK-lee-uh) The fluid-filled, snail-shaped, bony chamber in the inner ear that contains the basilar membrane and its hair cells (the sound receptors).

hair cells   Sensory receptors for hearing that are attached to the basilar membrane in the cochlea.

Theories of Hearing

3.10 What two major theories attempt to explain hearing?

How do the parts of the ear work together to produce auditory sensations? Scientists have proposed two theories to explain hearing.

In the 1860s, Hermann von Helmholtz helped develop **place theory.** This theory of hearing holds that each individual pitch a person hears is determined by the particular spot or place along the basilar membrane that vibrates the most. Observing the living basilar membrane, researchers verified that different locations do indeed vibrate in response to differently pitched sounds (Ruggero, 1992). Even so, place theory seems to apply only to frequencies above 150 Hz.

Another attempt to explain hearing is **frequency theory.** According to this theory, the hair cells vibrate the same number of times per second as the sounds that reach them. Thus, a tone of 500 Hz would stimulate the hair cells to vibrate 500 times per second. However, frequency theory cannot account for frequencies higher than 1,000 Hz because individual neurons linked to the hair cells cannot fire more than about 1,000 times per second. So, even if a receptor vibrated as rapidly as the sound wave associated with a higher tone, the information necessary to perceive the pitch wouldn't be faithfully transmitted to the brain. Consequently, frequency theory seems to be a good explanation of how we hear low-frequency tones (below 500 Hz), but place theory better describes the way in which tones with frequencies above 1,000 Hz are heard (Matlin & Foley, 1997). Both frequency and location are involved when we hear sounds whose frequencies are between 500 and 1,000 Hz.

Hearing Loss

Did you know that every individual has a fairly high risk of suffering from some kind of hearing loss? About one infant in every 1,000 in the United States is born with a moderate to severe hearing loss, usually due to circumstances of birth (especially prematurity or lack of oxygen during birth) or to genetic defects (CDC, 2003). Many other children suffer from milder hearing losses, many of which occur after birth as a result of disease or exposure to excessive noise. And hearing loss affects many older Americans as well. In fact, hearing loss affects normal communication in 10% of people 65 or older who have a prior history of normal hearing (Willems, 2000). There are several different kinds of hearing loss, many of which are treatable or entirely preventable.

Conductive hearing loss, or *conduction deafness*, usually is caused by disease or by injury to the eardrum or to the bones of the middle ear, preventing sound waves from being conducted to the cochlea. Almost all conductive hearing loss can be repaired medically or surgically. And, in rare cases, a person can be fitted with a hearing aid that bypasses the middle ear, using bone conduction to send sound vibrations to the cochlea.

Most adults with hearing loss suffer from *sensorineural hearing loss*, which involves damage to either the cochlea or the auditory nerve. Large numbers of the cochlea's delicate hair cells, which transduce sound waves into neural impulses, may be damaged or destroyed. If the damage is not too severe, a conventional hearing aid may reduce the effects of this type of hearing loss (Bramblett, 1997). And cochlear implants may help restore hearing in many cases of sensorineural hearing loss, even when the individual is totally deaf. But hearing aids and implants are useless if the damage is to the auditory nerve, which connects the cochlea to the brain; in such cases, the hearing loss is usually total.

Many of the cases of hearing loss in older adults appear to be caused by lifelong exposure to excessive noise rather than by aging (Rabinowitz, 2000). Cross-cultural research supports the view that noise is a factor in age-related hearing loss. Older persons in one culture, the Mabaan tribe in the Sudan in Africa, don't appear to suffer much hearing loss as they age. In fact, when hearing tests were conducted on Mabaan tribe members, some of the 80-year-olds could hear as well as 20-year-olds from industrialized countries. The Mabaan pride themselves on their sensitive hearing, and an important tribal custom is never raising one's voice. Even tribal festivals and celebrations are quiet affairs, featuring dancing and soft singing accompanied by stringed instruments rather than drums (Bennett, 1990).

Noise-induced hearing loss is not just a problem of the elderly. In the workplace, government agencies regulate the amount of noise to which workers can be exposed because the risk of permanent damage to their hearing is great. In the United States, the Occupational Health and Safety Administration requires employers to provide workers with ear protection in work environments in which sound levels regularly exceed 90 decibels (Noise Pollution Council, 2003). Children's hearing can be damaged by toys emitting decibel levels of this magnitude and, as you might suspect, fireworks can potentially damage anyone's hearing. Likewise, decibel levels at some concerts exceed threshold levels for possible ear damage. Furthermore, when a person wearing headphones or ear buds regularly cranks up the volume on her MP3 or CD player, she

3.11 What are some of the major causes of hearing loss?

▲ Members of some Sudanese tribes play stringed instruments rather quietly during celebrations. Perhaps because they are not exposed to much noise, these people generally have very sharp hearing.

place theory   The theory of hearing that holds that each individual pitch a person hears is determined by the particular location along the basilar membrane of the cochlea that vibrates the most.

frequency theory   The theory of hearing that holds that hair cell receptors vibrate the same number of times per second as the sounds that reach them.

greatly increases her risk of hearing loss. For these reasons, doctors have noted that the vast majority of cases of hearing loss are 100% preventable simply by managing the amount of noise to which one is exposed (Rabinowitz, 2000).

Remember It | Hearing

1. The pitch of a sound is chiefly determined by _____.

2. Loudness is chiefly determined by _____.

3. Decibels are units used to measure _____.

4. Match the part of the ear with the structures it contains.

   _____ (1) ossicles
   _____ (2) pinna, auditory canal
   _____ (3) cochlea, hair cells

   a. outer ear
   b. middle ear
   c. inner ear

5. The sensory receptors for hearing are found in the _____.

6. Two major theories that explain hearing are _____ theory and _____ theory.

Answers: 1. frequency; 2. amplitude; 3. loudness; 4. (1) b, (2) a, (3) c; 5. cochlea; 6. frequency, place

---

The Other Senses: Smell, Taste, Touch, and Balance

Clearly, our sensory experiences would be extremely limited without vision and hearing, but what about the chemical senses—smell and taste? The sensory receptors in the skin provide us with a great deal of information, too, including our experiences of both pleasure and pain. The capacity to sense our position in space helps us maintain balance and move from one place to another.

Smell

3.12 What path does a smell message take from the nose to the brain?

If you suddenly lost your sense of smell, you might think, "This isn't so bad. I can't smell flowers or food, but, on the other hand, I no longer have to endure the foul odors of life." But your *olfactory system*—the technical name for the organs and brain structures involved in the sense of smell—aids your survival. You smell smoke and can escape before the flames of a fire envelop you. Your nose broadcasts an odor alarm to the brain when certain poisonous gases or noxious fumes are present. Smell, aided by taste, provides your line of defense against putting spoiled food or drink into your body. And, believe it or not, every single individual gives off a unique scent, which is genetically determined (Axel, 1995).

The Mechanics of Smell. Did you know that the human olfactory system is capable of sensing and distinguishing 10,000 different odors? **Olfaction,** the sense of smell, is a chemical sense. You cannot smell a substance unless some of its molecules vaporize—pass from a solid or liquid into a gaseous state. Heat speeds up the vaporization of molecules, which is why food that is cooking has a stronger and more distinct odor than uncooked food. When odor molecules vaporize, they become airborne and make their way up each nostril to the **olfactory epithelium.** The olfactory epithelium consists of two 1-square-inch patches of tissue, one at the top of each nasal cavity; together these patches contain about 10 million olfactory neurons, which are the receptor cells for smell. Each of these neurons contains only one of the 1,000 different types of odor receptors (Bargmann, 1996). Because humans are able to detect some 10,000 odors, each of the 1,000 types of odor receptors must be able to respond to more than one kind of odor molecule. Moreover, some odor molecules trigger more than one type of odor receptor (Axel, 1995). The intensity of a smell stimulus—how strong or weak it is—is apparently determined by the number of olfactory neurons firing at the same time (Freeman, 1991). **Figure 3.7** shows a diagram of the human olfactory system.

olfaction (ol-FAK-shun) The sense of smell.

olfactory epithelium Two 1-square-inch patches of tissue, one at the top of each nasal cavity, which together contain about 10 million olfactory neurons, the receptors for smell.

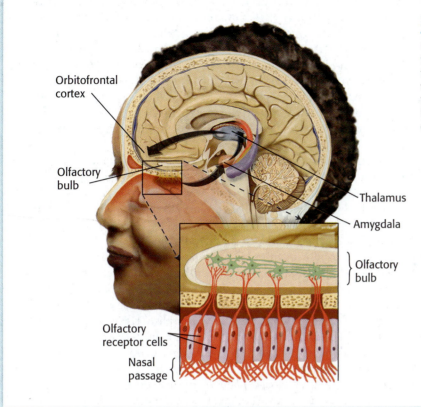

Figure 3.7 **The Olfactory System**

Odor molecules travel up the nostrils to the olfactory epithelium, which contains the receptor cells for smell. Olfactory receptors are special neurons whose axons form the olfactory nerve. The olfactory nerve relays smell messages to the olfactory bulbs, which pass them on to the thalamus, the orbitofrontal cortex, and other parts of the brain.

Orbitofrontal cortex

Olfactory bulb

Thalamus

Amygdala

Olfactory bulb

Olfactory receptor cells

Nasal passage

Have you ever wondered why dogs have a keener sense of smell than humans? Not only do many dogs have a long snout, but, in some breeds, the olfactory epithelium can be as large as the area of a handkerchief and can contain up to 20 times as many olfactory neurons as in humans (Engen, 1982). It is well known that dogs use scent to recognize not only other members of their species, but also the humans they live with. And humans have this ability, too. The mothers of newborns can recognize their own babies by smell within hours after birth. But can humans recognize the scents of other species—their own pets, for example? Yes, to a remarkable degree. When presented with blankets permeated with the scents of dogs, some 89% of the dog owners easily identified their own dog by smell (Wells & Hepper, 2000).

Olfactory neurons are different from all other sensory receptors: They both come into direct contact with sensory stimuli and reach directly into the brain. These neurons have a short life span; after functioning for only about 60 days, they die and are replaced by new cells (Buck, 1996).

The axons of the olfactory neurons relay a smell message directly to the **olfactory bulbs**—two brain structures the size of matchsticks that rest above the nasal cavities (refer to Figure 3.7). From the olfactory bulbs, the message is relayed to the thalamus and the orbitofrontal cortex, which distinguish the odor and relay that information to other parts of the brain.

The process of sensing odors is the same in every individual, but there are large differences in sensitivity to smells. For example, perfumers and whiskey blenders can distinguish subtle variations in odors that are indistinguishable to the average person. Young people are more sensitive to odors than older people, and nonsmokers are more sensitive than smokers (Matlin & Foley, 1997).

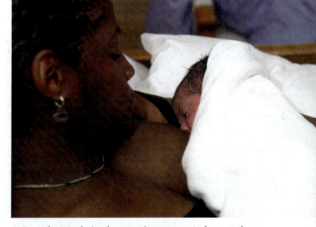

▲ Every human being has a unique scent. In fact, mothers and their newborn babies can recognize each other's scents within hours of birth.

olfactory bulbs   Two matchstick-sized structures above the nasal cavities, where smell sensations first register in the brain.

Smell and Memory. Has a particular smell ever triggered a memory for you? In his novel *Remembrance of Things Past*, the French novelist Marcel Proust told the story of a character who claimed to have accessed all of his childhood memories by simply smelling a "petite Madeline" (a small cake or cookie) dipped in a cup of tea. But is there any evidence to support this idea? Indeed, brain-imaging studies of human olfactory functioning have established key connections among smell, emotion, and memory (Hertz, 2004; Pause & Krauel, 2000; Zald & Pardo, 2000). Interestingly, the brain's encoding system for smell-related memories appears to bypass the hippocampus, a structure involved in most other kinds of memories (Kaut et al., 2003).

So, you might be thinking, would my memory for psychology information be better if I splashed on a distinctive cologne while studying and then applied the same scent to my body just prior to taking an exam? Maybe, but you should be aware that the ability to associate odors with memories appears to peak between 6 and 10 years of age (Chu and Downes, 2000). Therefore, using scents as memory-enhancers, as Proust's character did, may work best for childhood memories.

Another piece of the odor-memory puzzle comes from research examining the sense of smell in Alzheimer's patients. Researchers have found that measures of olfactory function in the elderly strongly predict the onset of age-related memory problems (Royall et al., 2002; Swan & Carmelli, 2002). Those who show the greatest loss of olfaction are more likely to develop dementia. Recall from the discussion of correlation in Chapter 1 that it would be erroneous to conclude that a deficient sense of smell *causes* dementia or that improving older adults' sense of smell, or somehow preventing loss of olfactory function, will protect them against dementia. At the very least, however, these studies suggest that measurement of olfactory function in older adults may be a useful way of identifying those who are at greater risk for developing dementia, prior to their having exhibited any symptoms.

Pheromones. Many animals excrete chemicals called **pheromones,** which can have a powerful effect on the behavior of other members of the same species. For example, the "queen" of an ant colony emits an odor that identifies her as such to all subordinate colony members (Vander Meer & Alonso, 2002). Animals also use pheromones to mark off territories and to signal sexual receptivity. A female mouse in heat will find the pheromone secreted from a gland on the penis of a male mouse irresistible; the same pheromone will enrage another male mouse. Higher mammals, such as monkeys, also make use of pheromones in their sexual behavior. In some animals, pheromones serve as cues for the adoption of antipredator behaviors such as hiding (Kiyokawa et al., 2006; Sullivan et al., 2002).

Humans produce and respond to pheromones as well. When people are exposed to the hormone *androsterone*, which acts as a pheromone, physiological functions such as heart rate are affected and mood states change (DeBortoli et al., 2001). Another interesting area of pheromone research involves *menstrual synchrony*, the tendency of the menstrual cycles of women who live together to synchronize over time. In one study of women living in college dormitories, researchers found that 38% of roommate pairs developed synchronous cycles after 3 months of living together (Morofushi et al., 2000). Roommates who were synchronized showed greater olfactory sensitivity to androsterone than those who were not synchronized.

Other studies suggest that humans may respond both biochemically and behaviorally to pheromones. In one study, researchers analyzed the saliva of 66 young men who had used an inhalant to sniff copulines—pheromones found in female vaginal secretions (Holden, 1996). The secretions were obtained during three different times in the menstrual cycle, but those taken at ovulation were the only ones to cause a rise in testosterone levels in the men's saliva. The men apparently recognized, though not consciously, which of the women were most likely to be fertile. In another fascinating study, researchers randomly sprayed chairs in a waiting room with a male pheromone. When study participants en-

▲ Individual differences in sensitivity to pheromones contribute to variations in menstrual synchrony among women who live in college dormitories.

pheromones Chemicals excreted by humans and other animals that can have a powerful effect on the behavior of other members of the same species.

tered the room, researchers noted that homosexual men and heterosexual women (based on self-reported sexual orientation) were more likely to choose sprayed than unsprayed chairs (Pause, 2004). Research has also shown that men exposed to male pheromones display greater interest in male-oriented magazines than at times when they are not under the influence of these substances (Ebster & Kirk-Smith, 2005). Studies like these suggest that pheromones may play some kind of role in the maintenance of gender role identity and in sexual attraction.

Taste

Do you think you would enjoy life without the tastes of fresh-baked bread, crispy fried chicken, or luscious chocolate ice cream? Of course, even without a sense of taste, you would still feel the texture and temperature of foods you put in the mouth. And you might be surprised to learn that much of the pleasure you attribute to the sense of taste actually arises from smells, which are due to odor molecules forced up the nasal cavity by the action of the tongue, cheeks, and throat when you chew and swallow. So, without a sense of taste, your sense of smell would provide you with some taste sensations. Still, life without the ability to fully experience the tastes of the foods we love would, no doubt, be less enjoyable.

3.13 What are the primary taste sensations, and how are they detected?

The Five Basic Tastes. Psychology textbooks have long maintained that **gustation,** the sense of taste, produces four distinct kinds of taste sensations: sweet, sour, salty, and bitter. This is true. But recent research suggests that there is a fifth taste sensation in humans (Herness, 2000). This fifth taste sensation, called *umami*, is triggered by the substance glutamate, which, in the form of monosodium glutamate (MSG), is widely used as a flavoring in Asian foods (Matsunami et al., 2000). Many protein-rich foods, such as meat, milk, aged cheese, and seafood, also contain glutamate.

All five taste sensations can be detected on all locations of the tongue. Indeed, even a person with no tongue could still taste to some extent, thanks to the taste receptors found in the palate, in the mucus lining of the cheeks and lips, and in parts of the throat, including the tonsils. When tastes are mixed, the specialized receptors for each type of flavor are activated and send separate messages to the brain (Frank et al., 2003., Sugita & Shiba, 2005). In other words, your brain perceives the two distinctive flavors present in sweet and sour sauce quite separately. This analytical quality of the sense of taste prevents your being fooled into eating spoiled or poisoned food when the characteristic taste of either is combined with some kind of pleasant flavor.

The Taste Receptors. If you look at your tongue in a mirror, you will see many small bumps called *papillae*. There are four different types of papillae, and three of them have **taste buds** along their sides (see **Figure 3.8**). Each taste bud is composed of 60 to 100 receptor cells. But the life span of the taste receptors is very short—only about 10 days—and they are continually being replaced.

Taste Sensitivities. Research indicates that humans can be divided into three groups based on taste sensitivity for certain sweet and bitter substances: nontasters, medium tasters, and supertasters (Yackinous & Guinard, 2002). Nontasters are unable to taste certain sweet and bitter compounds, but they do taste most other substances, although with less sensitivity. Supertasters taste these sweet and bitter compounds with far stronger intensity than other people. Researchers are currently investigating links between taste sensitivity, eating behaviors, and health status variables, such as obesity. For example, supertasters who are particularly sensitive to the chemical that gives fruits and vegetables a

▲ When a cold interferes with your ability to smell, you may not be able to taste even the spiciest foods.

gustation   The sense of taste.

taste buds   Structures in many of the tongue's papillae that are composed of 60 to 100 receptor cells for taste.

Figure 3.8 The Tongue's Papillae and Taste Buds

(a) A photomicrograph of the surface of the tongue shows several papillae. (b) This vertical cross-section through a papillae reveals the location of the taste buds and taste receptors.

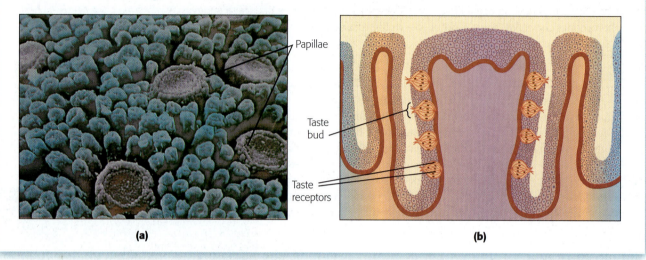

(a)   (b)

bitter taste eat less salad than medium tasters and nontasters (Yackinous & Guinard, 2002). Still, supertasters appear no more likely to be overweight than medium tasters or nontasters. In fact, among individuals who report that they never deliberately restrict their diets to try to lose weight, supertasters of the bitter chemical have less body fat than medium tasters or nontasters (Tepper & Ullrich, 2002). So, researchers know that taste sensitivity is linked to food preferences, but they do not yet understand how these preferences may be connected to nutritional status.

Touch

3.14 How does the skin provide sensory information?

How important is the sense of touch? Classic research in the mid-1980s demonstrated that premature infants who were massaged for 15 minutes three times a day gained weight 47% faster than other premature infants who received only regular intensive care treatment (Field et al., 1986). The massaged infants were more responsive and were able to leave the hospital about 6 days earlier on average than those who were not massaged. Thus, the sense of touch is not only one of the more pleasant aspects of life, but it is also critical to our survival. And it may be just as important to adult as to infant survival. For instance, you may feel a poisonous spider crawling up your arm and flick it away before it can inflict a deadly bite. The other skin sense—pain—is also vital because it serves as an early warning system for many potentially deadly conditions, as you'll learn in this section.

Your natural clothing, the skin, is the largest organ of your body. It performs many important biological functions, while also providing much of what is known as sensual pleasure. **Tactile** information is conveyed to the brain when an object touches and depresses the skin, stimulating one or more of the several distinct types of receptors found in the nerve endings. These sensitive nerve endings in the skin send the touch message through nerve connections to the spinal cord. The message travels up the spinal cord and through the brainstem and the midbrain, finally reaching the somatosensory cortex, as shown in **Figure 3.9**. (Recall from Chapter 2 that the somatosensory cortex is the strip of tissue at the front of the parietal lobes where touch, pressure, temperature, and pain register.) Once the somatosensory cortex has been activated, you become aware of where and how hard you have been touched. In the 1890s, one of the most prominent researchers of the tactile sense, Max von Frey, discovered the *two-point threshold*—the measure of how far apart two points must be before they are felt as two separate touches.

If you could examine the skin from the outermost to the deepest layer, you would find a variety of nerve endings that differ markedly in appearance. Most or all of these

tactile   Pertaining to the sense of touch.

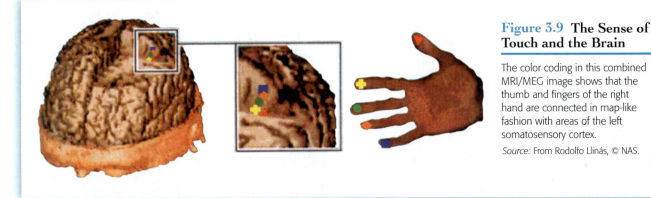

Figure 3.9 **The Sense of Touch and the Brain**

The color coding in this combined MRI/MEG image shows that the thumb and fingers of the right hand are connected in map-like fashion with areas of the left somatosensory cortex.

Source: From Rodolfo Llinás, © NAS.

nerve endings appear to respond in some degree to all different types of tactile stimulation. The more densely packed with these sensory receptors a part of the body's surface is, the more sensitive it is to tactile stimulation.

Pain

Although the tactile sense delivers a great deal of pleasure, it brings us pain as well. Pain motivates us to tend to injuries, to restrict activity, and to seek medical help. Pain also teaches us to avoid pain-producing circumstances in the future. Chronic pain—pain that persists for 3 months or more—continues long after it serves any useful function and is itself a serious medical problem for some 34 million Americans (Brownlee & Schrof, 1997; Pal, 2005). The three major types of chronic pain are low-back pain, headache, and arthritis pain. For its victims, chronic pain is like a fire alarm that no one can turn off.

Scientists are not certain how pain works, but one major theory that attempts to answer this question is the *gate-control theory* of Ronald Melzack and Patrick Wall (1965, 1983). These researchers contend that there is an area in the spinal cord that can act like a "gate" and either block pain messages or transmit them to the brain. Only so many messages can go through the gate at any one time. You feel pain when pain messages carried by small, slow-conducting nerve fibers reach the gate and cause it to open. Large, fast-conducting nerve fibers carry other sensory messages from the body, and these can effectively tie up traffic at the gate so that it will close and keep many of the pain messages from getting through. What is the first thing you do when you stub your toe or pound your finger with a hammer? If you rub or apply gentle pressure to the injury, you are stimulating the large, fast-conducting nerve fibers, which get their message to the spinal gate first and block some of the pain messages from the slower nerve fibers. Applying ice, heat, or electrical stimulation to the painful area also stimulates the large nerve fibers and closes the spinal gate.

The gate-control theory also accounts for the fact that psychological factors, both cognitive and emotional, can influence the perception of pain. Melzack and Wall (1965, 1983) contend that messages from the brain to the spinal cord can inhibit the transmission of pain messages at the spinal gate and thereby affect the perception of pain. This explains why some people can undergo surgery under hypnosis and feel little or no pain. It also explains why soldiers injured in battle or athletes injured during games can be so distracted that they do not experience pain until some time after the injury.

Psychological and Cultural Influences on the Experience of Pain. Chronic pain rates vary across cultures, as you can see in **Figure 3.10**. Why? Researchers don't have a definitive answer. However, they do know that the experience of pain has a physical and an emotional component, both of which vary from person to person. Animal studies showing that biochemical changes take place in the cells of the amygdala when chronic pain is experienced support the notion that pain and emotion are linked (Narita et al., 2006). Thus, pain experts distinguish between pain and suffering—suffering being the affective, or emotional, response to pain. Sullivan and others (1995) found that people

3.15 What is the function of pain, and how is pain influenced by psychological factors, culture, and endorphins?

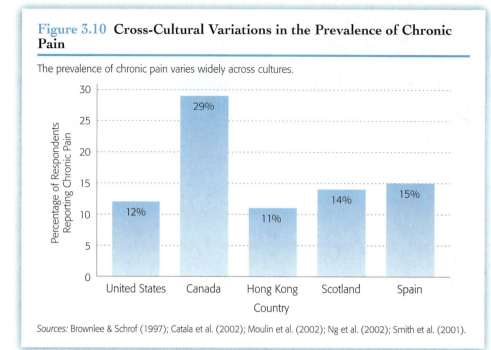

Figure 3.10 Cross-Cultural Variations in the Prevalence of Chronic Pain

The prevalence of chronic pain varies widely across cultures.

Sources: Brownlee & Schrof (1997); Catala et al. (2002); Moulin et al. (2002); Ng et al. (2002); Smith et al. (2001).

suffered most from pain when they harbored negative thoughts about it, feared its potential threat to their well-being, and expressed feelings of helplessness. So, cross-cultural variations in chronic pain may be linked to differences in people's emotional states.

Culture also influences the way pain is experienced and expressed. The most often cited work on pain and culture is that of Zborowski (1952), who compared the responses to pain of Italian, Jewish, Irish, and native-born Anglo-Saxon patients in a large hospital in New York. Among the four groups, Jewish and Italian patients responded more emotionally and showed heightened expressions of pain.

Culture even influences the experience and expression of pain during childbirth. The Chinese value silence, and Chinese women enduring the pain of childbirth typically do not engage in loud and highly emotional responses for fear they will dishonor themselves and their families (Weber, 1996). In stark contrast are some Pakistani women who believe that the greater their suffering and the louder their response to the pain, the more caring their husbands will be during the following weeks (Ahmad, 1994).

Endorphins. Americans spend more money trying to get rid of pain than for any other medical purpose. More than 20% of adults in the United States take some kind of pain relief medication several times a week (Turunen et al., 2005). About 8% of them take nonprescription pain relievers exclusively. Another 8% take only prescription pain relievers several days a week, and nearly 5% take both prescription and nonprescription medicine with the same frequency. The body produces its own natural painkillers, the **endorphins,** which block pain and produce a feeling of well-being. Endorphins are released when you are injured, when you experience stress or extreme pain, and when you laugh, cry, or exercise. Recent findings suggest that the release of endorphins that occurs during acupuncture treatments may be one of the factors involved in individuals who respond favorably to such treatments for conditions such as chronic back pain (Cabýoglu, Ergene, & Tan, 2006).

Some people release endorphins even when they only *think* they are receiving pain medication but are being given, instead, a placebo in the form of a sugar pill or an injection of saline solution. Asthma, high blood pressure, and even heart disease can respond to placebo "treatment" (Brown, 1998). Why? Apparently, when patients believe that they have received a drug for pain, that belief stimulates the release of their own natural pain relievers, the endorphins.

endorphins (en-DOR-fins) The body's own natural painkillers, which block pain and produce a feeling of well-being.

Balance and Movement

The senses you've learned about so far provide you with valuable information about your environment. But what if you could see, hear, smell, taste, and sense touch perfectly well, but your ability to orient yourself in space was disrupted? For instance, what if you couldn't sense how high to raise a hammer in order to hit a nail? You might hit yourself in the head with the hammer. How would you keep from falling if you couldn't sense whether you were standing up straight or leaning to one side? You would be forever bumping into walls as you rounded corners. Fortunately, the kinesthetic and vestibular senses keep you apprised of exactly where all parts of your body are and how the location of your body is related to your physical environment.

The **kinesthetic sense** provides information about (1) the position of body parts in relation to each other and (2) the movement of the entire body or its parts. This information is detected by receptors in the joints, ligaments, and muscles. The other senses, especially vision, provide additional information about body position and movement, but the kinesthetic sense works well on its own. Thanks to the kinesthetic sense, we are able to perform smooth and skilled body movements without visual feedback or a studied, conscious effort. (But why do we perceive ourselves as stationary in a moving car? More on this later in the chapter.)

The **vestibular sense** detects movement and provides information about the body's orientation in space. The vestibular sense organs are located in the semicircular canals and the *vestibular sacs* in the inner ear. The **semicircular canals** sense the rotation of your head, such as when you are turning your head from side to side or when you are spinning around (see **Figure 3.11**). Because the canals are filled with fluid, rotating movements of the head in any direction send the fluid coursing through the tubelike semicircular canals. In the canals, the moving fluid bends the hair cells, which act as receptors and send neural impulses to the brain. Because there are three canals, each positioned on a different plane, rotation in a given direction will cause the hair cells in one canal to bend more than the hair cells in the other canals.

The semicircular canals and the vestibular sacs signal only changes in motion or orientation. If you were blindfolded and had no visual or other external cues, you would not be able to sense motion once your speed reached a constant rate. For example, in an airplane, you would feel the takeoff and the landing, as well as any sudden changes in speed. But once the plane leveled off and maintained a fairly constant cruising speed, your vestibular organs would not signal the brain that you are moving, even if you were traveling at a rate of hundreds of miles per hour.

3.16 What kinds of information do the kinesthetic and vestibular senses provide?

kinesthetic sense   The sense providing information about the position of body parts in relation to each other and the movement of the entire body or its parts.

vestibular sense   (ves-TIB-yu-ler) The sense that detects movement and provides information about the body's orientation in space.

semicircular canals   Three fluid-filled tubular canals in the inner ear that sense the rotation of the head.

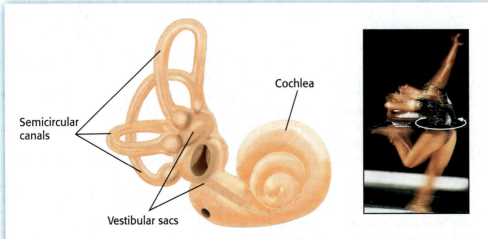

Figure 3.11 Sensing Balance and Movement

You sense the rotation of your head in any direction because the movement sends fluid coursing through the tubelike semicircular canals in the inner ear. The moving fluid bends the hair cell receptors, which, in turn, send neural impulses to the brain.

Cochlea

Semicircular canals

Vestibular sacs

Remember It   The Other Senses: Smell, Taste, Touch, and Balance

1. The technical name for the process or sensation of smell is _____.

2. The olfactory, or smell, receptors are located in the _____.

3. The primary taste sensations are _____, _____, _____, _____, and _____.

4. Each _____ contains from 60 to 100 receptor cells for taste.

5. The part of the brain that is responsible for interpreting tactical information is the _____.

6. _____ in the skin respond to all kinds of tactile stimuli.

7. _____ are the body's own natural painkillers.

8. The _____ sense provides information about the position of body parts in relation to each other.

9. Vestibular sense organs are located in the _____ and the _____ in the inner ear.

Answers: 1. olfaction; 2. olfactory epithelium; 3. sweet, salty, sour, bitter, and umami (for glutamate); 4. taste bud; 5. somatosensory cortex; 6. Nerve endings; 7. Endorphins; 8. kinesthetic; 9. semicircular canals, vestibular sacs

Principles of Perception

Earlier in the chapter, you learned why an apple appears to be red. But why do we think of an apple as having a somewhat spherical shape, like that of a ball? And how do we tell the difference between a picture of an apple and the real thing—that is, the difference between two-dimensional and three-dimensional objects? Recall that *perception* is the process by which sensory information is actively organized and interpreted by the brain. Sensations are the raw materials of human experiences; perceptions are the finished products.

Perceptual Organization

3.17 What are the principles that govern perceptual organization?

Are our perceptions random and haphazard in nature, or do our brains provide us with rules for interpreting sensory experiences? Researchers addressing this question have found a few principles that appear to govern perceptions in all human beings.

Gestalt Principles of Perceptual Organization. The Gestalt psychologists maintained that people cannot understand the perceptual world by breaking down experiences into tiny parts and analyzing them separately. When sensory elements are brought together, something new is formed. That is, the whole is more than just the sum of its parts. The German word **Gestalt** has no exact English equivalent, but it roughly refers to the whole form, pattern, or configuration that a person perceives. The Gestalt psychologists claimed that sensory experience is organized according to certain basic principles of perceptual organization:

- *Figure-ground.* As we view the world, some object (the figure) often seems to stand out from the background (the ground) (see **Figure 3.12**).
- *Similarity.* Objects that have similar characteristics are perceived as a unit. In **Figure 3.13(a)**, dots of a similar color are perceived as belonging together to form horizontal rows on the left and vertical columns on the right.
- *Proximity.* Objects that are close together in space or time are usually perceived as belonging together. Because of their spacing, the lines in **Figure 3.13(b)** are perceived as four pairs of lines rather than as eight separate lines.
- *Continuity.* We tend to perceive figures or objects as belonging together if they appear to form a continuous pattern, as in **Figure 3.13(c)**.
- *Closure.* We perceive figures with gaps in them to be complete. Even though parts of the figure in **Figure 3.13(d)** are missing, we use closure and perceive it as a triangle.

Gestalt (geh-SHTALT) A German word that roughly refers to the whole form, pattern, or configuration that a person perceives.

Figure 3.12 Reversing Figure and Ground

In this illustration, you can see a white vase as a figure against a black background, or two black faces in profile on a white background. Exactly the same visual stimulus produces two opposite figure-ground perceptions.

Perceptual Constancy. When you say good-bye to friends and watch them walk away, the image they cast on your retina grows smaller and smaller until they finally disappear in the distance. So how does your brain know that they are still the same size? Scientists call this phenomenon **perceptual constancy.** Thanks to perceptual constancy, when you watch someone walk away, the information that the retina sends to the brain (the sensation that that person is shrinking in size) does not fool the perceptual system. As objects or people move farther away, you continue to perceive them as being about the same size. This perceptual phenomenon is known as *size constancy*. You do not make a literal interpretation about the size of an object from its retinal image— the image of the object projected onto the retina. If you did, you would believe that objects become larger as they approach and smaller as they move away.

The shape or image of an object projected onto the retina changes according to the angle from which it is viewed. But your perceptual ability includes *shape constancy—* the tendency to perceive objects as having a stable or unchanging shape, regardless of changes in the retinal image resulting from differences in viewing angle. In other words, you perceive a door as rectangular and a plate as round from whatever angle you view them (see **Figure 3.14**).

We normally see objects as maintaining a constant level of brightness, regardless of differences in lighting conditions—a perceptual phenomenon known as *brightness constancy*. Nearly all objects reflect some part of the light that falls on them, and white objects reflect more light than black objects. However, a black asphalt driveway at noon in bright sunlight actually reflects more light than a white shirt does indoors at night in dim lighting. Nevertheless, the driveway still looks black, and the shirt still looks white. Why? We learn to infer the brightness of objects by comparing it with the brightness of all other objects viewed at the same time.

perceptual constancy The phenomenon that allows us to perceive objects as maintaining stable properties, such as size, shape, and brightness, despite differences in distance, viewing angle, and lighting.

Figure 3.13 Gestalt Principles of Grouping

Gestalt psychologists proposed several principles of perceptual grouping, including similarity, proximity, continuity, and closure.

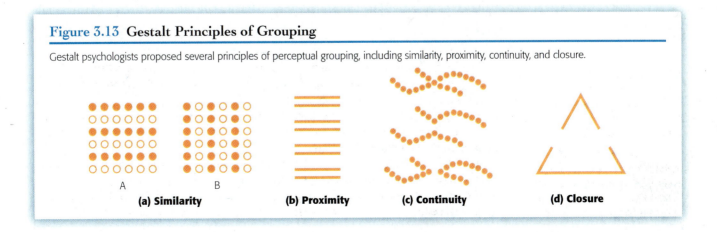

(a) Similarity   (b) Proximity   (c) Continuity   (d) Closure

Figure 3.14 Shape Constancy

The door projects very different images on the retina when viewed from different angles. But because of shape constancy, you continue to perceive the door as rectangular.

Depth Perception

3.18 What are some of the binocular and monocular depth cues?

Depth perception is the ability to perceive the visual world in three dimensions and to judge distances accurately. We judge how far away objects and other people are. We climb and descend stairs without stumbling and perform numerous other actions requiring depth perception. Depth perception is three-dimensional. Yet each eye is able to provide only a two-dimensional view. The images cast on the retina do not contain depth; they are flat, just like a photograph. How, then, do we perceive depth so vividly?

Binocular Depth Cues. Some cues to depth perception depend on both eyes working together. These are called **binocular depth cues,** and they include convergence and binocular disparity. *Convergence* occurs when the eyes turn inward to focus on nearby objects—the closer the object, the greater the convergence. Hold the tip of your finger about 12 inches in front of your nose, and focus on it. Now, slowly begin moving your finger toward your nose. Your eyes will turn inward so much that they virtually cross when the tip of your finger meets the tip of your nose. Many psychologists believe that the tension of the eye muscles as they converge conveys to the brain information that serves as a cue for depth perception. Fortunately, the eyes are just far enough apart, about $2\frac{1}{2}$ inches or so, to give each eye a slightly different view of the objects being focused on and, consequently, a slightly different retinal image. The difference between the two retinal images, known as *binocular disparity* (or *retinal disparity*), provides an important cue for depth perception (see **Figure 3.15**). The farther away from the eyes (up to 20 feet or so) the objects being looked at, the less is the disparity, or difference, between the two retinal images. The brain integrates the two slightly different retinal images and creates the perception of three dimensions.

Monocular Depth Cues. Close one eye, and you will see that you can still perceive depth. The visual depth cues perceived with one eye alone are called **monocular depth cues.** The following is a description of seven monocular depth cues, many of which have been used by artists in Western cultures to give the illusion of depth to their paintings.

depth perception The ability to perceive the visual world in three dimensions and to judge distances accurately.

binocular depth cues Depth cues that depend on both eyes working together.

monocular depth cues (mah-NOK-yu-ler) Depth cues that can be perceived by one eye alone.

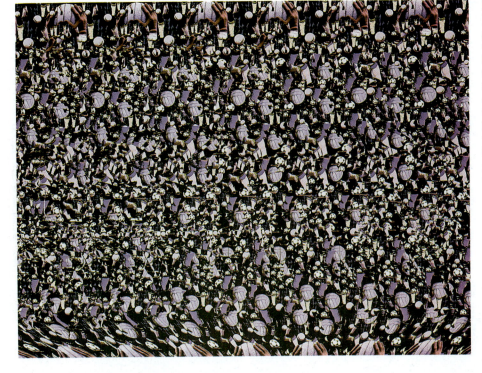

Figure 3.15 **Retinal Disparity and Viewing a Stereogram**

Retinal disparity enables most of us to perceive 3-D images in stereograms. Place this picture against the tip of your nose and then very, very slowly move the book straight back from your face. Look at the image without blinking. A 3-D picture of soccer players and their fans will suddenly appear.

- *Interposition.* When one object partly blocks your view of another, you perceive the partially blocked object as being farther away.
- *Linear perspective.* Parallel lines that are known to be the same distance apart appear to grow closer together, or converge, as they recede into the distance.
- *Relative size.* Larger objects are perceived as being closer to the viewer, and smaller objects as being farther away.
- *Texture gradient.* Objects close to you appear to have sharply defined features, and similar objects that are farther away appear progressively less well-defined or fuzzier in texture.
- *Atmospheric perspective* (sometimes called *aerial perspective*). Objects in the distance have a bluish tint and appear more blurred than objects close at hand.
- *Shadow or shading.* When light falls on objects, they cast shadows, which add to the perception of depth.
- *Motion parallax.* When you ride in a moving vehicle and look out the side window, the objects you see outside appear to be moving in the opposite direction and at different speeds; those closest to you appear to be moving faster than those in the distance. Objects very far away, such as the moon and the sun, appear to move in the same direction as the viewer.

Photos illustrating each of these cues are shown in **Figure 3.16**.

Motion Perception

Imagine you're sitting in a bus looking through the window at another bus parked parallel to the one in which you are sitting. Suddenly, you sense your bus moving; then, you realize that it is not your bus that moved but the one next to it. In other words, your ability to perceive the motion of objects has been fooled in some way. This example illustrates the complexity of motion perception, a process that is primarily visual, but that also involves auditory and kinesthetic cues. False motion perceptions are so

3.19 How does the brain perceive real and apparent motion?

Figure 3.16 Monocular Depth Cues

Interposition
When one object partially blocks your view of another, you perceive the partially blocked object as being farther away.

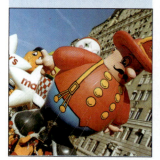

Linear Perspective
Parallel lines are the same distance apart but appear to grow closer together, or converge, as they recede into the distance.

Relative Size
Larger objects are perceived as being closer to the viewer, and smaller objects as being farther away.

Texture Gradient
Objects close to you appear to have sharply defined features, and similar objects farther away appear progressively less well defined, or fuzzier in texture.

Atmospheric Perspective
Objects in the distance have a bluish tint and appear more blurred than objects close at hand (sometimes called *aerial perspective*).

Shadow or Shading
When light falls on objects, they cast shadows, which add to the perception of depth.

Motion Parallax
When you ride in a moving train and look out the window, the objects you see outside appear to be moving in the opposite direction and at different speeds; those closest to you appear to be moving faster than those in the distance.

common that psychologists have conducted a great deal of research to find out how the brain perceives real and apparent motion. These researchers use the term **real motion** to refer to perceptions of motion tied to movements of real objects through space. In contrast, the term **apparent motion** signifies perceptions of motion that seem to be psychologically constructed in response to various kinds of stimuli.

Real Motion. When objects move in the field of vision, they project images that move across the retina. As you might expect, research indicates that motion detection is caused by brain mechanisms linked to the retina, the edges of which appear to be especially sensitive to motion, just as the fovea is specialized for detail and color (Bach & Hoffman, 2000). However, if you walk across a room with your eyes fixed on an object—your sofa, for example—the object will move across your retina. So, movement of an image across the retina isn't sufficient for motion detection. Your own kinesthetic sense contributes to judgments of motion. Generally, you know whether you're moving or not. But have you ever watched a train go by while sitting still? It's not unusual to have the feeling that your head is moving as you watch the railroad cars whiz by. So, your kinesthetic sense is also linked to your perceptions of move-

real motion Perceptions of motion tied to movements of real objects through space.

apparent motion Perceptions of motion that seem to be psychologically constructed in response to various kinds of stimuli.

ment outside your own body. Brain-imaging studies show that such stimuli activate the vestibular cortex, just as real body movements do (Nishiike et al., 2001).

One of the most important contributors to our understanding of motion perception is psychologist James Gibson. Gibson points out that our perceptions of motion appear to be based on fundamental, but frequently changing, assumptions about stability (Gibson, 1994). Our brains seem to search for some stimulus in the environment to serve as the assumed reference point for stability. Once the stable reference point is chosen, all objects that move relative to that reference point are judged to be in motion. For example, in the bus situation, your brain assumes that the other bus is stable, and when the motion sensors linked to your retina detect movement, it concludes that your bus is moving. In the train situation, your brain assumes that the train is stable, and so your head must be moving. And when you're driving a car, you sense the car to be in motion relative to the outside environment. But your brain uses the inside of the car as the stable point of reference for your own movements. Only your movements in relation to the seat, steering wheel, and so on are sensed as motion by your brain.

Apparent Motion. In one type of apparent motion study, several stationary lights in a dark room are flashed on and off in sequence, causing participants to perceive a single light is moving from one spot to the next. This type of apparent motion, called the phi phenomenon, was first discussed by Max Wertheimer (1912), one of the founders of Gestalt psychology. How many neon signs have you seen that caused you to perceive motion? The neon lights don't move; they simply flash on and off in a particular sequence. When you watch a motion picture, you are also perceiving this kind of apparent motion, often called *stroboscopic motion*.

The fact that the eyes are never really completely still also contributes to perceptions of apparent motion. For instance, if you stare at a single unmoving light in a dark room for a few seconds, the light will appear to begin moving, a phenomenon called the autokinetic illusion. However, if you look away from the light and then return to watching it, it will again appear to be stable. (Could this phenomenon account for some sightings of "unidentified flying objects"?) Two lights placed close to one another will appear to move together, as if they are linked by an invisible string. What is really happening is that your eyes, not the lights, are moving. Because of the darkness of the room, the brain has no stable visual reference point to use in deciding whether the lights are actually moving or not (Gibson, 1994). But when the room is lit up, the brain immediately "fixes" the error because it has a stable visible background for the lights.

Puzzling Perceptions

Not only can we perceive motion that doesn't exist, we can also perceive objects that aren't present in a stimulus and misinterpret those that are.

Ambiguous and Impossible Figures. When you are faced for the first time with an *ambiguous figure*, you have no experience to call on. Your perceptual system is puzzled and tries to resolve the uncertainty by seeing the ambiguous figure first one way and then another, but not both ways at once. You never get a lasting impression of ambiguous figures because they seem to jump back and forth beyond your control. In some ambiguous figures, two different objects or figures are seen alternately. The best known of these, "Old Woman/Young Woman," by E. G. Boring, is shown in **Figure 3.17(a)**. If you direct your gaze to the left of the drawing, you are likely to see an attractive young woman, her face turned away. But the young woman disappears when you suddenly perceive the image of the old woman. Such examples of object ambiguity offer striking evidence that perceptions are more than the mere sum of sensory parts. It is hard to believe that the same drawing (the same sum of sensory parts) can convey such dramatically different perceptions.

At first glance, many impossible figures do not seem particularly unusual—at least not until you examine them more closely. Would you invest your money in a company that manufactured the three-pronged device shown in **Figure 3.17(b)**? Such an object

3.20 What are three types of puzzling perceptions?

phi phenomenon Apparent motion that occurs when several stationary lights in a dark room are flashed on and off in sequence, causing the perception that a single light is moving from one spot to the next.

autokinetic illusion Apparent motion caused by the movement of the eyes rather than the movement of the objects being viewed.

Figure 3.17 Some Puzzling Perceptions

(a) Do you see an old woman or a young woman? (b) Why couldn't you build a replica of this three-pronged device? (c) Which horizontal line appears to be longer? (d) Which bar, A or B, is longer?

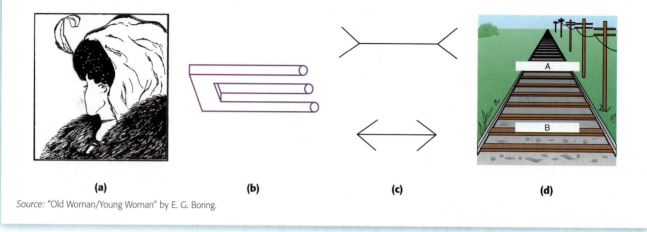

(a)   (b)   (c)   (d)

Source: "Old Woman/Young Woman" by E. G. Boring.

could not be made as pictured because the middle prong appears to be in two different places at the same time. However, this type of impossible figure is more likely to confuse people from Western cultures. Classic research in the 1970s showed that people in some African cultures do not represent three-dimensional visual space in their art, and they do not perceive depth in drawings that contain pictorial depth cues. These people see no ambiguity in drawings similar to the three-pronged trident, and they can draw the figure accurately from memory much more easily than people from Western cultures can (Bloomer, 1976).

Illusions. An **illusion** is a false perception or a misperception of an actual stimulus in the environment. We can misperceive size, shape, or the relationship of one element to another. We need not pay to see illusions performed by magicians. Illusions occur naturally, and we see them all the time. An oar in the water appears to be bent where it meets the water. The moon looks much larger at the horizon than it does overhead. Why? One explanation of the *moon illusion* involves relative size. This idea suggests that the moon looks very large on the horizon because it is viewed in comparison to trees, buildings, and other objects. When viewed overhead, the moon cannot be directly compared with other objects, and it appears smaller.

In **Figure 3.17(c)**, the two lines are the same length, but the diagonals extending outward from both ends of the upper line make it look longer than the lower line, which has diagonals pointing inward, a phenomenon known as the *Müller-Lyer illusion*. The *Ponzo illusion* also plays an interesting trick on our estimation of size. Look at **Figure 3.17(d)**. Contrary to your perceptions, bars A and B are the same length. Again, perceptions of size and distance, which we trust and which are normally accurate in informing us about the real world, can be wrong. If you saw two obstructions like the ones in the illusion on real railroad tracks, the one that looks larger would indeed be larger. So the Ponzo illusion is not a natural illusion but a contrived one. In fact, all these illusions are really misapplications of principles that nearly always work properly in normal everyday experience.

Cultural Differences in the Perception of Visual Illusions. Because responses to a number of illusions are universal, many psychologists believe they are inborn. However, British psychologist R. L. Gregory believed that susceptibility to the Müller-Lyer and other such illusions is not innate. Rather, the culture in which people live is responsible to some extent for the illusions they perceive. To test whether susceptibility to the Müller-Lyer and similar illusions is due to experience, Segall and others (1966) tested 1,848 adults and children from 15 different cultures in Africa, the Philippines,

illusion A false perception or a misperception of an actual stimulus in the environment.

and the United States. Included were a group of Zulus from South Africa and a group of Illinois residents. The study revealed that "there were marked differences in illusion susceptibility across the cultural groups included in this study" (Segall, 1994, p. 137). People from all the cultures showed some tendency to perceive the Müller-Lyer illusion, indicating a biological component, but experience was clearly a factor. Zulus, who have round houses and see few corners of any kind, are not fooled by this illusion. Illinois residents saw the illusion readily, while the Zulu tribespeople tended not to see it.

Early cross-cultural researchers suggested that race might offer an explanation for the cultural differences in perceptions of illusions (Pollack, 1970). But an important study by Stewart (1973) in response to these claims provided evidence that it is fundamentally culture, not race, that drives perceptions of illusions. When two groups of schoolchildren from Illinois (60 African Americans and 60 Whites) were shown the Müller-Lyer and other illusions, no significant differences were found in susceptibility to the illusions. And in Zambia, researchers tested five different groups of Black African schoolchildren using the same illusions. Children's tendency to see the illusions had nothing to do with race but was strongly influenced by culture. Those children who lived in areas where buildings had angles, edges, corners, and doors were likely to be fooled by the illusions; those who lived in remote villages with primarily round houses were not.

In another classic cross-cultural study of illusions, Pedersen and Wheeler (1983) studied perceptions of the Müller-Lyer illusion among two groups of Navajos. The group who lived in rectangular houses and had experienced corners, angles, and edges tended to see the illusion. The members of the other group, like the Zulus, tended not to see it because they lived in round houses.

▲ Some visual illusions seem to be culture-dependent. For example, Zulus and people from other cultures in which the houses lack straight sides and corners do not perceive the Müller-Lyer illusion.

Remember It   Principles of Perception

1. Retinal disparity and convergence are two _____ depth cues.

2. Match each example with the appropriate monocular depth cue.

   ____ (1) one building partly blocking your view of another
   ____ (2) railroad tracks converging in the distance
   ____ (3) closer objects appearing to move faster than objects farther away
   ____ (4) small objects appearing to be farther away

   a. motion parallax
   b. linear perspective
   c. interposition
   d. relative size

3. The apparent motion produced by several lights flashing off and on in sequence is known as the _____.

4. The apparent motion produced by movements of the eyes is known as the _____.

5. A(n) _____ is a misinterpretation of a real stimulus.

6. Responses to many illusions are _____, but perceptions of others are influenced by _____.

Answers: 1. binocular; 2. (1) c, (2) b, (3) a, (4) d; 3. phi phenomenon; 4. autokinetic illusion; 5. illusion; 6. universal, culture

---

Influences on Perception

How we perceive sensory information is often determined by factors—such as the Gestalt principle of perceptual organization—that vary little from individual to individual. But individual differences can influence perceptions as well. Consequently, many sensory experiences are interpreted differently by various people.

Prior Knowledge

The knowledge we possess about a given sensory stimulus influences how we perceive it. Prior knowledge sometimes enhances perception, but it can lead to errors as well.

Bottom-Up and Top-Down Processing. Look at this array of letters and numbers. How would you go about trying to use your prior knowledge to make sense of it?

DP

6-4-3

If you don't immediately recognize the array, you might begin trying to decipher it by guessing what the letters "DP" stand for, a classic example of **bottom-up processing,** or *data-driven* processing. This strategy involves looking for patterns in individual bits of information that can be interpreted using prior knowledge. For example, bottom-up processing might lead you to call up compound nouns (nouns made up of two words) from your memory such as "Detroit Police" or "data projector" that the letters might stand for. Perhaps you would try to decide which of these two possible meanings of "DP" was more feasible based on the information given in "6-4-3." Ultimately, you would probably give up and declare the array either meaningless or indecipherable.

Suppose we told you that the array has something to do with baseball. Now, if you have some knowledge of the game, you might try to think of baseball terms that could be represented by the letters "DP." In so doing, you would be using **top-down processing,** or *concept-driven* processing. In top-down processing, prior knowledge limits the range of one's guesses by providing a "whole" that can serve as a context for individual bits of information. Thus, given that baseball is the context for the array, neither "Detroit Police" nor "data projector" will fit. Of course, if you know how to score a baseball game, you probably instantly moved into top-down processing mode when you saw the array. No doubt, you recognized the array as representing a double play (DP) in which the third baseman (6) threw the ball to the second baseman (4) who, in turn, threw it to the first baseman (3) to get two runners out.

This example might lead you to think that bottom-up processing seldom leads to accurate perceptions. However, there are some situations in which only bottom-up processing will work. A "find the differences" activity, such as the one in **Figure 3.18**, provides a good example of a task that can only be accomplished through bottom-up processing. Why? Top-down processing causes you to perceive the scene as a whole and, as a result, to overlook details. To find the differences, you have to look at the items individually, without allowing the picture to contextualize them.

Perceptual Set. If you ordered raspberry sherbet and it was colored green, would it still taste like raspberry, or might it taste more like lime? Would you eagerly bite into a hamburger patty to which someone had added green food coloring, or would you be a bit more cautious? The **perceptual set**—what we expect to perceive—determines, to a large extent, what we actually see, hear, feel, taste, and smell. Such expectations are, of course, based on prior knowledge (that lime sherbert is usually green and green meat is usually spoiled). Such expectations do seem to influence perception. So, green raspberry sherbert might, indeed, taste a bit like lime, and a green hamburger might smell and taste spoiled.

In a classic study of perceptual set, psychologist David Rosenhan (1973) and some of his colleagues were admitted as patients to various mental hospitals with "diagnoses" of schizophrenia. Once admitted, they acted normal in every way. The purpose? They wondered how long it would take the doctors and the hospital staff to realize that they were not mentally ill. But the doctors and the staff members saw what they expected to see and not what actually occurred. They perceived everything the pseudo-patients said and did, such as note taking, to be symptoms of their illness. But the real patients were not fooled; they were the first to realize that the psychologists were not really mentally ill.

bottom-up processing Information processing in which individual components of a stimulus are combined in the brain and prior knowledge is used to make inferences about these patterns.

top-down processing Information processing in which previous experience and conceptual knowledge are applied in order to recognize the nature of a "whole" and then logically deduce the individual components of that whole.

perceptual set An expectation of what will be perceived, which can affect what actually is perceived.

Figure 3.18 A Bottom-Up Processing Task

A bottom-up processing strategy is the best approach to some kinds of tasks because top-down processing prevents you from processing the details in the two scenes pictured.

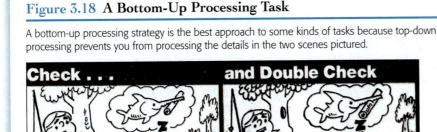

Attention

In some cases, linking sensations to meanings—the essence of the process of perception—requires very little mental effort. For instance, when reading familiar words, the sensation of seeing the word and the perception of its meaning occur almost simultaneously (Heil et al., 2004). Likewise, while we are driving, perceiving that the other objects on the road with us are cars takes very little mental effort because we are so familiar with them. In other words, connecting the sensation of seeing a car with the perception that the object is a car is an *automatic* (non-effortful) mental process. However, more mental effort is required to determine which cars we should watch most closely. When we engage in this kind of mental effort, the process of *attention* is at work. **Attention** is defined as the process of sorting through sensations and selecting some of them for further processing. Without attention, perception of all but the most familiar sensations would be impossible.

Of course, we cannot pay attention to everything at once. Thus, in a complex perceptual task, such as the everyday experience of driving in traffic, it's important to realize that attention carries certain perceptual costs. Research examining the phenomenon of **inattentional blindness** has helped to illustrate these costs (Mack, 2003; Mack & Rock, 1998; Most et al., 2001; Simons & Rensink, 2005). Inattentional blindness occurs when we shift our attention from one object to another and, in the process, fail to notice changes in objects to which we are not directly paying attention (Woodman & Luck, 2003). In many studies of inattentional blindness, experimenters have presented participants with a scene and asked them to attend to a particular element in it. For example, Daniel Simons and colleagues (e.g., Simons & Chabris, 1999) showed participants a videotape of a basketball game in which one team wore white uniforms and the other team wore black uniforms. Participants were instructed to count how many times the ball was passed from one player to another, either on the white team or on the black team. Under such conditions, about one-third of participants typically failed to later recall the appearance on the screen of even extremely incongruent stimuli (for example, a man dressed in a gorilla costume). The inattentional blindness happens even when the incongruous stimulus is present on the screen for a long period of time. Simon's research helps us understand why we

3.22 What is gained and what is lost in the process of attention?

▲ When you look at this photograph, you can easily notice the gorilla-costumed figure. However, this photo is actually a frame from a video used in Simons's inattentional blindness studies. Participants are shown the video after being told to keep track of how many times the basketball is passed from one person to another. Under these conditions, participants typically fail to notice when the gorilla-costumed figure enters the scene. You can view clips from Simons's videos at http://viscog.beckman.uiuc.edu/grafs/demos/15.html.

sometimes exclaim, "Where did that car come from?" when a car we had been ignoring suddenly swerves into our path.

Similar costs arise when we attend to auditory sensations. Suppose you are standing in a crowded room in which a large number of conversations are going on simultaneously. What would happen if someone mentioned your name? Research shows that you would zero in on the conversation that included your name and ignore others. This *cocktail party phenomenon* was documented in classic research by E. C. Cherry (1953). Remember, perception is the process of attaching meaning to sensations—and what is more meaningful to a person than his or her own name? Thus, when you hear your name, you assume that whatever is to follow will be personally meaningful to you. The process of attending to the conversation that included your name, however, would prevent you from adequately perceiving other conversations. Thus, you might fail to pick up on other conversations that might have more meaning for you but are free from obvious attentional cues such as your name.

Although attending to a stimulus is associated with deficits in the ability to attend to other stimuli, attention is clearly not an all-or-nothing process. We can, and often do, process more than one simulus, at a time. Indeed, research shows that we are capable of accurately perceiving some sensations to which we do not pay direct attention. For example, in the same series of classic studies that led to the discovery of the cocktail party phenomenon, E. C. Cherry (1953) discovered that listeners who were presented with different verbal messages in either ear could remember the content of only the message to which the experimenter directed their attention (e.g., "Pay attention to the message in your left ear"). Nevertheless, they were able to remember many things about the unattended message, such as whether it had been delivered by a male or a female.

Social Perception

3.23 Do we perceive physical objects and social stimuli in the same way?

Finally, do the rules of perceptual processing you've learned so far apply to social stimuli as well as physical objects? The traditional view holds that perceptual processes in the brain are organized according to the kind of process—vision, hearing, smell, taste, touch, or kinesthetic sense—needed to perceive a particular stimulus. Thus, looking at a face or a cat should elicit the same kind of response from the brain because both are visual stimuli. It is true that visual perception occurs primarily in the same parts of the brain, no matter what you are looking at. But brain-imaging studies show that patterns of neural activation within those areas vary according to the types of objects being viewed. For example, there is one pattern for faces and another for cats (Haxby et al., 2001). These differences exist in the brains of other primates as well (Tsao, Freiwald, Tootell, & Livingstone, 2006).

Perception of human faces appears to be particularly complex and distinctive from perceptions of other kinds of visual stimuli. Researcher James Haxby and his colleagues suggest that there is a "core system" of face perception that uses the universal features of the human face (eyes, nose, and mouth) to make judgments about people's identities (Haxby et al., 2002). We move beyond the core system when we engage in verbal and nonverbal communication with others and, in so doing, activate a larger neural network. Other researchers have found equally distinctive neural systems for processing images of human body parts (Downing et al., 2001).

The way we combine information from two sensory modalities—a process known as *cross-modal perception*—also differs for nonsocial and social stimuli. For example, how would your brain respond to the sight of an approaching train paired with the sound of a departing train? Research indicates that, when judging motion based on conflicting visual and auditory cues, we tend to rely on the auditory input (Meyer & Wuerger, 2001). So, your brain would decide that the train was moving away rather than approaching.

In the case of social perception, the opposite is true. Facial expressions, the visual cues for emotional perceptions, often take priority over the auditory cues associated with a person's speech intonation and volume, as well as the actual words spoken.

attention   The process of sorting sensations and selecting some for further processing.

inattentional blindness   The phenomenon in which we shift our focus from one object to another and, in the process, fail to notice changes in objects to which we are not directly paying attention.

Thus, a person who exhibits an angry face but speaks in a happy voice will typically be judged to be angry rather than happy (Vroomen et al., 2001). Perhaps this is why one old song suggests that we "put on a happy face."

Unusual Perceptual Experiences

All of the principles of perception and the influences on perception you have learned about up to this point involve stimuli that are above the absolute threshold. What happens when we encounter stimuli that are below our sensory thresholds? Furthermore, is it possible to perceive without sensing any stimuli; that is, does *extrasensory perception* exist?

Subliminal Perception. For decades, psychologists have studied a phenomenon known as **subliminal perception,** the capacity to perceive and respond to stimuli that are presented below the threshold of awareness. Neuroimaging studies show that the brain does, indeed, respond physiologically to subliminally presented stimuli (Brown, 2004; Bernat et al., 2001). Moreover, subliminal information can influence behavior to some degree. For example, when people are subliminally exposed to a picture of one person hitting another, they are more likely to judge a consciously perceived neutral scene, such as two people talking in a restaurant, as involving some kind of aggression (Todorov & Bargh, 2002).

But how strongly does subliminal perception affect behavior? You might remember the infamous "rats" commercial that the Republican party ran during the 2000 presidential campaign, in which the word *bureaucrats* was reduced to *rats* for about $\frac{1}{30}$ of a second. Democrats accused Republicans of attempting to subliminally influence voters against Albert Gore, the Democratic party candidate. The use of messages presented below the threshold of awareness in advertising, often called *subliminal persuasion,* has been around for decades. However, most research on subliminal perception suggests that, although the phenomenon does exist, it probably cannot produce the kinds of behavior changes claimed by the proponents of its use for advertising purposes (Greenwald, 1992).

Similarly, people who want to lose weight may purchase audiotapes containing subliminal messages such as "I will eat less" embedded in recordings of music or ocean waves in the hopes that listening to the tapes will help them control their appetite. Recordings of this kind are also marketed to people who want to quit smoking. However, experimental, placebo-controlled studies have found that such subliminal messages have no effect on behavior (Greenwald, 1992; Greenwald et al., 1991; Russell et al., 1991).

Extrasensory Perception. **Extrasensory perception (ESP)** is defined as gaining information about objects, events, or another person's thoughts through some means other than the known sensory channels. Several different kinds of ESP have been proposed to exist. *Telepathy* means gaining awareness of the thoughts, feelings, or activities of another person without the use of the senses—in other words, reading a person's mind. *Clairvoyance* means gaining information about objects or events without use of the senses, such as knowing the contents of a letter before opening it. *Precognition* refers to an awareness of an event before it occurs. Most of the reported cases of precognition in everyday life have occurred while people were dreaming.

Many studies of ESP employ the *Ganzfeld procedure,* a study design in which two individuals, a "sender" and a "receiver," are placed in separate rooms. The rooms are specially designed to minimize distractions and to facilitate deep concentration. Experimenters provide senders with messages that they are supposed to attempt to transmit to receivers. Some studies using the Ganzfeld technique have suggested that ESP exists and that some people are more capable of sending and receiving extrasensory messages than others (Ben & Honorton, 1994). However, in almost all cases, attempts at replication of these studies have failed (Milton & Wiseman, 2001). Thus, most psychologists remain skeptical about the existence of ESP.

3.24 What have studies of subliminal and extrasensory perception shown?

subliminal perception The capacity to perceive and respond to stimuli that are presented below the threshold of awareness.

extrasensory perception (ESP) Gaining information about objects, events, or another person's thoughts through some means other than the known sensory channels.

Remember It | Influences on Perception

1. When you approach a problem by using prior knowledge to analyze its components, you are using _____ processing.

2. When you approach a problem by using prior knowledge to make assumptions about the nature of the solution, you are using _____ processing.

3. _____ refers to what people expect to perceive.

4. When individuals focus on one of several moving objects in their visual field, they often exhibit _____.

5. When visual and auditory information are in conflict, individuals tend to rely on _____ sensations when processing social information.

6. Studies of subliminal perception show that the brain (*does/does not*) respond to stimuli that are presented below the threshold of awareness.

7. ESP is studied with the _____ procedure.

Answers: 1. bottom-up; 2. top-down; 3. Perceptual set; 4. inattentional blindness; 5. visual; 6. does; 7. Ganzfeld

Apply It | How Dangerous Is It to Talk on a Cell Phone While Driving?

When you read about the research demonstrating inattentional blindness, you may have thought of an everyday experience that many of us have, that of talking on a cell phone while driving. As Simons' research showed, when we concentrate on one set of stimuli in the environment, we may be functionally "blind" to others. Interestingly, though, surveys suggest that we are more concerned about other drivers' cell phone use than our own. In one study, researchers found that just 6% of drivers reported that their cell phone use had caused them to get into a potentially dangerous situation on the road. Remarkably, when participants were asked whether another driver's cell phone use had ever put them at risk, 66% said yes (Troglauer, Hels, & Christens, 2006). As much as we would like to believe that cell phones affect other drivers' behavior but not our own, research clearly shows that talking on a cell phone, or engaging in other kinds of attention-demanding tasks, results in potentially dangerous changes in our behind-the-wheel behavior.

Behavioral Effects of Cell Phone Use

Most experiments examining cell phone use while driving take place in laboratories in which participants use driving simulators. Cell phone use is usually the independent variable; that is, experimental subjects talk on the cell phone while driving, but control group subjects do not. The simulators are programmed to provide drivers with challenges such as changes from city streets to freeways, cars that stop suddenly, long- and short-interval traffic lights, pedestrians that step off the curb into traffic, and so on. These variations in driving conditions constitute a set of independent variables that may interact with cell phone use. For instance, cell phone use may cause changes in behavior in one kind of driving situation but not in others. The dependent, or outcome variables are items such as changes in speed, reaction time to changes in driving conditions, potential moving violations, and compensatory behaviors such as slamming on the brakes.

Experiments of this type show that cell phone use clearly affects drivers' behavior (Beede & Kass, 2006; Liu & Lee, 2006). Drivers tend to slow down when talking on the phone. They also

have slower reaction times and often drift outside the lines of the lane in which they are driving. Lapses in attention are common as well, often causing drivers to make errors in judgment such as stopping at green lights. Stop signs are missed by many drivers, some of whom slam on their brakes when they notice they are part of the way through an intersection at which they were supposed to stop. Note, too, that these effects have been observed just as often in studies using hands-free phones as conventional hand-held models (Strayer & Drews, 2004). However, one study suggested that hands-free phone use gave drivers a false sense of safety (Langer, Holzner, Magnet, & Kopp, 2005). Thus, experimental studies show definitively that, on average, cell phone use impairs driving ability.

Criticisms of Cell Phone Use Research

Despite the clear findings of these studies, critics have attacked cell phone use studies on several fronts. First, they say, other attention-demanding tasks impair driving behaviors just as much as cell phone use does. One study found, for example, that searching for a radio station while driving produced the same kinds of detrimental effects on drivers' behavior as cell phone use (Horberry, et al., 2006). Another demonstrated that the same kinds of effects on driving behavior occurred whether a person was talking on a cell phone or talking to a passenger in the car (Amado & Ulupinar, 2005).

Another frequent criticism of cell phone studies involves the nature of the cell phone task itself. In most studies, participants do not engage in a real conversation on their cell phones. Instead of trying to simulate real-world conversations, experimenters transmit math problems to drivers that they are supposed to solve in their heads within a limited time frame. So, critics ask, when was the last time anyone used a cell phone to work math problems in the real world? To bolster their argument, these critics have carried out their own studies in which participants engaged in an actual conversation with someone they knew. In these experiments, drivers displayed far less impairment than in studies involving telephonically transmitted math problems (Rakauskas, Gugerty, & Ward, 2004).

A third criticism of cell phone use studies involves their failure to consider practice effects. Critics say that people become more proficient at multi-tasking with practice, a factor that isn't taken into account in most experiments. Advocates of the practice-makes-less-dangerous position have done their own studies in which changes in participants' driving behaviors have been charted across several simulator sessions involving the same kinds of distractors. These studies show that, indeed, multi-tasking does improve with repetition in that deleterious effects on driving behaviors are less evident in later sessions (Shinar, Tractinsky, & Compton, 2005). Individuals who have more experience with talking while engaged in attention-demanding tasks, such as airline pilots, also perform more proficiently in cell phone use experiments than participants who have less experience in such situations (Hunton & Rose, 2005).

Others have noted that real-world drivers often take actions to reduce distractions (Pöysti, Rajalin, & Summala, 2005). For instance, a driver might turn off the radio while talking on the cell phone and turn it back on when the conversation is over. Another might respond to every caller with a message such as, "I'm driving right now. I'll call you back as soon as I'm off the road." The point these critics are making is that drivers are well aware of the potentially risk-enhancing effects of behavior changes caused by distractions. As a result, they actively work to manage the number of demands on their attention while driving.

The Take-Away Message

How should you apply all of this information to your own driving decisions? In summary, experiments show that cell phone use and other activities place demands on drivers' attention that can cause them to change their driving behavior. These changes in behavior may result in actions that can increase the chances of, at best, a traffic ticket, or, at worst, getting into an accident. Although practice may help, intentional management of the number of attention-demanding tasks in which you engage while driving may be the best approach to risk reduction. And the best task management strategy may involve pulling off the road when you need to use your cell phone.

Summary and Review

The Process of Sensation p. 83

3.1 What is the difference between the absolute threshold and the difference threshold? p. 84

The absolute threshold is the minimum amount of sensory stimulation that can be detected 50% of the time. The difference threshold is a measure of the smallest increase or decrease in a physical stimulus that can be detected 50% of the time.

3.2 How does transduction enable the brain to receive sensory information? p. 84

For each of the senses, the body has sensory receptors that detect and respond to sensory stimuli. Through the process of transduction, the receptors change the sensory stimuli into neural impulses, which are then transmitted to precise locations in the brain.

Vision p. 86

3.3 How does each part of the eye function in vision? p. 86

The cornea bends light rays inward through the pupil—the small, dark opening in the eye. The iris dilates and contracts the pupil to regulate the amount of light entering the eye. The lens changes its shape as it focuses images of objects at varying distances on the retina, a thin layer of tissue that contains the sensory receptors for vision. The cones detect color and fine detail; they function best in adequate light. The rods are extremely sensitive and enable vision in dim light.

3.4 What path does visual information take from the retina to the primary visual cortex? p. 88

The rods and the cones transduce light waves into neural impulses that pass from the bipolar cells to the ganglion cells, whose axons form the optic nerve beyond the retinal wall of each eye. At the optic chiasm, the two optic nerves come together, and some of the nerve fibers from each eye cross to the opposite side of the brain. They synapse with neurons in the thalamus, which transmit the neural impulses to the primary visual cortex.

3.5 How do we detect the difference between one color and another? p. 90

The perception of color results from the reflection of particular wavelengths of the visual spectrum from the surfaces of objects. For example, an object that appears to be red reflects light of longer wavelengths than one that appears to be blue.

3.6   What two major theories attempt to explain color vision? p. 90

Two major theories that attempt to explain color vision are the trichromatic theory and the opponent-process theory.

3.7   Do individuals with color blindness see the world in black and white? p. 91

No, color blindness is the inability to distinguish certain colors from one another, rather than the total absence of color vision.

Hearing p. 92

3.8   What determines the pitch and loudness of a sound, and how is each quality measured? p. 92

The pitch of a sound is determined by the frequency of the sound waves, which is measured in hertz. The loudness of a sound is determined largely by the amplitude of the sound waves, which is measured in decibels.

3.9   How do the outer ear, middle ear, and inner ear function in hearing? p. 93

Sound waves enter the pinna, the visible part of the outer ear, and travel to the end of the auditory canal, causing the eardrum to vibrate. This sets in motion the ossicles in the middle ear, which amplify the sound waves. The vibration of the oval window causes activity in the inner ear, setting in motion the fluid in the cochlea. The moving fluid pushes and pulls the hair cells attached to the thin basilar membrane, which transduce the vibrations into neural impulses. The auditory nerve then carries the neural impulses to the brain.

3.10   What two major theories attempt to explain hearing? p. 94

Two major theories that attempt to explain hearing are place theory and frequency theory.

3.11   What are some of the major causes of hearing loss? p. 95

Some causes of hearing loss are excessive noise, disease, circumstances of birth, genetic defects, injury, and aging.

The Other Senses: Smell, Taste, Touch, and Balance p. 96

3.12   What path does a smell message take from the nose to the brain? p. 96

The act of smelling begins when odor molecules reach the smell receptors in the olfactory epithelium, at the top of the nasal cavity. The axons of these receptors relay the smell message to the olfactory bulbs. From there, the smell message travels to the thalamus and the orbito-frontal cortex, which distinguish the odor and relay that information to other parts of the brain.

3.13   What are the primary taste sensations, and how are they detected? p. 99

The primary taste sensations are sweet, salty, sour, and bitter, along with a newly discovered one for glutamate, called umami. The receptor cells for taste are found in the taste buds on the tongue and in other parts of the mouth and throat.

3.14   How does the skin provide sensory information? p. 100

Sensitive nerve endings in the skin convey tactile information to the brain when an object touches and depresses the skin. The neural impulses for touch sensations ultimately register in the brain's somatosensory cortex.

3.15   What is the function of pain, and how is pain influenced by psychological factors, culture, and endorphins? p. 101

Pain can be a valuable warning and a protective mechanism, motivating people to tend to an injury, to restrict activity, and to seek medical help. Negative thinking can influence the perception of pain. Some cultures encourage individuals to suppress (or exaggerate) emotional reactions to pain. Endorphins are natural painkillers produced by the body, which block pain and produce a feeling of well-being.

3.16   What kinds of information do the kinesthetic and vestibular senses provide? p. 103

The kinesthetic sense provides information about the position of body parts in relation to one another and movement of the entire body or its parts. This information is detected by sensory receptors in the joints, ligaments, and muscles. The vestibular sense detects movement and provides information about the body's orientation in space. Sensory receptors in the semicircular canals and the vestibular sacs sense changes in motion and the orientation of the head.

Principles of Perception p. 104

3.17   What are the principles that govern perceptual organization? p. 104

The Gestalt principles of perceptual organization include figure-ground, similarity, proximity, continuity, and closure. Perceptual constancy is the tendency to perceive objects as maintaining the same size, shape, and brightness, despite changes in lighting conditions or changes in the retinal image that result when an object is viewed from different angles and distances.

3.18   What are some of the binocular and monocular depth cues? p. 106

The binocular depth cues include convergence and binocular disparity, which depend on both eyes working together for depth perception. The monocular depth cues, those that can be perceived by one eye, include interposition, linear perspective, relative size, texture gradient, atmospheric perspective, shadow or shading, and motion parallax.

3.19   How does the brain perceive real and apparent motion? p. 107

The brain perceives real motion by comparing the movement of images across the retina to information derived from the spatial orientation senses. Apparent motion is the result of a psychological response to specific kinds of stimuli, such as flashing lights. The brain may also mistakenly perceive eye movement as object movement.

3.20 What are three types of puzzling perceptions? p. 109

Three types of puzzling perceptions are ambiguous figures, impossible figures, and illusions.

Influences on Perception p. 111

3.21 How does prior knowledge influence perception? p. 112

Individuals use bottom-up and top-down processing to apply their prior knowledge to perceptual problems. Expectations based on prior knowledge may predispose people to perceive sensations in a particular way.

3.22 What is gained and what is lost in the process of attention? p. 113

Attention enables the brain to focus on some sensations while screening others out. Unattended stimuli may be missed altogether or incorrectly perceived.

3.23 Do we perceive physical objects and social stimuli in the same way? p. 114

Research suggests that the neural systems and rules for processing information about social stimuli are distinct from those for physical objects.

3.24 What have studies of subliminal and extrasensory perception shown? p. 115

Subliminal perception has subtle influences on behavior but appears to be ineffective at persuading people to buy products or to vote in certain ways.

Thinking Critically about Psychology

1. Vision and hearing are generally believed to be the two most highly prized senses. How would your life change if you lost your sight? How would your life change if you lost your hearing? Which sense would you find more traumatic to lose? Why?
2. Using what you have learned about how noise contributes to hearing loss, prepare a statement indicating what you think should be done to control noise pollution, even to the extent of banning certain noise hazards. Consider the workplace, the home, automobiles and other vehicles, toys, machinery, rock concerts, and so on.
3. Based on your own point of view, choose one of these statements and explain why you agree with it: (1) Research on subliminal perception could be exploited to help people learn to behave in ways that are more beneficial to themselves and to society. For example, subliminal anti-drug messages could be embedded in popular television programs. (2) Secretly embedding subliminal messages in entertainment media violates individuals' freedom of choice; therefore, this practice should be illegal.

Key Terms

absolute threshold, p. 84
accommodation, p. 87
afterimage, p. 90
amplitude, p. 92
apparent motion, p. 108
attention, p. 113
audition, p. 93
autokinetic illusion, p. 109
binocular depth cues, p. 106
blind spot, p. 88
bottom-up processing, p. 112
brightness, p. 90
cochlea, p. 94
color blindness, p. 91
cones, p. 87
cornea, p. 86
decibel (dB), p. 92
depth perception, p. 106
difference threshold, p. 84
endorphins, p. 102
extrasensory preception (ESP) p. 115
feature detectors, p. 89
fovea, p. 88

frequency, p. 92
frequency theory, p. 95
Gestalt, p. 104
gustation, p. 99
hair cells, p. 94
hue, p. 90
illusion, p. 110
inattentional blindness, p. 113
inner ear, p. 93
just noticeable difference (JND), p. 84
kinesthetic sense, p. 103
lens, p. 87
middle ear, p. 93
monocular depth cues, p. 106
olfaction, p. 96
olfactory bulbs, p. 97
olfactory epithelium, p. 96
opponent-process theory, p. 90
optic nerve, p. 89
outer ear, p. 93
perception, p. 82
perceptual constancy, p. 105
perceptual set, p. 112

pheromones, p. 98
phi phenomenon, p. 109
place theory, p. 95
primary visual cortex, p. 89
real motion, p. 108
retina, p. 87
rods, p. 87
saturation, p. 90
semicircular canals, p. 103
sensation, p. 82
sensory adaptation, p. 85
sensory receptors, p. 85
subliminal perception, p. 115
tactile, p. 100
taste buds, p. 99
timbre, p. 93
top-down processing, p. 112
transduction, p. 85
trichromatic theory, p. 90
vestibular sense, p. 103
visible spectrum, p. 86
Weber's law, p. 84

Chapter 4

States of Consciousness

Continued

Psychoactive Drugs

4.18 How do drugs affect the brain's neurotransmitter system?

4.19 What are some risk and protective factors for substance abuse?

4.20 What is the difference between physical and psychological drug dependence?

4.21 What are the effects of stimulants, depressants, and hallucinogens on behavior?

4.22 What are the pros and cons of using herbal remedies?

When you hear the word *cult,* you probably think of a group of people. Thus, it might surprise you to learn that some psychologists believe that a cult can involve as few as two people. In a *cult of two,* a dominant individual controls a submissive partner through emotional and/or physical abuse and social isolation (Flora, 2003). Moreover, the dominant person convinces the submissive one that the pair has a mission, often divinely appointed, that only they can fulfill. Sometimes the mission involves violence.

According to several experts, the relationship of John Allen Muhammad and Lee Boyd Malvo was cultic in nature (Eichel & Martin, 2004). Muhammad and Malvo were the infamous "Beltway Snipers" whose random shootings, cryptic crime scene clues, and demands for a $10 million ransom terrorized people in the Washington, D.C., area for three weeks in October 2002. At the time of their arrest, the two were 42 and 17 years old, respectively. Their capture and the trials that followed sparked public speculation about the nature of their relationship and the role it might have played in their homicidal shooting spree.

According to the psychiatrists who testified on Malvo's behalf, Muhammad was the dominant member of the pair. These psychiatrists explained that, as a young child, Malvo had learned to put himself into a *dissociative state,* a condition in which an individual loses self-awareness, to steel himself against the frequent beatings his mother gave him and her abandonment of him (Bender, 2004; Jackman, 2003). By the time Malvo reached his early teens, dissociation had become his primary way of managing stress, and he had developed an intense longing for a warm, attentive parent. These tendencies, experts said, rendered him vulnerable to anyone who might exploit him by filling the parental void in his life. Muhammad entered Malvo's life when the boy was 15 years old and began doing just that. Over the course of several moves, from Antigua to Florida to the state of Washington, a deep bond developed between the two, and they began posing as father and son.

As the "father" and "son" drifted from one temporary residence to another, Muhammad began to lecture Malvo about his belief that the two had been divinely called to become soldiers in a holy army. The older man claimed that the holy army's mission was to destroy the United States of America because of this country's history of oppressing people of color. Muhammad argued that his own years in the U.S. Army qualified him for service, but Malvo, he said, needed to be trained. In his role as Malvo's trainer, Muhammad controlled the boy's diet, forced him to endure long sessions of rigorous physical exercise, and taught him how to shoot a gun.

In February 2002, Muhammad ordered Malvo to kill a Tacoma woman to demonstrate his readiness for combat. Malvo dutifully obeyed, but he was emotionally distraught after the shooting. To escape from his distress, the boy turned to the dissociation strategy he had used to numb himself to his mother's abuse. The expert witnesses at Malvo's trial claimed that the result of his dissociative response to the shooting was that he was no longer capable of independent thought or action. Effectively, he had become Muhammad's puppet.

In the summer of 2002, Muhammad and Malvo embarked on a road trip with a stolen rifle stashed in the trunk of their car. They believed the trip was their first divinely sanctioned mission. After numerous shootings in several states and the District of Columbia, at least 12 of which were fatal, the "mission" came to an end on October 24, 2002, when Muhammad and Malvo were arrested while sleeping in their car at a Maryland rest stop.

Once in custody, Malvo laughed when he recounted stories of the killings and refused to criticize Muhammad. He revealed little about his relationship with the older man to his court-appointed psychiatrists. As time went on, however, the boy's demeanor changed. The psychiatrists theorized that, without Muhammad's influence, Malvo's true self was beginning to emerge from the dissociative state he had entered months earlier. By the time Malvo had been in jail for several months, he was able to talk openly about the techniques Muhammad had used to indoctrinate him and about his role in the shootings.

In the fall of 2003, a Virginia jury sentenced Muhammad to death for one of the pair's fatal shootings. Malvo confessed to the killings, but entered a plea of not guilty by reason of insanity. His attorneys argued that the dissociative state induced by Malvo's cultic relationship with Muhammad absolved him of legal responsibility for the killings. However, the jury disagreed and sentenced him to life in prison. By that time, Malvo's long separation from Muhammad and the psychiatric treatment he received in jail had helped him recognize that pleading guilty to the other Beltway Sniper killings was in his best interest. He reached a particularly

significant turning point when, in May 2006, he agreed to testify against his former mentor in Muhammad's trial for the murders that the two had committed in the state of Maryland.

The degree to which one person can alter another's self-awareness in the way that advocates for the cult-of-two hypothesis claim is a hotly debated topic among mental health professionals (Anthony, 1999; Baron, 2000; Hassan, 2000; Richardson & Introvigne, 2001; Zimbardo, 2002). Some argue that cultic relationships can almost totally subsume an individual's identity in the way that expert witnesses at Malvo's trial claimed. Others state that there is no scientific evidence to support such claims. Still other experts agree that cult-of-two relationships exist, but they do not believe that these relationships absolve submissive partners from moral responsibility for crimes they commit at the behest of dominant partners. Before the debate can be resolved, psychologists need to learn a great deal more about the nature of human awareness, or *consciousness*, in order to answer such questions definitively. Nevertheless, what we do know about consciousness can help you better understand many of your everyday experiences.

What Is Consciousness?

What if, in the course of a middle-of-the-night phone call, your mother told you that your grandmother had had a stroke and had been in a coma for a short while, but then had regained consciousness? You would most likely understand your mother to mean that your grandmother was in a state of unawareness of her own and others' activities but then returned to a state of awareness, or wakefulness. One way of understanding the meaning of consciousness is to think of it in contrast to its opposite, unconsciousness. But, is that all there is to consciousness—simply being awake? What about when you arrive home from shopping but have no recollection of the drive from the mall to your home. Certainly, you were awake, so the reason you don't remember is *not* that you were unconscious. Thus, **consciousness** is defined as everything of which we are aware at any given time—our thoughts, feelings, sensations, and perceptions of the external environment.

The early psychologists held widely varying views of the nature of consciousness. William James likened consciousness to a flowing stream (the stream of consciousness) that sometimes is influenced by the will and sometimes is not. Sigmund Freud emphasized the notion that unconscious wishes, thoughts, and feelings are hidden from consciousness because they evoke too much anxiety. In contrast to both James and Freud, behaviorist John Watson urged psychologists to abandon the study of consciousness, claiming that it could not be studied scientifically. Because of the

4.1 How have psychologists' views about consciousness changed since the early days of psychology?

consciousness Everything of which we are aware at any given time—our thoughts, feelings, sensations, and external environment.

strong influence of behaviorism, especially in the United States, psychologists did not study consciousness for several decades (Nelson, 1996).

In recent decades, though, psychological researchers have returned to the study of consciousness, in examining physiological rhythms, sleep, and **altered states of consciousness** (changes in awareness produced by sleep, meditation, hypnosis, and drugs). Modern brain-imagining techniques have allowed psychologists to accumulate a large body of evidence leading to a better understanding of the neurological basis of consciousness. Consequently, today's psychologists think about consciousness largely in neurobiological terms. In other words, psychologists tend to equate the subjective experience of consciousness with objective observations of what's actually happening in the brain during states such as sleep and hypnosis (Parvizi & Damasio, 2001).

Remember It | What Is Consciousness?

1. A synonym for consciousness is _____.

2. Because of the influence of _____, psychologists avoided the study of consciousness for several decades.

3. Today's psychologists focus on the _____ aspects of consciousness.

4. Changes in awareness associated with sleep, meditation, hypnosis, and drugs are called _____.

Answers: 1. awareness; 2. behaviorism; 3. neurobiological; 4. altered states of consciousness

Circadian Rhythms

Do you find yourself nodding off in the middle of your afternoon classes? If so, you may be experiencing one of several different types of disturbances of **circadian rhythms,** the regular fluctuation of bodily functions within each 24-hour period. These rhythms tie our bodily functions to the earth's light-dark cycle such that we are most alert during the daytime hours and least so when it is dark. Disruptions in circadian rhythms occur in a variety of situations, but before considering these, let's take a look at how they operate most of the time.

The Influence of Circadian Rhythms

4.2 Which physiological and psychological functions are influenced by circadian rhythms?

Circadian rhythms play a critical role in the timing of life-sustaining processes in virtually all organisms, from humans and other vertebrates to plants, and even single-cell life forms (Kay, 1997). Physiological functions such as blood pressure, heart rate, appetite, secretion of hormones and digestive enzymes, sensory acuity, elimination, and even the body's response to medication all follow circadian rhythms (Hrushesky, 1994; Morofushi et al., 2001). Many psychological functions—including learning efficiency, the ability to perform a wide range of tasks, and even moods—ebb and flow according to these daily rhythms (Boivin et al., 1997; Johnson et al., 1992; Manly et al., 2002). Indeed, the circadian timing system is involved in the 24-hour variation of virtually every physiological and psychological variable researchers have studied (Kunz & Herrmann, 2000).

Two circadian rhythms of particular importance are the sleep/wakefulness cycle and the daily fluctuation in body temperature. Normal human body temperature ranges from a low of about 97–97.5°F between 3:00 and 4:00 A.M. to a high of about 98.6°F between 6:00 and 8:00 P.M. People sleep best when their body temperature is at its lowest, and they are most alert when their body temperature is at its daily high point. Alertness also follows a circadian rhythm, one that is quite separate from the sleep/wakefulness cycle (Monk, 1989). For most people, alertness decreases between 2:00 and 5:00 P.M. and between 2:00 and 7:00 A.M. (Webb, 1995).

altered state of consciousness Changes in awareness produced by sleep, meditation, hypnosis, and drugs.

circadian rhythm (sur-KAY-dee-un) Within each 24-hour period, the regular fluctuation from high to low points of certain bodily functions and behaviors.

The Suprachiasmatic Nucleus

In their studies of circadian rhythms in mammals, researchers have found that the biological clock is the **suprachiasmatic nucleus (SCN),** located in the brain's hypothalamus (Ginty et al., 1993; Ralph, 1989; Ruby et al., 2002; Takahashi et al., 2003). The SCN, a pair of tiny brain structures, each about the size of a pinhead, controls the timing of circadian rhythms (Moore-Ede, 1993).

But the ebb and flow of circadian rhythms is not strictly biological. Environmental cues also play a part. The most significant environmental cue is bright light, particularly sunlight. Specialized cells (photoreceptors) in the retina at the back of each eye respond to the amount of light reaching the eye and relay this information via the optic nerve to the SCN. The SCN acts on this information by signaling the pineal gland, located in the center of the brain. In response, the pineal gland secretes the hormone *melatonin* from dusk to shortly before dawn, for a total of about 9 hours, but does not secrete it during daylight (Kripke et al., 2005). Melatonin induces sleep, perhaps through its ability to lower the activity of neurons in the SCN (Barinaga, 1997).

Other types of cells may also respond to daily light-dark cycles. Researchers studying vertebrates less complex than humans have found that exposing some of the animals' bodily organs to light sets the "circadian clock" and maintains circadian rhythms. When certain single cells from these vertebrates are placed in cultures in the laboratory, they respond directly to light-dark cycles (Abe et al., 2002; Whitmore et al., 2000). Such findings provide some of the supporting evidence for using light exposure to treat certain kinds of disruptions of circadian functioning. As you'll learn in the next section, other kinds of disruptions are best managed by simple changes in behavior.

4.3 How do biological and environmental variables influence circadian rhythms?

Disruptions in Circadian Rhythms

Disruptions in circadian rhythms can be quite troublesome, but there are effective coping strategies for each kind of disturbance.

Delayed Sleep Phase Syndrome (DSPS). *Delayed sleep phase syndrome (DSPS)* is the most common disturbance of circadian rhythms among adolescents and young adults (Cataletto & Hertz, 2005). Researchers believe that DSPS is brought on by the hormonal changes of puberty but is maintained by adolescents' social pressure to stay up late (Hansen, Janssen, Schiff, & Zee, 2005; Millman, 2005). Once the pattern is established, individuals with DSPS find it difficult to fall asleep before 3:00 A.M., even when they have no particular reason for staying up late. Individuals with DSPS sleep about the same number of hours as those with more typical rhythms, and, as a result, their natural awakening time is usually around noon. Despite having slept for 8 or more hours, however, most individuals with DSPS become so sleepy in the afternoon that they can't stay awake.

College students with DSPS struggle to keep up in morning classes and may accommodate by avoiding enrolling in them. However, the afternoon sleepiness that is associated with DSPS prevents these students from doing their best in afternoon classes as well. The good news is that DSPS need not be a permanent condition. Researchers have found that it can be reversed by avoiding social activities and meals in the early morning hours (midnight to 3:00 A.M.) and gradually moving bedtime back. For example, if a student's habitual bedtime is 3:00 A.M., she should try going to bed at 2:30 for several days. Once the 2:30 bedtime becomes habitual, then she can move the time back to 2:00, then 1:30, and so on, until she achieves her desired waking-up time and an acceptable degree of daytime alertness.

4.4 How do disruptions in circadian rhythms affect the body and the mind?

Advanced Sleep Phase Syndrome (ASPS). Many elderly adults have the opposite problem, a disturbance in circadian rhythms called *advanced sleep phase syndrome (ASPS)* (Cataletto & Hertz, 2005). Such individuals fall asleep at extraordinarily early times, sometimes as early as 6:00 P.M., and, predictably, they wake up between 2:00 and 3:00 A.M. Like DSPS sufferers, adults with this sleep-wake pattern get sleepy during the middle

suprachiasmatic nucleus (SCN)
A pair of tiny structures in the brain's hypothalamus that control the timing of circadian rhythms; the biological clock.

of the day. They may accommodate by avoiding social activities in the evening hours, a pattern that can be problematic because it is out-of-phase with the culture at large. The cause of ASPS is unknown, but it can be managed by reversing the approach described above for DSPS, that is, by gradually moving bedtime to later and later times.

▲ Research indicates that frequent flyers, such as these airline employees, are just as likely to suffer from jet lag when crossing several time zones as travelers who are on their first intercontinental journey.

Jet Lag. Suppose you fly from Chicago to London, and the plane lands at 12:00 A.M. Chicago time, about the time you usually go to sleep. At the same time that it is midnight in Chicago, it is 6:00 A.M. in London, almost time to get up. The clocks, the sun, and everything else in London tell you it is early morning, but you still fell like it is midnight. You are experiencing jet lag.

Chronic jet lag, such as that experienced by many airline pilots and flight attendants, produces memory deficits that may be permanent (Cho, 2001; Cho et al., 2000). You might think that airline employees who regularly fly across time zones would adjust to their schedules. However, research indicates that experienced airline workers are just as likely to suffer from jet lag as passengers on their first intercontinental flight (Criglington, 1998).

Researchers have found that travelers can prevent jet lag to some degree by slowly advancing their sleep schedules about an hour a day for several days before they leave home (Eastman et al., 2005). Of course, such strategies can't be employed by all travelers, especially those who travel long distances within relatively short time spans. For instance, a flight attendant might cross several time zones within a period of just a couple of days. For these travelers, exposure to bright sunlight during the early morning hours and avoidance of bright lights during the evening may restore circadian rhythms (Edwards et al., 2000; Zisapel, 2001).

▲ People who work at night experience disruptions in their circadian rhythms that can cause physical and psychological problems.

Shift Work. Similarly, alertness and performance deteriorate if people work during **subjective night,** when their biological clock is telling them to go to sleep (da Silva Borges & Fischer, 2003). During subjective night, energy and efficiency are at their lowest points, reaction time is slowest, productivity is diminished, and industrial accidents are significantly higher. In one study, more than 17% of a group of commercial long-haul truck drivers admitted to having experienced "near misses" while dozing off behind the wheel (Häkkänen & Summala, 1999). Furthermore, shift workers get less sleep overall than nonshift workers (Bonnefond et al., 2006). Some studies show that the deleterious effects of shift work persist for months or even years after shift work ends (Rouch, Wild, Ansiau, & Marquie, 2005).

Moving work schedules forward from days to evenings to nights makes adjustment easier because people find it easier to go to bed later and wake up later than doing the reverse. And rotating shits every 3 weeks instead of every week lessens the effect on sleep even more (Pilcher et al., 2000). Some researchers are investigating the use of a new wakefulness drug called *modafinil* that helps people remain alert without the side effects of stimulants such as caffeine (Wesensten et al., 2002). Others have used a device called a "light mask" to reset shift workers' biological clocks. This mask allows researchers to control the amount of light to which the closed eyelids of research participants are exposed. The findings of light mask studies suggest that exposing participants to bright light during the last 4 hours of sleep is an effective treatment for the kinds of sleep-phase delays experienced by

subjective night   The time during a 24-hour period when the biological clock is telling a person to go to sleep.

shift workers (Cole et al., 2002). Thus, this device may become important in the treatment of sleep disorders associated with shift work.

Circadian Timing and Neurological Disorders

Given the neurological basis of circadian rhythms, do you think there might be any link between these rhythms and brain injuries, neurological diseases, or psychiatric disorders? Consider the case of V.D., a 54-year-old man who sustained a head injury after falling off a scaffold (Florida Institute for Neurologic Rehabilitation, Inc., 2002). One of the many trauma-related symptoms V.D. has is difficulty in both falling asleep and waking up. Problems like this are common in head-injury patients (Thaxton & Myers, 2002), perhaps because such injuries, as well as a number of neurological diseases and psychiatric disorders, are associated with disturbances in circadian functioning (Kashihara et al., 1999; Kirveskari et al. 2001; Kropyvnytskyy et al., 2001). Consequently, like many shift workers, many head-injury patients suffer from disturbed sleep-wakefulness cycles. Experts suggest that these sleep-wakefulness problems are a major source of stress for patients and should be treated with the same methods used to reset the circadian clocks of shift workers.

Research examining the link between circadian rhythms and neurological disorders may lead to new ways of diagnosing Alzheimer's disease. Abnormal circadian rhythms are common in Alzheimer's patients (Harper et al., 2001; Harper et al., 2006; Volicer et al., 2001). But individuals with non-Alzheimer's types of dementia, as well as those whose self-reported memory problems are the result of normal aging, are less likely to exhibit circadian disturbances. Thus, researchers believe that tracking patients' daily variations in body temperature and other circadian variables (e.g., heart rate) may provide a fairly simple way of distinguishing those with Alzheimer's from those with other types of dementia (Cromie, 2001). The distinction is important because different kinds of dementia respond to different kinds of treatment. One study of autopsies performed on individuals suspected of having Alzheimer's disease found that almost a third did not have the disease, suggesting that current methods of diagnosis are inadequate (Cromie, 2001).

Understanding disturbances in circadian timing may also be important in helping caregivers manage Alzheimer's patients. One consequence of the atypical circadian rhythms exhibited by Alzheimer's sufferers is a phenomenon called *sundowning*, a tendency to exhibit more symptoms of the disease in the afternoon and nighttime hours (Volicer et al., 2001). Caring for an Alzheimer's patient who exhibits sundowning causes many caregivers to develop their own sleep disturbances. Thus, researchers hope to learn how to modify these patterns for the benefit of both Alzheimer's patients and their caregivers.

4.5 How can research linking circadian rhythms and neurological disorders be put to practical use?

Remember It   Circadian Rhythms

1. The two circadian rhythms of particular importance are the sleep/wakefulness cycle and the daily fluctuation in _____.

2. People sleep best when their body temperature is at its _____ point in the 24-hour cycle.

3. The structure that serves as the body's biological clock is the _____.

4. Exposure to _____ helps many travelers overcome the effects of jet lag.

5. Alertness and performance deteriorate when people work during _____.

6. _____ is a hormone that is believed to regulate the biological clock.

Answers: 1. body temperature; 2. lowest; 3. suprachiasmatic nucleus (SCN); 4. bright light; 5. subjective night; 6. Melatonin

Sleep

As noted earlier, the sleep/wakefulness cycle is a circadian rhythm. But what actually happens during our periods of sleep? In the early 20th century, there was little understanding of what goes on during the state of consciousness known as sleep. Then, in the 1950s, several universities set up sleep laboratories where people's brain waves, eye movements, chin-muscle tension, heart rate, and respiration rate were monitored through a night of sleep. From analyses of sleep recordings, known as *polysomnograms,* researchers discovered the characteristics of two major types of sleep.

Why Do We Sleep?

4.6 What is the difference between the restorative and circadian theories of sleep?

Are you one of those people who regards sleep as a waste of time—especially when you have a term paper due the next day? (Of course, you wouldn't be facing a sleepless night if you hadn't procrastinated about the paper in the first place!) In fact, consistent sleep habits are probably important to getting good grades. Why?

Two complementary theories have been advanced to explain why we need to sleep. Taken together, they provide us with a useful explanation. One, the **restorative theory of sleep,** holds that being awake produces wear and tear on the body and the brain, while sleep serves the function of restoring body and mind (Gökcebay et al., 1994). There is now convincing evidence for this theory: The functions of sleep do include the restoration of energy and the consolidation of memory (Kunz & Herrmann, 2000). The second explanation, the **circadian theory of sleep,** sometimes called the *evolutionary theory,* is based on the premise that sleep evolved to keep humans out of harm's way during the dark of night, possibly preventing them from becoming prey for some nocturnal predator.

Alexander Borbely (1984; Borbely et al., 1989) explains how a synthesis of the circadian and restorative theories can be used to explain the function of sleep. That people feel sleepy at certain times of day is consistent with the circadian theory. And that sleepiness increases the longer a person is awake is consistent with the restorative theory. In other words, the urge to sleep is partly a function of how long a person has been awake and partly a function of the time of day (Webb, 1995).

restorative theory of sleep The theory that the function of sleep is to restore body and mind.

circadian theory of sleep The theory that sleep evolved to keep humans out of harm's way during the night; also known as the evolutionary theory.

Types of Sleep

4.7 How do NREM and REM sleep differ?

The two major types of sleep are NREM (non–rapid eye movement) sleep and REM (rapid eye movement) sleep. During **NREM** (pronounced "NON-rem") **sleep,** there are no rapid eye movements. Heart rate and respiration are slow and regular, there is little body movement, and blood pressure and brain activity are at their lowest points of the 24-hour period. **REM sleep,** sometimes called "active sleep," is anything but calm, and it constitutes 20–25% of a normal night's sleep in adults. During the REM state, there is intense brain activity. In fact, within 1 to 2 minutes after REM sleep begins, brain metabolism increases, and brain temperature rises rapidly (Krueger & Takahashi, 1997). Epinephrine is released into the system, causing blood pressure to rise and heart rate and respiration to become faster and less regular. Ulcer patients may secrete 3 to 20 times as much stomach acid as during the day and may awaken with stomach pains (Webb, 1975). In contrast to this storm of internal activity, there is an external calm during REM sleep. The large muscles of the body—arms, legs, trunk—become paralyzed (Chase & Morales, 1990). Some researchers suggest that this paralysis prevents people from acting out their dreams. In a rare condition known as *REM sleep behavior disorder,* individuals are not paralyzed during REM sleep. Consequently, they may become violent, causing injury to themselves and their bed partners and damage to their homes (Broughton & Shimizu, 1995; Moldofsky et al., 1995).

Observe a sleeper during the REM state, and you will see her or his eyes darting around under the eyelids. Eugene Azerinsky first discovered these bursts of rapid eye

NREM sleep Non–rapid eye movement sleep, which consists of four sleep stages and is characterized by slow, regular respiration and heart rate, little body movement, an absence of rapid eye movements, and blood pressure and brain activity that are at their 24-hour low points.

REM sleep A type of sleep characterized by rapid eye movements, paralysis of large muscles, fast and irregular heart and respiration rates, increased brain-wave activity, and vivid dreams.

movements in 1952, and William Dement and Nathaniel Kleitman (1957) made the connection between rapid eye movements and dreaming. It is during REM sleep that the most vivid dreams occur. When awakened from REM sleep, 80% of people report that they had been dreaming (Carskadon & Dement, 1989). And, if you awaken during REM sleep and remain awake for several minutes, you may not go back into REM sleep for at least 30 minutes. This is why most people have had the disappointing experience of waking in the middle of a wonderful dream and trying to get back to sleep quickly and into the dream again, but failing to do so.

Almost from birth, regardless of the content of their dreams, males have a full or partial erection during REM sleep, and females experience vaginal swelling and lubrication. Because sleepers are more likely to awaken naturally at the end of a period of REM sleep than during NREM sleep, men usually wake up with an erection (Campbell, 1985). In males suffering from impotence, the presence of an erection during REM sleep, even occasionally, indicates that the impotence is psychological; the consistent absence of an erection indicates that the impotence is likely to be physiological in origin.

Sleep Cycles

You may be surprised to learn that sleep follows a fairly predictable pattern each night. We all sleep in cycles. During each **sleep cycle,** which lasts about 90 minutes, a person has one or more stages of NREM sleep, followed by a period of REM sleep. Let's look closely at a typical night of sleep for a young adult.

The first sleep cycle begins with a few minutes in Stage 1 sleep, sometimes called "light sleep." Stage 1 is actually a transition stage between waking and sleeping. Irregular waves, some of which are alpha waves, are characteristic of Stage 1. **Sleep spindles,** which are brain waves characterized by alternating short periods of calm and flashes of intense activity, appear in Stage 2, the phase in which we spend about 50% of each night's sleep. The appearance of sleep spindles in the electroencephalogram (EEG) usually means that the individual is in transition from the light sleep of Stage 1 to a state of much deeper sleep. Consequently, sleepers are much more difficult to awaken in Stage 2 than in Stage 1. As sleep gradually becomes deeper, brain activity slows, and more delta waves (slow waves) appear in the EEG. When the EEG registers 20% delta waves, sleepers enter Stage 3 sleep, the beginning of **slow-wave sleep** (or deep sleep). Delta waves continue to increase, and when they reach more than 50%, people enter **Stage 4 sleep**—the deepest sleep, from which they are hardest to awaken (Carskadon & Rechtschaffen, 1989; Cooper, 1994). Perhaps you have taken an afternoon nap and woke up confused, not knowing whether it was morning or night, a weekday or a weekend. If so, you probably awakened during Stage 4 sleep.

In Stage 4 sleep, delta waves may reach nearly 100% on the EEG, but after about 40 minutes in this stage, brain activity increases and the delta waves begin to disappear. Sleepers ascend back through Stage 3 and Stage 2 sleep, then enter their first REM period, which lasts 10 or 15 minutes. At the end of this REM period, the first sleep cycle is complete, and the second sleep cycle begins. Unless people awaken after the first sleep cycle, they go directly from REM into Stage 2 sleep. They then follow the same progression as in the first sleep cycle, through Stages 3 and 4 and back again into REM sleep.

After the first two sleep cycles of about 90 minutes each (3 hours total), the sleep pattern changes, and sleepers usually get no more Stage 4 sleep. From this point on, during each 90-minute sleep cycle, people alternate mainly between Stage 2 and REM sleep for the remainder of the night. With each sleep cycle, the REM period (and therefore dreaming time) gets progressively longer. The last REM period of the night may last 30 to 40 minutes. Most people have about five sleep cycles (7 to 8 hours) and average 1 to 2 hours of slow-wave sleep and 1 to 2 hours of REM sleep. **Figure 4.1** shows the progression through NREM and REM sleep during a typical night.

4.8 What is the progression of NREM stages and REM sleep in a typical night of sleep?

sleep cycle A period of sleep lasting about 90 minutes and including one or more stages of NREM sleep, followed by REM sleep.

sleep spindles Sleep Stage 2 brain waves that feature short periods of calm interrupted by brief flashes of intense activity.

slow-wave sleep Deep sleep; associated with Stage 3 and Stage 4 sleep.

Stage 4 sleep The deepest stage of NREM sleep, characterized by an EEG pattern of more than 50% delta waves.

Figure 4.1 Brain-Wave Patterns Associated with Different Stages of Sleep

By monitoring brain-wave activity on an EEG throughout a night's sleep, researchers have identified the brain-wave patterns associated with different stages of sleep. As sleepers progress through the four NREM stages, the brain-wave pattern changes from faster, smaller waves in Stages 1 and 2 to the slower, larger delta waves in Stages 3 and 4.

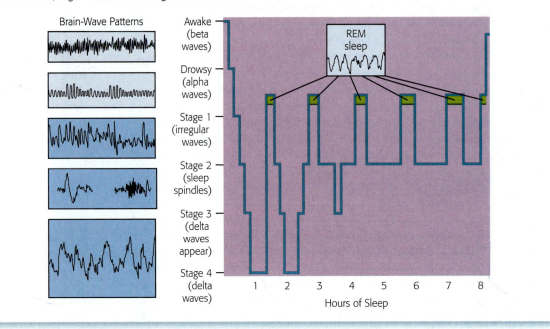

REM Sleep and Memory

You may have already found out through personal experience that studying all night before a big exam can cause you to yawn frequently and nod off when you take the actual test. But did you know that you can also short-circuit the learning process by engaging in this popular, though ineffective, method of exam preparation? Researchers say that REM sleep aids in information processing, helping people sift through daily experiences in order to organize and store in memory information that is relevant to them (Walker & Stickgold, 2006). Animal studies provide strong evidence for a relationship between REM sleep and learning (Hennevin et al., 1995; Smith, 1995; Winson, 1990). However, research also suggests that animals become tolerant of REM sleep deprivation after 4 days or so and return to pre-deprivation levels of learning performance (Kennedy, 2002). Thus, the final verdict on the necessity of REM sleep for efficient learning has yet to be reached.

In humans, researchers have found that sleep may be critical to the consolidation of memories after learning. Several experiments have shown that participants' performance on previously acquired motor and verbal tasks improves after a period of normal sleep (Fenn et al., 2003; Nader, 2003; Walker et al., 2003). Other studies have suggested that the brain carries out the important function of memory consolidation during REM sleep. Karni and others (1994) found that research participants who were learning a new perceptual skill showed an improvement in performance, with no additional practice, 8 to 10 hours later if they had a normal night's sleep or if the researchers disturbed only their NREM sleep. Performance did not improve, however, in those who were deprived of REM sleep. Naps that are long enough to include both slow-wave and REM sleep also appear to enhance learning (Walker & Stickgold, 2005).

There is no doubt that REM sleep serves an important function, even if psychologists do not know precisely what that function is. The fact that newborns show such a high percentage of REM sleep has led to the conclusion that this type of sleep is necessary for maturation of the brain during infancy (Marks et al., 1995). Furthermore, when people are deprived of REM sleep as a result of general sleep loss or illness, they will make up for the deprivation by getting an increased amount of REM sleep afterward, a phenomenon called **REM rebound.** Because the intensity of REM sleep is increased during a REM rebound, nightmares often occur. Alcohol, amphetamines, cocaine, and LSD suppress REM sleep, and withdrawal from these drugs results in a REM rebound (Porte & Hobson, 1996).

Variations in Sleep

Have you ever compared notes with a friend about how much sleep it takes to make you feel alert and rested the next day? If so, you have probably noticed that the amount of sleep people get varies a lot from one person to another. But how much sleep do we need? Many of us have heard that 8 hours of sleep are required for optimal health. Research suggests that this is not true. In a longitudinal study begun in 1982, more than a million Americans were asked about their sleep habits. Twenty years later, people who reported sleeping 6 or fewer hours per night, along with those who slept more than 8, showed somewhat higher death rates than adults who slept about 7 hours each night (Kripke et al., 2002).

Do such findings mean that we should all strive to sleep exactly 7 hours each night? Not at all, because these findings are correlational. We cannot infer from them that differences in amount of sleep cause differences in death rates. People who have diseases that result in early death may sleep less because of their symptoms or because of anxiety about their health status. Moreover, such studies deal with averages. There is considerable individual variation in the amount of sleep people need, and, for each individual, a certain amount of sleep may be sufficient at one point in life but insufficient at another.

Sleep requirements vary with age as well. In general, the older people are, the less sleep they require (see **Figure 4.2**). The proportions of NREM and REM sleep vary with age as well. Infants and young children have the highest percentages of REM and slow-wave sleep (Mindell, 1999). However, infants and children also have more erratic sleep patterns than individuals in other age groups (Millman, 2005). By contrast, children from age 6 to puberty are the most consistent sleepers and wakers. They fall asleep easily, sleep soundly for 10 to 11 hours at night, and feel awake and alert during the day. Moreover, they tend to fall asleep and wake up at about the same time every day.

As people age, the quality and quantity of sleep usually decrease (Reyner & Horne, 1995). In one large study of 9,000 participants aged 65 and over, only 12% reported no sleep problems (Foley et al., 1995). Older adults have more difficulty falling asleep than younger people do and typically sleep more lightly. Moreover, they spend more time in bed but less time asleep, averaging about 6 hours of sleep a night (Prinz et al., 1990). However, although slow-wave sleep decreases substantially from age 30 to age 50 (Mourtazaev et al., 1995; Van Cauter, 2000), the percentage of REM sleep stays about the same (Moran & Stoudemire, 1992).

Sleep Deprivation

What is the longest you have ever stayed awake—about 48 hours? According to the *Guinness Book of World Records*, Robert McDonald stayed awake 453 hours and 40 minutes (almost 19 days) in a 1986 rocking-chair marathon. Unlike McDonald, most people have missed no more than a few consecutive nights of sleep, perhaps studying for final exams. If you have ever missed two or three nights of sleep, you may remember experiencing difficulty concentrating, lapses in attention, and general irritability. Research indicates that even the rather small amount of sleep deprivation associated with delaying your bedtime on weekends leads to decreases in cognitive performance and increases in negative mood on Monday morning (Yang & Spielman, 2001). Thus, the familiar phenomenon of the "Monday morning blues" may be the result of staying up late on Friday and Saturday nights.

4.10 How do age and individual differences influence people's sleep patterns?

▲ How much sleep does the average person need? The need for sleep varies across individuals, but these people are obviously not getting enough!

4.11 How does sleep deprivation affect behavior and neurological functioning?

REM rebound The increased amount of REM sleep that occurs after REM deprivation; often associated with unpleasant dreams or nightmares.

Figure 4.2 Average Hours of Daily Sleep Across the Life Span

The number of hours devoted to sleep in each 24-hour period decreases dramatically across the lifespan.

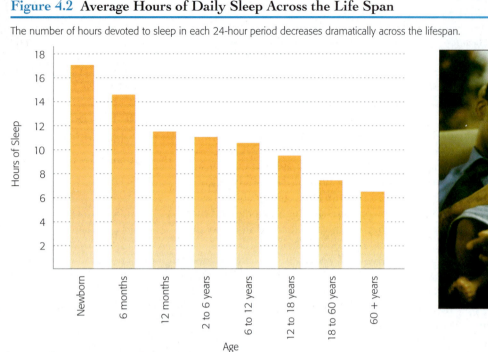

Sources: Foley, Ancoli-Israel, Britz, & Walsh, 2004; Iglowstein, Jenni, Molinari, & Largo, 2003; Hansen, Janssen, Schiff, & Zee, 2005; Millman, 2005; Mindell, 1999; Ohayan, Carskadon, Guilleminault, & Vitiello (2004).

After 60 hours without sleep, cognitive performance declines substantially. Some people deprived of this much sleep even have minor hallucinations. Most people who try to stay awake for long periods of time will experience **microsleeps,** 2- to 3-second lapses from wakefulness into sleep. You may have experienced a microsleep if you have ever caught yourself nodding off for a few seconds in class or on a long automobile trip. Note that if you do become sleepy while driving, you should not rely on a blast of cold air or higher volume on your radio to keep you awake for more than about 30 minutes (Reyner & Horne, 1998).

Researchers have known for some time that sleep deprivation impairs a variety of cognitive functions, such as the retrieval of recently learned information from memory, in both children and adults (Harrison & Horne, 2000; Raz et al., 2001; Sadeh et al., 2003). But the specific brain areas that are most (and least) active when sleep-deprived and non–sleep-deprived individuals perform cognitive tasks remained unidentified until recently.

Drummond and others (2000) used brain-imaging techniques to map the patterns of brain activity during a verbal learning task in two groups of participants: those in an experimental group who were deprived of sleep for about 35 hours, and those in a control group who slept normally. In the control group, the prefrontal cortex was highly active, as were the temporal lobes. As expected, on average, these rested participants scored significantly higher on the learning task than did their sleep-deprived counterparts. Surprisingly, however, areas of the prefrontal cortex were even more active in the sleep-deprived participants than in those who slept normally. Moreover, the temporal lobes that were so active in the rested group were almost totally inactive in the sleep-deprived group. The parietal lobes of the latter group became highly active, however, as if to compensate for their sleep-deprived condition. And, the more active the parietal lobes were, the higher a sleep-deprived participant scored on the learning task.

This study, which was the first to use brain-imaging techniques to examine the effects of sleep deprivation on verbal learning, indicates that the cognitive functions used in such learning are significantly impaired by sleep deprivation. It also shows that there are compensatory mechanisms in the parietal lobes that can reduce this impairment to some degree (Drummond et al., 2000).

microsleep   A brief lapse (2 to 3 seconds long) from wakefulness into sleep, usually occurring when a person has been sleep-deprived.

Dreams

What does a young woman mean when she says, "I met the guy of my dreams last night?" Or how about a telemarketer who promises you a "dream vacation" in exchange for listening to a sales pitch? Most of the time, we think of dreaming as a pleasant, imaginative experience. But when a fellow student exclaims, "That exam was a nightmare!" he or she means, of course, that the exam was somewhat less than pleasant, like a frightening dream. Good or bad, just exactly what is a dream?

The vivid dreams people remember and talk about are usually **REM dreams,** the type that occur almost continuously during each REM period. But people also have **NREM dreams,** which occur during NREM sleep, although these are typically less frequent and less memorable than REM dreams (Foulkes, 1996). REM dreams have a storylike or dreamlike quality and are more visual, vivid, and emotional than NREM dreams (Hobson, 1989). Blind people who lose their sight before age 5 usually do not have visual dreams, although they do have vivid dreams involving the other senses.

The Content of Dreams. What do people dream about? Griffith and others (1958) asked 250 college students about the themes of their dreams. The most common themes, reported by 70% or more of the sample, were about falling, being attacked or chased, trying repeatedly to do something, and studying. How many of these have you dreamed about?

Because dreams are notoriously hard to remember, the features that stand out tend to be those that are bizarre or emotional. Indeed, individuals who suffer from delusional disorders, such as schizophrenia, report more bizarre dreams than do individuals without such disorders (Watson, 2001). However, researchers don't know whether the dreams of people with these mental illnesses really are more bizarre or if their disorders cause them to focus more on the dreams' bizarre qualities.

REM Sleep, Dreaming, and the Brain. Brain-imaging studies suggest that the general perception that events in REM dreams are stranger and more emotion-provoking than waking experiences is probably true. The areas of the brain responsible for emotions, as well as the primary visual cortex, are active during REM dreams (Braun et al., 1998). By contrast, the prefrontal cortex, the more rational part of the brain, is suppressed during REM sleep, suggesting that the bizarre events that happen in REM dreams result from the inability of the brain to structure perceptions logically during that type of sleep. Areas associated with memory are also suppressed during REM sleep, which may explain why REM dreams are difficult to remember.

Furthermore, in the cortex different neurotransmitters are dominant during wakefulness and REM sleep (Gottesmann, 2000). When we are awake, powerful inhibiting influences exert control over the functioning of the cortex, keeping us anchored to reality, less subject to impulsive thoughts and acts, and more or less "sane." These inhibiting influences are maintained principally by cortical neurons that are responding to serotonin and norepinephrine. These neurotransmitters are far less plentiful during REM dreaming, when a higher level of dopamine causes other cortical neurons to show intense activity. This uninhibited, dopamine-stimulated activity of the dreaming brain has been likened to a psychotic mental state (Gottesmann, 2000).

Some researchers have questioned an assumption held by many sleep experts that dreaming is simply the brain's effort to make sense of the random firing of neurons that occurs during REM sleep. There is mounting evidence, says British researcher Mark Solms (2000), that dreaming and REM sleep, while normally occurring together, are not one and the same. The REM state is controlled by neural mechanisms in the brainstem, whereas areas in the forebrain provide the neural pathway for the complex and often vivid mental experiences we call dreams. In fact, vivid REM dreams are associated with distributions of activity in the forebrain that are very similar to those exhibited by individuals with delusional disorders while they are awake (Schwartz & Maquet, 2002). These findings suggest the network of neurons associated with dreaming can be activated regardless of whether an individual is asleep.

4.12 What have researchers learned about dreams, their content, their biological basis, and their controllability?

REM dream A type of dream occurring almost continuously during each REM period and having a storylike quality; typically more vivid, visual, and emotional than NREM dreams.

NREM dream A type of dream occurring during NREM sleep that is typically less frequent and memorable than REM dreams.

Lucid Dreaming. Have you ever been troubled by a frightening, recurring dream? People who have such dreams seem to experience a greater number of minor physical complaints, greater stress, and more anxiety and depression than other people do (Brown & Donderi, 1986). Is there anything that can be done to stop recurring dreams? Although most adults do not believe that the content of dreams can be controlled (Woolley & Boerger, 2002), some people have been taught to deliberately control dream content in order to stop unwanted, recurrent dreams. In **lucid dreams,** people attempt to exert control over a dream while it is in progress. Research suggests that individuals who are good at controlling their thoughts when awake are also successful at lucid dreaming (Blagrove & Hartnell, 2000). Lucid dreaming has even been advocated as an intervention for depression, although its effects appear to be inconsistent among depressed individuals (Newell & Cartwright, 2000), perhaps because the ability to control thoughts is impaired in many of these people. *Try It* introduces you to a technique for lucid dreaming.

lucid dream   A dream that an individual is aware of dreaming and whose content the individual is often able to influence while the dream is in progress.

manifest content   Freud's term for the content of a dream as recalled by the dreamer.

latent content   Freud's term for the underlying meaning of a dream.

Try It   Lucid Dreaming

Next time you wake up during a dream, try the following steps to see if you can engage in lucid dreaming.

1. Relax.
2. Close your eyes and focus on an imaginary spot in your field of vision.
3. Focus on your intention on having a lucid dream.
4. Tell yourself that you're going to dream about whatever you want.
5. Imagine yourself in a dream of the type you want to have.
6. Repeat the steps until you fall asleep.

Interpreting Dreams

4.13 How do the views of contemporary psychologists concerning the nature of dreams differ from those of Freud?

You may have wondered whether dreams, especially those that frighten us or that recur, have hidden meanings. Sigmund Freud believed that dreams function to satisfy unconscious sexual and aggressive desires. Because such wishes are unacceptable to the dreamer, they have to be disguised and therefore appear in dreams in symbolic forms. Freud (1900/1953a) claimed that objects like sticks, umbrellas, tree trunks, and guns symbolize the male sex organ; objects such as chests, cupboards, and boxes represent the female sex organ. Freud differentiated between the **manifest content** of a dream—the content of the dream as recalled by the dreamer—and the **latent content** —or the underlying meaning of the dream—which he considered more significant.

In recent years, there has been a major shift away from the Freudian interpretation of dreams. Now there is a greater focus on the manifest content—the actual dream itself—which is seen as an expression of a broad range of the dreamer's concerns rather than as an expression of sexual impulses (Webb, 1975). And, from an evolutionary viewpoint, dreams are viewed as a mechanism for simulating threatening and dangerous events so that the dreamer can "rehearse" and thus enhance her or his chances for survival (Revensuo, 2000).

Well-known sleep researcher J. Allan Hobson (1988) rejects the notion that nature would equip humans with the capability of having dreams that would require a specialist to interpret. Hobson and McCarley (1977) advanced the **activation-synthesis hypothesis of dreaming.** This hypothesis suggests that dreams are simply the brain's attempt to make sense of the random firing of brain cells during REM sleep. Just as people try to make sense of input from the environment during their waking hours, they try to find meaning in the conglomeration of sensations and memories that are generated internally by this random firing of brain cells. Hobson (1989) believes that dreams also have psychological significance, because the meaning a person imposes on the random mental activity reflects that person's experiences, remote memories, associations, drives, and fears. (As noted earlier, some researchers have questioned Hobson's position.)

▲ If you dream you are trapped in a virtual reality matrix, does your dream mean that you have problems in your relationship with your parents, or perhaps an unconscious fear of video games? Freud might think so, but it's more likely that your dream resembles a movie you saw recently.

Sleep Disorders

So far, our discussion has centered on a typical night for a typical sleeper. But what about the significant number of people who report sleep problems (Rosekind, 1992)?

Parasomnias. Do you walk or talk in your sleep? Or have you ever had a relative or roommate who did so? Psychologists use the term *parasomnia* to refer to such behaviors. **Parasomnias** are sleep disturbances in which behaviors and physiological states that normally occur only in the waking state take place during sleep (Schenck & Mahowald, 2000). For example, sleepwalking **(somnambulism)** occurs during a partial arousal from Stage 4 sleep in which the sleeper does not come to full consciousness. Sleepwalkers may get up and roam through the house, or simply stand for a short time and then go back to bed. Occasionally, they get dressed, eat a snack, or go to the bathroom. Some sleepwalkers have even been known to drive during an episode (Schenck & Mahowald, 1995). Typically, though, there is no memory of the episode the following day (Moldofsky et al., 1995).

Sleep terrors also happen during partial arousal from Stage 4 sleep. Sleep terrors usually begin with a piercing scream. The sleeper springs up in a state of panic—eyes open, perspiring, breathing rapidly, with the heart pounding at two or more times the normal rate (Karacan, 1988). Episodes usually last from 5 to 15 minutes, and then the person falls back to sleep. Up to 5% of children have sleep terrors (Keefauver & Guilleminault, 1994), but only about 1% of adults experience them (Partinen, 1994). Parents should not be unduly alarmed by sleep terrors in young children, but episodes that continue through adolescence into adulthood are more serious (Horne, 1992). Sleep terrors in adults often indicate extreme anxiety or other psychological problems.

Unlike sleep terrors, **nightmares** are very frightening dreams that occur during REM sleep and are likely to be remembered in vivid detail. The most common themes are falling and being chased, threatened, or attacked. Nightmares can be a reaction to traumatic life experiences (Krakow & Zadra 2006). They are more frequent at times of high fevers, anxiety, and emotional upheaval. REM rebound during drug withdrawal or following long periods without sleep can also produce nightmares. Whereas sleep terrors occur early in the night during Stage 4 sleep, anxiety nightmares occur toward morning, when the REM periods are longest. Frequent nightmares may be associated with psychological maladjustment (Berquier & Aston, 1992).

Sleeptalking **(somniloquy)** can occur during any sleep stage and is more frequent in children than in adults. There is no evidence at all that sleeptalking is related to a physical or psychological disturbance—not even to a guilty conscience. Sleeptalkers rarely reply to questions, and they usually mumble words or phrases that make no sense to the listener.

Major Sleep Disorders. Some sleep disorders can be so debilitating that they affect a person's entire life. For instance, **narcolepsy** is an incurable sleep disorder characterized by excessive daytime sleepiness and uncontrollable attacks of REM sleep, usually lasting 10 to 20 minutes (American Psychiatric Association, 1994). People with narcolepsy, who number from 250,000 to 350,000 in the United States alone, tend to be involved in accidents virtually everywhere—while driving, at work, and at home (Broughton & Broughton, 1994). Narcolepsy is caused by an abnormality in the part of the brain that regulates sleep, and it appears to have a strong genetic component (Billiard et al., 1994; Partinen et al., 1994). Some dogs are subject to narcolepsy, and much has been learned about the genetics of this disorder from research on canine subjects (Lamberg, 1996). Although there is no cure for narcolepsy, stimulant medications improve daytime alertness in most patients (Guilleminault, 1993; Mitler et al., 1994). Experts also recommend scheduled naps to relieve sleepiness (Garma & Marchand, 1994).

Over 1 million Americans—mostly obese men—suffer from another sleep disorder, **sleep apnea.** Sleep apnea consists of periods during sleep when breathing stops, and the individual must awaken briefly in order to breathe (White, 1989). The major symptoms of sleep apnea are excessive daytime sleepiness and extremely loud snoring, often accompanied by snorts, gasps, and choking noises. A person with sleep apnea will drop off to sleep, stop breathing altogether, and then awaken struggling for breath. After gasping several breaths in a semi-awakened state, the person falls back to sleep and stops breath-

4.14 What are the various disorders that can trouble sleepers?

activation-synthesis hypothesis of dreaming The hypothesis that dreams are the brain's attempt to make sense of the random firing of brain cells during REM sleep.

parasomnias Sleep disturbances in which behaviors and physiological states that normally take place only in the waking state occur while a person is sleeping.

somnambulism Sleepwalking; a parasomnia that occurs during partial arousal from Stage 4 sleep.

sleep terrors A sleep disturbance that occurs during partial arousal from Stage 4 sleep, in which the sleeper springs up in a state of panic.

nightmares Frightening dreams that occur during REM sleep and are likely to be remembered in vivid detail.

somniloquy Sleeptalking; a parasomnia that can occur during any sleep stage.

narcolepsy An incurable sleep disorder characterized by excessive daytime sleepiness and uncontrollable attacks of REM sleep.

sleep apnea A sleep disorder characterized by periods during sleep when breathing stops and the individual must awaken briefly in order to breathe.

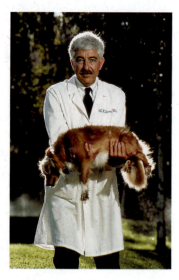

▲ Sleep researcher William Dement holds a dog that is experiencing a narcoleptic sleep attack. Much has been learned about narcolepsy through research with dogs.

ing again. People with severe sleep apnea may partially awaken as many as 800 times a night to gasp for air. Alcohol and sedatives aggravate the condition (Langevin et al., 1992).

Severe sleep apnea can lead to chronic high blood pressure, heart problems, and even death (Lavie et al., 1995). Neuroscientists have also found that sleep apnea may cause mild brain damage (Macey et al., 2002). Physicians sometimes treat sleep apnea by surgically modifying the upper airway (Sher et al., 1996). When the surgery is effective, sleep apnea sufferers not only sleep better, they also exhibit higher levels of performance on tests of verbal learning and memory (Dahloef et al., 2002). These findings suggest that the interrupted sleep experienced by individuals with this disorder affects cognitive as well as physiological functioning.

Approximately one-third of adults in the United States suffer from **insomnia,** a sleep disorder characterized by difficulty falling or staying asleep, waking too early, or sleep that is light, restless, or of poor quality. Any of these symptoms can lead to distress and impairment in daytime functioning (Costa E Silva et al., 1996; Roth, 1996; Sateia et al., 2000). Transient (temporary) insomnia, lasting 3 weeks or less, can result from jet lag, emotional highs (as when preparing for an upcoming wedding) or lows (losing a loved one or a job), or a brief illness or injury that interferes with sleep (Reite et al., 1995). Much more serious is chronic insomnia, which lasts for months or even years and plagues about 10% of the adult population (Roth, 1996). The percentages are even higher for women, the elderly, and people suffering from psychiatric and medical disorders (Costa E Silva et al., 1996). Chronic insomnia may begin as a reaction to a psychological or medical problem but persist long after the problem is resolved. Individuals with chronic insomnia experience "higher psychological distress [and] greater impairments of daytime functioning, are involved in more fatigue-related accidents, take more sick leave, and utilize health care resources more often than good sleepers" (Morin & Wooten, 1996, p. 522).

Remember It   Sleep

1. The two main theories that attempt to explain the function of sleep are the _____ and the _____ theories.

2. In _____ sleep, heart rate and respiration are slow and regular.

3. There is intense brain activity and large muscle paralysis during _____ sleep.

4. Match each NREM sleep stage with its characteristics.
   - _____ (1) Transition between waking and sleeping
   - _____ (2) The deepest sleep occurs
   - _____ (3) The beginning of slow-wave sleep
   - _____ (4) About 50% of each night's sleep

   a. Stage 1
   b. Stage 2
   c. Stage 3
   d. Stage 4

5. During _____ sleep, the brain consolidates and organizes memories.

6. _____ and _____ have the highest percentages of REM and slow-wave sleep of any age group.

7. The least memorable dreams occur during _____ sleep.

8. The _____ hypothesis suggests that dreams are the brain's attempt to make sense of the random firing of brain cells during REM sleep.

9. Match each sleep problem with its description or associated symptom.
   - _____ (1) Uncontrollable sleep attacks during the day
   - _____ (2) Very frightening REM dream
   - _____ (3) Cessation of breathing during sleep
   - _____ (4) Difficulty falling or staying asleep

   a. Narcolepsy
   b. Sleep apnea
   c. Insomnia
   d. Nightmare

Answers: 1. restorative, circadian (evolutionary); 2. NREM; 3. REM; 4. (1) a, (2) d, (3) c, (4) b; 5. REM; 6. Infants, young children; 7. NREM; 8. activation-synthesis; 9. (1) a, (2) d, (3) b, (4) c

insomnia A sleep disorder characterized by difficulty falling or staying asleep, by waking too early, or by sleep that is light, restless, or of poor quality.

Meditation and Hypnosis

We all have to sleep. Even if you fight it, your body will eventually force you to sleep. But there are other forms of altered consciousness that we may experience only if we choose to do so. Meditation and hypnosis are two of these.

Meditation

Do you know that a mental and physical relaxation technique can actually induce an altered state of consciousness? **Meditation** (the concentrative form) is a group of techniques that involve focusing attention on an object, a word, one's breathing, or one's body movements in order to block out all distractions, to enhance well-being, and to achieve an altered state of consciousness. Some forms of concentrative meditation, such as yoga, Zen, and transcendental meditation (TM), have their roots in Eastern religions and are practiced by followers of those religions to attain a higher spiritual state. In the United States, these approaches are often used to increase relaxation, reduce arousal, or expand consciousness (Wolsko et al., 2004). Brain-imaging studies support the conclusion that meditation, in addition to being relaxing, induces an altered state of consciousness (Cahn & Polich, 2006; Newberg et al., 2001).

Neuroscientists at the University of Wisconsin suspect that meditation may lead to permanent changes in the parts of the brain that integrate the functions of the frontal and parietal lobes (Lutz et al., 2004). Their research focuses on Tibetan Buddhist monks who have practiced deep meditation for many years. So far, neuroimaging studies have suggested that several areas of the brain may be permanently changed by the long-term practice of meditation. However, these findings are preliminary. Much research remains to be done before neuroscientists will have a complete understanding of how such neurological changes affect meditators' cognitive or emotional functioning.

Meditation has benefits beyond relaxation and stress relief. Researchers have found that regular meditation helps individuals, even those who are severely depressed, learn to control their emotions (Segal et al., 2001). Such findings have implications for professionals whose clients are interested in alternative approaches to mental health care. They are also helpful to mental health professionals who practice in non-Western societies where meditation is highly valued, such as India (Clay, 2002). Studies demonstrating the mental health benefits of meditation provide justification for its inclusion in culturally sensitive therapy (see Chapter 15).

But what about physical health? Meditation may be helpful here as well. It appears that meditation may lower blood pressure, cholesterol levels, and other measures of cardiovascular health (Seeman et al., 2003). Thus, researchers think that meditation may be an important component of a comprehensive approach to preventing and treating cardiovascular disease (Fields et al., 2002). Keep in mind, though, that meditation isn't a "quick fix" for either mental or physical health problems. Deriving benefits from meditation requires self-discipline and commitment (Murray, 2002). Use the steps in *Try It* to learn how to induce a relaxation state that is very similar to that experienced by those who meditate; practice the technique until you become proficient in it. You will then be ready to incorporate it into your daily routine.

4.15 What are the benefits of meditation?

▲ The altered state of consciousness associated with meditation appears to have health benefits.

meditation (concentrative) A group of techniques that involve focusing attention on an object, a word, one's breathing, or one's body movements in order to block out all distractions, to enhance well-being, and to achieve an altered state of consciousness.

Try It   The Relaxation Response

Find a quiet place and sit in a comfortable position.

1. Close your eyes.
2. Relax all your muscles deeply. Beginning with your feet and moving slowly upward, relax the muscles in your legs, buttocks, abdomen, chest, shoulders, neck, and finally your face. Allow your whole body to remain in this deeply relaxed state.
3. Now concentrate on your breathing, and breathe in and out through your nose. Each time you breathe out, silently say the word *one* to yourself.
4. Repeat this process for 20 minutes. (You can open your eyes to look at your watch periodically but don't use an alarm.) When you are finished, remain seated for a few minutes—first with your eyes closed, then with them open.

Hypnosis

People have been fascinated by the subject of hypnosis for centuries. Let's first consider the scientific basis of this phenomenon. **Hypnosis** may be formally defined as a procedure through which one person, the hypnotist, uses the power of suggestion to induce changes in thoughts, feelings, sensations, perceptions, or behavior in another person, the subject. Under hypnosis, people suspend their usual rational and logical ways of thinking and perceiving and allow themselves to experience distortions in perceptions, memories, and thinking. They may experience positive hallucinations, in which they see, hear, touch, smell, or taste things that are not present in the environment. Or they may have negative hallucinations, in which they fail to perceive things that are actually present.

About 80–95% of people are hypnotizable to some degree, but only 5% can reach the deepest levels of the hypnotic state (Nash & Baker, 1984). The ability to become completely absorbed in imaginative activities is characteristic of highly hypnotizable people (Nadon et al., 1991). Silva and Kirsch (1992) found that individuals' fantasy-proneness and their expectation of responding to hypnotic suggestions are predictors of their hypnotizability.

Myths about Hypnosis. There are many misconceptions about hypnosis, some of which probably stem from its long association with stage entertainers. Have you ever believed one of these myths?

- *Hypnotized people are under the complete control of the hypnotist and will violate their moral values if told to do so.* Hypnosis is not something that is done to people. Subjects retain the ability to refuse to comply with the hypnotist's suggestions, and they will not do anything that is contrary to their true moral beliefs.
- *People can demonstrate superhuman strength and perform amazing feats under hypnosis.* Subjects are not stronger or more powerful under hypnosis (Druckman & Bjork, 1994).
- *Memory is more accurate under hypnosis.* Although it is true that hypnotized subjects supply more information and are more confident of their recollections, the information is often inaccurate (Dywan & Bowers, 1983; Kihlstrom & Barnhardt, 1993; Nogrady et al., 1985; Weekes et al., 1992). And in the process of trying to help people recall certain events, hypnotists may instead create in them false memories, or *pseudomemories* (Lynn & Nash, 1994; Yapko, 1994).
- *People under hypnosis will reveal embarrassing secrets.* Hypnosis is not like a truth serum. Subjects can keep secrets or lie under hypnosis.
- *People under hypnosis can relive an event that occurred when they were children and can function mentally as if they were that age.* Careful reviews of studies on hypnotic age regression have found no evidence to support this claim. "Although hypnotically regressed subjects may undergo dramatic changes in demeanor and subjective experience, their performance is not accurately childlike" (Nash, 1987, p. 50).

▲ A hypnotized person is in a state of heightened suggestibility. This hypnotherapist may therefore be able to help the woman control chronic or postsurgery pain.

hypnosis A procedure through which one person, the hypnotist, uses the power of suggestion to induce changes in thoughts, feelings, sensations, perceptions, or behavior in another person, the subject.

Medical Uses of Hypnosis. Hypnosis has come a long way from the days when it was used mainly by entertainers. It is now recognized as a viable technique to be used in medicine, dentistry, and psychotherapy (Lynn et al., 2000). Hypnosis is accepted by the American Medical Association, the American Psychological Association, and the American Psychiatric Association. Hypnosis has been particularly helpful in the control of pain (Hilgard, 1975; Kihlstrom, 1985; Liossi; 2006; Montgomery et al., 2000). Experimental studies have shown that patients who are hypnotized and exposed to suggestions designed to induce relaxation prior to surgery experience less postsurgery pain than do non-hypnotized patients (Montgomery et al., 2002).

Hypnosis has also been used successfully to treat a wide range of disorders, including high blood pressure, bleeding, psoriasis, severe morning sickness, and the side effects of chemotherapy. Other problems that have responded well to hypnosis are asthma, severe insomnia, some phobias (Orne, 1983), dissociative identity disorder (Kluft, 1992), and posttraumatic stress disorder (Cardena, 2000). Furthermore, there are studies suggesting that hypnosis can be useful in treating warts (Ewin, 1992), pain due to severe burns (Patterson & Ptacek, 1997), repetitive nightmares (Kingsbury, 1993), and sexual dysfunctions such as inhibited sexual desire and impotence (Crasilneck, 1992; Hammond, 1992). Suppose you are overweight, or you smoke or drink heavily. Could a visit to a hypnotist rid you of overeating or other bad habits? Probably not. Hypnosis has been only moderately effective in weight control and virtually useless in overcoming drug and alcohol abuse or nicotine addiction (Abbot et al., 2000; Green & Lynn, 2000; Orne, 1983).

For the most hypnotizable people, hypnosis can be used instead of a general anesthetic in surgery. In one remarkable case, a young Canadian dentist had gallbladder surgery, using only hypnosis. From the time of the first incision until the operation was over, the patient maintained a steady pulse rate and blood pressure. Unbelievably, he claimed that he felt nothing that could be described as pain, only a tugging sensation (Callahan, 1997). Did this patient have the world's greatest hypnotist? No, most experts in hypnosis believe that "hypnotic responsiveness depends more on the efforts and abilities of the person hypnotized than on the skill of the hypnotist" (Kirsch & Lynn, 1995, p. 846).

Theories of Hypnosis. According to the sociocognitive theory of hypnosis the behavior of a hypnotized person is a function of that person's expectations about how subjects behave under hypnosis. People are motivated to be good subjects, to follow the suggestions of the hypnotist, and to fulfill the social role of the hypnotized person as they perceive it (Spanos, 1986, 1991, 1994). Does this mean that hypnotized people are merely acting or faking it? No, "most hypnotized persons are neither faking nor merely complying with suggestions" (Kirsch & Lynn, 1995, p. 847). In fact, using the single most effective and reliable indicator of deception in the laboratory—skin conductance, which indicates emotional response by measuring perspiration—Kinnunen and others (1994) found that 89% of supposedly hypnotized people had been truly hypnotized.

Ernest Hilgard (1986, 1992) has proposed a theory to explain why hypnotized individuals can accomplish very difficult acts, even undergoing surgery without anesthesia. According to his neodissociation theory of hypnosis, hypnosis induces a split, or dissociation, between two aspects of the control of consciousness: the planning function and the monitoring function. During hypnosis, it is the planning function that carries out the suggestions of the hypnotist and remains a part of the subject's conscious awareness. The monitoring function monitors or observes everything that happens to the subject, but without his or her conscious awareness. Hilgard called the monitoring function, when separated from conscious awareness, "the hidden observer."

Bowers and his colleagues (Bowers, 1992; Woody & Bowers, 1994) have proposed a view of hypnosis as an authentic altered state of consciousness. Their theory of dissociated control maintains that hypnosis does not induce a splitting of different aspects of consciousness, as Hilgard's model suggests. Rather, they believe that hypnosis weakens the control of the executive function over other parts (subsystems) of consciousness, allowing the hypnotist's suggestions to contact and influence those subsystems directly. Bowers further believes that the hypnotized person's responses are automatic and involuntary, like reflexes, and not controlled by normal cognitive functions (Kirsch & Lynn, 1995). And, indeed, some research supports this viewpoint (Bowers & Woody, 1996; Hargadon et al., 1995).

Although the majority of hypnosis researchers seem to support the sociocognitive theory, most clinicians, and some influential researchers in the field, apparently believe that hypnosis is a unique altered state of consciousness (Kirsch & Lynn, 1995; Nash, 1991; Woody & Bowers, 1994). Kihlstrom (1986) has suggested that a more complete picture of hypnosis could emerge from some combination of the sociocognitive and neodissociation theories. Even though researchers still have theoretical

sociocognitive theory of hypnosis A theory suggesting that the behavior of a hypnotized person is a function of that person's expectations about how subjects behave under hypnosis.

neodissociation theory of hypnosis A theory proposing that hypnosis induces a split, or dissociation, between two aspects of the control of consciousness: the planning function and the monitoring function.

theory of dissociated control The theory that hypnosis is an authentic altered state of consciousness in which the control the executive function exerts over other subsystems of consciousness is weakened.

differences, hypnosis is being increasingly used in clinical practice and in selected areas of medicine and dentistry.

Culture and Altered States of Consciousness

In every culture around the world, and throughout recorded history, human beings have found ways to induce altered states of consciousness (Ward, 1994). Some means of inducing altered states that are used in other cultures may seem strange and exotic to most Westerners. Entering ritual trances and experiencing spirit possession are seen in many cultures in religious rites and tribal ceremonies. Typically, people induce ritual trance by flooding the senses with repetitive chanting, clapping, or singing; by whirling in circles until they achieve a dizzying speed; or by burning strong, pungent incense.

Cross-cultural conflicts can occur when the practices of one culture are judged to be deviant by members of another culture. Many such conflicts arise when non-Western practices overlap with Western-based opinions about normal behavior and mental illness. For example, one religious practice that shows overlaps with the diagnostic criteria employed by mental health professionals is that of *mediumship*. Practitioners of a religion called *Kardecism Spiritism*, a belief system that is popular among Brazilians, turn to mediums for help in communicating with spirits. Mediums undergo specialized training in *dissociation,* or the detachment of oneself from material reality, in order to open themselves to the spirit world. Research has shown that some mediums have difficulty restricting this practice to *séances,* the religious ceremonies in which the living communicate with the spirit world through mediums. Thus, clinicians have suggested that the practice of severing psychological connections with the material world may be detrimental to the long-term mental health of some mediums (Negro, Palladino-Negro, & Louza, 2002).

▲ The ritualized spinning dance of the whirling dervishes produces an altered state of consciousness that is recognized as part of their religious practice.

In the United States, the use of an illegal drug called *peyote* by members of the Native American Church, sometimes called *peyotism,* is controversial (Jones, 2005). Court rulings established long ago that church members have the right to use the drug in their religious ceremonies. However, some mental health professionals have argued that the religious use of peyote may lead to the development of substance abuse problems among church members. They point out that peyote is a powerful hallucinogen even in very small doses. Moreover, these critics say, Native American Church members consume peyote during their rituals for the express purpose of inducing hallucinations, a behavior that satisfies one of several criteria for a formal diagnosis of substance abuse.

In response to these critics, advocates for the use of peyote in the Native American Church argue that church officials take care to regulate the dosages of the drug that are available for consumption during their rituals. In support of this claim, advocates cite the fact that there has never been a reported case of peyote overdose resulting from a church ceremony (Jones, 2005). The church's official doctrines also condemn substance dependence as a moral failing. As a result, advocates say, dependence is unlikely to develop. Furthermore, studies have shown that the practitioners of peyotism show no long-term effects from use of the drug (Halpern et al., 2005). Consequently, peyotism advocates say that mental health professionals who characterize the religious use of the drug as substance abuse are perpetuating stereotypes that have plagued Native Americans for centuries.

The fact that so many different means of altering consciousness are practiced by members of so many cultures around the world has led some experts to wonder whether "there may be a universal human need to produce and maintain varieties of conscious experiences" (Ward, 1994, p. 60). This may be why some people use drugs to deliberately induce altered states of consciousness.

Remember It — Meditation and Hypnosis

1. Researchers have found that meditation may be useful in prevention and treatment of _____.
2. About _____ of people can attain a deep state of hypnosis.
3. Information recalled while under hypnosis is often _____.
4. The three main theories proposed to explain hypnosis are the _____, _____, and _____.

Answers: 1. cardiovascular disease; 2. 5%; 3. inaccurate; 4. sociocognitive theory, neodissociation theory, theory of dissociated control

Psychoactive Drugs

The last time you took a pain reliever or an antibiotic, you probably didn't think of yourself as engaging in a mind-altering experience. However, all chemical substances, even the pain reliever you take for a headache and the penicillin your doctor prescribes to cure an ear or sinus infection, affect the brain because they alter the functioning of neurotransmitters (Munzar et al., 2002). As you can probably guess, most such substances have no noticeable effect on your state of consciousness. Some drugs, however, have especially powerful effects on the brain and induce dramatically altered states of consciousness.

A **psychoactive drug** is any substance that alters mood, perception, or thought. When psychoactive drugs, such as antidepressants, are approved for medical use, they are called *controlled substances*. The term *illicit* denotes psychoactive drugs that are illegal. Many *over-the-counter drugs*, such as antihistamines and decongestants, as well as many herbal preparations, are psychoactive. And, certain foods, such as chocolate, may also alter our moods (Dallard et al., 2001). Note to restaurant servers: Giving customers a piece of chocolate along with their checks increases tips (Strohmetz et al., 2002).

How Drugs Affect the Brain

Did you know that all kinds of physical pleasure have the same neurological basis? Whether derived from sex, a psychoactive chemical, or any other source, a subjective sense of physical pleasure is brought about by an increase in the availability of the neurotransmitter dopamine in a part of the brain's limbic system known as the *nucleus accumbens* (Gerrits et al., 2002; Robinson et al., 2001). Thus, it isn't surprising that researchers have found that a surge of dopamine is involved in the rewarding and motivational effects produced by most psychoactive drugs (Carlson, 1998), including marijuana, heroin (Tanda et al., 1997), and nicotine (Pich et al., 1997; Pontieri et al., 1996). Why, then, does the altered state associated with alcohol feel different from that associated with nicotine or marijuana? The effect drugs have on the dopamine system is just the beginning of a cascade of effects that involve the brain's entire neurotransmitter system. Each drug influences the whole system differently and is associated with a distinctive altered state of consciousness. Consider a few examples of how different drugs act on neurotransmitters and the associated beneficial effects:

- Opiates such as morphine and heroin mimic the effects of the brain's own endorphins, chemicals that have pain-relieving properties and produce a feeling of well-being. For this reason, opiates are useful in pain management.
- Depressants such as alcohol, barbiturates, and benzodiazepines (Valium and Librium, for example) act on GABA receptors to produce a calming, sedating effect (Harris et al., 1992). Thus, depressants can play a role in reducing a patient's nervousness prior to undergoing a medical procedure.

4.18 How do drugs affect the brain's neurotransmitter system?

psychoactive drug Any substance that alters mood, perception, or thought; called a controlled substance if approved for medical use.

- Stimulants such as amphetamines and cocaine mimic the effects of epinephrine, the neurotransmitter that triggers the sympathetic nervous system. The effects of the sympathetic nervous system include suppressed hunger and digestion; this is why "diet pills" typically contain some kind of stimulant, such as caffeine.

However, as we all know, drugs don't always have solely beneficial effects. Why? Because too much of a good thing, or the wrong combination of good things, can lead to disaster. For example, opiates, when taken regularly, will eventually completely suppress the production of endorphins. As a result, natural pain management systems break down, and the brain becomes dependent on the presence of opiates to function normally. Similarly, if ingestion of too much alcohol, or of a combination of alcohol and other depressants, floods the brain with GABA, consciousness will be lost and death may follow. And excessive amounts of a stimulant can send heart rates and blood pressure levels zooming; death can even result from the ingestion of a single, large dose.

Risk and Protective Factors for Substance Abuse

4.19 What are some risk and protective factors for substance abuse?

What motivates people to abuse psychoactive drugs when the possible side effects can be so devastating? One possibility is that many people are unaware of just how harmful these drugs can be (Johnston et al., 1997). Or drug abusers may believe that they aren't ingesting enough of a particular drug to cause permanent harm to their bodies. Other, possibly more important, factors may also underlie substance abuse.

Neurobiological Factors. The pleasant physiological state produced by stimulation of the nucleus accumbens is one reason for substance abuse. But pleasure seeking alone doesn't fully explain drug abuse. Brain-imaging studies have also shown that the irrationality caused by drugs' effects on brain structures other than the nucleus accumbens is also a contributing factor (Porrino & Lyons, 2000; Volkow & Fowler, 2000). It is now known that the irrational behavior of substance abusers is associated with changes in the orbitofrontal cortex and other brain structures to which it is connected. Impaired decision making, irresistible craving for the abused substance, and the willingness to do anything to get it are all sustained, in part, by this drug-disabled brain area (London et al., 2000).

Where is the orbitofrontal cortex? Point your index finger between your eyes where your nose meets your skull. You are pointing directly toward your orbitofrontal cortex, which lies at the very front of the cortex at its lowermost point, just behind the eye sockets. This brain structure is anatomically connected to the association areas for all five of your senses, to structures in the limbic system (such as the amygdala, which has so much to do with emotions), and to other regions in the frontal cortex that handle decision making (Bechara et al., 2000). Thus, the orbitofrontal cortex is intimately involved in everything you see, hear, touch, taste, and smell, in the emotions you feel, and even in the decisions you make. Now, imagine what happens when this brain area is abnormally activated by illicit drugs. It is no wonder that addictive behavior is so irrational.

Heredity. Individual differences in the way people respond physiologically to drugs also contribute to substance abuse. For example, some people feel intoxicated after drinking very small amounts of alcohol, whereas others require a much larger "dose." People who have to drink more to experience intoxication are more likely to become alcoholics. Genetic researchers are currently searching for the gene or genes that contribute to low response to alcohol (Schuckit et al., 2001).

The genetic underpinnings of alcoholism and other addictions appear to involve physiological differences beyond those associated with drug responses. Neuroscientist Henri Begleiter and his colleagues have accumulated a large body of evidence suggesting that the brains of alcoholics respond differently to visual and auditory

▲ Would you be surprised to learn that these two physically pleasurable experiences stimulated the same part of the brain?

stimuli than do those of nonalcoholics (Hada et al., 2000; Porjesz et al., 2005; Prabhu et al., 2001). Further, many relatives of alcoholics, even children and adults who have never consumed any alcohol in their lives, display the same types of response patterns (Hada et al., 2001; Zhang et al., 2001). And relatives of alcoholics who display these patterns are more likely to become alcoholics themselves or to suffer from other types of addictions (Anokhin et al., 2000; Bierut et al., 1998). Begleiter has suggested that the kinds of brain-imaging techniques he uses in his research may someday be used to determine which relatives of alcoholics are genetically predisposed to addiction and which are not (Porjesz et al., 1998).

Psychological and Social Factors. Psychological factors also strongly influence a person's response to a drug. Impulsivity, for instance, is associated with both experimentation with drugs and addiction (Simons & Carey, 2002). And stress-related variables, both early in life and in adulthood, are reliable predictors of substance abuse (Gordon, 2002; Sussman & Dent, 2000). For example, recent research indicates that family violence strongly predicts drug use (Easton et al., 2000). One study found that females are much more likely than males to use drugs to cope with family dysfunction and the symptoms that arise from internalizing various forms of abuse (Dakof, 2000).

The earlier adolescents start using drugs (most start with alcohol and nicotine), the more likely they are to progress to more serious drugs and full-blown addiction (Kandel & Davies, 1996; Zinkernagel et al., 2001). As you can see in Figure 4.3 (on the next page), the proportion of teens who have tried illegal drugs is lower than it was among the then-teenaged "Baby Boomers" who were surveyed 30 years ago (Johnston et al., 2001). Furthermore, recent surveys show that rates of substance abuse and dependence continue to be far higher among members of the Baby Boom generation, even though they are now middle-aged, than in other cohorts (Sherer, 2006). Still, most experts regard current levels of adolescent drug use to be unacceptable.

Adolescents who use drugs seek out peers who also use and, in turn, are influenced by those peers (Curran et al., 1997). In a 16-year longitudinal study that followed 552 seventh, eighth, and ninth graders into adulthood, Newcomb (1997) found that drug use and abuse in adolescents was associated with a number of problem behaviors, including "cigarette use, alcohol abuse, . . . precocious sexual involvement, academic problems, frequency of various sexual activities, deviant attitudes, and delinquent behavior" (p. 65). Substance abuse among adolescents is also related to the propensity to take risks, and a significant percentage of risk-taking drug users (15%) reported suffering injuries while engaging in substance use (Spirito et al., 2000).

Protective Factors. Several protective factors tend to lower the risk of drug use by young people. These include parental support, behavioral coping skills, academic and social competence (Newcomb, 1997; Wills & Cleary, 1996; Wills et al., 1996), and traditional religious beliefs (Kendler et al., 1997). In addition, adolescents who belong to a peer group that values academic and personal competence are less likely to use drugs (Piko, 2006). Cultural variables contribute to protection from drug abuse as well. In one study of more than 400 California teens, researchers found that adolescents of Chinese and Asian/Pacific Island backgrounds were far more likely to abstain from alcohol than peers in other groups (Faryna & Morales, 2000) (see Figure 4.4). Remarkably, 9% of European American and 12% of Latin American youths reported using alcohol every day. Researchers attribute these differences to healthy social influences, such as an environment that promotes abstinence and a greater likelihood of having an intact family among Americans of Chinese and Asian/Pacific Island backgrounds. Also, young Asian Americans spend more time with their families and less time with friends and other peers, thus minimizing potentially bad influences and peer group pressures (Au & Donaldson, 2000).

Figure 4.3 **Results of a Survey of 8th, 10th, and 12th Graders about Their Use of Any Illicit Drug during the Previous 12 Months**

The graph shows the percentage of high school seniors for 1976 through 2004 and the percentages of 8th and 10th graders for 1991 through 2004 who reported using any illicit (illegal) drug during the previous 12 months. After declining steeply from 1982 to 1992, the use of illicit drugs began to increase dramatically in 1992 and continued to climb until 1997. Then, drug use decreased slightly in 1997 and 1998 but began to creep upward again in 1999 and then decreased again in 2004.

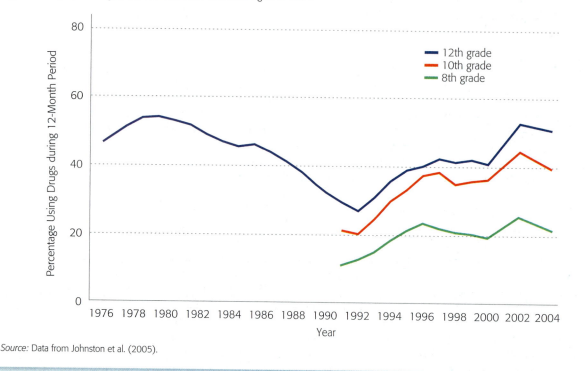

Source: Data from Johnston et al. (2005).

Drug Addiction

4.20 What is the difference between physical and psychological drug dependence?

The journey from first use to abuse of a drug may be long or very short. *Substance abuse* may be defined as continuing drug use that interferes with a person's major life roles at home, in school, at work, or elsewhere and contributes to legal difficulties or any psychological problems (American Psychiatric Association, 1994). Four factors influence the addictive potential of a drug:

- how fast the effects of the drug are felt
- how pleasurable the drug's effects are in producing euphoria or in extinguishing pain
- how long the pleasurable effects last
- how much discomfort is experienced when the drug is discontinued (Medzerian, 1991)

The pleasurable effects of the most addictive drugs are felt almost immediately, and they are short-lived. For example, the intense, pleasurable effects of crack cocaine are felt in 7 seconds and last only about 5 minutes. The addictive potential of an addictive drug is higher if it is injected rather than taken orally, and slightly higher still if it is smoked rather than injected.

Physical Dependence. Some drugs create a physical or chemical dependence; others create a psychological dependence. **Physical drug dependence** comes about as a result of the body's natural ability to protect itself against harmful substances by developing a **drug tolerance.** This means that the user becomes progressively less affected by the drug and must take larger and larger doses to get the same effect or high (Ramsay & Woods, 1997). Tolerance occurs because the brain adapts to the presence of the drug by

physical drug dependence A compulsive pattern of drug use in which the user develops a drug tolerance coupled with unpleasant withdrawal symptoms when the drug use is discontinued.

drug tolerance A condition in which the user becomes progressively less affected by the drug and must take larger and larger doses to maintain the same effect or high.

Figure 4.4 Alcohol Use Among Adolescents of Diverse Ethnicities

In this study involving more than 400 California high school students, researchers found that those with Chinese and Asian/Pacific Island backgrounds were less likely to use alcohol than were their peers from other ethnic groups. The researchers suggested that differences in cultural values and family structure help to account for these differences. Chinese American and Asian American/Pacific Islander teens were more likely to come from homes in which both parents were present. Further, European American, Latin American, and African American teens spent more time with peers than with their families, but the reverse was true for the Chinese American and Asian American/Pacific Islander high school students.

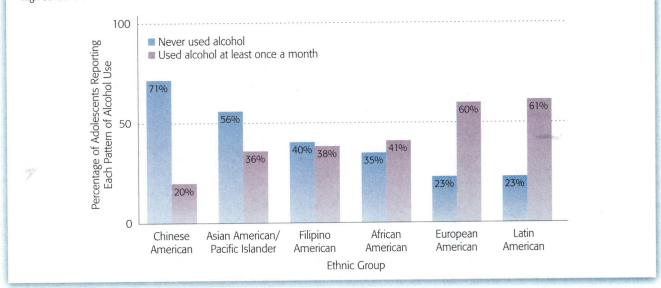

responding less intensely to it. In addition, the liver produces more enzymes to break down the drug. The various bodily processes adjust in order to continue to function with the drug present in the system.

Once drug tolerance is established, a person cannot function normally without the drug. If the drug is taken away, the user begins to suffer withdrawal symptoms. The **withdrawal symptoms,** both physical and psychological, are usually the exact opposite of the effects produced by the drug. For example, withdrawal from stimulants leaves a person exhausted and depressed; withdrawal from tranquilizers leaves a person nervous and agitated. Since taking the drug is the only way to escape these unpleasant symptoms, withdrawal can lead to relapse into addiction. Moreover, the lasting behavioral and cognitive effects of abused substances on the brain also often interfere with attempts to stop using the substances. Among other effects, researchers have learned that addiction is associated with attention and memory deficits, loss of the ability to accurately sense the passage of time, and decreased capacity to plan and control behavior (Bates et al., 2002; Buhusi & Meck, 2002; Lyvers, 2000). Abusers need all of these skills to overcome addiction and rebuild their lives, but regaining them once drug abuse has stopped takes time and determination.

Psychological Dependence. There is more to drug addiction than physical dependence. **Psychological drug dependence** is a craving or irresistible urge for the drug's pleasurable effects, and it is more difficult to combat than physical dependence (O'Brien, 1996). Some experts believe that drug cravings are controlled by a neural network that operates independently from and competes with a different network that controls deliberative decision making (Bechara, 2005). The drug-craving network acts on impulse that is largely influenced by the desire for immediate gratification. By contrast, the decision-making network identifies the consequences of potential actions and makes conscious decisions to engage in constructive behaviors and to avoid those that are destructive. This model of competing neural networks may explain why individuals who suffer from addiction often relapse despite their knowledge of the painful consequences that may occur as a result of doing so. Continued use of drugs to

withdrawal symptoms The physical and psychological symptoms (usually the exact opposite of the effects produced by the drug) that occur when a regularly used drug is discontinued and that terminate when the drug is taken again.

psychological drug dependence A craving or irresistible urge for a drug's pleasurable effects.

which an individual is physically addicted is influenced by the psychological component of the habit. There are also drugs that are probably not physically addictive but may create psychological dependence.

Learning processes are important in the development and maintenance of psychological dependence. For example, drug-taking cues—the people, places, and things associated with using—can produce a strong craving for the abused substance (Hillebrand, 2000). In fact, some researchers have found that people addicted to opiates selectively pay attention to drug-related cues, ignoring virtually all non-drug cues any time the drug cues are present (Lubman et al., 2000). However, "selective attention" probably isn't the most descriptive term for what is happening in a drug addict's brain. PET scans of cocaine addicts' brains indicate that such cues arouse a cue-specific neural network, which may explain why it is difficult for addicts to divert their attention from them (Bonson et al., 2002). These findings underscore the necessity of changes in addicts' physical and social environment in the treatment of both physical and psychological drug dependence.

The Behavioral Effects of Psychoactive Drugs

4.21 What are the effects of stimulants, depressants, and hallucinogens on behavior?

Have you ever advised a friend to "switch to decaf"? This advice comes from a bit of drug knowledge we all share: Caffeine can make us jumpy. But what are the specific behavioral effects associated with other kinds of drugs? Let's begin with a look at the stimulants, the group to which caffeine belongs.

Stimulants. **Stimulants,** often called "uppers," speed up activity in the central nervous system, suppress appetite, and can make a person feel more awake, alert, and energetic. Stimulants increase pulse rate, blood pressure, and respiration rate, and they reduce cerebral blood flow (Mathew & Wilson, 1991). In higher doses, stimulants make people feel nervous, jittery, and restless, and they can cause shaking or trembling and interfere with sleep.

Caffeine. Coffee, tea, cola drinks, chocolate, and more than 100 prescription and over-the-counter drugs contain caffeine. Caffeine makes people more mentally alert and can help them stay awake (Wesensten et al., 2002). When moderate to heavy caffeine users abstain, they suffer withdrawal symptoms such as nervousness, instability, headaches, drowsiness, and decreased alertness. Using EEGs and sonograms, researchers looked at the effects of caffeine withdrawal symptoms on the brain and were able to correlate the symptoms with significant increases in blood pressure and in the velocity of blood flow in all four of the cerebral arteries. The EEGs also showed an increase in slower brain waves, which correlates with decreased alertness and drowsiness (Jones et al., 2000).

Nicotine. Like caffeine, nicotine increases alertness, but few people who have tried to quit smoking doubt its addictive power. (The many serious health problems associated with smoking are discussed in Chapter 12.) Many treatment methods that are advertised as being helpful to smokers trying to quit appear to have limited value. For example, Green and Lynn (2000) reviewed the results of 59 studies of hypnosis and smoking and concluded that hypnosis cannot be considered effective in helping smokers break the habit. However, experiments have shown that over-the-counter nicotine patches help about one in five smokers quit and enable many others to cut down on the number of cigarettes they smoke (Jolicoeur et al., 2003).

Amphetamines. Amphetamines increase arousal, relieve fatigue, improve alertness, suppress the appetite, and give a rush of energy. Animal research suggests that amphetamines stimulate the release of dopamine in the frontal cortex as well as in the nucleus accumbens, which may account for some of their desirable cognitive effects such as increases in attention span and concentration (Frantz et al., 2002). In high doses (100 milligrams or more), however, amphetamines can cause confused and disorganized behavior, extreme fear and suspiciousness, delusions and hallucinations, aggressiveness and antisocial behavior, even manic behavior and paranoia (Thirthalli & Benegal, 2006). The powerful amphetamine methamphetamine (known as "crank" or "speed") comes in a smokable form ("ice"), which is highly addictive and can be fatal.

▲ Amphetamines affect the parts of the brain that control attention and concentration, as well as the nucleus accumbens. This helps explain why these stimulants are useful in the treatment of attention problems in schoolchildren.

stimulants A category of drugs that speed up activity in the central nervous system, suppress appetite, and can cause a person to feel more awake, alert, and energetic; also called "uppers."

Withdrawal from amphetamines leaves a person physically exhausted; he or she will sleep for 10 to 15 hours or more, only to awaken in a stupor, extremely depressed and intensely hungry. Stimulants constrict the tiny capillaries and the small arteries. Over time, high doses can stop blood flow, causing hemorrhaging and leaving parts of the brain deprived of oxygen. In fact, victims of fatal overdoses of stimulants usually have multiple hemorrhages in the brain.

Cocaine. Cocaine, a stimulant derived from coca leaves, can be sniffed as a white powder, injected intravenously, or smoked in the form of crack. The effects of snorting cocaine are felt within 2 to 3 minutes, and the high lasts 30 to 45 minutes. The euphoria from cocaine is followed by an equally intense crash, marked by depression, anxiety, agitation, and a powerful craving for more of the drug.

Cocaine stimulates the reward, or "pleasure," pathways in the brain, which use the neurotransmitter dopamine (Landry, 1997). With continued use, these reward systems fail to function normally, and the user becomes incapable of feeling any pleasure except from the drug. The main withdrawal symptoms are psychological—the inability to feel pleasure and the craving for more cocaine.

Cocaine constricts the blood vessels, raises blood pressure, speeds up the heart, quickens respiration, and can even cause epileptic seizures in people who have no history of epilepsy (Pascual-Leone et al., 1990). Over time, or even quickly in high doses, cocaine can cause heart palpitations, an irregular heartbeat, and heart attacks, and high doses can cause strokes in healthy young individuals. Chronic cocaine use can also result in holes in the nasal septum (the ridge of cartilage running down the middle of the nose) and in the palate (the roof of the mouth) (Armstrong & Shikani, 1996; Sastry et al., 1997).

Animals become addicted more readily to cocaine than to any other drug, and those who are addicted to multiple substances prefer cocaine when offered a choice of drugs (Manzardo, et al., 2002). Given unlimited access to cocaine, animals will lose interest in everything else, including food, water, and sex, and will rapidly and continually self-administer cocaine. They tend to die within 14 days, usually from cardiopulmonary collapse (Gawin, 1991). Cocaine-addicted monkeys will press a lever as many as 12,800 times to get one cocaine injection (Yanagita, 1973).

Crack, or "rock," the most dangerous form of cocaine, can produce a powerful dependency in several weeks. Users who begin with cocaine in powder form are likely to progress to crack, while users who start on crack are more likely to continue using it exclusively. When both powder and crack are used interchangeably, a mutual reinforcement seems to occur, and the user develops a dependence on both forms of cocaine (Shaw et al., 1999).

Depressants. Another class of drugs, the **depressants** (sometimes called "downers"), decrease activity in the central nervous system, slow down bodily functions, and reduce sensitivity to outside stimulation. Within this category are the sedative-hypnotics (alcohol, barbiturates, and minor tranquilizers) and the narcotics (opiates). When different depressants are taken together, their sedative effects are additive and, thus, potentially dangerous.

Alcohol. The more alcohol a person consumes, the more the central nervous system is depressed. As drinking increases, the symptoms of drunkenness mount—slurred speech, poor coordination, staggering. Men tend to become more aggressive (Pihl et al., 1997) and more sexually aroused (Roehrich & Kinder, 1991) but less able to perform sexually (Crowe & George, 1989). (We will discuss the health consequences of alcohol abuse in detail in Chapter 12.) Alcohol also decreases the ability to form new memories (Kirchner & Sayette, 2003; Ray & Bates, 2006). That's why an episode of heavy drinking is often followed by a "morning after," during which the drinker is unable to remember the events that occurred while he or she was under the influence of alcohol. Interestingly, though, alcohol placebos have similar effects on memory function, so a drinker's expectations contribute to alcohol's effects to some extent (Assefi & Garry, 2003).

Barbiturates. Barbiturates depress the central nervous system, and, depending on the dose, a barbiturate can act as a sedative or a sleeping pill. People who abuse barbiturates become drowsy and confused, their thinking and judgment suffer, and their coordination

depressants A category of drugs that decrease activity in the central nervous system, slow down bodily functions, and reduce sensitivity to outside stimulation; also called "downers."

▲ Some people feel intoxicated after drinking very small amounts of alcohol, while others require a much larger "dose." People who have to drink more to experience intoxication are more likely to become alcoholics.

and reflexes are affected (Henningfield & Ator, 1986). Barbiturates can kill if taken in overdose, and a lethal dose can be as little as only three times the prescribed dose. Alcohol and barbiturates, when taken together, are a potentially fatal combination.

Minor Tranquilizers. The popular minor tranquilizers, the *benzodiazepines,* came on the scene in the early 1960s and are sold under the brand names Valium, Librium, Dalmane, and, more recently, Xanax (also used as an antidepressant). About 90 million prescriptions for minor tranquilizers are filled each year. Benzodiazepines are prescribed for several medical and psychological disorders. Abuse of these drugs is associated with both temporary and permanent impairment of memory and other cognitive functions (Paraherakis et al., 2001). (A more detailed discussion of tranquilizers can be found in Chapter 15.)

Narcotics. Narcotics are derived from the opium poppy and produce both pain-relieving and calming effects. Opium affects mainly the brain, but it also paralyzes the intestinal muscles, which is why it is used medically to treat diarrhea. If you have ever taken paregoric, you have had a tincture (extract) of opium. Because opium suppresses the cough center, it is used in some cough medicines. Morphine and codeine, natural constituents of opium, may be found in some drugs prescribed for pain relief. Such drugs, including Oxycontin and Vicodin, are addictive and are sold illegally to millions of people in the United States every year (Drug Enforcement Administration, 2003).

A highly addictive narcotic derived from morphine is heroin. Heroin addicts describe a sudden "rush" of euphoria, followed by drowsiness, inactivity, and impaired concentration. Withdrawal symptoms begin about 6 to 24 hours after use, and the addict becomes physically sick. Nausea, diarrhea, depression, stomach cramps, insomnia, and pain grow worse and worse until they become intolerable—unless the person gets another "fix."

Hallucinogens. The hallucinogens, or *psychedelics,* are drugs that can alter and distort perceptions of time and space, alter mood, and produce feelings of unreality. As the name implies, hallucinogens also cause hallucinations, sensations that have no basis in external reality (Andreasen & Black, 1991; Malik & D'Souza, 2006; Miller & Gold, 1994; Thirthalli & Benegal, 2006). Rather than producing a relatively predictable effect like most other drugs, hallucinogens usually magnify the mood of the user at the time the drug is taken. And, contrary to the belief of some, hallucinogens hamper rather than enhance creative thinking (Bourassa & Vaugeois, 2001).

Marijuana. THC (tetrahydrocannabinol), the ingredient in marijuana that produces the high, remains in the body "for days or even weeks" (Julien, 1995). Marijuana impairs attention and coordination and slows reaction time, and these effects make operating complex machinery such as an automobile dangerous, even after the feeling of intoxication has passed. Marijuana can interfere with concentration, logical thinking, and the ability to form new memories. It can produce fragmentation in thought and confusion in remembering recent occurrences (Herkenham, 1992). A 17-year longitudinal study of Costa Rican men supports the claim that long-term use of marijuana has a negative impact on short-term memory and the ability to focus sustained attention (Fletcher et al., 1996). Many of the receptors for THC are in the hippocampus, which explains why the drug affects memory (Matsuda et al., 1990).

Chronic use of marijuana has been associated with loss of motivation, general apathy, and decline in school performance, referred to as *amotivational syndrome* (Andreasen & Black, 1991). Studies comparing marijuana users who began before age 17 with those who started later show that early marijuana use is associated with a somewhat smaller brain volume and a lower percentage of the all-important gray matter in the brain's cortex. Marijuana users who started younger were also shorter and weighed less than users who started when older (Wilson et al., 2000). Further, marijuana smoke contains many of the same carcinogenic chemicals as cigarette smoke.

narcotics A class of depressant drugs derived from the opium poppy that produce both pain-relieving and calming effects.

hallucinogens (hal-LU-sin-o-jenz) A category of drugs that can alter and distort perceptions of time and space, alter mood, produce feelings of unreality, and cause hallucinations; also called *psychedelics.*

However, an advisory panel of the National Institute on Drug Abuse, after reviewing the scientific evidence, concluded that marijuana shows promise as a treatment for certain medical conditions. It has been found effective for treating the eye disease glaucoma, for controlling nausea and vomiting in cancer patients receiving chemotherapy, and for improving appetite and curtailing weight loss in some AIDS patients (Fackelmann, 1997). But there is a continuing controversy over whether marijuana should be legalized for medical purposes. Moreover, the U.S. Food and Drug Administration has stated unequivocally that smoked marijuana has no known medical benefits and should continue to be regarded as a dangerous drug (FDA, 2006).

LSD (lysergic acid diethylamide). LSD is lysergic acid diethylamide, sometimes referred to simply as "acid." The average LSD "trip" lasts for 10 to 12 hours and usually produces extreme perceptual and emotional changes, including visual hallucinations and feelings of panic (Miller & Gold, 1994). On occasion, bad LSD trips have ended tragically in accidents, death, or suicide. Former LSD users sometimes experience *flashbacks,* brief recurrences of previous trips that occur suddenly and without warning. Some develop a syndrome called *hallucinogen persisting perception disorder (HPPD),* in which the visual cortex becomes highly stimulated whenever the individuals shut their eyes, causing them to experience chronic visual hallucinations whenever they try to sleep (Abraham & Duffy, 2001).

Designer Drugs. Designer drugs are so called because they are specially formulated to mimic the pleasurable effects of other drugs without, supposedly, their negative side effects. STP (for Serenity, Tranquility, and Peace) and MDMA (methylene-dioxymethamphetamine, commonly known as Ecstasy) are two common designer drugs. All designer drugs are derived from amphetamines but have hallucinogenic as well as stimulant effects. One reason for their popularity is that most are metabolized by the body differently than are the drugs they imitate (Drug Free Workplace, 2002). As a result, conventional drug tests do not detect the presence of designer drugs in an individual's system. As drug testing has become more common prior to employment and on a random basis in workplaces and some schools, designer drugs have become more popular.

▲ Many Americans believe that the use of marijuana for medical purposes ought to be legal. However, the U.S. Food and Drug Administration insists that there are no legitimate medical uses for smoked marijuana (FDA, 2006). They point out that the active ingredient in marijuana, THC, is available in pill form and can be legally prescribed to patients by any licensed physician in the United States.

MDMA is often used at rave dances. Users of MDMA describe a wonderfully pleasant state of consciousness, in which even the most backward, bashful, self-conscious people shed their inhibitions (U.S. Department of Health and Human Services, 2001). Pretenses melt away, and the users become "emotionally synthesized" with other ravers and with the music and the lighting effects. Users feel that the drug allows them to be who they "really are." They report an immediate and deep acceptance and understanding of others; interpersonal barriers disappear, along with emotional and sexual inhibitions. It is said that the frequent, spontaneous outbursts of mass hugging and kissing make MDMA users feel that they are accepted, even loved. But there is a price to be paid for entering this "joyous" state.

MDMA is known to impair a variety of cognitive functions, including memory, sustained attention, analytical thinking, and self-control (National Institute on Drug Abuse, 2001). More specifically, the drug is believed to have devastating effects on the critically important neurotransmitter serotonin, by depleting the brain's serotonin receptors. Serotonin, as you learned in Chapter 2, influences cognitive performance (including memory), as well as moods, sleep cycles, and the ability to control impulses (Reneman et al., 2000; Volkow & Fowler, 2000). Overdoses of MDMA can be fatal (Drug Enforcement Administration, 2003).

Moreover, MDMA seems to impair the capacity for judging social cues in frequent users. In one study, Ecstasy users were more likely than nonusers to incorrectly classify the actions of others as having aggressive intent (Hoshi et al., 2006). As you will learn in Chapter 16, poor social judgments of this type are thought to be the cognitive basis of some acts of aggression. Thus, by changing the way Ecstasy users think about social cues, the drug may indirectly increase their proclivity for aggressive behavior.

Review and Reflect provides a summary of the effects and withdrawal symptoms of the major psychoactive drugs.

Review and Reflect — The Effects and Withdrawal Symptoms of Some Psychoactive Drugs

Psychoactive Drug	Effects	Withdrawal Symptoms
Stimulants		
Caffeine	Produces wakefulness and alertness; increases metabolism but slows reaction time	Headache, depression, fatigue
Nicotine (tobacco)	Effects range from alertness to calmness; lowers appetite for carbohydrates; increases pulse rate and other metabolic processes	Irritability, anxiety, restlessness, increased appetite
Amphetamines	Increase metabolism and alertness; elevate mood, cause wakefulness, suppress appetite	Fatigue, increased appetite, depression, long periods of sleep, irritability, anxiety
Cocaine	Brings on euphoric mood, energy boost, feeling of excitement; suppresses appetite	Depression, fatigue, increased appetite, long periods of sleep, irritability
Depressants		
Alcohol	First few drinks stimulate and enliven while lowering anxiety and inhibitions; higher doses have a sedative effect, slowing reaction time, impairing motor control and perceptual ability	Tremors, nausea, sweating, depression, weakness, irritability, and in some cases hallucinations
Barbiturates	Promote sleep, have calming and sedative effect, decrease muscular tension, impair coordination and reflexes	Sleeplessness, anxiety; sudden withdrawal can cause seizures, cardiovascular collapse, and death
Tranquilizers (e.g., Valium, Xanax)	Lower anxiety, have calming and sedative effect, decrease muscular tension	Restlessness, anxiety, irritability, muscle tension, difficulty sleeping
Narcotics	Relieve pain; produce paralysis of intestines	Nausea, diarrhea, cramps, insomnia
Hallucinogens		
Marijuana	Generally produces euphoria, relaxation; affects ability to store new memories	Anxiety, difficulty sleeping, decreased appetite, hyperactivity
LSD	Produces excited exhilaration, hallucinations, experiences perceived as insightful and profound	None Known
MDMA (Ecstasy)	Typically produces euphoria and feelings of understanding others and accepting them; lowers inhibitions; often causes overheating, dehydration, nausea; can cause jaw clenching, eye twitching, and dizziness	Depression, fatigue, and in some cases a "crash," during which the person may be sad, scared, or annoyed

Apply It — The Brain's Internal Timer

Have you ever been in this situation? You stop at a red light and wait patiently for it to change to green. As time goes on, you start to think that the light has been red for an unusually long period of time. You look around at other drivers, wondering if they have the same impression. Finally, you decide that the light is malfunctioning and cautiously proceed through the intersection even though the light is still red. What happened?

Earlier in the chapter you learned about your brain's circadian clock, the one that keeps your sleep/wake cycles in tune with the earth's day/night cycle. But did you know there are actually several kinds of clocks in the brain? One of them is an interval timer, much like the wind-up or digital device in your kitchen that you use to remind yourself to take a pizza out of the oven before it burns. This timer is the neurological mechanism that gives your higher brain centers information such as "The light has been red too long," so that you can decide what, if any, action to take.

How the Timer Switches On and Off

The brain's interval timer consists of a network of neurons in the cerebral cortex that fire randomly and independently until something gets their attention (Wright, 2002). When an attention-getting stimulus that has time characteristics (e.g., a traffic light) occurs, the substantia nigra sends out a pulse of dopamine that signals these neurons to fire simultaneously. This simultaneous firing becomes a neurological marker for the beginning of the event. When the event ends, the substantia nigra does the same thing, creating a marker for the end of the event. In some cases, the brain's timer compares its measurements to standards stored in your memory. This is what happens when you are sitting at a traffic light and have the impression that the light has been red too long.

When you concentrate deeply, as happens when you are absorbed in a movie, the timer turns itself off. You find yourself wondering where the time went when you come out of the concentration state. The timer also switches off when you are in an emergency situation or when you are experiencing deep emotions. By contrast, when you are bored, your brain's interval timer alerts you to every passing second, and time seems to creep by.

Accuracy of the Brain's Timer

How accurate is the brain's interval timer? Here's a prime illustration. Your alarm goes off, and you look at the clock. You decide to allow yourself to sleep 10 more minutes. You think of resetting the alarm but decide not to because, "I'll wake up," you assure yourself. Remarkably, you wake up again, look at the clock, and note that you have slept for about 10 minutes, just as you planned. But on other occasions, you wake up to find that you have slept for 2 hours rather than 10 minutes. Thus, you have probably learned by experience that sometimes the brain's timer works well, but at others it fails miserably.

Some of the timer's errors appear to be wired-in (Wright, 2002). One such inherent error is its tendency to underestimate time. Limitations on how many tasks our brains can handle at one time also contribute to the unreliability of the brain's timer. In one study, experimental group participants were instructed to read aloud for a fixed period of time (Tracy et al., 1998). Control group subjects did nothing during the period. When the time expired, participants in both groups were asked to estimate how long the interval had been. Experimental group participants gave estimates that were more variable and, on average, much less accurate than those in the control group.

As noted, the substantia nigra and the neurotransmitter dopamine are critical to the operation of the brain's timer. Thus, anything that affects either the substantia nigra or dopamine also affects the timer. For example, you may recall from Chapter 2 that Parkinson's disease is associated with dysfunction in the substantia nigra. Predictably, researchers have found that individuals who suffer from this condition perform more poorly on tasks involving time estimation than people who don't have the disease (Wright, 2002). Similarly, individuals with schizophrenia, a psychiatric disorder in which dopamine function is impaired, also have difficulty estimating time intervals (Davalos, Kisley, & Freedman, 2005).

Distortions of time perception are also common among people who use drugs, because, as you learned in this chapter, drugs affect the brain's dopamine system. Most drugs give users a sense of expanded time; one minute may seem like an hour (Bauer, 2001; Lieving et al., 2006). In one study, when researchers instructed participants to wait for a brief period of time (e.g., 5 seconds) before pressing a lever, marijuana users typically pressed the lever before the specified number of seconds had elapsed, whereas nonusers were able to accurately estimate short intervals under such conditions (McDonald, Schleifer, Richards, & deWit, 2003).

The Brain's Timer in Everyday Life

Experiences that demonstrate the effects of learning on the brain's timer, such as the traffic light example, suggest that you can exploit the adaptability of the brain's timer to become a better test-taker. By taking practice tests and timing yourself, you can "teach" your brain's timer to more accurately estimate how long it will take you to complete exams of varying lengths and types. As a result of this improved time-estimation ability, you will be able to make better judgments about pacing yourself during real exams.

However, if you want to spend a few more minutes in dreamland when you wake up on the morning of an exam, don't rely on the brain's timer to wake you up, even if you have practiced doing so. Think back to the chapter's discussion of sleep cycles to understand why. Once you go back to sleep, your brain begins a new sleep cycle, one that will last 90 minutes or so if it isn't interrupted. Note that Stage 1, the drowsiness phase, lasts only a few minutes. If your brain slips into the deeper sleep of Stage 2 before the internal timer wakes you up, you are likely to sleep through the exam. Thus, instead of relying on your brain's internal timer, turn to your alarm clock, one of the many devices humans have invented to compensate for the inaccuracies of our built-in neurological timers.

Herbal Remedies and Supplements

Have you ever heard a radio or television commercial touting a "natural" remedy that works just as well as some prescription drug? Such advertisements are becoming more frequent because public interest in alternative approaches to health care has grown tremendously in the past few years. One survey of college students found that about half used herbal supplements (Newberry, et al., 2001). The use of herbs as medicines is an ancient practice that is still very common in some cultures.

4.22 What are the pros and cons of using herbal remedies?

▲ Herbal supplements are growing in popularity. However, the effectiveness of most of them has not been tested scientifically.

Many herbs have the same kinds of effects on the brain as drugs do. However, the kinds of placebo-controlled studies that are common in pharmacological research are still rare in research on herbal treatments. In the few studies that have been done, researchers have found that many herbal preparations do live up to their claims. Both kava and valerian can make you feel calmer and help you sleep (Mischoulon, 2002; Wheatley, 2001). Kava, however, is toxic to the liver, and valerian acts more slowly and less reliably than conventional treatments for anxiety and insomnia (Wheatley, 2005). Other herbs appear to be effective in treating attention deficit disorder (Lyon et al., 2001) and in relieving symptoms of premenstrual syndrome and menopause (Chavez & Spitzher, 2002).

Many people think that something called "natural" must be safe. But research has yet to establish effective and safe dosages for herbal treatments. The dosage issue is an important one because excessive consumption of herbal supplements has been linked to allergic reactions, heightened risk for sunburn, asthma, liver failure, hypertension, mania, depression, and potentially dangerous interactions with prescription medications (Escher et al., 2001; Halemaskel et al., 2001; Pyevich & Bogenschutz, 2001; Rivas-Vasquez, 2001).

Other problems arise from the fact that, in the United States, supplements are regulated as foods rather than as drugs. This means that consumers cannot be sure that the contents of an herbal product are consistent with the label on the container. For example, some women use black cohosh to relieve hot flashes and other symptoms of menopause (Geller & Studee, 2005). The effectiveness of the North American strain of this plant is believed to be derived from several compounds the plant contains that are similar to female hormones. In a test of the authenticity of products labeled "black cohosh," researchers analyzed 11 products to determine how much of the herb each product actually contained (Jiang et al., 2006). They found that three of the products contained an Asian variant of the plant that does not have any of the compounds that are believed to be effective in the treatment of menopausal symptoms. Another product contained a mixture of the Asian and North American plants. The seven products that contained authentic North American black cohosh varied greatly in chemical composition. Some had generous amounts of the supposed symptom-relieving compounds, whereas others did not. Yet, all 11 of these products satisfied government regulations for food product labeling. By contrast, both prescription and over-the-counter pharmaceuticals must be labeled precisely as to their active ingredients.

Clearly, many of us find herbal preparations to be helpful. However, we need to keep in mind that their ability to affect both mind and body shouldn't be underestimated just because they seem more "natural" than manufactured drugs.

Remember It   Psychoactive Drugs

1. All addictive drugs increase the effect of the neurotransmitter _____ in the _____.

2. The irrationality associated with substance abuse is probably caused by the effects of drugs on the _____.

3. Physical dependence on a drug begins with the development of _____, followed by _____ whenever the drug is discontinued.

4. Classify each drug by matching it with the appropriate category.

_____ (1) marijuana
_____ (2) caffeine
_____ (3) Ecstasy
_____ (4) STP
_____ (5) heroin
_____ (6) LSD
_____ (7) amphetamine
_____ (8) cocaine
_____ (9) nicotine
_____ (10) alcohol

a. depressant
b. stimulant
c. narcotic
d. hallucinogen
e. designer drug

Answers: 1. dopamine, nucleus accumbens; 2. orbitofrontal cortex; 3. drug tolerance, withdrawal symptoms; 4. (1) d, (2) b, (3) e, (4) e, (5) a, (6) d, (7) b, (8) b, (9) b, (10) a

✸ Summary and Review

What Is Consciousness? p. 123

4.1   How have psychologists' views about consciousness changed since the early days of psychology? p. 123

Early psychologists saw consciousness, or awareness, as psychological in nature. Freud distinguished between conscious and unconscious experiences. James emphasized the continuous flow of thought and feeling in consciousness. Today's pschologists view consciousness as a neurobiological phenomenon, rather than an exclusively psychological one.

Circadian Rhythms p. 124

4.2   Which physiological and psychological functions are influenced by circadian rhythms? p. 124

Circadian rhythms regulate all vital life functions (e.g., heart rate, blood pressure), as well as learning efficiency and moods. These rhythms also affect sleep patterns and alertness.

4.3   How do biological and environmental variables influence circadian rhythms? p. 125

The suprachiasmatic nucleus (SCN) is the body's biological clock, which regulates circadian rhythms and signals the pineal gland to secrete or suppress secretion of melatonin, a hormone that acts to induce sleep. The amount of melatonin released by the pineal gland depends on the amount of light perceived by specialized photoreceptor cells on the retina.

4.4   How do disruptions in circadian rhythms affect the body and the mind? p. 125

Delayed sleep phase syndrome and advanced sleep phase syndrome cause people to fall asleep either very late or very early, respectively. Jet lag and shift work disrupt circadian rhythms, which can lead to sleep difficulties as well as reduced alertness during periods of wakefulness.

4.5   How can research linking circadian rhythms and neurological disorders be put to practical use? p. 127

Individuals with neurological disorders show distinctive circadian rhythms, and restoring them to normal circadian functioning may help both the patients and their caregivers.

Sleep p. 128

4.6   What is the difference between the restorative and circadian theories of sleep? p. 128

The restorative theory of sleep claims that being awake causes stress on the body and the brain; repairs are made during sleep. The circadian (evolutionary) theory maintains that circadian rhythms, which evolved to protect humans from predators during the night, dictate periods of sleep and alertness.

4.7   How do NREM and REM sleep differ? p. 128

During NREM sleep, heart rate and respiration are slow and regular, and blood pressure and brain activity are at a 24-hour low point; there is little body movement and no rapid eye movements. During REM sleep, the large muscles of the body are paralyzed, respiration and heart rate are fast and irregular, brain activity increases, and rapid eye movements and vivid dreams occur.

4.8   What is the progression of NREM stages and REM sleep in a typical night of sleep? p. 129

During a typical night of sleep, a person goes through about five sleep cycles, each lasting about 90 minutes. The first sleep cycle contains Stages 1, 2, 3, and 4 of NREM sleep as well as a period of REM sleep; the second contains Stages 2, 3, and 4 of NREM sleep and a period of REM sleep. In the remaining sleep cycles, the sleeper alternates mainly between Stage 2 and REM sleep, with each sleep cycle having progressively longer periods of REM.

4.9   What does research tell us about the link between REM sleep and memory? p. 130

REM appears to be essential to the consolidation of memories. It may also be the period during which the brain erases unnecessary memories and reorganizes those that are deemed essential.

4.10   How do age and individual differences influence people's sleep patterns? p. 131

Infants and young children have the longest sleep time and largest percentages of REM and slow-wave sleep. Children from age 6 to puberty sleep best. The elderly typically have shorter total sleep time, more awakenings, and substantially less slow-wave sleep.

4.11   How does sleep deprivation affect behavior and neurological functioning? p. 131

Sleep deprivation can lead to lapses in concentration and emotional irritability. Microsleeps are common among the sleep-deprived. Research examining the effects of sleep deprivation on verbal learning have shown that sleep deprivation may lead to suppression of neurological activity in the temporal lobes.

4.12   What have researchers learned about dreams, their content, their biological basis, and their controllability? p. 133

REM dreams have a storylike or dreamlike quality and are more visual, vivid, and emotional than NREM dreams. Common dream themes include falling or being attacked or chased. During REM dreams, areas of the brain responsible for emotions and the primary visual cortex are active, but the neurotransmitters serotonin and norepinephrine are less plentiful. Lucid dreaming is a set of techniques that enable dreamers to exert cognitive control over the content of their dreams.

4.13 How do the views of contemporary psychologists concerning the nature of dreams differ from those of Freud? p. 134

Freud believed that dreams carry hidden meanings and function to satisfy unconscious sexual and aggressive desires. He claimed that the manifest content of dreams differs from their latent content. Today, some psychologists support the activation-synthesis hypothesis, which claims that dreams are the brain's attempt to make sense of the random firing of brain cells during REM sleep.

4.14 What are the various disorders that can trouble sleepers? p. 135

Parasomnias such as somnambulism and sleep terrors occur during a partial arousal from Stage 4 sleep, and the person does not come to full consciousness. In a sleep terror, the sleeper awakens in a panicked state with a racing heart. Episodes last 5 to 15 minutes, and then the person falls back to sleep. Nightmares are frightening dreams that occur during REM sleep and are usually remembered in vivid detail. Somniloquy (sleeptalking) can occur during any sleep stage and is more common in children than adults. The symptoms of narcolepsy include excessive daytime sleepiness and sudden attacks of REM sleep. Sleep apnea is a serious sleep disorder in which a sleeper's breathing stops and the person must awaken briefly to breathe. Its major symptoms are excessive daytime sleepiness and extremely loud snoring. Insomnia is a sleep disorder characterized by difficulty falling or staying asleep, by waking too early, or by sleep that is light, restless, or of poor quality.

Meditation and Hypnosis p. 136

4.15 What are the benefits of meditation? p. 137

Meditation is used to promote relaxation, reduce arousal, or expand consciousness. It may also help prevent and treat cardiovascular disease.

4.16 What are the effects of hypnosis, and how do theorists explain them? p. 138

Hypnosis is a procedure through which a hypnotist uses the power of suggestion to induce changes in the thoughts, feelings, sensations, perceptions, or behavior of a subject. It has been used most successfully for the control of pain. The three main theories proposed to explain hypnosis are the sociocognitive theory, the neodissociation theory, and the theory of dissociated control.

4.17 What is the connection between altered states of consciousness and culture? p. 140

Practices in many cultures allow individuals to deliberately induce altered states, often as part of tribal ceremonies or religious rituals.

Psychoactive Drugs p. 141

4.18 How do drugs affect the brain's neurotransmitter system? p. 141

Psychoactive drugs increase the availability of dopamine in the nucleus accumbens. Beyond that, each drug has a unique influence on a specific neurotransmitter or group of neurotransmitters.

4.19 What are some risk and protective factors for substance abuse? p. 142

Risk factors for substance abuse include craving for the drug, genetics, impulsivity, association with drug-using peers, family violence, and sexual abuse. Age is a risk factor: The younger a teen is when he or she first uses drugs, the more likely he or she is to abuse them. Protective factors include parental support, behavioral coping skills, academic and social competence, and traditional religious beliefs. Cultural background may also have a protective effect.

4.20 What is the difference between physical and psychological drug dependence? p. 144

With physical drug dependence, the user develops a drug tolerance, and so larger and larger doses of the drug are needed to get the same effect or high. Withdrawal symptoms appear when the drug is discontinued and disappear when the drug is taken again. Psychological drug dependence involves an intense craving for the drug's pleasurable effects.

4.21 What are the effects of stimulants, depressants, and hallucinogens on behavior? p. 146

Stimulants (amphetamines, cocaine, caffeine, and nicotine) speed up activity in the central nervous system, suppress appetite, and make a person feel more awake, alert, and energetic. Depressants decrease activity in the central nervous system, slow down bodily functions, and reduce sensitivity to outside stimulation. Depressants include sedative-hypnotics (alcohol, barbiturates, and minor tranquilizers) and narcotics (opiates such as opium, codeine, morphine, and heroin), which have both pain-relieving and calming effects. Hallucinogens—including marijuana, LSD, and MDMA—can alter and distort perceptions of time and space, alter mood, produce feelings of unreality, and cause hallucinations.

4.22 What are the pros and cons of using herbal remedies? p. 151

Many herbs affect the brain in much the same way as drugs do. Some herbs have been shown to help in the treatment of anxiety, insomnia, depression, attention deficit disorder, premenstrual syndrome, and menopause symptoms. However, effective dosage guidelines have yet to be established, and excessive consumption of herbal supplements can have very serious effects on health.

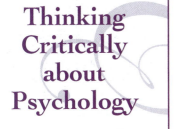

Thinking Critically about Psychology

1. Suppose you have been hired by a sleep clinic to formulate a questionnaire for evaluating patients' sleep habits. List ten questions you would include in your questionnaire.

2. Luanne is a full-time student who wants to find a way to keep up with her class load while working full-time. She decides to work the 11:00 P.M. to 7:00 A.M. shift at a hospital, then attend morning classes. After her classes end at noon, she intends to sleep from 1:00 P.M. until 7:00 P.M., at which time she will get up and study until it is time to leave for work. Based on what you have learned about circadian rhythms in this chapter, what kinds of problems do you think Luanne will encounter in trying to carry out her plan?

3. You have been asked to make a presentation to seventh and eighth graders about the dangers of drugs. What are the most persuasive general arguments you can give to convince them not to start using drugs? What are some convincing, specific arguments against each of these drugs: alcohol, marijuana, cocaine, and MDMA?

Key Terms

activation-synthesis hypothesis of dreaming, p. 134
altered state of consciousness, p. 124
circadian rhythm, p. 124
circadian theory of sleep, p. 128
consciousness, p. 123
depressants, p. 147
drug tolerance, p. 144
hallucinogens, p. 148
hypnosis, p. 138
insomnia, p. 136
latent content, p. 134
lucid dream, p. 134
manifest content, p. 134
meditation (concentrative), p. 137
microsleep, p. 132

narcolepsy, p. 135
narcotics, p. 148
neodissociation theory of hypnosis, p. 139
nightmares, p. 135
NREM dream, p. 133
NREM sleep, p. 128
parasomnias, p. 135
physical drug dependence, p. 144
psychoactive drug, p. 141
psychological drug dependence, p. 145
REM dream, p. 133
REM rebound, p. 130
REM sleep, p. 128
restorative theory of sleep, p. 128
sleep apnea, p. 135

sleep cycle, p. 129
sleep spindles, p. 129
sleep terrors, p. 135
slow-wave sleep, p. 129
sociocognitive theory of hypnosis, p. 139
somnambulism, p. 135
somniloquy, p. 135
Stage 4 sleep, p. 129
stimulants, p. 146
subjective night, p. 126
suprachiasmatic nucleus (SCN), p. 125
theory of dissociated control, p. 139
withdrawal symptoms, p. 145

Chapter 5

Learning

Imagine that you are a cybernetic human who has narrowly escaped from the final battle in an alien war against planet Earth, only to find yourself marooned on a mysterious space station known as *The World of Psychology,* or *WP6E,* as it is more often called. To get back to Earth, you must unlock the secrets of WP6E. You soon learn that WP6E is inhabited by a ruthless alien army made up of killing machines who will stop at nothing to protect their secrets, even if they must resort to destroying every living being in the galaxy, including themselves, by means of a merciless horde of parasites. Your task seems impossible, but you have many weapons at your disposal. Do you think you are up to the challenge?

If you are one of the millions of college students who enjoy playing the video game *Halo,* these words have a familiar ring. Of course, learning psychology isn't among the obstacles that the game's heroes have to overcome. Suppose, though, that your psychology course was structured like a role-playing video game. Do you think you would learn more than you might from a conventional course?

Many educators argue that video game design principles should be incorporated into computer-assisted and online courses (Dickey, 2005; Hitch, 2005; Prensky, 2000; Riegle, 2005). To critics who scoff at the idea of game-based instruction, proponents point out that educational board games, for example, are a staple of both elementary and secondary classrooms. Thus, advocates say, using video games in classrooms represents nothing more than an update of an instructional resource that has been employed by teachers throughout the ages.

One of the most vocal advocates of applying video game design principles to instruction, Professor Rod Riegle of Illinois State University, launched what he claims to be the first role-playing game (RPG) online course in 2000. Riegle's undergraduate education course features an interactive learning environment that includes sights, sounds, and language that are similar to those found in fantasy-based electronic games. Students are cast as "Change Agents" who must do battle against "Status Quo," a fictional character who represents forces in education that oppose new technologies and methods of instruction. Assignments consist of four hierarchical quests that require mastery of progressively difficult concepts and technological skills. When each quest is completed to Riegle's satisfaction, he awards students a title. "Future Lords" are students who have completed Quest 1 and "Hidden Masters" are those who have finished Quest 2. Those who have completed Quest 3 are known as "Infonauts," and their class-

mates who have finished Quest 4 are called "CyberGuides." (You can take a guest tour of Dr. Riegle's course at http://www.coe.ilstu.edu/rpriegle/eaf228/.)

Professor Riegle's course is very popular among students at Illinois State University. However, before other educators adopt Riegle's strategies, most of them want to know how game-based instruction affects students' learning. Experiments carried out by Richard Mayer, an educational psychologist at the University of California at Santa Barbara who has studied the effects of media on learning for more than 20 years, can provide some hints. Mayer's studies suggest that a game-based learning environment such as Riegle's RPG course could be quite effective if the instructor takes care to ensure that the structure of the course itself does not distract students from the content that they are expected to learn (Harp & Mayer, 1998; Mayer, Heiser, & Lonn, 2001; Moreno, Mayer, Spires, & Lester, 2001). Research also indicates that instructors must consider the nature of the subject matter they teach. For some kinds of content, particularly complex scientific principles, Mayer's studies show that conventional strategies (e.g., lectures and demonstrations) are more effective than a game-based approach (Mayer, Hegarty, Mayer, & Campbell, 2005).

When applying Mayer's well-designed experimental studies to questions about game-based instruction in college courses, however, we must remember that the behavior of research participants in laboratory studies may tell us little, if anything, about students' behavior outside the laboratory. As every teacher knows, there is no instructional strategy that can overcome lack of student engagement. Unless students participate in class and complete their assignments, they are unlikely to learn much of anything. Thus, the strongest argument in favor of game-based instruction is its potential for enhancing student engagement (Dickey, 2005). To understand how a course that is structured like a video game might increase student engagement, we must understand why video games are engaging. Here's how the principles of learning that you will read about in this chapter can be used to explain how video games attract and hold players' interest:

- *Learning through association of stimuli:* The cues associated with games—their names, images, and sounds—trigger the emotions players experience while playing them, a set of feelings that are implied when we use the word "fun."
- *Learning through rewards:* With every new game, players experience both success and failure, and the consequences of their actions are immediate. Rewards of this kind exert a powerful influence on future behavior.
- *Learning through discovery:* The "Aha!" experiences that happen when players suddenly realize how to predict the appearance of an obstacle, learn how to escape from a trap, or find a shortcut from one level to the next have an important role in the "fun" experience of playing a video game.
- *Learning through exploration:* Whether players win or lose, each time they play a game, they become more familiar

with its features. This knowledge helps them develop and execute effective strategies.

- *Learning through observation:* Playing video games with friends is yet another source of learning that keeps players coming back for more. Internet sites and magazines devoted to game-playing strategies are also important sources of observational learning. A possible downside of this principle is that players may imitate risky behaviors exhibited by a game's characters (e.g., reckless driving).

Applying learning principles to explain why video games are engaging calls attention to the practical value of psychological research. However, be forewarned that you will read about many experiments in this chapter that seem to be far removed from everyday learning experiences. Remember, though, that the goal of psychologists is to identify general principles that explain and predict behavior across a variety of situations. Thus, the principles in this chapter can be used to explain diverse learned behaviors—from those exhibited by maze-running laboratory rats to those of the 48% of college students who admit that they sometimes play video games when they should be studying and the 30% or so who say that they even play games while in class (Jones, 2003).

Psychologists define **learning** as a relatively permanent change in behavior, knowledge, capability, or attitude that is acquired through experience and cannot be attributed to illness, injury, or maturation. Several parts of this definition warrant further explanation. First, defining learning as a "relatively permanent change" excludes temporary changes that could result from illness, fatigue, or fluctuations in mood. Second, limiting learning to changes that are "acquired through experience" excludes some readily observable changes in behavior that occur as a result of brain injuries or certain diseases. Also, certain observable changes that occur as individuals grow and mature have nothing to do with learning. For example, technically speaking, infants do not *learn* to crawl or walk. Basic motor skills and the maturational plan that governs their development are a part of the genetically programmed behavioral repertoire of every species. The first kind of learning we'll consider is classical conditioning.

Classical Conditioning: The Original View

Why do images of Adolf Hitler, the mere mention of the IRS, and the sight of an American flag waving in a gentle breeze evoke strong emotional responses? Each stirs up our emotions because it carries certain associations: Hitler with evil, the IRS with paying taxes, and the American flag with national pride. How do such associations occur?

learning A relatively permanent change in behavior, knowledge, capability, or attitude that is acquired through experience and cannot be attributed to illness, injury, or maturation.

Classical conditioning is a type of learning through which an organism learns to associate one stimulus with another. A **stimulus** (the plural is *stimuli*) is any event or object in the environment to which an organism responds. People's lives are profoundly influenced by the associations learned through classical conditioning, which is sometimes referred to as *respondent conditioning*, or *Pavlovian conditioning*.

Pavlov and Classical Conditioning

5.1 What kind of learning did Pavlov discover?

Ivan Pavlov (1849–1936) organized and directed research in physiology at the Institute of Experimental Medicine in St. Petersburg, Russia, from 1891 until his death 45 years later. There, he conducted his classic experiments on the physiology of digestion, which won him a Nobel Prize in 1904—the first time a Russian received this honor.

Pavlov's contribution to psychology came about quite by accident. To conduct his study of the salivary response in dogs, Pavlov made a small incision in the side of each dog's mouth. Then he attached a tube so that the flow of saliva could be diverted from inside the animal's mouth, through the tube, and into a container, where the saliva was collected and measured. Pavlov's purpose was to collect the saliva that the dogs would secrete naturally in response to food placed inside the mouth. But he noticed that, in many cases, the dogs would begin to salivate even before the food was presented. Pavlov observed drops of saliva collecting in the containers when the dogs heard the footsteps of the laboratory assistants coming to feed them. He observed saliva collecting when the dogs heard their food dishes rattling, saw the attendant who fed them, or spotted their food. How could an involuntary response such as salivation come to be associated with the sights and sounds involved in feeding? Pavlov spent the rest of his life studying this question. The type of learning he studied is known today as classical conditioning.

Just how meticulous a researcher Pavlov was is reflected in this description of the laboratory he planned and built in St. Petersburg more than a century ago:

> The windows were covered with extra thick sheets of glass; each room had double steel doors which sealed hermetically when closed; and the steel girders which supported the floors were embedded in sand. A deep moat filled with straw encircled the building. Thus, vibration, noise, temperature extremes, odors, even drafts were eliminated. Nothing could influence the animals except the conditioning stimuli to which they were exposed. (Schultz, 1975, pp. 187–188)

classical conditioning A type of learning through which an organism learns to associate one stimulus with another.

stimulus (STIM-yu-lus) Any event or object in the environment to which an organism responds; plural is *stimuli*.

▶ Ivan Pavlov (1849–1936) earned fame by studying the conditioned reflex in dogs.

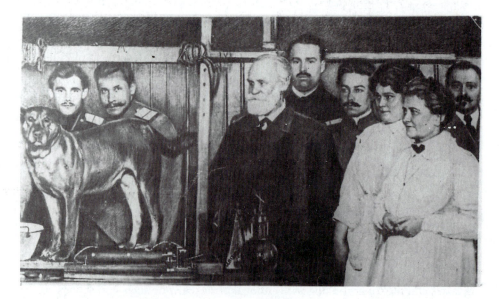

The dogs were isolated inside soundproof cubicles and placed in harnesses to restrain their movements. From an adjoining cubicle, an experimenter observed the dogs through a one-way mirror. Food and other stimuli were presented, and the flow of saliva measured by remote control (see **Figure 5.1**). What did Pavlov and his colleagues learn?

The Process of Classical Conditioning

Classical conditioning involves several components. It begins with some kind of built-in connection between a stimulus and a response.

5.2 How is classical conditioning accomplished?

The Reflex.   A **reflex** is an involuntary response to a particular stimulus. Two examples are salivation in response to food placed in the mouth and the eyeblink response to a puff of air (Green & Woodruff-Pak, 2000). There are two kinds of reflexes: conditioned and unconditioned. Think of the term *conditioned* as meaning "learned" and the term *unconditioned* as meaning "unlearned." Salivation in response to food is an unconditioned reflex because it is an inborn, automatic, unlearned response to a particular stimulus.

When Pavlov observed that his dogs would salivate at the sight of food or the sound of rattling dishes, he realized that this salivation reflex was the result of learning. He called these learned involuntary responses **conditioned reflexes.**

The Conditioned and Unconditioned Stimulus and Response.   Pavlov (1927/1960) used tones, bells, buzzers, lights, geometric shapes, electric shocks, and metronomes in his conditioning experiments. In a typical experiment, food powder was placed in the dog's mouth, causing salivation. Because dogs do not need to be conditioned

Figure 5.1 The Experimental Apparatus Used in Pavlov's Classical Conditioning Studies

In Pavlov's classical conditioning studies, the dog was restrained in a harness in the cubicle and isolated from all distractions. An experimenter observed the dog through a one-way mirror and, by remote control, presented the dog with food and other conditioning stimuli. A tube carried the saliva from the dog's mouth to a container where it was measured.

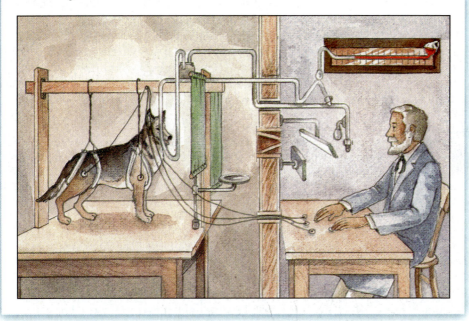

reflex   An involuntary response to a particular stimulus, such as the eyeblink response to a puff of air or salivation when food is placed in the mouth.

conditioned reflex   A learned involuntary response.

unconditioned response (UR)   A response that is elicited by an unconditioned stimulus without prior learning.

to salivate to food, salivation to food is an unlearned response, or **unconditioned response (UR).** Any stimulus, such as food, that without prior learning will automatically elicit, or bring forth, an unconditioned response is called an **unconditioned stimulus (US).**

Following is a list of some common unconditioned reflexes, showing their two components: the unconditioned stimulus and the unconditioned response.

Unconditioned Reflexes

Unconditioned Stimulus (US)	Unconditioned Response (UR)
food	salivation
loud noise	startle response
light in eye	contraction of pupil
puff of air in eye	eyeblink response

Pavlov demonstrated that dogs could be conditioned to salivate to a variety of stimuli never before associated with food, as shown in **Figure 5.2** (on page 163). During the conditioning process, the researcher would present a neutral stimulus such as a musical tone shortly before placing food powder in the dog's mouth. The food powder would cause the dog to salivate. Pavlov found that after the tone and the food were paired many times, usually 20 or more, the tone alone would elicit salivation (Pavlov, 1927/1960, p. 385). Pavlov called the tone the learned stimulus, or **conditioned stimulus (CS),** and salivation to the tone the learned response, or **conditioned response (CR).**

Higher-Order Conditioning. Once a connection between a conditioned stimulus and a conditioned response has been learned, new stimuli can be introduced by pairing them with the conditioned stimulus. This process creates a series of signals and is known as **higher-order conditioning.** The sequence of events that occurs when you go to a laboratory for a blood test provides a good example of higher-order conditioning. First, you sit in a chair next to a table on which are arranged materials such as needles, syringes, and such. Next, some kind of constricting device is tied around your arm, and the nurse or technician pats on the surface of your skin until a vein becomes visible. Each step in the sequence tells you that the unavoidable "stick" of the needle and the pain, which is largely the result of reflexive muscle tension, is coming. The stick itself is the unconditioned stimulus, to which you reflexively respond. But all the steps that precede it are conditioned stimuli that cause you to anticipate the pain of the stick itself. And with each successive step, a conditioned response occurs, as your muscles respond to your anxiety by contracting a bit more in anticipation of the stick. As you may have inferred, higher order conditioning can occur in any situation in which the same sequence of stimuli precedes exposure to a stimulus to which you respond reflexively. For instance, you may begin to shiver, a reflexive response to exposure to frigid temperatures, as you put on layers of clothing, your heavy winter coat, and your boots before going out on a snowy day. Can you think of other examples of stimuli sequences that precede reflexive responses?

Changing Conditioned Responses

After conditioning an animal to salivate to a tone, what would happen if you continued to sound the tone but no longer paired it with food? What would happen if you sounded a tone of a higher or lower pitch than the one that was used to initially condition the animal?

Extinction and Spontaneous Recovery. Pavlov studied the first of these questions by withholding food from the dogs after sounding the tone to which they had been conditioned to salivate. He found that without the food, salivation to the tone became weaker and weaker and then finally disappeared altogether—a process known as **extinction.** After the response had been extinguished, Pavlov allowed the dog to rest for 20 minutes and then brought it back to the laboratory. He found that the dog would again salivate to the tone. Pavlov called this recurrence

---

unconditioned stimulus (US)
A stimulus that elicits a specific unconditioned response without prior learning.

conditioned stimulus (CS) A neutral stimulus that, after repeated pairing with an unconditioned stimulus, becomes associated with it and elicits a conditioned response.

conditioned response (CR) The learned response that comes to be elicited by a conditioned stimulus as a result of its repeated pairing with an unconditioned stimulus.

higher-order conditioning
Conditioning that occurs when conditioned stimuli are linked together to form a series of signals.

5.3 What kinds of changes in stimuli and learning conditions lead to changes in conditioned responses?

extinction In classical conditioning, the weakening and eventual disappearance of the conditioned response as a result of repeated presentation of the conditioned stimulus without the unconditioned stimulus.

Figure 5.2   Classically Conditioning a Salivation Response

A neutral stimulus (a tone) elicits no salivation until it is repeatedly paired with the unconditioned stimulus (food). After many pairings, the neutral stimulus (now called the conditioned stimulus) alone produces salivation. Classical conditioning has occurred.

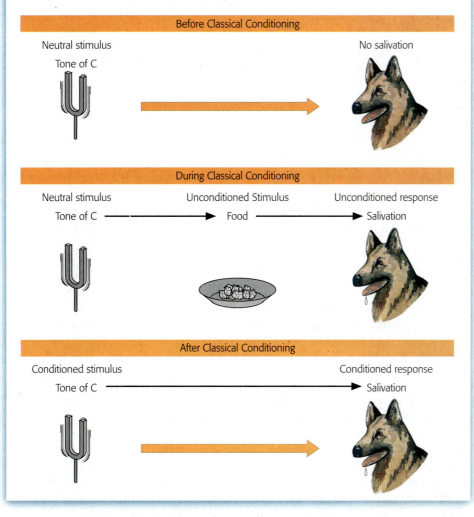

spontaneous recovery. But the spontaneously recovered response was weaker and shorter in duration than the original conditioned response. **Figure 5.3** shows the processes of extinction and spontaneous recovery.

Some research indicates that extinction is context-specific (Bouton, 1993; Bouton & Ricker, 1994). When a conditioned response is extinguished in one setting, it can still be elicited in other settings in which extinction training has not occurred. Pavlov did not discover this because his experiments were always conducted in the same setting.

Generalization and Discrimination.   Assume that you have conditioned a dog to salivate when it hears the tone middle C played on the piano. Would it also salivate if you played B or D? Pavlov found that a tone similar to the original conditioned stimulus would produce the conditioned response (salivation), a phenomenon called **generalization.** But the salivation decreased the farther the tone was from the original conditioned stimulus, until the tone became so different that the dog would not salivate at all.

Pavlov was able to demonstrate generalization using other senses, such as touch. He attached a small vibrator to a dog's thigh and conditioned the dog to salivate

spontaneous recovery   The reappearance of an extinguished response (in a weaker form) when an organism is exposed to the original conditioned stimulus following a rest period.

generalization   In classical conditioning, the tendency to make a conditioned response to a stimulus that is similar to the original conditioned stimulus.

▲ Smell and taste are closely associated because the smell of a particular food is a signal for its taste and the physical sensations associated with eating it. Consequently, a food's odor is a conditioned stimulus that elicits the same emotional and even physiological responses as the food itself. In fact, seeing a photo of someone smelling a particularly pungent food may also act as a conditioned stimulus. When you look at this photo, can you imagine how the peach smells? When you imagine the smell, do you recall the food's taste and texture? Are you starting to get hungry?

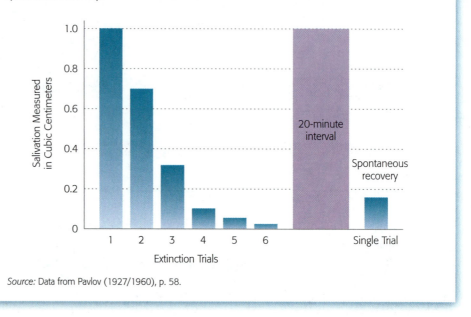

Figure 5.3 Extinction of a Classically Conditioned Response

When a classically conditioned stimulus (a tone) was presented in a series of trials without the unconditioned stimulus (food), Pavlov's dogs salivated less and less until there was virtually no salivation. But after a 20-minute rest, one sound of the tone caused the conditioned response to reappear in a weakened form (producing only a small amount of salivation), a phenomenon Pavlov called *spontaneous recovery.*

Source: Data from Pavlov (1927/1960), p. 58.

when the thigh was stimulated. Once generalization was established, salivation also occurred when other parts of the dog's body were stimulated. But the farther away the point of stimulation was from the thigh, the weaker the salivation response became (see **Figure 5.4**).

It is easy to see the value of generalization in daily life. For instance, if you enjoyed being in school as a child, you probably feel more positively about your college experiences than your classmates who enjoyed school less. Because of generalization, we do not need to learn a conditioned response to every stimulus that may differ only slightly from an original one. Rather, we learn to approach or avoid a range of stimuli similar to the one that produced the original conditioned response.

Let's return to the example of a dog being conditioned to a musical tone to trace the process of **discrimination,** the learned ability to distinguish between similar stimuli so that the conditioned response occurs only to the original conditioned stimuli but not to similar stimuli.

Step 1. The dog is conditioned to salivate in response to the tone C.

Step 2. Generalization occurs, and the dog salivates to a range of musical tones above and below C. The dog salivates less and less as the tone moves away from C.

Step 3. The original tone C is repeatedly paired with food. Neighboring tones are also sounded, but they are not followed by food. The dog is being conditioned to discriminate. Gradually, the salivation response to the neighboring tones (A, B, D, and E) is extinguished, whereas salivation to the original tone C is strengthened.

Like generalization, discrimination has survival value. Discriminating between the odors of fresh and spoiled milk will spare you an upset stomach. Discriminating between a rattlesnake and a garter snake could save your life.

discrimination The learned ability to distinguish between similar stimuli so that the conditioned response occurs only to the original conditioned stimulus but not to similar stimuli.

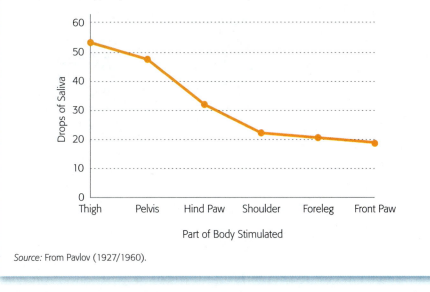

Figure 5.4 Generalization of a Conditioned Response

Pavlov attached small vibrators to different parts of a dog's body. After conditioning salivation to stimulation of the dog's thigh, he stimulated other parts of the dog's body. Due to generalization, the salivation also occurred when other body parts were stimulated. But the farther away from the thigh the stimulus was applied, the weaker the salivation response.

Source: From Pavlov (1927/1960).

John Watson and Emotional Conditioning

In 1919, John Watson (1878–1958) and his assistant, Rosalie Rayner, conducted a now-famous study to prove that fear could be classically conditioned. The subject of the study, known as Little Albert, was a healthy and emotionally stable 11-month-old infant. When tested, he showed no fear except of the loud noise Watson made by striking a hammer against a steel bar near his head.

In the laboratory, Rayner presented Little Albert with a white rat. As Albert reached for the rat, Watson struck the steel bar with a hammer just behind Albert's head. This procedure was repeated, and Albert "jumped violently, fell forward and began to whimper" (Watson & Rayner, 1920, p. 4). A week later, Watson continued the experiment, pairing the rat with the loud noise five more times. Then, at the sight of the white rat alone, Albert began to cry.

When Albert returned to the laboratory 5 days later, the fear had generalized to a rabbit and, somewhat less, to a dog, a seal coat, Watson's hair, and a Santa Claus mask (see **Figure 5.5**). After 30 days, Albert made his final visit to the laboratory. His fears were still evident, although they were somewhat less intense. Watson concluded that conditioned fears "persist and modify personality throughout life" (Watson & Rayner, 1920, p. 12).

Although Watson had formulated techniques for removing conditioned fears, Albert moved out of the city before they could be tried on him. Since Watson apparently knew that Albert would be moving away before these fear-removal techniques could be applied, he clearly showed a disregard for the child's welfare. The American Psychological Association now has strict ethical standards for the use of human and animal participants in research experiments and would not sanction an experiment such as Watson's.

Some of Watson's ideas for removing fears laid the groundwork for certain behavior therapies used today. Three years after his experiment with Little Albert, Watson and a colleague, Mary Cover Jones (1924), found 3-year-old Peter, who, like Albert, was afraid of white rats. He was also afraid of rabbits, a fur coat, feathers, cotton, and a fur rug. Peter's fear of the rabbit was his strongest fear, and this became the target of Watson's fear-removal techniques. Peter was brought into the laboratory, seated in a high chair, and given candy to eat. A white rabbit in a wire cage was brought into the

5.4 How did Watson demonstrate that fear could be classically conditioned?

Figure 5.5 The Conditioned Fear Response

Little Albert's fear of a white rat was a conditioned response that was generalized to other stimuli, including a rabbit and, to a lesser extent, a Santa Claus mask.

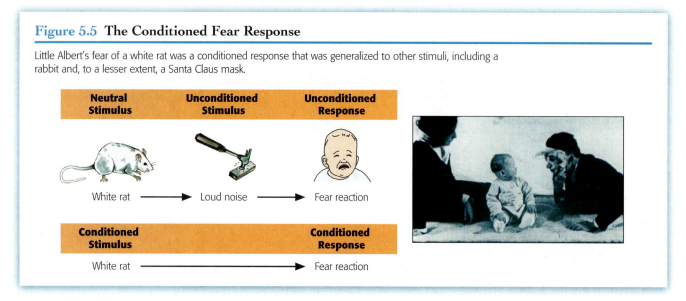

room but kept far enough away from Peter that it would not upset him. Over the course of 38 therapy sessions, the rabbit was brought closer and closer to Peter, who continued to enjoy his candy. Occasionally, some of Peter's friends were brought in to play with the rabbit at a safe distance from Peter so that he could see firsthand that the rabbit did no harm. Toward the end of Peter's therapy, the rabbit was taken out of the cage and eventually put in Peter's lap. By the final session, Peter had grown fond of the rabbit. What is more, he had lost all fear of the fur coat, cotton, and feathers, and he could tolerate the white rats and the fur rug.

So far, we have considered classical conditioning primarily in relation to Pavlov's dogs and Watson's human subjects. How is classical conditioning viewed today?

Remember It   Classical Conditioning: The Original View

1. Classical conditioning was discovered by _____.

2. A dog's salivation in response to a musical tone is a(n) _____ response.

3. The weakening of a conditioned response that occurs when a conditioned stimulus is presented without the unconditioned stimulus is called _____.

4. Five-year-old Mia was bitten by her grandmother's labrador retriever. She won't go near that dog but seems to have no fear of other dogs, even other labradors. Her behavior is best explained by the principle of _____.

5. For _____ conditioning to occur, conditioned stimuli are linked together to form a series of signals.

6. In Watson's experiment with Little Albert, the white rat was the _____ stimulus, and Albert's crying when the hammer struck the steel bar was the _____ response.

7. Albert's fear of the white rat transferred to a rabbit, a dog, a fur coat, and a mask, in a learning process known as _____.

Answers: 1. Pavlov; 2. conditioned; 3. extinction; 4. discrimination; 5. higher-order; 6. conditioned, unconditioned; 7. generalization

Classical Conditioning: The Contemporary View

Which aspect of the classical conditioning process is most important? Pavlov believed that the critical element in classical conditioning was the repeated pairing of the conditioned stimulus and the unconditioned stimulus, with only a brief interval between the two. Beginning in the late 1960s, though, researchers began to discover exceptions to some of the general principles Pavlov had identified.

The Cognitive Perspective

Robert Rescorla (1967, 1968, 1988; Rescorla & Wagner, 1972) is largely responsible for changing how psychologists view classical conditioning. Rescorla was able to demonstrate that the critical element in classical conditioning is not the repeated pairing of the conditioned stimulus and the unconditioned stimulus. Rather, the important factor is whether the conditioned stimulus provides information that enables the organism to reliably *predict* the occurrence of the unconditioned stimulus. How was Rescorla able to prove that prediction is the critical element?

Using rats as his subjects, Rescorla used a tone as the conditioned stimulus and a shock as the unconditioned stimulus. For one group of rats, the tone and shock were paired 20 times—the shock always occurred during the tone. The other group of rats also received a shock 20 times while the tone was sounding, but this group also received 20 shocks that were not paired with the tone. If the only critical element in classical conditioning were the number of pairings of the conditioned stimulus and the unconditioned stimulus, both groups of rats should have developed a conditioned fear response to the tone, because both groups experienced exactly the same number of pairings of tone and shock. But this was not the case. Only the first group, for which the tone was a reliable predictor of the shock, developed the conditioned fear response to the tone. The second group showed little evidence of conditioning, because the shock was just as likely to occur without the tone as with it. In other words, for this group, the tone provided no additional information about the shock.

But what about Pavlov's belief that almost any neutral stimulus could serve as a conditioned stimulus? Later research revealed that organisms' biological predispositions can limit the associations they can form through classical conditioning.

The way your body learns to respond to distinctive food flavors provides an everyday example that illustrates Rescorla's work. For instance, researchers have found that the pancreas quickly adapts to food cues (e.g., Stockhorst et al., 1999). Most of the time, the presence of a sweet taste on the tongue (a CS) reliably predicts a rise in blood sugar (a UCS). As a result of the repeated pairing of the sweet taste and the ensuing rise in blood sugar, the pancreas "learns" to pump out insulin in response to the sweet taste (a CR) rather than waiting for the actual rise in blood sugar to occur (a UCR). But what happens when you "confuse" the pancreas by consuming artificial sweeteners, that is, sweet tastes that do not predict a rise in blood sugar? Extinction occurs because the sweet taste has lost its predictive meaning to your pancreas. As a result, your pancreas will excrete insulin only in response to actual rises in blood sugar (the original UCS) rather than immediately upon the tongue's sensation of a sweet taste.

▲ The sweet taste of sugary treats conditions the pancreas to release insulin before an actual rise in blood sugar occurs. In keeping with Rescorla's research, this happens because the sweet taste reliably predicts the rise in blood sugar. Such conditioning may be extinguished when we consume artificial sweeteners. Why?

Biological Predispositions

Remember that Watson conditioned Little Albert to fear the white rat by pairing the presence of the rat with the loud noise of a hammer striking against a steel bar. Do you think Watson could just as easily have conditioned a fear response to a flower or a piece of ribbon? Probably not. Research has shown that humans are more easily conditioned to fear stimuli, such as snakes, that can have very real negative effects on their well-being (Ohman & Mineka, 2003). Moreover, fear of snakes and other potentially threatening animals is just as common in apes and monkeys as in humans, suggesting a biological predisposition to develop these fearful responses.

5.5 According to Rescorla, what is the critical element in classical conditioning?

5.6 What did Garcia and Koelling discover about classical conditioning?

taste aversion The intense dislike and/or avoidance of a particular food that has been associated with nausea or discomfort.

According to Martin Seligman (1972), most common fears "are related to the survival of the human species through the long course of evolution" (p. 455). Seligman (1970) has suggested that humans and other animals are prepared to associate only certain stimuli with particular consequences. One example of this preparedness is the tendency to develop **taste aversions**—the intense dislike and/or avoidance of particular foods that have been associated with nausea or discomfort.

Experiencing nausea and vomiting after eating a certain food is often enough to condition a long-lasting taste aversion. You may have had some personal experience with this phenomenon if you have ever thrown up after eating spaghetti, chili, or some other food with a very distinctive taste and smell. If so, you know that, for weeks afterward, just the smell of the offending food was sufficient to prompt a wave of nausea. Researchers have found that taste aversions can be classically conditioned when the delay between the conditioned stimulus (food or drink) and the unconditioned stimulus (nausea) is as long as 12 hours.

In a classic study on taste aversion, Garcia and Koelling (1966) exposed rats to a three-way conditioned stimulus: a bright light, a clicking noise, and flavored water. For one group of rats, the unconditioned stimulus was being exposed to either X-rays or lithium chloride, either of which produces nausea and vomiting several hours after exposure; for the other group, the unconditioned stimulus was an electric shock to the feet. The rats that were made ill associated the flavored water with the nausea and avoided it at all times, but they would still drink unflavored water when the bright light and the clicking sound were present. The rats receiving the electric shock continued to prefer the flavored water over unflavored water, but they would not drink at all in the presence of the bright light or the clicking sound. The rats in one group associated nausea only with the flavored water; those in the other group associated electric shock only with the light and the sound.

Garcia and Koelling's research established two exceptions to traditional ideas of classical conditioning. First, the finding that rats formed an association between nausea and flavored water ingested several hours earlier contradicted the principle that the conditioned stimulus must be presented shortly before the unconditioned stimulus. Second, the finding that rats associated electric shock only with noise and light and nausea only with flavored water revealed that animals are apparently biologically predisposed to make certain associations and that associations cannot be readily conditioned between just any two stimuli.

▼ Chemotherapy treatments can result in a conditioned taste aversion, but providing patients with a "scapegoat" target for the taste aversion can help them maintain a proper diet.

Knowledge about conditioned taste aversion is useful in solving other problems as well. Bernstein and others (1982; Bernstein, 1985) devised a technique to help cancer patients avoid developing aversions to desirable foods. A group of cancer patients were given a novel-tasting, maple-flavored ice cream before chemotherapy. The nausea caused by the treatment resulted in a taste aversion to the ice cream. The researchers found that when an unusual or unfamiliar food becomes the "scapegoat," or target for a taste aversion, other foods in the patient's diet may be protected, and the patient will continue to eat them regularly. So, cancer patients should refrain from eating preferred or nutritious foods prior to chemotherapy. Instead, they should be given an unusual-tasting food shortly before treatment. As a result, they are less likely to develop aversions to foods they normally eat and, in turn, are more likely to maintain their body weight during treatment.

Classical Conditioning in Everyday Life

5.7 **What types of everyday responses can be subject to classical conditioning?**

Do certain songs have special meaning because they remind you of a current or past love? Do you find the scent of a particular perfume or after-shave pleasant or unpleasant because it reminds you of a certain person? Many of our emotional responses, whether positive or negative, result from classical conditioning. Clearly, classical conditioning is an important, even essential, component of the array of learning capacities characteristic of humans. Indeed, recent research suggests that the inability to acquire classically conditioned responses may be the first sign of Alzheimer's disease, a sign that appears prior to any memory loss (Woodruff-Pak, 2001).

Fear Responses.   You may have a fear or phobia that was learned through classical conditioning. For example, many people who have had painful dental work develop a dental phobia. Not only do they come to fear the dentist's drill, but they develop anxiety in response to a wide range of stimuli associated with it—the dental chair, the waiting room, even the building where the dentist's office is located. In the conditioning of fear, a conditioned stimulus (CS), such as a tone, is paired with an aversive stimulus (US), such as a foot shock, in a new or unfamiliar environment (context). After just one pairing, an animal exhibits a long-lasting fear of the CS and of the context.

Drug Use.   Through classical conditioning, environmental cues associated with drug use can become conditioned stimuli and later produce the conditioned responses of drug craving (Field & Duka, 2002; London et al., 2000). The conditioned stimuli associated with drugs become powerful, often irresistible forces that lead individuals to seek out and use those substances (Porrino & Lyons, 2000). Consequently, drug counselors strongly urge recovering addicts to avoid any cues (people, places, and things) associated with their past drug use. Relapse is far more common in those who do not avoid such associated environmental cues.

Advertising.   Advertisers seek to classically condition consumers when they show products being used by great-looking models or celebrities or in situations where people are enjoying themselves. Advertisers reason that if the "neutral" product is associated with people, objects, or situations consumers particularly like, in time the product will elicit a similarly positive response. Pavlov found that presenting the tone just before the food was the most efficient way to condition salivation in dogs. Television advertisements, too, are most effective when the products are presented before the beautiful people or situations are shown (van den Hout & Merckelbach, 1991).

The Immune System.   Research indicates that even the immune system is subject to classical conditioning (Ader, 1985; Exton et al., 2000). In the mid-1970s, Robert Ader was conducting an experiment with rats, conditioning them to avoid saccharin-sweetened water. Immediately after drinking the sweet water (which rats consider a treat), the rats were injected with a tasteless drug (cyclophosphamide) that causes severe nausea. The conditioning worked, and from that time on, the rats would not drink the sweet water, with or without the drug. Attempting to reverse the conditioned response, Ader force-fed the sweet water to the rats for many days; later, unexpectedly, many of them died. Ader was puzzled, because the sweet water was in no way lethal. When he checked further into the properties of the tasteless drug, he learned that it suppresses the immune system. A few doses of an immune-suppressing drug paired with sweetened water had produced a conditioned response. As a result, the sweet water alone continued to suppress the immune system, causing the rats to die. Ader and Cohen (1982) successfully repeated the experiment, with strict controls to rule out other explanations. The fact that a neutral stimulus such as sweetened water can produce effects similar to those of an immune-suppressing drug shows how powerful classical conditioning can be.

Bovbjerg and others (1990) found that in some cancer patients undergoing chemotherapy, environmental cues in the treatment setting (context) eventually came to elicit nausea and immune suppression. These were the same conditioned responses that the treatment alone had caused earlier. Other researchers showed that classical conditioning could be used to suppress the immune system in order to prolong the survival of mice heart tissue transplants (Grochowicz et al., 1991). And not only can classically conditioned stimuli suppress the immune system, they can also be used to boost it (Exton et al., 2000; Markovic et al., 1993).

Grow Moore.

got milk?

▲ Classical conditioning has proved to be a highly effective tool for advertisers. Here, a neutral product (milk) is paired with an image of an attractive celebrity.

Factors Influencing Classical Conditioning

5.8 Why doesn't classical conditioning result every time unconditioned and conditioned stimuli occur together?

In summary, four major factors facilitate the acquisition of a classically conditioned response:

1. *How reliably the conditioned stimulus predicts the unconditioned stimulus.* The neutral stimulus must reliably predict the occurrence of the unconditioned stimulus. A tone that is always followed by food will elicit more salivation than one that is followed by food only some of the time. Likewise, the cues associated with a video game that is consistently entertaining will elicit pleasant emotions, and the cues associated with academic subject matter that you dislike will trigger unpleasant ones.

2. *The number of pairings of the conditioned stimulus and the unconditioned stimulus.* In general, the greater the number of pairings, the stronger the conditioned response. But one pairing is all that is needed to classically condition a taste aversion or a strong emotional response to cues associated with some traumatic event, such as an earthquake or rape.

3. *The intensity of the unconditioned stimulus.* If a conditioned stimulus is paired with a very strong unconditioned stimulus, the conditioned response will be stronger and will be acquired more rapidly than if the conditioned stimulus were paired with a weaker unconditioned stimulus (Gormezano, 1984). For example, a life-threatening car crash is more likely than a minor fender-bender to condition you to feel anxious when you are near the location where the accident occurred.

4. *The temporal relationship between the conditioned stimulus and the unconditioned stimulus.* Conditioning takes place fastest if the conditioned stimulus occurs shortly before the unconditioned stimulus. For instance, as a misbehaving child, you probably learned how long it would take your parent to execute a disciplinary action after exhibiting his or her first anger cue (e.g., a louder voice or a distinctive way of saying your name). If the interval was short, you probably learned to respond immediately to the initial anger cue (a CS) in order to avoid the disciplinary action (a UCS).

Remember It   Classical Conditioning: The Contemporary View

1. According to Rescorla, the most critical element in classical conditioning is _____.

2. Garcia and Koelling's research suggests that classical conditioning is influenced by _____.

3. Conditioning of a _____ contradicts the general principle of classical conditioning that the unconditioned stimulus should occur immediately after the conditioned stimulus and the two should be paired repeatedly.

4. In everyday life, _____ and _____ are often acquired through classical conditioning.

5. Classical conditioning can suppress or boost the _____.

Answers: 1. prediction; 2. biological predispositions; 3. taste aversion; 4. fears, phobias; 5. immune system

Operant Conditioning

Understanding the principles of classical conditioning can provide a great deal of insight into human behavior. But is there more to human learning than simply responding reflexively to stimuli? Think about a ringing telephone, for example. Do you respond to this stimulus because it has been paired with a natural stimulus of some kind or because of a consequence you anticipate when you hear it? The work of two psychologists, Edward L. Thorndike and B. F. Skinner, helps answer this question.

Thorndike and the Law of Effect

Have you ever watched a dog learn how to turn over a trash can, or a cat learn how to open a door? If so, you probably observed the animal fail several times before finding just the right physical technique for accomplishing the goal. According to American psychologist Edward Thorndike (1874–1949), **trial-and-error learning** is the basis of most behavioral changes. Based on his observations of animal behavior, Thorndike formulated several laws of learning, the most important being the law of effect (Thorndike, 1911/1970). The **law of effect** states that the consequence, or effect, of a response will determine whether the tendency to respond in the same way in the future will be strengthened or weakened. Responses closely followed by satisfying consequences are more likely to be repeated. Thorndike (1898) insisted that it was "unnecessary to invoke reasoning" to explain how the learning took place.

In Thorndike's best-known experiments, a hungry cat was placed in a wooden box with slats, which was called a *puzzle box.* The box was designed so that the animal had to manipulate a simple mechanism—pressing a pedal or pulling down a loop—to escape and claim a food reward that lay just outside the box. The cat would first try to squeeze through the slats; when these attempts failed, it would scratch, bite, and claw the inside of the box. In time, the cat would accidentally trip the mechanism, which would open the door. Each time, after winning freedom and claiming the food reward, the cat was returned to the box. After many trials, the cat learned to open the door almost immediately after being placed in the box.

Thorndike's law of effect was the conceptual starting point for B. F. Skinner's work in operant conditioning.

The Process of Operant Conditioning

Most people in the United States know something about B. F. Skinner (1904–1990) because his ideas about learning have strongly influenced American education, parenting practices, and approaches to business management. Skinner's research, and his explanation of his findings, suggested that behavior change, or learning, often results from **operant conditioning,** a type of learning in which the frequency of a voluntary behavior changes as the result of the consequences that the behavior produces. In his research, Skinner demonstrated operant conditioning by deliberately manipulating the consequences that occurred when animals carried out certain behaviors. For example, laboratory rats learned to press levers to get food because Skinner administered food to them whenever they did so. Thus, Skinner concluded that behavior that is reinforced—that is, followed by rewarding consequences—tends to be repeated. A **reinforcer** is anything that strengthens or increases the probability of the response it follows.

Operant conditioning permits the learning of a broad range of new responses. For example, humans can learn to modify their brain-wave patterns through operant conditioning if they are given immediate positive reinforcement for the brain-wave changes that show the desired direction. Such operantly conditioned changes can result in better performance on motor tasks and faster responses on a variety of cognitive tasks (Pulvermüller et al., 2000).

Shaping Behavior.   Have you ever attended a show that featured trained animals? Trainers use a process called **shaping,** in which animals learn their tricks in small steps rather than all at once. B. F. Skinner (1904–1990) demonstrated that shaping is particularly effective in conditioning complex behaviors. With shaping, rather than waiting for the desired response to occur and then reinforcing it, a researcher (or parent or animal trainer) reinforces any movement in the direction of the desired response, thereby gradually guiding the responses toward the ultimate goal.

Skinner designed a soundproof apparatus, commonly called a **Skinner box,** with which he conducted his experiments in operant conditioning. One type of box is equipped with a lever, or bar, that a rat presses to gain a reward of food pellets or

5.9 What did Thorndike conclude about learning by watching cats try to escape from his puzzle box?

trial-and-error learning Learning that occurs when a response is associated with a successful solution to a problem after a number of unsuccessful responses.

law of effect   One of Thorndike's laws of learning, which states that the consequence, or effect, of a response will determine whether the tendency to respond in the same way in the future will be strengthened or weakened.

5.10 What is the process by which behaviors are acquired through operant conditioning?

▲ B. F. Skinner shapes a rat's bar-pressing behavior in a Skinner box.

water from a dispenser. A record of the animal's bar pressing is registered on a device called a *cumulative recorder*, also invented by Skinner. Through the use of shaping, a rat in a Skinner box is conditioned to press a bar for rewards. It may be rewarded first for simply turning toward the bar. The next reward comes only when the rat moves closer to the bar. Each step closer to the bar is rewarded. Next, the rat must touch the bar to receive a reward; finally, it is rewarded only when it presses the bar.

Shaping—rewarding **successive approximations** of the desired response—has been used effectively to condition complex behaviors in people as well as other animals. Parents may use shaping to help their children develop good table manners, praising them each time they show an improvement. Teachers often use shaping with disruptive children, reinforcing them at first for very short periods of good behavior and then gradually expecting them to work productively for longer and longer periods. Through shaping, circus animals have learned to perform a wide range of amazing feats, and pigeons have learned to bowl and play Ping-Pong.

Of course, the motive of the shaper is very different from that of the person or animal whose behavior is being shaped. The shaper seeks to change another's behavior by controlling its consequences. The motive of the person or animal whose behavior is being shaped is to gain rewards or avoid unwanted consequences.

Extinction.   What happens when reinforcement is no longer available? In operant conditioning, **extinction** occurs when reinforcers are withheld. A rat in a Skinner box will eventually stop pressing a bar when it is no longer rewarded with food pellets.

In humans and other animals, the withholding of reinforcement can lead to frustration or even rage. Consider a child having a temper tantrum. If whining and loud demands do not bring the reinforcer, the child may progress to kicking and screaming. If a vending machine takes your coins but fails to deliver candy or soda, you might shake the machine or even kick it before giving up. When we don't get something we expect, it makes us angry.

The process of *spontaneous recovery*, which we discussed in relation to classical conditioning, also occurs in operant conditioning. A rat whose bar pressing has been extinguished may again press the bar a few times when it is returned to the Skinner box after a period of rest.

Generalization and Discrimination.   Skinner conducted many of his experiments with pigeons placed in a specially designed Skinner box. The box contained small illuminated disks that the pigeons could peck to receive bits of grain from a food tray. Skinner found that **generalization** occurs in operant conditioning, just as in classical conditioning. A pigeon reinforced for pecking at a yellow disk is likely to peck at another disk similar in color. The less similar a disk is to the original color, the lower the rate of pecking will be.

Discrimination in operant conditioning involves learning to distinguish between a stimulus that has been reinforced and other stimuli that may be very similar. Discrimination develops when the response to the original stimulus is reinforced but responses to similar stimuli are not reinforced. For example, to encourage discrimination, a researcher would reinforce the pigeon for pecking at the yellow disk but not for pecking at the orange or red disk. Pigeons have even been conditioned to discriminate between a cubist-style Picasso painting and a Monet with 90% accuracy. However, they weren't able to tell a Renoir from a Cézanne ("Psychologists' pigeons . . . ," 1995).

Certain cues come to be associated with reinforcement or punishment. For example, children are more likely to ask their parents for a treat when the parents are smiling than when they are frowning. A stimulus that signals whether a certain response or behavior is likely to be rewarded, ignored, or punished is called a **discriminitive stimulus.** If a pigeon's peck at a lighted disk results in a reward but a peck at an unlighted disk does not, the pigeon will soon be pecking exclusively at the lighted disk. The presence or absence of the discriminative stimulus—in this case, the lighted disk—will control whether the pecking takes place.

Why do children sometimes misbehave with a grandparent but not with a parent, or make one teacher's life miserable yet be model students for another? The children

---

operant conditioning   A type of learning in which the frequency of a voluntary behavior changes because of the consequences that the behavior produces.

reinforcer   Anything that follows a response and strengthens it or increases the probability that it will occur.

shaping   An operant conditioning technique that consists of gradually molding a desired behavior (response) by reinforcing any movement in the direction of the desired response, thereby gradually guiding the responses toward the ultimate goal.

Skinner box   A soundproof chamber with a device for delivering food to an animal subject; used in operant conditioning experiments.

successive approximations   A series of gradual steps, each of which is more similar to the final desired response.

extinction   In operant conditioning, the weakening and eventual disappearance of the conditioned response as a result of the withholding of reinforcement.

generalization   In operant conditioning, the tendency to make the learned response to a stimulus similar to that for which the response was originally reinforced.

discriminative stimulus   A stimulus that signals whether a certain response or behavior is likely to be rewarded, ignored, or punished.

may have learned that in the presence of some people (the discriminative stimuli), their misbehavior will almost certainly lead to punishment, but in the presence of certain other people, it may even be rewarded.

Reinforcement

5.11 What are the effects of positive reinforcement and negative reinforcement?

How did you learn the correct sequence of behaviors involved in using an ATM machine? Simple—a single mistake in the sequence will prevent you from getting your money, so you learn to do it correctly. What about paying bills on time? Doesn't prompt payment allow you to avoid those steep late-payment penalties? In each case, your behavior is reinforced, but in a different way.

Positive and Negative Reinforcement. **Reinforcement** is a key concept in operant conditioning and may be defined as an increase in behavior that occurs as a result of a consequence. Another way to say this is that reinforcement involves learning or increasing the frequency of a behavior in order to make something happen. Reinforcement can be either positive or negative. These terms are used in their mathematical sense in operant conditioning. Thus, *positive* is equivalent to *added*, and *negative* is equivalent to *subtracted* or *removed*.

Combining the two concepts you have just learned yields the definition of **positive reinforcement:** an increase in behavior that results from an added consequence. For instance, performing the correct sequence of behaviors at the ATM machine is the only way to obtain money. Thus, you are careful to get the sequence right (increased behavior) because doing so will cause the machine to dispense the money (added consequence) that you need. Here are a few more examples of positive reinforcement:

- Rat learns to press a lever (increased behavior) to obtain a food pellet (added consequence)
- College student studies more often (increased behavior) after getting an A on an exam for which she studied more than usual (added consequence)
- Person buys more lottery tickets (increased behavior) after hitting a $100 jackpot (added consequence)

You may have already predicted the definition of **negative reinforcement** because it follows logically from the definitions of its constituent terms (negative + reinforcement). It simply means an increase in behavior (reinforcement) that is brought about by the subtraction of something that is typically unpleasant. Stated differently, negative reinforcement involves learning or increasing a behavior in order to make something unpleasant go away. For instance, you take cough medicine (learned behavior) to make your coughing go away (removed consequence). Here are a few more examples:

- Rat learns to press a lever (increased behavior) to turn off an annoying stimulus such as a loud buzzer (removed consequence)
- College student studies more often (increased behavior) in order to avoid getting another F on an exam (removed consequence)
- Individual calls his mother more often (increased behavior) in order to keep the mother from nagging him (removed consequence)

Primary and Secondary Reinforcers. Are all reinforcers created equal? Not necessarily. A **primary reinforcer** is one that fulfills a basic physical need for survival and does not depend on learning. Food, water, sleep, and termination of pain are examples of primary reinforcers. And sex is a powerful reinforcer that fulfills a basic physical need for survival of the species. Fortunately, learning does not depend solely on primary reinforcers. If that were the case, people would need to be hungry, thirsty, or sex starved before they would respond at all. Much observed human behavior occurs in response to secondary reinforcers. A **secondary reinforcer** is acquired or learned through association with other reinforcers. Some secondary reinforcers (money, for example) can be exchanged at a later time for other reinforcers. Praise, good grades, awards, applause, attention, and signals of approval, such as a smile or a kind word, are all examples of secondary reinforcers.

reinforcement An increase in the frequency of a behavior that occurs as the result of the consequence that the behavior produces.

positive reinforcement An increase in a behavior that occurs as the result of an added consequence.

negative reinforcement An increase in a behavior that occurs because increasing the behavior results in the termination of an unpleasant condition or stimulus.

primary reinforcer A reinforcer that fulfills a basic physical need for survival and does not depend on learning.

secondary reinforcer A reinforcer that is acquired or learned through association with other reinforcers.

Schedules of Reinforcement

Think about the difference between an ATM machine and a slot machine. Under the right conditions, you can get money from either of them. But the ATM machine gives you a reinforcer every time you use the right procedure, while the slot machine does so only intermittently. How is your behavior affected in each case?

Initially, Skinner conditioned rats by reinforcing each bar-pressing response with a food pellet. Reinforcing every correct response, known as **continuous reinforcement,** is the kind of reinforcement provided by an ATM machine, and it is the most effective way to condition a new response. However, after a response has been conditioned, partial or intermittent reinforcement is often more effective in maintaining or increasing the rate of response. How many people punch buttons on ATM machines just for fun? And how long will you keep on trying to get money from an ATM machine that hasn't responded to a couple of attempts in which you know you did everything right? Yet people will spend hours playing slot machines without being rewarded. **Partial reinforcement** (the slot machine type) is operating when some but not all responses are reinforced. In real life, reinforcement is almost never continuous; partial reinforcement is the rule.

Partial reinforcement may be administered according to any of several types of **schedules of reinforcement.** Different schedules produce distinct rates and patterns of responses, as well as varying degrees of resistance to extinction when reinforcement is discontinued. The effects of reinforcement schedules can vary somewhat with humans, depending on any instructions given to participants that could change their expectations (Lattal & Neef, 1996).

The two basic types of schedules are ratio and interval schedules. Ratio schedules require that a certain number of responses be made before one of the responses is reinforced. With interval schedules, a given amount of time must pass before a reinforcer is administered. These types of schedules are further subdivided into fixed and variable categories. (See **Figure 5.6.**)

▲ Recall that negative reinforcement involves learning a behavior in order to make something unpleasant go away. For many students, studying with classmates (learned behavior) reduces test anxiety (removed consequence). Thus, for these students, test anxiety is an important source of negative reinforcement, one that encourages them to engage in effective study behaviors.

The Fixed-Ratio Schedule.   On a **fixed-ratio schedule,** a reinforcer is given after a fixed number of correct, nonreinforced responses. If the fixed ratio is set at 30 responses (FR-30), a reinforcer is given after 30 correct responses. When wages are paid to factory workers according to the number of units produced and to migrant farm workers for each bushel of fruit they pick, those payments are following a fixed-ratio schedule.

The fixed-ratio schedule is a very effective way to maintain a high response rate, because the number of reinforcers received depends directly on the response rate. The faster people or animals respond, the more reinforcers they earn and the sooner they earn them. When large ratios are used, people and animals tend to pause after each reinforcement but then return to the high rate of responding.

▲ Two examples of variable-ratio schedules of reinforcement: Gamblers can't predict when the payoff (reinforcement) will come, so they are highly motivated to keep playing. Likewise, many computer users find themselves in the predicament of knowing they should stop playing solitaire and get to work, but they just can't seem to tear themselves away from the game. Why? The power of variable-ratio reinforcement motivates them to stick with the game until the next win, and the next, and the next. . . .

The Variable-Ratio Schedule.   The pauses after reinforcement that occur with a high fixed-ratio schedule normally do not occur with a variable-ratio schedule. On a **variable-ratio schedule,** a reinforcer is given after a varying number of nonreinforced responses, based on an average ratio. With a variable ratio of 30 responses (VR-30), people might be reinforced one time after 10 responses, another after 50, another after 30 responses, and so on. It would not be possible to predict exactly which responses will be reinforced, but reinforcement would occur 1 in 30 times, on average.

Variable-ratio schedules result in higher, more stable rates of responding than do fixed-ratio schedules. Skinner (1953) reported that on this type of schedule, "a pigeon may respond as rapidly as five times per second and maintain this rate for many hours" (p. 104). The best example of the power of the variable-ratio schedule is found in the gambling casino. Slot machines, roulette wheels, and most other games of

Figure 5.6 Four Types of Reinforcement Schedules

Skinner's research revealed distinctive response patterns for four partial reinforcement schedules (the reinforcers are indicated by the diagonal marks). The ratio schedules, based on the number of responses, yielded a higher response rate than the interval schedules, which are based on the amount of time elapsed between reinforcers.

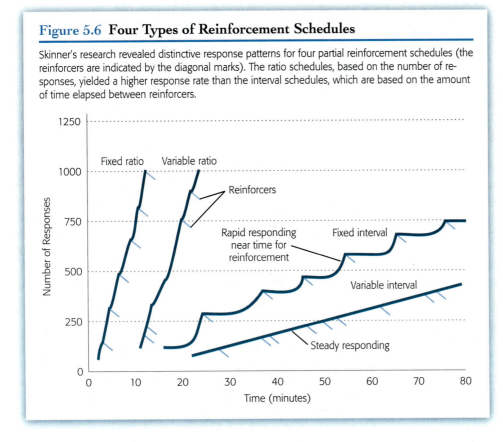

chance pay on this type of schedule. Success experiences in video games also operate on a variable-ratio schedule. In general, the variable-ratio schedule produces the highest response rate and the most resistance to extinction. That's why gamblers spend hours depositing coins into slot machines and students find it difficult to stop playing a video game even when they know they should be writing a paper or preparing for an exam.

The Fixed-Interval Schedule. On a **fixed-interval schedule,** a specific period of time must pass before a response is reinforced. For example, on a 60-second fixed-interval schedule (FI-60), a reinforcer is given for the first correct response that occurs 60 seconds after the last reinforced response. People who are on salary, rather than paid an hourly rate, are reinforced on the fixed-interval schedule.

Unlike ratio schedules, reinforcement on interval schedules does not depend on the number of responses made, only on the one correct response made after the time interval has passed. Characteristic of the fixed-interval schedule is a pause or a sharp decline in responding immediately after each reinforcement and a rapid acceleration in responding just before the next reinforcer is due.

The Variable-Interval Schedule. Variable-interval schedules eliminate the pause after reinforcement typical of the fixed-interval schedule. On a **variable-interval schedule,** a reinforcer is given after the first correct response following a varying time of nonreinforced responses, based on an average time. Rather than being given every 60 seconds, for example, a reinforcer might be given after a 30-second interval, with others following after 90-, 45-, and 75-second intervals. But the average time elapsing between reinforcers would be 60 seconds (VI-60). This schedule maintains remarkably stable and uniform rates of responding, but the response rate is typically lower than that for ratio schedules, because reinforcement is not tied directly to the number of

continuous reinforcement Reinforcement that is administered after every desired or correct response; the most effective method of conditioning a new response.

partial reinforcement A pattern of reinforcement in which some but not all correct responses are reinforced.

schedule of reinforcement A systematic process for administering partial reinforcement that produces a distinct rate and pattern of responses and degree of resistance to extinction.

fixed-ratio schedule A schedule in which a reinforcer is given after a fixed number of correct, nonreinforced responses.

variable-ratio schedule A schedule in which a reinforcer is given after a varying number of nonreinforced responses, based on an average ratio.

fixed-interval schedule A schedule in which a reinforcer is given following the first correct response after a specific period of time has elapsed.

variable-interval schedule A schedule in which a reinforcer is given after the first correct response that follows a varying time of nonreinforcement, based on an average time.

responses made. Random drug testing in the workplace is an excellent example of application of the variable-interval schedule that appears to be quite effective.

The *Review and Reflect* below summarizes the characteristics of the four schedules of reinforcement.

Review and Reflect   Reinforcement Schedules Compared

Schedule of Reinforcement	Response Rate	Pattern of Responses	Resistance to Extinction
Variable-ratio schedule	Highest response rate	Constant response pattern, no pauses.	Most resistance to extinction.
Fixed-ratio schedule	Very high	Steady response with low ratio. Brief pause after each reinforcement with very high ratio.	The higher the ratio, the more resistance to extinction.
Variable-interval schedule	Moderate	Stable, uniform response.	More resistance to extinction than fixed-interval schedule with same average interval.
Fixed-interval schedule	Lowest response rate	Long pause after reinforcement, followed by gradual acceleration.	The longer the interval, the more resistance to extinction.

The Effect of Continuous and Partial Reinforcement on Extinction. One way to understand extinction in operant conditioning is to consider how consistently a response is followed by reinforcement. On a continuous schedule, a reinforcer is expected without fail after each correct response. When a reinforcer is withheld, it is noticed immediately. But on a partial-reinforcement schedule, a reinforcer is not expected after every response. Thus, no immediate difference is apparent between the partial-reinforcement schedule and the onset of extinction.

When you put money in a vending machine and pull the lever but no candy or soda appears, you know immediately that something is wrong with the machine. But if you were playing a broken slot machine, you could have many nonreinforced responses before you would suspect the machine of malfunctioning.

Partial reinforcement results in greater resistance to extinction than does continuous reinforcement (Lerman et al., 1996). This result is known as the **partial-reinforcement effect.** There is an inverse relationship between the percentage of responses that have been reinforced and resistance to extinction. That is, the lower the percentage of responses that are reinforced, the longer extinction will take when reinforcement is withheld. The strongest resistance to extinction ever observed occurred in one experiment in which pigeons were conditioned to peck at a disk. Holland and Skinner (1961) report that "after the response had been maintained on a fixed ratio of 900 and reinforcement was then discontinued, the pigeon emitted 73,000 responses during the first 4½ hours of extinction" (p. 124).

Parents often wonder why their children continue to whine in order to get what they want, even though the parents usually do not give in to the whining. Unwittingly, parents are reinforcing whining on a variable-ratio schedule, which results in the most persistent behavior. This is why experts always caution parents to be consistent. If parents never reward whining, the behavior will stop; if they give in occasionally, it will persist and be extremely hard to extinguish.

Reward seeking is indeed a powerful motivating force for both humans and animals. There is little doubt that rewards are among the most important of the influences that shape behavior (Elliott et al., 2000). However, the results of more than 100 studies suggest that the overuse of tangible rewards may have certain long-term negative effects, such as undermining people's intrinsic motivation to regulate their own behavior (Deci et al., 1999).

partial-reinforcement effect
The greater resistance to extinction that occurs when a portion, rather than all, of the correct responses are reinforced.

Factors Influencing Operant Conditioning

What factors, other than reinforcement schedules, influence learning from consequences? We have seen that the schedule of reinforcement influences both response rate and resistance to extinction. Three other factors affect response rate, resistance to extinction, and how quickly a response is acquired:

5.13 Why don't consequences always cause changes in behavior?

1. *The magnitude of reinforcement.* In general, as the magnitude of reinforcement increases, acquisition of a response is faster, the rate of responding is higher, and resistance to extinction is greater (Clayton, 1964). For example, in studies examining the influence of cash incentives on drug addicts' ability to abstain from taking the drug, researchers have found that the greater the amount of the incentive, the more likely the addicts are to abstain over extended periods of time (Dallery et al., 2001; Katz et al., 2002).

2. *The immediacy of reinforcement.* In general, responses are conditioned more effectively when reinforcement is immediate. As a rule, the longer the delay before reinforcement, the more slowly a response is acquired (Church, 1989; Mazur, 1993). (See Figure 5.7). In animals, little learning occurs when there is any delay at all in reinforcement, because even a short delay obscures the relationship between the behavior and the reinforcer. In humans, a reinforcer sometime in the future is usually no match for immediate reinforcement in controlling behavior. Overweight people have difficulty changing their eating habits partly because of the long delay between their behavior change and the rewarding consequences of weight loss.

3. *The level of motivation of the learner.* If you are highly motivated to learn to play tennis, you will practice more and learn faster than if you have no interest in the game. Skinner (1953) found that when food is the reinforcer, a hungry animal will learn faster than a full animal. To maximize motivation, he used rats that had been deprived of food for 24 hours and pigeons that were maintained at 75–80% of their normal body weight.

Punishment

You may be wondering about one of the most common types of consequences, punishment. **Punishment** is the opposite of reinforcement. Thus, it is a decrease in the frequency of a behavior that follows some kind of consequence.

5.14 How does punishment affect behavior?

Positive and Negative Punishment.   Like reinforcement, punishment can involve either positive (added) or negative (removed) consequences. In **positive punishment,** behavior decreases after the addition of a consequence, usually an unpleasant one. For example, a driver avoids taking a particular route (decreased behavior) because it has caused him to become bogged down in traffic jams in the past (added consequence). Here are a few more examples:

- Rat stops pressing a lever (decreased behavior) when doing so causes a loud, annoying buzzing sound (added consequence)
- Student stops staying up late (decreased behavior) after sleeping through an important exam (added consequence)

Students sometimes confuse negative reinforcement and positive punishment because both involve unpleasant stimuli. However, negative reinforcement increases behavior, whereas positive punishment decreases the behavior that it follows. The simplest examples are those that happen in the context of laboratory experiments. In a negative reinforcement experiment, a rat might be put into a cage with an electrical current running through its metal floor, causing an unpleasant sensation on the rat's feet. By pressing a lever, the rat can turn off the current. After some trial and error, the rat stands on his hind legs and uses his front paws to keep the lever in the depressed position, thus eliminating the electric shocks. His lever-pressing behavior has increased (reinforcement) as a result of the removal of the unpleasant shock sensation.

punishment   A decrease in the frequency of a behavior caused by some kind of consequence.

positive punishment   A decrease in behavior that results from an added consequence.

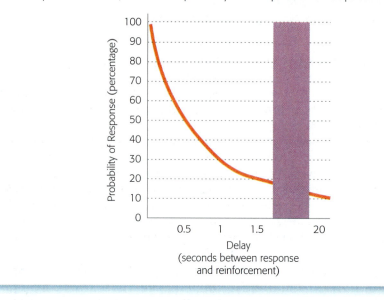

Figure 5.7 **The Effect of a Delay in Reinforcement on the Conditioning of a Response**

In general, responses are conditioned more effectively when reinforcement is immediate. The longer the delay in reinforcement, the lower the probability that a response will be acquired.

In a positive punishment experiment, the lever would turn on the electricity instead of turning it off. As a result, the rat would learn to not press the lever (a decrease in behavior) because he gets a shock when he does so.

Negative punishment happens when a behavior decreases after the removal of a consequence. The consequence usually involves the loss of something desirable. For example, a driver who speeds less often (decreased behavior) after suffering through a 6-month suspension of his license (removed consequence) has experienced negative punishment. Here are few more examples:

- Rat stops pressing a lever (decreased behavior) when doing so causes a dish of food to disappear from its cage (removed consequence)
- Teenager stops coming home late (decreased behavior) after parents take away his going-out privileges for two weeks (removed consequence)

The Disadvantages of Punishment. Thus, if punishment can suppress behavior, why do so many people oppose its use? A number of potential problems are associated with the use of punishment:

1. According to Skinner, punishment does not extinguish an undesirable behavior; rather, it suppresses that behavior when the punishing agent is present. But the behavior is apt to continue when the threat of punishment is removed and in settings where punishment is unlikely. If punishment (imprisonment, fines, and so on) reliably extinguished unlawful behavior, there would be fewer repeat offenders in the criminal justice system.
2. Punishment indicates that a behavior is unacceptable but does not help people develop more appropriate behaviors. If punishment is used, it should be administered in conjunction with reinforcement or rewards for appropriate behavior.
3. The person who is severely punished often becomes fearful and feels angry and hostile toward the punisher. These reactions may be accompanied by a desire to retaliate or to avoid or escape from the punisher and the punishing situation. Many runaway teenagers leave home to escape physical abuse. Punishment that involves a loss of privileges is more effective than physical punishment and engenders less fear and hostility (Walters & Grusec, 1977).

negative punishment A decrease in behavior that results from a removed consequence.

4. Punishment frequently leads to aggression. Those who administer physical punishment may become models of aggressive behavior, by demonstrating aggression as a way of solving problems and discharging anger. Children of abusive, punishing parents are at greater risk than other children of becoming aggressive and abusive themselves (Widom, 1989).

If punishment can cause these problems, what can be done to discourage undesirable behavior?

Alternatives to Punishment.   Are there other ways to suppress behavior? Many psychologists believe that removing the rewarding consequences of undesirable behavior is the best way to extinguish a problem behavior. According to this view, parents should extinguish a child's temper tantrums not by punishment but by never giving in to the child's demands during a tantrum. A parent might best extinguish problem behavior that is performed merely to get attention by ignoring it and giving attention to more appropriate behavior. Sometimes, simply explaining why a certain behavior is not appropriate is all that is required to extinguish the behavior.

Using positive reinforcement such as praise will make good behavior more rewarding for children. This approach brings with it the attention that children want and need—attention that often comes only when they misbehave.

It is probably unrealistic to believe that punishment will ever become unnecessary. If a young child runs into the street, puts a finger near an electrical outlet, or reaches for a hot pan on the stove, a swift punishment may save the child from a potentially disastrous situation.

Making Punishment More Effective.   When punishment is necessary (e.g., to stop destructive behavior), how can we be sure that it will be effective? Research has revealed several factors that influence the effectiveness of punishment: its timing, its intensity, and the consistency of its application (Parke, 1977).

1. Punishment is most effective when it is applied during the misbehavior or as soon afterward as possible. Interrupting the problem behavior is most effective because doing so abruptly halts its rewarding aspects. The longer the delay between the response and the punishment, the less effective the punishment is in suppressing the response (Camp et al., 1967). When there is a delay, most animals do not make the connection between the misbehavior and the punishment. For example, anyone who has tried to housebreak a puppy knows that it is necessary to catch the animal in the act of soiling the carpet for the punishment to be effective. With humans, however, if the punishment must be delayed, the punisher should remind the perpetrator of the incident and explain why the behavior was inappropriate.

2. Ideally, punishment should be of the minimum severity necessary to suppress the problem behavior. Animal studies reveal that the more intense the punishment, the greater the suppression of the undesirable behavior (Church, 1963). But the intensity of the punishment should match the seriousness of the misdeed. Unnecessarily severe punishment is likely to produce the negative side effects mentioned earlier. The purpose of punishment is not to vent anger but, rather, to modify behavior. Punishment meted out in anger is likely to be more intense than necessary to bring about the desired result. Yet, if the punishment is too mild, it will have no effect. Similarly, gradually increasing the intensity of the punishment is not effective because the perpetrator will gradually adapt, and the unwanted behavior will persist (Azrin & Holz, 1966). At a minimum, if a behavior is to be suppressed, the punishment must be more punishing than the misbehavior is rewarding. In human terms, a $200 ticket is more likely to suppress the urge to speed than a $2 ticket.

3. To be effective, punishment must be applied consistently. A parent cannot ignore misbehavior one day and punish the same act the next. And both parents should react to the same misbehavior in the same way. An undesired response will be suppressed more effectively when the probability of punishment is high. Would you be tempted to speed if you saw a police car in your rearview mirror?

▲ What strategies other than punishment might a parent use to get this child to behave more appropriately?

▲ Culture shapes ideas about punishment. Because ideas about what is and is not humane punishment have changed in Western society, public humiliation is no longer considered to be an appropriate punishment, regardless of its potential for reducing crime.

Culture and Punishment. Do you think stoning is an appropriate punishment for adultery? Probably not, unless you come from a culture in which such punishments are acceptable. Punishment is used in every culture to control and suppress people's behavior. It is administered when important values, rules, regulations, and laws are violated. But not all cultures share the same values or have the same laws regulating behavior. U.S. citizens traveling in other countries need to be aware of how different cultures view and administer punishment. For example, selling drugs is a serious crime just about everywhere. In the United States, it carries mandatory prison time; in some other countries, it is a death penalty offense.

Can you imagine being beaten with a cane as a legal punishment for vandalism? A widely publicized 1994 incident involving a young man named Michael Fay continues to serve as one of the best real-life examples of the sharp differences in concepts of crime and punishment between the United States and Singapore. Fay, an 18-year-old American living in Singapore, was arrested and charged with 53 counts of vandalism, including the spray painting of dozens of cars. He was fined approximately $2,000, sentenced to 4 months in jail, and received four lashes with a rattan cane, an agonizingly painful experience. In justifying their system of punishment, the officials in Singapore were quick to point out that their city, about the same size as Los Angeles, is virtually crime-free. Among Americans, sentiment about the caning was mixed. Some, including Fay's parents, viewed it as barbarous and cruel. But many Americans (51% in a CNN poll) expressed the view that caning might be an effective punishment under certain circumstances. What do you think?

Escape and Avoidance Learning

5.15 When is avoidance learning desirable, and when is it maladaptive?

Remember the earlier example about paying bills on time to avoid late fees? Learning to perform a behavior because it prevents or terminates an aversive event is called *escape learning*, and it reflects the power of negative reinforcement. Running away from a punishing situation and taking a pain reliever to relieve a pounding headache are examples of escape behavior. In these situations, the aversive event has begun, and an attempt is being made to escape it.

Avoidance learning, in contrast, depends on two types of conditioning. Through classical conditioning, an event or condition comes to signal an aversive state. Drinking and driving may be associated with automobile accidents and death. Because of such associations, people may engage in behaviors to avoid the anticipated aversive consequences. Making it a practice to avoid riding in a car with a driver who has been drinking is sensible avoidance behavior.

Much avoidance learning is maladaptive, however, and occurs in response to phobias. Students who have had a bad experience speaking in front of a class may begin to fear any situation that involves speaking before a group. Such students may avoid taking courses that require class presentations or taking leadership roles that necessitate public speaking. Avoiding such situations prevents them from suffering the perceived dreaded consequences. But the avoidance behavior is negatively reinforced and thus strengthened through operant conditioning. Maladaptive avoidance behaviors are very difficult to extinguish, because people never give themselves a chance to learn that the dreaded consequences probably will not occur, or that they are greatly exaggerated.

There is an important exception to the ability of humans and other animals to learn to escape and avoid aversive situations: <mark>Learned helplessness</mark> is a passive resignation to aversive conditions, learned by repeated exposure to aversive events that are inescapable or unavoidable. The initial experiment on learned helplessness was conducted by Overmeier and Seligman (1967). Dogs in the experimental group were strapped into harnesses from which they could not escape and were exposed to electric shocks. Later, these same dogs were placed in a box with two compartments separated by a low barrier. The dogs then experienced a series of trials in which a warn-

avoidance learning Learning to avoid events or conditions associated with aversive consequences or phobias.

learned helplessness A passive resignation to aversive conditions that is learned through repeated exposure to inescapable or unavoidable aversive events.

ing signal was followed by an electric shock administered through the box's floor. However, the floor was electrified only on one side, and the dogs could have escaped the electric shocks simply by jumping the barrier. Surprisingly, the dogs did not do so. Dogs in the control group had not previously experienced the inescapable shock and behaved in an entirely different manner and quickly learned to jump the barrier when the warning signal sounded and thus escaped the shock. Seligman (1975) later reasoned that humans who have suffered painful experiences they could neither avoid nor escape may also experience learned helplessness. Then, they may simply give up and react to disappointment in life by becoming inactive, withdrawn, and depressed (Seligman, 1991).

◀ Learned helplessness may result from traumatic experiences over which we have no control.

Applications of Operant Conditioning

You have probably realized that operant conditioning is an important learning process that we experience almost every day. Operant conditioning can also be used intentionally by one person to change another person's or an animal's behavior.

5.16 What are some applications of operant conditioning?

Shaping the Behavior of Animals. The principles of operant conditioning are used effectively to train animals not only to perform entertaining tricks but also to help physically challenged people lead more independent lives. Dogs and monkeys have been trained to help people who are paralyzed or confined to wheelchairs, and for years, seeing-eye dogs have been trained to assist the blind.

Through the use of shaping, animals at zoos, circuses, and marine parks have been conditioned to perform a wide range of amazing feats. After conditioning thousands of animals from over 38 different species to perform numerous feats for advertising and entertainment purposes, Breland and Breland (1961) concluded that biological predispositions in various species can affect how easily responses can be learned. When an animal's instinctual behavior runs counter to the behavior being conditioned, the animal will eventually resume its instinctual behavior, a phenomenon known as *instinctual drift*. For example, picking up coins and depositing them in a bank is a task that runs counter to the natural tendencies of raccoons and pigs. In time, a raccoon will hold the coins and rub them together instead of dropping them in the bank, and the pigs will drop them on the ground and push them with their snouts.

biofeedback The use of sensitive equipment to give people precise feedback about internal physiological processes so that they can learn, with practice, to exercise control over them.

Biofeedback. Training your dog to roll over is one thing, but can you train yourself to control your body's responses to stress? For years, scientists believed that internal responses such as heart rate, brain-wave patterns, and blood flow were not subject to operant conditioning. It is now known that when people are given very precise feedback about these internal processes, they can learn, with practice, to exercise control over them. **Biofeedback** is a way of getting information about internal biological states. Biofeedback devices have sensors that monitor slight changes in these internal responses and then amplify and convert them into visual or auditory signals. Thus,

▲ With biofeedback devices, people can see or hear evidence of internal physiological states and learn how to control them through various mental strategies.

people can see or hear evidence of internal physiological processes, and by trying out various strategies (thoughts, feelings, or images), they can learn which ones routinely increase, decrease, or maintain a particular level of activity.

Biofeedback has been used to regulate heart rate and to control migraine and tension headaches, gastrointestinal disorders, asthma, anxiety tension states, epilepsy, sexual dysfunctions, and neuromuscular disorders such as cerebral palsy, spinal cord injuries, and stroke (Kalish, 1981; L. Miller, 1989; N. E. Miller, 1985).

Behavior Modification.   Can operant conditioning help you get better grades? Perhaps, if you apply its principles to your study behavior. **Behavior modification** is a method of changing behavior through a systematic program based on the learning principles of classical conditioning, operant conditioning, or observational learning (which we will discuss soon). The majority of behavior modification programs use the principles of operant conditioning. The *Try It* below challenges you to come up with your own behavior modification plan.

Try It   Using Behavior Modification

Use conditioning to modify your own behavior.

1. *Identify the target behavior.* It must be both observable and measurable. You might choose, for example, to increase the amount of time you spend studying.

2. *Gather and record baseline data.* Keep a daily record of how much time you spend on the target behavior for about a week. Also note where the behavior takes place and what cues (or temptations) in the environment precede any slacking off from the target behavior.

3. *Plan your behavior modification program.* Formulate a plan and set goals to either decrease or increase the target behavior.

4. *Choose your reinforcers.* Any activity you enjoy more can be used to reinforce any activity you enjoy less. For example, you could reward yourself with a movie after a specified period of studying.

5. *Set the reinforcement conditions and begin recording and reinforcing your progress.* Be careful not to set your reinforcement goals so high that it becomes nearly impossible to earn a reward. Keep in mind Skinner's concept of shaping through rewarding small steps toward the desired outcome. Be perfectly honest with yourself and claim a reward only when you meet the goals. Chart your progress as you work toward gaining more control over the target behavior.

behavior modification   A method of changing behavior through a systematic program based on the learning principles of classical conditioning, operant conditioning, or observational learning.

token economy   A program that motivates socially desirable behavior by reinforcing it with tokens that can be exchanged for desired items or privileges.

Many institutions, such as schools, mental hospitals, homes for youthful offenders, and prisons, have used behavior modification programs with varying degrees of success. Such institutions are well suited for the use of these programs because they provide a restricted environment in which the consequences of behavior can be more strictly controlled. Some prisons and mental hospitals use a **token economy**—a program that motivates socially desirable behavior by reinforcing it with tokens. The tokens (poker chips or coupons) may later be exchanged for desired items such as candy or cigarettes and privileges such as weekend passes, free time, or participation in desired activities. People in the program know in advance exactly what behaviors will be reinforced and how they will be reinforced. Token economies have been used effectively in mental hospitals to encourage patients to attend to grooming, to interact with other patients, and to carry out housekeeping tasks (Ayllon & Azrin, 1965, 1968). Although the positive behaviors generally stop when the tokens are discontinued, this does not mean that the programs are not worthwhile. After all, most people who are employed would probably quit their jobs if they were no longer paid.

Many classroom teachers and parents use *time out*—a behavior modification technique in which a child who is misbehaving is removed for a short time from sources of positive reinforcement. (Remember, according to operant conditioning, a behavior that is no longer reinforced will extinguish.)

Behavior modification is also used successfully in business and industry to increase profits and to modify employee behavior related to health, safety, and job performance. In order to keep their premiums low, some companies give annual rebates to employees who do not use up the deductibles in their health insurance plan. To encourage employees to take company-approved college courses, some companies offer tuition reimbursement to employees who complete such courses with acceptable grades. Many companies promote sales by giving salespeople bonuses, trips, and other prizes for increasing sales. One of the most successful applications of behavior modification has been in the treatment of psychological problems ranging from phobias to addictive behaviors. In this context, behavior modification is called behavior therapy (discussed in Chapter 15).

Remember It — Operant Conditioning

1. The process of reinforcing successive approximations of a behavior is known as _____.

2. When reinforcers are withheld, _____ of a response occurs.

3. Taking a pain reliever to relieve a headache is an example of _____ reinforcement; studying to get a good grade on a test is an example of _____ reinforcement.

4. Glen and Megan are hired to rake leaves. Glen is paid $1 for each bag of leaves he rakes; Megan is paid $4 per hour. Glen is paid according to a _____ schedule; Megan is paid according to a _____ schedule.

5. Negative reinforcement _____ behavior, while punishment _____ behavior.

6. Victims of spousal abuse who have repeatedly failed to escape or avoid the abuse may eventually passively resign themselves to it, a condition known as _____.

7. The use of sensitive electronic equipment to monitor physiological processes in order to bring them under conscious control is called _____.

8. Applying learning principles to eliminate undesirable behavior and/or encourage desirable behavior is called _____.

Answers: 1. shaping; 2. extinction; 3. negative, positive; 4. fixed-ratio, fixed-interval; 5. strengthens, suppresses; 6. learned helplessness; 7. biofeedback; 8. behavior modification

---

Cognitive Learning

By now, you are probably convinced of the effectiveness of both classical and operant conditioning. But can either type of conditioning explain how you learned a complex mental function such as reading? Behaviorists such as Skinner and Watson believed that any kind of learning could be explained without reference to internal mental processes. Today, however, a growing number of psychologists stress the role of mental processes. They choose to broaden the study of learning to include such **cognitive processes** as thinking, knowing, problem solving, remembering, and forming mental representations. According to cognitive theorists, understanding these processes is critically important to a more complete, more comprehensive view of learning. We will consider the work of three important researchers in the field of cognitive learning: Wolfgang Köhler, Edward Tolman, and Albert Bandura.

cognitive processes (COG-nuh-tiv) Mental processes such as thinking, knowing, problem solving, remembering, and forming mental representations.

Learning by Insight

Have you ever been worried about a problem, only to have a crystal clear solution suddenly pop into your mind? If so, you experienced an important kind of cognitive learning first described by Wolfgang Köhler (1887–1967). In his book *The Mentality of Apes* (1925), Köhler described experiments he conducted on chimpanzees confined in caged areas. In one experiment, Köhler hung a bunch of bananas inside the caged area but overhead, out of reach of the chimps; boxes and sticks were left around the cage. Köhler observed the chimps' unsuccessful attempts to reach the bananas by jumping up or swinging sticks at them. Eventually, the chimps solved the problem by piling the boxes on top of one another and climbing on the boxes until they could reach the bananas.

Köhler observed that the chimps sometimes appeared to give up in their attempts to get the bananas. However, after an interval, they returned with the solution to the problem, as if it had come to them in a flash of **insight.** They seemed to have suddenly

5.17 What is insight, and how does it affect learning?

insight The sudden realization of the relationship between elements in a problem situation, which makes the solution apparent.

realized the relationship between the sticks or boxes and the bananas. Köhler insisted that insight, rather than trial-and-error learning, accounted for the chimps' successes, because they could easily repeat the solution and transfer this learning to similar problems. In human terms, a solution gained through insight is more easily learned, less likely to be forgotten, and more readily transferred to new problems than a solution learned through rote memorization (Rock & Palmer, 1990). Brain-imaging studies indicate that insight learning is associated with a unique pattern of interaction involving several different brain areas (Jing, 2004).

Latent Learning and Cognitive Maps

5.18 What did Tolman discover about the necessity of reinforcement?

Like Köhler, Edward Tolman (1886–1959) held views that differed from the prevailing ideas on learning. First, Tolman (1932) believed that learning could take place without reinforcement. Second, he differentiated between learning and performance. He maintained that **latent learning** could occur; that is, learning could occur without apparent reinforcement and not be demonstrated until the organism was motivated to do so. A classic experimental study by Tolman and Honzik (1930) supports this position.

Three groups of rats were placed in a maze daily for 17 days. The first group always received a food reward at the end of the maze. The second group never received a reward, and the third group did not receive a food reward until the 1F-1th day. The first group showed a steady improvement in performance over the 17-day period. The second group showed slight, gradual improvement. The third group, after being rewarded on the 11th day, showed a marked improvement the next day and, from then on, outperformed the rats that had been rewarded daily (see **Figure 5.8**). The rapid improvement of the third group indicated to Tolman that latent learning had occurred—that the rats had actually learned the maze during the first 11 days but were not motivated to display this learning until they were rewarded for it.

Skinner was still in graduate school in 1930 when Tolman provided this exception to a basic principle of operant conditioning—that reinforcement is required for learning new behavior. The rats in the learning group did learn something before reinforcement and without exhibiting any evidence of learning by overt, observable behavior. But what did they learn? Tolman concluded that the rats had learned to form a **cognitive map,** a mental representation or picture, of the maze but had not demonstrated their learning until they were reinforced. In later studies, Tolman showed how rats quickly learn to rearrange their established cognitive maps and readily find their way through increasingly complex mazes.

The very notion of explaining the rats' behavior with the concept of cognitive maps is counter to Skinner's most deeply held belief—that mental processes do not explain the causes of behavior. But the concepts of cognitive maps and latent learning have a far more important place in psychology today than was true in Tolman's lifetime. They provide a cognitive perspective on operant conditioning. Recall that, at the beginning of the chapter, we pointed out that you learn more about a video game each time you play it, regardless of whether you succeed or fail. Like Tolman's rats, such learning helps you form a mental map of the game that enables you to more effectively pursue desired reinforcers, such as moving from one level to the next, the next time you play.

latent learning Learning that occurs without apparent reinforcement and is not demonstrated until the organism is motivated to do so.

cognitive map A mental representation of a spatial arrangement such as a maze.

observational learning Learning by observing the behavior of others and the consequences of that behavior; learning by imitation.

modeling Another name for observational learning.

Observational Learning

5.19 How do we learn by observing others?

Have you ever wondered why you slow down when you see another driver getting a speeding ticket? In all likelihood, no one has ever reinforced you for slowing down under these conditions, so why do you do it?

Principles of Observational Learning. Psychologist Albert Bandura (1986) contends that many behaviors or responses are acquired through observational learning, or as he calls it, *social-cognitive learning.* **Observational learning,** sometimes called **modeling,** results when people observe the behavior of others and note the consequences of that behavior. Thus, you slow down when you see another driver getting a ticket because

Figure 5.8 Latent Learning

Rats in Group 1 were rewarded every day for running the maze correctly, while rats in Group 2 were never rewarded. Group 3 rats were rewarded only on the 11th day and thereafter outperformed the rats in Group 1. The rats had "learned" the maze but were not motivated to perform until rewarded, demonstrating that latent learning had occurred.

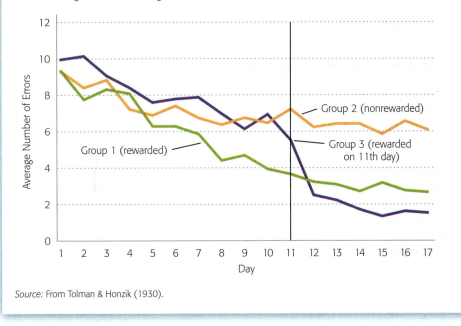

Source: From Tolman & Honzik (1930).

you assume their consequence will also be your consequence. The same process is involved when we see another person get a free soft drink by hitting the side of a vending machine. We assume that if we hit the machine, we will also get a free drink.

A person who demonstrates a behavior or whose behavior is imitated is called a **model.** Parents, movie stars, and sports personalities are often powerful models for children. The effectiveness of a model is related to his or her status, competence, and power. Other important factors are the age, sex, attractiveness, and ethnicity of the model. Whether learned behavior is actually performed depends largely on whether the observed models are rewarded or punished for their behavior and whether the observer expects to be rewarded for the behavior (Bandura, 1969, 1977a). Recent research has also shown that observational learning is improved when several sessions of observation (watching the behavior) precede attempts to perform the behavior and are then repeated in the early stages of practicing it (Weeks & Anderson, 2000).

But repetition alone isn't enough to cause an observer to learn from a model: An observer must be physically and cognitively capable of performing the behavior in order to learn it. In other words, no matter how much time you devote to watching Serena Williams play tennis or Tiger Woods play golf, you won't be able to acquire skills like theirs unless you possess physical talents that are equal to theirs. Likewise, it is doubtful that a kindergartener will learn geometry from watching her high-school-aged brother do his homework. Furthermore, the observer must pay attention to the model and store information about the model's behavior in memory. Ultimately, to exhibit a behavior learned through observation, the observer must be motivated to perform the behavior on her or his own.

A model does not have to be a person. For example, when you buy a piece of furniture labeled "assembly required," it usually comes with diagrams and instructions showing how to put it together. Typically, the instructions break down the large task of assembling the piece into a series of smaller steps. Similarly, Chapter 1 includes an explanation of the SQ3R method that provides step-by-step instructions on how to incorporate the features of this textbook, such as the questions in the chapter outlines, into an organized study method. These instructions serve as a model, or plan, for you

model The individual who demonstrates a behavior or whose behavior is imitated.

▲ Aggressive behaviors aren't the only kinds of behaviors people can learn from watching television. Rachael Ray became famous by showing millions of viewers how to add creativity to everyday activities such as preparing family meals.

to follow in studying each chapter. As is true of learning from human models, you must believe that imitating this kind of verbal model will be beneficial to you. Moreover, you must remember the steps and be capable of applying them as you read each chapter. You will be more likely to keep using the SQ3R method if your experiences motivate you to do so. That is, once you use the model and find that it helps you learn the information in a chapter, you will be more likely to use it for another chapter.

Types of Observational Learning.   One way people learn from observation is to acquire new responses, a kind of learning called the **modeling effect.** Do you remember learning how to do math problems in school? Most likely, when your teachers introduced a new kind of problem, they demonstrated how to solve them on a chalkboard or overhead projector. Your task was then to follow their procedures, step by step, until you were able to work the new problems independently. For you and your classmates, solving each new kind of problem was a new behavior acquired from a model.

Another kind of observational learning is particularly common in unusual situations. Picture yourself as a guest at an elaborate state dinner at the White House. Your table setting has more pieces of silverware than you have ever seen before. Which fork should be used for what? How should you proceed? You might decide to take your cue from the First Lady. In this case, you wouldn't be learning an entirely new behavior. Instead, you would be using a model to learn how to modify a known behavior (how to use a fork) to fit the needs of an unfamiliar situation. This kind of observational learning is known as the **elicitation effect.**

Sometimes, models influence us to exhibit behaviors that we have previously learned to suppress, a process called the **disinhibitory effect.** For example, we have all learned not to belch in public. However, if we are in a social setting in which others are belching and no one is discouraging them from doing so, we are likely to follow suit. And adolescents may lose whatever resistance they have to drinking, drug use, or sexual activity by seeing or hearing about peers or characters in movies or television shows engaging in these behaviors without experiencing any adverse consequences.

However, we may also suppress a behavior upon observing a model receive punishment for exhibiting it (**inhibitory effect**). This is the kind of observational learning we are displaying when we slow down upon seeing another driver receiving a ticket. When schoolchildren see a classmate punished for talking out, the experience has a tendency to suppress that behavior in all of them. Thus, a person does not have to experience the unfortunate consequences of dangerous or socially unacceptable behaviors in order to avoid them.

Fears, too, can be acquired through observational learning. Gerull and Rapee (2002) found that toddlers whose mothers expressed fear at the sight of rubber snakes and spiders displayed significantly higher levels of fear of these objects when tested later than did control group children whose mothers did not express such fears. Conversely, children who see "a parent or peer behaving nonfearfully in a potentially fear-producing situation may be 'immunized'" to feeling fear when confronting a similar frightening situation at a later time (Basic Behavioral Science Task Force, 1996, p. 139).

The following *Review and Reflect* compares the three types of cognitive learning we've discussed.

modeling effect   Learning a new behavior from a model through the acquisition of new responses.

elicitation effect   Exhibiting a behavior similar to that shown by a model in an unfamiliar situation.

disinhibitory effect   Displaying a previously suppressed behavior because a model does so without receiving punishment.

inhibitory effect   Suppressing a behavior because a model is punished for displaying the behavior.

Review and Reflect   Cognitive Learning

Type of Learning	Major Contributors	Classic Research
Insight Sudden realization of how to solve a problem	Wolfgang Köhler	Observations of chimpanzees' attempts to retrieve bananas suspended from the tops of their cages
Latent learning Learning that is hidden until it is reinforced	Edward Tolman	Comparisons of rats that were rewarded for learning to run a maze with others that were allowed to explore it freely
Observational learning Learning from watching others	Albert Bandura	Comparisons of children who observed an adult model behaving aggressively with those who did not observe such an aggressive model

Learning from Media

How much of your day is spent in the presence of information that is flowing from some kind of electronic source? Many people nowadays are exposed to such information almost every waking minute. There is even a 24/7 cable television channel just for babies these days ("Round-the-clock baby TV . . . ," 2006).

Effects of the Multi-tasking Environment.   The various kinds of electronic information media that are common in today's world comprise what some researchers call an *electronic multi-tasking environment* in which we attempt to manage several different sources of information at once (Rideout, Roberts, & Foehr, 2005). In one observational study of college computer labs, researchers found that many college students worked on papers and other assignments in a split-screen format, with one part of the screen devoted to their work and another to a game (Jones, 2003). And many of these students were listening to music on their MP3 players at the same time.

Research examining the effects on learning of the multi-tasking environment is still too preliminary to support definitive conclusions, but the questions being examined are likely to be of great interest to people who spend their days juggling multiple information sources. One such question concerns the degree to which the brain adapts to multiple sources of information by changing its attentional strategies (e.g., Zhang et al., 2005). Another has led researchers to examine the possibility that simultaneous exposure to multiple information sources degrades learning from any one of those sources (e.g., Law, Logie, & Pearson, 2006). Other hypotheses currently being investigated include the possibility that keeping track of multiple streams of information induces anxiety (e.g., Bailey & Konstan, 2006).

By contrast, researchers have been studying the effects of the content of information media for decades. Much of the information provided through modern media differs little from what was available via other means in the past. For example, many electronic games employ fictional themes that are found in oral storytelling traditions that have been around for millennia (e.g., heroes versus villains). What concerns psychologists about newer media is that they provide consumers with information that is more immediately accessible and realistic than older forms of communication.

Television and Other Entertainment Media.   More than four decades ago, Albert Bandura raised concerns regarding the impact of televised violence on children's behavior with a classic series of studies. Bandura suspected that aggression and violence

5.20 What has research shown regarding the influence of media violence on aggressive feelings and behavior?

▲ In Bandura's observational learning research, children learned to copy aggression by observing adult models act aggressively toward a Bobo doll.

on television programs, including cartoons, tend to increase aggressive behavior in children. His pioneering work has greatly influenced current thinking on these issues. In several classic experiments, Bandura demonstrated how children are influenced by exposure to aggressive models. One study involved three groups of preschoolers. Children in one group individually observed an adult model punching, kicking, and hitting a 5-foot, inflated plastic "Bobo Doll" with a mallet, while uttering aggressive phrases (Bandura et al., 1961, p. 576). Children in the second group observed a nonaggressive model who ignored the Bobo Doll and sat quietly assembling Tinker Toys. The children in the control group were placed in the same setting with no adult present. Later, each child was observed through a one-way mirror. Those children exposed to the aggressive model imitated much of the aggression and also engaged in significantly more nonimitative aggression than did children in either of the other groups. The group that observed the nonaggressive model showed less aggressive behavior than the control group.

A further study compared the degree of aggression in children following exposure to (1) an aggressive model in a live situation, (2) a filmed version of the same situation, or (3) a film depicting an aggressive cartoon character using the same aggressive behaviors in a fantasylike setting (Bandura et al., 1963). A control group was not exposed to any of the three situations of aggression. The groups exposed to aggressive models used significantly more aggression than the control group. The researchers concluded that "of the three experimental conditions, exposure to humans on film portraying aggression was the most influential in eliciting and shaping aggressive behavior" (p. 7).

Bandura's research sparked interest in studying the effects of violence and aggression portrayed in other entertainment media. For example, researchers have also shown in a variety of ways—including carefully controlled laboratory experiments with children, adolescents, and young adults—that violent video games increase aggressive behavior (Anderson & Bushman, 2001). Moreover, the effects of media violence are evident whether the violence is presented in music, music videos, or advertising or on the Internet (Villani, 2001). Such research has spawned a confusing array of rating systems that parents may refer to when choosing media for their children. However, researchers have found that labeling media as "violent" may enhance children's desire to experience it, especially in boys over the age of 11 years (Bushman & Cantor, 2003).

But, you might argue, if televised violence is followed by appropriate consequences, such as an arrest, it may actually teach children not to engage in aggression. However, experimental research has demonstrated that children do not process information about consequences in the same ways as adults do (Krcmar & Cooke, 2001). Observing consequences for aggressive acts does seem to help preschoolers learn that violence is morally unacceptable. By contrast, school-aged children appear to judge the rightness or wrongness of an act of violence on the basis of provocation; that is, they believe that violence demonstrated in the context of retaliation is morally acceptable even if it is punished by an authority figure.

Remarkably, too, recently published longitudinal evidence shows that the effects of childhood exposure to violence persist well into the adult years. Psychologist L. Rowell Huesman and his colleagues (2003) found that individuals who had watched the greatest number of violent television programs in childhood were the most likely to have engaged in actual acts of violence as young adults. This study was the first to show that observations of media violence during childhood are linked to real acts of violence in adulthood. Brain-imaging studies suggest that these long-term effects may be the result of patterns of neural activation that underlie emotionally laden behavioral scripts that children learn while watching violent programming (Murray et al., 2006).

But just as children imitate the aggressive behavior they observe on television, they also imitate the prosocial, or helping, behavior they see there. Programs such as

Mister Rogers' Neighborhood and *Sesame Street* have been found to have a positive influence on children. And, hopefully, the findings of Huesman and his colleagues also apply to the positive effects of television.

Electronic Games.   In recent years, concerns about media violence have shifted away from television and toward an emphasis on electronic games. This shift has occurred because children and teenagers now spend as much time playing these games as they do watching television ("Children spend more time . . . ," 2004). Adults also devote a considerable amount of time to gaming. For instance, 70% of college students and 40% of adults in their twenties, thirties, and forties tell researchers that they play computer, online, or video games regularly (Jones, 2003; "Survey: Four in 10 . . . ," 2006). Psychologists wonder what players learn from these games, especially those that encourage them to assume the roles of characters who are rewarded for engaging in aggressive behavior (Schneider, Lang, Shin, & Bradley, 2004; Walsh, Gentile, VanOverbeke, & Chasco, 2002).

▲ Portrayals on television showing violence as an acceptable way to solve problems tend to encourage aggressive behavior in children.

A number of studies have shown that playing violent games increases feelings of hostility and decreases sensitivity to violent images (Anderson & Bushman, 2001; Anderson & Dill, 2000; Arriaga et al., 2006; Bushman & Huesman, 2006; Carnagey & Anderson, 2005). Researchers have also found that such games influence the physiological correlates of hostile emotions and aggressive behavior. These correlates include particular patterns of brain activation, hormonal secretions, and vital functions such as heart rate and respiration (Brady & Matthews, 2006; Hébert et al., 2005; Wang & Perry, 2006; Weber, Ritterfeld, & Mathiak, 2006). Research has also consistently shown that individuals with aggressive behavioral histories more strongly prefer and are more emotionally responsive to violent games than their nonaggressive peers (Anderson & Dill, 2000).

Despite these findings, some psychologists argue that violent electronic games allow individuals, especially adolescent and young adult males, to express socially unacceptable feelings in a socially acceptable and safe manner (Jansz, 2005). They point out that these games are most often played in groups and are a central shared activity in many young males' peer relationships (Jansz & Martens, 2005). Consequently, learning to channel aggressive impulses into competitive play among friends, even when such play involves simulated violence, may be an essential part of the social development of adolescent males.

Like television, video games can be used to teach positive messages and skills. For example, researchers at the University of Michigan have found that video games are an effective medium through which to teach teenagers how to drive more safely (UMTRI, 2003). Furthermore, playing video games appears to enhance women's spatial cognitive skills, a domain in which females typically perform more poorly than males (Terlecki & Newcombe, 2005).

Finally, did you know that psychology is a vital part of the video game design process? Designers consult psychological theories and research to learn how to create realistic characters (Poznanski & Thagard, 2005). The knowledge that designers have accumulated from the translation of psychological principles into programming codes that enable video game characters to behave in believable ways is being used to "humanize" all kinds of virtual environments. For instance, such knowledge may facilitate the replacement of today's text-based online banking web sites with virtual tellers who are just as adept at interacting with customers as their real-world counterparts.

Remember It   Cognitive Learning

1. The sudden realization of the relationship between the elements in a problem situation that results in the solution to the problem is called _____.

2. Learning not demonstrated until the organism is motivated to perform the behavior is called _____ learning.

3. Grant has been afraid of mice for as long as he can remember, and his mother has the same paralyzing fear. Grant most likely acquired his fear through _____ learning.

4. Match each psychologist with the subject(s) of his research.

____ (1) Edward Tolman   a. observational learning
____ (2) Albert Bandura   b. cognitive maps
____ (3) Wolfgang Köhler   c. learning by insight
                         d. latent learning

Answers: 1. insight; 2. latent; 3. observational; 4. (1) b, d, (2) a, (3) c

Apply It   How to Win the Battle against Procrastination

Have you often thought that you could get better grades if only you had more time? Do you often find yourself studying for an exam or completing a term paper at the last minute? If so, it makes sense for you to learn how to overcome the greatest time waster of all—procrastination. Research indicates that academic procrastination arises partly out of a lack of confidence in one's ability to meet expectations (Wolters, 2003). Once procrastination has become established as a behavior pattern, it often persists for years (Lee, Kelly, & Edwards, 2006). Nevertheless, anyone can overcome procrastination, and gain self-confidence in the process, by using behavior modification techniques. Systematically apply the following suggestions to keep procrastination from interfering with your studying:

• *Identify the environmental cues that habitually interfere with your studying.* Television, computer or video games, and even food can be powerful distractors that consume hours of valuable study time. However, these distractors can be useful positive reinforcers to enjoy *after* you've finished studying.

• *Schedule your study time and reinforce yourself for adhering to your schedule.* Once you've scheduled it, be just as faithful to your schedule as you would be to a work schedule set by an employer. And be sure to schedule something you enjoy immediately following the study time.

• *Get started.* The most difficult part is getting started. Give yourself an extra reward for starting on time and, perhaps, a penalty for starting late.

• *Use visualization.* Much procrastination results from the failure to consider its negative consequences. Visualizing the consequences of not studying, such as trying to get through an exam you haven't adequately prepared for, can be an effective tool for combating procrastination.

• *Beware of jumping to another task when you reach a difficult part of an assignment.* This procrastination tactic gives you the feeling that you are busy and accomplishing something, but it is, nevertheless, an avoidance mechanism.

• *Beware of preparation overkill.* Procrastinators may actually spend hours preparing for a task rather than working on the task itself. For example, they may gather enough library materials to write a book rather than a five-page term paper. This enables them to postpone writing the paper.

• *Keep a record of the reasons you give yourself for postponing studying or completing important assignments.* If a favorite rationalization is "I'll wait until I'm in the mood to do this," count the number of times in a week you are seized with the desire to study. The mood to study typically arrives after you begin, not before.

Don't procrastinate! Begin now! Apply the steps outlined here to gain more control over your behavior and win the battle against procrastination.

✸ Summary and Review

Classical Conditioning: The Original View
p. 159

5.1 What kind of learning did Pavlov discover? p. 160

Pavlov's study of a conditioned reflex in dogs led him to discover a model of learning called classical conditioning.

5.2 How is classical conditioning accomplished? p. 161

In classical conditioning, a neutral stimulus (a tone in Pavlov's experiments) is presented shortly before an unconditioned stimulus (food in Pavlov's experiments), which naturally elicits, or brings forth, an unconditioned response (salivation for Pavlov's dogs). After repeated pairings, the conditioned stimulus alone (the tone) comes to elicit the conditioned response.

5.3 What kinds of changes in stimuli and learning conditions lead to changes in conditioned responses? p. 162

If the conditioned stimulus (tone) is presented repeatedly without the unconditioned stimulus (food), the conditioned response (salivation) eventually disappears, a process called extinction. Generalization occurs when an organism makes a conditioned response to a stimulus that is similar to the original conditioned stimulus. Discrimination is the ability to distinguish between similar stimuli.

5.4 How did Watson demonstrate that fear could be classically conditioned? p. 165

Watson showed that fear could be classically conditioned by presenting a white rat to Little Albert along with a loud, frightening noise, thereby conditioning the child to fear the white rat.

Classical Conditioning: The Contemporary View
p. 166

5.5 According to Rescorla, what is the critical element in classical conditioning? p. 167

Rescorla found that the critical element in classical conditioning is whether the conditioned stimulus provides information that enables the organism to reliably predict the occurrence of the unconditioned stimulus.

5.6 What did Garcia and Koelling discover about classical conditioning? p. 167

Garcia and Koelling conducted a study in which rats formed an association between nausea and flavored water ingested several hours earlier. This represented an exception to the principle that the conditioned stimulus must be presented shortly before the unconditioned stimulus.

5.7 What types of everyday responses can be subject to classical conditioning? p. 168

Types of responses acquired through classical conditioning include positive and negative emotional responses (including likes, dislikes, fears, and phobias), responses to environmental cues associated with drug use, and conditioned immune system responses.

5.8 Why doesn't classical conditioning result every time unconditioned and conditioned stimuli occur together? p. 170

Whenever unconditioned and conditioned stimuli occur close together in time, four factors determine whether classical conditioning results: (1) how reliably the conditioned stimulus predicts the unconditioned stimulus, (2) the number of pairings of the conditioned stimulus and unconditioned stimulus, (3) the intensity of the unconditioned stimulus, and (4) the amount of time that elapses between the conditioned stimulus and the unconditioned stimulus and the order in which they occur.

Operant Conditioning p. 170

5.9 What did Thorndike conclude about learning by watching cats try to escape from his puzzle box? p. 171

Thorndike concluded that most learning occurs through trial and error. He claimed that the consequences of a response determine whether the tendency to respond in the same way in the future will be strengthened or weakened (the law of effect).

5.10 What is the process by which behaviors are acquired through operant conditioning? p. 171

In operant conditioning, behaviors change as a result of the consequences they produce. In one kind of operant conditioning, shaping, complex behaviors are learned in small steps. In extinction, behaviors disappear when the consequences they formerly produced are no longer available.

5.11 What are the effects of positive reinforcement and negative reinforcement? p. 173

Both positive (added) and negative (subtracted, removed) reinforcement increase behavior. In positive reinforcement, a behavior occurs more frequently because it produces a desired consequence. In negative reinforcement, a behavior is learned because it makes an undesirable condition or stimulus go away.

5.12   What are the four types of schedules of reinforcement, and which type is most effective? p. 174

The four types of schedules of reinforcement are the fixed-ratio, variable-ratio, fixed-interval, and variable-interval schedules. The variable-ratio schedule provides the highest response rate and the most resistance to extinction. The partial-reinforcement effect is the greater resistance to extinction that occurs when responses are maintained under partial reinforcement, rather than under continuous reinforcement.

5.13   Why don't consequences always cause changes in behavior? p. 177

In operant conditioning, response rate, resistance to extinction, and how quickly a response is acquired are influenced by the magnitude of reinforcement, the immediacy of reinforcement, and the motivation level of the learner. If the incentive is minimal, the reinforcement delayed, or the learner minimally motivated, consequences will not necessarily cause behavior changes.

5.14   How does punishment affect behavior? p. 177

Punishment happens when either an added (positive) or a removed (negative) consequence leads to a reduction in the frequency of a behavior. Generally, punishment does not help people develop more appropriate behaviors, and it can cause fear, anger, hostility, and aggression in the punished person. Punishment is most effective when it is given immediately after undesirable behavior, when it is consistently applied, and when it is just intense enough to suppress the behavior.

5.15   When is avoidance learning desirable, and when is it maladaptive? p. 180

Avoidance learning is desirable when it leads to a beneficial response, such as buckling a seat belt to stop the annoying sound of a buzzer. It is maladaptive when it occurs in response to fear. For example, fear of speaking to a group may lead you to skip class on the day your oral report is scheduled.

5.16   What are some applications of operant conditioning? p. 181

Applications of operant conditioning include training animals to provide entertainment or to help physically challenged people, using biofeedback to gain control over internal physiological processes, and using behavior modification techniques to eliminate undesirable behavior and/or encourage desirable behavior in individuals or groups.

Cognitive Learning p. 183

5.17   What is insight, and how does it affect learning? p. 183

Insight is the sudden realization of the relationship of the elements in a problem situation that makes the solution apparent; this solution is easily learned and transferred to new problems.

5.18   What did Tolman discover about the necessity of reinforcement? p. 184

Tolman demonstrated that rats could learn to run to the end of a maze just as quickly when allowed to explore it freely as when they were reinforced with food for getting to the end. His hypothesis was that the rats formed a cognitive map of the maze.

5.19   How do we learn by observing others? p. 184

Learning by observing the behavior of others (called models) and the consequences of that behavior is known as observational learning. We learn from models when we assume that the consequences they experience will happen to us if we perform their behaviors.

5.20   What has research shown regarding the influence of media violence on aggressive feelings and behavior? p. 187

Violence in both television programs and electronic games can induce feelings of hostility and lessen viewers' and players' capacity for empathy. However, games may provide young adult males with socially acceptable outlets for such feelings.

Thinking Critically about Psychology

1. Compare and contrast the principles of classical and operant conditioning. What are the essential differences between these two types of learning?
2. Think of a behavior of a friend, family member, or professor that you would like to change. Using what you know about classical conditioning, operant conditioning, and observational learning, formulate a detailed plan for changing the targeted behavior.
3. State the arguments for and against this proposition: "Colleges have spent millions of dollars to provide students with sophisticated computer facilities. Their goal in doing so was to help students learn more effectively. Thus it is wrong for students to use these facilities to play games, and any student who is caught doing so should lose his or her computer-use privileges."

Key Terms

avoidance learning, p. 180
behavior modification, p. 182
biofeedback, p. 181
classical conditioning, p. 160
cognitive map, p. 184
cognitive processes, p. 183
conditioned reflex, p. 161
conditioned response (CR), p. 162
conditioned stimulus (CS), p. 162
continuous reinforcement, p. 174
discrimination, p. 164
discriminative stimulus, p. 172
disinhibitory effect, p. 186
elicitation effect, p. 186
extinction (in classical conditioning), p. 162
extinction (in operant conditioning), p. 172
fixed-interval schedule, p. 175
fixed-ratio schedule, p. 174
generalization (in classical conditioning), p. 163

generalization (in operant conditioning), p. 172
higher-order conditioning, p. 162
inhibitory effect, p. 186
insight, p. 183
latent learning, p. 184
law of effect, p. 171
learned helplessness, p. 180
learning, p. 159
model, p. 185
modeling, p. 184
modeling effect, p. 186
negative punishment, p. 178
negative reinforcement, p. 173
observational learning, p. 184
operant conditioning, p. 171
partial reinforcement, p. 174
partial reinforcement effect, p. 176
positive punishment, p. 177
positive reinforcement, p. 173
primary reinforcer, p. 173
punishment, p. 177

reflex, p. 161
reinforcement, p. 173
reinforcer, p. 171
schedule of reinforcement, p. 174
secondary reinforcer, p. 173
shaping, p. 171
Skinner box, p. 171
spontaneous recovery, p. 163
stimulus, p. 160
successive approximations, p. 172
taste aversion, p. 168
token economy, p. 182
trial-and-error learning, p. 171
unconditioned response (UR), p. 161
unconditioned stimulus (US), p. 162
variable-interval schedule, p. 175
variable-ratio schedule, p. 174

Chapter 6

Memory

Have you ever visited a place where you lived when you were a child and found that it seemed smaller than you remembered it? This happens because we attach our own perspectives to the objective features of the information we commit to memory. For instance, your perception of the ratio of the size of your childhood home to the size you were when you lived there is attached to your memories of the house itself. Today, the size ratio is different because you are much larger; hence, your perception that the house is smaller.

Such distortions of memory are common and rarely affect our daily lives in any meaningful way. By contrast, the kinds of cognitive distortions that are experienced by some individuals who suffer from neurological disorders can make it impossible for them to conduct their lives in the same way that they did before they became ill. The writings of neurologist Oliver Sacks include case descriptions of many such individuals. For instance, in *An Anthropologist on Mars,* Sacks recounts the story of Franco Magnani, a man who became a world-renowned artist after a neurological illness left him with vivid images of the places he had known as a child as well as an obsession to paint them (Chatterjee, 2004; Sacks, 1995). Here is his story.

Franco Magnani was born in 1934 in Pontito, an ancient village in the hills of Tuscany. His father died when Franco was eight, and soon after that, Nazi troops occupied his village. The Magnani family lived through many years of hardship, at times facing starvation. After the war, Magnani worked as a furniture maker in Pontito until 1958, when economic conditions in his hometown forced him to seek employment as a cook at the posh resorts on the coast of the Mediterranean Sea. Magnani was successful in his new career, and moved on to serve in the kitchens of several luxury cruise ships. These positions allowed him to travel all over the world. Still, he never lost his fascination with an image he had seen as a young child, that of the Golden Gate Bridge in San Francisco. He fulfilled a life-long dream when he emigrated to America in 1965 and settled in the fabled City by the Bay.

Shortly after his arrival in America, Franco contracted a viral illness that caused him to have a very high fever for several days. When the fever lifted, Franco's body recovered, but his mind was forever changed. Although he did not know it at the time, the virus had left him with a condition known as *Waxman-Geschwind syndrome* (Trevisol-Bittencourt & Troiano, 2000; Waxman & Geschwind, 1975). This syndrome includes a variety of symptoms—changes in personality, loss of interest in sex, and moodiness, among others—but the one that became most relevant for Magnani was the tendency to experience vivid, detailed mental images that resemble photographs. Patients report that these images pop into their minds randomly and are not subject to any kind of intentional control. Sometimes they happen during dreams, as they did in Magnani's case, and some people who have them are obsessively compelled to draw the images. Remarkably, all of Magnani's visions were scenes from his hometown, a place he had not seen for many years. When the visions appeared, Magnani complied with the obsessive desires to draw the scenes that accompanied the visions. He soon discovered that he had also somehow acquired the skills needed to turn his visions into stunning works of art, even though he had never had any artistic training and had only a passing interest in painting prior to his illness.

Magnani's first painting depicted the house in which he had grown up. When he completed the painting, he sent a photograph of it to his mother. Magnani's mother was amazed at the photographic detail in her son's painting, and her enthusiastic response to it encouraged Magnani to paint more scenes of Pontito and the surrounding countryside. Working entirely from the vivid mental images produced by Waxman-Gerschwind syndrome, Magnani painted a series of such pictures and opened a small gallery in San Francisco to display his work.

In 1987, photographer Susan Schwartzenberg traveled to Italy to photograph the scenes that Magnani had painted. Magnani's paintings and Schwartzenberg's photographs were put on display at the Exploratorium, a museum in San Francisco. The exhibition, Sacks's 1995 book, and an updated version of the exhibition that took place in 1998 brought Magnani worldwide acclaim. Now in his seventies and known as "Il Pittore della Memoria" in Italy, Magnani continues to paint his still-frequent visions. "The Memory Artist" lives in a small town in the San Francisco area and continues to display his paintings at his gallery called "Pontito."

cooking that exist in his memory. Clearly, too, the painting is imbued with a warmth that is not evident in the photo. This warmth, no doubt, emanates from the artist's fondness for the places he paints and for a time that is long gone. In fact, Sacks speculates that the paintings represent Magnani's attempt to reconstruct the Pontito that existed prior to its corruption—as he and his family viewed it—by the Nazi occupation. Thus, the scenes Magnani painted depict elements that never could have been represented in a photograph. They are the unique product of his memories and the social and emotional context in which they were formed. (You can see more of Magnani's work at http://francomagnani.com/ and more comparisons of his paintings to Schwartzenberg's photographs at http://www.exploratorium.edu/memory/magnani/index.html.)

Comparisons of Magnani's paintings to photographs of the same scenes suggest several observations about human memory. For example, look at the pictures above. On the left is a photograph of the house in which the artist grew up. On the right is his painting of the house. As you can see, the painting is a very accurate rendering of the house, but it differs from the photograph in several striking ways. For one, Magnani probably had never seen his mother preparing a meal in the way he has portrayed it in the painting. Instead, the scene he paints represents an inference derived from the connections among the house, his experiences as a young boy, and his mother's

As Magnani's paintings suggest, human memory does not function like a camera. Instead, our memory system combines objective knowledge with subjective feelings, thoughts, and perspectives to construct our remembrances. In this chapter, you will read about the fascinating processes that, together, make up human memory.

The Structure of Human Memory

How do our minds create memories? Psychologists have been studying memory for more than a century. However, the need to break down the memory process into its constituent parts that was necessitated by the invention of modern computers and computer programming has opened the doors to psychologists' understanding of how the human memory system works.

The Information-Processing Approach

Most current studies aimed at understanding human memory are conducted within a framework known as **information-processing theory** (Klaatsky, 1984). This approach makes use of modern computer science and related fields to provide models that help psychologists understand the processes involved in memory (Kon & Plaskota, 2000; Bishop, 2005). In keeping with the computer analogy, information-processing theorists sometimes apply such terms as "hardware" (e.g., brain structures that are involved in memory) and "software" (e.g., learned memory strategies) to various aspects of the human memory system.

Note that information-processing theory is a perspective, or general framework, that yields *microtheories* that explain specific memory processes or outcomes using the general principles of the information-processing approach. One such microtheory might explain how study participants remember lists of words in laboratory experiments,

6.1 How does the information-processing approach describe the structure of human memory?

information-processing theory
An approach to the study of mental structures and processes that uses the computer as a model for human thinking.

▲ Sensory memory holds a visual image, such as a lightning bolt, for a fraction of a second—just long enough for you to perceive a flow of movement.

6.2 **What are the characteristics of sensory memory?**

encoding   The process of transforming information into a form that can be stored in memory.

storage   The process of keeping or maintaining information in memory.

consolidation   A physiological change in the brain that allows encoded information to be stored in memory.

retrieval   The process of bringing to mind information that has been stored in memory.

memory   The process of encoding, storage, consolidation, and retrieval of information.

whereas another might focus on how our memories keep track of everyday tasks such as "I have to remember to go to the library after class."

The general principles of the information-processing approach to memory include the notion that memory involves three distinct processes. The first process, **encoding,** is the transformation of information into a form that can be stored in memory. For example, if you witness a car crash, you might try to form a mental picture of it to enable yourself to remember it. The second memory process, **storage,** involves keeping or maintaining information in memory. In order for encoded information to be stored, some physiological change must take place in the brain—a process called **consolidation.** The final process, **retrieval,** occurs when information stored in memory is brought to mind. To remember something, you must perform all three processes—encode the information, store it, and then retrieve it. Thus, **memory** is a cognitive process that includes encoding, storage, consolidation, and retrieval of information (see **Figure 6.1**).

The information-processing approach is not associated with any one theorist. However, there are several theorists who have been especially influential about whom you will learn in this chapter. Two ground-breaking theorists, Richard Atkinson and Richard Shiffrin, proposed the model of memory that almost all researchers employ (Atkinson & Shiffrin, 1968; Shiffrin, 1999). Their model characterizes memory as three different, interacting memory systems: sensory memory, short-term memory, and long-term memory. We will examine each of these three memory systems, which are shown in **Figure 6.2**, in detail.

Sensory Memory

Imagine yourself driving down a city street. How many separate pieces of information are you sensing? You are probably seeing, hearing, feeling, and smelling millions of tiny bits of information every minute. But how many of them do you remember? Very few, most likely. That's because, although virtually everything we see, hear, or otherwise sense is held in **sensory memory,** each piece of information is stored only for the briefest period of time. As shown in Figure 6.2, sensory memory normally holds visual images for a fraction of a second and sounds for about 2 seconds (Crowder, 1992; Klatzky, 1980). Visual sensory memory lasts just long enough to keep whatever you are viewing from disappearing when you blink your eyes. You experience auditory sensory memory when the last few words someone has spoken seem to echo briefly in your head. So, sensory memory functions a bit like a strainer; that is, most of what flows into it immediately flows out again.

Exactly how long does visual sensory memory last? Glance at the three rows of letters shown below for a fraction of a second, and then close your eyes. How many of the letters can you recall?

X   B   D   F
M   P   Z   G
L   C   N   H

Most people can correctly recall only four or five of the letters when they are briefly presented. Does this indicate that visual sensory memory can hold only four or five letters at a time? To find out, researcher George Sperling (1960) briefly flashed

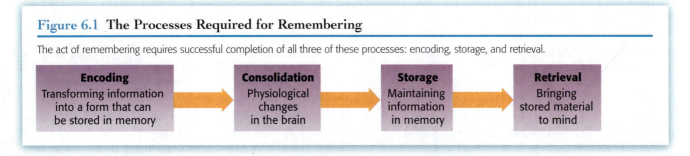

Figure 6.1 The Processes Required for Remembering

The act of remembering requires successful completion of all three of these processes: encoding, storage, and retrieval.

Encoding	**Consolidation**	**Storage**	**Retrieval**
Transforming information into a form that can be stored in memory	Physiological changes in the brain	Maintaining information in memory	Bringing stored material to mind

Figure 6.2 Characteristics of and Processes Involved in the Three Memory Systems

The three memory systems differ in what and how much they hold and for how long they store it.

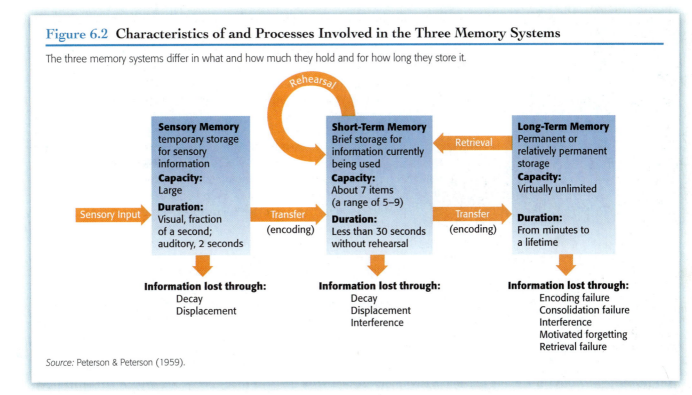

Source: Peterson & Peterson (1959).

12 letters, as shown on page 198, to participants. Immediately upon turning off the display, he sounded a high, medium, or low tone that signaled the participants to report only the top, middle, or bottom row of letters. Before they heard the tone, the participants had no way of knowing which row they would have to report. Yet Sperling found that, when the participants could view the rows of letters for $\frac{15}{1000}$ to $\frac{1}{2}$ second, they could report correctly all the items in any one row nearly 100% of the time. But the items faded from sensory memory so quickly that during the time it took to report three or four of them, the other eight or nine had already disappeared.

sensory memory The memory system that holds information from the senses for a period of time ranging from only a fraction of a second to about 2 seconds.

Short-Term Memory

So, you might be thinking, if almost everything flows out of sensory memory, how do we ever remember anything? Fortunately, our ability to attend allows us to grab onto some sensory information and send it to the next stage of processing, **short-term memory (STM).** Whatever you are thinking about right now is in your STM (see Figure 6.2). Unlike sensory memory, which holds virtually the exact sensory stimulus, short-term memory usually codes information according to sound. For example, the letter *T* is coded as the sound "tee," not as the shape T.

6.3 What happens to information in short-term memory?

Capacity. Short-term memory has a very limited capacity—about seven (plus or minus two) different items or bits of information at one time. This is just enough for phone numbers and ordinary zip codes. (Nine-digit zip codes strain the capacity of most people's STM.) When short-term memory is filled to capacity, displacement can occur. In **displacement,** each new, incoming item pushes out an existing item, which is then forgotten. Think of what happens when the top of your desk gets too crowded. Things start to "disappear" under other things; some items even fall off the desk. So, you can remember that short-term memory is the limited component of the memory system by associating it with the top of your desk: The desk is limited in size, causing you to lose things when it gets crowded, and the same is true of short-term memory.

One way to overcome the limitation of seven or so bits of information is to use a strategy that George A. Miller (1956), a pioneer in memory research, calls **chunking**— organizing or grouping separate bits of information into larger units, or chunks. A

short-term memory (STM) The memory system that codes information according to sound and holds about seven (from five to nine) items for less than 30 seconds without rehearsal; also called working memory.

displacement The event that occurs when short-term memory is filled to capacity and each new, incoming item pushes out an existing item, which is then forgotten.

chunking A memory strategy that involves grouping or organizing bits of information into larger units, which are easier to remember.

▲ Suppose the person with whom this driver is talking is giving her directions. As you can see, the driver has no way to write down the directions, and her short-term memory is trying to juggle the tasks of driving and talking on the phone while also trying to understand and remember the directions. If you have ever been in this situation, you probably learned the hard way that your performance on at least one of the tasks suffered because of the limitation of short-term memory.

chunk is an easily identifiable unit such as a syllable, a word, an acronym, or a number (Cowan, 1988). For example, nine digits, such as 5 2 9 7 3 1 3 2 5, can be divided into three more easily memorized chunks, 529 73 1325. (Notice that this is the form of social security numbers in the United States.)

Anytime you chunk information on the basis of knowledge stored in long-term memory, that is, by associating it with some kind of meaning, you increase the effective capacity of short-term memory (Lustig & Hasher, 2002). As a result, chunking is just as useful in remembering large amounts of information as it is to remembering telephone numbers and similar items. For instance, the headings, subheadings, and margin questions in this textbook help you sort information into manageable chunks. Thus, you will remember more material from each chapter if you use these elements as organizers for your notes and as cues to recall information when you are reviewing for an exam.

Duration. Items in short-term memory are lost in less than 30 seconds unless you repeat them over and over to yourself. This process is known as **rehearsal.** But rehearsal is easily disrupted. It is so fragile, in fact, that an interruption can cause information to be lost in just a few seconds. Distractions that are stressful are especially likely to disrupt short-term memory. And a threat to survival certainly does, as researchers showed when they pumped the odor of a feared predator, a fox, into a laboratory where rats were performing a task requiring short-term memory—the rats' performance plummeted (Morrison et al., 2002; Morrow et al., 2000).

How long does short-term memory last if rehearsal is prevented? In a series of early studies, participants were briefly shown three consonants (such as H, G, and L) and then asked to count backward by threes from a given number (738, 735, 732, and so on) (Peterson & Peterson, 1959). After intervals lasting from 3 to 18 seconds, participants were instructed to stop counting backward and recall the three letters. Following a delay of 9 seconds, the participants could recall an average of only one of the three letters. After 18 seconds, there was practically no recall whatsoever. An 18-second distraction had completely erased the three letters from short-term memory.

Short-term memory and working memory. Allan Baddeley (1998) has suggested that short-term memory is one component of a broader system of temporary storage structures and processes known as **working memory.** Simply put, working memory is the memory subsystem with which you work on information to understand it, remember it, or use it to solve a problem or to communicate with someone. Baddeley argues that STM is largely speech-based. Consequently, other kinds of information (e.g., visual) that we need to carry out an information-processing task are sent to other components of the working memory system for temporary storage while the STM is engaged in processing verbal information. Research shows that the prefrontal cortex is the site that is activated when we are using our working memories (Courtney et al., 1997; Rao et al., 1997).

So, just what kind of "work" goes on in working memory? One of the most important working memory processes is the application of *memory strategies,* such as chunking. Using a memory strategy involves manipulating information in ways that make it easier to remember. We use some memory strategies almost automatically, but others require more effort. For example, sometimes we repeat information over and over again until we can recall it easily. (Remember learning those multiplication tables in elementary school?) This strategy, sometimes called **maintenance rehearsal,** may work well for remembering telephone numbers, license plate numbers, and even the multiplication tables, especially when combined with chunking. However, it isn't the best way to remember more complex information, such as the kind you find in a textbook. For this kind of information, the best memory is probably **elaborative rehearsal,** which involves relating new information to something you already know.

How does elaborative rehearsal work? Here is an example. Suppose you are taking a French class and have to learn the word *éscaliers,* which is equivalent to *stairs* in En-

rehearsal The act of purposely repeating information to maintain it in short-term memory.

working memory The memory subsystem that we use when we try to understand information, remember it, or use it to solve a problem or communicate with someone.

maintenance rehearsal Repeating information in short-term memory until it is no longer needed; may eventually lead to storage of information on long-term memory.

elaborative rehearsal A memory strategy that involves relating new information to something that is already known.

glish. You might remember the meaning of *éscaliers* by associating it with the English word *escalator*.

Levels of Processing in Working Memory.   Maintenance and elaborative rehearsal were first described by memory researchers Fergus Craik and Robert Lockhart (1972) in the context of their *levels-of-processing* model of memory (Baddeley, 1998). Their model proposed that maintenance rehearsal involves "shallow" processing (encoding based on superficial features of information such as the sound of a word), whereas elaborative rehearsal involves "deep" processing (encoding based on the meaning of information). They hypothesized that deep processing is more likely than shallow processing to lead to long-term retention.

The levels-of-processing hypothesis was tested in classic research by Craik and Tulving (1975). They had participants answer "yes" or "no" to questions asked about words just before the words were flashed to them for $\frac{1}{5}$ of a second. The participants had to process the words in three ways: (1) visually (is the word in capital letters?); (2) acoustically (does the word rhyme with another particular word?); and (3) semantically (does the word make sense when used in a particular sentence?). Thus, this test required shallow processing for the first question, deeper processing for the second question, and still deeper processing for the third question. Later retention tests showed that the deeper the level of processing, the higher the accuracy of memory. But this conclusion is equally valid for the three-system model. Some brain-imaging studies with fMRI revealed that semantic (deeper) encoding causes greater activity in the left prefrontal cortex (Gabrieli et al., 1996). Other studies of how brain activity is related to depth of (semantic) processing reveal two kinds of memory-related activity: information search and information retrieval (Rugg et al., 2000).

Long-Term Memory

What happens next? If information is processed effectively in short-term memory, it makes its way to long-term memory. **Long-term memory (LTM)** is a person's vast storehouse of permanent or relatively permanent memories (refer to Figure 6.2). There are no known limits to the storage capacity of this memory system, and long-term memories can last for years, some of them for a lifetime. Information in long-term memory is usually stored in semantic form, although visual images, sounds, and odors can be stored there, as well. Memory researchers often divide long-term memory into two subsystems, declarative and nondeclarative memory.

Declarative Memory.   The memory system stores facts, information, and personal life events that can be brought to mind verbally or in the form of images and then declared or stated in **declarative memory.** This long-term memory subsystem holds information that we intentionally and consciously recollect. There are two types of declarative memory: episodic memory and semantic memory.

Episodic memory is the type of declarative memory that records events as they have been subjectively experienced (Wheeler et al., 1997). It is somewhat like a mental diary, a record of the episodes of your life—the people you have known, the places you have seen, and the personal experiences you have had. According to Canadian psychologist Endel Tulving (1989), "episodic memory enables people to travel back in time, as it were, into their personal past, and to become consciously aware of having witnessed or participated in events and happenings at earlier times" (p. 362). Using episodic memory, a person might make this statement: "I remember being in Florida on my vacation last spring, lying on the sand, soaking up some rays, and listening to the sound of the waves rushing to the shore."

Semantic memory, the other type of declarative memory, is memory for general knowledge, or objective facts and information. Semantic memory is involved when a

long-term memory (LTM)   The memory system with a virtually unlimited capacity that contains vast stores of a person's permanent or relatively permanent memories.

declarative memory   The subsystem within long-term memory that stores facts, information, and personal life events that can be brought to mind verbally or in the form of images and then declared or stated; also called explicit memory.

6.4 **What kinds of information are stored in the subsystems of long-term memory?**

◄ Declarative memories involve facts, information, and personal life events, such as a trip to a foreign country. Nondeclarative memory encompasses motor skills, such as the expert swing of professional golfer Tiger Woods. Once learned, such movements can be carried out with little or no conscious effort.

episodic memory   (ep-ih-SOD-ik) The type of declarative memory that records events as they have been subjectively experienced.

semantic memory   The type of declarative memory that stores general knowledge, or objective facts and information.

▲ Have you heard it said that you never forget how to ride a bicycle? It's true because, although implicit memories such as motor skills take a lot of time to acquire, once learned, they are seldom forgotten.

nondeclarative memory The subsystem within long-term memory that stores motor skills, habits, and simple classically conditioned responses; also called implicit memory.

priming The phenomenon by which an earlier encounter with a stimulus (such as a word or a picture) increases the speed or accuracy of naming that stimulus or a related stimulus at a later time.

person recalls that Florida is bounded by the Atlantic Ocean on the east and the Gulf of Mexico on the west. It is not necessary to have ever been to Florida to know these facts. Consequently, semantic memory is more like an encyclopedia or a dictionary than a personal diary.

Memory researcher Endel Tulving (1995) points out that the two types of declarative memory do not function independently. For instance, your memory of being on a beach in Florida (episodic) relies upon your understanding of what a beach is (semantic). Likewise, the experience of actually being there (episodic) undoubtedly enhanced your general knowledge of the state (semantic).

However, researchers have recently demonstrated that some people who have suffered selective damage to their long-term semantic memory can still learn and remember using episodic memory (Graham et al., 2000). Patients with "semantic dementia" perform poorly on semantic tasks, such as picture naming, giving examples of general categories (e.g., household items), and sorting words or pictures into specified categories (e.g., living versus nonliving things). Yet their episodic memory is mainly unaffected (Hodges et al., 1995; Snowden et al., 1996). Although episodic and semantic memory are connected, episodic memory can store perceptual information without direct aid from or dependence on semantic memory (Graham et al., 2000).

Nondeclarative Memory. **Nondeclarative memory** (also called *implicit memory*) is the subsystem within long-term memory that stores motor skills, habits, and simple classically conditioned responses (Squire et al., 1993). Motor skills are acquired through repetitive practice and include such things as eating with a fork, riding a bicycle, or driving a car. Although acquired slowly, once learned, these skills become habit, are quite reliable, and can be carried out with little or no conscious effort. For example, you probably use the keyboard on a computer without consciously being able to name the keys in each row from left to right. **Figure 6.3** shows the two subsystems of long-term memory.

Associated with nondeclarative, or implicit, memory is a phenomenon known as **priming,** by which an earlier encounter with a stimulus (such as a word or a picture) increases the speed or accuracy of naming that stimulus or a related stimulus at a later time. Such improvement occurs without the person's conscious awareness of having previously seen or heard the stimulus. For example, a researcher might flash the word *elephant* on a computer screen so briefly that it is not consciously perceived by a viewer. But if asked later to name as many animals as come to mind, the viewer is quite likely to include "elephant" on the list (Challis, 1996).

Priming can influence not only performance, but preferences and behavior as well. Individuals exposed briefly (even subliminally) to pictures of abstract art showed greater preferences for that type of art than did others who did not see the pictures. And in one study, participants subliminally exposed to faces of real people later interacted with those people more than did individuals not exposed to the photos (Basic Behavioral Science Task Force, 1996).

Remember It   The Structure of Human Memory

1. Transforming information into a form that can be stored in memory is the process of _____; bringing to mind the material that has been stored is the process of _____.

2. Match each memory system with the best description of its capacity and the duration of time it holds information.
   - ____ (1) sensory memory
   - ____ (2) short-term memory
   - ____ (3) long-term memory
   - a. virtually unlimited capacity; long duration
   - b. large capacity; short duration
   - c. very limited capacity; short duration

3. Declarative memory includes information that can be put into _____ form.

4. Information that you use to ride a bicycle is stored in _____ memory.

Answers: 1. encoding, retrieval; 2. (1) b, (2) c, (3) a; 3. verbal; 4. nondeclarative

Figure 6.3 Subsystems of Long-Term Memory

Declarative memory can be divided into two subsystems: episodic memory, which stores memories of personally experienced events, and semantic memory, which stores facts and information. Nondeclarative memory consists of motor skills acquired through repetitive practice, habits, and simple classically conditioned responses.

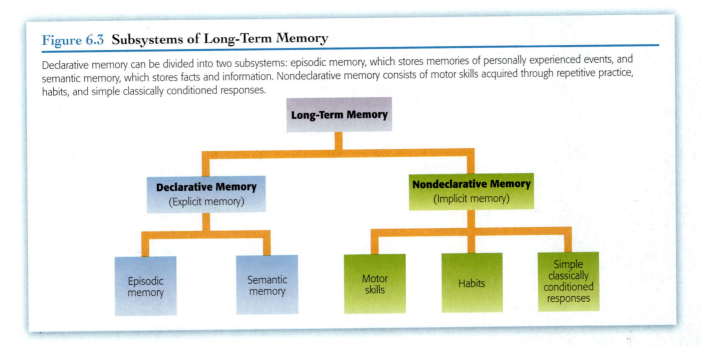

The Nature of Remembering

How many times have you recognized someone without being able to recall his or her name? Or perhaps you have tried to recall a telephone number and been able to remember only the first and last numbers. The processes that caused these apparent memory lapses represent two of the various principles that govern how we go about remembering things.

Three Types of Memory Tasks

Your experiences with your own memory have probably taught you that recalling information is far more difficult than recognizing that you have seen or heard it before. A great deal of memory research has focused on understanding the differences between these two processes.

6.5 What are the three methods used by psychologists to measure memory?

Recall.   Do you do well on essay tests? Most students prefer other kinds of exams, because essay tests usually require test takers to recall a lot of information. In **recall,** a person must produce required information simply by searching memory. Trying to remember someone's name, the items on a shopping list, or the words of a speech or a poem is a recall task. Which of the following test questions do you think is more difficult?

What are the three basic memory processes?
Which of the following is *not* one of the three basic memory processes?
a. encoding   b. storage   c. retrieval   d. relearning

Most people think the second question is easier because it requires only recognition, whereas the first involves recall.

A recall task may be made a little easier if cues are provided to jog memory. A **retrieval cue** is any stimulus or bit of information that aids in retrieving a particular memory. Think about how you might respond to these two test questions:

What are the four basic memory processes?
The four processes involved in memory are e _____ , s _____ , c _____ , and r _____ .

Both questions require you to recall information. However, most students would find the second question easier to answer because it includes four retrieval cues.

Sometimes *serial recall* is required; that is, information must be recalled in a specific order. This is the way you learned your ABCs, memorized poems, and learned any sequences that had to be carried out in a certain order. Serial recall is often easier than

recall   A memory task in which a person must produce required information by searching memory.

retrieval cue   Any stimulus or bit of information that aids in retrieving particular information from long-term memory.

▲ Are you better at remembering faces than names? Have you ever wondered why? It's because the task involves recognition rather than recall. You must recall the name but merely recognize the face.

recognition A memory task in which a person must simply identify material as familiar or as having been encountered before.

relearning method A measure of memory in which retention is expressed as the percentage of time saved when material is relearned compared with the time required to learn the material originally.

savings score The percentage of time saved when relearning material compared with the amount of time required for the original learning.

6.6 **What happens when information must be recalled in a particular order?**

serial position effect The finding that, for information learned in a sequence, recall is better for the beginning and ending items than for the middle items in the sequence.

primacy effect The tendency to recall the first items in a sequence more readily than the middle items.

free recall, or remembering items in any order. In serial recall, each letter, word, or task may serve as a cue for the one that follows. Indeed, research suggests that, in recall tasks, order associations are more resistant to distractions than meaningful associations are (Howard, 2002).

You may fail to recall information in a memory task even if you are given many retrieval cues, but this does not necessarily mean that the information is not in long-term memory. You might be able to remember it if a recognition task is used.

Recognition. **Recognition** is exactly what the name implies. A person simply recognizes something as familiar—a face, a name, a taste, a melody. Multiple-choice, matching, and true/false questions are examples of test items based on recognition. The main difference between recall and recognition is that a recognition task does not require you to supply the information but only to recognize it when you see it. The correct answer is included along with other items in a recognition question.

Recent brain-imaging studies have discovered that the hippocampus plays an extensive role in memory tasks involving recognition and that the degree of hippocampal activity varies depending on the exact nature of the task. When the task is recognizing famous faces, widespread brain activity takes place in both hemispheres, involving the prefrontal and temporal lobes and including the hippocampus and the surrounding hippocampal region. Less widespread brain activity is observed during the recognition of recently encoded faces or the encoding of faces seen for the first time (Henson et al., 2002). Studies with monkeys whose brain damage is limited to the hippocampal region show conclusively that this region is absolutely essential for normal recognition tasks (Teng et al., 2000; Zola et al., 2000).

Relearning. There is another, more sensitive way to measure memory. With the **relearning method,** retention is expressed as the percentage of time saved when material is relearned relative to the time required to learn the material originally. Suppose it took you 40 minutes to memorize a list of words, and 1 month later you were tested on those words, using recall or recognition. If you could not recall or recognize a single word, would this mean that you had absolutely no memory of anything on the list? Or could it mean that the recall and recognition tasks were not sensitive enough to measure what little information you may have stored? How could a researcher measure such a remnant of former learning? Using the relearning method, a researcher could time how long it would take you to relearn the list of words. If it took 20 minutes to relearn the list, this would represent a 50% savings over the original learning time of 40 minutes. The percentage of time saved—the **savings score**—reflects how much material remains in long-term memory.

College students demonstrate the relearning method each semester when they study for comprehensive final exams. Relearning material for a final exam takes less time than it took to learn the material originally.

The Serial Position Effect

What would happen if you were introduced to a dozen people at a party? You would most likely recall the names of the first few people you met and the last one or two, but forget many of the names in the middle. The reason is the **serial position effect**—the finding that, for information learned in a sequence, recall is better for items at the beginning and the end than for items in the middle of the sequence.

Information at the beginning of a sequence is subject to the **primary effect**—the tendency to recall the first items in a sequence more readily than the middle items. Such information is likely to be recalled because it already has been placed in long-term memory. Information at the end of a sequence is subject to the **recency effect**—the tendency to recall the last items in a sequence more readily than those in the middle. This information has an even higher probability of being recalled because it is still in short-term memory. The poorer recall of information in the middle of a sequence occurs because that information is no longer in short-term memory and has not yet been placed in long-term memory. The serial position effect lends strong support to the notion of separate systems for short-term and long-term memory (Postman & Phillips, 1965).

Context and Memory

Have you ever stood in your living room and thought of something you needed from your bedroom, only to forget what it was when you got there? Did the item come to mind again when you returned to the living room? Tulving and Thompson (1973) suggest that many elements of the physical setting in which a person learns information are encoded along with the information and become part of the memory. If part or all of the original context is reinstated, it may serve as a retrieval cue. That is why returning to the living room elicits the memory of the object you intended to get from the bedroom. In fact, just visualizing yourself in the living room might do the trick (Smith et al., 1978). (*Hint:* Next time you're taking a test and having difficulty recalling something, try visualizing yourself in the room where you studied.)

Godden and Baddeley (1975) conducted one of the early studies of context and memory with members of a university diving club. Participants memorized a list of words when they were either 10 feet underwater or on land. They were later tested for recall of the words in the same environment or in a different environment. Words learned underwater were best recalled underwater, and words learned on land were best recalled on land. In fact, when the divers learned and recalled the words in the same context, their scores were 47% higher than when the two contexts were different (see **Figure 6.4**).

In a more recent study of context-dependent memory, participants viewed videotapes and then were tested on their memory of the videos in two separate interviews conducted 2 days apart. The memory context was the same for all the participants, with one exception. Half the participants were questioned by different interviewers, whereas the other half were questioned by the same interviewer in both sessions. As you might expect, participants who were questioned twice by the same interviewer (same context) performed better than the other participants on the memory task (Bjorklund et al., 2000).

6.7 How do environmental conditions and emotional states affect memory?

recency effect   The tendency to recall the last items in a sequence more readily than those in the middle.

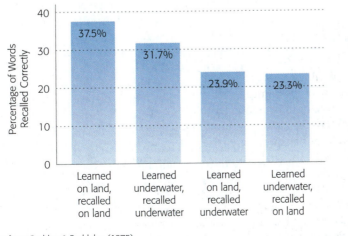

Figure 6.4 Context-Dependent Memory

Godden and Baddeley showed the strong influence of environmental context on recall. Divers who memorized a list of words, either on land or underwater, had significantly better recall in the same physical context in which the learning had taken place.

Source: Data from Godden & Baddeley (1975).

Odors can also supply powerful and enduring retrieval cues for memory. In a study by Morgan (1996), participants were placed in isolated cubicles and exposed to a list of 40 words. At the same time, they were exposed to different kinds of odors. They were instructed to perform a cognitive task using the words but were not asked to remember them. Then, back in the cubicle 5 days later, participants were unexpectedly tested for recall of the 40 words. Experimental participants who experienced a pleasant odor during learning and again when tested 5 days later had significantly higher recall than did control participants who did not experience the odor during both learning and recall.

People also tend to recall information better if they are in the same emotional state as when the information was encoded. Psychologists call this the **state-dependent memory effect.** For example, when researchers exposed college students to spiders and/or snakes while they were learning lists of words (presumably an anxiety-inducing experience!), the students recalled more words when the creatures were also present during tests of recall (Lang et al., 2001). Adults who are clinically depressed tend to recall more negative life experiences (Clark & Teasdale, 1982) and are likely to recall their parents as unloving and rejecting (Lewinsohn & Rosenbaum, 1987). Moreover, a meta-analysis of 48 studies revealed a significant relationship between depression and memory impairment. And recognition and recall were more impaired in younger depressed patients than in older ones (Burt et al., 1995). But, as depression lifts, the tendency toward negative recall and associated memory impairments reverses itself.

Memory as Reconstruction

Wilder Penfield, a Canadian neurosurgeon, claimed that all experiences leave a permanent record in the brain (Penfield, 1969). However, research suggests that the views of Sir Francis Bartlett (1886–1969), a pioneering memory researcher, are probably closer to the truth. Bartlett asserted that memory is a **reconstruction**—an account pieced together from a few highlights, using information that may or may not be accurate (Loftus & Loftus, 1980).

Schemas and Memory. Bartlett proposed that reconstructive memory processes are influenced by **schemas**—frameworks of knowledge and assumptions we have about people, objects, and events. In most cases, schemas are helpful to memory because they aid in processing large amounts of material by providing frameworks into which people can incorporate new information. For instance, suppose you read the headline, "Dog Saves Boy from Drowning." What facts would you expect to be included in the story? You might expect to read about where the incident took place; perhaps it happened at a beach or in a neighborhood swimming pool. But you would be unlikely to expect to read about a canine rescue that occurred in a bathtub. Why?—because schemas are based on situational averages. Drownings occur most often in bodies of water in which people swim. Thus the schema evoked by the headline would cause you to picture the incident taking place in the setting that would be most likely.

Of course, schemas can also lead to inaccuracies in memory. Bartlett studied this phenomenon by giving participants stories to read and drawings to study; then, after varying time intervals, he had them reproduce the original material. Accurate reports were rare. The participants seemed to reconstruct the material they had learned, rather than actually remember it. They recreated the stories, making them shorter and more consistent with their own individual viewpoints. They adapted puzzling features of the stories to fit their own expectations and often changed details, substituting more familiar objects or events. Errors in memory increased with time, and Bartlett's participants were not aware that they had partly remembered and partly invented the material. Ironically,

state-dependent memory effect The tendency to recall information better if one is in the same pharmacological or psychological state as when the information was encoded.

reconstruction An account of an event that has been pieced together from a few highlights, using information that may or may not be accurate.

schemas The integrated frameworks of knowledge and assumptions a person has about people, objects, and events, which affect how the person encodes and recalls information.

6.8 What is meant by the statement "Memory is reconstructive in nature"?

▼ When people recall an event, such as a car accident, they are actually reconstructing it from memory by piecing together bits of information that may or may not be totally accurate.

the parts his participants. had created were often the parts they most adamantly claimed to have remembered (Bartlett, 1932).

Bartlett concluded that people systematically distort the facts and the circumstances of experiences. Information already stored in long-term memory exerts a strong influence on how people remember new information and experiences. As Bartlett (1932) put it, "the past is being continually remade, reconstructed in the interest of the present" (p. 309).

Distortion in Memory.   When people reconstruct memories, they do not purposely try to distort the actual experience—unless, of course, they are lying. But people tend to omit some details that actually occurred and to supply other details from their own schemas. The tendency toward systematic distortion of actual events has been proven many times. The following *Try It* demonstrates distortion in memory.

Try It   Creating a False Memory

Read this list of words aloud at a rate of about one word per second. Then close your book, and write down all the words you can remember.

| bed | wake | snore | dream | yawn | tired |
| nap | awake | doze | rest | snooze | slumber |

Now check your list. Did you "remember" the word *sleep*?
Many people do, even though it is not one of the words on the list (Deese, 1959).

The *Try It* shows that we are very likely to alter or distort what we see or hear to make it fit with what we believe to be true, in other words, our schemas. All the words on the list are related to sleep, so it seems logical that *sleep* should be one of the words. In experiments using word lists similar to the one in the *Try It*, between 40% and 55% of the participants "remembered" a key related word that was not on the list (Roediger & McDermott, 1995). If you added the word *sleep* when doing the *Try It*, you created a false memory, which probably seemed as real to you as a true memory (Dodson et al., 2000).

The tendency to distort makes the world more understandable and enables people to organize their experiences into their existing systems of beliefs and expectations. But this tendency often causes gross inaccuracies in what people remember. Research has shown that autobiographical memories are particularly subject to reconstruction in ways that cause pleasant events to be better remembered than unpleasant ones and memories of unpleasant events to become more pleasant over time. Researchers call this kind of distortion *positive bias* (Wood & Conway, 2006). A study of college students' memories of their high school grades demonstrated this sort of bias. Nearly all the students accurately remembered the A's they made, while only 29% remembered their D's (Barhrick et al., 1996).

Remarkably, research suggests that memories of even the most horrific experiences can be influenced by positive bias. In several studies carried out in the 1980s, holocaust survivors' recollections of their experiences in Nazi concentration camps were compared to reports they had given to war crimes investigators during and immediately after World War II (1939–1945). In one case, a man reported in the 1940s that he had personally witnessed prisoners being drowned by concentration camp guards. In the 1980s, however, he claimed that no such incident had occurred and even denied having given the earlier report (Baddeley, 1998). Why are our memories subject to such positive bias? Researchers speculate that positive bias may be important to regulation of current states of emotional well-being (Kennedy, Mather, & Carstensen, 2004). In other words, our current need for emotional well-being is a schema we use to selectively process our memories of past events.

Remember It   The Nature of Remembering

1. Match each task with the corresponding method of measuring memory:

   _____ (1) identifying a suspect in a lineup

   _____ (2) answering a fill-in-the-blank question on a test

   _____ (3) having to study less for a comprehensive final exam than for all of the previous exams put together

   _____ (4) answering a matching or multiple-choice question on a test

   _____ (5) reciting one's lines in a play

   a. recognition
   b. relearning
   c. recall

2. When children learn the alphabet, they often can recite "A, B, C, D, . . ." and ". . . , W, X, Y, Z" before they can recite the letters in between. This is because of the _____.

3. The _____ happens when individuals acquire information while in a pharmacologically altered state of consciousness or when experiencing a particular emotion.

4. When a person uses _____ to process information, both encoding and retrieval can be affected.

Answers: 1. (1) a, (2) c, (3) b, (4) a, (5) c; 2. serial position effect; 3. state-dependent memory effect; 4. schemas

Memory in Everyday Life

Most of what you have learned so far in this chapter is based on laboratory experiments. Such studies provide psychologists with vital information about memory, but some researchers have ventured beyond the laboratory to find out how memory works in everyday settings, such as when we have a shocking emotional experience. Researchers have also examined how well (or how poorly) our memories function when we are confronted with information that represents a cultural framework different from our own. Other researchers, including those who study eyewitness testimony, have used laboratory experiments to demonstrate that the inaccuracy of human memory can sometimes lead to tragic results. Unfortunate consequences can also follow from incidents in which people believe that they have recovered a "lost" memory when, in fact, they have invented a false memory.

Flashbulb and Photographic Memories

6.9 What does research say about flashbulb and photographic memories?

Do you remember where you were and what you were doing when you heard about the tragic events of September 11, 2001? Most people do. Likewise, most people over age 50 claim to have vivid memories of exactly when and where they received the news of the assassination of President John F. Kennedy. And many of their parents have very clear memories of learning about the attack on Pearl Harbor on December 7, 1941, which marked the entry of the United States into World War II. This type of extremely vivid memory is called a **flashbulb memory** (Bohannon, 1988). Brown and Kulik (1977) suggest that a flashbulb memory is formed when a person learns of an event that is very surprising, shocking, or highly emotional. You might have a flashbulb memory of when you received the news of the death or the serious injury of a close family member or a friend.

Pillemer (1990) argues that flashbulb memories do not constitute a completely different type of memory. Rather, he suggests, all memories can vary on the dimensions of emotion, consequentiality (the importance of the consequences of the event), and rehearsal (how often people think or talk about the event afterwards). Flashbulb memories rank high in all three dimensions and thus are extremely memorable.

However, several studies suggest that flashbulb memories are not as accurate as people believe them to be. Neisser and Harsch (1992) questioned university freshmen about the televised explosion of the space shuttle *Challenger* the following morning. When the same students were questioned again 3 years later, one-third gave accounts that differed

flashbulb memory An extremely vivid memory of the conditions surrounding one's first hearing the news of a surprising, shocking, or highly emotional event.

markedly from those given initially, but these individuals were extremely confident about their recollections. Further, flashbulb memories appear to be forgotten at about the same rate and in the same ways as other kinds of memories (Curci et al., 2001).

Often, we believe that our flashbulb memories are photographic in nature, but studies showing that these memories include subtle inaccuracies suggest otherwise. Psychologists doubt that there are more than a few rare cases of truly photographic memories. That is why examples such as those provided by Franco Magnani's art-work stand out so sharply.

Some studies do suggest, however, that children are more likely than adults to have photographic memories. It appears that about 5% of children are capable of generat-ing such memories, the result of a process psychologists call **eidetic imagery** (Haber, 1980). These children can retain the image of a visual stimulus, such as a picture, for several minutes after it has been removed from view and use this retained image to answer questions about the visual stimulus.

Children with eidetic imagery generally have no better long-term memory than oth-ers their age. And virtually all children with eidetic imagery lose it before adulthood. One exceptional case, however, is Elizabeth, a teacher and a skilled artist. She can create on canvas an exact duplicate of a remembered scene in all its rich detail. Just as remark-able is her ability to retain visual images of words. "Years after having read a poem in a foreign language, she can fetch back an image of the printed page and copy the poem from the bottom line to the top line as fast as she can write" (Stromeyer, 1970, p. 77).

Memory and Culture

Sir Frederick Bartlett (1932) believed that some impressive memory abilities operate within a social or cultural context and cannot be completely understood as a process. He stated that "both the manner and matter of recall are often predominantly determined by social influences" (p. 244). Studying memory in a cultural context, Bartlett (1932) de-scribed the amazing ability of the Swazi people of Africa to remember the slight differences in individual characteristics of their cows. One Swazi herdsman, Bartlett claimed, could remember details of every cow he had tended the year be-fore. Such a feat is less surprising when you consider that the key component of traditional Swazi culture is the herds of cattle the people tend and depend on for their living. Do the Swazi people have super memory powers? Bartlett asked young Swazi men and young European men to recall a mes-sage consisting of 25 words. In this case, the Swazi had no better recall ability than the Europeans.

Among many tribal peoples in Africa, the history of the tribe is preserved orally by specialists, who must be able to encode, store, and retrieve huge volumes of historical data (D'Azevedo, 1982). Elders of the Iatmul people of New Guinea are also said to have committed to memory the lines of descent for the various clans of their people, stretching back for many generations (Bateson, 1982). The unerring memory of the elders for the kinship patterns of their people are used to resolve disputed property claims (Mistry & Rogoff, 1994).

Barbara Rogoff, an expert in cultural psychology, maintains that such phenomenal, prodigious memory feats are best explained and understood in their cultural context (Rogoff & Mistry, 1985). The tribal elders perform their impressive memory feats be-cause it is an integral and critically important part of the culture in which they live. Most likely, their ability to remember nonmeaningful information would be no better than your own.

A study examining memory for location among a tribal group in India, the Asur, who do not use artificial lighting of any kind, provides further information about the influence of culture on memory (Mishra & Singh, 1992). Researchers hypothesized that members of this group would perform better on tests of memory for locations

▲ Eyewitnesses to the aftermath of the terrorist attacks on the World Trade Center almost certainly formed flashbulb memories of the horrific events they witnessed. Do you re-member where you were and what you were doing when you heard the news on September 11, 2001?

6.10 How does culture influence memory?

▲ In many traditional cultures, elders are oral historians, remembering and passing on the details of tribal traditions and myths as well as ge-nealogical data.

eidetic imagery (eye-DET-ik) The ability to retain the image of a visual stimulus for several minutes after it has been removed from view and to use this retained image to answer questions about the visual stimulus.

than on memory tests involving word pairs, because, without artificial light, they have to remember where things are in order to be able to move around in the dark without bumping into things. When the tribe members were tested, the results supported this hypothesis: They remembered locations better than word pairs.

In classic research, cognitive psychologists have also found that people more easily remember stories set in their own cultures than those set in others, just as they more easily recognize photographs of people of their own ethnic group than they do of others (Corenblum & Meissner, 2006). In one of the first of these studies, researchers told women in the United States and Aboriginal women in Australia a story about a sick child (Steffensen & Calker, 1982). Participants were randomly assigned to groups for whom story outcomes were varied. In one version, the girl got well after being treated by a physician. In the other, a traditional native healer was called in to help the girl. Aboriginal participants better recalled the story with the native healer, while the American women were more accurate in their recall of the story in which a physician treated the girl. Most likely, these results reflect the influence of culturally based schemas. Aboriginal participants' schemas led them to expect a story about a sick child to include a native healer, and the story that fit with these expectations was easier for them to understand and remember. Just the opposite was true for the Western participants.

Culture also affects autobiographical memory. People in Western cultures, which emphasize the individual more than the society as a whole, focus on the emotional aspects of event memories. By contrast, individuals in socially oriented cultures emphasize emotions much less, especially emotions such as anger that can disrupt relationships (Fivush & Nelson, 2004).

Eyewitness Testimony

6.11 What conditions reduce the reliability of eyewitness testimony?

In 1999, the U.S. Department of Justice prepared the first set of national guidelines for the collection of eyewitness evidence in the United States (Wells et al., 2000). Research attesting to the inaccuracy of such testimony rendered these guidelines necessary (Loftus, 1993a, 2003; Villegas, 2005). According to one of the leading researchers in this area, Elizabeth Loftus, studies on the reconstructive nature of human memory suggest that eyewitness testimony is highly subject to error, and that it should always be viewed with caution (Loftus, 1979).

Fortunately, eyewitness mistakes can be minimized. Eyewitnesses to crimes typically identify suspects from a lineup. If shown photographs of a suspect before viewing the lineup, eyewitnesses may mistakenly identify that suspect in the lineup because the person looks familiar. Research suggests that it is better to have an eyewitness first describe the perpetrator and then search for photos matching that description than to have the eyewitness start by looking through photos and making judgments as to their similarity to the perpetrator (Pryke et al., 2000).

The composition of the lineup is also important. Other subjects in a lineup must resemble the suspect in age, body build, and certainly race. Even then, if the lineup does not contain the guilty party, eyewitnesses may identify the person who most closely resembles the perpetrator (Gonzalez et al., 1993). Eyewitnesses are less likely to make errors if a sequential lineup is used—that is, if the members of the lineup are viewed one after the other, rather than simultaneously (Loftus, 1993a). Some police officers and researchers prefer a "showup," in which the witness sees only one suspect at a time and indicates whether or not that person is the perpetrator. There are fewer misidentifications with a showup, but also more failures to make a positive identification (Wells, 1993).

Eyewitnesses are more likely to identify the wrong person if the person's race is different from their own. According to Egeth (1993), misidentifications are approximately 15% higher in cross-race than in same-race identifications. Misidentification is also somewhat more likely to occur when a weapon is used in a crime. The witnesses may pay more attention to the weapon than to the physical characteristics of the criminal (Steblay, 1992).

▲ The composition of this police lineup is consistent with research findings that suggest that all individuals in a lineup should be similar to the suspect with respect to age, race, body build, and other physical characteristics.

Even the questioning of witnesses after a crime can influence what they later remember. Because leading questions can substantially change a witness's memory of an event, it is critical that the interviewers ask neutral questions (Leichtman & Ceci, 1995). Misleading information supplied after the event can result in erroneous recollections of the actual event, a phenomenon known as the *misinformation effect* (Kroll et al., 1988; Loftus, 2005; Loftus & Hoffman, 1989). Loftus (1997) and her students have conducted "more than 20 experiments involving over 20,000 participants that document how exposure to misinformation induces memory distortion" (p. 71). Furthermore, after eyewitnesses have repeatedly recalled information, whether it is accurate or inaccurate, they become even more confident when they testify in court because the information is so easily retrieved (Shaw, 1996).

Witnessing a crime is highly stressful. How does stress affect eyewitness accuracy? Research suggests that eyewitnesses do tend to remember the central, critical details of the event, even though their arousal is high, but the memory of less important details suffers (Burke et al., 1992; Christianson, 1992).

Furthermore, the confidence eyewitnesses have in their testimony is not necessarily an indication of its accuracy (Loftus, 1993a; Sporer et al., 1995). In fact, eyewitnesses who perceive themselves to be more objective have more confidence in their testimony, regardless of its accuracy, and are more likely to include incorrect information in their verbal descriptions (Geiselman et al., 2000). When witnesses make incorrect identifications with great certainty, they can be highly persuasive to judges and jurors alike. "A false eyewitness identification can create a real-life nightmare for the identified person, friends, and family members. . . . False identifications also mean that the actual culprit remains at large—a double injustice" (Wells, 1993, p. 568).

The Repressed Memory Controversy

Do you believe that unconscious memories of childhood abuse can lead to serious psychological disorders? Perhaps because of the frequency of such cases in fictional literature, on television, and in movies, many people in the United States apparently do believe that so-called repressed memories can cause problems in adulthood (Stafford & Lynn, 2002). Such beliefs have also been fostered by self-help books such as *The Courage to Heal*, published in 1988, by Ellen Bass and Laura Davis. This bestselling book became the "bible" for sex abuse victims and the leading "textbook" for some therapists who specialized in treating them. Bass and Davis not only sought to help survivors who remember having suffered sexual abuse, but also reached out to other people who had no memory of any sexual abuse and tried to help them determine whether they might have been abused. They suggested that "if you are unable to remember any specific instances . . . but still have a feeling that something abusive happened to you, it probably did" (p. 71). They offered a definite conclusion: "If you think you were abused and your life shows the symptoms, then you were" (p. 22). And they freed potential victims of sexual abuse from the responsibility of establishing any proof: "You are not responsible for proving that you were abused" (p. 37).

6.12 What is the controversy regarding the recovery of repressed memories of childhood sexual abuse?

Recovered Memories or False Memories? Many psychologists are skeptical about such "recovered" memories, claiming that they are actually false memories created by the suggestions of therapists. Critics "argue that repression of truly traumatic memories is rare" (Bowers & Farvolden, 1996, p. 355). Moreover, they maintain that "when it comes to a serious trauma, intrusive thoughts and memories of it are the most characteristic reaction" (p. 359). Repressed-memory therapists believe, however, that healing hinges on their patients' being able to recover their repressed memories.

Critics further charge that recovered memories of sexual abuse are suspect because of the techniques therapists usually use to uncover them—namely, hypnosis and guided imagery. As you have learned (in Chapter 4), hypnosis does not improve the accuracy of memory, only the confidence that what one remembers is accurate. And a therapist using guided imagery might tell a patient something similar to what Wendy Maltz (1991) advocates in her book:

Spend time imagining that you were sexually abused, without worrying about accuracy, proving anything, or having your ideas make sense. . . . Ask yourself . . . these questions: What time of day is it? Where are you? Indoors or outdoors? What kind of things are happening? (p. 50)

Can merely imagining experiences in this way lead people to believe that those experiences had actually happened to them? Yes, according to some studies. Many research participants who are instructed to imagine that a fictitious event happened do, in fact, develop a false memory of that imagined event (Hyman et al., 1995; Hyman & Pentland, 1996; Loftus & Pickrell, 1995; Mazzoni & Memon, 2003; Worthen & Wood, 2001).

False childhood memories can also be experimentally induced. Garry and Loftus (1994) were able to implant a false memory of being lost in a shopping mall at 5 years of age in 25% of participants aged 18 to 53, after verification of the fictitious experience by a relative. Repeated exposure to suggestions of false memories can create those memories (Zaragoza & Mitchell, 1996). Further, researchers have found that adults who claim to have recovered memories of childhood abuse or of abduction by extraterrestrials are more vulnerable to experimentally induced false memories than are adults who do not report such recovered memories (McNally, 2003). So, individual differences in suggestibility may play a role in the recovery of memories.

Infantile Amnesia. Critics are especially skeptical of recovered memories of events that occurred in the first few years of life; in part because the hippocampus, vital in the formation of episodic memories, is not fully developed then. And neither are the areas of the cortex where memories are stored (Squire et al., 1993). Furthermore, young children, who are still limited in language ability, do not store semantic memories in categories that are accessible to them later in life. The relative inability of older children and adults to recall events from the first few years of life is referred to as **infantile amnesia.**

In light of these developmental limitations, is it possible that some individuals cannot recall incidents of childhood sexual abuse? Widom and Morris (1997) found that 64% of a group of women who had been sexually abused as children reported no memory of the abuse in a 2-hour interview 20 years later. Following up on women who had documented histories of sexual victimization, Williams (1994) found that 38% of them did not report remembering the sexual abuse some 17 years later. Memories of abuse were better when the victimization took place between the ages of 7 and 17 than when it occurred in the first 6 years of life. Keep in mind, however, that it is possible that some of these women may have remembered the abuse but, for whatever reason, chose not to admit it. Further, there is some indication that individuals who are traumatized develop an attentional style that involves distracting oneself from potentially unpleasant stimuli (DePrince & Freyd, 2004). It is this attentional style, some researchers argue, that prevents such individuals from forming memories of abuse that can be easily recalled.

Does it matter whether an abuse victim recalls the episode? Recall that Freud argued that repressed memories inhabit the unconscious mind and stir up troublesome emotions. His psychoanalytic therapy was geared toward helping patients recall repressed memories in order to improve their mental health. However, it turns out that victims who have no memory of abusive episodes for which there is reliable objective evidence, such as police reports, appear to be no less mentally healthy or unhealthy than their counterparts who remember these episodes (McNally et al., 2006).

The American Psychological Association (1994), the American Psychiatric Association (1993), and the American Medical Association (1994) have issued status reports on memories of childhood abuse. The position of all three groups is that current evidence supports both the possibility that repressed memories exist and the likehood that false memories can be constructed in response to suggestions of abuse. Moreover, individuals who hold false memories are often fully convinced that they are accurate because of the details such memories contain and the strong emotions associated with them (Dodson et al., 2000; Gonsalves et al., 2004; Henkel et al., 2000, 2004; Loftus, 2004; Loftus & Bernstein, 2005; McNally et al., 2004). Neuroimaging studies suggest that engaging in visually vivid mental replays of false memories may serve to strengthen them all the more (Lindsay et al., 2004). Thus, many experts recommend that recovered memories of abuse should be verified independently before they are accepted as facts.

infantile amnesia The relative inability of older children and adults to recall events from the first few years of life.

Biology and Memory

Obviously, a person's vast store of memories must exist physically somewhere in the brain. But where?

The Hippocampus and Hippocampal Region

Researchers continue to identify specific locations in the brain that house and mediate functions and processes in memory. One important source of information comes from people who have suffered memory loss resulting from damage to specific brain areas. One especially significant case is that of H.M., a man who suffered from such severe epilepsy that, out of desperation, he agreed to a radical surgical procedure. The surgeon removed the part of the brain believed to be causing H.M.'s seizures—the medial portions of both temporal lobes, containing the amygdala and the **hippocampal region,** which includes the hippocampus itself and the underlying cortical areas. It was 1953, and H.M. was 27 years old.

After his surgery, H.M. remained intelligent and psychologically stable, and his seizures were drastically reduced. But unfortunately, the tissue cut from H.M.'s brain housed more than the site of his seizures. It also contained his ability to use working memory to store new information in long-term memory. Although the capacity of his short-term memory remains the same and he remembers life events that were stored before the operation, H.M. suffers from **anterograde amnesia.** He has not been able to remember a single event that has occurred since the surgery. And though H.M. is in his 80s, as far as his conscious long-term memory is concerned, it is still 1953 and he is still 27 years old.

Surgery affected only H.M.'s declarative, long-term memory—his ability to store facts, personal experiences, names, faces, telephone numbers, and the like. But researchers were surprised to discover that he could still form nondeclarative memories; that is, he could still acquire skills through repetitive practice, although he could not remember having done so. For example, since the surgery, H.M. has learned to play tennis and improve his game, but he has no memory of ever having played (Milner, 1966, 1970; Milner et al., 1968).

Animal studies support the conclusion that the parts of H.M.'s brain that were removed are critical to working memory function (Ragozzino et al., 2002). Moreover, other patients who have suffered similar brain damage show the same types of memory loss (Squire, 1992).

Most research supports the hypothesis that the hippocampus is especially important in forming episodic memories (Eichenbaum, 1997; Eichenbaum & Fortin, 2003; Gluck & Myers, 1997;

6.13 What roles do the hippocampus and the hippocampal region play in memory?

hippocampal region A part of the limbic system, which includes the hippocampus itself and the underlying cortical areas, involved in the formation of semantic memories.

anterograde amnesia The inability to form long-term memories of events occurring after a brain injury or brain surgery, although memories formed before the trauma are usually intact and short-term memory is unaffected.

▲ In the film *50 First Dates*, Drew Barrymore's character suffered from a memory disorder very much like that of H.M.

Spiers et al., 2001). Semantic memory, however, depends not only on the hippocampus, but also on the other parts of the hippocampal region (Hoenig & Acheef, 2005; Vargha-Khadem et al., 1997). Once stored, memories can be retrieved without the involvement of the hippocampus (Gluck & Myers, 1997; McClelland et al., 1995). Consequently, many researchers argue that neurological underpinnings of episodic and semantic memories are entirely separate (e.g., Tulving, 2002). But the degree to which the brain processes associated with episodic and semantic memories can be clearly distinguished is being questioned by some neuroscientists. Research involving older adults who suffer from semantic dementia due to frontal lobe damage shows that many of them suffer from deficiencies in episodic memory (Nestor et al., 2002). Moreover, other studies show that damage to the temporal and occipital lobes can also affect episodic memory (Wheeler & McMillan, 2001).

An interesting study (Maguire et al., 2000) suggests that the hippocampus may serve special functions in addition to those already known. A part of the hippocampus evidently specializes in navigational skills by helping to create intricate neural spatial maps. Using magnetic resonance imaging (MRI) scans, researchers found that the rear (posterior) region of the hippocampus of London taxi drivers was significantly larger than that of participants in a matched control group whose living did not depend on navigational skills (see **Figure 6.5**). In addition, the more time spent as a taxi driver, the greater the size of this part of the hippocampus. Further, in many small mammals and birds, the size of the hippocampus increases seasonally, as navigational skills and spatial maps showing where food is hidden become critical for survival (Clayton, 1998; Colombo & Broadbent, 2000). Moreover, recent animal studies show that the hippocampus also plays an important role in the reorganization of previously learned spatial information (Bilkey & Clearwater, 2005; Lee & Kesner, 2002).

Thus, research has established that the hippocampus is critically important for storing and using mental maps to navigate in the environment. And the observed size increase in the hippocampus of the more experienced London taxi drivers confirms that brain plasticity in response to environmental demands can continue into adulthood. These findings also raise the possibility of *neurogenesis* (the growth of new neurons) in the adult hippocampus.

We have considered how researchers have identified and located some of the brain structures that play a role in memory. But what happens within these brain structures as they change, reshape, and rearrange to make new memories?

Neuronal Changes and Memory

6.14 Why is long-term potentiation important?

Some researchers are exploring memory at deeper levels than the structures of the brain. Some look at the actions of single neurons; others study collections of neurons and their synapses and the neurotransmitters whose chemical action begins the process of recording and storing a memory. The first close look at how memory works in single neurons was provided by Eric Kandel and his colleagues, who traced the effects of learning and memory in the sea snail *Aplysia* (Dale & Kandel, 1990). Using tiny electrodes implanted in several single neurons in this snail, the researchers mapped the neural circuits that are formed and maintained as the animal learns and remembers. They also discovered the different types of protein synthesis that facilitate short-term and long-term memory (Sweatt & Kandel, 1989). Kandel won a Nobel Prize in 2000 for his work.

But the studies of learning and memory in *Aplysia* reflect only simple classical conditioning, which is a type of nondeclarative memory. Other researchers studying mammals report that physical changes occur in the neurons and synapses in brain regions involved in declarative memory (Lee & Kesner, 2002).

As far back as the 1940s, Canadian psychologist Donald O. Hebb (1949) argued that learning and memory must involve the enhancement of transmission at the synapses between neurons. The most widely studied model for learning and memory at the level of the neurons meets the requirements of the mechanism Hebb described

Figure 6.5 MRI Scans Showing the Larger Size of the Posterior Hippocampus in the Brain of an Experienced Taxi Driver

The posterior (rear) hippocampus of an experienced London taxi driver, shown in red in MRI scan (a), is significantly larger than the posterior hippocampus of a research participant who was not a taxi driver, shown in red in scan (b).

(a)   (b)

Source: Adapted from Maguire et al. (2000).

(Fischbach, 1992). **Long-term potentiation (LTP)** is an increase in the efficiency of neural transmission at the synapses that lasts for hours or longer (Bliss & Lomo, 2000; Martinez & Derrick, 1996; Nguyen et al., 1994). (*To potentiate* means "to make potent, or to strengthen.") Long-term potentiation does not take place unless both the sending and the receiving neurons are activated at the same time by intense stimulation. Also, the receiving neuron must be depolarized (ready to fire) when the stimulation occurs, or LTP will not happen. LTP is common in the hippocampal region, which, as you have learned, is essential in the formation of declarative memories (Eichenbaum & Otto, 1993).

If the changes in synapses produced by LTP are the same changes that take place during learning, then blocking or preventing LTP should interfere with learning. And it does. When Davis and others (1992) gave rats a drug that blocks certain receptors in doses large enough to interfere with a maze-running task, they discovered that LTP in the rats' hippocampi was also disrupted. In contrast, Riedel (1996) found that LTP was enhanced and the rats' memory improved when a drug that excites those same receptors was administered shortly after maze training.

These studies have led researchers to search for associations between long-term potentiation and disorders that are known to disrupt neurotransmitter activity and to be associated with memory functioning. Depression, for instance, has been found to interfere with long-term potentiation (Froc & Racine, 2005). Other disorders that are suspected to have biochemical links to long-term potential include bipolar disorder, Alzheimer's disease, and Parkinson's disease (Francis, 2003; Friedrich, 2005; Ueki et al., 2006). However, controversy continues as to whether the relatively long-lasting increase in synaptic efficiency that constitutes LTP is the result of an increase in the amount of neurotransmitter released, an increase in the number of receptors at the synapses, or both (Bennett, 2000).

Hormones and Memory

The strongest and most lasting memories are usually those fueled by emotion. Research by Cahill and McGaugh (1995) suggests that there may be two pathways for forming memories—one for ordinary information and another for memories that are fired by emotion. When a person is emotionally aroused, the adrenal glands release the hormones epinephrine (adrenalin) and norepinephrine (noradrenaline) into the bloodstream. Long known to be involved in the "fight or flight response," these hormones enable humans to survive, and they also imprint powerful and enduring memories of the circumstances surrounding threatening situations. Such emotionally laden

6.15 How do hormones influence memory?

long-term potentiation (LTP)
An increase in the efficiency of neural transmission at the synapses that lasts for hours or longer.

▲ The strongest and most lasting memories are usually fueled by emotion. That's why most people have vivid memories of the events and circumstances that surround the experience of falling in love.

memories activate the amygdala (known to play a central role in emotion) and other parts of the memory system. This widespread activation in the brain may be the most important factor in explaining the intensity and durability of flashbulb memories.

Other hormones may have important effects on memory. Excessive levels of the stress hormone *cortisol*, for example, have been shown to interfere with memory in patients who suffer from diseases of the adrenal glands, the site of cortisol production (Jelicic & Bonke, 2001). Furthermore, people whose bodies react to experimenter-induced stressors, such as forced public speaking, by releasing higher than average levels of cortisol perform less well on memory tests than those whose bodies release lower than average levels in the same situations (Al'absi et al., 2002).

Estrogen, the female sex hormone, appears to improve working memory efficiency (Dohanich, 2003). This hormone, along with others produced by the ovaries, also plays some role in the development and maintenance of synapses in areas of the brain known to be associated with memory (e.g. the hippocampus). This finding caused researchers to hypothesize that hormone replacement therapy might prevent or reverse the effects of Alzheimer's disease (Dohanich, 2003). However, recent research shows that postmenopausal women who take a combination of synthetic estrogen and progesterone, the two hormones that regulate the menstrual cycle, may actually increase their risk of developing dementia (Rapp et al., 2003; Shumaker et al., 2003). Some researchers have explained these seemingly contradictory findings by claiming that the timing of estrogen replacement is the most critical factor in its effect on memory function (Marriott & Wenk, 2004). They think that women who take estrogen before developing symptoms of Alzheimer's disease may be more likely to benefit from it than those who receive hormone replacement therapy after they have been diagnosed with the disorder. Most researchers agree, though, that much more research is needed before there will be a definitive answer about the possible role of hormone treatment in the prevention and treatment of dementia.

Remember It   Biology and Memory

1. The hippocampus is involved primarily in the formation of _____ memories; the rest of the hippocampal region is involved primarily in the formation of _____ memories.

2. H.M. retained his ability to add to his _____ memory.

3. _____ is the long-lasting increase in the efficiency of neural transmission at the synapses; it may be the basis for learning and memory at the level of the neurons.

4. Memories of circumstances surrounding threatening situations that elicit the "fight or flight response" activate the _____.

Answers: 1. episodic, semantic; 2. nondeclarative; 3. Long-term potentiation; 4. amygdala

Forgetting

Wouldn't it be depressing if you remembered in exact detail every bad thing that ever happened to you? Most people think of forgetting as a problem to be overcome, but it's not always unwelcome. Still, when you need to remember particular information to answer an exam question, forgetting can be very frustrating.

Ebbinghaus and the First Experimental Studies on Forgetting

6.16 What did Ebbinghaus discover about forgetting?

Hermann Ebbinghaus (1850–1909) conducted the first experimental studies on learning and memory. Realizing that some materials are easier than others to understand and remember, Ebbinghaus faced the task of finding items that would all be equally difficult to memorize. So he invented the **nonsense syllable,** a consonant-vowel-consonant combination that is not an actual word. Examples are LEJ, XIZ, LUK, and

ZOH. Using nonsense syllables in his research largely accomplished Ebbinghaus's goal. But did you notice that some of the syllables sound more like actual words than others and would, therefore, be easier to remember?

Ebbinghaus (1885/1964) conducted his studies on memory using 2,300 nonsense syllables as his material and himself as the only participant. He carried out all his experiments at about the same time of day in the same surroundings, eliminating all possible distractions. Ebbinghaus memorized lists of nonsense syllables by repeating them over and over at a constant rate of 2.5 syllables per second, marking time with a metronome or a ticking watch. He repeated a list until he could recall it twice without error, a measure he called *mastery*.

Ebbinghaus recorded the amount of time or the number of trials it took to memorize his lists to mastery. Then, after different periods of time had passed and forgetting had occurred, he recorded the amount of time or number of trials needed to relearn the same list to mastery. Ebbinghaus compared the time or number of trials required for relearning with that for original learning and then computed the percentage of time saved. This savings score represented the percentage of the original learning that remained in memory.

Ebbinghaus learned and relearned more than 1,200 lists of nonsense syllables to discover how rapidly forgetting occurs. Figure 6.6 shows his famous curve of forgetting, which consists of savings scores at various time intervals after the original learning. The curve of forgetting shows that the largest amount of forgetting occurs very quickly, after which forgetting tapers off. Of the information Ebbinghaus retained after a day or two, very little more would be forgotten even a month later. But, remember, this curve of forgetting applies to nonsense syllables. Meaningful material is usually forgotten more slowly, as is material that has been carefully encoded, deeply processed, and frequently rehearsed.

What Ebbinghaus learned about the rate of forgetting is relevant for everyone. Do you, like most students, cram before a big exam? If so, don't assume that everything you memorize on Monday can be held intact until Tuesday. So much forgetting occurs within the first 24 hours that it is wise to spend at least some time reviewing the material on the day of the test. The less meaningful the material is to you, the more you will forget and the more necessary a review is. Recall from Chapter 4 that the quantity and quality of sleep you get between studying and taking the test also influence how much you will remember.

When researchers measured psychology students' retention of names and concepts, they found that the pattern of forgetting was similar to Ebbinghaus's curve. Forgetting of names and concepts was rapid over the first several months, leveled off in approximately 36 months, and remained about the same for the next 7 years (Conway et al., 1991).

The Causes of Forgetting

Why do we fail to remember, even when we put forth a lot of effort aimed at remembering? There are many reasons.

Encoding Failure.   When you can't remember something, could it be because the item was never stored in memory to begin with? Of course, there is a distinction between forgetting and not being able to remember. *Forgetting* is the inability to recall something that you could recall previously. But often when people say they cannot remember, they have not actually forgotten. The inability to remember is sometimes a result of **encoding failure**—the information was never put into long-term memory in the first place.

Of the many things we encounter every day, it is surprising how little we actually encode. Can you recall accurately, or even recognize, something you have seen thousands of times before? Read the *Try It* on the next page to find out.

In your lifetime, you have seen thousands of pennies, but unless you are a coin collector, you probably have not encoded the details of a penny's appearance. If you did poorly on the *Try It*, you have plenty of company. After studying a large group of participants, Nickerson and Adams (1979) reported that few people could reproduce a penny from recall. In fact, only a handful of participants could even recognize an

6.17 What causes forgetting?

nonsense syllable   A consonant-vowel-consonant combination that does not spell a word and is used in memory research.

encoding failure   A cause of forgetting that occurs when information was never put into long-term memory.

Figure 6.6 Ebbinghaus's Curve of Forgetting

After memorizing lists of nonsense syllables similar to those at left, Ebbinghaus measured his retention after varying intervals of time using the relearning method. Forgetting was most rapid at first, as shown by his retention of only 58% after 20 minutes and 44% after 1 hour. Then, the rate of forgetting tapered off, with a retention of 34% after 1 day, 25% after 6 days, and 21% after 31 days.

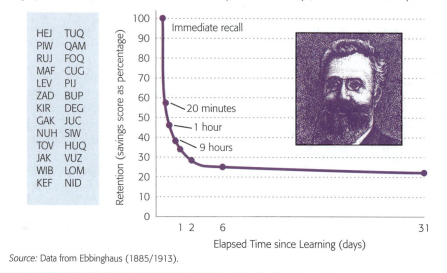

Source: Data from Ebbinghaus (1885/1913).

Try It   A Penny for Your Thoughts

On a sheet of paper, draw a sketch of a U.S. penny from memory using recall. In your drawing, show the direction in which President Lincoln's image is facing and the location of the date, and include all the words on the "heads" side of the penny. Or try the easier recognition task and see if you can recognize the real penny in the drawings shown here. (From Nickersen & Adams, 1979.)

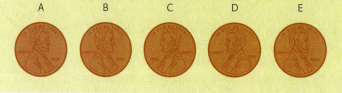

accurate drawing of a penny when it was presented along with incorrect drawings. (The correct penny is the one labeled A in the *Try It*.)

When preparing for tests, do you usually take on a passive role? Do you merely read and reread your textbook and your notes and assume that this process will eventually result in learning? If you don't test yourself by reciting the material, you may find that you have been the unwilling victim of encoding failure. Textbook features such as margin questions and end-of-section reviews can help you by providing structure for rehearsing information to ensure that is encoded.

Decay.   **Decay theory,** probably the oldest theory of forgetting, assumes that memories, if not used, fade with time and ultimately disappear entirely. The word *decay* implies a physiological change in the neurons that recorded the experience. According to this theory, the neuronal record may decay or fade within seconds, days, or even much longer periods of time.

Most psychologists now accept that decay, or the fading of memories, is a cause of forgetting in sensory and short-term memory but not in long-term memory. There does not appear to be a gradual, inevitable decay of long-term memories. In one study,

decay theory   The oldest theory of forgetting, which holds that memories, if not used, fade with time and ultimately disappear altogether.

Harry Bahrick and others (1975) found that after 35 years, participants could recognize 90% of their high school classmates' names and photographs, the same percentage as for recent graduates.

Interference. A major cause of forgetting that affects people every day is **interference.** Whenever you try to recall any given memory, two types of interference can hinder the effort. Information or associations stored either *before* or *after* a given memory can interfere with the ability to remember it (see **Figure 6.7**). Interference can reach either forward or backward in time to affect memory—it gets us coming and going. Also, the more similar the interfering associations are to the information a person is trying to recall, the more difficult it is to recall the information (Underwood, 1964).

Proactive interference occurs when information or experiences already stored in long-term memory hinder the ability to remember newer information (Underwood, 1957). For example, Laura's romance with her new boyfriend, Todd, got off to a bad start when she accidentally called him "Dave," her former boyfriend's name. One explanation for proactive interference is the competition between old and new responses (Bower et al., 1994).

Retroactive interference happens when new learning interferes with the ability to remember previously learned information. The more similar the new material is to that learned earlier, the more interference there is. For example, when you take a psychology class, it may interfere with your ability to remember what you learned in your sociology class, especially with regard to theories (e.g., psychoanalysis) that are shared by the two disciplines but applied and interpreted differently. However, research shows that the effects of retroactive interference are often temporary (Lustig, Konkel, & Jacoby, 2004). In fact, after some time has passed, the old information may be better remembered than the material that was learned more recently. So, the material a student learned in a previous sociology course may appear to fade when she encounters similar information presented in a somewhat different light in a psychology course. In the long run, though, her sociology knowledge may outlast what she learned in psychology.

Consolidation Failure. *Consolidation* is the process by which encoded information is stored in memory. When a disruption in this process occurs, a long-term memory usually does not form. **Consolidation failure** can result from anything that causes a person to lose consciousness—a car accident, a blow to the head, a grand mal epileptic seizure, or an electroconvulsive shock treatment given for severe depression. Memory loss of the experiences that occurred shortly before the loss of consciousness is called **retrograde amnesia.**

Researchers Nader and others (2000) demonstrated that conditioned fears in rats can be erased by infusing into the rats' brains a drug that prevents protein synthesis (such synthesis is necessary for memory consolidation). Rats experienced a single pairing of a tone (the conditioned stimulus, CS) and a foot shock (the unconditioned stimulus, US). Later, the rats were exposed to the sound of the tone alone (CS) and showed a fear response, "freezing" (becoming totally immobile as if frozen with fright). Clearly, the rats remembered the feared stimulus. Twenty-four hours later, the rats were again exposed to the tone alone, and it elicited fear, causing them to freeze. Immediately, the drug anisomycin, which prevents protein synthesis in the brain, was infused into the rats' amygdalae (the part of the brain that processes fear stimuli). After the drug was infused, the rats were shocked again, but they showed no fear response (freezing). The rats in the study had already consolidated the memory of the fear, but it was completely wiped out after the drug prevented protein synthesis from occurring. This means that fear memories, once activated, must be "reconsolidated," or they may disappear.

This finding has positive implications. If fear memories can be activated and then wiped out with drugs that prevent protein synthesis, a new therapy may be on the horizon for people who suffer from debilitating fears (Nader et al., 2000).

We have discussed ways to avoid forgetting, but there are occasions when people may want to avoid remembering—times when they want to forget.

interference A cause of forgetting that occurs because information or associations stored either before or after a given memory hinder the ability to remember it.

consolidation failure Any disruption in the consolidation process that prevents a long-term memory from forming.

retrograde amnesia (RET-ro-grade) A loss of memory for experiences that occurred shortly before a loss of consciousness.

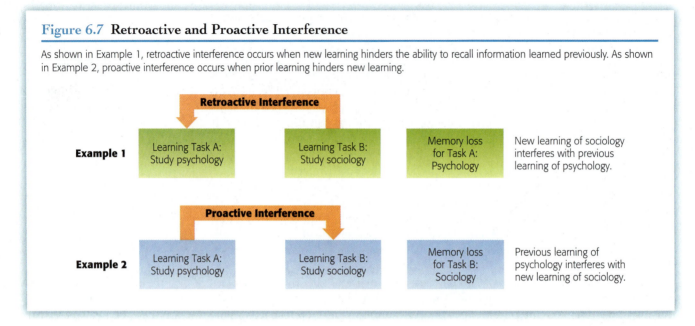

Figure 6.7 Retroactive and Proactive Interference

As shown in Example 1, retroactive interference occurs when new learning hinders the ability to recall information learned previously. As shown in Example 2, proactive interference occurs when prior learning hinders new learning.

Retroactive Interference

Example 1

Learning Task A: Study psychology → Learning Task B: Study sociology → Memory loss for Task A: Psychology — New learning of sociology interferes with previous learning of psychology.

Proactive Interference

Example 2

Learning Task A: Study psychology → Learning Task B: Study sociology → Memory loss for Task B: Sociology — Previous learning of psychology interferes with new learning of sociology.

motivated forgetting Forgetting through suppression or repression in order to protect oneself from material that is painful, frightening, or otherwise unpleasant.

repression Completely removing unpleasant memories from one's consciousness, so that one is no longer aware that a painful event occurred.

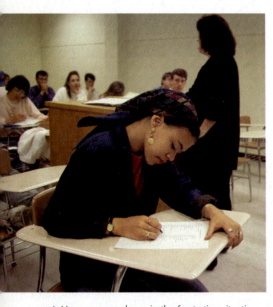

▲ Have you ever been in the frustrating situation of knowing that you know the answer to an exam question but being unable to recall it? If so, you have experienced retrieval failure.

Motivated Forgetting. Victims of rape or physical abuse, war veterans, and survivors of airplane crashes or earthquakes all have had terrifying experiences that may haunt them for years. These victims are certainly motivated to forget their traumatic experiences, but even people who have not suffered any trauma use **motivated forgetting** to protect themselves from experiences that are painful, frightening, or otherwise unpleasant.

With one form of motivated forgetting, *suppression*, a person makes a conscious, active attempt to put a painful, disturbing, anxiety- or guilt-provoking memory out of mind, but the person is still aware that the painful event occurred. With another type of motivated forgetting, **repression,** unpleasant memories are literally removed from consciousness, and the person is no longer aware that the unpleasant event ever occurred (Freud, 1922). People who have **amnesia** (partial or complete memory loss) that is not due to loss of consciousness or brain damage have repressed the events they no longer remember. Motivated forgetting is probably used by more people than any other method to deal with unpleasant memories. It seems to be a natural human tendency to forget the unpleasant circumstances of life and to remember the pleasant ones (Linton, 1979; Meltzer, 1930).

Prospective forgetting—not remembering to carry out some intended action (e.g., forgetting to go to your dentist appointment)—is another type of motivated forgetting. People are most likely to forget to do the things they view as unimportant, unpleasant, or burdensome. They are less likely to forget things that are pleasurable or important to them (Winograd, 1988).

However, as you probably know, prospective forgetting isn't always motivated by a desire to avoid something. Have you ever arrived home and suddenly remembered that you had intended to go to the bank to deposit your paycheck? Or you may have seen a review of a concert in the newspaper and suddenly remembered that you had intended to buy a ticket for it. In such cases, prospective forgetting is more likely to be the result of interference or consolidation failure.

Retrieval Failure. How many times has this experience happened to you? While taking a test, you can't remember the answer to a question that you are sure you know. Often, people are certain they know something, but are not able to retrieve the information when they need it. This type of forgetting is called **retrieval failure.**

Endel Tulving (1974) claims that much of what people call forgetting is really an inability to locate the needed information. The information is in long-term memory, but the person cannot retrieve it. In his experiments, Tulving found that participants could recall a large number of items they seemed to have forgotten if he provided retrieval cues to jog their memory. For example, odors often provide potent reminders of experiences from the past, and certain odors can serve as retrieval cues for information that was learned when those odors were present (Schab, 1990).

A common experience with retrieval failure is known as the *tip-of-the-tongue (TOT) phenomenon* (Brown & McNeil, 1966). You have surely experienced trying to recall a name, a word, or some other bit of information, knowing that you knew it but not able to come up with it. You were on the verge of recalling the word or name, perhaps aware of the number of syllables and the beginning or ending letter. It was on the tip of your tongue, but it just wouldn't quite come out.

amnesia A partial or complete loss of memory due to loss of consciousness, brain damage, or some psychological cause.

prospective forgetting Not remembering to carry out some intended action.

retrieval failure Not remembering something one is certain of knowing

---

Remember It   Forgetting

1. _Herman Ebbinghaus_ invented the nonsense syllable, conceived the relearning method for retention, and plotted the curve of forgetting.

2. Match each cause of forgetting with the appropriate example.

   _____ (1) encoding failure
   _____ (2) consolidation failure
   _____ (3) retrieval failure
   _____ (4) repression
   _____ (5) interference

   a. failing to remember the answer on a test until after you turn the test in
   b. forgetting a humiliating childhood experience
   c. not being able to describe the back of a dollar bill
   d. calling a friend by someone else's name
   e. waking up in the hospital and not remembering you had an automobile accident

3. To minimize interference, it is best to follow learning with _____.

4. According to the text, the major cause of forgetting is _____.

Answers: 1. Ebbinghaus, 2. (1) c, (2) e, (3) a, (4) b, (5) d; 3. sleep; 4. interference

---

Improving Memory

Have you ever wished there was a magic pill you could take before studying for an exam, one that would make you remember everything in your textbook and lecture notes? Sorry, but there are no magic formulas for improving your memory. Remembering is a skill that, like any other, requires knowledge and practice. In this section, we consider several study habits and techniques that can improve your memory.

Are you the kind of person who has a place for everything in your home or office, or do you simply toss things anywhere and everywhere? If you're the everything-in-its-place type, you probably have an easier time finding things than do people who are the "wherever" type. Memory works the same way. How information is organized strongly influences your ability to remember it.

6.18 How can organization, overlearning, spaced practice, and recitation improve memory?

For example, almost anyone can name the months of the year in about 10 seconds, but how long would it take to recall them in alphabetical order? These 12 well-known items are much harder to retrieve in alphabetical order, because they are not organized that way in memory. Similarly, you are giving your memory an extremely difficult task if you try to remember large amounts of information in a haphazard fashion. Try to organize items you want to remember in alphabetical order, or according to categories, historical sequence, size, or shape, or in any other way that will make retrieval easier for you.

Do you still remember the words to songs that were popular when you were in high school? Can you recite many of the nursery rhymes you learned as a child even though you haven't heard them in years? You probably can because of **overlearning,** practicing or studying material beyond the point where it can be repeated once without error. Suppose you wanted to memorize a list of words, and you studied until you could recite them once without error. Would this amount of study or practice be sufficient? Research suggests that people remember material better and longer if they overlearn it (Ebbinghaus, 1885/1964). A pioneering study in overlearning by Krueger (1929) showed very substantial long-term gains for participants who engaged in 50% and 100% overlearning (see **Figure 6.8**). Furthermore, overlearning makes material more resistant to interference and is perhaps the best insurance against stress-related forgetting. So, the next time you study for a test, don't stop studying as soon as you think you know the material. Spend another hour or so going over it, using features of your textbook such as margin questions and end-of-section review questions; you will be surprised at how much more you will remember.

Most students have tried cramming for examinations, but spacing study over several sessions is generally more effective than **massed practice,** learning in one long practice session without rest periods (Glover & Corkill, 1987). You will remember more with less total study time if you engage in **spaced practice,** learning in short practice sessions with rest periods in between. Long periods of memorizing make material particularly subject to interference and often result in fatigue and lowered concentration. Also, when you space your practice, you probably create new memories that may be stored in different places, thus increasing your chances for recall. The spacing effect applies to learning motor skills as well as to learning facts and information. Music students can tell you that it is better to practice for half an hour each day, every day, than to practice many hours in a row once a week.

Furthermore, recent research suggests that significant improvement in learning results when spaced study sessions are accompanied by short, frequent tests of the material being studied (Cull, 2000). Thus, you should be doing well in this course if you are answering the questions in the *Remember It* boxes at the ends of sections in this textbook.

Do you ever reread a chapter just before a test? Research over many years shows that you will recall more if you increase the amount of recitation in your study. For example, it is better to read a page or a few paragraphs and then recite or practice recalling what you have just read. Then, continue reading, stop and practice reciting again, and so on. When you study for a psychology test and review the assigned chapter, try to answer each of the questions in the *Summary and Review* section at the end of the chapter. Then, read the material that follows each question and check to see if you answered the question correctly. This will be your safeguard against encoding failure. Don't simply read each section and assume that you can answer the question. Test yourself before your professor does.

A. I. Gates (1917) tested groups of students who spent the same amount of time in study, but who spent different percentages of that time in recitation and rereading. Participants recalled two to three times more if they increased their recitation time up to 80% and spent only 20% of their study time rereading.

The *Review and Reflect* on the following page provides examples for each of the memory improvement techniques discussed in this section.

overlearning   Practicing or studying material beyond the point where it can be repeated once without error.

massed practice   Learning in one long practice session without rest periods.

spaced practice   Learning in short practice sessions with rest periods in between.

Figure 6.8 Overlearning

When a person learns material only to the point of one correct repetition, forgetting is very rapid. Just 22% is retained after 1 day, 3% after 4 days, and 2% after 14 days. When participants spend 50% more time going over the material, the retention increases to 36% after 1 day, 30% after 4 days, and 21% after 14 days.

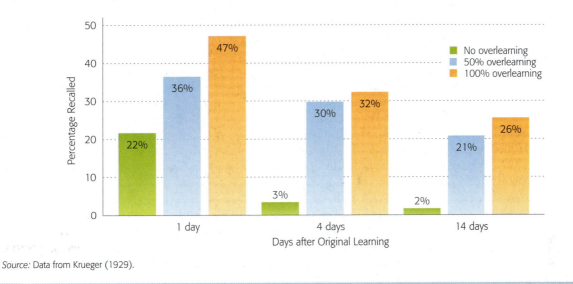

Source: Data from Krueger (1929).

Review and Reflect   Examples of Strategies for Improving Memory

Strategy	Example
Organization	Write each heading and subheading of a textbook chapter on an index card; take notes on each section and subsection on the cards; keep them in order by chapter and use them to review for exams.
Overlearning	Memorize information that is easily organized into a list (e.g., the functions associated with the left and right cerebral hemispheres) until you can recall each item on the list automatically without error.
Spaced practice	When you have an hour to study, break it up into three 15-minute study periods with 5-minute breaks between them.
Recitation	After you finish studying this *Review and Reflect* table, close your eyes and see how much of the information you can repeat aloud.

Remember It   Improving Memory

1. When studying for an exam, it is best to spend:
   a. more time reciting than rereading.
   b. more time rereading than reciting.
   c. equal time rereading and reciting.
   d. all of the time reciting rather than rereading.

2. The ability to recite a number of nursery rhymes from childhood is probably due mainly to _____.

Answers: 1. a; 2. overlearning

Apply It   Improving Memory with Mnemonic Devices

You are probably no more acutely aware of the difference between recognition and recall than when you are taking an exam. "I know I read about this in the textbook," you say to yourself, indicating that you do, indeed, recognize the subject matter of the question. However, you simply can't recall enough of it to answer the question. Facilitating recall is what studying for an exam is all about. This is true because even test questions that require primarily recognition processes (i.e., matching, multiple choice) are made easier by your being able to recall the relevant information. There are a few *mnemonic devices* that can greatly improve your capacity for recall (Bower, 1973; Higbee, 1977; Roediger, 1980). Learning to use them takes a bit of practice. If you take the time to do so, you are likely to find that these strategies render the task of recalling information much easier.

Rhyme

Rhymes are a common aid to remembering material that otherwise might be difficult to recall. Perhaps as a child you learned to recite "*i* before *e* except after *c*" when you were trying to spell a word containing that vowel combination.

Here are two couplets that could be applied to remembering the section of this chapter devoted to memory improvement.

Organizing helps recall, but overlearning's best of all.

Spacing practice is the best, because it gives your brain a rest.

The Method of Loci

The *method of loci* is a mnemonic device that can be used when you want to remember a list of items such as a grocery list, or when you give a speech or a class report and need to make your points in order without using notes. The word *loci* (pronounced "LOH-sye") is the plural form of *locus*, which means "location" or "place."

Figure 6.9 shows how to use the method of loci. Select any familiar place—your home, for example—and simply associate the items to be remembered with locations there. Progress in an orderly fashion: For example, visualize the first item or idea you want to remember in its place on the driveway, the second in the garage, the third at the front door, and so on, until you have associated each item you want to remember with a specific location. You may find it helpful to conjure up oversized images of the items that you place at each location. When you want to recall the items, take an imaginary walk starting at the first place—the first item will pop into your mind. When you think of the second place, the second item will come to mind, and so on.

The method of loci would be a very effective way to remember the characteristics of the various components of the memory system. You could associate the name of each component and its characteristics with different rooms in your home or areas of a single room. The sensory memory and its description could be pictured on your bed, and the short-term

Figure 6.9 The Method of Loci

Begin by thinking of locations, perhaps in your home, that are in a sequence. Then, visualize one of the items to be remembered in each location.

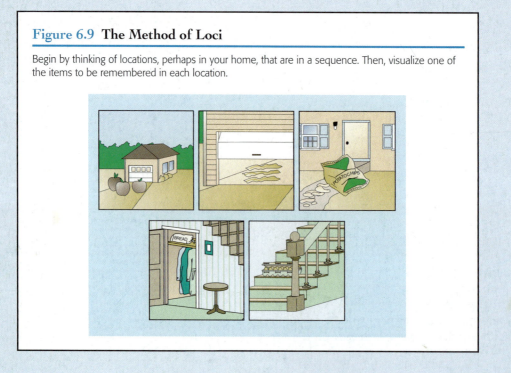

memory would be associated with your desk. A chair in the room could be the association object for long-term memory, with the back of the chair devoted to declarative memory and its seat associated with nondeclarative memory.

The First-letter Technique

Another useful technique is to take the first letter of each item to be remembered and form a word, a phrase, or a sentence with those letters (Matlin, 1989). For example, suppose you had to memorize the seven colors of the visible spectrum in their proper order:

Red

Orange

Yellow

Green

Blue

Indigo

Violet

You could make your task easier by using the first letter of each color to form the name Roy G. Biv. Three chunks are easier to remember than seven different items.

Think about a first- and last-name combination like Roy G. Biv that you could make up to remember the four processes involved in memory—encoding, consolidation, storage, and retrieval. How about "Eduardo Carlos Sanchez Rodriguez"? You might also use the first letters of these four terms in a sentence such as "Ed calls Sue regularly" that would be reminiscent of the expression "please excuse my dear Aunt Sally" that you may have learned to help you remember the order of operations in an algebra problem (parentheses, exponents, multiplication, division, addition, and subtraction).

Summary and Review

The Structure of Human Memory p. 197

6.1 How does the information-processing approach describe the structure of human memory? p. 197

The information-processing approach uses the computer as an analogy to describe human cognition. It conceptualizes memory as involving the processes of encoding, consolidation, storage, and retrieval. The model proposes that information flows through a three-part system—sensory memory, short-term memory, and long-term memory.

6.2 What are the characteristics of the sensory memory? p. 198

Sensory memory holds information coming in through the senses for up to 2 seconds, just long enough for the nervous system to begin to process it.

6.3 What happens to information in short-term memory? p. 199

Short-term (working) memory holds about seven (plus or minus two) unrelated items of information for less than 30 seconds without rehearsal. Short-term memory also acts as a mental workspace for carrying out any mental activity.

6.4 What kinds of information are stored in the subsystems of long-term memory? p. 201

The subsystems of long-term memory are (1) declarative memory, which holds facts and information (semantic memory) along with personal life experiences (episodic memory); and (2) nondeclarative memory, which consists of motor skills, conditioned behaviors, and other types of memories that are difficult or impossible to put into verbal form.

The Nature of Remembering p. 203

6.5 What are the three methods used by psychologists to measure memory? p. 203

Three methods of measuring retention of information in memory are (1) recall, where information must be supplied with few or no retrieval cues; (2) recognition, where information must simply be recognized as having been encountered before; and (3) the relearning method, which measures retention in terms of time saved when relearning material compared with the time required to learn it originally.

6.6   What happens when information must be recalled in a particular order? p. 204

The serial position effect is the tendency, when recalling a list of items, to remember the items at the beginning of the list (primacy effect) and the items at the end of the list (recency effect) better than items in the middle.

6.7   How do environmental conditions and emotional states affect memory? p. 205

People tend to recall material more easily if they are in the same physical location during recall as during the original learning. The state-dependent memory effect is the tendency to recall information better if one is in the same pharmacological or psychological state as when the information was learned.

6.8   What is meant by the statement "Memory is reconstructive in nature"? p. 206

Memory does not work like a video recorder. People reconstruct memories, piecing them together from a few highlights and using information that may or may not be accurate. Sir Frederick Bartlett found that people systematically reconstruct and distort memories to fit information already stored in memory. Bartlett suggested that reconstructive memory involves the application of schemas, or integrated frameworks of prior knowledge and assumptions, during the encoding and retrieval phases of remembering.

Memory in Everyday Life p. 208

6.9   What does research say about flashbulb and photographic memories? p. 208

Flashbulb memories, which are formed when a person learns of events that are surprising, shocking, or highly emotional, may not be as accurate as people believe they are. Researchers have also found that some of the details in flashbulb memories change over time. Something similar to photographic memory, called eidetic imagery, appears to exist in about 5% of children.

6.10   How does culture influence memory? p. 209

The existence of oral historians in some cultures suggests that the ability to remember certain kinds of material may be influenced by culture. The status of the role and the importance of the particular information to members of the culture motivate individuals to store and retrieve large amounts of such information. Their memory for other kinds of information, however, is no better than that of others. In addition, we more easily remember stories set in our own culture.

6.11   What conditions reduce the reliability of eyewitness testimony? p. 210

The reliability of eyewitness testimony is reduced when witnesses view a photograph of the suspect before viewing the lineup, when members of a lineup don't sufficiently resemble each other; when members of a lineup are viewed at the same time rather than one by one, when the perpetrator's race is different from that of the eyewitness, when a weapon has been used in the crime, and when leading questions are asked to elicit information from the witness.

6.12   What is the controversy regarding the recovery of repressed memories of childhood sexual abuse? p. 211

Critics argue that therapists using hypnosis and guided imagery to help their patients recover repressed memories of childhood sexual abuse are actually implanting false memories in those patients. Therapists who use these techniques believe that a number of psychological problems can be treated successfully by helping patients recover repressed memories of sexual abuse.

Biology and Memory p. 213

6.13   What roles do the hippocampus and the hippocampal region play in memory? p. 213

The hippocampus itself is involved primarily in the formation of episodic memories; the rest of the hippocampal region is involved in forming semantic memories.

6.14   Why is long-term potentiation important? p. 214

Long-term potentiation (LTP) is a long-lasting increase in the efficiency of neural transmission at the synapses. LTP is important because it may be the basis for learning and memory at the level of the neurons.

6.15   How do hormones influence memory? p. 215

Memories of threatening situations tend to be more powerful and enduring than ordinary memories, because of the hormones associated with the strong emotions aroused in such situations.

Forgetting p. 216

6.16   What did Ebbinghaus discover about forgetting? p. 216

In conducting the first experimental studies of learning and memory, Ebbinghaus invented the nonsense syllable, used the relearning method as a test of memory, and plotted the curve of forgetting. He discovered that the largest amount of forgetting occurs very quickly, then it tapers off.

6.17 What causes forgetting? p. 217

Encoding failure happens when an item is perceived as having been forgotten but, in fact, was never stored in memory. Information that has not been retrieved from memory for a long time may fade and ultimately disappear entirely (decay theory). Consolidation failure results from a loss of consciousness as new memories are being encoded. Interference occurs when information or associations stored either before or after a given memory hinder the ability to remember it. Sometimes, we forget because we don't want to remember something, a process called motivated forgetting. Other times, an item is stored in memory, but we are unable to retrieve it (retrieval failure).

Improving Memory p. 221

6.18 How can organization, overlearning, spaced practice, and recitation improve memory? p. 221

Organization, as in using outlines based on chapter headings, provides retrieval cues for information. Overlearning means practicing or studying material beyond the point where it can be repeated once without error. You remember overlearned material better and longer, and it is more resistant to interference and stress-related forgetting. Short study sessions at different times (spaced practice) allow time for consolidation of new information. Recitation of newly learned material is more effective than simply rereading it.

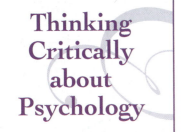

Thinking Critically about Psychology

1. Based on what you learned in this chapter, formulate a plan that you can put into operation to help improve your memory and avoid the pitfalls that cause forgetting.
2. If you were serving on a jury in a trial in which the prosecution's case rested entirely upon eyewitness testimony, how would you weigh that evidence in light of what you have learned in this chapter?
3. How does information in a textbook make its way from the sensory to the long-term memory and back again when you need to use it to answer a question on an exam?

Key Terms

amnesia, p. 220
anterograde amnesia, p. 213
chunking, p. 220
consolidation, p. 198
consolidation failure, p. 219
decay theory, p. 218
declarative memory, p. 201
displacement, p. 199
eidetic imagery, p. 209
elaborative rehearsal, p. 200
encoding, p. 198
encoding failure, p. 217
episodic memory, p. 201
flashbulb memory, p. 208
hippocampal region, p. 213
infantile amnesia, p. 212
information processing theory, p. 197

interference, p. 219
long-term memory (LTM), p. 201
long-term potentiation (LTP), p. 215
maintenance rehearsal, p. 200
massed practice, p. 222
memory, p. 198
motivated forgetting, p. 220
nondeclarative memory, p. 202
nonsense syllable, p. 217
overlearning, p. 222
primacy effect, p. 204
priming, p. 202
prospective forgetting, p. 220
recall, p. 203
recency effect, p. 204
recognition, p. 204
reconstruction, p. 206

rehearsal, p. 200
relearning method, p. 204
repression, p. 220
retrieval, p. 198
retrieval cue, p. 203
retrieval failure, p. 221
retrograde amnesia, p. 219
savings score, p. 204
schemas, p. 206
semantic memory, p. 201
sensory memory, p. 198
serial position effect, p. 204
short-term memory (STM), p. 199
spaced practice, p. 222
state-dependent memory effect, p. 206
storage, p. 198
working memory, p. 200

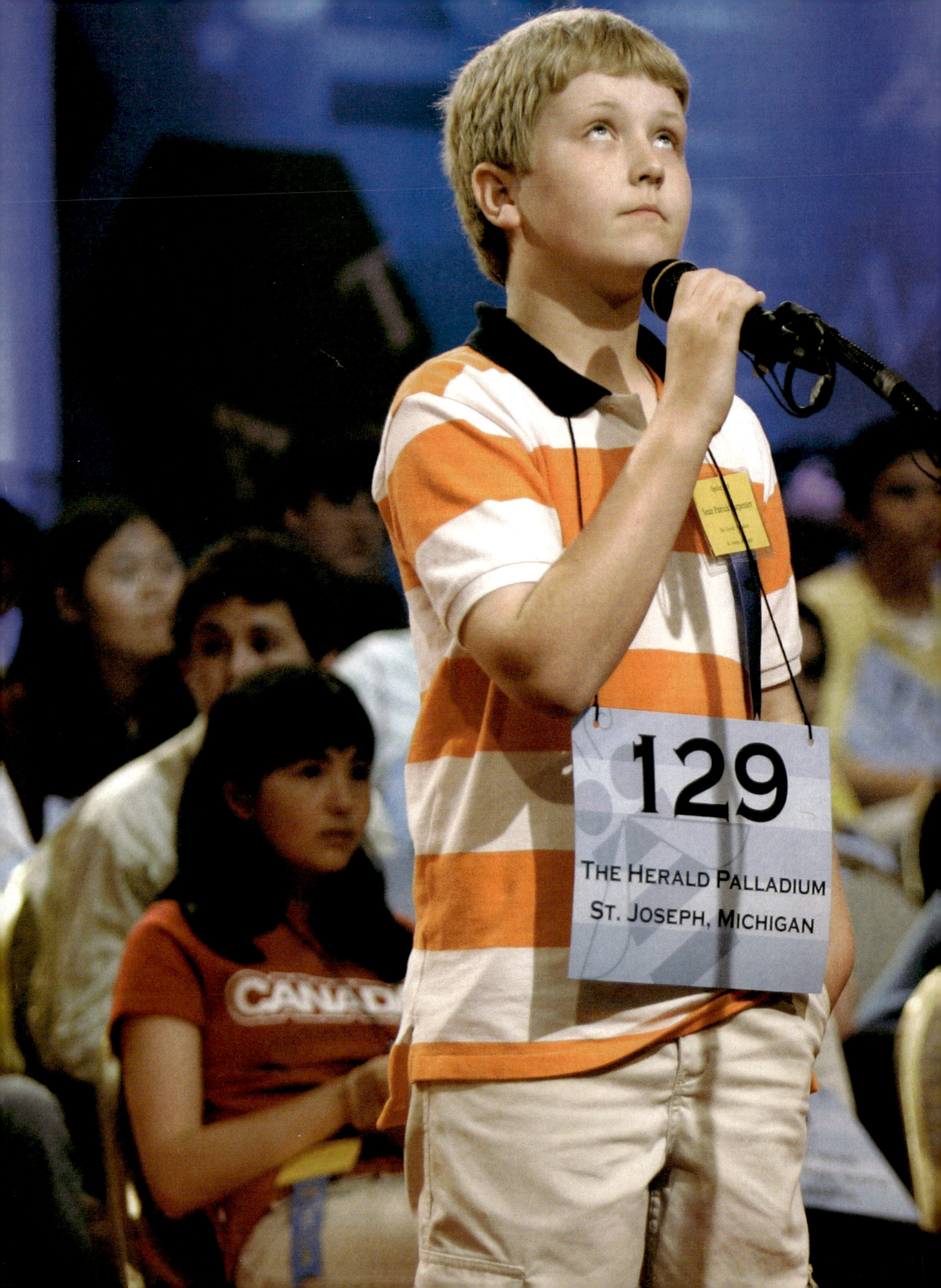
129
THE HERALD PALLADIUM
ST. JOSEPH, MICHIGAN
CANADA

Chapter 7

Cognition, Language, and Intelligence

Continued

You have probably heard stories about people with severe cognitive disabilities who exhibit some kind of remarkable talent despite their intellectual limitations. Many of these individuals can carry out complex calculations in their heads; others are gifted artists or musicians. Consider the inspiring story of one such person, Japanese composer Hikari Oe.

When their first son was born, prize-winning Japanese novelist Kinzaburo Oe and his wife were overjoyed (Cameron, 1998). Their joy turned to grief, though, when doctors told them that their newborn son's brain was herniated outside of his skull, and only a dangerous operation, one that would leave the boy with mental retardation and vulnerable to other neurological difficulties, could save his life. The doctors' recommendation that the couple allow the child to die peacefully did little to lift Oe's spirits. Instead of taking their advice, Oe turned to doctors who had spent their lives treating survivors of the atomic bomb that was dropped on the Japanese city of Hiroshima at the end of World War II. These doctors agreed that the child would likely be severely disabled by the surgery, but they encouraged Oe and his wife to adopt the view that human life is precious and that hope and joy can be found even in the most dire of circumstances. With that philosophical outlook, Oe named the boy Hikari, the Japanese word for "light," and told surgeons to operate on his son.

As the doctors had predicted, it was quite clear by the time Hikari was just a few years old that he had mental retardation. He also suffered from epileptic seizures and had extremely poor vision. In addition, Hikari appeared to be incapable of forming social relationships. Still, Oe gained inspiration from his own and his wife's efforts to reach the boy. His writing became embued with a sense of hope that can be developed only in the midst of a human tragedy. As a result, his career prospered, and his work achieved worldwide acclaim. Soon, two more children, both healthy and normal, were born into the Oe family.

When Hikari was about 6 years old, his parents noticed that he had an unusual ability to memorize and sing songs, though his ability to speak and to understand language was quite limited. They decided to give him piano lessons and found a teacher who was willing to take on the challenging student. As the teacher worked with Hikari, it became apparent that the child had remarkable musical gifts. Within months, he was playing difficult classical pieces with ease. Moreover, he began to improvise on classical forms to create his own pieces. Though she doubted the effort would be successful, Hikari's piano teacher decided to try to teach him musical notation so that he could write down his compositions. To her surprise, he mastered the difficult skill of writing classical music in a relatively short time. Today, as a middle-aged man, Hikari Oe is an accomplished and celebrated composer of classical music. Yet his scores on standardized tests of intelligence are far below average, and he is unable to live independently.

Hikari Oe is just one of the thousands of individuals with mental retardation and other severe mental disabilities who display *savant syndrome*, the exhibition of remarkable talents in the context of a severe disability. Psychologists have studied savants such as Hikari for more than a hundred years, yet do not yet know why some abilities in these individuals become accentuated while others are destroyed. Studying savants has led to the development of new theories of normal intellectual functioning that have led psychologists to look beyond conventional intelligence tests in the quest for an accurate definition of human intelligence.

In earlier chapters, we discussed the cognitive processes of sensation, perception, and memory. In this chapter, we first consider several other cognitive processes. We begin by discussing the universal intellectual tools that we use to make sense of the world—reasoning, imagery, and concepts—and discuss how we put these tools to work to make decisions, solve problems, and develop technological devices that mirror our own thought processes. Next, we turn to another vital cognitive tool: language. Finally, we end with a discussion of intelligence, creativity, and other aspects of cognitive functioning that vary from one person to another.

Intelligence is just one of several aspects of intellectual functioning. You have read about several others in earlier chapters—sensation, perception, and memory, to name a few. In this chapter, you will learn more about how our brains manage intellectual tasks. We begin by considering the very nature of thinking itself.

Cognition

Cognition is a collective term that refers to the mental processes involved in acquiring, storing, retrieving, and using information (Matlin, 1989). It includes our ability to contemplate abstract issues such as truth and justice as well as the strategies we use to make decisions and solve problems. It turns out, too, that tasks our minds handle with ease have proven to be nearly impossible for computers to learn how to do.

cognition The mental processes that are involved in acquiring, storing, retrieving, and using information and that include sensation, perception, memory, imagery, concept formation, reasoning, decision making, problem solving, and language.

Reasoning

Perhaps you remember Mr. Spock from the original *Star Trek* series. Mr. Spock's inability to experience emotions enabled him to dispassionately apply logic to activities as varied as defeating Captain Kirk in a friendly game of chess to rescuing the starship *Enterprise* from the clutches of the Klingons. The ancient Greek philosopher Aristotle probably would have applauded the cognitive model provided to millions of television viewers by Mr. Spock. Aristotle devised a system of *formal logic*, which he believed would enable thinkers to separate cognitive processes from emotions and other extraneous influences that might cause them to reach conclusions inconsistent with the facts upon which they claim to be based. Thus, from this perspective,

7.1 What is the difference between deductive and inductive reasoning?

reasoning is a form of thinking in which valid conclusions are drawn from a set of facts. Aristotle's system has served as the foundation of the scientific method for more than two thousand years and is the basis of the critical thinking strategies you read about in Chapter 1. Here are the rules of formal logic.

◄ In the original *Star Trek* series, Mr. Spock often chastised other members of the *Enterprise* crew for allowing emotions rather than logic to rule their thinking. Mr. Spock's emphasis on precise logic and emotional objectivity was in line with the goals of Aristotle's system of deductive and inductive reasoning.

Reasoning by Deduction. **Deductive reasoning** is reasoning from the general to the specific, or drawing particular conclusions from general principles. Aristotle introduced a formal method for deductive reasoning—the syllogism. A syllogism is a scheme for logical reasoning in which two statements known as *premises* (the major premise and the minor premise) are followed by a valid conclusion. The power of the syllogism is not in its content but in its form. It is organized in such a way that the conclusion must be true if both premises are true and if the premises follow the rules of formal logic.

Consider this syllogism:

Major premise: All standard cars have four wheels.
Minor premise: Maria's vehicle is a standard car.
Conclusion: Therefore, Maria's vehicle has four wheels.

reasoning A form of thinking in which conclusions are drawn from a set of facts.

deductive reasoning Reasoning from the general to the specific, or drawing particular conclusions from general principles.

Clearly, the conclusion is valid because the entire class of standard cars fits within the larger class of four-wheeled vehicles. Maria's vehicle is within "standard cars" and thus also within the larger class, "four-wheeled vehicles."

Now consider this syllogism, which does not adhere to the rules of formal logic:

Major premise: All standard cars have four wheels.
Minor premise: Maria's vehicle has four wheels.
Conclusion: Therefore, Maria's vehicle is a standard car.

The conclusion is invalid. Even though the major and minor premises are both true, a valid conclusion does not follow from them. The minor premise is too general to be used deductively: Some trucks and other vehicles, such as tractors, also have four wheels. Therefore, we cannot logically conclude that Maria's vehicle is a standard car.

Reasoning by Induction. **Inductive reasoning** is a form of reasoning in which general conclusions are drawn from particular facts or individual cases. This kind of reasoning results in conclusions that *might* be true. Therefore, premises can be judged to be false on the basis of conclusions, but they cannot be judged to be true. Thus, inductive reasoning stands in sharp contrast to deductive reasoning, in which true premises always yield true conclusions.

For example, given the number series 737373737, what would you predict the next number to be? A reasonable conclusion would be that the next number will be 3. The premise of this conclusion is a general rule derived from the series: 7 is always followed by 3. If the next number is 5, you know the premise is false. However, if the next number is 3, you still don't know whether the premise is true because its predictions may not hold up in the future. You only know that it was supported in this particular instance.

Formal Logic in Everyday Life. Many people have difficulty with reasoning problems. One reason for our difficulties is that prior beliefs can cause us to question the conclusions we reach through deductive and inductive reasoning (Evans, Handley, & Harper, 2001; Wang & Li, 2003). It seems that we prefer to hold on to these beliefs rather than surrender them to the demands of logic.

Nevertheless, research indicates that instruction and practice strongly influence our ability to use formal logic. For example, scientists have found that 12- to 14-year-olds exhibit impressive reasoning skills when researchers ask them to complete logical exercises that are similar to ones that they have learned how to do in school. By contrast, when investigators instruct them to use logic to solve everyday problems, children of these ages often perform poorly (Artman, Cahan, & Avni-Babad, 2006). College students and other adults also benefit from formal instruction in logic (Leshowitz et al., 2002).

Building up a store of information helps us reason more effectively as well (Johnson-Laird, 2001). Consequently, baseball fans can reason more logically when thinking about the probabilities of a given team's winning a league championship than when considering problems about which they have little relevant knowledge. Of course, emotions and prior beliefs may influence the fans' thinking when they analyze their favorite team's chances of winning that championship. Fans may so strongly wish that their team will succeed that they can easily fashion "logical" arguments in their team's favor in the face of facts that strongly suggest otherwise, such as the team's lack of an effective pitching staff. Thus, although there is no doubt about our ability to engage in Mr. Spock-style logic, we often fall short of Aristotle's ideal. Thankfully, we possess a number of cognitive tools that help to make our cognitive efforts more efficient even when they are not purely logical.

Imagery

7.2 How does imagery help us think?

Can you imagine hearing a recording of your favorite song or someone calling your name? In doing such a thing, you take advantage of your own ability to use mental **imagery,**—that is, to represent or picture a sensory experience.

According to psychologist Stephen Kosslyn (1988), we mentally construct our images of objects one part at a time. Stored memories of how the parts of an object look

inductive reasoning Reasoning in which general conclusions are drawn from particular facts or individual cases.

imagery The representation in the mind of a sensory experience—visual, auditory, gustatory, motor, olfactory, or tactile.

are retrieved and assembled in working memory to form a complete image. Such images can be directly analogous to the real world or they can be creative. In the *Apply It* box in Chapter 6, you read about several mnemonic devices that rely on imagery. Such images can be extremely helpful to memory. For example, to remember that the independent variable is the one in an experiment that is manipulated by the experimenter, you might imagine a puppeteer with a large "I" on his forehead manipulating a marionette.

Images can also be helpful in learning or maintaining motor skills. Brain-imaging studies show that, in general, the same brain areas are activated whether a person is actually performing a given task or mentally rehearsing the same task using imagery (Fourkas, Ionta, & Aglioti, 2006; Lotze et al., 1999; Richter et al., 2000; Stephan et al., 1995). Thus, it isn't surprising that professionals whose work involves repetitive physical actions, such as musicians and athletes, use imaging effectively. One remarkable demonstration of the power of imagery may be found in the case of professional pianist Liu Chi Kung, who was imprisoned for 7 years during China's cultural revolution. He mentally rehearsed all the pieces he knew every day and was able to play them all immediately following his release (Garfield, 1986).

▲ Many professional athletes use visualization to improve performance.

Concepts

The ability to form concepts is another important aid to thinking. A **concept** is a mental category used to represent a class or group of objects, people, organizations, events, situations, or relations that share common characteristics or attributes. *Furniture, tree, student, college,* and *wedding* are all examples of concepts. As fundamental units of thought, concepts are useful tools that help us to order our world and to think and communicate with speed and efficiency.

Formal and Natural Concepts. Thanks to our ability to use concepts, we are not forced to consider and describe everything in great detail before we make an identification. If you see a hairy, brown-and-white, four-legged animal with its mouth open, tongue hanging out, and tail wagging, you recognize it immediately as a representative of the concept *dog. Dog* is a concept that stands for a class of animals that share similar characteristics or attributes, even though they may differ in significant ways. Great Danes, dachshunds, collies, Chihuahuas, and other breeds—you recognize all these varied creatures as fitting into the concept *dog.* Moreover, the concepts we form do not exist in isolation, but rather in hierarchies. For example, dogs represent one subset of the concept *animal;* at a higher level, animals are a subset of the concept *living things.* Thus, concept formation has a certain logic to it.

Psychologists identify two basic types of concepts: formal (also known as artificial) concepts and natural (also known as fuzzy) concepts. A **formal concept** is one that is clearly defined by a set of rules, a formal definition, or a classification system. Most of the concepts we form and use are **natural concepts,** acquired not from definitions but through everyday perceptions and experiences. Eleanor Rosch, a leading cognition researcher, and her colleagues studied concept formation in its natural setting and concluded that in real life, natural concepts (such as *fruit, vegetable,* and *bird*) are somewhat fuzzy, not clear-cut and systematic (Rosch, 1973, 1978).

Many formal concepts are acquired in school. For example, we learn that an equilateral triangle is one in which all three sides are the same size. We acquire many natural concepts through experiences with examples, or positive instances of the concept. When children are young, parents may point out examples of a car—the family car, the neighbor's car, cars on the street, and pictures of cars in books. But if a child points to some other type of moving vehicle and says "car," the parent will say, "No, that's a

7.3 What kinds of concepts help us manage information?

concept A mental category used to represent a class or group of objects, people, organizations, events, situations, or relations that share common characteristics or attributes.

formal concept A concept that is clearly defined by a set of rules, a formal definition, or a classification system; also known as an artificial concept.

natural concept A concept acquired not from a definition but through everyday perceptions and experiences; also known as a fuzzy concept.

▶ A prototype is an example that embodies the most typical features of a concept. Which of the animals shown here best fits your prototype for the concept of *bird*?

truck," or "This is a bus." *Truck* and *bus* are negative instances, or nonexamples, of the concept *car*. After experience with positive and negative instances of the concept, a child begins to grasp some of the properties of a car that distinguish it from other wheeled vehicles.

Prototypes and Exemplars. How do we use concepts in our everyday thinking? One view suggests that, in using natural concepts, we are likely to picture a **prototype** of the concept—an example that embodies its most common and typical features. Your *bird* prototype is more likely to be robin or a sparrow than either a penguin or a turkey: Those birds can fly, whereas penguins and turkeys can't. Nevertheless, both penguins and turkeys are birds. Thus, not all examples of a natural concept fit it equally well. This is why natural concepts often seem less clear-cut than formal ones. Nevertheless, the prototype most closely fits a given natural concept, and other examples of the concept most often share more attributes with that prototype than with the prototype of any other concept.

A more recent theory of concept formation suggests that concepts are represented by their **exemplars**—individual instances, or examples, of a concept that are stored in memory from personal experience (Estes, 1994). So, if you work with penguins or turkeys every day, your exemplar of *bird* might indeed be a penguin or a turkey. By contrast, most people encounter robins or sparrows far more often than penguins or turkeys (except the roasted variety!). Thus, for the majority of people, robins or sparrows are exemplars of the *bird* concept.

As noted earlier, the concepts we form do not exist in isolation, but rather in hierarchies, or nested categories. Thus, concept formation has a certain orderliness about it, just as the process of *decision making* does—or, at least, sometimes does.

prototype An example that embodies the most common and typical features of a concept.

exemplars The individual instances, or examples, of a concept that are stored in memory from personal experience.

Decision Making

7.4 What are the roles of systematic processes, heuristics, framing, and intuition in decision making?

Do you recall the last time you made an important decision? Would you describe the process you used to make the decision as a logical one? Psychologists define **decision making** as the process of considering alternatives and choosing among them.

Systematic Decision Making. Some psychologists and other scientists with an interest in decision making—particularly economists—maintain that humans use **systematic decision making** processes. This approach involves examining all possible alternatives and then choosing the one that will be most beneficial to them. However, psychologists have pointed out that, in everyday life, we rarely engage in this sort of formal, systematic approach to decision making. One factor that motivates us to seek other methods of making decisions is the amount of time required by the systematic approach. There are several other limits on this kind of decision making.

decision making The process of considering alternatives and choosing among them.

systematic decision making Making a decision after carefully considering all possible alternatives.

Limits on Systematic Decision Making. Many contemporary studies of decision making trace their roots to the concept of *bounded rationality* that psychologist Herbert

Simon proposed in 1956. Bounded rationality simply means that boundaries, or limitations, around the decision-making process prevent it from being entirely systematic. One important limitation is the size of working memory. We can think about only so much at any given time. Another limitation is our inability to predict the future. For example, if you are considering marrying someone, how do you know that you will still feel the same way about him or her 20 years from now? Obviously, you can't know, so you have to make an educated guess. For the past several decades, research on decision making has focused on how we form such educated guesses.

In one of the most important early studies of decision making along these lines, psychologist Amos Tversky (1972) suggested that we deal with the limitations on decision making by using a strategy he called **elimination by aspects.** With this approach, the factors on which the alternatives are to be evaluated are ordered from most important to least important. Any alternative that does not satisfy the most important factor is automatically eliminated. The process of elimination continues as each factor is considered in order. The alternative that survives is the one chosen. For example, if the most important factor for your apartment search was that you could afford a maximum rent of $800 per month, then you would automatically eliminate all the apartments that rented for more than that. If the second most important factor was availability of parking, you would then look at the list of apartments that cost $800 or less per month and weed out those without appropriate parking. You would then continue with your third most important factor and so on, until you had trimmed the list down.

Heuristics. Of course, decision making is often less systematic than Tversky's model suggests. For instance, have you ever decided to leave home a bit earlier than necessary so as to allow time for a possible traffic jam? Such decisions are often based on **heuristics**—rules of thumb that are derived from experience. Several kinds of heuristics exist. One that has been studied a great deal is the **availability heuristic,** a rule stating that the probability of an event corresponds to the ease with which the event comes to mind. Thus, a decision to leave home early to avoid a possible traffic jam may result from having been stuck in one recently. Another type of heuristic is the **representativeness heuristic,** a decision strategy based on how closely a new situation resembles a familiar one. For instance, a decision about whether to go out with someone you have just met may be based on how much the person resembles someone else you know.

The **recognition heuristic,** a strategy in which the decision-making process terminates as soon as a factor that moves one toward a decision has been recognized, has also been the subject of much research. Suppose you are voting and the only information you have is the list of candidates for a particular office on the ballot. If you recognize one of the candidates' names as being that of a woman, and you have a predisposition toward seeing more women elected to public office, the recognition heuristic may cause you to decide to vote for the female candidate.

Psychologists have debated the importance of recognition in making decisions. For instance, Gerd Gigerenzer and his colleagues (Gigerenzer et al., 1999; Goldstein & Gigerenzer, 2002) maintain that recognition heuristics enable decision makers to engage in a "fast and frugal" process that leads to rapid decisions that require little cognitive effort. Their research involving computer models of human decision-making processes suggests that the recognition heuristic is just as likely to lead to good decisions as to more time-consuming processes. Thus, Gigerenzer argues that the recognition heuristic is our preferred cognitive decision-making tool most of the time because of its efficiency.

elimination by aspects A decision-making approach in which alternatives are evaluated against criteria that have been ranked according to importance.

heuristic (yur-RIS-tik) A rule of thumb that is derived from experience and used in decision making and problem solving, even though there is no guarantee of its accuracy or usefulness.

availability heuristic A cognitive rule of thumb that says that the probability of an event or the importance assigned to it is based on its availability in memory.

representativeness heuristic A thinking strategy based on how closely a new object or situation is judged to resemble or match an existing prototype of that object or situation.

recognition heuristic A strategy in which decision making stops as soon as a factor that moves one toward a decision has been recognized.

▲ How do you decide which fast-food restaurant to patronize when you want a quick bite to eat? Chances are you use a representativeness heuristic, a prototype that guides your expectations about how long it will take to get your food and what it will taste like. Fast-food chains use the same ingredients and food preparation methods at every location in order to maintain patrons' representativeness heuristics as guides for their future fast-food buying decisions.

Other researchers have challenged Gigerenzer's assertion about the importance of the recognition heuristic (Lee & Cummins, 2004; Newell & Shanks, 2003, 2004; Richter & Späth, 2006). Their studies have shown that research participants use recognition heuristics only when they have little or no information about alternative choices and must make a decision in a very limited amount of time. Even under these conditions, all of the participants in a study do not use heuristics. Some individuals, for reasons that are not yet known, prefer to use more time-consuming, logically based strategies even in circumstances in which they have little information or time to make a decision. As a consequence, many psychologists believe that research on decision making needs to address the nature of such individual differences as well as any universals that may exist in the use of heuristics (Lee & Cummins, 2004; Newell, 2005).

Psychologists agree, however, that heuristics can sometimes lead to illogical decisions and, in turn, to tragic outcomes. For example, immediately after the terrorist attacks of September 11, 2001, Gigerenzer hypothesized that the number of deaths due to traffic accidents in the United States would increase dramatically in the ensuing weeks (Gigerenzer, 2004). Why? Gigerenzer believed that memories of the attacks would serve as availability heuristics that would cause people to choose to travel by car rather than by plane, despite the fact that their chances of being the target of a terrorist attack were far less than those associated with getting into an automobile accident. To test his hypothesis, Gigerenzer compared police records of fatal car crashes during September, October, and November of 2001 to the same records for the same months in 1996 through 2000. He found that substantially more such accidents occurred in the months immediately after September 11 than during the same period in the five previous years.

The take-away message from the scholarly debate about the role of heuristics in decision making is that there is little doubt that such strategies help us make rapid decisions with little mental effort, but they can also lead to errors. The challenge we face in everyday decision making is to accurately assess the degree to which a heuristic strategy is appropriate for a given decision. For instance, in the voting booth, we would probably agree that it would be better to base one's decision on information about candidates' positions on issues than to make last-minute decisions on the basis of characteristics such as gender that we may be able to infer from their names.

Framing. Whether we use heuristics or more time-consuming strategies, we should be aware that the manner in which information is presented can affect the decision-making process. For example, **framing** refers to the way information is presented so as to emphasize either a potential gain or a potential loss as the outcome. To study the effects of framing on decision making, Kahneman and Tversky (1984) presented the following options to a group of participants. Which program would you choose?

> The United States is preparing for the outbreak of a dangerous disease, which is expected to kill 600 people. There have been designed two alternative programs to combat the disease. If program A is adopted, 200 people will be saved. If program B is adopted, there is a one-third probability that all 600 will be saved and a two-thirds probability that no people will be saved.

The researchers found that 72% of the participants selected the "sure thing" of program A over the "risky gamble" of program B. Now consider the options as they were reframed:

> If program C is adopted, 400 people will die. If program D is adopted, there is a one-third probability that nobody will die and a two-thirds probability that all 600 people will die.

Which program did you choose? Of research participants given this version of the problem, 78% chose program D. A careful reading will reveal that program D has exactly the same consequences as program B in the earlier version. How can this result be explained? The first version of the problem was framed to focus attention on the number of lives that could be saved. And when people are primarily motivated to achieve gains (save lives), they are more likely to choose a safe option over a risky one, as 72% of the participants did. The second version was framed to focus attention on the 400 lives that would be lost. When trying to avoid losses, people appear much more willing to choose a risky option, as 78% of the participants were.

framing The way information is presented so as to emphasize either a potential gain or a potential loss as the outcome.

Intuition. What if you had to make an on-the-spot decision about whether you would rather purchase an $18,000 car and receive a $1,000 rebate or buy a $17,000 car? What would your decision be? Perhaps *intuition* would lead you to choose the car with the rebate even though both options require you to pay the same amount of money for a car. **Intuition** produces rapidly formed judgments based on "gut feelings." These gut feelings often lead us to decide in favor of options that appear to offer us some kind of gain, such as a rebate on the purchase of a car. Information-processing researchers argue that intuition is based on a mental representation of the gist of a body of information rather than on its factual details (Reyna, 2004). The gist of a car dealer's advertisement for a $1,000 rebate on an $18,000 automobile is "you'll save money if you buy it here," not "$18,000 − $1,000 = $17,000; therefore, it doesn't matter where you buy the car." Furthermore, researchers have found that intuition can lead to errors in reasoning about decisions that carry far greater risks than those associated with buying a car. Researchers have found that intuitive thought processes can cause physicians to overestimate the degree to which condoms reduce the risk of sexually transmitted diseases (Adam & Reyna, 2005; Reyna & Adam, 2003). Study participants' assessments of the comparative risks of sexual behavior with and without condoms tended to ignore infections that have modes of transmission other than sexual intercourse (e.g., chlamydia).

intuition   Rapidly formed judgments based on "gut feelings" or "instincts."

problem solving   Thoughts and actions required to achieve a desired goal that is not readily attainable.

Review and Reflect   Approaches to Decision Making

Approach	Description
systematic decision making	Consideration of all possible alternatives prior to making a decision.
elimination by aspects	Factors on which alternatives are to be evaluated are ordered from most to least important; any alternatives that do not satisfy the most important factor are eliminated; elimination of alternatives then continues factor by factor until one choice remains.
availability heuristic	Information that comes easily to mind determines the decision that is made.
representativeness heuristic	The decision is based on how closely an object or situation resembles or matches an existing prototype.
recognition heuristic	A rapid decision based on recognition of one of the alternatives.
framing	Potential gains and losses associated with alternatives are emphasized and influence the decision.
intuition	Decisions are motivated by "gut feelings" that may be influenced by perceptions of gains.

Problem Solving

How do you usually try to solve a problem? Perhaps you use the *trial-and-error method*; that is, you try one method after another until you find one that works. More likely, you have found that other strategies are more effective. In fact, the process of decision making you have just been reading about shares many features with **problem solving,** the thoughts and actions required to achieve a desired goal.

7.5 **What are some basic approaches to problem solving, and how do they differ?**

Heuristics and Algorithms. Most of us find heuristics to be just as useful for solving problems as they are for making decisions. For instance, the **analogy heuristic** involves comparing a problem to others you have encountered in the past. The idea is that if strategy A worked with similar problems in the past, it will be effective for solving a new one.

Another heuristic that is effective for solving some problems is **working backward,** sometimes called the *backward search*. This approach starts with the solution, a known condition, and works back through the problem. Once the backward search has revealed the steps to be taken and their order, the problem can be solved. Try working backwards to solve the water lily problem in the *Try It* (on page 238).

analogy heuristic   A rule of thumb that applies a solution that solved a problem in the past to a current problem that shares many features with the past problem.

working backward   A heuristic strategy in which a person discovers the steps needed to solve a problem by defining the desired goal and working backward to the current condition; also called *backward search*.

Try It   Water Lily Problem

Water lilies double the area they cover every 24 hours. At the beginning of the summer there is one water lily on a pond. It takes 60 days for the pond to become covered with water lilies. On what day is the pond half covered? (From Fixx, 1978.)

Answer: The most important fact is that the lilies double in number every 24 hours. If the pond is to be completely covered on the 60th day, it has to be half covered on the 59th day.

Source: From *Solve It: A Perplexing Profusion of Puzzles* by James F. Fixx, 1978.

▲ Many of us are hampered in our efforts to solve problems in daily life because of functional fixedness—the failure to use familiar objects in novel ways to solve problems.

means–end analysis A heuristic strategy in which the current position is compared with the desired goal and a series of steps are formulated and taken to close the gap between them.

algorithm A systematic, step-by-step procedure, such as a mathematical formula, that guarantees a solution to a problem of a certain type if applied appropriately and executed properly.

functional fixedness The failure to use familiar objects in novel ways to solve problems because of a tendency to view objects only in terms of their customary functions.

mental set The tendency to apply a familiar strategy to the solution of a problem without carefully considering the special requirements of that problem.

Another popular heuristic strategy is **means–end analysis,** in which the current position is compared with a desired goal, and a series of steps are formulated and then taken to close the gap between the two (Sweller & Levine, 1982). Many problems are large and complex and must be broken down into smaller steps or subproblems before a solution can be reached. If your professor assigns a term paper, for example, you probably do not simply sit down and write it. You must first determine how you will approach the topic, research the topic, make an outline, and then write the sections over a period of time. At last, you will be ready to assemble the complete term paper, write several drafts, and put the finished product in final form before handing it in and receiving your A.

When you adopt a heuristic strategy, it may or may not lead to a correct solution. By contrast, an **algorithm** is a problem-solving strategy that always leads to a correct solution if it is applied appropriately. For example, the formula you learned in school for finding the area of a rectangle (width × length) is an algorithm.

Of course, you have to know an algorithm and be able to match it with appropriate problems to use it. Likewise, heuristics must be based on prior knowledge. Thus, one important obstacle to effective problem solving is lack of appropriate knowledge. There are several others.

Impediments to Problem Solving. In some cases, we are hampered in our efforts to solve problems in daily life because of **functional fixedness** —the failure to use familiar objects in novel ways to solve problems. We tend to see objects only in terms of their customary functions. Just think of all the items you use daily—tools, utensils, and other equipment—that help you perform certain functions. Often, the normal functions of such objects become fixed in your thinking so that you do not consider using them in new and creative ways (German & Barrett, 2005).

Suppose you wanted a cup of coffee, but the glass carafe for your coffeemaker was broken. If you suffered from functional fixedness, you might come to the conclusion that there was nothing you could do to solve your problem at that moment. But, rather than thinking about the object or utensil that you don't have, think about the function that it needs to perform. What you need is something to catch the coffee, not necessarily the specific type of glass carafe that came with the coffeemaker. Could you catch the coffee in a bowl or cooking utensil, or even in coffee mugs?

Another impediment to problem solving, similar to functional fixedness but much broader, is mental set. **Mental set** is a mental rut in one's approach to solving problems, the tendency to continue to use the same old method even though another approach might be better. Perhaps you hit on a way to solve a problem once in the past and continue to use the same technique in similar situations, even though it is not highly effective or efficient. People are much more susceptible to mental set when they fail to consider the special requirements of a problem. Not surprisingly, the same people who are subject to mental set are also more likely to have trouble with functional fixedness when they attempt to solve problems (McKelvie, 1984).

Finally, you may have heard the expression "two heads are better than one." With regard to problem solving, this proverb may indeed be true. Researchers have found that groups of 2 to 5 people produce better solutions to problems than any of the individual group members came up with (Laughlin et al., 2006). Thus, the next time you are faced with a perplexing problem, the best strategy may be to enlist the aid of your friends, family, or classmates in finding a workable solution.

◄ World champion Garry Kasparov contemplates a move against Deep Blue, an IBM computer that exhibited artificial intelligence in the area of top-level chess play.

Artificial Intelligence

In the previous section you learned that mathematical formulas are algorithms, or problem-solving strategies that always lead to a correct solution. Another kind of algorithm tests all possible solutions and then executes the one that works best. In most situations, the limits of human working memory render this kind of algorithm difficult, if not impossible, to employ. By contrast, computers are capable of completing such an algorithm, and doing so in a matter of seconds. This particular feature of computer "thinking" has been well illustrated by artificial intelligence programs that have been designed to match the skills of human experts in games such as chess. You may have heard of the series of chess matches that pitted renowned player Garry Kasparov against IBM computers named "Deep Blue" and "Deep Junior." The best Kasparov has been able to do is to play the computers to a draw.

If a computer can beat a human at chess, does it mean that computers process information in exactly the same way as the human brain does? Not necessarily. However, computer scientists hope to design artificial intelligence that accomplishes that goal. Programs designed to mimic human brain functioning are called artificial neural networks (ANNs). Such networks have proved very useful in computer programs designed to carry out highly specific functions within a limited domain, known as expert systems. One of the first expert systems was MYCIN, a program used by physicians to diagnose blood diseases and meningitis. For the most part, expert systems

offer the greatest benefits when acting as assistants to humans. For example, medical diagnosis programs are most often used to confirm doctors' hypotheses or to generate possible diagnoses that have not occurred to them (Brunetti et al., 2002). Remember, too, that any expert system relies on the accumulated knowledge of human experts. Thus, it is impossible for computers to totally replace human professionals.

Moreover, many cognitive tasks that humans find relatively easy to perform are actually quite difficult to teach a computer to

do. Many aspects of language processing, for instance, are extremely difficult for computers to manage (Athanasselis et al., 2005). For example, what kind of scene comes to mind when you hear the word *majestic*? Perhaps you see a range of snow-capped mountains. Computer scientists are currently working to develop programs that can

---

7.6 **What are some important applications of artificial intelligence technologies?**

artificial intelligence The programming of computer systems to simulate human thinking in solving problems and in making judgments and decisions.

artificial neural networks (ANNs) Computer systems that are intended to mimic the human brain.

expert systems Computer programs designed to carry out highly specific functions within a limited domain.

◄ If expert systems that include ANNs can make medical diagnoses, why are human doctors still needed? The reason is that humans can make subtle judgments that are difficult for computers. For instance, a doctor may detect a subtle change in facial expression that suggests that the patient may not be telling the truth. Language can be an obstacle to computer-based diagnoses as well. How would you tell a computer that you feel a "catch" in your back whenever you raise your arms? Hundreds of lines of programming would be required to program a computer to understand this expression, something that a doctor would instantly comprehend.

enable computers to retrieve images on the basis of such vague, abstract cues (Kuroda, 2002). As you will see in the next section, although we use it effortlessly most of the time, human language is an extremely complex phenomenon.

Remember It | Cognition

1. Syllogisms involve _____ reasoning.
2. Imagining an action stimulates the same brain areas that are active when actually engaging in the action. (true/false)
3. A(n) _____ is the most typical example of a concept.
4. Heuristics have both desirable and undesirable effects on decision making. (true/false)

5. A(n) _____ is a problem-solving strategy that guarantees a correct answer.
6. Computer systems intended to mimic the functioning of the human brain are called _____.

Answers: 1. deductive; 2. true; 3. prototype; 4. true; 5. algorithm; 6. artificial neural networks

Language

Can we think without using language? Research on imagery indicates that we can. But, without language, each of us would live in a largely solitary and isolated world, unable to communicate or receive much information. Scientists define **language** as a means of communicating thoughts and feelings, using a system of socially shared but arbitrary symbols (sounds, signs, or written symbols) arranged according to rules of grammar.

Think for a minute about how amazing language really is. It allows us to form and comprehend a virtually infinite number of meaningful sentences. If this were not the case, we would be limited to merely repeating statements we had heard or read. Moreover, language is not bound by space or time. Language enables us to communicate about things that are abstract or concrete, present or not present, and about what has been, is now, or conceivably might be. Thanks to language, we can profit from the experience, the knowledge, and the wisdom of others, and we can benefit others with our own. Language makes available the wisdom of the ages from every corner of the world. In Chapter 8, we will discuss how language is acquired by infants. Here, we explore the structure and the components of this amazing form of human communication.

The Structure of Language

7.7 What are the necessary components of any language?

Psycholinguistics is the study of how language is acquired, produced, and used and how the sounds and symbols of language are translated into meaning. Psycholinguists devote much effort to the study of the structure of language and the rules governing its use. These vital components of language are phonemes, morphemes, syntax, semantics, and pragmatics.

Phonemes. The smallest units of sound in a spoken language are known as **phonemes.** Phonemes form the basic building blocks of a spoken language. Three phonemes together form the sound of the word *cat*—the c (which sounds like k), a, and t. Phonemes do not sound like the single letters of the alphabet as you recite them, a-b-c-d-e-f-g, but like the sounds of the letters as they are used in words, like the b in *boy*, the p in *pan*, and so on. The sound of the phoneme c in the word *cat* is different from the sound of the phoneme c in the word *city*.

Letters combined to form sounds, such as *th* in *the* and *ch* in *child*, are also phonemes. The same sound (phoneme) may be represented by different letters in different words, as the a in *stay* and the *ei* in *sleigh*. And, as you saw with c, the same letter can serve as different phonemes. The letter a, for example, is sounded as four different phonemes in *day, cap, watch*, and *law*.

How many phonemes are there? About 100 or so different sounds could serve as phonemes, but most languages have far fewer. English uses about 45 phonemes, whereas some languages may have as few as 15 and others as many as 85 (Solso,

language A means of communicating thoughts and feelings, using a system of socially shared but arbitrary symbols (sounds, signs, or written symbols) arranged according to rules of grammar.

psycholinguistics The study of how language is acquired, produced, and used, and how the sounds and symbols of language are translated into meaning.

phonemes The smallest units of sound in a spoken language.

1991). However, phonemes do not provide meaning. Meaning is conveyed by the next component of a language, the morphemes.

Morphemes. Morphemes are the smallest units of meaning in a language. In almost all cases in the English language, a morpheme is made of two or more phonemes. But a few phonemes also serve as morphemes, such as the article *a* and the personal pronoun *I*. Many words in English are single morphemes—*book, word, learn, reason,* and so on. In addition to root words, morphemes may also be prefixes (such as *re-* in *relearn*) or suffixes (such as *-ed* to show past tense, as in *learned*). The word *reasonable* consists of two morphemes: *reason* and *able.* The addition of the prefix *un-* (another morpheme) forms *unreasonable,* reversing the meaning. The letter *s* gives a plural meaning to a word and is thus a morpheme. The morpheme *book* (singular) becomes two morphemes, *books* (plural).

So, morphemes, singly and in combination, form the words in a language and provide meaning. But single words alone do not constitute a language. A language also requires rules for structuring, or putting together, words in orderly and meaningful fashion. This is where syntax enters the picture.

Syntax. Syntax is the aspect of grammar that specifies the rules for arranging and combining words to form phrases and sentences. For example, an important rule of syntax in English is that adjectives usually come before nouns. English speakers refer to the residence of the U.S. President as the White House. But in Spanish, the noun usually comes before the adjective, and Spanish speakers would say, "la Casa Blanca" (the House White). In English, we ask, "Do you speak German?" But speakers of German would ask, "Sprechen sie Deutsch?" (Speak you German?). So, the rules of word order, or syntax, differ from one language to another.

It is important to point out here that *grammar* includes both the rules for combining morphemes and those that govern syntax. For example, the rules for combining morphemes determine the difference between "sock" and "socks." The difference between "Is it here?" and "Here it is." involves syntax. Both kinds of rules contribute to the grammar of a language.

Semantics. Semantics refers to the meaning derived from morphemes, words, and sentences. The same word can have different meanings, depending on how it is used in sentences: "I don't mind." "You mind your manners." "He has lost his mind."

The noted linguist and creative theorist Noam Chomsky (1986, 1990) maintained that the ability to glean a meaningful message from a sentence is stored in a different area of the brain than are the words used to compose the sentence. Moreover, he distinguished between the surface structure and the deep structure of a sentence. The surface structure of a sentence refers to the literal words that are spoken or written (or signed). The deep structure is the underlying meaning of the sentence.

In some sentences, the surface structure and the deep structure are the same. This is true of the sentence "Lauren read the book." But if this sentence is rewritten in the passive voice—"The book was read by Lauren"—the surface structure changes, yet the deep structure remains the same. Alternatively, a single sentence may have one or more different deep structures. For example, in the sentence "John enjoys charming people," two competing deep structures produce ambiguity. Does John enjoy people who are charming, or does he enjoy exercising his charm on other people?

Pragmatics. How do you know whether a person is making a statement or asking a question? The pragmatic characteristics of a language help you tell the difference. Pragmatics is defined as the characteristics of spoken language that help you decipher the social meaning of utterances. For example, one aspect of pragmatics is *prosody,* or intonation. Every language has prosodic rules that are followed when producing statements or questions. In English, statements fall in intonation at the end, while questions rise. So, if someone sitting near you in an airport says to you, "newspaper," with rising intonation at the end of the word, you know that she is saying "Would you like this newspaper?" Other nonverbal cues may accompany the question. She may be holding a newspaper out to you or motioning to a newspaper lying on a table. Such gestures represent another aspect of pragmatics.

morphemes The smallest units of meaning in a language.

syntax The aspect of grammar that specifies the rules for arranging and combining words to form phrases and sentences.

semantics The meaning derived from morphemes, words, and sentences.

surface structure The literal words of a sentence that are spoken or written (or signed).

deep structure The underlying meaning of a sentence.

pragmatics The characteristics of spoken language, such as intonation and gestures, that indicate the social meaning of utterances.

Language and Thinking

If language is unique to humans, then does it drive human thinking? Does the fact that you speak English mean that you reason, think, and perceive your world differently than does someone who speaks Spanish, or Chinese, or Swahili? According to one hypothesis presented about 50 years ago, it does. Benjamin Whorf (1956) put forth his **linguistic relativity hypothesis,** suggesting that the language a person speaks largely determines the nature of that person's thoughts. According to this hypothesis, people's worldview is constructed primarily by the words in their language. As proof, Whorf offered his classic example: The languages used by the Eskimo people have a number of different words for snow—"*apikak,* first snow falling; *aniv,* snow spread out; *pukak,* snow for drinking water"—while the English-speaking world has but one word, *snow* (Restak, 1988, p. 222). Whorf claimed that such a rich and varied selection of words for various snow types and conditions enabled Eskimos to think differently about snow than do people whose languages lack such a range of words.

Eleanor Rosch (1973) tested whether people whose language contains many names for colors would be better at thinking about and discriminating among colors than people whose language has only a few color names. Her participants were English-speaking Americans and the Dani, members of a remote tribe in New Guinea whose language has only two names for colors—*mili* for dark, cool colors and *mola* for bright, warm colors. Rosch showed members of both groups single-color chips of 11 colors—black, white, red, yellow, green, blue, brown, purple, pink, orange, and gray—for 5 seconds each. Then, after 30 seconds, she had the participants select the 11 colors they had viewed from an assortment of 40 color chips. Did the Americans outperform the Dani participants, for whom brown, black, purple, and blue are all *mili,* or dark? No. Rosch found no significant differences between the Dani and the Americans in discriminating, remembering, or thinking about those 11 basic colors. Rosch's study did not support the linguistic relativity hypothesis.

Clearly, however, it would be a mistake to go too far in the opposite direction and assume that language has no influence on how people think. Thought both influences and is influenced by language, and language appears to reflect cultural differences more than it determines them (Pinker, 1994; Rosch, 1987).

Learning a Second Language

Do you speak more than one language? Most native-born Americans speak only English. But in many other countries around the world, the majority of citizens speak two or even more languages (Snow, 1993). In European countries, most students learn English in addition to the languages of the countries bordering their own. Dutch is the native language of the Netherlands, but all Dutch schoolchildren learn German, French, and English. College-bound German students also typically study three languages (Haag & Stern, 2003). What about the effect of learning two languages on the process of language development itself?

Research suggests that there are both advantages and disadvantages to learning two languages early in life. One of the pluses is that among preschool and school-age children, **bilingualism,** fluency in two languages, is associated with better *metalinguistic skills,* the capacity to think about language (Bialystok et al., 2000; Mohanty & Perregaux, 1997). On the downside, even in adulthood, bilingualism is sometimes associated with decreased efficiency in memory tasks involving words (Gollan & Silverberg, 2001; McElree et al., 2000). However, bilinguals appear to develop compensatory strategies that allow them to make up these inefficiencies. Consequently, they often perform such tasks as accurately as monolinguals, though they may respond more slowly. Many people would argue, however, that the advantages associated with fluency in two languages are worth giving up a bit of cognitive efficiency.

So, you may ask, what about people who did not have the good fortune to grow up bilingual? Is it still possible to become fluent in a second language after reaching adulthood? Researchers have found that there is no age at which it is impossible to

linguistic relativity hypothesis
The notion that the language a person speaks largely determines the nature of that person's thoughts.

bilingualism   Fluency in at least two languages.

acquire a new language. Although it is true that those who begin earlier reach higher levels of proficiency, age is not the only determining factor. Kenji Hakuta and his colleagues (2003) used census data to examine relationships among English proficiency, age at entry into the United States, and educational attainment for Chinese- and Spanish-speaking immigrants. The results of their study are shown in **Figure 7.1**. As you can see, even when immigrants entered the United States in middle and late adulthood, their ability to learn English was predicted by their educational backgrounds. And other studies have shown that the more you know about your first language—its spelling rules, grammatical structure, and vocabulary—the easier it will be for you to learn another language (Meschyan & Hernandez, 2002).

It may be that children attain second-language fluency more easily than adults simply because they practice more. Older individuals may rely more on passive strategies such as listening to others' conversations or watching television to pick up a new language. Research has shown that passive listening can help us learn new vocabulary, but it is of no help in learning grammar (Van Lommel, Laenen, & d'Ydewalle, 2006). In fact, listening to others speak actually appears to cause us to forget the grammatical knowledge that we already have. This may happen because natural conversation includes fragmentary expressions rather than complete sentences. For example, a friend might say to you, "How long did you study for the psychology exam?" In reply, you would probably say "about three hours" rather than "I studied about three hours for the psychology exam." Thus, when you take a foreign language class, some of the required exercises may seem silly. (How often does anyone say something like "Here is my aunt's big yellow pencil" or "There is Lucy's beautiful blue hat" in real life?) Yet, they are essential to your acquisition of the language's grammar.

There is one clear advantage to learning two languages earlier in life, however. People who are younger when they learn a new language are far more likely to be able to speak it with an appropriate accent (McDonald, 1997). One reason for this difference between early and late language learners may have to do with slight variations in neural processing in Broca's area, the area of the brain that controls speech production. Research by Kim and others (1997) suggests that bilinguals who learned a second language early (younger than age 10 or 11) rely on the same patch of tissue in Broca's area

▲ Growing up in a bilingual home provides distinct advantages in adolescence and adulthood. Spanish and English are the languages spoken by the majority of bilinguals in the United States.

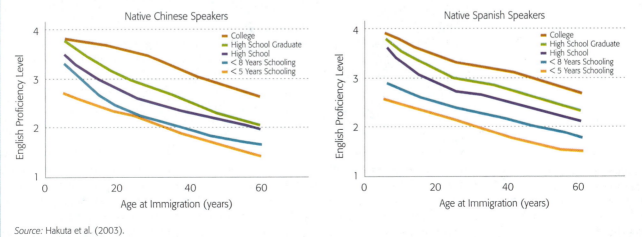

Figure 7.1 **English Proficiency in Chinese- and Spanish-Speaking Immigrants to the United States**

These research results, based on census data involving more than 2 million individuals, suggest that it is never too late to learn a second language.

Source: Hakuta et al. (2003).

for both of the languages they speak. In those who learned a second language at an older age, two different sections of Broca's area are active while they are performing language tasks—one section for the first language and another for the second language. Yet, the two sections are very close, only $\frac{1}{3}$ inch apart.

Animal Communication

7.10 **What does research indicate about animals' capacity for language?**

Ask people what capability most reliably sets humans apart from all other animal species, and most will answer "language." And for good reason. As far as scientists know, humans are the only species to have developed this rich, varied, and complex system of communication.

Studies with Chimpanzees. As early as 1933 and 1951, researchers attempted to teach chimpanzees to speak by raising the chimps in their homes. These experiments failed because the vocal tract in chimpanzees and the other apes is not adapted to human speech, so researchers turned to sign language. Psychologists Allen and Beatrix Gardner (1969) took in a 1-year-old chimp named Washoe and taught her sign language. Washoe learned signs for objects and certain commands, such as *flower, give me, come, open,* and *more.* By the end of her fifth year, she had mastered about 160 signs (Fleming, 1974).

Psychologist David Premack (1971) taught another chimp, Sarah, to use an artificial language he developed. Its symbols consisted of magnetized chips of various shapes, sizes, and colors, as shown in **Figure 7.2**. Premack used operant conditioning techniques to teach Sarah to select the magnetic chip representing a fruit and place it on a magnetic language board. The trainer would then reward Sarah with the fruit she had requested. Sarah mastered the concepts of similarities and differences, and eventually she could signal whether two objects were the same or different with nearly perfect accuracy (Premack & Premack, 1983). Even more remarkable, Sarah could view a whole apple and a cut apple and, even though she had not seen the apple being cut, could match the apple with the utensil needed to cut it—a knife.

At the Yerkes Primate Research Center at Emory University, a chimp named Lana participated in a computer-controlled language training program. She learned to press keys imprinted with geometric symbols that represented words in an artificial language called Yerkish. Researcher Sue Savage-Rumbaugh and a colleague (1986; Rumbaugh, 1977) varied the location, color, and brightness of the keys, so Lana had to learn which symbols to use no matter where they were located. One day, her trainer Tim had an orange that she wanted. Lana had available symbols for many fruits—apple, banana, and so on—but none for an orange. Yet there was a symbol for the color orange. So Lana improvised and signaled, "Tim give apple which is orange."

Furthermore, researcher Herbert Terrace (1979, 1981) and his co-workers taught sign language to a chimp they called Nim Chimpsky (after the famed linguist Noam Chomsky) and reported Nim's progress from the age of 2 weeks to 4 years. Nim learned 125 symbols, which is respectable, but does not amount to language, according to Terrace (1985, 1986). Terrace believed that chimps like Nim and Washoe were simply imitating their trainers and making responses to get reinforcers, according to the laws of operant conditioning, not the laws of language. Finally, Terrace suggested that the studies with primates were probably influenced by experimenter bias; trainers might unconsciously tend to interpret the behavior of the chimps as more indicative of progress toward developing language than it really was. However, Terrace had not heard of Kanzi when he expressed his skepticism.

Kanzi's Amazing Language Skills. As impressive as the feats of Washoe, Sarah, Lana, and Nim Chimsky were, the linguistic skills that were acquired by a bonobo chimp named Kanzi eclipsed them all. During the mid-1980s, researchers had taught Kanzi's mother to press symbols representing words. Her progress was not remarkable; but her infant son Kanzi, who stood by and observed her during training, was

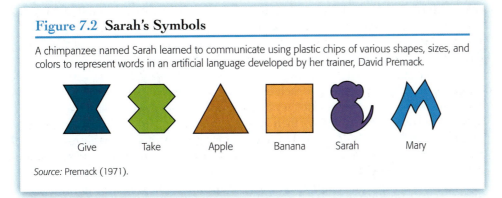

Figure 7.2 Sarah's Symbols

A chimpanzee named Sarah learned to communicate using plastic chips of various shapes, sizes, and colors to represent words in an artificial language developed by her trainer, David Premack.

| Give | Take | Apple | Banana | Sarah | Mary |

Source: Premack (1971).

learning rapidly (thanks to observational learning, discussed in Chapter 5). When Kanzi had a chance at the symbol board, his performance quickly surpassed that of his mother and of every other chimp the researchers had tested.

Kanzi demonstrated an advanced understanding (for chimps) of spoken English and could respond correctly even to new commands, such as "Throw your ball to the river," or "Go to the refrigerator and get out a tomato" (Savage-Rumbaugh, 1990; Savage-Rumbaugh et al., 1992). By the time Kanzi was 6 years old, a team of researchers who worked with him had recorded more than 13,000 "utterances" and reported that Kanzi could communicate using some 200 different geometric symbols (Gibbons, 1991). Kanzi could press symbols to ask someone to play chase with him and even ask two others to play chase while he watched. And if Kanzi signaled someone to "chase" and "hide," he was insistent that his first command, "chase," be done first (Gibbons, 1991). Kanzi was not merely responding to nearby trainers whose actions or gestures he might have copied. He responded just as well when requests were made over earphones so that no one else in the room could signal to him purposely or inadvertently.

Chimpanzees' Use of Numerical Symbols. More recent research suggests that chimpanzees may be able to learn numerical as well as linguistic symbols (Beran, 2004; Beran & Rumbaugh, 2001). Researchers trained two chimpanzees to use a joystick to move dots on a computer screen. Then, the chimps were taught to collect specific numbers of dots in association with Arabic numerals. In other words, when *3* was displayed on the screen, the chimp was supposed to use its joystick to move three dots from one location to another. Although the chimps learned the task, they tended to perform poorly with quantities in excess of six or seven. Afterward, the researchers ceased practicing with them because they wanted to find out whether the animals would remember the associations over extended periods of time. When they were retested 6 months later, the chimps were able to perform the task quite well, although they made more errors than when they were first trained. After 3 years, the researchers tested them again and found that they still remembered the symbol–quantity associations.

▲ From their studies of communication among chimps and other animals, researchers have gained useful insights into the nature of language. The pygmy chimp Kanzi became skilled at using a special symbol board to communicate.

Studies with Other Species. Most animal species studied by language researchers are limited to motor responses such as sign language, gestures, using magnetic symbols, or pressing keys on symbol boards. But these limitations do not extend to some bird species such as parrots, which are capable of making humanlike speech sounds. One remarkable case is Alex, an African gray parrot that not only mimics human speech but also seems to do so intelligently. Able to recognize and name various colors, objects, and shapes, Alex answers questions about them in English. Asked "Which object is green?" Alex easily names the green object (Pepperberg, 1991, 1994b). And he can count as well. When asked such questions as "How many red blocks?" Alex answers correctly about 80% of the time (Pepperberg, 1994a). Recent studies even suggest that Alex may be able to add (Pepperberg, 2006).

Research with sea mammals such as whales and dolphins has established that they apparently use complicated systems of grunts, whistles, clicks, and other sounds to communicate within their species (Herman, 1981; Savage-Rumbaugh, 1993). Researchers at the University of Hawaii have trained dolphins to respond to fairly complex commands requiring an understanding of directional and relational concepts. Dolphins can learn to pick out an object and put it on the right or left of a basket, for example, and comprehend such commands as "in the basket" and "under the basket" (Chollar, 1989).

Remember It   Language

1. Match each description with the correct component of language.

   (1) _____ the smallest units of meaning   a. pragmatics
   (2) _____ the meaning of utterances   b. syntax
   (3) _____ grammatical rules   c. morphemes
   (4) _____ the social aspects of language   d. semantics
   (5) _____ the smallest units of sound   e. phonemes

2. Sentences are more likely to be ambiguous if they have two or more _____ structures.

3. According to the _____, thinking can be limited by language.

4. The ability to reach high levels of proficiency when learning a second language _____ as people get older.

5. Chimpanzees can communicate with humans using symbols or _____.

Answers: 1. (1) c, (2) d, (3) b, (4) a, (5) e; 2. deep; 3. linguistic relativity hypothesis; 4. declines; 5. sign language

---

Intelligence

Have you ever stopped to think what you really mean when you say someone is "intelligent"? Do you mean that the person learns quickly or that he or she can solve problems that appear to mystify others? Spending a few minutes thinking about intelligence in this way will help you realize that defining intelligence in ways that can be measured is quite a challenge.

The Nature of Intelligence

7.11 How do the views of Spearman, Thurstone, Gardner, and Sternberg differ with regard to the definition of intelligence?

A task force of experts from the American Psychological Association (APA) defined **intelligence** as possessing several basic facets: an individual's "ability to understand complex ideas, . . . to adapt effectively to the environment, . . . to learn from experience, to engage in various forms of reasoning, and to overcome obstacles by taking thought" (Neisser et al., 1996, p. 77). As you will see, however, there's more to intelligence than this simple definition suggests.

The APA's definition of intelligence includes several factors, such as the ability to understand complex ideas and the capacity for adapting to the environment. But are these manifestations of a single entity or truly separate abilities? This question has fascinated psychologists for more than a century.

English psychologist Charles Spearman (1863–1945) observed that people who are bright in one area are usually bright in other areas as well. In other words, they tend to be generally intelligent. Spearman (1927) came to believe that intelligence is composed of a general ability that underlies all intellectual functions. Spearman concluded that intelli-

intelligence An individual's ability to understand complex ideas, to adapt effectively to the environment, to learn from experience, to engage in various forms of reasoning, and to overcome obstacles through mental effort.

gence tests tap this ***g* factor,** or general intelligence, and a number of *s* factors, or specific intellectual abilities. Spearman's influence can be seen in those intelligence tests, such as the Stanford–Binet, that yield one IQ score to indicate the level of general intelligence.

Another early researcher in testing, Louis L. Thurstone (1938), rejected Spearman's notion of general intellectual ability, or *g* factor. After analyzing the scores of many participants on some 56 separate ability tests, Thurstone identified seven **primary mental abilities:** verbal comprehension, numerical ability, spatial relations, perceptual speed, word fluency, memory, and reasoning. He maintained that all intellectual activities involve one or more of these primary mental abilities. Thurstone and his wife, Thelma G. Thurstone, developed their Primary Mental Abilities Tests to measure these seven abilities. Thurstone believed that a single IQ score obscured more than it revealed. He suggested that a profile showing relative strengths and weaknesses on the seven primary mental abilities would provide a more accurate picture of a person's intelligence.

Harvard psychologist Howard Gardner (Gardner & Hatch, 1989) also denies the existence of a *g* factor. Instead, he proposes eight independent forms of intelligence, or *frames of mind*, as illustrated in **Figure 7.3**. The eight frames of mind are linguistic, logical-mathematical, spatial, bodily-kinesthetic, musical, interpersonal, intrapersonal, and naturalistic.

Gardner (1983) first developed his theory by studying patients with different types of brain damage that affect some forms of intelligence but leave others intact. He also studied reports of people with *savant syndrome*, who show a combination of mental retardation and unusual talent or ability. (You'll read more about this phenomenon later in this chapter.) Gardner also considered how various abilities and skills have been valued differently in other cultures and periods of history. Furthermore, Gardner continues to refine his model. In recent years, he has proposed that a ninth type of intelligence, one that he calls *existential intelligence*, deals with the spiritual realm and enables us to contemplate the meaning of life (Halama & Strízenec, 2004).

***g* factor**   Spearman's term for a general intellectual ability that underlies all mental operations to some degree.

primary mental abilities
According to Thurstone, seven relatively distinct capabilities that singly or in combination are involved in all intellectual activities.

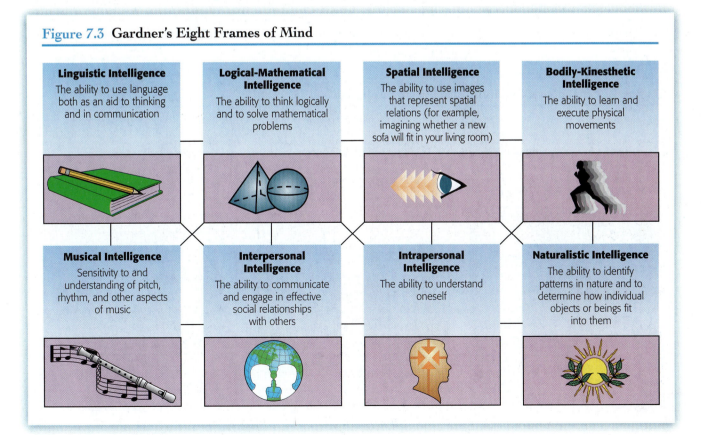

Figure 7.3 Gardner's Eight Frames of Mind

Linguistic Intelligence
The ability to use language both as an aid to thinking and in communication

Logical-Mathematical Intelligence
The ability to think logically and to solve mathematical problems

Spatial Intelligence
The ability to use images that represent spatial relations (for example, imagining whether a new sofa will fit in your living room)

Bodily-Kinesthetic Intelligence
The ability to learn and execute physical movements

Musical Intelligence
Sensitivity to and understanding of pitch, rhythm, and other aspects of music

Interpersonal Intelligence
The ability to communicate and engage in effective social relationships with others

Intrapersonal Intelligence
The ability to understand oneself

Naturalistic Intelligence
The ability to identify patterns in nature and to determine how individual objects or beings fit into them

Perhaps the most controversial aspect of Gardner's theory is his view that all forms of intelligence are of equal importance. In fact, different cultures asign varying degrees of importance to the types of intelligence. For example, linguistic and logical mathematical intelligences are valued most in the United States and other Western cultures; bodily-kinesthetic intelligence is more highly prized in cultures that depend on hunting for survival.

Psychologist Robert Sternberg (2000) is also critical of heavy reliance on Spearman's *g* factor for measuring intelligence. But Sternberg is not merely a critic; he has developed his own theory of intelligence. Sternberg (1985a, 1986a) has formulated a **triarchic theory of intelligence** which proposes that there are three types of intelligence (see **Figure 7.4**). The first type, *componential intelligence*, refers to the mental abilities most closely related to success on conventional IQ and achievement tests. He claims that traditional IQ tests measure only componential, or analytical, intelligence.

The second type, *experiential intelligence*, is reflected in creative thinking and problem solving. People with high experiential intelligence are able to solve novel problems and deal with unusual and unexpected challenges. Another aspect of experiential intelligence is finding creative ways to perform common daily tasks more efficiently and effectively.

The third type, *contextual intelligence*, or practical intelligence, might be equated with common sense or "street smarts." People with high contextual intelligence are survivors, who capitalize on their strengths and compensate for their weaknesses. They either adapt well to their environment, change the environment so that they can succeed, or, if necessary, find a new environment.

Sternberg and others (1995) argue that IQ-test performance and real-world success are based on two different types of knowledge: *formal academic knowledge*, or the knowledge we acquire in school, and *tacit knowledge*. Unlike formal academic knowledge, tacit knowledge is action-oriented and is acquired without direct help from others. According to Sternberg, tacit knowledge is more important to successful real-world performance. Research supports Sternberg's contention that the two forms of knowledge are different (Taub et al., 2001; Grigorenko et al., 2004). However, investigators have found that measures of formal academic knowledge, such as traditional IQ tests, better predict real-world success than do Sternberg's tests of practical intelli-

triarchic theory of intelligence
Sternberg's theory that there are three types of intelligence: componential (analytical), experiential (creative), and contextual (practical).

Figure 7.4 Sternberg's Triarchic Theory of Intelligence

According to Sternberg, there are three types of intelligence: componential, experiential, and contextual.

Componential Intelligence
Mental abilities most closely related to success on traditional IQ and achievement tests

Experiential Intelligence
Creative thinking and problem solving

Contextual Intelligence
Practical intelligence or "street smarts"

gence. Sternberg and those who agree with him contend that imperfections in the tests themselves are responsible for such results. Thus, in recent years, Sternberg and his colleagues have focused on developing a reliable and valid intelligence test that measures each of the three hypothesized types of intelligence (Sternberg et al., 2001; Sternberg, 2003a, 2003b).

Sternberg's ideas have become popular among educators. Several studies have shown that teaching methods designed to tap into all three types of intelligence can be effective with students who are low achievers (Grigorenko et al., 2002). In such instruction, teachers emphasize the practical relevance of formal academic knowledge and help students apply it to real-world problems.

The following *Review and Reflect* summarizes the various theories of intelligence.

▲ These soccer players would probably get high scores on a measure of the ability Gardner calls *bodily-kinesthetic intelligence.*

Review and Reflect   Theories of Intelligence

Theory	Description
Spearman's *g* factor	Intelligence consists of a single factor known as *g*, which represents a general intellectual ability.
Thurstone's primary mental abilities	Intelligence has seven separate components: verbal comprehension, numerical ability, spatial relations, perceptual speed, word fluency, memory, and reasoning.
Gardner's frames of mind	There are eight independent forms of intelligence: linguistic, logical-mathematical, spatial, bodily-kinesthetic, musical, interpersonal, intrapersonal, and naturalistic.
Sternberg's triarchic theory	There are three types of intelligence: componential, experiential, and contextual.

Measuring Intelligence

The first successful effort to measure intelligence resulted not from a theoretical approach, but as a practical means of solving a problem.

The Binet–Simon Intelligence Scale. In 1903, the French government formed a special commission to look for a way of assessing the intellectual potential of individual school children. One of the commission members, Alfred Binet (1857–1911), with the help of his colleague, psychiatrist Theodore Simon, developed a variety of tests that eventually became the first intelligence test, the *Binet–Simon Intelligence Scale*, first published in 1905.

The Binet–Simon Scale used a type of score called *mental age*. A child's mental age was based on the number of items she or he got right as compared with the average number right for children of various ages. In other words, if a child's score equaled the average for 8-year-olds, the child was assigned a mental age of 8, regardless of her or his chronological age (age in years). To determine whether children were bright, average, or retarded, Binet compared the children's mental and chronological ages. A child who was mentally 2 years ahead of his or her chronological age was considered bright; one who was 2 years behind was considered retarded. But there was a flaw in Binet's scoring system. A 4-year-old with a mental age of 2 is far more retarded than a 12-year-old with a mental age of 10. How could a similar degree of retardation at different ages be expressed?

7.12 What did Binet, Terman, and Wechsler contribute to the study of intelligence?

▲ Working with psychiatrist Theodore Simon to develop a test for evaluating children's intelligence, Alfred Binet (shown here) began testing Parisian students in 1904.

The Stanford–Binet Intelligence Scale. German psychologist William Stern (1914) provided an answer. In 1912, he devised a simple formula for calculating an index of intelligence—*the intelligence quotient*. But it was American psychologist Lewis M. Terman, a professor at Stanford University, who perfected this new way of scoring intelligence tests. In 1916, Terman published a thorough revision of the Binet–Simon scale, consisting of items adapted for use with American children. Terman also established new **norms,** or age-based averages, based on the scores of large numbers of children. Within 3 years, 4 million American children had taken Terman's revision, known as the *Stanford–Binet Intelligence Scale*. It was the first test to make use of Stern's concept of the **intelligence quotient (IQ).** (Terman also introduced the abbreviation *IQ*.) Terman's formula for calculating an IQ score was

$$\frac{\text{Mental age}}{\text{Chronological age}} \times 100 = \text{IQ}$$

For example,

$$\frac{14}{10} \times 100 = 140 \text{ (superior IQ)}$$

The highly regarded Stanford–Binet is an individually administered IQ test for those aged 2 to 23. It contains four subscales: verbal reasoning, quantitative reasoning, abstract visual reasoning, and short-term memory. An overall IQ score is derived from scores on the four subscales, and the test scores correlate well with achievement test scores (Laurent et al., 1992). Intelligence testing became increasingly popular in the United States in the 1920s and 1930s, but it quickly became obvious that the Stanford–Binet was not useful for testing adults. The original IQ formula could not be applied to adults, because at a certain age people achieve maturity in intelligence. According to the original IQ formula, a 40-year-old with the same IQ test score as the average 20-year-old would be considered mentally retarded, with an IQ of only 50. Obviously, something was wrong with the formula when applied to populations of all ages.

To address this problem, psychologist David Wechsler developed the first individual intelligence test for individuals over the age of 16 (Wechsler, 1939). Rather than being based on mental and chronological ages, scores on the *Wechsler Adult Intelligence Scale (WAIS)* were based on how much an individual deviated from the average score for adults. Wechsler's new IQ score was so well received that he subsequently published similarly scored tests for children (*Wechsler Intelligence Scale for Children, WISC*) and preschoolers (*Wechsler Preschool and Primary Scale of Intelligence, WPPSI*).

Modern Intelligence Tests. Both Terman's and Wechsler's tests continue to be among the most frequently used of all psychological tests. Psychologists have revised each of them several times. The Stanford–Binet is now known as the SB-V, meaning the fifth revision of the original scale. The current editions of Wechsler's scales are the WAIS-III, WISC-IV, and the WPPSI-III. These scales have changed somewhat since their introduction and now yield several types of scores, a feature of modern intelligence tests that is perhaps best exemplified by the WISC-IV.

When psychologists who work in schools need to find out why a particular child is exhibiting learning problems, they most often turn to the WISC-IV for guidance in determining the child's intellectual strengths and weaknesses. The scale consists of 15 separate subtests. Five of these tests, those that make up the *verbal comprehension index*, measure verbal skills such as vocabulary. The remaining 10 tests demand nonverbal types of thinking, such as arranging pictures to tell a story and repeating digits back to an examiner. The nonverbal tests are divided among the *perceptual reasoning index, processing speed index,* and *working memory index*. Each of these indexes measures a different kind of nonverbal intelligence and generates its own IQ score. The WISC-IV also provides a comprehensive *full scale IQ* score that takes all four types of tests into account. Many psychologists find comparisons of the different

norms Standards based on the range of test scores of a large group of people who are selected to provide the bases of comparison for those who take the test later.

intelligence quotient (IQ) An index of intelligence, originally derived by dividing mental age by chronological age and then multiplying by 100, but now derived by comparing an individual's score with the scores of others of the same age.

Table 7.1 Typical Subtests on the Wechsler Intelligence Scale for Children (WISC-III)

Verbal Subtest	Sample Item	Performance Subtest	Sample Item
Information	How many wings does a bird have?	Picture arrangement	Arrange a series of cartoon panels to make a meaningful story.
Digit span	Repeat from memory a series of digits, such as 3 1 0 6 7 4 2 5, after hearing it once.	Picture completion	What is missing from these pictures?
General comprehension	What is the advantage of keeping money in a bank?	Block design	Copy designs using blocks
Arithmetic	If 2 apples cost 15¢, what will be the cost of a dozen apples?		
Similarities	In what way are a lion and a tiger alike?		
Vocabulary	This test consists simply of asking, "What is a _____?" or "What does _____ mean?" The words cover a wide range of difficulty or familiarity.	Object assembly	Put together a jigsaw puzzle.
		Digit symbol	Fill in the missing symbols:

kinds of IQ scores generated by the WISC-IV to be helpful in gaining insight into a child's learning difficulties.

Individual intelligence tests such as the Stanford–Binet and the Wechsler scales must be given to one person at a time by a psychologist or educational diagnostician. For testing large numbers of people in a short period of time (often necessary due to budget limitations), group intelligence tests are the answer. Group intelligence tests such as the *California Test of Mental Maturity*, the *Cognitive Abilities Test*, and the *Otis–Lennon Mental Ability Test* are widely used.

Requirements of Good Tests

Both individual and group tests of intelligence are judged according to the same criteria. First, they must provide consistent results. What if your watch gains 6 minutes one day and loses 3 or 4 minutes the next day? It would not be reliable. You want a watch you can rely on to give the correct time day after day. Like a watch, an intelligence test must have **reliability;** the test must consistently yield nearly the same score when the same person is tested and then retested on the same test or an alternative form of the test. The higher the correlation between the two scores, the more reliable the test.

Tests can be highly reliable but worthless if they are not valid. **Validity** is the ability or power of a test to measure what it is intended to measure. For example, a thermometer is a valid instrument for measuring temperature; a bathroom scale is valid for measuring weight. But no matter how reliable your bathroom scale is, it will not take your temperature. It is valid only for weighing.

Aptitude tests are designed to predict a person's probable achievement or performance at some future time. Selecting students for admission to college or graduate schools is based partly on the predictive validity of aptitude tests such as the SAT, the American College Testing Program (ACT), and the Graduate Record Examination (GRE). How well do SAT scores predict success in college? The correlation between SAT scores and the grades of first year college students is about .40 (Cullen, Hardison & Sackett, 2004; Linn, 1982).

Once a test is proven to be valid and reliable, the next requirement is **standardization.** There must be standard procedures for administering and scoring the test. Exactly the same directions must be given, whether written or oral, and the

7.13 Why are reliability, validity, standardization, and cultural bias important in intelligence testing?

reliability The ability of a test to yield nearly the same score when the same people are tested and then retested on the same test or an alternative form of the test.

validity The ability of a test to measure what it is intended to measure.

aptitude test A test designed to predict a person's achievement or performance at some future time.

standardization Establishing norms for comparing the scores of people who will take a test in the future; administering tests using a prescribed procedure.

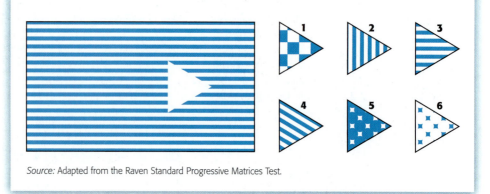

Figure 7.5 An Example of an Item on a Culture-Fair Test

This culture-fair test item does not penalize test takers whose language or cultural experiences differ from those of the urban middle or upper classes. Test takers select, from the six samples on the right, the patch that completes the pattern. Patch number 3 is the correct answer.

Source: Adapted from the Raven Standard Progressive Matrices Test.

same amount of time must be allowed for every test taker. But even more important, standardization means establishing norms by which all scores are interpreted. A test is standardized by administering it to a large sample of people who are representative of those who will be taking the test in the future. The group's scores are analyzed, and then the average score, standard deviation, percentile rankings, and other measures are computed. These comparative scores become the norms used as the standard against which all other scores on that test are measured.

One criticism that continues to plague advocates of IQ testing is the suggestion that minority children and those for whom English is a second language are at a disadvantage when they are assessed on conventional tests because their cultural backgrounds differ from that assumed by the tests' authors. In response, attempts have been made to develop **culture-fair intelligence tests** designed to minimize cultural bias. The questions do not penalize individuals whose cultural experience or language differs from that of the mainstream or dominant culture. See **Figure 7.5** for an example of the type of test item found on a culture-fair test. Research shows that such tests are moderately correlated with other measures of intellectual ability such as the SAT (Frey & Detterman, 2004). Likewise, high-IQ minority children are more likely to be identified as gifted when culture-fair tests are used than when school officials use conventional IQ tests to screen students for inclusion in programs for the gifted (Shaunessy et al., 2004).

The Bell Curve

7.14 What does the term "bell curve" mean when applied to IQ test scores?

You may have heard of a bell curve and wondered just exactly what it is. When large populations are measured on intelligence or on physical characteristics, such as height or blood pressure, a graph of the frequencies of all the test scores or results usually conforms to a bell-shaped distribution known as the *normal curve*, or sometimes as the *bell curve*. The majority of the scores cluster around the mean (average). The more the scores deviate, or the farther away they are, from the mean—either above or below— the fewer there are. And the curve is perfectly symmetrical, that is, there are just as many scores above as below the mean.

The average IQ test score for all people in the same age group is arbitrarily assigned an IQ score of 100. On the Wechsler intelligence tests, approximately 50% of the scores are in the average range, between 90 and 110. About 68% of the scores fall between 85 and 115, and about 95% fall between 70 and 130. About 2% of the scores are above 130, which is considered superior, and about 2% fall below 70, in the range of mental retardation (see **Figure 7.6**).

culture-fair intelligence test An intelligence test that uses questions that will not penalize those whose culture differs from the mainstream or dominant culture.

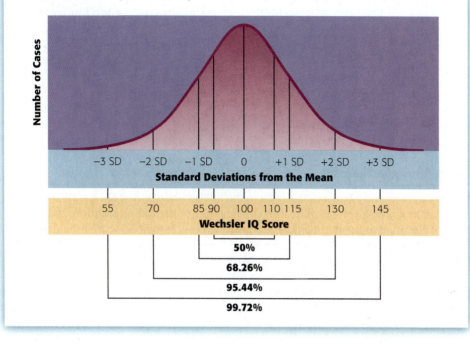

Figure 7.6 The Normal Curve

When a large number of IQ test scores are compiled and graphed, they are typically distributed in a normal (bell-shaped) curve. On the Wechsler scales, the average or mean IQ score is set at 100. About 68% of the scores fall between 15 IQ points (1 standard deviation) above and below 100 (from 85 to 115), and about 95.5% of the scores fall between 30 points (2 standard deviations) above and below 100 (from 70 to 130).

Giftedness

What is the meaning of variations in IQ scores? One way of examining this question is to study individuals whose scores lie at one extreme or the other of the bell curve.

Terman's Study of "Genius." In 1921, Lewis Terman (1925) launched a longitudinal study, now a classic, in which 1,528 students with "genius" IQs were measured at different ages throughout their lives. The participants, 857 males and 671 females, had an average IQ of 151, with Stanford–Binet scores ranging from 135 to 200. Terman assumed that the Stanford–Binet measured innate intelligence and that IQ was fixed at birth (Cravens, 1992).

Terman's early findings put an end to the myth that mentally superior people are more likely to be physically inferior. In fact, Terman's gifted participants excelled in almost all of the abilities he studied—intellectual, physical, emotional, moral, and social. Terman also exploded many other myths about the mentally gifted (Terman & Oden, 1947). For example, you may have heard the saying that there is a thin line between genius and madness. Actually, Terman's gifted group enjoyed better mental health than the general population. Also, you may have heard that mentally gifted people are long on "book sense" but short on "common sense." In reality, Terman's participants earned more academic degrees, achieved higher occupational status and higher salaries, were better adjusted both personally and socially, and were healthier than their less mentally gifted peers. However, most women at that time did not pursue careers outside of the home, so the findings related to occupational success applied primarily to the men. Terman (1925) concluded that "there is no law of compensation whereby the intellectual superiority of the gifted is offset by inferiorities along nonintellectual lines" (p. 16).

7.15 How do the gifted differ from the general population?

The Terman study continues today, with the surviving participants in their 80s or 90s. In a report on Terman's study, Shneidman (1989) states its basic findings—that "an unusual mind, a vigorous body, and a relatively well-adjusted personality are not at all incompatible" (p. 687).

Who Are the Gifted? Beginning in the early 1920s, the term *gifted* was used to describe the intellectually superior, those with IQs in the upper 2–3% of the U.S. population. Today, the term also includes both the exceptionally creative and those who excel in the visual or performing arts.

Traditionally, special programs for the gifted have involved either acceleration or enrichment. *Acceleration* enables students to progress at a rate that is consistent with their ability. Students may skip a grade, progress through subject matter at a faster rate, be granted advanced placement in college courses, or enter college early. *Enrichment* aims to broaden students' knowledge by giving them special courses in foreign language, music appreciation, and the like or by providing special experiences designed to foster advanced thinking skills.

Mental Retardation

7.16 What two criteria must a person meet to be classified as having mental retardation?

At the opposite end of the bell curve from the intellectually gifted are the 2% of the U.S. population whose IQ scores place them in the range of **mental retardation.** Individuals are not classified as having mental retardation unless (1) their IQ score is below 70 and (2) they have a severe deficiency in everyday adaptive functioning—the ability to care for themselves and relate to others (Grossman, 1983). Degrees of retardation range from mild to profound. Individuals with IQs ranging from 55 to 70 have mild retardation; from 40 to 55, moderate retardation; from 25 to 40, severe retardation; and below 25, profound retardation. Table 7.2 shows the level of functioning expected for various categories of mental retardation.

Among the many causes of mental retardation are brain injuries, chromosomal abnormalities such as Down syndrome, chemical deficiencies, and hazards present during fetal development. And studies continue to document the enduring mental deficits produced by early exposure to lead (Garavan et al., 2000; Morgan et al., 2000).

Before the late 1960s, children with mental retardation in the United States were educated almost exclusively in special schools. Since then, there has been a move-

mental retardation Subnormal intelligence reflected by an IQ below 70 and by adaptive functioning that is severely deficient for one's age.

Table 7.2 Mental Retardation as Measured on the Wechsler Scales

Classification	IQ Range	Percentage of Individuals with Mental Retardation	Characteristics of Retarded Persons at Each Level
Mild	55–70	90%	Are able to grasp learning skills up to 6th-grade level. May become self-supporting and can be profitably employed in various vocational occupations.
Moderate	40–55	6%	Probably are not able to grasp more than 2nd-grade academic skills but can learn self-help skills and some social and academic skills. May work in sheltered workshops.
Severe	25–40	3%	Can be trained in basic health habits; can learn to communicate verbally. Learn through repetitive habit training.
Profound	Below 25	1%	Have rudimentary motor development. May learn very limited self-help skills.

ment toward **inclusion**—educating students with mental retardation in regular schools. Inclusion, or *mainstreaming*, may involve placing these students in general classes for part of the day or in special classrooms in regular schools.

Resources spent on training programs for individuals with mental retardation are proving to be sound investments. Such programs, which rely heavily on behavior modification techniques, are making it possible for some citizens with mental retardation to become employed workers who earn the minimum wage or better. Everyone benefits—the individual, the family, the community, and society as a whole.

◄ Individuals with mental retardation can learn to do many kinds of jobs that are both beneficial to society and personally rewarding to themselves.

Remember It   Intelligence

1. Match each theory of intelligence to its author
   - (1) primary mental abilities
   - (2) frames of mind
   - (3) *g* factor
   - (4) triarchic theory of intelligence
   - a. Sternberg
   - b. Thurstone
   - c. Spearman
   - d. Gardner

2. On modern intelligence tests, IQ scores are based on _____.

3. A test that gives consistent results has _____, whereas one that measures what it claims to measure has _____.

4. Fifty percent of individuals score between _____ and _____ on intelligence tests.

5. The research of _____ challenged the view that individuals with high IQs are physically inferior to others.

6. People are considered to have mental retardation if they are clearly deficient in adaptive functioning and their IQ is below _____.

Answers: 1. (1) b, (2) d, (3) c, (4) a; 2. how much an individual deviates from the average score of others who are the same age; 3. reliability, validity; 4. 90, 110; 5. Terman; 6. 70

Explaining Differences in Cognitive Abilities

We use several words to refer to people we believe to be intellectually superior—*bright*, *clever*, *intelligent*, *smart*, and so on. Likewise, we have just as many words to describe our peers who seem to possess less intelligence than others. In fact, the presence of these terms in our vocabularies demonstrates that a wide range of differences in intellectual functioning are readily apparent in our everyday interactions with other people. What accounts for these differences?

The Heritability of Intelligence

Do you think of intelligence as an inherited or a learned characteristic? Even though it has been debated for about 140 years, the **nature-nurture debate** is still very much alive. British researcher Sir Francis Galton (1822–1911) coined this term when he initiated the debate over whether intelligence is predominantly the result of heredity (nature) or the environment (nurture) (Galton, 1874). After studying many prominent English families, Galton concluded that intelligence is inherited—that nature, not nurture, is responsible for intelligence. Environmentalists disputed Galton's claim and just as strongly insisted that intelligence is the product of one's environment—the

inclusion   Educating students with mental retardation in regular schools by placing them in classes with general students for part of the day or in special classrooms in regular schools; also known as *mainstreaming*.

nature-nurture debate   The debate over whether intelligence (or another trait) is primarily the result of heredity (nature) or the environment (nurture).

7.17 What is the nature-nurture debate regarding intelligence, and why are twin studies important to it?

▲ The IQ scores of adopted children have been found to correlate more strongly with those of their biological parents than with those of their adoptive parents. However, the correlation is far from perfect, leaving ample opportunity for adoptive parents to influence the cognitive functioning of their children.

result of nurture. Today, most psychologists agree that both nature and nurture contribute to intelligence, but they continue to debate the relative contributions of these two factors (Petrill, 2003).

You should remember from Chapter 2 that behavioral genetics is the field of study in which scientists attempt to determine the relative contributions of nature and nurture to variables such as intelligence. Many of the most important studies in the field involve twins. Twins, whether identical or fraternal, who are raised together have similar environments. If identical twins raised together are found to be more alike on a certain trait than are fraternal twins raised together, then that trait is assumed to be more influenced by heredity. But if identical and fraternal twins from similar environments do not differ on a trait, then that trait is assumed to be influenced more by environment. The **heritability** of a trait is a measure of the degree to which a characteristic is estimated to be influenced by heredity.

Minnesota—home of the twin cities and the Minnesota Twins—is also, fittingly, the site of the most extensive U.S. study of identical and fraternal twins. The Minnesota Center for Twin and Adoption Research has assembled the Minnesota Twin Registry, which in 1998 included more than 10,000 twin pairs (Bouchard, 1998). Since 1979, Minnesota researchers, headed by Thomas Bouchard, have studied about 60 pairs of fraternal twins and 80 pairs of identical twins who were reared apart. Of all the traits Bouchard and his colleagues studied, the most heritable trait turned out to be intelligence. Bouchard (1997) reported that various types of twin studies have consistently yielded heritabilities of .60 to .70 for intelligence. (A heritability of 1.00 would mean that all of the variation in intelligence is due to genes.)

Not all researchers agree with Bouchard's estimate of the heritability of intelligence. Combining data from a number of twin studies, Plomin and others (1994) found the heritability estimate for general intelligence to be .52. Similar findings emerged from meta-analyses using dozens of adoption studies and twin studies involving more than 10,000 pairs of twins. These analyses concluded that the heritability of general cognitive ability was about .50 (McClearn et al., 1997). Psychologists who consider environmental factors as the chief contributors to differences in intelligence also take issue with Bouchard's findings. They claim that most separated identical twins are raised by adoptive parents who have been matched as closely as possible to the biological parents. This fact, the critics say, could account for the similarity in the identical twins' IQ scores. In response to his critics, Bouchard (1997) points out that children who are not related biologically but are raised in the same home are no more similar in intelligence once they reach adulthood than are complete strangers.

Researchers also use the **adoption study method,** an approach that involves studying children who were adopted very early in life. Adoption studies reveal that children adopted shortly after birth have IQs more closely resembling those of their biological parents than those of their adoptive parents. The family environment has an influence on IQ early in life, but that influence seems to diminish with age. Twin and adoption studies indicate that, as people reach adulthood, genetic factors are most closely correlated with IQ (Loehlin et al., 1988, McCartney, et al., 1990; Plomin & Rende, 1991). In fact, the influence of genes seems to increase predictably as people age, with a heritability of .30 in infancy, .40 in childhood, .50 in adolescence, and about .60 in adulthood (McGue et al., 1993). A large study in Sweden of pairs of identical twins and same-sex fraternal twins who had been reared together and had reached the age of 80 or more revealed a heritability estimate of .62 for general cognitive ability (McClearn et al., 1997).

Bouchard and others (1990) claim that "although parents may be able to affect their children's rate of cognitive skill acquisition, they may have relatively little influence on the ultimate level attained" (p. 225). A great deal of convincing research does argue for the importance of genes in determining intelligence, including language skills (Craig & Plomin, 2006; Plomin & Dale, 2000). But a great deal of room is still left for environmental forces to have a significant influence. Thus, the nature-nurture debate remains unresolved.

heritability   A measure of the degree to which a characteristic is estimated to be influenced by heredity.

adoption study method   A method researchers use to assess the relative effects of heredity and environment by studying children who were adopted very early in life.

Intelligence: Fixed or Changeable?

Clearly, the high degree of similarity in the intelligence scores of identical twins who have been reared apart makes a strong case for the powerful influence of genetics. But it's important to keep in mind that none of us inherits a specific IQ score. Instead, our genes probably set the boundaries of a fairly wide range of possible performance levels, called the *reaction range*. Our environments determine where we end up within that range.

7.18 What kinds of evidence suggest that IQ is changeable?

Adoption Studies. In general, the IQ scores of adopted children tend to resemble those of their biological parents more than those of their adopted parents. However, almost three decades ago, Sandra Scarr and Richard Weinberg (1976) found a different pattern among adopted children whose biological and adoptive parents differed both in race and in socioeconomic status. Their study involved 130 Black and biracial children who had been adopted by highly educated, upper-middle-class White families; 99 of the children had been adopted in the first year of life. The adoptees were fully exposed to middle-class cultural experiences and vocabulary, the "culture of the tests and the school" (p. 737).

How did the children perform on IQ and achievement tests? The average IQ score of the 130 adoptees was 106.3. And their achievement test scores were slightly above the national average, not below. On average, the earlier the children were adopted, the higher their IQs were. The mean IQ score of the 99 early adoptees was 110.4, about 10 IQ points above the average for Whites. Studies in France have also shown that IQ scores and achievement are substantially higher when children from lower-class environments are adopted by middle-class and upper-middle-class families (Duyme, 1988; Schiff and Lewontin, 1986).

Early Childhood Interventions. In addition to these adoption studies, research examining the effects of preschool programs involving infants and young children from poor families clearly indicates that early educational experiences can affect intellectual functioning (Brooks-Gunn, 2003; Schellenberg, 2004). Some of the best known of these interventions have been carried out by developmental psychologist Craig Ramey (Burchinal et al., 1997; Campbell & Ramey, 1994; Ramey, 1993; Ramey & Campbell, 1987; Ramey & Ramey, 2004). And unlike many studies of early interventions, Ramey's research focuses on true experiments—so we know that the outcomes are caused by the interventions.

In one of Ramey's programs, 6- to 12-month-old infants of low-IQ, low-income mothers were randomly assigned either to an intensive, 40-hour-per-week day-care program that continued throughout the preschool years or to a control group that received only medical care and nutritional supplements. When the children reached school age, half

▲ Developmental psychologist Craig Ramey has used the experimental method to show that early childhood education can raise the IQs of disadvantaged children.

in each group (again based on random assignment) were enrolled in a special after-school program that helped their families learn how to support school learning with educational activities at home. Ramey followed the progress of children in all four groups through age 12, giving them IQ tests at various ages.

Figure 7.7 shows that children who participated in Ramey's infant and preschool program scored higher on IQ tests than their peers who received either no intervention or only the school-age intervention. Perhaps more important, during the elementary school years, about 40% of the control group participants had IQ scores classified

Figure 7.7 Ramey's Infant Intervention Program

The positive effects of Ramey's intervention program for young children were still evident when participants reached age 12.

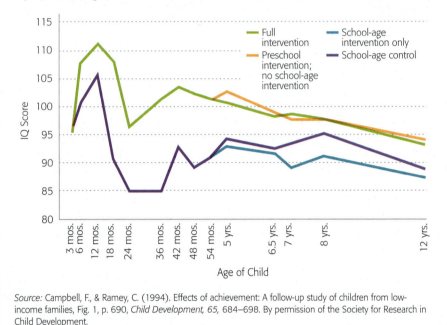

Source: Campbell, F., & Ramey, C. (1994). Effects of achievement: A follow-up study of children from low-income families, Fig. 1, p. 690, *Child Development, 65,* 684–698. By permission of the Society for Research in Child Development.

as borderline or retarded (scores below 85), compared to only 12.8% of those who were in the infant program. Further, recent research shows that the cognitive advantage enjoyed by the infant intervention group has persisted into adulthood (Campbell et al., 2001, 2002). Clearly, Ramey's work shows that the environment has great potential to influence IQ scores.

Changes in Standard of Living. The IQ scores of Americans and of citizens of other developed nations have gained about 3 points per decade since 1940, a finding most often attributed to widespread changes in the standard of living. James Flynn (1987, 1999; Dickens & Flynn, 2001) analyzed 73 studies involving some 7,500 participants ranging in age from 12 to 48 and found that "every Binet and Wechsler sample from 1932 to 1978 has performed better than its predecessor" (p. 225). Studies in developing countries, such as Kenya, have shown that IQ gains can happen over much shorter periods of time when the standard of living improves drastically (Daley et al., 2003). The consistent improvement in IQ scores over time that accompanies an increase in the standard of living is known as the *Flynn effect*.

Some researchers suggest that the Flynn effect is caused by those parts of IQ tests that measure learning rather than the *g* factor (Flynn, 2003; Kane & Oakland, 2000). In other words, from their perspective, people today possess more knowledge but do not necessarily possess a greater quantity of intelligence, as Spearman defined it. In support of their view, these psychologists point out that average scores on the Wechsler subtests of arithmetic, vocabulary, and general information have not changed over time. These subtests, they argue, are more strongly correlated with *g* than are the subtests that show changes in average scores. Recent studies in Europe, too, have suggested that IQ scores may actually be declining since Flynn first began studying historical trends in the early 1980s. Researchers have found that these score trends are correlated with declining enrollments in secondary schools (Teasdale & Owen, 2005). These findings bolster the argument that the Flynn effect is the result of learning rather than actual increases in intelligence. In response to these criticisms, Flynn claims that the similarities subtest on the Wechsler scales, the one on which scores have changed the most, reflects the kind of thinking and problem solving needed in modern society. Therefore, he claims, the gains are still real and socially significant, regardless of whether they represent gains in g (Flynn, 2003).

Some observers suggest that physiological variables underlie the association between improved standards of living and IQ score gains. They claim that improved nutrition and prenatal care are responsible for gains in neurological functioning that have resulted in increased IQ scores (Flynn, 2003). However, Flynn argues that such changes should affect those at the bottom of the IQ scale more than those at the top. He points out that there has been just as much change among high scorers as among those whose scores are below average. Consequently, Flynn argues that more general cultural changes, such as the increased popularity of cognitively demanding leisure activities, have produced these gains.

Another general cultural change, noted by Zajonc and Mullally (1997), is decreased family size. According to their research, first- and second-born children tend to do better on intelligence and achievement tests than do children born later in larger families. The decrease in average family size has increased the proportions of first-borns and second-borns in the population as a whole.

Like Flynn, some psychologists believe that changes in standards of living may also be narrowing the Black-White IQ gap. Researcher Ken Vincent (1991) presents data suggesting that the gap is smaller (about 7 or 8 IQ points) among younger children than among older children and adults. Vincent (1993) attributes the rapid mean gains by African American children to environmental changes in economic and educational opportunity. These conclusions are supported by studies in which low-income families are given vouchers to pay for housing in more affluent neighborhoods (Leventhal & Brooks-Gunn, 2003). Although these studies do not deal directly with IQ, they have demonstrated that children whose families move from low- to moderate-income neighborhoods demonstrate significant gains in academic functioning within a very short period of time.

Race and IQ

The nature–nurture debate has also been important in the discussion of race differences in intelligence test scores. Historically, most studies have shown that Blacks score, on average, about 15 points lower than Whites on standardized IQ tests in the United States (e.g., Loehlin et al., 1975; Rushton & Jensen, 2005). Other studies have shown similar differences for Blacks and Whites in other nations (e.g., Rushton & Jensen, 2003). But why? Two publications addressing this question stimulated heated debate about the link between race and intelligence in the scientific community and the general public.

In 1969, psychologist Arthur Jensen published an article in which he attributed the IQ gap to genetic differences between the races. Further, he claimed that the genetic influence on intelligence is so strong that the environment cannot make a significant difference. Jensen even went so far as to claim that Blacks and Whites possess qualitatively different kinds of intelligence.

The late psychologist Richard Herrnstein (1930–1994) and political scientist Charles Murray added fresh fuel to the controversy in the mid-1990s with their book *The Bell Curve* (Herrnstein & Murray, 1994). They argued that IQ differences among individuals and between groups explain how those at the top of the ladder in U.S. society got there and why those on the lower rungs remain there. Herrnstein and Murray largely attributed the social ills of modern society—including poverty, welfare dependency, crime, and illegitimacy—to low IQ, which they implied is primarily genetic and largely immune to change by environmental intervention. Yet, their own estimate was that 60% of IQ is genetically inherited, "which, by extension, means that IQ is about 40% a matter of environment" (p. 105). That 40% would seem to leave a lot of room for improvement.

Beliefs such as those expressed by Jensen and Herrnstein and Murray run counter to the results of the studies carried out by Craig Ramey and others that you read about in the preceding section. Such studies suggest that racial differences are more likely to result from poverty and lack of access to educational opportunities than from genetics.

7.19 What arguments have been advanced to explain racial differences in IQ scores?

Moreover, a new testing technique called *dynamic assessment* supports the environmental explanation. In dynamic assessment, examinees are taught the goal and format of each IQ subtest before they are actually tested. The rationale behind the technique is the assumption that children from middle-class backgrounds have more experience with testing procedures and better understand that the goal of testing is to demonstrate competency. Studies of dynamic assessment show that it significantly increases the number of minority children who achieve above-average IQ scores (Lidz & Macrine, 2001).

In recent years, psychologists have begun to investigate another variable called *stereotype threat* that may help explain racial differences in IQ scores. The stereotype threat theory was first proposed by psychologist Claude Steele (Steele & Aronson, 1995). According to Steele, when minority individuals hear discussions of group differences in IQ scores, they may assume that their own intellectual ability is inferior to that of individuals in the majority group. Therefore, when faced with an IQ test, they "disengage," to avoid the threat of being stereotyped as having limited intellectual ability. This disengagement becomes a self-fulfilling prophecy: It causes individuals to obtain low scores, thereby appearing to validate the stereotype. Research has shown that programs designed to help people talk about and overcome the degree to which they sense stereotype threat when they take cognitive ability tests helps them achieve higher scores (Good et al., 2003). Other psychologists have pointed out that although studies have shown that stereotype threat does exist, it explains only a fraction of the total average score differences among racial groups (Sackett et al., 2004).

Before leaving the topic of race and IQ, stop and consider why the debates spawned by findings showing that one group has a higher average IQ than another group have stirred so much emotional intensity. One reason might be that in Western societies such as the United States intellectual ability is highly valued.

Culture, IQ, and Achievement

7.20 How do cultures vary in their views about the importance of intelligence, and how do those differences influence achievement?

When it comes to group differences in IQ scores, those that exist across racial groups in the United States are quite small by comparison to global variations. Psychologist Richard Lynn (2006) has studied cross-national differences in intelligence for more than 30 years. By combining the results of hundreds of studies, Lynn has estimated IQs to be highest in the industrialized economies of Hong Kong, Japan, and Korea, followed closely by European nations, Canada, and the United States. Lynn claims that the average IQ of Asian groups is around 105, and European and North American groups have average IQs of about 100. Note that only a few points separate the average IQs of these groups. By contrast, Lynn estimates average IQs to be 30 to 40 points lower among people in some cultural groups whose economies are based on hunting and agriculture.

Given the wide variations in standards of living around the world, Lynn's findings may not surprise you. And you would probably not be surprised by studies showing that school children in the industrialized world fare better on achievement tests than their peers in nonindustrialized nations. However, cross-national studies of mathematics and science achievement show that students in Asian nations outscore their counterparts in Europe and North America despite the similarities in general intellectual ability that exist across these groups (NCES, 2003). Some researchers suspect that cultural beliefs about ability and effort are at least partially responsible for these differences (Li, 2003).

Cultural Beliefs. In a classic study of cultural beliefs about the importance of intelligence, the late educational psychologist Harold Stevenson (1925–2005) and his colleagues (1986) interviewed the parents of their study participants. The Chinese and Japanese mothers considered academic achievement to be the most important pursuit of their children, whereas American parents did not value it as a central concern. The Asian, but not the American, families structured their home activities to promote academic achievement as soon as their first child started elementary school.

Significantly, too, the Asian parents downplayed the importance of innate ability but emphasized the value of hard work and persistence (Stevenson, 1992). American parents, in contrast, believed more firmly in genetic limitations on ability and achievement. More recent research indicates that as preschoolers, children in the United States display beliefs about the effort-achievement connection that are similar to those of Asian children (Heyman et al., 2003). However, apparently as a result of both adult and peer influence, by the time they reach the age of 11 years, American children have acquired the belief that achievement results more from ability than effort (Altermatt & Pomerantz, 2003; Heyman et al., 2003). As Stevenson states, "when [adults] believe success in school depends for the most part on ability rather than effort, they are less likely to foster [children's] participation in activities related to academic achievement" (1992, p. 73). As a result, the ability-achievement belief affects the amount of academic effort put forth by the children and becomes a self-fulfilling prophecy.

▲ Asian students consistently score higher on math achievement tests than do their American counterparts. Cultural beliefs and parenting practices explain some of this difference, but variations in teaching methods across the two cultures are contributing factors.

In follow-up studies, Stevenson and others (1993) found that the achievement gap between Asian and American students persisted over a 10-year period. Some critics of Stevenson's work have argued that cross-national differences in high school achievement are explained in part by the fact that the American students spend more time working at part-time jobs and socializing than their Asian counterparts do (Fuligni & Stevenson, 1995; Larson & Verma, 1999). However, a comparison of German and Japanese students found that German teens, like their American agemates, are less likely to attribute academic success to effort (Randel et al., 2000). Moreover, German students' achievement test scores were found to be lower than those of Japanese teens. These findings support the contention that Western beliefs about ability and learning contribute to cross-national differences in achievement.

Teaching Methods. Obviously, differences in cultural values do not tell us the whole story regarding cross-national differences in math achievement. However, these differences may be the impetus behind other cross-national variations that contribute just as much or more to the math achievement gap as do the values themselves. That is, because Asian cultures value ability less than their American and European counterparts, parents and teachers in those countries may do a better job of teaching math and science skills to children and of inspiring children to work hard to learn them. For instance, in Singapore, an Asian nation with consistently high math achievement scores, parents begin teaching their children about numbers and the relationships among numbers long before the children enter school (Sharpe, 2002). Moreover, Singaporean parents specifically tailor this home teaching, and their selection of formal preschool experiences, to the mathematics curricula of the early grades in public schools. Consequently, by the tender age of 5 or 6, Singaporean youngsters are already ahead of their peers in other nations.

Teaching methods, too, can vary widely from one country to another. In one frequently cited study, Stigler and Stevenson (1991) observed math teachers in Japan, Taiwan, and the United States. They found that the Asian teachers spent more time on each kind of problem and did not move on to another until they were certain that students understood the first. By contrast, the American teachers introduced many kinds of problems within a single class period and did not allow time for students to master any of them. More recent studies have produced similar findings (NCES, 2003).

Another important aspect of math teaching, emphasis on computational fluency, has been found to contribute to math achievement differences both across cultures and across classrooms within the United States (Geary et al., 1999; Kail & Hall, 1999).

Computational fluency is the ability to produce answers to simple calculations automatically. Many critics of teaching practices in the United States claim that math curricula in American elementary schools seldom include criteria that encourage students to develop computational fluency (Murray, 1998). As a result, these critics say, elementary school students in the United States are not adequately prepared to tackle the more advanced mathematical concepts of algebra, geometry, and calculus. Cross-national studies of calculator use support such conclusions. Japanese eighth-grade algebra students are far less likely to use calculators than their American peers (NCES, 2003). It is possible that Japanese students' superior computational fluency frees up working memory space such that they are better able than American students to manage multi-step problems and to see connections among different kinds of math problems.

Remember It — Explaining Differences in Cognitive Abilities

1. IQ tests are good predictors of _____ success.

2. Twin studies suggest that variation in IQ scores is strongly influenced by _____.

3. The studies of Weinberg and Scarr suggest that IQ is _____.

4. The finding that early childhood intervention programs can improve IQ scores is associated with the research of _____.

5. The _____ refers to the historical change in average IQ scores that has accompanied improved standards of living.

6. The work of Stevenson and his colleagues suggests that Western cultures associate intellectual achievement with _____, while Asian cultures attribute academic success to _____.

Answers: 1. academic; 2. heredity; 3. changeable; 4. Ramey; 5. Flynn effect; 6. ability, effort.

Beyond Intelligence

Perhaps the most important contribution of Gardner, Sternberg, and others who have suggested multi-component models of intelligence is their emphasis on the notion that there are many aspects of cognitive functioning that are not captured by standardized tests of intelligence. Such tests cannot measure how well we relate to others, for example. Nor can they assess our ability to use our imaginations to escape the limitations of present reality. Likewise, there are no tests that can predict which individuals with cognitive disabilities will develop remarkable talents like those exhibited by Hikari Oe.

Emotional Intelligence

7.21 What are the components of emotional intelligence?

Whether one is male or female, the understanding we possess about our own and others' emotions influences how we think about ourselves and manage our interactions with others. **Emotional intelligence** is the ability to apply knowledge about emotions to everyday life (Salovey & Pizarro, 2003). Two leading researchers in the field, Peter Salovey and David Pizarro, argue that emotional intelligence is just as important to many important outcome variables, including how we fare in our chosen careers, as the kind of intelligence that is measured by IQ tests. Research supports this view, showing that emotional intelligence is unrelated to IQ scores (Lam & Kirby, 2002; van der Zee et al., 2002). At the same time, emotional intelligence is correlated with both academic and social success (Rozell et al., 2002).

Emotional intelligence includes two sets of components. The first, known as the *personal* aspects of emotional intelligence, includes awareness and management of our own emotions. People who are able to monitor their feelings as they arise are less

emotional intelligence The ability to apply knowledge about emotions to everyday life.

likely to be ruled by them. However, managing emotions does not mean suppressing them; nor does it mean giving free rein to every feeling. Instead, effective management of emotions involves expressing them appropriately. Emotion management also involves engaging in activities that cheer us up, soothe our hurts, or reassure us when we feel anxious.

The *interpersonal* aspects of emotional intelligence make up the second set of components. *Empathy*, or sensitivity to others' feelings, is one such component. One key indicator of empathy is the ability to read others' nonverbal behavior—the gestures, vocal inflections, tones of voice, and facial expressions of others. Another of the interpersonal components is the capacity to manage relationships. However, it is related to both the personal aspects of emotional intelligence and to empathy. In other words, to effectively manage the emotional give-and-take involved in social relationships, we have to be able to manage our own feelings and be sensitive to those of others.

▲ A person with high emotional intelligence shows empathy, recognizing nonverbal signals from others and making appropriate responses.

In a recent study, men were found to process emotions, especially positive ones, predominantly in the left hemisphere of the brain, whereas women were found to use both cerebral hemispheres more equally for processing emotions (Coney & Fitzgerald, 2000). This finding could account for some of the emotional difference between the genders. You can test your own "EQ" in the following *Try It*.

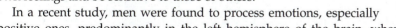

Try It — Find Your EQ

Emotional intelligence may be just as important to success in your chosen career as your actual job skills. Take this short test to assess your EQ by checking one response for each item.

1. I'm always aware of even subtle feelings as I have them.
   ___ Always ___ Usually ___ Sometimes ___ Rarely ___ Never

2. I can delay gratification in pursuit of my goals instead of getting carried away by impulse.
   ___ Always ___ Usually ___ Sometimes ___ Rarely ___ Never

3. Instead of giving up in the face of setbacks or disappointments, I stay hopeful and optimistic.
   ___ Always ___ Usually ___ Sometimes ___ Rarely ___ Never

4. My keen sense of others' feelings makes me compassionate about their plight.
   ___ Always ___ Usually ___ Sometimes ___ Rarely ___ Never

5. I can sense the pulse of a group or relationship and state unspoken feelings.
   ___ Always ___ Usually ___ Sometimes ___ Rarely ___ Never

6. I can soothe or contain distressing feelings, so that they don't keep me from doing things I need to do.
   ___ Always ___ Usually ___ Sometimes ___ Rarely ___ Never

Score your responses as follows: Always = 4 points, Usually = 3 points, Sometimes = 2 points, Rarely = 1 point, Never = 0 points. The closer your total number of points is to 24, the higher your EQ probably is.

Creativity

Have you ever known a person who was intellectually bright, but lacked creativity? **Creativity** can be thought of as the ability to produce original, appropriate, and valuable ideas and/or solutions to problems.

Creativity and IQ. Research indicates that there is only a weak to moderate correlation between creativity and IQ (Lubart, 2003). Remember the mentally gifted individuals studied by Lewis Terman? Not one of them has produced a highly creative work (Terman & Oden, 1959). No Nobel laureates, no Pulitzer prizes. Geniuses, yes; creative geniuses, no. Thus, high intelligence does not necessarily mean high creativity.

Genuine creativity rarely appears in the form of sudden flashes (Haberlandt, 1997). For the most part, creative ideas that come to conscious awareness have been incubating for some time.

7.22 How does creativity differ from other forms of cognition, and how has it been measured?

creativity The ability to produce original, appropriate, and valuable ideas and/or solutions to problems.

There are basically four stages in the creative problem-solving process (Goleman et al., 1992):

1. *Preparation*—searching for information that may help solve the problem
2. *Incubation*—letting the problem "sit" while the relevant information is digested
3. *Illumination*—being suddenly struck by the right solution
4. *Translation*—transforming the insight into useful action

The incubation stage, perhaps the most important part of the process, takes place below the level of awareness.

▲ One characteristic of creative people is intrinsic motivation. They enjoy the process of creation for its own sake—the end result may be a whimsical toy rather than a practical tool.

Creative Thinking. What is unique about creative thought? According to psychologist J. P. Guilford (1967), who studied creativity for several decades, creative thinkers are highly proficient at divergent thinking. **Divergent thinking** is the ability to produce multiple ideas, answers, or solutions to a problem for which there is no agreed-on solution (Guilford, 1967). More broadly, divergent thinking is novel, or original, and involves the synthesis of an unusual association of ideas; it is flexible, switching quickly and smoothly from one stream of thought or set of ideas to another; and it requires fluency, or the ability to formulate an abundance of ideas (Csikszentmihalyi, 1996). In contrast to divergent thinking, Guilford defined *convergent thinking* as the type of mental activity measured by IQ and achievement tests; it consists of solving precisely defined, logical problems for which there is a known correct answer.

However, divergent and convergent thinking are not always separate phenomena. Both are required for most cognitive tasks. For example, to be creative, a person must develop divergent thinking, but convergent thinking is required to discriminate between good and bad ideas (Csikszentmihalyi, 1996). Similarly, solving precisely defined problems can involve divergent thinking, as one tries to think of possible solutions.

Researchers are identifying the different brain areas involved in convergent and divergent thinking. In general, convergent thinking is characterized by greater activity in the left frontal cortex, while divergent thinking is marked by higher levels of activity in the right frontal cortex (Razoumnikova, 2000). Other studies show that processes involved in convergent thinking, such as searching for patterns in events, are carried out in the left hemisphere (Wolford et al., 2000). Studies by Carlsson and others (2000) that measured regional cerebral blood flow (rCBF) revealed striking differences in frontal lobe activity between participants who were engaged in highly creative thinking and those who were not. **Figure 7.8(a)** shows the frontal lobe activity during highly creative thinking. There is activity in both hemispheres but a significantly greater amount in the right frontal cortex. In contrast, **Figure 7.8(b)** shows that during periods when no creative thinking is occurring, the left frontal lobe is highly active, and there is very little activity in the right hemisphere.

Measuring Creativity. How might individual differences in creativity be measured? Tests designed to measure creativity emphasize original approaches to arriving at solutions for open-ended problems or to producing artistic works (Gregory, 1996). One creativity test, the Unusual Uses Test, asks respondents to name as many uses as possible for an ordinary object (such as a brick). Another measure of creativity is the Consequences Test, which asks test takers to list as many consequences as they can that would be likely to follow some basic change in the world (such as the force of gravity being reduced by 50%). And researchers Mednick and Mednick (1967), who reasoned that the essence of creativity consists of the creative thinker's ability to fit together ideas that to the noncreative thinker might appear remote or unrelated, created the Remote Associates Test (RAT).

Creative Individuals. Psychologists studying exceptionally creative individuals (e.g., Bloom et al., 1985) have learned that they share a number of characteristics that distinguish them from less creative individuals. Most creative individuals have these characteristics:

divergent thinking The ability to produce multiple ideas, answers, or solutions to a problem for which there is no agreed-on solution.

Figure 7.8 Maps of Regional Cerebral Blood Flow (rCBF)

(a) Highly creative thinking is associated with activity in both hemispheres, but with significantly higher levels in the right hemisphere (red indicates activity). (b) During thinking that is not creative, activity is largely restricted to the left hemisphere.

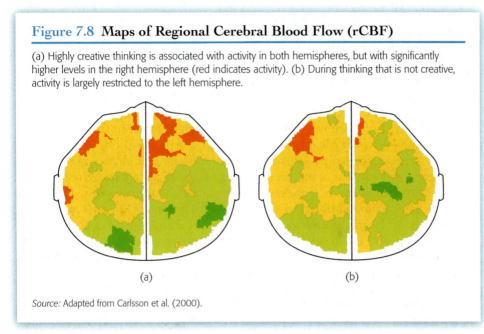

(a)   (b)

Source: Adapted from Carlsson et al. (2000).

- Curiosity and inquisitiveness
- Openness to new experiences
- Expertise in a specific area that has been built up over years of study and practice
- Tendency to be an independent thinker
- Self-motivation

Finally, creative endeavor requires hard work and persistence in the face of failure. For instance, Albert Einstein published 248 papers on his theory of relativity before it was finished, and Mozart, when he died at age 35, had created 609 musical compositions (Haberlandt, 1997).

Savant Syndrome

Finally, in our quest to understand intellectual functioning, we return to the phenomenon so strikingly illustrated by the story of Hikari Oe at the beginning of the chapter. As noted, Oe is a prime example of **savant syndrome,** an unusual combination of mental retardation and genius. It is a condition that allows an individual whose level of general intelligence is very low to perform certain highly creative or difficult mental feats. The term is derived from the French term for such a person: *idiot savant* (*idiot* means "poorly informed or untutored" and *savant* means "wise one"). Savants demonstrate high levels of performance in a variety of domains. Some are exceptionally gifted in musical performance. Others can identify the day of the week corresponding to any specific date in the past or in the future. Still others can carry out complex calculations in their heads. Arthur is such a person.

> "Arthur, how much is 6,427 times 4,234?" Arthur turned his head in my direction and said slowly but without hesitation, "27 million, 211 thousand, 918." His voice was stilted but precise. His eyes never lost their blank stare, and now he returned to gazing into space, without seeing anything, a handsome, impassive 8-year-old. (Rimland, 1978, p. 69)

Arthur can multiply multidigit numbers in his head faster than you could do it on a calculator, and he never makes a mistake. Yet, his measured IQ is extremely low.

The puzzle of savant syndrome is slowly being unraveled by scientists. For instance, psychologists have known for a long time that the prevalence of *absolute pitch,*

7.23 How do savants differ from other people?

savant syndrome A condition that allows an individual whose level of general intelligence is very low to perform highly creative or difficult mental feats.

the ability to identify musical tones merely by hearing them, is greater among individuals with autism than in the general population. Recently, though, researchers have found that people with autism are more sensitive than other people to sounds, and to changes in pitch, in general (Bonnel et al., 2003). Moreover, savants who can rapidly determine day-date associations in the past and future, known as *calendrical savants*, appear to have enhanced abilities to calculate and to associate all kinds of verbal and numerical stimuli (Cowan et al., 2003; Pring & Hermelin, 2002).

Another take on the nature of savant syndrome can be found in the work of Australian cognitive scientist Allan Snyder. He has long maintained that everyone possesses the talents exhibited by savants, particularly those that involve rapid mental calculations. His view is that the damaged brains of savants allow such abilities to come to the surface, whereas, in the healthy brain, they are overridden by higher cognitive functions. A ground-breaking study provided support for Snyder's hypothesis. In this study, Snyder and his colleagues used magnetic impulses to repress the parts of healthy individuals' brains that group and categorize information (Snyder et al., 2006). With these brain areas suppressed, participants were able to rapidly perform complex calculations in their heads in much the same way as savants do.

Does such research mean that nature gives advantages to individuals with cognitive disabilities that are withheld from those who don't have such disabilities? No, because the kinds of talents exhibited by savants are remarkable, but they are not adaptive in the sense that they help persons with mental retardation or autism function in the world. Remember, Hikari Oe is a great composer, but he lacks the cognitive skills that are needed for everyday tasks such as balancing a checkbook. As a result, although he is musically gifted, he cannot live independently. The healthy brain develops in ways that render us capable of functioning effectively in all kinds of situations, even when the cost of such development is the repression of narrow skills such as rapid mental calculation. Thus, the study carried out by Snyder and his colleagues and others like it will undoubtedly help neuroscientists better understand intelligence and creativity in normal individuals and in savants such as Hikari Oe. Furthermore, Snyder is also attempting to develop techniques that may enable normal people to tap into the hidden talents that he believes their brains possess. You can learn more about these techniques at http://www.centreforthemind.com.

Remember It   Beyond Intelligence

1. Identify the category in which each component of emotional intelligence belongs.

    (1) empathy
    (2) awareness of one's own emotions
    (3) self-motivation
    (4) ability to handle relationships

    a. personal
    b. interpersonal

2. Creativity and IQ scores are _____ related.

3. Match each stage of the creative process with its associated activity.

    _____ (1) preparation
    _____ (2) incubation
    _____ (3) illumination
    _____ (4) translation

    a. letting the problem "sit" while digesting information
    b. transforming the new insight into useful action
    c. searching for relevant information
    d. being suddenly struck by the right solution

4. Divergent thinking is associated with activity in the _____ of the brain.

5. Fred is autistic but can play any piece of music he hears on the piano immediately after listening to it. Fred exhibits _____.

Answers: 1. (1) b, (2) a, (3) a, (4) b; 2. weakly; 3. (1) c, (2) a, (3) d, (4) b; 4. right frontal cortex; 5. savant syndrome

Apply It   How to Build a Powerful Vocabulary

Of all the cognitive skills humans possess, none is more important for clarity of thinking and academic success than vocabulary. How, then, can you build a more powerful vocabulary? The best way is to realize that almost all words belong to larger networks of meaning, and to understand that your mind is already geared toward organizing information in terms of meaning. Thus, with a little effort, you can greatly increase your vocabulary by supporting the kind of learning your brain is already trying to do. Here are a few techniques you can apply.

- *Learn to think analytically about words you already know and relate new words to them.* What do the words *antiseptic* and *septic tank* have in common? You use an *antiseptic* to prevent bacterial infection of a wound; a *septic tank* is used for removing harmful bacteria from water containing human waste. A logical conclusion would be that *septic* has something to do with bacteria. Knowing this, what do you think a doctor means when she says that a patient is suffering from *sepsis*? By linking *sepsis* to *septic tank* and *antiseptic,* you can guess that she is referring to some kind of bacterial infection.

- *Be aware of word connections that may be hidden by spelling differences.* You may know that both *Caesar* and *Czar* refer to some kind of ruler or leader. But you may not know that they are exactly the same word, spoken and spelled somewhat differently in Ancient Rome (*Caesar*) and in Russia (*Czar*). Now, if you're taking a history class in which you learn about *Kaiser* Wilhelm, who led Germany during World War I, thinking analytically about his title may help you

realize that it is exactly the same word as *Caesar* and *Czar,* with a German spelling. Here's another example: Can you guess something about the location and climate of the nation of Ecuador by relating its name to a word that differs from it only slightly in spelling?

- *Use your knowledge of word parts to actively seek out new words.* Don't learn new words one at a time. Instead, be on the lookout for "word families"—root words and prefixes and suffixes. Here is one important root word: *spect*, which means "look," "look at," "watch," and "see." And *spect* appears in dozens of different words, such as *inspect*. What do you do when you *inspect* something? You look closely at it. Equipped with this knowledge, other *spect* words may start to come to mind, along with an entirely new way of thinking about their meanings: *spectacular, spectator, spectacle, spectacles, perspective, prospect, respect, disrespect, retrospect, suspect,* and so on. The word *circumspect* may be new to you. Look it up in a dictionary, and think about how the literal meaning of the word ("look around") relates to the way this word is frequently used. And, when you read Chapter 1, do you think it would have been easier to understand and remember the meaning of Wundt's research method, *introspection*, if you had thought about the *spect* part of the word? Probably so.

A strong vocabulary based on root words and prefixes and suffixes will yield the word power that will "literally" profit you in many ways. If you put this Apply It into practice, you will be able to build a powerful vocabulary.

❋ Summary and Review

Cognition p. 231

7.1 What is the difference between deductive and inductive reasoning? p. 231

Deductive reasoning involves reasoning from the general to the specific, or drawing particular conclusions from general principles. In inductive reasoning, general conclusions are drawn from particular facts or individual cases.

7.2 How does imagery help us think? p. 232

Imagery is helpful for learning new skills and for practicing those we already know. It can also help us store and retrieve information.

7.3 What kinds of concepts help us manage information? p. 233

Concepts are categories that allow us to quickly comprehend information. Rules and definitions determine formal concepts, whereas natural concepts arise out of everyday experiences. We also match information with prototypes, or examples, that include most or all of the features associated with the concepts they represent. Exemplars are examples of concepts with which we have the most familiarity.

7.4   What are the roles of systematic processes, heuristics, framing, and intuition in decision making? p. 234

Systematic processes involve considering all possible options prior to making a decision. Sometimes we use priorities to eliminate some of these options to speed up the decision-making process. By contrast, heuristics, or "rules of thumb," allow us to make decisions quickly, with little effort. Framing causes us to weigh a decision's gains and losses, and intuition relies on "gut feelings."

7.5   What are some basic approaches to problem solving, and how do they differ? p. 237

Analogy, working backward, and means-end analysis are problem-solving heuristics that may or may not lead to a correct solution. An algorithm is a strategy that always yields a correct solution.

7.6   What are some important applications of artificial intelligence technologies? p. 239

Artificial neural networks (ANNs) are used to simulate human thinking. They process information like human experts and learn from experience.

Language p. 240

7.7   What are the necessary components of any language? p. 240

The components of language are (1) phonemes, (2) morphemes, (3) syntax, (4) semantics, and (5) pragmatics.

7.8   In what ways does thinking influence language? p. 242

In general, thinking has a greater influence on language than language has on thinking. Whorf's linguistic relativity hypothesis has not been supported by research.

7.9   What are the advantages of learning a second language in childhood or adulthood? p. 242

People who learn a second language when they are younger than age 10 or 11 usually speak it without an accent. However, adolescents and adults know more about their own languages, and they can use this knowledge when they are learning a second one.

7.10   What does research indicate about animals' capacity for language? p. 244

Chimpanzees can learn to use sign language to communicate. Birds that can vocalize have been taught to use words to communicate. For the most part, research indicates that animals string symbols together rather than create true sentences.

Intelligence p. 246

7.11   How do the views of Spearman, Thurstone, Gardner, and Sternberg differ with regard to the definition of intelligence? p. 246

Spearman believed that intelligence is composed of a general ability factor (*g*) and a number of specific abilities (*s*). Thurstone proposed seven primary mental abilities. Gardner claims that there are eight kinds of intelligence, and Sternberg's triarchic theory proposed that three types exist.

7.12   What did Binet, Terman, and Wechsler contribute to the study of intelligence? p. 249

Binet developed the first standardized intelligence test. Terman adapted Binet's test for use in the United States and adopted Stern's "intelligence quotient" or "IQ" as the scoring system for the new test. Wechsler developed tests for children and adults. Scores in Wechsler's tests are based on deviation from age-based averages.

7.13   Why are reliability, validity, standardization, and cultural bias important in intelligence testing? p. 251

Reliable tests yield consistent results. Tests are valid if they predict appropriate outcome variables. Standardization is necessary so that individuals' scores can be compared. Cultural bias threatens the validity of a test, so test makers must reduce it as much as possible.

7.14   What does the term "bell curve" mean when applied to IQ test scores? p. 252

Graphing the frequencies of a large number of IQ scores produces a symmetrical curve (the normal curve) shaped like a bell. Exactly 50% of IQ scores fall above and below the average score of 100 on this curve.

7.15   How do the gifted differ from the general population? p. 253

Terman's longitudinal study revealed that, in general, gifted individuals enjoy better physical and mental health and are more successful than members of the general population.

7.16   What two criteria must a person meet to be classified as having mental retardation? p. 254

To be classified as having mental retardation, an individual must have an IQ score below 70 and show a severe deficiency in everyday adaptive functioning.

Explaining Differences in Cognitive Abilities p. 255

7.17   What is the nature-nurture debate regarding intelligence, and why are twin studies important to it? p. 255

The nature–nurture debate concerns the relative contributions of heredity and environment to variations in IQ test scores. Studies involving identical twins are important to this debate because twins have exactly the same genes. Research has shown that identical twins' IQs are more similar than those of other siblings even when the twins are raised in different families.

7.18 What kinds of evidence suggest that IQ is changeable? p. 257

Adoption studies have shown that infants from disadvantaged environments adopted into middle-class families have higher IQs than infants who remain in disadvantaged homes. Early educational experiences may also raise IQ scores. Also, IQ scores have been steadily rising over the past 70 years, presumably because of changes in standards of living.

7.19 What arguments have been advanced to explain racial differences in IQ scores? p. 259

Some researchers claim that racial differences result from genetics. Others argue that poverty, lack of educational opportunities, familiarity with testing situations, and stereotype threat explain these differences.

7.20 How do cultures vary in their views about the importance of intelligence, and how do those differences influence achievement? p. 260

Asian cultures appear to emphasize effort more than ability. As a result, Asian parents may encourage their children to work harder than do parents in Western societies where ability is considered to be more impor-

tant than effort. Such beliefs may also influence teaching methods. Parental and educational practices that are derived from cultural beliefs may lead to cross-cultural differences in achievement.

Beyond Intelligence p. 262

7.21 What are the components of emotional intelligence? p. 262

The components of emotional intelligence include awareness of one's own emotions, an ability to manage those emotions, self-motivation, empathy, and the ability to handle relationships.

7.22 How does creativity differ from other forms of cognition, and how has it been measured? p. 263

Guilford suggests that creativity involves divergent thinking. Tests used to measure creativity include the Unusual Uses Tests, the Consequences Test, and the Remote Associates Test.

7.23 How do savants differ from other people? p. 265

Savants are individuals whose level of general intelligence is very low but who can perform certain highly creative or difficult mental feats.

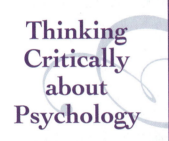

Thinking Critically about Psychology

1. Review the three basic approaches to decision making discussed in this chapter. Which approach do you think is most practical and efficient for making everyday decisions?
2. Based on what you have learned in this chapter, prepare arguments for and against raising a child in a bilingual environment and for and against requiring all school children in the United States to learn a second language.
3. Which of the theories of intelligence best fits your notion of intelligence? Why?

Key Terms

Chapter 8

Child Development

Continued

Do you look forward to graduation? Most college students do. You can probably imagine what the members of the class of 2006 of the University of Massachusetts at Boston were thinking on a rainy day in early June as they sat in their caps and gowns anxiously awaiting the moment when they would receive their diplomas. They listened attentively to speeches by U.S. Senator Barack Obama and other dignitaries, but, from time to time, their thoughts undoubtedly strayed to the prospect of beginning a new chapter in their lives. Many also probably reflected on the hard work and determination that had been required to attain their degrees. Few among them, though, looked back to the sorts of obstacles that had once faced one of their classmates, 29-year-old Panther Alier. Just five years earlier, Alier had been one of several thousand African refugees who had immigrated to the United States after spending more than a dozen years living in refugee camps; he was a member of a group called "The Lost Boys of the Sudan." Here is a brief account of their ordeal.

From the late 1980s to the early 1990s, government-backed forces bent on imposing Islamic law on the entire population of the Sudan drove millions of Christian and animist families from their homes. These desperate families headed for the Kenyan and Ethiopian borders in hope of finding refuge. Sadly, tens of thousands of the refugees died, and their deaths left many children without parents. These children, some of whom were as young as four years of age, knew that they faced certain death if they returned home. Lacking adults to support them, the children banded together, with the older children protecting the younger ones, and kept on the move. Little did they know that they would spend years walking in the hostile East African desert, a deadly hot and dry land more than twice the size of Texas. Many starved to death or died from disease, bad water, or tainted or poisonous food. Often, at night, a howling pack of hyenas would stalk a group of boys. On some occasions, as many as five boys in a group would be lost to these predators. The terrified survivors could do nothing but climb a tree and watch until the hyenas had finished turning their human prey into small piles of cleaned bones.

Miraculously, thousands of these children, many of whom were girls despite the popular moniker of "Lost Boys," made it to refugee camps in Kenya and Ethiopia. In the camps, relief workers fed them, treated their injuries, and set up makeshift schools to educate them. Nevertheless, it would be several more years before the United Nations and other organizations would succeed in finding permanent homes for them.

Panther Alier was 10 years old when he arrived at an Ethiopian refugee camp. During the four years he spent at the camp, he learned to read and write. After Alier moved on to a refugee camp in northern Kenya, he completed high school. In 2001, when Alier was selected by a United Nations committee to be relocated to the United States, he wasn't sure that he wanted to go. He feared losing contact with the surviving members of his family, but the older adults in the camp urged him to take advantage of the educational opportunities that they believed life in America would offer him. Trusting their advice, Alier set out on yet another journey, one that would take him to the radically different cultural setting of twenty-first-century America.

The Lost Boys were resettled in communities throughout the United States. The younger ones were adopted into families, and many of the older boys lived together in group homes. Many of those who had already reached adulthood, like Alier, were sent to Boston. With the help of

organizations such as Boston's Sudanese Education Fund, many of these boys enrolled in college. Although the task of adapting to life on an American college campus was challenging, many of those who persevered and succeeded in graduating view the hardships they endured as part of a longer journey. As Alier put it, "Had I stayed and lived in my village in southern Sudan, my life would be completely different from what it is today. I would be a cattle keeper or farmer . . . I would be illiterate" (*Boston Globe*, 2006).

For some of the Lost Boys, however, things have not turned out so well. The move to America brought on a confusing mixture of feelings of relief, joy, sadness, and anger. One of the boys, Alephonsien Deng, reports that he had no idea how angry he was about what had happened to his family until he was free from the stresses associated with living in a refugee camp (*Newsweek*, 2005). For a long time, he resented the happiness he saw in American society, knowing that there was so

much misery among the Sudanese refugees he had left behind. Fortunately, Deng resolved these issues and is now living happily in southern California. For other Lost Boys, however, emotional turmoil brought on by the multiple traumas they experienced as young children has driven them into substance abuse and depression (*Salon*, 2005).

The variety of outcomes experienced by the Lost Boys challenges the view that childhood is a fragile period of life in which potentially damaging influences can easily push an individual toward a poor outcome. Certainly, it is preferable for children to have positive experiences, but in many cases of deprivation and even outright abuse, there appear to be compensating forces at work that moderate the influence of negative factors. The Lost Boys, for example, developed intense emotional bonds with one another that may have protected them to some degree from the damaging effects of their experiences. But why didn't these bonds protect all of them? Why did some experience stunning successes after immigrating to the United States, while others were unable to escape the emotional chains of their traumatic memories? Psychologists study such questions in their research on child development, as you will learn in this chapter.

Developmental Psychology: Basic Issues and Methodology

Developmental psychology is the study of how humans grow, develop, and change throughout the life span. Some developmental psychologists specialize in the study of a particular age group on the continuum from infancy, childhood, and adolescence, through early, middle, and late adulthood, to the end of the life span. Others concentrate on a specific area of interest, such as physical, cognitive, or language development or emotional or moral development.

developmental psychology The study of how humans grow, develop, and change throughout the life span.

Controversial Issues in Developmental Psychology

In turning to the study of development, we encounter two age-old questions. First, which is more important, heredity or environment? Second, does development happen in stages?

Nature and Nurture. In Chapter 7 you read about the nature-nurture debate regarding differences in intelligence. Among developmental psychologists, interest in these

8.1 What three issues are frequently debated among developmental psychologists?

▲ This baby appears to have one of several protective factors, that of an easygoing personality.

two sets of factors extends far beyond the domain of intelligence. Obviously, heredity imposes some limits on what a person can become. The best possible home environment, education, and nutrition are not enough to produce an Albert Einstein or a Marilyn Mach vos Savant (whose 230 IQ is the highest ever recorded). But parental neglect, poor nutrition, ill health, abuse, and lack of education can prevent even the brightest child from becoming the best his or her genes would allow. Still, many individuals have achieved normal or exceptional lives despite childhood deprivation.

Some developmental psychologists have argued that the best way to resolve the nature-nurture debate—and to explain why some children exhibit *resilience* (the capacity to bounce back) in response to unsupportive or harmful environments—is to think of each child as being born with certain *vulnerabilities*, such as a difficult temperament or a genetic disorder (Masten, 2001; Masten et al., 1999). Each child is also born with some *protective factors*, such as high intelligence, good coordination, or an easygoing personality, that tend to increase resilience. Through childhood and adolescence, vulnerabilities and protective factors interact with variables in the environment so that the same environment can have different effects, depending on the characteristics of each child. For example, a shy child who has few friends might be damaged more by parental emotional abuse than one who is more outgoing and has a greater number of relationships outside the family.

Stages or No Stages? We often say that a child who is acting out in some way is going through a "phase" or a "stage." But are there really phases or stages in development that differ qualitatively? This is one of the most important questions in developmental psychology. To understand how developmentalists think about this question, consider what happens as children become taller. Children change *quantitatively* as they grow taller. In other words, the characteristic of height is the same at all ages. Older children simply have more of it than those who are younger. However, changes in other developmental variables—logical thinking, for example—occur in stages. Such changes are *qualitative* in nature. In other words, the logic of a 10-year-old is completely different from that of a 3-year-old. The older child doesn't just have more logic; he thinks in an entirely different way. In this chapter, we will explore one of the most important stage theories in developmental psychology: Piaget's theory of cognitive development. In Chapter 9, you will read about Erikson's psychosocial stages and Kohlberg's stages of moral reasoning.

Developmentalists also attempt to answer questions about the extent to which personal traits, such as intelligence and personality, are stable over time. How do developmental psychologists study changes over the lifespan?

Approaches to Studying Developmental Change

8.2 What methods do developmental psychologists use to investigate age-related changes?

How would you go about finding out how individuals change with age? You could follow a group of people as they get older, or you could compare individuals of different ages. Developmental psychologists use both approaches in their research.

In a **longitudinal study,** the same group of participants is followed and measured at different ages, over a period of years. Such studies allow researchers to observe age-related changes in individuals. There are some drawbacks to a longitudinal study, however. It is time-consuming and expensive, and participants may drop out of the study or die, possibly leaving the researcher with a biased sample.

A **cross-sectional study** is a less expensive and less time-consuming method in which researchers compare groups of participants of different ages to determine age-related differences in some characteristics. But, in a cross-sectional study, differences across age groups are based on group averages, so this approach cannot be used to answer certain questions. For example, it could not be used to determine if individual temperament is stable over time. Moreover, certain relevant differences in groups of participants may have less to do with the participants' ages than with the eras in which they grew up, a problem known as the *cohort effect*. **Figure 8.1** compares longitudinal and cross-sectional studies.

Development is a fascinating and remarkable process that begins even before birth, and we will trace its course from the very beginning.

longitudinal study   A type of developmental study in which the same group of participants is followed and measured at different ages.

cross-sectional study   A type of developmental study in which researchers compare groups of participants of different ages on various characteristics to determine age-related differences.

Figure 8.1 A Comparison of Longitudinal and Cross-Sectional Studies

To study age-related changes using a longitudinal study, researchers examine the same group of participants at several times over an extended period. When using a cross-sectional study, researchers examine and compare groups of different ages at one point in time.

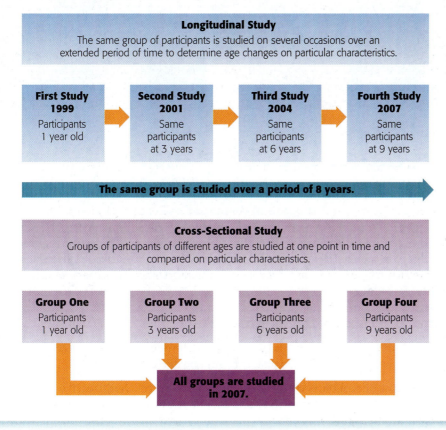

Longitudinal Study
The same group of participants is studied on several occasions over an extended period of time to determine age changes on particular characteristics.

First Study 1999	Second Study 2001	Third Study 2004	Fourth Study 2007
Participants 1 year old	Same participants at 3 years	Same participants at 6 years	Same participants at 9 years

The same group is studied over a period of 8 years.

Cross-Sectional Study
Groups of participants of different ages are studied at one point in time and compared on particular characteristics.

Group One	Group Two	Group Three	Group Four
Participants 1 year old	Participants 3 years old	Participants 6 years old	Participants 9 years old

All groups are studied in 2007.

▲ To find out about developmental changes, is it better to compare older and younger people, like those in this photo, or to begin studying individuals when they are young and follow them as they age? Developmental psychologists use both approaches, and each has advantages and disadvantages.

Remember It   Developmental Psychology

1. Developmental psychologists study changes that happen during
 a. childhood.
 b. adulthood.
 c. old age.
 d. the entire lifespan.

2. One of the controversies in developmental psychology is whether development occurs in _____.

3. The finding that older children think more logically than younger children is an example of a(n) _____ change.

4. Identify the characteristics of cross-sectional studies with the letter c and the characteristics of longitudinal studies with the letter l.
 _____ (1) Groups of different ages are tested at the same time.
 _____ (2) A single group is studied at different times.
 _____ (3) The less expensive of the two research methods.
 _____ (4) The method that can reveal individual change over time.
 _____ (5) Participants may drop out or die.
 _____ (6) Differences may be due to factors other than development, such as the era in which participants grew up.

Answers: (1) d; 2. stages; 3. qualitative; 4. (1) c, (2) l, (3) c, (4) l, (5) l, (6) c

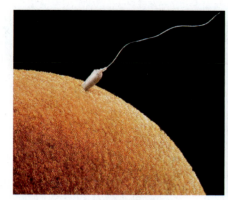

▲ This sequence of photos shows the fertilization of an egg by a sperm (left), an embryo at 7 weeks (center), and a fetus at 22 weeks (right).

Prenatal Development

Many people divide the 9 months of pregnancy into *trimesters,* three periods of 3 months' duration: The first begins at conception and ends at 3 months, the second spans the period from 3 to 6 months, and the third extends from 6 to 9 months. However, the division of pregnancy into trimesters is arbitrary and has no significance with regard to prenatal development. Moreover, you may be surprised to learn, by the time the first trimester of pregnancy is over, the third stage of prenatal development has already begun.

Stages of Prenatal Development

8.3 What happens in each of the three stages of prenatal development?

Each of the three stages of **prenatal development,** or development from conception to birth, is marked by a specific event at its beginning and another at its end.

Conception. Conception occurs the moment a sperm cell fertilizes the ovum (egg cell), forming a single-celled **zygote.** You should remember from Chapter 2 that the zygote carries the full complement of 46 chromosomes (23 from the father's sperm and 23 from the mother's ovum) that are necessary for the development of a human being. These chromosomes carry genes, the biochemical instructions that determine many of the new individual's characteristics, such as eye color and genetic disorders. Other genetic instructions, in combination with environmental influences, will shape the individual's development throughout the lifespan. These include genes that influence intelligence, personality, and the development of chronic health conditions such as diabetes and heart disease.

Sometimes, for an unknown reason, the zygote divides into two cells, resulting in identical, or *monozygotic,* twins. There are even cases of identical triplets, quadruplets, and quintuplets. In fact, the famous Dionne quintuplets, born in Canada in the 1930s, were identical. There are also times when two (or more) eggs unite with two (or more) sperm, resulting in fraternal, or *dizygotic,* twins.

The Germinal, Embryonic, and Fetal Stages. Conception usually takes place in one of the fallopian tubes, and within the next 2 weeks, the zygote travels to the uterus and attaches itself to the uterine wall. During this 2-week period, called the *germinal stage,* rapid cell division occurs. Once the zygote is successfully attached, the germinal stage is over. At the end of this stage, the zygote is only the size of the period at the end of this sentence.

The second stage is the *embryonic stage,* during which the developing human organism, now called an **embryo,** forms all of the major body systems, organs, and structures. Lasting from the beginning of week 3 through week 8, this period begins when the zygote attaches itself to the uterine wall and ends when the first bone cells form. Only 1 inch long and weighing $\frac{1}{7}$ of an ounce, the embryo already resembles a human being, with limbs, fingers, toes, and many internal organs that have begun to function.

The final stage of prenatal development, the *fetal stage,* lasts from the beginning of week 9, when bone cells begin to form, until birth. The developing human organism

prenatal development Development that occurs between conception and birth and consists of three stages (germinal, embryonic, and fetal).

zygote The single cell that forms when a sperm and egg unite.

embryo The developing human organism during the period from week 3 through week 8, when the major systems, organs, and structures of the body develop.

Table 8.1 Stages of Prenatal Development

Stage	Time After Conception	Major Activities of the Stage
Germinal	1 to 2 weeks	Zygote attaches to the uterine lining. At 2 weeks, zygote is the size of the period at the end of this sentence.
Embryonic	3 to 8 weeks	Major systems, organs, and structures of the body develop. Stage ends when first bone cells appear. At 8 weeks, embryo is about 1 inch long and weighs $\frac{1}{7}$ of an ounce.
Fetal	9 weeks to birth (38 weeks)	Rapid growth and further development of the body structures, organs, and systems.

is now called a **fetus,** and it experiences rapid growth and further development of body structures, organs, and systems. **Table 8.1** summarizes the stages of prenatal development.

Fetal Behavior

Would you be surprised to learn that a human fetus is very responsive to sounds as early as the 25th week of gestation (Joseph, 2000)? Over the past few decades, scientists have learned a great deal about the behavior of fetuses because of the availability of such technologies as ultrasonography, which allow them to observe fetal behavior directly. Thus, we know that fetal responses to sound are both physical, such as turning the head toward a sound, and neurological (Moore et al., 2001).

8.4 What have scientists learned about fetal behavior in recent years?

Several studies of newborns have shown that they remember sounds to which they were exposed as fetuses. In one frequently cited study, researchers DeCasper and Spence (1986) had 16 pregnant women read *The Cat in the Hat* to their developing fetuses twice a day during the final 6 weeks of pregnancy. A few days after birth, the infants could adjust their sucking on specially designed, pressure-sensitive nipples to hear their mother reading either *The Cat in the Hat* or *The King, the Mice, and the Cheese,* a story they had never heard before. By their sucking behavior, the infants showed a clear preference for the familiar sound of *The Cat in the Hat.* Other research has demonstrated that newborns remember such prenatal stimuli as their mother's heartbeats, the odor of the amniotic fluid, and music they heard in the womb (Kisilevsky et al., 2003; Righetti, 1996; Schaal et al., 1998).

Does prenatal learning contribute to intellectual development in infancy or even later in childhood? Researchers don't yet know the answer to this question (Bornstein et al., 2002). However, experiments are currently under way in which the cognitive development of children who were systematically exposed to prenatal stimuli is being compared to that of children not so exposed. In one of these studies, pregnant women strapped small speakers to their abdomens during the later weeks of pregnancy in order to expose their babies to many hours of classical music (Lafuente et al., 1997). Babies who were exposed to the music prior to birth were found to be more advanced in cognitive development at 6 months of age than infants in the control group, who were not exposed to the music (Lafuente et al., 1997). Of course, the long-term significance of such findings is unknown.

Stable individual differences are also evident during prenatal development. For instance, fetuses exhibit a wide range of differences in activity level. Longitudinal research has demonstrated that highly active fetuses grow into young children who are very active (DiPietro et al., 2002). Moreover, in the elementary school years, parents and teachers are more likely to label such children "hyperactive." By contrast, low levels of fetal activity are associated with mental retardation (Accardo, et al., 1997).

Some sex differences appear early in prenatal development as well. One such difference is the frequent finding that male fetuses, on average, are more physically active than females (DePietro et al., 1996a, 1996b). Another difference is that female fetuses appear to be more responsive than male fetuses to sounds and other external stimuli (Groome et al., 1999).

fetus The developing human organism during the period from week 9 until birth, when rapid growth and further development of the structures, organs, and systems of the body occur.

Negative Influences on Prenatal Development

8.5 What are some negative influences on prenatal development, and when is their impact greatest?

Most of the time, prenatal development progresses smoothly and ends in the birth of a normal, healthy infant. However, there are a few factors that increase the risks of various kinds of problems. Maternal illness, for one, can interfere with the process. A chronic condition such as diabetes, for example, can cause problems that may include retardation or acceleration of fetal growth (Levy-Shiff et al., 2002).

When the mother suffers from a viral disease such as rubella, chicken pox, or HIV, she may deliver an infant with physical and behavioral abnormalities (Amato, 1998; Kliegman, 1998). Some of these effects, such as the heart problems that are associated with rubella, can be lifelong. In addition, these viral diseases can be passed from mother to child. In the case of HIV, prenatal transmission of the virus is likely to lead to the development of full-blown AIDS in the child after birth. Viruses and other harmful agents, including drugs, X-rays, and environmental toxins, that can have a negative impact on prenatal development are called **teratogens.**

teratogens Viruses and other harmful agents that can have a negative impact on prenatal development.

A teratogen's impact depends on both its intensity and the time during prenatal development when it is present. (See **Figure 8.2**). Drugs, environmental hazards such as X-rays and toxic waste, and diseases such as rubella generally have their most devas-

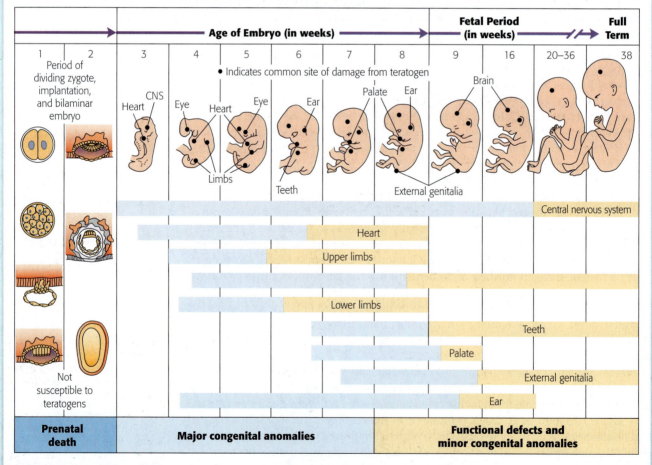

Figure 8.2 Critical Periods in the Prenatal Development of Various Body Parts

Critical periods in the prenatal development of various body parts. The light blue portion of each line signifies the period during which any teratogen is likely to produce a major structural deformity in that particular body part. The gold part of each line shows the period in which more minor problems may result. The embryonic period is generally the time of greatest vulnerability.

(*Source:* Moore, K. L. and Persaud T., *The Developing Human: Clinically Oriented Embryology*, 5th ed. © 1993 by permission from Elsevier.)

tating consequences during the embryonic stage. During this time, there are critical periods when certain body structures develop. If drugs or infections interfere with development during a critical period, a particular body structure will not form properly, nor will it develop later (Kopp & Kaler, 1989). For example, maternal alcohol intake early in prenatal development can lead to facial deformities as well as mental retardation and behavior problems, a condition known as **fetal alcohol syndrome.** Exposure to teratogens during the fetal stage is more likely to result in various types of intellectual and social impairments than to cause physical abnormalities. Table 8.2 lists a number of teratogens and other factors that may negatively affect prenatal development.

One of the most serious effects of teratogens is that they increase the risks of low birth weight, a birth weight less than 5.5 pounds. There are two types of low-birth-weight infants: preterm and small-for-date. *Preterm infants* are those who are born early, specifically, before 38 weeks of gestation. *Small-for-date infants* are those who have birth weights lower than expected for their gestational age. Of the two types, small-for-date infants are more likely to die or have permanent disabilities because their size is the result of some prenatal factor, such as maternal malnutrition, that caused them to grow too slowly. By contrast, preterm infants have experienced appropriate growth rates but may have organs, especially the lungs, that are not yet ready to function independently.

Finally, things sometimes go wrong during the birth process. When infants are exposed to life-threatening complications during birth, such as collapse of the umbilical cord, they are at increased risk of experiencing many negative developmental outcomes. For example, lack of sufficient oxygen can damage the brain. Moreover, birth complications are related to behavior problems, such as excessive aggressiveness, later in childhood and adolescence (Arseneault et al., 2002).

▲ Drinking alcohol during pregnancy can result in the birth of an infant with fetal alcohol syndrome, a permanent condition that involves mental retardation and physical and behavioral abnormalities.

Table 8.2 Negative Influences on Prenatal Development

Teratogens	Possible Effects on Fetus
Maternal Diseases/ Conditions	
Malnutrition	Poor growth, mental retardation
Diabetes	Growth abnormalities
Rubella	Heart defects, blindness, deafness
Herpes	Nerve damage; disease can be transmitted to fetus
HIV	Disease can be transmitted to fetus
Cancer	Fetal or placental tumor
Hepatitis B	Hepatitis
Chlamydia	Conjunctivitis, pneumonia
Syphilis	Blindness, deafness, mental retardation
Gonorrhea	Blindness
Drugs	
Alcohol	Fetal alcohol syndrome (FAS; facial deformities, mental retardation, behavior problems), ADHD
Heroin	Addiction, tremors, erratic sleep patterns, vomiting, prematurity
Cocaine	Prematurity, physical defects, sleep difficulties, tremors
Marijuana	Tremors, sleep difficulties, ADHD
Tobacco	Low birth weight, sudden infant death syndrome, ADHD
Caffeine	Consumption of more than 300 mg/day (about 3 cups of brewed coffee) linked to low birth weight
Diet pills	Low birth weight

Source: Amato (1998); Kliegman (1998); Huizink & Mulder (2006).

critical period A period during the embryonic stage when certain body structures are developing and can be harmed by negative influences in the prenatal environment.

fetal alcohol syndrome A condition that is caused by maternal alcohol intake early in prenatal development and that leads to facial deformities as well as mental retardation.

low birth weight A weight at birth of less than 5.5 pounds.

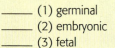

Remember It | Prenatal Development

1. Match each stage of prenatal development with its description.

   _____ (1) germinal
   _____ (2) embryonic
   _____ (3) fetal

   a. first 2 weeks of life
   b. rapid growth and further development of body structures and systems
   c. development of major systems, organs, and structures of the body

2. Fetal variations in _____ are related to the diagnosis of hyperactivity during childhood.

3. Because many body structures are at critical periods of development during this time, a teratogen is most likely to cause defects during the _____ stage.

Answers: 1. (1) a, (2) c, (3) b; 2. activity level; 3. embryonic

Infancy

One of the pioneers of psychology, William James, made many notable contributions to the field. However, he could not have been more wrong when he claimed that the newborn perceives the world "as one great blooming, buzzing confusion" (James, 1890, p. 462). To the contrary, newborns enter the world ready and eager to take in all of its sights and sounds in an organized fashion.

Reflexes and Motor Development

8.6 How do the motor behaviors of a newborn compare to those of an older infant?

If you have observed the behavior of a newborn baby, you probably noticed that his or her movements seem fairly erratic when compared to those of an older infant. During the first few days after birth, the movements of **neonates** (newborn babies up to 1 month old) are dominated by **reflexes,** which are inborn, unlearned, automatic responses to certain stimuli. These behaviors are needed to ensure survival in their new world. Sucking, swallowing, coughing, and blinking are some important behaviors that newborns can perform right away. Newborns will move an arm, a leg, or other body part away from a painful stimulus and will try to remove a blanket or cloth placed over the face. Stroke a baby on the cheek, and you will trigger the *rooting reflex*—the baby opens its mouth and actively searches for a nipple.

Neonates also have some reflexes that serve no apparent function and are believed to be remnants of humans' evolutionary past. As the brain develops, some behaviors that were initially reflexive (controlled by structures in the hindbrain) gradually come under the voluntary control of parts of the forebrain. The presence of these reflexes at birth and their disappearance between the 2nd and 4th months of age provide researchers with a means of assessing development of the nervous system.

In time, most reflexes give way to more deliberate, coordinated motor behavior. Most motor milestones (shown in Figure 8.3) result from **maturation,** each infant's own genetically determined, biological pattern of development. Although infants follow their own individual timetables, the basic motor skills usually appear in a particular sequence. Physical and motor development proceeds from the head downward to the trunk and legs. So, babies lift their heads before they sit, and they sit before they walk. Development also proceeds from the center of the body outward—trunk to shoulders to arms to fingers. Thus, control of the arms develops before control of the fingers.

But what about experience? What influence does it exert on motor development? The rate at which the motor milestones are achieved is delayed when an infant is

neonate A newborn infant up to 1 month old.

reflexes Inborn, unlearned, automatic responses (such as blinking, sucking, and grasping) to certain environmental stimuli.

maturation Each infant's own genetically determined, biological pattern of development.

Figure 8.3 **The Progression of Motor Development**

Most infants develop motor skills in the sequence shown. The ages indicated are only averages, so normal, healthy infants may develop any of these milestones a few months earlier or several months later than the average.

Lifts head up
2 months

Rolls over
3 months

Sits propped up
3 months

Sits without support
6 months

Stands holding on
7 months

Walks holding on
9 months

Stands momentarily
10 months

Stands alone
11 months

Walks alone
12 months

Walks backwards
14 months

Walks up steps
17 months

Kicks ball forward
18 months

Source: Frankenburg et al. (1992).

subjected to extremely unfavorable environmental conditions, such as severe malnutrition or illness. And experiences that restrict infants' freedom of movement, including cultural practices such as strapping babies to "papoose" boards, also delay motor development. However, once babies are free to move about, they quickly acquire the same level of motor skill development as others their age who have not been restricted.

Experience may also accelerate motor development. In some African cultures, mothers use special motor training techniques that enable their infants to attain some of the major motor milestones earlier than most infants in the United States (Kilbride & Kilbride, 1975; Super, 1981). But maturation limits the effects of experience. No amount of training will cause a one-month-old infant to walk; when the baby is near the typical age for walking, special exercises may facilitate acquisition of the skill. Moreover, speeding up infant motor development has no effect on a child's future physical abilities.

Sensory and Perceptual Development

8.7 What are the sensory and perceptual abilities of a newborn?

Did you know that the five senses, although not fully developed, are functional at birth? Moreover, a newborn already has preferences for certain types of stimuli.

Vision. At birth, an infant's vision is about 20/600, and it doesn't approach the 20/20 level until the child is about 2 years old (Courage & Adams, 1990; Held, 1993). Newborns focus best on objects about 9 inches away, and they can follow a slowly moving object. By 2 to 3 months of age, most infants prefer human faces to other visual images (Fantz, 1961; see **Figure 8.4**). Although newborns prefer colored stimuli to gray ones, they can't distinguish all of the colors adults normally can until they are about 2 months old (Franklin, Pilling, & Davies, 2005).

Depth Perception. Gibson and Walk (1960) designed an apparatus called the **visual cliff** (shown in the photograph on the left) to measure infants' ability to perceive depth. When 36 babies, aged 6 to 14 months, were placed on the center board, most could be coaxed by their mothers to crawl to the shallow side, but only three would crawl onto the deep side. Gibson and Walk concluded that most babies "can discriminate depth as soon as they can crawl" (p. 64). Campos and others (1970) also found that 6-week-old infants had distinct changes in heart rate when they faced the deep side of the cliff, but no change when they faced the shallow side. The change in heart rate indicated interest or apprehension and showed that the infants could perceive depth.

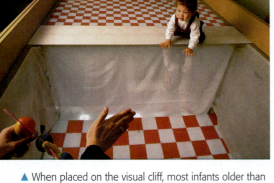

▲ When placed on the visual cliff, most infants older than 6 months will not crawl out over the deep side, indicating that they can perceive depth.

Hearing and Other Senses. At birth, a newborn's hearing is much better developed than her or his vision. An infant is able to turn the head in the direction of a sound and shows a general preference for female voices. Newborns also prefer their own mother's voice to that of an unfamiliar female (DeCasper & Fifer, 1980; Kisilevsky et al., 2003), but a preference for the father's voice over a strange male voice does not develop until later.

Neonates are able to discriminate among and show preferences for certain odors and tastes (Bartoshuk & Beauchamp, 1994; Leon, 1992). They show a favorable response to sweet tastes and are able to differentiate between salty, bitter, and sour solutions. Newborns are also sensitive to pain (Porter et al., 1988) and are particularly responsive to touch, reacting positively to stroking and fondling.

Learning

8.8 What types of learning occur in infancy?

Earlier in the chapter, you read that learning takes place even in the womb, so you won't be surprised to hear that several types of learning are evident in newborns. The simplest evidence of learning in infants is the phenomenon of **habituation.** When presented with a new stimulus, infants respond with a general quieting, their heart rate slows, and they fixate on the stimulus. But when they become accustomed to the stimulus, they stop responding—that is, they habituate to it. Later, if the familiar stimulus is presented along with a new stimulus, the infants will usually pay more attention to the new stimulus, indicating that they remember the original stimulus but prefer the new one.

Using habituation, Swain and others (1993) demonstrated that 3-day-old newborns could retain in memory for 24 hours a speech sound that had been presented repeatedly to them the day before. When the same sound was repeated the following day, the babies quickly showed habituation by turning their head away from the familiar sound and toward a novel sound. And infants 2 to 3 months old can form memories of their past experiences that last for days, and even longer as they get older (Rovee-Collier, 1990). Other researchers have demonstrated both classical conditioning and operant conditioning in infants (Lipsitt, 1990).

By the tender age of 12 months, infants appear to be quite capable of learning through observation as well. Research reported by German scientists indicates that babies of this age learn a great deal about causes and effects from observing the actions of others. For example, they learn that pulling on a handle opens a drawer and flip-

visual cliff An apparatus used to measure infants' ability to perceive depth.

habituation A decrease in response or attention to a stimulus as an infant becomes accustomed to it.

Figure 8.4 Results of Fantz's Study

Using a device called a *viewing box* to observe and record infants' eye movements, Fantz (1961) found that they preferred faces to black-and-white abstract patterns.

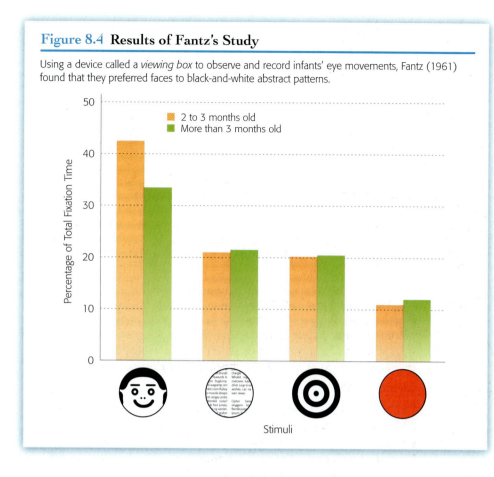

ping a switch causes a light to go on or off. Apparently, they can learn just as much from watching televised models as they do from watching live models. In a classic study, Meltzoff (1988) showed babies a videotape of an adult playing with a toy in an unusual way. The next day, when presented with the toy, the babies imitated the actions they observed the models performing in the video.

Temperament

Have you ever heard the parent of a newborn describe him or her as "shy" or "outgoing" and thought they were reading more into their infant's behaviors than was warranted? You might have been wrong, because research shows that such differences among infants can be identified even in the earliest days of life. In fact, current thinking and research in developmental psychology suggest that each baby is born with an individual behavioral style or characteristic way of responding to the environment—a particular **temperament.**

Differences in Temperament. One of the most important studies of temperament began in 1956. Alexander T. Thomas, Stella C. Chess, and Herbert B. Birch (1970) studied a group of 2- to 3-month-old infants and followed them into adolescence and adulthood. They found that "children do show distinct individuality in temperament in the first weeks of life independently of their parents' handling or personality style" (p. 104). Three general types of temperament emerged from the study: easy, difficult, and slow-to-warm-up.

- *Easy children*—40% of the group—had generally pleasant moods, were adaptable, approached new situations and people positively, and established regular sleeping, eating, and elimination patterns.
- *Difficult children*—10% of the group—had generally unpleasant moods, reacted negatively to new situations and people, were intense in their emotional reactions, and showed irregularity of bodily functions.

8.9 What is temperament, and what are the three temperament types identified by Thomas, Chess, and Birch?

temperament A person's behavioral style or characteristic way of responding to the environment.

- *Slow-to-warm-up children*—15% of the group—tended to withdraw, were slow to adapt, and were prone to negative emotional states. The remaining 35% of the children studied were too inconsistent to categorize.

Researchers now view infants as possessing different degrees of several dimensions of temperament. An individual baby might be higher than average in all of them, or high in some and low in others, or below average for all of the dimensions. Although there is still debate over the definitions of these proposed dimensions of temperament, a few of them that are accepted by almost all developmental psychologists are listed in Table 8.3.

Origins and Significance of Temperamental Differences. Research indicates that temperament is strongly influenced by heredity (e.g., Caspi, 2000; Plomin, 2001; Saudino, 2005). However, environmental factors, such as parents' child-rearing style, also affect temperament (Richter et al., 2000). For example, mothers' responses to toddlers can serve to either increase or decrease shyness (Rubin et al., 2002). When mothers criticize toddlers' shy behavior, it increases; by contrast, toddlers of mothers who are more tolerant of their children's shyness become more outgoing as they get older.

Studies suggest that the various dimensions of temperament can predict behavioral problems that may appear later in childhood or in adolescence (Chess, 2005; Pierrehumbert et al., 2000). Children who are impulsive at a young age tend to become aggressive, danger-seeking, impulsive adolescents (Hart et al., 1997), with strong negative emotions (Caspi & Silva, 1995). Temperament affects future behavior by influencing parenting practices as well. For instance, parents of temperamentally irritable children are more likely than other parents to exhibit inconsistent parenting practices (Lengua & Kovacs, 2005). Ultimately, it is this interplay between an infant's inborn temperament and his family's responses to it that shapes his personality.

Attachment

8.10 What did the research of Harlow, Bowlby, and Ainsworth reveal about the process of infant-caregiver attachment?

You may have noticed that once they reach a certain age, most babies cry or protest when separated from their parents. The cultural emphasis on individualism and independence may lead some adults in the United States and other Western nations to see such behavior as a sign that an infant is developing an undesirable trait. But this view is wrong. One of the most important concepts in developmental psychology is **attachment,** the early, close relationship formed between infant and caregiver (Lamb & Lewis, 2005). In fact, failure to develop an attachment relationship in infancy can seriously compromise later development.

Attachment in Infant Monkeys. For many years, it was believed that the main ingredient in infant-caregiver attachment was the fact that the caregiver provides the infant with the nourishment that sustains life. However, a series of classic studies conducted by psychologist Harry Harlow on attachment in rhesus monkeys suggests that physical nourishment alone is not enough to bind infants to their primary caregivers. To systematically investigate the nature of attachment and the effects of maternal deprivation on infant monkeys, Harlow constructed two surrogate (artificial) monkey "mothers." One was a plain wire-mesh cylinder with a wooden head; the other was a wire-mesh cylinder that was padded, covered with soft terrycloth, and fitted with a somewhat more monkey-like head. A baby bottle could be attached to either surrogate mother for feeding.

Newborn monkeys were placed in individual cages where they had equal access to a cloth surrogate and a wire surrogate. The source of their nourishment (cloth or wire surrogate) was unimportant. "The infants developed a strong attachment to the cloth mothers and little or none to the wire mothers" (Harlow & Harlow, 1962, p. 141). Harlow found that it was contact comfort—the comfort supplied by bodily contact—rather than nourishment that formed the basis of the infant monkey's attachment to its mother.

If infant monkeys were placed with the cloth mother for the first $5\frac{1}{2}$ months of life, their attachment was so strong that it persisted even after an 18-month separation. Their attachment to the cloth mother was almost identical to the attachment normal

attachment The early, close relationship formed between infant and caregiver.

Table 8.3   Dimensions of Temperament

Activity level	Quantity and quality of physical movement; how often and how strongly a baby moves
Sociability *or* Approach	A tendency to move toward rather than away from new people and things; often accompanied by positive emotion
Inhibition *or* Shyness	A tendency to respond with fear or withdrawal to new people or situations or to situations in which there is too much stimulation (e.g., a children's birthday party)
Negative emotionality	A tendency to respond with anger, fussing, loudness, or irritability
Effortful control	The ability to stay focused and manage attention and effort; to persist until a task is complete

monkeys have to their real mothers. However, unlike real mothers, the cloth mothers were unresponsive, so the emotional development of monkeys attached to cloth mothers was quite different from that of their peers who had access to real mothers. Monkeys with cloth mothers would not interact with other monkeys, and they showed inappropriate aggression. Their sexual behavior was grossly abnormal, and they would not mate. If impregnated artificially, they became terrible mothers, whose behavior ranged from ignoring their babies to violently abusing them (Harlow et al., 1971). The only aspect of development not affected was learning ability. Thus, Harlow concluded that contact comfort might be sufficient for attachment, but something more was required for normal emotional development: active affection and responsiveness.

The Development of Attachment in Humans. Numerous studies have supported Harlow's conclusion that parental affection and responsiveness are necessary for the development of attachment in human infants (e.g., Posada et al., 2002). The primary caregiver holds, strokes, and talks to the baby and responds to the baby's needs. In turn, the baby gazes at, listens to, and moves in synchrony with the caregiver's voice. Even crying can promote attachment: The caregiver is motivated to relieve the baby's distress and feels rewarded when the crying stops. Like Harlow's monkeys, babies cling to their mothers and, when old enough to crawl, will move to stay near them.

The infant's attachment to the mother develops over time and is usually quite strong by age 6 to 8 months (Bowlby, 1969). According to developmentalist John Bowlby, attachment behavior serves the evolutionary function of protecting the infant from danger (Bretherton, 1992). Once the attachment has formed, infants begin to show **separation anxiety**—fear and distress when the parent leaves them. Occurring from about 8 to 24 months of age, separation anxiety peaks between 12 and 18 months of age (Fox & Bell, 1990). Infants who previously voiced no distress when left with a babysitter may now scream when their parents leave.

At about 6 or 7 months of age, infants develop a fear of strangers called **stranger anxiety,** which increases in intensity until about $12\frac{1}{2}$ months and then declines in the second year (Marks, 1987). Stranger anxiety is greater in an unfamiliar setting, when the parent is not close at hand, and when a stranger abruptly approaches or touches the child. Interestingly, stranger anxiety is not directed at unfamiliar children until age 19 to 30 months (P. K. Smith, 1979).

Ainsworth's Attachment Categories. Practically all infants reared in a family develop an attachment to a familiar caregiver by the age of 2 years. But there are vast differences in the quality of attachment. In a classic study of mother-child attachment, the late Mary Ainsworth (1913–1999) observed mother-child interactions in the home during the infants' first year and then again at age 12 months in a laboratory, using a procedure called the "strange situation" (Ainsworth 1973, 1979). Based on infants' reactions to their mothers after brief periods of separation, Ainsworth and others (1978; Main & Solomon, 1990) identified four patterns of attachment: *secure, avoidant, resistant,* and *disorganized/ disoriented*. **Table 8.4** describes these attachment patterns.

▲ Harlow found that infant monkeys developed a strong attachment to a cloth-covered surrogate mother and little or no attachment to a wire surrogate mother—even when the wire mother provided nourishment.

separation anxiety   The fear and distress shown by infants and toddlers when the parent leaves, occurring from 8 to 24 months and reaching a peak between 12 and 18 months.

stranger anxiety   A fear of strangers common in infants at about 6 or 7 months of age, which increases in intensity until about $12\frac{1}{2}$ months and then declines.

Table 8.4 Attachment Patterns

Pattern	Prevalence	Description
Secure	About 65% of infants	Infants show distress on separation from mother and happiness when mother returns; use mother as safe base for exploration.
Avoidant	About 20% of infants	Infants do not show distress when mother leaves and are indifferent when mother returns.
Resistant	Approximately 10% of infants	Infants may cling to mother before she leaves and show anger when mother returns; may push mother away; do not explore environment when mother is present; difficult to comfort when upset.
Disorganized/ Disoriented	About 5% of infants	Infants may show distress when mother leaves and alternate between happiness, indifference, and anger when mother returns; often look away from mother or look at her with expressionless face.

▲ What are some of the benefits of a secure attachment?

Secure attachment is the most common pattern across cultures. However, cross-cultural research revealed a higher incidence of insecure attachment in Israel, Japan, and West Germany than in the United States (Collins & Gunnar, 1990). Thus, Ainsworth's procedure may not be valid for all cultures.

Origins and Significance of Attachment Differences. Some studies show that depression in the mother is related to insecure attachment (Hipwell et al., 2000). Infant temperament is associated with attachment quality as well (Szewczyk-Sokolowski, Bost, & Wainwright, 2005). Easy infants are more likely to be securely attached than are difficult or slow-to-warm-up babies.

Other researchers have studied infant-caregiver attachment in foster families. In these settings, the primary factor affecting attachment seems to be the age of the infant at the time of placement in a foster home. Children who were less than 1 year old at the time of placement tended to develop secure attachments, whereas those who were older than 1 year at placement were more likely to develop insecure attachments (Stovall and Dozier, 2000).

Variations in the quality of infant attachment persist into adulthood and predict behavior (Tideman et al., 2002). In childhood and adolescence, securely attached infants are likely to be more socially competent than less securely attached infants (Weinfield et al., 1997). Their interactions with friends tend to be more harmonious and less controlling (Park & Waters, 1989). Attachment style also seems to have an impact on the quality of adult love relationships (Collins, 1996). In addition, secure attachment seems to protect infants from the potentially adverse effects of risk factors such as poverty (Belsky & Fearon, 2002). And parents who were securely attached infants are more responsive to their own babies (van IJzendoorn, 1995).

The Father-Child Relationship

8.11 How do fathers affect children's development?

Father-child interactions have enduring influences on children. On the negative side, children whose fathers exhibit antisocial behavior, such as deceitfulness and aggression, are more likely to demonstrate such behavior themselves (Jaffee et al., 2003). More often, though, fathers exert a positive influence on their children's development. For instance, children who experience regular interaction with their fathers tend to have higher IQs and to do better in social situations and at coping with frustration than children lacking such interaction. They also persist longer in solving problems and are less impulsive and less likely to become violent (Adler, 1997; Bishop & Lane, 2000; Roberts & Moseley, 1996). Positive father-son relationships are also associated with parenting behavior by sons when they have children of their own (Shears et al., 2002). In other words, research supports the commonsense notion that fathers serve as important role models for the fathering skills that will be exhibited by their sons later in life.

Because the effects of fathers on children's development are generally positive, father absence is associated with many undesirable developmental outcomes. For example, children in homes without fathers experience poorer school performance, lower grade point average, lower school attendance, and higher dropout rate. Father absence is also related to children's reduced self-confidence in problem solving, low self-esteem, depression, suicidal thoughts, and behavioral problems such as aggression and delinquency (Bishop & Lane, 2000). And, for girls, father absence predicts early sexual behavior and teenage pregnancy (Ellis et al., 2003).

▲ Fathers tend to engage in more physical play with their children than mothers. However, many fathers today share basic child-care responsibilities, such as feeding and diaper changing, with mothers.

The presence or absence of the father may affect development because mothers and fathers interact differently with infants and children. In general, fathers do not appear to be as affectionate as mothers (Berndt et al., 1993; Hoosain & Roopnarine, 1994). However, fathers engage in more exciting and arousing physical play with children (McCormick & Kennedy, 2000). Mothers are more likely to cushion their children against overstimulation, while fathers tend to pour it on, producing a wider range of arousal. Fathers tend "to get children worked up, negatively or positively, with fear as well as delight, forcing them to learn to regulate their feelings" (Lamb, quoted in Roberts & Moseley, 1996, p. 53).

Some developmentalists believe that fathers are more supportive than mothers of children's confidence and identity development (Moradi, cited in Adler, 1997). A mother may instill a sense of caution in a child, but a father may encourage the child (especially if male) to be more daring. For example, fathers allow infants to crawl farther away, up to twice as far as mothers usually do. And fathers remain farther away as the infant explores novel stimuli and situations. Mothers tend to move in closer when the child confronts the unknown.

Ideally, children need both sets of influences. Moreover, when the mother and the father have a good relationship, fathers tend to spend more time with and interact more with their children (Matta & Knudson-Martin, 2006; Willoughby & Glidden, 1995). However, about 28% of American children live apart from their biological fathers today compared to 17.5% who did in 1960 (U.S. Census Bureau, 2005).

Remember It   Infancy

1. _____ is the main factor in motor development.

2. _____ is better developed at birth than vision.

3. Two-month-old Carter was entranced by the multicolored ball in his crib for a couple of days, but then seemed to lose interest. This phenomenon is called _____.

4. Children who have pleasant moods and positive attitudes toward new situations and people have _____ temperaments.

5. Ainsworth found that most infants showed _____ attachment.

6. Fathers help children develop a sense of _____.

Answers: 1. Maturation; 2. Hearing; 3. habituation; 4. easy; 5. secure; 6. individual identity

Piaget's Theory of Cognitive Development

Can you determine what is happening in this scenario? A parent gives his 3-year-old a cookie. When the child bites into the cookie, it breaks into several pieces. The child begins to cry and complains that his cookie is now "ruined" and demands a new one. The parent responds that the cookie is still the same whether broken or not, but the child is inconsolable until the parent provides him with an intact cookie. Why was the parent unable to convince the 3-year-old that a broken cookie is just as good as an unbroken one? Thanks to the work of Swiss psychologist Jean Piaget (pronounced "PEE-ah-ZHAY"), psychologists have gained insights about how children think and solve problems. After reading this section, see if you can understand why the parent's logic had little effect on the 3-year-old.

Schemes: The Foundation of Cognitive Development

8.12 How did Piaget use the concepts of scheme, assimilation, and accommodation to explain cognitive development?

The primary way in which human knowledge develops, according to Piaget, is through the application of a mental process called organization. Through organization, we use specific experiences to make inferences that can be generalized to new experiences. These inferences result in the construction of schemes—plans of action to be used in similar circumstances. For instance, once you've experienced the series of actions involved in using a fast-food restaurant's drive-through service, you can construct a drive-through scheme and apply it to any such restaurant. Each time you use this scheme at a different restaurant, there will be a few differences from your experience at other places, but the basic plan of action you follow will be the same. The point is that you don't have to start from scratch every time you go to a new fast-food restaurant; the mental process of organization has provided you with a general plan of action—a scheme—to follow.

The essence of cognitive development, for Piaget, is the refinement of schemes. For example, an infant who has had experience playing with rubber balls has constructed a scheme that she uses whenever she encounters a ball-like object. The scheme leads her to expect that anything resembling a ball will bounce. Consequently, when she is presented with a plum, her ball scheme (her mental plan of action to be applied to ball-like objects) leads her to throw the plum to the floor, expecting it to bounce. Piaget used the term assimilation to refer to the mental process by which new objects, events, experiences, and information are incorporated into existing schemes.

Of course, plums don't bounce, so what happens to the ball scheme? According to Piaget, a mental process called equilibration is at work when the results of our actions conflict with our expectations. Equilibration is a characteristic of human intelligence that motivates us to keep our schemes in balance with the realities of the environment. So, when the infant sees that the plum doesn't bounce, her ball scheme changes (although she may try bouncing plums a few more times just to be sure!). This change of scheme will result in a better intellectual adaptation to the real world (a better *equilibrium*, to use Piaget's term), because the revised scheme includes the knowledge that some ball-like objects bounce but others do not. Piaget used the term accommodation for the mental process of modifying existing schemes and creating new ones to incorporate new objects, events, experiences, and information.

Accommodation, however, is not the end of the process. As a result of her discovery that plums don't bounce, the infant will be motivated to experiment on every ball-like object she sees (back to assimilation again) so that she can learn to discriminate between those that bounce and those that don't. The goal of her actions is to add to the scheme a set of rules that can be used to tell the difference between bouncing and non-bouncing balls (accommodation). One such rule might be "if you can eat it, it doesn't bounce." Once a workable set of rules is constructed, her ball scheme will be finished (or *equilibrated*, in Piaget's terms), and she will stop trying to bounce every round ob-

organization   Piaget's term for a mental process that uses specific experiences to make inferences that can be generalized to new experiences.

scheme   A plan of action, based on previous experiences, to be used in similar circumstances.

assimilation   The mental process by which new objects, events, experiences, and information are incorporated into existing schemes.

equilibration   The mental process that motivates humans to keep schemes in balance with the real environment.

accommodation   The mental process of modifying existing schemes and creating new ones in order to incorporate new objects, events, experiences, and information.

Figure 8.5 Assimilation, Accommodation, and Equilibration

(1) Toddler assimilates a ball to her ball scheme. (2)Toddler assimilates a plum to her ball scheme. (3) Toddler accommodates the ball scheme to include the observation that some round objects bounce, but others don't. (4) Toddler seeks to equilibrate her ball scheme through experimentation with other round objects. (5) Toddler achieves equilibration when her scheme for spheres enables her to appropriately assimilate all kinds of round objects.

ject that comes her way. Children develop cognitively through this back-and-forth process of using schemes to act on the world (assimilation), changing them when things don't go as expected (accommodation), and acting on the world with the new schemes until they fit reality (equilibration). **Figure 8.5** shows how an infant's "round object" scheme would change as she discovers the distinguishing characteristics of balls that bounce (e.g. tennis balls) and ball-shaped fruit (e.g. plums).

Piaget's Stages of Cognitive Development

Piaget's primary research method was to observe children in natural settings, formulate hypotheses about their behavior, and devise problems that would allow him to test his hypotheses. He and his research assistants presented these problems to children individually, posing questions to gain insight into how each child thought about a problem and to determine whether he or she could give the right answer. Piaget's problems have been used by thousands of developmental psychologists, working in

8.13 What occurs during each of Piaget's stages of cognitive development?

▶ According to Piaget, this infant has not yet developed object permanence—the understanding that objects continue to exist even when they are out of sight. He makes no attempt to look for the toy after the screen is placed in front of it.

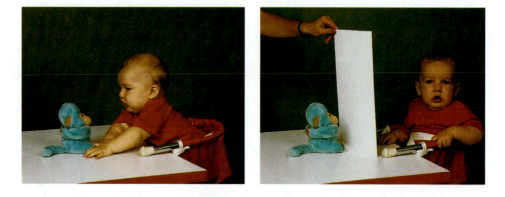

many different cultures. The result of all this research is the discovery that logical thinking in human beings develops in a universal sequence.

Piaget thought of this sequence as a series of universal *stages,* each of which represents a better set of schemes (Piaget, 1963, 1964; Piaget & Inhelder, 1969). In recent years, Piaget's notion of stages, and their relationship to children's ages, has been challenged by other developmentalists. However, the sequence of development for cognitive skills that he first discovered remains one of the most enduring sets of findings in all of psychology. So, before we explore the debate about stages and ages, we will discuss that sequence using Piaget's terminology.

The Sensorimotor Stage (Ages Birth to 2 Years). In the sensorimotor stage, infants gain an understanding of the world through their senses and their motor activities (actions or body movements). The child learns to respond to and manipulate objects and to use them in goal-directed activity. These manipulations are physical at first but become transformed into "mental action" and representational thought in the second half of the stage (Beilin & Fireman, 1999).

The major achievement of the sensorimotor stage is the development of **object permanence,** which is the realization that objects (including people) continue to exist even when they are out of sight. The concept of object permanence develops gradually and is complete when the child is able to represent objects mentally in their absence. The attainment of this ability marks the end of the sensorimotor period.

The Preoperational Stage (Ages 2 to 6 Years). The ability to mentally represent objects at the end of the sensorimotor stage makes it possible for the infant to construct a scheme for symbolic representation—that is, the idea that one thing can stand for another. For example, the word *ball* can stand for all round objects; a half-eaten piece of toast can stand for a car when the infant pushes it around and makes a motor sound; a doll can represent an imaginary baby that may be rocked and fed. The development and refinement of schemes for symbolic representation is the theme of the preoperational stage.

The ability to use symbols greatly advances the child's ability to think beyond what was possible in the sensorimotor stage. However, the child's ability to use logic is still quite restricted. Thinking is dominated by perception, and children at this stage exhibit *egocentrism* in thought. They believe that everyone sees what they see, thinks as they think, and feels as they feel. And they may display *animistic thinking,* the belief that inanimate objects are alive (e.g., "Why is the moon following me?").

The preoperational stage is so named because children are not yet able to perform mental operations (manipulations) that follow logical rules. If you know a child of preschool age and have the parents' permission, try the experiment illustrated in the *Try It* on the next page.

Piaget proposed that young children have difficulty with logic because of a flaw in their thinking that he called **centration,** the tendency to focus on only one dimension of a stimulus. For example, in the *Try It,* the child focuses on the tallness of the glass and fails to notice that it is also narrower. And the child with the broken cookie, discussed earlier, can only think of the cookie in its present state, not the fact that it still has the same mass and makeup as before it broke.

sensorimotor stage Piaget's first stage of cognitive development (ages birth to 2 years), in which infants gain an understanding of their world through their senses and their motor activities; culminates with the development of object permanence and the beginning of representational thought.

object permanence The realization that objects continue to exist even when they are out of sight.

preoperational stage Piaget's second stage of cognitive development (ages 2 to 6 years), which is characterized by the development and refinement of schemes for symbolic representation.

centration A preoperational child's tendency to focus on only one dimension of a stimulus.

Try It   Conservation of Volume

Show a preschooler two glasses of the same size and then fill them with the same amount of juice. After the child agrees they are the same, pour the juice from one glass into a taller, narrower glass and place that glass beside the other original one. Now ask the child if the two glasses have the same amount of juice, or if one glass has more than the other. Children at this stage will in-

sist that the taller, narrower glass has more juice, although they will quickly agree that you neither added juice nor took any away.

Now, repeat the procedure with a school-aged child. The older child will be able to explain that even though there appears to be more liquid in the taller glass, pouring liquid into a different container doesn't change its quantity.

Because of egocentrism and centration, children in the preoperational stage have problems understanding any activity that is governed by rules. Two young children playing a board game may move their pieces around randomly on the board and have little or no sense of what it means to win. The end of the stage is marked by a shift in play preferences that may first be seen in shared pretending. A group of children playing "house" may make up rules such as "the smallest one has to be the baby."

Another piece of evidence that a child is leaving this stage is his realization that costumes and masks don't change his identity. A 3-year-old may be frightened by seeing himself in a mirror wearing a Halloween mask. He may be unsure as to whether the mask causes him to temporarily become the character it represents. By contrast, most 5-year-olds think masks are fun because they know that changing their outward appearance doesn't change who they are on the inside. Piaget would say that they are beginning to make the transition to a more mature form of thought.

The Concrete Operations Stage (Ages 6 to 11 or 12 Years). In the third stage, the **concrete operations stage,** children gradually construct schemes that allow them to *decenter* their thinking—that is, to attend to two or more dimensions of a stimulus at the same time. These schemes also allow them to understand **reversibility,** the fact that when only the appearance of a substance has been changed, it can be returned to its original state. So, the child in this stage who works on the problem in the *Try It* can think about both the height and the width of the liquid in the two containers and can mentally return the poured juice to the original glass. As a result, the child realizes that the two glasses of juice are equal, a concept Piaget called **conservation**—the understanding that a given quantity of matter (a given number, mass, area, weight, or volume of matter) remains the same if it is rearranged or changed in its appearance, as long as nothing is added or taken away. Children's ability to apply concrete operational schemes to different kinds of quantities develops gradually (see **Figure 8.6**).

concrete operations stage
Piaget's third stage of cognitive development (ages 6 to 11 or 12 years), during which a child acquires the concepts of reversibility and conservation and is able to attend to two or more dimensions of a stimulus at the same time.

reversibility   The fact that when only the appearance of a substance has been changed, it can be returned to its original state.

conservation   The understanding that a given quantity of matter remains the same if it is rearranged or changed in its appearance, as long as nothing is added or taken away.

Figure 8.6 Piaget's Conservation Tasks

Piaget's research involved several kinds of conservation tasks. He classified children's thinking as concrete operational with respect to a particular task if they could correctly solve the problem and provide a concrete operational reason for their answer. For example, if a child said, "The two circles of marbles are the same because you didn't add any or take any away when you moved them," the response was judged to be concrete operational. Conversely, if a child said, "The two circles are the same, but I don't know why," the response was not classified as concrete operational.

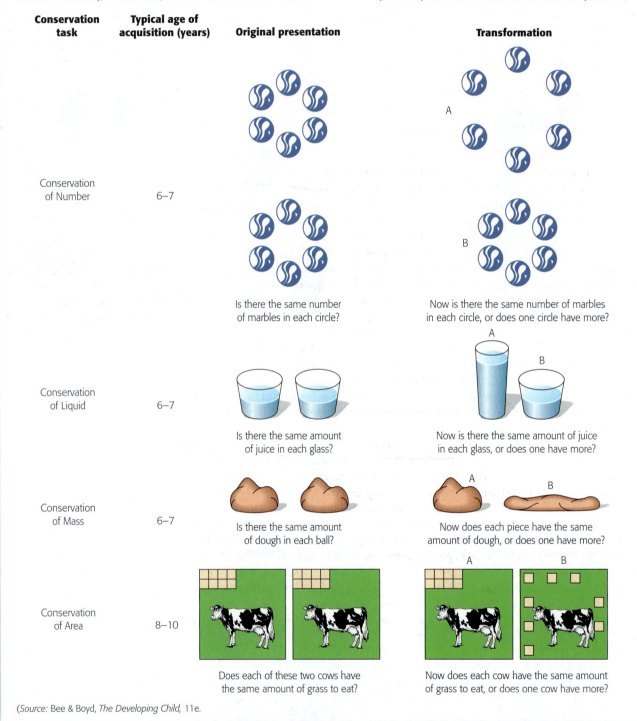

Conservation task	Typical age of acquisition (years)	Original presentation	Transformation
Conservation of Number	6–7	Is there the same number of marbles in each circle?	Now is there the same number of marbles in each circle, or does one circle have more?
Conservation of Liquid	6–7	Is there the same amount of juice in each glass?	Now is there the same amount of juice in each glass, or does one have more?
Conservation of Mass	6–7	Is there the same amount of dough in each ball?	Now does each piece have the same amount of dough, or does one have more?
Conservation of Area	8–10	Does each of these two cows have the same amount of grass to eat?	Now does each cow have the same amount of grass to eat, or does one cow have more?

(*Source:* Bee & Boyd, *The Developing Child*, 11e.)

Children at this stage, however, are able to apply logical operations only to problems that can be tested in the real world. For example, consider this deductive reasoning problem: If John has three apples, and Lucy has two, how many do they have together? A child can verify a proposed solution of "five" by taking three objects, combining them with two others, and counting the total. Now, consider a deductive problem that cannot be tested in the real world: If Farmer Brown has three green sheep, and one of them is named Suzie, what color is Suzie? Given this problem, a child in Piaget's concrete operations stage is likely to say that Suzie is white or gray or that he or she doesn't know the answer. The child may also propose a concrete explanation for the color of the sheep: "Suzie is green because she's been rolling around in the grass" (Rosser, 1994). The child's confusion results from the fact that there are no green sheep in the real world. Thus, even though children in this stage are quite good at applying logical schemes to problems with real-world referents, they can't yet think logically about hypothetical or abstract problems. In fact, according to Piaget, when children can respond correctly to problems with unreal elements like green sheep, they have equilibrated the concrete operations stage and are moving on to the next one.

The Formal Operations Stage (Ages 11 or 12 Years and Beyond). To get beyond the concrete operations stage, children must construct a scheme that allows them to coordinate present reality with other possible realities. Let's say, for example, that Joe is a 16-year-old who doesn't have a car but who imagines himself buying one. Of course, when he was younger, he could imagine owning a car. However, he couldn't construct a mental bridge between the reality of not having a car and the imagined goal of getting one that would actually result in his owning a car. The schemes of Piaget's fourth and final stage, the **formal operations stage,** allow him to do so. Joe can use these schemes to apply logical thinking to a series of hypothetical propositions that will result in a plan for buying a car: "If I get a job that pays $X \ldots$; if I save all my money for X months $\ldots$; if I can find a car for X amount of money $\ldots$," and so on. Joe's plan may be flawed because of his lack of financial experience, but it will be a plan that is far superior, in a logical sense, to any he might have constructed a few years earlier.

Because of their ability to construct an imaginary reality that is linked to present reality, adolescents exhibit types of thinking that are virtually nonexistent in younger children. One is the kind of thinking required for scientific experimentation. Adolescents can formulate a hypothesis and devise a way of testing it: "I think Jennifer likes me. I'll say 'hi' to her at lunch today, and, if she smiles at me, I'll know she likes me."

Even though formal operational schemes represent a huge leap in cognitive development, they still must be put to work in the real world (just like the infant's ball scheme) in order to become equilibrated. Teenagers' attempts to do this have varying results. Teens display a type of thinking Piaget called *naive idealism* (Piaget & Inhelder, 1969) when they come up with elaborate plans to end world hunger or to achieve total disarmament. Naive idealism may also be evident in their personal plans, as when two 17-year-olds plan to marry immediately after high school graduation and use their earnings from their minimum wage jobs both to live on and to attend college. Adults have a hard time convincing adolescents that they are wrong because the plans are so perfectly worked out in the adolescents' own minds. Did you construct any seemingly perfect plan in your teen years that didn't go quite as you thought it would when you tried to put it into action?

Another manifestation of teenagers' newly constructed formal operational schemes is *adolescent egocentrism* (Elkind, 1967, 1974). Do you remember, as a teenager, picturing how your friends would react to the way you looked when you made your grand entrance at a big party? At this stage of life, it never occurs to teens that most of the people at the party are preoccupied not with others, but with the way they themselves look and the impression they are making. This *imaginary audience* of admirers (or critics) that adolescents conjure up exists only in their imagination, "but in the young person's mind, he/she is always on stage" (Buis & Thompson, 1989, p. 774).

▲ Formal operational thinking enables teenagers to create an "imaginary audience" in their minds. What thoughts do you think are running through this teenaged girl's mind as she contemplates the reaction of an imaginary peer audience to her appearance?

formal operations stage Piaget's fourth and final stage of cognitive development (ages 11 or 12 years and beyond), which is characterized by the ability to apply logical thinking to abstract problems and hypothetical situations.

Teenagers also have an exaggerated sense of their own uniqueness, known as the *personal fable*. They cannot fathom that anyone has ever felt as deeply as they feel or has ever loved as they love. Some psychologists claim that this compelling sense of personal uniqueness may cause adolescents to believe that they are somehow indestructible and protected from the misfortunes that befall others, such as unwanted pregnancies, auto accidents, or drug overdoses. However, research suggests that the personal fable may also lead to exaggerated estimates of risk (Quadrel et al., 1993). For the formal operational teenager, hypothesized reality, whether good or bad, is the basis for many behavioral choices.

Piaget's stages of cognitive development are summarized in the *Review and Reflect* below.

Review and Reflect   Piaget's Stages of Cognitive Development

Stage		Description
Sensorimotor (0 to 2 years)		Infants experience the world through their senses, actions, and body movements. At the end of this stage, toddlers develop the concept of object permanence and can mentally represent objects in their absence.
Preoperational (2 to 6 years)		Children are able to represent objects and events mentally with words and images. They can engage in imaginary play (pretend), using one object to represent another. Their thinking is dominated by their perceptions, and they are unable to consider more than one dimension of an object at the same time (centration). Their thinking is egocentric; that is, they fail to consider the perspective of others.
Concrete operations (6 to 11 or 12 years)		Children at this stage become able to think logically in concrete situations. They acquire the concepts of conservation and reversibility, can order objects in a series, and can classify them according to multiple dimensions.
Formal operations (11 or 12 years and beyond)		At this stage, adolescents learn to think logically in abstract situations, learn to test hypotheses systematically, and become interested in the world of ideas. Not all people attain full formal operational thinking.

An Evaluation of Piaget's Contribution

8.14 What are some important criticisms of Piaget's work?

Although Piaget's genius and his monumental contribution to scientists' knowledge of mental development are rarely disputed, some of his findings and conclusions have been criticized.

Piaget's Methods. Today's developmental psychologists point out that Piaget relied on observation and on the interview technique, which depends on verbal responses. Newer techniques requiring nonverbal responses—sucking, looking, heart-rate changes, reaching, and head turning—have shown that infants and young children are more competent than Piaget proposed (Flavell, 1992; Johnson, 2000). For example, recent research indicates that an infant's knowledge of hidden objects may be more advanced than Piaget originally believed (Hespos & Baillargeon, 2006; Johnson et al., 2003; Mareschal, 2000). And there is some evidence that awareness of object permanence may begin as early as 3 $\frac{1}{2}$ months (Baillargeon & DeVos, 1991).

Critique of Stages. Few developmental psychologists believe that cognitive development takes place in the general stagelike fashion proposed by Piaget. If it did, children's cognitive functioning would be similar across all cognitive tasks and content areas (Flavell, 1992). *Neo-Piagetians* believe that there are important general patterns in cognitive development, but there is also more variability in how children perform on certain tasks than Piaget described (Case, 1992). This variability results from expertise children acquire in different content areas through extensive practice and experience (Flavell, 1992). Even adults who use formal operational reasoning fall back on concrete operational thinking when they approach a task outside their areas of expertise.

Cross-Cultural Research. Cross-cultural studies have verified the sequence of cognitive development, but they have also revealed differences in the rate of such development. Whereas the children in Piaget's research began to acquire the concept of conservation between ages 5 and 7, Australian Aboriginal children show this change between the ages of 10 and 13 (Dasen, 1994). Yet the Aboriginal children function at the concrete operations stage earlier on spatial tasks than on quantification (counting) tasks, and the reverse is true for Western children.

Formal Operational Thought. Another criticism comes from research showing that formal operational thought is not universal. Not only do many people fail to show formal operational thinking, but those who do attain it usually apply it only in those areas in which they are most proficient (Ault, 1983; Martorano, 1977). And in non-Western cultures, some studies of adults have found no evidence of formal operational thinking. Consequently, some psychologists have suggested that formal operational thought may be more a product of formal education and specific learning experiences than of a universal developmental process, as Piaget hypothesized.

According to Flavell (1996), "Piaget's greatest contribution was to found the field of cognitive development as we currently know it" (p. 200). And Piaget's theories remain works in progress because of their continuing impact on psychology and education (Beilin & Fireman, 1999).

Remember It Piaget's Theory of Cognitive Development

1. Which statement reflects Piaget's thinking about the stages of cognitive development?
   a. All people pass through the same stages but not necessarily in the same order.
   b. All people progress through the stages in the same order but not at the same rate.
   c. All people progress through the stages in the same order and at the same rate.
   d. Very bright children sometimes skip stages.

2. Eight-month-old Amala spots a dead bug on the living room floor, picks it up, and puts it in her mouth. She is using the mental process Piaget called _____ .

3. Four-year-old Madeleine rolls a ball of clay into a sausage shape to "make more" clay. Her actions demonstrate that she has not acquired the concept of _____ .

4. Not all individuals reach Piaget's _____ stage.

5. Match the stage with the relevant concept.

   _____ (1) abstract thought
   _____ (2) conservation, reversibility
   _____ (3) object permanence
   _____ (4) egocentrism, centration

   a. sensorimotor stage
   b. preoperational stage
   c. concrete operations stage
   d. formal operations stage

Answers: 1. b; 2. assimilation; 3. conservation; 4. formal operations; 5. (1) d, (2) c, (3) a, (4) b

Other Approaches to Cognitive Development

As you might imagine, developmental psychologists have proposed other ways of looking at cognitive development that differ somewhat from Piaget's approach. Two important frameworks are Vygotsky's sociocultural theory and the information-processing approach.

Vygotsky's Sociocultural View

8.15 In Vygotsky's view, how do private speech and scaffolding contribute to cognitive development?

Have you ever noticed children talking to themselves as they assemble a puzzle or paint a picture? Russian psychologist Lev Vygotsky (1896–1934) believed that this and other spontaneous language behaviors exhibited by children are important to the process of cognitive development. Vygotsky maintained that human infants come equipped with basic skills such as perception, the ability to pay attention, and certain capacities of memory not unlike those of many other animal species (Vygotsky 1934/1986). During the first 2 years of life, these skills grow and develop naturally through direct experiences and interactions with the child's sociocultural world. In due course, children develop the mental ability to represent objects, activities, ideas, people, and relationships in a variety of ways, but primarily through language (speech). With their new ability to represent ideas, activities, and so on through speech, children are often observed "talking to themselves." Vygotsky believed that talking to oneself—*private speech*—is a key component in cognitive development. Through private speech, children can specify the components of a problem and verbalize steps in a process to help them work through a puzzling activity or situation. As young children develop greater competence, private speech fades into barely audible mumbling and muttering, and finally becomes simply thinking.

► This father teaching his daughter to ride a bike is using Vygotsky's technique called *scaffolding*. A parent or teacher provides direct and continuous instruction at the beginning of the learning process and then gradually withdraws from active teaching as the child becomes more proficient at the new task or skill.

Vygotsky saw a strong connection among social experience, speech, and cognitive development. He also maintained that a child's readiness to learn resides within a *zone of proximal development* (*proximal* means "potential"). This zone, according to Vygotsky, is a range of cognitive tasks that the child cannot yet perform alone but can learn to perform with the instruction and guidance of a parent, teacher, or more advanced peer. This kind of help, in which a teacher or parent adjusts the quality and degree of instruction and guidance to fit the child's present level of ability or performance, is often referred to as *scaffolding*. In scaffolding, direct instruction is given, at first, for unfamiliar tasks (Maccoby, 1992). But as the child shows increasing competence, the teacher or parent gradually withdraws from direct and active teaching, and the child may continue toward independent mastery of the task.

The Information-Processing Approach

8.16 What three cognitive abilities have information-processing researchers studied extensively?

The information-processing approach sees the human mind as a system that functions like a computer (see Chapters 1 and 6). Psychologists who use this approach view cognitive development as a gradual process through which specific information-processing skills are acquired, rather than a series of cognitive "leaps," as Piaget's stage theory suggests (Klahr, 1992; Kuhn, 1992). Researchers using the information-processing approach have done extensive work on age-related changes in three cognitive abilities: processing speed, memory, and metacognition.

Processing Speed. Developmental psychologist Robert Kail (Kail & Miller, 2006) has found that processing speed increases dramatically as children move from infancy through childhood. This increase in speed is evident in a number of tasks, including perceptual-motor tasks such as responding quickly to a stimulus (e.g., pushing a button when a tone is heard) and cognitive tasks such as mental arithmetic. Increased processing speed is also associated with improved memory. Thus, age differences in this variable may explain why younger children are less efficient learners than those who are older.

Memory. Short-term memory develops dramatically during an infant's first year. Babies under 8 months of age who watch an object being hidden have trouble remembering its location if they are distracted for a short time and are not allowed to reach for the object immediately—out of sight, out of short-term memory. At 15 months, though, children's short-term memory has developed to the point that they can remember where an object is hidden even when they are not allowed to reach for it until 10 seconds have passed (Bell & Fox, 1992).

Children increasingly use strategies for improving memory as they mature cognitively. One universal strategy for holding information in short-term memory is *rehearsal*, or mentally repeating information over and over. You use rehearsal when you silently repeat a new phone number long enough to dial it. Although certain aspects of rehearsal may be observed in preschoolers, in general, they have not learned how to use this strategy effectively to help them retain information (Bjorklund & Coyle, 1995). Rehearsal becomes a more valuable strategy for storing information by the time children reach age 6, and the majority of children use rehearsal routinely by age 8 (Lovett & Flavell, 1990).

Organization is a very practical strategy for storing information in such a way that it can be retrieved without difficulty. By about age 9, children tend to use organization to help them remember. *Elaboration*, another useful strategy, is not widely used until age 11 or older (Schneider & Pressley, 1989). Elaboration requires creating relationships or connections between items that are to be remembered but have no inherent connection.

Metacognition. A fundamental developmental task for children is coming to understand that people differ greatly in what they know and believe (Miller, 2000). Reaching a level of cognitive maturity in which an individual is aware of his or her own thoughts and has an understanding about how thinking operates involves acquiring what is referred to as a *theory of mind*. More broadly, the process of thinking about how you or others think is known as *metacognition*. We use metacognition when we see ourselves and others as having various mental states such as beliefs, perceptions, and desires (Johnson, 2000). Children learn very young (at about 3 years of age) that people, including themselves, have different mental states during thinking, remembering, forgetting, pretending, wishing, imagining, guessing, and daydreaming. In short, they can distinguish between thinking and other mental states.

Some research suggests that children as young as 18 months of age are aware when adults are imitating their behavior, gestures, or words and have been observed purposely testing the adults to see if the "imitation" will continue (Aspendorf et al., 1996). Children older than $2\frac{1}{2}$ years know the difference between reality and pretending. And 3-year-olds typically know that thinking is an activity that occurs inside one's head and that they can think about something without seeing, hearing, or touching it (Flavell et al., 1995).

Development of theory of mind and metacognition is related to children's language skills: The more advanced they are in language, the greater their ability to think about their own and others' thoughts (Astington & Jenkins, 1999; Deak et al., 2003). Parental statements about others' thoughts appear to bolster children's theory of mind development as well (Ruffman et al., 2006). In addition, theory of mind seems to grow when children engage in shared pretending with others their age (Tan-Niam et al., 1998). The importance of social interactions to metacognition is also illustrated by research showing that children with disorders that interfere with social interactions—such as deafness, autism, and schizophrenia—lag far behind others their age in the development of theory of mind (Jarrold et al., 2000; Lundy, 2002; Pilowsky et al., 2000; Sarfati, 2000).

Language Development

Think about how remarkable it is that, at birth, an infant's only means of communication is crying, but at age 17, an average high school graduate has a vocabulary of 80,000 words (Miller & Gildea, 1987). From age 18 months to 5 years, a child acquires about 14,000 words, an amazing average of 9 new words per day (Rice, 1989). But children do much more than simply add new words to their vocabulary. In the first 5 years of life, they also acquire an understanding of the way words are put together to form sentences (syntax) and the way language is used in social situations.

The Sequence of Language Development

8.17 What is the sequence of language development from babbling through the acquisition of grammatical rules?

Have you ever tried to learn another language? It's difficult, isn't it? Yet children acquire most of their language without any formal teaching and discover the rules of language on their own. They do so during the first 3 years of life, in a sequence shown in Table 8.5. The process begins in the early weeks of life with *cooing,* the familiar "ooh" and "aah" sounds uttered by all babies. At about 6 months, cooing begins to evolve into **babbling.** Babbling is the vocalization of *phonemes,* the basic units of sound in any language. By about 1 year of age, babies have restricted the sounds they utter to those that fit the language they are learning. So a 1-year-old French baby's babbling sounds different from that of a 1-year-old Chinese baby. In fact, babies of this age can no longer hear subtle distinctions between sounds that differentiate the accents of one language from that of another (Werker & Desjardins, 1995). This is why Japanese speakers may have difficulty distinguishing between the [l] and [r] sounds in English.

Sometime during the second year, infants begin to use words to communicate. Single words may function as whole sentences, called *holophrases* by linguists. Depending on the context, an infant who says "cookie" might mean "I want a cookie" or "This is a cookie" or "Where is the cookie?"

Once children know about 50 words, they stop using holophrases and start combining words into two-word sentences. As is true for holophrases, the meanings of these two-word sentences have to be determined using the child's tone of voice, intonation, and the context in which they are spoken as clues. The utterance "eat cookie" may mean many different things.

By the end of the second year, most children use nearly 300 words (Brown, 1973). However, they don't always use them correctly. Sometimes, as when a child uses "doggie" to refer to all four-legged animals, they exhibit **overextension.** They may also display **underextension,** or the failure to apply a word to other members of the class to which it applies. For example, the family beagle is a "doggie," but the German shepherd next door is not.

Children's language advances considerably between 2 and 3 years of age as they begin to use sentences of three words, which linguists call **telegraphic speech** (Brown,

babbling Vocalization of the basic units of sound (phonemes).

overextension The application of a word, on the basis of some shared feature, to a broader range of objects than is appropriate.

underextension The restriction of a word to only a few, rather than to all, members of a class of objects.

telegraphic speech Short sentences that follow a rigid word order and contain only three or so essential content words.

Table 8.5 Language Development during the First 3 Years of Life

Age	Language Activity
2–3 months	Makes cooing sounds when alone; responds with smiles and cooing when talked to.
20 weeks	Mixes various vowel and consonant sounds with cooing.
6 months	Babbles; utters phonemes of all languages.
8 months	Focuses on the phonemes, rhythm, and intonation of native tongue.
12 months	Says single words; mimics sounds; understands some words.
18–20 months	Uses two-word sentences; has vocabulary of about 50 words; overextension common.
24 months	Has vocabulary of about 270 words; acquires suffixes and function words in a fixed sequence.
30 months	Uses telegraphic speech.
36 months	Begins acquisition of grammar rules; overregularization common.

1973). These short sentences follow a rigid word order and contain only essential content words, leaving out plurals, possessives, conjunctions, articles, and prepositions. Telegraphic speech reflects the child's understanding of *syntax*—the rules governing how words are ordered in a sentence. When a third word is added to a sentence, it is usually the word missing from the two-word sentence (for example, "Mama eat cookie").

After age 3, children experience a phase linguists refer to as the *grammar explosion*, meaning that they acquire the grammatical rules of language very rapidly. Most become fluent speakers by about age 5. But they still make errors. One kind of error is **overregularization,** which happens when children inappropriately apply grammatical rules for forming plurals and past tenses to irregular nouns and

▲ Children exhibit overextension when they refer to all four-legged animals as "doggie" or "kitty."

verbs. For example, a 3-year-old might say "I breaked my cookie," to which the parent replies "You mean you broke your cookie." In response, the child overcorrects and says "I broked it" or even "I brokeded it." Sometimes, parents and teachers worry about overregularization errors, but they actually represent an advance in language development since they indicate that a child has acquired some grammatical rules. Through observation and practice, the child will learn which words do not follow the rules.

Theories of Language Development

Exactly how does language development happen? The same sequence of language development can be found in every culture in the world, but there has been considerable debate about how best to explain it.

Learning Theory. Learning theorists have long maintained that language is acquired in the same way as other behaviors are acquired—as a result of learning through reinforcement and imitation. B. F. Skinner (1957) asserted that language is shaped through reinforcement. He claimed that parents selectively criticize incorrect speech and reinforce correct speech through praise, approval, and attention. Thus, the child's utterances are progressively shaped in the direction of grammatically correct speech. Others believe that children acquire vocabulary and sentence construction mainly through imitation (Bandura, 1977a).

8.18 How do learning theory and the nativist position explain the acquisition of language?

overregularization The act of inappropriately applying the grammatical rules for forming plurals and past tenses to irregular nouns and verbs.

▲ Deaf mothers use sign language to communicate with their young children, but they do so in *motherese*, signing slowly and with frequent repetitions.

Problems arise, however, when learning theory is considered the sole explanation for language acquisition. Imitation cannot account for patterns of speech such as telegraphic speech or for systematic errors such as overregularization. Children do not hear telegraphic speech in everyday life, and "I comed" and "he goed" are not forms commonly used by parents. There are also problems with reinforcement as the major cause of language acquisition. Parents seem to reward children more for the content of the utterance than for the correctness of the grammar (Brown et al., 1968). And parents are much more likely to correct children for saying something untrue than for making a grammatical error.

The Nativist Position. The nativist view asserts that the language learning process is an inborn characteristic of all members of the human species, quite similar to the developmental sequence of motor milestones you read about earlier in this chapter (Lenneberg, 1967). For the nativists, the only environmental factor required for language development is the presence of language. Neither instruction nor reinforcement is necessary.

Nativist and linguist Noam Chomsky (1968) maintains that the brain contains a *language acquisition device (LAD),* which enables children to sort the stream of speech they hear around them in ways that allow them to discover grammar rules. So, a child listening to English quickly figures out that adjectives (such as *big*) usually precede the nouns they describe (such as *house*). By contrast, a child learning Spanish infers the opposite, the noun *casa* comes before the adjective *grande*.

Chomsky also suggests that the LAD determines the sequence of language development—babbling at about 6 months, the one-word stage at about 1 year, and the two-word stage at 18 to 20 months. In fact, although English- and Spanish-speaking children learn different rules for adjective-noun order, they apply those rules to their own speech at the same point in their development. Thus, the universality of the sequence of language development supports the nativist view. Morever, research demonstrating that deaf children exposed to sign language from birth proceed along the same schedule also supports this view (Meier, 1991; Petitto & Marentette, 1991).

Nature and Nurture: An Interactionist Perspective. The interactionist perspective acknowledges the importance of both learning and an inborn capacity for acquiring language (MacWhinney, 2005). One's first language, after all, is acquired in a social setting, where the experiences one has must have some influence on language development. And, of course, heredity plays a role in every human capability.

Recent research reveals that language learning proceeds in a piecewise fashion, which calls into question the assumptions of Chomsky's nativist approach (Tomasello, 2000). Children learn the concrete language expressions they hear around them, and then they imitate and build on those. One way parents support the language-learning process is by adjusting their speech to their infant's level of development. Parents often use *motherese*—highly simplified speech with shorter phrases and sentences and simpler vocabulary, which is uttered slowly, at a high pitch, and with exaggerated intonation and much repetition (Fernald, 1993). Deaf mothers communicate with their infants in a similar way, signing more slowly and with exaggerated hand and arm movements and frequent repetition (Masataka, 1996).

phonological awareness
Sensitivity to the sound patterns of a language and how they are represented as letters.

Learning to Read

8.19 What is phonological awareness, and why is it important?

Learning spoken language seems to be largely a natural process, but what about learning to understand written language? As you might expect, many aspects of the development of spoken language are critical to the process of learning to read. **Phonological awareness,** or sensitivity to the sound patterns of a language and how they are represented as letters, is particularly important. Children who can answer questions such as "What would *bat* be if you took away the [b]?" by the age of 4 or so learn to read more rapidly than peers who cannot (de Jong & van der Leij, 2002). Moreover, children who have good phonological awareness skills in their first language learn to read more easily even if reading instruction takes place in an entirely new language (McBride-Chang & Treiman, 2003; Mumtaz & Humphreys, 2002; Quiroga et al., 2002). And blind children who have poor phonological awareness skills are slower at learning to read Braille than are their peers with better skills (Gillon & Young, 2002).

Children seem to learn phonological awareness skills through word play. Among English-speaking children, learning nursery rhymes facilitates the development of these skills (Layton et al., 1996). Japanese parents foster phonological awareness in their children by playing a game called *shiritori*, in which one person says a word and another must supply a word that begins with its ending sound (Serpell & Hatano, 1997). Activities in which parents and children work together to read or write a story also foster the development of phonological awareness (Aram & Levitt, 2002).

The formal reading instruction that children receive when they start school helps them improve their phonological awareness skills (Shu et al., 2000). Once children have mastered the basic symbol-sound decoding process, they become better readers by learning about root words, suffixes, and prefixes (Nagy, Berninger, & Abbott, 2006). Teachers also facilitate the development of reading comprehension by helping children learn skills such as identifying the main idea of a passage or story (Pressley & Wharton-McDonald, 1997). Moreover, at every stage in the process, children benefit from exposure to good stories, both those they read on their own and those that are read to them by parents and teachers.

▲ Reading to children and engaging them in word play helps them acquire phonological awareness.

Remember It   Language Development

1. Match each utterance with the linguistic term that describes it.

   _____ (1) "ba-ba-ba"
   _____ (2) "He eated the cookies."
   _____ (3) "Mama see ball."
   _____ (4) "oo," "ah"
   _____ (5) "kitty," meaning a lion
   _____ (6) "ball," meaning "look at the ball"

   a. telegraphic speech
   b. holophrase
   c. overregularization
   d. babbling
   e. overextension
   f. cooing

2. The nativist position suggests that language ability is largely _____.

3. When asked to supply a word that rhymes with *cat*, 3-year-old Jenny says "hat." Jenny's response indicates that she has developed _____.

Answers: 1. (1) d, (2) c, (3) a, (4) f, (5) e, (6) b; 2. innate; 3. phonological awareness

Social Development

To function effectively and comfortably in society, children must acquire the patterns of behavior considered to be desirable and appropriate. The process of learning socially acceptable behaviors, attitudes, and values is called **socialization.** Although parents play the major role in socialization, peers, school, the media, and religion are also important influences.

socialization The process of learning socially acceptable behaviors, attitudes, and values.

The Parents' Role in the Socialization Process

Have you ever read William Golding's novel *Lord of the Flies*? The story implies that, without adult influence, children will grow up to be ignorant of important facts about the natural and social world, subject to superstitious beliefs, cruel to one another, and highly aggressive. Do you agree with this view?

Most people, whether laypersons or psychologists, believe that parents' role in the socialization process is to set examples, to teach, and to provide discipline. Research supports this view and has demonstrated that parents are usually most effective when

8.20 What are the three parenting styles identified by Baumrind, and which does she find most effective?

▲ What aspect of authoritative parenting might this mother be demonstrating?

they are loving, warm, nurturing, and supportive (Maccoby & Martin, 1983). In fact, a longitudinal study that followed individuals from age 5 to age 41 revealed that "children of warm, affectionate parents were more likely to be socially accomplished adults who, at age 41, were mentally healthy, coping adequately, and psychosocially mature in work, relationships, and generativity" (Franz et al., 1991, p. 593). Families are dysfunctional when the roles are reversed, and the children nurture and control their parents (Maccoby, 1992).

To be effective, socialization must ultimately result in children having the ability to regulate their own behavior. The attainment of this goal is undermined when parents control their children's behavior by asserting power over them (Maccoby, 1992). Diane Baumrind (1971, 1980, 1991) studied the continuum of parental control and identified three parenting styles: authoritarian, authoritative, and permissive. She related these styles to different patterns of behavior in predominantly White, middle-class children.

Authoritarian Parents. Authoritarian parents make arbitrary rules, expect unquestioned obedience from their children, punish misbehavior (often physically), and value obedience to authority. Rather than giving a rationale for a rule, authoritarian parents consider "because I said so" a sufficient reason for obedience. Parents using this style tend to be uncommunicative, unresponsive, and somewhat distant. Baumrind (1967) found preschool children disciplined in this manner to be withdrawn, anxious, and unhappy.

Parents' failure to provide a rationale for rules makes it hard for children to see any reason for following them. Saying "Do it because I said so" or "Do it, or you'll be punished" may succeed in making the child do what is expected when the parent is present, but it is ineffective when the parent is not around. The authoritarian style has been associated with low intellectual performance and lack of social skills, especially in boys (Maccoby & Martin, 1983). However, research suggests that there are some circumstances in which authoritarian parenting is beneficial to children's development. For instance, children of authoritarian parents who live in impoverished neighborhoods display more favorable developmental outcomes than their peers whose parents are more permissive (Steinberg, Blatt-Eisengart, & Cauffman, 2006).

Authoritative Parents. Authoritative parents set high but realistic and reasonable standards, enforce limits, and, at the same time, encourage open communication and independence. They are willing to discuss rules and supply rationales for them. Knowing why the rules are necessary makes it easier for children to internalize them and to follow them, whether their parents are present or not. Authoritative parents are generally warm, nurturing, supportive, and responsive, and they show respect for their children and their opinions. Their children are usually mature, happy, self-reliant, self-controlled, assertive, socially competent, and responsible. The authoritative parenting style is associated with higher academic performance, independence, higher self-esteem, and internalized moral standards in middle childhood and adolescence (Aunola et al., 2000; Lamborn et al., 1991; Steinberg et al., 1989).

The positive effects of authoritative parenting have been found across all ethnic groups in the United States (Querido et al., 2002; Steinberg, Blatt-Eisengart, & Cauffman, 2006; Steinberg & Dornbusch, 1991). The one exception is that the authoritarian style is more strongly associated with academic achievement among first-generation Asian immigrants (Chao, 2001). Developmental psychologist Ruth Chao suggests that this finding may be explained by the traditional idea in Asian culture that making a child obey is an act of affection. Moreover, strict parenting tends to be tem-

authoritarian parents Parents who make arbitrary rules, expect unquestioned obedience from their children, punish misbehavior, and value obedience to authority.

authoritative parents Parents who set high but realistic and reasonable standards, enforce limits, and encourage open communication and independence.

pered by emotional warmth in Asian families, so the children probably get the idea that their parents expect unquestioning obedience because they love them (Chao, 2001).

Permissive Parents. Although they are rather warm and supportive, **permissive parents** make few rules or demands and usually do not enforce those that are made. They allow children to make their own decisions and control their own behavior. Children raised in this manner are often immature, impulsive, and dependent, and they seem to have less self-control and be less self-reliant (Steinberg, Blatt-Eisengart, & Cauffman, 2006).

Neglecting Parents. Based on their own research, developmental psychologists Eleanor Maccoby and John Martin (1983) identified a fourth parenting style, in addition to the three proposed by Baumrind. **Neglecting parents** are permissive and are not involved in their children's lives. Infants of neglecting parents are more likely than others to be insecurely attached and to continue to experience difficulties in social relationships throughout childhood and into their adult years. Lack of parental monitoring during adolescence places children of neglecting parents at increased risk of becoming delinquent, of using drugs or alcohol, or of engaging in sexual activity in the early teen years (Maccoby & Martin, 1983; Patterson et al., 1992; Pittman & Chase-Lansdale, 2001).

permissive parents Parents who make few rules or demands and usually do not enforce those that are made; they allow children to make their own decisions and control their own behavior.

neglecting parents Parents who are permissive and are not involved in their children's lives.

Peer Relationships

The stereotypical view of peer influence is that it is negative. But is this belief justified? Probably not. For one thing, interest in peers seems to be an innate response. Infants begin to show an interest in each other at a very young age. At only 6 months of age, they already demonstrate an interest in other infants by looking, reaching, touching, smiling, and vocalizing (Vandell & Mueller, 1980). Friendships begin to develop by 3 or 4 years of age, and relationships with peers become increasingly important. These early relationships are usually based on shared activities; two children think of themselves as friends while they are playing together. By middle childhood, friendships tend to be based on mutual trust (Dunn et al., 2002), and membership in a peer group is usually seen as central to a child's happiness. Peer groups are usually composed of children of the same race, sex, and social class (Schofield & Francis, 1982). Moreover, during the school years, peer groups tend to be homogeneous with regard to academic achievement (Chen et al., 2003).

8.21 How do peers contribute to the socialization process?

The peer group serves a socializing function by providing models of behavior, dress, and language. It is a continuing source of both reinforcement for appropriate behavior and punishment for deviant behavior. The peer group also provides an objective measure against which children can evaluate their own traits and abilities—how smart or how good at sports they are, for example. In their peer groups, children learn how to get along with age-mates—how to share and cooperate, develop social skills, and regulate aggression.

Physical attractiveness is a major factor in peer acceptance even in children as young as 3 to 5, although it seems to be more important for girls than for boys (Krantz, 1987; Langlois, 1985). Negative traits are often inappropriately attributed to unattractive children. Athletic

▲ Children who are rejected or neglected by their peers are at risk of developing feelings of loneliness, unhappiness, and alienation.

ability and academic success in school are also valued by the peer group. The more popular children are usually energetic, happy, cooperative, sensitive, and thoughtful. Popular children have social skills that lead to positive social outcomes and facilitate the goals of their peers. But they are also able to be assertive and aggressive when the situation calls for it (Murphy & Faulkner, 2006; Newcomb et al., 1993). Popular children tend to have parents who use an authoritative parenting style (Dekovic & Janssens, 1992).

Low acceptance by peers can be an important predictor of later mental health problems (Kupersmidt et al., 1990). Most often excluded from the peer group are neglected children, who are shy and withdrawn, and rejected children, who typically exhibit aggressive and inappropriate behavior and who are likely to start fights (Dodge, Cole, et al., 1990). Rejection by peers is linked to feelings of loneliness, unhappiness, alienation, and poor achievement; in middle childhood, it is linked with delinquency and dropping out of school (Asher & Paquette, 2003; Gazelle & Ladd, 2003; Kupersmidt & Coie, 1990; Parker & Asher, 1987).

Television as a Socializing Agent

8.22 What are some of the positive and negative effects of television?

How important was television to you when you were growing up? For most children in the industrialized world, television is a powerful influence. We discussed the impact of televised aggression on children in Chapter 5 in the context of Bandura's theory of observational learning. Here, we turn our attention to the other aspects of television's effects on learning and development.

Cognitive Effects. You may have watched the program *Sesame Street* when you were a young child. With the program now approaching the ripe old age of 40, hundreds of studies have documented its positive effects on cognitive development (Augustyn, 2003). Although the program's educational content targets 3- and 4-year-olds, studies

show that it and other such educational shows (e.g., *Dora the Explorer*, *Blues Clues*) have positive effects on toddlers' cognitive development as well (Linebarger & Walker, 2005). However, there is also evidence showing that children younger than age 3 pay attention to different elements of programs than older preschoolers do (Valkenberg & Vroone, 2004). Thus, programming developed with the viewing characteristics of infants and toddlers in mind might be a more effective means of enhancing their cognitive development.

An increasing number of programs and videos for the under-2 viewing audience have appeared in the past decade (e.g., *Barney, Sesame Beginnings, Baby Einstein*). Despite the popularity of these programs and videos, the American Academy of Pediatrics (AAP) continues to recommend that children watch no television whatsoever until they are at least 2 years of age (AAP, 2002). Their position was supported by a study linking early television viewing to the development of attention deficit/hyperactivity disorder (ADHD) later in childhood (Christakis, Zimmerman, DiGiuseppe, & McCarty, 2004). However, the study was a correlational one in which a measure of behavior (time watching television) at one age was used to predict another measure of behavior (ADHD scale scores) at a later age. As such, its interpretation was subject to all the usual limitations of any correlational study. Further research is required before any definitive conclusions can be drawn regarding the possible long-term effects of television on children's attention processes.

▲ Although the American Association of Pediatrics recommends that children do not watch television until after age 2, videos and television programs aimed at infants and toddlers have become increasingly popular over the last few years.

Social and Emotional Development. Recall from Chapter 5 that there is a substantial amount of evidence showing that children imitate the aggressive behavior of models they view on television. However, there is also a large body of evidence suggesting that television programs specifically designed to teach prosocial behavior can positively affect children's social development (Mares & Woodard, 2005). One such program was found to be an effective strategy for decreasing ethnic stereotyping among Israeli and Palestinian children (Cole et al., 2003).

Nevertheless, the research literature contains hints that television can have undesirable effects on children's emotions. Studies involving children who had no direct connection to the September 11 terrorist attacks, for example, have found that children who have seen videos of the attacks on television worry about the possibility that a similar attack will be perpetrated on their own cities (Lengua, Long, Smith, & Meltzoff, 2005). Thus, some experts argue that when children view such events on television prior to an age at which they are cognitively capable of understanding them, it causes the youngsters to view the world as a frightening, unpredictable place.

Moreover, developmental psychologists have found that children's emotions are easily manipulated by advertising. Children as young as 12 months exhibit positive emotions when researchers present them with toys that they have seen featured in researcher-created television commercials (Mumme & Fernald, 2003). In an apt demonstration of the emotional power of advertising, the son of one of the authors of this textbook responded to a parental refusal to buy a certain type of cereal with this tearful protest: "But the kids on TV look so happy when they eat it. Don't you want me to be happy?" Such reactions are common in children, and raise concerns among both psychologists and parents that television advertising may cause children to develop a worldview in which happiness is linked to material possessions.

Finally, studies show that television viewing is linked to both sleep problems and obesity in children (Owens et al., 2000; Tuncer & Yalcin, 2000). These findings, in combination with the various studies showing negative effects on children's psychological development, suggest that parents should closely monitor their children's viewing habits. If possible, they should strive to ensure that, on balance, the programs their children watch create opportunities for the positive effects of television to outweigh those that are less desirable.

Culture and Child Development

You learned earlier that first-generation Asian immigrants tend to display an authoritarian parenting style because of beliefs rooted in the traditional Asian cultures from which they emigrated. This is one example of the influence of culture on children's development. But just how do such variables as cultural beliefs influence individual children?

The late developmental psychologist Urie Bronfenbrenner (1917–2005) proposes that the environment in which a child grows up is a system of interactive, layered **contexts of development** (Bronfenbrenner, 1979, 1989, 1993). (See **Figure 8.7**). At the core of the system are what he calls *microsystems*, which include settings in which the child has personal experience (e.g., the family). The next layer, known as *exosystems*, includes contexts that the child does not experience directly but that affect the child because of their influence on microsystems (e.g., parents' jobs). Finally, the *macrosystem* includes all aspects of the larger culture.

The ideas and institutions of the macrosystem filter down to the child through the exosystems and microsystems. Bronfenbrenner's explanation of the process can be best understood by using this question as an example: Why do some cultures provide public schools for all children and require them to attend whereas other cultures do not, and how does this cultural difference affect individual children? One reason for cross-cultural variations in schooling might be that, at the level of the macrosystem, societies with public schools believe strongly in the value of education for all people. At the exosystem level, this belief is put into practice when governmental authorities allocate funds for schools and make laws requiring parents to enroll their children. In

8.23 How does Bronfenbrenner explain the influence of culture on children's development?

contexts of development
Bronfenbrenner's term for the interrelated and layered settings (family, neighborhood, culture, etc.) in which a child grows up.

Figure 8.7 Bronfenbrenner's Contexts of Development

Bronfenbrenner's theory proposes that children grow up in an environment of interconnected and layered contexts that have significant effects on their development.

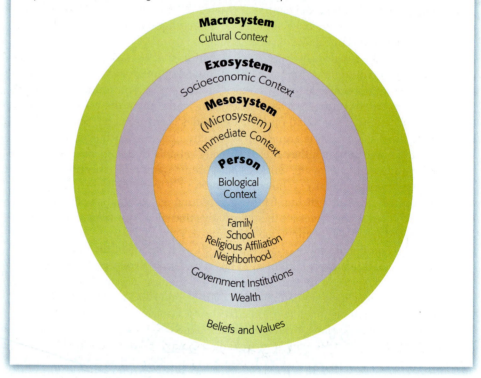

a culture in which there is no such belief, or the belief is present but there are no funds to pay for public education, there will be no schools.

Even so, the microsystem may ultimately determine whether a culture's beliefs and practices regarding education will reach the individual child. In countries without public schools, wealthy parents may send their children to private schools, middle-class parents may pinch pennies to do likewise, and poor parents may do their best to teach their children at home. In countries with a public school system—some parents may choose not to enroll their children, even at the risk of facing legal sanctions. They might do so because they need the children to stay home to care for younger siblings or to do agricultural work. Or they may have ideological reasons for keeping their children at home. A child's own abilities, attitudes, and behaviors may also determine the individual effects of the macrosystem and exosystem. A child who has a learning disability will respond to school differently than a child who doesn't have learning problems. A child's like or dislike of the school environment and her or his ability to behave appropriately in the classroom will also contribute to the impact of schooling on that child's individual development. Conversely, in a culture without public schools, a child who is very curious and determined may find ways to educate herself or himself. Thus, every level of the system is involved in determining whether and how cultural variables affect individual children.

Clearly, the values and decisions associated with each level of Bronfenbrenner's system have a strong and lasting impact on children's development. With regard to schooling, developmental psychologists know that formal education is strongly associated with progression through Piaget's stages of cognitive development as well as with the acquisition of information-processing skills (Mishra, 1997). Children who attend school advance more rapidly through the concrete operations stage and have more memory strategies than do their peers who do not go to school. And, as teens and adults, those with formal education are more likely to develop formal operational thinking. Obviously, children benefit most when all contexts of development work together toward the same goals for them.

Remember It   Social Development

1. Match each approach to discipline with the related parenting style.

_____ (1) expecting unquestioned obedience

_____ (2) setting high standards, giving rationale for rules

_____ (3) setting few rules or limits

_____ (4) lack of involvement in children's lives

a. permissive
b. authoritative
c. authoritarian
d. neglecting

2. The _____ can have either a negative or a positive effect on development.

3. Which is not an effect of television on children?
   a. reducing racial and sexual stereotypes
   b. shortening attention span
   c. contributing to childhood obesity
   d. increasing aggressive behavior through exposure to televised violence

4. Identify each of the following as belonging to one of Bronfenbrenner's contexts of development.

_____ (1) a child's parents

_____ (2) cultural beliefs about punishment

_____ (3) public funding for day care centers

_____ (4) the social status of a family's neighborhood

_____ (5) a racial group's sense of ethnic identity

a. macrosystem
b. exosystem
c. microsystem

Answers: 1. (1) c, (2) b, (3) a, (4) d; 2. peer group; 3. a; 4. (1) c, (2) a, (3) b, (4) b, (5) a

Apply It   Choosing a Nonparental Care Arrangement

Surveys show that most young adults plan to have both a career and a family (Galinsky et al., 2000). One of the most daunting tasks associated with balancing work and family is that of choosing a nonparental care arrangement for an infant or young child. Here is a systematic approach that may help you reduce the stress associated with making this important decision.

Step 1: Define Your Parenting Goals

Child psychologist Sandra Scarr (1997) suggests that nonparental care is best thought of as an extension of your own parenting priorities. Thus, it's worthwhile to spend some time thinking about your parenting goals before you start your search. Think about the kind of home environment you plan to provide for your child's early years and look for the nonparental care arrangement that best matches it.

Step 2: Understand the Limitations of Research

All research on nonparental care is correlational, meaning that it is inappropriate to infer causation. For example, if a study shows that children who attend day care centers get higher scores on vocabulary tests than children who stay at home, there is no way to tell whether the center-based care caused the difference. It may be that working parents engage in more activities that encourage language development than nonworking parents or that they have more money for books, videos, and educational toys. If either is the case, then the observed "effect" of center-based care is really a parenting effect.

Remember, too, that research is based on averages. Familiarity with the research on nonparental care can be immensely helpful in your search for a high-quality arrangement. However, keep in mind that a research finding regarding a developmental outcome that is associated with nonparental care—desirable or undesirable—may or may not turn out to be valid for your child. That's why the next step is so vital.

Step 3: Know Your Child's Temperament and Preferences

Research suggests that temperament interacts with care arrangements (Crockenberg & Leerkes, 2005; Wachs, Gurkas, & Kontos, 2004). For example, slow-to-warm-up children may be overwhelmed by the sheer number of children in a day care center (Watamura et al., 2003). Thus, it helps to know what kind of temperament your child has and the kinds of situations in which she is most comfortable.

A child's likes and dislikes are important as well. For a picky eater, a care arrangement in which the child can have her beloved peanut butter and banana sandwich at every meal may be more practical than a center where she will only be offered food that she will refuse to eat. Similarly, an active child may be happiest in a situation in which children can go outdoors whenever their caregivers sense that they need to burn off some energy.

Step 4: Consider the Research

Despite the limitations of correlational research, the importance of child care to families and to society in general has motivated psychologists to conduct thousands of studies aimed at identifying the differences between high- and low-quality nonparental care (see Feine, 2002 for a summary). Here are a few criteria that most experts recommend taking into account:

- *Health practices*: Take note of hand-washing rules (for both children and caregivers), food-handling practices, and the nutritional quality of meals.
- *Caregiver–child ratio, sensitivity, stability, and training*: Look for a low ratio of adults to children, sensitive responses to children's behavior, low turnover, and formal training requirements for all caregivers.
- *Group size*: Smaller is generally better, especially for infants.
- *Appropriate learning environment*: Look for toys, games, books, activities, and a daily routine that are appropriate for your child's age group.
- *History*: If the facility is licensed, check to see whether it has ever been cited for violating state or local regulations. If the facility is not licensed, ask the owner or manager for references.

Step 5: Evaluate Your Choice

The evaluation process shouldn't stop once you have made your choice. Drop in unexpectedly from time to time to see how things are going, and keep track of personnel changes. Above all, do not hesitate to withdraw your child if you become dissatisfied or uncomfortable in any way with the arrangement you have chosen.

✺ Summary and Review

Developmental Psychology: Basic Issues and Methodology p. 273

8.1 **What three issues are frequently debated among developmental psychologists? p. 273**

Many questions in developmental psychology are rooted in the nature-nurture controversy. Others stem from the assertion that development occurs in stages. Another point of debate is whether certain characteristics, such as personality traits, remain stable across the entire lifespan.

8.2 **What methods do developmental psychologists use to investigate age-related changes? p. 274**

To investigate age-related changes, developmental psychologists use the longitudinal study and the cross-sectional study. In longitudinal research, a single group of individuals is studied at different ages. Cross-sectional research compares groups of participants of different ages at the same time.

Prenatal Development p. 276

8.3 **What happens in each of the three stages of prenatal development? p. 276**

In the germinal stage, from conception to 2 weeks, the egg is fertilized, and the zygote attaches itself to the uterine wall. During the embryonic stage, from week 3 to week 8, all of the major systems, organs, and structures form. In the fetal stage, from week 9 until birth, the fetus experiences rapid growth and body systems, structures, and organs continue their development.

8.4 **What have scientists learned about fetal behavior in recent years? p. 277**

Fetuses can hear and remember sounds that they hear repeatedly. Some individual and sex differences in behavior are evident during prenatal development.

8.5 **What are some negative influences on prenatal development, and when is their impact greatest? p. 278**

Some common negative influences on prenatal development include certain prescription and nonprescription drugs, psychoactive drugs, environmental hazards, poor maternal nutrition, and maternal illness. Their impact depends on their timing during pregnancy. Exposure is most harmful when it occurs during critical periods of development for the various body structures.

Infancy p. 280

8.6 **How do the motor behaviors of a newborn compare to those of an older infant? p. 280**

The motor behavior of newborns is dominated by reflexes. As maturation proceeds, controlled motor skills, such as grasping and walking, develop. Experience can retard or accelerate motor development, but the sequence of motor milestones is universal.

8.7 **What are the sensory and perceptual abilities of a newborn? p. 282**

All of a newborn's senses are functional at birth, and the infant already shows preferences for certain odors, tastes, sounds, and visual patterns.

8.8 **What types of learning occur in infancy? p. 282**

Newborns are capable of habituation, and they can acquire new responses through classical and operant conditioning and observational learning.

8.9 **What is temperament, and what are the three temperament types identified by Thomas, Chess, and Birch? p. 283**

Temperament refers to an individual's behavioral style or characteristic way of responding to the environment. The three temperament types identified by Thomas, Chess, and Birch are easy, difficult, and slow-to-warm-up. Current research indicates that dimensions of temperament include activity level, sociability inhibition, negative emotionality, and effortful control.

8.10 **What did the research of Harlow, Bowlby, and Ainsworth reveal about the process of infant-caregiver attachment? p. 284**

Harlow found that the basis of attachment in infant monkeys is contact comfort, and that monkeys raised with surrogate mothers show normal learning ability but abnormal social, sexual, and emotional behavior. According to Bowlby, the infant has usually developed a strong attachment to the mother at age 6 to 8 months. Ainsworth identified four attachment patterns in infants: secure, avoidant, resistant, and disorganized/disoriented.

8.11 **How do fathers affect children's development? p. 286**

Fathers' patterns of interaction with children differ from those of mothers. Thus, mothers and fathers exert unique influences on children's development, and, ideally, children need both influences. Children who interact regularly with their fathers tend to have higher IQs, do better in social situations, and manage frustration better than children lacking such interaction. Father absence is associated with low self-esteem, depression, suicidal thoughts, behavioral problems, and teen pregnancy.

Piaget's Theory of Cognitive Development p. 288

8.12 **How did Piaget use the concepts of scheme, assimilation, and accommodation to explain cognitive development? p. 288**

Piaget proposed that humans construct schemes, or general action plans, on the basis of experiences. Schemes change through assimilation and accommodation until they work effectively in the real world.

8.13 **What occurs during each of Piaget's stages of cognitive development? p. 289**

During the sensorimotor stage (ages birth to 2 years), infants understand their world through their senses and motor activities and develop object permanence. Children at the preoperational stage (ages 2 to 6 years) are increasingly able to represent objects and events mentally, but they exhibit egocentrism and centration. When working real-world problems, children at the concrete operations stage (ages 6 to 11 or 12 years) are able to apply logical operations only to problems that can be tested in the real world. At the formal operations stage (ages 11 or 12 years and beyond), adolescents are able to apply logical thinking to abstract problems and hypothetical situations.

8.14 **What are some important criticisms of Piaget's work? p. 294**

Piaget may have underestimated the cognitive skills of infants and young children. Formal operations do not appear in all individuals or in all cultures.

Other Approaches to Cognitive Development p. 296

8.15 **In Vygotsky's view, how do private speech and scaffolding contribute to cognitive development? p. 296**

Private speech, or self-guided talk, helps children to specify the components of a problem and verbalize the steps in a process to help them solve it. Scaffolding is a process in which a teacher or parent adjusts the quality and degree of instruction or guidance to fit the child's present level of ability. It allows a child to gradually perform a task independently.

8.16 **What three cognitive abilities have information-processing researchers studied extensively? p. 296**

The three cognitive abilities studied extensively by information-processing researchers are processing speed, memory, and metacognition.

Language Development p. 298

8.17 **What is the sequence of language development from babbling through the acquisition of grammatical rules? p. 298**

Babbling begins at age 6 months, followed by single words or holophrases sometime during the second year, two-word sentences at ages 18 to 20 months, and telegraphic speech between 2 and 3 years of age, and then the acquisition of grammatical rules.

8.18 **How do learning theory and the nativist position explain the acquisition of language? p. 299**

Learning theory suggests that language is acquired through imitation and reinforcement. The nativist position is that language ability is largely innate, because it is acquired in stages that occur in a fixed order at the same ages in most children throughout the world.

8.19 **What is phonological awareness, and why is it important? p. 300**

Phonological awareness is sensitivity to the sound patterns of a language and how those patterns are represented as letters. Children who acquire good phonological awareness skills before going to school have an easier time learning to read than do peers with lower skill levels.

Social Development p. 301

8.20 **What are the three parenting styles identified by Baumrind, and which does she find most effective? p. 301**

The three parenting styles identified by Baumrind are authoritarian, authoritative, and permissive. She claims the authoritative style is the most effective.

8.21 **How do peers contribute to the socialization process? p. 303**

The peer group serves a socializing function by modeling and reinforcing behaviors it considers appropriate, by punishing inappropriate behaviors, and by providing an objective measure against which children can evaluate their own traits and abilities.

8.22 **What are some of the positive and negative effects of television? p. 304**

Television can increase prosocial behavior, imaginative play, and vocabulary and improve prereading and number skills. But it can also lead to aggressive behavior, obesity, racial and sexual stereotyping, and a shortened attention span.

8.23 **How does Bronfenbrenner explain the influence of culture on children's development? p. 305**

Bronfenbrenner thinks of the environment in which a child grows up as a system of interactive, layered contexts of development. Cultural influences, found at the macrosystem level, filter down to the individual child through the exosystems and microsystems in which the child lives. A child's own characteristics are also part of the microsystem and contribute to how much or how little of the cultural effects actually influence her or his development.

Thinking Critically about Psychology

1. Suppose there were something similar to a driver's license for parents, and that each prospective parent had to pass a parenting education course in order to get such a license. Based on what you have learned in this chapter, what kinds of information would you recommend including in such a course?
2. Using Baumrind's categories, classify the parenting style your parents used in raising you. Cite examples of techniques they used that support your classification.
3. If a pregnant woman uses drugs that are potentially harmful to a fetus, do you think she should be prosecuted for child maltreatment? Why or why not?

Key Terms

accommodation, p. 288
assimilation, p. 288
attachment, p. 284
authoritarian parents, p. 302
authoritative parents, p. 302
babbling, p. 298
centration, p. 290
concrete operations stage, p. 291
conservation, p. 291
contexts of development, p. 305
critical period, p. 279
cross-sectional study, p. 274
developmental psychology, p. 273
embryo, p. 276
equilibration, p. 288

fetal alcohol syndrome, p. 279
fetus, p. 277
formal operations stage, p. 293
habituation, p. 282
longitudinal study, p. 274
low birth weight, p. 279
maturation, p. 280
neglecting parents, p. 303
neonate, p. 280
object permanence, p. 290
organization, p. 288
overextension, p. 298
overregularization, p. 299
permissive parents, p. 303
phonological awareness, p. 300

prenatal development, p. 276
preoperational stage, p. 290
reflexes, p. 280
reversibility, p. 291
scheme, p. 288
sensorimotor stage, p. 290
separation anxiety, p. 285
socialization, p. 301
stranger anxiety, p. 285
telegraphic speech, p. 298
temperament, p. 283
teratogens, p. 278
underextension, p. 298
visual cliff, p. 282
zygote, p. 276

Chapter 9

Adolescence and Adulthood

If you were asked to make predictions about a person based solely on the knowledge that he or she was over 100 years of age, what would your forecast be? If you were to say that the person is likely to be incapacitated in some way, statistically speaking, you would be on target. However, perhaps the most important concept to grasp when it comes to understanding human aging is that age and variability are correlated. That is, the older we get, the more we vary from one another. Thus, there is considerably more variability among the elderly than any other age group, and that variability yields some remarkable deviations from the average among our oldest citizens.

Consider Tom Spear, who, at the advanced age of 104, still plays 18 holes of golf three times a week. And then there's Lily Hearst, age 103, who swims eight laps a day, does yoga, and gives piano lessons. Spear and Hearst are just two of more than 1,000 centenarians (people who have lived a century or more) whose longevity has been studied by Dr. Thomas Perls and his colleagues at the New England Centenarian Study located at Boston University Medical School. Perls and his colleagues are gathering data about all aspects of centenarians' lives. So far, they have learned that:

- Most centenarians have a long history of regular physical activity.
- The majority have remained mentally active by pursuing work or hobbies that they enjoy.
- Until the age of 90, 90% of centenarians are able to live independently, and 75% do so until the age of 95.
- Many centenarians have experienced long periods of deprivation and hardship. Some were born as slaves; others survived the Holocaust.
- Worldwide, women centenarians outnumber men by a ratio of nine to one.
- Very few centenarians are obese, and most are lean, especially the men.
- A substantial history of smoking is rare.
- Centenarians tend to be optimistic and are able to shrug off worries.
- A good sense of humor seems to be a common trait.
- Most centenarians have one or more parents, siblings, or grandparents who also lived a very long time.
- Many centenarians enjoy close family relationships, and quite a few of them live within daily visiting distance of family members.
- Centenarians are less likely to develop cognitive disabilities than their peers who die at younger ages.

Perls has developed an online quiz that can help you determine your own chances of living to 100 (www.livingto100.com/quiz.cfm). But the scientific study of old age has ramifications that go far beyond our individual concerns about aging. Centenarians are the fastest-growing segment of the population in developed countries. In the United States, for example, there are about 60,000 centenarians; if current trends continue, there will be more than 800,000 by the year 2050. In the rest of the world, the odds of reaching 100 are considerably lower, but the United Nations predicts that improvements in public health will rapidly increase the proportion of centenarians who live in developing countries. The UN estimates that there will be more than 3 million centenarians in the world by 2050. Social scientists and politicians alike have raised concerns about the costs, both social and economic, of caring for this unprecedented number of elderly individuals. For these reasons, understanding the aging process and those who seem to defy it is vital to our future.

The study of aging has also influenced the way psychologists think about the entire scope of human development. Historically, psychologists considered childhood and adolescence to be periods of change culminating in physical, social, and intellectual maturity. Next, most believed, came several decades of behavioral and psychological stability in adulthood. Finally, the conventional wisdom said, old age ushered in an era of rapid decline that resulted in death. Today, psychologists' approach to all of these periods is strongly influenced by the belief that change happens throughout the human lifespan.

The Lifespan Perspective

You may recall being introduced to the concept of *psychological perspectives* back in Chapter 1. To review, a perspective is a general point of view used for explaining people's behavior and thinking. In recent years, as our understanding of lifelong change has expanded, developmental scientists have adopted the **lifespan perspective,** the view that developmental changes happen throughout the entire human lifespan, literally from "womb to tomb" (Baltes et al., 1980). Thus, understanding change in adulthood is just as important as understanding change in childhood and adolescence. Moreover, research based in many disciplines—anthropology, sociology, economics, political science, and biology, as well as psychology—is required to fully comprehend human development. One of the most important theoretical influences for the lifespan perspective has been Erikson's theory of psychosocial development.

▲ The lifespan perspective is the view that changes across all developmental domains—physical, cognitive, and social—occur throughout the entire human lifespan, from conception to death.

Erikson's Psychosocial Theory

Erik Erikson (1902–1994) proposed the only major theory of development to include the entire lifespan. According to Erikson, individuals progress through eight **psychosocial stage** during the lifespan. As **Table 9.1** shows, each stage is defined by a conflict that arises from the individual's relationship with the social environment and that must be resolved satisfactorily in order for healthy development to occur. The stages are named for the contrasting outcomes that result, depending on how the conflict is resolved (Erikson, 1980). Although failure to resolve a particular conflict impedes later development, the resolution may occur at a later stage and reverse any damage done previously.

Erikson proposed that the adult personality is built upon successful resolutions of earlier conflicts. For instance, an infant will be better off in adulthood, Erikson claimed, if he leaves infancy with a greater tendency toward trust than toward mistrust. Likewise, an individual's prospects for developing a healthy adult personality improve if he acquires autonomy, initiative, and industry in the next three childhood stages. Erikson also viewed adolescence as the time in life when an individual must acquire an understanding of her place in the world, that is, a sense of personal identity, with which to approach the developmental tasks of adulthood.

The adult stages in Erikson's theory are not as strongly tied to age as those that occur in childhood and adolescence. For example, the need for intimacy arises in accordance with a particular culture's expectations regarding mating, and the need to contribute to the next generation is shaped by cultural expectations regarding child-rearing. Finally, the approach of death signals the adult's entry into the final stage in which he seeks to establish a sense of having had a meaningful life—Erikson called this ego integrity.

As you can see, the scope of Erikson's theory is quite broad. Consequently, most researchers who are interested in Erikson's ideas focus on a single stage and either the positive or negative outcome it can produce. Two such outcomes that have been studied extensively, and that have particular relevance to our discussion of adolescence and adulthood, are identity and generativity.

9.1 How does Erikson's theory of psychosocial development differ from other developmental theories?

lifespan perspective   The view that developmental changes happen throughout the human lifespan and that interdisciplinary research is required to fully understand human development.

psychosocial stages   Erikson's eight developmental stages through which individuals progress during their lifespan; each stage is defined by a conflict involving the individual's relationship with the social environment, which must be resolved satisfactorily in order for healthy development to occur.

Table 9.1 Erikson's Psychosocial Stages of Development

Stage	Ages	Description
Trust vs. mistrust	Birth to 1 year	Infants learn to trust or mistrust depending on the degree and regularity of care, love, and affection provided by parents or caregivers.
Autonomy vs. shame and doubt	1 to 3 years	Children learn to express their will and independence, to exercise some control, and to make choices. If not, they experience shame and doubt.
Initiative vs. guilt	3 to 6 years	Children begin to initiate activities, to plan and undertake tasks, and to enjoy developing motor and other abilities. If not allowed to initiate or if made to feel stupid and considered a nuisance, they may develop a sense of guilt.
Industry vs. inferiority	6 years to puberty	Children develop industriousness and feel pride in accomplishing tasks, making things, and doing things. If not encouraged or if rebuffed by parents and teachers, they may develop a sense of inferiority.
Identity vs. role confusion	Adolescence	Adolescents must make the transition from childhood to adulthood, establish an identity, develop a sense of self, and consider a future occupational identity. Otherwise, role confusion can result.
Intimacy vs. isolation	Young adulthood	Young adults must develop intimacy—the ability to share with, care for, and commit themselves to another person. Avoiding intimacy brings a sense of isolation and loneliness.
Generativity vs. stagnation	Middle adulthood	Middle-aged people must find some way of contributing to the development of the next generation. Failing this, they may become self-absorbed and emotionally impoverished and reach a point of stagnation.
Ego integrity vs. despair	Late adulthood	Individuals review their lives, and if they are satisfied and feel a sense of accomplishment, they will experience ego integrity. If dissatisfied, they may sink into despair.

The Identity Crisis

9.2 How did Marcia expand on Erikson's ideas about the adolescent identity crisis?

Erikson's proposal that the process of identity development is central to adolescent development is one of his most important contributions to the field of developmental psychology. He coined the term **identity crisis** to refer to the emotional turmoil a teenager experiences when trying to establish a sense of personal identity. In other words, the adolescent in the midst of Erikson's identity crisis is trying to answer the question "Who am I?" As you probably know from personal experience, this is no easy task.

Most of the research on identity development has employed a model suggested by psychologist James Marcia (1966, 1980). Marcia proposed that the identity formation process has two key parts: a crisis and a commitment. For Marcia, a "crisis" is an event or gradually emerging feeling of unrest that calls for a decision requiring reexamination of prior beliefs. The outcome of this reexamination is a commitment to some specific role or belief system. The distress a high school senior feels when she contemplates what she will do after graduation and the decision at which she arrives exemplify Marcia's notions of crisis and commitment.

Marcia suggested that the elements of crisis and commitment occur together as shown in **Figure 9.1**. These intersections of high and low crisis with high and low commitment produce four possible identity statuses. Here is a brief overview of them:

▲ Research suggests that the identity crisis extends into the adult years. How do you think attending college affects the identity development process?

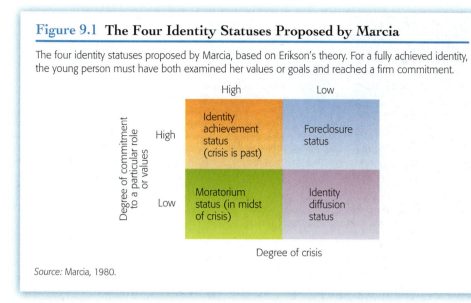

Figure 9.1 The Four Identity Statuses Proposed by Marcia

The four identity statuses proposed by Marcia, based on Erikson's theory. For a fully achieved identity, the young person must have both examined her values or goals and reached a firm commitment.

Source: Marcia, 1980.

- *Identity achievement:* The young person has been through a crisis and has reached a commitment to ideological or occupational goals.
- *Moratorium:* A crisis is in progress, but no commitment has yet been made.
- *Foreclosure:* A young person makes a commitment by accepting a culturally or socially defined option without having gone through a crisis.
- *Identity diffusion:* The young person is neither in crisis nor has reached a commitment.

Research indicates that Marcia's statuses are useful for classifying the state of a given individual's search for a personal identity. However, most studies find that the process occurs later than Erikson's theory would suggest. According to Erickson, the identity versus role confusion stage lasts from puberty to about age 18. By contrast, research shows that the identity development process doesn't begin in earnest until the late teens and that it continues into the twenties. This may happen because cognitive development plays an important role in identity formation (Klaczynski, Fauth, & Swanger, 1998). That is, a teenager must have attained Piaget's formal operational stage of cognitive development (see Chapter 8) before she has access to the kind of abstract thinking that is required for identity development. Moreover, Marcia himself has pointed out that the quest for personal identity reappears from time to time throughout adulthood (Marcia, 2002). Thus, even if a teenager succeeds in reaching Marcia's identity achieved status, she is likely to reconsider her commitment some time in the future.

Generativity

Like the concept of identity crisis, Erikson's notion of *generativity*, the desire to contribute something to the next generation, is an enduring feature of his theory. According to Erikson, generativity arises out of an individual's sense of personal mortality and appears after the person has made some kind of commitment regarding her lifelong pattern of intimate relationships. Generativity can be manifested as bringing up children, mentoring co-workers, writing or producing artwork, doing volunteer work, or any other activity that gives a person a sense of having left the world changed in some way as a result of having lived. As such, generativity is the predominant theme of adulthood, preoccupying our thoughts and motivating our actions for several decades.

A number of studies provided support for the importance of generativity in adulthood. In one such study, researchers found that generativity increased in middle adulthood (Zucker et al., 2002). However, it did not decline in late adulthood.

9.3 In what ways does generativity shape the lives of adults?

identity crisis The emotional turmoil a teenager experiences when trying to establish a sense of personal identity.

▶ According to Erikson, in middle adulthood, people develop generativity—an interest in guiding the next generation.

The oldest group of study participants, with an average age of 66, cited generativity concerns as being important to them just as frequently as the middle-aged group did. Thus, generativity may be more characteristic of middle than of early adulthood, as Erikson suggested, but it appears to continue to be important in late adulthood.

Differences in generativity, as Erikson predicted, are related to variations in behavior. For example, a study involving parents of adolescents found that those with the most acute sense of generativity were more likely than those with lower levels of generativity to display an authoritative parenting style. However, the relationship between generativity and authoritative parenting was much stronger for mothers than for fathers (Pratt et al., 2001). Thus, Erikson's conflict for middle age may be more applicable to women than to men.

There is also some research support for Erikson's claim that generativity is related to mental health in middle age. In a study of midlife adults, generativity was positively related to satisfaction in life and work, and it was a strong predictor of emotional well-being (Ackerman et al., 2000). In another study, which measured middle-aged women's sense of being burdened by caring for elderly parents, those who exhibited the highest levels of generativity felt the least burdened (Peterson, 2002).

Erikson's lifespan perspective was a key factor that influenced 20th-century developmentalists to look more closely at the transition from childhood to adulthood commonly known as *adolescence*.

Remember It   The Lifespan Perspective

1. According to Erikson, the poor resolution of conflicts in early stages affects an individual's ability to _____.

2. Match each description of child behavior with the appropriate psychosocial stage.

   _____ (1) needs consistent attention to physical, social, and emotional needs
   _____ (2) initiates play and motor activities, asks questions
   _____ (3) strives for sense of independence
   _____ (4) undertakes projects, makes things

   a. trust vs. mistrust
   b. autonomy vs. shame and doubt
   c. initiative vs. guilt
   d. industry vs. inferiority

3. Match each description of adolescent or adult behavior with the appropriate psychosocial stage.

   _____ (1) searches for a life partner
   _____ (2) seeks to answer the question "Who am I?"
   _____ (3) concerned with influencing future generations
   _____ (4) reflects on life's accomplishments to achieve a sense of satisfaction

   a. identity vs. role confusion
   b. intimacy vs. isolation
   c. generativity vs. stagnation
   d. ego integrity vs. despair

4. Most research on Erikson's theory has focused on his concepts of _____ and _____.

Answers: 1. resolve conflicts in later stages; 2. (1) a, (2) c, (3) b, (4) d; 3. (1) b, (2) a, (3) c, (4) d; 4. identity, generativity

Adolescence

What personal associations do you have with the beginning of adolescence? You might remember your first day of secondary school, or the realization that the clothing and shoes sold in children's stores no longer fit you, or perhaps your first serious "crush." In some cultures, young teens participate in formal ceremonies known as *rites of passage*, which publicly mark the passage from childhood to adulthood. In the Western industrialized world, however, there is a long transitional period between childhood and adulthood, which is marked by many less formal experiences, such as a first job, that help young people acquire the skills necessary to live independently. The term **adolescence** refers to this developmental stage that begins at puberty.

The concept of adolescence did not exist until 1904, when psychologist G. Stanley Hall first wrote about it in his book by that name. He portrayed adolescence as characterized by "storm and stress," resulting from the biological changes that occur during the period. Anna Freud (1958), daughter of Sigmund Freud, even considered a stormy adolescence a necessary part of normal development. And though it does appear to be true that turbulent, unsettled periods occur more often in adolescence than in any other period of human development, Hall and Freud overstated the case (Arnett, 1999).

The somewhat exaggerated claims of Hall and Freud about the emotional upheavals of adolescence have probably contributed to a number of negative stereotypes. Many see adolescence as a period of emotional instability, punctuated by inevitable associations with socially deviant peers and experimentation with risky behaviors, such as alcohol abuse and unprotected sexual intercourse. However, the truth is that most teens are psychologically healthy and have primarily positive developmental experiences (Takanishi, 1993). Most enjoy good relationships with their families and friends, and researchers say that the majority of them are happy and self-confident (Diener & Diener, 1996). Perhaps few teens have the experiences stereotypically associated with adolescence because most are too busy doing exactly what they should be doing during these years: learning the skills they will need for adulthood.

▲ Contrary to popular belief, adolescence is not stormy and stressful for most teenagers.

Puberty

Finding the dividing line between adolescence and adulthood is far more difficult than determining when adolescence begins. A dramatic series of physiological changes clearly mark, at least in a physical sense, the transition from childhood to adolescence. **Puberty** is a collective term that includes all of these changes. Thus, puberty is not a single event. Rather, it is a period of several years' duration that is marked by rapid physical growth and physiological changes and that culminates in sexual maturity. Although the average onset of puberty is at age 10 for girls and age 12 for boys, the normal range extends from 7 to 14 for girls and from 9 to 14 for boys (Adelman & Ellen, 2002).

The Physical Changes of Puberty. Puberty begins with a surge in hormone production, which, in turn, causes a number of physical changes. For instance, do you remember outgrowing a new pair of shoes in just a few days or weeks during your early teen years? Such experiences are common because the most startling change during puberty is the marked acceleration in growth known as the *adolescent growth spurt*. On the average, the growth spurt occurs from age 10 to 13 in girls and about 2 years later in boys, from age 12 to 15 (Tanner, 1990). Because various parts of the body grow at

9.4 **What physical and psychological changes occur as a result of puberty?**

adolescence The developmental stage that begins at puberty and encompasses the period from the end of childhood to the beginning of adulthood.

puberty A period of several years in which rapid physical growth and physiological changes occur, culminating in sexual maturity.

different rates, the adolescent often has a lanky, awkward appearance. Girls attain their full height between ages 16 and 17, and boys, between ages 18 and 20.

During puberty, the reproductive organs in both sexes mature, and **secondary sex characteristics** appear—those physical characteristics that are not directly involved in reproduction but distinguish the mature male from the mature female. In girls, the breasts develop and the hips round; in boys, the voice deepens, and facial and chest hair appears; and in both sexes, pubic and underarm (axillary) hair grows.

The major landmark of puberty for males is the first ejaculation, which occurs, on average, at age 13 (Adelman & Ellen, 2002). For females, it is *menarche,* the onset of menstruation, which occurs, on average, between ages 12 and 13, although the normal range is considered to extend from 10 to 16 (Tanner, 1990). The age of menarche is influenced by heredity, but a girl's diet and lifestyle contribute as well. Regardless of genes, a girl must have a certain proportion of body fat to attain menarche. Consequently, girls who eat high-fat diets and who are not physically active begin menstruating earlier than girls whose diets contain less fat and whose activities involve fat-reducing exercise (e.g., ballet, gymnastics). And girls living in poor countries where they experience malnutrition or in societies in which children are expected to perform physical labor also begin menstruating at later ages.

The Timing of Puberty. The timing of puberty can have important psychological and social consequences. Early-maturing boys, taller and stronger than their classmates, have an advantage in sports and in capturing attention from girls. They are likely to have a positive body image, to feel confident, secure, independent, and happy, and to be successful academically as well (Alsaker, 1995; Blyth et al., 1981; Peterson, 1987). Late-maturing boys often show the opposite effects: poor body image, less confidence, and so on.

However, early puberty isn't always positive for boys. For example, some researchers have found that boys who enter puberty earlier than their peers do are also more likely to engage in aggressive behavior. This trend has been observed across diverse cultural settings, from African American boys who live in low-income neighborhoods in the United States to Finnish youths who live in suburban areas (Ge et al., 2002; Kaltiala-Heino et al., 2003).

For girls, early maturation brings increased self-consciousness and, often, dissatisfaction with their developing bodies (Ohring et al., 2002). Consequently, early-maturing girls are more likely than their peers to develop bulimia and other eating disorders (Kaltiala-Heino et al., 2001). In addition, they may have to deal with the sexual advances of older boys before they are emotionally or psychologically mature (Peterson, 1987). In addition to having earlier sexual experiences and more unwanted pregnancies than late-maturing girls, early-maturing girls are more likely to be exposed to alcohol and drug use (Caspi et al., 1993; Lanza & Collins, 2002). And those who have had such experiences tend to perform less well academically than their agemates (Stattin & Magnusson, 1990).

Sexuality. Puberty, of course, brings with it the capacity for sexual intercourse. Before the 1960s, the surging sex drive of adolescents was held in check primarily by societal influences. Parents, religious leaders, the schools, and the media were united in delivering the same message: Premarital sex is wrong. Then, sexual attitudes began to change. Today, as **Figure 9.2** shows, high school students in the United States are very sexually active, with about 25% of them having had four or more sex partners by the time they are seniors (CDC, 2000). Still, research has demonstrated that sex education that includes the message that postponing sex until adulthood is a good decision can reduce teen pregnancy rates (Doniger et al., 2001).

Teen Pregnancy. In the United States, approximately 9% of young women become pregnant before the age of 20 (CDC, 2006). Stereotypes surrounding the issue of teen pregnancy often focus on tragic cases involving very young teens, but less than 1% of teen pregnancies involve girls younger than 15. Moreover, the rate of pregnancy among 18- and 19-year-olds is three times that of 15- to 17-year-olds.

secondary sex characteristics
Those physical characteristics that are not directly involved in reproduction but distinguish the mature male from the mature female.

Figure 9.2 **Sexual Activity among High School Students in the United States**

This graph is based on surveys of more than 15,000 high school students conducted in 2003.

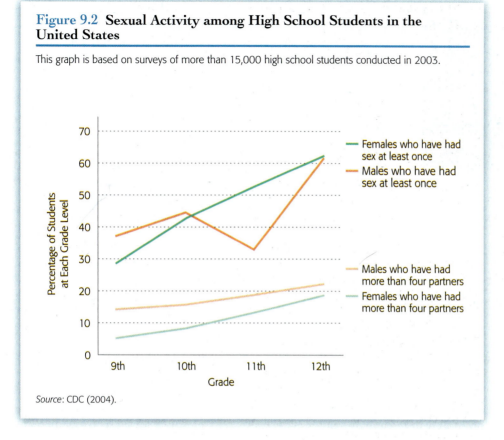

Source: CDC (2004).

When pregnancy occurs in the life of a secondary school student, her chances of completing high school drop substantially (Kirby, 2001). Thus, parents, teachers, and policymakers need to do everything possible to prevent teen pregnancy. Recent statistics suggest that such efforts have paid dividends in recent years as the percentage of teenagers who are sexually active has declined somewhat, and the rates of contraceptive use among those who are sexually active have increased (CDC, 2006).

However, teen pregnancy does not inevitably lead to poor outcomes. Parents who provide teenaged mothers with financial and emotional support increase their daughters' chances of finishing school (Birch, 1998). School programs such as on-campus day care and parenting classes can also help pregnant teenagers stay on track. Supportive families and school programs yield benefits for society as well as for teen mothers and their children. Teenaged mothers who graduate from high school are less likely than their peers who drop out to require long-term public assistance, such as food stamps and welfare payments (Morris et al., 2003).

Cognitive Development

In Chapter 8, you read about Piaget's formal operations stage, in which teenagers acquire the capacity to think hypothetically. Many other improvements in cognitive abilities also occur during these years.

A classic study of the processing of expository text (the type of text you are reading right now), conducted by psychologists Ann Brown and Jeanne Day (1983), illustrates these changes quite well. Experimenters asked 10-, 13-, 15-, and 18-year-olds to read and summarize a 500-word passage (about the same as a page in a typical college textbook). The researchers predicted that participants would use four rules in writing summaries: (1) Delete trivial information; (2) use categories to organize information (e.g., use terms such as *animals* rather than specific names of animals); (3) incorporate topic sentences from the text's paragraphs; and (4) invent topic sentences for paragraphs that lacked them. All participants, regardless of age, included more general information than details in their summaries, suggesting that they had all used

9.5 **What cognitive abilities develop during adolescence?**

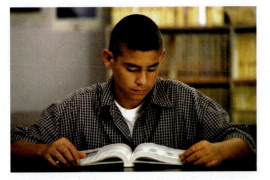

▲ Advances in information processing enable teenagers to more easily grasp the logic of expository text, the kind of language used in textbooks, than they could have just a few years earlier.

the first rule. However, there was far less evidence suggestive of the remaining three rules in the summaries of the 10- and 13-year-olds than in those written by the 15- and 18-year-olds. In addition, only the 18-year-olds used topic sentences consistently.

Other research has shown that metamemory skills also improve dramatically during adolescence (Winsler & Naglieri, 2003). **Metamemory** is the ability to think about and control one's own memory processes. In one frequently cited early study, researchers instructed 10- and 14-year-olds to engage in an activity for precisely 30 minutes and provided them with a clock to keep track of time (Ceci & Bronfenbrenner, 1985). A much greater proportion of the 14-year-olds than the 10-year-olds periodically checked the clock to determine how many minutes had elapsed since they had begun the activity. As you might expect, fewer than half of the 10-year-olds succeeded in stopping on time, compared to more than 75% of the 14-year-olds. The difference between the two groups was most likely the more efficient working memories of the teenagers. In other words, the 14-year-olds were able to keep both the time limit and the activity in mind at the same time. By contrast, the 10-year-olds' working memories were less able to manage the dual demands of keeping up with elapsed time while also engaging in an activity.

These results, along with many other similar ones, indicate that teenagers are much more able than children to organize information efficiently. As a result, adolescents are more effective learners than children are. Moreover, information-processing skills continue to improve well into late adolescence and early adulthood. So, you are far better equipped to handle the intellectual demands of college than you would have been just a few years ago. And it isn't just because you have more knowledge. You manage the knowledge you have, as well as new information you encounter, in an entirely different way.

Moral Development

9.6 **What are the differences among Kohlberg's three levels of moral reasoning?**

Does the clear cognitive advantage of adolescents over children also extend to other domains such as moral reasoning? What about teenagers' capacity to think about moral issues? Lawrence Kohlberg (1981, 1984, 1985) believed, as did Piaget before him, that moral reasoning is closely related to cognitive development and that it, too, evolves in stages. Kohlberg (1969) studied moral development by presenting a series of moral dilemmas to male participants from the United States and other countries. Here is one of his best-known dilemmas:

> In Europe a woman was near death from a special kind of cancer. There was one drug the doctors thought might save her. It was a form of radium that a druggist in the same town had recently discovered. The drug was expensive to make, and the druggist was charging ten times what it cost him. He paid $200 for the radium and charged $2,000 for a small dose of the drug. The sick woman's husband, Heinz, went to everyone he knew to borrow the money, but he could only get together $1,000, which was half of what the drug cost. He told the druggist that his wife was dying and asked him to sell it cheaper or let him pay later. But the druggist said, "No, I discovered the drug, and I am going to make money from it." So Heinz got desperate and broke into the man's store to steal the drug for his wife (Colby et al., 1983, p. 77).

What moral judgment would you make about this dilemma? Should Heinz have stolen the drug? Why or why not? Kohlberg was less interested in whether the participants judged Heinz's behavior right or wrong than in the reasons for their responses. He found that moral reasoning could be classified into three levels, with each level having two stages.

The Levels of Moral Reasoning. Kohlberg's first level of moral reasoning is the **preconventional level**, where moral reasoning is governed by the standards of others rather than the individual's own internalized standards of right and wrong. An act is judged good or bad based on its physical consequences. In Stage 1, "right" is what-

metamemory The ability to think about and control one's own memory processes.

preconventional level Kohlberg's first level of moral reasoning, in which moral reasoning is governed by the standards of others rather than the person's own internalized standards of right and wrong; acts are judged as good or bad based on their physical consequences.

ever avoids punishment. In Stage 2, "right" is whatever is rewarded, benefits the individual, or results in a favor being returned. "You scratch my back, and I'll scratch yours" is the type of thinking common at this stage.

At Kohlberg's second level of moral reasoning, the ==conventional level,== the individual has internalized the standards of others and judges right and wrong in terms of those standards. In Stage 3, sometimes called the *good boy–nice girl orientation*, "good behavior is that which pleases or helps others and is approved by them" (Kohlberg, 1968, p. 26). In Stage 4, the orientation is toward "authority, fixed rules, and the maintenance of the social order. Right behavior consists of doing one's duty, showing respect for authority, and maintaining the given social order for its own sake" (p. 26).

Kohlberg believed that a person must function at Piaget's concrete operations stage to reason morally at the conventional level. Thus, theoretically at least, conventional moral reasoning should appear some time between the ages of 6 and 12. However, Kohlberg's research and that of others demonstrated that moral reasoning lags behind cognitive development. Consequently, most school-age children, though proficient at concrete operational thinking, do not yet reason about moral dilemmas at the conventional level, as shown in **Figure 9.3**.

Kohlberg's highest level of moral reasoning is the ==postconventional level.== At this level, people weigh moral alternatives, realizing that at times laws may conflict with basic human rights. In Stage 5, the person believes that laws are formulated to protect both society and the individual and should be changed if they fail to do so. In Stage 6, ethical decisions are based on universal ethical principles, which emphasize respect for human life, justice, equality, and dignity for all people. People who reason morally at Stage 6 believe that they must follow their conscience, even if it results in a violation of the law.

According to Kohlberg, postconventional moral reasoning requires the ability to think at Piaget's stage of formal operations. However, attainment of formal operational thought does not guarantee that an individual will reach Kohlberg's postconventional level. Postconventional reasoning is strongly related to education and is most often found among middle-class, college-educated adults.

The *Review and Reflect* on the next page summarizes Kohlberg's six stages of moral reasoning.

conventional level Kohlberg's second level of moral reasoning, in which the individual has internalized the standards of others and judges right and wrong in terms of those standards.

postconventional level Kohlberg's highest level of moral reasoning, in which moral reasoning involves weighing moral alternatives and realizing that laws may conflict with basic human rights.

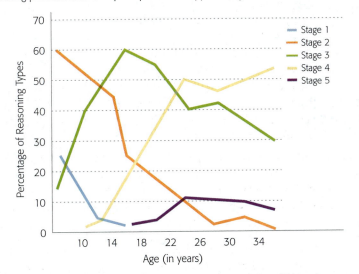

Figure 9.3 **Changes in Moral Reasoning from Childhood to Early Adulthood**

Researchers Ann Colby and Lawrence Kohlberg studied changes in participants' responses to the Heinz dilemma and similar moral problems over more than 20 years. As you can see, preconventional reasoning predominated until participants were approaching adolescence.

Source: Colby et al. (1983), Figure 1, p. 46. Copyright: The Society for Research in Child Development.

Review and Reflect Kohlberg's Stages of Moral Reasoning

Level	Stage
Level I: Preconventional level Moral reasoning is governed by the standards of others; an act is good or bad depending on its physical consequences—whether it is punished or rewarded.	**Stage 1** The stage in which behavior that avoids punishment is right. Children obey out of fear of punishment. **Stage 2** The stage of self-interest. What is right is what benefits the individual or gains a favor in return. "You scratch my back, and I'll scratch yours."
Level II: Conventional level The child internalizes the standards of others and judges right and wrong according to those standards.	**Stage 3** The morality of mutual relationships. The "good boy–nice girl orientation." Child acts to please and help others. **Stage 4** The morality of the social system and conscience. Orientation toward authority. "Right" is doing one's duty, respecting authority, and maintaining the social order.
Level III: Postconventional level Moral conduct is under internal control; this is the highest level and the mark of true morality.	**Stage 5** The morality of contract; respect for individual rights and laws that are democratically agreed on. Rational valuing of the wishes of the majority and the general welfare. Belief that society is best served if citizens obey the law. **Stage 6** The morality of universal ethical principles. The person acts according to internal standards, independent of legal restrictions or opinions of others. The highest stage of the highest level of moral reasoning.

The Development of Moral Reasoning. Kohlberg claimed that people progress through his stages of moral reasoning one stage at a time, in a fixed order. As you learned earlier, moral and cognitive development are correlated, but attaining a high level of cognitive development does not guarantee advanced moral reasoning. And, as Kohlberg came to realize, discussion of moral dilemmas does not reliably improve moral behavior. He eventually agreed that direct teaching of moral and ethical values is necessary and compatible with his theory (Higgins, 1995; Power et al., 1989).

Inconsistencies between moral judgment as measured by Kohlberg's dilemmas and everyday moral decision making have led to the development of additional qualifications of Kohlberg's theory. Psychologists Dennis Krebs and Kathy Denton point out that people exhibit lower levels of reasoning in response to real-life dilemmas than they do when formulating judgments about the hypothetical scenarios used in Kohlberg's research (Krebs & Denton, 2005). Krebs and Denton argue that hypothetical dilemmas tap cognitive development, whereas those we experience in real life call for reasoning based on our culture's standards for social cooperation. Moreover, when reasoning about our own actions, say Krebs and Denton, our judgments are often tainted by a "self-righteous bias" in which we view our own behavior as more morally justifiable than that of others. Thus, their modification of Kohlberg's model asserts that the development of everyday moral judgment is strongly influenced by both social standards and the integration of self-interest with those standards.

Research on Kohlberg's Theory. In a review of 45 studies of Kohlberg's theory conducted in 27 countries, Snarey (1985) found support for the universality of Stages 1 through 4 and for the invariant sequence of these stages in all groups studied. Although extremely rare, Stage 5 was found in almost all samples from urban or middle-class populations and was absent in all of the tribal or village folk societies studied. More recent research conducted by Snarey (1995) supports the conclusions reached a decade earlier.

In a cross-cultural study of the moral reasoning of adults and children from India and the United States, Miller and Bersoff (1992) found great differences between the two cultures. The postconventional moral reasoning common in India stresses interpersonal responsibilities over obligations to further justice. In contrast, Americans emphasize individual rights over responsibilities to others. Such findings, along with Snarey's observations about Stage 5 reasoning, suggest that Kohlberg's postconventional level of moral reasoning may be more strongly associated with culture than are his lower levels.

Gilligan's Alternative Approach. Kohlberg indicated that the majority of women remain at Stage 3, while most men attain Stage 4. Do men typically attain a higher level of moral reasoning than women? Carol Gilligan (1982) asserts that Kohlberg's theory is gender-biased. Not only did Kohlberg fail to include females in his original research, Gilligan points out, but he limits morality to abstract reasoning about moral dilemmas. Moreover, Kohlberg's highest level, Stage 6, emphasizes justice and equality but not mercy, compassion, love, or concern for others. Gilligan suggests that females, more than males, tend to view moral behavior in terms of compassion, caring, and concern for others. More recent evidence suggests that females do tend to emphasize care and compassion in resolving moral dilemmas, whereas males tend to stress justice or at least give it equal standing with caring (Garmon et al., 1996; Wark & Krebs, 1996). And researchers other than Kohlberg have found that females score as high as males in moral reasoning (Walker, 1989).

Parental Relationships

You may recall from Chapter 8 that many teens use their newfound cognitive abilities to devise idealistic plans, which give rise to many parent-teen conflicts. For instance, a 14-year-old might protest against doing algebra homework because he envisions himself becoming a professional athlete, who would, of course, have no need for algebra. Parents counter that, athlete or not, algebra is required for high school graduation and the homework, therefore, must be done. You probably had some arguments with your parents during your high school years, but research does not support the view that adolescents' relationships with their parents are dominated by conflicts. In fact, secure attachments to parents, along with effective parenting practices, are just as critical to a teen's development as they are to that of an infant or child (Allen et al., 2003; Cassidy et al., 2003; Galambos et al., 2003).

> **9.7** What outcomes are often associated with the authoritative, authoritarian, and permissive parenting styles?

Of the three parenting styles discussed in Chapter 8 (authoritative, authoritarian, and permissive), the authoritative style is most effective and the permissive least effective for adolescents (Baumrind, 1991; Steinberg et al., 1994). In a study of about 2,300 adolescents, those with permissive parents were more likely to use alcohol and drugs and to have conduct problems and less likely to be engaged in school than were those with authoritative or authoritarian parents (Lamborn et al., 1991). The authoritarian style was related to more psychological distress and less self-reliance and self-confidence in adolescents. The authoritative parenting style was associated with psychosocial competence for adolescents of all racial and ethnic groups and with academic success for those who are White and middle-class (Aunola et al., 2000; Steinberg et al., 1994). But the authoritarian rather than the authoritative style has been found to be associated with high academic achievement by Asian American and African American adolescents (Steinberg, 1992). Why? With regard to Asian American teens, Steinberg (1992) suggests that authoritarian parenting is tied to parents' strong belief that a child's accomplishments are attributable to both the child's own efforts and those of his family. In the case of African American adolescents, though, authoritarian parenting may help overcome potentially negative peer influences. According to Steinberg (1992), "African American students are more likely than others to be caught in a bind between performing well in school and being popular among their peers" (p. 728). Thus, when peer values and norms do not support academic pursuits, African American parents may

▲ Most adolescents and their parents have good relationships and enjoy doing things together.

adopt an authoritarian approach because they believe it will best serve their child's long-term interests.

Other research suggests that the relationship between parenting style and developmental outcomes is more complex than researchers once believed. For instance, when parents become increasingly authoritarian in response to their teenage children's deviant behavior, researchers have found that the deviant behavior decreases (Galambos et al., 2003). Also, firm parental control over teenagers' behavior helps to counteract the adverse effects of peers who engage in deviant behavior. Further, parents who monitor the activities and relationships of teenagers who have a history of delinquency increase those teens' chances of getting their lives on a more positive developmental track (Laird et al., 2003). So, good parenting for teens may not necessarily mean adoption of any single style. Instead, it may be more important for parents to be flexible and to exhibit the style of parenting that is most appropriate for their own teenager.

The Peer Group

9.8 What are some of the beneficial functions of the adolescent peer group?

Clearly, parents are important to adolescent development, but friends can also be a vital source of emotional support and approval. Indeed, interactions with peers may be critical while young people are fashioning their identities. Adolescents can try out different roles and observe the reactions of their friends to their behavior and their appearance. The peer group provides teenagers with a standard of comparison for evaluating their own attributes as well as a vehicle for developing social skills (Berndt, 1992). For example, an academically inclined teen is likely to gravitate to a peer group with academic interests (Altermatt & Pomerantz, 2003). Associating with academically successful peers will reinforce this teenager's achievement. In such cases, then, peer influence complements parental influence.

Unfortunately, teens also receive reinforcement for undesirable behaviors from their peers. For instance, aggressive teens tend to associate with peers who are equally aggressive (Espelage et al., 2003). And, like the peers of academically inclined teens, the friends of teens who are aggressive reinforce their behavior. Moreover, associating with peers who use tobacco, alcohol, or other substances increases the odds that a teenager will adopt these practices (Cleveland & Wiebe, 2003). In these cases, peer influence and parental influence are in opposition. Still, as noted earlier, when parents adapt their approaches to parenting to a teenager's behavior and his or her peer associations, their influence can counteract the negative effects of deviant peers (Laird et al., 2003). Thus, peer influences can render parenting more complex when children reach their teen years, but peer influence does not generally outweigh the effects of good parenting.

Emerging Adulthood

9.9 What are the neurological and psychosocial characteristics of emerging adulthood?

Physically speaking, the body is fully mature by age 18. There are varied legal definitions of adulthood—voting age, drinking age, and the like. But what are the psychological and social criteria that distinguish an adolescent from an adult? In search of an answer to this question, developmental psychologist Jeffrey Arnett has proposed that the educational, social, and economic demands of modern culture have given rise to a new developmental period he calls **emerging adulthood,** the period from the late teens to the early twenties when individuals experiment with options prior to taking on adult roles (Arnett, 2000). Arnett's studies and those of other researchers indicate that, at least in the United States, young people do not tend to think of themselves as having fully attained adulthood until the age of 25 or so (Galambos, Turner, & Tilton-Weaver, 2005).

Neuroimaging studies have provided some support for the notion that emerging adulthood is a unique period of life. These studies suggest that the parts of the brain that underlie rational decision making, impulse control, and self-regulation mature during these years (Crone et al., 2006; Gogtay et al., 2004). As a result, early on in this phase of life, individuals make poorer decisions about matters such as risky behaviors

emerging adulthood The period from the late teens to early twenties when individuals explore options prior to committing to adult roles.

(e.g., unprotected sex) than they do when these brain areas reach full maturity in the early to mid-twenties.

The neurological changes of the emerging adult period combine with cultural demands to shape the psychosocial features of this period of development. Researcher Glenn Roisman and his colleagues have hypothesized that emerging adults must address developmental tasks in five domains: academic, friendship, conduct, work, and romantic (Roisman et al., 2004). Roisman's research suggests that skills within the first three of these domains transfer easily from adolescence to adulthood. Useful study skills (academic) acquired in high school, for instance, are just as helpful in college. Likewise, the skills needed to make and keep friends (friendship) are the same in both periods, and the process of adapting to rules (conduct) is highly similar as well.

By contrast, emerging adults must approach the work and romantic domains differently than they did as adolescents, according to Roisman. Certainly, many teenagers have jobs and are involved in romances. However, the cultural expectations associated with emerging adulthood require them to commit to a career path that will enable them to achieve full economic independence from their families. Likewise, emerging adults must make decisions about the place of long-term romantic relationships in their present and future lives as well as participate in such relationships. As predicted by his hypothesis, Roisman's findings and those of other researchers suggest that emerging adults experience more adjustment difficulties related to these two domains than they do in the academic, friendship, and conduct domains (Korobov & Thorne, 2006).

Finally, psychologists speculate that the tendency of emerging adults to push the limits of the independence from their families that most acquire in the late teens contributes to the remarkable neurological changes that occur during this phase. Thus, the road that leads to fulfillment of the developmental tasks outlined by Roisman is often a bumpy one. The hope of most parents and teachers of emerging adults is that each of these bumps further opens, rather than closes, the doors of opportunity.

▲ We often hear discussions of peer influences in the teenage years, with some being identified as beneficial and others as detrimental. However, a research methodologist would object to the use of the word "influence" with regard to such findings. Why? (*Hint:* Think about the difference between experimental and correlational research.)

Remember It — Adolescence

1. According to _____ and _____, adolescence is a period of storm and stress.

2. _____ sex characteristics are physical characteristics that are not directly involved in reproduction.

3. The ability to consciously monitor memory function, known as _____, dramatically improves during adolescence.

4. Match each rationale for engaging in a behavior with one of Kohlberg's levels of moral reasoning.

   _____ (1) to avoid punishment or gain a reward
   _____ (2) to ensure that human rights are protected
   _____ (3) to gain approval or follow the law

   a. conventional level
   b. preconventional level
   c. postconventional level

5. For adolescents, the most effective parenting style is the _____ style; the least effective is the _____ style.

6. Peers can be an important source of _____ for teens.

7. _____ is a period between adolescence and adulthood when an individual explores options.

Early and Middle Adulthood

When do you think a person attains adulthood? An 18-year-old is physically and legally an adult. However, a full-fledged adult—in the social sense of the term—is an individual who is living independently from his or her parents. But, as noted earlier, considerable change can occur in the adult years. Clearly, a 25-year-old differs from a 45-year-old in important ways. To help in studying developmental differences among adults, psychologists divide adulthood into early, middle, and late periods. We consider the early and middle periods in this section and the late period in the next section. Generally, developmentalists regard the years from ages 20 to 40 as *early adulthood* and those from ages 40 to 65 as *middle adulthood*. Several physical, cognitive, and social changes occur across these years.

Physical Changes

9.10 What is the difference between primary and secondary aging?

You probably won't be surprised to learn that adults in their 20s are in their top physical condition. It is in this decade that physical strength, reaction time, reproductive capacity, and manual dexterity all peak. During the 30s, there is a slight decline in these physical capacities, which is barely perceptible to most people other than professional athletes. People in their 40s and 50s often complain about a loss of physical vigor and endurance.

Researchers divide the events associated with aging into two categories: *primary aging* and *secondary aging*. Primary aging is biological and generally unavoidable. For example, one unavoidable change in the mid- to late 40s is the development of **presbyopia,** a condition in which the lenses of the eyes no longer accommodate adequately for near vision, and reading glasses or bifocals are often required for reading. Secondary aging is the result of poor health-related habits and lifestyle choices. For instance, the loss of strength many adults experience as they get older is more likely to be from lack of exercise than biological aging processes. Thus, declines associated with advancing age are attributable to the combination of primary and secondary aging. Moreover, changing controllable factors, such as diet and exercise, may slow down these declines. (You'll read more about this intriguing idea in Chapter 12.)

One important milestone of primary aging for women during middle age is **menopause,** the cessation of menstruation, which usually occurs between ages 45 and 55 and marks the end of reproductive capacity. Although life expectancy for females in developed countries increased by 30 years during the 20th century, the span of their fertile years, during which conception is possible, has not increased. The duration of women's reproductive capability is apparently unaffected by the factors that control longevity (Brody et al., 2000).

The most common symptom associated with menopause and the accompanying sharp decrease in the level of estrogen is hot flashes, sudden feelings of being uncomfortably hot. Some women also experience symptoms such as anxiety, irritability, and/or mood swings, and about 10% become depressed. However, most women do not experience psychological problems in connection with menopause (Busch et al., 1994; Matthews, 1992).

Although men do not have a physical event equivalent to menopause, they do experience a gradual decline in testosterone from age 20 until about age 60. During late middle age, many men also experience a reduction in semen production and in the sex drive. Still, in contrast to women, men are capable of fathering a child throughout their lives. However, the DNA carried by their sperm show increasing amounts of fragmentation as they get older (Wyrobek, 2006). Scientists have not yet determined if or how damage of this kind is linked to either male fertility or pregnancy outcomes.

presbyopia (prez-bee-O-pee-uh) A condition, developing in the mid- to late 40s, in which the lenses of the eyes no longer accommodate adequately for near vision, and reading glasses or bifocals are required for reading.

menopause The cessation of menstruation, which usually occurs between ages 45 and 55 and marks the end of reproductive capacity.

Intellectual Abilities

Are there any middle-aged adults in your psychology class? If so, do you think they will perform as well as younger students? The answer might depend on the kind of learning required. Younger adults outperform older adults on tests requiring speed or rote memory. On tests measuring general information, vocabulary, reasoning ability, and social judgment, however, older participants usually do better than younger ones because of their greater experience and education (Horn, 1982). Adults actually continue to gain knowledge and skills over the years, particularly when they lead intellectually challenging lives. Thus, it isn't surprising that most middle-aged college students are academically successful.

Intellectual gains across early and middle adulthood have been documented in longitudinal studies. For example, psychologist Walter Schaie (2005) analyzed data from the Seattle Longitudinal Study, which assessed the intellectual abilities of some 5,000 participants. Many of the participants were tested six times over the course of 50 years. Schaie found that in five areas—verbal meaning, spatial orientation, inductive reasoning, numerical reasoning, and word fluency—participants showed modest gains from young adulthood to their mid-40s (see **Figure 9.4**). Decline did not occur, on average, until after age 60, and even then the decline was modest until participants were in their 80s. Even at age 81, half of the participants showed no decline over the previous 7 years. The study also revealed several gender differences: Females performed better on tests of verbal meaning and inductive reasoning, whereas males tended to do better on tests of numerical reasoning and spatial orientation.

Further, in a classic study of intellectual productivity, Dennis (1968) looked at the productivity of 738 persons who had lived at least 79 years and had attained eminence as scholars, scientists, or artists. For almost every one of these individuals, the decade of the 40s was most productive. Historians, philosophers, and literary scholars enjoyed high productivity from their 40s all the way through their 70s. Scientists were highly productive from their 40s through their 60s, but showed a significant decline in productivity in their 70s. Those in the arts peaked earliest and showed a dramatic decline in their 70s. Of course, the researchers did not interview Michelangelo, Pablo Picasso, Georgia O'Keeffe, Duke Ellington, Irving Berlin, or any of the many other individuals who have been artistically potent and vital into their 80s and 90s.

The work of both Schaie and Dennis challenges many of our assumptions about intellectual decline in adulthood. Research that appears over the next few years may challenge those views to an even greater degree as the Baby Boomers, the large cohort of children born between 1946 and 1964, move through middle age and into late adulthood. The most recent entrants to the Seattle Longitudinal Study have included children and grandchildren of Schaie's original participants. Generational comparisons suggest that Baby Boomers will enter late adulthood with higher levels of intellectual

9.11 In what ways do cognitive functions change between the ages of 20 and 60?

▼ Ironically, the oldest members of the Baby Boom generation, those who once proclaimed "Never trust anyone over 30," are on the verge of entering late adulthood. Two well-known Boomers are President Bill Clinton and Senator Hillary Rodham Clinton. What characteristics of this generation make it likely that they will alter psychologists' understanding of how intellectual abilities change in middle and old age?

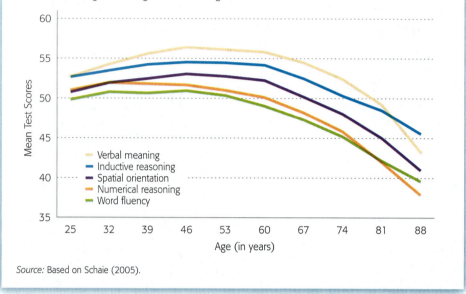

Figure 9.4 Age Differences in Performance on Tests of Five Mental Abilities

This graph shows the average scores of participants in the Seattle Longitudinal Study on tests of five mental abilities. Participants were tested seven times over a period of 50 years and showed gains from young adulthood until their mid-40s. Very little decline occurred until after age 60. Even so, half were still exhibiting normal cognitive functioning into their 80s.

Source: Based on Schaie (2005).

ability than did their parents' generation. Of course, it remains to be seen whether Baby Boomers will maintain this cognitive advantage over prior generations as they become progressively more subject to physiological aging processes. Schaie predicts that they will, for two reasons (Schaie & Willis, 2005). First, Boomers are better educated than their parents, with 89% having graduated from high school and 30% having college degrees compared to 68% and 15%, respectively, among the older generation (U.S. Census Bureau, 2004). Second, Boomers may be more mentally active in old age than their parents were, because most will remain in the workforce past the traditional retirement age of 65 (Harvard School of Public Health, 2004). Moreover, they have established a pattern of returning to college whenever they need to acquire new job skills or to develop an interest in a hobby (*Newsweek*, 2006). As you will see in the next section, the college environment can have a significant impact on both intellectual and social development, an effect that probably holds true regardless of a student's age.

The Impact of College Attendance

9.12 How does attending college affect adult development?

Have you ever wondered whether college is really worth the trouble? The answer is yes, if the measure of worth is income. As you can see in **Figure 9.5**, some college is better than none, but there is a clear income advantage for degree-holders. These income differences exist because, compared to nongraduates, college graduates get more promotions, are less likely to experience long periods of unemployment, are less likely to be discriminated against on the basis of race or gender, and are regarded more favorably by potential employers (Pascarella & Terenzi, 1991). But college attendance has benefits beyond increased income.

College Attendance and Development. The longer individuals attend college, even if they don't graduate, the more likely they are to be capable of formal operational thinking and other forms of abstract logical thought (Lehman & Nisbett, 1990; Pascarella, 1999). Years of attendance is also correlated with how efficiently people manage problems in their everyday lives, such as balancing family and work

Figure 9.5 Level of Education and Income

These statistics make it clear that, the longer you stay in school, the more money you are likely to earn.

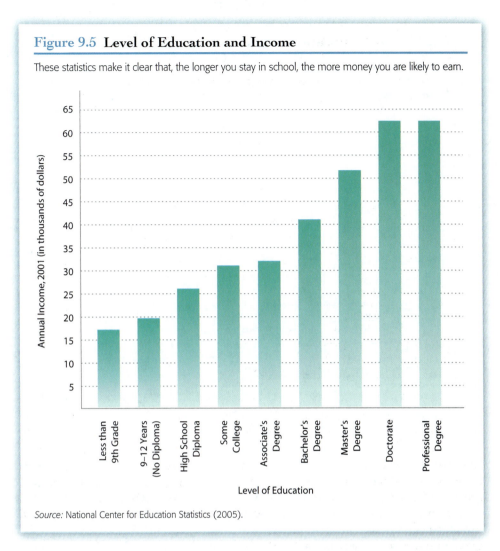

Source: National Center for Education Statistics (2005).

schedules. Longitudinal studies show that these cognitive gains happen between the first and later years of college. Such findings mean that two individuals who are of equal intellectual ability, as measured by acceptance by a college or university, are likely to diverge from one another in cognitive skills if one leaves school while the other persists.

College attendance influences social development as well. For many students, college is their first opportunity to meet people of ethnicities and nationalities that are different from theirs. And students, particularly those who live on campus, learn to establish social networks that eventually replace parents as their primary source of emotional support. The extensive opportunities for social interaction may explain associations that researchers (Chickering & Reisser, 1993; Pascarella & Terenzi, 1991) have found among college attendance, capacity for empathy, and moral reasoning.

Gender, Race, and College Completion. At all degree levels, women are more likely than men to graduate (NCES, 1997). Why? One reason is that female students use more effective study strategies than their male counterparts do (Braten & Olaussen, 1998; Pearsall et al., 1997). In addition, male students are more likely to cheat and to be negatively influenced by peers in making decisions about behaviors such as binge drinking (Senchak et al., 1998; Thorpe et al., 1999).

Race is linked to graduation rates as well, as you can see in **Figure 9.6**. Note, however, that these data refer to degree completion within a six-year time frame. Economic pressures often force students from disadvantaged groups to leave college

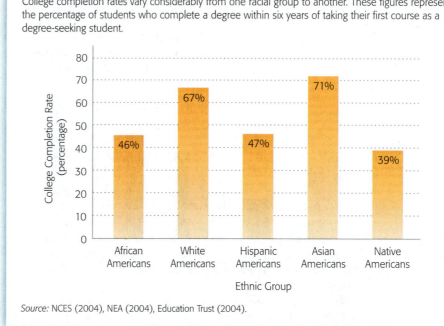

Figure 9.6 **Degree Completion Rates in the United States**

College completion rates vary considerably from one racial group to another. These figures represent the percentage of students who complete a degree within six years of taking their first course as a degree-seeking student.

Source: NCES (2004), NEA (2004), Education Trust (2004).

temporarily or to reduce the number of credit hours they take each semester. As a result, these students may be less likely to finish college in six years than more economically advantaged Asian and White students (Seidman, 2005). In response to the needs of such groups, many colleges have developed programs aimed at retaining these students and providing them with the support they need to complete their degrees.

Of course, economic reasons alone cannot fully explain race differences in college completion. Many factors, including the "fit" between a particular student and the college she chooses to attend matter as well (Seidman, 2005). Research examining college completion among African Americans at historically Black institutions can provide us with a few glimpses into how the sense of belongingness contributes to the educational success of minority students. These studies indicate that African American students who attend historically Black institutions show more gains in both cognitive and social competence than their peers who attend predominantly White colleges (Flowers, 2002; Flowers & Pascarella, 1999). In addition, attending historically Black colleges may help African American students achieve a stronger sense of racial identity, a factor which is correlated with persistence in college (Rowley, 2000). Thus, when these students graduate, they may be better prepared for the demands of graduate and professional programs than are peers who graduate from colleges where African Americans are in the minority.

Since its inception just over 30 years ago, the tribal college movement led by Native American educators has sought to provide the same type of culturally sensitive learning environment for reservation-dwelling Native Americans that historically Black colleges provide for African American students (American Indian Higher Education Consortium, 1999). By higher education standards, however, tribal colleges are newborns. Many European universities have existed for 800 years or more, and several universities in the United States have been in existence for more than 300 years. Moreover, the oldest historically Black colleges were founded in the first half of the nineteenth century. Thus, it is far too soon to determine whether the tribal college movement has been successful. Suffice to say that it represents an important step toward recognizing that Native American youth who grow up on reservations are most likely to thrive academically in settings in which they feel a sense of belonging and commitment.

Lifestyle Patterns in Adulthood

Surveys indicate that 49.7% of households in the United States are headed by a married couple (U. S. Census Bureau, 2006). However, in the 1960s, married couples headed nearly 80% of all households. As you will learn, several factors have contributed to changes in the proportions of all of the various households types that are represented in Figure 9.7 on page 334. Regardless of household type, though, the keys to an individual's sense of well-being appear to be satisfaction with his or her life situation and the maintenance of a supportive social network.

Singles. The primary reason for recent changes in the proportion of married-couple households is that more people are now living alone than in the past, and they are doing so for a larger proportion of their adult years. As you can see in Figure 9.7, 27% of adults in the United States live alone (U. S. Census Bureau, 2006). By contrast, only 13% of adults lived by themselves in 1960.

Most single-person households today are headed by a young adult. The number of such households has increased because young adults nowadays tend to marry at later ages than earlier cohorts did. Equally important, though, is the growing number of single-person households that belong to senior citizens. As life expectancy increases, and as the general health of the elderly population improves, it is likely that the proportion of single-person households that are headed by a divorced, widowed, or never-married older adult will increase.

Several researchers have documented the existence of negative stereotypes about singlehood (DePaulo & Morris, 2005). Single adults are often assumed to be unhappy and desperately searching for a life partner. Yet most singles are satisfied with their status and do not seek to change it (Davies, 2003). Moreover, stereotypes notwithstanding, many singles do have an intimate partner but prefer to continue living alone.

Cohabiting Couples. Some single people choose to cohabit with their intimate partners. In the United States, nearly 5% of all households are headed by a cohabiting opposite-sex couple. An additional 1% of households are headed by a cohabiting same-sex couple.

Because many people regard cohabitation as a trial marriage, you may be surprised to learn that the divorce rate for couples who cohabit before marrying is actually higher than that of couples who do not live together (Heaton, 2002). Research suggests that a pattern of emotionally negative, unsupportive communication is more likely to develop among cohabiting than among married couples. After the wedding, couples who have lived together often carry these patterns over into their marriages, a tendency that many observers believe explains their higher divorce rate (Cohan & Kleinbaum, 2002).

However, these findings may be somewhat misleading in that they often do not take into account the firmness of couples' intention to marry. More careful studies show that couples who undertake a cohabiting relationship with a clear understanding by both partners that the arrangement is a prelude to marriage differ little in relationship satisfaction or stability from those who do not cohabit before marriage (Kline et al., 2004; Teachman, 2003).

Marriage. The mating culture of today's singles is not as oriented toward marriage as it was in the past. The extensive research conducted by David Popenoe and other investigators with the National Marriage Project at Rutgers University suggests several reasons for this trend (Whitehead & Popenoe, 2005). One is the popularity of cohabitation noted earlier. Moreover, attitudes toward single parenting are such that about half of adults no longer believe that marriage is a necessary prerequisite to becoming a parent. The age at first marriage has risen dramatically over the past five decades as well. In 1960, the median age at first marriage was 20 for females and 23 for males; today, the median age is 26 for females and 27 for males (Whitehead & Popenoe, 2005).

Despite these trends, Popenoe's analyses suggest that more than 80% of adults will marry at least once in their lives. Marriage confers significant economic benefits on spouses, as you might suspect (Whitehead & Popenoe, 2005). Moreover, research

9.13 What are some current trends in lifestyle patterns among young adults?

▲ Have you made friends with someone online? Many young adults use the Internet as a way of meeting potential friends and romantic partners.

Figure 9.7 Household Compostion in the United States

Government surveys indicate that households in the United States are now about evenly divided between those that are headed by a married couple and living arrangements that involve other kinds of relationships. However, a broader interpretation of the data suggests that "coupled" households continue to be more common among adults than those that are headed by singles (54% versus 46%). Furthermore, many individuals in the single-person-household and single-parent-household groups were previously married or partnered, and many of them will be so again in the future. And, no doubt, many of them have partners who also live in single-person households. Thus, partnering continues to be an important facet of adult life in the United States.

Source: Data from U. S. Census Bureau (2006).

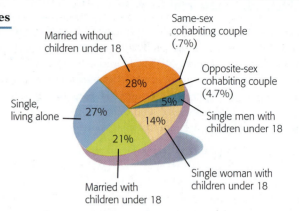

Married without children under 18 — 28%

Same-sex cohabiting couple (.7%)

Opposite-sex cohabiting couple (4.7%)

5%

Single, living alone — 27%

14%

Single men with children under 18

Single woman with children under 18

21%

Married with children under 18

indicates that marriage is associated with numerous physical and mental health benefits (e.g., lower rates of depression) for both men and women (Bierman, Fazio, & Milkie, 2006; Umberson et al., 2006). However, some studies suggest that an unhappy, stress-filled marriage may actually be detrimental to the health of one or both spouses (Umberson et al., 2006).

Nevertheless, there is evidence that some kinds of stressful marital interactions eventually turn out to benefit the health of both partners. For instance, spouses tend to pressure one another about health-related behaviors. In one study, researchers found that marijuana smoking was a continuing source of arguments between smoking and nonsmoking spouses (Leonard & Hornish, 2005). The typical result of these long-term arguments was that the partner who smoked marijuana eventually gave up cannabis in order to preserve marital harmony. Interestingly, wives appear to be more adept at exerting this kind of pressure than are husbands. This gender difference may help explain findings showing that health disparities between single and married men are greater than those that exist for single and married women (Bell & Bell, 2005; Markey et al., 2005).

Divorce. Today's divorce rate is far higher than that which existed 50 years ago. However, in recent years, this trend seems to have leveled off and may even be reversing itself. In 1960, there were 9 divorces per 1,000 married women age 15 or older. In 1980, the rate was 23 divorces for every 1,000 married women over the age of 15. The most recent statistics indicate that the divorce rate has been falling since 1980 and has reached 17 divorces per 1,000 married women over age 15. The marriages most likely to fail are marriages between teenagers, nonreligious marriages in which the bride was pregnant, and marriages of people whose parents had divorced (Popenoe & Whitehead, 2000). But the marriages that do survive are not necessarily happy. Many couples stay together for reasons other than love: because of religious beliefs, for the sake of the children, for financial reasons, or out of fear of facing the future alone.

Divorce often radically alters the course of an adult's life, especially for a woman. For one thing, women who have children often experience a reduced standard of living after divorce. For another, both women and men must often find new networks of friends and often new places to live. On a positive note, research shows that the new friendship networks of divorced mothers help them cope with the effects of divorce (Albeck & Kaydar, 2002). Their networks are larger than those of married women, and the relationships are emotionally closer.

Parenthood. Several studies have shown that marital satisfaction declines after the birth of the first child (Belsky et al., 1989; Cowan & Cowan, 1992; Hackel & Ruble, 1992). The problem appears to center mainly on the division of work—that is, who does what. Even though men are helping with children more than in the past, child

▲ Parenthood can cause stress and conflict in a marriage, but it is also immensely satisfying for most couples.

care still generally ends up being primarily the responsibility of the woman. Unless she holds very traditional views of gender roles, a woman's dissatisfaction after the birth of the first child often relates to the discrepancy between how much help with child care and housework she expected from her husband and how much help she actually receives (Hackel & Ruble, 1992). Thus, you probably won't be surprised to learn that researchers have found that equitable sharing of responsibilities results in a more satisfying marriage (Erel & Burman, 1995). Sharing responsibilities may be especially important when both parents work outside the home. (Tsang, Harvey, Duncan, & Sommer, 2003).

The Myths of Middle Age. As noted at the beginning of the chapter, stereotypes abound for each phase of life. For instance, you may have heard the term *mid-life crisis* to describe the angst middle-aged people feel over their lost youth. Research refutes the idea that middle-aged people go through such a crisis, however. More often, individuals between the ages of 40 and 60 are more likely than either younger or older adults to experience what psychologist David Almeida calls *stressor overload* (Clay, 2003). This condition arises when middle-aged people must balance the demands of mentoring teenaged and young adult children with those associated with caring for aging parents, managing their own careers, finding time for intimate relationships, and looking ahead to retirement. Surprisingly, though, Almeida has found that successful management of these challenges enhances middle-aged adults' sense of competence (Serido, Almeida, & Wethington, 2004).

Another frequent observation about middle age is the idea that parents experience an *empty nest syndrome* when their grown children leave home. Contrary to this popular stereotype, parents often appreciate the opportunity to reexamine their identity that is afforded by their children's departure from home (Noriko, 2004; Norris & Tindale, 1994). Moreover, analyses show that the presence of an empty nest has little or no relationship to the appearance of mental disorders such as depression at mid-life (Schmidt et al., 2004). Thus, the concept of an empty nest syndrome seems to have little basis in reality.

▲ When their children leave home to go to college or get a job, most parents do not experience the sadness associated with the "empty nest syndrome" but instead are able to adjust successfully.

Reinke's Life Course for Women. Some theorists believe that theory and research examining adult development have focused more on models that apply to men than on those that may better explain women's experiences. Reinke and her colleagues (1985) interviewed 124 middle-class women aged 30 to 60 to gain information about their marriages, families, employment, life satisfactions and dissatisfactions, and life changes. The researchers found major transitional periods in which participants seemed to reappraise their lives and consider changes. Some of these transitional periods were related to specific chronological ages, but the researchers believe that married women's development is best viewed in terms of six phases in the family cycle: (1) the no-children phase, (2) the starting-a-family/preschool phase, (3) the school-age phase, (4) the adolescent phase, (5) the launching phase (beginning when the first child leaves home and ending when the last child leaves), and (6) the postparental phase. Changes were reliably associated with each of the six family-cycle phases, regardless of whether women had experienced major transitions. Although Reinke's research is now more than 20 years old, it continues to be relevant to women who seek to balance work and family roles. Many such women make career decisions based on how the consequences of such decisions will affect their families (Hill, Märtinson, Ferris, & Baker, 2004). These women also frequently make family decisions (e.g., when to have a child) with an eye toward how such decisions will affect their careers. As a result, they are likely to experience the same kinds of reappraisals as Reinke's participants did at similar points in their lives.

Remember It   Early and Middle Adulthood

1. Most people reach their physical peak while they are in their _____.

2. From the 20s to the 40s, intellectual performance tends to _____.

3. While attending college, young adults form _____ that serve as the primary source of social support.

4. About _____ percent of adults in the United States marry at least once.

5. Marriage is associated with advantages in _____ and _____.

6. Since 1980, divorce rates have (risen, fallen).

Answers: 1. 20s; 2. increase; 3. social networks; 4. 80; 5. income, health 6. fallen

Later Adulthood

What are your perceptions of old age? The statistics in the *Try It* below might surprise you. As we noted at the outset of this chapter, the most remarkable characteristic of later adulthood is the degree of variability that exists across individuals. Some of us do quite well in our later years, and others suffer from devastating losses.

Try It   Stereotypes about Later Adulthood

Estimate the percentages of people older than age 65 in the United States who exhibit these indicators of well-being:

1. Live alone or with a spouse
2. Have incomes above the poverty level
3. Interact with family at least once every two weeks
4. Need no help with daily activities
5. Need no assistive devices (e.g., cane, wheelchair)

6. Go out to eat at least once every two weeks
7. Attend religious services regularly
8. Are sexually active

Sources: FIFARS (2000, 2004); Gingell et al. (2003).

Answers: 1. 94%; 2. 90%; 3. 90%; 4. 89%; 5. 85%; 6. 60%; 7. 50%; 8. 50%

Physical Changes in Later Adulthood

9.14 What are some physical changes associated with later adulthood?

Do you know which age group in the United States is increasing in size most rapidly? You have probably heard that it is the elderly. But did you know that it is the oldest group of elders, those over the age of 85, that is increasing at the most rapid rate (U.S. Census Bureau, 2005)? This is the phenomenon to which social scientists are referring when they speak of the "graying" of society. Not only are the elderly more numerous than ever, but more of them are enjoying life in relatively good health (Morley & van den Berg, 2000). In fact, the majority of older adults are active, healthy, and self-sufficient (Schaie & Willis, 1996). Still, the effects of primary aging are far more evident in later than in middle adulthood.

Primary and Secondary Aging Effects. One primary aging effect is **general slowing,** a process in which the reductions in the speed of neural transmission lead to a slowing of physical and mental functions. General slowing results from the breakdown of the myelin sheaths of individual neurons in the brain (Birren & Fisher, 1995; Peters et al., 1994; Wickelgren, 1996). It is also influenced by the deaths of the neurons themselves, a process that causes the brain to shrink somewhat and the cortex to thin (Joynt, 2000; Salat et al., 2004). A decrease in the rate at which the body supplies oxygen to the brain also helps explain general slowing (Mehagnoul-Schipper et al., 2002).

general slowing A process in which the reduction in the speed of neural transmission leads to a slowing of physical and mental functions.

Neuroscientists point out that these features of normal neurological aging do not necessarily lead to changes in the quality of an individual's mental performance (Joynt, 2000). In fact, such changes can be observed in the brains of elderly people who function quite competently. Furthermore, the brain has a number of compensatory mechanisms. For instance, the capacity of neurons for developing new synapses appears to continue until death. And the brain's redundancy—that is, its tendency to create multiple neuronal networks to serve all kinds of physical and mental functions—also helps to moderate the effects of primary aging.

By contrast, there is little doubt that primary aging affects sensory functioning (Joynt, 2000). Vision, hearing, and all the other senses decline with age. However, most senior citizens find ways to compensate for sensory changes. For instance, reading glasses or corrective surgery can prevent increasing levels of farsightedness from interfering with elders' daily activities. Likewise, there are many kinds of hearing aids to help offset hearing losses. Similarly, older adults' problems with mobility can be addressed in a variety of ways. For example, there are special grips available for pens and pencils that can help seniors with joint pain to write more comfortably. Likewise, there is a vast array of products designed to prevent falls in bath areas.

With regard to secondary aging, research shows that it is never too late to make lifestyle changes that will enhance one's health. Experimental studies in which experimental groups exercise while control groups engage in some kind of non-physical activity (e.g., nutrition education) are especially telling in this regard. Most such studies indicate that elders who exercise get better scores on measures of physical functioning (e.g., muscular strength, blood pressure, heart rate) than those who do not (e.g., Blumenthal et al., 1991; Carmeli, Reznick, Coleman, & Carmeli, 2000; Tsang & Hui-Chan, 2003). Remarkably, interventions as short as two weeks in duration are sufficient to produce such differences (Small, 2005). Such findings have implications for cognitive functioning as well. Schaie's longitudinal studies show that cardiovascular health is the best physical predictor of intellectual ability in old age, and, of course, exercise is known to increase cardiovascular fitness (Schaie, 2005).

Sex and the Senior Citizen. Are you surprised to learn that people in their 90s are sexually active? Older adults are less sexually active than those who are younger, but not by much. Surveys indicate that more than 70% of adults over age 65 in the United States are still sexually active. Moreover, in a survey of adults aged 80 to 102 who were not taking medication, 70% of the men and 50% of the women admitted fantasizing about intimate sexual relations often or very often. And 63% of the men and 30% of the women were doing more than fantasizing—they were still having sex (McCarthy, 1989).

Declines in testosterone associated with aging in both men and women are partly responsible for diminished sexual activity and pleasure. However, research suggests that older adults compensate for these primary aging effects with sexual experimentation. For example, elderly women are more likely to be willing to watch sexually explicit films with their partners than are younger women (Purnine & Carey, 1998). Clearly, sexual activity remains an important component of adults' lives, no matter how old they are. Moreover, the reasons for engaging in sexual activity do not change with age. Thus, it appears that elders have just as much need for love, affection, and physical intimacy as younger adults do (Kamel, 2001).

Successful Aging. A recent concept in *gerontology* (the scientific study of aging) is that of successful aging. First proposed by gerontologists John Rowe and Robert Kahn (1998), the *successful aging perspective* provides researchers with a comprehensive theoretical framework from which to derive hypotheses about aging. Essentially, Rowe and Kahn maintain that successful aging is a function of an elderly individual's status and characteristics across three domains: physical health, cognitive functioning, and social engagement. Individuals are deemed as having aged successfully if they effectively integrate their levels of functioning in the three domains. In other words, if an elderly woman has a physical ailment that limits her activities, she may compensate for this limitation in the cognitive domain by reading more or listening to music.

Cognitive Changes in Later Adulthood

9.15 What happens to mental ability in later adulthood?

Intellectual decline in later adulthood is not inevitable. Older adults who keep mentally and physically active tend to retain their mental skills. They do well on tests of vocabulary, comprehension, and general information, and their ability to solve practical problems is generally higher than that of young adults. And they are just as capable as younger adults at learning new cognitive strategies (Saczynski et al., 2002).

Researchers often distinguish between two types of intelligence (Horn, 1982): **Crystallized intelligence**—verbal ability and accumulated knowledge—tends to increase over the lifespan. **Fluid intelligence**—abstract reasoning and mental flexibility—peaks in the early 20s and declines slowly as people age. The rate at which people process information also slows gradually with age (Hertzog, 1991; Lindenberger et al., 1993; Salthouse, 1996; Schaie, 2005). This explains, in part, why older adults perform more poorly on mental tasks requiring speed. When tasks do not involve speed, however, elderly adults perform just as well as those who are younger.

Several factors are positively correlated with good cognitive functioning in the elderly. They are education level (Vander Elst et al., 2006), a complex work environment, a long marriage to an intelligent spouse, and a higher income (Schaie, 2005). Gender is a factor as well: Women not only outlive men; they generally show less cognitive decline during old age. A study by Shimamura and others (1995) revealed that people who continue to lead intellectually stimulating and mentally active lives are far less likely to suffer mental decline as they age. Moreover, there is some evidence that physical exercise positively affects cognitive functioning in old age (Colcombe & Kramer, 2003; Small, 2005).

▲ Older adults take more time to learn new skills, but, once learned, they apply new skills as accurately as those who are younger.

Alzheimer's Disease—the Most Common Dementia

9.16 How does Alzheimer's disease affect the brain?

Athough most older adults are in full possession of their intellectual faculties, the rapid population growth among the elderly has brought an increase in the number of individuals who suffer from severe, age-related cognitive disabilities. As adults get older, the likelihood that they will develop one of several dementias increases. The **dementias** are a group of neurological disorders in which problems with memory and thinking affect an individual's emotional, social, and physical functioning. Dementias are not part of normal aging, but both their incidence and severity increase with age (He et al., 2005; Head et al., 2005). Dementias are caused by physical deterioration of the brain. They can result from cerebral arteriosclerosis (hardening of the arteries in the brain), chronic alcoholism, or irreversible damage by a series of small strokes. But about half of all cases of dementia result from **Alzheimer's disease,** a progressive and incurable disorder that involves widespread degeneration and disruption of brain cells.

At first, victims of Alzheimer's disease show a gradual impairment in memory and reasoning, and in their efficiency in carrying out everyday tasks. Many have difficulty finding their way around in familiar locations. Alzheimer's patients, even in early stages, have difficulty with temporal memory (time sequences), especially when distractors are present (Putzke et al., 2000). As the disorder progresses, Alzheimer's patients become increasingly unable to care for themselves. Even motor skills, habits, and simple classically conditioned responses are eventually lost (Bäckman et al., 2000). If Alzheimer's patients live long enough, they reach a stage where they do not respond when spoken to and no longer recognize even their spouse or children.

Compared with healthy people of similar age, Alzheimer's patients in one study averaged 68% fewer neurons in parts of the hippocampus, the area of the brain important in the formation and retention of memories (West et al., 1994). Alzheimer's pa-

crystallized intelligence A type of intelligence comprising verbal ability and accumulated knowledge, which tend to increase over the lifespan.

fluid intelligence A type of intelligence comprising abstract reasoning and mental flexibility, which peak in the early 20s and decline slowly as people age.

dementias A group of neurological disorders in which problems with memory and thinking affect an individual's emotional, social, and physical functioning; caused by physical deterioration of the brain.

Alzheimer's disease A progressive and incurable disorder that involves widespread degeneration and disruption of brain cells, resulting in dementia.

tients also show memory impairment beyond that involving the hippocampal region (Hamann et al., 2002; Kensinger et al., 2002). Autopsies of Alzheimer's patients reveal that the cerebral cortex as well as the hippocampus contain neurons clogged with twisted, stringy masses (called *neurofibrillary tangles*) and surrounded by dense deposits of proteins and other materials (called *plaques*) (de Leon et al., 1996; Peskind, 1996; Riley et al., 2002).

◄ As Alzheimer's disease worsens, those afflicted with it need constant reminders of the locations and names of common household items if they are to perform any routine tasks.

Heredity is a major factor in early-onset Alzheimer's, which accounts for about 10% of the disease's victims and develops before age 65—in some cases, as early as the 40s. Heredity is also a major factor in late-onset Alzheimer's, which generally affects people over 65 (Bergem et al., 1997). Alzheimer's has been linked to genes on 4 of the 23 human chromosomes (Selkoe, 1997).

Results from a study of older Americans from various ethnic groups who were suffering from Alzheimer's disease showed that African Americans were less debilitated by the disease than were their Asian, White, and Hispanic counterparts. Compared to the other ethnic groups, African Americans had less depression, less anxiety, and fewer sleep problems (Chen et al., 2000).

Can Alzheimer's disease be delayed? According to researchers, a high IQ coupled with lifelong intellectual activity may delay or lessen the symptoms of Alzheimer's in those who are at risk for the disease (Alexander et al., 1997; Wilson & Bennett, 2003). Unfortunately, though, research aimed at finding ways to prevent or cure the disease have yielded little in the way of positive findings. Vitamins, anti-inflammatory drugs, and the female hormone estrogen have all been ruled out as potential cures or preventives for Alzheimer's disease. However, scientists say that a new vaccine that prevents the development of neurofibrillary tangles shows promise in animal research. A similar vaccine was used in trials with humans a few years ago, but studies were terminated because the vaccine caused swelling in the brains of participants. Investigators now believe that they have solved the swelling problem and will soon reinitiate clinical trials with human beings (Okura et al., 2006).

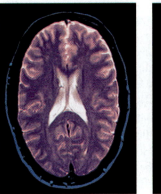 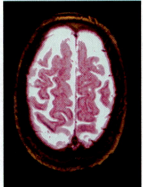

◄ Compared with a normal adult brain (left), the brain of an Alzheimer's patient (right) has a smaller volume and many twisted, stringy masses called *neurofibrillary tangles*.

Social Development and Adjustment in Later Adulthood

Life satisfaction in older adults appears to be most strongly related to good health, as well as to a feeling of control over one's life (Schulz & Heckhausen, 1996). Elders who tend to have an optimistic outlook on life also report higher levels of satisfaction (Hagberg et al., 2002; Litwin, 2005; Mehlsen, 2005). Further, the incidence of optimism itself increases as adults age, perhaps from the tendency to recall fewer negative experiences (Charles et al., 2003). Adequate income, participation in religious and social activities, and a satisfactory marital relationship are also associated with

9.17 What does research indicate about older adults' life satisfaction?

Figure 9.8 Percent of People Aged 65 and Over in Poverty by Living Arrangement, Race, and Hispanic Origin: 2003[1]

Seniors in the United States vary widely in economic status. Note, however, that the highest poverty rates are found among single women.

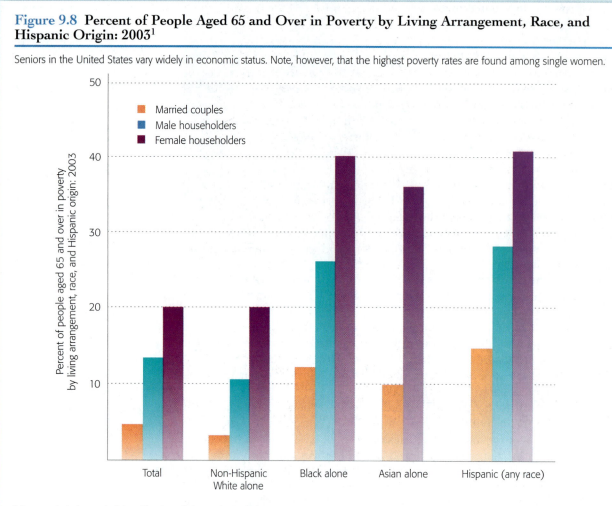

[1] Does not include people living with other relatives and nonrelatives.
Note: The reference population for these data is the civilian noninstitutionalized population.
Source: He et al. (2005).

high levels of life satisfaction in later adulthood (Harlow & Cantor, 1996; Litwin, 2006; Pinquart & Sörensen, 2000).

Contrary to some stereotypes, older adults vary widely in economic status. About 10.5% of Americans over age 65 live below the poverty line, and among them are disproportionately high numbers of African Americans (25.4%) and Hispanic Americans (23.5%) (He et al., 2005). However, as you can see in **Figure 9.8**, married seniors are less likely than singles to be poor, with single African American and Hispanic American women experiencing the highest poverty rates of all groups. Moreover, elderly persons, especially those with cognitive or physical impairments who are struggling to live on small incomes, are especially vulnerable to financial exploitation (Tueth, 2000). But many adults in the 65-plus group live comfortably. With homes that are paid for and no children to support, people over 65 tend to view their financial situation more positively than do younger adults.

Yet old age undoubtedly involves many losses. Health declines, friends die, and some older adults who do not wish to retire must do so because of company policies or for health reasons. When life becomes more burdensome than enjoyable, an older person can fall victim to depression, a serious problem that affects about 15% of the elderly and can even be deadly. White males over age 75 have the highest suicide rate of any age group in the United States (U.S. Census Bureau, 1997). But the rate of major depression seems to be lower among the elderly than among younger persons (Benazzi, 2000).

Another factor affecting life satisfaction involves older adults' career-related decisions. Most older adults in the United States (about 88%) are retired (U.S. Census Bureau, 2001). Despite stereotypes, most of them are happy to leave work and do not experience a great deal of stress in adjusting to retirement. Generally, the people most reluctant to retire are those who are better educated, hold high-status jobs with a good income, and find fulfillment in their work. Bosse and others (1991) found that only 30% of retirees reported finding retirement stressful, and most of those were likely to be in poor health and to have financial problems.

Another common event that may affect life satisfaction for older adults is the loss of a spouse. For most people, losing a spouse is the most stressful event in a lifetime. Disruption of sleep patterns is one of the many physical effects associated with this loss (Steeves, 2002). These physical effects take their toll on the bereaved elderly and lead to tiredness and anxiety. In addition, both widows and widowers are at a greater risk for health problems due to suppressed immune function and have a higher mortality rate, particularly within the first 6 months, than their age-mates who are not bereaved (Martikainen & Valkonen, 1996).

Cultural Differences in Care for the Elderly

As you have learned, the United States, along with some other industrialized countries, will soon have a great many more elderly people to care for and not enough young people to serve as their caretakers. How will these changes affect Americans in different ethnic groups? Can we learn some lessons about elder care from other cultures?

9.18 In what ways do the experiences of older adults differ across cultures?

Older African Americans as well as older Asian and Hispanic Americans are more likely to live with and be cared for by their adult children than are other elderly Americans. African Americans are more likely than White Americans to regard elderly persons with respect and to feel that children should help their older parents (Mui, 1992). Still, multigenerational households are by no means commonplace in the United States, regardless of ethnicity. For the most part, older Americans have a strong preference for maintaining their independence and living in their own homes (Bengston, 1990; He et al., 2005). However, elders in the United States often relocate after retirement to be closer to their children (He et al., 2005). The preference of American older adults for independent living is manifested in the high rates of emotional distress elders experience when they must depend on their children for financial support (Nagumey, Reich, & Newsome, 2004).

In contrast to trends in the United States, elders in Asian nations are likely to be distressed if they live alone rather than with their children (Chou, Chi, & Chow, 2004; McDonald, 2004; Min, 2004). Their distress arises out of the Asian tradition of *filial piety*, the notion that younger generations have an obligation to care for their elders. Because of this tradition, many Asian countries have very limited retirement programs for senior citizens. Thus, multigenerational households are a financial necessity in Japan, Korea, and other Asian nations, and, as a result, grandparents play a vital role in the everyday lives of their grandchildren.

However, social systems based on filial piety do not always work the way they are supposed to. In China, for example, widespread neglect and abuse of the elderly led the government to enact laws that impose fines on families that fail to care for their elderly members (Lijia, 2000). Retirement homes are available for older Chinese adults, but most families do not want to deal with their costs or with the social shame that comes from relegating one's parents to such a facility. Furthermore, with China's booming economy, many young and middle-aged adults are simply too busy working to provide the care their disabled elders require. These problems have led to the

▶ Older African Americans and older members of other minority groups are more likely than older White Americans to live with relatives. However, among all ethnic groups in the United States, aging adults prefer to maintain their independence by living alone. This pattern of living arrangements contrasts sharply with that in many other cultures around the world.

development of an innovative system in which Chinese youth serve as volunteer caregivers for elderly adults in exchange for credits that they can use to obtain similar voluntary helpers in their own later years (Peterson, 2006).

Death and Dying

9.19 According to Kübler-Ross, what stages do terminally ill patients experience as they come to terms with death?

Death, of course, can come at any age. Still, for most people, one of the developmental tasks of old age is to accept the inevitability of death and to prepare for it. Research suggests that impending death may lead to certain psychological responses that are common to dying individuals of all ages.

Kübler-Ross on Death and Dying. As a professor at the University of Colorado, the late Elisabeth Kübler-Ross (1926–2004) stunned her class of first-year medical students when she interviewed a young woman with a terminal disease during the first class meeting of the term (Blaylock, 2005). The students listened intently as Kübler-Ross questioned the woman about her feelings and her strategies for coping with the prospect of dying from a disease that had already seriously eroded her quality of life. Her purpose in doing so was to inspire her students look beyond the pathology of such cases to find the human patient who was struggling to cope with her fate. She extended that goal beyond the confines of her own classes with her landmark book *On Death and Dying* (1969), based on interviews with about 200 terminally ill people. In it she proposed five stages people go through in coming to terms with death.

In the first stage, *denial,* most patients react to the diagnosis of their terminal illness with shock and disbelief. (Surely, the doctors must be wrong.) The second stage, *anger,* is marked by feelings of resentment toward and envy of those who are young and healthy. In the third stage, *bargaining,* the person attempts to postpone death in return for a promise of "good behavior." An individual may offer God some special service or a promise to live a certain kind of life in exchange for an opportunity to attend a child's wedding or a grandchild's graduation. The fourth stage, *depression,* brings a great sense of loss and may take two forms: depression over past losses and depression over impending losses. Given enough time, patients may reach the final stage, *acceptance,* in which they stop struggling against death and contemplate its coming without fear or despair. Kübler-Ross claims that immediate family members also go through stages similar to those experienced by the patient.

Critics deny the universality of Kübler-Ross's proposed stages and their invariant sequence (Butler & Lewis, 1982; Kastenbaum, 1992). Each person is unique. The reactions of all terminally ill people cannot be expected to conform to some rigid sequence of stages. Nevertheless, the place of Kübler-Ross's work in awakening the health care community to the notion that empathy and compassion ought to guide the treatment of individuals who are dying has not been challenged.

Decisions about Death. Death comes too soon for most people, but not soon enough for others. Some who are terminally ill and subject to intractable pain may welcome an end to their suffering. Today, physician-assisted suicide ("requested death") has become the focus of a social movement (McInerney, 2000). The state of Oregon legalized physician-assisted suicide in 1997. Most patients who "request" death cite as their reasons loss of control of bodily functions, loss of autonomy, and inability to take part in activities that make life enjoyable (Sullivan, Hedberg, et al., 2000). However, when Oregon physicians provide such patients with prescriptions for lethal doses of drugs, the patients often do not fill the prescriptions, illustrating that the desire to live is a powerful motivator even among people who wish to escape from pain and suffering (Meers, 2006).

To avoid leaving surviving family members with staggering medical bills, many people write living wills. Under the terms of a typical living will, hospitals and medical professionals are not to use heroic measures or life-support systems to delay the death of a patient who cannot possibly recover, but may linger indefinitely in a comatose state.

A rapidly growing alternative to hospitals and nursing homes is hospice care. *Hospices* are agencies that care for the needs of the dying in ways that differ from traditional hospital care. A hospice follows a set of guidelines attuned to patients' personal needs and preferences. These guidelines include the following:

- The patient and his or her family will control decisions about the patient's care.
- The patient's pain will be managed so that the patient's remaining time is more livable.
- Professional personnel will be available as needed, at any time of the day or night.
- Facilities will be less clinical and more homelike than typical hospital environments are.
- Family members may work with the hospice team as caregivers.
- Family members may receive counseling before and after the patient dies and be helped through the grieving process.

Bereavement. Many of us have experienced the grieving process—the period of bereavement that follows the death of a loved one and sometimes lingers long after the person has gone. Contrary to what many believe, bereaved individuals who suffer the most intense grief initially, who weep inconsolably and feel the deepest pain, do not get through their bereavement more quickly than others (Bonanno et al., 1995). According to one proposed model for how married people cope with bereavement, the grieving spouse at times actively confronts and at other times avoids giving full vent to grief. This dual-process coping, with periods of grieving and periods of relief, seems effective in dealing with the stress of losing a spouse (Stroebe & Schut, 1999).

Researchers have also studied bereavement in those who care for loved ones dying of AIDS. Folkman and her colleagues (1996) interviewed male partners who were caregivers for AIDS patients. From several interviews conducted both before and after the patient's death, they concluded that the gay partners experienced basically the same grieving process as married heterosexuals in similar circumstances did.

Death and dying are not easy subjects to discuss, but doing so helps us remember that each day alive should be treasured like a precious gift.

Remember It   Later Adulthood

1. Which of the following statements is true of older adults as compared to younger adults?
   a. They are less satisfied with life.
   b. They are less likely to be poor.

2. Alzheimer's disease is associated with neurons clogged with _____ and surrounded by _____.

3. Younger adults outperform older adults on cognitive tasks requiring _____.

4. According to Kübler-Ross, the first stage experienced by terminally ill patients in coming to terms with death is _____; the last stage is _____.

5. An agency that is an alternative to a hospital or nursing home as a provider of care for the dying is a _____.

Answers: 1. b; 2. neurofibrillary tangles, plaques; 3. speed; 4. denial, acceptance; 5. hospice

Apply It   Building a Good Relationship

Decide whether each of the following statements about intimate relationships is true or false:

- The best relationships are free from conflict.
- Voicing complaints to one's partner undermines happiness in the relationship.
- Anger in all its forms is a negative emotion that is destructive in a relationship.
- The best way to maintain a relationship is to have a realistic view of one's partner.

All of these statements are true, right? Wrong. Every one of them is false. In studies of couples married 20 years or more, John Gottman (1994) and his colleagues gained some interesting insights on how different aspects of conflict affect relationship quality. You can learn more about Gottman's work and take several different kinds of relationship quizzes at http://www.gottman.com. Here are a few key findings from his studies and those of other researchers.

Complaints

A complaint is limited to a specific situation and states how you feel: "I am upset because you didn't take out the garbage tonight." Complaints may actually make a relationship stronger. In fact, Gottman believes that complaining "is one of the healthiest activities that can occur in a marriage" (1994, p. 73). Why? Because it is better to express your feelings through complaints than to let them seethe until they crystallize into deep-seated resentment.

This is not to say that all complaining is useful. Cross-complaining, in which you counter your partner's complaint with one of your own and ignore what your partner has said, obviously serves no useful purpose. And spouting off a long list of complaints all at once—what Gottman calls "kitchen-sinking" —is not productive either.

Criticism

A complaint is likely to begin with "I," but criticisms typically begin with "you": "You never remember to take out the trash. You promised you would do it, and you broke your promise again." Criticisms also tend to be global, often including the word *always* or *never:* "You never take me anywhere"; "You're always finding fault with me." Criticizing thus goes beyond merely stating a feeling; a criticism is an accusation, sometimes even a personal attack. Frequent criticism can destroy a relationship.

Contempt

Even more damaging than criticism is contempt. As Gottman points out, "what separates contempt from criticism is the intention to insult and psychologically abuse your partner" (1994, p. 79). Contempt basically adds insult to criticism. The insult can take a variety of forms, including name calling, hostile humor, mockery, and body language such as sneering and rolling the eyes. According to Gottman, words such as *jerk, fat,* and *stupid* "are such dangerous assault weapons that they ought to be outlawed" (1994, p. 80).

Anger

Whereas criticism and contempt definitely have negative effects on relationships, anger does not. Anger has negative effects on a relationship only if it is expressed along with criticism or contempt. In fact, according to Gottman, "expressing anger and disagreement—airing a complaint—though rarely pleasant, makes the [relationship] stronger in the long run than suppressing the complaint" (1994, p. 73).

Hints for Resolving Conflicts

Learning to manage conflicts is essential to good relationships (Fincham, 2003). But how can you solve a conflict without resorting to complaining, criticism, contempt, and anger? Try applying these guidelines for resolving conflicts:

- *Be gentle with complaints*. Kindness works wonders when stating a complaint. And remember to avoid criticism.
- *Don't get defensive when your partner makes requests*. Remain positive, and comply willingly and as quickly as possible.
- *Stop conflicts before they get out of hand*. Don't let negative thoughts about your partner grow into criticism or contempt. Do whatever it takes to put the brakes on negativity. Relive in your memory the happiest moments you and your partner have spent together.

Finally, it helps to have a positive, even idealistic, perception of one's partner. Research by Sandra Murray and her colleagues (1996a, 1996b) has shown that in the best relationships partners overlook each other's faults and embellish each other's virtues. A full and accurate assessment of one's partner's imperfections leads to dissatisfaction.

✸ Summary and Review

The Lifespan Perspective p. 315

9.1 How does Erikson's theory of psychosocial development differ from other developmental theories? p. 315

Most developmental theories focus on childhood. By contrast, Erikson believed that individuals progress through eight psychosocial stages that span the entire period from birth to death. Each stage is defined by a conflict involving the individual's relationship with the social environment. A positive resolution of each conflict makes it more likely that an individual will be successful in later stages.

9.2 How did Marcia expand on Erikson's ideas about the adolescent identity crisis? p. 316

Marcia proposed four identity statuses to classify differences in identity among adolescents. Each status represents a particular kind of intersection between crisis and commitment. The four statuses are identity achieved (high crisis/high commitment), moratorium (high crisis/low commitment), foreclosure (low crisis/high commitment), and identity diffusion (low crisis/low commitment).

9.3 In what ways does generativity shape the lives of adults? p. 317

According to Erikson, the need for generativity motivates adults to find ways to contribute to the next generation. Research provides some support for his suggestion that adults who achieve their generativity goals are mentally healthier than those who do not.

Adolescence p. 319

9.4 What physical and psychological changes occur as a result of puberty? p. 319

Puberty is characterized by the adolescent growth spurt, further development of the reproductive organs, and the appearance of the secondary sex characteristics. Early maturation provides enhanced status for boys, because of their physical advantage in sports and greater attractiveness to girls. Late maturation puts boys at a disadvantage in these areas, resulting in a lack of confidence that can persist into adulthood. Early-maturing girls are often self-conscious and dissatisfied with their bodies. They are also more likely to be exposed prematurely to alcohol and drug use and to have early sexual experiences and unwanted pregnancies.

9.5   What cognitive abilities develop during adolescence? p. 321

Teenagers acquire hypothetical thinking in Piaget's formal operations stage. Their advanced information-processing skills, compared to those of preadolescents, allow them to better organize text and to keep track of their own memory processes.

9.6   What are the differences among Kohlberg's three levels of moral reasoning? p. 322

At the preconventional level, moral reasoning is governed by the standards of others, and the physical consequences of an act determine whether it is judged as good or bad. At the conventional level of moral reasoning, judgments of right and wrong are based on the internalized standards of others. Postconventional moral reasoning involves weighing moral alternatives and realizing that laws may conflict with basic human rights.

9.7   What outcomes are often associated with the authoritative, authoritarian, and permissive parenting styles? p. 325

Authoritative parenting is most effective and is associated with psychosocial competence in all groups and with academic success in White middle-class teens. Adolescents with authoritarian parents are typically the most psychologically distressed and the least self-reliant and self-confident. Permissive parenting is least effective and is often associated with adolescent drug use and behavior problems.

9.8   What are some of the beneficial functions of the adolescent peer group? p. 326

The adolescent peer group (usually composed of teens with similar interests) provides a vehicle for developing social skills and a standard of comparison against which teens' attributes can be evaluated.

9.9   What are the neurological and psychosocial characteristics of emerging adulthood? p. 326

The parts of the brain that are involved in decision making and self-control mature between the late teens and early twenties. Emerging adults use skills they acquired earlier in life to accomplish developmental tasks in the academic, conduct, and friendship domains. New skills are required for tasks in the work and romantic domains.

Early and Middle Adulthood p. 328

9.10   What is the difference between primary and secondary aging? p. 328

Primary aging is caused by biological processes and is unavoidable; secondary aging results from poor health-related behaviors and lifestyle choices. Physical changes associated with middle age are a loss of physical vigor and endurance, a need for reading glasses,

and the end of reproductive capacity (menopause) in women and a decline in testosterone levels in men.

9.11   In what ways do cognitive functions change between the ages of 20 and 60? p. 329

Although younger people tend to do better on mental tasks requiring speed or rote memory, the intellectual performance of adults shows modest gains until the mid-40s. A modest decline occurs from the 60s to the 80s.

9.12   How does attending college affect adult development? p. 330

Adults who attend college earn more money and possess better cognitive skills than those who do not. They also exhibit higher levels of moral reasoning and empathy. College helps some adults sharpen their self-perceptions, and it influences social development as well.

9.13   What are some current trends in lifestyle patterns among young adults? p. 333

About 53% of the U.S. population live in households headed by a married couple with or without children under 18. Couples are waiting longer to get married and to have children. Marital satisfaction often declines after the birth of the first child, and many married women with children under age 6 hold full-time or part-time jobs outside the home. Research indicates that most middle-aged adults are happy, rather than distressed, when their children leave home.

Later Adulthood p. 336

9.14   What are some physical changes associated with later adulthood? p. 336

Physical changes associated with later adulthood include a general slowing of behavior, a decline in sensory capacity and in heart, lung, kidney, and muscle function, and an increase in chronic conditions such as arthritis, heart problems, and high blood pressure.

9.15   What happens to mental ability in later adulthood? p. 338

Crystallized intelligence tends to increase over the lifespan; fluid intelligence peaks in the early 20s and declines slowly as people age. Although older adults perform cognitive tasks more slowly, if they keep mentally and physically active, they can usually maintain their mental skills as long as their health holds out.

9.16   How does Alzheimer's disease affect the brain? p. 338

Alzheimer's disease is an incurable form of dementia characterized by a progressive deterioration of intellect and personality, resulting from widespread degeneration of brain cells.

9.17 **What does research indicate about older adults' life satisfaction? p. 339**

Life satisfaction in old age is related to good health, a sense of control over one's life, optimism, adequate income, social and religious involvement, and marital satisfaction.

9.18 **In what ways do the experiences of older adults differ across cultures? p. 341**

In the United States, older adults are more likely to live with family members if they are Hispanic, Asian, or African American. However, older Americans of all ethnic groups are more likely to live alone than are their peers in other countries around the world.

9.19 **According to Kübler-Ross, what stages do terminally ill patients experience as they come to terms with death? p. 342**

Kübler-Ross maintains that terminally ill patients go through five stages in coming to terms with death: denial, anger, bargaining, depression, and acceptance.

Thinking Critically about Psychology

1. Look back at Marcia's four identity statuses. Which do you think best describes the present state of your own sense of personal identity? Have you experienced others? If so, what were the circumstances?
2. Choose two of Erikson's stages and use everyday examples to explain how accomplishing the tasks of the earlier stage supports development in the stage that follows.
3. In your view, what are the strengths and weaknesses of Kohlberg's theory of moral development?

Key Terms

adolescence, p. 319
Alzheimer's disease, p. 338
conventional level, p. 323
crystallized intelligence, p. 338
dementias, p. 338
emerging adulthood, p. 326

fluid intelligence, p. 338
general slowing, p. 336
identity crisis, p. 316
lifespan perspective, p. 315
menopause, p. 328
metamemory, p. 322

postconventional level, p. 323
preconventional level, p. 322
presbyopia, p. 328
psychosocial stages, p. 315
puberty, p. 319
secondary sex characteristics, p. 320

Chapter 10

Motivation and Emotion

Continued

The miniature spaceship traveling faster than the speed of light hurtled through space on its way to planet Earth bearing a male infant who had been launched into space by his parents who hoped to save him from the impending destruction of their planet. They programmed the ship to travel to Earth because they knew that the terrestrial environment would provide the cells of the boy's body with the nourishing radiation they required. When the ship landed, a childless couple took the boy to raise as their own.

You probably recognize the infant as none other than Kal-El of Krypton, better known as Superman, the iconic warrior who fights for truth, justice, and the American way. But have you ever stopped to wonder *why* Superman fights for truth and justice? Why doesn't he use his powers for personal gain? These were the questions posed to Mark Waid, an accomplished comic book writer and well-known authority on the history of Superman, when DC Comics hired him in 2002 to refresh the story of Superman's origins for a 21st century audience in a 12-part series called *Superman: Birthright* (Waid, 2005).

To develop motivations for the character of Superman, Waid turned to the work of humanistic psychologist Abraham Maslow. According to Maslow's hierarchy of needs, shown in **Figure 10.1**, individuals must satisfy their needs for physiological well-being and for safety before they are motivated by the higher needs of belongingness and esteem. Once these have been satisfied, the motive for self-actualization, the need to fulfill one's full potential, emerges, and it is then, says Maslow, that people are at their best and at their happiest.

Clearly, Waid realized, Superman was fully self-sufficient with regard to physiological and safety needs. However, because he had grown up in the world of humans and had acquired their values and modes of thinking, Wade thought that the superhero (in the guise of his alter ego, Clark Kent) would

▲ Most people know that Superman is faster than a speeding bullet and able to leap tall buildings in a single bound, but what motivates him to fight for truth and justice? Why doesn't he use his superpowers to gain wealth and power?

have to negotiate the belongingness level just as any other person would.

In search of himself and his place in the world, the 18-year-old Kent in Waid's story embarked on a seven-year search for personal identity during which he traveled the world as a freelance journalist. He learned to love the profession of journalism and decided that his life's work would be in that field. His career choice having been made, one aspect of Clark Kent's quest for belongingness was satisfied. How, though, could he meaningfully integrate his superpowers into his life? Kent gained two insights during his travels that helped to answer this question.

First, from a bold African social leader, Kent learned that his plight was no different than that of any human who is uncertain about how his or her abilities can best be used. In other words, he learned that self-esteem comes from ascertaining the purpose for which one has been uniquely prepared and committing oneself to fulfilling it. When Kent realized that this notion could be applied to his superpowers and the potential they offered him for serving others, he took an important step toward achieving belongingness.

Kent's second major insight came from the electronic history book that his natural parents had packed in his spaceship. He had taken the book with him on his journey, although he could not read the words it contained. While traveling, he searched its images of Krypton's past for anything that might

Figure 10.1 Maslow's Hierarchy of Needs

According to humanistic psychologist Abraham Maslow, "higher" motives, such as the need for esteem, go unheeded when "lower" motives, such as the need for safety, have not been met.

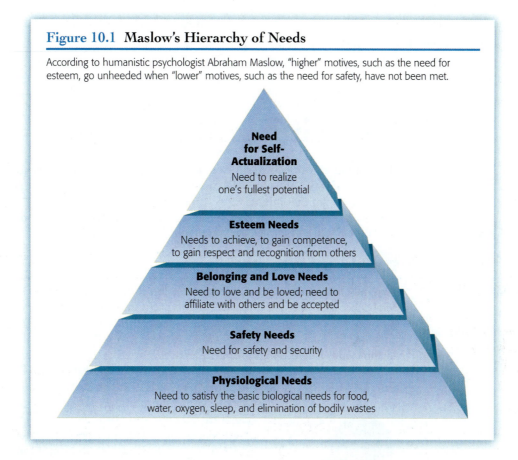

give him insight into his natural origins. He was struck by the prominence of a mysterious symbol that he recognized as the same one that had been on the cloth in which his adoptive parents had found him swaddled. Kent determined that this symbol had been of great importance to the society into which he had been born. Ultimately, for Kent, the symbol came to represent all of the valiant characteristics he saw in the people whose images appeared in the book. Thus, he decided that he would use it to symbolize his desire to live up to the ideals of the culture from which he had come through its incorporation into the uniform he would wear when using his superpowers.

As a result of these insights, Kent knew that using his superpowers to help the citizens of his adopted home in a fight for truth and justice was the only means by which he could achieve both belongingness and esteem. Through the persona of Clark Kent, he would learn to better understand them. Furthermore, the common ground between his true self, the person who would later become known as "Superman," and his human neighbors would be that their enemies would be his enemies.

What Waid's Clark Kent had learned, in summary, was that belongingness does not require being like everyone else. Instead, it involves finding the unique role in which one is best suited to serve. Furthermore, self-esteem comes from accept-

ing this role and making an unwavering commitment to it. Having achieved these insights, Kent was ready to respond to Maslow's ultimate motivating force, the drive for self-actualization. Pseudo-Earthman Clark Kent was poised to become the best journalist he could be, and the super-strong, super-fast, super-intelligent visitor from beyond was primed to discover the full extent of his gifts and the good that he might achieve through them.

Perhaps you can see parallels between Clark Kent's quest for belongingness and your own. At this point in your life, you have probably gotten beyond the self-conscious, I-don't-fit-in-anywhere feelings of adolescence. But do you get butterflies in your stomach when you consider the prospect of looking for your place in the world beyond your family, friends, and college campus? According to Maslow, the desire to quell those butterflies is exactly what will push you to resolve your dilemma. Like Clark Kent, it is likely that you will learn that you don't have to adopt other people's values or goals to fit in. You simply have to find out how to use your unique characteristics in ways that allow you to develop the sense of social connectedness that Maslow believed to be vital to your well-being. From there, you can move on to the greater challenges of finding esteem and, finally, seeking self-actualization.

Maslow's hierarchy of needs is just one of several approaches psychologists have developed to explain why people do what they do. In this chapter you will learn about these the-ories, the research that supports them, and the related topic of human emotion. We will begin by thinking about how to define motivation in order to make it amenable to scientific study.

Explaining Motivation

The first step toward the scientific study of any phenomenon is to establish a workable definition of it. For psychologists, **motivation** is a very broad term that encompasses all the processes that initiate, direct, and sustain behavior. As such, it takes in a lot of mental and behavioral territory. To make the task of studying motivation more manageable, we will break the topic down into its constituent parts.

motivation   All the processes that initiate, direct, and sustain behavior.

The Components of Motivation

10.1   How do the three components of motivation work together to influence behavior?

Generally, psychologists consider motivation to have three components: activation, persistence, and intensity. To understand each, think about the role of motivation in studying for an exam. In the *activation* phase, you take the first steps required to achieve your goal of being prepared for the exam. You find out what will be covered on the exam; locate the appropriate material in your textbook, notes, and other resources; and develop a study plan. *Persistence* is the faithful and continued effort put forth in working toward a goal. In other words, this phase of motivation requires that you put your plan into action and stick to it even in the face of distractions and obstacles. *Intensity* refers to the focused energy and attention applied in order to achieve the goal. When you study, do you get caught up in your interest in the subject matter or in the emotional roller coaster that comes from thinking about the alternate possibilities of success and failure? Either way, it's the intensity component of motivation that's at work.

In addition to breaking motivation into its component parts, researchers can further their understanding of motivation by working from a precise definition of the term *motive*, a concept that is narrower than the full scope of motivation itself. A **motive** is a need or desire that energizes and directs behavior toward a goal. The motives that might compel a student to study for an exam are many. The student might derive self-esteem from getting good grades, or she might desire to escape from the anxiety that comes from a failing grade. Either motive would push her in the direction of moving through the motivational steps outlined above. Thus, two people could exhibit exactly the same behavior on the basis of very different motives.

▲ Which is the more powerful motivator in a game of poker, the gratification that comes from devising a successful strategy (intrinsic motivation) or the money you get when you win (extrinsic motivation)? As is true of many activities, poker is an engaging hobby (or profession, depending on your skill level) that involves both intrinsic and extrinsic motivators.

Intrinsic and Extrinsic Motivation

10.2   What is the difference between intrinsic and extrinsic motivation?

motives   Needs or desires that energize and direct behavior toward a goal.

intrinsic motivation   The desire to behave in a certain way because it is enjoyable or satisfying in and of itself.

As noted earlier, motives direct behavior toward a goal. Motives can arise from something inside yourself, such as when you keep studying because you find the subject matter interesting. Such activities are pursued as ends in themselves, simply because they are enjoyable, not because any external reward is attached. This type of motivation is known as **intrinsic motivation.**

Other motives originate from outside, as when some external stimulus, or **incentive,** pulls or entices you to act. When the desire to get a good grade—or to avoid a bad grade—causes you to study, the grade is serving as this kind of external incentive. When we act so as to gain some external reward or to avoid some undesirable consequence, we are pulled by **extrinsic motivation.**

According to B. F. Skinner, a reinforcer is a consequence that increases the frequency of a behavior. Once the link between a behavior and a reinforcer has been established, the expectation of receiving the reinforcer again serves as an incentive to perform the behavior. For example, the prospect of getting a generous tip serves as an incentive for restaurant servers to serve their customers promptly and courteously.

In real life, the motives for many activities are both intrinsic and extrinsic. You may love your job, but you would probably be motivated to leave if your salary, an important extrinsic motivator, were taken away. Although grades are extrinsic motivators, outstanding grades—especially when earned on a particularly difficult assignment or exam—usually bring with them a sense of pride in a job well done (an intrinsic motivator). Table 10.1 gives examples of intrinsic and extrinsic motivation.

Biological Approaches to Motivation

Perhaps you have heard the term *instinct* used to explain why spiders spin webs or birds fly south in the winter. An instinct is a fixed behavior pattern that is characteristic of every member of a species and is assumed to be genetically programmed. Thus, instincts represent one kind of biological motivation. Psychologists generally agree that no true instincts motivate human behavior. However, most also agree that biological forces underlie some human behaviors.

One biological approach to motivation, **drive-reduction theory,** was popularized by Clark Hull (1943). According to Hull, all living organisms have certain biological needs that must be met if they are to survive. A need gives rise to an internal state of tension called a **drive,** and the person or organism is motivated to reduce it. For example, when you are deprived of food or go too long without water, your biological need causes a state of tension—in this case, the hunger or thirst drive. You become motivated to seek food or water to reduce the drive and satisfy your biological need.

Drive-reduction theory is derived largely from the biological concept of **homeostasis**—the tendency of the body to maintain a balanced, internal state to ensure physical survival. Body temperature, blood sugar level, water balance, blood oxygen level—in short, everything required for physical existence—must be maintained in a state of equilibrium, or balance. When such a state is disturbed, a drive is created to restore the balance, as shown in Figure 10.2. But drive-reduction theory cannot fully account for the broad range of human motivation. It cannot explain why some people, often called *sensation seekers* by psychologists, love the thrill they experience when engaging in activities that produce states of tension—such as skydiving or bungee-jumping.

Drive-reduction theorists cannot explain sensation seeking because the theory assumes that humans are always motivated to reduce tension. Other theorists argue just the opposite, that humans are sometimes motivated to increase tension. These theorists use the term **arousal** to refer to a person's state of alertness and mental and physical activation. Arousal levels can range from no arousal (when a person is comatose),

incentive   An external stimulus that motivates behavior (for example, money or fame).

extrinsic motivation   The desire to behave in a certain way in order to gain some external reward or to avoid some undesirable consequence.

10.3 How do drive-reduction and arousal theory explain motivation?

drive-reduction theory   A theory of motivation suggesting that biological needs create internal states of tension or arousal—called drives—which organisms are motivated to reduce.

drive   An internal state of tension or arousal that is brought about by an underlying need and that an organism is motivated to reduce.

homeostasis   The natural tendency of the body to maintain a balanced internal state in order to ensure physical survival.

arousal   A state of alertness and mental and physical activation.

Table 10.1   Intrinsic and Extrinsic Motivation

	Description	Examples
Intrinsic motivation	An activity is pursued as an end in itself because it is enjoyable and rewarding.	A person anonymously donates a large sum of money to a university to fund scholarships for deserving students.
		A child reads several books each week because reading is fun.
Extrinsic motivation	An activity is pursued to gain an external reward or to avoid an undesirable consequence.	A person agrees to donate a large sum of money to a university for the construction of a building, provided it will bear the family name.
		A child reads two books each week to avoid losing TV privileges.

▲ People vary greatly in the amount of arousal they can tolerate. For some people, the heightened level of arousal they experience when hanging from the surface of a sheer cliff like this one is enjoyable. Others prefer less arousing activities.

to moderate arousal (when pursuing normal day-to-day activities), to high arousal (when excited and highly stimulated). **Arousal theory** states that people are motivated to maintain an optimal level of arousal. If arousal is less than the optimal level, we do something to stimulate it; if arousal exceeds the optimal level, we seek to reduce the stimulation.

When arousal is too low, **stimulus motives**—such as curiosity and the motives to explore, to manipulate objects, and to play—cause humans and other animals to increase stimulation. Think about sitting in an airport or at a bus stop, or any other place where people are waiting. How many people do you see playing games on their cell phones or personal digital assistants (PDAs)? Waiting is boring; in other words, it provides no sources of arousal. Thus, people turn to electronic games to raise their level of arousal.

There is often a close link between arousal and performance. According to the **Yerkes-Dodson law,** performance on tasks is best when the person's arousal level is appropriate to the difficulty of the task. Performance on simple tasks is better when arousal is relatively high. Tasks of moderate difficulty are best accomplished when arousal is moderate; complex or difficult tasks, when arousal is lower (see **Figure 10.3**). But performance suffers when arousal level is either too high or too low for the task. For instance, how often have you heard about great athletes who "choke" in critical situations compared to those who "come through" under pressure? Perhaps high-pressure situations push the athletes who choke past the optimal point of arousal but have just the opposite effect on the reliable athletes.

The relationship between arousal and performance is most often explained in terms of attention. Low arousal allows the mind to wander, so performance declines for tasks that require concentration, such as taking a test. By contrast, high arousal interferes with concentration by taking up all the available space in working memory. The ideal level of arousal for test taking, then, is an amount that is sufficient to keep the mind from wandering but not so great as to interfere with the

arousal theory A theory of motivation suggesting that people are motivated to maintain an optimal level of alertness and physical and mental activation.

stimulus motives Motives that cause humans and other animals to increase stimulation when the level of arousal is too low (examples are curiosity and the motive to explore).

Yerkes-Dodson law The principle that performance on tasks is best when the arousal level is appropriate to the difficulty of the task: higher arousal for simple tasks, moderate arousal for tasks of moderate difficulty, and lower arousal for complex tasks.

Figure 10.2 Drive-Reduction Theory

Drive-reduction theory is based on the biological concept of homeostasis—the natural tendency of a living organism to maintain a state of internal balance, or equilibrium. When the equilibrium becomes disturbed (by a biological need such as thirst), a drive (an internal state of arousal or tension) emerges. Then, the organism is motivated to take action to satisfy the need, thus reducing the drive and restoring equilibrium.

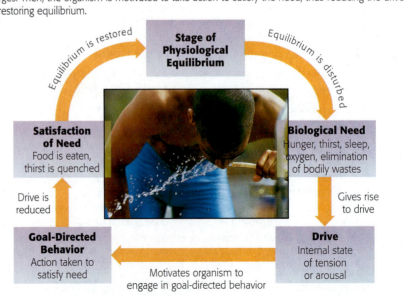

Equilibrium is restored → **Stage of Physiological Equilibrium** → Equilibrium is disturbed

Satisfaction of Need
Food is eaten, thirst is quenched

Biological Need
Hunger, thirst, sleep, oxygen, elimination of bodily wastes

Drive is reduced

Gives rise to drive

Goal-Directed Behavior
Action taken to satisfy need

Motivates organism to engage in goal-directed behavior

Drive
Internal state of tension or arousal

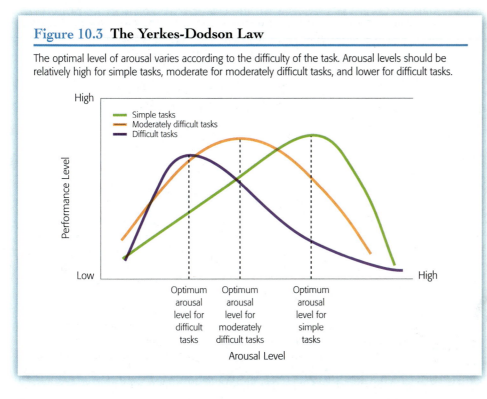

Figure 10.3 **The Yerkes-Dodson Law**

The optimal level of arousal varies according to the difficulty of the task. Arousal levels should be relatively high for simple tasks, moderate for moderately difficult tasks, and lower for difficult tasks.

memory demands of taking the test. Critics of this theory have argued that arousal is merely one of many variables that influence attention (Hanoch & Vitouch, 2004). Moreover, they point out that the Yerkes-Dodson law is based primarily on animal research (Hancock & Ganey, 2003). For these reasons, they caution against generalizing arousal theory to complex human behaviors such as test performance without taking into account other factors that influence how humans allocate attention.

Remember It   Explaining Motivation

1. In Maslow's view, _____ and _____ needs must be met before a person can be motivated by needs for social belonging, esteem, and self-actualization.

2. When you engage in an activity in order to gain a reward or to avoid an unpleasant consequence, your motivation is _____.

3. Drive-reduction theory focuses primarily on _____ needs and the drives they produce.

4. According to arousal theory, people seek _____ levels of arousal.

Answers: 1. physiological, safety; 2. extrinsic; 3. biological; 4. optimal

---

Two Primary Drives: Hunger and Thirst

Do you think Maslow was right when he suggested that physiological needs must be met before higher goals can motivate our behavior? For instance, do you find it difficult to concentrate on studying, a behavior motivated by your esteem needs, when you are feeling hunger pangs? Most people would probably agree that at times, physiological drives demand our full attention, although we don't often think of them as being psychologically important. Physiological drives are usually referred

primary drive A state of tension or arousal that arises from a biological need and is unlearned.

to as **primary drives,** those that are unlearned and that serve to satisfy biological needs. Two of the most important primary drives are thirst and hunger.

Thirst

10.4 Under what conditions do the two types of thirst occur?

Thirst is a basic biological drive, for all animals must have a continuous supply of fluid. Adequate fluid is critical because the body itself is about 75% water. Without any intake of fluids, a person can survive only about 4 or 5 days.

There are two types of thirst. *Extracellular thirst* occurs when fluid is lost from the body tissues. If you are exercising heavily or doing almost anything in hot weather, you will perspire and lose bodily fluid. Bleeding, vomiting, and diarrhea also rob your body of fluid. In addition, alcohol increases extracellular fluid loss. This is why people awaken with a powerful thirst after drinking heavily the night before.

Intracellular thirst involves the loss of water from inside the body cells. When you eat a lot of salty food, the water-sodium balance in the blood and in the tissues outside the cells is disturbed, so the cells release some of their own water into surrounding tissues to restore the balance. As the body cells become dehydrated, thirst is stimulated and you drink to increase their water volume (Robertson, 1983). This explains why so many bars offer customers free salted nuts, chips, or pretzels—to stimulate their thirst for more drinks.

Internal and External Hunger Cues

10.5 How do internal and external hunger cues influence eating behavior?

You probably won't be surprised to learn that hunger, the other major primary drive, is a bit more complex than thirst. We'll look at hunger and eating from a biological perspective, before turning to its psychological and social aspects. What happens in the body to make you feel hungry, and what causes *satiety*—the feeling of being full or satisfied?

lateral hypothalamus (LH) The part of the hypothalamus that acts as a feeding center to incite eating.

ventromedial hypothalamus (VMH) The part of the hypothalamus that acts as a satiety (fullness) center to inhibit eating.

The Hypothalamus. Researchers have found two areas of the hypothalamus that are of central importance in regulating eating behavior and thus affect the hunger drive (Steffens et al., 1988). As researchers discovered long ago, the **lateral hypothalamus (LH)** acts as a feeding center to incite eating. Stimulating the feeding center causes animals to eat even when they are full (Delgado & Anand, 1953). And when the feeding center is destroyed, animals initially refuse to eat (Anand & Brobeck, 1951).

The **ventromedial hypothalamus (VMH)** apparently acts as a satiety (fullness) center that inhibits eating (Hernandez & Hoebel, 1989). If the satiety center is electrically stimulated, animals stop eating (Duggan & Booth, 1986). If the VMH is surgically removed, animals soon eat their way to gross obesity (Hetherington & Ranson, 1940; Parkinson & Weingarten, 1990).

More recent studies have suggested that referring to the LH as the brain's hunger center and the VMH as its satiety center fails to convey the subtle ways in which the neurons in these organs influence eating and body weight (King, 2006; Pinel, 2007). For one thing, animals eventually recover from LH damage and resume eating (Teitelbaum, 1957). Similarly, the effects of VMH damage are not permanent. A rat whose VMH is damaged will eventually stop overeating. In addition, damage to the VMH renders laboratory rats less willing to work (i.e., press a lever) in order to get food and more particular about what kinds of foods they are willing to eat. Thus, on balance, it's difficult to see how damage to the VMH alone might lead to obesity. Therefore, although the hypothalamus clearly plays a role in eating behavior, researchers have yet to determine precisely how its role is shaped by both its own neurons and biochemical signals from other components of the body's hunger management system.

▲ A rat whose satiety center has been destroyed can weigh up to six times as much as a normal rat—in this case, 1,080 grams, enough to exceed the capacity of the scale.

Other Internal Hunger and Satiety Signals. Other body structures and processes contribute to feelings of hunger and satiety. For example, the fuller the stomach, even when the substance with which it is filled is a non-nourishing one such as water, the less hunger we feel. (Remember this the next time you are trying to curb your appetite.) Moreover, some of the substances secreted by the gastrointestinal tract during digestion, such as the hormone cholecystokinin (CCK), act as satiety signals (Geary, 2004).

Changes in blood sugar level and the hormones that regulate it also contribute to sensations of hunger. Blood levels of glucose are monitored by nutrient detectors in the liver that send this information to the brain (Friedman et al., 1986). Hunger is stimulated when the brain receives the message that blood levels of glucose are low. Similarly, insulin, a hormone produced by the pancreas, chemically converts glucose into energy that is usable by the cells. Elevations in insulin cause an increase in hunger, in food intake, and in a desire for sweets (Rodin et al., 1985). In fact, chronic oversecretion of insulin stimulates hunger and often leads to obesity.

External Signals. Sensory cues such as the taste, smell, and appearance of food stimulate the appetite. For many, the hands of a clock alone, signaling mealtime, are enough to prompt a quest for food. Even eating with others tends to stimulate people to eat more than they would if they were eating alone (de Castro & de Castro, 1989). For some individuals, simply seeing or thinking about food can cause an elevated level of insulin, and such people have a greater tendency to gain weight (Rodin, 1985).

Table 10.2 summarizes the factors that stimulate and inhibit eating.

▲ Just the sight of mouth-watering foods can make us want to eat, even when we aren't actually hungry.

Explaining Variations in Body Weight

Obviously, body weight can vary tremendously from one individual to another, even when two people are the same size in other dimensions, such as height and shoe size. Extremes in either fatness or thinness can pose health risks, as you'll learn in Chapter 12. In some cases, these extremes result from variations in the hunger-satiety system itself rather than simply from differences in eating and exercise patterns. Before considering the various factors that affect variations in body weight, we will consider how such variations are measured.

10.6 What are some factors that account for variations in body weight?

The Body Mass Index. Health care professionals classify individuals' body weights using a measure of weight relative to height called the **body mass index** or **BMI.** A BMI less than 18.5 is considered underweight, while one in excess of 25 is classified as overweight. To calculate your BMI, use this formula or use the BMI calculator at http://www.cdc.gov/nccdphp/dnpa/bmi/index.htm:

$$[\text{weight in pounds}/(\text{height in inches} \times \text{height in inches})] \times 703$$

Understanding variations in body weight has become an important public health topic in recent years because of the link between excessive weight and health problems such as heart disease and arthritis (National Center for Health Statistics, 2004). As you can see in **Figure 10.4**, the prevalence of overweight (BMI between 25 and 29.9) and **obesity** (BMI over 30) have risen dramatically over the past three decades. Nearly one-third of adults in the United States are obese, and another third are overweight. There are several proposed causes for both normal variations in weight and obesity (NCES, 2004).

body mass index (BMI)   A measure of weight relative to height.

obesity   BMI more than 30

Table 10.2 Biological and Environmental Factors That Inhibit and Stimulate Eating

	Biological	Environmental
Factors that inhibit eating	Activity in ventromedial hypothalamus	Unappetizing smell, taste, or appearance of food
	Raised blood glucose levels	Acquired taste aversions
	Distended (full) stomach	Learned eating habits
	CCK (hormone that acts as satiety signal)	Desire to be thin
	Sensory-specific satiety	Reaction to stress or unpleasant emotional state
Factors that stimulate eating	Activity in lateral hypothalamus	Appetizing smell, taste, or appearance of food
	Low blood levels of glucose	Acquired food preferences
	Increase in insulin	Being around others who are eating
	Stomach contractions	Foods high in fat and sugar
	Empty stomach	Learned eating habits
		Reaction to boredom, stress, or unpleasant emotional state

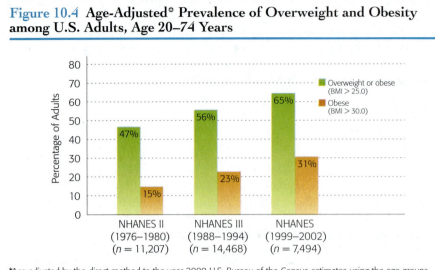

Figure 10.4 Age-Adjusted* Prevalence of Overweight and Obesity among U.S. Adults, Age 20–74 Years

*Age-adjusted by the direct method to the year 2000 U.S. Bureau of the Census estimates using the age groups 20–39, 40–59, and 60–74 years.
Source: National Center for Health Statistics (2004).

Heredity. Across all weight classes, from very thin to very obese, children adopted from birth tend to resemble their biological parents more than their adoptive parents in body size. A review of studies encompassing more than 100,000 participants found that 74% of identical twin pairs had similar body weights. Only 32% of fraternal twins, however, had comparable body weights. The researchers reported an estimated heritability for body weight of between .50 and .90 (Barsh et al., 2000).

A gene map for human obesity has been constructed; it contains information about 15 different chromosome regions (Perusse et al., 1999). More than 40 genes appear to be related to obesity and the regulation of body weight (Barsh et al., 2000). Moreover, these genes interact in complex ways (Grigorenko, 2003), and so genetically based obesity isn't simply a matter of inheriting a gene or two from one's parents. At present, scientists don't know why one person who has a particular obesity-related genetic profile is obese, whereas another is not. Once the functioning of such genes is clearly understood, perhaps new weight-loss drugs or even high-tech treatments such as gene therapy can be developed to fight obesity more effectively than currently available methods.

Hormones. But what exactly do people inherit that affects body weight? Researchers Friedman and others identified the hormone *leptin*, which affects the hypothalamus and may be an element in the regulation of body weight (Friedman, 1997, 2000; Geary, 2004; Kochavi et al., 2001). Leptin is produced by the body's fat tissues, and the amount produced is a direct measure of body fat: The more leptin produced, the higher the level of body fat. Decreases in body fat cause lower levels of leptin in the body, and lower levels of leptin stimulate food intake. When leptin levels increase sufficiently, energy expenditure exceeds food intake, and people lose weight. Obese mice injected with leptin lost 30% of their body weight within 2 weeks (Halaas et al., 1995). In humans, a mutation of the leptin receptor gene can cause obesity as well as pituitary abnormalities (Clément et al., 1998; Farooqi & O'Rahilly, 2005). Changes in the body's leptin levels can affect the immune and reproductive systems, as well as the processes involved in bone formation. Thus, leptin appears to have a role in linking nutrition to overall human physiology (Friedman, 2000).

Metabolic Rate. The rate at which the body burns calories to produce energy is called the **metabolic rate,** and it may also be subject to genetic influences. Physical activity uses up only about one-third of your energy intake; the other two-thirds is consumed

metabolic rate (meh-tuh-BALL-ik) The rate at which the body burns calories to produce energy.

by the maintenance processes that keep you alive. When there is an imbalance between energy intake (how much you eat) and output (how much energy you use), your weight changes. Generally, if your caloric intake exceeds your daily energy requirement, you gain weight. If your daily energy requirement exceeds your caloric intake, you lose weight.

Researchers studying human metabolism from the perspective of thermodynamics have learned that obesity can result when energy intake (eating) exceeds energy expenditure (body heat and exercise) by only a small amount over an extended time period (Lowell & Spiegelman, 2000). There are, however, significant individual differences in the efficiency with which energy is burned. Even if two people are the same age and weight and have the same build and level of activity, one may be able to consume more calories each day without gaining weight.

Fat-Cell Theory. Fat-cell theory proposes that obesity is related to the number of fat cells (adipose cells) in the body. It is estimated that people of normal weight have between 25 and 35 billion fat cells, whereas those whose weight is twice normal may have between 100 and 125 billion fat cells (Brownell & Wadden, 1992). The number of fat cells is determined by both genes and eating habits (Grinker, 1982). These cells serve as storehouses for liquefied fat. When a person loses weight, he or she does not lose fat cells themselves, but rather the fat that is stored in them; the cells simply shrink (Dietz, 1989).

Researchers once believed that all the fat cells a person would ever have were formed early in life. This is no longer the accepted view. Moreover, researchers at Harvard Medical School have discovered the mechanisms that regulate the development of new fat cells in the body (Rosen et al., 2002). Do their findings mean that an anti-obesity drug might be developed that short-circuits the development of fat cells? Perhaps, but the poor overall health of the genetically engineered mice in the Harvard study who produced no fat cells suggests otherwise. Simply put, the body needs fat to store energy, and it needs these stores of energy to stay healthy. Researchers also point out that when we interfere with the development of fat in the places where we don't want it, such as on our hips and thighs, we cause the body to store it in places where it can do far more damage, such as in our livers (Cromie, 2002).

Set-Point Theory. Set-point theory suggests that humans are genetically programmed to carry a certain amount of body weight (Levin, 2005; Keesey, 1988). Set point—the weight the body normally maintains when one is trying neither to gain nor to lose weight—is affected by the number of fat cells in the body and by metabolic rate, both of which are influenced by the genes (Gurin, 1989). Yet, people with a genetic propensity to be thin can become overweight if they overeat steadily for long periods, because they will gradually develop more and more fat cells.

According to set-point theory, an internal homeostatic system functions to maintain set-point weight, much as a thermostat works to keep temperature near the point at which it is set. When body weight falls below set point, appetite increases, whether an individual is lean, overweight, or average. When weight climbs above set point, appetite decreases so as to restore the original weight. The rate of energy expenditure is also adjusted to maintain the body's set-point weight (Keesey & Powley, 1986). When people gain weight, metabolic rate increases (Dietz, 1989). But when they restrict calories to lose weight, the metabolic rate lowers, causing the body to burn fewer calories and thus making further weight loss more difficult. Increasing the amount of physical activity—exercising during and after weight loss—is the best way to lower the set point so that the body will store less fat (Forey et al., 1996).

Researchers think that fat cells send biochemical messages to the hypothalamus indicating how much energy is stored in them (Hallschmid et al., 2004). Presumably, the genes influence what the hypothalamus "believes" to be the appropriate amount of energy to store. One of the most important current lines of research in this area aims to identify these biochemical messages and influence them in ways that will lower the set-points of obese individuals (Hallschmid et al., 2004).

▲ Because of the health risks associated with obesity, some people, such as *Today* personality Al Roker, resort to a surgical solution. Gastric bypass surgery reduced the capacity of Roker's stomach, thereby limiting the amount of food he can consume at any one time. As a result, Roker's weight has decreased dramatically.

fat cells   Cells (also called *adipose cells*) that serve as storehouses for liquefied fat in the body; their number is determined by both genes and eating habits, and they decrease in size but not in number with weight loss.

set point   The weight the body normally maintains when one is trying neither to gain nor to lose weight.

Weight Loss Strategies

10.7 Why is it almost impossible to maintain weight loss by cutting calories alone?

Are you currently on some kind of weight-loss diet? If so, you have a lot of company. National surveys show that nearly 60% of Americans are actively attempting to lose weight (Sutherland, 2002). All types of weight-reduction diets—no matter what approach they use—result in some weight loss in most people who try them (French et al., 1999; Serdula et al., 1993; Wadden, 1993). However, the weight loss is often temporary. Why?

The complexities of the processes involved in appetite regulation and energy metabolism explain why diets often do not work (Campbell & Dhand, 2000). To be effective, any weight-loss program must help people decrease energy intake (eat less), increase energy expenditure (exercise more), or both (Bray & Tartaglia, 2000). Unfortunately, most people who are trying to lose weight focus only on cutting calories. At first, when overweight people begin to diet and cut their calories, they do lose weight. But after a few pounds are shed initially, the dieter's metabolic rate slows down as if to conserve the remaining fat store because fewer calories are being consumed (Hirsch, 1997). Besides making it more difficult to lose weight, this reduction in metabolic rate drains the dieter's energy such that he or she is less able to exercise. This effect appears to be particularly pronounced with today's popular low-carbohydrate diets (Butki et al., 2003).

Understanding the complexities of the hunger regulation system can help an overweight person realize that successful weight loss involves more than simply counting calories. For instance, calories eaten in the form of fat are more likely to be stored as body fat than are calories eaten as carbohydrates. Miller and others (1990) found that even when obese and thin people have the same caloric intake, thin people derive about 29% of their calories from fats, whereas obese people average 35% from fat. So, the composition of the diet may have as much to do with weight gain as the amount of food eaten and the lack of exercise. Counting and limiting the grams of fat or more effectively balancing proteins and carbohydrates may be more beneficial than counting calories in helping a person achieve and maintain a desirable body weight.

As you may have inferred from the foregoing discussion, for individuals who are not obese, the principles of successful dieting are fairly simple. There is no need to spend your hard-earned money on special foods, food supplements, or the latest celebrity or fad diet. In fact, the Mayo Clinic in Rochester, Minnesota, is one of many health care institutions that have posted everything you need to know about weight loss on the Internet (Mayo Clinic, 2005). **Table 10.3** summarizes the strategies the clinic recommends for achieving and maintaining a healthy weight. At their web site, you can enter your own personal information and get a customized weight loss plan that includes recipes and menus (see https://www.mayoclinic.com/health/weight-loss/HQ01625).

Most individuals who are obese require the help of a physician to attain a healthy weight. For one thing, many suffer from other health problems, such as diabetes, that are linked to their weight problems in complex ways. Thus, any weight loss program they undertake must be managed in such a way that does not aggravate other conditions. Children who are obese (11–25% of all children in the United States) also require medical assistance to lose weight, because caloric restriction diets can interfere with their growth (Overby, 2002).

Finally, for unknown reasons, some people who suffer from obesity appear to be unable to reverse the trend of continual weight gain. For these individuals, *gastric bypass surgery*, a procedure in which the size of the stomach is reduced, may be the only alternative. Candidates for gastric bypass surgery must have a BMI in excess of 40. Individuals with BMIs ranging from 35 to 39 may be considered for the surgery if they have a weight-related health problem such as diabetes or high blood pressure. Among more than 80% of patients, gastric bypass surgery results in both weight reduction below the obesity threshold and improvements in weight-related health conditions (Schauer et al., 2000). However, physicians stress that any person who undergoes the surgery must be willing to commit to postoperative lifestyle changes, including following a healthy diet and exercise regimen. These changes are needed because, even with reduced stomach capacity, it is quite possible to return to an obese state after a period of post operative weight loss. Moreover, gastric bypass surgery is associated with risks such as the possi-

Table 10.3 Six Weight Loss Strategies from the Mayo Clinic

Make a commitment.
Approach weight loss as an effortful task, one in which you are likely to have some setbacks.
Be determined to persist toward your weight loss goal.

Get emotional support.
Share your goals with people whom you know will support and encourage you. If possible, participate in an informal weight-loss support group, or suggest to a friend who also wants to lose weight that the two of you become "accountability partners."

Set realistic goals.
Do some research to determine your body type and a target weight that is appropriate for you. A realistic timeframe is important as well. Permanent weight loss is best achieved over a long, rather than a short, period of time with a reasonable diet and exercise program that you can stick to.

Enjoy healthier foods.
Making permanent changes in your everyday diet is the best way to insure that the pounds you shed during dieting won't reappear as soon as you return to your normal eating patterns. The Mayo Clinic states, too, that extreme calorie restriction—less than 1,200 calories per day for women and 1,400 for men—is detrimental to you health.

Get active, stay active.
There is simply no way around the fact that increased activity is vital to the success of any weight loss plan. Find a physical activity that you enjoy, or do something that you enjoy (e.g., listening to music) while engaging in a calorie-burning activity, to motivate yourself to exercise.

Change your lifestyle.
Devise your entire plan, eating, exercise, and all, with the idea in mind that you are designing a lifelong strategy for weight maintenance.

Source: Mayo Clinic (2005).

bility of postoperative infection. In general, the heavier the patient is, the greater the risk of postsurgical complications (Livingston et al., 2002).

Eating Disorders

Eating disorders constitute a category of mental disorder in which eating and dieting behaviors go far beyond the common, everyday experiences of overeating and dieting. Sadly, there has been an increase in the incidence of these disorders in recent years (American Psychiatric Association, 2000).

Anorexia Nervosa. Anorexia nervosa is characterized by an overwhelming, irrational fear of gaining weight or becoming fat, compulsive dieting to the point of self-starvation, and excessive weight loss. Some anorexics lose as much as 20–25% of their original body weight.

Anorexia typically begins in adolescence, and most of those afflicted are females. About 1% of females between ages 12 and 40 suffer from this disorder (Johnson et al., 1996). The greater prevalence of eating disorders among females appears to be a general phenomenon, rather than a culturally specific one. In a large sample of Norwegian adults, for example, women were twice as likely as men to have an eating disorder (Augestad, 2000). Although it has been established that females are significantly more at risk for eating disorders than males are, a study of the relationship of eating problems to self-concept and other emotional/behavioral measures found that 20% of the females and, surprisingly, 10% of the males in a sample of 471 college students had symptoms of anorexia. This study, although small, suggests that eating disorders may be more prevalent among males than has been thought (Nelson et al., 1999).

10.8 What are the symptoms of anorexia nervosa and bulimia nervosa?

anorexia nervosa An eating disorder characterized by an overwhelming, irrational fear of gaining weight or becoming fat, compulsive dieting to the point of self-starvation, and excessive weight loss.

▲ Mary Kate Olsen is one of many young women who have struggled with anorexia. Individuals with anorexia usually have a distorted body image that causes them to believe they are overweight when they are actually dangerously underweight.

There are important differences between dieting, or even obsessive dieting, and anorexia nervosa. For one, perception of their body size is grossly distorted among people with anorexia. No matter how emaciated they become, they continue to perceive themselves as fat. Researchers have learned that such unrealistic perceptions may result from a general tendency toward distorted thinking in individuals with anorexia (Tchanturia et al., 2001). Moreover, an unusually high rate of psychological disorders has been found among people with anorexia (Dyl et al., 2006; Milos et al., 2002). These findings suggest that, for some sufferers, anorexia may be only one component of a larger set of problems.

Frequently, individuals with anorexia not only starve themselves but also exercise relentlessly in an effort to accelerate the weight loss. Further, most are fascinated with food and the process of preparing it (Faunce, 2002). Many become skilled in giving the appearance of eating while not actually swallowing food. To accomplish this, some individuals with anorexia habitually chew and spit out their food, often with such dexterity that others with whom they eat don't notice (Kovacs et al., 2002).

Among young females with anorexia, progressive and significant weight loss eventually results in amenorrhea (cessation of menstruation). Some also develop low blood pressure, impaired heart function, dehydration, electrolyte disturbances, and sterility (American Psychiatric Association, 2006), as well as decreases in the gray matter volume in the brain, which are thought to be irreversible (Lambe et al., 1997). Moreover, prolonged self-starvation produces changes in the lining of the stomach that can make it extremely difficult for individuals with anorexia to recover normal functioning of the digestive system even after they have begun eating normally (Ogawa et al., 2004). Unfortunately, up to 20% of those suffering from anorexia nervosa eventually die of starvation or complications from organ damage (Brotman, 1994).

It is difficult to pinpoint the cause of this disorder. Most individuals with anorexia are well behaved and academically successful (Vitousek & Manke, 1994). Psychological risk factors for eating disorders include being overly concerned about physical appearance, worrying about perceived attractiveness, and feeling social pressure in favor of thinness (Whisenhunt et al., 2000). Some investigators believe that young women who refuse to eat are attempting to control a portion of their lives, which they may feel unable to control in other respects.

Anorexia is very difficult to treat. Most sufferers are steadfast in their refusal to eat, while insisting that nothing is wrong with them. The main thrust of treatment, therefore, is to get the anorexic individual to gain weight. The patient may be admitted to a hospital, fed a controlled diet, and given rewards for small weight gains and increases in food intake. The treatment usually includes some type of psychotherapy and/or a self-help group. Some studies show that anti-depressant drugs may help in the treatment of anorexia (Barbarich et al., 2004). Others suggest that protein-rich supplements help individuals with anorexia regain their normal appetites (Latner & Wilson, 2004). Multi-dimensional treatment programs, that is, those that include a combination of medication, nutritional therapy, and psychotherapy may prove to be most successful (Bean et al., 2004). However, no matter what treatment approach is used, most individuals with anorexia experience relapses (Hogan & McReynolds, 2004).

Bulimia Nervosa. Up to 50% of anorexics also develop **bulimia nervosa,** a chronic disorder characterized by repeated and uncontrolled (and often secretive) episodes of binge eating (American Psychiatric Association, 2000). Individuals who are not anorexic may also develop bulimia. Many individuals with bulimia come from families in which family members make frequent negative comments about others' physical appearances (Crowther et al., 2002).

An episode of binge eating has two main features: (1) the consumption of much larger amounts of food than most people would eat during the same period of time, and (2) a feeling that one cannot stop eating or control the amount eaten. Binges—which generally involve foods that are rich in carbohydrates, such as cookies, cake, and candy—are frequently followed by purging. Purging consists of self-induced vomiting and/or the use of large quantities of laxatives and diuretics. People with bu-

bulimia nervosa An eating disorder characterized by repeated and uncontrolled (and often secretive) episodes of binge eating.

limia may also engage in excessive dieting and exercise. Athletes are especially susceptible to this disorder. But many bulimics are of average size and purge after an eating binge simply to maintain their weight.

Bulimia nervosa can cause a number of physical problems. The stomach acid in vomit eats away at the teeth and may cause them to rot, and the delicate balance of body chemistry is destroyed by excessive use of laxatives and diuretics. Bulimia can also cause a chronic sore throat as well as a variety of other symptoms, including dehydration, swelling of the salivary glands, kidney damage, and hair loss. The disorder also has a strong emotional component: The person with bulimia is aware that the eating pattern is abnormal and feels unable to control it. Depression, guilt, and shame accompany both binging and purging.

Bulimia nervosa tends to appear in the late teens and affects about 1 in 25 women (Kendler et al., 1991). Like those with anorexia, individuals with bulimia have high rates of obsessive-compulsive disorder (Milos et al., 2002). Further, perhaps as many as a third of them have engaged in other kinds of self-injurious behavior, such as cutting themselves intentionally (Paul et al., 2002). About 10–15% of all bulimics are males, and homosexuality or bisexuality seems to increase the risk for bulimia in males (Carlat et al., 1997). In addition, researchers are finding evidence of a cultural component to bulimia. Westernized attitudes in Turkey, for example, are clashing with the country's traditional values and, according to researchers, creating an increase in cases of bulimia (Elal et al., 2000). Apparently, some Turkish citizens succumb to Western media pressure to have an ultrathin body.

Bulimia, like anorexia, is difficult to treat. Sometimes treatment is complicated by the fact that a person with an eating disorder is likely to have a personality disorder as well or be too shy to interact effectively with therapists (Goodwin & Fitzgibbon, 2002; Rosenvinge et al., 2000). Some behavior modification programs have helped extinguish bulimic behavior (Traverso et al., 2000), and cognitive-behavioral therapy has been used successfully to help people with bulimia modify their eating habits and their abnormal attitudes about body shape and weight (Wilson & Sysko, 2006). Antidepressant drugs have been found to reduce the frequency of binge eating and purging in some individuals with bulimia (Monteleone et al., 2005).

Remember It   Two Primary Drives: Hunger and Thirst

1. All of the following are hunger signals except
   a. activity in the lateral hypothalamus
   b. low levels of glucose in the blood
   c. the hormone CCK
   d. a high insulin level

2. Your _____ rate is responsible for how fast your body burns calories to produce energy.

3. According to _____ theory, the body works to maintain a certain weight.

4. Effective weight loss programs must include _____ as well as reduced caloric intake.

5. Compulsive dieting to the point of self-starvation is the defining symptom of _____

Answers: 1. c; 2. metabolic; 3. set-point; 4. exercise; 5. anorexia nervosa

---

Social Motives

Now we turn from biological motives to those that are social in nature. For instance, when you feel lonely, you may call a friend or go to your favorite coffee house. The need for *affiliation*, as psychologists call it, is one kind of **social motive.** Unlike the primary drives, social motives are learned through experience and interaction with others. This group of motives includes achievement motivation and the kinds of motivations most of us experience in the workplace.

social motives Motives (such as the needs for affiliation and achievement) that are acquired through experience and interaction with others.

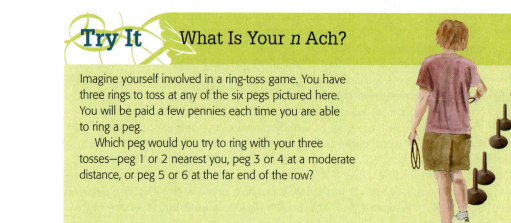

Try It   What Is Your *n* Ach?

Imagine yourself involved in a ring-toss game. You have three rings to toss at any of the six pegs pictured here. You will be paid a few pennies each time you are able to ring a peg.

Which peg would you try to ring with your three tosses—peg 1 or 2 nearest you, peg 3 or 4 at a moderate distance, or peg 5 or 6 at the far end of the row?

Achievement Motivation

10.9 How do need for achievement theory and goal orientation theory explain achievement motivation?

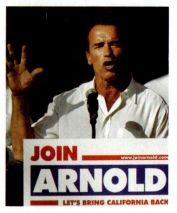

▲ People with a high need for achievement relish opportunities to take on new challenges. For example, after successful careers in acting and in business, Arnold Schwarzenegger was elected governor of California.

need for achievement (*n* Ach) The need to accomplish something difficult and to perform at a high standard of excellence.

goal orientation theory The view that achievement motivation depends on which of four goal orientations (mastery/approach, mastery/avoidance, performance/approach, performance/avoidance) an individual adopts.

Maslow's hierarchy suggests that achievement motivation, one of many esteem needs, will appear somewhat spontaneously as soon as lower needs are met. Other theorists have explained this important dimension of human motivation differently.

The Need for Achievement In early research, Henry Murray (1938) developed the *Thematic Apperception Test (TAT)*, which consists of a series of pictures of ambiguous situations. The person taking the test is asked to create a story about each picture—to describe what is going on in the picture, what the person or persons pictured are thinking about, what they may be feeling, and what is likely to be the outcome of the situation. The stories are presumed to reveal the test taker's needs and the strength of those needs. One of the motives identified by Murray was the **need for achievement** (abbreviated *n* Ach), or the motive to accomplish something difficult and to maintain high standards of performance. The need for achievement, rather than being satisfied with accomplishment, seems to grow as it is fed.

Researchers David McClelland and John Atkinson have conducted many studies of the need for achievement (McClelland, 1958, 1961, 1985; McClelland et al., 1953). People with a high *n* Ach pursue goals that are challenging, yet attainable through hard work, ability, determination, and persistence. Goals that are too easy, those anyone can reach, offer no challenge and hold no interest because success would not be rewarding (McClelland, 1985). Impossibly high goals and high risks are not pursued because they offer little chance of success and are considered a waste of time. The goals of those with high *n* Ach are self-determined and linked to perceived abilities; thus, these goals tend to be realistic (Conroy et al., 2001).

By contrast, people with low *n* Ach, the researchers claim, are not willing to take chances when it comes to testing their own skills and abilities. They are motivated more by their fear of failure than by their hope and expectation of success. This is why they set either ridiculously low goals, which anyone can attain, or impossibly high goals (Geen, 1984). After all, who can fault a person for failing to reach a goal that is impossible for almost anyone? Complete the *Try It* above, which describes a game that is said to reveal a high or low need for achievement.

Goal Orientation Theory. An approach known as **goal orientation theory** provides a somewhat different view of achievement motivation. According to this perspective, achievement motivation varies according to which of four goal orientations an individual adopts (Wolters, 2004). Here's how each of the orientations might affect a college student. Students with a *mastery/approach* orientation will study and engage in other behaviors (e.g., attend class) so as to increase their knowledge and overcome challenges. Those who have a *mastery/avoidance* orientation will exhibit whatever behaviors

---

Table 10.4 Goal Orientations

Mastery/Approach
Working to attain something of self-determined intrinsic value (e.g., knowledge).

Mastery/Avoidance
Working to avoid an outcome that threatens self-worth (e.g., failing a course).

Performance/Approach
Doing just enough work to ensure that one's performance will be superior to that of others (e.g., working for an A in a difficult class to feel superior to others in a class or being satisfied with a D because most other students are failing).

Performance/Avoidance
Limiting efforts in order to avoid surpassing the performance of others (e.g., getting mediocre grades to fit in with a peer group).

Note: Mastery involves working toward a personally meaningful goal. *Performance* involves working toward a goal defined by social comparison. *Approach* means that the goal helps the individual move toward something that is desirable. *Avoidance* means that the goal helps the individual move away from something that is undesirable.

---

are necessary to avoid failing to learn (a different outcome than a failing grade, by the way). Students with a *performance/avoidance* orientation will measure their performance against that of other students and are motivated to work to the point where they are at least equal to their peers. Finally, those who have a *performance/approach* orientation try to surpass the performance of their peers in an attempt to enhance their own sense of self-worth. (**Table 10.4** summarizes the four goal orientations. Stop for a minute and think about which orientation best describes your own.)

Research indicates that college and high school students who adopt either of the mastery orientations are less likely to procrastinate than their peers who adopt either of the performance orientations (Wolters, 2003, 2004). However, a mastery orientation doesn't necessarily mean that a student will get good grades (Harackiewicz et al., 2002). It appears that the performance/approach orientation is more strongly associated with high grades than any of the others (Church et al., 2001).

Work Motivation

What motivates workers to perform well, or to perform poorly, on the job? Psychologists who apply their knowledge in the workplace are known as **industrial/organizational (I/O) psychologists.** (You'll read more about their field in Chapter 17.) Although I/O psychologists are interested in many aspects of the workplace—organizational design, decision making, personnel selection, training and evaluation, work-related stress—they are vitally interested in work motivation and job performance. **Work motivation** can be thought of as "the conditions and processes that account for the arousal, direction, magnitude, and maintenance of effort in a person's job" (Katzell & Thompson, 1990, p. 144). Two of the most effective ways to increase employee motivation and improve performance are reinforcement and goal setting.

To use reinforcement, I/O psychologists help design behavior modification techniques to increase performance and productivity. Reinforcers or incentives include bonuses, recognition awards, praise, time off, posting of individual performance, better offices, more impressive titles, and/or promotions. Companies may discourage ineffective behaviors through such measures as docking the pay of employees who miss work.

Using goal setting to increase performance involves establishing specific, difficult goals, which leads to higher levels of performance than simply telling people to do their best in the absence of assigned goals (Latham & Pinder, 2005). An organization can enhance employees' commitment to goals by (1) having them participate in the goal setting, (2) making goals specific, attractive, difficult, and attainable, (3) providing feedback on performance, and (4) rewarding the employees for attaining the goals (Katzell & Thompson, 1990).

10.10 What kinds of conditions affect work motivation?

industrial/organizational (I/O) psychologists Psychologists who apply their knowledge in the workplace and are especially interested in work motivation and job performance.

work motivation The conditions and processes responsible for the arousal, direction, magnitude, and maintenance of effort of workers on the job.

▲ Clearly stated goals and recognition for accomplishing them motivates employees to make a company's goals their own.

Several theories have been applied to research on work motivation. According to one of these—*expectancy theory*—motivation to engage in a given activity is determined by (1) *expectancy,* a person's belief that more effort will result in improved performance; (2) *instrumentality,* the person's belief that doing a job well will be noticed and rewarded; and (3) *valence,* the degree to which a person values the rewards that are offered. Several studies have supported expectancy theory by showing that employees work harder when they believe that more effort will improve their performance, when they think that a good performance will be acknowledged and rewarded, and when they value the rewards that are offered (Fairbank et al., 2003; Tubbs et al., 1993; van Eerde & Thierry, 1996).

The aspects of a job workers consider most rewarding are interesting work, good pay, sufficient resources and authority, and friendly and cooperative co-workers. Conversely, some factors undermine job satisfaction. For one, workers become dissatisfied when their workload is increased beyond their perceived capacity to perform (Yousef, 2002). For another, job satisfaction declines when workers believe that there is no fair, systematic process for resolving grievances (Kickul et al., 2002).

Remember It   Social Motives

1. Social motives are acquired through _____.
2. Individuals who have a high need for achievement set goals that are of _____ difficulty.

3. Industrial/organizational psychologists use reinforcement and goal setting to increase _____.

Answers: 1. learning; 2. moderate; 3. employee motivation

Understanding Emotion

emotion An identifiable feeling state involving physiological arousal, a cognitive appraisal of the situation or stimulus causing that internal body state, and an outward behavior expressing the state.

What do you do when you feel angry? For most people, anger leads to some kind of action directed toward the source of the anger. So, an important component of motivation is emotion—and not just anger. Think about the kinds of actions that result from feelings of disgust or sadness or fear. In fact, the root of the word *emotion* means "to move," indicating the close relationship between emotion and motivation. But what, precisely, are emotions?

Explaining the Components of Emotions

10.11 What are the three components of emotions?

An **emotion** is an identifiable feeling state, something we all recognize when we feel it. But how can subjective feelings be studied? Typically, psychologists have studied emotions in terms of three components: the physical, the cognitive, and the behavioral (Wilken et al., 2000). The physical component is the physiological arousal (the internal body state) that accompanies the emotion. The cognitive component, the way we perceive or interpret a stimulus or situation, determines the specific emotion we feel. The behavioral component of emotions is their outward expression.

The three components appear to be interdependent. For instance, in one study, participants who were better at detecting changes in heart rate (the physical component) rated their subjective experiences of emotion (the cognitive component) as being more intense than did participants who were less able to detect such physical changes (Wilken et al., 2000). Thus, any satisfactory explanation of emotion must consider these interdependencies.

Theories of Emotion

The idea that an emotion has components seems to make sense, but in exactly what sequence do we experience the physical, cognitive, and behavioral components? As you might suspect, there is a long-standing debate among psychologists about which component comes first in the overall experience of emotion.

The James-Lange Theory. American psychologist William James (1884) argued that the sequence of events in an emotional experience is exactly the reverse of what subjective experience tells us. James claimed that only after an event causes physiological arousal and a physical response does the individual perceive or interpret the physical response as an emotion. In other words, saying something stupid causes you to blush, and you interpret your physical response, blushing, as an emotion, embarrassment. James (1890) went on to suggest that "we feel sorry because we cry, angry because we strike, afraid because we tremble" (p. 1066).

At about the same time that James proposed his theory, a Danish physiologist and psychologist, Carl Lange, independently formulated a very similar theory. The two have been combined into the **James-Lange theory of emotion** (Lange & James, 1922), which suggests that different patterns of arousal in the autonomic nervous system produce the different emotions people feel, and that the physiological arousal appears before the emotion is perceived (see **Figure 10.5**).

But if physical arousal causes what we know as emotion, there would have to be distinctly different bodily changes associated with each emotion. Otherwise, you wouldn't know whether you were sad, embarrassed, frightened, or happy.

The Cannon-Bard Theory. Another early theory of emotion that challenged the James-Lange theory was proposed by Walter Cannon (1927), who did pioneering work on the fight-or-flight response and the concept of homeostasis. Cannon claimed that the bodily changes caused by the various emotions are not sufficiently distinct to allow people to distinguish one emotion from another.

Cannon's original theory was later expanded by physiologist Philip Bard (1934). The result, the **Cannon-Bard theory of emotion,** suggests that the following chain of events occurs when we feel an emotion: Emotion-provoking stimuli are received by the senses and then relayed simultaneously to the cerebral cortex, which provides the conscious mental experience of the emotion, and to the sympathetic nervous system, which produces the physiological state of arousal. In other words, your feeling of emotion (fear, for example) occurs at about the same time that you experience physiological arousal (a pounding heart). One does not cause the other.

The Schachter-Singer Theory. Stanley Schachter believed that the early theories of emotion left out a critical component—the subjective cognitive interpretation of why a state of arousal has occurred. Schachter and his colleague, Jerome Singer, proposed a two-factor theory (Schachter & Singer, 1962). According to the **Schachter-Singer theory of emotion,** two things must happen in order for a person to feel an emotion: (1) The person must first experience physiological arousal; (2) there must then be a cognitive interpretation or explanation of the physiological arousal so that the person can label it as a specific emotion. Thus, Schachter concluded, a true emotion can occur only if a person is physically aroused and can find some reason for it. When people are in a state of physiological arousal but do not know why they are aroused, they tend to label the state as an emotion that is appropriate to their situation at the time.

Some attempts to replicate the findings of Schachter and Singer have been unsuccessful (Marshall & Zimbardo, 1979). Also, the notion that arousal is general rather

10.12 According to the various theories of emotion, what sequence of events occurs when an individual experiences an emotion?

James-Lange theory of emotion The theory that emotional feelings result when an individual becomes aware of a physiological response to an emotion-provoking stimulus (for example, feeling fear because of trembling).

Cannon-Bard theory of emotion The theory that an emotion-provoking stimulus is transmitted simultaneously to the cerebral cortex, providing the conscious mental experience of the emotion, and to the sympathetic nervous system, causing the physiological arousal.

Schachter-Singer theory of emotion A two-factor theory stating that for an emotion to occur, there must be (1) physiological arousal and (2) a cognitive interpretation or explanation of the arousal, allowing it to be labeled as a specific emotion.

Figure 10.5 The James-Lange Theory of Emotion

The James-Lange theory of emotion is the exact opposite of what subjective experience tells us. If a dog growls at you, the James-Lange interpretation is that the dog growls, your heart begins to pound, and only after perceiving that your heart is pounding do you conclude that you must be afraid.

Stimulus situation → Physiological arousal, action → Experience of emotion based on interpretation of arousal and action

Fear

A dog growls at you. → Your heart pounds; you run. → "My heart is racing and I'm running. I must be afraid."

than specific has been questioned by later researchers who have identified some distinctive patterns of arousal for some of the basic emotions (Ekman et al., 1983; Levenson, 1992; Scherer & Wallbott, 1994).

The Lazarus Theory. The theory of emotion that most heavily emphasizes the cognitive aspect has been proposed by the late Richard Lazarus (1922–2002) (Ekman & Campos, 2003). According to the **Lazarus theory of emotion,** a cognitive appraisal is the first step in an emotional response, and all other aspects of an emotion, including physiological arousal, depend on that cognitive appraisal. This theory is most compatible with the subjective experience of an emotion's sequence of events—the sequence that James reversed long ago. Faced with a stimulus, an event, a person first appraises it. This cognitive appraisal determines whether the person will have an emotional response and, if so, what type of response. The physiological arousal and all other aspects of the emotion flow from the appraisal. In short, Lazarus contends that emotions are provoked when cognitive appraisals of events or circumstances are positive or negative—but not neutral.

Critics of the Lazarus theory have pointed out that some emotional reactions occur too rapidly to pass through a cognitive appraisal (Zajonc, 1980, 1984). Lazarus (1984, 1991a, 1991b) has responded that some mental processing occurs without conscious awareness. And there must be some form of cognitive realization, however brief, or else a person would not know what he or she is responding to or what emotion to feel. Further, researchers have found that reappraisal, or changing one's thinking about an emotional stimulus, is related to a reduction in physiological response (Gross, 2002). By contrast, suppression of emotional behavior without cognitive reappraisal is not.

The following *Review and Reflect* summarizes the four major theories of emotion: James-Lange, Cannon-Bard, Schachter-Singer, and Lazarus.

Lazarus theory of emotion The theory that a cognitive appraisal is the first step in an emotional response and all other aspects of an emotion, including physiological arousal, depend on it.

Review and Reflect   Theories of Emotion

Theory	View	Example
James-Lange theory	An event causes physiological arousal. You experience an emotion only *after* you interpret the physical response.	You are walking home late at night and hear footsteps behind you. Your heart pounds and you begin to tremble. You interpret these physical responses as *fear*.
Cannon-Bard theory	An event causes a physiological and an emotional response simultaneously. One does not cause the other.	You are walking home late at night and hear footsteps behind you. Your heart pounds, you begin to tremble, *and* you feel afraid.
Schachter-Singer theory	An event causes physiological arousal. You must then be able to identify a reason for the arousal in order to label the emotion.	You are walking home late at night and hear footsteps behind you. Your heart pounds and you begin to tremble. You know that walking alone at night can be dangerous, and so you feel afraid.
Lazarus theory	An event occurs, a cognitive appraisal is made, and then the emotion and physiological arousal follow.	You are walking home late at night and hear footsteps behind you. You think it could be a mugger. So you feel afraid, and your heart starts to pound and you begin to tremble.

Emotion and the Brain

What happens in the brain when we experience an emotion? More than any other emotion, fear has stimulated research by neuroscientists (LeDoux, 1996, 2000). And the brain structure most closely associated with fear is the amygdala (see Figure 10.6). Information comes to the amygdala directly from all of the senses and is acted on there immediately, without initial involvement of the primary "thinking" area of the brain, the cortex. But, as with reflex actions, the cortex does become involved as soon as it "catches up" with the amygdala (LeDoux, 2000). Thus, an emotion can be stirred up even before the cortex knows what is going on.

10.13 **What brain structure processes the emotion of fear?**

Figure 10.6 Neuroimaging of Emotions

PET scans show distinct patterns of brain activation for the various emotions. Red areas show areas of activation, and purple areas show areas of deactivations.

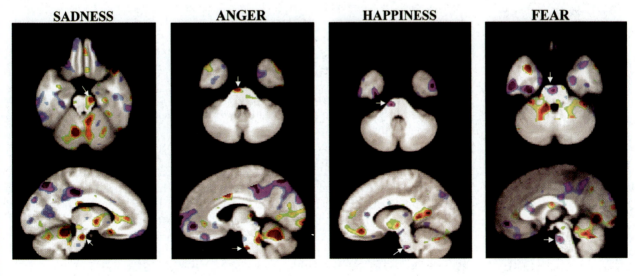

SADNESS   ANGER   HAPPINESS   FEAR

Source: Damasio (2000).

When the emotion of fear first materializes, much of the brain's processing is non-conscious. We become conscious of it later, of course, but the amygdala is activated before we are aware that a threat is present (Damasio, 1994, 1999). Interestingly, the amygdala becomes more highly activated when a person looks at photos of angry or fearful-looking faces than it does when the person views photos of happy faces (LeDoux, 2000; Wright et al., 2006).

Emotions may also be lateralized. Researchers using electroencephalographs to track mood changes have found that reductions in both anxiety and depression are associated with a shift in electrical activity from the left to the right side of the brain. Perception of others' emotions appears to be lateralized on the right side of the brain. This pattern of lateralization may be more pronounced in females than in males. In one study, participants listened to emotional expressions alternately with the left and right ears. (Recall that the left ear sends auditory signals to the right side of the brain, while the right ear sends them to the left side.) A left-ear advantage for accurate identification of a speaker's emotional state was evident only for women (Voyer & Rodgers, 2002). Another interesting and possibly related finding is that women who describe themselves as being high in emotional expressivity are more likely to turn the left side of their face to the camera when asked to pose for a picture than those who report less emotional sensitivity (Nicholls et al., 2002). Researchers speculate that their behavior is motivated by an unconscious sense of the left-ear advantage in emotional perception.

Remember It   Understanding Emotion

1. Emotion involves _____, _____, and _____ components.

2. The _____ theory of emotion holds that you feel a true emotion only when you become physically aroused and can identify some cause for the arousal.

3. The _____ theory suggests that you would feel fearful *because* you were trembling.

4. The _____ theory suggests that the feeling of an emotion and the physiological response to an emotional situation occur at about the same time.

5. The _____ theory suggests that the physiological arousal and the emotion flow from a cognitive appraisal of an emotion-provoking event.

6. When fear strikes, the _____ is activated before the _____.

Answers: 1. physical, cognitive, behavioral; 2. Schachter-Singer; 3. James-Lange; 4. Cannon-Bard; 5. Lazarus; 6. amygdala, cerebral cortex

Expressing Emotion

Who taught you how to smile and frown? No one did, of course. Expressing emotions comes as naturally to humans as breathing. And the facial expressions of certain basic emotions are similar in all cultures.

The Range of Emotion

10.14 What are basic emotions?

How many emotions are there? Two leading researchers on emotion, Paul Ekman (1993) and Carroll Izard (1992), insist that there are a limited number of basic emotions. **Basic emotions** are unlearned and universal; that is, they are found in all cultures, are reflected in the same facial expressions, and emerge in children according to their biological timetable of development. Fear, anger, disgust, surprise, happiness or joy, and sadness or distress are usually considered basic emotions.

In studying the range of emotion, Ekman (1993) has suggested that emotions should be considered as families. The anger family might range from annoyed to irritated, angry, livid, and, finally, enraged. Furthermore, if perceived as a family, anger should also include various forms of its expression, according to Ekman (1993). Resentment, for example, is a form of anger "in which there is a sense of grievance" (p. 386). Other forms are indignation and outrage, which seem to be justifiable anger focused on a wrongful or unjust action against self or others. Vengefulness is anger that retaliates, or gets revenge for an injustice or misdeed by another. In its most intense form, anger may be expressed as blind rage, in which a person loses control and may commit brutal atrocities against the target of the rage. Just as there are many words in the English language to describe the variations in the range of any emotion, there are subtle distinctions in the facial expression of a single emotion that convey its intensity (Ekman, 1993).

basic emotions Emotions that are unlearned and universal, that are reflected in the same facial expressions across cultures, and that emerge in children according to their biological timetable of development; fear, anger, disgust, surprise, happiness, and sadness are usually considered basic emotions.

The Development of Facial Expressions

Emotional expressions are natural, but what patterns are associated with their development? Newborn babies don't even smile, but 1-year-olds exhibit almost as many facial expressions as older children and adults. Like the motor skills of crawling and walking, facial expressions of emotions develop according to a biological timetable of maturation. Even newborns are capable of expressing some emotions—specifically, distress, pleasure, and interest in the environment. By 3 months of age, babies can express happiness and sadness (Lewis, 1995), and laughter appears somewhere between 3 and 4 months (Provine, 1996). Between the ages of 4 and 6 months, the emotions of anger and surprise appear, and by about 7 months, infants show fear. The self-conscious emotions do not emerge until later. Between 18 months and 3 years, children begin to show first empathy, envy, and embarrassment, followed by shame, guilt, and pride (Lewis, 1995).

The consistency of emotional development across individual infants and across cultures supports the idea that emotional expression is inborn. Another strong indication that the facial expressions of emotion are biologically determined comes from research on children who have been blind and deaf since birth. Their smiles and frowns, laughter and crying, and facial expressions of anger, surprise, and pouting are the same as those of children who can hear and see (Eibl-Eibesfeldt, 1973).

10.15 How does the development of facial expressions in infants suggest a biological basis for emotional expression?

The Universality of Facial Expressions

Do you think that facial expressions have the same meaning for every individual and in every culture? Use the photos in the *Try It* below to find out whether people you know agree about what these facial expressions mean.

The relationship between emotions and facial expressions was first studied by Charles Darwin (1872/1965). He believed that the facial expression of emotion was an aid to survival, because it enabled people to communicate their internal states and react to emergencies before they developed language. Darwin maintained that most emotions, and the facial expressions that convey them, are genetically inherited and

10.16 What evidence is there to suggest that facial expressions have the same meanings all over the world?

Try It   Recognizing Basic Emotions

Look carefully at the six photographs. Which basic emotion is portrayed in each? Match the photograph with the letter of the basic emotion it conveys.

a. happiness   b. sadness   c. fear   d. anger   e. surprise   f. disgust

 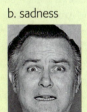 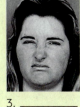   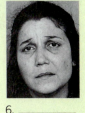

1. _____.   2. _____   3. _____   4. _____   5. _____   6. _____

Answers: 1. d; 2. c; 3. f; 4. e; 5. a; 6. b

▲ Even infants who are blind or deaf smile and frown, suggesting that facial expressions are biologically programmed, universal expressions of emotion.

characteristic of the entire human species. To test his belief, he asked missionaries and people of different cultures around the world to record the facial expressions that accompany the basic emotions. Based on those data, he concluded that facial expressions were similar across cultures. Modern researchers agree that Darwin was right.

Other researchers have found evidence for universality as well as for cultural variations. Scherer and Wallbott (1994) found very extensive overlap in the patterns of emotional experiences reported across cultures in 37 different countries on 5 continents. They also found important cultural differences in the ways emotions are elicited and regulated and in how they are shared socially. Recent research suggests that Asians pay more attention to indicators of emotion, such as tone of voice, than Westerners do (Ishii et al., 2003).

Moreover, each culture appears to have an "accent" for facial expressions (Marsh et al., 2003). This accent is a pattern of minute muscle movements that are used by most members of a culture when they exhibit a particular facial expression. In other words, there is a Japanese way to make a happy face, an American way to make a happy face that is somewhat different, and a German way of making a happy face that differs from both. In fact, these differences are enough to influence perceptions of emotion even when individuals come from very similar cultural backgrounds. In one classic study, researchers found that White Americans more quickly identified the facial expressions of other White Americans than did White Europeans (Izard, 1971).

Cultural Rules for Displaying Emotion

10.17 How do display rules for emotions differ across cultures?

display rules Cultural rules that dictate how emotions should generally be expressed and when and where their expression is appropriate.

Do you remember what you did at age 8 when you opened Aunt Sally's birthday gift and discovered it was a hideous sweater you would never wear? You probably said "yuck," or something similar. But what happened when you had a similar experience at age 18? By then, you had learned to smile and pretend you loved Aunt Sally's gift. In other words, you had learned a **display rule**—a cultural rule that dictates how an emotion should generally be expressed and when and where its expression is appropriate (Ekman, 1993; Ekman & Friesen, 1975; Scherer & Wallbott, 1994).

Often, a society's display rules require people to give evidence of certain emotions that they may not actually feel or to disguise their true feelings. For example, we are expected to look sad at funerals, to hide disappointment when we lose at games, and to refrain from making facial expressions of disgust if the food we are served tastes bad. In one study, Cole (1986) found that when 3-year-old girls were given an unattractive gift, they smiled nevertheless. They had already learned a display rule and signaled an emotion they very likely did not feel. Davis (1995) found that among 1st, 2nd, and 3rd graders, girls were better able to hide disappointment than boys were.

Different cultures, neighborhoods, and even families may have very different display rules. Display rules in Japanese culture dictate that negative emotions must be disguised when other people are present (Ekman, 1972; Matsumoto et al., 2005; Triandis, 1994). In many societies in the West, women are expected to smile often, whether they feel happy or not. And in East Africa, young males from traditional Masai society are expected to appear stern and stony-faced and to "produce long, unbroken stares" (Keating, 1994). Thus, the emotions people show are sometimes not truly felt, but merely reflect compliance with display rules.

Not only can emotions be displayed and not felt, they can also be felt and not displayed (Russell, 1995). Consider Olympic medalists waiting to receive their gold, silver, or bronze medals. Though brimming with happiness, the athletes display few smiles until their medals have been presented and they are interacting with the authorities and responding to the crowd (Fernández-Dols & Ruiz-Belda, 1995). Further, researchers have learned that in the United States, teens conform to unspoken display rules acquired from peers that discourage public displays of emotion. The

▲ There are many situations in which people must disguise their emotions to comply with the display rules of their culture, which dictate when and how feelings should be expressed. For example, these Buckingham palace guards are expected to remain expressionless, even if it means hiding their true feelings.

resulting subdued emotional expressions can cause them to appear aloof, uncaring, and even rude to parents and other adults (Salisch, 2001). Psychologists speculate that conformity to these peer-based display rules may be the basis of much miscommunication between teens and their parents and teachers.

Most of us learn display rules very early and abide by them most of the time. Yet you may not be fully aware that the rules you have learned dictate where, when, how, and even how long certain emotions should be expressed. You will learn more about reading emotions and detecting the probable motives of others when we explore nonverbal behavior—the language of facial expressions, gestures, and body positions—in Chapter 16.

Emotion as a Form of Communication

Often, we communicate emotions in order to motivate others to action. If you communicate sadness or distress, then people close to you are likely to be sympathetic and try to help. Emotional expressions allow infants to communicate their feelings and needs before they are able to speak.

10.18 Why is emotion considered a form of communication?

In an early study, Katherine Bridges (1932) observed emotional expression in Canadian infants over a period of months. She reported that the first emotional expression to appear is that of distress. In survival terms, the expression of distress enables helpless newborns to get the attention of their caretakers so that their needs can be met. More recent research indicates that adults are quite adept at interpreting infants' nonverbal emotional signals; they can even correctly determine whether a baby is looking at a new or familiar object by simply observing the change in the baby's facial expression and body language (Camras et al., 2002).

Do you feel happier when you are around others who are happy? You may already know that emotions are contagious. Mothers seem to know this intuitively when they display happy expressions in an effort to improve their babies' moods (Keating, 1994). Researchers have found that mothers in many cultures—Trobriand Island, Yanomamo, Greek, German, Japanese, and American—attempt to regulate the moods of their babies through facial communication of emotions (Kanaya et al., 1989; Keller et al., 1988; Termine & Izard, 1988).

From an evolutionary perspective, there is survival value in the ability to interpret various states instantly and reliably and then emulate them. In many species, if a single member of the group or herd senses a predator and communicates the emotion of fear, the other members also become afraid, which prepares them to flee for their lives. For humans, too, quick and accurate recognition of facial expressions that communicate anger or a threat clearly has adaptive value. And research indicates that such recognition is indeed fast and efficient (Fox et al., 2000; Horstmann, 2003).

Humans begin to perceive the emotions of others early in the first year of life and use this information to guide behavior. Infants pay close attention to the facial expressions of others, especially their mothers. And when they are confronted with an ambiguous situation, they use the mother's emotion as a guide to whether they should approach or avoid the situation. This phenomenon is known as *social referencing* (Klinnert et al., 1983).

But what happens when false and thus deceptive emotions are being conveyed? Evolutionary psychologists, who study how humans adapt their behavior for the purpose of passing on their genes (as noted in Chapter 1), have presented evidence indicating that both males and females use emotional deception in the context of mating behavior. In a study involving some 200 male and female university students, women admitted that they had flirted with, smiled at, and played up to men, leading them on when they had no romantic interest in the men or any intention of having sex with them. Men admitted intentionally deceiving women

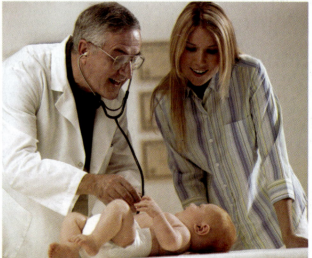

▲ Infants use their parents' facial expressions to guide them as to whether they should feel secure or frightened in unfamiliar situations. What emotional message do you think this baby is receiving?

about the depth of their emotional commitment. Asked whether they had ever exaggerated the depth of their feelings for a partner in order to get sex, more than 70% of the male students said yes, compared with 39% of the female students. When asked whether they thought that a man had ever exaggerated his feelings to get sex, a staggering 97% of the female students said yes (Buss, 1994, 1999).

The Art and Science of Lie Detection

10.19 What has research revealed about behavioral, physiological, and neurological measures of deception?

Given the findings regarding women's realistic assessments of men's willingness to lie in order to obtain sexual favors, doesn't it stand to reason that women would be good at detecting such lies? As it happens, hundreds of studies have shown that neither men nor woman are particularly good at detecting deception.

Human Lie Detectors. The strategies most people use to assess truthfulness are no more effective than simply flipping a coin: Heads-you're lying; Tails-you're telling the truth (Lock, 2004). Surprisingly, too, research about professionals whose work often depends on assessing another person's truthfulness has produced mixed results. Some studies have shown that individuals who are experienced in the detection of lies, such as law enforcement officers, do better than the rest of us (Ekman & O'Sullivan, 1991; Ekman, O'Sullivan, & Frank, 1999). However, there have also been studies showing that these experts perform just as poorly as inexperienced people do (Akehurst, Bull, Vrij, & Kohnken, 2004; Leach et al., 2004).

Despite these discouraging findings, there may be exceptions to the proposition that humans are poor lie detectors. One such exception is the finding that experienced law enforcement officers perform better on lie detection tests when they observe videotapes of actual criminal interrogations than when they observe videotaped actors who have been instructed by researchers to lie (Mann, Vrij, & Bull, 2004). Thus, laboratory studies do not tell the full story about humans' lie detecting abilities. More studies involving real-world lie detection must be done before we can make a final judgment on the matter.

Studies also indicate that there are a few gifted individuals who are extraordinarily good at catching liars. Psychologist Paul Ekman, whose work on emotion you read about earlier in the chapter, suggests that these people are better able than the rest of us to detect *microemotions*, facial expressions that last no longer than one twenty-fifth of a second. Ekman's frequently cited study of microemotion detection showed that participants who were good at detecting microemotions were also good at detecting deception (Ekman & O'Sullivan, 1991).

polygraph A lie-detecting device that detects changes in heart rate, blood pressure, respiration rate, and skin conductance response.

Our inability to identify deception may be caused by the inconsistencies in liars' behavior. Although many people believe that there are common signs of lying, such as looking away or fidgeting, there are actually very few consistencies across deceivers. On average, liars may pause more often or blink less often while speaking than truth-tellers do, but these behaviors do not correlate perfectly with deception (Lock, 2004). Thus, for some time, scientists have thought that it might be possible to design a machine that can do a better job than we do of distinguishing between liars and truth-tellers.

Physiological Measures of Deception. One lie-detecting device that is familiar to most of us is the **polygraph,** a machine that detects changes in heart rate, blood pressure, respiration rate, and skin conductance response. The assumption behind the use of the polygraph is that lying causes changes in these physiological functions that can be accurately measured and recorded

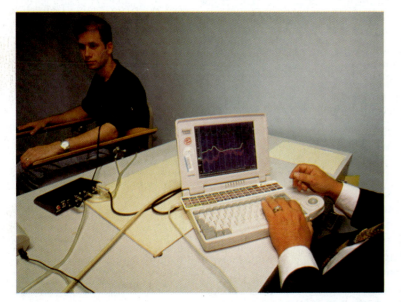

▲ About one-third of truthful individuals are wrongly accused of lying by a polygraph machine. Although polygraph results are not admissible as evidence in court, the technique continues to be important to criminal investigations.

by the device (Rosenfeld, 1995). However, some experts say that the percentage of innocent people who are falsely accused of lying by polygraphs may be as high as one out of three (Kleinmuntz & Szucko, 1984). They also point out that one out of four liars is judged by these machines to be telling the truth. Moreover, habitual liars can lie without causing physiological arousal in their bodies, so polygraphs are unable to distinguish between their false and truthful statements.

Voice stress analysis devices work on a similar principle, namely, that lying affects physiological variables which, in turn, influence the voice in ways that can be measured reliably. A variety of such devices are currently available. However, voice analysis has proven to be far less accurate than even the polygraph (National Research Council, 2003).

The less-than-satisfactory reliability of physiologically based lie detectors has led to increasing restrictions on their use. However, polygraphs continue to be important investigative tools. Their usefulness derives from investors' understanding that they do not pinpoint specific false statements. Instead, they give hints about areas of an investigation that merit further scrutiny or a more detailed round of questioning with an interviewee.

Neurological Measures of Deception. Neurological measures of deception are far more accurate than those that are based on physiological measures. Both electroencephalography (EEG) and fMRI have been used to test hypotheses about correlations between brain function and deception. Studies involving EEG lie-detection technology, known as *brain fingerprinting*, have produced near-perfect rates of lie detection (Farwell & Smith, 2001). Likewise, fMRI scans tend to be extremely reliable at detecting deception (Kozel et al., 2005).

In the future, will every police station have its own neuroimaging laboratory? Such a prospect is unlikely. Not only are these techniques cumbersome and expensive, but researchers do not yet have a full understanding of their utility as lie detectors. One possibility that needs to be studied is whether there are behaviors other than lying that trigger the same neurological reactivity patterns as deception.

Nevertheless, EEG technology has been used in criminal justice settings (*The Economist*, 2004). In one case, the tests helped to keep a guilty man in prison. In another, an innocent man was cleared of a crime for which a jury had convicted him. Thus, the use of neurological lie detection is likely to become more frequent, although not commonplace, in the future.

Remember It   Expressing Emotion

1. The basic emotions emerge in children as a result of their _____ of development.

2. Each culture appears to have its own pattern of minute _____ that are used to exhibit a particular facial expression.

3. Because of cultural _____, people sometimes express emotions they do not really feel.

4. According to evolutionary pychologists, both men and women use _____ in their mating behaviors.

5. Polygraph examinations measure _____.

6. Brain fingerprinting uses _____ technology.

Answers: 1. biological timetable; 2. muscle movements; 3. display rules; 4. emotional deception; 5. physiological responses; 6. EEG

Experiencing Emotion

How is the expression of emotion related to the experience of emotion? Some researchers go so far as to suggest that the facial expression alone can actually produce the feeling.

The Facial-Feedback Hypothesis

10.20 How do facial expressions influence internal emotional states?

Do you think that making particular facial expressions can affect your emotions? Nearly 130 years ago, Darwin wrote, "Even the simulation of an emotion tends to arouse it in our minds" (1872/1965, p. 365). Researcher Sylvan Tomkins (1962, 1963) went a step further. He claimed that the facial expression itself—that is, the movement of the facial muscles producing the expression—triggers both the physiological arousal and the conscious feeling associated with the emotion. The notion that the muscular movements involved in certain facial expressions produce the corresponding emotions is called the **facial-feedback hypothesis** (Izard, 1971, 1977, 1990; Strack et al., 1988).

In classic research using 16 participants (12 professional actors and 4 scientists), Ekman and colleagues (1983) documented the effects of facial expressions on physiological indicators of emotion. The participants were guided to contract specific muscles in the face so that they could assume the facial expressions of six basic emotions—surprise, disgust, sadness, anger, fear, and happiness. They were never actually told to smile, frown, or put on an angry face, however. The participants were monitored by electronic instruments, which recorded physiological changes in heart rate, galvanic skin response (to measure perspiring), muscle tension, and hand temperature. Measurements were taken as the participants made each facial expression. The participants were also asked to imagine or relive an experience in which they had felt each of the six emotions.

Ekman reported that a distinctive physiological response pattern emerged for each of the emotions of fear, sadness, anger, and disgust, whether the participants relived an emotional experience or simply made the corresponding facial expression. In fact, in some cases the physiological measures of emotion were greater when the actors and scientists made the facial expression than when they imagined an emotional experience (Ekman et al., 1983). The researchers found that both anger and fear accelerate heart rate, but fear produces colder fingers than does anger.

If facial expressions can activate emotions, is it possible that intensifying or weakening a facial expression might intensify or weaken the corresponding feeling state? Izard (1990) believes that learning to self-regulate emotional expression can help in controlling emotions. You might learn to change the intensity of an emotion by inhibiting, weakening, or amplifying its expression. Or you might change the emotion itself by simulating the expression of another emotion. Izard proposes that this approach to the regulation of emotion might be a useful adjunct to psychotherapy. Regulating or modifying an emotion by simulating an expression of its opposite may be effective if the emotion is not unusually intense.

Does it really matter whether we control our emotions? You may have heard that "venting" emotions, a process known as *catharsis*, is good for mental health. In reality, the opposite is true. Venting anger makes a person angrier and may even make him or her more likely to express the anger aggressively (Bushman, 2002). Better control of emotions is associated with a lower incidence of drug problems (Simons & Carey, 2002). Presumably, the better we are at controlling our own emotions, the less likely we are to resort to chemical means of regulating them.

facial-feedback hypothesis The idea that the muscular movements involved in certain facial expressions produce the corresponding emotions (for example, smiling makes one feel happy).

Gender Differences in Experiencing Emotion

10.21 In what ways do males and females differ with regard to emotions?

Do females and males differ significantly in the way they experience their emotions? Do women tend to be more intensely emotional than men? According to evolutionary psychologists, the answer to both questions is yes. Intense emotions are frequently experienced in the context of sexual behavior, and evolutionary psychologist David Buss (1999, 2000b) has reported that women are far more likely than men to feel anger when their partner is sexually aggressive. Men, on the other hand, experience greater anger than women do when their partner withholds sex.

There are other gender differences with respect to the emotion of anger. According to the evolutionary perspective, your answer to the following question is likely to be gender-specific: What emotion would you feel first if you were betrayed or harshly criticized by another person? When asked to respond to this question, male research participants in a classic study were more likely to report that they would feel angry; female participants were more likely to say that they would feel hurt, sad, or disappointed (Brody, 1985). Of course, both males and females express anger, but typically not in the same ways. Women are just as likely as men to express anger in private (at home) but much less likely than men to express it publicly (Cupach & Canary, 1995).

Men and women appear to have different ways of regulating angry feelings as well. In one study, researchers made remarks to participants that were designed to make them angry (Knobloch-Westerwick & Alter, 2006). Half of the participants were led to believe that they would have a chance to retaliate against the experimenters. The researchers offered participants the opportunity to read news stories on a computer while they waited for the next phase of the study to begin. Participants did not know that the researchers were tracking the kinds of news stories they chose to read. At the end of the reading period, the researchers found that men who believed they would get to retaliate against the experimenters were more likely to read negative than positive news stories. By contrast, women who were in the retaliation opportunity group chose to read mostly positive stories. The researchers hypothesized that men's focus on negative stories helped them maintain their state of anger in order to be prepared to retaliate. And they believe women used the reading session as an opportunity to dissipate their feelings of anger by reading positive stories.

In a recent study, men were found to process emotions, especially positive ones, predominantly in the left hemisphere of the brain, while women were found to use both cerebral hemispheres more equally for processing emotions (Coney & Fitzgerald, 2000). This finding could account for some of the emotional difference between the genders.

▲ Do you think that gender differences in experiencing emotions affect the ways in which men and women argue? If so, how?

Emotion and Cognition

You learned in Chapter 6 that an individual's emotional state can affect the way the person remembers a particular event. For example, when people feel sad, they recall more negative events than when they are happy. Thus, emotion is clearly an integral part of human thought processes. So, what happens when, instead of trying to recall the past, we think about the future while in one emotional state or another?

There is a good deal of evidence suggesting that emotions help us formulate risk assessments and develop appropriate behavioral responses (Lerner & Tiedens, 2006; Schupp et al., 2003). In fact, emotion allows us to detect risk more quickly than we could using rational thought alone (Dijksterhuis & Aarts, 2003). Suppose you get on a bus late one night and see a passenger methodically sharpening a knife. Will you engage in a cool-headed logical analysis of the likelihood that he will use his knife to attack you? Probably not. Chances are, your emotions will steer you toward the more efficient course of staying clear of the threatening passenger or getting off the bus as soon as you can.

The connection between emotion and risk assessment was demonstrated particularly well in a series of studies conducted by psychologist Jennifer Lerner and several colleagues. They examined how people's emotional responses to the terrorist attacks

10.22 How does emotion influence thought?

of September 11, 2001, influenced their ability to assess the risk of future events of the same kind (Lerner et al., 2003). First, Lerner and her associates examined whether naturally occurring individual differences in emotional responses to the attacks were related to differences in risk perception. Their first surveys were carried out within 9 to 23 days of the attacks. They found that people who responded with anger, as measured on a "desire for vengeance" scale, were less likely to believe that another major attack would occur within a year than were those who responded with fear. And they found that the initial emotional reactions continued to predict differences in risk assessment 6 to 10 weeks later.

Next, this group of researchers asked whether experimentally induced emotions would color risk perceptions in the same way. To examine this question, the researchers randomly assigned participants to conditions in which they were exposed to stimuli designed to elicit specific emotions. For instance, in the anger condition, the participants were first asked to explain what about the attacks made them most angry; these participants then watched a video portraying celebrations of the attacks in Middle Eastern countries. In the fear condition, participants were first asked what about the attacks made them most afraid; next, they were shown a video depicting postal workers taking measures to protect themselves from anthrax exposure. After the questions and videos, participants in both groups were asked to predict the probability that at some time within the next 12 months, they personally would be victimized by terrorism and that there would be attacks on other Americans. Lerner and her colleagues (2003) found that the the probability estimates, both personal and general, given by participants in the fear group were higher than those given by participants in the anger group.

What would cause an angry person to be more optimistic than a fearful person? One clue may lie in the participants' views of possible policy responses to terrorist attacks. Anger, both naturally occurring and experimentally induced, was associated with endorsement of specific actions against potential perpetrators of terrorism, such as strict policies requiring immediate deportation of individuals who enter the United States illegally. By contrast, fear, again both naturally and experimentally induced, was associated with precautionary approaches such as universal vaccinations against possible biological weapons. Thus, it is possible that the anger-optimism link arises from confidence, whether justified or not, in concrete measures directed toward people who are perceived as potentially threatening.

Love

10.23 How does Sternberg's triangular theory of love account for the different kinds of love?

What emotion do you think has the most positive influence on our experiences? Most people would say that love is the most life-enhancing of all emotions. Although people often use the term rather loosely or casually ("I *love* ice cream," "I *love* to dance"), love is usually experienced as a deep and abiding affection for parents, children, and, ideally, friends, neighbors, and other fellow humans. There is also love of country and love of learning. But what about romantic love? Is it different from other forms of this emotion?

Robert Sternberg (1986b, 1987), whose triarchic theory of intelligence was discussed in Chapter 7, has also proposed a **triangular theory of love.** Its three components are intimacy, passion, and commitment. Sternberg explains intimacy as "those feelings in a relationship that promote closeness, bondedness, and connectedness" (1987, p. 339). Passion refers to those drives in a loving relationship "that lead to romance, physical attraction, [and] sexual consummation" (1986b, p. 119). The commitment component consists of (1) a short-term aspect, the decision that one loves another person, and (2) a long-term aspect, a commitment to maintaining that love over time.

Sternberg proposes that these three components, singly and in various combinations, produce seven different kinds of love (see **Figure 10.7**).

triangular theory of love
Sternberg's theory that three components—intimacy, passion, and commitment—singly, and in various combinations produce seven different kinds of love.

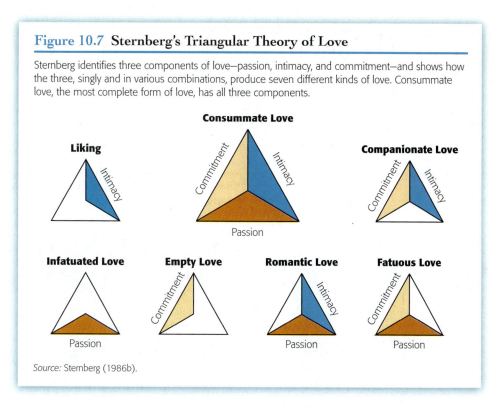

Figure 10.7 Sternberg's Triangular Theory of Love

Sternberg identifies three components of love—passion, intimacy, and commitment—and shows how the three, singly and in various combinations, produce seven different kinds of love. Consummate love, the most complete form of love, has all three components.

Source: Sternberg (1986b).

1. *Liking* includes only one of the love components—intimacy. In this case, liking is not used in a trivial sense. Sternberg says that this intimate liking characterizes true friendships, in which a person feels a bondedness, a warmth, and a closeness with another but not intense passion or long-term commitment.

2. *Infatuated love* consists solely of passion and is often what is felt as "love at first sight." But without the intimacy and the commitment components of love, infatuated love may disappear suddenly.

3. *Empty love* consists of the commitment component without intimacy or passion. Sometimes, a stronger love deteriorates into empty love, in which the commitment remains, but the intimacy and passion have died. In cultures in which arranged marriages are common, relationships often begin as empty love.

4. *Romantic love* is a combination of intimacy and passion. Romantic lovers are bonded emotionally (as in liking) and physically through passionate arousal.

5. *Fatuous love* has the passion and the commitment components but not the intimacy component. This type of love can be exemplified by a whirlwind courtship and marriage in which a commitment is motivated largely by passion, without the stabilizing influence of intimacy.

6. *Companionate love* consists of intimacy and commitment. This type of love is often found in marriages in which the passion has gone out of the relationship, but a deep affection and commitment remain.

7. *Consummate love* is the only type of love that includes all three components—intimacy, passion and commitment. **Consummate love** is the most complete form of love, and it represents the ideal love relationship for which many people strive but which apparently few achieve. Sternberg cautions that maintaining a consummate love may be even harder than achieving it. He stresses the importance of translating the components of love into action. "Without expression," he warns, "even the greatest of loves can die" (1987, p. 341).

▲ According to Sternberg, romantic love has both emotional and physical components.

consummate love According to Sternberg's theory, the most complete form of love, consisting of all three components—intimacy, passion, and commitment.

Remember It   Experiencing Emotion

1. The idea that making a happy, sad, or angry face can actually trigger the physiological response and the feeling associated with the emotion is called the _____.

2. Women and men experience and regulate feelings of _____ differently.

3. Sternberg's theory claims that the three components of romantic love are _____, _____, and _____.

4. According to Sternberg, the most complete form of love is _____ love.

Answers: 1. facial-feedback hypothesis; 2. anger; 3. intimacy, passion, commitment; 4. consummate

Apply It   The Quest for Happiness

"Life, Liberty and the pursuit of Happiness"—these ringing words from the Declaration of Independence are familiar to most of us, and most of us would agree that happiness is a desirable goal. But what exactly is happiness, and how can one attain it? These questions are not as easily answered as you might expect.

Happiness is closely related to life satisfaction—people who feel happy also tend to believe that their lives are satisfying. Of course, there are factors in everyone's life that can't be changed, and some of them can result in unhappiness. However, people can use certain strategies to exercise greater control over the way they respond emotionally to their life situations.

Remove Your Rose-Colored Glasses

Optimism, that is, having a generally positive outlook on life, is an important factor in maintaining a sense of well-being. However, do you know what it means to "see the world through rose-colored glasses"? The expression derives from a French metaphor, *voire la vie en rose* (to see life in pink), that means to see things more favorably than they really are. Psychologist Daniel Gilbert has studied the connection between decision making and happiness (Gilbert et al., 2006). He points out that we are often disappointed when we make decisions based on what we believe will make us happy. For example, the belief that a new house will make us happy motivates us to save money, spend time searching for a house, and go through the stressful experience of moving. But within a very short time, we discover that the new house did not bring us the bliss we expected. Gilbert says that we do the same thing in relationships. In pursuit of happiness, we date, marry, have affairs, divorce, have children, reconcile with estranged relatives, cut off communication with troublesome relatives, join clubs to find new friends, and on and on, only to find that we revert to our original emotional state after all is said and done.

Does our tendency to overestimate the amount of happiness a given life change will bring us, that is, to see our world through rose-colored glasses, mean that happiness is impossible? No, in fact, some degree of dissatisfaction with our present state of affairs is probably necessary to keep us motivated to ccontinue improving ourselves and our life situations. However, Gilbert's findings do mean that keeping our expectations in balance may be critical to enjoying the happiness we do experience. So, how do we avoid becoming trapped in the never-ending cycle that comes from the notion that happiness will be found on the other side of our next big decision?

Count Your Blessings

Perhaps we can avoid the hope-disappointment cycle Gilbert describes by learning to be more appreciative of that which we already have. Psychologist Martin Seligman and his colleagues (2005) have used a number of exercises geared toward increasing people's sense of well-being by getting them to focus on the positive aspects of their experiences. One such exercise is "Three Good Things." Seligman instructs participants in his studies to keep a journal in which they record three positive things that happen each day. They have found that participants report feeling happier after having kept the "three good things" journal for only a week. Furthermore, those who continue the practice after their participation in the study has ended report enduring effects.

Likewise, we can take a cue from research examining the attitudes of contented older adults. Such elders have been found to judge their current state of well-being by comparing themselves to others who are doing more poorly (Frieswijk, Buunk, Steverink, & Slaets, 2004). Thus, although elderly characters who proclaim, "It could be worse!" are often the targets of humor in television and movie scripts, it turns out that it is precisely the attitude embodied in this expression that enables older adults to cope with the trials and tribulations of aging.

Keep Busy

You will also feel happier if you get so caught up in an activity that you become oblivious to your surroundings. Psychologists refer to this state as *flow*. To be in flow is to be unself-consciously absorbed (Csikszentmihalyi, 1990). People who are engaged in some activity that engages their skills—whether it is work, play, or simply driving a car—report more positive feelings.

You may not be able to control every aspect of your life situation, but you do have some control over how you respond to it.

✳ Summary and Review

Explaining Motivation p. 352

10.1 How do the three components of motivation work together to influence behavior? p. 352

Activation is the component of motivation in which an individual takes the first steps toward a goal. Persistence is the component of motivation that enables a person to continue to work toward the goal even when he or she encounters obstacles. The intensity component of motivation refers to the energy and attention a person must employ to reach a goal.

10.2 What is the difference between intrinsic and extrinsic motivation? p. 352

With intrinsic motivation, an act is performed because it is satisfying or pleasurable in and of itself; with extrinsic motivation, an act is performed in order to gain a reward or to avert an undesirable consequence.

10.3 How do drive reduction and arousal theory explain motivation? p. 353

Drive-reduction theory suggests that a biological need creates an unpleasant state of emotional arousal that compels the organism to engage in behavior that will reduce the arousal level. Arousal theory suggests that the aim of motivation is to maintain an optimal level of arousal.

Two Primary Drives: Hunger and Thirst p. 355

10.4 Under what conditions do the two types of thirst occur? p. 356

Extracellular thirst results from a loss of fluid from the body tissues. This can be caused by perspiring, vomiting, bleeding, diarrhea, or excessive intake of alcohol. Intracellular thirst results from loss of water inside the body cells. This can be caused by excessive intake of salt, which disturbs the water-sodium balance in the blood and tissues.

10.5 How do internal and external hunger cues influence eating behavior? p. 356

The lateral hypothalamus (LH) signals us to eat when we are hungry, and the ventromedial hypothalamus (VMH) motivates us to stop eating when we are full. Other internal hunger signals are low blood glucose levels and high insulin levels. Some satiety signals are high blood glucose levels and the presence in the blood of other satiety substances (such as CCK) that are secreted by the gastrointestinal tract during digestion. External hunger cues, such as the taste, smell, and appearance of food, eating with other people, and the time of day, can cause people to eat more food than they actually need.

10.6 What are some factors that account for variations in body weight? p. 357

Variations in body weight are influenced by genes, hormones, metabolic rate, activity level, number of fat cells, and eating habits. Fat-cell theory claims that individuals who are overweight have more fat cells in their bodies. Set-point theory suggests that an internal homeostatic system functions to maintain body weight by adjusting appetite and metabolic rate.

10.7 Why is it almost impossible to maintain weight loss by cutting calories alone? p. 360

It is almost impossible to maintain weight loss by cutting calories alone because a dieter's metabolic rate slows down to compensate for the lower intake of calories. Exercise both prevents the lowering of metabolic rate and burns up additional calories.

10.8 What are the symptoms of anorexia nervosa and bulimia nervosa? p. 361

The symptoms of anorexia nervosa are an overwhelming, irrational fear of being fat, compulsive dieting to the point of self-starvation, and excessive weight loss. The symptoms of bulimia nervosa are repeated and uncontrolled episodes of binge eating, usually followed by purging.

Social Motives p. 363

10.9 How do need for achievement theory and goal orientation theory explain achievement motivation? p. 364

Murray's need for achievement theory claims that individuals vary in their need to accomplish something difficult and to perform at a high standard of excellence. Goal orientation theory asserts that individuals vary in their adoption of mastery and performance goals. Mastery goals measure achievement against a desired level of knowledge acquisition. Performance goals measure personal achievement against that of others.

10.10 What kinds of conditions affect work motivation? p. 365

Conditions such as support from supervisors, fair pay, and good relationships with coworkers influence work motivation. It is also influenced by workers' beliefs about their competency.

Understanding Emotion p. 366

10.11 What are the three components of emotions? p. 366

The three components of emotions are the physiological arousal that accompanies the emotion, the cognitive appraisal of the stimulus or situation, and the outward behavioral expression of the emotion.

10.12 According to the various theories of emotion, what sequence of events occurs when an individual experiences an emotion? p. 367

According to the James-Lange theory of emotion, environmental stimuli produce a physiological response, and then awareness of this response causes the emotion to be experienced. The Cannon-Bard theory suggests that emotion-provoking stimuli received by the senses are relayed simultaneously to the cortex, providing the mental experience of the emotion, and to the sympathetic nervous system, producing physiological arousal. The Schachter-Singer theory states that for an emotion to occur, (1) there must be physiological arousal, and (2) the person must perceive some reason for the arousal in order to label the emotion. According to the Lazarus theory, an emotion-provoking stimulus triggers a cognitive appraisal, which is followed by the emotion and the physiological arousal.

10.13 What brain structure processes the emotion of fear? p. 369

The emotion of fear is processed by the amygdala, without initial involvement of the brain's cortex.

Expressing Emotion p. 370

10.14 What are basic emotions? p. 370

The basic emotions (happiness, sadness, disgust, and so on) are those that are unlearned and universal and that emerge in children according to their biological timetable of development.

10.15 How does the development of facial expressions in infants suggest a biological basis for emotional expression? p. 371

The facial expressions of different emotions develop in a particular sequence in infants and seem to be the result of maturation rather than learning. The same sequence occurs even in children who have been blind and deaf since birth.

10.16 What evidence is there to suggest that facial expressions have the same meanings all over the world? p. 371

Charles Darwin first studied the universality of facial expressions because he believed that the ability to read others' emotions was an aid to survival. His research demonstrated that facial expressions are similar across cultures. Later studies confirmed Darwin's findings but also indicated that there is variation across cultures in the ways emotions are elicited and regulated and how they are shared socially.

10.17 How do display rules for emotions differ across cultures? p. 372

The customs of an individual's culture determine when, where, and under what circumstances various emotions are exhibited. Children learn these rules as they mature so that, as adults, they will be able to suppress and exhibit emotions in accordance with the rules of their cultures. Violating a culture's display rules can cause a person's behavior to be interpreted as rude or offensive.

10.18 Why is emotion considered a form of communication? p. 373

Emotions enable people to communicate desires, intentions, and needs more effectively than just words alone and thus make it more likely that others will respond.

10.19 What has research revealed about behavioral, physiological, and neurological measures of deception? p. 374

Behavioral measures show that people are poor lie detectors and that there are few consistent behaviors that distinguish truth-tellers from liars. Physiological measures such as the polygraph may be useful in investigations, but they are not reliable enough to pinpoint false statements. Neurological measures based on EEG and fMRI technology are more accurate than physiological measures and may become more frequently used in the future.

Experiencing Emotion p. 375

10.20 How do facial expressions influence internal emotional states? p. 376

The facial-feedback hypothesis suggests that the muscular movements involved in certain facial expressions trigger corresponding emotions (for example, smiling triggers happiness).

10.21 In what ways do males and females differ with regard to emotions? p. 376

When exposed to similar stimuli, men and women respond with different emotions. Moreover, emotions such as anger and jealousy are linked to different experiences in males and females. Women may be better than men at interpreting emotions and often serve as the "emotional managers" in relationships. Men process emotion predominately in the left hemisphere of the brain, whereas women use both cerebral hemispheres.

10.22 How does emotion influence thought? p. 377

Emotional states affect memory. Emotions also influence attention and allow us to make rapid assessments of threatening conditions. Fear increases our perceptions of risk, while anger reduces them.

10.23 How does Sternberg's triangular theory of love account for the different kinds of love? p. 378

In his triangular theory of love, Sternberg proposes that, singly and in various combinations, three components—intimacy, passion, and commitment—produce seven different kinds of love: liking, infatuated, empty, romantic, fatuous, companionate, and consummate love.

Thinking Critically about Psychology

1. Which of the four types of goal orientations best describes your own pattern of motivation? To what extent do you exhibit different goal orientations in different situations?
2. Prepare arguments for and against this statement: "In criminal prosecutions, technological measures of the truthfulness of the accused should carry more weight than other kinds of evidence."
3. Arousal theory is often proposed to explain risk-taking behaviors that have undesirable outcomes, such as experimentation with drugs. How can we use the theory to explain risk-taking behaviors that offer the possibility of a desirable outcome, such as starting your own business?

Key Terms

anorexia nervosa, p. 361
arousal, p. 353
arousal theory, p. 354
basic emotions, p. 370
body mass index (BMI), p. 357
bulimia nervosa, p. 362
Cannon-Bard theory of emotion, p. 367
consummate love, p. 379
display rules, p. 372
drive, p. 353
drive-reduction theory, p. 353
emotion, p. 366
extrinsic motivation, p. 352

facial-feedback hypothesis, p. 376
fat cells, p. 359
goal orientation theory, p. 364
homeostasis, p. 353
incentive, p. 352
industrial/organizational (I/O) psychologists, p. 365
intrinsic motivation, p. 352
James-Lange theory of emotion, p. 367
lateral hypothalamus (LH), p. 356
Lazarus theory of emotion, p. 368
metabolic rate, p. 358
motivation, p. 352

motive, p. 352
need for achievement (n Ach), p. 364
obesity, p. 357
primary drive, p. 356
polygraph, p. 374
Schachter-Singer theory of emotion, p. 367
set point, p. 359
social motives, p. 363
stimulus motives, p. 354
triangular theory of love, p. 378
ventromedial hypothalamus (VMH), p. 356
work motivation, p. 365
Yerkes-Dodson law, p. 354

Chapter 11

Human Sexuality and Gender

Continued

Sexual Dysfunctions

11.15 What are the defining features of two sexual desire disorders?

11.16 What are the defining features of the sexual arousal disorders?

11.17 How do orgasmic and sexual pain disorders affect men's and women's sexual experiences?

Sexually Transmitted Diseases

11.18 What are the major bacterial sexually transmitted diseases, and how are they treated?

11.19 What viral diseases are transmitted through sexual contact?

11.20 In what ways can HIV/AIDS affect an individual's physical and psychological health?

Can you guess the gender of a mystery person based entirely on his or her behavior in sexual relationships? Try your hand with this description. This mystery person became sexually active at 13 years of age. Now an adult, he or she prefers short-term to long-term sexual partners. When no longer interested in a partner, Mr. or Ms. X simply stops communicating with him or her.

You might be surprised to learn that these are the typical behaviors of heterosexual women of the Mosuo, a group that inhabits the rugged mountains of southwestern China (Yuan, 2000). The Mosuo culture is matriarchal in structure; that is, it is organized around maternal relationships. Each Mosuo household is headed by a female leader called a "Duba" to whom all of the members of the household are biologically related in some way. Dubas control all the family's wealth, and there are special rites of passage for 13-year-old girls in which they are recognized as the society's future leaders. The Mosuo have no corresponding rites of passage for boys.

Heterosexual relationships among the Mosuo are polyandrous, meaning that one woman may have several male partners at the same time. These relationships take the form of "walking marriages." A walking marriage begins when a Mosuo woman invites a potential mate to visit her home during the night. Eager to make a good impression, the man goes to the woman's home bearing the best gift he can afford. If the woman finds the man to be pleasing, sexual relations occur. At dawn, the man goes back to his Duba's home and may only return to the woman's home if she chooses to invite him again. However, women are not obligated to form permanent relationships with men, and they can have as many nighttime visitors as they desire.

When a child is conceived, there is no need for a Mosuo woman to know exactly who her child's father is, because wealth is inherited through mothers rather than fathers. Furthermore, men are obligated to care for their sisters' children rather than their own. Thus, biological fathers have no formal role in rearing their children and are not economically responsible for them.

Do these Mosuo customs seem odd to you? Most of the world's cultures, including that of the United States, arose from patriarchal systems in which men are dominant. What is familiar to us often shapes our ideas about what is natural as well as how things *should be*, from a moral perspective. For instance, people who are socialized in a patriarchal culture may believe that sexual aggression perpetrated by males against females is a manifestation of "natural" male sexual impulses (Jewkes, Penn-Kekana, & Rose-Junius, 2005). Likewise, a patriarchal culture's belief that women are "naturally" submissive may unwittingly contribute to such behavior.

Despite the insight we might gain from considering cross-cultural differences in sexual behavior, it is important to keep in mind that the culture of the Mosuo includes many gender-based practices that are similar to those that are common in other societies. Consider the customary division of labor among the Mosuo. Men do the heavier agricultural and maintenance tasks, and women attend to housework (Gatsua, 2003). Studies show that a similar division of labor exists in the United States today. Recent surveys comparing stay-at-home mothers to stay-at-home fathers have shown that a gender-based division of labor is maintained regardless of which parent takes time off from work to raise the children (Salary.com, 2006a, 2006b). Overall, these surveys showed that the activities of stay-at-home fathers and mothers are very similar. However, one interesting difference emerged. Stay-at-home dads, on average, spent more time doing household maintenance tasks than their female counterparts. Stay-at-home moms differed from stay-at-home dads in the average amount of time they devoted to housework. Surveys of families in which both parents work show a similar pattern in after-work and weekend activities. Such findings show that patriarchal and matriarchal cultures are not complete mirror images of one another with regard to gender-based expectations.

It is also important to know that, although there are no cultural mandates regarding permanent relationships, many such relationships do develop among the Mosuo. In fact, the term "friend marriage" is used by the Mosuo to refer to such partnerships (Yuan, 2000). These relationships often develop when a couple conceives a child. Apparently, even though Mosuo men are not obligated to care for their offspring, most are interested in their children's upbringing. Similarly, most fathers in patriarchal societies are motivated to support their children both economically and emotionally by the bonds of affection that they share with them. Thus, the motivating forces behind father-child relationships in both cultures go beyond cultural prescriptions regarding economic support.

Considerations of cross-cultural differences and similarities highlight the need to separate nature from nurture when we study variations in sexual behavior both across and within cultures. Of course, sex represents only one arena of experience in which gender is relevant. Everyday observations of men and women—and of boys and girls—suggest that the two genders dress differently, are attracted to different leisure and occupational activities, experience emotions differently, and, perhaps, think differently. But are these observations really accurate? Are males and females really as different as we often judge them to be? If so, are these differences "natural," or do they arise from social experiences? As you'll learn in this chapter, psychologists are interested in finding out the relevance and significance of "maleness" and "femaleness" in every area of life.

Sex, Gender, and Gender Roles

Do you use the words *sex* and *gender* interchangeably? Most people do, but the words have different meanings. Generally speaking, *sex* is a biological term. Thus, for the sake of clarity, the term **biological sex**—the physiological status of being male or female—is often used by psychologists and others who study this aspect of human experience. By contrast, **gender** is more commonly used to refer to the psychological and social variables associated with one's sex. As you might imagine, there is considerable debate about how the two are related.

biological sex Physiological status as male or female.

gender (JEN-der) The psychological and sociocultural definition of masculinity or femininity, based on the expected behaviors for males and females.

Biological Sex

As you learned in Chapter 2, the **sex chromosomes,** XX in females and XY in males, determine one's biological sex. Information on these chromosomes contributes the development of the genitalia and other aspects of biological sex. Sometimes the process goes awry, and a child is born with features that make it difficult to identify his or her sex. Before exploring these cases, we will outline the milestones of sex development experienced by most children.

11.1 How does biological sex develop both typically and atypically?

The Development of Biological Sex. In the early weeks of prenatal development, the **gonads,** or sex glands, of the male and female fetus are identical. During the 7th week of prenatal development, a single gene found only on the Y chromosome (Capel, 2000) and known as *Sry*, sets in motion the forces that lead to the development of testes in male fetuses (Hanley et al., 2000). If the Sry gene is absent or not functioning, ovaries

sex chromosomes The pair of chromosomes that determines the biological sex of a person (XX in females and XY in males).

gonads The sex glands; the ovaries in females and the testes in males.

will develop about 12 weeks after conception (Wertz & Herrmann, 2000). But the story does not end here.

The presence or absence of **androgens,** or male sex hormones, determines whether an embryo develops male or female **genitals,** also called the **primary sex characteristics.** In the male embryo, androgens produced and secreted by the primitive testes cause the male genitals—the penis, testes, and scrotum—to develop. If androgens are not present, female genitals—the ovaries, uterus, and vagina—develop (Breedlove, 1994). A genetic male (XY) can develop female genitals if androgens are absent, and a genetic female (XX) can develop male genitals if an abnormally high level of androgens is present. But androgens affect more than the physical development of the genitals. These hormones also have a tremendous influence on the brain during fetal development, causing the brains of males and females to begin to develop in somewhat different ways Lazar, 2000.

At puberty, the hypothalamus sends a signal to the pituitary gland, which in turn sets in motion the maturing of the genitals and the appearance of the **secondary sex characteristics.** These are the physical characteristics that are associated with sexual maturity but not directly involved in reproduction: pubic and underarm hair in both sexes, breasts in females, and facial and chest hair and a deepened voice in males.

Atypical Development. A very small proportion of children are born with some degree of genital ambiguity. Most of these cases are caused by excessive or deficient levels of androgens between the 9th and 13th weeks of prenatal development (Styne & Glaser, 1998). The process of determining in which sex a child with ambiguous genitalia should be reared is called **sex assignment.** In most such cases, the ambiguous anatomy turns out to consist of normal genitals with a distorted appearance (i.e., enlarged clitoris in females, undersized penis in males). In cases of this kind, the distorted genitals are accompanied by normal internal sex organs. Thus, sex assignment decisions are fairly straightforward (Styne & Glaser, 1998). Doctors use surgery, hormones, or both to achieve greater consistency between the child's internal organs and external appearance.

In a few cases, an infant is born with a condition known as **intersex.** These children possess some or all of the anatomical and physiological characteristics of both sexes. Chromosomal defects are responsible for most cases of intersex. Rarely, the condition results from the fusion of two fertilized eggs, one of which is XX and the other of which is XY (Dewald et al., 1980; Wright & Wales, 2004).

Of intersexuals, 10% are **true hermaphodites** who have both testicular and ovarian internal tissues (Whitman-Elia & Queenan, 2005). Sex assignment decisions for hermaphrodite children can be challenging and can require extensive testing of the child's internal organs, gonadal tissue, and chromosomal status. In recent years, the Intersex Society of North America (ISNA), a support group for intersexuals, has raised awareness of the issues they face both in childhood and adulthood (Dreger, 2006). As individuals who have grown up with various kinds of intersexual conditions, the members of the ISNA insist that the intersexual child's long-term psychological well-being should be the top priority in sex assignment decisions. They point out that genital surgery is almost never medically necessary. Therefore, they suggest that children be allowed time to manifest their psychological gender before undergoing irreversible surgeries or hormone treatments. Taking a wait-and-see approach to sex assignment, the ISNA says, will increase the chances of achieving a match between sex and gender and will also allow intersexual children sufficient time to develop the cognitive maturity needed to participate in sex assignment decisions.

Psychological Gender

As you learned at the beginning of this chapter, the Mosuo expect girls to grow up to be leaders, and they are provided with rites of passage that make them mindful of their future positions. By contrast, patriarchal cultures expect boys to assume leadership positions in adulthood and socialize them accordingly. Cultural expectations for males and females are called **gender roles.** Gender roles include psychological as well as be-

androgens Male sex hormones.

genitals (JEN-uh-tulz) The internal and external reproductive organs of males or females.

primary sex characteristics The internal and external reproductive organs; the genitals.

secondary sex characteristics The physical characteristics that appear at puberty and are associated with sexual maturity but not directly involved in reproduction.

sex assignment The decision to bring up a child with ambiguous genitalia as either a male or female.

intersex The condition in which a person's internal organs differ from his or her external genitalia.

true hermaphrodite An individual who has both ovarian and testicular tissue.

gender roles Cultural expectations about the behaviors appropriate to each gender.

11.2 What is the relationship between sex and gender?

havioral components. A culture's gender role for males is referred to as the *masculine* gender role, and its gender role for females is referred to as the *feminine* gender role.

The integration of culturally defined masculine and feminine gender roles into one's sense of self underlies the development of ==gender identity,== the psychological experience of feeling male or female. Most boys grow up with a masculine gender identity that helps them to be comfortable with the behaviors that their cultures regard as acceptable for males. Likewise, most female children develop a feminine gender identity that is consistent with behaviors in the cultures in which they are raised. We will discuss how this process occurs a bit later. Now, though, what do you think happens when a person's sex and his or her gender identity do not match? In other words, what are the consequences of having male sex combined with female gender identity or female sex combined with male gender identity?

A person who is **transgendered** has a gender identity that is the opposite of his or her biological sex. Thus, the person has a strong desire to be the opposite sex. Some studies suggest that transgendered individuals may have been exposed to atypical amounts of androgens in the womb (Lippa, 2005a). But most do not have such histories, so the cause of transgenderism remains a mystery.

In an effort to bring congruence to their lives, some transgendered individuals wear clothing and display behaviors that are more typical of the opposite sex. Those who live as the opposite gender on a full-time basis are known as **transsexuals.** Some transsexuals are so anguished by the conflict between their sex and their gender identity that they undergo **sex reassignment**—a process involving hormonal treatment, reconstructive surgery, and psychological counseling—in order to achieve a match between the two. Research shows that, following sex reassignment, transsexuals are generally satisfied with the results and seldom regret their decision (Lawrence, 2003).

The phenomenon of transgenderism illustrates the fact that biological sex and psychological gender are distinct entities. Moreover, biological sex is clearly categorical; that is, people are *either* male *or* female, rare cases of intersexual status notwithstanding. By contrast, psychological gender seems to vary by degrees. As noted, most girls grow up to be comfortable with their culture's feminine gender role, but they do not all conform to that gender role to the same degree. The same is true for boys. Thus, one of the most widely researched questions in psychology concerns the process through which children develop their understanding of cultural gender roles and integrate that understanding into their own sense of self.

Early Theories of Gender Role Development

How do you think children acquire gender roles? When we look at early theories of gender role development, we find that the ideas of all the major schools of psychology are represented.

Psychoanalytic Theory. Psychoanalytic theory proposes that gender role development is a largely unconscious process governed by the child's emotions. According to Freud, children's ideas about gender arise out of a conflict concerning their feelings toward their parents. They want to bond to the opposite-sex parent, but fear the jealous reaction of the same-sex parent. To resolve the conflict, they connect to the same-sex parent, adopting his or her gender-related ideas and behavior. At the same time, they defer their love for the opposite-sex parent in the hope that someday they will be able to achieve a sexual relationship with a partner who is similar to him or her. The idea is that the better job they do of becoming like the same-sex parent, the more likely it is that they will be able to attract a partner who is like the opposite-sex parent (a popular song in the early 20th century was even titled "I Want a Girl Just Like the Girl Who Married Dear Old Dad").

Masculinity and Femininity as Opposites. Freud put forward several interesting ideas about gender, but many researchers believe that the scientific study of gender

11.3 How did the early theorists explain gender role development?

gender identity   The sense of being male or female; acquired between ages 2 and 3.

transgendered   The condition in which an individual's biological sex and psychological gender do not match.

transsexual   An individual who lives as the opposite gender on a full-time basis.

sex reassignment   Assignment to the opposite sex after living for a period of time as the other sex.

▲ Gender socialization begins early in life, when girls and boys learn to engage in activities that are considered typically female or male.

roles began in earnest when Lewis Terman, the author of the *Stanford-Binet Scale of Intelligence*, and his colleague Catherine Cox Miles (1936) proposed that masculinity and femininity are two endpoints of a single dimension. To get a better understanding of this concept, think about height. Short people are at one end of the height continuum, and tall people are at the other. Thus, shortness and tallness are opposites. This is how Terman and Miles thought of gender roles. From their perspective, the more femininity a person has, the less masculinity she has, and vice versa. The expression *masculinity-femininity* is often used to refer to this idea.

Terman and Miles developed the *Attitude Interest Analysis Survey (AIAS)* to measure masculinity-femininity. The name of the test was intended to prevent test takers from guessing what Terman and Miles were trying to measure. Among psychologists, the test is usually referred to as the *Terman-Miles MF Test*. It included many different kinds of items, with each "feminine" answer being scored −1 and each "masculine" answer scored +1. Here are two test questions similar to those on the MF test. The signs in parentheses show how each answer would be scored.

Which word, a or b, is the best associate for the word in capital letters?
BALL   a. dance (−1)   b. game (+1)

Which profession do you find most appealing?
Nurse (−1)   Mechanic (+1)   Teacher (−1)   Architect (+1)

An individual's MF score was calculated by summing the scores of all of his or her answers to the more than 400 items on the test. With half the answers scored negatively and half positively, a person who chose mostly "feminine" answers received a negative score, and one who chose mostly "masculine" answers received a positive score. (You have probably noticed the implications of this scoring system: feminine = negative, masculine = positive.)

Many psychologists of the day recognized the shortcomings of the MF test and criticized it quite severely, especially for the shallow way in which it approached masculinity and femininity (Rosenzweig, 1938). Nevertheless, the assumption that masculinity and femininity are opposites became the accepted way of thinking about gender roles among most researchers (Bem, 1974). Although this view is no longer dominant among psychologists, there are several personality tests in use today that have MF scales that are similar to the one created by Terman and Miles.

Learning Theories. In contrast to the ideas of Freud and other psychologists who accepted the notion that masculinity-femininity was a measurable trait, learning theorists argued that gender roles were nothing more than learned behavior. As such, girls acquire "feminine" behaviors and boys acquire "masculine" behaviors because their parents and peers reinforce them for doing so. Later, social learning theorists such as Walter Mischel also argued that children acquire gender roles through imitation of models (Mischel, 1966). Mischel and others pointed out that children are usually reinforced for imitating behaviors considered appropriate for their gender. When behaviors are not appropriate (a boy puts on lipstick, or a girl pretends to shave her face), children are quickly informed, often in a tone of reprimand, that boys or girls do not do that. However, there is little evidence that parents reinforce behavior that is gender-role appropriate often enough to account for the early age at which children begin to exhibit gender typing (Fagot, 1995). Developmental psychologists have found that boys in father-absent homes exhibit the same levels of gender-typed behavior as boys in father-present homes do (Stevens et al., 2002). Thus, imitation and reinforcement probably play some part in gender role development, but they do not provide a full explanation of this phenomenon.

Cognitive-Developmental Theory. Lawrence Kohlberg, whose theory of moral development you read about in Chapter 8, strongly challenged Freud's ideas about gender roles as well as the assumptions of a masculinity-femininity test (Kohlberg, 1966; Kohlberg & Ullian, 1974). He was equally critical of the view that reinforcement and imitation of models determine children's gender roles. Kohlberg argued that an understanding of gender is a prerequisite to gender role development. According to Kohlberg, children go through a series of stages in acquiring the concept of gender. Between ages 2 and 3, children acquire gender identity, the sense of being a male or a female. Between ages 4 and 5, children grasp the concept of **gender stability,** awareness that boys are boys and girls are girls for a lifetime. Finally, between ages 6 and 8, children acquire **gender constancy,** the understanding that gender does not change, regardless of the activities people engage in or the clothes they wear. Moreover, according to Kohlberg, when children realize that their gender is permanent, they are motivated to seek out same-sex models and learn to act in ways considered appropriate for that gender.

▲ Children are often reinforced for imitating the gender-typed behaviors of adults.

Cross-cultural studies reveal that Kohlberg's stages of gender identity, gender stability, and gender constancy occur in the same order in cultures as different as those in Samoa, Kenya, Nepal, and Belize (Munroe et al., 1984). Moreover, progression through the stages is correlated with other advances in cognitive development (Trautner et al., 2003). However, Kolberg's theory fails to explain why many gender-role appropriate behaviors and preferences are observed in children as young as age 2 or 3, long before gender constancy is acquired (Bussey & Bandura, 1999; Jacklin, 1989; Martin & Little, 1990).

gender stability   The awareness that gender is a permanent characteristic; acquired between ages 4 and 5.

gender constancy   The understanding that activities and clothes do not affect gender stability; acquired between ages 6 and 8.

The Multi-Dimensional Approach to Gender Roles

An enormous leap forward in the study of gender roles occurred when several psychologists, most notably Sandra Bem (1974, 1977, 1985), proposed that gender roles include both masculine and feminine dimensions. The relative balance between these dimensions, argued Bem, determines an individual's gender role. The idea that masculinity and femininity are separate dimensions, together with the proposition that an individual's gender role is a combination of the two, is known as the *multi-dimensional approach* to gender roles.

To demonstrate the usefulness of the multi-dimensional approach, Bem (1974) developed an instrument known as the *Bem Sex Role Inventory (BSRI)*. People who take the BSRI describe themselves in terms of adjectives that Bem's preliminary studies showed were perceived as stereotypically masculine, feminine, or neutral by both men and women. A few such descriptors are shown in **Table 11.1**. As you can see in **Figure 11.1**,

11.4 How does the multi-dimensional approach explain gender roles?

Table 11.1 Items from the Bem Sex Role Inventory

Masculine	Feminine	Neutral
Aggressive	Loyal	Conscientious
Athletic	Compassionate	Adaptable
Self-reliant	Yielding	Sincere
Willing to take a stand	Sympathetic	Truthful
Forceful	Soft spoken	Helpful

Source: Bem (1974).

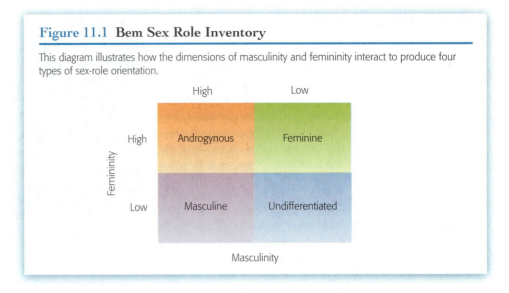

Figure 11.1 Bem Sex Role Inventory

This diagram illustrates how the dimensions of masculinity and femininity interact to produce four types of sex-role orientation.

Bem's scoring system classifies those who identify with neither masculine nor feminine gender roles as *undifferentiated*. Those who are higher on masculinity than femininity are classified as *masculine*, whereas those with the reverse pattern are assigned to the *feminine* category. Test takers who score high on both scales are deemed **androgynous.**

Since its introduction in the mid-1970s, the BSRI has been used extensively by gender role researchers throughout the world. They have discovered a wide variety of associations between Bem's gender role categories and other variables of interest. Here are a few examples of the results of recent studies.

- A French study showed that androgynous men were more likely to help their female partners with domestic tasks such as housework and child care than men in other categories (Gana et al., 2001).
- Israeli men and women in the feminine category were found to be more likely to be involved in voluntary charity work than individuals in the other three categories (Karniol & Grosz, 2003).
- British researchers found that, compared to those in other categories, men and women in the masculine classification had the highest levels of the male hormone testosterone (Deady, Smith, Sharp, & Al-Dujaili, 2006).
- A Turkish study suggested that individuals in the masculine category get more traffic tickets than those in other groups (Ozkan & Lajunen, 2005).

Researchers have also used the BSRI to examine possible associations between gender roles and individual differences in variables such as self-esteem and general mental health. Bem (1975) hypothesized that androgynous individuals should demonstrate superior adjustment compared to individuals in the other three categories. Studies that have tested Bem's hypothesis have shown that for both males and females, masculine traits are the most strongly associated with self-esteem, adjustment, creativity, and mental health (Aube & Koestner, 1992; Hittner & Daniels, 2002; Moeller-Leimkuehler et al., 2002). To the extent that androgynous people possess masculine traits, they are likely to be better adjusted and to have higher self-esteem than people who are feminine or undifferentiated.

However, both Bem's concept of androgyny and the BSRI have been criticized for a variety of reasons. For example, researcher Janet Spence argued that the terms *instrumentality* and *expressiveness* should be used rather than *masculinity* and *femininity* because the continued use of these terms by psychologists serves to perpetuate cultural stereotypes (Spence, Helmreich, & Stapp, 1974). Others, including Bem herself in later work, suggested that the BSRI and other such tests measure personality rather than gender roles (Lippa, 2005a). Nevertheless, the multidimensional approach revolutionized the study of gender roles and continues to be important today.

androgyny (an-DROJ-uh-nee) A combination of desirable masculine and feminine characteristics in one person.

Gender Schema Theory

In addition to introducing the concept of androgyny into psychologists' discussion of gender roles, Sandra Bem also played an important role in the development of current theories of gender role development. **Gender schema theory,** as Bem's approach is called, proposes that the characteristics of the information-processing system influence how children acquire and use information about the gender-based expectations of their cultures (Bem 1981; Martin & Halverson, 1981; Martin & Ruble, 2002). Here is a brief overview of the process of gender role development as the gender schema theorists view it.

As you learned in Chapter 6, long-term memory employs structures called *schemas* to organize information in memory. Bem and other gender schema theorists assert that children begin to organize gender-related information into such schemas at about the same time they consistently label themselves as boys or girls, around age 2 or so. Soon afterward, motivated by the information-processing system's need to refine these schemas, children begin to show strong preferences for sex-appropriate toys and clothing, and to favor same-sex friends over those of the other sex (Powlishta, 1995). While children are constructing rules that can help them determine what should and should not to be part of their gender schemas, they tend to think somewhat rigidly about gender-appropriate behaviors. A 4-year-old may say, for example, that a boy who plays with dolls should be punished. Once children have a clearer understanding of the arbitrariness of some of the associations between sex and activity preferences that they observe in others, they think more flexibly. Consequently, a 9-year-old boy knows that most boys don't play with dolls; however, he also knows that boys who cross such boundaries are not breaking any sort of moral rule and will argue that such behaviors do not merit punishment by either peers or adults. At the same time, the older child knows that some gender-related phenomena, such as women bearing children, are fixed by nature. Children's schemas for gender roles, once fully developed, enable them to distinguish between the arbitrary and natural components of gender-related expectations.

As you can see, like their predecessor Lawrence Kohlberg, gender schema theorists regard the cognitive aspects of gender role development as a subset of general cognitive development (Martin & Ruble, 2002). Accordingly, they suggest that gender schemas develop early in life because biological sex is a highly obvious, either-or category that young children can easily grasp. For a while, children operate under the false premise that the psychological and social aspects of gender are just as easily classified. But, just as they overcome the weaknesses in logical thinking that you learned about in Chapter 8, children eventually get past these limitations (Trautner et al., 2005). Thus, the egalitarian-minded parent of a young child who has rigid ideas about what boys and girls should and should not do probably doesn't need to worry that the child will grow up to be intolerant. The parents should simply continue to challenge the child's statements and encourage him or her to develop a broader perspective. Over time, the child will come to realize that many aspects of gender roles have more to do with cultural beliefs than they do with any essential qualities of males and females. Of course, evolutionary theorists take a somewhat different view, as you will see.

Evolutionary Theory

In recent years, evolutionary theory has gained a prominent place in explanations of gender differences. Support for this approach comes from studies showing that females and males display similar mating patterns across widely varying cultures. To put it succinctly, men tend to prefer youthful, physically attractive mates, whereas women tend to seek men who have the skills to provide for their physical needs (Buss, 1994).

To explain these findings, evolutionary theorists propose that natural selection has shaped both male and female mating strategies to foster the survival of offspring. Men, they say, use attractiveness as an indicator of health in a potential mate. Moreover, they behave assertively because they know that women are looking for a mate

11.5 How do gender roles develop according to gender schema theorists?

gender schema theory   A theory suggesting that young children are motivated to attend to and behave in ways consistent with gender-based standards and stereotypes of their culture.

11.6 What do evolutionary theories say about the contribution of natural selection to gender roles?

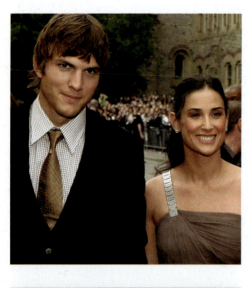

▲ Which one of these couples best conforms to the predictions of evolutionary theory? Which is more representative of sociocultural theory?

who can protect and provide for them. In contrast, women look for stable, committed mates who are good providers. At the same time, they know that men seek attractive mates, so they focus on that attribute in themselves rather than on developing the skills needed for self-sufficiency.

You might be thinking that the evolutionary explanation makes sense for early humans who lived in caves, but what about today? Evolutionary theorists argue that the same factors are at work among modern humans. They hypothesize that men are motivated to enter higher-paying fields because their earning power will help them attract a youthful, fertile female. For their part, evolutionists say, women's career decisions are less influenced by financial concerns than are those of men, because they know that it is their attractiveness and not their earning power that will enable them to attract a stable, committed, economically successful mate.

Furthermore, some evolutionary theorists have argued that the gender-based play preferences of toddlers and children result from an innate biological preparedness, shaped by natural selection, to assume these mating roles in adulthood (Alexander, 2003). Thus, boys engage in mock fighting because, in the future, they will have to demonstrate to desirable females that they have the capacity to take care of them. Girls play with dolls and put on make-up because, in the future, they will have to maximize their physical appearance to attract a mate and use their nurturing skills to raise children.

Researchers who approach gender differences from a sociocultural perspective question whether women's reported mate preferences are thoroughly biological in nature. Researcher Alice Eagly, for example, cites research demonstrating that gender differences in mate preferences are significantly smaller when economic and social conditions for males and females are more equal, as they are becoming in developed countries in the 21st century (Eagly & Wood, 1999). In other words, when women are economically dependent on men, the mating "rules" described by evolutionary psychologists may apply; however, gender differences in mate preferences decline as women gain independence. Under conditions of equality, physical attractiveness in a mate would be likely to be just as important to women as to men. And a woman's earning capacity might be more highly valued by men.

Research supports Eagly's view. Studies show that in societies with egalitarian attitudes about gender roles, marital status and income are correlated. Longitudinal, prospective research has shown that the higher a woman's economic status is, the more likely she is to get married (Ono, 2003). Furthermore, studies show that over the past several years, men's interest in the earning power of potential mates has risen (Buss, Shackelford, Kirkpatrick, & Larsen, 2001). So, today's men may be looking for more in their mates than good looks and child-bearing potential.

Finally, some psychologists have criticized the tendency of evolutionary theory to exaggerate differences between males and females (Barrett & Hyde, 2001). They suggest that so-called masculine and feminine characteristics are linked to the contexts in which behavior occurs rather than to internal traits that have been shaped by natural selection. For example, comforting a grieving co-worker elicits stereotypically "feminine" nurturing behavior from both men and women. Likewise, rectifying an error on one's electric bill brings stereotypically "masculine" assertiveness to the fore in both genders. These theorists argue that we should not make the mistake of thinking that any characteristic is the exclusive domain of one gender or the other. This, say these critics, is the erroneous conclusion that can be inferred from evolutionary theory's emphasis on gender roles and gender differences as products of the forces of nature.

The various theoretical explanations of gender role development are summarized in the following *Review and Reflect*.

Review and Reflect   Theories of Gender Role Development

Theory	Factors Proposed to Explain Gender Role Development
Psychoanalytic theory	Emotional conflicts brought about by attempts to bond with opposite-sex parent
Masculinity-femininity approach	Masculinity and femininity are opposite ends of the same measurable trait
Learning theory	Role models, imitation, and reinforcement
Cognitive developmental theory	Series of stages necessary to develop concept of gender
Multi-dimensional approach	Masculinity and femininity are separate variables; balance between them defines gender role
Gender schema theory	Information-processing system determines how concepts about gender develop
Evolutionary theory	Male and female roles are influenced by natural selection

Remember It   Sex, Gender, and Gender Roles

1. The sex chromosomes in a male are _____; while the sex chromosomes in a female are _____.

2. If _____ are not present, female genitals will develop, regardless of whether the sex chromosomes are those of a male or a female.

3. _____ individuals have reproductive tissue of both sexes.

4. The psychological sense of being male or female is called _____.

5. A person who is transgendered perceives a mismatch between _____ and _____.

6. Match each theoretical perspective with its explanation of gender role development.

   _____ (1) gender schema theory
   _____ (2) multi-dimensional approach
   _____ (3) social learning theory
   _____ (4) psychoanalytic theory
   _____ (5) cognitive developmental theory
   _____ (6) evolutionary theory

   a. role models and reinforcement
   b. stages in understanding of gender concepts
   c. natural selection shaped gender roles
   d. unconscious emotional conflicts
   e. information processing
   f. masculinity and femininity are independent

Answers: 1. XY, XX; 2. androgens; 3. Intersex; 4. gender identity; 5. sex, gender identity; 6. (1) e, (2) f, (3) a, (4) d, (5) b, (6) c

Gender Differences

Suppose you had to participate in a debate in which you were assigned to argue in favor of one of these propositions: (1) There are no differences whatsoever between males and females. (2) There are no similarities whatsoever between males and females. To which side would you hope to be assigned? Of course, the truth about gender differences lies between these two extremes. Nevertheless, some of the variables shown in Table 11.2 for which researchers have found zero or near-zero differences across males and females may be surprising to you. Before we examine gender differences, we need to explore the cognitive processes that are involved in turning information about these differences into gender stereotypes.

Table 11.2 Meta-Analyses of Gender Differences

Variables with Zero or Near-Zero Gender Differences

Math concepts	Self-disclosure
Math problem solving	Impulsiveness
Reading comprehension	Outgoingness
Vocabulary	Life satisfaction
Verbal reasoning	Happiness
Abstract reasoning	Self-esteem

Variables with Moderate to Large Differences Favoring Males

Mechanical reasoning	Computer self-efficacy
Mental rotation	Assertiveness
Science achievement	Helping when watched
Intrusive interruptions	Physical aggression
Tolerance of academic cheating	Verbal aggression

Variables with Moderate to Large Differences Favoring Females

Spelling	Smiling
Perceptual speed	Indirect aggression
Language ability	Trust
Speech production	Aggreeableness

Source: Hyde (2005).

Thinking about Gender Differences

11.7 How does the information-processing system create gender stereotypes?

How many times have you heard someone say that "Women do X, but men do Y"? Unless these statements are made in reference to an obvious physical difference between males and females (e.g., only women bear children), they are probably the products of **stereotypes,** the assumption that all or most members of a group are alike. Stereotypes result from the human information-processing system's reliance upon schemas. Schemas are based on averages. For instance, our schema for birthday parties includes cake, ice cream, gifts, and so on, because, if we lump together all the birthday parties we have attended, the "average" party included such items.

Because of this tendency to schematize information, when we hear about an average difference between males and females, our information-processing system often translates the information into a dichotomous statement such as "Men do X, but women do Y." Moreover, once we construct a stereotype, we pay more attention to information that confirms it than to information that challenges it (Maas et al., 2005; Wigboldus et al., 2003). For these reasons, people who want to avoid thinking stereotypically about gender have to keep their cognitive guard up, so to speak, in order to avoid creating and applying such stereotypes (Barbera, 2003; Oakhill, Garnham, & Reynolds, 2005).

Another characteristic of the information-processing system—its love of efficiency—also contributes to stereotypes. As illustrated in **Figure 11.2**, there is a large difference between the average heights of adult males and adult females, and the distributions of these variables within genders don't overlap match. This is true of many other physical variables as well, such as arm strength (Hyde, 2005). In the interest of efficiency, our information-processing system may, at times, generalize what we know about physical differences between men and women to gender differences in other domains. Without realizing it, when we hear a news report stating that males score higher than females on tests of math ability, we assume that the distributions of math ability look like those for height. This leads to the categorical inference "*Most* males

stereotype The assumption that all members of a group are alike.

Figure 11.2 Gender Differences in Height and Math Ability

The distributions in (a) show that the height ranges for men and women do not overlap much. Those in (b) show that the distributions of math ability for males and females overlap a great deal. Yet, we are more likely to make stereotypical statements about math ability than we are about height.

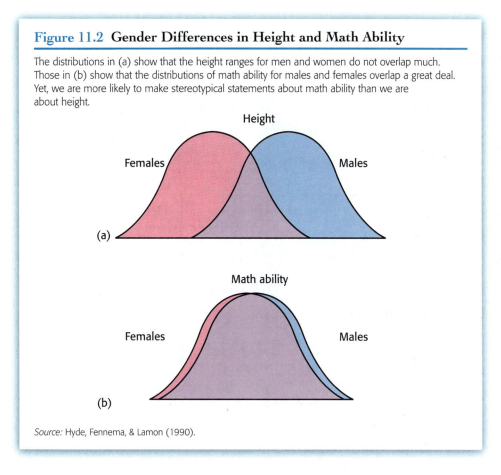

(a)

Height

Females   Males

(b)

Math ability

Females   Males

Source: Hyde, Fennema, & Lamon (1990).

▲ Everyone knows that, on average, men are taller than women. Why don't we lump all men and women into discrete categories based on those averages and create a gender stereotype such as "men are tall, and women are short" as we often do for psychological variables?

are better than *most* females at math." Why do we make this categorical inference? Because this statement accurately describes some physical differences between men and women, we wrongfully generalize it to the news about math ability. However, as you can see in the second set of distributions in Figure 11.2 that were derived from a meta-analysis of dozens of studies of gender differences in math ability, the average gender difference is actually quite small (Hyde, Fennema, & Lamon, 1990).

Cultural values and beliefs also lend weight to stereotypes. For example, math ability is a highly valued commodity in our increasingly technological society. As such, it is associated with the culturally powerful professions of science and engineering. Thus, the categorical inference that *all* men have more math ability than *all* women do, fits neatly into cultural perceptions of men as powerful and women as weak (Glick et al., 2004).

Finally, the best way to avoid developing gender stereotypes as you learn about gender differences is to understand that there is always more variability within each gender than there is between males and females. Important, too, is the understanding that a gender difference at one age doesn't necessarily imply that the difference is present throughout life (Hyde, 2005). Thus, as you read through the discussion of gender differences, keep your anti-stereotyping guard up.

Cognitive Abilities

There is some evidence that men and women have different intellectual strengths. **Figure 11.3** shows some types of problems on which each gender tends to excel. There tends to be more variation in such abilities among males than among females (that is, the range of test scores is typically greater for males).

Gender Differences in Verbal Ability. You have probably heard that females have the advantage over males in verbal ability. With regard to vocabulary size, females have a small advantage, which shows up as soon as children begin speaking (Hyde, 2005; Lutchmaya et al., 2002). Girls also outperform boys on reading achievement

11.8 For what cognitive abilities have gender differences been found?

Figure 11.3 Problem-Solving Tasks Favoring Women and Men

(a) A series of problem-solving tasks on which women generally do better than men.
(b) Problem-solving tasks on which men do better.

Women tend to perform better than men on tests of perceptual speed, in which subjects must rapidly identify matching items—for example, pairing the house on the far left with its twin:

In addition, women remember whether an object, or a series of objects, has been displaced:

On some tests of ideational fluency—for example, those in which subjects must list objects that are the same color—and on tests of verbal fluency—in which participants must list words that begin with the same letter—women outperform men:

Women do better on precision manual tasks—that is, those involving fine motor coordination—such as placing the pegs in holes on a board:

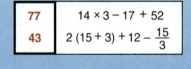

And women do better than men on mathematical calculation tests:

| 77 | 14 × 3 − 17 + 52 |
| 43 | 2 (15 + 3) + 12 − $\frac{15}{3}$ |

(a)

Men tend to perform better than women on certain spatial tasks. They do well on tests that involve mentally rotating an object or manipulating it in some fashion, such as imagining turning this three-dimensional object:

or determining where the holes punched in a folded piece of paper will fall when the paper is unfolded:

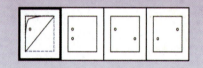

Men also are more accurate than women in target-directed motor skills, such as guiding or intercepting projectiles:

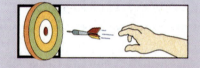

They do better on disembedding tests, in which they have to find a simple shape, such as the one on the left, once it is hidden within a more complex figure:

And men tend to do better than women on tests of mathematical reasoning:

| 1,100 | If only 60 percent of seedlings will survive, how many must be planted to obtain 660 trees? |

(b)

Source: Kimura (1992).

tests throughout the school years (Hedges & Nowell, 1995; Freeman, 2005). Spelling and writing are strengths for girls as well. However, on college entrance tests, such as the SAT, males tend to outscore females on verbal tasks by about 10 points (College Board, 1998).

Math and Spatial Ability. As noted earlier, boys display slightly higher levels of ability in mathematics than girls (Hyde, 2005). Likewise, they get slightly higher scores on math achievement tests in some studies, but these differences are quite small (Freeman, 2004). Nevertheless, girls get higher math grades than boys (Duckworth & Seligman, 2006; Kenney-Benson et al., 2006).

National testing programs in the United States suggest that the stereotypical male advantage may exist only at the very highest levels of ability. For example, more high school boys than girls take advanced placement exams in math and physics (Freeman, 2004). Moreover, boys outscore girls on these exams. Similarly, although female high school students' scores have been rising for several years, their male counterparts tend to score about 30 points higher on the math sections of the SAT (College Board, 1998).

In college, women get better grades in math classes than men do, on average. However, when researchers look at just those students who take math courses as part of a math- or science-based major (e.g., engineering, computer science), this pattern is reversed. Men in such programs tend to get higher math grades than the women in these programs do (College Board, 1998).

It has been hypothesized that gender differences in performance on spatial tasks contributes to gender differences in math performance. Differences favoring males in spatial tasks such as mental rotation are among the largest of all gender differences that researchers have found (Hyde, 2005). However, these differences do not appear until adolescence, so they do not explain any gender differences favoring males that show up earlier.

Explaining Cognitive Differences. Many factors have been proposed to explain gender differences in cognitive abilities. Most recently, explanations based on gender differences in brain function have been proposed. Researchers have found that the brains of women function most efficiently when engaged in verbal tasks, while those of men do so when they are carrying out a spatial task (Neubauer et al., 2005). One hypothesized reason for such observations is gender differences in exposure to androgens in the developing male and female brains. Some studies involving children have shown an association between levels of androgens and performance on cognitive tasks (e.g., Azurmendi et al., 2005). But these studies often show that androgen levels predict individual differences within each gender to a greater degree than they predict differences between males and females (Fink et al., 2006). Consequently, these hypotheses require more testing before we will have the final word on their usefulness.

By contrast, it seems clear that differences in how boys and girls are socialized contribute to cognitive gender differences. For example, as stereotypes would predict, parents often expect their sons to do better than their daughters in math (Tiedemann, 2000). Longitudinal research by psychologist Jacqueline Eccles has shown that parents' beliefs about their 6-year-old children's abilities predict those children's beliefs about their own abilities at age 17 (Fredricks & Eccles, 2002). Moreover, parents are influential in teaching girls who excel in math to think of themselves as "hard workers" and boys who are good at math to view themselves as "talented" (Ratty et al., 2002).

This difference in socialization may pay dividends for girls when it comes to grades in math classes. Researchers have discovered that girls are more likely to take an effortful approach to their work in these classes and, as a result, they develop more effective learning strategies than boys do (Kenney-Benson et al., 2006). Studies have also shown that girls, on average, are more self-disciplined than boys, a difference that some researchers believe explains the common finding that girls get higher grades than boys do in all school subjects (Duckworth & Seligman, 2006; Else-Quest et al., 2006).

Children's activity choices may also contribute to gender differences. In one study, researchers asked 5th-graders how often they participated in out-of-school math activities such as math-based computer games (Simpkins, Davis-Kean, & Eccles, 2006). They found that boys were more likely than girls to engage in such activities. Moreover,

▲ Research shows that girls are influenced by "you can do it" verbal messages, so they may find this poster depicting World War II icon "Rosie the Riveter" to be inspirational. Rosie's image was used by the U.S. government to recruit women to work in short-handed factories during the war. Most of the 3 million women who responded to the call were already employed in low-paying jobs and jumped at the chance to improve their standard of living that skilled factory work offered them. When men returned home from the war, many "Rosies" lost their jobs both because the country no longer needed as many industrial workers and because of the gender stereotypes of the day.

engagement in out-of-school math activities predicted both boys' and girls' high school achievement test scores. The researchers interpreted their findings to mean that boys, on average, are more interested in math, and that interest in math, both for boys and girls, is one of several factors that influences achievement.

Interestingly, other researchers have found a similar, but opposite, gender difference for reading achievement. That is, elementary school girls tend to be more interested than boys are in reading, and interest predicts achievement in both genders (Pecjak & Pedlaj, 2005). Of course, we are still left with questions about why boys and girls have different interests, but these studies do show that motivational factors play some role in gender differences in achievement.

Similarly, researchers have found that video game experience improves spatial task scores in both males and females (Terlecki & Newcombe, 2005). Yet, males spend more time playing these games than females do. Research from the newly emerging field of media psychology provides some possible clues as to why.

Nonverbal cues in advertisements are designed to foster rapid *for-me/not-for-me* decisions by consumers with regard to the products that are advertised in them (Chandler, 2002). As such, advertisements take advantage of obvious categories such as gender, race, and age. With regard to gender, dark or primary colors, odd camera angles, hard-driving electric guitars, deep voices, and rapidly moving, sharply focused images signal viewers that a product is intended for males (Griffiths & Chandler, 1998). By contrast, pastel colors, conventional angles, catchy jingles, high voices, and slowly moving, slightly blurry images are used to capture females' attention.

By the time children reach the age of 6 or 7, most are quite skilled at classifying advertisements by gender on the basis of these cues (Pike & Jennings, 2005). Moreover, they express more interest in products that they perceive to be gender-congruent than in those they believe to be intended for the opposite gender. These nonverbal cues are so powerful that children will say that a toy advertised with "male" nonverbal cues is for boys even if a girl is shown playing with it in a commercial.

Consequently, the ways in which video game systems and the games themselves are advertised may send girls a nonverbal "this-is-not-for-you" message. And there are some studies that show that girls, on average, are more responsive to such messages than boys are (Usher & Pajares, 2006). Thus, girls who conform to the gender-based expectations implied by these nonverbal messages may be missing out on opportunities to develop their spatial abilities. The good news, though, is that girls also appear to be more responsive than boys to persuasive messages that tell them "you can do it." Such research suggests that parents and teachers should encourage girls to engage in more activities that enhance spatial abilities. (You will read more about nonverbal messages in advertisements when we discuss persuasion in Chapter 16: Social Psychology).

Gender Differences in Social Behavior and Personality

11.9 What gender differences are found in social behavior and personality?

You may already be familiar with one important gender difference in social behavior: Most researchers agree that greater physical aggression in males is one of the most consistent and significant gender differences (Hyde, 2005). However, females are aggressive, just in a different way: Girls and women are more likely than their male peers to use indirect forms of aggression, such as gossip, spreading rumors, and rejecting, ignoring, or avoiding the target of aggression (Björkqvist et al., 1992). Thus, it isn't true to say that males are aggressive and females aren't.

Females appear to have strengths in the area of communication. Researchers have consistently found that, compared to men, women appear to be more open, trusting, and agreeable. Women also consistently outperform men on tasks involving facial recognition (La France et al., 2003; Lewin & Herlitz, 2002).

Explaining Social and Personality Differences. The hormonal hypothesis mentioned earlier has been advanced to explain social and personality gender differences in addition to cognitive differences. In one unusual prospective study, researchers measured androgen levels in the amniotic fluid surrounding male and female fetuses (Knickmeyer et al., 2006). Four years later, the children were given tests of social reasoning. The researchers found that prenatal androgens predicted children's understanding of intentional and unintentional behavior. Interestingly, androgen levels predicted this variable both across genders and among boys. The relationship was an inverse one, so lower levels of androgens were associated with better performance on the task that required children to identify intentional behavior. Again, like the earlier study we cited, this one suggests that hormone levels may be important predictors of individual differences within each gender.

Social factors are likely contributors to gender differences in the domains of social behavior and personality as well. For instance, earlier you read about the influence of video games on gender differences in spatial cognition. You may recall from Chapter 5 that when such games have violent content, they increase males' aggressive behavior. Thus, boys who play such games may be experiencing gains in the cognitive domain at the expense of increased risks in the social arena.

Moreover, stereotypes may lead parents to expect girls to be better behaved and easier to get along with than they do boys. These expectations may explain why researchers have found that parents are more likely to punish girls than boys for being aggressive (Martin & Ross, 2005). Similarly, studies have shown that parents are less likely to monitor the activities of their teen-aged sons than they are those of their daughters (Richards et al., 2004). Such findings have prompted some researchers to suggest that improved parental monitoring might decrease the rates of risky behaviors such as substance abuse among both male and female teenagers. However, psychologists have noted that assumptions about the nature of male behavior have caused researchers to focus almost exclusively on the parenting factors that are associated with these behaviors in boys and to simply generalize their findings to girls without actually studying them (Granic & Patterson, 2006). Thus, as you can see, researchers themselves can be influenced by stereotypes.

▲ Boys show higher levels of physical aggression, but girls tend to use indirect forms of aggression, such as gossiping about and rejecting others.

Remember It　　Gender Differences

1. The information-processing system uses _____ as the basis of schemas.

2. For each cognitive ability, indicate whether males or females, in general, tend to score higher on tests of that ability.

   _____ (1) writing
   _____ (2) science
   _____ (3) spatial ability
   _____ (4) reading comprehension
   _____ (5) mathematics

   a. males
   b. females

3. Varying levels of exposure of the brain to _____ have been proposed as an explanation for gender differences in cognitive abilities.

4. Physical aggression is more common among _____.

5. Parents are more likely to punish (*daughters/sons*) for aggressive behavior.

Answers: 1. averages; 2. (1) b, (2) a, (3) a, (4) b, (5) a; 3. androgens; 4. males; 5. sons.

Sexual Attitudes and Behavior

Almost six decades have passed since Indiana University professor Alfred Kinsey shocked the world by publishing a two-volume study that detailed the sexual attitudes and behaviors of thousands of men and women. Kinsey's *Sexual Behavior in the Human Male* (1948) and *Sexual Behavior in the Human Female* (1953) shattered many widely held beliefs about sexuality. For one, he revealed that men and women were equally capable of sexual arousal and orgasm. Although his work has been called into question by many other researchers on both theoretical and methodological grounds, most admit that the topic of sexuality is discussed more openly now because of Kinsey's landmark research findings.

Gender and Cultural Differences

Do you think that men and women have different ideas about sex? Research suggests that they do. Studies have also shown that sexual beliefs and behaviors vary across culture as well.

Gender Differences. Research shows that, on average, men are more interested in sex and think about it more often than women do (Peplau, 2003). They are also more likely than women to emphasize the physical aspects of sexual intercourse and to have more permissive attitudes toward casual sexual encounters (Baldwin & Baldwin, 1997; Dantzker & Eisenman, 2003). The results of a comprehensive survey of more than 1,500 adults sponsored by the television program *Primetime Live* (Langer, Arnedt, & Sussman, 2004) found similar patterns of differences.

The *Primetime Live* survey also found that several factors contribute to adults' satisfaction with their sex lives. These factors include the frequency of orgasm, sexual adventurousness, and general satisfaction with the relationship within which sex occurs. Perhaps because of the link between relationship and sexual satisfaction, adults who are in committed relationships reported greater satisfaction with their sex lives than singles did.

The findings in **Table 11.3** suggest that males and females have different views about how important and enjoyable sex is. Nevertheless, the gender gap has narrowed considerably since the mid-20th century. Psychologists Brooke Wells and Jean Twenge analyzed the results of attitude surveys from 1943 to 1999 (Wells & Twenge, 2006). They found that among women, approval rates for premarital sex had risen dramatically, from 30% in the early years of their study to 91% in 1999. Behavior, too, had changed. Twenge's analysis showed that about 13% of teenaged girls admitted to being sexually active during the 1950s. By the 1990s, the proportion had increased to 47%. Thus, even though recent surveys show that there are still gender differences in both sexual attitudes and behavior, the historical perspective helps us see that, over time, this gender gap has narrowed considerably. However, critics of such studies say that what has really changed is people's willingness to talk about their sexual experiences rather than their actual attitudes and behavior (Dobson & Baird, 2006).

Cultural Differences. Willingness to talk about sex has helped researchers learn more about variation in sexual attitudes and behavior across cultures as well as across genders. **Table 11.4** shows a few highlights of the Durex Global Sex Survey (2005). The survey included males and females age 16 and older in 41 countries. As you can see, the frequency of intercourse in the year prior to the study varied widely, from a low of 45 times in Japan to a high of 138 times in Greece. Rates of satisfaction with one's sex life varied widely as well. The survey found that adults in the 30- to 44-year-old age range were the most sexually active, probably because they were more likely than members of other age groups to have a cohabiting or marital partner.

Perhaps the reasons behind the reports of relatively high rates of sexual activity are simple: People enjoy sex, and attitudes have changed such that they feel free to do so. But what explains the low rate of sexual activity in Japan? Japanese officials, concerned about their country's plummeting birth rate and growing number of elderly, blame long work days, the high cost of raising children, and the increasing number of women who choose to focus on their careers rather than to become mothers (Reuters, 2006). Of course, these trends are found throughout the industrialized world, so they cannot explain why Japanese sexual activity rates are lower than those of other nations.

Cross-national differences in perceived sex drive cannot explain this difference either. The Durex survey found that both Chinese and Japanese adults are about twice as likely as those in Western nations to agree with the statement "I do not have a high

Table 11.3 Selected Findings from the *Primetime Live* Poll (2004)

	Men	Women
Think about sex at least once a day	70%	33%
Think about sex several times a day	43%	13%
Enjoy sex a great deal	83%	59%
Ever had sex on the first date	47%	17%
Believe it's okay to have sex for purely physical reasons	35%	18%
Approve of premarital sex	68%	54%
Equate participation in online sex chats to sexual infidelity	54%	72%
Equate perusal of online sexual material to sexual infidelity	25%	42%
Prefer to have the lights off during sex	27%	51%
Ever been unfaithful	21%	11%
Always have an orgasm	74%	30%
Median number of lifetime sex partners	8	3

Source: *Primetime Live poll: American sex survey analysis.* http://abcnews.go.com/Primetime/PollVault/story?id=156921&page=1

sex drive." Yet, Chinese adults have sex twice as often as the Japanese. Thus, an adequate explanation for Japan's low rate of sexual activity has yet to be discovered.

Cross-cultural differences in sexual attitudes and behavior go beyond variations in the frequency of intercourse. In some societies, the practice of *female circumcision* or *female genital mutilation* is a cultural tradition (World Health Organization, 2000). In this procedure, a girl's genital tissue is surgically altered by a traditional practitioner. The belief that doing so will help to insure that she will remain a virgin until marriage is the basis for this practice. However, girls who undergo this procedure are likely to develop scars that interfere with urination and cause pain during intercourse. These scars may also interfere with childbirth.

Because of the health consequences of female genital mutilation, the World Health Organization has worked in regions where the practice is common to educate people about its detrimental effects (WHO, 2000). These regions include various parts of Africa, the Middle East, and southern Asia. Human rights organizations have made the elimination of this practice by nations in these regions a top priority. Many Western

Table 11.4 Selected Findings from the Durex Global Sex Survey

Country	Frequency of Intercourse in the Past Year	Percentage Who are Satisfied with their Sex Lives
Greece	138	43%
United States	113	52%
Chile	112	50%
South Africa	109	46%
Canada	108	46%
Italy	106	36%
Israel	100	36%
China	96	22%
Sweden	92	45%
Japan	45	24%

Source: *Durex Global Sex Survey 2005.* http://www.durex.com/cm/gss2005results.asp

governments have passed laws that make financial aid to these nations dependent upon their efforts to eliminate female genital mutilation. To date, many governments in the regions in which female genital mutilation is traditionally practiced have banned the procedure. However, it is a tradition that is proving difficult to eliminate, as many people believe so strongly in the benefits of the procedure that they defy these laws.

Sexual Desire and Arousal

11.11 According to Masters and Johnson, what are the phases of the human sexual response cycle?

For most people, intimate relationships are not restricted to the physical realm, and the physiological aspects of sex are critical to its enjoyment. In 1954, Dr. William Masters and Dr. Virginia Johnson conducted the first laboratory investigations of the human sexual response and its culmination in coitus (penile-vaginal intercourse). They monitored volunteer participants, who engaged in sex while connected to electronic sensing devices. Masters and Johnson (1966) concluded that both males and females experience a sexual response cycle with four phases (see Figure 11.4).

Excitement. The excitement phase is the beginning of the sexual response cycle. Visual cues such as watching a partner undress are more likely to initiate the excitement phase in men than in women. Tender, loving touches coupled with verbal expressions of love arouse women more readily than visual stimulation. And men can become aroused almost instantly, while arousal for women may be a more gradual, building process. For both partners, muscular tension increases, heart rate quickens, and blood pressure rises. As additional blood is pumped into the genitals, the male's penis becomes erect, and the female feels a swelling of the clitoris. Vaginal lubrication occurs as the inner two-thirds of the vagina expands and its inner lips enlarge. In women, especially, the nipples harden and stand erect.

coitus (KOY-tus) Penile-vaginal intercourse.

sexual response cycle According to Masters and Johnson, the typical pattern of the human sexual response in both males and females, consisting of four phases: excitement, plateau, orgasm, and resolution.

excitement phase The first stage of the sexual response cycle, characterized by an erection in males and a swelling of the clitoris and vaginal lubrication in females.

Plateau. After the excitement phase, the individual enters the plateau phase, when excitement builds steadily. Blood pressure and muscle tension increase still more, and breathing becomes heavy and more rapid. The man's testes swell, and drops of liquid, which could contain live sperm cells, may drip from the penis. The outer part of the woman's vagina swells as the increased blood further engorges the area in preparation for orgasm. The clitoris withdraws under the clitoral hood, its skin covering, and the breasts become engorged with blood.

plateau phase The second stage of the sexual response cycle, during which muscle tension and blood flow to the genitals increase in preparation for orgasm.

Orgasm. The orgasm, the shortest of the phases, is the highest point of sexual pleasure, marked by a sudden discharge of accumulated sexual tension. Involuntary muscle contractions may seize the entire body during orgasm, and the genitals contract rhythmically. Orgasm is a two-stage experience for the male. In the first stage, he is aware that ejaculation is near and that he can do nothing to stop it; the second stage consists of the ejaculation itself, when semen is released from the penis in forceful spurts. The experience of orgasm in women builds in much the same way as for men. Marked by powerful, rhythmic contractions, the female's orgasm usually lasts longer than that of the male.

orgasm The third stage of the sexual response cycle, marked by a sudden discharge of accumulated sexual tension and involuntary muscle contractions.

resolution phase The final stage of the sexual response cycle, during which the body returns to an unaroused state.

Resolution. The orgasm gives way to the resolution phase, a tapering-off period, when the body returns to its unaroused state. Men experience a refractory period in the resolution phase, during which they cannot have another orgasm. The refractory period may last from only a few minutes for some men to as much as several hours for others. Women do not have a refractory period and may, if restimulated, experience another orgasm right away.

estrogen (ES-truh-jen) A female sex hormone that promotes the secondary sex characteristics in females and controls the menstrual cycle.

progesterone (pro-JES-tah-rone) A female sex hormone that plays a role in the regulation of the menstrual cycle and prepares the lining of the uterus for pregnancy.

Hormones. The sexual response cycle is strongly influenced by hormones. The sex glands manufacture hormones—estrogen and progesterone in the ovaries, and androgens in the testes. The adrenal glands in both sexes also produce small amounts of these hormones. Estrogen promotes the secondary sex characteristics in females and controls the menstrual cycle; progesterone aids in the regulation of the menstrual cycle and prepares the lining of the uterus for pregnancy. Females have considerably more estrogen and progesterone than males do, so these are known as the female sex hormones. Males have considerably more androgens, the male sex hormones.

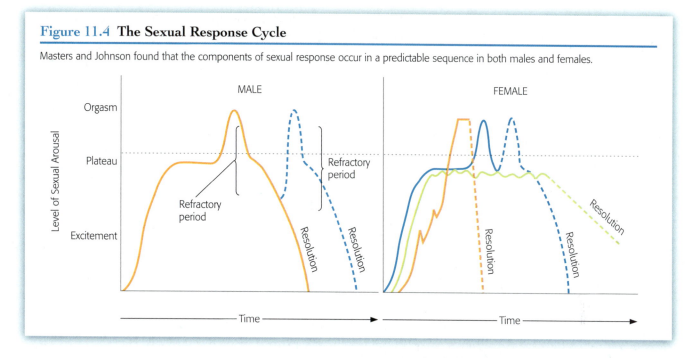

Figure 11.4 The Sexual Response Cycle

Masters and Johnson found that the components of sexual response occur in a predictable sequence in both males and females.

Testosterone, the most important androgen, influences the development and maintenance of male sex characteristics as well as sexual motivation. Males must have a sufficient level of testosterone in order to maintain sexual interest and have an erection. Females, too, need small amounts of testosterone in the bloodstream to maintain sexual interest and responsiveness (Anderson & Cyranowski, 1995). Deficiencies in sexual interest and activity can sometimes be reversed in men or women with the use of testosterone patches or ointments (Meyer, 1997).

Psychological Factors. Psychological factors play a large role in sexual arousal. Part of the psychological nature of sexual behavior stems from the preferences and practices people learn from their culture. And cultural norms for sexual behavior vary widely, covering everything from the age at which initiation of sexual behavior is proper to the partners, conditions, settings, positions, and specific sexual acts that are considered acceptable. Moreover, what is perceived as sexually attractive in males and females may differ dramatically from culture to culture.

Fantasy and External Stimuli. Sexual fantasies also influence sexual arousal. Men's fantasies generally involve more specific visual imagery, whereas women's fantasies have more emotional and romantic content. Although 95% of males and females admit to having sexual fantasies, about 25% experience strong guilt about them (Leitenberg & Henning, 1995). However, research seems to suggest an association between a higher incidence of sexual fantasies and a more satisfactory sex life and fewer sexual problems.

External stimuli, such as images in magazines or movies, can also influence arousal. Men are more likely to seek out such sources of stimulation. Some studies reveal that people may come to value their partner and relationship less after exposure to erotic sexual material. Also, people may feel disappointed with their own sexual performance after comparing it to performances by actors.

Of course, there is much more to sex than the physical response. According to Masters and Johnson, a couple's "total commitment, in which all sense of obligation is linked to mutual feelings of loving concern, sustains a couple sexually over the years" (1975, p. 268). Research supports this assertion: Both men and women experience greater sexual satisfaction in relationships that are emotionally satisfying and supportive (Greeff & Malherbe, 2001; Waite & Joyner, 2001).

▲ Psychological factors play an important role in sexual attraction and arousal. Such factors involve preferences and attitudes we learn from our culture.

testosterone (tes-TOS-tah-rone)
The most important androgen, which influences the development and maintenance of male sex characteristics and sexual motivation and, in small amounts, maintains sexual interest and responsiveness in females.

Remember It   Sexual Attitudes and Behavior

1. _____ tend to have more permissive attitudes toward premarital sex than _____ do.

2. The belief that _____ will ensure that a girl will remain a virgin is found in some traditional cultures.

3. The human sexual response cycle consists of _____ phases.

4. With regard to the sexual response cycle, the most important sex hormone in both men and women is _____.

Answers: 1. Men, women; 2. female genital mutilation; 3. four; 4. testosterone

Sexual Orientation

So far, we have discussed many aspects of human sexual response and sexual arousal, but we have not considered **sexual orientation**—the direction of an individual's sexual preference, erotic feelings, and sexual activity. In heterosexuals, the human sexual response is oriented toward members of the opposite sex; in homosexuals, toward those of the same sex; and in bisexuals, toward members of both sexes.

Homosexuality has been reported in all societies throughout recorded history (Carrier, 1980; Ford & Beach, 1951). Kinsey and his associates (1948, 1953) estimated that 4% of their male respondents had had exclusively homosexual relations throughout life, and about 2–3% of their female participants had been in mostly or exclusively lesbian relationships. Findings from the ABC *Primetime Live* survey (Langer, Arnedt, & Sussman, 2004) discussed earlier concur with Kinsey's data. About 5% of respondents indicated that they were homosexual. However, the survey did not provide any details as to the breakdown of gays and lesbians among this 5% or the degree to which these respondents were actively involved in same-sex relationships.

In what is still said to be the most comprehensive survey of homosexual practices to date, Laumann and others (1994) reported that the percentages of people who identified themselves as homosexual or bisexual were 2.8% of men and 1.4% of women. But 5.3% of men and 3.5% of women said that they had had a sexual experience with a person of the same sex at least once since puberty. And even larger percentages of those surveyed—10% of males and 9% of females—said that they had felt some same-sex desires.

However, other surveys suggest that a completely accurate measure of the prevalence of homosexuality may still be lacking. For one thing, a truly exclusive homosexual orientation appears to be rare. For example, Sell and his colleagues (1995) reanalyzed the results of a 1988 Harris Poll to include both homosexual attraction and behavior. They found that 6% of the male and 3–4% of the female respondents identified themselves as predominantly homosexual in both attraction and behavior. However, only 1% of these poll respondents claimed to have had no sexual contact whatever with members of the opposite sex in the previous 5 years.

sexual orientation The direction of one's sexual preference, erotic feelings, and sexual activity—toward members of the opposite sex (heterosexuality), toward one's own sex (homosexuality), or toward both sexes (bisexuality).

Determinants of Sexual Orientation

11.12 What are the various factors that have been suggested as possible determinants of a gay or lesbian sexual orientation?

Psychologists continue to debate whether sexual orientation is biologically determined or acquired through learning and experience. Although Freud argued that homosexuality results from early childhood experiences (Mitchell, 2002), many psychologists believe that biological factors largely determine sexual orientation (Bailey & Pillard, 1994; Isay, 1989; LeVay, 1993). Still others lean toward an interaction theory, which holds that both nature and nurture play a part (Breedlove, 1994; Byne, 1994; Patterson, 1995).

Hormones. Could hormones play a role? Some researchers have suggested that exposure to androgens during prenatal development, or at any other time in development, might influence sexual orientation (Collaer & Hines, 1995; McFadden, 2002). A few studies have revealed an increase in the incidence of lesbianism among females who had been exposed prenatally to synthetic estrogen (Meyer-Bahlburg et al., 1995).

In the last few years, research examining the relationship between prenatal hormones and sexual orientation has focused on associations between these hormones and inconsistencies between the left and right sides of the body. One such difference involves the ratio of the second and fourth fingers on the left and right hands (Rahman & Wilson, 2003a). It has long been known that fluctuations of androgen levels in the prenatal environment can produce these inconsistencies. Thus, researchers reason that if prenatal androgens contribute to sexual orientation, then such physical inconsistencies should occur more frequently in homosexuals than in heterosexuals. Studies have shown that this is indeed the case (Rahman, 2005; Rahman & Wilson, 2003a).

Brain Structure. Neuroscientist Simon LeVay (1991) reported that an area in the hypothalamus governing sexual behavior is about twice as large in heterosexual men as in homosexual men. This part of the hypothalamus, no larger than a grain of sand, is about the same size in heterosexual females as in homosexual males. LeVay admits that his research offers no direct evidence that the brain differences he found cause homosexuality (LeVay & Hamer, 1994), and critics were quick to point out that all of the gay men included in his research sample died of AIDS. It is known that AIDS is associated with abnormalities in certain brain areas. Therefore, some researchers questioned whether the brain differences LeVay observed might have resulted from AIDS, rather than being associated with sexual orientation (Byne, 1993b). Others have suggested that the brain differences could be either the cause or the consequence of variables as yet unidentified that may interact with the brain in determining sexual orientation.

Genetic Influences. In early research on the influence of heredity on sexual orientation, Bailey and Pillard (1991) studied gay males who had twin brothers. They found that 52% of the gay identical twins and 22% of the gay fraternal twins had a gay twin brother. Among adoptive brothers of the gay twins, however, only 11% shared a homosexual orientation. In a similar study, Whitam and others (1993) found that 66% of the identical twins and 30% of the fraternal twins of gay males studied were also gay. Such studies indicate a substantial genetic influence on sexual orientation, but suggest that nongenetic influences are at work as well.

Bailey and Benishay (1993) found that 12.1% of their lesbian participants had a sister who was also lesbian, compared with 2.3% of heterosexual female participants. Bailey and others (1993) report that in a study of lesbians, 48% of their identical twins, 16% of their fraternal twins, 14% of their nontwin biological sisters, and 6% of their adopted sisters were also lesbian. Bailey and Pillard (1994) claim that according to their statistical analysis, the heritability of sexual orientation is about 50%.

Hamer and others (1993) found that brothers of gay participants had a 13.5% chance of also being gay. Furthermore, male relatives on the mother's side of the family, but not on the father's side, had a significantly higher rate of homosexuality. This led the researchers to suspect that a gene influencing sexual orientation might be located on the X chromosome, the sex chromosome contributed by the mother. After studying the DNA on the X chromosomes of 40 pairs of gay brothers, the researchers found that 33 of the pairs carried matching genetic information on the end tip of the X chromosome. However, no particular gene has been singled out among the several hundred genes carried on that end tip. And precisely how the gene might influence sexual orientation is not known (LeVay & Hamer, 1994; Rahman & Wilson, 2003). Some researchers have questioned the validity of Hamer's findings, and a colleague has charged that Hamer excluded from the study some pairs of brothers whose sexual orientations contradicted his findings (Horgan, 1995).

▲ Ellen DeGeneres sparked controversy when she revealed that she was a lesbian on her sitcom *Ellen* in 1997. Today, she is the host of an award-winning talk show, and is one of only two women, along with megastar Oprah Winfrey, on the Harris Poll's list of America's favorite television personalities (Harris Poll, 2004).

▲ Social attitudes towards homosexuality vary widely around the world. In the United States, court rulings in Massachusetts have paved the way for same-sex couples to marry. Same-sex couples can be legally partnered in civil unions in Vermont and in domestic partnerships in many cities. In Canada, same-sex marriage is legal throughout the country, as it is in the Netherlands, Spain, and Belgium. By contrast, homosexual behavior is illegal in many nations of Africa and southern Asia, and those who engage in such behavior are subject to the death penalty in Saudi Arabia, Iran, the Sudan, and Mauritania.

homophobia   An intense, irrational hostility toward or fear of homosexuals.

11.13 How have attitudes toward homosexuality changed in recent decades?

Gene-Environment Interactions. Studies examining the relationship between prenatal exposure to androgens and sexual orientation have added a new twist to the discussion of the genetic determinants of homosexuality. One particularly intriguing study involved identical twins in which one or both twins were lesbian (Hall & Love, 2003). Researchers found that when both twins were lesbian, the ratios of their index and ring fingers (an indicator of prenatal androgen exposure) were more similar to those that are typical for men than to those that are typical for women. However, in the pairs in which one twin was lesbian but the other was not, the typical male finger ratio pattern was found only in the lesbian twin.

This study points to the possible influence of the prenatal environment on gene expression. It is possible that prenatal androgens "turned on" or "turned off" the genes that contribute to sexual orientation in these pairs of twins. But why would these hormones influence the genes in one member of a pair of twin fetuses but not in the other? Researchers do not yet have an answer to this question, and many studies will be required before they do. However, such questions about the complex interactions of genetic and environmental factors are at the forefront of current research in behavioral genetics, with regard to both sexual orientation and other variables that are known to have some genetic component.

Childhood Experiences of Gay Men and Lesbians. What evidence is there that homosexuality is linked to some kind of formative experience in childhood? In classic research examining this question, Alan P. Bell, Martin Weinberg, and Sue Kiefer Hammersmith (1981) conducted extensive face-to-face interviews with 979 homosexual participants (293 women, 686 men) and 477 heterosexual controls. The researchers found no single condition of family life or childhood experience that in and of itself appeared to be a factor in either homosexual or heterosexual development. But, as children, the homosexuals they interviewed did not feel that they were like others of their sex.

Using meta-analysis, Bailey and Zucker (1995) found that cross-gender behavior exhibited in early childhood could be a predictor of homosexuality for both females and males. In one study, Bailey and others (1995) found a strong association between sexual orientation and sex-typed behavior in childhood, as recalled by both gay men and their mothers. However, some gay men exhibited masculine sex-typed behavior, and some heterosexual men were "feminine" boys. In another study, Phillips and Over (1995) found that lesbian women were more likely to recall imagining themselves as males, preferring boy's games and being called "tomboys." Yet, some heterosexual women recalled childhood experiences similar to those of the majority of lesbians, and some lesbians recalled experiences more like those of the majority of heterosexual women.

Clearly, there are no certain predictors of homosexuality. And so, researchers continue to disagree on the genesis of sexual orientation. Psychologist Charlotte Patterson (1995) suggests that the relationship between sexual orientation and human development can be studied more profitably as a complex interaction of nature and nurture.

Social Attitudes toward Gays and Lesbians

The American Psychiatric Association considered homosexuality a disorder until 1973, but now views it as such only if the individual considers it a problem. Thanks to such changes, more gay men and lesbians are "coming out," preferring to acknowledge and express their sexual orientation. Such individuals appear to be as healthy psychologically as heterosexuals (Strickland, 1995).

Homophobia is an intense, irrational hostility toward or fear of homosexuals that can lead to discrimination against gays and lesbians, or even motivate acts of violence against them. Fortunately, most people's views of homosexuality stop short of full-blown homophobia, although negative attitudes toward homosexuality are still common in U.S. society (Herek, 2002). Generally, men are more likely to express such views. For instance, in one survey, 54% of women believed that homosexuality is morally acceptable, while only 45% of men approved of same-sex relationships (Pew Research Center, 2006).

Importantly, though, most people are opposed to discrimination based on sexual orientation. (Moreover, such discrimination is illegal.) Surveys show that more than three-quarters of Americans believe that homosexuality should not be a factor in hiring public school teachers (Herek, 2002). Similarly, an overwhelming majority of Americans, including those who are strongly opposed to homosexual behavior, adamantly support the rights of homosexuals to speak out and to try to influence public policy. Thus, objections to homosexuality appear to be focused on the behavior itself and not on those who exhibit it.

Gay and Lesbian Relationships

Social changes have enabled researchers to learn more about same-sex relationships. One thing that has been learned is that, as is true for heterosexuals, gay and lesbian committed couples report greater satisfaction with their sex lives than do singles (Home & Biss, 2005). Interestingly, though, studies also show that monogamy is less important to most gay couples than it is to either lesbian or heterosexual couples (Garza-Mercer, Christenson, & Doss, 2006).

11.14 In what ways do gay and lesbian relationships resemble those of heterosexuals?

Some observers suggest that the openness of gay relationships is an adaptation to the finding that males, both heterosexual and homosexual, desire sex more frequently than females do (Buss, 1998). That is, if a gay man in a committed relationship is unhappy with the frequency of sex, he is likely to be free to look elsewhere for sex without threatening the existence of the relationship. By contrast, a heterosexual man usually doesn't have that option because of women's expectations with regard to fidelity. Predictably, research shows that heterosexual men are more dissatisfied with the frequency of sex in their relationships than adults in any other group, and heterosexual couples have more conflicts about sexual frequency than either gay or lesbian couples.

Consistent with these findings are studies showing that lesbian couples tend to value monogamy more highly than either heterosexual or gay couples (Garza-Mercer, Christensen, & Doss, 2006). Like women in heterosexual relationships, they often value emotional closeness as highly as they do sexual contact with their partners. Moreover, lesbians experience more distress over their partner's unfaithfulness than do adults in other groups.

Remember It Sexual Orientation

1. Sexual _____ is the direction of a person's sexual preference.
2. Statistics suggest that homosexuality is twice as common in _____ as in _____.
3. Indicate whether or not each of the statements about the origins of homosexuality is supported by research.
   _____ (1) Homosexual and heterosexual adults have different levels of sex hormones.
   _____ (2) Homosexual men and women are more likely than heterosexuals to recall cross-gender childhood experiences.
   _____ (3) Genetics may play a role in sexual orientation.
   _____ (4) Differences between homosexual and heterosexual individuals are not evident before puberty.
   _____ (5) Exposure to androgens during prenatal development may influence an individual's sexual orientation.

   a. supported by research
   b. not supported by research

Answers: 1. orientation; 2. males, females; 3. (1) b, (2) a, (3) a, (4) b, (5) a

Sexual Dysfunctions

Have you seen advertisements for drugs or herbal preparations that enhance sexual performance? The prevalence of such ads should tell you that the desire to improve the quality of one's sexual experiences is common. Further, a sizable number of women and men are plagued by serious sexual dysfunctions, which eliminate or at least decrease the pleasures of sex. A **sexual dysfunction** is a persistent or recurrent problem that causes marked distress and interpersonal difficulty and may involve any or a combination of the following: sexual desire, sexual arousal or the pleasure associated with sex, or orgasm.

Sexual Desire Disorders

> **11.15** What are the defining features of two sexual desire disorders?

Disorders of sexual desire involve a lack of sexual desire and/or an aversion to genital sexual contact. One of the most common complaints of people who see sex therapists is low or nonexistent sexual desire or interest in sexual activity. This condition is known as **hypoactive sexual desire disorder** (Beck, 1995). Such people may be unreceptive to the sexual advances of their partners, or they may participate despite their lack of desire. Loss of desire or lack of interest can stem from depression, emotional stress, marital dissatisfaction, or repeated unsuccessful attempts at intercourse. In men who are middle-aged and older, a decline in sexual interest may be related to a decline in testosterone levels that occurs with aging (Brody, 1995).

A more severe problem is **sexual aversion disorder,** a dislike and avoidance of genital contact with a sexual partner (American Psychiatric Association, 2000). People with this condition experience emotions ranging from anxiety or fear to disgust when confronted with a sexual situation. In some cases, a sexual aversion stems from a sexual trauma such as rape or incest.

Sexual Arousal Disorders

> **11.16** What are the defining features of the sexual arousal disorders?

Some individuals have a normal interest in sex but are unable to become aroused. A woman with **female sexual arousal disorder** may not feel sexually aroused in response to sexual stimulation (American Psychiatric Association, 2000). The problem may stem from the trauma of rape or childhood sexual abuse, from resentment toward one's partner, or from vaginal dryness due to reduced estrogen production.

A common sexual dysfunction reported in men is **erectile dysfunction,** the repeated inability to have or sustain an erection firm enough for coitus. This disorder *impotence* can take different forms: the inability to have an erection at all, having one but losing it, or having a partial erection that is not adequate for intercourse. Some men have firm erections under some conditions but not under others (with one sexual partner but not with another, or during masturbation but not during intercourse). The term *erectile dysfunction* does not apply to the failures all males have on occasion as a result of fear, anxiety, physical fatigue, illness, or drinking too much alcohol.

It is quite difficult to determine the prevalence of erectile dysfunction. Statistics for such conditions are usually derived from medical records kept in health clinics and doctors' offices. However, because erectile dysfunction is not a life-threatening condition, many men do not consult a physician for help with the condition, perhaps out of embarrassment or the belief that medical treatment will not make a difference.

Recent studies show that the availability of the drug sildenafil (Viagra) has been helpful to sufferers of erectile dysfunction in several ways. First, the drug is quite effective in helping men with this condition achieve and maintain an erection (Rosen, 1996). Second, the publicity surrounding the availability of sildenafil has increased the number of men who seek treatment for erectile dysfunction (Kaye & Jick, 2003). As a result, the impact of erectile dysfunction on many men's lives has been greatly reduced, and researchers have a much better idea about how prevalent erectile dysfunction actually is. Studies carried out after the introduction of sildenafil suggest that as

---

sexual dysfunction A persistent or recurrent problem that causes marked distress and interpersonal difficulty and that may involve some combination of the following: sexual desire, sexual arousal or the pleasure associated with sex, or orgasm.

hypoactive sexual desire disorder A sexual dysfunction marked by low or nonexistent sexual desire or interest in sexual activity.

sexual aversion disorder A sexual dysfunction characterized by an aversion to and active avoidance of genital contact with a sexual partner.

female sexual arousal disorder A sexual dysfunction in which a woman may not feel sexually aroused in response to sexual stimulation or may be unable to achieve or sustain an adequate lubrication-swelling response to sexual excitement.

erectile dysfunction A sexual dysfunction in which a man experiences the repeated inability to have or sustain an erection firm enough for coitus; also known as erectile dysfunction or impotence.

many as one-third of men in the United States suffer from some degree of erectile dysfunction (Laumann, Paik, & Rosen, 1999).

The availability of sildenafil has improved the lives of men in other ways. For one, researchers in the United Kingdom have found that the increased presence of erectile dysfunction patients in health clinics has led to declines in the rates of some types of heart disease among British men (Kay & Jick, 2003). This has occurred because heart problems are among the physical causes of erectile dysfunction that doctors always look for in men who are diagnosed with this problem. In addition, erectile dysfunction is one of the side effects of antidepressant drugs. Consequently, men who suffer from depression often refuse to take them. Since the advent of sildenafil, doctors have learned that the drug moderates the side effects of antidepressants, thus enabling many men who have depression to find relief from their depressive symptoms without the threat of erectile dysfunction (Nurnberg et al., 1999).

Antidepressants cause problems with sexual arousal among women as well. Sildenafil helps some female patients with depression overcome this side effect (Nurnberg et al., 1999). These findings led scientists to examine the possible benefits of the drug for women who suffer from sexual dysfunctions with other causes. However, these studies have had disappointing results (Harris, 2004). Thus, the search for effective treatments for women's sexual arousal disorders continues.

Orgasmic and Sexual Pain Disorders

The most common sexual dysfunction in women is **female orgasmic disorder,** a persistent inability to reach orgasm or a delay in reaching orgasm despite adequate sexual stimulation. Some women with this disorder have never been able to reach orgasm; others who were formerly orgasmic no longer can achieve orgasm. Some women are able to have orgasms only under certain circumstances or during certain types of sexual activity, whereas others have orgasms only from time to time. Recent twin studies suggest that such variations may have a genetic basis (Dawood et al., 2005). Women with this disorder may be uninterested in sex, or they may still find it exciting, satisfying, and enjoyable, despite the lack of orgasms.

In **male orgasmic disorder,** there is an absence of ejaculation, or ejaculation occurs only after strenuous effort over an extremely prolonged period. Sometimes, both partners may nearly collapse from exhaustion before the male finally reaches orgasm or gives up. The delay in or absence of ejaculation usually occurs during intercourse, rather than during manual or oral stimulation or during masturbation. Suspected causes include alcoholism or use of drugs (illicit or prescription), stressful or traumatic life situations, and fear of impregnating one's partner (Kaplan, 1974).

The most common sexual dysfunction in males is **premature ejaculation,** a chronic or recurring orgasm disorder in which orgasm and ejaculation occur with little stimulation, before, during, or shortly after penetration and before the man wishes (American Psychiatric Association, 2000). This condition may have its origins in early sexual experiences that called for quick ejaculation, such as hurried masturbation. However, biological factors may be more important. Some research suggests that SSRI antidepressants (those that increase the action of the neurotransmitter serotonin) are effective in helping some men with this problem (Balon, 1996; Rowland et al., 2003).

Sexual pain disorders are common in women but infrequent in men (Rosen & Leiblum, 1995). **Dyspareunia,** genital pain associated with sexual intercourse, is much more common in women. Inadequate lubrication is the major cause, although vaginal infections, sexually transmitted diseases, and various psychological factors may also be involved.

Vaginismus is a sexual pain disorder in which involuntary muscle contractions tighten and even close the vagina, making intercourse painful or impossible. The problem may stem from a rigid religious upbringing in which sex was looked on as sinful and dirty. It may also stem from past experiences of extremely painful intercourse or from a fear of men, rape, or other traumatic experiences associated with intercourse (Kaplan, 1974).

11.17 How do orgasmic and sexual pain disorders affect men's and women's sexual experiences?

female orgasmic disorder A sexual dysfunction in which a woman is persistently unable to reach orgasm or delays in reaching orgasm, despite adequate sexual stimulation.

male orgasmic disorder A sexual dysfunction in which a man experiences the absence of ejaculation, or ejaculation occurs only after strenuous effort over a prolonged period.

premature ejaculation A chronic or recurring orgasmic disorder in which orgasm and ejaculation occur with little stimulation, before, during, or shortly after penetration and before the man wishes; the most common sexual dysfunction in males.

dyspareunia (dis-PAH-roo-nee-yah) A sexual pain disorder marked by genital pain associated with sexual intercourse; more common in females than in males.

vaginismus (VAJ-ah-NIZ-mus) A sexual pain disorder in which involuntary muscle contractions tighten and even close the vagina, making intercourse painful or impossible.

Remember It   Sexual Dysfunctions

Match each sexual disorder with the appropriate description.

_____ (1) male erectile disorder
_____ (2) vaginismus
_____ (3) premature ejaculation
_____ (4) female orgasmic disorder
_____ (5) female sexual arousal disorder
_____ (6) hypoactive sexual desire disorder

a. inability to reach orgasm
b. inability to control ejaculation
c. lack of sexual interest
d. inability to have or maintain an erection
e. an involuntary closing of the vagina
f. inability to feel sexually excited and to lubricate sufficiently

Answers: 1. d; 2. e; 3. b; 4. a; 5. f; 6. c

Sexually Transmitted Diseases

What is the most common infectious disease in the United States? You might be surprised to learn that it isn't the common cold or the flu. It's a sexually transmitted disease called *chlamydia* (CDC, 2005a).

Sexually transmitted diseases (STDs) are infections spread primarily through intimate sexual contact. Each year, about 19 million Americans contract a sexually transmitted disease. Half of these cases involve young people ages 15 to 24 (Cates et al., 2004). Minority populations in U.S. inner cities are experiencing an epidemic in STDs as well. Worldwide, more than 300 million people contract curable STDs each year (WHO, 2001). Millions more are diagnosed each year with incurable STDs—including about 5 million cases of HIV/AIDS (NIH, 2003).

The incidence of many sexually transmitted diseases has increased dramatically since the early 1970s. This can be explained in part by more permissive attitudes toward sex and an increase in sexual activity among young people (Turner et al., 1995). Another factor is the greater use of nonbarrier methods of contraception such as the pill. Barrier methods, such as condoms and vaginal spermicide, provide some protection against STDs. Some of the more serious sexually transmitted diseases are bacterial infections such as chlamydia, gonorrhea, and syphilis, which are curable, and viral infections such as genital warts, genital herpes, and AIDS, which are not curable. However, all STDs are preventable, but do you know how to prevent them? Take the quiz in *Try It* to find out.

sexually transmitted diseases (STDs) Infections that are spread primarily through intimate sexual contact.

Try It   Mayo Clinic STD Quiz: What You Don't Know Can Hurt You

Answer these questions True or False. (Note: full explanations of the answers to these questions can be found at http://mayoclinic.com/health/stds/QZ00037)

1. The rate of STDs in the United States is on the rise.

2. Condoms—so long as they're still wrapped—will stay effective even if carried around for months at a time in your wallet.

3. Animal skin (lambskin) condoms protect against pregnancy, but don't protect you from STDs, such as HIV/AIDS.

4. You should lubricate condoms with petroleum jelly or baby oil to reduce their risk of tearing.

5. When condoms fail, it's usually because of incorrect use.

6. If you have a history of genital herpes, you can infect your partner even when you don't have symptoms of the disease.

7. Having regular Pap tests will prevent cervical cancer.

8. You can't get an STD from oral sex.

9. Taking birth control pills eliminates your need for a condom.

10. STDs aren't life-threatening.

Answers: 1. T; 2. F; 3. T; 4. F; 5. T; 6. T; 7. F; 8. F; 9. F; 10. F

Bacterial STDs

There are many types of bacteria that cause sexually transmitted diseases. Fortunately, in most cases, bacterial STDs, including chlamydia, gonorrhea, and syphilis, can be cured with antibiotics.

Chlamydia is a highly infectious disease. Rates of infection among young people are especially high. For example, studies involving teenagers confined to juvenile detention centers have found that as many as 14% of them test positive for chlamydia (CDC, 2005). And in 2004, about 6% of women aged 15 to 24 who visited family planning clinics were found to have the disease (CDC, 2005a).

Men with chlamydia are likely to have symptoms that alert them to the need for treatment, but they suffer no adverse reproductive consequences from the infection. Women, on the other hand, typically have only mild symptoms or no symptoms at all when chlamydia begins in the lower reproductive tract. Therefore, the infection often goes untreated and spreads to the upper reproductive tract, where it can cause **pelvic inflammatory disease (PID).** PID often produces scarring of tissue in the fallopian tubes, which can result in infertility or an *ectopic pregnancy*—in which the fertilized ovum is implanted outside of the uterus (Temmerman, 1994; Weström, 1994).

In 2004, in the United States, 330,132 cases of **gonorrhea** were reported to the Centers for Disease Control; this number represented nearly 113.5 cases for every 100,000 people in the U.S. population. The rate dropped from 133 cases per 100,000 people in 2000 (CDC, 2005a). Within the first 2 weeks after contracting gonorrhea, 95% of men develop a puslike discharge from the penis and experience painful urination (Schwebke, 1991a). Most seek treatment and are cured. If there are no symptoms present or if the individual does not seek treatment within 2 to 3 weeks, the infection may spread to the internal reproductive organs and eventually cause sterility. The bad news for women is that 50–80% of women who contract gonorrhea do not have early symptoms. The infection spreads from the cervix through the other internal reproductive organs, causing inflammation and scarring. Gonorrhea can be cured with antibiotics but public health officials are concerned about the growing number of antibiotic-resistant strains of the bacteria that cause the disease (CDC, 2005a).

About 8,000 cases of **syphilis** were reported in the United States in 2004 (CDC, 2005a). Unfortunately, the prevalence of this deadly disease began to rise in 2000 after more than fifty years of decline. The increase, say public health officials, is largely confined to urban areas and is due to skyrocketing syphilis rates among gay men (CDC, 2005a). Remarkably, syphilis rates among gay male patients in STD clinics more than doubled from 1999 (4%) to 2004 (10%). Around the world, prostitution is a major factor in rising syphilis rates. In China, for example, some 15% of female sex workers are infected with syphilis (Ruan, 2006). Because of the prevalence of syphilis among selected groups, public health officials believe that prevention programs geared toward the needs and behaviors of each particular group will be most effective.

Left untreated, syphilis progresses in predictable stages. In the primary stage, a painless sore, or chancre (pronounced "SHANK-er"), appears where the spirochete ("SPY-ro-keet"), the microorganism that causes syphilis, entered the body. This sore may go unnoticed, but even without treatment, it will heal. In the second stage of syphilis, a painless rash appears on the body, usually accompanied by a fever, sore throat, loss of appetite, fatigue, and headache. Again, without treatment, these symptoms eventually disappear. Then, the spirochetes enter the various tissues and organs of the body, where they may be inactive for anywhere from several years to a lifetime. About 30–50% of people with untreated syphilis enter the final and terrible third stage, in which blindness, paralysis, heart failure, mental illness, and death result.

A pregnant woman in any stage of syphilis will infect the fetus. But syphilis can be stopped at any point in its development, except in the third stage, with strong doses of penicillin (CDC, 2005a).

11.18 What are the major bacterial sexually transmitted diseases, and how are they treated?

chlamydia (klah-MIH-dee-uh) A highly infectious bacterial STD that is found in both sexes and can cause infertility in females.

pelvic inflammatory disease (PID) An infection in the female pelvic organs, which can result from untreated chlamydia or gonorrhea and can cause pain, scarring of tissue, and even infertility or an ectopic pregnancy.

gonorrhea (gahn-ah-REE-ah) A bacterial STD that, in males, causes a puslike discharge from the penis and painful urination; if untreated, females can develop pelvic inflammatory disease and possibly infertility.

syphilis A bacterial STD that progresses through three predictable stages; if untreated, it can eventually be fatal.

Viral STDs

11.19 What viral diseases are transmitted through sexual contact?

Unlike the bacterial infections, the viral infections—genital warts, genital herpes, and AIDS—are incurable. Moreover, they can lead to more serious diseases, including cancer. For example, **genital warts** are caused by the **human papillomavirus (HPV).** Even after the warts are removed or disappear spontaneously, the virus remains latent in the body for years and may eventually cause genital cancer, particularly cervical cancer (Koutsky et al., 1992; Tinkle, 1990). Prevalence studies in the United States show that 25% of women between 20 and 29 years of age, and 10% of women 30 and over, are infected with HPV (Stone et al., 2002).

Recently, the Food and Drug Administration approved a vaccine that officials believe will protect young women against four types of HPV (CDC, 2006a). However, the vaccine is only licensed for use in females between the ages of 9 and 26, and researchers do not yet know how long the vaccine's protective effects will last. Moreover, officials point out that there are other forms of HPV against which the vaccine offers no protection. For these reasons, public health officials state that women who get the vaccine should continue to be vigilant about safe sex practices and routine medical screening.

According to the Centers for Disease Control and Prevention (CDC, 2001b), 20% of adults in the United States, or about 45 million people, are infected with the virus that causes most cases of **genital herpes** (CDC, 2001b). The type 2 virus—herpes simplex— produces 80–90% of the cases of genital herpes and is transmitted through direct contact with infected genitals. However, the type 1 virus—the herpes virus more commonly associated with cold sores and fever blisters in the mouth—can also cause genital herpes and can be transmitted via oral or genital sex.

In genital herpes, painful blisters form on the genitals (or around the anus in homosexual men), fill with pus, and then burst, leaving open sores. It is at this point that a person is most contagious. After the blisters heal, the virus travels up nerve fibers to an area around the base of the spinal cord, where it remains in a dormant state but can flare up anew at any time. The first herpes episode is usually the most severe (Apuzzio, 1990); recurring attacks are typically milder and briefer. Although genital herpes is most contagious during an outbreak, it can be transmitted even when an infected person has no symptoms (Dawkins, 1990).

genital warts Growths on the genitals that are caused by the human papillomavirus (HPV).

human papillomavirus (HPV) A virus that causes genital warts; also believed to contribute to cervical cancer.

genital herpes An STD that is caused by the herpes simplex virus and results in painful blisters on the genitals; presently incurable, the infection usually recurs and is highly contagious during outbreaks.

Acquired Immune Deficiency Syndrome (AIDS)

11.20 In what ways can HIV/AIDS affect an individual's physical and psychological health?

No sexually transmitted disease has more devastating consequences than **acquired immune deficiency syndrome (AIDS).** The *New England Journal of Medicine* published an interactive timeline that chronicled the history of this dreaded disease from its discovery in 1981 to its 25th anniversary in 2006 (Sepkowitz, 2006). As you can see from the timeline's highlights in Figure 11.5, the number of AIDS cases around the world rose dramatically over these years as researchers worked to find a cure for the disease and more effective ways of preventing its spread. To date, 25 million have died from AIDS (Merson, 2006). Furthermore, more than 40 million people are currently infected with the virus that causes AIDS. Two-thirds of these people live in sub-Saharan Africa (Merson, 2006). In the United States, there are more than 1 million such individuals, 80% of whom are male (Sepkowitz, 2006).

How much do you know about AIDS? Find out by completing the *Try It* on the next page.

AIDS is caused by the **human immunodeficiency virus (HIV),** often referred to as the *AIDS virus.* When a person is first infected, HIV enters the bloodstream. This initial infection usually causes no symptoms, and the immune system begins to produce HIV antibodies. It is these antibodies that are detected in a blood test for AIDS. Individuals then progress to the asymptomatic carrier state, in which they experience no symptoms whatsoever and thus can unknowingly infect others.

HIV attacks the immune system until it becomes essentially nonfunctional. The diagnosis of AIDS is made when the immune system is so damaged that victims develop rare forms of cancer or pneumonia or other opportunistic infections. Such infections are

acquired immune deficiency syndrome (AIDS) A devastating and incurable illness that is caused by HIV and progressively weakens the body's immune system, leaving the person vulnerable to opportunistic infections that usually cause death.

human immunodeficiency virus (HIV) The virus that causes AIDS.

Try It   Knowledge about AIDS

1. AIDS is a single disease. (true/false)
2. AIDS symptoms vary widely from country to country, and even from risk group to risk group. (true/false)
3. Those at greatest risk for getting AIDS are people who have sex without using condoms, drug users who share needles, and infants born to AIDS-infected mothers. (true/false)

4. AIDS is one of the most highly contagious diseases. (true/false)
5. One way to avoid contracting AIDS is to use an oil-based lubricant with a condom. (true/false)

Answers:
1. False: AIDS is not a single disease. Rather, a severely impaired immune system leaves a person with AIDS highly susceptible to a whole host of infections and diseases.
2. True: In the United States and Europe, AIDS sufferers may develop Kaposi's sarcoma (a rare form of skin cancer), pneumonia, and tuberculosis. In Africa, people with AIDS usually waste away with fever, diarrhea, and symptoms caused by tuberculosis.
3. True: Those groups are at greatest risk. Screening of blood donors and testing of donated blood have greatly reduced the risk of contracting AIDS through blood transfusions. Today, women make up the fastest-growing group of infected people worldwide, as AIDS spreads among heterosexuals, especially in Africa.
4. False: AIDS is not among the most highly infectious diseases. You cannot get AIDS from kissing, shaking hands, or using objects handled by people who have AIDS.
5. False: *Do not* use oil-based lubricants, which can eat through condoms. Latex condoms with an effective spermicide are safer. Learn the sexual history of any potential partner, including HIV test results. Don't have sex with prostitutes.

not usually serious in people with normal immune responses, but in those with a very impaired immune system, they can be very serious and even life-threatening. At this point, patients typically experience progressive weight loss, weakness, fever, swollen lymph nodes, and diarrhea; 25% develop a rare cancer that produces reddish-purple spots on the skin. Other infections develop as the immune system weakens further.

Before developing a full-blown case of AIDS, some people develop less severe symptoms related to immune system dysfunction, such as unexplained fevers, chronic diarrhea, and weight loss. The average time from infection with HIV to advanced AIDS is about 10 years. But three individuals shown in Figure 11.5 have defied the odds. Basketball great Magic Johnson, former Playboy Playmate Rebekka Armstrong, and Olympic diver Greg Louganis are among the thousands of people who have lived with HIV for more than 10 years without having developed AIDS. All three made lifestyle changes when they were diagnosed with the virus. These changes have undoubtedly contributed to their good health. Likewise, they have probably taken advantage of the many drug treatments developed by medical researchers to help HIV-positive people ward off full-blown AIDS.

The long search for effective treatments for HIV has produced two major victories. First, the discovery that drugs such as AZT can prevent the transmission of HIV from a pregnant woman to her fetus has saved thousands of lives. During the 1990s, nearly 2000 infants were diagnosed with HIV each year. Thanks to widespread prenatal HIV screening and to the availability of these preventive drugs, just under 100 infants were diagnosed with HIV in 2004 (CDC, 2006b).

Second, the advent of *antiretroviral drugs* has probably prevented millions of deaths from AIDS by interfering with HIV's ability to invade healthy cells, the process through which HIV destroys its victims' immune systems. At present, the United Nations—aided by the World Bank, governments throughout the industrialized world, corporations, charitable foundations, and celebrity spokespersons, such as U2 singer Bono—is working to provide the funding needed to supply antiretroviral drugs to developing regions in which HIV-infection rates are particularly high, such as sub-Saharan Africa (Global Fund to Fight AIDS, Tuberculosis, and Malaria, 2006; Merson, 2006).

The Transmission of AIDS. Researchers believe that HIV is transmitted primarily through the exchange of blood, semen, or vaginal secretions during sexual contact or when IV (intravenous) drug users share contaminated needles or syringes. In the United States, about 25% of those with AIDS are IV drug users, but homosexual men represent the largest number of HIV carriers and AIDS cases (CDC, 2001c). Anal intercourse is more dangerous than coitus, because rectal tissue often tears during penetration, allowing HIV ready entry into the bloodstream. However, it is a mistake to view

Figure 11.5 Milestones from the History of HIV/AIDS

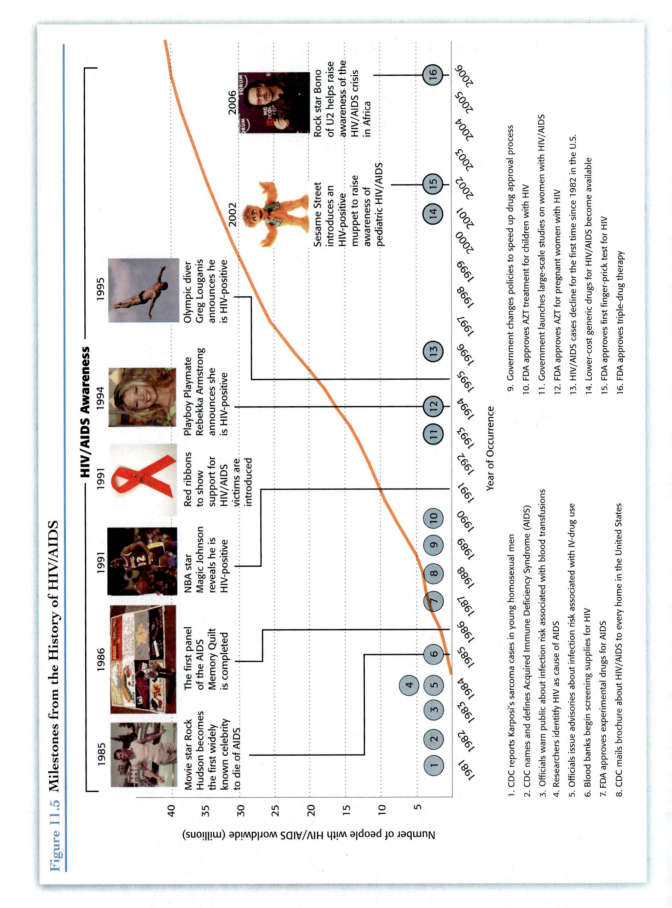

HIV/AIDS Awareness

1985	1986	1991	1991	1994	1995	2002	2006

Movie star Rock Hudson becomes the first widely known celebrity to die of AIDS

The first panel of the AIDS Memory Quilt is completed

NBA star Magic Johnson reveals he is HIV-positive

Red ribbons to show support for HIV/AIDS victims are introduced

Playboy Playmate Rebekka Armstrong announces she is HIV-positive

Olympic diver Greg Louganis announces he is HIV-positive

Sesame Street introduces an HIV-positive muppet to raise awareness of pediatric HIV/AIDS

Rock star Bono of U2 helps raise awareness of the HIV/AIDS crisis in Africa

Number of people with HIV/AIDS worldwide (millions)

Year of Occurrence

1. CDC reports Karposi's sarcoma cases in young homosexual men
2. CDC names and defines Acquired Immune Deficiency Syndrome (AIDS)
3. Officials warn public about infection risk associated with blood transfusions
4. Researchers identify HIV as cause of AIDS
5. Officials issue advisories about infection risk associated with IV-drug use
6. Blood banks begin screening supplies for HIV
7. FDA approves experimental drugs for AIDS
8. CDC mails brochure about HIV/AIDS to every home in the United States
9. Government changes policies to speed up drug approval process
10. FDA approves AZT treatment for children with HIV
11. Government launches large-scale studies on women with HIV/AIDS
12. FDA approves AZT for pregnant women with HIV
13. HIV/AIDS cases decline for the first time since 1982 in the U.S.
14. Lower-cost generic drugs for HIV/AIDS become available
15. FDA approves first finger-prick test for HIV
16. FDA approves triple-drug therapy

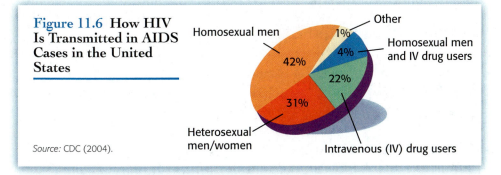

Figure 11.6 How HIV Is Transmitted in AIDS Cases in the United States

Homosexual men 42%

Other 1%

Homosexual men and IV drug users 4%

Intravenous (IV) drug users 22%

Heterosexual men/women 31%

Source: CDC (2004).

AIDS as a disease confined to gay men; about 30% of AIDS suffers are women. **Figure 11.6** illustrates the rates of infection in the United States in 2004 for four different modes of transmission: (1) male/male sexual relations; (2) male/female sexual relations; (3) intravenous drug use; and (4) male/male sexual relations combined with intravenous drug use. You may be surprised to learn that almost a third of new HIV cases in that year resulted from heterosexual contact.

Researchers have recently discovered that circumcision substantially reduces the risk of HIV transmission (Auvert et al., 2005). In response, public health officials in many of the developing nations that have large populations of HIV-positive men, such as Uganda, have begun educating them about the procedure along with other ways of reducing their risk of infection (Cassell, Halperin, Shelton, & Stanton, 2006). Screening and treatment for other STDs are vital to the prevention of HIV (CDC, 2004) as well. Research has shown that the presence of another STD in an HIV-infected person causes him or her to have higher levels of the communicable form of the virus in his or her bodily fluids. Anyone who has sex with such a person is, therefore, at a greatly increased risk of becoming infected with HIV.

The Psychological Impact of HIV Infection and AIDS. What are the psychological effects on people who struggle to cope with this fearsome disease? The reaction to the news that one is HIV-positive is frequently shock, bewilderment, confusion, or disbelief (Bargiel-Matasiewicz et al., 2005). Another common reaction is anger—at past or present sexual partners, family members, health care professionals, or society in general. Often, a person's response includes guilt, a sense of being punished for homosexuality or drug abuse. Other people exhibit denial, ignoring medical advice and continuing to act as if nothing has changed in their lives. Then, of course, there is fear—of death, of mental and physical deterioration, of rejection by friends, family, and co-workers, of sexual rejection, of abandonment. Experiencing emotional swings ranging from shock to anger to guilt to fear can lead to serious clinical depression and apathy (Tate et al., 2003). Once apathy sets in, HIV patients may become less likely to comply with treatment (Dorz et al., 2003).

Once AIDS develops, a sequence of events that devastates the brains of 40% of its victims is set in motion (Thompson et al., 2005). The cortex of an AIDS victim gradually thins as the disease gains ground in its attack on the sufferer's immune system. Motor and language impairments often result from slow deterioration of the areas of the cortex that are involved in these functions. Cortical thinning causes some AIDS patients to develop *AIDS-related dementia*, a disorder that is similar to Alzheimer's disease. Researchers say that some people who are HIV-positive but who have not developed full-blown AIDS show cortical thinning to some extent as well. Thus, studies are currently underway to determine the best way to approach this effect of the virus.

To cope psychologically, AIDS patients and those infected with HIV, and their loved ones, need education and information about the disease. They can be helped by psychotherapy, self-help groups, and medications such as antidepressants and anti-anxiety drugs. Self-help groups and group therapy may serve as an extended family for some patients. A concern voiced by most patients in psychotherapy is whether to tell others, and if so, what to tell them and how. Patients may feel a compelling need to confide in others and, at the same time, to conceal their condition.

Remember It | Sexually Transmitted Diseases

1. If left untreated, _____, a bacterial STD, can be fatal.
2. Genital _____ causes painful blisters on the genitals and is usually recurring, highly contagious during outbreaks, and incurable.
3. The two STDs most likely to cause infertility in women are _____ and _____.
4. HIV eventually causes a breakdown of the _____ system.
5. The group in the United States at highest risk of being infected with HIV is _____.

Answers: 1. syphilis; 2. herpes; 3. chlamydia, gonorrhea; 4. immune; 5. homosexual men

Apply It | Rules for Internet Dating

Internet dating has been around ever since the World Wide Web became widely available in the mid-1990s. However, online daters were often stigmatized as "desperate." Things have changed, and researchers have found that nearly two-thirds of adults in the United States view online dating as one of many mainstream options for meeting potential mates (Madden & Lenhart, 2006).

A veteran of the online dating scene, Suzanne Schlosberg, author of *The Curse of the Singles Table: A True Tale of 1001 Nights without Sex* (2004) claims to be one of the world's leading experts on Internet dating, having initiated more than 50 dating relationships with men via online meeting places. Significantly, too, Schlosberg met her husband on the Internet. Now officially retired from the single life, Suzanne hopes that the strategies she developed for online dating can be helpful to others. Her insights are available in the form of rules for Internet dating for both men and women at her web site http://www. suzanneschlosberg.com. Schlosberg claims that men and women need different rules because they tend to make different kinds of dating mistakes. Still, she notes that both sets of rules offer enlightenment for both men and women. Likewise, many of the principles expressed in Schlosberg's rules are just as applicable to same-sex relationships as they are to heterosexuals. Here are the highlights. In deference to cultural conventions, ladies go first.

Eight Simple Rules for Internet Dating for Women

- *Seek out potential matches rather than wait for them to e-mail you.*
  Schlosberg argues that women are more selective than men and that their selectivity increases the chances that a romance that begins online will endure.
- *Don't lie about anything. Ever.*
  Schlosberg advises women to avoid beginning relationships on false premises by posting "glamour" photos that make them look like cover models for the *Sports Illustrated* swimsuit issue.
- *Don't have more than five e-mail exchanges before either making a date or cutting the person loose.*
  Such limitations will help you avoid revealing too much information to people who might not turn out to be worthy of your trust, says Schlosberg.
- *Don't talk on the phone before meeting.*
  Schlosberg believes that what you really need to know about a potential partner is whether the two of you will "click" in person, so, she says, why waste time talking on the phone?

- *Meet for coffee first—no dinners!*
  Coffee dates, claims Schlosberg, allow potential partners to extend the date if there is a mutual attraction or to make a socially comfortable hasty exit if need be.
- *Arrive early, buy your own drink, bring a newspaper and have an exit line.*
  When a woman buys her own drink before the man arrives, she spares herself and the man from addressing questions about who should pay. The newspaper gives her something to do if the guy doesn't show up, and the exit line helps her avoid social awkwardness if she decides that the man does not fit her criteria for an acceptable match.
- *Change your search criteria every few weeks.*
  Making such changes alters the pool of potential dates, says Schlosberg.
- *Keep your expectations low.*
  Remember, says Schlosberg, no matter how perfect a man's profile may seem, everything may change when you meet him in person, so you may have to go through dozens of such meetings before finding a good match.

Nine Simple Rules for Internet Dating for Men

- *Don't send generic e-mails.*

  Dating and selling low-interest auto loans don't have much in common, according to Schlosberg, so men shouldn't use mass marketing e-mail techniques to find a girlfriend.

- *Don't brag.*

  Schlosberg points out that an online boast such as "I recently paid off all of my credit cards" will be undermined when your dream girl finds out that you still have 50 years to pay on your $250,000 student loan.

- *Reveal something interesting about yourself in your profile*

  Women, Schlosberg says, are looking for insight into your personality (i.e., your hobbies, favorite movies, etc.), not just basics such as your hair color and height.

- *Don't say you're looking for a woman who "likes to laugh" or "likes to have fun."*

  Do you know anyone who doesn't like to laugh or have fun? asks Schlosberg.

- *Don't specify a hair color or a weight limit or breast size that you're looking for in a woman.*

  Let women know that you are interested in more than just their looks, Schlosberg recommends.

- *Do your homework before a date.*

  Committing a woman's profile to memory will help you avoid making embarrassing admissions such as "Sorry, I got you mixed up with the girl I hooked up with last night" when you misstate her profession or the town in which she grew up.

- *Ask questions.*

  Everyone, including the women you go out with, perceives you more positively when you display more interest in getting to know them than you do in talking about yourself.

- *Don't talk about your other Internet dates while on an Internet date.*

  Telling sob stories with the tag line, "I thought we were meant for each other, but she dumped me" will interfere with your ability to make judgments about the person with whom you are exploring the possibility of a future relationship, Schlosberg recommends.

- *Don't say "I'll call you" if you don't intend to.*

  Schlosberg advises men to say something like "see you on-line" if they have no intention of continuing a relationship.

  The kinds of strategies suggested by Suzanne Schlosberg may increase the chances that you will find yourself among the 20% or so of men and women who develop long-term relationships with partners whom they have met online (Gavin, Scott, & Duffield, 2005). At the very least, such guidelines will help you make the most of the opportunities the Internet offers for widening your social network. Even if you don't end up with a romantic partner, you may make some new friends and gain some insight into your own psychosocial make-up in the process.

Summary and Review

Sex, Gender, and Gender Roles p. 387

11.1 How does biological sex develop both typically and atypically? p. 387

The primary sex characteristics of a fetus resemble those of a female until acted upon by male hormones that are released in response to the Sry gene located on the Y chromosome. The hormones of puberty cause the primary sex characteristics to mature and also lead to the appearance of the secondary sex chacteristics. In rare cases, the balance of hormones is disturbed during prenatal development, and a child is born with ambiguous genitalia. Intersexual infants are those who are born with sexual features of both sexes. Sex assignment is the process of determining whether a child with ambiguous genitalia should be brought up as male or female.

11.2 What is the relationship between sex and gender? p. 388

Biological sex is categorical, whereas psychological gender varies by degree. In transgendered individuals, sex and gender are not the same.

11.3 How did the early theorists explain gender role development? p. 389

Freud focused on children's bond with the same-sex parent. Terman and Miles viewed masculinity and femininity as opposites and developed a test to measure them. Learning theorists explained gender roles as the result of reinforcement and modeling. Cognitive-developmental theorists emphasized the stages of gender identity, gender stability, and gender constancy.

11.4 How does the multi-dimensional approach explain gender roles? p. 391

Bem argued that an individual's gender role is influenced by the balance between the independent dimensions of masculinity and femininity. She proposed that people who are high in both are androgynous, a condition that she believed to be associated with adjustment and mental health. She devised a test to measure masculinity and femininity that classifies test-takers into four categories: masculine, feminine, androgynous, and undifferentiated.

Sexually Transmitted Diseases p. 412

11.18 **What are the major bacterial sexually transmitted diseases, and how are they treated? p. 413**

The major sexually transmitted diseases caused by bacteria are chlamydia, gonorrhea, and syphilis. All can be cured with antibiotics. However, chlamydia and gonorrhea pose a particular threat to women because, unlike men, women with these infections typically have no symptoms or very mild symptoms, making prompt diagnosis and treatment less likely. If the infection spreads, it may result in infertility or an ectopic pregnancy.

11.19 **What viral diseases are transmitted through sexual contact? p. 414**

Viral STDs include genital warts, genital herpes, and AIDS. Viral infections presently are not curable. Genital herpes causes painful blisters on the genitals, is usually recurring, and is highly contagious during outbreaks.

11.20 **In what ways can HIV/AIDS affect an individual's physical and psychological health? p. 414**

HIV gradually renders the immune system nonfunctional. The diagnosis of AIDS is made when the person succumbs to various opportunistic infections. Persons with HIV must take precautions against transmitting the infection to others. Thinning of the cortex leads to declines in cognitive functioning in some individuals who have HIV or AIDS. Psychotherapy, self-help groups, and antidepressant medication can be helpful to those coping with HIV.

Thinking Critically about Psychology

1. What are some of the potential problems with information about sexual behavior and attitudes derived from surveys?
2. List the most persuasive arguments you can think of to justify each of the following: (1) Today it is easier to be a man than a woman. (2) Today it is easier to be a woman than a man.
3. To what extent did gender stereotypes affect the way your parents brought you up?

Key Terms

acquired immune deficiency syndrome (AIDS), p. 414
androgens, p. 388
androgyny, p. 392
biological sex, p. 387
chlamydia, p. 413
coitus, p. 404
dyspareunia, p. 411
erectile disfunction, p. 410
estrogen, p. 405
excitement phase, p. 404
female orgasmic disorder, p. 411
female sexual arousal disorder, p. 410
gender, p. 387
gender constancy, p. 391
gender identity, p. 389
gender roles, p. 388
gender schema theory, p. 393
gender stability, p. 391

genital herpes, p. 414
genital warts, p. 414
genitals, p. 388
gonads, p. 387
gonorrhea, p. 413
homophobia, p. 408
human immunodeficiency virus (HIV), p. 414
human papillomavirus (HPV), p. 414
hypoactive sexual desire disorder, p. 410
intersex, p. 388
male orgasmic disorder, p. 411
orgasm, p. 404
pelvic inflammatory disease (PID), p. 413
plateau phase, p. 404
premature ejaculation, p. 411
primary sex characteristics, p. 388
progesterone, p. 404

resolution phase, p. 404
secondary sex characteristics, p. 388
sex assignment, p. 388
sex chromosomes, p. 387
sex reassignment, p. 389
sexual aversion disorder, p. 410
sexual dysfunction, p. 410
sexual orientation, p. 406
sexual response cycle, p. 404
sexually transmitted diseases (STDs), p. 412
stereotype, p. 396
syphilis, p. 413
testosterone, p. 405
true hermaphrodite, p. 388
transgendered, p. 389
transsexual, p. 389
vaginismus, p. 411

Chapter 12

Health and Stress

Continued

Lifestyle and Health

12.18 **Why is smoking the most dangerous health-threatening behavior?**

12.19 **What are some health risks of alcohol abuse?**

12.20 **How does diet influence health?**

12.21 **What are some benefits of regular aerobic exercise?**

12.22 **What are the benefits and risks associated with alternative medicine?**

Lance Armstrong was, in his own words, "born to race bikes." As a teenager, and the child of a divorced working mother in Plano, Texas, he trained and competed hard. On weekends, he rode his bicycle so far that he sometimes had to phone his mother to pick him up. Armstrong's dedication to his training was so single-minded that he neglected his schoolwork and nearly failed his senior year of high school, but he managed to squeak by. After high school, his life was a whirlwind of amateur competitions, the 1992 Olympics, and then the professional cycling circuit.

In his first professional race, Armstrong came in dead last, but he won ten titles the following year. By 1996, he was a household name in Europe and was gaining fame in the United States as well—heady stuff for any 25-year-old. It seemed that everything was going his way. But one fall day, Armstrong experienced an excruciating pain. Shockingly, tests revealed that he had advanced testicular cancer that had spread to his lungs and his brain. Doctors recommended surgeries to remove his malignant testicle and the cancer in his brain. Following those procedures, he would undergo an aggressive course of chemotherapy. The physicians told Armstrong that, even with the best treatment, he had less than a 50-50 chance to recover. This young, powerful man who had been on top of the world just days before now faced his own mortality.

The chemotherapy weakened Armstrong severely, and he lost 20 pounds. However, his years of training gave him great reserves of physical strength and, at least as importantly, his will was strong. Armstrong has said cancer caused him to take a hard look at himself. He realized that he had relied on his tremendous natural physical abilities and had not learned the discipline, strategy, and teamwork that would be necessary to become a truly great cyclist. He had never given himself the full opportunity to train. He would start, then stop, then start again just a month before a big race. His natural ability was so great that he still won many races, but not the long-distance ones for which more skill is required. Now that Armstrong could take nothing for granted, he realized how important it was to develop into the best cycler he could be. He had a strong network of family and friends he could count on for emotional support. And, even in the midst of his own treatment, he wanted to do something for others. To this end, he established the Lance Armstrong Foundation to help other cancer victims and raise awareness about the importance of early detection. "Having cancer," he says, "was the best thing that ever happened to me."

Armstrong believes that his dedication to rebuilding his health and turning a tragedy into opportunity helped him to recover rapidly. His oncologist described the cyclist as "the most willful person I have ever met . . . he wasn't *willing* to die." Just 5 months after the diagnosis, he began to train again and vowed to return better than ever. But his sponsors, doubtful that he would ever be able to achieve this goal, dropped him. Armstrong signed a much less lucrative contract with another sponsor and continued to train, but his initial efforts left him exhausted and depressed. Afraid of failing, afraid that his strength would never rebound, afraid of a humiliating loss, afraid that his cancer would return, again and again Armstrong had to fight the desire to quit when things were too tough. One day, riding high in the mountains of North Carolina, he felt his unquenchable spirit return. A few days earlier, his coach had had to coax him to try just one more race. Now he was on top of the world again, spoiling for a competition.

Armstrong won his first post-cancer race in 1998, but his real comeback arrived in 1999, when he won Tour de France, a grueling 21 days of riding totaling 2,110 miles. He became an inspiration and a role model to young people and cancer survivors around the world. In 2001, 5 years after his diagnosis, Armstrong was pronounced cancer free. He undergoes regular testing to ensure that the disease has not recurred. He also continues to work with his foundation. In 2005, Armstrong won his seventh Tour de France race, setting a world record.

Why would someone say, as Armstrong did, that cancer was the best thing that ever happened to him? Such statements represent a deliberate choice to view what anyone would agree is a "stressor" as an opportunity for growth. As you will learn in this chapter, the way that individuals view their challenges in life greatly influences whether they succeed in overcoming them. We will begin by considering the various sources of stress in our lives.

In this chapter, we explore many aspects of health and stress. We begin our exploration by looking at stress, which is necessary for survival, but which, if chronic and excessive, can become disabling or even deadly.

Sources of Stress

What do you mean when you say you are "stressed out"? Most psychologists define **stress** as the physiological and psychological response to a condition that threatens or challenges an individual and requires some form of adaptation or adjustment. Stress is associated with the **fight-or-flight response,** in which the body's sympathetic nervous system triggers the release of hormones that prepare the body to fight or escape from a threat (see Chapter 2). Most of us frequently experience other kinds of **stressors,** stimuli or events that are capable of producing physical or emotional stress.

stress The physiological and psychological response to a condition that threatens or challenges a person and requires some form of adaptation or adjustment.

fight-or-flight response A response to stress in which the sympathetic nervous system triggers the release of hormones that prepare the body to fight or flee.

stressor Any stimulus or event capable of producing physical or emotional stress.

Social Readjustment Rating Scale (SRRS) Holmes and Rahe's measure of stress, which ranks 43 life events from most to least stressful and assigns a point value to each.

Life Events: Big and Small

Researchers Holmes and Rahe (1967) developed the **Social Readjustment Rating Rating Scale (SRRS)** to measure stress by ranking different life events from most to least stressful and assigning a point value to each event. Life events that produce the greatest life changes and require the greatest adaptation are considered the most stressful, regardless of whether the events are positive or negative. The 43 life events on the scale range from death of a spouse (assigned 100 stress points) to minor law violations such as getting a traffic ticket (11 points). Find your life stress score by completing the *Try It* on the following page.

Holmes and Rahe claim that there is a connection between the degree of life stress and major health problems. People who score 300 or more on the SRRS, the researchers say, run about an 80% risk of suffering a major health problem within the next 2 years. Those who score between 150 and 300 have a 50% chance of becoming ill within a 2-year period (Rahe et al., 1964). More recent research has shown that the weights given to life events by Holmes and Rahe continue to be appropriate for adults in North America and that SRRS scores are correlated with a variety of health indicators (De Coteau, Hope, & Anderson, 2003; Dohrenwend, 2006; Hobson & Delunas, 2001; Scully et al., 2000).

12.1 What was the Social Readjustment Rating Scale designed to reveal?

▲ Even positive life events, such as getting married, can cause stress.

Try It · Finding a Life Stress Score

To assess your level of life changes, check all of the events that have happened to you in the past year. Add up the points to derive your life stress score. (Based on Holmes & Masuda, 1974.)

Rank	Life Event	Life Change Unit Value	Your Points
1	Death of spouse	100	_____
2	Divorce	73	_____
3	Marital separation	65	_____
4	Jail term	63	_____
5	Death of close family member	63	_____
6	Personal injury or illness	53	_____
7	Marriage	50	_____
8	Getting fired at work	47	_____
9	Marital reconciliation	45	_____
10	Retirement	45	_____
11	Change in health of family member	44	_____
12	Pregnancy	40	_____
13	Sex difficulties	39	_____
14	Gain of new family member	39	_____
15	Business readjustment	39	_____
16	Change in financial state	38	_____
17	Death of close friend	37	_____
18	Change to different line of work	36	_____
19	Change in number of arguments with spouse	35	_____
20	Taking out loan for major purchase (e.g., home)	31	_____
21	Foreclosure of mortgage or loan	30	_____
22	Change in responsibilities at work	29	_____
23	Son or daughter leaving home	29	_____
24	Trouble with in-laws	29	_____
25	Outstanding personal achievement	28	_____
26	Spouse beginning or stopping work	26	_____
27	Beginning or ending school	26	_____
28	Change in living conditions	25	_____
29	Revision of personal habits	24	_____
30	Trouble with boss	23	_____
31	Change in work hours or conditions	20	_____
32	Change in residence	20	_____
33	Change in schools	20	_____
34	Change in recreation	19	_____
35	Change in church activities	19	_____
36	Change in social activities	18	_____
37	Taking out loan for lesser purchase (e.g., car or TV)	17	_____
38	Change in sleeping habits	16	_____
39	Change in number of family get-togethers	15	_____
40	Change in eating habits	15	_____
41	Vacation	13	_____
42	Christmas	12	_____
43	Minor violation of the law	11	_____

Life stress score: _____

Some researchers have questioned whether a high score on the SRRS is a reliable predictor of future health problems (Krantz et al., 1985; McCrae, 1984). One of the main shortcomings of the SRRS is that it assigns a point value to each life change without taking into account how an individual copes with that stressor. One study found that SRRS scores did reliably predict disease progression in multiple sclerosis patients (Mohr et al., 2002). But the patients who used more effective coping strategies displayed less disease progression than did those who experienced similar stressors but coped poorly with them.

Daily Hassles and Uplifts

Which is more stressful—major life events or those little problems and frustrations that seem to crop up every day? Richard Lazarus believes that the little stressors, which he calls **hassles,** cause more stress than major life events do (Lazarus & DeLongis, 1983). Daily hassles include irritating, frustrating experiences such as standing in line, being stuck in traffic, waiting for an appliance or utility repair technician to come to your home, and so on. Relationships are another frequent source of hassles, such as when another person misunderstands us or when coworkers or customers are hard to get along with. Likewise, environmental conditions such as traffic noise and pollution are among the daily hassles reported by city dwellers (Moser & Robin, 2006).

To illustrate the usefulness of Lazarus's approach to studying stress, Kanner and others (1981) developed the Hassles Scale to assess various categories of hassles. Unlike the Holmes and Rahe scale, the Hassles Scale takes into account that items may or may not represent stressors to individuals and that the amount of stress produced by an item varies from person to person. People completing the scale indicate the items that have been a hassle for them and rate the severity of those items on a 3-point scale. Table 12.1 shows the ten hassles most frequently reported by the students that Kanner and his colleagues originally surveyed in 1981. Do you think these are still relevant today?

DeLongis and others (1988) studied 75 American couples over a 6-month period and found that daily stress (as measured on the Hassles Scale) related significantly to present and future "health problems such as flu, sore throat, headaches, and backaches" (p. 486). Research also indicates that minor hassles that accompany stressful major life events, such as those measured by the SRRS, are sometimes better predictors of a person's level of psychological distress than the major events themselves (Pillow et al., 1996).

12.2 What roles do hassles and uplifts play in the stress of life, according to Lazarus?

hassles   Little stressors, including the irritating demands that can occur daily, that may cause more stress than major life changes do.

Table 12.1 **The Ten Most Common Hassles for College Students**

Hassle	Percentage of Times Checked
1. Troubling thoughts about future	76.6
2. Not getting enough sleep	72.5
3. Wasting time	71.1
4. Inconsiderate smokers	70.7
5. Physical appearance	69.9
6. Too many things to do	69.2
7. Misplacing or losing things	67.0
8. Not enough time to do the things you need to do	66.3
9. Concerns about meeting high standards	64.0
10. Being lonely	60.8

Source: Kanner et al. (1981).

According to Lazarus, **uplifts,** or positive experiences in life, may neutralize the effects of many hassles. Lazarus and his colleagues also constructed an Uplifts Scale. As with the Hassles Scale, people completing this scale make a cognitive appraisal of what they consider to be an uplift. Items viewed as uplifts by some people may actually be stressors for others. For middle-aged people, uplifts are often health- or family-related (Pinquart & Sörensen, 2004), whereas for college students uplifts often take the form of having a good time (Kanner et al., 1981).

Conflicts and Controllability

12.3 How do choice-related conflicts and lack of control contribute to stress?

One of the benefits of the times in which we are living is that we have many choices. However, making choices can be stressful. Having to choose between one thing and another, or among several alternatives, creates **conflict,** the stress that arises from knowing that choosing one alternative means foregoing another.

Do you experience anxiety, for example, when you have to decide which movie to see or which new restaurant to try? Choosing between two desirable alternatives often creates an **approach-approach conflict,** that is, one in which you must choose between two equally desirable options. Some approach-approach conflicts are minor, such as deciding which movie to see. Others can have major consequences, such as the conflict between building a promising career or interrupting that career to raise a child. In an **avoidance-avoidance conflict,** a person must choose between two undesirable alternatives. For example, you may want to avoid studying for an exam, but at the same time you want to avoid failing the test. An **approach-avoidance conflict** involves a single choice that has both desirable and undesirable features. The person facing this type of conflict is simultaneously drawn to and repelled by a choice—for example, wanting to take a wonderful vacation but having to empty a savings account to do so.

Situations in which we perceive ourselves to have no choice can be stressful as well. What happens when your professor walks into the classroom and says "Today we are going to have a pop quiz"? Your heart probably starts to beat a little faster, a sure sign that a fight-or-flight response has been triggered. If you have had such an experience, then you won't be surprised to learn that humans who are warned of a stressor before it occurs and have a chance to prepare themselves for it experience less stress than those who must cope with an unexpected stressor.

Our physical and psychological well-being is profoundly influenced by the degree to which we feel a sense of control over our lives (Rodin & Salovey, 1989). In classic research, Langer and Rodin (1976) studied the effects of control on nursing-home residents. Residents in one group were given some measure of control over their lives, such as choices in arranging their rooms and in the times they could see movies. They showed improved health and well-being and had a lower death rate than another group who were not given such control. Within 18 months, 30% of the residents given no choices had died, compared with only 15% of those who had been given some control over their lives.

Research has also shown that both children and adults expect to experience more stress when faced with unexpected negative life events, such as the sudden death of a loved one, than when dealing with stress generated by more controllable stressors, such as low grades (Hasan & Power, 2004). It is likely, then, that our expectations about unpredictable stressors may influence the manner in which we respond to them. Studies that distinguish between perceived and actual control support this hypothesis. In one such study, experimenters exposed participants to an annoying noise (e.g., a randomly sounded buzzer), but offered them the opportunity to control the intensity of the noise (Bollini et al., 2004). Even though all participants had an equal opportunity to exert some degree of control over the stressor, only those who had a general belief in their own ability to moderate the effects of stressors appeared to benefit. These participants were found to have lower levels of the stress hormone *cortisol* than

uplifts The positive experiences in life, which may neutralize the effects of many hassles.

conflict The stress that arises from knowing that choosing one alternative means foregoing another.

approach-approach conflict A conflict arising from having to choose between equally desirable alternatives.

avoidance-avoidance conflict A conflict arising from having to choose between undesirable alternatives.

approach-avoidance conflict A conflict arising when the same choice has both desirable and undesirable features.

participants who lacked confidence in their ability to control stressors. Thus, perceived control may be at least as important as actual control in the relationship between the predictability of stressors and our responses to them.

Stress in the Workplace

Perhaps there is no more troublesome source of stress than the workplace. Everyone who works is subject to some job-related stress, but the amount and sources of the stress differ, depending on the type of job and the kind of organization. Albrecht (1979) suggests that if people are to function effectively and find satisfaction on the job, the following nine variables must fall within their comfort zone (see also **Figure 12.1**):

- *Workload.* Too much or too little to do can cause people to feel anxious, frustrated, and unrewarded.
- *Clarity of job description and evaluation criteria.* Anxiety arises from confusion about job responsibilities and performance criteria or from a job description that is too rigidly defined to leave room for individual initiative.
- *Physical variables.* Temperature, noise, humidity, pollution, amount of workspace, and the physical positions (standing or sitting) required to carry out job duties should fall within a person's comfort zone.
- *Job status.* People with very low-paying, low-status jobs may feel psychological discomfort; those with celebrity status often cannot handle the stress that fame brings.
- *Accountability.* Accountability overload occurs when people have responsibility for the physical or psychological well-being of others but only a limited degree of control (air-traffic controllers, emergency room nurses and doctors); accountability underload occurs when workers perceive their jobs as meaningless.
- *Task variety.* To function well, people need a comfortable amount of variety and stimulation.
- *Human contact.* Some workers have virtually no human contact on the job (forest-fire lookouts); others have almost continuous contact with others (welfare and employment office workers). People vary greatly in how much interaction they enjoy or even tolerate.
- *Physical challenge.* Jobs range from being physically demanding (construction work, professional sports) to requiring little to no physical activity. Some jobs (firefighting, police work) involve physical risk.
- *Mental challenge.* Jobs that tax people beyond their mental capability, as well as those that require too little mental challenge, can be frustrating.

▲ Air-traffic controllers have an extremely high-stress job. The on-the-job stress they experience increases the risk of coronary disease and stroke.

Workplace stress can be especially problematic for women because of sex-specific stressors, including sex discrimination and sexual harassment in the workplace and difficulties in combining work and family roles. These added stressors have been shown to increase the negative effects of occupational stress on the health and well-being of working women (Swanson, 2000).

Job stress can have a variety of consequences. Perhaps the most frequently cited is reduced effectiveness on the job. But job stress can also lead to absenteeism, tardiness, accidents, substance abuse, and lower morale. Chronic stress can also lead to work-related **burnout** (Freudenberger & Richelson, 1981). People with burnout lack energy and feel emotionally drained and are pessimistic about the possibility of changing their situations. People who feel that their work is unappreciated are more subject to burnout than others. For example, one survey suggested that nearly half of the social workers in the United Kingdom suffer from burnout, and the sense of being unappreciated was the best predictor of the condition (Evans et al., 2006).

12.4 **For people to function effectively and find satisfaction on the job, what nine variables should fall within their comfort zone?**

burnout Lack of energy, exhaustion, and pessimism that result from chronic stress.

Figure 12.1 Variables in Work Stress

For a person to function effectively and find satisfaction on the job, these nine variables should fall within the person's comfort zone.

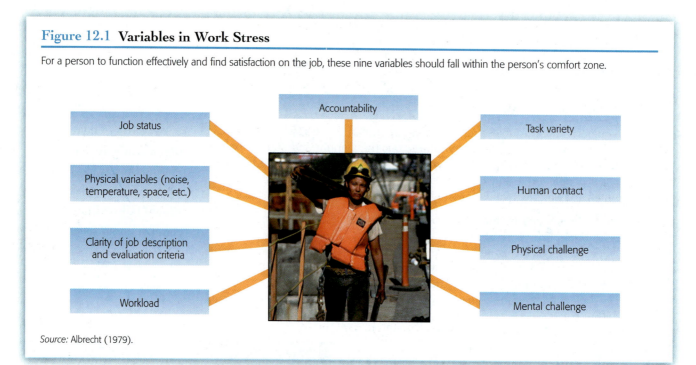

Job status

Accountability

Task variety

Physical variables (noise, temperature, space, etc.)

Human contact

Clarity of job description and evaluation criteria

Physical challenge

Workload

Mental challenge

Source: Albrecht (1979).

Catastrophic Events

12.5 How do people typically react to catastrophic events?

Catastrophic events such as the terrorist attacks of September 11, 2001, the deadly Indian Ocean tsunami of 2004, and the devastating hurricanes that hit the Gulf Coast of the United States in 2005 are stressful both for those who experience them directly and for people who learn of them via news media. Most people are able to manage the stress associated with such catastrophes. However, for some, these events lead to **posttraumatic stress disorder (PTSD)**, a prolonged and severe stress reaction to a catastrophic event (such as a plane crash or an earthquake) or to severe, chronic stress (such as that experienced by soldiers engaged in combat or residents of neighborhoods in which violent crime is a daily occurrence) (Kilpatrick et al., 2003).

People with posttraumatic stress disorder often have flashbacks, nightmares, or intrusive memories that make them feel as though they are actually re-experiencing the traumatic event. They suffer increased anxiety and startle easily, particularly in response to anything that reminds them of the trauma (Green et al., 1985). Many survivors of war or catastrophic events experience *survivor guilt* because they lived while others died; some feel that perhaps they could have done more to save others. Extreme combat-related guilt in Vietnam veterans is a risk factor for suicide or preoccupation with suicide (Hendin & Haas, 1991). One study of women with PTSD revealed that they were twice as likely as women without PTSD to experience first-onset depression and three times as likely to develop alcohol problems (Breslau et al., 1997). PTSD sufferers also experience cognitive difficulties, such as poor concentration (Vasterling et al., 2002).

Traumatic events that are of a more individual and personal nature can also lead to the development of PTSD. Survivors of childhood cancer and their parents, for example, sometimes develop the disorder (Bruce, 2006). Likewise, victims of sexual violence and child abuse are also at risk of developing PTSD (Filipas & Ullman, 2006; NCIPC, 2002).

posttraumatic stress disorder (PTSD) A prolonged and severe stress reaction to a catastrophic event or to severe, chronic stress.

Racism and Stress

12.6 How might historical racism affect the health of African Americans?

A significant source of chronic stress is being a member of a minority group in a majority culture. A study of White and African American participants' responses to a questionnaire about ways of managing stress revealed that a person may experience racial stress from simply being one of the few or only members of a particular race in any of a variety of settings, such as a classroom, the workplace, or a social situation (Plummer & Slane, 1996). The feelings of stress experienced in such situations can be intense, even in the absence of racist attitudes, discrimination, or any other overt evidence of racism.

Some theorists have proposed that a phenomenon called *historical racism*—experienced by members of groups that have a history of repression—can also be a source of stress (Troxel et al., 2003). Researchers interested in the effects of historical racism have focused primarily on African Americans. Many of these researchers claim that the higher incidence of high blood pressure among African Americans is attributable to stress associated with historical racism. Surveys have shown that African Americans experience more race-related stress than members of other minority groups do (Utsey et al., 2002). Those African Americans who express the highest levels of concern about racism display higher levels of cardiovascular reactivity to experimentally induced stressors, such as sudden loud noises, than do peers who express less concern (Bowen-Reid & Harrell, 2002). Thus, there may indeed be a link between perceptions of historical racism and high blood pressure.

▲ A strong sense of ethnic identity helps African Americans cope with the stress that may arise from living with racism.

The experience of racism may also interact with immune system functioning. In a recent study, researchers asked African Americans to write brief memoirs about their personal experiences with racism prior to receiving flu vaccine shots (Stetner, Chen, & Miller, 2006). Participants in a control group wrote about a neutral topic. Blood samples taken before administration of the vaccine that were compared to those drawn 1 to 3 months later showed differences across groups. The vaccine was least effective for the participants who wrote about racism.

The risks associated with historical racism are offset by protective factors in some African Americans. Specifically, a strong sense of ethnic identity appears to moderate the effects of racial stress (Utsey et al., 2002). But some studies show that personal characteristics, such as hostility, may increase the effects of racial stress (Fang & Myers, 2001; Raeikkoenen et al., 2003). So, the relationship between historical racism and cardiovascular health is probably fairly complex and varies considerably across individuals. Moreover, some researchers believe that the association must be studied more thoroughly in other historically repressed groups, such as Native Americans, before firm conclusions can be drawn (Belcourt-Dittloff & Stewart, 2000).

Socioeconomic Status and Stress

The term **socioeconomic status** is often used to refer to differences in income levels, but it includes much more than just financial resources. Occupation and education are also important components of socioeconomic status, as is the more subjective variable of social status. These variables interact to influence the status that is assigned to an individual, and these interactions can vary differently from one setting to another. For example, in some neighborhoods, police officers have low status even though they may have more education and higher incomes than the people who live in the communities they serve. In other neighborhoods, police officers have high status despite having less education and lower incomes than many members of the community. Thus, socioeconomic status is a fairly complex variable.

Despite these complexities, large-scale studies of health and other variables of interest often rely on data such as income and educational level to sort people into socioeconomic status categories. When this technique is used, as you can probably predict, people who are low in socioeconomic status are usually found to more frequently suffer from stress-related health conditions such as colds and the flu. In addition, health risk factors such as high levels of LDL cholesterol are typically more common among them (Goodman et al., 2005). However, in studies that distinguish between objective status and self-perceived status, researchers sometimes find that perceived status actually predicts health outcome better than objective measures such as income and education (Singh-Manoux, Marmot, & Adler, 2005).

12.7 How are socioeconomic status and health related?

socioeconomic status A collective term for the economic, occupational, and educational factors that influence an individual's relative position in society.

To understand how objective and perceived status differ from each other, imagine an older woman who dropped out of high school to get married at the age of 16 and whose only income is her meager Social Security check. By objective standards, she has low socioeconomic status. But suppose she is known as a pillar of her community, that she owns her home and has lived in it for 50 years. Furthermore, imagine that she teaches Sunday School, and is known by her neighbors as the first person one should turn to for help in a time of need. Clearly, within the context of her community, she has high status. And, as a psychologically well-adjusted person, she is aware of her position in that community. At the same time, she knows that her status within the context of the larger society is much lower than what she enjoys in her own community. Still, her community-based status and her realistic perception of it probably serve as protective factors that offset the risk factors associated with being of low socioeconomic status with regard to the larger culture.

Closer scrutiny of the variables associated with socioeconomic status reveals other factors that help us interpret links between socioeconomic status and health. For example, one frequent finding is that people of lower socioeconomic status have higher levels of stress hormones than people of higher status (Cohen, Doyle, & Baum, 2006). Looking further into this relationship, researchers have identified several behavioral and social factors among such people that help to explain the relationship between status and stress hormones. These factors included higher rates of smoking, more limited social networks, and less regular patterns of eating as compared to people at higher levels of socioeconomic status. This is not to say that these factors apply to everyone who has a low income, but they are found more frequently among those who are economically disadvantaged. Their presence affects the averages of health variables among low-income groups, thus creating correlations between socioeconomic status and these variables.

Finally, unemployment is another aspect of socioeconomic status that is related to stress and health. People who are forced out of their jobs experience heightened risks of stress-related illnesses in the months that follow (Crowley, Hayslip, & Hobdy, 2003; He, Colantonio, & Marshall, 2003; Isaksson et al., 2004). These effects are found among people of low, middle, and high socioeconomic status, by the way. This consistency is the result of the financial strain that accompanies the loss of income and the uncertainty about the future that is part of the experience of looking for a new job. These aspects of unemployment are stressful no matter how much money people made in their former jobs. However, unemployment is also stressful because it diminishes people's sense of control over what happens to them. And as you learned earlier in this chapter, perceived control is a good predictor of responses to stress.

Remember It   Sources of Stress

1. According to Holmes and Rahe, health may be adversely affected if a person experiences many stressful _____ in a short period of time.
2. According to Lazarus, _____ typically cause more stress than major life events do.
3. Rich cannot decide whether to go out with friends or stay home and study for tomorrow's test. This is an example of an _____ conflict.
4. The belief that one has _____ over a situation can moderate the effects of stress.
5. The nine variables proposed by Albrecht to account for most job-related stress are _____, _____, _____, _____, _____, _____, _____, _____, and _____.
6. _____ is a prolonged and severe stress reaction that can result from experiencing a catastrophic event.
7. Some researchers have found links between _____ and high blood pressure in African Americans.
8. Socioeconomic status includes _____, _____, and _____.

Answers: 1. life events; 2. hassles; 3. approach-avoidance; 4. control; 5. workload, job status, physical variables, clarity of job description, accountability, task variety, human contact, physical challenge, mental challenge; 6. Posttraumatic stress disorder; 7. historical racism; 8. income, occupation, education

Responding to Stress

How do you respond to stress? Psychologists have different views of the ways in which people respond to stressful experiences. Each approach can help us gain insight into our own experiences and, perhaps, deal more effectively with stress.

Selye and the General Adaptation Syndrome

Hans Selye (1907–1982), the researcher most prominently associated with the effects of stress on health, established the field of stress research. At the heart of Selye's concept of stress is the **general adaptation syndrome (GAS),** the predictable sequence of reactions that organisms show in response to stressors. It consists of three stages: the alarm stage, the resistance stage, and the exhaustion stage (Selye, 1956). (See **Figure 12.2.**)

The first stage of the body's response to a stressor is the **alarm stage,** in which the adrenal cortex releases hormones called *glucocorticoids* that increase heart rate, blood pressure, and blood-sugar levels, supplying a burst of energy that helps the person deal with the stressful situation (Pennisi, 1997). Next, the organism enters the **resistance stage,** during which the adrenal cortex continues to release glucocorticoids to help the body resist stressors. The length of the resistance stage depends both on the intensity of the stressor and on the body's power to adapt. If the organism finally fails in its efforts to resist, it reaches the **exhaustion stage,** at which point all the stores of deep energy are depleted, and disintegration and death follow.

Selye found that the most harmful effects of stress are caused by the prolonged secretion of glucocorticoids, which can lead to permanent increases in blood pressure, suppression of the immune system, weakening of muscles, and even damage to the hippocampus (Stein-Behrens et al., 1994). Thanks to Selye, the connection between extreme, prolonged stress and certain diseases is now widely accepted by medical experts.

12.8 **What is the general adaptation syndrome?**

Figure 12.2 The General Adaptation Syndrome

The three stages in Selye's general adaptation syndrome are (1) the alarm stage, during which there is emotional arousal and the defensive forces of the body are mobilized for fight or flight; (2) the resistance stage, in which intense physiological efforts are exerted to resist or adapt to the stressor; and (3) the exhaustion stage, when the organism fails in its efforts to resist the stressor.

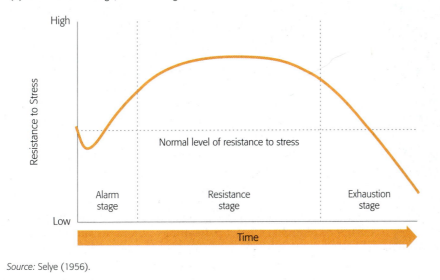

Source: Selye (1956).

general adaptation syndrome (GAS) The predictable sequence of reactions (alarm, resistance, and exhaustion stages) that organisms show in response to stressors.

alarm stage The first stage of the general adaptation syndrome, in which the person experiences a burst of energy that aids in dealing with the stressful situation.

resistance stage The second stage of the general adaptation syndrome, when there are intense physiological efforts to either resist or adapt to the stressor.

exhaustion stage The third stage of the general adaptation syndrome, which occurs if the organism fails in its efforts to resist the stressor.

Lazarus's Cognitive Theory of Stress

12.9 **What are the roles of primary and secondary appraisals when a person is confronted with a potentially stressful event?**

Is it the stressor itself that upsets us, or the way we think about it? The late Richard Lazarus (1922–2002) contended that it is not the stressor that causes stress, but a person's perception of it. According to Lazarus, when people are confronted with a potentially stressful event, they engage in a cognitive process that involves a primary and a secondary appraisal (1966; Lazarus & Folkman, 1984). A **primary appraisal** is an evaluation of the meaning and significance of the situation—whether its effect on one's well-being is positive, irrelevant, or negative. An event appraised as stressful could involve (1) harm or loss, that is, damage that has already occurred; (2) threat, or the potential for harm or loss; or (3) challenge, that is, the opportunity to grow or to gain. An appraisal of threat, harm, or loss can occur in relation to anything important to you—a friendship, a part of your body, your property, your finances, your self-esteem. When people appraise a situation as involving threat, harm, or loss, they experience negative emotions such as anxiety, fear, anger, and resentment (Folkman, 1984). An appraisal that sees a challenge, on the other hand, is usually accompanied by positive emotions such as excitement, hopefulness, and eagerness.

During **secondary appraisal,** if people judge the situation to be within their control, they make an evaluation of available resources—physical (health, energy, stamina), social (support network), psychological (skills, morale, self-esteem), material (money, tools, equipment), and time. Then, they consider the options and decide how to deal with the stressor. The level of stress they feel is largely a function of whether their resources are adequate to cope with the threat, and how severely those resources will be taxed in the process. **Figure 12.3** summarizes the Lazarus and Folkman psychological model of stress. Research supports their claim that the physiological, emotional, and behavioral reactions to stressors depend partly on whether the stressors are appraised as challenging or threatening.

primary appraisal A cognitive evaluation of a potentially stressful event to determine whether its effect is positive, irrelevant, or negative.

secondary appraisal A cognitive evaluation of available resources and options prior to deciding how to deal with a stressor.

Coping Strategies

12.10 **What is the difference between problem-focused and emotion-focused coping?**

If you're like most people, the stresses you have experienced have helped you develop some coping stratgies. **Coping** refers to a person's efforts through action and thought to deal with demands perceived as taxing or overwhelming. **Problem-focused coping** is direct; it consists of reducing, modifying, or eliminating the source of stress itself. If you are getting a poor grade in history and appraise this as a threat, you may study harder, talk over your problem with your professor, form a study group with other class members, get a tutor, or drop the course.

Emotion-focused coping involves reappraising a stressor in order to reduce its emotional impact. If you lose your job, you may decide that it isn't a major tragedy and instead view it as a challenge, an opportunity to find a better job with a higher salary. Despite what you may have heard, ignoring a stressor—one form of emotion-focused coping—can be an effective way of managing stress. Researchers studied 116 people who had experienced heart attacks (Ginzburg et al., 2002). All of the participants reported being worried about suffering another attack. However, those who tried to ignore their worries were less likely to exhibit anxiety-related symptoms such as nightmares and flashbacks. Other emotion-focused strategies, such as keeping a journal in which you write about your worries and track how they change over time, may be even more effective (Pennebaker & Seagal, 1999; Solano et al., 2003).

A combination of problem-focused and emotion-focused coping is probably the best stress-management strategy (Folkman and Lazarus, 1980). For example, a heart patient may ignore her anxiety (emotion-focused coping) while conscientiously adopting recommended lifestyle changes such as increasing exercise (problem-focused coping).

Some stressful situations can be anticipated in advance, allowing people to use a strategy called **proactive coping ,** which consists of

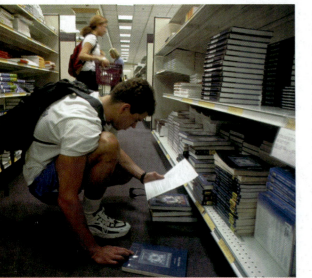

▲ Ordering your books online is one way of coping proactively with the stress you know you will experience if you wait until the last minute to buy your books.

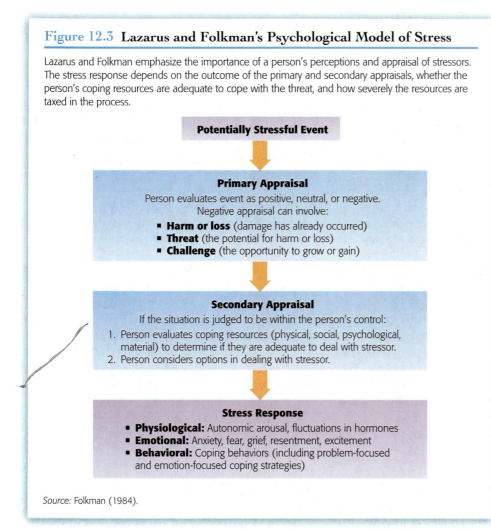

Figure 12.3 **Lazarus and Folkman's Psychological Model of Stress**

Lazarus and Folkman emphasize the importance of a person's perceptions and appraisal of stressors. The stress response depends on the outcome of the primary and secondary appraisals, whether the person's coping resources are adequate to cope with the threat, and how severely the resources are taxed in the process.

Potentially Stressful Event

Primary Appraisal
Person evaluates event as positive, neutral, or negative.
Negative appraisal can involve:
- **Harm or loss** (damage has already occurred)
- **Threat** (the potential for harm or loss)
- **Challenge** (the opportunity to grow or gain)

Secondary Appraisal
If the situation is judged to be within the person's control:
1. Person evaluates coping resources (physical, social, psychological, material) to determine if they are adequate to deal with stressor.
2. Person considers options in dealing with stressor.

Stress Response
- **Physiological:** Autonomic arousal, fluctuations in hormones
- **Emotional:** Anxiety, fear, grief, resentment, excitement
- **Behavioral:** Coping behaviors (including problem-focused and emotion-focused coping strategies)

Source: Folkman (1984).

efforts or actions taken in advance of a potentially stressful situation to prevent its occurrence or to minimize its consequences (Aspinwall & Taylor, 1997). Proactive copers anticipate and then prepare for upcoming stressful events and situations. For example, one certain stressor associated with attending college is that college bookstores are very busy at the beginning of the semester. To cope with this stress proactively, that is, to avoid the stress associated with standing in line with a heavy stack of books, you may order some of your books online or go to the bookstore well in advance of the start of the semester. Parents proactively cope, too, when they take along their children's favorite snacks and toys in anticipation of the children's becoming hungry and restless at a relative's home or a doctor's office.

The *Review and Reflect* below summarizes the key aspects of the various theories concerning humans' response to stress.

coping Efforts through action and thought to deal with demands that are perceived as taxing or overwhelming.

problem-focused coping A direct response aimed at reducing, modifying, or eliminating a source of stress.

emotion-focused coping A response involving reappraisal of a stressor to reduce its emotional impact.

proactive coping Active measures taken in advance of a potentially stressful situation in order to prevent its occurrence or to minimize its consequences.

Review and Reflect   Theories of Stress Responses

Theory	Description
Selye's general adaptation syndrome (GAS)	Three stages: alarm, resistance, and exhaustion
Lazarus's cognitive theory	Primary appraisal (evaluation of stressor), followed by secondary appraisal (evaluation of resources and options)
Coping strategies	Problem-focused coping, directed toward stressor; emotion-focused coping, directed toward the emotional response to the stressor

Health and Illness

Have you heard the term *wellness* and wondered exactly what was meant by it? This word is associated with a new approach to thinking about health, used by both professionals and laypersons. This approach encompasses a growing emphasis on lifestyle, preventive care, and the need to maintain wellness rather than thinking of health matters only when the body is sick. Health psychologists are discovering how stress, through its influence on the immune system, may affect people's health. They are also examining how personal and demographic factors are related to both illness and wellness.

Two Approaches to Health and Illness

12.11 How do the biomedical and biopsychosocial models differ in their approaches to health and illness?

biomedical model A perspective that explains illness solely in terms of biological factors.

biopsychosocial model A perspective that focuses on health as well as illness and holds that both are determined by a combination of biological, psychological, and social factors.

For many decades, the predominant view in medicine was the **biomedical model,** which explains illness in terms of biological factors. Today, physicians and psychologists alike recognize that the **biopsychosocial model** provides a fuller explanation of both health and illness (see **Figure 12.4**) (Engel, 1977, 1980; Schwartz, 1982). This model considers health and illness to be determined by a combination of biological, psychological, and social factors. Furthermore, it shows promise as a model for understanding and enhancing people's health and well-being. However, some advocates of the biopsychosocial approach have pointed out that the medical profession has been slow to recognize its value and continues to train physicians to focus almost exclusively on the physical aspects of illness and health (Scherger, 2005).

Growing acceptance of the biopsychosocial approach has given rise to a new subfield, **health psychology,** the subfield of psychology that uses psychological theory and research to promote individual and public health. Health psychology is particularly important today because several prevalent diseases, including heart disease and cancer, are related to unhealthy lifestyles and stress (Taylor & Repetti, 1997).

Coronary Heart Disease

12.12 What are the Type A, Type B, and Type D behavior patterns?

In order to survive, the heart muscle requires a steady, sufficient supply of oxygen and nutrients carried by the blood. Coronary heart disease is caused by the narrowing or the blockage of the coronary arteries, which supply blood to the heart muscle. Although coronary heart disease remains the leading cause of death in the United States, responsible for 24% of all deaths, deaths from this cause have declined 50% during the past 35 years (National Center for Health Statistics, 2005).

A health problem of modern times, coronary heart disease is largely attributable to lifestyle and is therefore an important field of study for health psychologists.

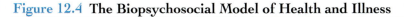

Figure 12.4 The Biopsychosocial Model of Health and Illness

The biopsychosocial model focuses on health as well as on illness and holds that both are determined by a combination of biological, psychological, and social factors. Most health psychologists endorse the biopsychosocial model.

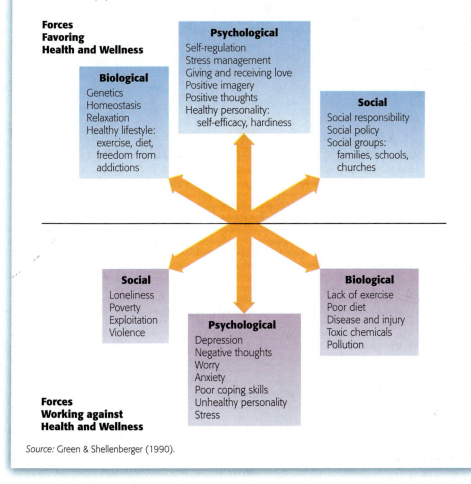

Forces Favoring Health and Wellness

Psychological
Self-regulation
Stress management
Giving and receiving love
Positive imagery
Positive thoughts
Healthy personality:
 self-efficacy, hardiness

Biological
Genetics
Homeostasis
Relaxation
Healthy lifestyle:
 exercise, diet,
 freedom from
 addictions

Social
Social responsibility
Social policy
Social groups:
 families, schools,
 churches

Social
Loneliness
Poverty
Exploitation
Violence

Biological
Lack of exercise
Poor diet
Disease and injury
Toxic chemicals
Pollution

Psychological
Depression
Negative thoughts
Worry
Anxiety
Poor coping skills
Unhealthy personality
Stress

Forces Working against Health and Wellness

Source: Green & Shellenberger (1990).

A *sedentary lifestyle*—one that includes a job at which one spends most of the time sitting and less than 20 minutes of exercise three times per week—is the primary modifiable risk factor contributing to death from coronary heart disease (Gallo et al., 2003). Other modifiable risk factors are high serum cholesterol level, cigarette smoking, and obesity.

Although not modifiable, another important risk factor is family history. The association between family history and coronary heart disease is both genetic and behavioral. For instance, individuals whose parents have high blood pressure, but who have not yet developed the disorder themselves, exhibit the same kinds of emotional reactivity and poor coping strategies as their parents (Frazer et al., 2002).

High levels of stress and job strain have also been associated with increased risk for coronary heart disease and stroke (Brydon, Magid, & Steptoe, 2006; Rosengren et al., 1991; Siegrist et al., 1990). Apparently, the effects of stress enter the bloodstream almost as if they were injected intravenously. Malkoff and others (1993) report that after an experimental group of participants had experienced laboratory-induced stress, their blood platelets (special clotting cells) released large amounts of a substance that promotes the buildup of plaque in blood vessels and may lead to heart attack and stroke. No changes were found in the blood platelets of unstressed control-group participants.

Personality type is also associated with an individual's risk of heart disease. After extensive research, cardiologists Meyer Friedman and Ray Rosenman (1974)

health psychology The subfield within psychology that is concerned with the psychological factors that contribute to health, illness, and recovery.

▲ Hostility is a key component of the Type A behavior pattern.

concluded that there are two types of personality: Type A, associated with a high rate of coronary heart disease, and Type B, commonly found in persons unlikely to develop heart disease. People with the **Type A behavior pattern** have a strong sense of time urgency and are impatient, excessively competitive, hostile, and easily angered. People with the **Type B behavior pattern** are relaxed and easygoing and are not driven by a sense of time urgency. They are not impatient or hostile and are able to relax without guilt. They play for fun and relaxation rather than to exhibit superiority over others. Yet, a Type B individual may be as bright and ambitious as a Type A person, and more successful as well.

Research indicates that the lethal core of the Type A personality is not time urgency but anger and hostility, which fuel an aggressive, reactive temperament (Smith & Ruiz, 2002). These associations have been found across cultures and in both men and women (Mohan, 2006; Olson et al., 2005).

However, careful studies have shown that anger and hostility may be part of a larger complex of variables that includes other forms of emotional distress (Kubzansky et al., 2006; Olson et al., 2005). When anger and hostility are considered as single variables, both prove to be predictive of coronary heart disease. However, when other distress variables, such as anxiety and cynicism, are added to them, statistical analyses suggest that it is the whole cluster of negative emotions that best predicts heart disease rather than any one of the variables alone.

The finding that negative emotions collectively predict coronary disease better than any one of the variables alone has led some researchers to propose a new classification, **Type D behavior pattern** ("D" for distress; Denollet, 1997). People with this profile exhibit a chronic pattern of emotional distress combined with a tendency to suppress negative emotions. In one study of men who were enrolled in a rehabilitative therapy program after having had a heart attack, those with the Type D profile were found to have four times the risk of death as other patients in the program (Sher, 2004). Researchers speculate that the high mortality rate of individuals with Type D personality may come from their body's heightened tendency to produce an inflammatory response to invasive medical procedures such as surgery (Pedersen & Denollet, 2003). However, more research is needed before the physiology associated with Type D personality will be fully understood.

Whatever the physiological link between personality and coronary disease, its relationship to both health behaviors and social support may turn out to be equally important. For example, individuals who, like those with Type D personality, tend to have a negative view of life, are less likely to abstain from tobacco after completing a smoking cessation program (Hooten et al., 2005). Furthermore, researchers have found that Type D personality in the partners of patients who have coronary heart disease impair these partners' ability to be supportive (Pedersen, van Domburg, & Theuns, 2004). As you can see, the ramifications of personality for heart disease may turn out to be quite comprehensive.

Type A behavior pattern
A behavior pattern marked by a sense of time urgency, impatience, excessive competitiveness, hostility, and anger; considered a risk factor in coronary heart disease.

Type B behavior pattern
A behavior pattern marked by a relaxed, easygoing approach to life, without the time urgency, impatience, and hostility of the Type A pattern.

Type D behavior pattern A behavior pattern marked by chronic emotional distress combined with a tendency to suppress negative emotions.

Cancer

12.13 How do psychological factors influence cancer patients' quality of life?

Cancer is the second leading cause of death in the United States, accounting for 20% of all deaths (National Center for Health Statistics, 2005). Cancer rates have dropped somewhat since the early 1990s. In 1990, 4.8% of the population was newly diagnosed with some type of cancer. In 2002, the rate was just 4.3%. Public health researchers attribute this decrease to a reduction in the number of people who smoke.

Cancer, a collection of diseases rather than a single illness, can invade cells in any part of a living organism—humans, other animals, and even plants. Normal cells in all parts of the body divide, but fortunately they have built-in instructions about when to stop dividing. Unlike normal cells, cancer cells do not stop dividing. And, unless caught in time and destroyed, they continue to grow and spread, eventually killing the organism. Health psychologists point out that an unhealthy diet, smoking, excessive alcohol consumption, promiscuous sexual behavior, or becoming sexually active in the early teens (especially for females) are all behaviors that increase the risk of cancer.

The half million people in the United States who are diagnosed with cancer each year have the difficult task of adjusting to a potentially life-threatening disease and the chronic stressors associated with it. Thus, researchers claim that cancer patients need more than medical treatment. Their therapy should include help with psychological and behavioral factors that can influence their quality of life. Although there is no evidence that such interventions affect the course of the disease itself, they have been shown to enable patients to maintain a positive emotional state and to cope more effectively with pain (Goodwin et al., 2001). Studies have also shown that psychotherapy initiated soon after the cancer diagnosis is made helps women cope with the changes in physical appearance that usually result from cancer treatment (Vos et al., 2006).

▲ This group of cancer patients is involved in art therapy, which is believed to lower the stress level associated with having a serious illness.

The Immune System and Stress

Composed of an army of highly specialized cells and organs, the immune system works to identify and search out and destroy bacteria, viruses, fungi, parasites, and any other foreign matter that may enter the body. The key components of the immune system are white blood cells known as **lymphocytes,** which include B cells and T cells. *B cells* are so named because they are produced in the bone marrow. *T cells* derive their name from the thymus gland where they are produced. All cells foreign to the body, such as bacteria, viruses, and so on, are known as *antigens*. B cells produce proteins called *antibodies*, which are highly effective in destroying antigens that live in the bloodstream and in the fluid surrounding body tissues (Paul, 1993). T cells are critically important for defeating harmful foreign invaders that have taken up residence inside the body's cells.

The immune system may turn on healthy cells or specific organs and attack them, as happens in autoimmune diseases such as juvenile diabetes, multiple sclerosis, rheumatoid arthritis, and lupus. Moreover, the system itself may be the target of a disease-causing organism. In Chapter 11, you learned about *acquired immune deficiency syndrome (AIDS)*, which is caused by the *human immunodeficiency virus (HIV)*. The virus attacks the T cells, gradually but relentlessly weakening the immune system until it is essentially nonfunctional. **Psychoneuroimmunology** is a field of study in which psychologists, biologists, and medical researchers combine their expertise to learn the effects of psychological factors—emotions, thinking, and behavior—on the immune system (Cohen, 1996). Researchers now know that the immune system is not just a means for fighting off foreign invaders. Rather, it is an incredibly complex, interconnected defense system working with the brain to keep the body healthy (Ader, 2000).

Psychological factors, emotions, and stress are all related to immune system functioning (Robles, Glaser, & Kiecolt-Glaser, 2005). The immune system exchanges information with the brain, and what goes on in the brain can apparently enhance or suppress the immune system. In one study, researchers gave volunteers nasal drops containing a cold virus. Within the next few days, symptoms of the viral infection rose sharply in some of the 151 women and 125 men who participated in the study, but less so or not at all in others. Participants with a rich social life in the form of frequent interactions with others—spouses, children, parents, co-workers, friends, and volunteer and religious groups—seemed to enjoy a powerful shield of protection against the virus infection. This pattern of protection held across age and racial groups, for both sexes, at all educational levels, and at every season of the year (Ader, 2000; Cohen et al., 1997).

12.14 What are the effects of stress on the immune system?

lymphocytes The white blood cells—including B cells and T cells—that are the key components of the immune system.

psychoneuroimmunology (sye-ko-NEW-ro-IM-you-NOLL-oh-gee) A field in which psychologists, biologists, and medical researchers combine their expertise to study the effects of psychological factors on the immune system.

Periods of high stress are correlated with increased symptoms of many infectious diseases, including oral and genital herpes, mononucleosis, colds, and flu. Stress can cause decreased levels of the immune system's B and T cells. Kiecolt-Glaser and others (1996) found that elderly men and women experiencing chronic stress as a result of years of caring for a spouse with Alzheimer's disease showed an impaired immune response to flu shots. Physicians have long observed that stress and anxiety can worsen autoimmune diseases. And "if fear can produce relapses [in autoimmune diseases], then even the fear of a relapse may become a self-fulfilling prophecy" (Steinman, 1993, p. 112). Stress is also associated with an increase in illness behaviors—reporting physical symptoms and seeking medical care (Cohen & Herbert, 1996; Cohen & Williamson, 1991).

Academic pressures, poor marital relationships and sleep deprivation have been linked to lowered immune response (Kiecolt-Glaser et al., 1987; Maier & Laudenslager, 1985). Several researchers have reported that severe, incapacitating depression is also related to lowered immune system activity (Herbert & Cohen, 1993; Robles, et al. 2006). For several months after the death of a spouse, the widow or widower suffers weakened immune system function and is at a higher risk of mortality. Severe bereavement weakens the immune system, increasing a person's chance of suffering from a long list of physical and mental ailments for up to 2 years following a partner's death (Prigerson et al., 1997).

Personal Factors Reducing the Impact of Stress and Illness

12.15 What four personal factors are associated with health and resistance to stress?

There are several personal factors that seem to offer protection against the effects of stress and illness.

Optimism. People who are generally optimistic tend to cope more effectively with stress, and this, in turn, may reduce their risk of illness (Seligman, 1990). An important characteristic optimists share is that they generally expect good outcomes. Such positive expectations help make them more stress-resistant than pessimists, who tend to expect bad outcomes. Researchers suspect that associations between optimism and resistance to stress are explained by the finding that, in response to similar stressors, optimists secrete lower levels of stress hormones than pessimists do (Lai et al., 2005). An especially lethal form of pessimism is hopelessness. A longitudinal study of a large number of Finnish men revealed that participants who reported feeling moderate to high hopelessness died from all causes at two to three times the rates of those reporting low or no hopelessness (Everson et al., 1996).

▲ Have you noticed that you get more colds during mid-terms and finals? If so, then your experience fits with research showing that stress is associated with an increased incidence of such illnesses.

Hardiness. Studying male executives with high levels of stress, psychologist Suzanne Kobasa (1979; Kobasa et al., 1982) found three psychological characteristics that distinguished those who remained healthy from those who had a high incidence of illness. The three qualities, which she referred to collectively as **hardiness,** are *commitment*, *control*, and *challenge*. Hardy individuals feel a strong sense of commitment to both their work and their personal life. They see themselves not as victims of whatever life brings, but as people who have control over consequences and outcomes. They act to solve their own problems, and they welcome challenges in life, viewing them not as threats but as opportunities for growth and improvement. Other researchers have found that the dimensions of hardiness are related to the sense of well-being among the elderly and parents of children who have severe disabilities (Ben-Zur, Duvdevany, & Lury, 2005; Smith, Young, & Lee, 2004).

hardiness A combination of three psychological qualities—commitment, control, and challenge—shared by people who can handle high levels of stress and remain healthy.

Religious Involvement. Another personal factor that contributes to resistance to stress and illness is religious faith (Dedert et al., 2004; Miller & Thoresen, 2003). One longitudinal study (conducted over a period of 28 years) revealed that frequent attendance at religious services is correlated with better health habits (Strawbridge et al., 1997). A meta-analysis of 42 separate studies combined data on some 126,000 individuals and revealed that religious involvement is positively associated with measures of physical health and lower rates of cancer, heart disease, and stroke (McCullough et al., 2000). Also, measures of religious involvement were reliable predictors of greater longevity when all causes of mortality were considered. The specific measures of religious involvement most closely related to a lower mortality rate were regular attendance at worship services, religious orthodoxy, and a personal sense of comfort and strength from one's religion (McCullough et al., 2000). This study and others have found the association between religious involvement and lower mortality to be stronger for women than for men (Hummer et al., 1999; Strawbridge et al., 1997).

Why is religious involvement linked to health? Researchers are currently examining a number of hypotheses (Powell et al., 2003). One proposal is that individuals who frequent religious services experience proportionately more positive emotions than those who do not attend. Another is that religious involvement provides people with a stronger form of social support than is available to those who are not religious. Essentially, this hypothesis claims that social support may be more meaningful, and more effective, when it comes from others who share your world view. Researchers have also proposed that religious practices, specifically meditation and prayer, may have positive effects on health-related physiological variables such as blood pressure (Seeman et al., 2003). Researchers have also noted that the association between religious practice and health-related behaviors such as smoking should not be overlooked (Timberlake et al., 2006). That is, at least part of the association between religion and health may derive from some members' adherence to religiously based prohibitions of behaviors that threaten health.

▲ A strong social support network can help a person recover faster from an illness.

Social Support. Another factor contributing to better health is **social support** (Cohen, 1988; Kaplan et al., 1994). Social support is support provided, usually in time of need, by a spouse, other family members, friends, neighbors, colleagues, support groups, or others. It can involve tangible aid, information, and advice, as well as emotional support. It can also be viewed as the feeling of being loved, valued, and cared for by those toward whom we feel a similar obligation.

Social support appears to have positive effects on the body's immune system as well as on the cardiovascular and endocrine systems (Bouhuys et al., 2004; Holt-Lunstad et al., 2003; Miller et al., 2002; Uchino et al., 1996). Social support may help encourage health-promoting behaviors and reduce the impact of stress so that people are less likely to resort to unhealthy methods of coping, such as smoking or drinking. Further, social support has been shown to reduce depression and enhance self-esteem in individuals who suffer from chronic illnesses such as kidney disease (Symister & Friend, 2003). And a large study of soldiers who had enlisted in the U.S. Army showed that a high level of social support from peers was an essential ingredient in reducing stress (Bliese & Castro, 2000). People with social support recover more quickly from illnesses and lower their risk of death from specific diseases. Social support may even increase the probability of surviving a heart attack because it buffers the impact of stress on cardiovascular function (Steptoe, 2000). A longitudinal study of 4,775 people over a 9-year period found that those low in social support died at twice the rate of those high in social support (Berkman & Syme, 1979).

In recent years, social support researchers have begun to distinguish between *perceived support,* the degree to which a person believes help is available when needed, and *received support,* the actual help a person receives from others. Interestingly, many have found that perceived support is more important than received support (Norris &

social support Tangible and/or emotional support provided in time of need by family members, friends, and others; the feeling of being loved, valued, and cared for by those toward whom we feel a similar obligation.

Kaniasty, 1996; Reinhardt et al., 2006). Other research has shown that high levels of perceived social support are associated with lower levels of depression and even with recovery from depression (Lara et al., 1997). Such perceived support may be more a function of individual personality than of the actual availability of family and friends who can offer help. One longitudinal study found that college-aged participants who had sociable, outgoing personalities were more likely to report having high levels of perceived social support later in adulthood (Von Dras & Siegler, 1997). These results underscore the importance of psychological variables in health.

Gender and Health

12.16 How do males and females differ with regard to health?

Most medical research in the past, primarily funded by the U.S. government, rejected women as participants in favor of men (Matthews et al., 1997). One area where the failure to study women's health care needs has been particularly evident is in research examining mortality risk following open-heart surgery. Women are more likely to die after such surgery than are men. To date, studies have shown that the gender gap in surgical survival narrows with age, but researchers are still investigating why women's postsurgical mortality rate is higher than men's (Vaccarino et al., 2002).

In general, however, men have higher death rates from all causes than women do, although women tend to be less healthy. These seemingly contradictory findings have puzzled researchers for decades (Rieker & Bird, 2005). The finding that women are more likely than men are to seek medical care explains some of this difference (Addis & Mahalik, 2003). However, differences in care-seeking fall short of fully explaining gender differences in illness and death.

In recent years, researchers have begun to examine how the progression of potentially fatal diseases varies across gender (Case & Paxson, 2004). For example, lung diseases that are caused by smoking afflict women and men about equally. However, for unknown reasons, men with these diseases are more seriously ill, as indicated by gender differences in the frequency of hospitalization, and males are more likely to die from them than are women. Researchers are looking at physiological gender differences such as hormone levels in search of explanations for these patterns. Some have also pointed out that interactions among gender differences in the physiological, psychological, and social domains must be examined as well (Rieker & Bird, 2005).

Race and Health

12.17 How does racial patterning contribute to health differences across groups?

Like gender, racial categories are associated with different patterns of health outcomes. Remember as you read that, as we have stated many times before, there is more variability within each of these groups than there is between them. In addition, the methods used to collect health statistics often obscure important variations among subgroups of the five major groups—White Americans, African Americans, Hispanic Americans, Asian Americans and Pacific Islanders, and Native Americans—whose health is tracked by government agencies. Here are a few highlights from the many findings in this area.

Group Differences in Health. African Americans have higher rates of many chronic conditions than do White Americans. For example, they have higher rates of diabetes, arthritis, and high blood pressure (National Center for Health Statistics, 2005). African Americans are 40% more likely than White Americans to die of heart disease and 30% more likely to die of cancer. Even when African and White Americans of the same age suffer from similar illnesses, the mortality rate of African Americans is higher (CDC, 2003a). And the rate of AIDS is more than three times higher among African Americans than among White Americans.

Hispanic Americans account for more than 20% of new tuberculosis cases in the United States (CDC, 2003a). Hypertension and diabetes are also more prevalent among Hispanic Americans than among non-Hispanic White Americans, but heart problems are less prevalent (CDC, 2005). Rates of diabetes are also dramatically higher among Native Americans than for other groups (CDC, 2005). In addition, the infant mortality rate among Native Americans is two times higher than among Whites (CDC, 2005).

Asian Americans, are comparatively healthy. However, there are wide disparities among subgroups. For example, Vietnamese women are five times more likely to suffer from cervical cancer than White women are (CDC, 2005). Similarly, the overall age-adjusted death rate for Asian American males is 40% lower than that for White American males, but their death rate from stroke is 8% higher.

Among Native Americans, cancer rates are higher than they are among other groups (NCHS, 2005). Public health officials attribute this difference to high smoking rates among Native Americans. As a result, Native Americans not only get more cancers than people in other groups, but also about 10% of them suffer from chronic lung diseases. Rates of diabetes are also dramatically higher among Native Americans than for other groups (CDC, 2003).

Explaining Group Differences. How can such differences be explained? One health-related factor that distinguishes racial groups is the incidence of poverty (Franks, Gold, & Fiscella, 2003). About a quarter of African Americans, Native Americans, and Hispanic Americans live in poverty (U.S. Census Bureau, 2004). Thus, we might conclude that variables related to poverty—nutritional status, access to health care, and education, for example—explain racial differences in health.

However, studies that provide us with a closer look at the links among race, income, and health suggest otherwise. For instance, in one study, researchers found that the general health of African American and White children from middle-class families was quite similar; however, the African American children had much higher rates of asthma than did the White children in the study (Weitzman, Byrd, & Auinger, 2005). Large-scale studies of health trends also show that poor White Americans and African Americans have similar rates of health-related activity limitations in old age (NCHS, 2005). However, the rate of such limitations is nearly 50% less among older Hispanic Americans who live in poverty.

Another interesting phenomenon that appears when researchers closely examine the connection between income and health is that this relationship can vary across groups. Such examples can be found in the research on obesity in males and females in different racial groups and different income groups (Chang, 2005). Among White American men, low income is associated with obesity, but among Mexican American and African American men, those with high incomes are more likely to be obese than those with who are poor. And the pattern is different among women. Like their male counterparts, White American women with higher incomes are less likely to be obese than those with lower incomes. African American women show an inconsistent pattern, with obesity rates rising faster among middle-income than high- or low-income groups. Among Mexican American women, there appears to be no association between income and obesity.

As these findings illustrate, group differences in socioeconomic factors do not fully account for group differences in health, so what other variables might contribute to them? Bioethics professor Pilar Ossorio and sociologist Troy Duster suggest that the phenomenon of *racial patterning* underlies such differences. Racial patterning is the tendency of groups of people to maintain their collective identities through shared behavior patterns. Moreover, groups tend to share certain aspects of living conditions that may have health consequences as well (e.g., the concentration of Hispanic Americans in the semi-tropical and desert regions of the southwestern United States). As a result of these patterns, risk and protective factors occur at different rates in different groups.

Here is an example of how racial patterning works with regard to a health risk. In the United States, Asian Americans, Pacific Islanders, and the Native American groups of the Pacific coast region consume larger quantities of fish than people in other groups. This pattern is derived from the traditional diets these groups have followed for many generations. However, today pollution of the oceans has resulted in the presence of high levels of mercury in fish. Consequently, individuals who eat a lot of fish are at risk for mercury poisoning. Moreover, when fish consumption distinguishes a particular racial group from others, comparative mercury levels may distinguish that group as well. This is precisely what researchers have found among Asian Americans, Pacific Islanders, and the Native Americans of the Pacific coast. That is, individuals in these groups tend to have higher average levels of mercury in their systems than people in other groups (Hightower, O'Hare, & Hernandez, 2006). Of course, such findings don't imply that all members of these groups consume a lot of fish or that they all have high levels of mercury. Rather, the prevalence of this pattern in these groups, as compared to others, skews group averages with regard to the risks associated with eating fish. Furthermore, to fully understand group differences, researchers must study each kind of outcome difference separately and determine which racially patterned variables best explain it. Consequently, it is likely to be some time before we have a comprehensive explanation of racial group differences in health.

Studying race differences in health and the patterns of behavior that contribute to them is important to the development of social policy and to improving behavioral scientists' understanding of the human experience. However, it is vital to remember that the health outcomes associated with lifestyle factors such as smoking, alcohol consumption, exercise, and diet are the same for all groups. Thus, taking steps to ensure that individuals across all racial groups are aware of these factors is likely to bring about improvements in health for all concerned (Beets & Pitetti, 2004; CDC, 2005).

Remember It   Health and Illness

1. The biomedical model focuses on _____; the biopsychosocial model also emphasizes _____.

2. Research suggests that the most harmful component of the Type A behavior pattern is _____.

3. Quality of life is associated with _____ among cancer patients.

4. Lowered immune response has been associated with _____.

5. Hardiness includes _____, _____, and _____.

6. In general, women are (healthier/less healthy) than men, and men are (more/less) likely to die from most diseases.

7. A phenomenon called _____ has been proposed to explain group differences in health.

Answers: 1. illness, health; 2. hostility; 3. optimism; 4. stress; 5. commitment, control, challenge; 6. less healthy, more 7. racial patterning

---

Lifestyle and Health

Think about your own health for a moment. What do you think is the greatest threat to your personal well-being and longevity? For most Americans, health enemy number one is their own habits—lack of exercise, too little sleep, alcohol or drug abuse, an unhealthy diet, and overeating. What can make someone change an unhealthy lifestyle? Perhaps vanity is the key. Researchers have found that people are more likely to adopt healthy behaviors if they believe behavioral change will make them look better or appear more youthful than if they simply receive information about the health benefits of the suggested change (Mahler et al., 2003). Still, there are some health-threatening behaviors that carry such grave risks that everyone ought to take them seriously. The most dangerous unhealthy behavior of all is smoking.

Smoking and Health

Smoking remains the foremost cause of preventable diseases and deaths in the United States (U.S. Department of Health and Human Services, 2000). That message appears to be taking root because the prevalence of smoking among American adults has been decreasing and is currently under 25% (National Center for Health Statistics, 2005). Moreover, smoking is more likely to be viewed as a socially unacceptable behavior now than in the past (Chassin et al., 2003). But there are wide variations in smoking habits according to gender and ethnic group. The highest rates of smoking are found among Native American men (33%) and women (31%), whereas the lowest rates are reported for Asian American men (17%) and women (6%) (NCHS, 2005).

12.18 Why is smoking the most dangerous health-threatening behavior?

Even though the prevalence of smoking is decreasing, every year more than 1 million young Americans become regular smokers, and more than 400,000 American adults die from diseases related to tobacco use (U.S. Department of Health and Human Services, 2000). Smoking increases the risk for heart disease, lung cancer, other cancers that are smoking-related, and emphysema. It is now known that smoking suppresses the action of T cells in the lungs, increasing susceptibility to respiratory tract infections and tumors (McCue et al., 2000).

Other negative consequences from smoking include the widespread incidence of chronic bronchitis and other respiratory problems; the deaths and injuries from fires caused by smoking; and the low birthweight and retarded

▲ There are many effective ways to quit smoking, but aiming for a "quit date" during a time period when they know their stress levels will be reduced may help some smokers follow through on their good intentions.

fetal development in babies born to smoking mothers. Furthermore, mothers who smoke during pregnancy tend to have babies who are at greater risk for anxiety and depression and are five times more likely to become smokers themselves (Cornelius et al., 2000). And millions of nonsmokers engage in *passive smoking* by breathing smoke-filled air—with proven ill effects. Research indicates that nonsmokers who are regularly exposed to *second-hand smoke* have a 30% greater risk of developing heart disease than those who are not exposed (National Center for Chronic Disease Prevention and Health Promotion, 2006).

There are many ways to quit smoking, but overall success rates for these methods, or for smoking cessation in general, can be somewhat misleading. There are many variables that affect success rates other than the desire to quit and the cessation method that a person chooses. Thus, if a study shows that only 20% of smokers using nicotine replacement, such as patches or chewing gum, succeed, reasons other than the purely physical aspects of nicotine addiction may be to blame (Rose, 2006).

The circumstances in smokers' lives may affect the outcome of their attempts to quit smoking. In one study involving more than 600 college students, researchers found that those who perceived that their lives were not very stressful had more success than other participants who felt more stress (Norman et al., 2006). Participants' overall success rate over the 18-month-long study was only 18%, but the low-perceived-stress group achieved a success rate of 52%. By contrast, only 13% of participants who perceived their lives to be highly stressful managed to quit in 18 months. The implication of these findings for others who want to quit smoking is that the often-heard recommendation that they choose a "quit date" is probably good advice. Planning a quit date to coincide with times of reduced stress, such as immediately after final exams, might be better than trying to quit at time of great stress.

Alcohol Abuse

12.19 What are some health risks of alcohol abuse?

Do you use alcohol regularly? Many Americans do. Recall from Chapter 4 that *substance abuse* is defined as continued use of a substance that interferes with a person's major life roles at home, in school, at work, or elsewhere and contributes to legal difficulties or any psychological problems (American Psychiatric Association, 2000). Alcohol is perhaps the most frequently abused substance of all, and the health costs of alcohol abuse are staggering—in fatalities, medical bills, lost work, and family problems.

When consumed to excess alcohol can damage virtually every organ in the body, but it is especially harmful to the liver and is the major cause of cirrhosis, one of the top 15 causes of death in the United States (CDC, 2002). Other causes of death are more common in alcoholics than in nonalcoholics as well. One Norwegian longitudinal study involving more than 40,000 male participants found that the rate of death prior to age 60 was significantly higher among alcoholics than nonalcoholics (Rossow & Amundsen, 1997). Alcoholics are about three times as likely to die in automobile accidents or of heart disease as nonalcoholics, and they have twice the rate of deaths from cancer.

Damage to the brains of alcoholics has been found by researchers using MRI scans (Daurignac et al., 2005). CT scans also show brain shrinkage in a high percentage of alcoholics, even in those who are young and in those who show normal cognitive functioning (Lishman, 1990). Moreover, heavy drinking can cause cognitive impairment that continues for several months after the drinking stops (Sullivan et al., 2002). The only good news in recent studies is that some of the effects of alcohol on the brain seem to be partially reversible with prolonged abstinence.

One of the aspects of alcohol use that many people overlook is the possibility that it will interfere with or enhance the effects of other substances. For example, both alcohol and the popular pain reliever acetaminophen (Tylenol) have the potential to harm the liver if taken to excess. The combination of the two greatly increases the risk of liver damage, so experts advise drinkers to abstain from alcohol when taking acetaminophen, and vice versa (NIAAA, 2004). Similarly, antihistamines should not be taken while consuming alcohol because the alcohol amplifies the drowsiness that often accompanies these medications.

Since the late 1950s, the American Medical Association has maintained that alcoholism is a disease, and once an alcoholic, always an alcoholic. According to this view, even a small amount of alcohol can cause an irresistible craving for more, leading alcoholics to lose control of their drinking (Jellinek, 1960). Thus, total abstinence is seen as the only acceptable and effective method of treatment. Alcoholics Anonymous (AA) also endorses both the disease concept and the total abstinence approach to treatment. And there is a drug that may make abstinence somewhat easier. Researchers report that the drug acamprosate helps prevent relapse in recovering alcoholics (Mason et al., 2006).

▲ At Case Western Reserve University, special living arrangements are available for students who are recovering from substance use problems. To be eligible to live in Recovery House, as it is called, students must develop an individual recovery plan in consultation with a university counselor. The plan includes participation in Alcoholics Anonymous groups and a commitment to sobriety. Officials at Case believe that the program prevents students with substance use problems from relapsing after they have expressed a desire to overcome these problems.

Some studies suggest a genetic influence on alcoholism and lend support to the disease model. For example, neuroscientist Henri Begleiter and his colleagues have accumulated a large body of evidence suggesting that the brains of alcoholics respond differently to visual and auditory stimuli than do the brains of nonalcoholics (Hada et al., 2000, 2001; Prabhu et al., 2001). Further, many relatives of alcoholics, even children and adults who have never consumed any alcohol in their lives, display the same types of response patterns (Kamarajan et al., 2006; Zhang et al., 2001). The relatives of alcoholics who do display these patterns are more likely to become alcoholics themselves or to suffer from other types of addictions (Anokhin et al., 2000; Bierut et al., 1998). Consequently, Begleiter has suggested that the brain-imaging techniques he uses in his research may someday be used to determine which relatives of alcoholics are genetically predisposed to addiction (Porjesz et al., 1998).

Diet

In Chapter 10, you learned about obesity as it relates to the primary motive of hunger and that a BMI in excess of 30 is considered obese. Obesity increases a person's chances of developing several chronic diseases (CDC, 2006b). These conditions include high blood pressure, type 2 diabetes, gallbladder disease, arthritis, and respiratory disorders. In addition, people who are obese are more likely to develop coronary heart disease and to have elevated levels of LDL cholesterol (the bad cholesterol that is associated with heart disease).

12.20 How does diet influence health?

Health problems may also develop in people whose diets have insufficient amounts of particular nutrients (CDC, 2006b). For example, a diet that is deficient in iron leads to *anemia*, a condition that impairs the blood's ability to deliver oxygen to the body's organs. Likewise, a diet that lacks sufficient calcium may cause degeneration of the bones. And among pregnant women, those whose diets lack folic acid are more likely to deliver infants with spinal defects.

People who regularly consume fast foods are at risk for both obesity and specific nutritional deficiencies. Thus, nutrition experts recommend that such food be eaten infrequently or not at all. To help consumers achieve this goal, experts have also developed several strategies for improving overall diet quality. One simple approach is the "5-a-day" plan in which people are advised to try to eat at least five servings of fruits and vegetables every day. Another involves reading the labels of processed foods and avoiding those that are high in saturated fats, transfats, and sodium, all of which are associated with high levels of LDL cholesterol. Labels can also guide people to foods that are high in monosaturated fats, a type of fat that may increase levels of HDL cholesterol (the good cholesterol).

For people who want more detailed information about what to eat, the U.S. Department of Health and Human Services publishes dietary guidelines every five years based on the latest nutritional research. The most recent edition of these guidelines was published in 2005 and is available at http://www.healthierus.gov/dietaryguidelines/. Note, however, that dietary recommendations are always accompanied by guidelines for physical exercise, because, when it comes to maintaining health, the two go hand in hand.

▲ Strength training moderates the effects of aging on older adults' muscles and bones.

Exercise

How much exercise do you get? Many studies show that regular exercise pays rich dividends in the form of physical and mental fitness. However, many people still express reluctance to exercise. Some simply prefer not to be physically active; others blame such factors as the cost of joining a health club or even the unpredictability of the weather for their lack of physical activity (Salmon et al., 2003). Such individuals are missing out on one of the simplest and most effective ways of enhancing one's health.

Aerobic exercise (such as running, swimming, brisk walking, bicycling, rowing, and jumping rope) is exercise that uses the large muscle groups in continuous, repetitive action and increases oxygen intake and breathing and heart rates. To improve cardiovascular fitness and endurance and to lessen the risk of heart attack, an individual should perform aerobic exercise regularly—five times a week for 20–30 minutes (CDC, 2006c). Individuals who engage in more than 3 hours of aerobic activity each week are more successful at losing excess weight and keeping it off than are those who exercise less (Votruba et al., 2000).

Exercise also appears to moderate the effects of aging on the body. Strength training, for example, has been found to reduce *sarcopenia*, an age-related process in which the muscles deteriorate (CDC, 2006c). Such training appears to prevent the loss of bone mass, or *osteoporosis*, as well. Moreover, physical exercise helps seniors with balance, coordination, and stamina.

Alternative Medicine

Do you take vitamins or herbal supplements in hopes of positively influencing your health? According to surveys, Americans spend billions of dollars each year on unconventional treatments—herbs, massage, self-help groups, megavitamins, folk remedies, and homeopathy—for a variety of illnesses and conditions. In one such survey, the National Science Foundation (NSF, 2002) found that 88% of Americans believe that there are valid ways of preventing and curing illnesses that are not recognized by medical professionals.

The National Science Foundation (2002) defines **alternative medicine** as any treatment or therapy that has not been scientifically demonstrated to be effective. Even a simple practice such as taking vitamins sometimes falls into this category. For instance, *scurvy* (a condition whose symptoms include bleeding gums and easy bruising) has been scientifically determined to be caused by vitamin C deficiency. So, taking vitamin C to prevent or cure scurvy is not considered an alternative therapy. However, if you take vitamin C to protect yourself against the common cold, you are using alternative medicine because vitamin C has not been scientifically proven to prevent colds.

If alternative treatments lack scientific support, why do so many people believe in them? One possibility is that it is easier to take a vitamin than to make a lifestyle change. But it is also true that people who do their own research about alternative therapies may happen upon effective treatments of which their physicians are unaware. However, most patients who use alternative treatments do not inform their physicians about them. Health professionals cite this tendency toward secrecy as a major risk factor in the use of alternative medicine (Yale-New Haven Hospital, 2003). They point out that many therapies, especially those that involve food supplements, have pharmacological effects that can interfere with treatments prescribed by physicians. Consequently, individuals who use alternative treatments should tell their physicians about them. Although doctors may be skeptical about the utility of the alternative treatments, they need to have this information about their patients in order to practice conventional medicine effectively. Moreover, faith in an alternative treatment may cause an individual to delay seeking necessary conventional medical treatment.

aerobic exercise (ah-RO-bik) Exercise that uses the large muscle groups in continuous, repetitive action and increases oxygen intake and breathing and heart rates.

alternative medicine Any treatment or therapy that has not been scientifically demonstrated to be effective.

Although it is true that some alternative therapies may be helpful in both preventing and treating illness, most health professionals agree that lifestyle changes bring greater health benefits than do any methods of alternative medicine. Unfortunately, many people resist making lifestyle changes because they see them as taking too long to be effective or being too difficult to carry out. A smoker may think, "I've been smoking so long, quitting now won't make a difference." An obese person may be so overwhelmed by the amount of weight loss necessary to attain an ideal weight that she or he gives up. However, Table 12.2 shows that the benefits of various lifestyle changes, some of which are fairly easy to achieve, can be well worth the effort. And remember, to be healthier, you don't have to make *all* of the changes. You might consider starting with just one. Even if you never make another change, you are likely to live longer and be healthier than you would have otherwise.

Table 12.2 Benefits of Lifestyle Changes

Lifestyle Change	Benefits
If overweight, lose just 10 pounds.	34% reduction in triglyceride levels; 16% decrease in total cholesterol; 18% increase in HDL ("good" cholesterol); significant reduction in blood pressure; decreased risk of diabetes, sleep apnea, and osteoarthritis (Still, 2001).
Add 20 to 30 grams of fiber to your diet each day.	Improved bowel function; reduced risk of colon cancer and other digestive-system diseases; decrease in total cholesterol; reduced blood pressure; improved insulin function in both diabetics and nondiabetics (HCF, 2003).
Engage in moderate physical activity every day (e.g., walk up and down stairs for 15 minutes; spend 30 minutes washing a car).	Reduced feelings of anxiety and sadness; increased bone density; reduced risk of diabetes, heart disease, high blood pressure, and many other life-shortening diseases (CDC, 1999).
Stop smoking at any age, after any number of years of smoking.	*Immediate:* improved circulation; reduced blood level of carbon monoxide; stabilization of pulse rate and blood pressure; improved sense of smell and taste; improved lung function and endurance; reduced risk of lung infections such as pneumonia and bronchitis. *Long-term:* reduced risk of lung cancer (declines substantially with each year of abstinence); decreased risk of other smoking-related illnesses such as emphysema and heart disease; decreased risk of cancer recurrence in those who have been treated for some form of cancer (National Cancer Institute, 2000).
Get recommended annual or 5-year screenings beginning at these ages	*Women:* (21) Chlamydia, cervical cancer, screenings if sexually active; (35), cholesterol test; (50) mammogram, colorectal exam; (65) vision, hearing tests *Men:* (30) EKG, cholesterol test; (40) PSA test for prostate cancer; (50) colorectal exam; (65) vision, hearing tests

Remember It   Lifestyle and Health

1. The greatest threat to Americans' health and longevity is a(n) _____.

2. _____ is the leading preventable cause of disease and death.

3. Excessive intake of _____ can damage virtually every organ in the body.

4. People whose diet includes a large quantity of fast food are at risk of developing _____ and _____.

5. Cardiovascular fitness and endurance can be improved through _____.

6. _____ may be a more effective way of enhancing health than turning to alternative medicine.

Answers: 1. unhealthy lifestyle; 2. Smoking; 3. alcohol; 4. obesity, nutritional deficiencies; 5. aerobic exercise; 6. Lifestyle changes

Apply It   Interpreting Health Information on the Internet

An increasing number of people are turning to the Internet for information about their health. Stereotypes might lead us to believe that the Internet is an important source of health information only in high-tech societies. However, surveys of teenagers in the developing African nation of Ghana found that 53% percent of adolescents in that country routinely use the Internet to research health-related topics (Borzekowski, Fobil, & Asante, 2006).

Many people use the Internet to search for information about health conditions they have or believe themselves to be at risk for. One study of 188 women with breast cancer found that about half of them used the Internet to find out more about the disease (Fogel et al., 2002). Surveys of older adults and HIV-positive individuals have shown that using the Internet helps them gain a sense of control over their health care decisions (Kalichman et al., 2003; McMellon & Schiffman, 2002). Chat rooms devoted to specific diseases may represent an important source of social support for patients, especially those suffering from rare disorders (Kummervold et al., 2002). And using email to coach and encourage patients in the management of chronic diseases such as diabetes has proven to be effective both for patients' health and for health care professionals' time management (McKay et al., 2002).

But how reliable is the information available on the Internet? In a large-scale study of health-related web sites sponsored by the American Medical Association, researchers found that the quality of information varied widely from one site to another (Eysenbach et al., 2002). A study of Internet-based advice for managing children's fever sponsored by the British Medical Association found that most web sites contained erroneous information. Moreover, in a follow-up study 4 years later, the researchers found that about half the sites were no longer available; those that remained showed little improvement in the quality of information.

Despite these difficulties, physicians' organizations acknowledge the potential value of the Internet in helping patients learn about and manage their own health. And because so many older adults are using the Internet to learn about health issues, the American Association of Retired Persons (2002) has published a list of points to keep in mind when surfing the Web for health information and advice:

- *Remember that there are no rules governing what is published on the Internet.* Unlike scientific journal articles, which are usually written and reviewed by experts in the field, Internet articles can be posted by anyone, without review of any kind. Without expert knowledge, it is extremely difficult to tell whether the information and advice these articles contain are valid.

- *Consider the source.* Generally, web sites sponsored by medical schools, government agencies, and public health organizations are reliable. Others, especially those promoting a health-related product, should be considered suspect.

- *Get a second opinion.* Ask your health care provider about Internet-based information, or read what's available from several different sources on the topic.

- *Examine references.* Sites that refer to credible sources (e.g., books, other web sites) that you can find on the Internet or in a library or bookstore are probably more reliable than sites that offer no references to support their advice.

- *How current is the information?* Health-related information changes frequently. Be certain that you are reading the most current findings and recommendations.

- *Is it too good to be true?* As in all areas of life, if something sounds too good to be true (e.g., a vitamin that cures cancer), it probably is. Try to find experimental, placebo-controlled studies that support any claims.

Using these guidelines, you can become a better consumer of Internet-based health information.

✳ Summary and Review

Sources of Stress p. 425

12.1 What was the Social Readjustment Rating Scale designed to reveal? p. 425

The SRRS assesses stress in terms of life events, positive or negative, that necessitate change and adaptation. Holmes and Rahe found a relationship between degree of life stress (as measured on the scale) and major health problems.

12.2 What roles do hassles and uplifts play in the stress of life, according to Lazarus? p. 427

According to Lazarus, daily hassles typically cause more stress than major life changes. Positive experiences in life—or uplifts—can neutralize the effects of many of the hassles, however.

12.3 How do choice-related conflicts and lack of control contribute to stress? p. 428

In an approach-approach conflict, a person must decide between equally desirable alternatives. In an avoidance-avoidance conflict, the choice is between two undesirable alternatives. In an approach-avoidance conflict, a person is both drawn to and repelled by a single choice. Stressors that are unpredictable and uncontrollable have greater impact than those that are predictable and controllable.

12.4 For people to function effectively and find satisfaction on the job, what nine variables should fall within their comfort zone? p. 429

The nine variables that should fall within a worker's comfort zone are workload, clarity of job description and evaluation criteria, physical variables, job status, accountability, task variety, human contact, physical challenge, and mental challenge.

12.5 How do people typically react to catastrophic events? p. 430

Most people cope quite well with catastrophic events. However, some people develop posttraumatic stress disorder (PTSD), a prolonged, severe stress reaction, often characterized by flashbacks, nightmares, or intrusive memories of the traumatic event.

12.6 How might historical racism affect the health of African Americans? p. 430

Some researchers believe that African Americans have greater levels of high blood pressure than members of other groups because of stress due to historical racism. African Americans who express high levels of concern about racism display larger cardiovascular responses to experimentally induced stressors than do their peers who express lower levels of concern.

12.7 How are socioeconomic status and health related? p. 431

People of low socioeconomic status have more stress-related health problems than those of higher status. Perceived status may predict these outcomes better than objective status. Unemployment is another status variable that is related to health.

Responding to Stress p. 433

12.8 What is the general adaptation syndrome? p. 433

The general adaptation syndrome (GAS) proposed by Selye is the predictable sequence of reactions that organisms show in response to stressors. It consists of the alarm stage, the resistance stage, and the exhaustion stage.

12.9 What are the roles of primary and secondary appraisals when a person is confronted with a potentially stressful event? p. 434

Lazarus maintains that when confronted with a potentially stressful event, a person engages in a cognitive appraisal process consisting of (1) a primary appraisal, to evaluate the relevance of the situation to one's well-being (whether it will be positive, irrelevant, or negative), and (2) a secondary appraisal, to evaluate one's resources and determine how to cope with the stressor.

12.10 What is the difference between problem-focused and emotion-focused coping? p. 434

Problem-focused coping is a direct response aimed at reducing, modifying, or eliminating the source of stress; emotion-focused coping involves reappraising a stressor in order to reduce its emotional impact.

Health and Illness p. 436

12.11 How do the biomedical and biopsychosocial models differ in their approaches to health and illness? p. 436

The biomedical model focuses on illness rather than on health and explains illness in terms of biological factors. The biopsychosocial model focuses on health as well as on illness and holds that both are determined by a combination of biological, psychological, and social factors.

12.12 What are the Type A, Type B, and Type D behavior patterns? p. 436

The Type A behavior pattern, often cited as a risk factor for coronary heart disease, is characterized by a sense of time urgency, impatience, excessive competitive drive, hostility, and easily aroused anger. The Type B behavior pattern is characterized by a relaxed, easygoing approach to life, without the time urgency, impatience, and hostility of the Type A pattern. People with the Type D behavior pattern experience high levels of negative emotions that they usually suppress.

12.13 How do psychological factors influence cancer patients' quality of life? p. 438

Cancer patients can improve their quality of life by maintaining an optimistic outlook, accepting the reality of their situation, and maintaining a sense of humor. Social support and psychotherapy can help them do so.

12.14 What are the effects of stress on the immune system? p. 439

Stress has been associated with lowered immune response and with increased symptoms of many infectious diseases.

12.15 What four personal factors are associated with health and resistance to stress? p. 440

Personal factors related to health and resistance to stress are optimism, hardiness, religious involvement, and social support.

12.16 How do males and females differ with regard to health? p. 442

Women are more likely than men to die following heart surgery. Generally, though, men are more likely than women to die from most diseases, but women are generally less healthy. When men and women have the same diseases, men are often more seriously ill. Researchers suspect these patterns may be caused by the unique physiology of each gender.

12.17 How does racial patterning contribute to health differences across groups? p. 442

Racial patterning produces correlations between race and health through its influence on group differences in risk and protective factors.

Lifestyle and Health p. 444

12.18 Why is smoking the most dangerous health-threatening behavior? p. 445

Smoking is considered the most dangerous health-related behavior because it is directly related to over 400,000 deaths each year, including deaths from heart disease, lung cancer, respiratory diseases, and stroke.

12.19 What are some health risks of alcohol abuse? p. 446

Alcohol abuse damages virtually every organ in the body, including the liver, stomach, skeletal muscles, heart, and brain. Alcoholics are three times as likely to die in motor vehicle accidents as nonalcoholics.

12.20 How does diet influence health? p. 447

Obesity is related to many chronic health conditions. Nutrient deficiencies also cause problems. Fast-food consumers are at risk for both obesity and dietary deficiencies. Guidelines based on the latest research are available to help people improve the quality of their diets.

12.21 What are some benefits of regular aerobic exercise? p. 448

Regular aerobic exercise reduces the risk of cardiovascular disease, increases muscular strength, moderates the effects of stress, makes bones denser and stronger, and helps one maintain a desirable weight.

12.22 What are the benefits and risks associated with alternative medicine? p. 448

Alternative medicine, or the use of any treatment that has not been proven scientifically to be effective, can benefit individuals who find alternative treatments that are effective. However, many patients increase their risk of poor outcomes by not telling their physicians about their use of alternative treatments. And some people delay seeking necessary conventional medical treatment because they believe that alternative approaches will work.

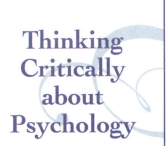

Thinking Critically about Psychology

1. In your view, which is more effective for evaluating stress: the Social Readjustment Rating Scale or the Hassle Scale? Explain the advantages and disadvantages of each.
2. Prepare two arguments: one supporting the position that alcoholism is a genetically inherited disease, and the other supporting the position that alcoholism is not a medical disease but results from learning.
3. Choose several stress-producing incidents from your life and explain the problem-focused and emotion-focused coping strategies you used. From the knowledge you have gained in this chapter, list other coping strategies that might have been more effective.

Key Terms

aerobic exercise, p. 448
alarm stage, p. 433
alternative medicine, p. 448
approach-approach conflict, p. 428
approach-avoidance conflict, p. 428
avoidance-avoidance conflict, p. 428
biomedical model, p. 436
biopsychosocial model, p. 436
burnout, p. 429
conflict, p. 428
coping, p. 434
emotion-focused coping, p. 434
exhaustion stage, p. 433

fight-or-flight response, p. 425
general adaptation syndrome (GAS), p. 433
hardiness, p. 440
hassles, p. 427
health psychology, p. 436
lymphocytes, p. 439
posttraumatic stress disorder (PTSD)
     p. 430
primary appraisal, p. 434
proactive coping, p. 439
problem-focused coping, p. 434
psychoneuroimmunology, p. 439
resistance stage, p. 433

secondary appraisal, p. 434
Social Readjustment Rating Scale (SRRS),
     p. 425
social support, p. 441
socioeconomic status, p. 431
stress, p. 425
stressor, p. 425
Type A behavior pattern, p. 438
Type B behavior pattern, p. 438
Type D behavior pattern, p. 438
uplifts, p. 428

Chapter 13

Personality Theory and Assessment

Perhaps you have heard of a song by Irish recording artist Ronan Keating that compares life to a ride at an amusement park. From a psychological perspective, this is an apt metaphor. Think about it. When you are riding on a roller coaster, as you are enjoying the thrills that go along with its ups and downs and its twists and turns, transient flashes of utter terror are balanced by the knowledge that, eventually, the ride will be over. When you exit the ride, you know that you will once again find yourself safely and securely on level ground, although you may feel a bit wobbly for a few minutes afterward. Soon, though, your body and mind will be back to normal and eager for the next set of thrills to which you will expose them. Similarly, when good news lifts your spirits or bad news dampens them, you know from experience that soon afterward you will return to your normal emotional state.

For a long time, psychologists used similar concepts to describe how people negotiate life's ups and downs in a theory known as the *hedonic treadmill* model (Brickman & Campbell, 1971). The idea behind the hedonic treadmill ("hedonic" has to do with pleasure) was that our emotional highs and lows vary around a neutral state to which we always return once those highs and lows have passed, or once we have become accustomed to them. For example, finding out that you made a good grade on an exam makes you happy for a while, but soon your mind adjusts to the news and moves on to concerns about future exams. There is little doubt among psychologists about the validity of the commonsense notion that emotional ups and downs are temporary states. However, recently, many psychologists have come to realize that there is probably no such thing as a universal neutral state to which all people return when these highs and lows end.

Instead of a neutral state, each of us has what psychologist Ed Diener and his colleagues refer to as an emotional *set point* (Diener, Lucas, & Scollon, 2006). Diener's revision of the hedonic treadmill assumes that when we are not in the midst of an emotional high or low, we function at our set point. Set points, says Diener, vary considerably across individuals. For some of us, the set point is one that endows us with a sense of optimism about what the future will bring. Others have a set point that is characterized by a pessimistic view of the future. These set point differences strongly influence how we experience life. Thus, people with an optimistic set point have an emotionally positive sense of their own well-being; in other words, these people are happy most of the time. By contrast, those whose set point is pessimistic tend to be in a continual state of malcontent.

How important is a person's emotional set point? Research suggests that it is very important. A remarkably comprehen-

sive recent study included an extensive review of the research on the impact of happiness on people's lives (Lyubomirsky et al., 2005). The correlational studies these researchers examined showed that people who were generally happy, that is, those with an optimistic set point, were more likely than their pessimistic peers to be successful in work and in relationships, probably because they were more sociable and more adept at resolving interpersonal conflicts. Happy people were also more likely to be both mentally and physically healthy. Similar results were found in longitudinal studies, demonstrating that happy people did not become so after they obtained success. Instead, happiness preceded success. Thus, it appears that having an optimistic set point is a distinctive advantage in life.

Diener has suggested that research examining the stability of the major components of our personalities supports his revision of the hedonic treadmill model. By **personality,** psychologists mean the characteristic patterns of thinking, feeling, and behaving that distinguish one person from another. One of the questions that has been addressed in the research to which Diener refers concerns the degree to which the various components of an individual's personality, including his or her emotional set point, is stable over the lifespan. Some psychologists assert that our personalities stabilize early in life and do not change much in the decades that follow. On the other side are psychologists who argue that personality does change.

Like most debates in psychology, this one has both an academic and an applied component. For academics, questions about the stability of personality are interesting in and of themselves, because the goal of psychology is to better understand mental processes and behaviors. For clinical and counseling psychologists, those who work with people who want to improve their own sense of well-being, questions about the possibility of personality change are important for a different reason. They want to know if it is possible to help pessimistic people change their set points so that they can function more effectively.

One of today's most influential clinical psychologists, Martin Seligman, not only enthusiastically endorses the idea that people can change their personalities, but also reports having made such a change himself. Seligman's metamorphosis was sparked by a conversation with his young daughter, Nikki. The precocious girl told her father, who was the president of the American Psychological Association at the time, that he ought to be able to stop being a grouch if she, a mere 5-year-old, had the strength of character needed to overcome her habit of constantly whining. Touched by his daughter's insight, Seligman resolved to abandon his grouchiness in favor of a more easy-going approach to life.

Shortly thereafter, Seligman initiated an effort to change what he viewed as the pessimistic nature of the field of psychology (Seligman & Csikszentmihalyi, 2000). Seligman argued that a new approach to both psychology and psychotherapy—one that emphasized strengths more than weaknesses—might

enable clinicians to prevent many kinds of mental disorders. As you learned in the Apply It feature at the end of Chapter 10 (see p. 380), Seligman's placebo-controlled experiments have shown that intentional, systematic efforts to change our outlook on life can cause us to feel more positively about our lives (Seligman et al., 2005). Thus, Seligman's studies provide compelling evidence in support of the view that personality is changeable.

The stability of personality is only one of many questions that psychologists have addressed regarding this important domain of individual differences. In this chapter, we will explore some of the theories that have been proposed to explain personality. As you will see, these theories differ widely, and you may wonder which one best captures the elusive concept of personality. You will probably find that it is best to think of the various theories as sources of different kinds of insights into personality rather than as mutually exclusive claims that must be judged as true or false. We will begin with the theory that established the study of personality as a central issue in the field of psychology, the psychoanalytic theory of Sigmund Freud.

Psychoanalytic Theories

When you hear the term **psychoanalysis,** do you picture a psychiatrist treating a troubled patient on a couch? Many people do, but the term refers not only to a therapy for treating psychological disorders devised by Sigmund Freud, but also to the influential personality theory he proposed. The central idea of psychoanalytic theory is that unconscious forces shape human thought and behavior.

personality A person's characteristic patterns of behaving, thinking, and feeling.

psychoanalysis (SY-co-ah-NAL-ih-sis) Freud's term for his theory of personality and his therapy for treating psychological disorders.

The Conscious, the Preconscious, and the Unconscious

Freud believed that there are three levels of awareness in consciousness: the conscious, the preconscious, and the unconscious. The **conscious** consists of whatever we are aware of at any given moment—thoughts, feelings, sensations, or memories. The **preconscious** is somewhat like long-term memory: It contains all the memories, feelings, experiences, and perceptions that we are not consciously thinking about at the moment, but that may be easily brought to consciousness.

13.1 What are the three levels of awareness in consciousness?

13.2 What are the roles of the id, the ego, and the superego?

▲ Sigmund Freud (1856–1939), with his daughter Anna.

The most important of the three levels is the **unconscious,** which Freud believed to be the primary motivating force of human behavior. The unconscious holds memories that once were conscious but were so unpleasant or anxiety-provoking that they were repressed (involuntarily removed from consciousness). The unconscious also contains all of the instincts (sexual and aggressive), wishes, and desires that have never been allowed into consciousness. Freud traced the roots of psychological disorders to these impulses and repressed memories.

The Id, the Ego, and the Superego

Freud also proposed three systems of personality. Figure 13.1 shows these three systems and how they relate to his conscious, preconscious, and unconscious levels of awareness. These systems do not exist physically; they are only concepts, or ways of looking at personality.

The **id** is the only part of the personality that is present at birth. It is inherited, primitive, inaccessible, and completely unconscious. The id contains (1) the life instincts, which are the sexual instincts and the biological urges such as hunger and thirst, and (2) the death instinct, which accounts for aggressive and destructive impulses (Freud, 1933/1965). Operating according to the *pleasure principle,* the id tries to seek pleasure, avoid pain, and gain immediate gratification of its wishes. The id is the source of the *libido,* the psychic energy that fuels the entire personality; yet, the id can only wish, image, fantasize and demand.

The **ego** is the logical, rational, realistic part of the personality. The ego evolves from the id and draws its energy from the id. One of the ego's functions is to satisfy the id's urges. But the ego, which is mostly conscious, acts according to the *reality principle.* It considers the constraints of the real world in determining appropriate times, places, and objects for gratification of the id's wishes. The art of the possible is its guide, and sometimes compromises must be made—such as settling for a McDonald's hamburger instead of steak or lobster.

When a child is age 5 or 6, the **superego,** the moral component of the personality, is formed. The superego has two parts: (1) The *conscience* consists of all the behaviors for which the child has been punished and about which he or she feels guilty; (2) the *ego ideal* comprises the behaviors for which the child has been praised and rewarded and about which he or she feels pride and satisfaction. At first, the superego reflects only the parents' expectations of what is good and right, but it expands over time to incor-

Figure 13.1 Freud's Conception of Personality

According to Freud, personality, which may be conceptualized as a giant iceberg, is composed of three structures: the id, the ego, and the superego. The id, completely unconscious, is wholly submerged, floating beneath the surface. The ego is largely conscious and visible, but partly unconscious. The superego also operates at both the conscious and unconscious levels.

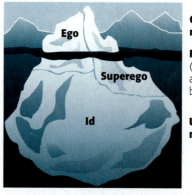

porate teachings from the broader social world. In its quest for moral perfection, the superego sets guidelines that define and limit the ego's flexibility. A harsher judge than any external authority, including one's parents, the superego judges not only behavior, but also thoughts, feelings, and wishes.

All would be well if the id, the ego, and the superego had compatible aims. But the id's demands for pleasure are often in direct conflict with the superego's desire for moral perfection. At times the ego needs some way to defend itself against the anxiety created by the excessive demands of the id and the harsh judgments of the superego. When it cannot solve problems directly, the ego may use a **defense mechanism,** a technique used to defend against anxiety and to maintain self-esteem. All people use defense mechanisms to some degree, but research supports Freud's view that the overuse of defense mechanisms can adversely affect mental health (Watson, 2002). Freud identified several different types of defense mechanisms. Table 13.1 lists their definitions and provides an example for each one.

As you probably know from your own experience, **repression** is the defense mechanism that people most frequently use. It involves removing painful or threatening memories, thoughts, or perceptions from consciousness and keeping them in the unconscious. It may also prevent unconscious sexual and aggressive impulses from breaking into consciousness. Several studies have shown that people do indeed try to repress unpleasant thoughts (Koehler et al., 2002). Freud believed that repressed thoughts lurk in the unconscious and can cause psychological disorders in adults. He thought that the way to cure such disorders was to bring the repressed material back to consciousness, and this was the basis for his system of therapy—psychoanalysis.

defense mechanism A means used by the ego to defend against anxiety and to maintain self-esteem.

repression A defense mechanism in which one involuntarily removes painful or threatening memories, thoughts, or perceptions from consciousness or prevents unconscious sexual and aggressive impulses from breaking into consciousness.

Table 13.1 Freud's Defense Mechanisms

Defense Mechanism	Description	Example
Repression	Involuntarily removing an unpleasant memory, thought, or perception from consciousness or barring disturbing sexual and aggressive impulses from consciousness	Jill forgets a traumatic incident from childhood.
Projection	Attributing one's own undesirable traits, thoughts, behavior, or impulses to another	A very lonely divorced woman accuses all men of having only one thing on their minds.
Denial	Refusing to acknowledge consciously the existence of danger or a threatening situation	Amy fails to take a tornado warning seriously and is severely injured.
Rationalization	Supplying a logical, rational, or socially acceptable reason rather than the real reason for an action or event	Fred tells his friend that he didn't get the job because he didn't have connections.
Regression	Reverting to a behavior that might have reduced anxiety at an earlier stage of development	Susan bursts into tears whenever she is criticized.
Reaction formation	Expressing exaggerated ideas and emotions that are the opposite of disturbing, unconscious impulses and desires	A former purchaser of pornography, Bob is now a tireless crusader against it.
Displacement	Substituting a less threatening object or person for the original object of a sexual or aggressive impulse	After being spanked by his father, Bill hits his baby brother.
Sublimation	Rechanneling sexual and aggressive energy into pursuits or accomplishments that society consider acceptable or even admirable	Tim goes to a gym to work out when he feels hostile and frustrated.

The Psychosexual Stages of Development

13.3 What are the psychosexual stages, and why did Freud consider them important in personality development?

The sex instinct, Freud said, is the most important factor influencing personality. It is present at birth and then develops through a series of **psychosexual stages.** Each stage centers on a particular part of the body that provides pleasurable sensations (an *erogenous zone*) and around which a conflict arises (Freud, 1905/1953b; 1920/1963b). If the conflict is not readily resolved, the child may develop a **fixation.** This means that a portion of the libido (psychic energy) remains invested at that particular stage, leaving less energy to meet the challenges of future stages. Overindulgence at any stage may leave a person psychologically unwilling to move on to the next stage, whereas too little gratification may leave the person trying to make up for unmet needs. Freud believed that certain personality characteristics develop as a result of difficulty at one or another of the stages.

Review and Reflect (below) summarizes Freud's psychosexual stages.

Review and Reflect Freud's Psychosexual Stages of Development

Stage		Part of the Body	Conflicts/Experiences	Adult Traits Associated with Problems at this Stage
Oral (birth to 1 year)		Mouth	Weaning Oral gratification from sucking, eating, biting	Optimism, gullibility, dependency, pessimism, passivity, hostility, sarcasm, aggression
Anal (1 to 3 years)		Anus	Toilet training Gratification from expelling and withholding feces	Excessive cleanliness, orderliness, stinginess, messiness, rebelliousness, destructiveness
Phallic (3 to 5 or 6 years)		Genitals	Oedipal conflict Sexual curiosity Masturbation	Flirtatiousness, vanity, promiscuity, pride, chastity
Latency (5 or 6 years to puberty)		None	Period of sexual calm Interest in school, hobbies, same-sex friends	
Genital (from puberty on)		Genitals	Revival of sexual interests Establishment of mature sexual relationships	

The Oral Stage (Birth to 1 Year). During the *oral stage*, the mouth is the primary source of an infant's sensual pleasure, which Freud (1920/1963b) considered to be an expression of infantile sexuality. The conflict at this stage centers on weaning. Too much or too little gratification may result in an oral fixation—an excessive preoccupation with oral activities such as eating, drinking, smoking, gum chewing, nail biting, and even kissing. (Freud's 20-cigars-a-day habit probably qualifies as an oral fixation, according to his theory.) Freud claimed that difficulties at the oral stage can result in certain personality traits: either excessive dependence, optimism, and gullibility (the tendency to believe anything) or extreme pessimism, sarcasm, hostility, and aggression.

The Anal Stage (1 to 3 Years). During the *anal stage*, children derive sensual pleasure, Freud believed, from expelling and withholding feces. But a conflict arises when toilet training begins, because this is one of parents' first attempts to have children give up or postpone gratification. When parents are harsh in their approach, children may rebel openly, defecating whenever and wherever they please. This may lead to an *anal expulsive personality*—someone who is sloppy, irresponsible, rebellious, hostile, and destructive. Other children may defy their parents and gain attention by withholding feces. They may develop an *anal retentive personality*, gaining security through what they possess and becoming stingy, stubborn, rigid, excessively neat and clean, orderly, and precise (Freud, 1933/1965).

The Phallic Stage (3 to 5 or 6 Years). During the *phallic stage*, children learn that they can derive pleasure from touching their genitals, and masturbation is common. They become aware of the anatomical differences in males and females. One of the most controversial features of Freud's theory is the central theme of the phallic stage, the ==Oedipus complex== (named after the central character in the Greek tragedy *Oedipus Rex*, by Sophocles). Freud claimed that, during the phallic stage, "boys concentrate their sexual wishes upon their mother and develop hostile impulses against their father as being a rival" (1925/1963a, p. 61). The boy usually resolves the Oedipus complex by identifying with his father and repressing his sexual feelings for his mother. With identification, the child takes on his father's behaviors, mannerisms, and superego standards; in this way, the superego develops (Freud, 1930/1962).

Freud proposed an equally controversial developmental process for girls in the phallic stage. When they discover they have no penis, girls in this stage develop "penis envy," and they turn to their father because he has the desired organ (Freud, 1933/1965). They feel sexual desires for him and develop jealousy and rivalry toward their mother. But eventually girls, too, experience anxiety as a result of their hostile feelings. They repress their sexual feelings toward the father and identify with the mother, leading to the formation of their superego (Freud, 1930/1962).

According to Freud, failure to resolve these conflicts can have serious consequences for both boys and girls: Tremendous guilt and anxiety may be carried over into adulthood and cause sexual problems, great difficulty relating to members of the opposite sex, or homosexuality.

The Latency Period (5 or 6 Years to Puberty). Following the stormy phallic stage, the *latency period* is one of relative calm. The sex instinct is repressed and temporarily sublimated in school and play activities, hobbies, and sports. During this period, children prefer same-sex friends and playmates.

The Genital Stage (from Puberty on). In the *genital stage*, the focus of sexual energy gradually shifts to the opposite sex for the vast majority of people, culminating in heterosexual love and the attainment of full adult sexuality. Freud believed that the few who reach the genital stage without having fixations at earlier stages can achieve the state of psychological health that he equated with the ability to love and work.

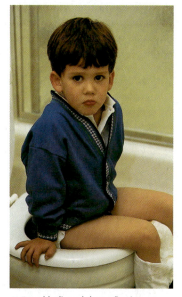

▲ Freud believed that a fixation at the anal stage, resulting from harsh parental pressure, could lead to an anal retentive personality—characterized by excessive stubbornness, rigidity, and neatness.

psychosexual stages A series of stages through which the sexual instinct develops; each stage is defined by an erogenous zone around which conflict arises.

fixation Arrested development at a psychosexual stage occurring because of excessive gratification or frustration at that stage.

Oedipus complex (ED-uh-pus) Occurring in the phallic stage, a conflict in which the child is sexually attracted to the opposite-sex parent and feels hostility toward the same-sex parent.

Evaluating Freud's Contribution

13.4 How are Freud's ideas evaluated by modern psychologists?

When was the last time you made a statement that was based on the assumption that sexual fulfillment is central to mental health? Or that a person can be motivated by impulses of which he or she is unaware? Perhaps you have opined that someone's current problems are the result of a long-forgotten childhood trauma or emotional conflict. If any of these statements is true for you, then you are a living example of the lasting influence of Freud's psychoanalytic theory on Western culture. In fact, you can tune in to any television or radio talk show, or pick up a popular magazine, and find many instances of such ideas.

Predictably, psychologists and other commentators on the human condition disagree as to whether Freudian ideas have benefited or harmed society. At one extreme, psychiatrist E. Fuller Torrey argues that the infusion of psychoanalytic concepts into Western culture has led to an overemphasis on sexual pleasure (Torrey, 1992). Torrey says that parenting recommendations based on psychoanalytic theory, such as those of Dr. Benjamin Spock, caused parents to be unnecessarily anxious that their child-rearing strategies might cause psychological harm to their children. Moreover, critics such as Torrey blame Freudian theory for the proliferation of "blame-the-parents" claims on behalf of defendants who are accused of crimes such as serial murder. (By the way, Torrey is equally critical of the behaviorists.)

At the opposite end of the spectrum, Freud's supporters argue that the popularization of his theory has made people more aware of the importance of sexuality in their lives and of the significance of early childhood experiences to later development. Supporters often claim, too, that critics mischaracterize Freud's ideas both in the popular media and in academic circles (Grant & Harari, 2005). Advocates also point out that Freud's theory played a seminal role in the development of every discipline that deals with human behavior, including psychology, sociology, anthropology, psychiatry, neuroscience, and social work, to name a few.

What about the scientific status of Freud's theory? Some have pointed out that Freud's work on defense mechanisms foreshadowed theories such as those of Lazarus in which cognitive appraisals are thought to shape emotional experiences (Fauerbach et al., 2002; Tori & Bilmes, 2002). In addition, some aspects of psychoanalytic theory, such as Freud's emphasis on family dynamics, continue to be important in explanations of psychological disorders (e.g., Pierenger, Fazekas, & Pierenger, 2005). Moreover, today's *psychodynamic* therapies are direct descendants of Freud's techniques (Bartlett, 2002; Houzel, 2004).

However, in Chapter 4 you learned that neurological approaches to dreaming have overtaken Freud's notions regarding symbolism in dreams. Likewise, in Chapter 6 you learned that, generally, people do not repress traumatic memories as Freud claimed. These challenges to psychoanalytic theory have arisen largely because of psychoanalysts' failure to adequately test the causal hypotheses found in psychoanalytic theory by means other than after-the-fact analyses of clinical case studies (Grünbaum, 2006). Moreover, a few observers claim that the unquestioning acceptance of Freud's theory by many therapists in the early decades of the 20th century went against Freud's own perception of psychoanalysis as a scientific theory that ought to be tested like any other.

When tests of Freud's hypotheses are available, the results show a mixed pattern. For instance, his suggestion that *catharsis*, the release of pent-up emotions, is good for one's psychological health has been refuted by studies showing that expressing negative emotions such as anger actually intensifies such feelings (Bushman, 2002). In contrast, his assertion that childhood trauma leads to the development of psychological disorders in adulthood has received partial support. One study found that more than 70% of women who had been sexually victimized in childhood were diagnosed with some kind of psychological disorder in adulthood (Katerndahl, Burge, & Kellogg, 2005). At the same time, though, studies show that individual differences among victims better predict adult outcomes than the experience of victimization itself (Eisold,

2005). Thus, many victims of sexual abuse display a greater degree of resilience—the capacity to overcome potentially damaging early experiences—than psychoanalytic theory might predict.

Finally, critics charge that much of Freud's theory defies scientific testing. Too much of the time, any act of behavior or even no act of behavior at all can be interpreted to support Freud's theory. How, for instance, can we ever test the idea that little boys are in love with their mothers and want to get rid of their fathers? How can we verify or falsify the idea that one component of personality is motivated entirely by the pursuit of pleasure? Chiefly because of the difficulty involved in finding scientific answers to such questions, there are very few strict Freudians among today's psychologists.

The Neo-Freudians

Is it possible to construct a theory of personality that builds on the strengths of Freud's approach and avoids its weaknesses? Several personality theorists, referred to as *neo-Freudians*, have attempted to do so. Most started their careers as followers of Freud, but then began to disagree on certain basic principles of psychoanalytic theory.

Carl Jung. One of the most important neo-Freudians, Carl Jung (1875–1961), did not consider the sexual instinct to be the main factor in personality, nor did he believe that the personality is almost completely formed in early childhood. For Jung (1933), middle age was an even more important period for personality development. Jung conceived of the personality as consisting of three parts: the ego, the personal unconscious, and the collective unconscious, as shown in **Figure 13.2**. He saw the ego as the conscious component of personality, which carries out normal daily activities. Like Freud, he believed the ego to be secondary in importance to the unconscious.

The **personal unconscious** develops as a result of one's own experience and is therefore unique to each person. It contains all the experiences, thoughts, and perceptions accessible to the conscious, as well as repressed memories, wishes, and impulses. The **collective unconscious,** the most inaccessible layer of the unconscious, contains the universal experiences of humankind throughout evolution. This is how Jung accounted for the similarity of certain myths, dreams, symbols, and religious beliefs in cultures widely separated by distance and time. Moreover, the collective unconscious contains what he called **archetypes,** inherited tendencies to respond to universal human situations in particular ways. Jung would say that the tendencies of people to believe in a god, a devil, evil spirits, and heroes all result from inherited archetypes that reflect the shared experience of humankind.

Jung also argued that each of us has qualities of the opposite sex within our unconscious, although usually in an underdeveloped state. The *anima* is Jung's term for the "inner feminine figure" within the unconscious of every man, and the *animus* is the "inner masculine figure" within the unconscious of every woman (Jung, 1961, p. 186). Both masculine and feminine qualities must be consciously acknowledged and integrated, Jung thought, for a healthy personality to develop.

The *self* represents the full development of the personality and is attained only when the opposing internal forces are integrated and balanced. The self encompasses the conscious and the unconscious, the persona, the shadow, the masculine and the feminine qualities, and the tendency toward extraversion or introversion (terms originated by Jung). *Extraversion* is the tendency to be outgoing, adaptable, and sociable; *introversion* is the tendency to focus inward and to be reflective, retiring, and nonsocial. Jung claimed that the integration and balancing of opposing internal forces begins in midlife. For some, this change may be accompanied by a *midlife crisis*, which Jung himself experienced. Because he emphasized personality development in midlife, many consider Jung to be the conceptual founder of the psychology of adult development (Moraglia, 1994).

13.5 How do the views of the neo-Freudians differ from those of Freud?

▲ Carl Gustav Jung (1875–1961)

personal unconscious In Jung's theory, the layer of the unconscious that contains all of the thoughts, perceptions, and experiences accessible to the conscious, as well as repressed memories, wishes, and impulses.

collective unconscious In Jung's theory, the most inaccessible layer of the unconscious, which contains the universal experiences of humankind throughout evolution.

archetype (AR-ka-type) Existing in the collective unconscious, an inherited tendency to respond to universal human situations in particular ways.

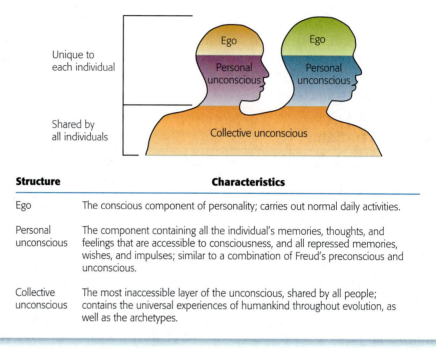

Figure 13.2 Jung's Conception of Personality

Like Freud, Jung saw three components in personality. The ego and the personal unconscious are unique to each individual. The collective unconscious accounts for the similarity of myths and beliefs in diverse cultures.

Structure	Characteristics
Ego	The conscious component of personality; carries out normal daily activities.
Personal unconscious	The component containing all the individual's memories, thoughts, and feelings that are accessible to consciousness, and all repressed memories, wishes, and impulses; similar to a combination of Freud's preconscious and unconscious.
Collective unconscious	The most inaccessible layer of the unconscious, shared by all people; contains the universal experiences of humankind throughout evolution, as well as the archetypes.

Alfred Adler Another neo-Freudian, Alfred Adler (1870–1937), emphasized the unity of the personality rather than the separate warring components of id, ego, and superego. Adler (1927, 1956) also maintained that the drive to overcome feelings of inferiority acquired in childhood motivates most of our behavior. He (1956) claimed that people develop a "style of life" at an early age—a unique way in which the child and later the adult will go about the struggle to achieve superiority. Sometimes inferiority feelings are so strong that they prevent personal development, a condition Adler called the *inferiority complex* (Dreikurs, 1953). Adler used this term to describe the motivating power of a self-concept that includes the idea that someone else, or everyone else, is better than we are. Thus, Adler's theory emphasizes a process he called *superiority striving* in which we try to equal or exceed the accomplishments of others whom we believe are superior to us. If we cannot accomplish this goal, we may find other ways of distinguishing ourselves. Adler is also known for his birth-order hypotheses, in which he viewed middle children as being more motivated by feelings of inferiority and superiority striving than either older or younger children are.

Karen Horney The work of neo-Freudian Karen Horney (1885–1952) centered on two main themes: the neurotic personality (Horney, 1937, 1945, 1950) and feminine psychology (Horney, 1967). Horney did not accept Freud's division of personality into id, ego, and superego, and she flatly rejected his psychosexual stages and the concepts of the Oedipus complex and penis envy. Furthermore, Horney thought Freud overemphasized the role of the sexual instinct and neglected cultural and environmental influences on personality. Although she stressed the importance of early childhood experiences, Horney (1939) believed that personality could continue to develop and change throughout life.

Horney argued forcefully against Freud's notion that a woman's desire to have a child and a man is nothing more than a conversion of the unfulfilled wish for a penis.

Horney (1945) believed that many of women's psychological difficulties arise from failure to live up to an idealized version of themselves. To be psychologically healthy, she claimed, women—and men, for that matter—must learn to overcome irrational beliefs about the need for perfection. Her influence may be seen in modern cognitive-behavioral therapies, which we will explore in Chapter 15.

Remember It   Psychoanalytic Theories

1. _____ is both a theory of personality and a therapy for the treatment of psychological disorders.

2. Freud considered the _____ to be the primary motivating force of human behavior.

3. According to Freud, the part of the personality that makes you want to eat, drink, and be merry is your _____.

4. You just found a gold watch in a darkened movie theater. Your _____ would urge you to turn it in to the lost-and-found.

5. The part of the personality that Freud believed determines appropriate ways to satisfy biological urges is the _____.

6. Match each psychosexual stage with its associated conflict or theme.

    _____ (1) oral stage   a. the Oedipus complex
    _____ (2) anal stage   b. the attainment of adult
    _____ (3) phallic stage   sexuality
    _____ (4) latency stage   c. weaning
    _____ (5) genital stage   d. toilet training
                                  e. preference for same-sex
                                     friends and playmates

7. In Jung's theory, the inherited part of the personality that stores the experiences of humankind is the _____ unconscious.

8. _____ believed that the basic human drive is to overcome and compensate for feelings of inferiority.

9. _____ believed that Freud was wrong about the concept of penis envy.

Answers: 1. Psychoanalysis; 2. unconscious; 3. id; 4. superego; 5. ego; 6. (1) c, (2) d, (3) a, (4) e, (5) b; 7. collective; 8. Alfred Adler; 9. Karen Horney

---

Humanistic Theories

In *humanistic psychology*, people are assumed to have a natural tendency toward growth and the realization of their fullest potential. Thus, humanistic personality theories are more optimistic than Freud's psychoanalytic theory. However, like Freud's theory, these perspectives are often criticized as being difficult to test scientifically.

Two Humanistic Theories

For humanistic psychologist Abraham Maslow (1908–1970), motivational factors are at the root of personality. You may remember from Chapter 10 that Maslow constructed a hierarchy of needs, ranging from physiological needs at the bottom upward to safety needs, belonging and love needs, esteem needs, and finally to the highest need—self-actualization (see Figure 10.1 on page 351). **Self-actualization** means developing to one's fullest potential. A healthy person is continually striving to become all that he or she can be.

In his research, Maslow found self-actualizers to be accurate in perceiving reality—able to judge honestly and to spot quickly the fake and the dishonest. Most of them believe they have a mission to accomplish or the need to devote their life to some

13.6 What are the contributions of humanistic theorists to the study of personality?

self-actualization Developing to one's fullest potential.

▲ Abraham Maslow (1908–1970)

larger good. Self-actualizers tend not to depend on external authority or other people but seem to be inner-driven, autonomous, and independent. Finally, the hallmark of self-actualizers is having frequently occurring *peak experiences*—experiences of deep meaning, insight, and harmony within themselves and with the universe. Current researchers have modified Maslow's definition of self-actualization to include effective personal relationships as well as peak experiences (Hanley & Abell, 2002).

According to another humanistic psychologist, Carl Rogers (1902–1987), our parents set up **conditions of worth,** or conditions on which their positive regard hinges. Conditions of worth force us to live and act according to someone else's values rather than our own. In our efforts to gain positive regard, we deny our true selves by inhibiting some of our behavior, denying or distorting some of our perceptions, and closing off parts of our experience. In so doing, we experience stress and anxiety, and our whole self-structure may be threatened.

For Rogers, a major goal of psychotherapy is to enable people to open themselves up to experiences and begin to live according to their own values rather than living by the values of others in an attempt to gain positive regard. He called his therapy *person-centered therapy,* preferring not to use the term *patient* (Rogers's therapy will be discussed further in Chapter 15). Rogers believed that the therapist must give the client **unconditional positive regard**—that is, unqualified caring and nonjudgmental acceptance, no matter what the client says, does, has done, or is thinking of doing. Unconditional positive regard is designed to reduce threat, eliminate conditions of worth, and bring the person back in tune with his or her true self. If successful, the therapy helps the client become what Rogers called a *fully functioning person,* one who is functioning at an optimal level and living fully and spontaneously according to his or her own inner value system.

conditions of worth Conditions on which the positive regard of others rests.

unconditional positive regard Unqualified caring and nonjudgmental acceptance of another.

Self-Esteem

13.7 What have psychologists learned about self-esteem?

No doubt you have heard discussions of the importance of self-esteem to one's mental health. Although humanists have been criticized for being unscientific and for seeing, hearing, and finding no evil within the human psyche, they have inspired the study of positive personality qualities, including altruism, cooperation, love, acceptance of others, and especially self-esteem. Complete the *Try It* below to estimate your current level of self-esteem.

Try It   Gauging Your Self-Esteem

For each statement below, choose the option that best reflects your feelings:

a. strongly agree   b. agree   c. neutral   d. disagree
e. strongly disagree

_____ **1.** I feel confident in most social situations.

_____ **2.** I believe I have something worthwhile to offer in life.

_____ **3.** I feel that others respect my opinion.

_____ **4.** I compare favorably with most people I know.

_____ **5.** I feel that, on the whole, other people like me.

_____ **6.** I deserve the love and respect of others.

Compute your score as follows: a = 4 points, b = 3, c = 2, d = 1, e = 0. A total score of 20–24 points indicates that you have excellent self-esteem; 15–19 means good, 10–14 is fair, and below 10 indicates that you could work on this quality.

How does self-esteem develop? One source of variations in self-esteem arises from comparisons of actual to desired traits. For example, a tone-deaf person who desires to be an accomplished musician might suffer from low self-esteem. However, most of us do not form a global idea about our own self-worth on the basis of a single area of competence. Instead, we view ourselves in terms of strengths and weaknesses. When our strengths lie in areas that we value and believe to be important, we have high self-esteem. Conversely, even outstanding achievements in areas we consider to be of little value may not affect our self-esteem. So, a person who is a great plumber, but who believes that being a good plumber isn't very important, is likely to have low self-esteem. At the same time, a person who feels incompetent because he has to pay a plumber a handsome sum to fix a leaking faucet might be in awe of the plumber's skill.

Developmental psychologists have found that self-esteem is fairly stable from childhood through the late adult years (Robins & Trzesniewski, 2005). So, the self-worth beliefs we adopt in childhood can affect us for a lifetime. Children and adolescents form ideas about their competencies in various domains—academics, sports, fine arts—that become increasingly stable across the elementary and secondary school years (Harter, 1990). And by age 7, most children have a sense of global self-esteem as well. These judgments come from both actual experiences and information provided by others. Thus, to develop high self-esteem, children need to experience success in domains they view as important and to be encouraged by parents, teachers, and peers to value themselves.

Remember It   Humanistic Theories

1. _____ maintained that human beings have a natural tendency toward self-actualization.

2. _____ believed that individuals require unconditional positive regard to become fully functioning persons.

3. Self-esteem results from the comparison of _____ to _____ characteristics.

Answers: 1. Abraham Maslow; 2. Carl Rogers; 3. actual, desired

---

Trait Theories

If you had to describe yourself in five words or less, how would you do it? Chances are, adjectives such as fun-loving, shy, generous, curious, smart, compassionate, and the like would come to mind. These descriptors represent the essence of what psychologists mean by the term *traits*. Formally, **traits** are defined as personal qualities or characteristics that make it possible for us to face a wide variety of situational demands and deal with unforeseen circumstances (De Raad & Kokkonen, 2000). *Trait theories* are attempts to explain personality and differences among people in terms of personal characteristics that are stable across situations.

Early Trait Theories

The early trait theories often focused on finding useful ways of classifying adjectives that people use to describe their own and others' personalities. As computer technology became increasingly available, trait theorists turned to sophisticated statistical strategies for grouping these descriptors. By the end of the 1960s, the idea that hundreds of personality descriptors could be grouped into clusters had become firmly entrenched among trait theorists.

Allport's Cardinal and Central Traits. One of the early trait theorists, Gordon Allport (1897–1967), claimed that each person inherits a unique set of raw materials for

13.8 What were some of the ideas proposed by early trait theorists?

trait A personal quality or characteristic, which is stable across situations, that is used to describe or explain personality.

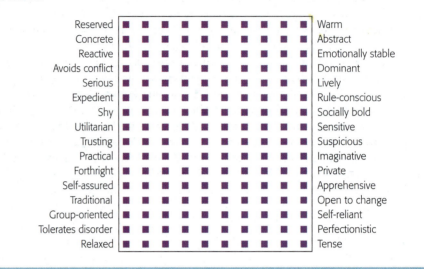

Figure 13.3 The 16PF Personality Profile

Results from Cattell's 16PF can be plotted on a chart like this one. The profile is represented by a line connecting an individual's score points on each dimension (e.g., reserved–warm). How would you draw your own profile? Circle the point along each of the dimensions, and connect them with a line to find out.

Reserved		Warm
Concrete		Abstract
Reactive		Emotionally stable
Avoids conflict		Dominant
Serious		Lively
Expedient		Rule-conscious
Shy		Socially bold
Utilitarian		Sensitive
Trusting		Suspicious
Practical		Imaginative
Forthright		Private
Self-assured		Apprehensive
Traditional		Open to change
Group-oriented		Self-reliant
Tolerates disorder		Perfectionistic
Relaxed		Tense

given traits, which are then shaped by experiences (Allport & Odbert, 1936). A *cardinal trait* is one that is viewed as the most defining trait of a person, one that can be found in almost all of the person's behavior. For example, people who seem to always be able to come up with witty punch lines and snappy comebacks are often described as "funny." Myths and legends about people are often built upon the assumption that the people they depict possessed an overriding cardinal trait. For instance, Abraham Lincoln is sometimes spoken of as "Honest Abe" because of popular stories about a few incidents involving his extraordinary honesty that supposedly took place when he was a young man. Practically speaking, however, few people have true cardinal traits. Instead, most of us are better described in terms of *central traits*, that is, a brief list of traits, rather than a single cardinal trait, that show up in most of our behaviors. If you were asked to write a letter of recommendation for a friend, you would include such traits. That is, you wouldn't just say that your friend is honest *or* hard-working *or* reliable. You would say that she is honest *and* hard-working *and* reliable.

Cattell's Surface and Source Traits. Raymond Cattell (1950) referred to observable qualities of personality as *surface traits*. Using observations and questionnaires, Cattell studied thousands of people and found certain clusters of surface traits that appeared together time after time. He thought these were evidence of deeper, more general, underlying personality factors, which he called *source traits*. People differ in the degree to which they possess each source trait. For example, Cattell claimed that intelligence is a source trait: Everyone has it, but the amount possessed varies from person to person.

Cattell found 23 source traits in normal individuals, 16 of which he studied in great detail. Cattell's Sixteen Personality Factor Questionnaire, commonly called the *16PF*, yields a personality profile (Cattell et al., 1950, 1977). This test continues to be widely used in research (e.g., Brody et al., 2000) and for personality assessment in career counseling, schools, and employment settings. Results from the 16PF are usually plotted on a graph such as that shown in **Figure 13.3**.

Eysenck's Three Factor Model. The early trait theories represented the beginning of a movement that continues to be important in personality research. Cattell's notion of personality factors was especially influential. Building on Cattell's notion of personality factors the late British psychologist Hans Eysenck (1916–1997) proposed a factor model that emphasized three dimensions and is sometimes called the *PEN* model (Eysenck, 1990). The first of the dimensions, psychoticism, is a continuum that represents an individual's link to reality. At one extreme are "psychotics," those who live in a world of hallucinations and delusions. At the other end are people whose thought processes are so rigidly tied to the material world that they lack creativity. The second dimension, extraversion, ranges from people who are outgoing to those who are shy. The third, neuroticism, describes emotional stability, with highly stable people at one end and anxious, irritable people at the other.

Eysenck proposed that all three of the PEN dimensions are rooted in neurological functioning. As a result, his theory has served as a useful framework for neurological studies of personality. For example, researchers have found a link between dopamine activity in the brain and extraversion (Wacker, Chavanon, & Stemmler, 2006). Studies using electroencephalography (EEG) have shown that neuroticism is correlated with a distinctive pattern of brain wave activity (Chi et al., 2005). In addition, Eysenck developed a series of personality tests that are still widely used by researchers and clinicians today (Miles & Hempel, 2004).

The Five-Factor Model

The most talked-about trait theory today is the **five-factor model,** the view that personality can be explained in terms of five broad dimensions, each of which is composed of a cluster of personality traits. The assertion that five factors are needed to account for personality, as opposed to Eysenck's three factors, dates back to the early 1960s (e.g., Norman, 1963). However, over the past two decades, the model has become most closely associated with the research of Robert McCrae and Paul Costa (1985). Another important five-factor model, known as the *Big Five*, proposed by psychologist Lewis Goldberg, varies somewhat from that of McCrae and Costa in its approach to measuring the factors (Goldberg, 1993). However, research based on both models supports the hypothesis that personality can be usefully described in terms of five factors. You will notice that the names of these factors can be easily remembered by using the acronym OCEAN.

Openness. Are you eager to try new things and consider new ideas? If so, then you might get a high score on a test that measures openness. This dimension contrasts individuals who seek out varied experiences and who are imaginative, intellectually curious, and broad-minded with those whose interests are narrower.

Openness may be an important factor in adapting to new situations. In one four-year study, researchers found that college students who scored high on this factor as freshmen adjusted to college life more easily than peers who scored lower (Harms, Roberts, & Winter, 2006). Apparently, students who were higher in openness were better able to adapt their own personality characteristics to the demands of the college environment than their low-scoring peers.

Conscientiousness. Do you always fold your laundry before putting it away? Individuals who score high on measures of conscientiousness pay more attention to such details than those who get lower scores. They are often viewed as reliable by others. By contrast, those at the lower end of this dimension may be perceived as lazy and undependable, but they also tend to be more spontaneous than people who get higher scores on this dimension. Thus, in some situations, such as a relaxing day at the beach, a nonconscientious person might be a more enjoyable companion than one who is concerned about details such as keeping sand off the blanket and reapplying sun block every fifteen minutes.

Research suggests that the components of conscientiousness include order, self-control, and industriousness (Roberts et al., 2005). Thus, it isn't surprising that conscientiousness is correlated with measures of health. Longitudinal studies, for example, suggest that, compared to peers who obtained low scores on measures of

13.9 What do five-factor theorists consider to be the most important dimensions of personality?

five-factor model A trait theory that attempts to explain personality using five broad dimensions, each of which is composed of a constellation of personality traits.

▲ Individuals who are high in extraversion and agreeableness are viewed more favorably in job interviews than those who score lower on these two dimensions of the five-factor model.

conscientiousness, children who were high in conscientiousness as elementary school students were less likely to be smokers or to be obese in middle adulthood (Hampson et al., 2006). Likewise, conscientiousness shows long-term links to the tendency to maintain health-protective factors, such as avoiding obesity, during middle adulthood (Brummett et al., 2006).

Conscientiousness also predicts both academic and job performance. Among elementary school students, those who are highest in conscientiousness tend to be the highest achievers later in high school (Shiner, 2000). Likewise, across the years of undergraduate and graduate school, assessments of conscientiousness during students' first year predict their standing at the end of their programs of study (Chamorro-Premuzic & Furnham, 2002; Lievens et al., 2003). Finally, variations in conscientiousness are correlated with measures of job performance among adults no matter what type of job is considered (Barrick, Mount, & Judge, 2001).

Extraversion. If you have a free evening, would you rather go to a party or stay home and read a book or watch a movie? Individuals who are high in extraversion prefer being around people. Chances are that anyone who is known as "the life of the party" is an extravert. Those at the opposite end of the continuum, introverts, may feel most comfortable when they are on their own.

Extraverts may have an easier time getting a job than their more introverted peers (Tay, Ang, & Dyne, 2006). Researchers have found that extraverts receive more job offers after being interviewed than do introverts. However, extraverts also may be more likely than introverts to engage in risky behaviors such as unprotected sex (Miller et al., 2004).

Agreeableness. Do people describe you as easygoing? Individuals who are high in agreeableness are often characterized in this way. This dimension is composed of a collection of traits that range from compassion to antagonism toward others. A person who is low in agreeableness would not be viewed as easygoing. Instead, this individual would be described as unfriendly, argumentative, cold, and perhaps vindictive.

Like conscientiousness, agreeableness is predictive of job performance (Witt et al., 2002). As you might guess, it is also related to employees' ability to function well in work teams (Stewart, Fulmer, & Barrick, 2005). Moreover, those who are most agreeable demonstrate the lowest amount of distress in response to work–family conflicts (Rantanen, Pulkkinen, & Kinnunen, 2005).

Neuroticism. If you see an 8-ounce glass that contains 4 ounces of water, is it half-empty or half-full? People who are high in neuroticism tend to be pessimistic and always see the negative aspects of situations—the "half-empty" interpretation of life. At the same time, they are prone to emotional instability because of their tendency to overreact to the kinds of daily annoyances that most people take in stride. For example, an individual who is high in neuroticism might be very demonstrative about his or her frustration while standing in a slow-moving line at the campus bookstore. When such behaviors are exhibited by neurotic characters in television shows (e.g., George Costanza on *Seinfeld*, Larry David on *Curb Your Enthusiasm*), they are often perceived as humorous by audiences and regarded sympathetically by other characters. However, in real life, individuals who are high in neuroticism have difficulty maintaining social relationships (Rogge et al., 2006).

Predictably, individuals who get high scores on measures of neuroticism receive low ratings on cooperativeness from their co-workers (Stewart, Fulmer, & Barrick, 2005). There is also evidence that high neuroticism impedes learning (Robinson & Tamir, 2005). It appears that the worrisome thoughts that result from neuroticism distract individuals with this characteristic from information that they are trying to learn, thereby interfering with the transfer of information from short- to long-term memory.

Origins and Stability of the Five Factors

How do you think the five factors describe your own personality? Whatever your profile, you are likely to have some ideas about how you acquired your personality traits and whether you have changed over the course of your life. These issues have been addressed in research on the five factors.

Heredity and Environment. As you learned in Chapter 7, one of the best known studies in psychology, the Minnesota twin study, revealed that the IQ scores of identical twins are strongly correlated (Bouchard, 1997). Using data from the same participants, Tellegen and others (1988) found that identical twins are also quite similar on several personality factors, regardless of whether they are raised together or apart. Other twin studies also indicate that heredity makes substantial contributions to individual differences in the five personality factors, as indicated in Figure 13.4 (Bouchard, 1994; Caspi, 2000; Johnson et al., 2004; Loehlin, 1992).

Note, however, that these correlations are not perfect, as is true of all genetic studies. Furthermore, the correlations vary considerably from one personality factor to another. Thus, it is likely that both heredity and environment contribute to the five factors. For instance, a conscientious student receives reinforcement for conscientiousness in the form of good grades, whereas one who is less so receives punishment in the form of poor grades. It is likely that such experiences amplify conscientiousness in those who are high in this factor and motivate those who are low in the factor to find ways of compensating.

The Five Factors across the Lifespan. If, as twin studies suggest, heredity strongly influences personality, then shouldn't we expect the five factors to remain stable across the lifespan? Some measures of personality in childhood are correlated to those that are taken in adulthood, consistent with the proposition that the five factors are determined very early in life, as a genetic explanation would predict (Caspi, 2000; Mc-Crae & Costa, 1990). Moreover, there is evidence that people's responses to measures of the five factors are largely consistent throughout the adult years (Roberts & Del-Vechio, 2000). However, like the correlations in the twin studies cited earlier, these cross-age correlations are far from perfect, suggesting that there are significant deviations from the general pattern of stability.

Careful analyses have shown that there are, indeed, subtle age-related changes in the five factors across the years of adulthood and that the patterns of change differ depending on which factor is considered (Terracciano et al., 2005). Studies that follow individuals into old age show that openness, extraversion, and neuroticism decline as adults age. Agreeableness increases, as does conscientiousness up until around age 70, when it begins to show declines.

How can we reconcile studies suggesting that the five factors are stable across the lifespan with others that show that age-related changes occur? Future research and improved ways of measuring the five factors may help psychologists find definitive answers to this question. For now, the most workable explanation seems to be that the five factors follow a general pattern of stability in most people, but that they are also subject to some degree of modification.

Culture and Personality Traits

Most advocates of the five-factor model assert that the factors are universal, but does research support this claim? Evidence for the universality of the five factors comes from research in which psychologists have successfully measured them in Canada, Finland, Poland, Germany, Russia, Hong Kong, Croatia, Italy, South Korea, China, Mexico, Scotland, India, and New Zealand (Gow et al., 2005; Guenole & Chernyshenko, 2005; McCrae et al., 2000; Paunonen et al., 1996; Rodriguez &

13.10 What does research say about the origins and stability of the five factors?

▲ Celebrities whose extraverted personalities help them make the transition from child to adult star, such as Lindsay Lohan, exemplify research findings showing that the five factors are stable throughout the lifespan in most individuals.

13.11 How does personality differ across cultures?

Figure 13.4 Estimated Influence of Heredity and Environment on the Big Five Personality Dimensions

The Minnesota study of twins reared apart yielded an average heritability estimate of .41 (41%) for the Big Five personality factors; the Loehlin twin studies, a heritability estimate of .42 (42%). Both studies found the influence of the shared environment to be only about .07 (7%). The remaining percentage represents a combination of nonshared environmental influences and measurement error.

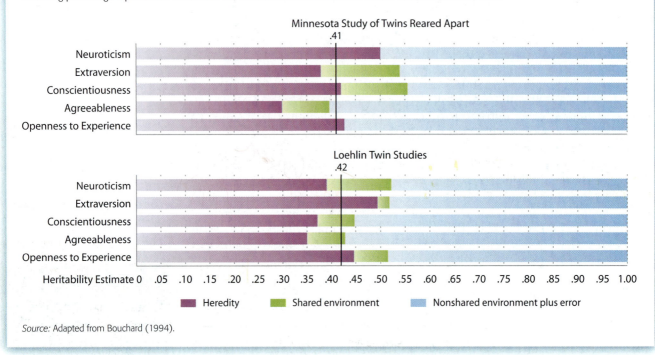

Source: Adapted from Bouchard (1994).

Church, 2003; Sahoo, Sahoo, & Harichandan, 2005; Zhang, 2002). Moreover, the five factors contribute to individual differences in adjustment among individuals who have experienced job-related moves from one culture to another (Shaffer et al., 2006). Studies of the five factors also show they predict outcomes such as health and academic performance similarly across ethnic groups within the United States (Worrell & Cross, 2004).

However, research also suggests that culture influences personality in ways that may not be captured by the five-factor model. In classic research, Hofstede (1980, 1983) analyzed questionnaire responses measuring the work-related values of more than 100,000 IBM employees in 53 countries around the world. Hofstede found four separate dimensions related to culture and personality, of which one, the **individualism/collectivism dimension** is of particular interest here. In individualist cultures, more emphasis is placed on individual achievement than on group achievement. High-achieving individuals are accorded honor and prestige in individualist cultures. People in collectivist cultures, on the other hand, tend to be more interdependent and to define themselves and their personal interests in terms of their group membership. Asians, for example, have highly collectivist cultures, and collectivism is compatible with Confucianism, the predominant religion of Eastern cultures. In fact, according to the Confucian values, the individual finds his or her identity in interrelatedness, as a part of the larger group. Moreover, this interrelatedness is an important ingredient of happiness for Asians (Kitayama & Markus, 2000).

Hofstede rank-ordered the 53 countries from the IBM study on each of the four dimensions. The United States ranked as the most individualist culture in the sample, followed by Australia, Great Britain, Canada, and the Netherlands. At the other end of the continuum were the most collectivist cultures: Guatemala, Ecuador, Panama, Venezuela, and Colombia—all Latin American countries.

individualism/collectivism dimension A measure of a culture's emphasis on either individual achievement or social relationships.

It is important to note that some psychologists warn against overemphasizing cultural differences in personality. For example, Constantine Sedikides and her colleagues have argued that the goal of all individuals, regardless of cultural context, is to enhance self-esteem (Sedikides et al., 2003). That is, even in collectivist cultures, the process of conforming to one's culture is motivated by an individualistic concern, the desire for self-esteem. Consequently, at least to some degree, an individualist orientation is universal. Furthermore, although members of different cultures display varying commitments to an individualistic philosophy, autonomy—a sense of personal control over one's life—predicts well-being in all cultures (Ryan et al., 2003).

◄ For these native Alaskans, participating in the traditional blanket toss ceremony is one manifestation of their culture's values related to community and cooperation.

Remember It   Trait Theories

1. According to Gordon Allport, the kind of trait that is a defining characteristic of one's personality is a _____ trait.

2. According to _____, the differences among people are explained by the number of source traits they possess.

3. _____ claimed that psychologists can best understand personality by assessing people on three major dimensions: psychoticism, extraversion, and neuroticism.

4. According to a growing consensus among trait theorists, there are _____ major dimensions of personality.

5. Many behavioral geneticists believe that as much as _____ of personality may be inherited.

6. People in collectivist cultures tend to be more _____ than people in individualist cultures.

Answers: 1. cardinal; 2. Raymond Cattell; 3. Hans Eysenck; 4. five; 5. 50%; 6. interdependent

Social-Cognitive Theories

Future research may demonstrate with certainty that the five factors are inherited, stable throughout life, and universal. However, they still do not provide psychologists with a complete explanation of the individual differences that are encompassed by the concept of personality. For instance, why are even the most extraverted individuals among us sometimes quiet and withdrawn? How do people who are disorganized—that is, who are low in conscientiousness—manage to complete tasks that require attention to detail, such as college research papers? Researchers who examine the influence of learning on personality have provided psychologists with some clues as to how these questions might be answered. For the most part, their hypotheses come from **social-cognitive theory,** the view that personality is a collection of learned behaviors that have been acquired through interactions with others.

social-cognitive theory The view that personality can be defined as a collection of learned behaviors acquired through social interactions

The Situation-Trait Debate

Over the past three decades, Walter Mischel has been among the most vocal critics of trait theories (1973). Mischel initiated the *situation-trait debate*, an ongoing discussion among psychologists about the relative importance of factors within the situation and factors within the person in accounting for behavior (Rowe, 1987). For instance,

13.12 What is the situation-trait debate about?

you probably wouldn't steal money from a store, but what if you saw a stranger unknowingly drop a $5 bill? Mischel and those who agree with him say that characteristics of the two situations dictate your behavior, not a trait such as honesty. Stealing from a store might require devising and carrying out a complicated plan, and it would carry a heavy penalty if you were caught, so you opt for honesty. Picking up a $5 bill is easy and may only result in embarrassment if you were caught, so you may do it. Mischel (1973, 1977) later modified his original position and conceded that behavior is influenced by both the person and the situation. Mischel views a trait as a conditional probability that a particular action will occur in response to a particular situation (Wright & Mischel, 1987).

Advocates for the trait side of the situation-trait debate point out that, as you learned earlier, longitudinal studies suggest that the five factors are relatively stable throughout life. Those who take the situational approach point to studies such as one in which researchers found that, contrary to the general pattern of decreasing neuroticism with age, women who lost important sources of social support displayed increases in neuroticism as they got older (Maiden et al., 2003). Thus, some participants in the debate have declared that, after three decades of research, both sides have been proven to be right, and that the truth about traits and situations is that both influence personality (Fleeson, 2004). Thus, both should be included in a comprehensive theory of this important domain of individual differences.

Reciprocal Determinism

13.13 How does Bandura's reciprocal determinism explain personality?

Social-cognitive theorist Albert Bandura, whose research on observational learning you learned about in Chapter 5, has proposed a comprehensive theory of personality that takes both traits and situations into account (1977a, 1986). Moreover, Bandura's model incorporates cognitive variables into the mix. Because the model includes so many variables and provides a systematic explanation of how these variables interact, it has generated a great deal of research and has helped psychologists better understand both consistencies and inconsistencies in personality.

Bandura has proposed that internal, environmental, and behavioral variables interact to influence personality. He calls this interaction **reciprocal determinism,** a term that conveys his view that mutual influences contribute to variations across all three types of variables. Internal variables, or *person* variables as they are usually called, include traits such as the five factors, information-processing variables such as short-term memory strategies, individual differences in intelligence, stages of cognitive and social development, learned expectancies about how the environment will respond to behaviors, and physiological factors such as neurological functioning. Environmental variables include social sources of information, the various kinds of consequences that are elicited by our behaviors, and the characteristics of specific situations. Behavioral variables are our actual behaviors. Here is an example of how reciprocal determinism might be used to explain how a student who is low in conscientiousness might become sufficiently conscientious to complete a research paper in a timely fashion (summarized in **Figure 13.5**).

First, when the student is thinking about how she will go about completing the research paper, person variables other than low conscientiousness will come into play. These variables include the student's memories of past experiences with research papers. In the past, she may have lost points on such assignments because her lack of conscientiousness caused her to miss deadlines. Thus, having developed an expectancy that the behavior of missing a deadline will result in a lower grade, the student resolves to make an intentional effort to get the paper done on time.

Second, a number of environmental factors will influence the student's attempts to achieve her goal of finishing the paper on time. For example, if the paper will be counted as half of her grade, she may be more likely to stick to her plan than if it will count only 10%. Similarly, instructions that are unclear may cause the student to be anxious about what the professor expects.

▲ Individuals who are high in self-efficacy pursue challenging goals and persist in their efforts until they reach them.

reciprocal determinism
Bandura's concept of a mutual influential relationship among behavior, cognitive factors, and environment.

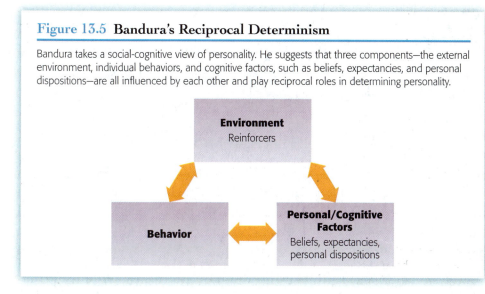

Figure 13.5 Bandura's Reciprocal Determinism

Bandura takes a social-cognitive view of personality. He suggests that three components—the external environment, individual behaviors, and cognitive factors, such as beliefs, expectancies, and personal dispositions—are all influenced by each other and play reciprocal roles in determining personality.

Third, the student's behaviors will influence the outcome of her research paper experience. On the one hand, she may respond to the professor's unclear instructions and the anxiety they cause by procrastinating. On the other hand, she may respond by asking the professor for clarification. Most likely, if she responds with procrastination, her trait of low conscientiousness will once again manifest itself as it has in the past. But choosing to seek clarification will help her break this pattern. As a result, her anxiety will diminish, and she will gain confidence in her ability to overcome a troublesome personality trait.

As this example illustrates, reciprocal determinism does a good job of explaining the mutual influences that occur among personal, environmental, and behavioral variables. Each of the three influences the other two. For Bandura, behavior is not exclusively caused by either personal variables, such as the five factors, or environmental influences, such as consequences. Instead, it is influenced by and, in turn, it influences variables within both the personal and environmental domains. Consequently, the three domains are inseparable components of a dynamic system of personality that adapts to whatever situational demands an individual faces.

Self-Efficacy and Locus of Control

Bandura has also proposed that **self-efficacy** is a key variable within the personal domain. Self-efficacy is the perception people have of their ability to perform competently whatever they attempt. Cross-cultural researchers examining self-efficacy in 25 countries found it to be an important individual difference in all of them (Scholz et al., 2002). According to Bandura, people high in self-efficacy approach new situations confidently, set high goals, and persist in their efforts because they believe success is likely. People low in self-efficacy, on the other hand, expect failure; consequently, they avoid challenges and typically give up on tasks they find difficult. Bandura's research has shown that people with high self-efficacy are less likely to experience depression than those with low self-efficacy (Bandura, 1997b).

Julian Rotter proposed a similar cognitive factor, **locus of control (LOC).** Some people see themselves as primarily in control of their behavior and its consequences. Rotter (1966, 1971, 1990) defined this perception as an *internal locus of control*. An internal LOC can emphasize either a stable trait or a variable factor. In our illustration involving a student who resolves to complete a research paper on time, for example, if the student fails and attributes her failure to low conscientiousness, she is exhibiting an internal LOC. If she attributes her failure to a lack of effort, however, she is also demonstrating an internal LOC. Research indicates that attributions to variable factors

13.14 What do self-efficacy and locus of control contribute to personality?

self-efficacy The perception a person has of his or her ability to perform competently whatever is attempted.

locus of control Rotter's concept of a cognitive factor that explains how people account for what happens in their lives—either seeing themselves as primarily in control of their behavior and its consequences (internal locus of control) or perceiving what happens to them to be in the hands of fate, luck, or chance (external locus of control).

that individuals view as controllable, such as effort, are more likely than attributions involving internal variables that are perceived to be uncontrollable, such as personality traits, to enhance an individual's chances of achieving a goal (Roesch & Weiner, 2001).

People who perceive that whatever happens to them is in the hands of fate, luck, or chance exhibit an *external locus of control* and may claim that it does not matter what they do because "whatever will be, will be." Rotter claimed that people with an external LOC are less likely to change their behavior as a result of reinforcement, because they do not see reinforcers as being tied to their own actions. Students who have an external LOC tend to be procrastinators and, thus, are less likely to be academically successful than those who have an internal LOC. Furthermore, external LOC is associated with lower levels of life satisfaction (Kirkcaldy et al., 2002). You can determine your own LOC in the *Try It* below.

Try It   Where Is Your Locus of Control?

For each statement, indicate whether you agree or disagree.

1. Heredity determines most of a person's personality.
2. Chance has a lot to do with being successful.
3. Whatever plans you make, something will always interfere.
4. Being at the right place at the right time is essential for getting what you want in life.
5. Intelligence is a given, and it cannot be improved.
6. If I successfully accomplish a task, it's because it was an easy one.
7. You cannot change your destiny.

8. School success is mostly a result of one's socioeconomic background.
9. People are lonely because they are not given the chance to meet new people.
10. Setting goals for yourself is of little use because nobody knows what might happen in the future to interfere with them.

Give yourself 1 point for each "agree" and 0 points for each "disagree." How close did you get to a score of 10? The closer your score to 10, the more external your locus of control.

Research suggests that both self-efficacy and locus of control are learned aspects of our personalities. Studies show, for example, that providing middle-school students with task-specific training, such as teaching them strategies for solving math problems, enhances their sense of self-efficacy with regard to such tasks (Poynton et al., 2006). Locus of control can be influenced by training as well. In one Chinese study, researchers taught middle-school students to attribute academic outcomes more to effort than to ability or to external variables (Guangyaun, 2005). Remarkably, when participants were retested 13 years later, the researchers found that they continued to demonstrate the positive effects of such training. Compared to control group subjects, those who received locus-of-control training were better at setting goals suited to their abilities and were more persistent in pursuing them.

Studies indicate that self-efficacy and locus of control contribute to important outcomes independently from the five personality factors. For example, both the personality factors and self-efficacy are correlated with the number of job offers a person receives after a round of interviews (Tay, Ang, & Dyne, 2006). Similarly, the five factors and locus of control make separate contributions to academic achievement (Hattrup, O'Connell, & Labrador, 2005). That is, a person who is high in conscientiousness is most likely to be a high achiever if she also has an internal locus of control.

As you can see, a model of personality that includes the five factors, self-efficacy, and locus of control provides us with a more comprehensive understanding of individual differences in personality than any of these variables does when considered alone. Moreover, Bandura's reciprocal determinism provides us with a useful explanation of how these variables and many others work together to produce the kind of behavior and mental processes that we typically think of as being a function of personality. Thus, as we noted at the outset of this chapter, the best strategy for understanding personality is to formulate a view that includes the strengths of all of the major perspectives.

Remember It   Social Cognitive Theories

1. The psychologist who is most often associated with the situation-trait debate is _____.

2. In Bandura's reciprocal determinism, personality is shaped by three sets of variables: _____, _____, and _____.

3. A person who believes that he can be successful at a task has high _____.

4. People who believe that luck determines what happens to them have an _____ locus of control, while those who believe their own efforts are more important than luck have an _____ locus of control.

Answers: 1. Walter Mischel; 2. personal, behavioral, environmental; 3. self-efficacy; 4. external, internal

---

Personality Assessment

Have you ever taken a personality test? You may have as part of a job application and screening process. Personality assessment is commonly used in business and industry to aid in hiring decisions, as you'll learn in Chapter 17. Various ways of measuring personality are used by clinical psychologists, psychiatrists, and counselors in the diagnosis of patients and in the assessment of progress in therapy.

Observation, Interviews, and Rating Scales

Psychologists use observation in personality assessment in a variety of settings—hospitals, clinics, schools, and workplaces. Behaviorists, in particular, prefer observation to other methods of personality assessment. Using an observational technique known as *behavioral assessment*, psychologists can count and record the frequency of particular behaviors. This method is often used in behavior modification programs in settings such as psychiatric hospitals, where psychologists may chart patients' progress toward reducing aggressive acts or other undesirable or abnormal behaviors. However, behavioral assessment is time-consuming, and behavior may be misinterpreted. Probably the most serious limitation is that the very presence of the observer can alter the behavior being observed.

Clinical psychologists and psychiatrists use interviews to help in the diagnosis and treatment of patients. Counselors use interviews to screen applicants for admission to college or other special programs, and employers use them to evaluate job applicants and employees for job promotions. Interviewers consider not only a person's answers to questions but the person's tone of voice, speech, mannerisms, gestures, and general appearance as well. Interviewers often use a *structured interview*, in which the content of the questions and even the manner in which they are asked are carefully planned ahead of time. The interviewer tries not to deviate in any way from the structured format so that more reliable comparisons can be made between different subjects.

Examiners sometimes use *rating scales* to record data from interviews or observations. Such scales are useful because they provide a standardized format, including a list of traits or behaviors to evaluate. A rating scale helps to focus the rater's attention on all the relevant traits to be considered so that none is overlooked or weighed too heavily. The major limitation of these scales is that the ratings are often subjective. A related problem is the *halo effect*—the tendency of raters to be excessively influenced in their overall evaluation of a person by one or a few favorable or unfavorable traits. Often, traits or attributes that are not even on the rating scale, such as physical attractiveness or similarity to the rater, heavily influence a rater's perception of an individual. To overcome these limitations, it is often necessary to have individuals rated by more than one interviewer.

13.15 How do psychologists use observations, interviews, and rating scales?

Personality Inventories

As useful as observations, interviews, and rating scales are, another method of measuring personality offers greater objectivity. This method is the **inventory,** a paper-and-pencil test with questions about an individual's thoughts, feelings, and behaviors, which measures several dimensions of personality and can be scored according to a standard procedure. Psychologists favoring the trait approach prefer the inventory because it reveals where people fall on various dimensions of personality, and it yields a personality profile.

The MMPI. The most widely used personality inventory is the **Minnesota Multiphasic Personality Inventory (MMPI)** or its revision, the MMPI-2. The MMPI is the most heavily researched personality test for diagnosing psychiatric problems and disorders (Butcher & Rouse, 1996). There have been more than 115 recognized translations of the MMPI, and it is used in more than 65 countries (Butcher & Graham, 1989).

Developed in the late 1930s and early 1940s by researchers J. Charnley McKinley and Starke Hathaway, the MMPI was originally intended to identify tendencies toward various types of psychiatric disorders. The researchers administered over 1,000 questions about attitudes, feelings, and specific symptoms to groups of psychiatric patients at the University of Minnesota hospital who had been clearly diagnosed with various specific disorders and to a control group of individuals who had no diagnosed disorders. They retained the 550 items that differentiated the specific groups of psychiatric patients from the group of participants considered to be normal.

Because the original MMPI had become outdated, the MMPI-2 was published in 1989 (Butcher et al., 1989). Most of the original test items were retained, but new items were added to more adequately cover areas such as alcoholism, drug abuse, suicidal tendencies, eating disorders, and the Type A behavior pattern. The MMPI had often been unreliable for African Americans, women, and adolescents (Levitt & Duckworth, 1984). Thus, new norms were established to reflect national census data and achieve a better geographical, racial, and cultural balance (Ben-Porath & Butcher, 1989).

Table 13.2 shows the ten clinical scales of the MMPI-2. Following are examples of items on the test, which are to be answered "true," "false," or "cannot say."

I wish I were not bothered by thoughts about sex.
When I get bored, I like to stir up some excitement.
In walking I am very careful to step over sidewalk cracks.
If people had not had it in for me, I would have been much more successful.

A high score on any of the scales does not necessarily mean that a person has a problem or a psychiatric symptom. Rather, the psychologist looks at the individual's MMPI profile—the pattern of scores on all the scales—and then compares it to the profiles of normal individuals and those with various psychiatric disorders.

inventory A paper-and-pencil test with questions about a person's thoughts, feelings, and behaviors, which measures several dimensions of personality and can be scored according to a standard procedure.

Minnesota Multiphasic Personality Inventory (MMPI) The most extensively researched and widely used personality test, which is used to screen for and diagnose psychiatric problems and disorders; revised as MMPI-2.

Table 13.2 The Clinical Scales of the MMPI-2

Scale Name	Interpretation
1. Hypochondriasis (Hs)	High scorers exhibit an exaggerated concern about their physical health.
2. Depression (D)	High scorers are usually depressed, despondent, and distressed.
3. Hysteria (Hy)	High scorers complain often about physical symptoms that have no apparent organic cause.
4. Psychopathic deviate (Pd)	High scorers show a disregard for social and moral standards.
5. Masculinity/femininity (Mf)	High scorers show "traditional" masculine or feminine attitudes and values.
6. Paranoia (Pa)	High scorers demonstrate extreme suspiciousness and feelings of persecution.
7. Psychasthenia (Pt)	High scorers tend to be highly anxious, rigid, tense, and worrying.
8. Schizophrenia (Sc)	High scorers tend to be socially withdrawn and to engage in bizarre and unusual thinking.
9. Hypomania (Ma)	High scorers are usually emotional, excitable, energetic, and impulsive.
10. Social introversion (S)	High scorers tend to be modest, self-effacing, and shy.

But what if someone lies on the test in order to appear mentally healthy? Embedded in the test to provide a check against lying are questions such as these:

Once in a while, I put off until tomorrow what I ought to do today.
I gossip a little at times.
Once in a while, I laugh at a dirty joke.

Most people would almost certainly have to answer "true" in response to such items—unless, of course, they were lying. Another scale controls for people who are faking psychiatric illness, as in the case of someone hoping to be judged not guilty of a crime by reason of insanity. Research seems to indicate that the validity scales in the MMPI-2 are effective in detecting test takers who were instructed to fake a psychological disturbance or to lie to make themselves appear more psychologically healthy (Bagby et al., 1994; Butcher et al., 1995). Even when given specific information about various psychological disorders, test takers could not produce profiles similar to those of people who actually suffered from the disorder (Wetter et al., 1993).

The MMPI-2 is reliable, easy to administer and score, and inexpensive to use. It is useful in the screening, diagnosis, and clinical description of abnormal behavior, but it does not reveal normal personality differences very well. A special form of the test, the MMPI-A, was developed for adolescents in 1992. The MMPI-A includes some items that are especially relevant to adolescents, such as those referring to eating disorders, substance abuse, and problems with school and family. The MMPI-2 has been translated for use in Belgium, Chile, China, France, Hong Kong, Israel, Korea, Italy, Japan, Norway, Russia, Spain, and Thailand (Butcher, 1992). Lucio and others (1994) administered the Mexican (Spanish) version of the MMPI-2 to more than 2,100 Mexican college students. They found the profiles of these students "remarkably similar" to profiles of U.S. college students.

The CPI. An important limitation of the MMPI-2, though, is that it was designed specifically to assess abnormality. By contrast, the **California Personality Inventory (CPI)** is a highly regarded personality test developed especially for normal individuals aged 13 and older. Similar to the MMPI, the CPI even has many of the same questions, but it does not include any questions designed to reveal psychiatric illness (Gough, 1987). The CPI is valuable for predicting behavior, and it has been "praised for its technical competency, careful development, cross-validation and follow-up, use of sizable samples and separate sex norms" (Domino, 1984, p. 156). The CPI was revised in 1987 to make it provide "a picture of the subject's life-style and the degree to which his or her potential is being realized" (McReynolds, 1989, p. 101). The CPI is particularly useful in predicting school achievement in high school and beyond, leadership and executive success, and the effectiveness of police, military personnel, and student teachers (Gregory, 1996).

The MBTI. The **Myers-Briggs Type Indicator (MBTI)** is another personality inventory that is useful for measuring normal individual differences. This test is based on Jung's personality theory. The MBTI is a forced-choice, self-report inventory that is scored on four separate bipolar dimensions:

Extraversion (E) ⟷ Introversion (I)
Sensing (S) ⟷ Intuition (N)
Thinking (T) ⟷ Feeling (F)
Judging (J) ⟷ Perceptive (P)

A person can score anywhere along a continuum for each of the four bipolar dimensions, and these individual scores are usually summarized according to a system of personality types. Sixteen types of personality profiles can be derived from the possible combinations of the four bipolar dimensions. For example, a person whose scores were more toward the Extraversion, Intuition, Feeling, and Perceptive ends of the four dimensions would be labeled an ENFP personality type, which is described as follows:

Relates more readily to the outer world of people and things than to the inner world of ideas (E); prefers to search for new possibilities over working with known facts and conventional ways of doing things (N); makes decisions and

California Personality Inventory (CPI) A highly regarded personality test developed especially for normal individuals aged 13 and older.

Myers-Briggs Type Indicator (MBTI) A personality inventory useful for measuring normal individual differences; based on Jung's theory of personality.

solves problems on the basis of personal values and feelings rather than relying on logical thinking and analysis (F); and prefers a flexible, spontaneous life to a planned and orderly existence (P). (Gregory, 1996)

The MBTI is popular in business and educational settings. Critics point to the absence of rigorous, controlled validity studies of the inventory (Pittenger, 2005). And it has also been criticized for being interpreted too often by unskilled examiners, who have been accused of making overly simplistic interpretations (Gregory, 1996). However, sufficiently sophisticated methods for interpreting the MBTI do exist, as revealed by almost 500 research studies to date (Allen, 1997). Many of these studies have shown that the MBTI personality types are associated with career choices and job satisfaction. For example, physicians who choose different specialties (e.g., pediatrics, surgery) tend to have different MBTI types (Stilwell et al., 2000). Consequently, the MBTI continues to enjoy popularity among career counselors.

Projective Tests

13.17 How do projective tests provide insight into personality, and what are some of the most commonly used projective tests?

Responses on interviews and questionnaires are conscious responses and, for this reason, are less useful to therapists who wish to probe the unconscious. Such therapists may choose a completely different technique called a projective test. A **projective test** is a personality test consisting of inkblots, drawings of ambiguous human situations, or incomplete sentences for which there are no obvious correct or incorrect responses. People respond by projecting their inner thoughts, feelings, fears, or conflicts onto the test materials.

The Rorschach. One of the oldest and most popular projective tests is the **Rorschach Inkblot Method** developed by Swiss psychiatrist Hermann Rorschach (ROR-shok) in 1921. It consists of 10 inkblots, which the test taker is asked to describe (see **Figure 13.6**). To develop his test, Rorschach put ink on paper and then folded the paper so that symmetrical patterns would result. Earlier, psychologists had used standardized series of inkblots to study imagination and other variables, but Rorschach was the first to use inkblots to investigate personality. He experimented with thousands of inkblots on different groups of people and found that ten of the inkblots could be used to discriminate among different diagnostic groups, such as manic depressives, paranoid schizophrenics, and so on. These ten inkblots—five black and white, and five with color—were standardized and are still widely used.

The Rorschach can be used to describe personality, make differential diagnoses, plan and evaluate treatment, and predict behavior (Ganellen, 1996; Weiner, 1997). It is second in popularity to the MMPI for use in research and clinical assessment (Butcher & Rouse, 1996). The test taker is shown the ten inkblots and asked to tell everything that he or she thinks about what each inkblot looks like or resembles. The examiner writes down the test taker's responses and then goes through the cards again, asking questions to clarify what the test taker has reported. In scoring the Rorschach, the examiner considers whether the test taker has used the whole inkblot in the description or only parts of it. The test taker is asked whether the shape of the inkblot, its color, or something else prompted the response. The examiner also considers whether the test taker sees movement, human figures or parts, animal figures or parts, or other objects in the inkblots.

Until the 1990s, the main problem with the Rorschach was that the results were too dependent on the interpretation and judgment of the examiner. In response to such criticisms, Exner (1993) developed the Comprehensive System, a more reliable procedure for scoring the Rorschach. It provides some normative data so that the responses of a person taking the test can be compared to those of others with known personality characteristics. Using this system, some researchers have found high agreement among different raters interpreting the same responses (interrater agreement) (McDowell & Acklin, 1996). Others believe that more research is necessary before it can be concluded that the Comprehensive System yields reliable and valid results (Wood et al., 1996). However, a number of meta-analyses indicate that the Rorschach Inkblot Method has "psychometric soundness and practical utility" (Weiner, 1996).

projective test A personality test in which people respond to inkblots, drawings of ambiguous human situations, or incomplete sentences by projecting their inner thoughts, feelings, fears, or conflicts onto the test materials.

Rorschach Inkblot Method (ROR-shok) A projective test composed of ten inkblots that the test taker is asked to describe; used to assess personality, make differential diagnoses, plan and evaluate treatment, and predict behavior.

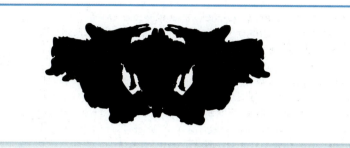
Figure 13.6 An Inkblot Similar to One Used for the Rorschach Inkblot Method

The Thematic Apperception Test. Another projective test is the **Thematic Apperception Test (TAT)** developed by Henry Murray and his colleagues in 1935 (Morgan & Murray, 1935; Murray, 1938). You may remember from Chapter 10 that researchers have used the TAT to study the need for achievement, but it is also useful for assessing other aspects of personality. The TAT consists of one blank card and 19 other cards showing vague or ambiguous black-and-white drawings of human figures in various situations. If you were taking the TAT, this is what you would be told:

> This is a test of your creative imagination. I shall show you a picture, and I want you to make up a plot or story for which it might be used as an illustration. What is the relation of the individuals in the picture? What has happened to them? What are their present thoughts and feelings? What will be the outcome? (Morgan & Murray, 1962, p. 532)

What does the story you write have to do with your personality or your problems or motives? Murray (1965) stresses the importance of "an element or theme that recurs three or more times in the series of stories" (p. 432). For example, if a person uses many story themes about illness, sex, fear of failure, aggression, power, or interpersonal conflict, such a recurring theme is thought to reveal a problem in the person's life. Murray (1965) also claims that the strength of the TAT is "its capacity to reveal things that the patient is unwilling to tell or is unable to tell because he [or she] is unconscious of them" (p. 427).

The TAT is time-consuming and difficult to administer and score. Although it has been used extensively in research, it suffers from the same weaknesses as other projective techniques: (1) It relies heavily on the interpretation skills of the examiner, and (2) it may reflect too strongly a person's temporary motivational and emotional states and not indicate more permanent aspects of personality.

Review and Reflect summarizes the various approaches to personality assessment.

Thematic Apperception Test (TAT) A projective test consisting of drawings of ambiguous human situations, which the test taker describes; thought to reveal inner feelings, conflicts, and motives, which are projected onto the test materials.

Review and Reflect Three Approaches to Personality Assessment

Method	Examples	Description
Observation and rating	Observation	Performance (behavior) is observed in a specific situation, and personality is assessed based on the observation.
	Interviews	In interviews, the responses to questions are taken to reveal personality characteristics.
	Rating scales	Rating scales are used to score or rate test takers on the basis of traits, behaviors, or results of interviews.
		Assessment is subjective, and accuracy depends largely on the ability and experience of the evaluator.

continued

continued

Method	Examples	Description
Inventories	Minnesota Multiphasic Personality Inventory-2 (MMPI-2)	Test takers reveal their beliefs, feelings, behavior, and/or opinions on paper-and-pencil tests.
	California Personality Inventory (CPI)	Scoring procedures are standardized, and responses of test takers are compared to group norms.
	Myers-Briggs Type Indicator (MBTI)	
Projective tests	Rorschach Inkblot Method	Test takers respond to ambiguous test materials and presumably reveal elements of their own personalities by what they report they see in inkblots, by themes they write about scenes showing possible conflict, or by how they complete sentences.
	Thematic Apperception Test (TAT)	
	Sentence completion method	Scoring is subjective, and accuracy depends largely on the ability and experience of the evaluator.

Remember It   Personality Assessment

1. In _____, psychologists ask a standard set of questions to assess an individual's personality.

2. Match each personality test with its description.

   _____ (1) MMPI-2   a. inventory used to diagnose psychopathology
   _____ (2) Rorschach   b. inventory used to assess normal personality
   _____ (3) TAT   c. projective test using inkblots
   _____ (4) CPI   d. projective test using drawings of ambiguous human situations
   _____ (5) MBTI   e. inventory used to assess personality types

3. George has an unconscious resentment toward his father. Which type of personality test might best detect this?

Answers: 1. structured interviews; 2. (1) a, (2) c, (3) d, (4) b, (5) e; 3. projective

Apply It   Personality Assessment in the Courtroom

In recent years, a number of high-profile criminal trials have increased public awareness of the field of *forensic psychology*, the branch of applied psychology that uses psychological knowledge and personality assessment techniques in judicial proceedings. Often, these high-profile trials involve a defendant who admits to having committed a heinous crime, but who claims to have been insane at the time. Insanity is a legal term, not psychological one, but psychological assessment techniques such as those you learned about in this chapter are often used both to support and refute such claims. However, there is one important difference. Being supportive of a person who is being assessed is an important aspect of non-forensic psychological assessment. During a forensic assessment, however, the psychologist usually remains detached and objective (Craig, 2005).

Insanity defense cases make up little, if any, of a typical forensic psychologist's workload. Instead, forensic psychologists spend most of their time dealing with cases that involve issues that seldom make headlines. Here is a brief overview of a few of the kinds of cases in which forensic psychologists are often involved.

Involuntary Commitment

Bill, a long-time alcoholic, had been living on the streets of a large city for 10 years when he began hearing voices that prompted him to dart in and out of traffic on a busy freeway on-ramp. Concerned for his safety, Bill's sister petitioned a judge to order her brother to be committed to a psychiatric hospital for treatment of his alcoholism and hallucinations. In response to her petition, the judge issued an order that authorized police to take Bill to a hospital to be assessed by a forensic psychologist.

In such cases, forensic psychologists use interviews, observations, and psychological tests to formulate a professional opinion regarding the individual's capacity for self-care and the degree to which he might be a danger to himself or others (National Mental Health Association, 2005). Assessing the potential for harm can be particularly challenging, and psychologists can be held legally responsible for failing to protect the community from dangerous individuals (Craig, 2005). Thus, if there is any reasonable indication that a patient might harm someone, for instance, if he has made a verbal threat against another person, then many forensic psychologists choose to commit the person, at least for a brief period of time.

Malingering

Several months ago, Marta suffered a head injury when a piece of lumber fell on her head at the home improvement store where she was employed. Her supervisor arranged for Marta to get medical treatment at company expense, and she was given paid leave time to recuperate from her injury. A few weeks later, her physician determined that she was able to resume work, but Marta protested that she was still too mentally confused to work and refused to go back. Consequently, the company fired her. Now Marta is suing the company for wrongful termination, back wages, and compensation for pain and suffering. The company's attorneys have hired a forensic psychologist to determine whether Marta is malingering, that is, to determine whether she is lying or exaggerating with regard to her condition in pursuit of financial gain.

In cases such as this, forensic psychologists are aided by the fact that most people, head injured or not, are unable to effectively manufacture the kinds of symptoms that neurologists observe in individuals who have actually experienced serious head injuries (Vickery et al., 2004). Furthermore, there are several neuropsychological assessments that have been specifically designed to distinguish between malingerers and those whose suffering is legitimate (Etherton et al., 2005; Henry, 2005). Other tests, such as the validity scales of the MMPI, are also often used (Boccaccini et al., 2006).

Competency to Stand Trial

In response to a neighbor's call, police arrived at the home of a 43-year-old woman named Lucy. They found her sitting in a lawn chair on the front porch, rocking back and forth and humming. According to the neighbors, Lucy had been sitting there day and night for more than a week. As the police were attempting to get Lucy to respond, they noticed an odor emanating from the house. They entered the house and found her husband's body in the couple's bedroom. A concrete block sat atop his crushed skull. When the police asked Lucy what had happened to her husband, she briefly stopped humming to say that she had killed him. Lucy's rocking, humming, and lack of responsiveness continued when in jail, hampering her attorney's efforts to develop a legal defense. The judge in her case called upon a forensic psychologist to determine whether Lucy was competent to stand trial.

Competency to stand trial involves several components (Redding, 2000). Defendants must be capable of making informed choices, so they must be able to understand and process information. They must also be capable of interacting with their attorneys in effective ways. In carrying out competency to stand trial (CST) assessments, psychologists typically use interviews, standardized personality and intelligence tests, and tests that have

been specifically developed to measure legal competency.

If Lucy's behavior is the result a psychological disorder that has caused her to lose touch with reality, then she may be found to be incompetent to stand trial (Viljoen et al., 2004). If a defendant who has been accused of a serious crime such as murder is found to be incompetent, she is typically confined to a psychiatric hospital. Her confinement usually continues until she becomes competent. While in the hospital, she can be legally forced to take medication that may, in the expert opinion of a psychiatrist, restore her competency (Mendoza, 2005). This is possible because, under the law, individuals who are committed to psychiatric hospitals because they have been judged incompetent to stand trial do not have the same rights as other patients.

Child Custody Evaluations

Mr. and Mrs. Romalo are getting a divorce. Both of them are seeking sole custody of their two children. The judge has requested that a forensic psychologist carry out a special kind of assessment known as a *child custody evaluation*.

Child custody evaluations require psychologists to assess both children and their parents (Craig, 2005). Psychological tests and observations of parent–child interactions are usually included in the evaluation (Acklin & Cho–Stutler, 2006). The goal of these assessments is to provide information that is relevant to the top priority in such proceedings—the best interests of the child. Usually, custody evaluations are required when children are too young to effectively determine and articulate what they believe will be in their best interests. At the conclusion of the evaluation, the forensic psychologist provides the court with his or her professional opinion regarding the short- and long-term impact on a child's life of placement with either parent.

Pursuing a Career in Forensic Psychology

If you aspire to become a forensic psychologist, it is likely to take you many years to fulfill all of the educational requirements (a doctoral degree, appropriate internship, and passing scores on licensing exams). But the path to a career in forensic psychology begins long before your first graduate class. Surveys show that most graduate programs in forensic psychology require applicants to have taken undergraduate courses in statistics, research methods, abnormal psychology, and experimental psychology (Helms & Mayhew, 2006). Many also recommend that prospective applicants take a course in psychological testing. Your application is also likely to be looked upon favorably if you have good undergraduate grades, some research experience, and favorable letters of recommendation from a few of your undergraduate professors. If a career in forensic psychology is your goal, keep these recommendations in mind as you work your way toward an undergraduate degree.

✳ Summary and Review

Psychoanalytic Theories p. 457

13.1 What are the three levels of awareness in consciousness? p. 457

The three levels of awareness in consciousness are the conscious, the preconscious, and the unconscious. The conscious mind includes everything we are thinking about at any given moment. The preconscious includes thoughts and feelings we can easily bring to mind. The unconscious contains thoughts and feelings that are difficult to call up because they have been repressed.

13.2 What are the roles of the id, the ego, and the superego? p. 458

The id is the primitive, unconscious part of the personality, which contains the instincts and operates on the pleasure principle. The ego is the rational, largely conscious system, which operates according to the reality principle. The superego is the moral system of the personality, consisting of the conscience and the ego ideal. A defense mechanism is a means used by the ego to defend against anxiety and to maintain self-esteem.

13.3 What are the psychosexual stages, and why did Freud consider them important in personality development? p. 460

Freud believed that the sexual instinct is present at birth and develops through a series of psychosexual stages, providing the driving force for all feelings and behaviors. The stages are the oral stage, anal stage, phallic stage (followed by the latency period), and genital stage. One of the most controversial features of Freud's stage theory is the Oedipus complex, a conflict that arises during the phallic stage, in which the child is sexually attracted to the opposite-sex parent and feels hostility toward the same-sex parent.

13.4 How are Freud's ideas evaluated by modern psychologists? p. 462

Freud is credited with calling attention to the unconscious, the importance of early childhood experiences, and the role of defense mechanisms. However, his theory is often criticized because it defies scientific testing.

13.5 How do the views of the neo-Freudians differ from those of Freud? p. 463

Jung conceived of the personality as having three parts: the ego, the personal unconscious, and the collective unconscious. Adler claimed that the predominant force of the personality is not sexual in nature but rather the drive to overcome and compensate for feelings of weakness and inferiority and to strive for superiority or significance. Horney took issue with Freud's sexist view of women and added the feminine dimension to the world of psychology.

Humanistic Theories p. 465

13.6 What are the contributions of humanistic theorists to the study of personality? p. 465

According to Maslow, the goal of personality development is to reach a level where most behavior is motivated by self-actualization, the drive to attain one's fullest potential. According to Rogers, individuals often do not become fully functioning persons because in childhood they did not receive unconditional positive regard from their parents. To gain positive regard, they had to meet their parents' conditions of worth.

13.7 What have psychologists learned about self-esteem? p. 466

The sense of self-esteem is influenced by comparisons of one's real self to one's desired self. Most people's self-esteem is based on what they perceive to be their strengths and weaknesses rather than on a single desired accomplishment or trait. By age 7, most children have a global sense of self-esteem and continue developing beliefs about their competencies in specific domains (e.g., sports) for several years.

Trait Theories p. 467

13.8 What were some of the ideas proposed by early trait theorists? p. 467

Allport defined a cardinal trait as a personal quality that pervades a person's personality to the point where he or she may become identified with that trait. A central trait is the type you might mention when writing a letter of recommendation. Cattell used the term *surface traits* to refer to observable qualities of personality. Source traits, which underlie the surface traits, are possessed in varying amounts by people. Eysenck considers the three most important dimensions of personality to be psychoticism, extroversion, and neuroticism.

13.9 What do five-factor theorists consider to be the most important dimensions of personality? p. 469

According to the five-factor model, personality is influenced by five dimensions. The Big Five are neuroticism, extroversion, conscientiousness, agreeableness, and openness to experience.

13.10 What does research say about the origins and stability of the five factors? p. 471

Both twin and adoption studies have shown that heredity strongly influences personality. However, some traits change over time.

13.11 How does personality differ across cultures? p. 471

The cultural dimension known as individualism/collectivism is associated with personality. Individualist cultures encourage people to view themselves as separate from others and to value independence and assertiveness. Collectivist cultures emphasize social connectedness among people and encourage individuals to define themselves in terms of their social relationships.

Social-Cognitive Theories p. 473

13.12 What is the situation-trait debate about? p. 473

The situation-trait debate concerns the degree to which situations influence the manifestation of personality traits.

13.13 How does Bandura's reciprocal determinism explain personality? p. 474

The external environment, behavior, and cognitive factors are the three components of reciprocal determinism, each influencing and being influenced by the others.

13.14 What do self-efficacy and locus of control contribute to personality? p. 475

Self-efficacy gives people the confidence they need to accomplish goals. An internal locus of control helps them do so as well. An external locus of control may lead to procrastination.

Personality Assessment p. 477

13.15 How do psychologists use observations, interviews, and rating scales? p. 477

During observations, psychologists count behaviors that may be representative of an individual's personality. They use structured interviews to compare the responses of one interviewee to those of others given under similar circumstances. Rating scales are used to quantify behaviors that occur during observations or interviews.

13.16 What is an inventory, and what are the MMPI-2 and the CPI designed to reveal? p. 478

An inventory is a paper-and-pencil test with questions about a person's thoughts, feelings, and behaviors, which measures several dimensions of personality and can be scored according to a standard procedure. The MMPI-2 is designed to screen and diagnose psychiatric problems, and the CPI is designed to assess the normal personality.

13.17 How do projective tests provide insight into personality, and what are some of the most commonly used projective tests? p. 480

In a projective test, people respond to inkblots, drawings of ambiguous human situations, or incomplete sentences by projecting their inner thoughts, feelings, fears, or conflicts onto the test materials. Examples are the Rorschach Inkblot Method and the Thematic Apperception Test (TAT).

Thinking Critically about Psychology

1. In your opinion, which of the major personality theories discussed in this chapter is the most accurate, reasonable, and realistic? Give reasons to support your answers.
2. Are personality traits mostly learned or inherited? Using what you have learned in this chapter and other evidence you can gather, make a case for each position. Support your answers with research and expert opinion.
3. Consider your own behavior and personality attributes from the standpoint of each of the theories: psychoanalysis, humanistic theory, trait theory, and social-cognitive theory. To which aspects of your personality can you apply each of the theories?

Key Terms

archetype, p. 463
California Personality Inventory (CPI), p. 479
collective unconscious, p. 463
conditions of worth, p. 466
conscious, p. 457
defense mechanism, p. 459
ego, p. 458
five-factor model, p. 469
fixation, p. 460
id, p. 458
individualism/collectivism dimension, p. 472

inventory, p. 478
locus of control, p. 475
Minnesota Multiphasic Personality Inventory (MMPI), p. 478
Myers-Briggs Type Indicator (MBTI), p. 479
Oedipus complex, p. 461
personal unconscious, p. 463
personality, p. 456
preconscious, p. 457
projective test, p. 480
psychoanalysis, p. 457
psychosexual stages, p. 460

reciprocal determinism, p. 474
repression, p. 459
Rorschach Inkblot Method, p. 480
self-actualization, p. 465
self-efficacy, p. 475
social-cognitive theory, p. 473
superego, p. 458
Thematic Application Test (TAT), p. 481
trait, p. 467
unconditional positive regard, p. 466
unconscious, p. 458

Chapter 14

Psychological Disorders

During her days at Wilson High School in Portland, Oregon, Tracy Moore discovered that she had a remarkable singing voice (Roberts, 2006). She longed to attend Musictech College in Minneapolis to pursue her goal of becoming a professional singer, but her parents insisted that she prove herself academically first. Moore spent a year at Western Oregon University, getting high grades in all kinds of classes. Encouraged by her success, Moore's parents allowed her to move to Minneapolis.

All seemed to be going well during Moore's first year at Musictech until she began hearing voices and started conversing with them, not knowing whether they were real or imagined. She became convinced that aliens were trying to take over her body and that her every move was being monitored by government intelligence agencies. On one occasion, she spent an entire day walking in circles in the belief that doing so would ward off the alien invaders. The other students began to stay away from her and to confront her about her strange behavior. Terrified, she called her parents for help, and they took her home.

Soon after returning to Portland, however, Moore slipped into a state in which she no longer realized that she was mentally ill. She insisted that her belief that aliens were taking over the world was true and that she had special knowledge of the take-over that other people couldn't understand. Moore's parents arranged for the 21-year-old to be hospitalized. Doctors determined that she was suffering from *schizophrenia*, a serious mental disorder in which a person loses contact with reality.

Once she was on medication, Moore's condition began to improve. However, her dream of becoming a singer gave way to more modest ambitions. The medicines required to control her bizarre thoughts also made it difficult for her to concentrate and to reason. Consequently, she found the demands of even the most menial jobs to be overwhelming. Moore feared that she would never get her life back. Her doctors experimented with various medicines and finally found one that helped bring Moore's symptoms under control without causing her to be confused. Slowly, her dream of a professional singing career began to re-emerge.

A fan of the program *American Idol*, Moore enlisted the help of a friend to make the long drive from Portland to Los Angeles to participate in the first round of auditions for the 2003 edition of the show. Of the 10,000 singers who tried out, she was one of only 250 who were chosen to advance to the next round. Three days later, Moore found herself among 50 vocalists who made the next cut. That meant that she would next be singing for the show's celebrity judges, Simon Cowell and Randy Jackson.

Before Moore sang, Cowell asked what her life's ambition was. She courageously told him that she was recovering from schizophrenia and hoped to raise money to fight the disease in the future. Moore reports that Cowell was stunned, although, in trademark fashion, he had no difficulty telling her that she lacked the talent needed to progress to the next level of competition. Nevertheless, he complimented her on her singing voice, and Moore vowed to come back the following year to try out again.

Once Moore returned to Portland, however, she suffered a setback, one that is common among those who suffer from serious psychological disorders. Without telling anyone, she stopped taking her medications. By the time those around her realized that something had gone terribly wrong, Moore was crippled once again by the debilitating delusion that the world was being taken over by aliens. Her suspicions of others made it almost impossible for her friends, family, and doctors to intervene. Moore believed that the medications they were urging her to take were poisonous. After intense struggles, she finally agreed to start taking the medicines again but, this time, they did not work as effectively for her as they had before. The more potent medications she was forced to take as a result caused such severe side-effects that Moore had to be hospitalized.

After more than a year of struggling with these side-effects and with the persistent symptoms of schizophrenia, Moore was well enough to live on her own. Her participation in the 2005 edition of *American Idol* was less successful than her first attempt. However, she has continued to sing, to write songs, and to raise money for organizations that provide support for those who suffer from schizophrenia.

Moore and her parents liken schizophrenia to chronic diseases such as diabetes for which there are no real cures. Such diseases have ups and downs that have to be carefully managed, but they are manageable. With this mindset, Tracy Moore now looks forward to a life that may not include the glamour of *American Idol*, but will be one in which maintaining a stable psychological state will be a priority. Moore realizes that both her music and her life depend on it.

What causes talented young people like Tracy Moore who have able minds and bright futures to become so caught up in false perceptions and beliefs that their lives are nearly, or sometime completely, destroyed? Psychologists don't yet have a definitive answer to this question, but they have learned a great deal about **psychological disorders** in recent years. This chapter explores the symptoms and possible causes of these mental processes or behavior patterns that cause emotional distress and/or substantial impairment in functioning. But first let's ask the obvious question: What is abnormal?

Defining Psychological Disorders

The belief that aliens were taking over the world was a prominent feature of Tracy Moore's struggles with schizophrenia. Perhaps you have heard devotees of some type of conspiracy theory express similar thoughts. However, most such people do not suffer from a psychological disorder. Why not? What separates a person who simply has unusual beliefs from another who has lost touch with reality?

What Is Abnormal?

The first step toward understanding psychological disorders is to grasp the difference between behavior that is out of the ordinary and behavior that is indicative of a psychological disorder. Psychologists think of human behavior as lying along a continuum from adaptive to maladaptive. Adaptive behaviors help us adjust to the demands of the settings in which we find ourselves. For example, studying for your psychology exam is an adaptive behavior. Maladaptive behaviors are the reverse; that is, they interfere with effective functioning. Thus, believing that aliens are taking over the world may be maladaptive if it interferes with adaptive behaviors such as studying.

Psychological disorders generally produce maladaptive behaviors, such as when Tracy Moore spent a day walking in circles. However, maladaptive behavior isn't

14.1 What criteria are used to determine whether behavior is abnormal?

psychological disorders Mental processes and/or behavior patterns that cause emotional distress and/or substantial impairment in functioning.

always a sign of a psychological disorder. To interpret the meaning of such behavior, mental health professionals must perform a comprehensive evaluation of all of the person's behaviors and the possible reasons behind them. Several questions are crucial to these evaluations:

- *Is the behavior considered strange within the person's own culture?* What is considered normal and abnormal in one culture is not necessarily considered so in another. In some cultures, it is normal for women to appear in public bare-breasted, but it would be abnormal for a female executive in an industrialized culture to go to work that way.
- *Does the behavior cause personal distress?* When people experience considerable emotional distress without any life experience that warrants it, they may be diagnosed as having a psychological or mental disorder. Some people may be sad and depressed, and some anxious; others may be agitated or excited, and still others frightened, or even terrified, by delusions and hallucinations.
- *How maladaptive is the person's behavior?* Some experts believe that the best way to differentiate between normal and abnormal behavior is to consider to what degree it leads to healthy or impaired functioning. Washing your hands before you eat is adaptive. Being reluctant to eat in situations in which you cannot wash your hands might be slightly maladaptive, depending upon whether it actually interferes with your need for food and other important aspects of your life. By contrast, washing your hands 100 times a day, and missing meals, classes, and work to do so is not only maladaptive, but it also prevents you from engaging in many adaptive behaviors.
- *Is the person a danger to self or others?* Another consideration is whether people pose any danger to themselves or others. To be committed to a mental hospital, a person must be judged both mentally ill and a danger to self or others.
- *Is the person legally responsible for his or her acts?* Often, the term *insanity* is used to label those who behave abnormally, but mental health professionals do not use this term. It is a legal term used by the courts to declare people not legally responsible for their acts. As noted in the *Apply It* at the end of Chapter 13, forensic psychologists are sometimes called to testify in such cases. However, the insanity defense is rarely successful.

▲ Abnormal behavior is defined by each culture. For example, homelessness is considered abnormal in some cultures and completely normal in others. Thus, the lack of a permanent dwelling place, in and of itself, is not necessarily indicative of a psychological disorder. The fact that homelessness is atypical in industrialized cultures renders it a possible indicator of a psychological disorder within those cultures. In contrast, in cultures in which moving from place to place is the customary way of life, the lack of a permanent home is not an indicator of a psychological disorder.

Classifying Psychological Disorders

In 1952, the American Psychiatric Association published a manual providing a diagnostic system for describing and classifying psychological disorders. Over the years, the manual has been revised several times. The most recent edition, the *Diagnostic and Statistical Manual of Mental Disorder,* 4th Edition, Text Revision, commonly known as the **DSM-IV-TR,** appeared in 2000. As of this writing, work was just beginning on the fifth edition that is scheduled for publication in 2011.

The *DSM-IV-TR* contains descriptions of about 300 specific psychological disorders and lists criteria that must be met in order to make a particular diagnosis. Further, the manual organizes these disorders into categories (see Table 14.1). The manual is used by researchers, therapists, mental health workers, and most insurance companies. This common language enables professionals to speak the same language when diagnosing, treating, researching, and conversing about a variety of psychological disorders (Clark et al., 1995). Moreover, the *DSM-IV-TR* provides clinicians with a multi-dimensional diagnostic system. This system is known as the *multi-axial system*

14.2 How do clinicians use the *DSM-IV-TR*?

DSM-IV-TR, 2000 *The Diagnostic and Statistical Manual of Mental Disorders,* 4th Edition, Text Revision, a manual published by the American Psychiatric Association, which describes the criteria used to classify and diagnose mental disorders.

Table 14.1 Major DSM-IV Categories of Mental Disorders

Disorder	Symptoms	Examples
Schizophrenia and other psychotic disorders	Disorders characterized by the presence of psychotic symptoms, including hallucinations, delusions, disorganized speech, bizarre behavior, and loss of contact with reality	Schizophrenia, paranoid type Schizophrenia, disorganized type Schizophrenia, catatonic type Delusional disorder, jealous type
Mood disorders	Disorders characterized by periods of extreme or prolonged depression or mania or both	Major depressive disorder Bipolar disorder
Anxiety disorders	Disorders characterized by anxiety and avoidance behavior	Panic disorder Social phobia Obsessive-compulsive disorder Posttraumatic stress disorder
Somatoform disorders	Disorders in which physical symptoms are present that are psychological in origin rather than due to a medical condition	Hypochondriasis Conversion disorder
Dissociative disorders	Disorders in which one handles stress or conflict by forgetting important personal information or one's whole identity, or by compartmentalizing the trauma or conflict into a split-off alter personality	Dissociative amnesia Dissociative fugue Dissociative identity disorder
Personality disorders	Disorders characterized by long-standing, inflexible, maladaptive patterns of behavior beginning early in life and causing personal distress or problems in social and occupational functioning	Antisocial personality disorder Histrionic personality disorder Narcissistic personality disorder Borderline personality disorder
Substance-related disorders	Disorders in which undesirable behavioral changes result from substance abuse, dependence, or intoxication	Alcohol abuse Cocaine abuse Cannabis dependence
Disorders usually first diagnosed in infancy, childhood, or adolescence	Disorders that include mental retardation, learning disorders, communication disorders, pervasive developmental disorders, attention-deficit and disruptive behavior disorders, tic disorders, and elimination disorders	Conduct disorder Autistic disorder Tourette's syndrome Stuttering
Eating disorders	Disorders characterized by severe disturbances in eating behavior	Anorexia nervosa Bulimia nervosa

Source: Based on *DSM-IV-TR* (American Psychiatric Association, 2000).

Table 14.2 The Multiaxial System

Axis	Description	Explanation
I	Clinical disorders	Psychological disorders or the main reason for an individual's visit to a clinician is recorded on Axis I. The clinician can enter as many diagnoses or problems as needed but, typically, designates one of them as primary.
II	Personality disorders Mental retardation	Axis II includes only two types of disorders, personality disorders and mental retardation. These two classes of disorders are separated because they usually call for special strategies for treating Axis I disorders.
III	General medical conditions	Any relevant health condition is recorded on Axis III. The clinician also notes any recommendations made to the person regarding the need to look for a medical cause for his or her psychological problems.
IV	Psychosocial, environmental problems	Life issues, such as strained romantic relationships, unemployment, or lack of social support that may be relevant to treatment are recorded on Axis IV.
V	Global assessment of functioning	Axis V usually includes a "global functioning" score ranging from 0 to 100 that describes the degree to which the person's psychological problems have affected his or her life.

Source: DSM-IV-TR, (American Psychological Association, 2000.)

and is described in Table 14.2. A complete description of any case includes information for each of the five axes.

Explaining Psychological Disorders

14.3 How do the various theoretical approaches explain the causes of psychological disorders?

What causes psychological disorders, and how can they be treated? This is the question addressed by the various theoretical approaches summarized in the *Review and Reflect* on the next page. Each perspective has its place in the description, analysis, and treatment of psychological disorders.

The *biological perspective* views abnormal behavior as arising from a physical cause, such as genetic inheritance, biochemical abnormalities or imbalances, structural abnormalities within the brain, and/or infection. Thus, its adherents favor biological treatments such as drug therapy.

The *biopsychosocial perspective* agrees that physical (biological) causes are of central importance but also recognizes the influence of psychological and social factors in the study, identification, and treatment of psychological disorders. Consequently, biopsychosocial psychologists often advocate treatment strategies that include both drugs and psychotherapy.

Originally proposed by Freud, the *psychodynamic perspective* maintains that psychological disorders stem from early childhood experiences and unresolved, unconscious conflicts, usually of a sexual or aggressive nature. The cause assumed by the psychodynamic approach also suggests the cure—psychoanalysis, which Freud developed to uncover and resolve such unconscious conflicts.

According to the *learning perspective*, psychological disorders are thought to be learned and sustained in the same way as any other behavior. According to this view, people who exhibit abnormal behavior either are victims of faulty learning or have failed to learn appropriate patterns of thinking and acting. Behavior therapists use the learning principles of classical and operant conditioning to eliminate distressing behavior and to establish new, more appropriate behavior in its place.

The *cognitive perspective* suggests that faulty thinking or distorted perceptions can contribute to some types of psychological disorders. Treatment based on this perspective is aimed at changing thinking, which presumably will lead to a change in behavior. Moreover, the cognitive perspective offers advice that may prevent psychological

Review and Reflect   Perspectives on Psychological Disorders

Perspective	Causes of Psychological Disorders	Treatment
Biological perspective	A psychological disorder is a symptom of an underlying physical disorder caused by a structural or biochemical abnormality in the brain, by genetic inheritance, or by infection.	Diagnose and treat like any other physical disorder Drugs, electroconvulsive therapy, or psychosurgery
Biopsychosocial perspective	Psychological disorders result from a combination of biological, psychological, and social causes.	An eclectic approach employing treatments that include both drugs and psychotherapy
Psychodynamic perspective	Psychological disorders stem from early childhood experiences and unresolved, unconscious sexual or aggressive conflicts.	Bring disturbing repressed material to consciousness and help patient work through unconscious conflicts Psychoanalysis
Learning perspective	Abnormal thoughts, feelings, and behaviors are learned and sustained like any other behaviors, or there is a failure to learn appropriate behaviors.	Use classical and operant conditioning and modeling to extinguish abnormal behavior and to increase adaptive behavior
Learning perspective		Behavior therapy Behavior modification
Cognitive perspective	Faulty thinking or distorted perceptions can cause psychological disorders.	Change faulty, irrational, and/or negative thinking Beck's cognitive therapy Rational-emotive therapy

disorders. For example, one step toward healthy thinking is to recognize and avoid five cognitive traps: (1) setting unrealistic standards for yourself; (2) negative "what if" thinking (such as "What if I lose my job?"); (3) turning a single negative event, such as a poor grade, into a catastrophe ("I'll never pass this course"); (4) judging anything short of perfection to be a failure; and (5) demanding perfection in yourself and others. If your happiness depends on any of these conditions, you are setting the stage for disappointment, or even depression.

Prevalence of Psychological Disorders

Would you be surprised to learn that psychological disorders are more common than many physical ailments? For instance, each year in the United States, less than 1% of adults, about 1.3 million people, are diagnosed with cancer (American Cancer Society, 2002). By contrast, 26% are diagnosed with a mental disorder of some kind (Kessler et al., 2005a).

> **14.4** How prevalent are psychological disorders?

Another way of thinking about the frequency of a disorder is to examine how likely an individual is to be diagnosed with it in his or her lifetime. The lifetime prevalence rate of cancer in the United States is about 30%; in other words, about 30% of Americans will be diagnosed with cancer sometime in their lives (NCHS, 2000). Again, mental disorders are more common, with a lifetime prevalence rate of nearly 50% (Kessler et al., 2005b). Lifetime rates of a few disorders are shown in Figure 14.1. Clearly, mental disorders represent a significant source of personal misery for individuals and of lost productivity for society. We will begin our study of psychological disorders with the category that occurs most frequently, one that you may have experienced yourself, the *anxiety disorders*.

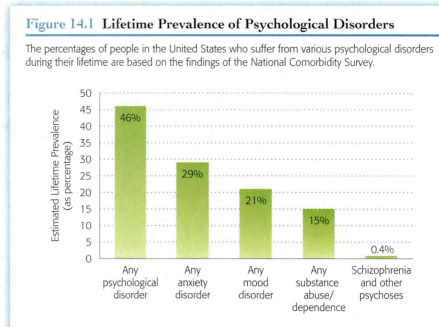

Figure 14.1 Lifetime Prevalence of Psychological Disorders

The percentages of people in the United States who suffer from various psychological disorders during their lifetime are based on the findings of the National Comorbidity Survey.

Source: Data from Bhugra (2005) & Kessler et al. (2005a).

Remember It   Defining Psychological Disorders

1. To be defined as abnormal, a person's behavior must be considered strange in the _____ in which it occurs.

2. The _____ lists criteria for diagnosing psychological disorders.

3. About _____ of people in the United States will suffer from a psychological disorder at some time in their lives.

4. Match the theoretical perspective with its suggested cause of abnormal behavior.

_____ (1) psychodynamic perspective
_____ (2) biological perspective
_____ (3) learning perspective
_____ (4) biopsychosocial perspective
_____ (5) cognitive perspective

a. faulty learning
b. unconscious, unresolved conflicts
c. genetic inheritance or biochemical or structural abnormalities in the brain
d. faulty thinking
e. combination of biological, psychological, and social factors

Answers: 1. culture; 2. *DSM-IV-TR*; 3. 50%; 4. (1) b, (2) c, (3) a, (4) e, (5) d

---

Anxiety Disorders

Did you know that Barbra Streisand, one of the most celebrated and successful singers in the history of American music, once suffered from a crippling case of stage fright that kept her off the stage for 27 years? Streisand's problems began when she forgot the words to a song during a concert in 1967. Afterwards, she was so afraid that the embarrassing situation would occur again that she was only able to sing in the tightly controlled conditions of a recording studio. In 1994, Streisand faced her fears and performed before a live audience. She has performed many times since then, although she still suffers from pre-performance jitters. Her case demonstrates that an exaggerated fear of what might happen in the future can have harmful effects on even the most talented and accomplished among us.

When thoughts about what might happen in the future (a state of mind referred to as *anxiety* by psychologists) become so intense and frequent that they interfere with a person's social or occupational functioning, worrying can develop into a serious psychological disorder. In fact, **anxiety disorders** are the most common category of mental disorders and account for more than 4 million doctor visits each year in the United States (NCHS, 2002b). We will begin our discussion of anxiety disorders by considering two kinds of anxious symptoms. Before you read on, take a minute now to complete the anxiety disorder checklist below.

Try It — Identifying Anxiety Disorders

Read each of the four descriptions below, and place a checkmark beside each description that sounds like you or someone you know.

_____ **1.** You are always worried about things, even when there are no signs of trouble. You have frequent aches and pains that can't be traced to physical illness or injury. You tire easily, and yet you have trouble sleeping. Your body is constantly tense.

_____ **2.** Out of the blue, your heart starts pounding. You feel dizzy. You can't breathe. You feel like you are about to die. You've had these symptoms over and over again.

_____ **3.** Every day, you fear you will do something embarrassing. You've stopped going to parties because you're afraid to meet new people. When other people look at you, you break out in a sweat and shake uncontrollably. You stay home from work because you're terrified of being called on in a staff meeting.

_____ **4.** You are so afraid of germs that you wash your hands repeatedly until they are raw and sore. You can't leave the house until you check the locks on every window and door over and over again. You are terrified that you will harm someone you care about. You just can't get those thoughts out of your head.

As you continue through this section of the chapter, you'll learn which anxiety disorders these symptoms represent. (From NIMH, 1999a.)

Panic Attacks and Agoraphobia

Feeling anxious is an extremely common experience. However, anxious feelings, even when they occur for unknown reasons and seem to be irrational, are not psychological disorders (American Psychiatric Association, 2000). Nevertheless, they may be symptomatic of a disorder (Morrison, 2001). When a person who is troubled by anxious feelings goes to a mental health professional for help, the clinician's first priority is to determine whether the feelings are symptoms of a psychological disorder. There are two types of anxious feelings for which people often seek professional help: panic attacks and agoraphobia.

14.5 What are the characteristics of panic attacks and agoraphobia?

Panic Attacks. Have you ever had a **panic attack,** a sudden feeling of fear in which your heart was pounding, your body was shaking, and you felt that you were choking? If so, then you may have believed that you were dying or "going crazy." Although panic attacks can be frightening, it's important to realize that they are very common, and, once again, they do not constitute a psychological disorder.

To determine whether an individual's panic attacks are symptomatic of a deeper problem, clinicians usually begin by determining whether an individual is having cued and uncued attacks (Morrison, 2001). Panicky feelings that have known cues, such as the feeling a person might get while driving through an intersection where she once had a traffic accident, are more often viewed as the result of learning rather than as signs of a disorder. By contrast, uncued attacks are more likely to be symptomatic of a psychological disorder.

anxiety disorders Psychological disorders characterized by frequent fearful thoughts about what might happen in the future.

panic attack An episode of overwhelming anxiety, fear, or terror.

Although researchers don't fully understand the process, uncued attacks appear to be brought about by a dysfunction in the autonomic nervous system's fight-or-flight system in which the brain misperceives a normal change in bodily functioning to be a danger signal (NAMI, 2003). For example, a person's heart rate normally increases after consuming a beverage that contains caffeine. For unknown reasons, in panic attack sufferers, this normal change may be perceived as a danger signal by the brain, thereby causing the sympathetic nervous system to put the body's autonomic systems on alert. Next, the panic attack sufferer's higher cognitive functions spring into action—"I'm having a heart attack! I'm going to die!"—thus amplifying the sensation of danger. These cognitive interpretations prolong the attack by short-circuiting the parasympathetic system's efforts to counteract the sympathetic system's influence on physiological functions. Thus, clinicians often treat panic attacks by teaching sufferers how to control their cognitive responses to the sensations that accompany these attacks.

Agoraphobia. The type of fear that is most likely to drive people to seek professional help is **agoraphobia.** A person with agoraphobia has an intense fear of being in a situation from which immediate escape is not possible or in which help would not be available if she or he should become overwhelmed by anxiety or experience. In some cases, a person's entire life is planned around avoiding feared situations such as busy streets, crowded stores, restaurants, and/or public transportation. An agoraphobic often will not leave home unless accompanied by a friend or family members, and, in severe cases, not even then.

Although agoraphobia can occur without panic attacks, it often begins during the early adult years with repeated panic attacks (American Psychiatric Association, 2000). The intense fear of having another attack causes the person to avoid any place or situation where previous attacks have occurred. Thus, although agoraphobia itself is not a psychological disorder, when it begins to interfere so dramatically with a person's everyday life, clinicians often find that it is one of many debilitating symptoms that a person is experiencing as a result of having developed an anxiety disorder.

Common Anxiety Disorders

14.6 How do the symptoms of four common anxiety disorders differ?

At the beginning of this section, you read about Barbra Streisand's 27-year battle with stage fright. She is among the millions of people who have struggled with and overcome one of four common anxiety disorders. These include generalized anxiety disorder, panic disorder, social phobia, and specific phobia.

Generalized Anxiety Disorder. **Generalized anxiety disorder** is the diagnosis given to people who are plagued by chronic, excessive worry for 6 months or more. These people expect the worst; their worrying is either unfounded or greatly exaggerated and, thus, difficult to control. They may be unduly worried about their finances, their own health or that of family members, their performance at work, or their ability to function socially. Their excessive anxiety may cause them to feel tense, tired, and irritable, and to have difficulty concentrating and sleeping. Other symptoms may include trembling, palpitations, sweating, dizziness, nausea, diarrhea, or frequent urination. This disorder affects twice as many women as men and leads to considerable distress and impairment (Brawman-Mintzer & Lydiard, 1996, 1997; Kranzler, 1996). The heritability of generalized anxiety disorder is estimated to be about 30% (Kendler et al., 1992). But, as troubling as this disorder is, it is less severe than panic disorder.

Panic Disorder. People who suffer from recurring panic attacks may be diagnosed with **panic disorder.** Panic disorder sufferers must cope with both repeated attacks and anxiety about the occurrence and consequences of further attacks. This anxiety can lead people to develop agoraphobia, as noted earlier. The presence of agoraphobia complicates clinicians' efforts to help people who suffer from panic disorder because confronting situations in which panic attacks are likely to occur is part of the process of learning to live with this persistent disorder. Obviously, clinicians have a much harder time getting sufferers with agoraphobia to take on this challenging aspect of

agoraphobia (AG-or-uh-FO-bee-ah) An intense fear of being in a situation from which escape is not possible or in which help would not be available if one experienced overwhelming anxiety or a panic attack.

generalized anxiety disorder An anxiety disorder in which people experience chronic, excessive worry for 6 months or more.

panic disorder An anxiety disorder in which a person experiences recurring, unpredictable episodes of overwhelming anxiety, fear, or terror.

their treatment. For this reason, panic disorder with agoraphobia is among the most debilitating of all psychological disorders.

Panic disorder can also have significant social and health consequences (Sherbourne et al., 1996). Panic disorder sufferers visit doctors' offices and emergency rooms quite frequently (Katon, 1996). However, most individuals with this disorder respond to a combination of medication and psychotherapy (Biondi & Picardi, 2003).

Social Phobia. Is there some situation or object of which you are dreadfully afraid? Perhaps you fear snakes, insects, heights, or closed-in spaces such as elevators. If so, then you have a **phobia,** a persistent, irrational fear of some specific object, situation, or activity that poses no real danger (or whose danger is blown out of proportion). Most people realize that their phobias are irrational, but they nevertheless feel compelled to avoid the feared situations or objects.

▲ People who have social phobia limit their interactions with others because of their fear of embarrassment.

People who suffer from **social phobia** are intensely afraid of any social or performance situation in which they might embarrass or humiliate themselves in front of others—by shaking, blushing, sweating, or in some other way appearing clumsy, foolish, or incompetent. Social phobia may take the specific form of *performance anxiety*. About one-third of social phobics only fear speaking in public (Kessler et al., 1998). And in a survey of 449 individuals who had not been formally diagnosed with social phobia, one-third said they would experience excessive anxiety if they had to speak in front of a large audience (Stein et al., 1996). If you are one of the millions who are afraid of public speaking, see the *Apply It* at the end of this chapter for advice on overcoming your fear.

Although less debilitating than agoraphobia, social phobia can be a disabling disorder (Stein & Kean, 2000). In its extreme form, it can seriously affect people's performance at work, preventing them from advancing in their careers or pursuing an education and severely restricting their social lives (Bruch et al., 2003; Greist, 1995; Stein & Kean, 2000). Often, those with social phobia turn to alcohol and tranquilizers to lessen their anxiety in social situations. Baseball legend Mickey Mantle, for example, used alcohol to calm himself when making public appearances (Jefferson, 1996).

Specific Phobia. A **specific phobia** is a marked fear of a specific object or situation. This general label is applied to any phobia other than agoraphobia and social phobia. Faced with the object or situation they fear, people afflicted with a specific phobia experience intense anxiety, even to the point of shaking or screaming. They will go to great lengths to avoid the feared object or situation. The categories of specific phobias, in order of frequency of occurrence, are (1) situational phobias (fear of elevators, airplanes, enclosed places, heights, tunnels, or bridges); (2) fear of the natural environment (fear of storms or water); (3) animal phobias (fear of dogs, snakes, insects, or mice); and (4) blood-injection-injury phobia (fear of seeing blood or an injury, or of receiving an injection) (Fredrikson et al., 1996). Two types of situational phobias—*claustrophobia* (fear of closed spaces) and *acrophobia* (fear of heights)—are the specific phobias treated most often by therapists.

Principles of learning are often used to treat phobias. A therapist may use classical conditioning principles to teach patients to associate pleasant emotions with feared objects or situations. For example, a child who fears dogs might be given ice cream while in a room where a dog is present. Behavior modification, in which patients are

phobia (FO-bee-ah) A persistent, irrational fear of some specific object, situation, or activity that poses little or no real danger.

social phobia An irrational fear and avoidance of any social or performance situation in which one might embarrass or humiliate oneself in front of others by appearing clumsy, foolish, or incompetent.

specific phobia A marked fear of a specific object or situation; a general label for any phobia other than agoraphobia and social phobia.

reinforced for exposing themselves to fearful stimuli, may also be useful. Observation of models who do not exhibit fear in response to the object or situation of which a phobic is afraid has also been an effective treatment technique. Finally, antidepressant drugs have been shown to help agoraphobics overcome their fears (Kampman et al., 2002).

Obsessive-Compulsive Disorder

14.7 **What thought and behavior patterns are associated with obsessive-compulsive disorder?**

What would your life be like if every time you left your home you were so fearful of having left your door unlocked that you had to go back and check it again and again? **Obsessive-compulsive disorder (OCD)** is an anxiety disorder in which a person suffers from recurrent obsessions or compulsions, or both. **Obsessions** are persistent, involuntary thoughts, images, or impulses that invade consciousness and cause a person great distress. People with obsessions might worry about contamination by germs or about whether they performed a certain act, such as turning off the stove or locking the door (Insel, 1990). Other types of obsessions center on aggression, religion, or sex. One minister reported obsessive thoughts of running naked down the church aisle and shouting obscenities at his congregation.

A person with a **compulsion** feels a persistent, irresistible, irrational urge to perform an act or ritual repeatedly. The individual knows such acts are senseless but cannot resist performing them without experiencing an intolerable buildup of anxiety—which can be relieved only by yielding to the compulsion. Many of us have engaged in compulsive behavior like stepping over cracks on the sidewalk, counting stairsteps, or performing little rituals from time to time. The behavior becomes a psychological problem only if the person cannot resist performing it, if it is very time-consuming, and if it interferes with the person's normal activities and relationships with others.

Compulsions exhibited by people with obsessive-compulsive disorder often involve cleaning and washing behaviors, counting, checking, touching objects, hoarding, and excessive organizing. These cleaning and checking compulsions affect 75% of OCD patients receiving treatment (Ball et al., 1996). Sometimes, compulsive acts or rituals seem to reflect superstitious thinking in that they must be performed faithfully to ward off some danger. People with OCD do not enjoy the endless counting, checking, or cleaning. They realize that their behavior is not normal, but they simply cannot help themselves, as shown in the following example.

▲ Like this woman, many people with obsessive-compulsive disorder take great pains to avoid contamination from germs and dirt.

> Mike, a 32-year-old patient, performed checking rituals that were preceded by a fear of harming other people. When driving, he had to stop the car often and return to check whether he had run over people, particularly babies. Before flushing the toilet, he had to check to be sure that a live insect had not fallen into the toilet, because he did not want to be responsible for killing a living thing. At home he repeatedly checked to see that the doors, stoves, lights, and windows were shut or turned off. . . . Mike performed these and many other checking rituals for an average of 4 hours a day. (Kozak et al., 1988, p. 88)

obsessive-compulsive disorder (OCD) An anxiety disorder in which a person suffers from recurrent obsessions and/or compulsions.

obsession A persistent, involuntary thought, image, or impulse that invades consciousness and causes great distress.

compulsion A persistent, irresistible, and irrational urge to perform an act or ritual repeatedly.

Mike's checking compulsion is quite extreme, but it has been estimated that perhaps 2–3% of the U.S. population will suffer from OCD at some time in life. Fairly similar rates have been reported in studies in Canada, Puerto Rico, Germany, Korea, and New Zealand (Weissman et al., 1994).

Studies have shown that early autoimmune system diseases, early strep infections, and changes in the brain caused by infection may predispose a person to develop OCD (Giedd et al., 2000; Hamilton & Swedo, 2001). Several twin and family studies suggest that a genetic factor is involved in the development of OCD as well (Nestadt et al., 2000; Rasmussen & Eisen, 1990). Genes affecting serotonin functioning are suspected of causing OCD in some people, many of whom are helped by antidepressant drugs that increase serotonin levels in the brain (Pigott, 1996).

Mood Disorders

Kay Redfield Jamison had just begun a promising career as a professor of psychiatry when she was confronted by a friend about her increasingly bizarre behavior (Jamison, 1995). Her marriage had fallen apart, her finances were in chaos, and, in private moments, Jamison often fancied herself to be traveling in outer space. Secretly, Jamison knew that her behavior was out of control and worried that it might cause her to lose her job. At her friend's urging, she consulted a psychiatrist and began taking medication for *bipolar disorder*, one of the mood disorders you will learn about in this section. Jamison's emotions stabilized in response to the medicine, but like many people who suffer from this disorder, she went through several periods during which she attempted to manage without it. Each time she returned to the cycle of chaotic highs followed by deep, suicidal lows. Finally, she realized that her life depended on the medicine and, today, she not only is psychologically stable, but also is regarded as one of the world's leading experts on the disorder with which she has struggled since her teenage years.

Bipolar disorder is just one of several **mood disorders,** which are characterized by extreme and unwarranted disturbances in emotion or mood. Like anxiety disorders, mood disorders are fairly common. We begin with the most common of them, major depressive disorder.

mood disorders   Disorders characterized by extreme and unwarranted disturbances in emotion or mood.

Major Depressive Disorder

People with **major depressive disorder** feel an overwhelming sadness, despair, and hopelessness, and they usually lose their ability to experience pleasure. They may have changes in appetite, weight, or sleep patterns, loss of energy, and difficulty in thinking or concentrating. Key symptoms of major depressive disorder are psychomotor disturbances (Sobin & Sackeim, 1997). For example, body movements, reaction time, and speech may be so slowed that some depressed people seem to be doing everything in slow motion. Others experience the opposite extreme and are constantly moving and fidgeting, wringing their hands, and pacing. Depression can be so severe that its victims suffer from delusions or hallucinations, which are symptoms of *psychotic depression*. And the more deeply a person descends into depression over an extended period, the more she or he withdraws from social activities (Judd et al., 2000).

14.8 What are the symptoms of major depressive disorder?

major depressive disorder   A mood disorder marked by feelings of great sadness, despair, and hopelessness.

According to the American Psychiatric Association (2000), 1 year after their initial diagnosis of major depressive disorder, 40% of patients are without symptoms; 40% are still suffering from the disorder; and 20% are depressed, but not enough to warrant a diagnosis of major depression. Slightly less than one-half of those hospitalized for major depressive disorder are fully recovered after 1 year (Keitner et al., 1992). For many, recovery is aided by antidepressant drugs. However, some studies show that psychotherapy can be just as effective (Hollon et al., 2002). Some people suffer only one major depressive episode, but 50–60% of patients will have a recurrence. Risk of recurrence is greatest for females (Winokur et al., 1993) and for individuals with an onset of depression before age 15 (Brown, 1996). Recurrences may be frequent or infrequent, and for 20–35% of patients, the episodes are chronic, lasting 2 years or longer.

Culture, Gender, and Depression

14.9 How are culture, gender, and depression related?

How is it possible to study depression, or any mental disorder for that matter, across cultures, since cultural context must be taken into consideration when defining abnormality? Indeed, it is extremely difficult to construct surveys or other instruments for measuring mental disorders that are valid in a variety of cultures (Girolamo & Bassi, 2003). Nevertheless, a few researchers have managed to produce a limited, but informative, body of data about cross-cultural differences in depression (Girolamo & Bassi, 2003). One large study involving participants from ten countries revealed that the lifetime risk for developing depression varied greatly around the world (see **Figure 14.2**), with Asian countries (Taiwan and Korea) having significantly lower rates of the disorder (Weissman et al., 1996). Researchers explain these differences as the result of cross-cultural differences in ideal emotional states (Tsai, Knutson, & Fung, 2006). The experience of depression in individuals who live in non-Asian cultures appears to be influenced by those culture's ideas about how people *ought* to feel.

In most countries, the rate of depression for females is about twice that of males (Culbertson, 1997). Before boys reach puberty, they are more likely than girls to be depressed, but a dramatic reversal of the gender-related depression rates takes place in adolescence (Cyranowski et al., 2000). Not only are women more likely than men to suffer from depression, they are also more likely to be affected by negative consequences as a result. Early-onset major depressive disorder adversely affects the educational attainment and earning power of women, but not men (Berndt et al., 2000). The National Task Force on Women and Depression suggests that the higher rate of depression in women is largely the result of social and cultural factors. In fulfilling her many roles—mother, wife, lover, friend, daughter, neighbor—a woman is likely to put the needs of others ahead of her own.

▲ Women who have a strong desire to be "Supermoms" may suffer from depression when conflicting demands cause them to be unable to live up to their own expectations.

Bipolar Disorder

14.10 What are the extremes of mood suffered by those with bipolar disorder?

bipolar disorder A mood disorder in which manic episodes alternate with periods of depression, usually with relatively normal periods in between.

Earlier you read that psychiatrist Kay Redfield Jamison has achieved a stable, successful life despite her struggles with bipolar disorder. Others with this devastating illness have not been so fortunate. For instance, you may have heard about a bizarre episode in which painter Vincent van Gogh cut off his own ear. Based on analyses of his artistic productivity and personal writings, mental health professionals believe that van Gogh suffered from **bipolar disorder** (Blumer, 2002). Individuals with bipolar disorder exhibit two radically different moods—the extreme highs of manic episodes (or *mania*) and the extreme lows of major depression—usually with relatively normal periods in between.

Figure 14.2 Lifetime Risk for Developing Depression in Ten Countries

The lifetime prevalence of depression for 38,000 men and women in ten different countries reveals that women are more susceptible to depression worldwide.

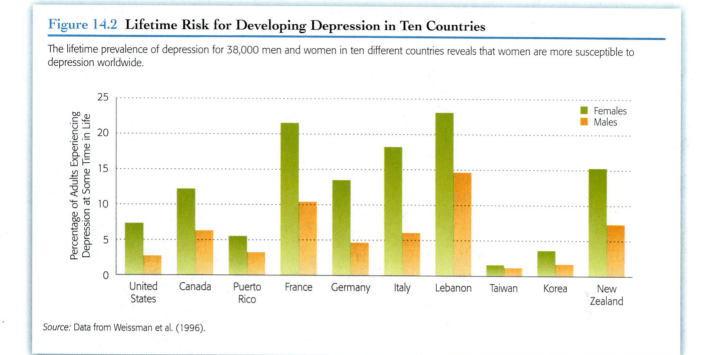

Source: Data from Weissman et al. (1996).

Van Gogh's ear-cutting episode occurred in the aftermath of a violent argument with another artist, Paul Gauguin, most likely in the context of a **manic episode.** Such episodes are marked by excessive euphoria, inflated self-esteem, wild optimism, and hyperactivity. People in a manic state have temporarily lost touch with reality and frequently have delusions of grandeur along with their euphoric highs. They may waste large sums of money on get-rich-quick schemes. If family members or friends try to stop them, they are likely to become irritable, hostile, enraged, or even dangerous; they may even harm themselves as van Gogh did. Quite often, patients must be hospitalized during manic episodes to protect them and others from the disastrous consequences of their poor judgment.

Van Gogh was hospitalized shortly after severing his ear. After his release from the hospital, and consistent with the modern-day diagnosis of bipolar disorder, his career was marked by intense bursts of creativity. In one 2-month period in 1889, he produced 60 paintings, some of which are regarded as his best works (Thomas & Bracken, 2001). Between these frantic periods of almost nonstop work, van Gogh experienced phases of deep despair, in which he could do no work at all. Tragically, he committed suicide at age 37.

Bipolar disorder is much less common than major depressive disorder, affecting about 1.2% of the U.S. population in any given year, and the lifetime prevalence rates are about the same for males and females (NIMH, 2001). Bipolar disorder tends to appear in late adolescence or early adulthood. About 90% of those with the disorder have recurrences, and about 50% experience another episode within a year of recovering from a previous one. The good news is that 70–80% of the patients return to a state of emotional stability (American Psychiatric Association, 2000), even though mild cognitive deficits, such as difficulty with planning, persist in many patients following a manic episode (Chowdhury et al., 2003). Still, in many cases, individuals with bipolar disorder can manage their symptoms, and thereby live a normal life, with the help of drugs such as lithium and divalproex. Moreover, psychotherapy can help them cope with the stress of facing life with a potentially disabling mental illness (Hollon et al., 2002).

manic episode (MAN-ik) A period of excessive euphoria, inflated self-esteem, wild optimism, and hyperactivity, often accompanied by delusions of grandeur and by hostility if activity is blocked.

Explaining Mood Disorders

14.11 What are some suggested causes of mood disorders?

There are many factors that contribute to the development of mood disorders. Biological factors appear to be central. However, an individual's life circumstances are important as well.

Neurological Correlates of Mood Disorders. PET scans have revealed abnormal patterns of brain activity in patients with mood disorders (George et al., 1993). Drevets and others (1997) located a brain area that may trigger both the sadness of major depression and the mania of bipolar disorder. A small, thimble-size patch of brain tissue in the lower prefrontal cortex (about 2–3 inches behind the bridge of the nose) is a striking 40–50% smaller in people with major depression. Earlier research established that this area of the brain plays a key role in the control of emotions. Moreover, the personality trait called *Neuroticism* is associated with both depression and abnormalities in the brain's serotonin levels (Fanous et al., 2002; Lesch, 2003). Research has shown that abnormal levels of serotonin are strongly linked to depression and to suicidal thoughts (Oquendo et al., 2003). Thus, individuals who are at the neurotic end of the Big Five personality dimension of Neuroticism may be predisposed to develop depression and to have suicidal thoughts.

Researchers have also found that the production, transport, and reuptake patterns for dopamine, GABA, and norepinephrine in people suffering from mood disorders differ from those in normal individuals (Kaladindi & McGuffin, 2003). Neurotransmitter abnormalities may reflect genetic variations, thus helping to explain the significant heritability rates for mood disorders. Based on a study of 1,721 identical and fraternal female twins, Kendler, Neale, Kessler, and others (1993) estimated the heritability of major depressive disorder to be 70% and the contribution of environment to be 30%.

Heredity. Evidence for a genetic basis for bipolar disorder is also strong. In one twin study, researchers found that 50% of the identical twins of bipolar sufferers had also been diagnosed with a mood disorder, compared to only 7% of fraternal twins (Kaladindi & McGuffin, 2003). Mounting evidence indicates that the genetic and neurological bases of bipolar disorder are more like those of schizophrenia than those of major depressive disorder (Molnar et al., 2003). These findings may explain why biological relatives of bipolar disorder sufferers are at increased risk of developing a number of mental disorders, while relatives of major depressive disorder sufferers display an increased risk only for that disorder (Kaladindi & McGuffin, 2003).

Stressors. Life stresses are also associated with depression. The vast majority of first episodes of depression strike after major life stress (Brown et al., 1994; Frank et al., 1994; Tennant, 2002). A longitudinal study of Harvard graduates that continued for over 40 years found that negative life events as well as family history played significant roles in the development of mood disorders (Cui & Vaillant, 1996). This seems particularly true of women, who are more likely to have experienced a severe negative life event just prior to the onset of depression (Spangler et al., 1996). Yet, recurrences of depression, at least in people who are biologically predisposed, often occur without significant life stress (Brown et al., 1994).

Suicide and Race, Gender, and Age

14.12 What are some of the risk factors for suicide?

Some depressed people commit the ultimate act of desperation—suicide. Mood disorders and schizophrenia, along with substance abuse, are major risk factors for suicide in all age groups (Mościcki, 1995; Pinikahana et al., 2003; Shaffer et al., 1996). Suicide risk also increases when people are exposed to particularly troubling life stressors, such as the violent death of a child (Murphy et al., 2003). There is also evidence that suicidal behavior runs in families (Brent et al., 1996; 2002). Even among people who have severe mood disturbances, such as bipolar disorder, those with a family history of suicide attempts are far more likely to kill themselves than are those without such history (Tsai et al., 2002).

Between 30,000 and 31,000 suicides are reported annually in the United States. Figure 14.3 shows the differences in U.S. suicide rates according to race, gender, and age (NCHS, 2001a, 2002a). As you can see, White Americans are more likely than African Americans to commit suicide. Native American suicide rates are similar to those of White Americans; rates for Hispanic Americans are similar to those of African Americans (NCHS, 2001b). Asian Americans have the lowest suicide rates of all ethnic groups in the United States (NCHS, 2002a).

You will also note in the Figure 14.3 that suicide rates are far lower for both White and African American women than for men. However, studies show that women are four times more likely than men to attempt suicide (Anderson, 2002). The higher rate of completed suicides in males is due to the methods men and women use. Emergency room records show that the rate of firearms use by suicide attempters and completers is 10 times higher in males than in females, while the rates of poisoning and drug overdose are higher in females (CDC, 2002). Consequently, a higher proportion of male suicide attempters succeed in killing themselves.

Although suicide rates among teens and young adults have increased in the past few decades, older Americans are at far greater risk for suicide than younger people. White males aged 85 and over have the highest recorded suicide rate, with over 75 suicides for every 100,000 people in that age group, about five times the average national suicide rate of 15.2 per 100,000 (U.S. Census Bureau, 1999). Poor general health, serious illness, loneliness (often due to the death of a spouse), and decline in social and economic status are conditions that may push many older Americans, especially those aged 75 and over, to commit suicide.

About 90% of individuals who commit suicide leave clues (Shneidman, 1994). They may communicate verbally: "You won't be seeing me again." They may provide behavioral clues, such as giving away their most valued possessions; withdrawing from friends, family, and associates; taking unnecessary risks; showing personality changes; acting and looking depressed; and losing interest in favorite activities. These warning signs should always be taken seriously. If you suspect you are dealing with a suicidal person, the best thing you can do is to encourage the person to get professional help. There are 24-hour suicide hotlines all over the country. A call might save a life.

▲ Evidence suggests that suicidal behavior tends to run in families. Les Franklin founded the Shaka Franklin Foundation for Youth, a suicide prevention organization, in memory of his son Shaka, who had killed himself. Ten years later, Franklin's other son, Jamon, also committed suicide.

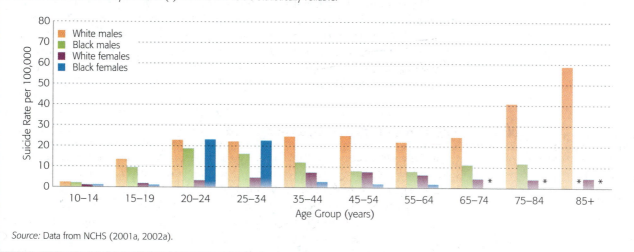

Figure 14.3 Differences in Suicide Rates According to Race, Gender, and Age

In every age group, the suicide rate is highest for White American males and second-highest for African American males. The general conclusion is that males are more likely to commit suicide than females, and that White Americans are more likely to do so than are African Americans. Suicide rates indicated by asterisks (*) are too low to be statistically reliable.

Source: Data from NCHS (2001a, 2002a).

Schizophrenia

The story of Tracy Moore at the beginning of the chapter introduced you to a few of the symptoms of **schizophrenia,** a serious psychological disorder characterized by loss of contact with reality, hallucinations, delusions, inappropriate or flat affect, some disturbance in thinking, social withdrawal, and/or other bizarre behavior. The state in which a person experiences such symptoms is known as a **psychosis.** People with mood disorders may have transient psychotic symptoms, sometimes causing them to be misdiagnosed with schizophrenia. However, people who have mood disorders are only subject to psychotic symptoms when they are in the altered mood states that define their disorders. By contrast, psychotic symptoms are the primary feature of schizophrenia and occur no matter what a sufferer's emotional state is (American Psychiatric Association, 2000). In Chapter 15 (Therapies), you will learn about the use of *antipsychotic drugs* in the treatment of psychotic symptoms in individuals who suffer from both schizophrenia and mood disorders.

Age, Gender, and Schizophrenia

14.13 How are age and gender linked to schizophrenia?

Schizophrenia typically first appears in a person's life in the late teens or early twenties, as it did in Tracy Moore's case. For this reason, most researchers think that normal developmental processes in the brain that happen in late adolescence set the stage for the appearance of the disease (Walker, 2004). Recall from Chapter 2 that the frontal lobes of the brain, the site of logic and planning, are the focus of neurological development during this period. Like these normal neurological changes, the symptoms of schizophrenia evolve gradually in most sufferers during what is known as the *prodromal phase* of the disease. Tracy Moore, for example, has stated that after she was diagnosed with the disorder, she realized that the intense mood swings and strange thoughts she experienced during her teen years were actually signs of an emergent case of schizophrenia.

Some researchers have suggested that full-blown schizophrenia might be prevented by prescribing antipsychotic drugs for teens who display signs of prodromal schizophrenia (Walker, 2004). However, this hypothesis is controversial. For one thing, it is not yet known whether these drugs will actually prevent the disease, and most antipsychotic drugs have undesirable side effects. Moreover, many teens display such signs, but do not develop schizophrenia. In fact, female teens who exhibit these signs appear to be more likely to ultimately develop mood disorders than they are to develop schizophrenia (Amminger et al., 2006). Therefore, there is no consensus among professionals regarding the appropriateness of treating the prodromal phase of schizophrenia.

As the findings regarding gender differences in the outcome of psychotic symptoms among teens suggest, gender differences exist among individuals with schizophrenia. For example, males tend to develop the disorder at an earlier age than females do (Takahashi et al., 2000). One reason for this age difference is that males are more likely

schizophrenia (SKIT-soh-FREE-nee-ah) A severe psychological disorder characterized by loss of contact with reality, hallucinations, delusions, inappropriate or flat affect, some disturbance in thinking, social withdrawal, and/or other bizarre behavior.

psychosis (sy-CO-sis) A condition characterized by loss of contact with reality.

to use substances that can cause schizophrenia, such as methamphetamine, early in life, and they appear to be more physiologically vulnerable to these substances than females are as well (Yen & Su, 2006). Furthermore, as you will learn later in this section, heredity contributes to schizophrenia. However, some studies suggest that different genes are linked to the disease in males and females (Sazci et al., 2005). Thus, it is possible that the genes that lead to the disease in males result in more severe symptoms than those that are associated with it in females.

Some studies suggest that males with schizophrenia are less responsive than females to the antipsychotic drugs that are used to treat schizophrenia (Takahashi et al., 2000). But other research suggests that this gender difference may vary across treatments. In a study involving the antipsychotic drug *amisulpride*, researchers found no behavioral differences between males and females, although the drug did produce greater changes in the blood chemistry of females than in that of males (Müller et al., 2006).

Positive Symptoms of Schizophrenia

The *positive symptoms* of schizophrenia are the abnormal behaviors that are present in people with the disorder. One of the clearest positive symptoms of schizophrenia is the presence of **hallucinations,** or imaginary sensations. Patients with schizophrenia may see, hear, feel, taste, or smell strange things in the absence of any stimulus in the environment, but hearing voices is the most common type of hallucination. Most often, the voices accuse or curse the patients or engage in a running commentary on their behavior. Visual hallucinations, less common than auditory hallucinations, are usually in black and white and commonly take the form of friends, relatives, God, Jesus, or the devil. People with schizophrenia also may experience exceedingly frightening and painful bodily sensations and feel that they are being beaten, burned, or sexually violated.

Having **delusions,** or false beliefs not generally shared by others in the culture, is another positive symptom of schizophrenia. Sufferers with **delusions of grandeur** may believe they are a famous person (the president or Moses, for example) or a powerful or important person who possesses some great knowledge, ability, or authority. Those with **delusions of persecution** have the false notion that some person or agency is trying to harass, cheat, spy on, conspire against, injure, kill, or in some other way harm them.

Another positive symptom is the loosening of associations, or *derailment*, that is evident when a person with schizophrenia does not follow one line of thought to completion but, on the basis of vague connections, shifts from one subject to another in conversation or writing. *Grossly disorganized behavior*, another positive symptom, can include such things as childlike silliness, inappropriate sexual behavior (masturbating in public), disheveled appearance, and peculiar dress. There may also be unpredictable agitation, including shouting and swearing, and unusual or inappropriate motor behavior, including strange gestures, facial expressions, or postures. People with schizophrenia may also display *inappropriate affect*; that is, their facial expressions, tone of voice, and gestures may not reflect the emotion that would be expected under the circumstances. A person might cry when watching a TV comedy and laugh when watching a news story showing bloody bodies at the scene of a fatal automobile accident.

Negative Symptoms of Schizophrenia

A *negative symptom* of schizophrenia is a loss of or deficiency in thoughts and behaviors that are characteristic of normal functioning. Negative symptoms include social withdrawal, apathy, loss of motivation, lack of goal-directed activity, very limited speech, slowed movements, poor hygiene and grooming, poor problem-solving abilities, and a distorted sense of time (Davalos et al., 2002; Hatashita-Wong et al., 2002; Skrabalo, 2000). Some who suffer from schizophrenia have *flat affect*, showing practically no emotional response at all, even though they often report feeling the emotion.

14.14 What are the major positive symptoms of schizophrenia?

hallucination An imaginary sensation.

delusion A false belief, not generally shared by others in the culture.

delusions of grandeur A false belief that one is a famous person or a powerful or important person who has some great knowledge, ability, or authority.

delusions of persecution A false belief that some person or agency is trying in some way to harm one.

14.15 What normal functions are reduced or absent in individuals with schizophrenia?

These patients may speak in a monotone, have blank and emotionless facial expressions, and act and move more like robots than humans.

Not all people with schizophrenia have negative symptoms. Those who do seem to have the poorest outcomes (Fenton & McGlashan, 1994). Negative symptoms are predictors of impaired overall social and vocational functioning. People with schizophrenia tend to withdraw from normal social contacts and retreat into their own world. They have difficulty relating to people, and often their functioning is too impaired for them to hold a job or even to care for themselves.

Types of Schizophrenia

14.16 What are the four types of schizophrenia?

▲ A person with catatonic schizophrenia may become frozen in an unusual position, like a statue, for hours at a time.

Even though various symptoms are commonly shared by people with schizophrenia, certain features distinguish one type of schizophrenia from another. For example, people with **paranoid schizophrenia** usually suffer from delusions of grandeur or persecution. They may be convinced that they have an identity other than their own—that they are the president, the Virgin Mary, or God—or that they possess great ability or talent. They may feel that they are in charge of the hospital or on a secret assignment for the government. Individuals with paranoid schizophrenia often show exaggerated anger and suspiciousness. If they have delusions of persecution and feel that they are being harassed or threatened, they may become violent in an attempt to defend themselves against their imagined persecutors. Usually, the behavior of a patient with paranoid schizophrenia is not so obviously disturbed as that of one with the catatonic or disorganized type, and the chance for recovery is better.

Disorganized schizophrenia, the most serious type, tends to occur at an earlier age than the other types and is marked by extreme social withdrawal, hallucinations, delusions, silliness, inappropriate laughter, grimaces, grotesque mannerisms, and other bizarre behavior. These patients show flat or inappropriate affect and are frequently incoherent. They often exhibit obscene behavior, may masturbate openly, and may swallow almost any kind of object or material. Disorganized schizophrenia results in the most severe disintegration of the personality, and its victims have the poorest chance of recovery (Fenton & McGlashan, 1991).

Persons with **catatonic schizophrenia** may display complete stillness and stupor or great excitement and agitation. Frequently, they alternate rapidly between the two. They may become frozen in a strange posture or position and remain there for hours without moving. **Undifferentiated schizophrenia** is the general term used when schizophrenic symptoms either do not conform to the criteria of any one type of schizophrenia or conform to more than one type.

Explaining Schizophrenia

14.17 What factors increase the risk of developing schizophrenia?

paranoid schizophrenia (PAIR-uh-noid) A type of schizophrenia characterized by delusions of grandeur or persecution.

disorganized schizophrenia The most serious type of schizophrenia, marked by extreme social withdrawal, hallucinations, delusions, silliness, inappropriate laughter, grotesque mannerisms, and other bizarre behavior.

Despite more than 100 years of research, the cause of schizophrenia remains a mystery. According to leading schizophrenia researcher Elaine Walker and her colleagues (2004), a key assumption underlying recent work on the puzzle of schizophrenia is that there is no single cause. Accordingly, over the past few decades, researchers have focused on a model of schizophrenia that includes both biological and experiential risk factors. This model assumes that these risk factors interact in complex ways such that an individual might have all of the relevant risk factors but never develop the disorder. The model is shown in **Figure 14.4**. As you can see, it includes several components. Walker and her team summarize these components as follows:

Constitutional Vulnerability. *Constitutional vulnerability* refers to the aspects of an individual's congenital (at birth) risk of developing schizophrenia that are attributable to factors within the person. As noted earlier, one such factor is gender; that is, males are more likely to develop schizophrenia than females are. Moreover, scientists have known for some time that heredity contributes to schizophrenia (Cannon et al., 1998;

Figure 14.4 How Risk Factors Lead to Schizophrenia

This diagram shows how many researchers today view the risk factors for schizophrenia. The central concept is "constitutional vulnerability." Prenatal and postnatal factors derived from both heredity and environmental factors cause some people to be born with a greater sensitivity to stress than others. Stress and neuromaturational processes interact with constitutional vulnerability to produce the symptoms of schizophrenia.

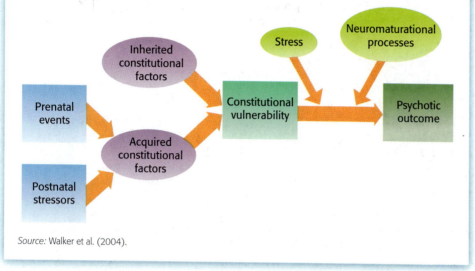

Source: Walker et al. (2004).

Gottesman, 1991; Kendler & Diehl, 1993; Owen & O'Donovan, 2003). **Figure 14.5** shows how the chance of developing schizophrenia varies with the degree of relationship to a person with schizophrenia. However, researchers do not yet know exactly what it is that vulnerable individuals inherit. It is possible that the genes that contribute to schizophrenia affect the structure of the developing fetal brain. On the other hand, they may shape later developmental processes or influence the actions of neurotransmitters such as dopamine in an individual's brain throughout life. Genes are also known to play a role in how well or how poorly individuals with schizophrenia respond to treatment with antipsychotic drugs (Yasui-Furukori et al., 2006).

Some aspects of constitutional vulnerability are acquired as a result of prenatal and/or postnatal experiences. These experiences include, for example, fetal exposure to maternal stress hormones and to substances such as alcohol and drugs that the mother ingests. They also include nutrients that the fetus receives from the mother as well as viruses and bacteria that cross the placenta. Postnatal stressors include birth trauma and other threats to the infant's health that occur during or immediately after birth.

Stress. Walker and her colleagues point out that there is no evidence suggesting that individuals who develop schizophrenia experience more stress than people who do not get the disease. Instead, researchers believe that the constitutional factors described above cause some individuals to be more vulnerable to stress than others. Thus, stress plays a role in the development of schizophrenia, but only among those who have the relevant constitutional vulnerability.

Furthermore, most researchers think that the physiological correlates of stress, not its psychological correlates, explain the common finding that schizophrenia typically appears in people's lives during periods of increased stress. Thus, the development of schizophrenia reflects something more fundamental than simply a failure to cope effectively with stress. Researchers hypothesize that the constitutional vulnerabilities of individuals who develop schizophrenia include some kind of neurological sensitivity to the biochemical changes that go along with being under stress. To use a crude analogy to illustrate this idea, stress hormones appear to flip switches in the brains of individuals who are constitutionally vulnerable to schizophrenia that they do not flip in the brains of others.

catatonic schizophrenia (KAT-uh-TAHN-ik) A type of schizophrenia characterized by complete stillness or stupor or great excitement and agitation; patients may assume an unusual posture and remain in it for long periods of time.

undifferentiated schizophrenia A catchall term used when schizophrenic symptoms either do not conform to the criteria of any one type of schizophrenia or conform to more than one type.

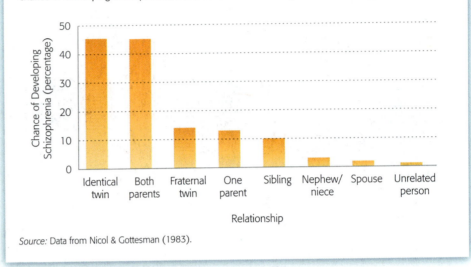

Figure 14.5 Genetic Similarity and Probability of Developing Schizophrenia

Research strongly indicates a genetic factor associated with schizophrenia. Identical twins have identical genes, and if one twin develops schizophrenia, the other twin has a 46% chance of also developing it. In fraternal twins, the chance is only 14%. A person with one schizophrenic parent has a 13% chance of developing schizophrenia, but a 46% chance if both parents are schizophrenic.

Source: Data from Nicol & Gottesman (1983).

Neuromaturational Processes. Walker reports that many studies have shown that the brains of individuals with schizophrenia differ both structurally and functionally from those of people who do not have the disorder. For example, levels of neural activity in the frontal lobes tend to be lower in the brains of people with schizophrenia than they are in others (Glantz & Lewis, 2000; Kim et al., 2000). Many individuals with schizophrenia have defects in the neural circuitry of the cerebral cortex and the limbic system (Benes, 2000; MacDonald et al., 2003; McGlashan & Hoffman, 2000). Further, on average, people with schizophrenia display slower than normal communication between the left and right hemispheres of the brain (Glorio et al., 2002).

Because schizophrenia is most often diagnosed in the late teens and early twenties, the theoretical model in Figure 14.4 assumes that the neurological correlates of schizophrenia are somehow linked to the neuromaturational processes that normally occur during late adolescence. Once the schizophrenia sets in, the progressive neurological deterioration that is part of the disease itself also induces changes in the brain. These changes include decreases in gray matter (see **Figure 14.6**) and in overall brain size along with deterioration of the cerebral cortex and the hippocampus.

According to Walker (2004), studies of the brains of individuals with schizophrenia after death have shown that the disease is associated with damage to the neurons themselves. Most such damage is found in the parts of the neurons that make up the brain's neurotransmitter system that you learned about in Chapter 2. Some researchers suggest that this damage leads to impaired communication between the emotional and intellectual parts of the brain. Others contend that the damaged neurons ineffectively govern the overall coordination of the brain's various functional sub-systems.

With regard to neurotransmitters themselves, Walker states that many studies suggest that dopamine plays an important role in schizophrenia, primarily because medications that are known to act on dopamine are usually helpful in the treatment of psychoses (Müller et al., 2006). However, the nature of the brain's neurotransmitter system is such that it is unlikely that deficiencies, excesses, or malfunctions that involve a single neurotransmitter can fully account for the complex features of schizophrenia. It is more likely, says Walker, that many other neurotransmitters, notably glutamate and GABA, also participate in the neurological processes that underlie the symptoms of schizophrenia.

Figure 14.6 Destruction of Gray Matter in the Brains of Adolescents Diagnosed with Schizophrenia

This figure dramatically depicts the devastating effects of schizophrenia on gray matter in the brains of its victims. The images on the first line of this figure show the average gray matter deficits in the brains of 15 adolescents who ranged from 12 to 15 years of age who had just been diagnosed with schizophrenia. Those on the second line represent the amount of gray matter they had lost to the disease five years later.

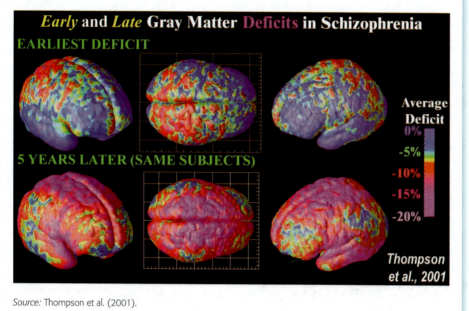

Source: Thompson et al. (2001).

Remember It Schizophrenia

1. Developmental changes in the brain during _____ may contribute to schizophrenia.

2. Match each symptom of schizophrenia with the appropriate example.

   _____ (1) delusions of grandeur

   _____ (2) hallucinations

   _____ (3) inappropriate affect

   _____ (4) delusions of persecution

   a. Bill believes he is Moses.

   b. Christina thinks her family is poisoning her food.

   c. Sal hears voices cursing him.

   d. Ophelia laughs at tragedies and cries when she hears a joke.

3. Match each subtype of schizophrenia with the appropriate example.

   _____ (1) paranoid schizophrenia

   _____ (2) disorganized schizophrenia

   _____ (3) catatonic schizophrenia

   _____ (4) undifferentiated schizophrenia

   a. Katy stands for hours in the same strange position.

   b. Vu believes that aliens are trying to kidnap him.

   c. Ethan makes silly faces, laughs a lot, and masturbates openly.

   d. Pam has symptoms of schizophrenia but does not fit any one type.

4. Researchers agree that there is no single cause of schizophrenia. (true/false)

Answers: 1. late adolescence; 2. (1) a, (2) c, (3) d, (4) b; 3. (1) b, (2) c, (3) a, (4) d; 4. true

Somatoform and Dissociative Disorders

In August, 2005, a homeless man who could not remember who he was or how he had gotten to their city pleaded with Chicago police to help him determine his identity. He believed that his name was Jay Tower, but he knew nothing more about himself. The police helped the desperate man send his fingerprints to the FBI, but these efforts were to no avail. Months later, one of the residents who lived in the same homeless shelter as Tower recognized him in a picture that was shown on the television program *America's Most Wanted* during February, 2006. The report claimed that the man in the picture was Ray Power, a New York attorney who had disappeared on August 1, 2005. Apparently, Power suffered from a form of amnesia known as *dissociative fugue*, one of several disorders you will read about in this section.

Somatoform Disorders

14.18 What are two somatoform disorders, and what symptoms do they share?

Have you heard the word *psychosomatic* applied to a symptom or illness? Laypersons usually use this term to refer to physical disorders of psychological origin. The *DSM-IV-TR* uses the term *somatoform disorder* to refer to such conditions. The **somatoform disorders** involve physical symptoms that are the result of psychological causes rather than any known medical condition. Although their symptoms are psychological in origin, patients are sincerely convinced that they spring from real physical disorders. People with somatoform disorders are not consciously faking illness to avoid work or other activities.

People with **hypochondriasis** are overly concerned about their health and fear that their bodily symptoms are a sign of some serious disease. A person with this somatoform disorder "might notice a mole and think of skin cancer or read about Lyme disease and decide it might be the cause of that tired feeling" (Barsky, 1993, p. 8). Yet, the symptoms are not usually consistent with known physical disorders, and even when a medical examination reveals no physical problem, people with hypochondriasis are not convinced. They may "doctor shop," going from one physician to another, seeking confirmation of their worst fears. Unfortunately, hypochondriasis is not easily treated, and there is usually a poor chance for recovery.

A person is diagnosed with a **conversion disorder** when there is a loss of motor or sensory functioning in some part of the body, which is not from a physical cause but which solves a psychological problem. A person may become blind, deaf, or unable to speak or may develop a paralysis in some part of the body. Many of Freud's patients suffered from conversion disorder, and he believed that they unconsciously developed a physical disability to help resolve an unconscious sexual or aggressive conflict.

Today, psychologists think that conversion disorder can act as an unconscious defense against any intolerable anxiety situation that the person cannot otherwise escape. For example, a soldier who desperately fears going into battle might escape the anxiety by developing a paralysis or some other physically disabling symptom. One reason for this hypothesis is that those with conversion disorder exhibit a calm and cool indifference to their symptoms, called "la belle indifference." Furthermore, many seem to enjoy the attention, sympathy, and concern their disability brings them.

somatoform disorders (so-MAT-uh-form) Disorders in which physical symptoms are present that are due to psychological causes rather than any known medical condition.

hypochondriasis (HI-poh-kahn-DRY-uh-sis) A somatoform disorder in which persons are preoccupied with their health and fear that their physical symptoms are a sign of some serious disease, despite reassurance from doctors to the contrary.

conversion disorder A somatoform disorder in which a person suffers a loss of motor or sensory functioning in some part of the body; the loss has no physical cause but solves some psychological problem.

Dissociative Disorders

14.19 How do the various dissociative disorders affect behavior?

Imagine how disconcerting it would be if you were unable to recognize your own leg. In his book *A Leg to Stand On*, neurologist Oliver Sacks (1984) described the case of a hospitalized man who could not feel or even recognize his own leg. This patient insisted that the leg wasn't even connected to his body, and his attempts to throw the leg out of his bed resulted in numerous falls. This unfortunate man was suffering from a profound disintegration of his physical and psychological self. Mental health professionals refer to this process as *dissociation*—the loss of one's ability to integrate all the components of self into a coherent representation of one's identity. In this case, the patient's dissociation was the result of an underlying physical illness. In many other instances, dissociation has a psychological rather than a physical cause.

In response to unbearable stress, some people develop a **dissociative disorder,** in which they lose the ability to consciously integrate their identities. Their consciousness becomes dissociated from their identity or their memories of important personal events, or both. For example, **dissociative amnesia** is a complete or partial loss of the ability to recall personal information or identify past experiences that cannot be attributed to ordinary forgetfulness or substance use. It is often caused by a traumatic experience—a psychological blow, so to speak—or a situation that creates unbearable anxiety causing the person to escape by "forgetting."

Several people previously thought to have been killed in the terrorist attacks on the World Trade Center on September 11, 2001, were discovered in mental hospitals many months later with diagnoses of dissociative amnesia (*Daily Hampshire Gazette*, 2002). They had been brought to hospitals on the day of the tragedy but were carrying no identification and were unable to remember their names or other identifying information. Extensive investigative work, including DNA testing in some cases, was required before they were identified. The fact that some were homeless people with schizophrenia who lived on the streets or in the subway stations near the World Trade Center made the task of identifying them all the more difficult. Such cases illustrate a puzzle concerning dissociative amnesia: Sufferers forget items of personal reference, such as their name, age, and address, and may fail to recognize their parents, other relatives, and friends, but they do not forget how to carry out routine tasks or how to read and write or solve problems, and their basic personality structure remains intact.

Even more puzzling than dissociative amnesia is **dissociative fugue.** In a fugue state, people like Ray Power, whose story you read at the beginning of this section, not only forget their identity they also travel away from home. Some take on a new identity that is usually more outgoing and uninhibited than their former identity. The fugue state may last for hours, days, or even months. The fugue is usually a reaction to some severe psychological stress, such as a natural disaster, a serious family quarrel, a deep personal rejection, or military service in wartime. Fortunately for most people, recovery from dissociative fugue is rapid, although they may have no memory of the initial stressor that brought on the fugue state. When people recover from the fugue, they often have no memory of events that occurred during the episode.

In **dissociative identity disorder (DID),** two or more distinct, unique personalities exist in the same individual, and there is severe memory disruption concerning personal information about the other personalities. In 50% of the cases, there are more than ten different personalities. The change from one personality to another often occurs suddenly and usually during stress. The personality in control of the body the largest percentage of time is known as the *host personality* (Kluft, 1984). The alternate personalities, or *alter personalities,* may differ radically in intelligence, speech, accent, vocabulary, posture, body language, hairstyle, taste in clothes, manners, and even handwriting and sexual orientation. In 80% of the cases of dissociative identity disorder, the host personality does not know of the alter personalities, but the alters have varying levels of awareness of each other (Putnam, 1989). The host and alter personalities commonly show amnesia for certain periods of time or for important life events such as a graduation or wedding. A common complaint is of "lost time"—periods for which a given personality has no memory because he or she was not in control of the body.

Dissociative identity disorder usually begins in early childhood but is rarely diagnosed before adolescence (Vincent & Pickering, 1988). About 90% of the treated cases have been women (Ross et al., 1989), and more than 95% of the patients reveal early histories of severe physical and/or sexual abuse (Coons, 1994; Putnam, 1992). The splitting off of separate personalities is apparently a way of coping with intolerable abuse. Researchers have found evidence to confirm the severe trauma and abuse suffered by many patients with DID (Gleaves, 1996). Dissociative identity disorder can be

dissociative disorders Disorders in which, under unbearable stress, consciousness becomes dissociated from a person's identity or her or his memories of important personal events, or both.

dissociative amnesia A dissociative disorder in which there is a complete or partial loss of the ability to recall personal information or identify past experiences.

dissociative fugue (FEWG) A dissociative disorder in which one has a complete loss of memory of one's entire identity, travels away from home, and may assume a new identity.

dissociative identity disorder (DID) A dissociative disorder in which two or more distinct, unique personalities occur in the same person, and there is severe memory disruption concerning personal information about the other personalities.

treated, often by psychotherapy, and some evidence indicates that DID patients respond well to treatment (Ellason & Ross, 1997).

Some individuals who have been charged with crimes have attempted to use dissociative identity disorder as a defense ("My other personality did it."). Such cases have demonstrated that symptoms of the disorder can be manufactured, and some of the cleverest individuals who do so can fool even highly trained mental health professionals, at least temporarily. Ultimately, in almost all cases, fakers are identified through the collaborative efforts of experienced professionals. However, these cases have also led to skepticism among both the public and some mental health professionals with regard to cases that do not involve crimes. Nevertheless, most professionals, and the *DSM-IV-TR*, agree that legitimate cases of DID do occur.

Another controversy surrounding the diagnosis of DID entails its possible association with child abuse. During the 1980s and 1990s, several studies indicated that almost all cases of DID were rooted in such experiences (Coons, 1994; Putnam, 1992). At the same time, other researchers countered that such findings were the result of an interaction between the suggestibility of fantasy-prone clients who claimed to have multiple personalities and the leading questions of overly zealous therapists intent on proving that DID was caused by abuse (Lilienfeld et al., 1999). The controversy continues today, but most experts acknowledge that the connection between abuse and DID is not an absolute one. That is, abuse does not lead to DID in every case, or even in most cases. Likewise, many cases of DID occur in individuals who do not have histories of abuse.

Remember It   Somatoform and Dissociative Disorders

1. Match each psychological disorder with the appropriate example.

_____ (1) dissociative identity disorder

_____ (2) dissociative fugue

_____ (3) dissociative amnesia

_____ (4) hypochondriasis

_____ (5) conversion disorder

a. Tyra is convinced she has some serious disease, although her doctors can find nothing physically wrong.
b. David is found far away from his hometown, calling himself by another name and having no memory of his past.
c. Theresa suddenly loses her sight, but doctors can find no physical reason for the problem.
d. Manuel has no memory of being in the boat with other family members on the day that his older brother drowned.
e. Nadia has no memory of blocks of time in her life and often finds clothing in her closet that she cannot remember buying.

2. _____ disorders involve physical symptoms that have psychological causes.

Answers: 1. (1) e, (2) b, (3) d, (4) a, (5) c; 2. Somatoform

Personality Disorders

Psychologist Martha Stout (2005), author of *The Sociopath Next Door*, claims that there are many people in the world who lack a conscience, but who have learned the outward behaviors expected by members of their culture. Such people are exclusively motivated by self-centered goals, and they use the good natures of others to get what they want. Stout cites the case of Dr. Doreen Littlefield (a fictitious name) to support her claim. For 14 years, "Dr." Littlefield posed as a licensed psychologist working in a large psychiatric hospital. In reality, the woman had neither a professional license nor a doctoral degree. Littlefield obtained her position as a result of having been recommended by two of her undergraduate psychology professors. Both men provided the references she asked for in exchange for Littlefield's promised silence about the sexual relationships they had been involved in with her. Once she had her job at the hospital, she developed chummy relationships with the clerical staff so that she could keep track of what the other therapists were doing. She used this information to undermine their work so that her own would look better by comparison. She even went so far as to destroy therapeutic relationships between other therapists and some of the patients in the hospital for the same purpose. When her lack of credentials was discovered by the hospital's management, Littlefield was quietly dismissed because they feared that publicly exposing her deception would provoke lawsuits by former and current patients. Apparently, Doreen Littlefield suffered from *antisocial personality disorder,* one of the disorders you will learn about in this section.

Characteristics of Personality Disorders

A **personality disorder** is a long-standing inflexible, maladaptive pattern of behaving and relating to others, which usually begins in childhood or adolescence. These disorders are among the most common of mental disorders; the *DSM-IV-TR* indicates that 10–15% of North Americans have one or more personality disorders. People who suffer from other disorders, especially mood disorders, are often diagnosed with personality disorders as well (Brieger et al., 2003; Joyce et al., 2003). In most cases, the causes of personality disorders have yet to be identified.

People with personality disorders are extremely difficult to get along with. As a result, most have unstable work and social histories. Some sufferers know that their behavior causes problems, yet they seem unable to change. But more commonly, they blame other people or situations for their problems. Thus, because medications have not proved to be very useful in the treatment of personality disorders, treatment options are few. After all, to seek and benefit from therapy, a person must realize that he or she has a problem and be somewhat cooperative with the therapist. Most individuals with personality disorders seek treatment only when forced to by legal authorities or family members and, once in therapy, seldom engage in the kind of self-reflection that is essential to successful psychotherapy.

Despite the apparently grim prognosis associated with personality disorders, research indicates that their features change over time. In one longitudinal study involving individuals who were diagnosed with personality disorders in adolescence, researchers found that, on average, these diagnoses were fairly stable over a 10-year period (Durbin & Klein, 2006). However, many individuals in the study no longer met the diagnostic criteria for personality disorders at the 10-year follow-up. Of course, these individuals may have been incorrectly diagnosed in the first place. However, the study also identified declines in specific features of these disorders, such as the high prevalence of neuroticism among personality disorder sufferers. Such trends support the view that, in some individuals, the psychological and behavioral factors that lead to a personality disorder diagnosis may be resolved to some degree or become less severe over time.

Types of Personality Disorders

There are several different types of personality disorders, and the criteria used to differentiate among them overlap considerably. Thus, the *DSM-IV-TR* groups personality disorders into *clusters,* as shown in Table 14.3. The individual disorders within each cluster have similarities.

Cluster A. All the personality disorders in Cluster A are characterized by odd behavior. Those who suffer from *paranoid personality disorder* display extreme suspiciousness, whereas those with *schizoid personality disorder* isolate themselves from others and appear to be unable to form emotional bonds. Individuals with *schizotypal personality disorder* are often mistakenly diagnosed as schizophrenic because their odd appearance, unusual thought patterns, and lack of social skills are also symptoms of schizophrenia.

Cluster B. Cluster B disorders are characterized by erratic, overly dramatic behavior, such as complaining loudly in a store about being slighted or insulted by a clerk. These disorders are associated with an increased risk of suicide (Lambert, 2003). A

14.20 What features are shared by all of the personality disorders?

14.21 What behaviors are associated with personality disorders in clusters A, B, and C?

personality disorder A long-standing, inflexible, maladaptive pattern of behaving and relating to others, which usually begins in early childhood or adolescence.

Table 14.3 Types of Personality Disorders

Personality Disorder	Symptoms
Cluster A: Odd behavior	
Paranoid	Individual is highly suspicious, untrusting, guarded, hypersensitive, easily slighted, lacking in emotion; holds grudges.
Schizoid	Individual isolates self from others; appears unable to form emotional attachments; behavior may resemble that of autistic children.
Schizotypal	Individual dresses in extremely unusual ways; lacks social skills; may have odd ideas resembling the delusions of schizophrenia.
Cluster B: Erratic, overly dramatic behavior	
Narcissistic	Individual has exaggerated sense of self-importance and entitlement; is self-centered, arrogant, demanding, exploitive, envious; craves admiration and attention; lacks empathy.
Histrionic	Individual seeks attention and approval; is overly dramatic, self-centered, shallow, demanding, manipulative, easily bored, suggestible; craves excitement; often, is attractive and sexually seductive.
Borderline	Individual is unstable in mood, behavior, self-image, and social relationships; has intense fear of abandonment; exhibits impulsive and reckless behavior and inappropriate anger; makes suicidal gestures and performs self-mutilating acts.
Antisocial	Individual disregards rights and feelings of others; is manipulative, impulsive, selfish, aggressive, irresponsible, reckless, and willing to break the law, lie, cheat, and exploit others for personal gain, without remorse; fails to hold jobs.
Cluster C: Anxious, fearful behavior	
Obsessive-compulsive	Individual is concerned with doing things the "right" way and is generally a perfectionist; relationships are emotionally shallow.
Avoidant	Individual fears criticism and rejection; avoids social situations in order to prevent being judged by others.
Dependent	Person overly dependent on others for advice and approval; may cling to lovers and friends, fearing abandonment.

pervasive desire to be the center of others' attention is characteristic of both *narcissistic personality disorder* and *histrionic personality disorder*, as is a lack of concern for others.

A more serious Cluster B disorder is *borderline personality disorder,* whose sufferers are highly unstable. Fear of abandonment is the primary theme of their social relationships. Consequently, they tend to cling to those for whom they feel affection. Once a relationship ends, however, the individual with borderline personality disorder views the former lover or friend as a mortal enemy. For the most part, though, people with this disorder direct their negative emotions toward themselves. They often harm themselves in bizarre ways, such as pulling out their hair or making tiny cuts in their forearms.

A significant proportion of patients with borderline personality disorder have histories of childhood abuse or disturbances in attachment relationships (Trull et al., 2003). Moreover, many of these patients suffer from mood disorders as well (Brieger et al., 2003). Thus, suicidal thoughts and behaviors are a major concern of therapists working with these patients. However, research indicates that antidepressant medication, combined with psychotherapy, can be effective in treating this disorder (Trull et al., 2003).

People who suffer from another Cluster B disorder, *antisocial personality disorder,* often violate others' rights and display little or no remorse for their actions. This pattern of behavior often begins in childhood or adolescence. Children and teenagers who have this disorder lie, steal, destroy property, run away, skip school, and may be physically cruel to others and to animals (Arehart-Treichel, 2002). Many of them drink excessively and engage in promiscuous sex. When children and teenagers are formally diagnosed with this disorder, it is known as *conduct disorder.*

In adulthood, most individuals with antisocial personality disorder cannot keep a job, act as responsible parents, honor financial commitments, or obey the law. However, individuals such as Doreen Littlefield, whose case you read about at the beginning of this section, represent a subset of those with antisocial personality disorder who display an exception to this pattern. As noted earlier, they follow the conventions of society to whatever degree is necessary in order to get what they want from others. They can "play the game," so to speak. Thus, the diagnosis of antisocial personality disorder applies equally to individuals who are overtly aggressive, uncaring, and lacking in conscience, and to those who have learned to artfully disguise these features of their personalities.

Brain-imaging studies suggest that people with antisocial personality disorder do not comprehend the emotional significance of words and images (Hare, 1995). They show the same level of brain arousal, measured by EEG recordings, whether they are confronting neutral stimuli (words such as *chair, table,* and *stone*) or emotionally charged stimuli (words such as *cancer, rape,* and *murder*). Such findings suggest that there is a neurophysiological basis for the lack of normal empathic responses shown by most individuals with this disorder (Habel et al., 2002). Some experts estimate that as many as 20% of people who are in prisons in the United States suffer from antisocial personality disorder.

Cluster C. Finally, Cluster C personality disorders are associated with fearful or anxious behavior. Individuals diagnosed with *obsessive-compulsive personality disorder* fear falling short of perfectionistic standards. Most have shallow emotional relationships because of their tendency to hold others to equally unrealistic standards of behavior. Order is important to them, but they do not experience the kinds of irrational obsessions and compulsions that dominate the lives of those who suffer from obsessive-compulsive disorder.

Two other Cluster C disorders, *avoidant personality disorder* and *dependent personality disorder*, represent opposite approaches to social relationships. A person with avoidant personality disorder shuns relationships because of excessive sensitivity to criticism and rejection. By contrast, someone with dependent personality disorder relies on others to an inappropriate degree. Such people can't make everyday decisions, such as what to have for dinner, without seeking others' advice and approval. Because of their dependency on others, they fear abandonment and tend to be "clingy" in social relationships.

Because the characteristics involved in personality disorders are quite similar to normal variations in personality, it is especially important when thinking about them to remember the criteria for abnormality discussed at the beginning of this chapter. For example, if a friend suspects a neighbor of poisoning his cat, and you think this an unreasonable suspicion, don't jump to the conclusion that your friend has paranoid personality disorder. This tendency toward suspiciousness is likely to be simply a personality trait your friend possesses.

Remember It   Personality Disorders

1. Match each cluster of personality disorders with its chief characteristic.

_____ (1) Cluster A   a. odd behavior
_____ (2) Cluster B   b. anxious, fearful behavior
_____ (3) Cluster C   c. overly dramatic behavior

2. Classify each of the following personality disorders as part of Cluster A, B, or C.

_____ (1) narcissistic personality disorder
_____ (2) obsessive-compulsive personality disorder
_____ (3) histrionic personality disorder
_____ (4) schizotypal personality disorder
_____ (5) schizoid personality disorder
_____ (6) paranoid personality disorder
_____ (7) antisocial personality disorder
_____ (8) dependent personality disorder
_____ (9) avoidant personality disorder
_____ (10) borderline personality disorder

Answers: 1. (1) a, (2) c, (3) b; 2. (1) B, (2) C, (3) B, (4) A, (5) A, (6) A, (7) B, (8) C, (9) C, (10) B

Disorders Diagnosed in Childhood

▶ Intensive educational programs help autistic children improve their language and social skills.

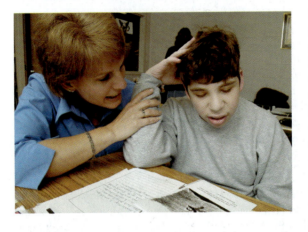

With the exception of the personality disorders, all of the disorders that you have learned about so far in this chapter apply to both children and adults. The criteria for anxiety and mood disorders, for example, are the same regardless of whether a case involves a child or an adult. Children can also suffer from schizophrenia, somatoform disorders, and dissociative disorders, although these categories are more often applied to adolescents than to children. But there are also a few potentially lifelong disorders that make their first appearance in childhood.

In this section, you will learn about two such disorders, *pervasive developmental disorders* and *attention deficit hyperactivity disorder*, both of which have shown a pattern of increasing prevalence over the past two decades for reasons that are as yet unknown (Newschaffer, Falb, & Gurney, 2005). Another aspect of these disorders that is poorly understood is the finding that males are four to five times more likely than females to be diagnosed with them (American Psychiatric Association, 2000). Currently, the most plausible explanation for this gender difference is that, as is true for schizophrenia, males possess some kind of genetic and/or prenatally acquired constitutional vulnerability to these disorders that distinguishes them from females. This hypothesis is supported by research showing that boys born to mothers who smoked or experienced high levels of stress hormones during pregnancy are more likely to be diagnosed with these disorders than are girls who are exposed to these risk factors (Rodriguez & Bohlin, 2005). However, it is also possible that boys and girls differ in the way they manifest these disorders, which, in turn, causes mental health professionals to be more likely to under-diagnose them in girls than in boys (Posserud, Lundervold, & Gillberg, 2006; Waschbusch & King, 2006). Despite the gender difference in prevalence, it is clear that these psychological disorders interfere with the development of boys and girls in similar ways.

Pervasive Developmental Disorders

14.22 How do pervasive developmental disorders affect children's development?

You may be familiar with the illustrious football career of retired Miami Dolphins quarterback Dan Marino, but did you know that he has a son who was diagnosed with *autistic disorder* at the age of 2? Autistic disorder is one of several **pervasive developmental disorders (PDDs)** that are also sometimes called *autism spectrum disorders*. The distinguishing feature of all PDDs is an inability to establish and maintain social relationships.

The social difficulties of individuals with PDDs usually derive from their poor communication skills and inability to understand the reciprocal, or "give-and-take," aspects of social relationships. Many of these children also exhibit odd, repetitive behaviors such as hand-flapping. Some develop attachments to objects and become extremely anxious, or even enraged, when separated from them. Others engage in self-injurious behaviors such as head-banging. In the United States, just under 1% of all

pervasive developmental disorders (PDDs) A group of disorders in which children exhibit severe disturbances in social relationships.

children have some kind of PDD (Kagan & Herschkowitz, 2005). The rates are similar in European countries (Lauritsen, Pedersen, & Mortensen, 2005). The two most frequently diagnosed PDDs are *autistic disorder* and *Asperger's disorder*.

Autistic Disorder. The distinguishing symptoms that are exhibited by children with autistic disorder include limited or nonexistent language skills, an inability to engage in reciprocal social relationships, and a severely limited range of interests (American Psychiatric Association, 2000). Most also have mental retardation, and are easily distracted, slow to respond to external stimuli, and highly impulsive (Calhoun & Dickerson Mayes, 2005). Some children are helped with symptoms of distractibility and impulsivity by the kinds of stimulant medications that are often prescribed for children with attention deficit/hyperactivity disorder (Posey et al., 2004).

Many parents of children with autism report having noticed their children's peculiarities during the first few months of life. What strikes these parents is their infants' apparent lack of interest in people. However, in most cases, the disorder cannot be definitively diagnosed until children's failure to develop normal language skills makes it apparent that they are on an atypical developmental path. This usually occurs between the first and second birthday.

Children with autism who are capable of some degree of normal verbal communication and whose cognitive impairments are minimal are often called *high-functioning*. However, these children's communicative abilities are quite poor because of their limited ability to engage in social cognition. For example, most never fully develop an ability to look at situations from other people's perspectives (Peterson, Wellman, & Liu, 2005). As a result, they typically fail to understand how their statements are perceived by listeners and are incapable of engaging in normal conversations. In addition, the pitch and intonation of their speech is often abnormal. Some utter repetitive phrases, often in robot-like fashion, that are inappropriate for the situation in which they occur.

Asperger's Disorder   About two in every 10,000 children in the United States is diagnosed with Asperger's disorder (Raja, 2006), a PDD that is often thought of as a mild form of autistic disorder. In fact, the diagnostic criteria for it are highly similar to those for autistic disorder (American Psychiatric Association, 2000). However, children with Asperger's disorder have age-appropriate language and cognitive skills and often obtain high scores on IQ tests. Despite their normal language skills, children with Asperger's disorder are incapable of engaging in normal social relationships because, like children with autism who are high-functioning, they usually do not develop the capacity to understand others' thoughts, feelings, and motivations (a theory of mind).

Because of their normal language and cognitive skills, most children with Asperger's disorder don't stand out from their peers until they reach the age at which children begin to engage in cooperative play between the second and third birthdays. However, normal children of this age vary widely, so children with Asperger's disorder are often assumed to be "late bloomers" or "going through a phase." Some are misdiagnosed with ADHD (Pozzi, 2003). Upon entering school, though, many begin to exhibit the odd behaviors that most people associate with pervasive developmental disorders. For example, they may become intensely focused on memorizing things that have little meaning to them, such as airline flight schedules. They may also engage in obsessive behaviors, such as counting and recounting the number of squares on a checkered tablecloth. By school age, their inability to form friendships like those of other children their age is also usually quite apparent.

Explaining Pervasive Developmental Disorders. Pervasive developmental disorders were once thought to be the result of poor parenting. However, although it is now well established that all of these disorders are of neurological origin (Kagan &

autistic disorder   A disorder in which children have very limited language skills compared to others of the same age along with an inability to engage in reciprocal social relationships, and a severely limited range of interests.

Asperger's disorder   A disorder in which children possess the same characteristics as those with autistic disorder but have intact language skills.

Herschkowitz, 2005), there is no single brain anomaly or dysfunction that is associated with PDDs. Even for the individual disorders within this category, researchers have not found a single definitive neurological marker. In a few cases, there are specific genetic defects that are known to lead to atypical neurological development and, in turn, to cause children to develop pervasive developmental disorders. For instance, *fragile X syndrome*, as you may recall from Chapter 2, can cause autistic disorder. For the most part, however, the cause of PDDs remains a mystery (Kagan & Herschkowitz, 2005).

Whatever the neurological mechanisms involved in PDDs are, twin studies suggest that these disorders are hereditary. Among identical twins, when one is diagnosed with a PDD, there is a 70–90% chance that the other twin will be diagnosed as well (Zoghbi, 2003). A wide variety of factors interact with genetic predispositions to trigger the appearance of these disorders (Rutter, 2005). When mothers are depressed, for example, infants have an increased risk of developing the symptoms of a PDD (Pozzi, 2003). However, media reports suggesting that immunizations may cause PDDs have proven to be unfounded (Rutter, 2005).

Treating Pervasive Developmental Disorders. There is no cure for autism. Even Dan Marino stops short of saying that his son is "cured" of the condition, although the young man is academically successful and plays high school football. However, as his case illustrates, there are effective treatments for the disorder. Such treatments are most successful when they are initiated prior to a child's third birthday and include intensive language and social skills training, along with behavior modification for self-injurious behaviors (Cohen, Amerine-Dickens, & Smith, 2006; Konstantareas, 2006; Luiselli & Hurley, 2005). But children who have PDDs vary widely in how well they respond to these treatments. The key to success, say experts, is that treatments have to be individually tailored to each child's unique needs (Autism Society of America, 2006).

The language skills of a child with a PDD are the best indicator of his or her prognosis in adulthood (American Psychiatric Association, 2000). A child's language and cognitive abilities are also good predictors of his or her response to treatment. Thus, children with Asperger's disorder have the best hope of attaining independence in adulthood. Thanks to their language and cognitive skills, many are capable of high levels of academic achievement.

Attention Deficit Hyperactivity Disorder

14.23 What are the features of attention deficit hyperactivity disorder?

If you had known popular recording artist Daniel Bedingfield during the early 1980s when he was just a preschooler, you might not have predicted a bright future for him. Bedingfield was diagnosed with **attention deficit hyperactivity disorder (ADHD)** at the tender age of four. Over the years, he learned to channel his energy into music, and Bedingfield became a star when a song he wrote and recorded on a computer in his bedroom, *Gotta Get Thru This*, became an international hit in 2001.

Prevalence and Characteristics of ADHD. Worldwide, experts estimate that 3 to 7% of children suffer from ADHD (NIMH, 2001). Some studies indicate that the prevalence of ADHD is as high as 18% in the United States (CDC, 2005). Many children with ADHD also have learning disabilities (Brook & Boaz, 2005). Some also display aggressive behavior and may be diagnosed with conduct disorder, the childhood version of antisocial personality disorder that you read about earlier in the previous section.

The hallmarks of ADHD are physical restlessness and problems with attention. However, experimental studies that employ laboratory tests of attention have shown that, on many attention tasks, children diagnosed with ADHD do not differ from non-diagnosed children (Lawrence et al., 2004). Nevertheless, children with

attention deficit hyperactivity disorder (ADHD) A disorder in which an individual shows both significant problems in focusing attention and physical hyperactivity.

ADHD differ from peers with regard to their capacity to sustain attention when engaged in real-world tasks that are boring and repetitive. They also seem to be less able than other children of the same age to control impulses. For these reasons, children with ADHD may function well in home settings in which they have the freedom to move from one engaging activity to another. By contrast, when these children enter school, their inattentive, impulsive, and highly active behaviors stand out. Consequently, the diagnosis is most often made during the early school years.

Explaining ADHD. Research suggests that ADHD is a neurological disorder (Kagan & Herschkowitz, 2005). Likewise, both twin and family studies show that the disorder is influenced by heredity (Thapar & Thapar, 2003; Thaper, O'Donovan, & Owen, 2005). The prenatal environment plays some role in the disorder, because, as noted in Chapter 8, children who are born to women who smoke or use drugs while pregnant are at higher risk for the disorder than infants who were not prenatally exposed to these substances.

However, research also clearly shows that the tendency toward ADHD symptoms is best thought of as a risk factor that may be amplified by other kinds of risk factors or balanced by protective factors (Chang & Burns, 2005). For example, a child's temperament can be either a risk or a protective factor with regard to ADHD. A child with a difficult temperament who has poor effortful control is more likely to be diagnosed with ADHD than one who is more easygoing (Chang & Burns, 2005). Likewise, young children who are extremely outgoing are at increased risk of being diagnosed with the disorder when they start school (Putnam & Stifter, 2005). However, high IQ and intrinsic motivation are important protective factors for children who are at risk of developing ADHD (Chang & Burns, 2005). And, like Daniel Bedingfield, many talented children with ADHD find out-of-school activities in which they excel that help to compensate for their academic struggles.

Treating ADHD. As we mentioned in Chapter 4, ADHD is often successfully treated with amphetamines such as methylphenidate. In fact, more than half of the school children in the United States who are diagnosed with ADHD, just over 2 million children, take these drugs (CDC, 2005). Placebo-controlled studies have consistently shown that the drugs have positive effects on the behavior of 70–90% of the children who take them (Pelham et al., 2002; Ridderinkhof et al., 2005).

Other treatments for ADHD have focused on parent training. Such efforts are based on the finding that many parents of children with ADHD display authoritarian parenting styles in which they manage children's behavior primarily through threats, coercion, and corporal punishment (Lange et al., 2005; McKee et al., 2004). In these training programs, researchers teach parents how to use more effective strategies. However, the results of these studies have been inconsistent (McKee et al., 2004). In most cases, changes in parenting techniques do not result in changes in the behavior of children with ADHD. Training studies are often cited in support of the proposition that medication is the best treatment for ADHD; however, in contrast to ADHD, parent training interventions are often successful in changing the behavior of children who suffer from other kinds of psychological disorders (Farley et al., 2005).

A growing number of adults are also taking medications for ADHD. Surveys show that about 4.4% of adults in the United States have the disorder (Kessler et al., 2006). However, the results of experimental studies regarding drug treatments for adult ADHD are mixed. Some studies suggest that the drugs that are effective for treating ADHD in children are equally so for adults (Turner et al., 2005). Others, by contrast, show that adults with ADHD are almost as likely to respond favorably to the placebos used in these studies as they are to respond favorably to authentic ADHD drugs (Carpentier et al., 2005). Consequently, more research is needed before researchers will know for certain whether drugs are the best treatment for ADHD in adults.

Remember It | Disorders Diagnosed in Childhood

1. Individuals with autistic disorder have _____.

2. Protective factors found in most children with Asperger's disorder include _____ and _____.

3. The hallmarks of ADHD are _____ and _____.

Answers 1. limited language and social skills; 2. normal language, normal cognitive skills; 3. restlessness, attention problems

Apply It | Overcoming the Fear of Public Speaking

Do you break out in a cold sweat and start trembling when you have to speak in public? If so, cheer up; you're in good company: Fear of public speaking is the number one fear reported by American adults in surveys. More people fear public speaking than flying, sickness, or even death (*CBS News*, July 31, 2002)!

What Causes It?

Fear of public speaking is a form of performance anxiety, a common type of social phobia. Much of the fear of public speaking stems from fear of being embarrassed or of being judged negatively by others. Some people cope with this fear by trying to avoid situations in which they may be required to speak in public. A more practical approach is to examine the incorrect beliefs that can cause the fear of public speaking and then take specific steps to overcome it. Here are some incorrect beliefs associated with public speaking (Orman, 1996):

- To succeed, a speaker has to perform perfectly. (Not true; no audience expects perfection.)

- A good speaker presents as many facts and details about the subject as possible. (Not true; all you need is two or three main points.)

- If some members of the audience aren't paying attention, the speaker needs to do something about it. (Not true; you can't please everyone, and it's a waste of time to try to do so.)

What Can You Do?

Some of the steps you can take to manage fear of public speaking deal with how you present yourself to your audience; others focus on what's going on inside you. Here are some of the many suggestions offered by experts at Toastmasters International (2003), an organization devoted to helping people improve their public speaking skills:

- *Know your material well.* Practice aloud, and revise your speech, if necessary.

- *Visualize your speech.* Imagine yourself giving your speech in a confident, clear manner.

- *Relax.* Reduce your tension by doing deep breathing or relaxation exercises.

- *Be familiar with the place where you will speak.* Arrive early, and practice using the microphone and any other equipment you plan to use.

- *Connect with the audience.* Greet some members of the audience as they arrive; then, when you give your speech, speak to the audience as though they were a group of your friends.

- *Project confidence through your posture.* Stand or sit in a self-assured manner, smile, and make eye contact with the audience.

- *Focus on your message, not on yourself.* Turn your attention away from your nervousness and focus on the purpose of your speech, which is to transmit information to your audience.

- *Remember that the audience doesn't expect you to be perfect.* Don't apologize for any problems you think you have with your speech. Just be yourself.

By applying these few simple tips, you can overcome nervousness and speak confidently on any topic—even on the spur of the moment.

✳ Summary and Review

Schizophrenia p. 504

14.13 How are age and gender linked to schizophrenia? p. 504

Schizophrenia is more frequently diagnosed during the late teens and early twenties. Males are more likely than females to be diagnosed with the disorder, and the disease follows a more serious course among them.

14.14 What are the major positive symptoms of schizophrenia? p. 505

The positive symptoms of people with schizophrenia are abnormal behaviors and characteristics, including hallucinations, delusions, derailment, grossly disorganized behavior, and inappropriate affect.

14.15 What normal functions are reduced or absent in individuals with schizophrenia? p. 505

The negative symptoms of schizophrenia represent loss of or deficiencies in thoughts and behavior that are characteristic of normal functioning. They include social withdrawal, apathy, loss of motivation, lack of goal-directed activity, very limited speech, slowed movements, flat affect, poor problem-solving abilities, a distorted sense of time, and poor hygiene and grooming.

14.16 What are the four types of schizophrenia? p. 506

The four types of schizophrenia are paranoid, disorganized, catatonic, and undifferentiated schizophrenia.

14.17 What factors increase the risk of developing schizophrenia? p. 506

Some risk factors for schizophrenia are a genetic predisposition, more stress and neurological abnormalities.

Somatoform and Dissociative Disorders p. 510

14.18 What are two somatoform disorders, and what symptoms do they share? p. 510

Somatoform disorders involve physical symptoms that cannot be identified as any of the known medical conditions. Hypochondriasis involves a persistent fear that bodily symptoms are the sign of some serious disease, and conversion disorder involves a loss of motor or sensory functioning in some part of the body, which has no physical cause but does solve a psychological problem.

14.19 How do the various dissociative disorders affect behavior? p. 510

People with dissociative amnesia have a complete or partial loss of memory of important personal events and/or their entire personal identity. In dissociative fugue, people forget their entire identity, travel away from home, and may assume a new identity somewhere else. In dissociative identity disorder, two or more distinct, unique personalities exist in the same person, and there is severe memory disruption concerning personal information about the other personalities.

Personality Disorders p. 512

14.20 What features are shared by all of the personality disorders? p. 513

People with personality disorders have long-standing, inflexible, maladaptive patterns of behavior that cause problems in their social relationships and at work.

14.21 What behaviors are associated with personality disorders in Clusters A, B, and C? p. 513

Cluster A disorders are characterized by odd behavior. The disorders in Cluster B involve erratic, overly dramatic behavior. Cluster C includes disorders that are associated with fearful and anxious behaviors.

Disorders Diagnosed in Childhood p. 516

14.22 How do pervasive developmental disorders affect children's development? p. 516

PDDs interfere with the development of communication skills and cause children to be unable to engage in normal social relationships. Children who are diagnosed with Asperger's disorder have a better prognosis than those who have autistic disorder because of their near-normal cognitive and language skills.

14.23 What are the features of attention deficit hyperactivity disorder? p. 518

ADHD includes both restlessness and attentional problems. It is most likely to be diagnosed when children enter school. The effectiveness of medications for ADHD together with the ineffectiveness of behavioral interventions suggests that this disorder has a physiological basis.

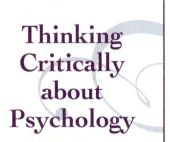

Thinking Critically about Psychology

1. Some psychological disorders are more common in women and some are more common in men. Give some possible reasons for such gender differences. Support your answer.
2. There is a continuing controversy over whether specific psychological disorders are chiefly biological in origin (nature) or result primarily from learning and experience (nurture). Select any two disorders from this chapter, and prepare arguments for both the nature and nurture positions for both disorders.
3. How do you think that you would respond to the news that your toddler had been diagnosed with a pervasive developmental disorder? What actions would you take to enhance your child's chances of leading as normal a life as possible?

Key Terms

agoraphobia, p. 496
anxiety disorders, p. 495
Asperger's disorder, p. 517
attention deficit hyperactivity disorder, p. 518
autistic disorder, p. 517
bipolar disorder, p. 500
catatonic schizophrenia, p. 506
compulsion, p. 498
conversion disorder, p. 510
delusion, p. 505
delusions of grandeur, p. 505
delusions of persecution, p. 505
disorganized schizophrenia, p. 506
dissociative amnesia, p. 511

dissociative disorders, p. 511
dissociative fugue, p. 511
dissociative identity disorder (DID), p. 511
DSM-IV-TR, p. 491
generalized anxiety disorder, p. 496
hallucination, p. 505
hypochondriasis, p. 510
major depressive disorder, p. 499
manic episode, p. 501
mood disorders, p. 499
obsession, p. 498
obsessive-compulsive disorder (OCD), p. 498
panic attack, p. 495

panic disorder, p. 496
paranoid schizophrenia, p. 506
personality disorder, p. 513
pervasive developmental disorders (PDDs), p. 516
phobia, p. 497
psychological disorders, p. 489
psychosis, p. 504
schizophrenia, p. 504
social phobia, p. 497
somatoform disorders, p. 510
specific phobia, p. 497
undifferentiated schizophrenia, p. 506

Chapter 15

Therapies

Insight Therapies

15.1 What are the basic techniques of psychoanalysis, and how are they used to help patients?

15.2 What problems commonly associated with major depression does interpersonal therapy focus on?

15.3 What are the role and the goal of the therapist in person-centered therapy?

15.4 What is the major emphasis of Gestalt therapy?

Relationship Therapies

15.5 How do traditional and integrated behavioral couple therapy differ?

15.6 What are the goals of family therapy?

15.7 What are some advantages of group therapy?

Behavior Therapies

15.8 How do behavior therapists modify clients' problematic behavior?

15.9 What behavior therapies are based on classical conditioning and observational learning theory?

Cognitive Therapies

15.10 What is the aim of rational emotive behavior therapy?

15.11 How does Beck's cognitive therapy help people overcome depression and panic disorder?

Biological Therapies

15.12 What are the advantages and disadvantages of using drugs to treat psychological disorders?

15.13 What are some of the issues involved in prescribing psychiatric drugs for children and adolescents?

15.14 What is electroconvulsive therapy (ECT) used for?

15.15 What is psychosurgery, and for what problems is it used?

Evaluating the Therapies

15.16 What therapy, if any, is most effective in treating psychological disorders?

Culturally Sensitive and Gender-Sensitive Therapy

15.17 What characterizes culturally sensitive and gender-sensitive therapy?

Suppose that one day, while waiting for a bus, you notice a poster that shows a distressed-looking person under the headline, "Imagine a life without fear." Intrigued, you move closer to read the fine print. It begins by explaining that the person depicted is anxious about making an important business presentation. The brief story reminds you of the nausea you felt when you had to give an oral report in class. Such individuals, the poster tells you, suffer from a hidden psychological disorder. However, a recent "medical breakthrough" has enabled many of them to overcome their anxiety. The message is sponsored by a nonprofit organization—the Campaign Against Social Fear. Encouraged that there may be help for you, you write down the web address and toll free number at the bottom of the poster.

You have just unknowingly been targeted by a pharmaceutical advertisement. Marketing strategies that employ public media like posters are known as "awareness-raising campaigns" (Plumer, 2005). They target consumer knowledge of disorders rather than knowledge of the products to treat them. Such campaigns have likely helped some individuals get much-needed help. However, critics charge that these strategies have made the featured disorders more prevalent.

A late 1990s campaign by pharmaceutical giant GlaxoSmithKline (GSK) provides a good example of awareness-raising tactics (Koerner, 2002). The campaign included posters quite similar to our fictional one that were ostensibly sponsored by the Social Anxiety Disorder Coalition (SADC), a nonprofit organization set up by GSK. Similarly disguised "public service announcements" appeared on television and radio. Through these media, the SADC alerted consumers to the possibility of becoming "allergic to people." To broaden the appeal of their message, these ads spoke of the ambiguous *social anxiety disorder (SAD)* (Moynihan & Cassells, 2005). Next came endorsements by celebrities and experts, along with press releases that inflated anxiety disorder statistics and touted the findings of studies funded by GSK.

With its awareness-raising campaign in full swing, GSK launched a more overt series of ads, which positioned Paxil as the treatment of choice for SAD (Koerner, 2002). Within one year, Paxil had become one of the top-selling psychiatric drugs in the United States, and other drug manufacturers had begun to adopt GSK's marketing strategies. The campaign was a re-markable success. But what were its effects on public health?

Critics of awareness-raising advertising claim that it leads to the "medicalization" of normal variation (Conrad & Leiter, 2004). Medicalization leads people to believe that challenging, but manageable personality traits are psychological disorders best treated with medication. People whose lives are negatively affected by such traits may consider medication their only alternative. As a result, many fail to seek out other equally effective therapies that don't involve the risks associated with psychiatric drugs (Pettus, 2006). Others regard drugs as the first line of defense in the fight for psychological health, and believe other therapies are last resorts. Trends among college students seeking help at on-campus psychological service centers exemplify such attitudes. At Bennington College in Vermont, about 40% of students who seek counseling are already taking psychiatric drugs (Young, 2003).

Defenders of awareness-raising campaigns point out that medicalizing a psychological difficulty may encourage sufferers to seek help. Some argue that such campaigns open consumers to the idea that psychological disorders have a biological basis. Consequently, advertising can educate consumers and remove the stigma often associated with psychological treatment (Pettus, 2006). Moreover, they say, advertising of this kind familiarizes consumers with the terminology for reporting symptoms to their health care providers. Many defenders of the awareness-raising approach also say that psychiatric drugs are safe enough that the benefits to legitimate sufferers far outweigh the potential costs to those who take them unnecessarily.

Like most people, you probably don't want to take psychiatric medications unnecessarily. So, how can you determine whether your problems are within the range of normal human experience or whether they represent a disorder for which medication is justified? The best strategy, and one that applies to any potential psychological disorder, is to refer back to the criteria for abnormality that you learned in Chapter 14.

First, look for a culture clash. If you come from a culture, or even a family, in which people are emotionally reserved, then being in an environment in which most people are outgoing and socially engaged may make you feel out of place. Second, think about how much distress your "problem" actually causes you. Are you really concerned about your shyness, or are you responding to the concerns of others? Third, determine whether your shyness interferes with adaptive behaviors that are vital to your goals. For example, do you accept zeroes on oral reports rather than endure the anxiety involved in doing them?

After thinking about your problem along these lines, if you conclude that you really might have an anxiety disorder, then, by all means, get help. However, remember that drugs are only one option. Moreover, many studies show that, depending on the disorder involved, the most useful therapy often combines drugs with other approaches.

Despite the dubious marketing practices of some drug manufacturers, there can be no doubt that psychiatric drugs have revolutionized the treatment of psychological disorders. In this chapter, you will learn about these drugs and the ways in which they have helped sufferers of many kinds of disorders. You will also learn about other kinds of biological treatments for psychological disorders. But before we turn to biological strategies for managing these disorders, we will introduce you to various kinds of psychotherapy, treatments that use psychological rather than biological means to treat emotional and behavioral disorders. The practice of **psychotherapy,** has grown and changed enormously since its beginnings more than 100 years ago, when Freud and his colleagues began using it.

Insight Therapies

Do you recall a form of learning called *insight* that you read about in Chapter 5? Such learning is the foundation of several approaches to psychotherapy. These approaches, fittingly enough, are collectively referred to as **insight therapies** because their assumption is that psychological well-being depends on self-understanding—understanding of one's own thoughts, emotions, motives, behavior, and coping mechanisms.

psychotherapy Any type of treatment for emotional and behavioral disorders that uses psychological rather than biological means.

insight therapies Approaches to psychotherapy based on the notion that psychological well-being depends on self-understanding.

Psychodynamic Therapies

Psychodynamic therapies attempt to uncover childhood experiences that are thought to explain a patient's current difficulties. The techniques associated with the first such therapy—Freud's **psychoanalysis**—are still used by psychodynamic therapists today (Epstein et al., 2001). One such technique is **free association,** in which the patient is asked to reveal whatever thoughts, feelings, or images come to mind, no matter how trivial, embarrassing, or terrible they might seem. The analyst then pieces together the free-flowing associations, explains their meanings, and helps patients gain insight into the thoughts and behaviors that are troubling them. But some patients avoid revealing certain painful or embarrassing thoughts while engaging in free association, a phenomenon Freud called *resistance*. Resistance may take the form of halting speech during free association, "forgetting" appointments with the analyst, or arriving late.

Dream analysis is another technique used by psychoanalysts. Freud believed that areas of emotional concern repressed in waking life are sometimes expressed in symbolic form in dreams. He claimed that patient behavior may have a symbolic quality as well. At some point during psychoanalysis, Freud said, the patient reacts to the analyst with the same feelings that were present in another significant relationship—usually with the mother or father. This reaction of the patient is called **transference.** Freud believed that encouraging patients to achieve transference was a essential part of psychotherapy. He claimed that transference allows the patient to relive troubling experiences from the past with the analyst as a parent substitute, thereby resolving any hidden conflicts.

15.1 What are the basic techniques of psychoanalysis, and how are they used to help patients?

psychodynamic therapies Psychotherapies that attempt to uncover childhood experiences that are thought to explain a patient's current difficulties.

psychoanalysis (SY-ko-uh-NAL-ul-sis) The first psychodynamic therapy, which was developed by Freud and uses free association, dream analysis, and transference.

free association A psychoanalytic technique used to explore the unconscious by having patients reveal whatever thoughts, feelings, or images come to mind.

▲ Freud's famous couch was used by his patients during psychoanalysis.

▲ Carl Rogers (at upper right) facilitates discussion in a therapy group.

transference An emotional reaction that occurs during psychoanalysis, in which the patient displays feelings and attitudes toward the analyst that were present in another significant relationship.

interpersonal therapy (IPT) A brief psychotherapy designed to help depressed people better understand and cope with problems relating to their interpersonal relationships.

humanistic therapies Psychotherapies that assume that people have the ability and freedom to lead rational lives and make rational choices.

Traditional psychoanalysis requires patients to participate in multiple sessions each week and can last for years. As psychodynamic methods evolved over the decades of the 20th century, this and other features of Freud's approach gave way to briefer, more sharply focused techniques. For example, many therapists today practice brief psychodynamic therapy, in which the therapist and patient decide on the issues to explore at the outset rather than waiting for them to emerge in the course of treatment. The therapist assumes a more active role and places more emphasis on the present than in traditional psychoanalysis. Brief psychodynamic therapy may require only one or two visits per week for as few as 12 to 20 weeks. In a meta-analysis of 11 well-controlled studies, Crits-Christoph (1992) found brief psychodynamic therapy to be as effective as other psychotherapies. More recent research has also shown brief psychodynamic therapy to be comparable to other forms of psychotherapy in terms of successful outcomes (Hager et al., 2000). Brief psychotherapy appears to be most effective with patients who do not have multiple psychological disorders, who lack significant social relationship problems, and who believe that the therapy will be effective (Crits-Christoph et al., 2004).

Interpersonal Therapy

15.2 What problems commonly associated with major depression does interpersonal therapy focus on?

Interpersonal therapy (IPT) is a brief psychodynamic therapy that has proven very effective in the treatment of depression (Elkin et al., 1989, 1995; Klerman et al., 1984). It can be carried out with individual clients or with groups (Mufson et al., 2004). IPT is designed specifically to help patients understand and cope with four types of interpersonal problems commonly associated with major depression:

1. *Unusual or severe responses to the death of a loved one.* The therapist and patient discuss the patient's relationship with the deceased person and feelings (such as guilt) that may be associated with the death.
2. *Interpersonal role disputes.* The therapist helps the patient to understand others' points of view and to explore options for bringing about change.
3. *Difficulty in adjusting to role transitions, such as divorce, career change, and retirement.* Patients are helped to see the change not as a threat but as a challenge that they can master and an opportunity for growth.
4. *Deficits in interpersonal skills.* Through role-playing and analysis of the patient's communication style, the therapist tries to help the patient develop the interpersonal skills necessary to initiate and sustain relationships.

▲ Therapists working with couples pay attention to the dynamics between the two people—how they communicate, act toward each other, and view each other.

Interpersonal therapy is relatively brief, consisting of 12 to 16 weekly sessions. A large study conducted by the National Institute of Mental Health found IPT to be an effective treatment even for severe depression and to have a low dropout rate (Elkin et al., 1989, 1995). Research also indicates that patients who recover from major depression can enjoy a longer period without relapse when they continue with monthly sessions of IPT (Frank et al., 1991).

Humanistic Therapies

Humanistic therapies assume that people have the ability and freedom to lead rational lives and make rational choices. **Person-centered therapy** (sometimes called *client-centered* therapy), developed by Carl Rogers (1951), is one of the most frequently used humanistic therapies. According to this view, people are innately good and if allowed to develop naturally, they will grow toward *self-actualization*—the realization of their inner potential. The humanistic perspective suggests that psychological disorders result when a person's natural tendency toward self-actualization is blocked either by himself or by others. In the 1940s and 1950s, person-centered therapy enjoyed a strong following among psychologists.

The person-centered therapist attempts to create an accepting climate, based on *unconditional positive regard* for the client. The therapist also empathizes with the client's concerns and emotions. When the client speaks, the therapist responds by restating or reflecting back her or his ideas and feelings. Using these techniques, the therapist allows the direction of the therapy sessions to be controlled by the client. Rogers rejected all forms of therapy that cast the therapist in the role of expert and clients in the role of patients who expect the therapist to prescribe something that "cures" their problem. Thus, person-centered therapy is called a **nondirective therapy.**

15.3 What are the role and the goal of the therapist in person-centered therapy?

person-centered therapy   A nondirective, humanistic therapy developed by Carl Rogers, in which the therapist creates an accepting climate and shows empathy, freeing clients to be themselves and releasing their natural tendency toward self-actualization.

nondirective therapy   Any type of psychotherapy in which the therapist allows the direction of the therapy sessions to be controlled by the client; an example is person-centered therapy.

Gestalt Therapy

Gestalt therapy, developed by Fritz Perls (1969), emphasizes the importance of clients' fully experiencing, in the present moment, their feelings, thoughts, and actions and then taking responsibility for them. The goal of Gestalt therapy is to help clients achieve a more integrated self and become more authentic and self-accepting. In addition, they learn to assume personal responsibility for their behavior rather than blaming society, past experiences, parents, or others.

Gestalt therapy is a **directive therapy,** one in which the therapist takes an active role in determining the course of therapy sessions and provides answers and suggestions to the client. The well-known phrase "getting in touch with your feelings" is a major objective of Gestalt therapy. Perls suggested that those of us who are in need of therapy carry around a heavy load of unfinished business, which may be in the form of resentment toward or conflicts with parents, siblings, lovers, employers, or others. If not resolved, these conflicts are carried forward into our present relationships. One method for dealing with unfinished business is the *empty chair technique* (Paivio & Greenberg, 1995). The client sits facing an empty chair and imagines, for example, that a wife, husband, father, or mother sits there. The client proceeds to tell the chair what he or she truly feels about that person. Then, the client moves to the empty chair and role-plays what the imagined person's response would be to what was said.

15.4 What is the major emphasis of Gestalt therapy?

Gestalt therapy   A therapy that was originated by Fritz Perls and that emphasizes the importance of clients' fully experiencing, in the present moment, their feelings, thoughts, and actions and then taking responsibility for them.

directive therapy   Any type of psychotherapy in which the therapist takes an active role in determining the course of therapy sessions and provides answers and suggestions to the patient; an example is Gestalt therapy.

Remember It   Insight Therapies

1. In psychoanalysis, the technique whereby a patient reveals every thought, idea, or image that comes to mind is called _____; the patient's attempt to avoid revealing certain thoughts is called _____.

2. Attempting to uncover childhood experiences that may explain a patient's current problems is the goal of _____ therapies.

3. A depressed person who would be *least* likely to benefit from interpersonal therapy (IPT) is one who

   a. is unable to accept the death of a loved one.
   b. has been depressed since his or her retirement.
   c. was sexually abused by a parent.
   d. feels isolated and alone because of difficulty making friends.

4. _____ therapy is the nondirective psychotherapy developed by Carl Rogers.

5. _____ therapy is a directive psychotherapy that emphasizes the importance of the client's fully experiencing, in the present moment, his or her thoughts, feelings, and actions.

Answers: 1. free association, resistance; 2. psychodynamic; 3. c; 4. Person-centered; 5. Gestalt

Relationship Therapies

Insight therapies focus on the self, which is not always the most appropriate approach to a psychological problem. **Relationship therapies** look at the individual's internal struggles in the context of his or her interpersonal relationships. Some deliberately create new relationships for people that can support them in their efforts to address their problems.

Couple Therapy

15.5 How do traditional and integrated behavioral couple therapy differ?

Some therapists work with couples to help them resolve problems. Couple therapy can take place during any phase of a relationship. For example, pre-marital sessions can help future spouses prepare for their life together and has been shown to be associated with marital satisfaction.

There are many approaches to pre-marital and other forms of couple therapy, but two models have become prominent in recent years because of experimental studies that attest to their effectiveness (Christensen et al., 2004; Snyder, Castellani, & Whisman, 2006). The older of the two, **traditional behavioral couple therapy (TBCT)** focuses on identification and modification of behaviors that contribute to a couple's conflicts (Jacobson & Margolin, 1979). For example, suppose that a wife complains that her husband is a poor listener. In response, the husband justifies his tendency to tune out as a reaction to his wife's habit of communicating in vague generalities. He further reports that she becomes defensive whenever he asks for clarification. A TBCT therapist would observe interactions between the couple to assess the accuracy of these complaints and to identify each spouse's communication strengths. Next, the therapist would work with each of them individually to modify the behaviors that contribute to the couple's communication difficulties. At the same time, the therapist would seek to enhance whatever behaviors each spouse exhibits that are helpful to the communication process.

A variation on TBCT, **integrated behavioral couple therapy (IBCT)** targets emotions as well as behaviors (Jacobson & Christensen, 1996). A central premise of IBCT is that couples' problems arise from changeable behaviors as well as the individual, and less changeable, personality traits of both partners. The five personality factors you learned about in Chapter 13 are examples of such traits (openness, conscientiousness, extroversion, agreeableness, and neuroticism). Thus, when couples complain about behaviors in their partners that reflect such traits, IBCT therapists seek to help them accept and adjust to each other's personalities rather than to try to change them.

In addition to helping couples achieve higher levels of relationship satisfaction, couple therapy has also been found to be useful in the treatment of psychological disorders. Sexual dysfunctions, for example, are sometimes best treated in the context of couple therapy (Gehring, 2003). It has also useful in the treatment of mood, anxiety, and substance use disorders (Snyder, Castellani, & Whisman, 2006; Walitzer & Demen, 2004).

relationship therapies Therapies that attempt to improve patients' interpersonal relationships or create new relationships to support patients' efforts to address psychological problems.

traditional behavioral couple therapy (TBCT) An approach to couple therapy that focuses on behavior change.

integrated behavioral couple therapy (IBCT) A type of couple therapy that emphasizes both behavior change and mutual acceptance.

family therapy Therapy involving an entire family, with the goal of helping family members reach agreement on changes that will help heal the family unit, improve communication problems, and create more understanding and harmony within the group.

Family Therapy

15.6 What are the goals of family therapy?

In **family therapy,** parents and children enter therapy as a group. The therapist pays attention to the dynamics of the family unit—how family members communicate, how they act toward one another, and how they view each other. The goal of the therapist is to help family members reach agreement on certain changes that will help heal the wounds of the family unit, improve communication patterns, and create more understanding and harmony within the group (Hawley & Weixz, 2003).

When accompanied by medication, family therapy can be beneficial in the treatment of schizophrenia and can prevent relapses (Heru, 2006). Patients with schizophrenia are more likely to relapse if their family members express emotions, attitudes, and behaviors that involve criticism, hostility, or emotional overinvolvement (Linszen et al., 1997). This pattern is labeled *high in expressed emotion*, or *high EE* (Falloon, 1988; Jenkins & Karno, 1992). Family therapy can help other family members modify their behavior toward the patient.

Family therapy also seems to be the most favorable setting for treating problem behaviors in teenagers. One variant, *functional family therapy (FFT),* has been helpful in the prevention and reduction of juvenile delinquency (Sexton & Alexander, 2000). FFT is carried out in three phases over a period of time that ranges from a few weeks to several months, depending on the severity of a teenager's problems and the response of the family to therapy.

In the first phase of FFT, the therapist works on engaging the family and motivating them to change. Doing so requires the establishment of trusting relationships between the parents and the therapist and between the teenager and the therapist. It also involves convincing all family members that their situation can be improved. In the second phase, the therapist works individually with family members to help them change the behaviors that contribute to their problems. For example, in this phase, the therapist might help parents learn to consistently enforce their rules and follow through with consequences for violations. In the final phase, therapists help the families of delinquents and the delinquents themselves to identify contextual variables that can help them maintain behavioral change. For example, parents might be encouraged to spend more time engaged in family activities so that the teenager has less time to spend with delinquent peers.

A similar approach, *multidimensional family therapy (MDFT)*, has proven to be useful in the treatment of teenagers' substance abuse problems (Liddle, 2002). A course of MDFT usually lasts about 6 months. In individual sessions, MDFT practitioners help teenagers learn decision-making skills and develop a sense of personal identity. Another goal of these sessions is to help teens develop an appreciation for how the present relates to the future through the exploration of the adolescents' educational and career goals. In their sessions with the therapist, parents are encouraged to resist the common tendency to disengage from substance-abusing teenagers and to appreciate their potential for positively influencing their children's lives. Parents also learn to identify and to modify behaviors that may be contributing to their children's problems. Family sessions are devoted to the development of effective communication skills.

group therapy A form of therapy in which several clients (usually 7 to 10) meet regularly with one or more therapists to resolve personal problems.

Group Therapy

Group therapy is a form of therapy in which several clients (usually 7 to 10) meet regularly with one or more therapists to resolve personal problems. Besides being less expensive than individual therapy, group therapy gives the individual a sense of belonging and opportunities to express feelings, to get feedback from other members, and to give and receive help and emotional support. Learning that others also share their problems helps people feel less alone and ashamed. A meta-analysis of studies comparing prisoners who participated in group therapy to those who did not found that group participation was helpful for a variety of problems, including anxiety, depression, and low self-esteem (Morgan & Flora, 2002).

15.7 What are some advantages of group therapy?

◀ Group therapy can give individuals a sense of belonging and an opportunity to give and receive emotional support.

A variant of group therapy is the *self-help group*. About 12 million people in the United States participate in roughly 500,000 self-help groups, most of which focus on a single problem such as substance abuse or depression. Self-help groups usually are not led by professional therapists. They are simply groups of people who share a common problem and meet to give and receive support.

One of the oldest and best-known self-help groups is Alcoholics Anonymous, which claims 1.5 million members worldwide. Other self-help groups patterned after Alcoholics Anonymous have been formed to help individuals overcome many other addictive behaviors, from overeating (Overeaters Anonymous) to gambling (Gamblers Anonymous). One study indicated that people suffering from anxiety-based problems were helped by participating in groups that used a multimedia self-help program called Attacking Anxiety. Of the 176 individuals who participated in the study, 62 were reported to have achieved significant improvement, and another 40 reported some improvement (Finch et al., 2000).

Remember It — Relationship Therapies

1. _____ behavioral couple therapy focuses on behavior change, while _____ behavioral couple therapy emphasizes mutual acceptance.
2. In family therapy, the therapist pays attention to the _____ of the family unit.
3. Match each description with the appropriate type(s) of therapy.
   ____ (1) led by professional therapists
   ____ (2) effective for supporting individuals recovering from alcoholism
   ____ (3) provides members with a sense of belonging
   ____ (4) less expensive than individual therapy but still provides contact with trained therapists

   a. group therapy
   b. self-help groups
   c. both group therapy and self-help groups

Answers: 1. Traditional, integrated; 2. dynamics; 3. (1) a, (2) b, (3) c, (4) a

Behavior Therapies

behavior therapy A treatment approach that is based on the idea that abnormal behavior is learned and that applies the principles of operant conditioning, classical conditioning, and/or observational learning to eliminate inappropriate or maladaptive behaviors and replace them with more adaptive responses.

behavior modification An approach to therapy that uses learning principles to eliminate inappropriate or maladaptive behaviors and replace them with more adaptive responses.

Sometimes, individuals seek help from a mental health professional because they want to rid themselves of a troublesome habit, such as procrastination or smoking. In such cases, psychotherapists may employ a behavioral approach.

A **behavior therapy** is a treatment approach consistent with the learning perspective on psychological disorders—that abnormal behavior is learned. Instead of viewing maladaptive behavior as a symptom of some underlying disorder, the behavior therapist sees the behavior itself as the disorder. If a person comes to a therapist with a fear of flying, that fear of flying is seen as the problem. Behavior therapies use learning principles to eliminate inappropriate or maladaptive behaviors and replace them with more adaptive responses—an approach referred to as **behavior modification.** The goal is to change the troublesome behavior, not to change the individual's personality structure or to search for the origin of the problem behavior.

Behavior Modification Techniques Based on Operant Conditioning

15.8 How do behavior therapists modify clients' problematic behavior?

Behavior modification techniques based on operant conditioning seek to control the consequences of behavior. Extinction of an undesirable behavior is accomplished by terminating, or withholding, the reinforcement that is maintaining that behavior (Lerman & Iwata, 1996). Behavior therapists also seek to reinforce desirable behavior in order to increase its frequency. Institutional settings such as hospitals, prisons, and school classrooms are well suited to behavior modification techniques, because they provide a restricted environment in which the consequences of behavior can be strictly controlled.

Some institutions use **token economies** that reward appropriate behavior with tokens such as poker chips, play money, gold stars, or the like. These tokens can later be exchanged for desired goods (candy, gum, cigarettes) and/or privileges (weekend passes, free time, participation in desirable activities). Sometimes, individuals are fined a certain number of tokens for undesirable behavior. Mental hospitals have successfully used token economies for decades with people suffering from chronic schizophrenia to improve their self-care skills and social interactions (Ayllon & Azrin, 1965, 1968). Similar interventions have been helpful in motivating clients at substance abuse clinics to remain abstinent (Petry et al., 2004).

Techniques based on operant conditioning have also been used to reduce the frequency of self-injurious behavior among children and adults with autism. They have also proven useful for encouraging hospitalized individuals with schizophrenia to maintain self-care routines such as brushing their teeth. And they have provided special education teachers and parents with effective strategies for teaching such skills to children with mental retardation. Although these techniques do not cure autism, schizophrenia, or mental retardation, they can increase the frequency of desirable behaviors and decrease the frequency of undesirable behaviors. For example, a large proportion of people who suffer from schizophrenia smoke cigarettes. Among this group, contingent monetary reinforcement has been found to be as effective as nicotine patches for the reduction of smoking (Tidey et al., 2002). In other words, smokers' receipt of the monetary reinforcers is linked to their smoking behavior (i.e., is contingent upon such behavior). Those who meet behavioral goals such as limiting themselves to one cigarette per day or getting through an entire day without smoking at all receive the reinforcers, but those who fail to do so do not receive them. Sometimes, modifying such behaviors enables the family members of people with schizophrenia to accept and care for them more easily.

Another effective method used to eliminate undesirable behavior, especially in children and adolescents, is **time out** (Kazdin & Benjet, 2003). Children are told in advance that if they engage in certain undesirable behaviors, they will be removed from the situation and will have to pass a period of time (usually no more than 15 minutes) in a place containing no reinforcers (no television, books, toys, friends, and so on). Theoretically, the undesirable behavior will stop if it is no longer followed by attention or any other positive reinforcers.

Behavior modification techniques can also be used by people who want to break bad habits such as smoking and overeating or to develop good habits such as a regular exercise regime. If you want to modify any of your behaviors, devise a reward system for desirable behaviors, and remember the principles of shaping. Reward gradual changes in the direction of your ultimate goal. If you are trying to develop better eating habits, don't try to change a lifetime of bad habits all at once. Begin with a small step, such as substituting frozen yogurt for ice cream. Set realistic weekly goals that you are likely to be able to achieve.

Behavior Therapies Based on Other Learning Theories

Behavior therapies based on classical conditioning can be used to rid people of fears and other undesirable behaviors. These therapies employ different means of exposing patients to feared objects or situations or to triggers that elicit undesirable behaviors such as substance abuse. Recent research also suggests that exposing individuals to such stimuli via *virtual reality* can be a useful addition to the standard ways in which such therapies are implemented (Mühlberger et al., 2006). Therapies of this type include systematic desensitization, flooding, exposure and response prevention, and aversion therapy.

▲ A time out is effective because it prevents a child from receiving reinforcers for undesirable behaviors.

token economy   A behavior modification technique that rewards appropriate behavior with tokens that can be exchanged later for desired goods and/or privileges.

time out   A behavior modification technique used to eliminate undesirable behavior, especially in children and adolescents, by withdrawing all reinforcers for a period of time.

15.9 What behavior therapies are based on classical conditioning and observational learning theory?

systematic desensitization A behavior therapy that is based on classical conditioning and used to treat fears by training clients in deep muscle relaxation and then having them confront a graduated series of anxiety-producing situations (real or imagined) until they can remain relaxed while confronting even the most feared situation.

Systematic Desensitization. One of the pioneers in the application of classical conditioning techniques to therapy, psychiatrist Joseph Wolpe (1958, 1973), reasoned that if he could get people to relax and stay relaxed while they thought about a feared object, person, place, or situation, they could conquer their fear. In Wolpe's therapy, known as **systematic desensitization,** clients are trained in deep muscle relaxation. Then, they confront a hierarchy of fears—a graduated series of anxiety-producing situations— either *in vivo* (in real life) or in their imagination, until they can remain relaxed even in the presence of the most feared situation. The technique can be used for everything from fear of animals to claustrophobia, social phobia, and other situational fears. In fact, you can use it on yourself, as illustrated in the following *Try It*.

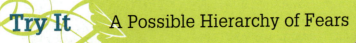

Try It   A Possible Hierarchy of Fears

Use what you have learned about systematic desensitization to create a step-by-step approach to help someone overcome a fear of taking tests. The person's hierarchy of fears begins with reading in the syllabus that a test will be given and culminates in actually taking the test. Fill in successive steps, according to a possible hierarchy of fears, that will lead to the final step. One set of possible steps is given below.

Suggested Answers: (1) Preparing for each class session by reading the assigned material and/or completing any homework assignments. (2) Attending each class session and taking notes on the material the test will cover. (3) Reviewing the new notes after each class period. (4) Reviewing all class materials beginning one week before the test. (5) Reciting key information from memory the day before the test. (6) Arriving early to take the test, having gotten a good night's sleep.

Taking the test in class

6. _____

5. _____

4. _____

3. _____

2. _____

1. _____

Reading in the syllabus that a test will be given on a certain day

Many experiments, demonstrations, and case reports confirm that systematic desensitization is a highly successful treatment for eliminating fears and phobias in a relatively short time (Kalish, 1981; Rachman & Wilson, 1980). It has proved effective for specific problems such as test anxiety, stage fright, and anxiety related to sexual disorders.

Flooding. Flooding, a behavior therapy used in the treatment of phobias, involves exposing clients to the feared object or event (or asking them to imagine it vividly) for an extended period, until their anxiety decreases. The person is exposed to the fear all at once, not gradually as in systematic desensitization. An individual with a fear of heights, for example, might have to go onto the roof of a tall building and remain there until the fear subsided.

Flooding sessions typically last from 30 minutes to 2 hours and should not be terminated until patients are markedly less afraid than they were at the beginning of the session. Additional sessions are required until the fear response is extinguished or reduced to an acceptable level. It is rare for a patient to need more than six treatment sessions (Marshall & Segal, 1988). *In vivo* flooding, the real-life experience, works faster and is more effective than simply imagining the feared object (Chambless & Goldstein, 1979; Marks, 1972). Thus, a person who fears flying would benefit more from taking an actual plane trip than from just thinking about one.

▲ Flooding can be a useful treatment for phobias, such as fear of dogs.

flooding A behavior therapy based on classical conditioning and used to treat phobias by exposing clients to the feared object or event (or asking them to imagine it vividly) for an extended period, until their anxiety decreases.

Exposure and Response Prevention. Exposure and response prevention has been successful in treating obsessive-compulsive disorder (Baer, 1996; Foa, 1995; Rhéaume & Ladouceur, 2000). The first component of this technique involves *exposure—*

exposing patients to objects or situations they have been avoiding because they trigger obsessions and compulsive rituals. The second component is *response prevention*, in which patients agree to resist performing their compulsive rituals for progressively longer periods of time.

Initially, the therapist identifies the thoughts, objects, or situations that trigger the compulsive ritual. For example, touching a doorknob, a piece of unwashed fruit, or a garbage bin might send people with a fear of contamination to the nearest bathroom to wash their hands. Patients are gradually exposed to stimuli that they find more and more distasteful and anxiety-provoking. They must agree not to perform the normal ritual (hand washing, bathing, or the like) for a specified period of time after each exposure. A typical treatment course—about ten sessions over a period of 3 to 7 weeks—can bring about considerable improvement in 60–70% of patients (Jenike, 1990). And patients treated with exposure and response prevention are less likely to relapse after treatment than those treated with drugs alone (Greist, 1992). Exposure and response prevention has also proved useful in the treatment of posttraumatic stress disorder (Cloitre et al., 2002).

Aversion Therapy. **Aversion therapy** is used to stop a harmful or socially undesirable behavior by pairing it with a painful, sickening, or otherwise aversive stimulus. Electric shock, emetics (which cause nausea and vomiting), or other unpleasant stimuli are paired with the undesirable behavior time after time until a strong negative association is formed and the person comes to avoid that behavior. Treatment continues until the bad behavior loses its appeal and becomes associated with pain or discomfort.

Alcoholics are sometimes given a nausea-producing substance such as Antabuse, which reacts violently with alcohol and causes a person to retch and vomit until the stomach is empty (Grossman & Ruiz, 2004). But for most problems, aversion therapy need not be so intense as to make a person physically ill. A controlled comparison of treatments for chronic nail biting revealed that mild aversion therapy—painting a bitter-tasting substance on the fingernails—yielded significant improvement (Allen, 1996).

Participant Modeling. Therapies derived from Albert Bandura's work on observational learning are based on the belief that people can overcome fears and acquire social skills through modeling. The most effective type of therapy based on observational learning theory is called **participant modeling** (Bandura, 1977a; Bandura et al., 1975, 1977). In this therapy, not only does the model demonstrate the appropriate response in graduated steps, but the client attempts to imitate the model step by step, while the therapist gives encouragement and support. Most specific phobias can be extinguished in only 3 or 4 hours of client participation in modeling therapy. For instance, participant modeling could be used to help someone overcome a fear of dogs. A session would begin with the client watching others petting and playing with a dog. As the client becomes more comfortable, he or she would be encouraged to join in. Alternatively, a client would be shown a video of people playing with a dog and then would be encouraged to play with a live dog.

exposure and response prevention A behavior therapy that exposes patients with obsessive-compulsive disorder to stimuli that trigger obsessions and compulsive rituals, while patients resist performing the compulsive rituals for progressively longer periods of time.

aversion therapy A behavior therapy in which an aversive stimulus is paired with a harmful or socially undesirable behavior until the behavior becomes associated with pain or discomfort.

participant modeling A behavior therapy in which an appropriate response to a feared stimulus is modeled in graduated steps and the client attempts to imitate the model step by step, encouraged and supported by the therapist.

Remember It   Behavior Therapies

1. Behavior therapies based on _____ conditioning are used to change behavior by reinforcing desirable behavior and removing reinforcers for undesirable behavior.
2. Behavior therapies based on _____ conditioning are sometimes used to rid people of fears and undesirable behaviors or habits.
3. Exposure and response prevention is a treatment for people with _____ disorder.
4. Match each therapy with the appropriate description.
   ____ (1) flooding
   ____ (2) aversion therapy
   ____ (3) systematic desensitization
   ____ (4) participant modeling

   a. practicing deep muscle relaxation during gradual exposure to a feared object
   b. associating a painful or sickening stimuli with undesirable behavior
   c. being exposed directly to a feared object until the fear response is reduced or eliminated
   d. imitating a model who is responding appropriately in a feared situation

Answers: 1. operant; 2. classical; 3. obsessive-compulsive; 4. (1) c, (2) b, (3) a, (4) d

Cognitive Therapies

Remember from earlier chapters that behavioral theories have often been criticized for ignoring internal variables such as thinking and emotion. As you might predict, behavior therapies are often criticized for the same reason. Cognitive psychologists argue that behaviors cannot be changed in isolation from the thoughts that produce them. Accordingly, they have developed cognitively based therapeutic approaches.

Cognitive therapies, based on the cognitive perspective, assume that maladaptive behavior can result from irrational thoughts, beliefs, and ideas, which the therapist tries to change. Cognitive therapies are also often referred to as *cognitive-behavioral approaches* because they combine the insights into behavior provided by cognitive psychology with the methodological approaches of behaviorism (Carson et al., 2000). That is, cognitive therapists seek to change the way clients think (cognitive), and they determine the effectiveness of their interventions by assessing changes in clients' behavior (behavioral). Cognitive-behavioral therapy has been shown to be effective in treating a wide variety of problems including anxiety disorders (Kellett et al., 2004), hypochondriasis (Martinez & Belloch, 2004), psychological drug dependence (Babor, 2004), and pathological gambling (Petry, 2002).

Rational Emotive Behavior Therapy

15.10 What is the aim of rational emotive behavior therapy?

Clinical psychologist Albert Ellis (1961, 1977, 1993) developed **rational emotive behavior therapy** in the 1950s. Ellis claims to have developed the technique as a way of addressing his own problems with incapacitating anxiety (Ellis, 2004a). This type of therapy is based on Ellis's *ABC theory.* The A refers to the activating event, the B to the person's belief about the event, and the C to the emotional consequence that follows. Ellis claims that it is not the event itself that causes the emotional consequence, but rather the person's belief about the event. In other words, A does not cause C; B causes C. If the belief is irrational, then the emotional consequence can be extreme distress, as illustrated in Figure 15.1.

Rational emotive behavior therapy is a directive form of psychotherapy designed to challenge clients' irrational beliefs about themselves and others. Most clients in rational emotive behavior therapy see a therapist individually, once a week, for 5 to 50 sessions. In Ellis's view, clients do not benefit from warm, supportive therapeutic approaches that help them feel better but do not address the irrational thoughts that underlie their problems (Ellis, 2004b). Instead, he argues that as clients begin to replace irrational beliefs with rational ones, their emotional reactions become more appropriate, less distressing, and more likely to lead to constructive behavior. For example, a client might tell a therapist that he is feeling anxious and depressed because of his supervisor's unreasonable demands. Using Ellis's model, the therapist would help the client distinguish between the supervisor's demands and the client's emotional reactions to them. The goal would be to help the client understand that his reactions to his supervisor's demands are the source of his anxiety and depression, not the demands themselves. Ultimately, the therapist would lead the client to the conclusion that while he may not be able to control his supervisor's demands, he is capable of controlling his emotional reactions to them. Once the client changes his thinking about the problem, the therapist helps him learn behavioral strategies, such as relaxation techniques, that can help him control his emotional reactions.

One meta-analysis of 28 studies showed that individuals receiving rational emotive behavior therapy did better than those receiving no treatment or a placebo, and about the same as those receiving systematic desensitization (Engels et al., 1993). Take a moment to apply Ellis's ideas to your own irrational thoughts in the *Try It* on the next page.

cognitive therapies Therapies that assume maladaptive behavior can result from irrational thoughts, beliefs, and ideas.

rational emotive behavior therapy A directive form of psychotherapy, developed by Albert Ellis and designed to challenge clients' irrational beliefs about themselves and others.

Figure 15.1   The ABCs of Rational Emotive Behavior Therapy

Rational emotive behavior therapy teaches clients that it is not the activating event (A) that causes the upsetting consequences (C). Rather, it is the client's beliefs (B) about the activating event. According to Albert Ellis, irrational beliefs cause emotional distress. Rational emotive behavior therapists help clients identify their irrational beliefs and replace them with rational ones.

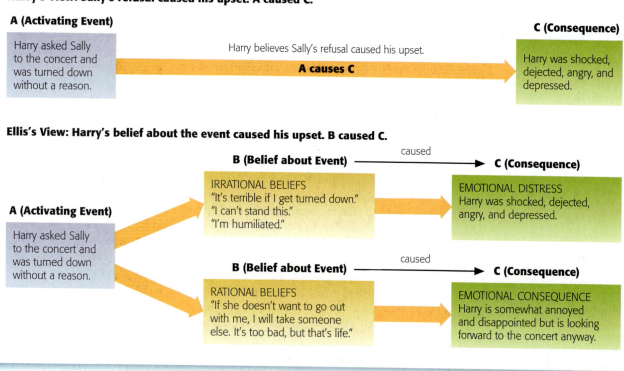

Harry's View: Sally's refusal caused his upset. A caused C.

A (Activating Event)

Harry asked Sally to the concert and was turned down without a reason.

Harry believes Sally's refusal caused his upset.
A causes C

C (Consequence)

Harry was shocked, dejected, angry, and depressed.

Ellis's View: Harry's belief about the event caused his upset. B caused C.

B (Belief about Event) ——— caused ———> **C (Consequence)**

IRRATIONAL BELIEFS
"It's terrible if I get turned down."
"I can't stand this."
"I'm humiliated."

EMOTIONAL DISTRESS
Harry was shocked, dejected, angry, and depressed.

A (Activating Event)

Harry asked Sally to the concert and was turned down without a reason.

B (Belief about Event) ——— caused ———> **C (Consequence)**

RATIONAL BELIEFS
"If she doesn't want to go out with me, I will take someone else. It's too bad, but that's life."

EMOTIONAL CONSEQUENCE
Harry is somewhat annoyed and disappointed but is looking forward to the concert anyway.

Try It   Dealing with Irrational Beliefs

Use what you have learned about Albert Ellis's therapy to identify—and perhaps even eliminate—an irrational belief that you hold about yourself.

First, identify an irrational belief, preferably one that causes some stress in your life. For example, maybe you feel that you must earn all A's in order to think of yourself as a good person.

Ask yourself the following questions, and write down your answers in as much detail as possible.

- Where does this belief come from? Can you identify the time in your life when it began?

- Why do you think this belief is true? What evidence can you think of that "proves" your belief?

- Can you think of any evidence to suggest that this belief is false? What evidence contradicts your belief? Do you know anyone who does not cling to this belief?

- How does holding this belief affect your life, both negatively and positively?

- How would your life be different if you stopped holding this belief? What would you do differently?

Beck's Cognitive Therapy

Psychiatrist Aaron T. Beck (1976) claims that much of the misery endured by a depressed and anxious person can be traced to *automatic thoughts*—unreasonable but unquestioned ideas that rule the person's life ("To be happy, I must be liked by everyone"; "If people disagree with me, it means they don't like me"). Beck (1991) believes that depressed persons hold "a negative view of the present, past, and future experiences" (p. 369). These individuals notice only negative, unpleasant things and jump to upsetting conclusions.

15.11 How does Beck's cognitive therapy help people overcome depression and panic disorder?

The goal of Beck's **cognitive therapy** is to help clients stop their negative thoughts as they occur and replace them with more objective thoughts. After identifying and challenging a client's irrational thoughts, the therapist sets up a plan and guides the client so that her or his personal experience can provide actual evidence in the real world to refute the false beliefs. Clients are given homework assignments, such as keeping track of automatic thoughts and the feelings evoked by them and then substituting more rational thoughts.

Cognitive therapy is brief, usually lasting only 10 to 20 sessions (Beck, 1976). This therapy has been researched extensively and is reported to be highly successful in the treatment of mild to moderately depressed individuals (Hollan, Stewart, & Strunk, 2006). There is some evidence that depressed people who have received cognitive therapy are less likely to relapse than those who have been treated with antidepressant drugs (Hallen, Stewart, & Strunk, 2006).

Cognitive therapy has also been shown to be effective for treating panic disorder (Addis et al., 2004; Barlow, 1997; Power et al., 2000). By teaching clients to change the catastrophic interpretations of their symptoms, cognitive therapy helps prevent the symptoms from escalating into panic. Studies have shown that after 3 months of cognitive therapy, about 90% of individuals with panic disorder are panic-free (Robins & Hayes, 1993). Not only does cognitive therapy have a low dropout rate and a low relapse rate, but clients often continue to improve even after treatment is completed (Öst & Westling, 1995). And cognitive therapy has proved effective for generalized anxiety disorder (Beck, 1993; Wetherell et al., 2003), OCD (Abramowitz, 1997), cocaine addiction (Carroll et al., 1994), insomnia (Quesnel et al., 2003), and bulimia (Agras et al., 2000). Some research even indicates that cognitive therapy is effective in treating both negative and positive symptoms of schizophrenia (Bach & Hayes, 2002; Lecomte & Lecomte, 2002; Sensky et al., 2000).

cognitive therapy A therapy designed by Aaron Beck to help patients stop their negative thoughts as they occur and replace them with more objective thoughts.

Remember It | Cognitive Therapies

1. Cognitive therapists believe that, for the most part, maladaptive behavior results from _____ beliefs and ideas.

2. _____ therapists challenge clients' beliefs.

3. The goal of cognitive therapy is to help clients replace _____ thoughts with more _____ thoughts.

4. Cognitive therapy has proved very successful in the treatment of _____ and _____.

Answers: 1. irrational; 2. Rational emotive behavior; 3. negative, objective; 4. panic disorder, depression

Biological Therapies

Do you know someone who takes or has taken a drug prescribed by a physician or psychiatrist as a means of overcoming a psychological problem? Chances are good that you do, because millions of people the world over are now taking various medications for just such reasons. Treatment with drugs is a cornerstone of the biological approach to therapy. Predictably, professionals who favor the biological perspective—the view that psychological disorders are symptoms of underlying physical problems—usually favor a **biological therapy.** The three main biological therapies are drug therapy, electroconvulsive therapy (ECT), and psychosurgery.

biological therapy A therapy (drug therapy, electroconvulsive therapy, or psychosurgery) that is based on the assumption that psychological disorders are symptoms of underlying physical problems.

Drug Therapy

15.12 What are the advantages and disadvantages of using drugs to treat psychological disorders?

The most frequently used biological treatment is drug therapy. Breakthroughs in drug therapy, coupled with the federal government's effort to reduce involuntary hospitalization of mental patients, lowered the mental hospital patient population in the United States from about 560,000 in 1955, when the drugs were introduced, to about 100,000 by 1990 (see Figure 15.2); this figure continued to drop throughout the 1990s. Furthermore, the average stay of patients who require hospitalization is now usually a matter of days.

Figure 15.2 Decrease in Patient Populations in State and County Mental Hospitals (1950–2000)

State and county mental hospital patient populations peaked at approximately 560,000 in 1955, the same year that antipsychotic drugs were introduced. These drugs, coupled with the federal government's efforts to reduce involuntary hospitalization of mental patients, resulted in a dramatic decrease in the patient population to fewer than 100,000 in 2000.

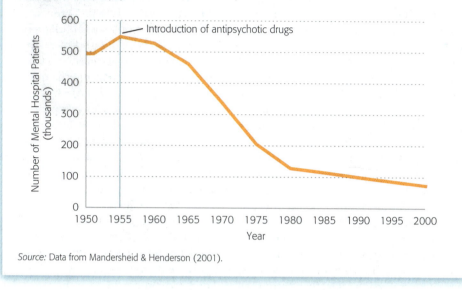

Source: Data from Mandersheid & Henderson (2001).

Antipsychotics. Antipsychotic drugs known as *neuroleptics* are prescribed primarily for schizophrenia. You may have heard of these drugs by their brand names— Thorazine, Stelazine, Compazine, and Mellaril. Their purpose is to control hallucinations, delusions, disorganized speech, and disorganized behavior (Andreasen et al., 1995). The neuroleptics work primarily by inhibiting the activity of the neurotransmitter dopamine. About 50% of patients have a good response to the standard antipsychotics (Bobes et al., 2003; Kane, 1996). The long-term use of typical antipsychotic drugs carries a high risk of a severe side effect, *tardive dyskinesia*—almost continual twitching and jerking movements of the face and tongue, and squirming movements of the hands and trunk (Glazer et al., 1993).

Newer antipsychotic drugs called *atypical neuroleptics* (clozapine, risperidone, olanzipine) can treat not only the positive symptoms of schizophrenia but the negative symptoms as well, leading to marked improvement in patients' quality of life (Lauriello et al., 2005; Worrel et al., 2000). Atypical neuroleptics target both dopamine and seratonin receptors (Kawanishi et al., 2000). About 10% of patients who take clozapine find the results so dramatic that they almost feel as though they have been reborn. Clozapine produces fewer side effects than standard neuroleptics, and patients taking it are less likely to develop tardive dyskinesia (Casey, 1996). It may also be more effective at suicide prevention than other antipsychotic drugs (Meltzer et al., 2003). However, clozapine is extremely expensive, and without careful monitoring, it can cause a fatal blood defect in 1–2% of patients who take it. For this reason, the levels of various liver enzymes and other substances in patients who take the drug must be regularly monitored (Erdogan et al., 2004). Risperidone appears to be effective and safe and also has fewer side effects than standard neuroleptics (Lauriello et al., 2005; Marder, 1996; Tamminga, 1996).

Antidepressants. Antidepressant drugs act as mood elevators for people who are severely depressed (Elkin et al., 1995) and are also helpful in the treatment of certain anxiety disorders. About 65–75% of patients who take antidepressants find themselves significantly improved, and 40–50% of those are essentially completely recovered (Frazer, 1997). It is important to note, though, that most antidepressant research

antipsychotic drugs Drugs used to control severe psychotic symptoms, such as delusions, hallucinations, disorganized speech, and disorganized behavior, by inhibiting dopamine activity; also known as neuroleptics.

antidepressant drugs Drugs that act as mood elevators for severely depressed people and are also prescribed to treat some anxiety disorders.

involves severely depressed patients—those who are most likely to show a significant change after treatment (Zimmerman et al., 2002). Thus, these studies may not apply to mildly depressed individuals. Moreover, research has shown that participants respond almost as frequently to placebo treatments as to real drugs (Walsh et al., 2002). In fact, EEG studies of patients who receive placebos have documented neurological changes that, while different from those in patients receiving real drugs, are associated with improvements in mood (Leuchter et al., 2002). Recall from Chapter 1 that placebo effects are attributable to the belief that a given treatment will help. Consequently, many researchers think that depressed patients' positive responses to antidepressant drugs result from a combination of the physiological effects of these medications on the brain and patients' confidence in the effectiveness of drug treatment.

The first-generation antidepressants are known as the *tricyclics* (amitriptyline, imipramine) (Nutt, 2000). The tricyclics work against depression by blocking the reuptake of norepinephrine and serotonin into the axon terminals, thus enhancing the action of these neurotransmitters in the synapses. But tricyclics can have some unpleasant side effects, including sedation, dizziness, nervousness, fatigue, dry mouth, forgetfulness, and weight gain (Frazer, 1997). Progressive weight gain (an average of more than 20 pounds) is the main reason people stop taking tricyclics, in spite of the relief these drugs provide from distressing psychological symptoms.

The second-generation antidepressants, the *selective serotonin reuptake inhibitors (SSRIs)*, block the reuptake of the neurotransmitter serotonin, increasing its availability at the synapses in the brain (Nutt, 2000; Vetulani & Nalepa, 2000). SSRIs (fluoxetine, clomipramine) have fewer side effects (Nelson, 1997) and are safer than tricyclics if an overdose occurs (Thase & Kupfer, 1996). SSRIs have been found to be promising in treating many disorders. Currently, the U.S. Food and Drug Administration lists depression, obsessive-compulsive disorder, bulimia nervosa, and panic disorder as the conditions for which it approves the use of most SSRIs (FDA, 2006).

However, SSRIs can cause sexual dysfunction, although normal sexual functioning returns when the drug is discontinued. Reports indicating that SSRIs, especially fluoxetine (Prozac), increase the risk of suicide have not been substantiated (Ham, 2003; Warshaw & Keller, 1996).

Another line of treatment for depression is the use of *monoamine oxidase (MAO) inhibitors* (sold under the names Ensam, Marplan, Nardil, and Parnate). By blocking the action of an enzyme that breaks down norepinephrine and serotonin in the synapses, MAO inhibitors increase the availability of these neurotransmitters. MAO inhibitors are usually prescribed for depressed patients who do not respond to other antidepressants (Thase et al., 1992). They are also effective in treating panic disorder (Sheehan & Raj, 1988) and social phobia (Marshall et al., 1994). However, MAO inhibitors have many of the same unpleasant side effects as tricyclic antidepressants, and patients taking MAO inhibitors must avoid certain foods or run the risk of stroke.

Lithium and Anticonvulsant Drugs. Lithium, a naturally occurring salt, is considered a wonder drug for 40–50% of patients suffering from bipolar disorder (Thase & Kupfer, 1996). It is said to begin to quiet the manic state within 5 to 10 days. This is an amazing accomplishment, because the average episode, if untreated, lasts about 3 to 4 months. A proper maintenance dose of lithium reduces depressive episodes as well as manic ones. Published reports over a period of three decades show that the clinical effectiveness of lithium for treating depression and bipolar disorder is unmatched (Ross et al., 2000). But 40–60% of those who take a maintenance dose will experience a recurrence (Thase & Kupfer, 1996). Also, monitoring of the level of lithium in the patient's blood every 2 to 6 months is necessary to guard against lithium poisoning and permanent damage to the nervous system (Schou, 1997).

Recent research suggests that *anticonvulsant drugs*, such as Depakote (divalproex), may be just as effective for managing bipolar symptoms as lithium, with fewer side effects (Kowatch et al., 2000). Moreover, many bipolar patients, especially those whose manic states include symptoms of psychosis, benefit from taking antipsychotic drugs

lithium A drug used to treat bipolar disorder, which at proper maintenance dosage reduces both manic and depressive episodes.

along with the anticonvulsants (Bowden et al., 2000; Sachs et al., 2002). Furthermore, a growing body of research suggests that long-term treatment with antipsychotic drugs may prevent recurrences of mania (Vieta, 2003).

Anti-Anxiety Drugs. The family of minor tranquilizers called *benzodiazepines* includes, among others, the well-known drugs sold as Valium and Librium and the newer high-potency drug Xanax (pronounced "ZAN-ax"). Used primarily to treat anxiety, benzodiazepines are prescribed more often than any other class of psychoactive drugs (Medina et al., 1993). They have been found to be effective in treating panic disorder (Davidson, 1997; Noyes et al., 1996) and generalized anxiety disorder (Lydiard et al., 1996).

Xanax, the largest selling psychiatric drug (Famighetti, 1997), appears to be particularly effective in relieving anxiety and depression. When used to treat panic disorder (Noyes et al., 1996), Xanax works faster and has fewer side effects than antidepressants (Ballenger et al., 1993; Jonas & Cohon, 1993). However, if patients discontinue treatment, relapse is likely (Rickels, Schweizer et al., 1993). There is a downside to Xanax. Many patients, once they no longer experience panic attacks, find themselves unable to discontinue the drug because they experience moderate to intense withdrawal symptoms, including intense anxiety (Otto et al., 1993). Valium seems to be just as effective as Xanax for treating panic disorder, and withdrawal is easier. Although withdrawal is a problem with benzodiazepines, the abuse and addiction potential of these drugs is fairly low (Romach et al., 1995).

Disadvantages of Drug Therapy. Beyond the drugs' unpleasant or dangerous side effects, it's important to note that drugs do not cure psychological disorders, so patients usually experience a relapse if they stop taking the drugs when their symptoms lift (Hollan, Stewart, & Strunk, 2006). Further, some studies suggest that the trend away from involuntary hospitalization brought about by the availability of antipsychotic and other psychiatric drugs has led to an increase in homelessness among people who suffer from chronic mental illnesses such as schizophrenia (Carson et al., 2000). Unfortunately, after being discharged from mental hospitals because they have shown favorable responses to antipsychotic drugs, many schizophrenic patients do not get adequate follow-up care. As a result, some stop taking their medications, relapse into psychotic states, and are unable to support themselves.

The various drugs you have learned about in this section are summarized in the *Review & Reflect* below.

Review and Reflect   Drugs Used to Treat Psychological Disorders

Type of Drug	Brand Names	Symptoms Treated
Neuroleptics	Compazine, Mellaril, Stelazine, Thorazine	Hallucinations, delusions
Atypical neuroleptics	Clozaril, Olanzapine, Risperdal	Hallucinations, delusions Negative symptoms of schizophrenia
Tricyclics	Elavil, Tofranil	Depressed mood/Anxiety
SSRIs	Celexa, Paxil, Prozac, Zoloft	Depressed mood/Anxiety
MAOIs	Ensam, Nardil, Parnate, Marplan	Depressed mood/Anxiety
Lithium	Eskalith, Lithobid	Mania
Anticonvulsants	Depakote, Depacon, Depakene	Mania
Benzodiazepines	Librium, Valium, Xanax	Anxiety

Psychiatric Drugs for Children and Adolescents

In Chapter 14, you learned about the use of stimulants among children who are diagnosed with attention-deficit/hyperactivity disorder. These are not the only psychiatric drugs that are used with children. In fact, surveys suggest that parents are far more willing to use such drugs to help children who are depressed or anxious than they are to agree to put their children on medication for problems such as ADHD (McLeod et al., 2004). Moreover, the number of children who are taking psychiatric drugs has increased dramatically over the past few years. Some estimates indicate that 5–6% of children in the United States take them (Zito et al., 2003). Here is a brief overview of how mental health professionals use these drugs in pediatric (under age 18) populations.

Typical and atypical neuroleptics appear to be effective in the treatment of psychotic symptoms among children and adolescents (Armenteros & Davies, 2006). The possible uses of these drugs in children who suffer from autistic disorder is also currently under study (King & Bostic, 2006). However, some experts caution that the safety of these drugs for children and teenagers has not been studied directly (Correll et al., 2006). Instead, their use in pediatric populations is founded on the assumption that the risks associated with these drugs that have been found in studies of adults, apply to children as well. Thus, although these drugs can be enormously helpful to children who are suffering from symptoms of schizophrenia, their responses to them must be monitored more frequently than those of adults.

Similarly, children and teenagers usually respond to antidepressants in the same ways that adults do. However, as is true of antipsycyhotics, clinicians must closely track children's responses to them. Concerns about a link between antidepressant treatment and suicidal thinking and nonfatal suicidal behaviors in children and adolescents have led officials in the United States and other countries to recommend that patients younger than 18 be carefully monitored during the first few weeks of treatment (U.S. Food and Drug Administration, 2004). Thus, the use of antidepressant medications among children remains controversial.

The diagnosis of bipolar disorder in children, and the implications for drug treatment that accompany it, is also controversial. At present, some clinicians believe that bipolar disorder is the most appropriate diagnosis for children who display sudden bouts of impulsive, explosive, and non-goal-directed aggressive behaviors that alternate with periods of depressed moods (Barzman et al., 2005). Accordingly, these professionals recommend that such children be treated with the same types of drugs that are effective for treating bipolar symptoms in adults. Studies show that these drugs are effective among children and teenagers (Findling et al., 2006; Patel et al., 2006).

However, some experts argue that true mania, a DSM-IV-TR criterion for the diagnosis of bipolar disorder is extremely rare among children, if it exists at all (Harris, 2005). Thus, these professionals display little enthusiasm for expanding the definition of mania to accommodate aggressive children, and they object to the routine use of drugs such as lithium and divalproex in children. All agree, however, that it is risky to generalize research results derived from studies with adults to children and advocate for more research examining questions about the diagnosis and treatment of mania in children.

Research and clinical experience have provided somewhat more guidance regarding the use of tranquilizers among children. In general, these drugs are administered to children only in unusual circumstances. For instance, children are sometimes given these medicines prior to surgery in order to make it easier for them to undergo preoperative procedures. However, even in these situations, physicians try to avoid using anti-anxiety medicines with children because of the potential for paradoxical effects. That is, some children respond to these medicines by becoming agitated and hyperactive rather than by calming down (Breggin & Cohen, 2000). Moreover, at least one study has found that access to handheld video games does a better job of calming children down before surgery than anti-anxiety medications do (Johnson, 2004).

Electroconvulsive Therapy

Antidepressant drugs are relatively slow-acting. A severely depressed patient needs at least 2 to 6 weeks to obtain relief, and 30% of these patients don't respond at all. This situation can be too risky for suicidal patients. **Electroconvulsive therapy (ECT)** is sometimes used with such patients. ECT has a bad reputation because it was misused and overused in the 1940s and 1950s. Nevertheless, when used appropriately, ECT is a highly effective treatment for major depression (Folkerts, 2000; Little et al., 2002; McCall et al., 2004; Sienaert et al., 2006).

For many years, ECT was performed by passing an electric current through both cerebral hemispheres, a procedure known as *bilateral ECT*. Today, electric current is administered to the right hemisphere only, and the procedure is called *unilateral ECT*. Research suggests that unilateral ECT is as effective as the more intense bilateral form but produces milder cognitive effects (Sackeim et al., 2000). Also, a patient undergoing ECT today is given anesthesia, controlled oxygenation, and a muscle relaxant.

Experts think that ECT changes the biochemical balance in the brain, resulting in a lifting of depression. Some psychiatrists and neurologists have spoken out against the use of ECT, claiming that it causes pervasive brain damage and memory loss. But advocates of ECT say that claims of brain damage are based on animal studies in which dosages of ECT were much higher than those now used in human patients. No structural brain damage from ECT has been revealed by studies comparing MRI or CT scans before and after a series of treatments (Reisner, 2003).

Toward the end of the 20th century, a new brain-stimulation therapy known as *rapid transcranial magnetic stimulation (rTMS)* was developed. This magnetic therapy is not invasive in any way. Performed on patients who are not sedated, it causes no seizures, no memory loss, and has no known side effects. Its therapeutic value is similar to that of ECT, and it is much more acceptable to the public (Loo, Schweitzer, & Pratt, 2006; Vetulani & Nalepa, 2000).

15.14 What is electroconvulsive therapy (ECT) used for?

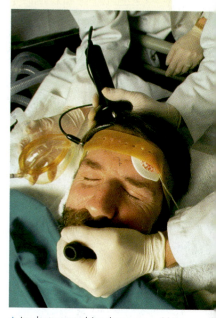

▲ In electroconvulsive therapy, a mild electric current is passed through the right hemisphere of the brain for 1 to 2 seconds, causing a brief seizure.

Psychosurgery

An even more drastic procedure than ECT is **psychosurgery**—brain surgery performed to alleviate serious psychological disorders, such as severe depression, severe anxiety, or obsessions, or to provide relief from unbearable chronic pain. The first experimental brain surgery for human patients, the *lobotomy*, was developed by Portuguese neurologist Egas Moniz in 1935 to treat severe phobias, anxiety, and obsessions. Surgeons performing a lobotomy would sever the neural connections between the frontal lobes and the deeper brain centers involved in emotion. But no brain tissue was removed. At first, the procedure was considered a tremendous contribution, and Moniz won the Nobel Prize in medicine in 1949. Eventually, however, it became apparent that this treatment left patients in a severely deteriorated condition.

Modern psychosurgery procedures result in less intellectual impairment because, rather than using conventional surgery, surgeons deliver electric currents through electrodes to destroy a much smaller, more localized area of brain tissue. In one procedure, called a *cingulotomy*, electrodes are used to destroy the *cingulum*, a small bundle of nerves connecting the cortex to the emotional centers of the brain. Several procedures, including cingulotomy, have been helpful for some extreme cases of obsessive-compulsive disorder (Baer et al., 1995; Lopes et al., 2004; Trivedi, 1996). But the results of psychosurgery are still not predictable, and the consequences—whether positive or negative—are irreversible. For these reasons, the treatment is considered experimental and absolutely a last resort (Glannon, 2006).

15.15 What is psychosurgery, and for what problems is it used?

electroconvulsive therapy (ECT) A biological therapy in which an electric current is passed through the right hemisphere of the brain; usually reserved for severely depressed patients who are suicidal.

psychosurgery   Brain surgery performed to alleviate serious psychological disorders or unbearable chronic pain.

Evaluating the Therapies

15.16 What therapy, if any, is most effective in treating psychological disorders?

If you look over the summaries of the various therapeutic approaches in this *Review and Reflect*, you will notice that there are many similarities among them. Several, for example, focus on helping clients reflect on their own thoughts and/or emotions. Analyses of therapy sessions representing different perspectives suggest that there is a core set of techniques that therapists use no matter which perspective they adopt, but these analyses also show that each therapeutic approach has elements that distinguish it from others (Gazzola & Stalikas, 2004; Trijsburg, Perry, & Semeniuk, 2004; Waldron & Helm, 2004).

Review and Reflect | Summary and Comparison of the Therapies

Type of Therapy	Perceived Cause of Disorder	Goals of Therapy	Methods Used	Primary Disorders or Symptoms Treated
Psycho-analysis	Unconscious sexual and aggressive urges or conflicts; fixations; weak ego	Help patient bring disturbing, repressed material to consciousness and work through unconscious conflicts; strengthen ego functions	Psychoanalyst analyzes and interprets dreams, free associations, resistance, and transference.	General feelings of unhappiness; unresolved problems from childhood
Person-centered therapy	Blocking of normal tendency toward self-actualization; incongruence between real and desired self; overdependence on positive regard of others	Increase self-acceptance and self-understanding; help patient become more inner-directed; increase congruence between real and desired self; enhance personal growth	Therapist shows empathy, unconditional positive regard, and genuineness, and reflects client's expressed feelings back to client.	General feelings of unhappiness; interpersonal problems
Interpersonal therapy	Difficulty with relationships and/or life transitions, as well as possible biological causes	Adjust to bereavement; overcome interpersonal role disputes; improve interpersonal skills; adjust to role transitions such as divorce, career change, and retirement	Therapist helps patient (1) release the past, (2) understand others' points of view and explore options for change, (3) view change as a challenge rather than a threat, and/or (4) improve interpersonal skills, using techniques such as role-playing.	Depression

Family therapy and couples therapy	Problems caused by faulty communication patterns, unreasonable role expectations, drug and/or alcohol abuse, and so on	Create more understanding and harmony within the relationships; improve communication patterns; heal wounds of family unit	Therapist sees clients individually or several family members at a time and explores such things as communication patterns, power struggles, and unreasonable demands and expectations.	Family problems such as marriage or relationship problems, troubled or troublesome teenagers, abusive relationships, drug or alcohol problems, schizophrenic family member
Behavior therapy	Learning of maladaptive behaviors or failure to learn appropriate behaviors	Extinguish maladaptive behaviors and replace with more adaptive ones; help patient acquire needed social skills	Therapist uses methods based on classical and operant conditioning and modeling, which include systematic desensitization, flooding, exposure and response prevention, and aversion therapy.	Fears, phobias, panic disorder, obsessive-compulsive disorder, bad habits
Cognitive therapy	Irrational and negative assumptions and ideas about self and others	Change faulty, irrational, and/or negative thinking	Therapist helps client identify irrational and negative thinking and substitute rational thinking.	Depression, anxiety, panic disorder, general feelings of unhappiness
Biological therapies	Underlying physical disorder caused by structural or biochemical abnormality in the brain; genetic inheritance	Eliminate or control biological cause of abnormal behavior; restore balance of neurotransmitters	Physician prescribes drugs such as antipsychotics, antidepressants, lithium, or tranquilizers; uses ECT or psychosurgery.	Schizophrenia, depression, bipolar disorder, anxiety disorders

But to what degree do the various therapies differ in effectiveness? In a classic study of therapeutic effectiveness, Smith and his colleagues (1980) analyzed the results of 475 studies, which involved 25,000 patients. Their findings revealed that psychotherapy was better than no treatment, but that no one type of psychotherapy was more effective than another. A subsequent reanalysis of the same data by Hans Eysenck (1994), however, showed a slight advantage for behavior therapies over other types. A study by Holloa and others (2002) found that cognitive and interpersonal therapies had an advantage over psychodynamic approaches for depressed patients.

But how do the patients themselves rate the therapies? To answer this question, *Consumer Reports* (1995) conducted the largest survey to date on patient attitudes toward psychotherapy. Martin Seligman (1995, 1996), a consultant for the study, summarized its findings:

- Overall, patients believed that they benefited substantially from psychotherapy.
- Patients seemed equally satisfied with their therapy, whether it was provided by a psychologist, a psychiatrist, or a social worker.
- Patients who were in therapy for more than 6 months did considerably better than the rest; generally, the longer patients stayed in therapy, the more they improved.
- Patients who took a drug such as Prozac or Xanax believed it helped them, but overall, psychotherapy alone seemed to work about as well as psychotherapy plus drugs.

Choosing a therapist with the type of training best suited to your problem can be crucial to how helpful the therapy turns out to be. Table 15.1 lists the various types of mental health professionals. One important difference among professionals, about which many people are confused, is that a **psychologist** has a doctoral degree in psychology, while a **psychiatrist** is a medical doctor. Historically, drug therapy has been available only from psychiatrists. At present, however, there is a movement that is gaining momentum in the United States to allow psychologists with special training in psychopharmacology to prescribe drugs. Only the U.S. military and two states, New Mexico and Louisiana, have authorized prescribing privileges for psychologists so far.

Regardless of training or theoretical orientation, all therapists are bound by ethical standards established by professional organizations and, in most cases, codified in state laws. Each profession (e.g., psychologists, social workers) has its own ethical standards, but certain features are common to all of them and are exemplified by the ethics code of the American Psychological Association (2002). One important standard is the requirement for *informed consent*. Therapists must inform clients of the cost and

psychologist A mental health professional who possesses a doctoral degree in psychology.

psychiatrist A mental health professional who is a medical doctor.

Table 15.1 Mental Health Professionals

Professional Title	Training	Services Provided
Psychiatrist	Medical degree (M.D. or O.D.); residency in psychiatry	Psychotherapy; drug therapy; hospitalization for serious psychological disorders
Psychoanalyst	M.D., Ph.D., or Psy.D.; additional training in psychoanalysis	Psychodynamic therapy
Clinical psychologist	Ph.D. or Psy.D.; internship in clinical psychology	Diagnosis and treatment of psychological disorders; can prescribe drugs in some settings after additional training; psychological testing
Counseling psychologist	Ph.D. or Ed.D.; internship in counseling psychology	Assessment and therapy for normal problems of life (e.g., divorce); psychological testing
School psychologist	Ph.D., Ed.D., or Ed.S.; internship in school psychology	Assessment and treatment of school problems in children and adolescents; psychological testing
Clinical or psychiatric social worker (M.S.W.)	Master's degree; internship in psychiatric social work	Diagnosis and treatment of psychological disorders; identification of supportive community services
Licensed professional counselor (L.P.C.)	Master's degree; internship in counseling	Assessment and therapy for normal problems of life; some psychological testing
Licensed marriage and family therapist (L.M.F.T.)	Master's degree; internship in couples therapy and family therapy	Assessment and therapy for relationship problems
Licensed chemical dependency counselor (L.C.D.C.)	Educational requirements vary from one state to another; often former addicts themselves	Treatment and education for substance abuse problems

expected duration of therapy prior to beginning any intervention. Moreover, clients must be informed of the legal limits of confidentiality. For example, if a client reveals that she or he has committed a crime, in most cases the therapist is obligated to report the confession to the appropriate authorities. In addition, some insurance companies require that therapists' notes be available for review without regard to clients' confidentiality.

The nature of the therapeutic relationship is also governed by ethical standards. Therapists are forbidden to engage in any kind of intimate relationship with a client or with anyone close to the client. They are also prohibited from providing therapeutic services to former intimate partners. When ending a therapeutic relationship, a therapist must counsel a client about the reason for terminating therapy and provide him or her with alternatives.

With regard to testing, therapists are ethically obligated to use tests that are reliable and valid. Moreover, they must have appropriate training for administering, scoring, and evaluating each test they use. They are also required to explain the purpose of testing to clients and to provide them with test results in a timely and confidential manner.

Remember It   Evaluating the Therapies

1. Match each problem or disorder with the most appropriate therapy.

  _____ (1) debilitating fears
  _____ (2) schizophrenia
  _____ (3) general unhappiness, interpersonal problems
  _____ (4) severe depression

  a. behavior therapy
  b. insight therapy
  c. drug therapy

2. The main difference between a psychologist and a psychiatrist is that the latter has a _____ degree.

Answers: 1. (1) a, (2) c, (3) b, (4) c; 2. medical

Culturally Sensitive and Gender-Sensitive Therapy

Think for a moment about the role played by culture and gender in our social relationships. Do you think it's possible that these variables could affect relationships between therapists and their clients?

Among most psychotherapists, there is a growing awareness of the need to consider cultural variables in diagnosing and treating psychological disorders (Bernal & Castro, 1994). In fact, the American Psychological Association recently published guidelines to help psychologists be more sensitive to cultural issues (APA, 2003). Similarly, many psychologists have expressed concern about the need for awareness of gender differences when practicing psychotherapy (Addis & Mahalik, 2003; Gehart & Lyle, 2001).

Culturally Sensitive Therapy.   According to Kleinman and Cohen (1997), people experience and suffer from psychological disorders within a cultural context that may dramatically affect the meaning of symptoms, outcomes, and responses to therapy. And cultural differences between therapist and client may undermine the *therapeutic alliance*, the bond between therapist and client that is known to be a factor in the effectiveness of psychotherapy (Blatt et al., 1996). Thus, many experts advocate an approach called **culturally sensitive psychotherapy** in which knowledge of clients' cultural backgrounds guides the choice of therapeutic interventions (Kumpfer et al., 2002).

Culturally sensitive therapists recognize that language differences between therapists and patients can pose problems (Santiago-Rivera & Altarriba, 2002). For example, a patient who speaks both Spanish and English but is more fluent in Spanish may exhibit hesitations, back-tracking, and delayed responses to questions when being interviewed in English. As a result, the therapist may erroneously conclude that this patient is suffering from the kind of disordered thinking that is often displayed by people with schizophrenia (Martinez, 1986). Such language differences may also affect patients' results on standardized tests used by clinicians. In one frequently cited study, researchers found that when a group of Puerto Rican patients took the Thematic Apperception Test (TAT) in English, their pauses and their choices of words were incorrectly interpreted as indications of psychological problems (Suarez, 1983). Thus, culturally sensitive therapists become familiar with patients' general fluency in the language in which they will be assessed prior to interviewing and testing them.

15.17 What characterizes culturally sensitive and gender-sensitive therapy?

▲ When therapist and client have the same racial or ethnic background, they are more likely to share cultural values and communication styles, which can facilitate the therapeutic process.

When working with recent immigrants to the United States, culturally sensitive therapists take into account the impact of the immigration experience on patients' thoughts and emotions (Lijtmaer, 2001; Sluzki, 2004; Smolar, 1999). Some researchers who have studied the responses of recent Asian immigrants to psychotherapy recommend that, prior to initiating diagnosis and treatment, therapists encourage patients who are immigrants to talk about the feelings of sadness they have experienced as a result of leaving their native culture, as well as their anxieties about adapting to life in a new society. Using this strategy, therapists may be able to separate depression and anxiety related to the immigration experience from true psychopathology.

Some advocates of culturally sensitive therapy point out that sometimes cultural practices can be used as models for therapeutic interventions. Traditional Native American *healing circles*, for example, are being used by many mental health practitioners who serve Native Americans (Garrett et al., 2001). Members of a healing circle are committed to promoting the physical, mental, emotional, and spiritual well-being of one another. Healing circle participants typically engage in member-led activities

culturally sensitive therapy   An approach to therapy in which knowledge of clients' cultural backgrounds guides the choice of therapeutic interventions.

such as discussion, meditation, and prayer. However, some more structured healing circles include a recognized Native American healer who leads the group in traditional healing ceremonies.

Culturally sensitive therapists also attempt to address group differences that can affect the results of therapy (Marlatt, 2005). For example, many studies have found that African Americans with mental disorders are less likely than White Americans with the same diagnoses to follow their doctor's or therapist's instruction about taking medications. (Fleck et al., 2002; Hazlett-Stevens et al., 2002). A culturally sensitive approach to this problem might be based on a therapist's understanding of the importance of kinship networks and community relationships in African American culture. A therapist might increase African American patients' compliance level by having the patient participate in a support group with other African Americans suffering from the same illness and taking the same medications (Muller, 2002). In addition, researchers and experienced therapists recommend that non–African American therapists and African American patients openly discuss their differing racial perspectives prior to beginning therapy (Bean et al., 2002).

Gender-Sensitive Therapy. Many psychotherapists note the need for **gender-sensitive therapy,** a therapeutic approach that takes into the account the effects of gender on both the therapist's and the client's behavior (Gehart & Lyle, 2001). To implement gender-sensitive therapy, therapists must examine their own gender-based prejudices. They may assume men to be more analytical, and women to be more emotional, for example. These stereotypical beliefs may be based on a therapist's socialization background or knowledge of research findings on gender differences.

Advocates of gender-sensitive therapy point out that knowledge of real differences between the sexes is important to the practice of gender-sensitive therapy. For instance, because of men's gender role socialization, interventions focused on emotional expression may be less effective for them than for women. Moreover, men may view seeking therapy as a sign of weakness or as a threat to their sense of masculinity (Addis & Mahalik, 2003). As a result, researchers advise therapists to try to avoid creating defensiveness in their male clients (Greer, 2005). Nevertheless, therapists must guard against using research findings as a basis for stereotyping either male or female clients. They have to keep in mind that there is more variation within each gender than across genders, and thus each man or woman must be considered as an individual.

Some therapists who are motivated by a sincere desire to be sensitive to gender issues may place too much emphasis on them and misinterpret clients' problems (Addis & Mahalik, 2003). For example, in one study, researchers found that therapists expect people who are working in nontraditional fields—female engineers and male nurses, for instance—to have more psychological problems (Rubinstein, 2001). As a result, therapists may assume that such clients' difficulties arise from gender role conflicts, when, in reality, their problems have completely different origins.

gender-sensitive therapy An approach to therapy that takes into account the effects of gender on both the therapist's and the client's behavior.

Remember It   Culturally Sensitive and Gender-Sensitive Therapy

1. _____ variables can influence the results of standardized tests used by psychologists.

2. Culturally sensitive therapy involves all of the following except:

    a. incorporation of cultural practices into therapeutic interventions.

    b. assessment of a client's language skills.

    c. avoidance of discussions of race and culture with clients.

    d. sensitivity to the emotions associated with living in a new culture.

3. Gender-sensitive therapy requires that therapists examine their own _____.

Answers: 1. Cultural; 2. c; 3. gender biases

Apply It   Is E-therapy Right for You?

If you were trying to overcome a substance abuse problem or needed help getting through a period of bereavement, would you turn to an online support group? Many people do. For example, researchers Taylor and Luce (2003) reported that, when Senator Edward Kennedy mentioned a web site for a particular support group on a nationally televised program, the site received more than 400,000 email inquiries over the next few days. But what about psychotherapy? Can online sessions with a trained therapist be just as effective as face-to-face therapy?

Some studies suggest that therapy delivered via the Internet can be highly effective (Kenwright & Marks, 2004). But people aren't waiting for scientific studies that demonstrate the effectiveness of these innovative treatments. Thousands have already turned to *e-therapy*—ongoing online interaction with a trained therapist (Alleman, 2002; Taylor & Luce, 2003). This form of therapy typically involves the exchange of email messages over a period of hours or days but can also include videoconferencing and telephone sessions (Day & Schneider, 2002).

Advantages of E-therapy

E-therapy enables clients to be much less inhibited than they might be in a face-to-face situation. It is also less expensive than traditional therapy (Roan, 2000). Another advantage is that the therapist and the client do not have to be in the same place at the same time. The client can write to the therapist whenever he or she feels like it and can keep records of "sessions" (email correspondence) to refer to later (Ainsworth, 2000; Stubbs, 2000). A therapist can also keep accurate records of communications with clients and can answer their questions at times of day when telephone calls are inconvenient, thus making his or her therapy practice more efficient (Andrews & Erskine, 2003). Researchers have found that e-therapy can be an especially helpful alternative to psychotherapy for people with any of several characteristics (Ainsworth, 2000; Postelet et al., 2005; Walker, 2000):

• They are often away from home or have full schedules.

• They cannot afford traditional therapy.

• They live in rural areas and do not have access to mental health care.

• They have disabilities.

• They are too timid or embarrassed to make an appointment with a therapist.

• They are good at expressing their thoughts and feelings in writing.

Disadvantages of E-therapy

Because of the anonymity of Internet interactions, it is easy for imposters to pose as therapists. So far, there is no system for regulating or licensing e-therapists. In addition, e-therapy poses some potential ethical problems, such as the possibility of breaches of confidentiality. But like all reputable therapists, the best e-therapists do everything they can to protect clients' privacy and confidentiality—except when it is necessary to protect them or someone else from immediate harm (Ainsworth, 2000). Perhaps the most serious drawback of e-therapy is the fact that the therapist cannot see the client and therefore cannot use visual and auditory cues to determine when the person is becoming anxious or upset. This reduces the effectiveness of treatment (Roan, 2000; Walker, 2000).

Another important limitation of e-therapy is that it is not appropriate for diagnosing and treating serious psychological disorders, such as schizophrenia or bipolar disorder (Manhal-Baugus, 2001). In addition, e-therapy is not appropriate for someone who is in the midst of a serious crisis. There are better ways to get immediate help, such as suicide hotlines.

Finding an E-therapist

If you wish to locate an e-therapist, the best place to start is www.metanoia.org. The site lists online therapists whose credentials have been checked by Mental Health Net. It provides information about the location of the therapist, the services offered, payment method, and so forth (Roan, 2000). When choosing a therapist, be sure to do the following (Ainsworth, 2000):

• Make sure the person's credentials have been verified by a third party.

• Get real-world contact information.

• Verify that you'll receive a personal reply to your messages.

• Find out in advance how much the therapist charges.

If you decide to contact an e-therapist, bear this in mind: Although e-therapy may be a good way to get started, if you have persistent problems, it would be wise in the long run to obtain traditional psychotherapy (Roan, 2000).

✺ Summary and Review

Insight Therapies p. 527

15.1 What are the basic techniques of psychoanalysis, and how are they used to help patients? p. 527

The techniques associated with psychoanalysis are free association, dream analysis, and transference. They are used to uncover the repressed memories, impulses, and conflicts presumed to be the cause of the patient's problems.

15.2 What problems commonly associated with major depression does interpersonal therapy focus on? p. 528

Interpersonal therapy (IPT) is designed to help depressed patients cope with unusual or severe responses to the death of a loved one, interpersonal role disputes, difficulty in adjusting to role transitions, and deficits in interpersonal skills.

15.3 What are the role and the goal of the therapist in person-centered therapy? p. 529

Person-centered therapy is a nondirective therapy in which the therapist provides empathy and a climate of unconditional positive regard. The goal is to allow the client to determine the direction of the therapy sessions and to move toward self-actualization.

15.4 What is the major emphasis of Gestalt therapy? p. 529

Gestalt therapy emphasizes the importance of clients' fully experiencing, in the present moment, their feelings, thoughts, and actions and taking personal responsibility for their behavior.

Relationship Therapies p. 530

15.5 How do traditional and integrated behavioral couple therapy differ? p. 530

TBCT focuses on changing the behaviors of partners that contribute to conflicts and enhancing behaviors that help resolve conflicts. IBCT does so as well, but it also emphasizes the need for partners to accept each other's differences in areas that are not amenable to change.

15.6 What are the goals of family therapy? p. 530

The goals of family therapy include helping family members improve communication patterns and create more interpersonal understanding and harmony.

15.7 What are some advantages of group therapy? p. 531

Group therapy is less expensive than individual therapy, and it gives people opportunities to express their feelings, get feedback from other group members, and give and receive help and emotional support.

Behavior Therapies p. 532

15.8 How do behavior therapists modify clients' problematic behavior? p. 532

Behavior therapists use operant conditioning techniques such as the use of reinforcement to shape or increase the frequency of desirable behaviors (token economies) and the withholding of reinforcement to eliminate undesirable behaviors (time out).

15.9 What behavior therapies are based on classical conditioning and observational learning theory? p. 533

Behavior therapies based on classical conditioning are systematic desensitization, flooding, exposure and response prevention, and aversion therapy. In participant modeling, an appropriate response to a feared stimulus is modeled in graduated steps, and the client is asked to imitate each step with the encouragement and support of the therapist.

Cognitive Therapies p. 536

15.10 What is the aim of rational emotive behavior therapy? p. 536

Rational emotive behavior therapy is a directive form of therapy whose aim is to challenge and modify a client's irrational beliefs, which are believed to be the cause of personal distress.

15.11 How does Beck's cognitive therapy help people overcome depression and panic disorder? p. 537

Beck's cognitive therapy helps people overcome depression and panic disorder by pointing out the irrational thoughts causing them misery and by helping them learn other, more realistic ways of looking at themselves and their experiences.

Biological Therapies p. 538

15.12 What are the advantages and disadvantages of using drugs to treat psychological disorders? p. 538

The use of drug therapy has reduced the number of patients in mental hospitals. Antipsychotic drugs control the major symptoms of schizophrenia by inhibiting the activity of dopamine. Antidepressants are helpful in the treatment of severe depression and certain anxiety disorders. Lithium and anticonvulsant drugs can control symptoms of manic episodes and can even out the mood swings in bipolar disorder. Some problems with the use of drugs are unpleasant or dangerous side effects, the difficulty in establishing the proper dosages, and the fact that relapse is likely if the drug therapy is discontinued. Also, the movement away from hospitalization has led to an increase in the number of homeless people with mental disorders.

15.13 What are some of the issues involved in prescribing psychiatric drugs for children and adolescents? p. 542

Most psychiatric drugs have proven to be as effective in the treatment of psychological disorders among children and teens as they are among adults. However, in most cases, the safety of these drugs has not been tested in studies that involve participants under age 18. Consequently, clinicians must monitor side effects in children more closely than they do in adults.

15.14 What is electroconvulsive therapy (ECT) used for? p. 543

The unilateral form of ECT is used to treat people with severe depression, especially those who are in imminent danger of committing suicide.

15.15 What is psychosurgery, and for what problems is it used? p. 543

Psychosurgery is brain surgery performed to relieve some severe, persistent, and debilitating psychological disorders or unbearable chronic pain. A highly controversial technique, psychosurgery is considered experimental and a last resort.

Evaluating the Therapies p. 544

15.16 What therapy, if any, is most effective in treating psychological disorders? p. 544

Although no one therapeutic approach has proved generally superior overall, specific therapies have proven to be most effective for treating particular disorders. For example, cognitive and interpersonal therapies are preferred for depressed patients.

Culturally Sensitive and Gender-Sensitive Therapy p. 547

15.17 What characterizes culturally sensitive and gender-sensitive therapy? p. 547

These approaches to therapy help mental health professionals be more aware of cultural variables and gender differences that may influence patients' responses to the therapy and the therapist as well as therapists' responses to patients. Patients' cultural backgrounds and practices may be useful in guiding the choice of therapeutic interventions.

Thinking Critically about Psychology

1. What are the major strengths and weaknesses of the following approaches to therapy: psychoanalysis, person-centered therapy, behavior therapy, cognitive therapy, and drug therapy?
2. From what you have learned in this chapter, prepare a strong argument to support each of these positions:
   a. Psychotherapy is generally superior to drug therapy in the treatment of psychological disorders.
   b. Drug therapy is generally superior to psychotherapy in the treatment of psychological disorders.
3. In selecting a therapist for yourself or advising a friend or family members, what are some important questions you would ask a therapist in an effort to determine whether he or she would be a good choice?

Key Terms

antidepressant drugs, p. 539
antipsychotic drugs, p. 539
aversion therapy, p. 535
behavior modification, p. 533
behavior therapy, p. 532
biological therapy, p. 538
cognitive therapies, p. 536
cognitive therapy, p. 538
culturally sensitive therapy, p. 547
directive therapy, p. 529
electroconvulsive therapy (ECT), p. 543
exposure and response prevention, p. 534
family therapy, p. 530
flooding, p. 534

free association, p. 527
gender-sensitive therapy, p. 548
Gestalt therapy, p. 529
group therapy, p. 531
humanistic therapies, p. 529
insight therapies, p. 527
integrated behavioral couple therapy (IBCT), p. 530
interpersonal therapy (IPT), p. 528
lithium, p. 540
nondirective therapy, p. 529
participant modeling, p. 535
person-centered therapy, p. 529
psychiatrist, p. 545

psychoanalysis, p. 527
psychodynamic therapies, p. 527
psychologist, p. 545
psychosurgery, p. 543
psychotherapy, p. 527
rational emotive behavior therapy, p. 536
relationship therapies, p. 530
systematic desensitization, p. 534
time out, p. 533
token economy, p. 533
traditional behavioral couple therapy (TBCT), p. 530
transference, p. 527

Chapter 16

Social Psychology

Continued

Are there any circumstances under which you could be persuaded to deliberately harm another person? Many people think they could never be persuaded to do such a thing. But a classic study suggests otherwise.

In the 1960s, an advertisement appeared in newspapers in New Haven, Connecticut, and other communities near Yale University. It read: "Wanted: Volunteers to serve as subjects in a study of memory and learning at Yale University." Many people responded to the ad, and 40 male participants between the ages of 20 and 50 were selected. Yet, instead of a memory experiment, a staged drama was planned. The cast of characters was as follows:

- The Experimenter: A 31-year-old high school biology teacher, dressed in a gray laboratory coat, who assumed a stern and serious manner

- The Learner: A middle-aged man (an actor and accomplice of the experimenter)

- The Teacher: One of the volunteers

The experimenter led the teacher and the learner into one room, where the learner was strapped into an electric-chair apparatus. The teacher was delivered a sample shock of 45 volts, supposedly for the purpose of testing the equipment and showing the teacher what the learner would feel. Next, the script called for the learner to complain of a heart condition and say that he hoped the electric shocks would not be too painful. The experimenter admitted that the stronger shocks would hurt but hastened to add, "Although the shocks can be extremely painful, they cause no permanent tissue damage" (Milgram, 1963, p. 373).

Then, the experimenter took the teacher to an adjoining room and seated him in front of an instrument panel with 30 lever switches arranged horizontally across the front. The first switch on the left, he was told, delivered only 15 volts, but each successive switch was 15 volts stronger than the previous one, up to the last switch, which carried 450 volts. The switches on the instrument panel were labeled with designations ranging from "Slight Shock" to "Danger: Severe Shock." The experimenter instructed the teacher to read a list of word pairs to the learner and then test his memory. When the learner made the right choice, the teacher was supposed to go on to the next pair. If the learner missed a question, the teacher was told to flip a switch and shock him, moving one switch to the right—delivering 15 additional volts—each time the learner missed a question.

The learner performed well at first but then began missing about three out of every four questions. The teacher began flipping the switches. When he hesitated, the experimenter urged him to continue. If he still hesitated, the experimenter said, "The experiment requires that you continue," or more strongly, "You have no other choice, you must go on" (Milgram, 1963, p. 374).

At the 20th switch, 300 volts, the script required the learner to pound on the wall and scream, "Let me out of here, let me out, my heart's bothering me, let me out!" (Meyer, 1972, p. 461). From this point on, the learner answered no more questions. If the teacher expressed concern or a desire to discontinue the experiment, the experimenter answered, "Whether the learner likes it or not, you must go on" (Milgram, 1963, p. 374). At the flip of the next switch—315 volts—the teacher heard only groans from the learner. Again, if the teacher expressed reluctance to go on, the experimenter said, "You have no other choice, you must go on" (Milgram, 1963, p. 374). If the teacher insisted on stopping at this point, the experimenter allowed him to do so.

How many of the 40 participants in the Milgram study do you think obeyed the experimenter to the end—450 volts? Not a single participant stopped before the 20th switch, at supposedly 300 volts, when the learner began pounding the wall. Amazingly, 26 participants—65% of the sample—obeyed the experimenter to the bitter end. But this experiment took a terrible toll on the participants. They "were observed to sweat, tremble, stutter, bite their lips, groan, and dig their fingernails into their flesh. These were characteristic rather than exceptional responses to the experiment" (Milgram, 1963, p. 375).

You have just read a description of a classic experiment in **social psychology,** the subfield that attempts to explain how the actual, imagined, or implied presence of others influences the thoughts, feelings, and behavior of individuals. A study like Milgram's could not be performed today because it would violate the American Psychological Association's code of ethics for researchers. Still, deception has traditionally been a part of social psychologists' research. To accomplish this deception, a researcher often must use one or more **confederates**—people who pose as participants in a psychology experiment but who are actually assisting the researcher, like the learner in the Milgram experiment. A **naive subject**—like the teacher in Milgram's study—is a person who has agreed to participate in an experiment but is not aware that deception is being used to conceal its real purpose. You will continue to see why it is often necessary to conceal the purpose of an experiment as you read about other classic studies in social psychology.

The range of topics that are of interest to social psychologists is quite broad. Taking note of the common issues that are found in all of the diverse questions that are addressed by social psychologists may help you better understand the field (Society for Personality and Social Psychology, 2006). First, like all psychologists, social psychologists are interested in how variables within individuals contribute to their responses to social influences. For example, introverts and extraverts may respond to group influences differently. Second, social psychologists are interested in group variables such as race and gender, as are other behavioral scientists. However, they are often more intrigued by groups that are defined by specific situations or circumstances. The social psychologist, for example, finds it interesting to examine the influence on your behavior of both the people with whom you happen to be waiting for a bus and the collection of people you more often associate with the concept of a "social group." Third, social psychologists want to know how interactions among individual and group variables shape behavior. For instance, suppose you are at a bus stop and notice a wallet lying on the sidewalk. Numerous variables will interact to either increase or decrease the chances that you will pick up the wallet: your own personality and values, the number of people at the bus stop, remarks made by others regarding the wallet, the physical condition of the wallet itself, the distance between you and the wallet, and so on. Alterations in any one or more of these variables are likely to produce different outcomes. Thus, the social psychologist seeks to identify hypotheses that can help to predict how changes in each of the variables will interact with changes in the others to produce variations in outcomes.

As you can see, social psychology is a fascinating topic. It is also one that touches on many of the most important aspects of our everyday lives. We begin by considering how we perceive and are perceived by others.

social psychology The subfield that attempts to explain how the actual, imagined, or implied presence of others influences the thoughts, feelings, and behavior of individuals.

confederate A person who poses as a participant in an experiment but is actually assisting the experimenter.

naive subject A person who has agreed to participate in an experiment but is not aware that deception is being used to conceal its real purpose.

Social Perception

What are the strategies we use to assess and make judgments of other people? Our ability to understand others is important because we live in a social world. The process we use to obtain critically important social information about others is known as *social perception* (Allison et al., 2000).

Impression Formation

16.1 Why are first impressions so important?

When we meet people for the first time, we begin forming impressions about them right away, and, of course, they are busily forming impressions of us. Naturally, we notice the obvious attributes first—gender, race, age, dress, and how physically attractive or unattractive someone appears (Shaw & Steers, 2001). Such attributes, combined with people's verbal and nonverbal behavior, play a part in establishing first impressions. Research shows that a firm handshake still makes a powerful first impression (Chaplin et al., 2000). It conveys that a person is positive, confident, and outgoing, not shy or weak-willed.

▶ What is your first impression of the person shown here?

Moods also play a part. When we are happy, our impressions of others are usually more positive than when we are unhappy.

A number of studies reveal that an overall impression or judgment of another person is influenced more by the first information that is received about that person than by information that comes later (Luchins, 1957). This phenomenon is called the **primacy effect.** It seems that we attend to initial information more carefully, and once an impression is formed, it provides the framework through which we interpret later information (Gawronski et al., 2002). Any information that is consistent with the first impression is likely to be accepted, thus strengthening the impression. Information that does not fit with the earlier information is more likely to be disregarded. Remember, any time you list your personal traits or qualities, always list your most positive qualities first. It pays to put your best foot forward—first.

primacy effect The tendency for an overall impression of another to be influenced more by the first information that is received about that person than by information that comes later.

Attribution

16.2 What is the difference between a situational attribution and a dispositional attribution?

Why do people do the things they do? To answer this question, we make **attributions**— that is, we assign or attribute causes to explain the behavior of others or of ourselves. One kind of attribution is called a **situational attribution** (an external attribution), in which we attribute a person's behavior to some external cause or factor operating within the situation. After failing an exam, you might say, "The test was unfair" or "The professor didn't give us enough time." Or you might make a **dispositional attribution** (an internal attribution) and attribute the behavior to some internal cause, such as a personal trait, motive, or attitude. For example, you might attribute a poor grade to lack of ability or to a poor memory. To some degree, attributions are influenced by informal psychological theories we develop through our observations of and interactions with people (Plaks, Grant, & Dweck, 2005). One such theory might be that children's behavior is primarily a function of parental discipline. Nevertheless, there are several other factors that influence whether we make situational or dispositional attributions.

We tend to use situational attributions to explain our own failures, because we are aware of factors in the situation that influenced us to act as we did (Jones, 1976, 1990; Jones & Nisbett, 1971). When we explain others' failures, we focus more on personal factors than on the factors operating within the situation (Gilbert & Malone, 1995; Leyens et

attribution An assignment of a cause to explain one's own or another's behavior.

situational attribution Attributing a behavior to some external cause or factor operating within the situation; an external attribution.

dispositional attribution Attributing a behavior to some internal cause, such as a personal trait, motive, or attitude; an internal attribution.

al., 1996; van Boven et al., 2003). The tendency to attribute our own shortcomings primarily to external, or situational, factors and those of others to internal, or dispositional, factors is known as the **actor-observer effect.** For instance, you may explain your own involvement in a traffic accident as the result of another driver's failure to yield to you (situational attribution). By contrast, you may say that another person's involvement in a similar accident was the result of his poor driving skills (dispositional attribution).

The tendency to attribute others' behavior to dispositional factors is sometimes referred to as the **fundamental attribution error.** This error comes into play in many everyday situations. For example, when we are waiting in line to make a purchase, witnessing an unsatisfactory transaction between the store clerk and a customer who is ahead of us may cause us to expect our own transaction to be unsatisfactory as well (Cowley, 2005). Why? Because the fundamental attribution error leads us to conclude that the clerk's incompetence was the source of the problem.

Similarly, our attributions about our own behavior are often influenced by the **self-serving bias.** We use the self-serving bias when we attribute our successes to dispositional causes and blame our failures on situational causes (Baumgardner et al., 1986; Brown & Rogers, 1991; Pansu & Gilibert, 2002). For example, if you interview for a job and get it, you tell yourself it is because you have the right qualifications; if someone else gets the job, it is probably because he or she knew the right people. The self-serving bias allows us to take credit for our successes and shift the blame for our failures to the situation. Research examining the attributions of professional athletes, for example, has shown that they attribute victories to internal traits, such as ability and effort, and losses to situational factors, poor officiating and the like (Roesch & Amirkhan, 1997). Interestingly, managers prefer job applicants who make dispositional attributions during interviews, especially when the attributions focus on effort rather than natural ability (Pansu & Gilibert, 2002).

Culture apparently contributes to attributional biases as well. In a series of studies, researchers compared Koreans' and Americans' situational and dispositional attributions for both desirable and undesirable behaviors (Choi et al., 2003). They found that Koreans, on average, made more situational attributions than Americans did, no matter what kind of behavior participants were asked to explain. The reason for the difference, according to the researchers, was that the Koreans took into account more information than the Americans did before making attributions.

actor-observer effect The tendency to attribute one's own behavior primarily to situational factors and the behavior of others primarily to dispositional factors.

fundamental attribution error The tendency to attribute others' behavior to dispositional factors.

self-serving bias The tendency to attribute one's successes to dispositional causes and one's failures to situational causes.

Remember It — Social Perception

1. Because of the _____, people pay closer attention to early information they receive about a person than to later information.
2. People tend to make _____ attributions to explain their own behavior and _____ attributions to explain the behavior of others. This tendency is called the _____.
3. Attributing a person's good grades to her intellectual ability is a _____ attribution.

Answers: 1. primacy effect; 2. situational, dispositional, self-serving bias; 3. dispositional

Attraction

proximity Physical or geographic closeness; a major influence on attraction.

mere-exposure effect The tendency to feel more positively toward a stimulus as a result of repeated exposure to it.

Think for a moment about your friends. What makes you like, or even fall in love with, one person and ignore or react negatively to someone else?

Factors Influencing Attraction

16.3 What factors contribute to attraction?

Several factors influence attraction. One is **proximity,** or physical or geographic closeness. Obviously, it is much easier to make friends with people who are close at hand. One reason proximity matters is the **mere-exposure effect,** the tendency to feel more positively toward a stimulus as a result of repeated exposure to it. People, food, songs, and clothing styles become more acceptable the more we are exposed to them. Advertisers rely on the positive effects of repeated exposure to increase people's liking for products and to create favorable opinions of political candidates.

Our own moods and emotions, whether positive or negative, can influence how much we are attracted to people we meet. We may develop positive or negative feelings toward others simply because they are present when very good or very bad things happen to us. Further, we tend to like the people who also like us—or who we *believe* like us—a phenomenon called *reciprocity* or *reciprocal liking*.

Beginning in elementary school and continuing through life, people are also more likely to pick friends of the same age, gender, race, and socioeconomic class. We tend to choose friends and lovers who have similar views on most things that are important to us. Similar interests and attitudes toward leisure-time activities make it more likely that time spent together is rewarding.

Physical Attractiveness

16.4 How important is physical attractiveness to attraction?

▲ The halo effect—the attribution of other favorable qualities to those who are attractive—helps explain why physical attractiveness is so important.

Perhaps no other factor influences attraction more than physical attractiveness. People of all ages have a strong tendency to prefer physically attractive people (Langlois et al., 2000). Even 6-month-old infants, when given the chance to look at a photograph of an attractive or an unattractive woman, man, or infant, will spend more time looking at the attractive face (Ramsey et al., 2004). How people behave, especially the simple act of smiling, influences our perceptions of their attractiveness (Reis et al., 1990). But physical appearance matters as well.

Based on studies using computer-generated faces, researchers Langlois and Roggman (1990) reported that perceptions of attractiveness are based on features that are approximately the mathematical average of the features in a general population. In addition, Perrett and others (1994) found that averaging faces tends to make them more symmetrical. Symmetrical faces and bodies are seen as more attractive and sexually appealing (Singh, 1995b; Thornhill & Gangestad, 1994).

In a review of 11 meta-analyses of cross-cultural studies of attractiveness, Langlois and others (2000) found that males and females across many cultures have similar ideas about the physical attractiveness of members of the opposite sex. When Asian, Hispanic American, and White American male students rated photographs of Asian, Hispanic, African American, and White females on attractiveness, Cunningham and others (1995) reported a very high mean correlation (.93) among the groups in attractiveness ratings. When African American and White American men rated photos of African American women, their agreement on facial features was also very high—a correlation of .94. Evolutionary psychologists suggest that this cross-cultural similarity is the result of a tendency, shaped by natural selection, to look for indicators of health in potential mates (Fink & Penton-Voak, 2002).

Why does physical attractiveness matter? When people have one trait that we either admire or dislike very much, we often assume that they also have other positive or negative traits—a phenomenon known as the **halo effect** (Nisbett & Wilson, 1977). Dion and others (1972) found that people generally attribute additional favorable qualities to those who are attractive. Attractive people are seen as more exciting, personable, interesting, and socially desirable than unattractive people. As a result, job interviewers are more likely to recommend highly attractive people (Dipboye et al., 1975). Similarly, when asked to rate pictures of women with regard to their likelihood of career success, research participants give higher ratings to those who are thin than to those who are overweight or obese (Wade & DiMaria, 2003).

Does this mean that unattractive people don't have a chance? Fortunately not. Eagly and her colleagues (1991) suggest that the impact of physical attractiveness is strongest in the perception of strangers. But once we get to know people, other qualities assume more importance. In fact, as we come to like people, they begin to look more attractive to us, and people with undesirable personal qualities begin to look less attractive.

halo effect The tendency to assume that a person has generally positive or negative traits as a result of observing one major positive or negative trait.

Romantic Attraction and Mating

You probably have heard that opposites attract, but is this really true? The **matching hypothesis** suggests that we are likely to end up with a partner similar to ourselves in physical attractiveness and other assets (Berscheid et al., 1971; Feingold, 1988; Walster & Walster, 1969). Furthermore, couples mismatched in attractiveness are more likely to end the relationship (Cash & Janda, 1984). It has been suggested that we estimate our social assets and realistically expect to attract someone with approximately equal assets. In terms of physical attractiveness, some people might consider a movie star or supermodel to be the ideal man or woman, but they do not seriously consider their ideal to be a realistic, attainable possibility. Fear of rejection keeps many people from pursuing those who are much more attractive than they are. But instead of marrying an extremely handsome man, a very beautiful woman may opt for money and social status. Extremely handsome men have been known to make similar "sacrifices." The matching hypothesis is generally applicable to friendships as well (Cash & Derlega, 1978), although it is more true of males than of females (Feingold, 1988).

But is a virtual clone of oneself the most desirable life partner? Not necessarily. Robert Winch (1958) proposes that men and women tend to choose mates with needs and personalities that are complementary rather than similar to their own. Winch sees complementary needs not necessarily as opposite, but as needs that supply what the partner lacks. A talkative person may seek a quiet mate who prefers to listen. There is some support for this view (Dryer & Horowitz, 1997). If you were to select a marriage partner, what qualities would attract you? Complete this *Try It* to evaluate your own preferences.

16.5 How do psychologists explain romantic attraction and mating?

▲ You are more likely to be attracted to someone who is similar to you than to someone who is your opposite.

 **Try It**   Choosing a Mate

In your choice of a mate, which qualities are most and least important to you? Rank these 18 qualities of a potential mate from most important (1) to least important (18) to you.

_____ Ambition and industriousness
_____ Chastity (no previous sexual intercourse)
_____ Desire for home and children
_____ Education and intelligence
_____ Emotional stability and maturity
_____ Favorable social status or rating
_____ Good cooking and housekeeping skills

_____ Similar political background
_____ Similar religious background
_____ Good health
_____ Good looks
_____ Similar education
_____ Pleasing disposition
_____ Refinement/neatness
_____ Sociability
_____ Good financial prospects
_____ Dependable character
_____ Mutual attraction/love

Compare your rankings from the *Try It* to those of men and women from 33 countries and five major islands around the world. Generally, men and women across those cultures rate these four qualities as most important in mate selection: (1) mutual attraction/love, (2) dependable character, (3) emotional stability and maturity, and (4) pleasing disposition (Buss et al., 1990). Aside from these first four choices, however, women and men differ somewhat in the attributes they prefer. According to the controversial views of evolutionary psychologist David Buss (1994), "Men prefer to mate with beautiful young women, whereas women prefer to mate with men who have resources and social status" (p. 239). These preferences, he claims, have been adaptive in human evolutionary history. To a male, beauty and youth suggest health and fertility—the best opportunity to send his genes into the next generation. To a female, resources

matching hypothesis The notion that people tend to have lovers or spouses who are similar to themselves in physical attractiveness and other assets.

and social status provide security for her and her children (Buss, 2000b). As was noted in Chapter 11, social role theorists maintain that gender differences in mate preferences are influenced by economic and social forces as well as evolutionary forces (Eagly & Wood, 1999).

Remember It   Attraction

1. Match each situation with the appropriate term.

_____ (1) Manny sees Susan at the library often and begins to like her.

_____ (2) Letitia assumes that because Carter is handsome, he must be popular and sociable.

_____ (3) Travis and Faith are going together and are both very attractive.

a. matching hypothesis
b. halo effect
c. mere-exposure effect

2. People are usually drawn to others who are _____ themselves.

3. Which attribute(s) do men and women across cultures view as most important in a prospective mate?
   a. mutual attraction/love
   b. dependable character
   c. emotional stability and maturity
   d. pleasing disposition
   e. all of the above

Answers: 1. (1) c, (2) b, (3) a; 2. similar to; 3. e

Conformity, Obedience, and Compliance

Do you think of yourself as independently minded? Most people do. In Western cultures in particular, individuality and independent thinking are highly valued. But what happened to your independent-mindedness the last time that someone talked you into doing something that you really didn't want to do? As you have probably learned through experience, we are all subject to social influences in one way or another.

Conformity

16.6 What did Asch find in his famous experiment on conformity?

If you are from a Western culture, no doubt you have learned to value your independence. However, there are times when following others' lead is beneficial both to ourselves as individuals and to a group to which we belong. For example, when you are driving, is it better for each motorist to act independently or to follow the conventions of traffic movement such as stopping at red lights? Of course, there are situations in which following others' lead can cause problems.

Two ways in which we subjugate our individual needs or wants to the goals of a group are through the process of *conformity* and by obeying *social norms*. **Conformity** is changing or adopting a behavior or an attitude in order to be consistent with the social norms of a group or the expectations of other people. **Social norms** are the standards of behavior and the attitudes that are expected of members of a particular group. Some conformity is necessary if we are to have a society at all. We cannot drive on the other side of the road anytime we please. And we conform to other people's expectations in order to have their esteem or approval, their friendship or love, or even their company (Christensen et al., 2004). In fact, researchers have found that teenagers who attend schools where the majority of students are opposed to smoking, drinking, and drug use are less likely to use these substances than are peers who attend school where the majority approves of these behaviors (Kumar et al., 2002).

The best-known experiment on conformity was conducted by Solomon Asch (1951, 1955), who designed the simple test shown in **Figure 16.1**. Eight male participants were seated around a large table and were asked, one by one, to tell the experimenter

conformity Changing or adopting a behavior or an attitude in order to be consistent with the social norms of a group or the expectations of other people.

social norms The attitudes and standards of behavior expected of members of a particular group.

which of the three lines matched the standard line. But only one of the eight was an actual participant; the others were confederates assisting the experimenter. There were 18 trials—18 different lines to be matched. During 12 of these trials, the confederates all gave the same wrong answer, which of course puzzled the naive participant. Remarkably, Asch found that 5% of the subjects conformed to the incorrect, unanimous majority all of the time, 70% conformed some of the time, but 25% remained completely independent and were never swayed by the group.

Varying the experiment with groups of various sizes, Asch found that the tendency to go along with the majority opinion remained in full force even when there was a unanimous majority of only 3 confederates. Surprisingly, unanimous majorities of 15 confederates produced no higher conformity rate than did those of 3. Asch also discovered that if just one other person voices a dissenting opinion, the tendency to conform is not as strong. When just one confederate in the group disagreed with the incorrect majority, the naive subjects' errors dropped drastically, from 32% to 10.4%.

Groupthink is the term social psychologist Irving Janis (1982) applied to the kind of conformity often seen in the decision-making processes of tightly knit groups. For example, the officers and soldiers who took part in the abuse of prisoners at Abu Ghraib during the first year of the Iraq War may have constituted such a group (Reicher & Haslam, 2004). When tightly-knit groups of this kind are more concerned with preserving group solidarity and uniformity than with objectively evaluating all possible alternatives in decision making, individual members may hesitate to voice any dissent. The group may also discredit opposing views from outsiders and begin to believe it is incapable of making mistakes. To guard against groupthink, Janis suggests that it is necessary to encourage open discussion of alternative views and the expression of any objections and doubts. He further recommends that outside experts sit in and challenge the views of the group. At least one group member should take the role of devil's advocate whenever a policy alternative is evaluated. Finally, to

▲ In this scene from Asch's experiment on conformity, all but one of the "subjects" were really confederates of the experimenter. They deliberately chose the wrong line to try to influence the naive subject (second from right) to go along with the majority.

groupthink The tendency for members of a tightly knit group to be more concerned with preserving group solidarity and uniformity than with objectively evaluating all alternatives in decision making.

Figure 16.1 Asch's Classic Study of Conformity

If you were one of eight participants in the Asch experiment who were asked to pick the line (1, 2, or 3) that matched the standard line shown above them, which line would you choose? If the other participants all chose line 3, would you conform and answer line 3?

Standard Line

1   2   3

Source: Based on Asch (1955).

avoid groupthink in workplace situations, managers should withhold their own opinions when problem-solving and decision-making strategies are being considered (Bazan, 1998).

Other research on conformity and the Big Five personality dimensions reveals that people who are low in Neuroticism but high in Agreeableness and Conscientiousness are more likely to conform than those who score oppositely on those dimensions (DeYoung et al., 2002). But, contrary to conventional wisdom, women are no more likely to conform than men (Eagly & Carli, 1981). And an individual's conformity is greater if the sources of influence are perceived as belonging to that person's own group (Abrams et al., 1990). Even so, those who hold minority opinions on an issue have more influence in changing a majority view if they present a well-organized, clearly stated argument and if they are especially consistent in advocating their views (Wood et al., 1994).

Obedience

16.7 What did researchers find when they varied the circumstances of Milgram's classic study of obedience?

Can you imagine a world in which each person always did exactly what he or she wanted, without regard for rules or respect for authority? We would stop at red lights only when we felt like it or weren't in a hurry. Someone might decide that he likes your car better than his own and take it. Or worse, someone might kill you because of an interest in your intimate partner.

Clearly, most people must obey most rules and respect those in authority most of the time if society is to survive and function. However, unquestioned obedience can cause humans to commit unbelievably horrible acts. One of the darkest chapters in human history arose from the obedience of officials in Nazi Germany, who carried out Adolph Hitler's orders to exterminate Jews and other "undesirables."

The study you read about at the beginning of this chapter demonstrated how far ordinary citizens would go to obey orders; remember, more than 60% of Milgram's participants delivered the "maximum" voltage, despite the pleading and eventual collapse of the "learner." Another researcher repeated the experiment in a three-room office suite in a run-down building rather than at prestigious Yale University. Even there, 48% of the participants administered the maximum shock (Meyer, 1972).

Milgram (1965) conducted a variation of the original experiment: Each trial involved three teachers, two of whom were confederates and the other, a naive participant. One confederate was instructed to refuse to continue after 150 volts, and the other confederate after 210 volts. In this situation, 36 out of 40 naive participants (90%) defied the experimenter before the maximum shock could be given, compared with only 14 out of 40 participants in the original experiment (Milgram, 1965). In Milgram's experiment, as in Asch's conformity study, the presence of another person who refused to go along gave many of the participants the courage to defy authority.

Compliance

16.8 What are three techniques used to gain compliance?

compliance Acting in accordance with the wishes, suggestions, or direct requests of other people.

foot-in-the-door technique A strategy designed to gain a favorable response to a small request at first, with the intent of making the person more likely to agree later to a larger request.

How often do you do what others want you to do? There are many times when people act, not out of conformity or obedience, but in accordance with the wishes, suggestions, or direct requests of others. This type of action is called **compliance.** One strategy people use to gain the compliance of others, the **foot-in-the-door technique,** is designed to gain a favorable response to a small request first. The intent is to make the person more likely to agree later to a larger request (the result desired from the beginning).

In a classic study of the foot-in-the-door technique, a researcher claiming to represent a consumers' group called a number of homes and asked whether the people answering the phone would mind responding to a few questions about the soap products they used. Then, a few days later, the same person called those who had agreed to the first request and asked if he could send five or six of his assistants to conduct an inventory of the products in their home. The researcher told the people that the inventory would take about 2 hours and that the inventory team would have to search all drawers, cabinets, and closets in the house. Nearly 53% of those asked preliminary questions agreed to the larger request, compared to 22% of a control group who were contacted only once with the larger request (Freedman & Fraser, 1966).

With the **door-in-the-face technique,** a large, unreasonable request is made first. The expectation is that the person will refuse but will then be more likely to respond favorably to a smaller request later (the result desired from the beginning). In one of the best-known studies on the door-in-the-face technique, college students were approached on campus. They were asked to agree to serve without pay as counselors to juvenile delinquents for 2 hours each week for a minimum of 2 years. As you would imagine, not a single person agreed (Cialdini et al., 1975). Then, the experimenters presented a much smaller request, asking if the students would agree to take a group of juveniles on a 2-hour trip to the zoo. Half the students agreed, a fairly high compliance rate. The researchers used another group of college students as controls, asking them to respond only to the smaller request, for the zoo trip. Only 17% agreed when the smaller request was presented alone.

Another method used to gain compliance is the **low-ball technique.** A very attractive initial offer is made to get people to commit themselves to an action, and then the terms are made less favorable. In a frequently cited study of this technique, college students were asked to enroll in an experimental course for which they would receive credit. After the students had agreed to participate, they were informed that the class would meet at 7:00 A.M. Control group participants were told about the class meeting time when first asked to enroll. More than 50% of the low-balled group agreed to participate, but only 25% of control participants did so (Cialdini et al., 1978).

Remember It   Conformity, Obedience, and Compliance

1. Match each example with the appropriate technique.

   _____ (1) Chantal agrees to sign a letter supporting an increase in taxes to fund construction of new schools. Later, she agrees to make 100 phone calls urging people to vote for the measure.

         a. door-in-the-face technique
         b. low-ball technique
         c. foot-in-the-door technique

   _____ (2) Bart refuses a phone request for a $20 donation but agrees to give $5.

   _____ (3) Hue agrees to babysit for her next-door neighbors and is then informed that their three nephews will be there, too.

2. What percentage of the participants in the original Asch study never conformed to the majority's unanimous incorrect response?

3. What percentage of the participants in Milgram's original obedience experiment administered what they thought was the maximum 450-volt shock?

4. When members of a group are more concerned with preserving group solidarity than with evaluating all possible alternatives in making a decision, _____ occurs.

Answers: 1. (1) c, (2) a, (3) b; 2. 25%; 3. 65%; 4. groupthink

---

Group Influence

Have you ever done something you really didn't want to do just to maintain harmony with a friend or friends? You may have seen a movie in which you really weren't interested.or gone to the beach when you would have preferred to stay home. Being part of a group often means giving up a bit of individuality, but the reward is the support and camaraderie of the group. Clearly, we behave differently in a variety of ways when we are part of a group, small or large. What happens when the group of which we are a part is made up of strangers? Do such groups influence our behavior as well?

door-in-the-face technique A strategy in which someone makes a large, unreasonable request with the expectation that the person will refuse but will then be more likely to respond favorably to a smaller request later.

low-ball technique A strategy in which someone makes a very attractive initial offer to get a person to commit to an action and then makes the terms less favorable.

Social Facilitation

16.9 How does social facilitation affect performance?

In certain cases, individual performance can be either helped or hindered by the mere physical presence of others. The term **social facilitation** refers to any effect on performance, whether positive or negative, that can be attributed to the presence of others. Research on this phenomenon has focused on two types of effects: (1) **audience effects,** the impact of passive spectators on performance, and (2) **co-action effects,** the impact on performance caused by the presence of other people engaged in the same task.

In one of the first studies in social psychology, Norman Triplett (1898) looked at co-action effects. He had observed in official records that bicycle racers pedaled faster when they were pedaling against other racers than when they were racing against the clock. Was this pattern of performance peculiar to competitive bicycling? Or was it part of a more general phenomenon whereby people would work faster and harder in the presence of others than when performing alone? Triplett set up a study in which he told 40 children to wind fishing reels as quickly as possible under one of two conditions: (1) alone, or (2) in the presence of other children performing the same task. He found that children worked faster when other reel turners were present. But later studies on social facilitation found that, in the presence of others, people's performance improves on easy tasks but suffers on difficult tasks (Michaels et al., 1982) (see **Figure 16.2**).

social facilitation Any positive or negative effect on performance that can be attributed to the presence of others, either as an audience or as co-actors.

Social Loafing

16.10 What is social loafing, and what factors reduce it?

Have you ever been assigned by a teacher or professor to work in a group and, at the end of the project, felt that you had carried more than your fair share of the workload? Such feelings are not uncommon. Researcher Bibb Latané used the term **social loafing** to refer to people's tendency to put forth less effort when working with others on a common task than they do when they are working alone (Latané et al., 1979). Social loafing occurs in situations in which no one person's contribution to the group can be identified and individuals are neither praised for a good performance nor blamed for a poor one (Williams et al., 1981). Social loafing is a problem in many workplaces, especially where employees have unlimited access to the Internet (Lim, 2002).

You may have noticed the phenomenon of social loafing if you ever had to do a group project for a class. Interestingly, though, achievement motivation influences social loafing (Hart et al., 2004). Researchers tested participants with regard to their levels of achievement motivation and then assigned them to pairs. Each pair was asked to generate as many uses for a knife as they could think of. The amount of effort exhibited by participants who were low in achievement motivation depended on their partner's effort. When paired with partners who worked hard, individuals with low achievement motivation contributed little; that is, they engaged in social loafing, but did the opposite when paired with others who didn't work. By contrast, participants who were high in achievement motivation worked hard at the task no matter what their partner's level of participation was.

▲ Studying in a group could lead to social loafing through a diffusion of responsibility effect.

In one experiment, Latané and others (1979) asked male students to shout and clap as loudly as possible, first alone and then in groups. In groups of two, individuals made only 71% of the noise they had made alone; in groups of four, each person put forth 51% of his solo effort; and with six persons, each made only a 40% effort. But Harkins and Jackson (1985) found that social loafing disappeared when participants in a group were led to believe that each person's output could be monitored and his or her performance evaluated. Even the possibility that the group performance may be evaluated against some standard can be sufficient to eliminate social loafing (Harkins & Szymanski, 1989).

audience effects The impact of passive spectators on performance.

co-action effects The impact on performance of the presence of other people engaged in the same task.

social loafing The tendency to put forth less effort when working with others on a common task than when working alone.

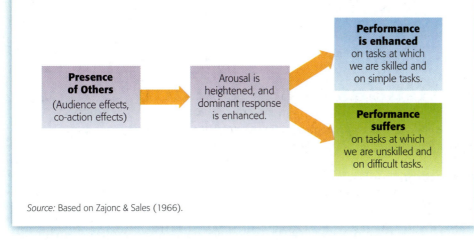

Figure 16.2 Social Facilitation: Performing in the Presence of Others

The presence of others (either as an audience or as co-actors engaged in the same task) may have opposite effects, either helping or hindering an individual's performance. Why? First, the presence of others heightens arousal, and, second, heightened arousal leads to better performance on tasks the individual is good at and worse performance on tasks that are difficult for him or her.

Presence of Others (Audience effects, co-action effects)

Arousal is heightened, and dominant response is enhanced.

Performance is enhanced on tasks at which we are skilled and on simple tasks.

Performance suffers on tasks at which we are unskilled and on difficult tasks.

Source: Based on Zajonc & Sales (1966).

Some 80 experimental studies have been conducted on social loafing in diverse cultures, including those of Taiwan, Japan, Thailand, India, China, and the United States. Social loafing on a variety of tasks was evident to some degree in all of the cultures studied. But it appears to be more common in individualistic Western cultures such as the United States (Karau & Williams, 1993).

Social Roles

Social roles are socially defined behaviors that are considered appropriate for individuals occupying certain positions within a given group. These roles can shape our behavior, sometimes quickly and dramatically. Consider a classic experiment in which psychologist Philip Zimbardo (1972) simulated a prison experience. College student volunteers were randomly assigned to be either guards or prisoners. The guards, wearing uniforms and carrying small clubs, strictly enforced harsh rules. The prisoners were stripped naked, searched, and deloused. Then, they were given prison uniforms, assigned numbers, and locked away in small, bare cells. The guards quickly adapted to their new role, some even to the point of becoming heartless and sadistic. One guard remembered forcing prisoners to clean toilets with their bare hands. And the prisoners began to act debased and subservient. The role playing became all too real—so much so that the experiment had to be ended in only 6 days.

Of course, social roles have positive effects on behavior as well. In classic research examining adolescents with learning disabilities, Palinscar and Brown (1984) reported that students' learning behaviors were powerfully affected by their being assigned to play either the "teacher" or the "student" role in group study sessions. Participants summarized reading assignments more effectively, and as a result learned more from them, when functioning as a teacher than when functioning as a student.

16.11 How do social roles influence individual behavior?

◀ Zimbardo's experiment simulated the prison environment by randomly assigning participants to the social roles of prison guards or inmates. The social roles influenced the participants' behavior: The prisoners began acting like real prisoners, and the prison guards, like real prison guards.

social roles Socially defined behaviors considered appropriate for individuals occupying certain positions within a given group.

Attitudes and Attitude Change

We use the word *attitude* frequently in everyday speech. We say that someone has a "bad attitude," for instance. But what is an attitude?

Attitudes

16.12 What are the three components of an attitude?

Essentially, **attitudes** are relatively stable evaluations of persons, objects, situations, or issues, along a continuum ranging from positive to negative (Petty et al., 1997). Most attitudes have three components: (1) a cognitive component, consisting of thoughts and beliefs about the attitudinal object; (2) an emotional component, made up of feelings toward the attitudinal object; and (3) a behavioral component, composed of predispositions concerning actions toward the object (Breckler, 1984). Think about your attitudes toward exercise, for example. On the positive side, you probably believe that exercise is a good thing to do. This is the cognitive component of your attitude. The emotional component may include feeling good about yourself after you work out, which just happens to be the behavioral component. On the negative side, you may believe that exercise is boring. Emotionally, your feelings about how you look in exercise clothing may make you want to avoid going to the gym altogether, which is, again, the behavioral component of your attitude. **Figure 16.3** illustrates these components of attitudes. Attitudes enable us to appraise people, objects, and situations, and provide structure and consistency in the social environment (Fazio, 1989). Attitudes also help us process social information (Pratkanis, 1989), guide our behavior (Sanbonmatsu & Fazio, 1990), and influence our social judgments and decisions (Jamieson & Zanna, 1989).

Some attitudes are acquired through firsthand experiences with people, objects, situations, and issues. Others are acquired when children hear parents, family, friends, and teachers express positive or negative attitudes toward certain issues or people. The mass media, including advertising, influence people's attitudes and reap billions of dollars annually for their efforts. As you might expect, however, the attitudes that people form through their own direct experience are stronger than those they acquire vicariously and are also more resistant to change (Wu & Shaffer, 1987). Once formed, however, attitudes tend to strengthen when we associate with others who share them (Visser & Mirabile, 2004).

Lively discussions of controversial topics, even when those discussions take place only with others who agree with us, may improve our ability to think analytically about our attitudes. Researchers Joseph Lao and Deanna Kuhn (2002) asked college students to engage in a series of six discussions about a controversial topic with another student. Participants were assigned to three experimental conditions. In one, all of their discussions involved a partner who agreed with them. In another, all of the partners disagreed. In the third condition, three discussion partners agreed and three disagreed with the participant. Six weeks later, Lao and Kuhn found that participants who had either discussed the topic with those who agreed with them or with an equal number of agreers and disagreers showed the greatest improvement in critical thinking about the topic. They inferred from these findings that discussing a controversial

attitude A relatively stable evaluation of a person, object, situation, or issue, along a continuum ranging from positive to negative.

Figure 16.3 The Three Components of an Attitude

An attitude is a relatively stable evaluation of a person, object, situation, or issue. Most of our attitudes have (1) a cognitive component, (2) an emotional component, and (3) a behavioral component.

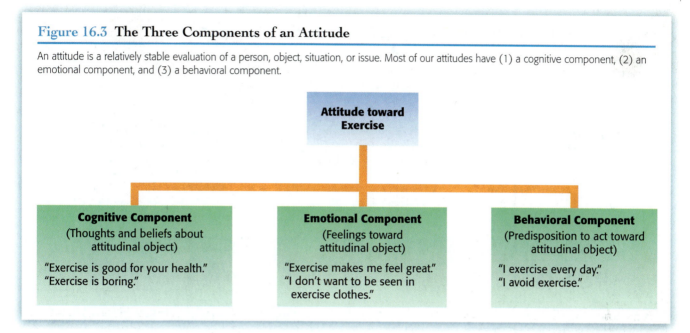

Attitude toward Exercise

Cognitive Component
(Thoughts and beliefs about attitudinal object)

"Exercise is good for your health."
"Exercise is boring."

Emotional Component
(Feelings toward attitudinal object)

"Exercise makes me feel great."
"I don't want to be seen in exercise clothes."

Behavioral Component
(Predisposition to act toward attitudinal object)

"I exercise every day."
"I avoid exercise."

issue with people who disagree with you is helpful only if it is balanced by discussions with others who share your views.

We often hear that attitude change is the key to behavior change. However, a number of studies in the mid–20th century showed that attitudes predict behavior only about 10% of the time (Wicker, 1969). People, for example, may express strong attitudes in favor of protecting the environment and conserving natural resources, yet not take their aluminum cans to a recycling center or join a carpool. However, attitudes are better predictors of behavior if they are strongly held, are readily accessible in memory (Bassili, 1995; Fazio & Williams, 1986; Kraus, 1995), and vitally affect the holder's interests (Sivacek & Crano, 1982).

Cognitive Dissonance

What happens when attitudes contradict one another, or when attitudes and behaviors are inconsistent? According to psychologist Leon Festinger (1957), if people discover that some of their attitudes are in conflict or that their attitudes are not consistent with their behavior, they are likely to experience an unpleasant state called **cognitive dissonance.** Psychologists believe that cognitive dissonance results from a desire to maintain self-esteem (Stone, 2003). People usually try to reduce the dissonance by changing the behavior or the attitude or by somehow explaining away the inconsistency or minimizing its importance (Aronson, 1976; Crano & Prislin, 2006; Festinger, 1957; Matz & Wood, 2005).

Smoking creates a perfect situation for cognitive dissonance. Faced with a mountain of evidence linking smoking to a number of diseases, what are smokers to do? The healthiest, but perhaps not the easiest, way to reduce cognitive dissonance is to change the behavior—quit smoking. Another way is to change the attitude, to convince oneself that smoking is not as dangerous as it is said to be. Smokers may also tell themselves that they will stop smoking long before any permanent damage is done, or that medical science is advancing so rapidly that a cure for cancer or emphysema is just around the corner. **Figure 16.4** illustrates the methods a smoker may use to reduce cognitive dissonance.

In classic research, Festinger and Carlsmith (1959) placed research participants alone in a room to play a boring game. Upon completing the game, participants were instructed to tell the next participants that the game was fun. Participants were

16.13 What is cognitive dissonance, and how can it be reduced?

cognitive dissonance The unpleasant state that can occur when people become aware of inconsistencies between their attitudes or between their attitudes and their behavior.

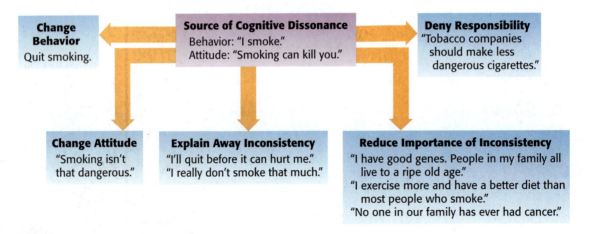

Figure 16.4 Methods of Reducing Cognitive Dissonance

Cognitive dissonance can occur when people become aware of inconsistencies in their attitudes or between their attitudes and their behavior. People try to reduce dissonance by (1) changing their behavior, (2) changing their attitude, (3) explaining away the inconsistency, or (4) reducing its importance. Here are examples of how a smoker might use these methods to reduce the cognitive dissonance created by his or her habit.

Change Behavior
Quit smoking.

Source of Cognitive Dissonance
Behavior: "I smoke."
Attitude: "Smoking can kill you."

Deny Responsibility
"Tobacco companies should make less dangerous cigarettes."

Change Attitude
"Smoking isn't that dangerous."

Explain Away Inconsistency
"I'll quit before it can hurt me."
"I really don't smoke that much."

Reduce Importance of Inconsistency
"I have good genes. People in my family all live to a ripe old age."
"I exercise more and have a better diet than most people who smoke."
"No one in our family has ever had cancer."

randomly assigned to two experimental groups. One group was paid $1 for following instructions, while the other was paid $20. Festinger and Carlsmith assumed that the conflict between participants' self-esteem and their lying behavior would cause cognitive dissonance. How could participants resolve this dissonance and get rid of the threat to self-esteem caused by lying? Just as Festinger and Carlsmith had hypothesized, participants who were paid $1 resolved the conflict by convincing themselves that the game really had been fun—a change in attitude. By contrast, participants who were paid $20 resolved the conflict by justifying their actions on the basis of having been paid a fairly large sum of money relative to the amount of effort it had required to lie to the next participant. Consequently, they did not view the lie as a threat to their self-esteem.

Persuasion

16.14 What are the elements of persuasion?

Have you ever tried to convince another person to agree with your political opinions or to do something you wanted them to do? **Persuasion** is a deliberate attempt to influence the attitudes and/or the behavior of another person. Attempts at persuasion are pervasive parts of work experience, social experience, and even family life. Researchers have identified four elements of persuasion: (1) the source of the communication (who is doing the persuading), (2) the audience (who is being persuaded), (3) the message (what is being said), and (4) the medium (the means by which the message is transmitted).

Some factors that make the source (the communicator) more persuasive are credibility, attractiveness, and likability. A credible communicator is one who has expertise (knowledge of the topic at hand) and trustworthiness (truthfulness and integrity). Other characteristics of the source—including physical attractiveness, celebrity status, and similarity to the audience—also contribute to our responses to the sources of persuasive messages.

Audience characteristics influence responses to persuasion as well. In general, people with low IQs are easier to persuade than those with high IQs (Rhodes & Wood, 1992). Evidence suggests that a one-sided message is usually most persuasive if the audience is not well informed on the issue, is not highly intelligent, or already agrees with the point of view. A two-sided message (where both sides of an issue are

persuasion A deliberate attempt to influence the attitudes and/or behavior of another person.

mentioned) works best when the audience is well informed on the issue, is fairly intelligent, or is initially opposed to the point of view. A two-sided appeal will usually sway more people than will a one-sided appeal (Hovland et al., 1949; McGuire, 1985). People also tend to scrutinize arguments that are contrary to their existing beliefs more carefully and to exert more effort refuting them; they are more likely to judge such arguments as being weaker than those that support their beliefs (Edwards & Smith, 1996).

A message can be well reasoned, logical, and unemotional ("just the facts"); it can be strictly emotional ("make their hair stand on end"); or it can be a combination of the two. Arousing fear seems to be an effective method for persuading people to quit smoking, get regular chest X-rays, and wear seat belts (Dillard & Anderson 2004). Appeals based on fear are most effective when the presentation outlines definite actions the audience can take to avoid the feared outcomes (Buller et al., 2000; Stephenson & Witte, 1998). However, nutritional messages are more effective when framed in terms of the benefits of dietary change rather than the harmful effects of a poor diet (van Assema et al., 2002).

Another important factor in persuasion is repetition. The more often a product or a point of view is presented, the more people will be persuaded to buy it or embrace it. Advertisers apparently believe in the mere-exposure effect, for they repeat their messages over and over (Bornstein, 1989). But messages are likely to be less persuasive if they include vivid elements (colorful language, striking examples) that hinder the reception of the content (Frey & Eagly, 1993).

▲ Celebrities enhance the persuasive powers of advertisements.

Remember It — Attitudes and Attitude Change

1. The three components of an attitude are _____, _____, and _____.

2. Changing an attitude can reduce cognitive _____.

3. Credibility relates most directly to a communicator's _____ and _____.

4. With a well-informed audience, _____ messages are more persuasive than _____ messages.

5. Appeals based on _____ are most effective if they provide definite actions that people can take to avoid dreaded outcomes.

Answers: 1. cognitive, emotional, behavioral; 2. dissonance; 3. expertise, trustworthiness; 4. two-sided, one-sided; 5. fear

Prosocial Behavior

Within a few days after Hurricane Katrina hit the Gulf Coast in 2005, Americans and others around the world had given more than $400 million to charities that pledged to use the money to help the storm's victims (Perry, Wallace, & Wilhelm, 2005). This giving supports our belief in the basic goodness of human beings. But what does it mean when people ignore others in need? In a now-famous case from 1964, New York City resident Kitty Genovese was murdered while her neighbors looked on, apparently indifferent to her plight. More recently, in early 2003, several people were caught on videotape doing nothing as a man who had just been shot lay dying in a gas station driveway (CNN.com, February 16, 2003). One person even stared at the victim for a few minutes and then calmly returned to the task of filling a can with kerosene. What causes such extreme variations in helping behavior?

Reasons for Helping

There are many kinds of **prosocial behavior**—behavior that benefits others, such as helping, cooperation, and sympathy. Such impulses arise early in life. Researchers agree that young children respond sympathetically to companions in distress, usually before their second birthday (Hay, 1994; Kochanska, 1993). The term **altruism** is usually reserved for behavior that is aimed at helping others, requires some self-sacrifice, and is not performed for personal gain. Batson and colleagues (1989) believe that we help out of *empathy*—the ability to take the perspective of others, to put ourselves in their place.

Commitment is another factor influencing altruism. We are more likely to behave in an altruistic fashion in the context of relationships to which we are deeply committed (Powell & Van Vugt, 2003). The influence of commitment is strongest when the cost of an altruistic act is high. For instance, you would probably be more likely to volunteer to donate a kidney to a family member than to a stranger.

The degree to which society values altruism is another variable that can influence individual decisions about altruistic behavior. Cultures vary in their norms for helping others—that is, their *social responsibility norms*. According to Miller and others (1990), people in the United States tend to feel an obligation to help family members, friends, and even strangers in life-threatening circumstances, but only family members in moderately serious situations. In contrast, in India the social responsibility norm extends to strangers whose needs are only moderately serious or even minor.

Whatever the motive for altruism, people who regularly engage in behavior that helps others reap significant benefits (Seenoo & Takagi, 2003). One interesting benefit is that, the more people help, the more altruistic they become. In other words, behaving altruistically generates or enhances an individual's altruistic attitudes. Along with this attitude change comes an increased appreciation for life. Thus, the costs of altruistic behavior are balanced by its benefits, both for those who are helped and for the helpers themselves.

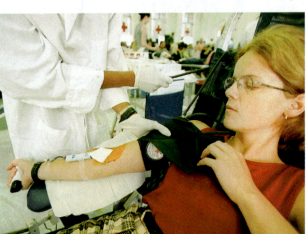

▲ Altruistic acts, such as donating blood, may be motivated by social responsibility norms.

The Bystander Effect

A variety of social circumstances contribute to the decision to help another person. One example is the **bystander effect:** As the number of bystanders at an emergency increases, the probability that the victim will receive help from them decreases, and the help, if given, is likely to be delayed. Psychologists have suggested that the bystander effect explains the failure of Kitty Genovese's neighbors to help her.

In now-classic research, Darley and Latané (1968a) placed a series of research participants alone in a small room and told them that they would be participating in a discussion group by means of an intercom system. Some participants were told that they would be communicating with only one other participant; some believed that two other participants would be involved; and some were told that five other people would participate. There really were no other participants in the study—only the prerecorded voices of confederates assisting the experimenter. Shortly after the discussion began, the voice of one confederate was heard over the intercom calling for help, indicating that he was having an epileptic seizure. Of the participants who believed that they alone were hearing the victim, 85% went for help before the end of the seizure. When participants believed that one other person heard the seizure, 62% sought help. But when they believed that four other people were aware of the emergency, only 31% tried to get help before the end of the seizure. **Figure 16.5** shows how the number of bystanders affects both the number of people who try to help and the speed of response.

prosocial behavior   Behavior that benefits others, such as helping, cooperation, and sympathy.

altruism   Behavior that is aimed at helping another, requires some self-sacrifice, and is not performed for personal gain.

bystander effect   A social factor that affects prosocial behavior: As the number of bystanders at an emergency increases, the probability that the victim will receive help decreases, and the help, if given, is likely to be delayed.

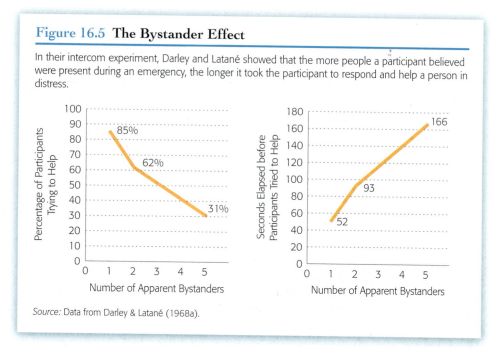

Figure 16.5 The Bystander Effect

In their intercom experiment, Darley and Latané showed that the more people a participant believed were present during an emergency, the longer it took the participant to respond and help a person in distress.

Source: Data from Darley & Latané (1968a).

Darley and Latané (1968a) suggest that, when bystanders are present in an emergency, they generally feel that the responsibility for helping is shared by the group, a phenomenon known as **diffusion of responsibility.** Consequently, each person feels less compelled to act than if she or he were alone and felt the total responsibility; each bystander thinks, "Somebody else must be doing something." Another reason for the bystander effect is the influence of other bystanders who appear calm. When others seem calm, we may conclude that nothing is really wrong and that no intervention is necessary (Darley & Latané, 1968b).

Ironically, though, with regard to catastrophes, such as the terrorist attacks of September 11, 2001, the Indonesian tsunami that occurred in 2004, and the numerous powerful hurricanes that have hit the coastal communities of the United States over the past several years, the bystander effect is greatly reduced. In fact, people are likely to put forth extraordinary effort to help others in such situations. A few pages back, we noted how much money people donated to Hurricane Katrina victims within the first few days after the storm made landfall. But this phenomenon is also seen in the countless individual acts of altruism that occur in the context of such events. Often, too, people who can't help directly witness the events via instantaneous communication media and contribute money to the families of victims within hours of these tragedies. Research on public responses to large-scale disasters predicts such responses (Shepperd, 2001).

▲ Why do people ignore someone who is unconscious on the sidewalk? Diffusion of responsibility is one possible explanation.

diffusion of responsibility The feeling among bystanders at an emergency that the responsibility for helping is shared by the group, making each person feel less compelled to act than if he or she alone bore the total responsibility.

Remember It   Prosocial Behavior

1. _____ involves making a sacrifice to help another person without expectation of reward.
2. As the number of bystanders at an emergency increases, the probability that the victim will receive help _____.
3. Cultural standards for helping others are called _____.

Answers: 1. Altruism; 2. decreases; 3. social responsibility norms

Aggression

One of the enduring themes of research in social psychology for many years has been the study of aggression. **Aggression** is the intentional infliction of physical or psychological harm on others. Aggression has many forms and takes place in a variety of locations—at home, at work, and even among drivers on the road.

Biological Factors in Aggression

16.17 What biological factors are thought to be related to aggression?

Sigmund Freud believed that humans have an aggressive instinct that can be turned inward as self-destruction or outward as aggression or violence toward others. Although many psychologists reject this view, they do concede that biological factors are involved. A meta-analysis of 24 twin and adoption studies of several personality measures of aggression revealed a heritability estimate of about .50 for aggression (Miles & Carey, 1997). Twin and adoption studies have also revealed a genetic link for criminal behavior (DiLalla & Gottesman, 1991). Cloninger and others (1982) found that adoptees with a criminal biological parent were four times as likely as members of the general population to commit crimes, whereas adoptees with a criminal adoptive parent were at twice the risk of committing a crime. But adoptees with both a criminal biological and a criminal adoptive parent were 14 times as likely to commit crimes, indicating the power of the combined influences of nature and nurture. Thus, many researchers believe that genes that predispose individuals to aggressive behavior may cause them to be more sensitive to models of aggressiveness in the environment (Rowe, 2003).

One biological factor that seems very closely related to aggression is a low arousal level of the autonomic nervous system (Raine, 1996). Low arousal level (low heart rate and lower reactivity) has been linked to antisocial and violent behavior (Brennan et al., 1997). People with a low arousal level tend to seek stimulation and excitement and often exhibit fearlessness, even in the face of danger.

Men are more physically aggressive than women (Green et al., 1996), and a correlation between high testosterone levels and aggressive behavior has been found in males (Archer, 1991; Dabbs & Morris, 1990). In fact, the primary biological variable related to domestic violence (both verbal and physical abuse) appears to be high testosterone levels, which are highly heritable (Soler et al., 2000). Harris and others (1996) found testosterone levels in male and female college students to be positively correlated with aggression and negatively corre-

▲ Alcohol impairs the brain's ability to process information, a condition that often leads to poor decisions. For this reason, alcohol is frequently involved in acts of aggression.

lated with prosocial behavior. Furthermore, violent behavior has been associated with low levels of the neurotransmitter serotonin (Gartner & Whitaker-Azimitia, 1996; Mitsis et al., 2000; Toot et al., 2004).

Brain damage, brain tumors, and temporal lobe epilepsy have all been related to aggressive and violent behavior (Mednick et al., 1988; van Elst et al., 2000). A study of 15 death row inmates revealed that all had histories of severe head injuries (Lewis et al., 1986). According to Eronen and others (1996), homicide rates are eight times higher among men with schizophrenia and ten times higher among men with antisocial personality disorder. The risk of violence is even greater when individuals with

aggression The intentional infliction of physical or psychological harm on others.

these disorders abuse alcohol (Hodgins et al., 1996; Tiihonen et al., 1997). In children, high levels of lead exposure (Needleman et al., 1996) and low IQ and problems paying attention (Loeber & Hay, 1997) are related to aggressive behavior and delinquency.

Alcohol and aggression are frequent partners. A meta-analysis of 30 experimental studies indicated that alcohol is related to aggression (Bushman & Cooper, 1990). The use of alcohol and other drugs that affect the brain's frontal lobes may lead to aggressive behavior in humans and other animals by disrupting normal executive functions (Lyvers, 2000). Ito and others (1996) found that alcohol intoxication is particularly likely to lead to aggression in response to frustration. People who are intoxicated commit the majority of murders, spouse beatings, stabbings, and instances of physical child abuse.

Review and Reflect summarizes the possible biological causes of aggression.

Review and Reflect   Possible Biological Causes of Aggression

Cause	Evidence
Heredity	If one identical twin is aggressive, there is a 50% chance that the other twin is aggressive as well. Adopted children's aggressive tendencies are more like those of their biological parents than their adopted parents.
Low arousal level	People with low levels of arousal seek stimulation and excitement to increase arousal.
High testosterone level	High levels of testosterone have been found to be correlated with some forms of aggression, such as intimate partner abuse, in both men and women.
Neurological disorders	Brain tumors and other neurological diseases have been linked to aggressive behavior.
Alcohol abuse	People who are intoxicated commit the majority of murders and most other violent crimes.

Other Influences on Aggression

Beyond biological factors, what other variables contribute to aggression? The **frustration-aggression hypothesis** suggests that frustration produces aggression (Dollard et al., 1939; Miller, 1941). If a traffic jam caused you to be late for an appointment and you were frustrated, would you lean on your horn, shout obscenities out of your window, or just sit patiently and wait? Frustration doesn't always cause aggression, but it is especially likely to do so if it is intense and seems to be unjustified (Doob & Sears, 1939; Pastore, 1950). Berkowitz (1988) points out that even if frustration is justified and not aimed specifically at an individual, it can cause aggression if it arouses negative emotions.

Aggression in response to frustration is not always focused on the actual cause of the frustration. If the preferred target is too threatening or not available, the aggression may be displaced. For example, children who are angry with their parents may take out their frustration on a younger sibling. Sometimes, members of minority groups or other innocent targets who are not responsible for a frustrating situation become targets of displaced aggression, a practice known as **scapegoating** (Koltz, 1983). For example, throughout American history, the most recent wave of immigrants—Irish and Italians in the late 19th century, the Vietnamese and other Asian groups in the 1970s, and, nowadays, Latinos—have been blamed for the economic struggles of people who were already living in the United States at the time.

People often become aggressive when they are in pain (Berkowitz, 1983) or are exposed to loud noise or foul odors (Rotton et al., 1979). Extreme heat has also been linked to aggression in several studies (Anderson & Anderson, 1996; Rotton & Cohn, 2000). These and other studies lend support to the *cognitive-neoassociationistic model* proposed by Berkowitz (1990), which suggests that anger and aggression result from aversive events and unpleasant emotional states, such as sadness, grief, and depression. The cognitive component of Berkowitz's model occurs when the angered person

16.18 What other factors contribute to aggression?

frustration-aggression hypothesis   The hypothesis that frustration produces aggression.

scapegoating   Displacing aggression onto members of minority groups or other innocent targets not responsible for the frustrating situation.

▲ Crowding may or may not be stressful, depending on the situation—waiting in a crowded airport terminal is more likely to be perceived as stressful than being part of a large crowd at a rally on Martin Luther King, Jr., Day.

appraises the aversive situation and makes attributions about the motives of the people involved. As a result of the cognitive appraisal, the initial reaction of anger can be intensified, reduced, or suppressed. This process makes the person either more or less likely to act on his or her aggressive tendency.

Personal space is an area surrounding each individual, much like an invisible bubble, that the person considers part of himself or herself and uses to regulate the closeness of interactions with others. Personal space serves to protect privacy and to regulate the level of intimacy with others. The size of personal space varies according to the person or persons with whom an individual is interacting and the nature of the interaction. When personal space is reduced, aggression can result.

Crowding—the subjective judgment that there are too many people in a confined space—often leads to higher physiological arousal, and males typically experience its effects more negatively than females do. The effects of crowding also vary across cultures and situations. Researchers have studied its effects on such diverse populations as male heads of households in India and middle-class male and female college students in the United States (Evans & Lepore, 1993). In both of these studies, psychological distress was linked to household crowding. Furthermore, studies in prisons have shown that the more inmates per cell, the greater the number of violent incidents (Paulus et al., 1988). However, keep in mind that a prison is an atypical environment with a population whose members have been confined precisely because they tend to be aggressive.

Finally, researchers Roy and Judy Eidelson have identified several beliefs that may lead members of a group of people to act aggressively toward outsiders (Eidelson & Eidelson, 2003). One such belief is a group's conviction that its members are superior to others, together with a sense of "chosenness" for a particular task. The view that one's own group has a legitimate grievance against outsiders can also spark aggression. Group members who believe themselves to be vulnerable may justify aggression as a form of defense. Similarly, those who are convinced that outsiders' promises to respect the rights of group members cannot be trusted may act aggressively. Finally, group members may resort to violence if they believe that aggression is the only strategy available to them for addressing grievances or protecting themselves. Group leaders play an important role in either encouraging or discouraging these beliefs among group members. So, positive leadership may be able to prevent intergroup aggression.

The Social Learning Theory of Aggression

16.19 According to social learning theory, what causes aggressive behavior?

personal space An area surrounding each person, much like an invisible bubble, that the person considers part of himself or herself and uses to regulate the level of intimacy with others.

crowding The subjective judgment that there are too many people in a confined space.

The *social learning theory of aggression* holds that people learn to behave aggressively by observing aggressive models and by having their aggressive responses reinforced (Bandura, 1973). It is well known that aggression is higher in groups and subcultures that condone violent behavior and accord high status to aggressive members. A leading advocate of the social learning theory of aggression, Albert Bandura (1976) claims that aggressive models in the subculture, the family, and the media all play a part in increasing the level of aggression in society.

Abused children certainly experience aggression and see it modeled day after day. And the rate of physical abuse is seven times greater in families where there is a stepparent (Daly & Wilson, 1996). "One of the most commonly held beliefs in both the scholarly and popular literature is that adults who were abused as children are more likely to abuse their own children" (Widom, 1989, p. 6). There is some truth to this belief. On the basis of original research and an analysis of 60 other studies, Oliver (1993) concludes that one-third of people who are abused go on to become abusers, one-third do not, and the final one-third may become abusers if their lives are highly stressful. Further, individuals who were sexually abused as children are more likely than others to become child sexual abusers as adults (Burton, 2003).

Most abusive parents, however, were not abused as children (Widom, 1989). Although abused and neglected children are at higher risk of becoming delinquent, criminal, or violent, the majority do not become abusive themselves (Widom & Maxfield, 1996). Several researchers suggest that the higher risk for aggression may not be solely the result of an abusive family environment but may be partly influenced by the genes (DiLalla & Gottesman, 1991). Some abused children become withdrawn and isolated rather than aggressive and abusive (Dodge et al., 1990).

As you learned in Chapter 5, the research evidence overwhelmingly supports a relationship between TV violence and viewer aggression (Coyne et al., 2004; Huesmann & Moise, 1996; Singer et al., 1999). And the negative effects of TV violence are even worse for individuals who are, by nature, highly aggressive (Bushman, 1995). Researchers have also found a correlation between playing violent video games and aggression (Anderson & Dill, 2000). Moreover, aggressiveness increases as more time is spent playing such games (Colwell & Payne, 2000). However, researchers in the Netherlands found that boys who choose aggressive video games tend to be more aggressive, less intelligent, and less prosocial in their behavior (Weigman & van Schie, 1998). So, the link between aggression and video games may be due to the tendency of aggressive individuals to prefer entertainment media that feature aggression.

Sexual Aggression

Sexual aggression is any kind of sexual contact in which one or more participants are either unable to give consent or are forced into participation (National Center for Injury Prevention and Control [NCIPC], 2002). Clearly, this definition is very broad and includes a number of different kinds of sexual contact, including the following:

16.20 What are some of the factors that contribute to sexual aggression?

- *Sexual assault*–forcing or coercing another person into engaging in any kind of sexual activity
- *Rape*–sexual assault that includes penetration
- *Date/acquaintance rape*–rape that occurs in the context of a social relationship
- *Sexual abuse*–sexual assault directed toward a vulnerable individual (e.g., a child or elderly person)

Women are far more likely than men to be victimized by sexual aggression (Murphy, 2003). In the United States, about 28% of women, compared to 8% of men, have experienced some type of sexual aggression by the time they reach college age (NCIPC, 2000). In most cases, the perpetrator is a current or former intimate partner. In the United States, rates of sexual aggression involving an intimate partner are among the highest in the world, as you can see in **Figure 16.6**.

Interestingly, the World Health Organization reports that the factors contributing to sexual violence against women are similar throughout the world (WHO, 2002a). In addition to these factors, shown in **Table 16.1** some other individual characteristics are associated with sexual aggression. For example, rapists are less able to empathize with their victims than are perpetrators of other kinds of crimes, a deficit that may arise from their own sexual victimization experiences in childhood (Fernandez & Marshall, 2003; Simons et al., 2002). Moreover, sex offenders are more likely than other criminal offenders to believe that men should be dominant over women (Murnen et al., 2002).

The desire for power over another may also play a role in sexual aggression in which children are targeted. Unfortunately, such acts occur all too commonly. In the United States, more than 100,000 cases of child sexual abuse are reported to authorities each year (NCIPC, 2002). Experts estimate that about 17% of women and 8% of men were sexually abused as children (Putnam, 2003). According to the World Health Organization, girls under the age of 15 are sexually assaulted more often than adult

sexual aggression Any kind of sexual contact in which one or more participants are either unable to give consent or are forced into participation.

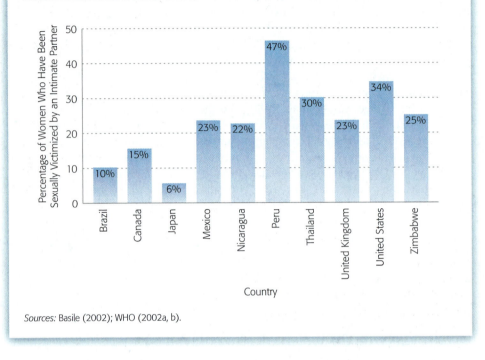

Figure 16.6 Percentages of Women Who Have Been Sexually Victimized by an Intimate Partner

A fairly large percentage of women all over the world have experienced sexual aggression within an intimate relationship. But percentages are much higher in some countries than in others, presumably because of differences in cultural factors, such as the economic status of women.

Sources: Basile (2002); WHO (2002a, b).

women in most countries (WHO, 2002b). In the United States, about 60% of sexual assault victims are females under age 15, and 29% are under age 10.

Some researchers have suggested that a tendency toward *pedophilia* (a preference for children as sexual partners) may be the result of hypersexuality due to a brain disorder, especially in the front part of the right frontal or temporal lobe (Burns & Swerdlow, 2003; Mendez et al., 2000). Therapies to treat those who sexually abuse children are likely to focus on deviant sexual fantasies, which are believed to serve as "triggers," pushing the abuser to act (Swaffer et al., 2000).

Table 16.1 Factors Contributing to Sexual Aggression against Women

Among Perpetrators	Among Victims
History of early sexual contact or victimization	Reluctance to report sexual violence to authorities
Extreme views about sex-role stereotypes	
Extreme views about sex-role stereotypes	Nonforceful verbal resistance of unwanted advances
Hostility toward women	
Fantasies about sexual violence	Extreme views about sex-role stereotypes
Involvement with pornography	Acceptance of rape myths
Association with sexually aggressive peers	Poverty
Acceptance of rape myths (e.g., women enjoy being raped)	Alcohol and/or drug use
Poverty	
Alcohol and/or drug use	

Sources: NCIPC (2000); WHO (2002b).

Prejudice and Discrimination

Do you know the difference between *prejudice* and *discrimination*? **Prejudice** consists of *attitudes* (usually negative) toward others based on their gender, religion, race, or membership in a particular group. Prejudice involves beliefs and emotions (not actions) that can escalate into hatred. **Discrimination** consists of *behavior*—actions (usually negative) toward others based on their gender, religion, race, or membership in a particular group. Many Americans have experienced prejudice and discrimination—minority racial groups (racism), women (sexism), the elderly (ageism), the handicapped, homosexuals, religious groups, and others. What are the roots of prejudice and discrimination?

The Roots of Prejudice and Discrimination

Social psychologists have proposed several theories to explain the psychological bases for prejudice and discrimination. Moreover, a number of studies have provided insight into their origins.

Realistic Conflict Theory. One of the oldest explanations as to how prejudice arose cites competition among various social groups that must struggle against each other for scarce resources—good jobs, homes, schools, and so on. Commonly called the **realistic conflict theory,** this view suggests that as competition increases, so do prejudice, discrimination, and hatred among the competing groups. Some historical evidence supports the realistic conflict theory. Prejudice and hatred were high between the American settlers and the Native Americans, who struggled over land during the westward expansion. The multitudes of Irish and German immigrants who came to the United States in the 1830s and 1840s felt the sting of prejudice and hatred from other Americans who were facing economic scarcity. But prejudice and discrimination are attitudes and actions too complex to be explained solely by economic conflict and competition.

In-Groups and Out-Groups. Prejudice can also spring from the distinct social categories into which people divide the world, employing an "us-versus-them" mentality (Turner et al., 1987). An **in-group** is a social group with a strong sense of togetherness, from which others are excluded. Members of college fraternities and sororities often exhibit strong in-group feelings. The **out-group** consists of individuals specifically identified by the in-group as not belonging. Us-versus-them thinking can lead to excessive competition, hostility, prejudice, discrimination, and even war. Prejudiced individuals are reluctant to admit outsiders to their racial in-group if there is the slightest doubt about the outsiders' racial purity (Blascovich et al., 1997).

16.21 What factors contribute to the development of prejudice and discrimination?

prejudice Attitudes (usually negative) toward others based on their gender, religion, race, or membership in a particular group.

discrimination Behavior (usually negative) directed toward others based on their gender, religion, race, or membership in a particular group.

realistic conflict theory The view that as competition increases among social groups for scarce resources, so do prejudice, discrimination, and hatred.

in-group A social group with a strong sense of togetherness, from which others are excluded.

out-group A social group made up of individuals specifically identified by the in-group as not belonging.

A famous study by Sherif and Sherif (1967) shows how in-group/out-group conflict can escalate into prejudice and hostility rather quickly, even between groups that are very much alike. The researchers set up their experiment at the Robber's Cave summer camp. Their subjects were 22 bright, well-adjusted, 11- and 12-year-old White middle-class boys from Oklahoma City. Divided into two groups and housed in separate cabins, the boys were kept apart for all their daily activities and games. During the first week, in-group solidarity, friendship, and cooperation developed within each of the groups. One group called itself the "Rattlers"; the other group took the name "Eagles."

During the second week of the study, competitive events were purposely scheduled so that the goals of one group could be achieved "only at the expense of the other group" (Sherif, 1958, p. 353). The groups were happy to battle each other, and inter-group conflict quickly emerged. Name-calling began, fights broke out, and accusations were hurled back and forth. During the third week of the experiment, the researchers tried to put an end to the hostility and to turn rivalry into cooperation. They simply brought the groups together for pleasant activities, such as eating meals and watching movies. "But far from reducing conflict, these situations only served as opportunities for the rival groups to berate and attack each other. . . . They threw paper, food and vile names at each other at the tables" (Sherif, 1956, pp. 57–58).

Finally, experimenters manufactured a series of crises that could be resolved only if all the boys combined their efforts and resources and cooperated. The water supply, sabotaged by the experimenters, could be restored only if all the boys worked together. After a week of several activities requiring cooperation, cut-throat competition gave way to cooperative exchanges. Friendships developed between groups, and before the end of the experiment, peace was declared. Working together toward shared goals had turned hostility into friendship.

Social-Cognitive Theory. According to the *social-cognitive theory*, people learn attitudes of prejudice and hatred the same way they learn other attitudes. If children hear their parents, teachers, peers, and others openly express prejudices toward different racial, ethnic, or cultural groups, they may be quick to learn such attitudes. And if parents, peers, and others reward children with smiles and approval for parroting their own prejudices (operant conditioning), children may learn these prejudices even more quickly. Phillips and Ziller (1997) suggest that people learn to be nonprejudiced in the same way.

Social cognition refers to the ways in which people typically process social information—the mental processes used to notice, interpret, and remember information about the social world. The very processes we use to simplify, categorize, and order the social world are the same processes that distort our views of it. Thus, as we explained with regard to gender stereotypes in Chapter 11, prejudice arises not only from heated negative emotions and hatred toward other social groups, but also from cooler cognitive processes that govern how we think and process social information (Kunda & Oleson, 1995).

One way people simplify, categorize, and order the world is by using stereotypes. **Stereotypes** are widely shared beliefs about the characteristic traits, attitudes, and behaviors of members of various social groups (racial, ethnic, or religious), including the assumption that "they" are usually all alike. Once a stereotype is in place, people tend to pay more attention to information that confirms their beliefs than to information that challenges them (Wigboldus et al., 2003).

Macrae and colleagues (1994) suggest that people apply stereotypes in their interactions with others because doing so requires less mental energy than trying to understand others as individuals. Stereotyping allows people to make quick, automatic (thoughtless) judgments about others and apply their mental resources to other activities (Forgas & Fiedler, 1996). Research by Anderson and others (1990) showed that participants could process information more efficiently and answer questions faster when they were using stereotypes.

Some research has revealed that people tend to perceive more diversity or more variability within the groups to which they belong (in-groups), but they see more similarity among members of other groups (out-groups) (Ostrom et al., 1993). For example, White Americans see more diversity among themselves but more sameness within groups of African Americans or Asian Americans. This tendency in thinking can also be based on

social cognition The mental processes that people use to notice, interpret, and remember information about the social world.

stereotypes Widely shared beliefs about the characteristic traits, attitudes, and behaviors of members of various social groups (racial, ethnic, or religious), including the assumption that the members of such groups are usually all alike.

gender, age, or any other characteristic. One study showed that a group of 100 young college students believed there was much more variability or diversity in their group than in a group of 100 elderly Americans, whom the students perceived to be much the same (Linville et al., 1989). And a study involving elderly adults showed that they perceived more variability within their own age group than among college students. Age stereotypes can be even more pronounced and negative than gender stereotypes (Kite et al., 1991).

The tendency to be less sensitive to variations among members of other groups may arise from a general tendency to look at people and situations from the perspective of one's own racial or cultural group. This tendency is often called **ethnocentrism.** In work settings, ethnocentrism may prevent us from realizing that coworkers from different backgrounds sometimes perceive the same incidents quite differently. For example, researchers have found that African Americans are more likely than Whites to perceive negative encounters between supervisors and subordinates of different races as being racial in nature (Johnson et al., 2003). To further complicate matters, members of each group believe such opinions are either right or wrong. Because of ethnocentrism, Whites will insist that their view is the correct one, whereas African Americans will take the same position about their view. To address this problem, many organizations provide workers with training geared toward helping them understand that such differences do not involve one view that is right and another that is wrong. Instead, each perspective is deserving of respect by the other.

▲ Can you perceive differences among the young girls shown here? Research shows that people typically perceive more variability among members of groups to which they belong and more similarity among members of groups with which they are unfamiliar.

Is Prejudice Decreasing?

Few people will readily admit to being prejudiced. Gordon Allport (1954), a pioneer in research on prejudice, said, "Defeated intellectually, prejudice lingers emotionally" (p. 328). Even those who are sincerely intellectually opposed to prejudice may still harbor some prejudiced feelings (Devine, 1989). However, most people feel guilty when they catch themselves having prejudiced thoughts or engaging in discriminatory behavior (Volis et al., 2002).

Is there any evidence that prejudice is decreasing in U.S. society? Gallup polls have revealed that White Americans became more racially tolerant over the final decades of the 20th century (Gallup & Hugick, 1990). When White Americans were asked in 1990 whether they would move if African Americans were to move next door to them, 93% said no, compared with 65% in 1965. Even if African Americans were to move into their neighborhood in great numbers, 68% of White Americans still said they would not move. Moreover, both White and African Americans overwhelmingly agree that conditions have improved for minorities in the United States over the past several decades (Public Agenda Online, 2002). However, there are still marked differences of opinion among ethnic groups as to whether racism continues to be a problem in the United States, as you can see in Figure 16.7. Moreover, studies show that fear of rejection continues to be a reason people cite when asked to explain why they don't engage in more social contact with others of different races (Shelton & Richeson, 2005).

Recall, too, that attitudes do not always predict behavior. In a recent study, researchers asked participants to judge whether a fictitious woman was qualified to be the president of a parent-teacher organization (Lott & Saxon, 2002). Participants were provided with information about the woman's occupation and education. In addition, they were told, based on random assignment, that the woman was Hispanic, Anglo-Saxon, or Jewish in ethnic origin. The experimenters found that participants who believed the woman to be Hispanic were more likely to say that she was not qualified for the position than those who thought her to be Anglo-Saxon or Jewish. Moreover, researchers have learned that teachers are more likely to attribute White children's behavior problems to situational factors and those of minority children to dispositional factors (Jackson, 2002).

Such studies suggest that racial stereotyping is still evident in the United States. But there are many things we can do to combat prejudice and discrimination.

16.22 What evidence suggests that prejudice and discrimination are decreasing?

ethnocentrism The tendency to look at situations from one's own racial or cultural perspective.

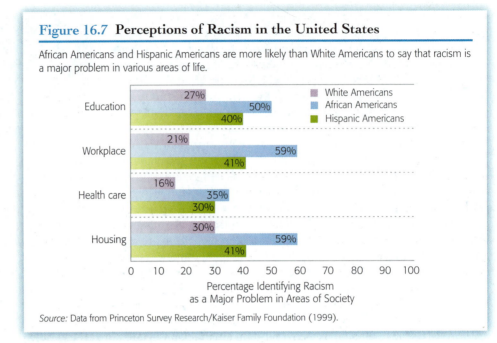

Figure 16.7 Perceptions of Racism in the United States

African Americans and Hispanic Americans are more likely than White Americans to say that racism is a major problem in various areas of life.

Source: Data from Princeton Survey Research/Kaiser Family Foundation (1999).

Unlearning Prejudice

16.23 What are some techniques for reducing prejudice?

As you learned from the Robber's Cave experiment (Sherif & Sherif, 1967), intergroup contact can sometimes lead to increased stereotyping. Under the right conditions, though, intergroup contact can reduce prejudice. College attendance, for example can provide a context in which students from diverse backgrounds study together, endure the same trials (midterms and finals), develop a shared sense of school spirit, join clubs in which members from different backgrounds share common goals, and so on.

Methods such as the *jigsaw technique,* a strategy that works well in college classrooms and as a game in less formal interactions, represent a more direct approach. Each participant in a jigsaw group is given a small amount of information and asked to teach it to other participants. The group must use all the individual pieces of information to solve a problem. This approach increases interaction among participants and helps them develop empathy for members of other ethnic and racial groups (Aronson, 1988; Aronson et al., 1978; Singh, 1991; Walker & Crogan, 1998). A side benefit is that it is an effective way of learning a new solution to a problem.

Many colleges and businesses conduct seminars and workshops designed to combat racism. In such settings, participants learn about racial and cultural perspectives that may differ from their own. They also learn to identify behaviors that may be construed as racist by others, even when that may not be what they intend. Researchers have found that such programs help to reduce automatic stereotyping among participants (Hill & Augoustinos, 2001; Rudman et al., 2001).

Remember It   Prejudice and Discrimination

1. Match each situation with the appropriate term.

   _____ (1) Darlene thinks all Whites are racists.

   _____ (2) Betty's salary is $5,000 less than that of her male counterparts.

   _____ (3) Bill doesn't like police officers.

   a. stereotypic thinking

   b. discrimination

   c. prejudice

2. Members of an in-group usually dislike people in a(n) _____.

3. The social-cognitive theory suggests that prejudice develops and is maintained through _____ and _____.

4. Prejudice and _____ may be means of bolstering one's self-image by disparaging others.

Answers: 1. (1) a, (2) b, (3) c; 2. out-group; 3. modeling, reinforcement; 4. discrimination

Apply It   Offender Profiling

Many people find criminal behavior to be a fascinating topic. Thus, whenever a particularly heinous crime occurs, news reports often include interviews with experts in *offender profiling* regarding the characteristics of the person or persons who committed the crime. "What kind of a person would commit such a horrific crime?" is often the central issue that is addressed in these interviews. But the answers to such questions aren't just intellectually interesting, they are an important investigative tool that often helps law enforcement officials catch criminals.

Modern offender profiling dates back to the time of the infamous serial killer "Jack the Ripper," who terrorized the city of London in the 1880s. Thomas Bond, a surgeon who assisted with the autopsy of one of the Ripper's victims developed a hypothetical description of his behavior that Bond hoped would help police capture the killer. As you probably know, Bond's profile and other investigative efforts failed to lead to an arrest. To this day, the identity of Jack the Ripper remains a mystery. Thus, offender profiling had a rather inauspicious beginning.

About a century after the Ripper's notorious killing spree, offender profiling was revolutionized by the results of numerous case studies of convicted criminals. From these studies, profilers gained insight into the characteristics of individuals who commit different kinds of crimes. A classic study in this genre was done by professional profilers John Douglas and Robert Ressler (Douglas et al., 1992). Douglas and Ressler spent three years interviewing 36 serial murderers and studying their crimes and their backgrounds. They are credited with having helped law enforcement officials understand the implications of organized and disorganized crime scenes. Typically, an organized crime scene with little physical evidence implies that the crime was planned and that the offender may be suffering from antisocial personality disorder. By contrast, a disorganized scene that is replete with physical evidence indicates a crime of passion and an offender that may

have been under the influence of an intense emotional state, a psychosis, or a judgment-impairing substance. During the 1980s, the organized/disorganized dichotomy became a standard crime scene analysis strategy among homicide investigators.

However, professional profilers are not psychologists. Many are, instead, experienced law enforcement officers. As a result, some psychologists have criticized their work as lacking grounding in psychological theory and research. Some of these critics have helped to develop theories and to conduct research that can be used to improve offender profiling. Many of them work in the field of *investigative psychology* that was founded in the early 1990s by British psychologist David Canter.

In one study, Canter and his colleagues analyzed 100 crime scenes of known serial murderers in order to test Douglas and Ressler's conclusions about organized and disorganized crime scenes (Canter et al., 2004). Canter and his team found that all serial murderers exhibit some degree of organization in their crimes. However, the crime scenes they studied suggested four different kinds of interaction patterns between killers and victims. The researchers called these patterns sexual control, mutilation, execution, and plunder. Once a crime scene has been classified according to one of these four subtypes, Canter's research suggests that correlations between these subtypes and other behaviors can help investigators make predictions about other aspects of the crime and the offender.

Although psychologists such as David Canter argue that research-based profiles are potentially more useful than those based on investigative experience, most acknowledge that the human element is also important in offender profiling. That is, investigators differ in their ability to use tools such as profiles. Thus, the most effective profile, many argue, is the one that is scientifically sound and can be put to use by an experienced, insightful investigator (Winerman, 2004).

Summary and Review

Social Perception p. 556

16.1   Why are first impressions so important? p. 556

First impressions are important because (1) people attend more carefully to the first information they receive about another person; and (2) once formed, an impression acts as a framework through which later information is interpreted.

16.2   What is the difference between a situational attribution and a dispositional attribution? p. 556

An attribution is an inference about the cause of one's own or another's behavior. In making a situational attribution, people attribute the cause of the behavior

to some factor operating within the situation. With a dispositional attribution, the inferred cause is internal, such as some personal trait, motive, or attitude. People tend to attribute their own shortcomings primarily to situational factors and those of others primarily to dispositional factors, a tendency known as the actor-observer effect.

Attraction p. 557

16.3   What factors contribute to attraction? p. 557

Proximity contributes to attraction because it is easier to develop relationships with people close at hand. Proximity also increases the likelihood that there will be repeated contacts, and there is a tendency to feel more positively toward a stimulus as a result of repeated exposure to it (the mere-exposure effect). Our moods and emotions influence how much we are attracted to those we meet. We also tend to like people who like us (reciprocity). Other factors that contribute to attraction are similarities in age, gender, race, and socioeconomic class and similar views and interests.

16.4   How important is physical attractiveness to attraction? p. 558

Physical attractiveness is a major factor in attraction for people of all ages. People attribute positive qualities to those who are physically attractive, a phenomenon called the halo effect.

16.5   How do psychologists explain romantic attraction and mating? p. 559

Psychologists have proposed the matching hypothesis to explain the finding that people are often attracted to others who are similar to themselves. Others argue that individuals choose mates whose characteristics complement their own. Evolutionary psychologists argue that men and women are attracted to one another on the basis of what each can contribute to the creation and support of a family.

Conformity, Obedience, and Compliance p. 560

16.6   What did Asch find in his famous experiment on conformity? p. 560

In Asch's classic study on conformity, 5% of the participants went along with the incorrect, unanimous majority all the time; 70% went along some of the time; and 25% remained completely independent.

16.7   What did researchers find when they varied the circumstances of Milgram's classic study of obedience? p. 562

Participants were almost as likely to obey experimenters when the study was repeated at a shabby office building rather than at Yale University. However, when participants were paired with confederates who refused to obey the experimenter, they were less likely to obey.

16.8   What are three techniques used to gain compliance? p. 562

Three techniques often used to gain compliance are the foot-in-the-door technique, the door-in-the-face technique, and the low-ball technique.

Group Influence p. 563

16.9   How does social facilitation affect performance? p. 564

When others are present, either as an audience or as co-actors, people's performance on easy tasks is usually improved through social facilitation. However, performance on difficult tasks is usually impaired.

16.10   What is social loafing, and what factors reduce it? p. 564

Social loafing is people's tendency to put forth less effort when they are working with others on a common task than when working alone. It is less likely to occur when individual output can be monitored or when people have a personal stake in the outcome.

16.11   How do social roles influence individual behavior? p. 565

Individual behavior can be guided by the expectations associated with certain social roles. The effects of such roles can be either negative or positive.

Attitudes and Attitude Change p. 566

16.12   What are the three components of an attitude? p. 566

An attitude usually has a cognitive, an emotional, and a behavioral component.

16.13   What is cognitive dissonance, and how can it be reduced? p. 567

Cognitive dissonance is an unpleasant state that can occur when people become aware of inconsistencies among their attitudes or between their attitudes and their behavior. People can reduce cognitive dissonance by changing the behavior or the attitude or by explaining away the inconsistency or minimizing its importance.

16.14   What are the elements of persuasion? p. 568

The four elements of persuasion are the source of the communication, the audience, the message, and the medium.

Prosocial Behavior p. 569

16.15   What motivates one person to help another? p. 570

Some prosocial behavior is motivated by altruism. In other cases, cultural norms influence helping behavior. We are more likely to help those in need if we are in a committed relationship with them or we perceive them to be similar to us.

16.16   What is the bystander effect, and why does it occur? p. 570

The bystander effect is a social factor that affects prosocial behavior: As the number of bystanders at an emergency increases, the probability that the victim will receive help decreases, and the help, if given, is likely to be delayed. The bystander effect may be due in part to diffusion of responsibility or the influence of other bystanders who seem calm.

Aggression p. 572

16.17   What biological factors are thought to be related to aggression? p. 572

Biological factors thought to be related to aggression are a genetic link in criminal behavior, low arousal levels, high testosterone levels, low levels of serotonin, and brain damage or certain brain disorders.

16.18 What other factors contribute to aggression? p. 573

The frustration-aggression hypothesis holds that frustration produces aggression and that this aggression may be directed at the person causing the frustration or displaced onto another target, as in scapegoating. Aggression has been associated with aversive conditions such as pain, heat, loud noise, and foul odors and with unpleasant emotional states such as sadness, grief, and depression. Invasions of privacy and crowding may also contribute to aggression. Finally, belief in the superiority of one's own group may lead to aggression toward outsiders.

16.19 According to social learning theory, what causes aggressive behavior? p. 574

According to social learning theory, people acquire aggressive responses by observing aggressive models, in the family, the subculture, and the media, and by having aggressive responses reinforced.

16.20 What are some of the factors that contribute to sexual aggression? p. 575

Factors that contribute to sexual aggression include abuse of alcohol and other substances, poverty, acceptance of rape myths, and a history of early sexual contact or victimization.

Prejudice and Discrimination p. 577

16.21 What factors contribute to the development of prejudice and discrimination? p. 577

Prejudice consists of attitudes (usually negative) toward others based on their gender, religion, race, or membership in a particular group. Discrimination consists of actions (usually negative) against others based on the same factors. Prejudice can arise out of competition for scarce resources or from people's tendency to divide the world into distinct social categories—in-groups and out-groups. According to social-cognitive theory, prejudice is learned in the same way that other attitudes are—through modeling and reinforcement.

16.22 What evidence suggests that prejudice and discrimination are decreasing? p. 579

White Americans are less likely to object to living in racially mixed neighborhoods than in the past. But ethnic groups still have varying views of the degree to which prejudice and discrimination continue to be problematic in the United States.

16.23 What are some techniques for reducing prejudice? p. 580

Prejudice declines when groups engage in social contact and work toward common goals. Specific strategies to reduce prejudice include the jigsaw technique and diversity education.

Thinking Critically about Psychology

1. Review the factors influencing impression formation and attraction discussed in this chapter. Prepare a dual list of behaviors indicating what you should and should not do if you wish to make a better impression on other people and to increase their liking for you.
2. Prepare a convincing argument supporting each of these positions:
   a. Aggression results largely from biological factors (nature).
   b. Aggression is primarily learned (nurture).
3. The ethical guidelines for research involving human participants that you read about in Chapter 1 did not exist when Milgram conducted his studies. If a researcher wanted to replicate his work today, how would the researcher have to change the study in order to comply with contemporary ethical guidelines?

Key Terms

actor-observer effect, p. 557
aggression, p. 572
altruism, p. 570
attitude, p. 566
attribution, p. 556
audience effects, p. 564
bystander effect, p. 570
co-action effects, p. 564
cognitive dissonance, p. 567
compliance, p. 562
confederate, p. 555
conformity, p. 560
crowding, p. 574
diffusion of responsibility, p. 571
discrimination, p. 577
dispositional attribution, p. 556

door-in-the-face technique, p. 563
ethnocentrism, p. 579
foot-in-the-door technique, p. 562
frustration-aggression hypothesis, p. 573
fundamental attribution error, p. 557
groupthink, p. 561
halo effect, p. 558
in-group, p. 577
low-ball technique, p. 563
matching hypothesis, p. 559
mere-exposure effect, p. 557
naive subject, p. 555
out-group, p. 577
personal space, p. 574
persuasion, p. 568
prejudice, p. 577

primacy effect, p. 556
prosocial behavior, p. 570
proximity, p. 557
realistic conflict theory, p. 577
scapegoating, p. 573
self-serving bias, p. 557
sexual aggression, p. 575
situational attribution, p. 556
social cognition, p. 578
social facilitation, p. 564
social loafing, p. 564
social norms, p. 560
social psychology, p. 555
social roles, p. 565
stereotypes, p. 578

Chapter 17

Psychology in the Workplace

What comes to mind when you hear the word *bully*? Perhaps you think of a school setting in which one child says to another, "Give me your lunch money, or I'll beat you up." But bullying extends beyond the school playground. Thus, psychologists have recently begun to study the phenomenon of bullying in the workplace.

Most researchers define a workplace bully as an employee who behaves in ways that cause harm to targeted co-workers. The motivations behind bullying are diverse. Some bullies are seeking to advance their own positions. Others are more focused on undermining the careers of others. However, in some cases, bullying seems to be more of a manifestation of an individual's personality than a means that he or she has adopted to achieve a particular goal.

The tactics employed by bullies may include yelling and name-calling as well as covert behaviors such as withholding information. In researchers' terminology, "targets" are the unfortunate victims of these behaviors. The institutional relationship between a bully and a target can be of any type, but bullying is probably most obvious when bullies are the targets' supervisors. In their book, *The Bully at Work,* psychologists Gary and Ruth Namie (2000) describe four types of "bully-bosses." See if you recognize any of them. (Note that although the Namies developed these types with bosses in mind, they could be applied to organizational leaders or any situation in which one person bullies another.)

According to the Namies, the *Constant Critic* is often the darling of upper management, thanks to his or her ability to wheedle performance improvements out of supervisees. The Constant Critic's tactics usually include inundating supervisees with massive amounts of information and then criticizing them for their failure to memorize every word of every memo he or she has ever generated. Constant Critics are also known for nitpicking and for making unreasonable, perfectionist demands of those whom they supervise. Predictably, supervisees are often blamed by Constant Critics for their own failures, and most are willing to lie to higher-level managers in order to be certain that the blame falls on the targeted supervisee.

Named for a World War II artillery rocket that emitted a distinctive whining sound before exploding, the *Screaming Mimi's* behavior often resembles that of their namesake. The sound of a slamming door often announces that the Screaming Mimi is in a volatile mood. This kind of bully-boss intimidates supervisees with angry, foot-stomping outbursts, verbal abuse, and threats. Screaming Mimis also constantly interrupt supervisees during conversations and meetings. These interruptions often take on a hostile tone. Screaming Mimis use intimidating nonverbal behaviors such as violating supervisees' personal space as well. They justify unreasonable demands with statements that are reminiscent of authoritarian parents: "Do it because I'm your boss, and I said so."

A third kind of bully boss, the *Gatekeeper,* must be in control at all times. Gatekeepers often institute policies that require their approval of all allocations of resources. For example, they may keep frequently needed supplies in a locked cabinet in their offices. When a supervisee requests a new box of paper clips from the Gatekeeper, she is likely to have to listen to a lecture on the cost of paper clips. In addition, gatekeepers include minor infractions (e.g., "on several occasions Mr. X was more than five minutes late for a meeting") in supervisees' performance evaluations. To intimidate a target, Gatekeepers often invoke the "silent treatment" and make it clear that they expect all supervisees to help them isolate the target. A Gatekeeper may also "accidentally" delete a supervisee's name from the department email list. Then, when the "deleted" supervisee misses a meeting, the gatekeeper reports the infraction to higher-ups with comments such as "How can you expect me to accomplish anything with such irresponsible people in my department?"

The *Two-Headed Snake* variety of bully-boss uses friendliness to get close to targets. The target of a Two-Headed Snake believes that the Snake is a friend, when, in reality, the Snake often makes disparaging remarks about the target to other supervisees and to higher-level managers. Two-Headed Snakes also use what the Namies call a "divide and conquer" strategy. They bestow favors on employees who are on the same level as the target for gathering information about the target. For example, a confederate of the Two-Headed Snake might encourage the target to make critical remarks about the supervisor that the confederate then reports back to the Snake.

Working under any type of bully-boss can be extremely stressful. Researchers have found that targets are prone to anxiety and depression. Long-term exposure to bullying tactics may even lead to post-traumatic stress disorder (Matthiesen & Einarsen, 2004). Targets may also experience physical symptoms such as frequent headaches and fatigue (Meyers, 2006).

The targets of bully-bosses often feel helpless because they fear that speaking out will lead to retaliation. Many times, these fears are justified (Cortina & Magley, 2003). Moreover, employees who complain about bullies are often told that they are overly sensitive. In effect, they are told to "get over it." Seeing bully-bosses promoted or given awards only adds to the frustration that many of their targets feel.

According to the Namies, there are some effective coping strategies that the target of a bully-boss can use to regain his or her psychological health. First, say the Namies, targets should give the bully's behavior a name—*bullying, intimidation, psychological harassment*, or whatever term the target thinks best fits. Second, the target should listen to his or her body's "fight-or-flight" message and do one or the other. The Namies recommend taking time off from work and consult-

ing with a mental health professional in order to decide which option (stay and fight versus move on to another organization) is best. They also recommend that the target use some of this time off to gather data about the impact of the bully-boss's behavior on the organization. This data may include information about employee turnover, absenteeism, or stress-related health costs. Even if the target decides to move on, say the Namies, he or she should present this information to the bully-boss's supervisor. The Namies' work with the victims of workplace bullies indicates that those who expose the bully before leaving their jobs recover from the effects of having been bullied more quickly than those who remain silent about their reason for resigning.

Using psychological principles to help organizations eliminate bullying and other behaviors that threaten the psychological health of employees is one of the many applications of industrial/organization (I/O) psychology. Specialists in this field apply psychological principles and research results to accomplish a variety of goals in all kinds of organizations—factories, retail stores, transportation companies, hospitals, the military, government and nonprofit agencies, and volunteer organizations. I/O psychology has three broad subfields: personnel psychology, organizational psychology, and human factors psychology. We'll look at each of these in some detail. Then, we'll consider gender issues and human diversity in today's workplace.

Personnel Psychology

Personnel psychology is the subfield of industrial/organizational psychology that deals with the design of appropriate and effective strategies for hiring, training, and evaluating employees.

Hiring Workers

If you owned a business and wanted to hire some help, where would you begin? Wouldn't it be best to start by thinking about exactly how many employees you need and what you need each of those employees to do for you?

Job Analysis. Personnel psychologists typically begin the hiring process with a **job analysis,** in which they determine the work that needs to be done and the skills required to do it. Think of a company that manufactures men's shirts, for example. Workers are needed to cut the various fabric pieces that will be sewn together and to do the stitching. But is it most efficient to have workers who both cut and sew, or is it better to have some workers who cut and others who sew? A thorough job analysis can determine whether the cutting and sewing tasks should be assigned to different categories of workers or to the same category. The end result of a job analysis is

industrial/organizational (I/O) psychologists Psychologists who apply psychological principles and research results in the workplace.

personnel psychology The branch of industrial/organizational psychology that deals with the design of appropriate and effective strategies for hiring, training, and evaluating employees.

17.1 What strategies do personnel psychologists use to hire the best workers?

job analysis An assessment by a personnel psychologist of a job category to determine the work that needs to be done and the skills required to do it.

a **job description,** an outline of the responsibilities associated with a given job category. An appropriate job description, based on a thorough job analysis, is a key ingredient in finding and hiring the best workers (Bowen, 2003).

Recruitment, Selection, and Testing. **Recruitment** involves the identification of appropriate candidates for a particular position. For example, a common recruitment strategy used by employers who want to hire new college graduates is participation in career fairs on college campuses. Employers may also use employment agencies, which screen and prequalify potential employees before the interview process. Many employers post their openings on Internet sites such as monster.com as well. In addition, there are Internet sites devoted to specific fields, such as bookjobs.com and mymusicjob.com, where job seekers can learn about employment opportunities in those industries.

Selection is the process of matching applicants to jobs. To facilitate the process, personnel psychologists develop appropriate assessment tools. One of these tools is the employment application itself. Personnel psychologists are often responsible for designing job applications that allow employers to obtain information about a candidate's prior work experience, educational background, and additional skills that are relevant to a position.

In some cases, personnel psychologists use psychological or other tests to aid in the selection process. These tests may measure general ability, a specific aptitude (e.g., mechanical ability), a physical skill (e.g., typing speed), or personality. Personnel psychologists are responsible for ensuring that the tests used by an organization and the procedures used to administer them are reliable and valid. Researchers have found that the validity of personality self-ratings, for example, can be enhanced by asking applicants to use the tests to describe themselves at work rather than in general (Hunthausen et al., 2003).

A new approach to pre-employment testing used by large corporations involves an **assessment center,** a facility devoted to testing job applicants, where work simulations and other comprehensive assessment tools can be used. At assessment centers, tests can be administered to large numbers of job applicants at once. These centers usually offer comfortable settings for comprehensive interviews, in which applicants interact with personnel psychologists, other human resource professionals, and individuals with whom they will work if hired. For example, in the assessment center of one major airline, pilot applicants are assessed by both personnel professionals and senior pilots (Damitz et al., 2003).

Assessment centers usually provide environments in which applicants can be tested in simulated work situations. One such simulation that has been used for more than 30 years is the **in-basket test** (Frederickson, 1962). In this test, applicants for managerial positions are given a stack of memos, reports, and other kinds of papers they might be expected to deal with on the job. They are expected to generate decisions based on the contents of this in-basket in a limited amount of time. Evaluation of an applicant's performance is based on both the quality of his or her decisions and the efficiency with which he or she uses the time allowed.

Because assessment centers incorporate work simulations into the selection process, they may yield more valid evaluations than those based solely on interviews and tests (Arthur et al., 2003). Moreover, when compared to conventional pre-employment procedures, assessment center evaluations better predict applicants'

▲ Many companies participate in career fairs at colleges and universities. Students who attend these events can learn about job opportunities that may be available to them after graduation and perhaps practice their interviewing skills.

job description An outline of the responsibilities associated with a given job category; the end result of a job analysis.

recruitment The identification of appropriate candidates for a particular position.

selection The process of matching applicants to jobs.

assessment center A facility devoted to testing job applicants using work simulations and other comprehensive assessment tools.

in-basket test A work simulation test in which applicants for managerial positions are given a stack of memos, reports, and other kinds of papers and expected to generate decisions based on their contents in a limited amount of time.

subsequent job performance. However, these centers are expensive to set up and maintain. Thus, organizations need to balance the cost of an assessment center against any gains it may offer in the selection process (Harel et al., 2003).

Interviews. Another important function of personnel psychologists is to design **structured interviews,** which consist of standardized interview questions and procedures that are used with all applicants for a position. Structured interviews are most useful when they are based on a sound job analysis, include questions that ask about specific job-related skills and experience, and involve more than one interviewer. Standardized questions help employers compare applicants fairly, by reviewing how they responded to the same questions. Once an interview has been completed, multiple interviewers can discuss points of agreement and disagreement about an applicant's responses.

Employee Training and Development

Many organizations provide formal training programs designed by personnel psychologists for their employees. One way of teaching job skills is through **on-the-job training,** an approach in which workers receive instruction while actually performing the job. A variation on on-the-job training is the **apprenticeship,** in which a novice employee is teamed with a more experienced one. Typically, the more experienced employee guides the novice toward gradual assumption of full responsibility for the work involved. In another approach, **off-the-job training,** employees watch videos or demonstrations and are expected to implement what they learn when back on the job.

Management training often involves **job rotation.** In this kind of training, employees spend relatively short periods of time performing the various jobs in an organization. A restaurant management trainee, for example, might spend a few weeks learning how to clear tables and wash dishes, then move on to working as a food server. Next, he might learn kitchen operations by working as a food preparer. From there, he might move on to beverage management, then to accounting procedures. The idea is that, when the job rotation process is finished, the potential manager will know how to perform every job in the restaurant.

Whatever the approach used, studies show that employees who are provided with training beyond that which is necessary to learn minimal job functions are more satisfied with their jobs and less likely to be absent than are employees who receive only minimal training (Landstad et al., 2001). Training in human relations can be especially helpful. Thus, a growing number of organizations are providing employees, especially those who will be placed in supervisory positions, with formal training in **conflict resolution,** a process of evaluating a conflict and identifying a strategy for resolving it (Lawrence et al., 2002). The following strategies are typical of those offered in conflict resolution training programs:

- *Avoidance.* Manager remains neutral and delegates responsibility for conflict resolution to the parties in conflict.
- *Accommodation.* Manager urges conflicting parties to minimize differences and highlight similarities.
- *Compromise.* Manager sees to it that all parties give up something of value to the other parties involved.
- *Authoritative command.* Manager asserts authority and reminds parties in conflict of their subordinate status.
- *Collaboration.* Manager and conflicting parties work together to gather information relevant to the conflict and to find a solution that is beneficial to everyone.

Complete the following *Try It* to get an idea of how these strategies can be applied to different kinds of workplace conflicts. (By the way, these conflict resolution strategies can also be applied effectively in relationships and settings outside the workplace.)

17.2 How do organizations train employees in job-related and interpersonal skills?

structured interviews
Standardized interview questions and procedures that are used with all applicants for a position.

on-the-job training An approach to training in which employees receive instruction while actually performing the job.

apprenticeship An approach to training in which a novice employee is teamed with a more experienced one.

off-the-job training An approach to training in which employees watch videos or demonstrations and are expected to implement what they learn when on the job.

job rotation An approach to training in which employees spend relatively short periods of time performing the various jobs in an organization.

conflict resolution A process in which a conflict is evaluated and an appropriate strategy for resolving it is identified.

How might a manager or supervisor implement the suggested conflict resolution strategy for each situation?

1. *Avoidance:* Two workers in a manufacturing facility disagree about where a trash can should be placed.

2. *Accommodation:* A new employee irritates co-workers by criticizing their actions and routines with the comment, "That's not the way we did it where I worked before."

3. *Compromise:* Cashiers in a busy retail store can't agree on which one of them should get to go on break first.

4. *Authoritative command:* An office employee is distressed because he is often asked to cover for a co-worker who is habitually tardy.

5. *Collaboration:* Teachers disagree about how to discipline disruptive students.

Evaluating Workers

17.3 What are some approaches used to evaluate workers?

Most organizations use a formal process to determine how well each employee is functioning in his or her job. This process is known as **performance appraisal.** In some cases, identifying an appropriate evaluation strategy is fairly straightforward. For example, an individual who is hired to sew shirts might be expected to produce a given number of shirts each day. If he produces fewer, he is judged as performing below expectations. If his production rate exceeds the target, he is judged as performing above expectations.

However, most jobs include performance expectations that are far less tangible than the number of shirts produced per day. To ensure that employee evaluations are as objective as possible, many organizations use **behavioral observation scales.** These instruments require respondents—the employee, co-workers, and/or the supervisor—to rate an employee's performance on observable behaviors. For instance, a supervisor might rate an employee on participation in meetings, which might be broken down into the behaviors of regular attendance and constructive responses.

Another approach to evaluation is known as **management by objectives (MBO).** With this strategy, subordinates and supervisors set performance goals together. In addition, they agree on how goal attainment will be measured and how much time will be allowed to reach each goal. Periodically, progress toward the goals is assessed. Employees' raises, bonuses, and promotions are often tied to this progress.

A relatively new evaluation strategy is **360-degree evaluation,** which combines worker performance ratings from supervisors, co-workers, subordinates, customers, and the workers themselves. Many people regard this approach as fairer and more meaningful than evaluations conducted exclusively by supervisors. However, research suggests that 360-degree evaluations have limited reliability and validity (Brett & Atwater, 2001; Hoffman et al., 2001; LeBreton et al., 2003). These limitations are largely due to discrepancies among ratings from various sources (Valle & Bozeman, 2002); self-ratings and supervisor ratings, for example, often vary considerably.

Whom do you think is a better evaluator of a worker's performance—the worker or the supervisor? In one study that addressed this question, researchers collected job performance ratings from workers and from their supervisors, co-workers in similar positions, and subordinates (Atkins & Wood, 2002). These ratings were used to predict how well the workers would perform in a work-simulation test. They found that the most accurate predictions came from supervisors and subordinates. Workers tended to overestimate their own abilities and those of their co-workers. In fact, some of the poorest performers on the work-simulation test received the highest self- and peer-rating scores.

performance appraisal A formal process used to determine how well an employee is functioning in his or her job.

behavioral observation scales Instruments for employee evaluation that require respondents to rate an employee's performance on observable behaviors.

management by objectives (MBO) An evaluation approach in which subordinates and supervisors set performance goals together and agree on how goal attainment will be measured and how much time will be allotted to reach each goal.

▶ In many workplaces, new employees learn job skills from co-workers who have more experience.

Nevertheless, some studies show that employees are better able to identify their strengths and weaknesses after receiving feedback on their work performance from several different sources (B. Green, 2002). Moreover, participating in 360-degree evaluations fosters positive attitudes among workers (Maurer et al., 2002). Thus, many experts argue that, despite its limitations, 360-degree evaluation can be useful for performance appraisal.

360-degree evaluation An evaluation strategy that combines worker performance ratings from supervisors, peers, subordinates, customers, and the workers themselves.

Remember It   Personnel Psychology

1. When employers set up booths at college career fairs, they are engaging in the process of _____.

2. The process of _____ often involves the use of psychological tests and structured interviews.

3. Match each of the following approaches to training with the appropriate description.

   _____ (1) off-the-job training   a. Employees receive instruction while actually performing the job.
   _____ (2) apprenticeship   b. A novice employee is teamed with a more experienced one.
   _____ (3) on-the-job training   c. Employees watch videos or demonstrations and implement what they learn afterward.

4. An evaluation technique in which workers receive feedback from multiple sources is known as the _____.

Answers: 1. recruitment; 2. selection; 3. (1) c, (2) b, (3) a; 4. 360-degree evaluation

---

Organizational Psychology

Experts define <mark>organizational psychology</mark> as the study of individuals and groups in formal organizations. We'll begin our discussion of organizational psychology with a brief look at the kinds of strategies managers use to get subordinates to do their work efficiently and effectively.

organizational psychology The study of individuals and groups in formal organizations.

scientific management An approach to management that assumes that workers and their supervisors operate more effectively and efficiently when job requirements are based on empirical data.

Approaches to Management

If you were hired as a manager in an organization, one of your key responsibilities would almost certainly be to ensure that your subordinates were doing their work. Determining the best way to get employees to complete their assigned tasks is the subject of a great deal of debate among I/O psychologists.

The assumption underlying <mark>scientific management,</mark> an approach developed by psychologist Frederick Taylor, is that workers and their supervisors work best when job requirements are based on empirical data. In the early 20th century, Taylor conducted <mark>time-motion studies,</mark> in which he examined the exact physical motions that were required to perform a given manufacturing function in the least amount of time. Once Taylor had completed a time-motion study of a particular task, he trained all workers who performed that task to do it in exactly the same way. Employers found that Taylor's approach resulted in significant gains in productivity among factory workers.

Today, scientific management is often referred to as **Theory X** (McGregor, 1960). This type of approach to management focuses on *work efficiency*, that is, on how well an employee performs specific job tasks. Critics of the Theory X approach claim that it ignores *psychological efficiency*, or the degree to which a job has a positive psychological impact on an employee. A theory of management that emphasizes psychological efficiency is often called <mark>Theory Y.</mark>

One frequent goal of Theory Y managers is <mark>job simplification,</mark> the process of standardizing the tasks associated with a particular job. For example, if you go to the kitchen area of a fast-food restaurant, you will probably see large posters showing exactly how

17.4 What is the difference between Theory X and Theory Y management approaches?

time-motion studies Research examining the exact physical motions required to perform a given manufacturing function in the least amount of time.

Theory X An approach to management that focuses on work efficiency, or how well an employee performs specific job tasks.

Theory Y An approach to management that emphasizes psychological efficiency, or the degree to which a job has a positive psychological impact on an employee.

job simplification The process of standardizing the tasks associated with a particular job.

▲ Quality circles often involve members from many departments who meet together regularly to devise ways of improving the quality of the organization's products or services.

job enrichment The process of changing a job so that it will be more intrinsically motivating.

participative management A management technique in which managers involve subordinates in the decision-making process.

self-managed teams A group of workers who have complete responsibility for planning, executing, and evaluating their work.

quality circle A group of employees who meet regularly to search for ways to increase a company's productivity, improve the quality of its products, or reduce its costs.

leadership The ability to get individuals or groups to do what the leader wants done.

charismatic leaders Leaders who rely on the sheer force of their personalities.

various food items are to be assembled. Advocates of this kind of job simplification claim that workers experience less job-related stress because of the clarity provided by the posters.

To lessen workers' boredom, managers may use another Theory Y strategy. **Job enrichment** is the process of changing a job so that it will be more intrinsically motivating, often by adding responsibilities that are normally assigned only to managers. For example, employees may be asked to evaluate the tasks they perform and to make suggestions as to how they could be done more efficiently. Job enrichment may also involve allowing employees greater freedom in determining how and when their work is performed. This flexibility results in higher levels of job satisfaction among workers (Culpan & Wright, 2002; Niehoff et al., 2001).

Another Theory Y strategy is **participative management,** in which managers involve subordinates in the decision-making process. A related technique is the organization of workers into **self-managed teams,** which have complete responsibility for planning, carrying out, and evaluating their work. All workers on a team are on the same level and are collectively accountable for achieving, or failing to achieve, specified goals. Organizing workers into self-managed teams can increase productivity (Glassop, 2002). However, research indicates that productivity increases are most likely under the following circumstances:

- Supervisors must allow the teams to manage themselves and resist the temptation to "micromanage" (Douglas, 2002).
- Team members must be committed to continuous learning and improvement (Bunderson & Sutcliffe, 2003; Druskat & Pescosolido, 2002).
- Team members must respect one another and share responsibility for leadership (Pearce & Sims, 2002).

Similar to a self-managed team is a **quality circle,** a group of employees who meet regularly to search for ways to increase a company's productivity, improve the quality of its products, or reduce its costs. Members may represent various departments in an organization or may be from the same department. Typically, quality circles are led by individuals who have received special training in team building and leadership. However, such leaders are not "supervisors" in the traditional sense of the term. Instead, they serve as facilitators, whose goal is to maximize participation by all members of the quality circle.

Leadership

17.5 What are several types of effective leaders, and how do psychologists explain effective leadership?

Every organization has managers, but managers are not always effective leaders. **Leadership** is defined as the ability to get individuals or groups to do what a leader wants done. What makes a good leader? To answer this question, psychologists have devised numerous classification systems identifying different kinds of leaders. The three types of leaders that we will discuss here are charismatic leaders, transactional leaders, and transformational leaders.

Charismatic Leaders. Charismatic leaders lead by the sheer force of their personalities. In many cases, charismatic leaders have a great need for power and extraordinary confidence in their ability to lead. They usually also believe passionately in the superiority of their goals over those of others and will pursue their goals even if it involves personal self-sacrifice (De Cremer, 2002). Charismatic leaders are typically highly persuasive and lead by convincing followers to share their passionate commitment to their goals. Cult leaders, as well as many of the darker figures in human history such as Adolf Hitler, are often of this type. But other charismatic leaders such as Martin Luther King, Jr., and Robert F. Kennedy have been positive forces. Moreover, leadership experts classify Franklin D. Roosevelt and Ronald Reagan, two U.S. presidents with very different political philosophies, as charismatic leaders (Deluga, 1998).

Transactional and Transformational Leadership. Much of the current research on leadership focuses on differences between transactional and transformational leaders. Transactional leaders focus on motivating followers to accomplish routine, agreed-on goals. In the workplace, transactional leaders are managers who think of job performance as a transaction in which workers receive wages in return for doing what is expected of them. As such, transactional leadership tends to maintain the organizational status quo, because it does not encourage either employees or leaders to do anything beyond what is explicitly required. Workers do their work, and leaders sign their paychecks.

By contrast, **transformational leaders** encourage followers to achieve excellence in the accomplishment of routine goals. They also motivate them to pursue goals that go beyond the status quo. Generally, good organizational leaders are able to combine transactional and transformational leadership to effectively manage an organization or a team (Al-Dmour & Al-Awamleh, 2002; Bass et al., 2003; Dvir et al., 2002; Kark et al., 2003).

The notion of transformational leadership has been most fully developed by organizational psychology researcher Bernard Bass. In general, Bass (1998) asserts that transformational leadership has four dimensions: The first dimension is *charisma*. The transformational leader's personality attracts followers and gives them a sense of pride in being part of the leader's organization. A good example of a transformational leader with charisma is Herb Kelleher, the founder of Southwest Airlines. Kelleher came on the airline scene in the 1970s with the idea that air travel should be as common as travel by city bus. Thus, it had to be inexpensive and reliable. Employees of the fledgling airline were won over by his confidence in the workability of his dream and believed themselves to be participants in an industry revolution. Southwest Airlines became and continues to be one of the most successful companies in its industry.

The second dimension of transformational leadership is *inspiration*, which involves the use of symbols to make organizational goals clear. For example, in 2001, United Parcel Service (UPS) began sponsoring a race car on the NASCAR circuit. In conjunction with their sponsorhip of the car, they launched a series of award-winning television commercials in which their familiar brown trucks were shown competing in NASCAR races. Linking the company's symbol, its trucks, with the concept of a race symbolized the company's goal: to deliver customers' packages as rapidly as possible.

The third dimension of transformational leadership is *intellectual stimulation,* which focuses on rational problem solving. Followers are encouraged to base decisions on data and logic rather than on emotion. For example, suppose two professors in a psychology department want to teach a course in I/O psychology, but there are only enough interested students to fill one section each semester. The logical solution, suggested by a transformational leader, would be that the professors teach the course in alternate semesters.

Finally, transformational leaders treat each follower as an individual, a leadership dimension called *individualized consideration*. They believe that the group or organization is best served by encouraging individual expression and personal growth. Business leaders exhibit individual consideration when they devise compensation schemes that allow all employees to share in a company's profits, based on their individual efforts.

This *Review and Reflect* summarizes the three types of leaders we've discussed.

▲ Charismatic leaders can motivate people to make significant changes. One such leader, Martin Luther King, Jr. (1927–1968), is often credited with being the driving force—through his personality, character, commitment, and example—behind the civil rights movement of the 1950s and 1960s in the United States.

transactional leaders Leaders who focus on motivating followers to accomplish routine, agreed-on goals.

transformational leaders
Leaders who encourage followers to achieve excellence in the accomplishment of routine goals and to pursue goals that go beyond the status quo.

Review and Reflect   Three Types of Leaders

Type	Characteristic
Charismatic	Lead by sheer force of personality
Transactional	Motivate followers to accomplish agreed-on goals
Transformational	Encourage followers to go beyond the status quo

▲ Many critics of President George W. Bush noted that he exhibited effective leadership behavior after the terrorist attacks of September 11, 2001. However, his leadership abilities were sharply criticized in the context of the government's poor response to the aftermath of Hurricane Katrina in 2005. The situational theory of leadership would explain this difference as the result of the perceived "fit" between President Bush's behavioral characteristics and the varying leadership demands of the two situations.

Explaining Differences in Leaders' Effectiveness. What makes leaders effective? One possible explanation, the **trait approach,** is that leaders possess intrinsic characteristics that help them influence others. In other words, the trait approach holds that some people are natural-born leaders. Cross-cultural studies showing that leaders in different societies demonstrate similar characteristics, such as problem-solving ability, support this view (Robie et al., 2001).

A different view of leadership is proposed by the **situational approach.** From this perspective, the effectiveness of a leader depends on the match between the leader's characteristics and the situations in which she or he is called upon to lead. For example, leadership researchers believe that the way in which U.S. President Franklin D. Roosevelt responded to the historical challenges that arose during his terms of office (the Great Depression and World War II) continues to shape positive perceptions of his leadership abilities. Similarly, prior to the terrorist attacks of September 11, 2001, many observers were critical of President George W. Bush's bluntness and rather direct way of expressing ideas. However, after the attacks, even his harshest critics acknowledged that these characteristics were assets that helped him build political support for changes in a variety of government policies. By contrast, these same characteristics were viewed negatively when President Bush exhibited them during the aftermath of Hurricane Katrina in 2005. Critics viewed him as lacking compassion for the storm's victims and as unwilling to accept responsibility for the shortcomings in the federal government's response to the disaster.

But can leadership be taught? The **behavioral approach** to explaining leadership effectiveness holds that it can be taught and is, in fact, the result of specific behaviors exhibited by leaders. Many researchers classify leadership behaviors under two broad categories: consideration and initiating structure. *Consideration* includes behaviors that communicate the leader's interest in followers as individuals. By contrast, *initiating structure* encompasses behaviors that focus on a task and the means employed to accomplish it. To be most effective, a leader must know when and how to demonstrate both kinds of behaviors (Schermerhorn et al., 2000).

Effective leadership behaviors can be acquired through formal training (Tjosvold et al., 2003). However, some studies show that personality traits determine how well leaders do at learning both consideration and initiating structure behaviors (Wang & Chen, 2002). Thus, training can help, but pre-existing characteristics appear to impose some limits on who can or cannot become an effective leader via formal training.

A recent variation on the behavioral approach to leadership is **leader-member exchange (LMX) theory,** which is based on the assumption that leaders and followers exert mutual influences on one another. Furthermore, LMX theory takes into account the emotional aspects of leader-follower relationships (Dasborough & Ashkanasy, 2002). According to advocates of LMX theory, leaders act differently toward individuals to whom they are closest (their in-group) than toward individuals with whom they do not have close relationships (their out-group).

But are leaders' exchanges with in-groups and out-groups really all that different? Research shows that leaders tend to assign more interesting tasks to in-group members. Moreover, in-group members often have more influence on a leader's decisions than do out-group members. Conversations between leaders and in-group members often include more personal statements than do conversations between leaders and out-group members. Further, as you may know from your own work experience, out-group members often resent in-group members and may even quit their jobs to escape unpleasant feelings of exclusion. Not surprisingly, in-group members experience higher levels of job satisfaction and get more raises and promotions than out-group members do.

trait approach A perspective on leadership that holds that leaders possess intrinsic characteristics that help them influence others.

situational approach A perspective that explains the effectiveness of leadership as depending on the match between a leader's characteristics and the situations in which she or he is called upon to lead.

behavioral approach A perspective that holds that leadership effectiveness can be taught and is the result of specific behaviors exhibited by leaders.

leader-member exchange (LMX) theory A behavioral perspective on leadership that assumes that leaders and followers exert mutual influences on one another and takes into account the emotional aspects of leader-follower relationships.

Organizational Culture and Climate

The term *culture* usually applies to a country or an ethnic group. An **organizational culture** is defined as a system of shared values, beliefs, and practices that evolves within an organization and influences the behavior of its members.

Surveys show that managers and their subordinates often think of organizational culture as involving purely physical aspects, such as who reports to whom and the physical layout of the workplace (Lurie & Riccucci, 2003). These are certainly elements of organizational culture. However, researchers point out that organizational culture has many of the same, sometimes hidden, elements that are found in larger cultures. For instance, *stories* are part of an organizational culture. These are stories about the founding and development of the organization as well as about how individuals in the organization attained their positions.

Researchers also say that, just as individuals are *socialized* into their respective cultures as children, new employees experience a parallel process of integration into an organizational culture. Familiarizing new employees with the stories of the organizational culture is an important part of a socialization process that occurs both formally and informally. When you start a new job, for example, you may receive a booklet or view a video detailing the company's history. Obviously, this is a kind of formal socialization. If a fellow employee takes you aside to give you the inside scoop on how others in the organization got to their current positions, you are experiencing informal socialization.

Organizational cultures also have both formal and informal *rites*, recurring events that carry specific meanings. For example, many organizations have annual ceremonies in which employees are recognized for their length of service or outstanding achievements. Formal recognition of this kind is associated with positive attitudes among employees (Markham et al., 2002). Less formal rites may characterize subgroups within an organization. For instance, a subgroup may have a habit of going to a particular restaurant for lunch every Friday. If a member of the subgroup invites a new employee to attend, the new employee may become part of that subgroup.

In addition to stories and rights, organizational cultures also have *symbols*, objects that transmit meaning to both insiders and outsiders. For instance, the distinctive vehicles of the U.S. Postal Service communicate to outsiders that the drivers are associated with the service. Moreover, the vehicles have significance for postal service employees because a letter carrier must complete training before being authorized to drive one and is then set apart from co-workers.

Finally, an organization's culture is often characterized by a management philosophy that employees believe sets the organization apart from others. *A management philosophy* is a broad statement of an organization's goals and the means that are used to attain them. For example, a retail electronics store may have a management philosophy that goes something like this: "We're going to be the best electronics store in town by putting customer service ahead of profits." This statement may be implemented in a policy of matching any other store's advertised price for an item the store sells. Employees' sense of belonging to an organization may be enhanced when they carry out such philosophically inspired policies.

The various components of an organization's culture work together to shape its organizational climate. **Organizational climate** refers to how employees perceive and respond emotionally to the culture of an organization. An emotionally positive organizational climate is associated with low employee turnover and high employee commitment to the organization's goals. One factor associated with organizational climate is the degree to which employees believe that the procedures used to evaluate them and to resolve their conflicts are fair (Brockner et al., 2003; De Cremer & van Knippenberg, 2003; Simons & Roberson, 2003). Another such factor is the confidence employees have in their managers' abilities (Goris et al., 2003). As you can probably guess, organizational climate influences workers' **job satisfaction,** the degree to which they feel positively about their jobs. (You will learn more about job satisfaction in the *Apply It* section at the end of this chapter.)

17.6 What is the relationship between organizational culture and organizational climate?

organizational culture   The system of shared values, beliefs, and practices that evolves within an organization and influences the behavior of its members.

organizational climate   Employees' perceptions and emotional responses to the culture of an organization.

job satisfaction   The degree to which an individual feels positively about his or her job.

Ethics in the Workplace

17.7 What are some key perspectives on workplace ethics?

Have you ever taken a pen or a notepad home from your workplace? Have you ever used your employer's telephone to make personal long distance calls? It might surprise you to learn that such actions by employees, though they may seem inconsequential, cost U.S. employers millions of dollars each year. For this reason, a growing number of organizations are promoting the concept of *workplace ethics*. But, as you'll see, ethical rules can be applied to the behavior of organizations as well to that of their employees.

Workplace ethics does not imply any single set of rules. Instead, there are guidelines that apply to different behaviors and issues. For example, with regard to individual behavior, the **moral-rights perspective** suggests that individuals within an organization should be guided by the same respect for basic rights endorsed by the larger culture. For example, most people agree that stealing is wrong. Further, you wouldn't take a pencil from your neighbor or use her car without permission, because you respect her property rights. Thus, say advocates of this perspective, you shouldn't do so at work either.

However, organizations often face decisions that are far more ethically complex. For example, how does a corporation decide whether to close an unprofitable manufacturing plant? What carries greater weight—the impact on workers if the plant is closed, or the impact on shareholders and workers in other locations if an unprofitable plant continues to operate? One approach to such dilemmas, called the **utilitarian perspective,** defines ethical behavior in terms of the greatest good for the greatest number of people. If a plant's closing will harm several hundred workers but will benefit thousands of shareholders and employees in other locations, the utilitarian approach says that it is ethical to close the plant and unethical to keep it open.

But, obviously, there is more to such decisions than just numbers. Consequently, the utilitarian perspective is often tempered by a sense of **organizational social responsibility,** a perspective based on the idea that an organization's policies should take into consideration the interests of the larger society of which it is a part. Thus, from this perspective, laying off several hundred workers provides a financial benefit to an organization, but it will also place a burden on taxpayers who will have to provide assistance to the displaced employees. When layoffs are unavoidable, however, socially responsible organizations try to minimize their impact both on the individuals involved and on society. For example, a company might provide job training, severance pay, and placement services for laid-off employees.

moral-rights perspective An approach to organizational ethics that suggests that individual behavior within an organization should be guided by the same respect for basic rights that is endorsed by the larger culture.

utilitarian perspective An approach to organizational ethics that defines ethical behavior in terms of the greatest good for the greatest number of people.

organizational social responsibility A perspective based on the idea that an organization's policies should take into consideration the interests of the larger society of which it is a part.

Remember It | Organizational Psychology

1. Worker satisfaction is more important in the _____ management approach than in the _____ management approach.

2. Barbara says that her boss is a great leader because he is so intelligent. Her assessment of her boss is consistent with the _____ approach to leadership effectiveness.

3. The degree to which employees perceive their company as fair to employees is a component of _____.

4. Proponents of _____ suggest that businesses should take into consideration the interests of the larger society.

Answers: 1. Theory Y, Theory X; 2. trait; 3. organizational climate; 4. organizational social responsibility

Human Factors Psychology

When the Iraq War began in 2003, soldiers who were on the front lines were often required to wear masks that protected them against chemical and biological weapons. Can you imagine what it would be like to carry out normal activities such as talking and eating while wearing one of these masks? Such questions are the primary concern of **human factors psychology,** often called **ergonomics.** One of the most important functions of human factors psychologists is to study and enhance the ways in which workers interact with the physical and social characteristics of a workplace.

▲ Human factors psychologists investigate how the physical aspects of work environments influence job performance. For instance, some have studied how well soldiers can function both with regard to their duties and to ordinary activities such as talking and eating while wearing protective gear (Krueger & Banderet, 1997). Their work has led to better designs for such equipment.

Workplace Design

Open Designs. Many workplaces today are arranged according to what human factors psychologists call an *open design*. In an open design, a large number of workers are placed in a very large space. Sometimes, there are partitions or other kinds of barriers between workers. Such designs allow organizations to use large spaces flexibly by rearranging individual workspaces as needed. Further, open designs are less expensive to construct because they have few walls and doors.

17.8 What are key aspects of workplace design?

However, many workers do not like open designs. For one thing, these workplaces are noisier than those with individual workspaces, and workers sometimes complain about interruptions and lack of privacy (Ettorre, 1995). Moreover, a private office is perceived as a status symbol, so employees in management positions expect to have rooms with doors. They argue that they need privacy to meet with their subordinates and to discuss decisions with their peers and superiors. Consequently, most open designs include at least a few private spaces, usually managers' offices and conference rooms.

▲ Cubicles and other features of an organization's physical layout are often designed by human factors psychologists. Using cubicles to define workers' spaces in large, open offices can add flexibility and save on construction costs. However, some workers complain about noise and a lack of privacy.

The Workspace Envelope. **Workspace envelope** refers to the three-dimensional space in which an individual worker performs the tasks that comprise his or her job. Some workspace envelopes are more comfortable than others. What makes the difference?

One factor to consider in the design of a workspace envelope is physical size. One of the most important contributions of human factors psychologists to workplace comfort is adjustable furniture. In many of today's workplaces, chairs, desks, and other features of the workspace envelope can be adjusted to fit about 95% of the population, men and women ranging from about 63 to 74 inches in height.

Many of the workspace envelope innovations introduced by human factors psychologists in recent years address aspects of computer use. Poor computer workstation designs are responsible for a growing number of workplace injuries such as chronic neck, shoulder, and wrist pain, as well as eyestrain and frequent headaches (Sarkis, 2000). As a result, some general guidelines for setting up a computer workstation have

human factors psychology The subfield of industrial/organizational psychology that deals with the ways in which workers interact with the characteristics of a workplace.

ergonomics Human factors psychology.

workspace envelope The three-dimensional space in which an individual worker performs the tasks that comprise his or her job.

▲ Artifactual communication is the process of using human-made objects to send messages to others. What kind of message does this woman's office convey?

been developed. For example, human factors experts suggest placing the monitor directly behind the keyboard. However, some studies suggest that allowing each worker to adjust the placement of all the physical elements of her or his workstation to suit personal preferences is a better way of reducing computer-use injuries (Krumm, 2001). Moreover, programming employees' computers with software that reminds them to take breaks and to practice exercises that reduce muscle fatigue and eyestrain can be an effective means of reducing such injuries (Krasowska, 1996).

Artifactual Communication. One important aspect of workplace design is **artifactual communication,** which is the use of objects to communicate nonverbal messages. (*Artifactual* means "made by human hands.") The location of an individual's office and its architectural and decorative features are one source of such messages. For example, large offices with windows are usually reserved for employees who hold managerial positions.

The size and architectural features of an office are part of its formal design and reflect an individual's relationship to the organization. However, the arrangement and condition of an individual's workspace can send messages as well. For instance, furniture placement and wall decorations can convey a feeling of welcome or coldness: "Come in; sit down and relax" or "Stand there and be intimidated; I'm too important to spend time with you." An office in which there are piles of paper everywhere, office supplies are strewn about, and the trash can is overflowing with soda cans and styrofoam cups may say, "I have more work to do than I can handle." By contrast, one in which papers are arranged in an organized way, office supplies are neatly stored in compartments or drawers, and there is little or no trash may say, "I'm in control."

The Quality of Work-Life Movement

17.9 What are some of the innovations associated with the quality of work life movement?

As you learned in Chapter 12, jobs can be highly stressful, especially when work and non-work roles are in conflict. For example, middle-aged adults sometimes find themselves in what some observers have termed a *generational sandwich* in which they are responsible for the care of both teenaged children and aging parents. The demands of the "sandwich" sometimes are in conflict with those of middle-aged adults' jobs, and workers find themselves constantly trying to figure out how they can be in more than one place at a time. Likewise, new parents experience such conflicts when they have to balance their desires to return to work with their concerns about nonparental care for their newborns. Interactions among work and non-work roles are at the core of **work-life balance,** one of the major emphases in contemporary human factors psychology.

Research has shown that work-life balance issues affect not only workers' mental and physical health, but also their job performance (Thompson, Brough, & Schmidt, 2006). Moreover, workers are more satisfied with their jobs when they believe that their supervisors share their views on work-life balance. Thus, many organizations today are searching for ways to help employees meet their work-life balance goals.

In order to address the work-life balance needs of today's employees, human factors psychologists have developed the **quality of work-life (QWL) movement.** Advocates of the QWL movement emphasize job and workplace designs based on analyses of the quality of employees' experiences in an organization. The idea is that when people are happier at work, they will be more productive. For example, the on-site child-care center is one innovation that has come about because of concern for the quality of work life. Even though providing on-site child-care can be expensive, QWL advocates argue that it will pay for itself in terms of reduced absences and lower stress levels among employees who are parents.

artifactual communication The use of objects to communicate nonverbal messages.

work-life balance The interactive influences among employees' work and non-work roles.

quality of work-life (QWL) movement An approach to reducing work-related stress by basing job and workplace design on analyses of the quality of employee experiences in an organization.

Another QWL innovation is **telecommuting.** Telecommuters work in their homes and are connected to their workplaces by computer, fax machine, and telephone. Some telecommuters work at home every day; others do so only one or two days each week. Allowing workers to telecommute accomplishes several organizational goals. For example, telecommuting reduces the number of workers who drive to work, thereby reducing pollution and the number of parking spaces the organization must provide. Further, telecommuting gives workers a great deal of flexibility and autonomy. They can choose whether to prepare written reports, for example, during normal working hours or in the middle of the night. This kind of flexibility can increase job satisfaction (Wilde, 2000). Moreover, telecommuting helps employees balance work and family responsibilities. It can also be helpful to employees with disabilities that make it difficult for them to get around. Government statistics in the United States show that 17% of employees now work at home (U.S. Bureau of Labor Statistics, 2005).

Two other innovations associated with the QWL movement are flextime and job sharing. *Flextime* involves allowing employees to create their own work schedules. Most organizations that use flextime have certain times (usually called "core hours") when all employees must be present. At other times, though, employees are free to come and go as long as their work is done and they put in the required number of hours. Many employees take advantage of the flextime option to reduce work-family conflicts (Sharpe et al., 2002). Others use this option to enhance their job performance by coming to the workplace at times when they believe they can be most productive. Further, flextime workers report that they experience less transportation-related stress—that is, they don't worry as much about rush-hour traffic jams and late trains or buses as they would if working a conventional schedule (Lucas & Heady, 2002). Researchers have found that flextime helps to build employee loyalty, thereby reducing turnover (Roehling et al., 2001).

Job sharing is a QWL innovation in which a full-time job is shared by two or more employees. For example, a receptionist's position might be filled by one person on Monday, Wednesday, and Friday and by another on Tuesday and Thursday. In fact, it's theoretically possible that the job could be filled by a different individual each day of the week. Employers have found job sharing to be a particularly effective way to help employees gradually return to full-time work after a leave of absence for reasons such as illness or pregnancy (Krumm, 2001).

As part of an effort to educate employers about the benefits associated with QWL policies and practices, the American Psychological Association (APA) has initiated a program in which organizations can apply to be considered for a Psychologically Healthy Workplace Award (APA, 2006). Honorees have included Versant (Wisconsin), ARUP Laboratories (Utah), The Comporium Group (South Carolina), IBM's T. J. Watson Research Laboratory (New York), Great River Health Systems (Iowa), and Green Chimneys School (New York). Applicants are assessed according to five sets of criteria:

- *Employee involvement:* worker participation in decision-making, self-managed work teams
- *Health and safety:* adequate health insurance, access to fitness centers and mental health services, training in workplace safety, promotion of healthy lifestyle choices
- *Employee growth and development:* opportunities for advancement, tuition reimbursement, skills enhancement training
- *Work-life balance:* flexible work schedules, assistance with child and elder care, family leave benefits
- *Employee recognition:* fair compensation, awards ceremonies, performance-based pay increases, and bonuses

▲ Assistance with child care is one of many quality of work-life (QWL) policies that have been implemented by some organizations in recent years.

telecommuting An arrangement in which employees work in their homes and are connected to their workplaces by computer, fax machine, and telephone.

Gender Issues at Work

One of the most profound changes in employment patterns has been the tremendous increase in the number of women in the workplace. By the end of the 20th century, women made up 47% of the civilian labor force in the United States (U.S. Census Bureau, 2001). However, there are important differences in the working lives of men and women.

Women's Work Patterns

17.10 In what ways do women's work patterns differ from those of men?

One consequence of the expansion of career opportunities for women has been the increasing representation of mothers in the workforce. In 1975, only 34% of women with children under the age of 3 were employed. By 2004, the proportion had increased to 57% (U.S. Bureau of Labor Statistics, 2005). Although there was a slight decline in the percentage of mothers who worked outside the home in the early years of the 21st century, more than 70% of mothers of children under age 18 are employed at least part-time. Thus, the experience of juggling family and work responsibilities is one aspect of work-life balance that is shared by the vast majority of women in the industrialized world.

One outcome of the increased participation of mothers in the work force has been that, in general, women's work patterns are less likely than those of men to be continuous. Most women move in and out of the workforce at least once, usually to spend time rearing children (Drobnic et al., 1999; Hofferth Curtin 2006).

Prior to actually having children, many women tell researchers that they intend to return to full-time work shortly after the birth of their first child. However, longitudinal research shows that many women change their plans after giving birth. In one study, researchers found that only 44% of female professionals followed through on their pre-pregnancy intention to return to full-time work shortly after giving birth (Abele, 2005). By contrast, very few of the male professionals that these researchers followed over the same period made any kind of change to their working conditions after becoming fathers.

Such findings often lead researchers to conclude that work-family conflict more strongly influences women's career decisions than those of men. Research showing that women are both more concerned about and more adept at integrating work and family roles than men are provides support for this view (Hoff et al., 2005; Wharton & Blair-Loy, 2006). However, some researchers point out that it may be more useful to think of work-family conflict as qualitatively different for mothers and fathers rather than important to one but not the other (McElwain, Korabik, & Rosin, 2005). Because of the traditional division of labor, they say, most of women's concerns about work-family conflicts involve situations in which family demands override those of work. For instance, a woman may worry that her decision to take time off from work for teacher-parent conferences will reduce her chances of advancing to a higher position. Among men, the pattern is the opposite; their work-family stress is more likely to involve prioritizing work over family than vice versa. For example, a father may regret that a business trip caused him to miss his daughter's dance recital.

Surveys showing that the division of work and family responsibilities among couples has changed very little in the last 30 years, despite the growing participation of mothers in the work force, support this view as well (Crompton, Brockman, & Lyonnette, 2005). For instance, fathers are seldom thought of as having a choice between working and staying home to rear children (Daly & Palkovitz, 2004). Like their fathers and grandfathers before them, they are expected to provide material support to their families even when their wives are pursuing their own lucrative careers. At the same time, although there is no denying the fact that women have many more life choices today than they did in the past, it is nonetheless true that mothers are the ones whose poor parenting skills or work-family priorities are likely to be blamed when children develop problems such as ADHD or substance abuse (Barnett, 2004; Jackson & Mannix, 2004; Singh, 2004). The prevalence of such views may influence women in the direction of prioritizing family over work. However, it is also important to note that many women willingly adapt their work lives to the demands of raising children simply because that is what they believe is best for their families rather than out of a sense of duty to culturally prescribed roles or the fear that they will be blamed if their children develop problems.

Gender Differences in On-the-Job Coping Styles

Like patterns of employment, patterns of job satisfaction among women are often more complex than those of men (Schieman & Taylor, 2001). This may be because men and women respond differently to work-related stress (Perho & Korhonen, 1999). Both sexes complain about the same stress factors: time pressure, getting along with co-workers, boring tasks, and fear of losing one's job. However, men typically address such problems directly by negotiating with supervisors and co-workers to bring about changes. In Chapter 12, you learned that this approach is known as *problem-focused coping*. By contrast, women tend to use *emotion-focused coping*. So, instead of confronting co-workers and supervisors directly, they often discuss job-related stressors with female co-workers. They may also adopt the kinds of defense mechanisms (e.g., repression) you learned about in Chapter 13.

At first glance, you might judge men's problem-focused coping strategies to be more effective than women's emotion-focused coping strategies. However, research has shown that the emotion-focused coping adopted by many female workers enables them to balance their dissatisfactions against their areas of contentment more effectively than their male co-workers do. For example, the statement "I don't enjoy working with spreadsheets all day long, but the 4-day work week in this company fits my needs" is more likely to come from a woman than a man. Thus, men may be more likely to improve their job satisfaction in situations where change is possible, but women probably cope more effectively when work stressors are difficult or impossible to change (Hattar-Pollara et al., 2003). Moreover, some research indicates that women are better able than men to assess the degree to which their skills and personality traits fit particular jobs, thus avoiding the stress associated with selecting an inappropriate career (Liff & Ward, 2001).

Gender Discrimination

At the beginning of the 21st century, women reportedly held 53% of the more than 20 million professional jobs in the United States. However, the majority of those jobs—such as public school teaching and nursing—pay only moderately well. Women hold only slightly over 28% of the more than 8 million higher-paying professional jobs in the United States. **Figure 17.1** charts the percentages of women who were holding various jobs through the end of the 20th century and shows women's earnings as a percentage of men's earnings for each job (Doyle, 2000).

In the late 1980s, the term **glass ceiling** was introduced into the American vocabulary by management consultant Ann Morrison and her colleagues (Morrison et al., 1987). Their book, *Breaking the Glass Ceiling*, claimed that women had entered the

17.11 How do men's and women's responses to job-related stress differ?

17.12 What evidence is there to suggest that women are breaking the glass ceiling?

glass ceiling An invisible, institutional barrier that prevents women from reaching the highest executive positions in organizations.

Figure 17.1 Representation of Women in Various Jobs and Professions in the United States, 1950–2000

Women steadily increased their representation in all sectors of the U.S. workforce over the last five decades of the 20th century.

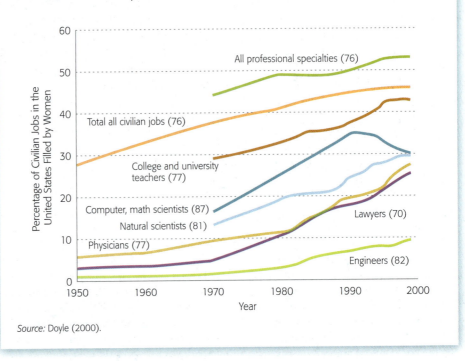

Source: Doyle (2000).

previously male-dominated world of business management but were unable to reach the highest executive positions because of institutional barriers such as sexism and the so-called good-old-boy network. At that time, there were only a handful of women serving as corporate CEOs in the United States.

Since the publication of Morrison's book, women have made many advances. As a result, the proportion of married women who earn more than their husbands increased from 18% in 1987 to 25% in 2003 (U.S. Bureau of Labor Statistics, 2005). Moreover, government statistics show that a higher proportion of women than men, 38% versus 32%, are employed in corporate management positions (U.S. Bureau of Labor Statistics, 2005). Women have also made inroads into the highest levels of leadership in educational institutions and government agencies (Addi-Raccah & Ayalon, 2002; Baker et al., 2002). Moreover, the number of female collegiate athletic directors rose dramatically during the 1990s (Whisenant et al., 2002). More women are found among the authors of studies in psychology today than in the past (McSweeney & Parks, 2002). Further, many women have avoided the glass ceiling by starting their own businesses in every area of the U.S. economy (U.S. Bureau of Labor Statistics, 2005; Weiler & Bernasek, 2001).

Despite these advances, gender stereotypes often taint evaluations of women's job performance (Lyness & Heilman 2006; Penny, 2001). And there are still a number of areas in which women have made few inroads. For example, even though more women now publish articles in psychology journals, women are still poorly represented among journal editors (McSweeney & Parks, 2002). Moreover, studies show that women are less likely than men to actively seek promotions to upper-level management positions because of potential conflicts between their work and family roles (Sarrio et al., 2002; van Vianen & Fischer, 2002). Thus, breaking the glass ceiling may ultimately require changes in attitudes about women's roles both at work and at home.

Sexual Harassment

As female representation in the workforce has increased, discussions about the appropriateness of various forms of sexual expression in the workplace have become more common. Specifically, concerns about sexual harassment have increased. **Sexual harassment** is a very broad term encompassing any kind of unwanted or offensive sexual expression in the workplace. Generally, sexual harassment complaints fall into two categories (Lovoy, 2001): In *quid pro quo* complaints, workers claim to have been offered something in exchange for sexual favors. *Hostile work environment* complaints involve inappropriate behavior of a sexual nature that creates an intolerable level of discomfort for the complainant. **Table 17.1** presents types of sexual harassment that give rise to these complaints.

Often, sexual harassment involves a supervisor and a subordinate, but it can also involve workers at the same level. Furthermore, although the stereotype associated with sexual harassment is that of a male worker harassing a female worker, sexual harassment can be male-to-female, female-to-male, male-to-male, or female-to-female. Further, in today's high-tech workplaces, the incidence of computer-based harassment is increasing dramatically (Cooper et al., 2002). "Cyber-harassers" use an organization's email system to send sexually explicit messages or even pornographic materials to co-workers. They may target individuals or send such items to everyone in the organization's email directory. Cyber-harassers often believe that their actions will be viewed as humorous rather than as harassing.

Research shows that sexual harassment has detrimental effects on employees' job satisfaction and may lead to higher turnover rates, increased absenteeism, and even higher levels of alcohol and drug abuse (Piotrkowski, 1998; Wislar et al., 2002). Sexual harassment is especially distressing when it is accompanied by aggressive or threatening behavior (Kinney, 2003). Most victims of sexual harassment cope with the stresses involved by using a combination of problem- and emotion-focused strategies (Magley, 2002). And, although sexual harassment affects victims in all racial and cultural groups in similar ways, a strong sense of ethnic identity helps minority men and women cope when they are victimized (Bergman & Drasgow, 2003; Shupe et al., 2002).

But what about sexual behaviors that may be regarded by most people as annoying, but don't quite rise to the level of illegality? Such behaviors include physical contact, such as an unsolicited backrub, or remarks of a sexual nature that are made within the context of jokes or small talk. Researchers have found that inappropriate sexual behaviors by co-workers are often cited as a major source of job stress, especially for women (Lyons, 2002). Moreover, women regard the climate of an organization more positively when leaders actively work to prevent inappropriate behavior of this kind and take action to stop it when it does occur (Offerman & Malamut, 2002).

17.13 What are the two categories of sexual harassment complaints?

sexual harassment Any kind of unwanted or offensive sexual expression in the workplace.

Table 17.1 Types of Sexual Harassment

Type	Example
Sexual bribery (quid pro quo)	A supervisor promises a raise to a subordinate in exchange for sexual intercourse.
Sexual coercion (quid pro quo)	A supervisor threatens to fire a subordinate who refuses to have intercourse with him.
Gender harassment (hostile work environment)	A female day-care worker belittles a male co-worker because she believes men are incapable of caring for children.
Seductive behavior (hostile work environment)	An employee sends email messages to a co-worker in which he describes in detail sexual fantasies involving both of them.
Sexual imposition (hostile work environment)	An employee displays pornographic pictures and refuses to remove them when asked to do so by co-workers.

To decrease the likelihood of sexual harassment, many organizations provide supervisors and workers with training in recognizing and combating it. Moreover, in the United States, federal labor laws require employers to take certain actions with regard to sexual harassment (Krumm, 2001). Employers must have written sexual harassment policies and distribute copies of them to employees. These policies must include a formal procedure for filing and reviewing sexual harassment complaints, which must be investigated and resolved in a timely manner.

Remember It   Gender Issues at Work

1. Women's work patterns are less likely than men's to be _____.

2. Men are less likely than women to use _____ coping strategies to address workplace stressors.

3. The _____ is often used to refer to the invisible barrier women face in advancing to top management positions.

4. Jane's boss offers to give her a raise if she will go out on a date with him. Jane might be justified in making a _____ complaint of sexual harassment.

Answers: 1. continuous; 2. emotion-focused; 3. glass ceiling; 4. quid pro quo

---

Human Diversity in the Workplace

In addition to training employees to recognize and combat sexual harassment, many organizations are providing employees with **diversity training** to help them acquire the human relations skills they need to function effectively in a diverse workplace. Before examining the content and effectiveness of diversity training, let's look at some of the factors that underlie diversity in today's society.

Race and Ethnicity in the Workplace

17.14 What is ethnocentrism, and how does it affect the workplace?

Often the terms *race* and *ethnicity* are used interchangeably. Although the distinctions between the two concepts are somewhat fuzzy, social scientists typically use *race* to refer to shared biological characteristics (e.g., skin color) and *ethnicity* to refer to shared social characteristics (e.g., language and customs). Thus, two people might be of the same race, but differ in ethnicity. For example, Germans and Italians are the same race but not the same ethnicity. Similarly, two individuals may share ethnicity but differ in race. In Latin America, for example, many people are descended from African slaves and, thus, have the same racial heritage as African Americans in the United States. But such individuals are ethnically Hispanic because they share the Spanish language and Spanish-based customs with Latin Americans who are of European and Native American descent.

According to most surveys, Americans of all races and ethnicities believe that intergroup relations are better today than at any time in U.S. history (Public Agenda, 2003a). But most say that there is still room for improvement. Researchers and diversity trainers agree that ethnocentrism can be an obstacle to improving race relations (Ensari, 2001; Hansen, 2003). *Ethnocentrism* is the tendency to look at situations from one's own racial or cultural perspective.

Most individuals are surprised to learn how great an influence ethnocentrism has on their everyday thinking and behavior (Danto, 2000). For instance, what do you expect to see when you open a box of "flesh-colored" adhesive bandages? If you are White, you will probably not perceive anything incongruous about the color of the bandages. It usually doesn't occur to most Whites that these common, everyday items

diversity training Formal training aimed at equipping workers with the human relations skills they need to function effectively in a diverse workplace.

are actually not flesh-colored for most of the world's population. Diversity training facilitators use such examples to illustrate how ethnocentrism affects everyday life.

The effects of ethnocentrism run far deeper than simply affecting how we perceive mundane items such as adhesive bandages. For example, ethnocentrism shapes interviewers' ideas about how interviewees should respond to questions, the meaning of their body language, and the appropriateness of interviewees' clothing. As a result, interviewers who get hgh scores on tests of ethnocentrism are more likely to recommmend hiring applicants of their own ethnicity than they are members of other groups (Neuliep, Hintz, & McCroskey, 2005).

▲ Employees of all races and ethnic groups may interpret interracial interactions ethnocentrically.

Similarly, ethnocentrism plays a role in co-worker conflict, because workers sometimes insist that the commonly held beliefs of members of their own ethnic group are right and that those of other groups are wrong. For example, as discussed in Chapter 16, African American workers are more likely than members of other ethnic groups to see conflicts with White co-workers as resulting from racism (Johnson et al., 2003). To counter this tendency, diversity trainers help workers understand that such differences are not a matter of right versus wrong. African Americans' views are shaped by real associations among career success variables, such as income, unemployment, and race. Similarly, the perspective of many White Americans derives from their belief that racism is no longer a significant problem in the United States (look back at Figure 16.7 on page 580; Kaiser Family Foundation, 1999). Thus, the differing views of African and White Americans are derived from looking at interpersonal interactions through different lenses, so to speak. And to think of either perspective as right or wrong is to oversimplify the rational and emotional processes that contribute to its development.

globalization The process through which workers all over the world have been brought into more frequent contact with one another as a result of advances in transportation and communications technology.

Cultural Diversity in the Workplace

Today's workforce is more culturally diverse than in the past. What factors have contributed to this change?

Globalization. One source of greater workplace diversity is **globalization,** the process through which workers all over the world have been brought into more frequent contact with one another as a result of advances in transportation and communications technology. Such advances mean that individuals whose workplaces are thousands of miles apart may communicate frequently with one another. It is no longer unusual for an employee of a firm in the United States to have daily interactions with suppliers in Japan, or customers in Poland, or fellow employees of the same firm who are based in Kenya.

17.15 What are some factors that have led to increased cultural diversity in the workplace?

Immigration. Immigration is another force behind increasing cultural diversity. A growing number of people are moving from Africa and Asia to Europe and North America seeking employment. In both Europe and North America, immigrants may be found in jobs ranging from unskilled labor to high-tech positions in computer science and engineering. Currently, more than 10% of U.S. residents, about 30 million people, were born in another country (U.S. Census Bureau, 2001).

Why Culture Matters in the Workplace. As you learned in Chapter 13, cultures differ with regard to the *individualism/collectivism dimension*, and this difference affects individuals' personalities. Individualist cultures place more emphasis on individual achievement than on group achievement. People in collectivist cultures, on the other hand, often define themselves in terms of their group membership. You may recall that American and European cultures tend to be individualist, whereas those found in Asia, Africa, and Latin America are often more collectivist. As you can see from **Figure 17.2**, people from collectivist cultures represented a far larger proportion of immigrants to the United States in 2001 than they did in the 1960s. Consequently, individualist versus collectivist conflicts are more likely to arise today than they were in the past.

▲ Differences in cultural values may cause management strategies that are successful in one culture to be less so in another.

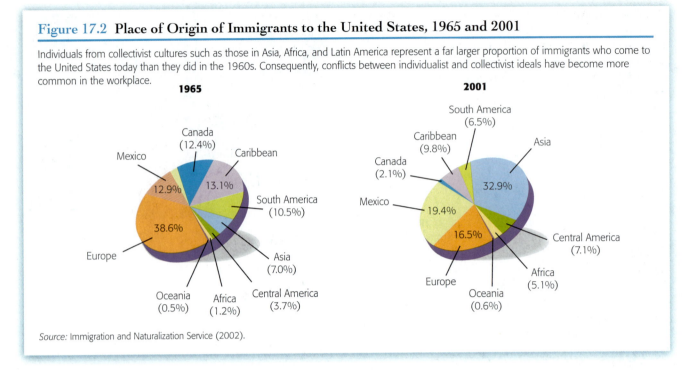

Figure 17.2 Place of Origin of Immigrants to the United States, 1965 and 2001

Individuals from collectivist cultures such as those in Asia, Africa, and Latin America represent a far larger proportion of immigrants who come to the United States today than they did in the 1960s. Consequently, conflicts between individualist and collectivist ideals have become more common in the workplace.

1965

- Canada (12.4%)
- Caribbean 13.1%
- South America (10.5%)
- Asia (7.0%)
- Central America (3.7%)
- Africa (1.2%)
- Oceania (0.5%)
- Europe 38.6%
- Mexico 12.9%

2001

- South America (6.5%)
- Caribbean (9.8%)
- Canada (2.1%)
- Mexico
- Europe
- Oceania (0.6%)
- Africa (5.1%)
- Central America (7.1%)
- Asia 32.9%
- 19.4%
- 16.5%

Source: Immigration and Naturalization Service (2002).

▲ Workplace diversity goes beyond race and ethnicity. The concept of diversity also includes gender, older workers, workers who vary in sexual orientation, and workers with disabilities.

17.16 What steps can organizations take to build a more diverse workforce?

One situation in which differences in individualism/collectivism become evident occurs when organizations attempt to implement in individualist cultures practices that have been successful in collectivist cultures, or vice versa. For example, *lean production* is a manufacturing management model that emphasizes cost control over all other considerations. This approach has been highly successful in Japan, but its implementation in North America and Europe has met with disappointing results. Why?

Researchers point to cultural differences between Japan and the West (Rafferty & Tapsell, 2001). They say that in the lean production model each worker is viewed as a component of a large system, a cog in a gigantic machine, so to speak. The individualist cultures of the West socialize people to value autonomy, so Western workers find the lean production approach to be psychologically stifling. Indeed, many critics who argue that the lean production model represents a return to a Theory X management approach are not surprised that this model has met with limited success in Western organizations (S. D. Green, 2002).

In response, lean production advocates argue that a clearly stated organizational goal can encourage workers to make meaningful contributions. In practice, though, organizations that implement the lean production model often become highly centralized, and upper-level managers receive credit for most of the organization's achievements. Western cultures tend to value individual recognition, whereas Asian cultures socialize individuals to associate their individual identities with those of the groups to which they belong (Matsumo, 2000). Thus, if a Japanese manufacturing plant becomes more cost-efficient, the Japanese worker takes pride in his employer's achievement. In contrast, the North American or European worker who makes a suggestion that leads to a reduction in costs wants to be personally recognized for her idea.

Promoting Diversity

The concept of workplace diversity involves more than just race and ethnicity. Gender, of course, is an additional consideration. Moreover, older workers and individuals who vary in sexual orientation are also represented in an organization that has a diverse workforce. Likewise, workers with disabilities increase the diversity of an organization.

There are many reasons for promoting diversity in an organization's workforce. One practical reason is that organizations can provide better services when they hire employees with racial and cultural backgrounds similar to those of their customers

(Cioffi, 2003). Another, perhaps more important, reason for seeking diversity is that it promotes a sense of fairness, one component of a positive organizational climate (Foley et al., 2002; Krysan & Farley, 2002). What's the best approach to achieving a diverse workforce?

Affirmative Action. One way that organizations can promote diversity is to actively seek to build an employee pool that includes members of as many racial and cultural groups as possible. This process is known as **affirmative action.** Many people view affirmative action as synonymous with fixed racial quotas (Arriola & Cole, 2001; Crosby, Iyer, & Sinchareon 2006). However, true affirmative action programs focus on opening up the recruitment, selection, and promotion processes in ways that enable women and minorities to gain access to positions in which they have been historically underrepresented. One component of such a program, for example, might involve sponsoring career fairs at historically African American colleges. Another would be to provide female and minority employees with special training opportunities to help them acquire leadership skills.

One key to accomplishing affirmative action goals involves keeping minority candidates involved in the job selection process. Researchers have found that minority applicants are more likely than White applicants to withdraw from the process (Ployhart et al., 2002), possibly because they are more likely to be anxious about pre-employment testing and to perceive the tests as invalid (Chan, 1997). Thus, organizations may be able to keep more minority group members in the applicant pool by providing them with data showing that the tests they will be required to take predict job performance equally well for Whites and minorities.

Training managers to avoid stereotypic thinking during interviews is also critical to building and maintaining a diverse workforce. This process, sometimes called *distortion management*, involves learning to recognize aspects of social information processing, such as stereotyping, when they happen and making conscious efforts to minimize their effects. Moreover, interviewers are legally forbidden to ask applicants about some topics, such as disability or marital status. For this reason, interviewers have to learn how to intentionally forget such information if interviewees mention it (Oien & Goernert, 2003).

Diversity Training. Once an organization has a diverse workforce, how can it help employees work together harmoniously? *Diversity training* is one approach. To be effective, diversity training must include information that can increase workers' awareness of ethnocentrism and the perspectives of different groups.

Once the goal of awareness has been achieved, diversity trainers often focus on the development of interaction skills. One common activity used for this purpose is called the *international meeting* (SIOP, 2002). Trainers divide participants into "cultures" and instruct them to adopt behaviors representing four categories of cultural norms: greetings, personal space, eye contact, and individualism/collectivism. For example, participants in one culture might greet others with handshakes, maintain a 6-inch personal space in conversations, avoid eye contact during social interactions, and display a collectivist orientation by always referring to themselves as group members rather than as individuals. By contrast, participants in another culture might greet others with a nod of the head, maintain a 2-foot personal distance, stare at people while talking to them, and demonstrate an individualist orientation by talking about themselves as individuals rather than as group members. After practicing the assigned norms, each participant is paired with a person from another culture. Each partner must introduce himself or herself to the other in a way consistent with the norms and find out one fact about that person. Afterward, participants discuss how they responded emotionally to the varying norms and how each of the behaviors influenced their views of others. As a result of this activity, participants become more aware of their own culture-based social behaviors and how they might be perceived by people from different cultural backgrounds.

Does diversity training really help? One study found that the effects of the training were dependent on trainees' personalities; those who were more open to new experiences benefited most (Lievens et al., 2003). Other research has suggested that men may be initially less open to diversity training than women are, but they derive

affirmative action A process through which organizations actively seek to build an employee pool that includes members of as many racial and cultural groups as possible.

similar benefits from it (Lin Lin & Rancer, 2003). Still, most studies show that, at the very least, diversity training helps workers who deal with culturally diverse suppliers, co-workers, or customers to feel more positively about their interactions with them (Cioffi, 2003). Moreover, learning to recognize ethnocentrism in their reactions to American ways of doing things appears to help immigrants to the United States cope with the stresses associated with working and living in an unfamiliar culture (Caruana & Chircop, 2001).

Remember It   Human Diversity in the Workplace

1. The tendency to assess a situation from one's own cultural perspective is known as _____ .

2. _____ and _____ are two factors that have led to increased diversity in the workplace.

3. Employers can increase workplace diversity by adjusting their _____ and _____ procedures.

Answers: 1. ethnocentrism; 2. Globalization, immigration; 3. recruitment, selection

Apply It   Where Are You in the Career Development Process?

Have you ever wondered what type of work you are best suited for? If so, you may want to begin your quest for an answer by looking at two models of career development, the process of choosing and adjusting to a particular career. Recommendations about what you might do to enhance your search for the ideal career can be derived from both. Ultimately, though, the degree to which you are satisfied with your career may depend on how you integrate your work into your life as a whole.

Holland's Personality Types

The work of John Holland has been very influential in shaping psychologists' ideas about personality and career. Holland proposes six basic personality types: realistic, investigative, artistic, social, enterprising, and conventional. His research shows that each of the six types is associated with work preferences. (The types and their associated work preferences are summarized in Table 17.2.) As Holland's theory predicts, people whose personality matches their job are also more likely to be satisfied with their work. Thus, a personality assessment may help you make an appropriate occupational choice and give you confidence about the decision (Francis-Smyth & Smith, 1997).

Super's Career Development Stages

Psychologist Donald Super proposed that career development happens in stages that begin in infancy (Super, 1971, 1986). First comes the growth stage (from birth to 14 years), in which you learn about your abilities and interests. Next is the exploratory stage, roughly between the ages of 15 and 24. According to Super, there's a lot of trial and error in this stage, so job changes happen frequently. Next is the establishment

stage (also called the stabilization stage), from 25 to 45. This stage begins with learning how things work in your career, the culture of your organization, and progression through the early steps of the career ladder. Sometimes, additional formal training is required during this stage. Setting goals is also important in this stage. You must decide how far you want to go and how you intend to get there. Mentoring by an experienced co-worker often helps you negotiate this stage successfully. Once an individual has become well established in a career, she or he enters the maintenance phase (age 45 through retirement), in which the goal is to protect and maintain the gains made in earlier years. Of course, in today's rapidly changing economy, people are often required to change careers. Thus, an individual may re-enter the exploratory stage at any time. As with most stage theories, the ages associated with Super's stages of career development are less important than the sequence of the stages.

Job Satisfaction

The career you choose may suit your personality perfectly, and you may progress through Super's stages with little difficulty. Does this mean that you will be happy in your work? Not necessarily. In fact, the key to job satisfaction probably lies outside of the career development process itself. Research shows, for example, that having a generally optimistic outlook on life predisposes us to be satisfied with our jobs (Diener et al., 2002). So learning to maintain a positive perspective on things may help you more in the long run than trying to find the perfect job. Additional insight can be gleaned from research linking age and job satisfaction. Younger people tend to be less satisfied in their work (Glenn & Weaver, 1986). Why? Many young people think middle-aged adults are happier in their jobs because they hold

Table 17.2 Holland's Personality Types and Work Preferences

Type	Personality Traits	Work Preferences
Realistic	Aggressive, masculine, physically strong, often with low verbal or interpersonal skills	Mechanical activities and tool use; often chooses a job such as mechanic, electrician, or surveyor
Investigative	Oriented toward thinking (particularly abstract thinking), organizing, and planning; low in social skills	Ambiguous, challenging tasks; often a scientist or engineer
Artistic	Intuitive, expressive, imaginative, impulsive, prefer flexibility	Unstructured, highly individual activity; often an artist
Social	Extraverted; people-oriented, sociable, and needing attention; avoids intellectual activity and dislikes highly ordered activity	Working with people in service jobs like nursing and education
Enterprising	Highly verbal and dominating; enjoys organizing and directing others; persuasive and a strong leader	Often chooses a career in sales
Conventional	Prefers structured activities and subordinate roles; likes clear guidelines; accurate and precise	May choose an occupation such as data entry

Source: Holland (1973, 1992).

higher-status positions and make more money than those who are younger. However, research suggests that the connection between job satisfaction and age exists because as people get older, work becomes less central to their lives (Tamir, 1982). Thus, finding the right balance between work and other pursuits in life may be the key ingredient in job satisfaction.

A Personal Definition of Success

You may be able to avoid the stresses associated with low levels of job satisfaction if you spend some time developing a personal definition of success. Is it wealth? A happy family? Social prestige? How much time do you want to devote to your work? What hobbies would you like to pursue? How important is having a family to you? Whatever your goals, thinking about them now and setting priorities may pay off in reduced stress in the future.

Summary and Review

Personnel Psychology p. 587

17.1 What strategies do personnel psychologists use to hire the best workers? p. 587

Personnel psychologists use job analysis, recruitment and selection, pre-employment testing, and interviewing to hire the best workers.

17.2 How do organizations train employees in job-related and interpersonal skills? p. 589

Organizations train employees through on-the-job training, apprenticeship, and off-the-job training. Management training often involves job rotation. Conflict resolution training is also useful for helping supervisors and employees get along in the workplace.

17.3 What are some approaches used to evaluate workers? p. 590

Performance appraisal, behavioral observation scales, management by objectives (MBO), and 360-degree evaluation are some approaches used for evaluating workers.

Organizational Psychology p. 591

17.4 What is the difference between Theory X and Theory Y management approaches? p. 591

The Theory X approach focuses on work efficiency, or how well an employee performs specific job tasks. The Theory Y approach focuses on psychological efficiency, or the degree to which a job has a positive psychological impact on a worker.

17.5 What are several types of effective leaders, and how do psychologists explain effective leadership? p. 592

Effective leaders may be charismatic, transactional, or transformational. The trait approach holds that effective leaders possess intrinsic characteristics that help them influence others. Advocates of the situational approach say that effective leadership depends on the match between a leader's characteristics and the situations in which she or he is called upon to lead. According to the behavioral approach, leadership can be taught and is the result of specific behaviors exhibited by leaders. Leader-member exchange (LMX) theory focuses on leaders' relationships with favored and nonfavored followers.

17.6 What is the relationship between organizational culture and organizational climate? p. 595

Organizational culture is the system of shared values, beliefs, and practices that evolves within an organization and influences the behavior of its members. Organizational climate refers to how employees perceive and respond emotionally to the culture of an organization.

17.7 What are some key perspectives on workplace ethics? p. 596

The moral-rights perspective suggests that individual behavior within an organization should be guided by the same respect for basic rights that is endorsed by the larger culture. The utilitarian perspective defines ethical behavior in terms of the greatest good for the greatest number of people. Organizational social responsibility is the idea that businesses and other organizations have an obligation to behave in ways that take into consideration the interests of the larger society of which they are a part.

Human Factors Psychology p. 597

17.8 What are key aspects of workplace design? p. 597

In an open design, a large number of workers are placed in a very large space. The workspace envelope is the three-dimensional space in which an individual worker performs the tasks that comprise his or her job. Office location and size convey information about an employee's status.

17.9 What are some of the innovations associated with the quality of work-life movement? p. 598

On-site child-care centers are one innovation that has arisen out of concern for the quality of work life. Telecommuters are able to work in their homes and are connected to their workplaces by computer, fax machine, and telephone. Flextime involves allowing employees to create their own work schedules. Job sharing is an innovation in which a full-time job is divided between two or more employees.

Gender Issues at Work p. 600

17.10 In what ways do women's work patterns differ from those of men? p. 600

Women's work patterns are less likely than those of men to be continuous, as many women move in and out of the workforce to bear and raise children.

17.11 How do men's and women's responses to job-related stress differ? p. 601

Men are more likely to use problem-focused coping to respond to job-related stress, while women typically rely on emotion-focused coping. As a result, men deal more effectively than women with job stressors that can be changed. By contrast, women are better able to cope with work situations in which change is impossible.

17.12 What evidence is there to suggest that women are breaking the glass ceiling? p. 601

One indication that the glass ceiling is breaking is that 33% of today's MBAs are women, and female representation in top corporate management positions has increased as women have accumulated work experience. About 18% of upper-level managers in U.S. corporations are women, and more women are attaining CEO positions every year. Research shows that well-qualified women are now two to four times as likely as men with equal qualifications to be promoted to top executive positions.

17.13 What are the two categories of sexual harassment complaints? p. 603

In *quid pro quo* complaints, workers claim to have been offered something in exchange for sexual favors. Hostile work environment complaints concern inappropriate behavior of a sexual nature that creates an intolerable level of discomfort for the complainant.

Human Diversity in the Workplace p. 604

17.14 What is ethnocentrism, and how does it affect the workplace? p. 604

Ethnocentrism is the tendency to look at situations from one's own racial or cultural perspective. Ethnocentrism may prevent workers from realizing that individuals from backgrounds different from theirs may view workplace interactions quite differently.

17.15 What are some factors that have led to increased cultural diversity in the workplace? p. 605

Globalization and immigration have increased cultural diversity in the workplace.

17.16 What steps can organizations take to build a more diverse workforce? p. 606

Organizations can promote diversity by actively seeking to build an employee pool that includes members of as many racial and cultural groups as possible. Such an approach is known as affirmative action. Training managers to avoid stereotypic thinking during interviews is also critical to building and maintaining a diverse workforce.

Thinking Critically about Psychology

1. What are your own plans for achieving a satisfactory work-life balance after you finish college?
2. In this chapter, you learned about the effects of ethnocentrism in the workplace. How do you think this way of thinking influences human behavior in other settings?
3. Develop and defend an argument in support of each of these statements:
   a. On average, women's earnings are lower than those of men because of women's discontinuous work patterns.
   b. On average, women's earnings are lower than those of men because of gender discrimination.

Key Terms

affirmative action, p. 607
apprenticeship, p. 589
artifactual communication, p. 598
assessment center, p. 588
behavioral approach, p. 594
behavioral observation scales, p. 590
charismatic leaders, p. 592
conflict resolution, p. 589
diversity training, p. 604
ergonomics, p. 597
glass ceiling, p. 601
globalization, p. 605
human factors psychology, p. 597
in-basket test, p. 588
industrial/organizational (I/O) psychologists, p. 587
job analysis, p. 587
job description, p. 588
job enrichment, p. 592

job rotation, p. 589
job satisfaction, p. 595
job simplification, p. 591
leader-member exchange (LMX) theory, p. 594
leadership, p. 592
management by objectives (MBO), p. 590
moral-rights perspective, p. 596
off-the-job training, p. 589
on-the-job training, p. 589
organizational climate, p. 595
organizational culture, p. 595
organizational psychology, p. 591
organizational social responsibility, p. 596
participative management, p. 592
performance appraisal, p. 590
personnel psychology, p. 587
quality circles, p. 592

quality of work-life (QWL) movement, p. 598
recruitment, p. 588
scientific management, p. 591
selection, p. 588
self-managed teams, p. 592
sexual harassment, p. 603
situational approach, p. 594
structured interviews, p. 589
telecommuting, p. 599
Theory X, p. 591
Theory Y, p. 591
360-degree evaluation, p. 590
time-motion studies, p. 591
trait approach, p. 594
transactional leaders, p. 593
transformational leaders, p. 593
utilitarian perspective, p. 596
work-life balance, p. 598
workspace envelope, p. 597

Appendix

Statistical Methods

Statistics, a branch of mathematics, enables psychologists and other scientists to organize, describe, and draw conclusions about the quantitative results of their studies. We will explore the two basic types of statistics that psychologists use—descriptive statistics and inferential statistics.

Descriptive Statistics

Descriptive statistics are statistics used to organize, summarize, and describe data. Descriptive statistics include measures of central tendency, variability, and relationship.

Measures of Central Tendency

A **measure of central tendency** is a measure or score that describes the center, or middle, of a distribution of scores. The most widely used and most familiar measure of central tendency is the **mean**, the arithmetic average of a group of scores. The mean is computed by adding all the single scores and dividing the sum by the number of scores.

Carl sometimes studies and does well in his classes, but he occasionally procrastinates and fails a test. Table A.1 shows how Carl performed on the seven tests in his psychology class last semester. Carl computes his mean score by adding up all his test scores and dividing the sum by the number of tests. Carl's mean, or average, score is 80.

The mean is an important and widely used statistical measure of central tendency, but it can be misleading when a group of scores contains one or several extreme scores. Table A.2 (on page A-2) lists the annual incomes of ten people in rank order. When an income of $1 million is averaged with several more modest incomes, the mean does not provide a true picture of the group. Therefore, when one

descriptive statistics Statistics used to organize, summarize, and describe data.

measure of central tendency A measure or score that describes the center, or middle, of a distribution of scores (example: mean, median, or mode).

mean The arithmetic average of a group of scores; calculated by adding all the single scores and dividing the sum by the number of scores.

Table A.1 Carl's Psychology Test Scores	
Test 1	98
Test 2	74
Test 3	86
Test 4	92
Test 5	56
Test 6	68
Test 7	86
Sum:	560
Mean: 560 ÷ 7 = 80	

Table A.2 Annual Income for Ten People

Subject	Annual Income
1	$1,000,000
2	$50,000
3	$43,000
4	$30,000
5	$28,000
6	$26,000
7	$22,000
8	$22,000
9	$16,000
10	$10,000
Sum:	$1,247,000

$28,000 and $26,000 → $27,000 = Median

$22,000 and $22,000] Mode

Mean: $1,247,000 ÷ 10 = $124,700
Median: $27,000
Mode: $22,000

or a few individuals score far above or below the middle range of a group, a different measure of central tendency should be used. The **median** is the middle score or value when a group of scores is arranged from highest to lowest. When there is an odd number of scores, the score in the middle is the median. When there is an even number of scores, the median is the average of the two middle scores. For the ten incomes arranged from highest to lowest in Table A.2, the median is $27,000, which is the average of the middle incomes, $28,000 and $26,000. The $27,000 median income is a truer reflection of the comparative income of the group than is the $124,700 mean.

Another measure of central tendency is the **mode.** The mode is easy to find because it is the score that occurs most frequently in a group of scores. The mode of the annual-income group in Table A.2 is $22,000.

Describing Data with Tables and Graphs

A researcher tested 100 students for recall of 20 new vocabulary words 24 hours after they had memorized the list. The researcher organized the scores in a **frequency distribution**—an arrangement showing the numbers of scores that fall within equal-sized class intervals. To organize the 100 test scores, the researcher decided to use intervals of 2 points each. Next, the researcher tallied the frequency (number of scores) within each 2-point interval. **Table A.3** presents the resulting frequency distribution.

The researcher then made a **histogram,** a bar graph that depicts the number of scores within each class interval in the frequency distribution. The intervals are plotted along the horizontal axis, and the frequency of scores in each interval is plotted along the vertical axis. **Figure A.1** shows the histogram for the 100 test scores.

Another common method of representing frequency data is the **frequency polygon.** As in a histogram, the class intervals are plotted along the horizontal axis and the frequencies are plotted along the vertical axis. However, in a frequency polygon, each class interval is represented by a graph point that is placed at the middle (midpoint) of the class interval so that its vertical distance above the horizontal axis shows the frequency of that interval. Lines are drawn to connect the points, as shown in **Figure A.2** (on page A-4). The histogram and the frequency polygon are simply two different ways of presenting data.

median   The middle score or value when a group of scores is arranged from highest to lowest.

mode   The score that occurs most frequently in a group of scores.

frequency distribution   An arrangement showing the numbers of scores that fall within equal-sized class intervals.

histogram   A bar graph that depicts the number of scores within each class interval in a frequency distribution.

frequency polygon   A line graph that depicts the frequency, or number, of scores within each class interval in a frequency distribution.

Table A.3 Frequency Distribution of 100 Vocabulary Test Scores

Class Interval	Tally of Scores in Each Class Interval	Number of Scores in Each Class Interval (Frequency)
1–2	|	1
3–4	||	2
5–6	Ⅲ |	6
7–8	Ⅲ Ⅲ Ⅲ |||	18
9–10	Ⅲ Ⅲ Ⅲ Ⅲ |||	23
11–12	Ⅲ ⅢⅢ Ⅲ |||	23
13–14	ⅢⅢ Ⅲ ||	17
15–16	Ⅲ |||	8
17–18	|	1
19–20	|	1

Measures of Variability

In addition to a measure of central tendency, researchers also need a measure of the **variability** of a set of scores—how much the scores spread out, away from the mean. Both groups in **Table A.4** (on page A-4) have a mean and a median of 80. However, the scores in Group II cluster tightly around the mean, while the scores in Group I vary widely from the mean.

The simplest measure of variability is the **range**—the difference between the highest and lowest scores in a distribution of scores. Table A.4 reveals that Group I has a range of 47, indicating high variability, while Group II has a range of only 7, showing low variability. Unfortunately, the range reveals only the difference between the lowest score and the highest score; it tells nothing about the scores in between.

The **standard deviation** is a descriptive statistic reflecting the average amount that scores in a distribution deviate, or vary, from their mean. The larger the standard deviation, the greater the variability in a distribution of scores. Refer to Table A.4 and note the standard deviations for the two distributions of test scores. In Group I, the

variability   How much the scores in a distribution spread out, away from the mean.

range   The difference between the highest score and the lowest score in a distribution of scores.

standard deviation   A descriptive statistic reflecting the average amount that scores in a distribution deviate, or vary, from their mean.

Figure A.1 A Frequency Histogram

Vocabulary test scores from the frequency distribution in Table A.3 are plotted here in the form of a histogram. Class intervals of 2 points each appear on the horizontal axis. Frequencies of the scores in each class interval are plotted on the vertical axis.

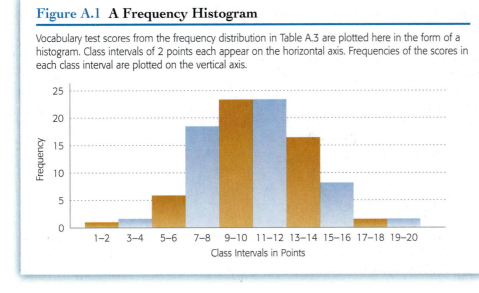

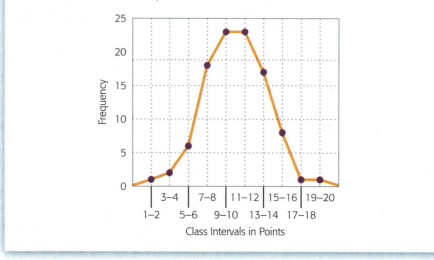

Figure A.2 A Frequency Polygon

Vocabulary test scores from the frequency distribution in Table A.3 are plotted here in the form of a frequency polygon. Class intervals of 2 points each appear on the horizontal axis. Frequencies of the scores in each class interval are plotted on the vertical axis.

relatively large standard deviation of 18.1 reflects the wide variability in that distribution. By contrast, the small standard deviation of 2.14 in Group II indicates that the variability is low, and you can see that the scores cluster tightly around the mean.

The Normal Curve

normal curve A symmetrical, bell-shaped frequency distribution that represents how scores are normally distributed in a population; most scores fall near the mean, and fewer and fewer scores occur in the extremes either above or below the mean.

Psychologists and other scientists often use descriptive statistics in connection with an important type of frequency distribution known as the **normal curve.** If a large number of people are measured on any of a wide variety of traits (such as height or IQ score), the great majority of values will cluster in the middle, with fewer and fewer individuals measuring extremely low or high on these variables. Note that slightly over 68% of the scores in a normal distribution fall within 1 standard deviation of the mean

Table A.4 Comparison of Range and Standard Deviation for Two Small Groups of Scores Having Identical Means and Medians

GROUP I			GROUP II		
TEST	SCORE		TEST	SCORE	
1	99		1	83	
2	99		2	82	
3	98		3	81	
4	80	Median	4	80	Median
5	72		5	79	
6	60		6	79	
7	52		7	76	
Sum:	560		Sum:	560	
Mean: $560 \div 7 = 80$			Mean: $560 \div 7 = 80$		
Median: 80			Median: 80		
Range: $99 - 52 = 47$			Range: $83 - 76 = 7$		
Standard deviation: 18.1			Standard deviation: 2.14		

(34.13% within 1 standard deviation above the mean, and 34.13% within 1 standard deviation below the mean). Almost 95.5% of the scores in a normal distribution lie between 2 standard deviations above and below the mean. And the vast majority of scores in a normal distribution—99.72%—fall between 3 standard deviations above and below the mean.

Using the properties of the normal curve and knowing the mean and the standard deviation of a normal distribution, we can find where any score stands (how high or low) in relation to all the other scores in the distribution. For example, on the Wechsler intelligence scales, the mean IQ is 100 and the standard deviation is 15. Thus, 99.72% of the population has an IQ score within 3 standard deviations above and below the mean, ranging from an IQ of 55 to an IQ of 145.

The Correlation Coefficient

A **correlation coefficient** is a number that indicates the degree and direction of relationship between two variables. Correlation coefficients can range from +1.00 (a perfect positive correlation) to .00 (no correlation) to −1.00 (a perfect negative correlation), as illustrated in **Figure A.3**. A **positive correlation** indicates that two variables vary in the same direction. An increase in one variable is associated with an increase in the other variable, or a decrease in one variable is associated with a decrease in the other. There is a positive correlation between the number of hours college students spend studying and their grades. The more hours they study, the higher their grades are likely to be. A **negative correlation** means that an increase in one variable is associated with a decrease in the other variable. There may be a negative correlation between the number of hours students spend watching television and studying. The more hours they spend watching TV, the fewer hours they may spend studying, and vice versa.

The sign (+ or −) in a correlation coefficient merely tells whether the two variables vary in the same or opposite directions. (If no sign appears, the correlation is assumed to be positive.) The number in a correlation coefficient indicates the relative strength

correlation coefficient   A numerical value indicating the strength and direction of relationship between two variables, which ranges from +1.00 (a perfect positive correlation) to −1.00 (a perfect negative correlation).

positive correlation   A relationship between two variables in which both vary in the same direction.

negative correlation   A relationship between two variables in which an increase in one variable is associated with a decrease in the other variable.

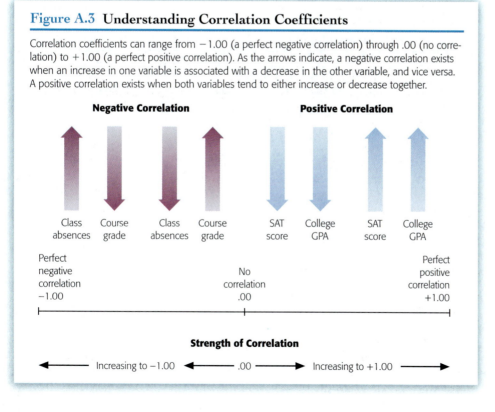

Figure A.3 Understanding Correlation Coefficients

Correlation coefficients can range from −1.00 (a perfect negative correlation) through .00 (no correlation) to +1.00 (a perfect positive correlation). As the arrows indicate, a negative correlation exists when an increase in one variable is associated with a decrease in the other variable, and vice versa. A positive correlation exists when both variables tend to either increase or decrease together.

of the relationship between the two variables—the higher the number, the stronger the relationship. For example, a correlation of −.70 is higher than a correlation of +.56; a correlation of −.85 is just as strong as one of +.85. A correlation of .00 indicates that no relationship exists between the variables. IQ and shoe size are examples of two variables that are not correlated.

Table A.5 shows the measurements of two variables—high school GPA and college GPA for 11 college students. Looking at the data, we can see that 6 of the 11 students had a higher GPA in high school, while 5 of the students had a higher GPA in college. A clearer picture of the actual relationship is shown by the scatterplot in Figure A.4. High school GPA (variable X) is plotted on the horizontal axis, and college GPA (variable Y) is plotted on the vertical axis.

One dot is plotted for each of the 11 students at the point where high school GPA, variable X, and college GPA, variable Y, intersect. For example, the first student is represented by a dot at the point where her high school GPA of 2.0 on the horizontal (x) axis and college GPA of 1.8 on the vertical (y) axis intersect. The scatterplot in Figure A.5 reveals a relatively high correlation between high school and college GPAs, because the dots cluster near the diagonal line. It also shows that the correlation is positive, because the dots run diagonally upward from left to right. The correlation coefficient for the high school and college GPAs of these 11 students is .71. If the correlation were perfect (1.00), all the dots would fall exactly on the diagonal line.

A scatterplot shows whether a correlation is low, moderate, or high and whether it is positive or negative. Scatterplots that run diagonally up from left to right reveal positive correlations. Scatterplots that run diagonally down from left to right indicate negative correlations. The closer the dots are to the diagonal line, the higher the correlation. It is important to remember that correlation does not demonstrate cause and effect. Even a perfect correlation (+1.00 or −1.00) does not mean that one variable causes or is caused by the other. Correlation shows only that two variables are related.

Not all relationships between variables are positive or negative. The relationships between some variables are said to be *curvilinear*. A curvilinear relationship exists when two variables correlate positively (or negatively) up to a certain point and then change direction. For example, there is a positive correlation between physical

Figure A.4 A Scatterplot

A scatterplot reveals a relatively high positive correlation between the high school and college GPAs of the 11 students listed in Table A.5. One dot is plotted for each of the 11 students at the point where high school GPA (plotted on the horizontal axis) and college GPA (plotted on the vertical axis) intersect.

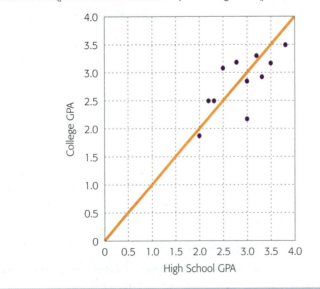

Table A.5 High School and College GPAs for 11 Students

Student	High School GPA (Variable X)	College GPA (Variable Y)
1	2.0	1.8
2	2.2	2.5
3	2.3	2.5
4	2.5	3.1
5	2.8	3.2
6	3.0	2.2
7	3.0	2.8
8	3.2	3.3
9	3.3	2.9
10	3.5	3.2
11	3.8	3.5

strength and age up to about 40 or 45 years of age. As age increases from childhood to middle age, so does the strength of handgrip pressure. But beyond middle adulthood, the relationship becomes negative, and increasing age is associated with decreasing handgrip strength. **Figure A.5** shows a scatterplot of this curvilinear relationship.

Inferential Statistics

Inferential statistics allow researchers (1) to make inferences about the characteristics of the larger population from their observations and measurements of a sample and (2) to derive estimates of how much faith or confidence can be placed in those inferences. In statistical theory, a **population** is the entire group that is of interest to researchers—the group to which they wish to apply their findings. For example, a population could be all the registered voters in the United States. Usually, researchers cannot directly measure and study the entire population of interest. Consequently, they make inferences about a population from a relatively small **sample** selected from that population. For researchers to draw conclusions about the larger population, the sample must be representative—that is, its characteristics must mirror those of the larger population. (See Chapter 1 for more information about representative samples.)

Statistical Significance

Suppose 200 students are randomly assigned either to an experimental group that will be taught psychology with innovative materials or to a control group that will receive traditional instruction. At the end of the semester, researchers find that the mean test scores of the experimental group are considerably higher than those of the control group. To conclude that the instructional methods caused the difference, the researchers must use **tests of statistical significance** to estimate how often the experimental results could have occurred by chance alone. The estimates derived from tests of statistical significance are stated as probabilities. A probability of .05 means that the experimental results would be expected to occur by chance no more than 5 times out of 100. The .05 level of significance is usually required as a minimum for researchers to conclude that their findings are statistically significant. Often the level of significance reached is even more impressive, such as the .01 level. The .01 level means that the probability is no more than 1 in 100 that the results occurred by chance.

inferential statistics Statistical procedures that allow researchers to make inferences about the characteristics of the larger population from observations and measurements of a sample and to derive estimates of how much confidence can be placed in those inferences.

population The entire group of interest to researchers and to which they wish to generalize their findings; the group from which a sample is selected.

sample The portion of any population that is selected for study and from which generalizations are made about the entire population.

tests of statistical significance Statistical tests that estimate the probability that a particular research result could have occurred by chance.

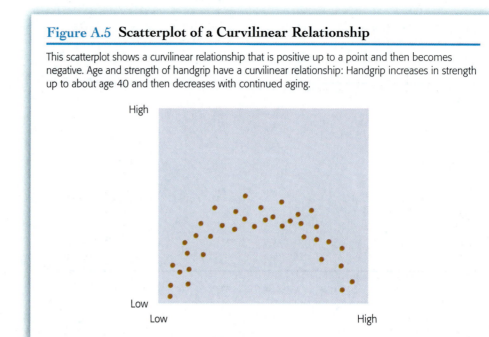

Figure A.5 Scatterplot of a Curvilinear Relationship

This scatterplot shows a curvilinear relationship that is positive up to a point and then becomes negative. Age and strength of handgrip have a curvilinear relationship: Handgrip increases in strength up to about age 40 and then decreases with continued aging.

The inferences researchers make are not absolute. They are based on probability, and there is always a possibility, however small, that experimental results could occur by chance. For this reason, replication of research studies is recommended.

References

Abbot, N. C., Stead, L. F., White, A. R., Barnes, J., & Ernst, E. (2000). Hypnotherapy for smoking cessation. *Cochrane Database System Review, 2*, CD001008.

Abe, M., Herzog, E., Yamazaki, S., Straume, M., Tei, H., Sakaki, Y., & Menaker, M. (2002). Circadian rhythms in isolated brain regions. *Journal of Neuroscience, 22*, 350–356.

Abele, A. (2005). Goals, gender-related self-concept, and work-life balance in long-term life pursuit: Findings from the Erlangen longitudinal study BELA-E. *Zeitscrift fur Arbeits und Organisationspsychologie, 49*, 176–186.

Abraham, H., & Duffy, F. (2001). EEG coherence in post-LSD visual hallucinations. *Psychiatry Research: Neuroimaging, 107*, 151–163.

Abramowitz, J. S. (1997). Effectiveness of psychological and pharmacological treatments for obsessive-compulsive disorder: A quantitative review. *Journal of Consulting and Clinical Psychology, 65*, 44–52.

Abrams, D., Wetherell, M., Cochrane, S., Hogg, M. A., & Turner, J. C. (1990). Knowing what to think by knowing who you are: Self-categorization and the nature of norm formation, conformity and group polarization. *British Journal of Social Psychology, 29*(Pt. 2), 97–119.

Accardo, P., Tomazic, T., Fete, T., Heaney, M., Lindsay, R., & Whitman, B. (1997). Maternally reported fetal activity levels and developmental diagnoses. *Clinical Pediatrics, 36*, 279–283.

Ackerman, S., Zuroff, D. C., & Moskowitz, D. S. (2000). Generativity in midlife and young adults: Links to agency, communion and subjective well-being. *International Journal of Aging and Human Development, 50*, 17–41.

Acklin, M., & Cho-Stutler, L. (2006). The science and art of parent-child observation in child custody evaluation. *Journal of Forensic Psychology Practice, 6*(1), 51–62.

Adam, M., & Reyna, V. (2005). Coherence and correspondence criteria for rationality: Experts' estimation of risks of sexually transmitted infections. *Journal of Behavioral Decision Making, 18*, 169–186.

Adams, J. H., Graham, D. I., & Jennett, B. (2000). The neuropathology of the vegetative state after an acute brain insult. *Brain, 123*, 1327–1338.

Addi-Raccah, Q., & Ayalon, H. (2002). Gender inequality in leadership positions of teachers. *British Journal of Sociology of Education, 23*, 157–177.

Addis, M., & Mahalik, J. (2003). Men, masculinity, and the contexts of help seeking. *American Psychologist, 58*, 5–14.

Addis, M., Hatgis, C., Krasnow, A., Jacob, K., Bourne, L., & Mansfield, A. (2004). Effectiveness of cognitive-behavioral treatment for panic disorder versus treatment as usual in a managed care setting. *Journal of Consulting & Clinical Psychology, 72*, 625–635.

Adelman, W., & Ellen, J. (2002). Adolescence. In A. Rudolph, R. Kamei, & K. Overby (Eds), *Rudolph's fundamental of pediatrics* (3rd ed., pp. 70–109). New York: McGraw-Hill.

Ader, R. (1985). CNS immune systems interactions: Conditioning phenomena. *Behavioral and Brain Sciences, 9*, 760–763.

Ader, R. (2000). On the development of psychoneuroimmunology. *European Journal of Pharmacology, 405*, 167–176.

Ader, R., & Cohen, N. (1982). Behaviorally conditioned immunosuppression and murine systemic *Lupus erythematosus. Science, 215*, 1534–1536.

Adesman, A. (1996). Fragile X syndrome. In A. Capute & P. Accardo (Eds.). *Developmental disabilities in infancy and childhood* (2nd ed., Vol. 2, pp. 255–269). Baltimore: Brookes.

Adler, A. (1927). *Understanding human nature.* New York: Greenberg.

Adler, A. (1956). In H. L. Ansbacher & R. R. Ansbacher (Eds.), *The individual psychology of Alfred Adler: A systematic presentation in selections from his writings.* New York: Harper & Row.

Adler, J. (1997, Spring/Summer). It's a wise father who knows. . . . *Newsweek* [Special Edition], p. 73.

Agras, W. S., Walsh, T., Fairburn, C. G., Wilson, T., & Kraemer, H. C. (2000). A multicenter comparison of cognitive-behavioral therapy and interpersonal psychotherapy for bulimia nervosa. *Archives of General Psychiatry, 57*, 459–466.

Ahmad, S. (1994, November). *Culturally sensitive caregiving for the Pakistani woman.* Lecture presented at the Medical College of Virginia Hospitals, Richmond, VA.

Ainsworth, M. (2000). ABCs of "internet therapy." *Metanoia* [Electronic version]. Retrieved from www.metanoia.org

Ainsworth, M. D. S. (1973). The development of infant-mother attachment. In B. Caldwell & H. Ricciuti (Eds.), *Review of child development research* (Vol. 3). Chicago: University of Chicago Press.

Ainsworth, M. D. S. (1979). Infant-mother attachment. *American Psychologist, 34*, 932–937.

Ainsworth, M. D. S., Blehar, M. C., Walters, E., & Wall, S. (1978). *Patterns of attachment.* Hillsdale, NJ: Erlbaum.

Akehurst, L., Bull, R., Vrij, A., & Kohnken, G. (2004). The effects of training professional groups and lay persons to use criterion-based content analysis to detect deception. *Applied Cognitive Psychology, 18*, 877–891.

Albeck, S., & Kaydar, D. (2002). Divorced mothers: Their network of friends pre- and post-divorce. *Journal of Divorce & Remarriage, 36*, 111–138.

Albert, M. L., & Helm-Estabrooks, N. (1988). Diagnosis and treatment of aphasia: Part II. *Journal of the American Medical Association, 259,* 1205–1210.

Albrecht, K. (1979). *Stress and the manager: Making it work for you.* Englewood Cliffs, NJ: Prentice-Hall.

Aldhous, P. (1992). The promise and pitfalls of molecular genetics. *Science, 257,* 164–165.

Al-Dmour, H., & Al-Awamleh, R. (2002). Effects of transactional and transformational leadership styles of sales managers on job satisfaction and self-perceived performance of sales people: A study of Jordanian manufacturing public shareholding companies. *Dirasat: Administrative Sciences, 29,* 247–261.

Alexander, G. (2003). An evolutionary perspective of sex-typed toy preferences: Pink, blue, and the brain. *Archives of Sexual Behavior, 32,* 7–14.

Alexander, G. E., Furey, M. L., Grady, C. L., Pietrini, P., Brady, D. R., Mentis, M. J., & Schapiro, M. B. (1997). Association of premorbid intellectual function with cerebral metabolism in Alzheimer's disease: Implications for the cognitive reserve hypotheses. *American Journal of Psychiatry, 154,* 165–172.

Alleman, J. (2002). Online counseling: The Internet and mental health treatment. *Psychotherapy: Theory, Research, Practice, Training, 39,* 199–209.

Allen, B. P. (1997). *Personality theories: Development, growth, and diversity* (2nd ed.). Boston: Allyn & Bacon.

Allen, G., Buxton, R. B., Wong, E. C., & Courchesne, E. (1997). Attentional activation of the cerebellum independent of motor involvement. *Science, 275,* 1940–1943.

Allen, J., McElhaney, K., Land, D., Kupermine, G., Moore, C., O'Beirne-Kelly, H., & Kilmer, S. (2003). A secure base in adolescence: Markers of attachment security in the mother-adolescent relationship. *Child Development, 74,* 292–307.

Allen, K. W. (1996). Chronic nailbiting: A controlled comparison of competing response and mild aversion treatments. *Behaviour Research and Therapy, 34,* 269–272.

Allison, T., Puce, A., & McCarthy, G. (2000). Social perception from visual cues: Role of the STS region. *Trends in Cognitive Sciences, 4,* 267–278.

Allport, G. W. (1954). *The nature of prejudice.* Reading, MA: Addison-Wesley.

Allport, G. W. (1961). *Pattern and growth in personality.* New York: Holt, Rinehart & Winston.

Allport, G. W., & Odbert, J. S. (1936). Trait names: A psycho-lexical study. *Psychological Monographs, 47*(1, Whole No. 211), 1–171.

Alsaker, F. D. (1995). Timing of puberty and reactions to pubertal changes. In M. Rutter (Ed.), *Psychosocial disturbances in young people* (pp. 37–82). New York: Cambridge University Press.

Altermatt, E., & Pomerantz, E. (2003). The development of competence-related and motivational beliefs: An investigation of similarity and influence among friends. *Journal of Educational Psychology, 95,* 111–123.

Amado, S., & Ulupinar, P. (2005). The effects of conversation on attention and peripheral detection: Is talking with a passenger and talking on the cell phone different? *Transportation Research, 8,* 383–395.

Amato, S. (1998). Human genetics and dysmorphy. In R. Behrman & R. Kliegman (Eds.), *Nelson essentials of pediatrics* (3rd ed., pp. 167–225). Philadelphia: W. B. Saunders.

American Academy of Pediatrics (AAP). (2002). *Television: How it affects children.* Retrieved July 2, 2004 from http://www.aap.org/family/tv1.htm.

American Association of Retired Persons. (2002). *Evaluating health information on the Internet: How good are your sources?* Retrieved November 1, 2002, from http://www.aarp.org/confacts/health/wwwhealth.html

American Cancer Society. (2002). *Cancer facts & figures/2002.* Retrieved November 10, 2002, from http://www.cancer.org/downloads/STT/CancerFacts&Figures2002TM

American Indian Higher Education Consortium. (1999). *Tribal colleges: An introduction.* Alexandria, VA: Author. Retrieved June 15, 2006 from http://www.aihec.org/documents/Research/intro.pdf

American Psychiatric Association. (1994). *Diagnostic and statistical manual of mental disorders* (4th ed.). Washington DC: Author.

American Psychiatric Association. (2000). *Practice guidelines for eating disorders.* Retrieved January 31, 2005 from http://www.psych.org.

American Psychiatric Association. (2000). *The Diagnostic and Statistical Manual of Mental Disorders* (4th ed., Text Revision). Washington, DC: Author.

American Psychiatric Association. (2006). *Practice guidelines for treatment of patients with eating disorders* (3rd edition). Retrieved October 12, 2006 from http://psych.org/psych_pract/treatg/pg/EatingDisorders3ePG_04-28-06.pdf

American Psychological Association (APA). (2002). Ethnical principles of psychologists and code of conduct. *American Psychologist, 57,* 1060–1073.

American Psychological Association (APA). (2003). *Graduate study in psychology.* Washington, DC: APA.

American Psychological Association (APA). (2003). Guidelines on multicultural education, training, research, practice, and organizational change for psychologists. *American Psychologist, 58,* 377–402.

American Psychological Association (APA). (2006). *The Psychologically Healthy Workplace Awards.* Retrieved July 28, 2006 from http://www.phwa.org/.

American Psychological Association. (1994). *Interim report of the APA Working Group on Investigation of Memories of Childhood Abuse.* Washington, DC: Author.

American Psychological Association. (1995). Psychology: Scientific problem-solvers—Careers for the 21st century. Retrieved March 7, 2002, from http://www.apa.org/students/brochure/outlook.html#bachelors

American Psychological Association. (2000). Psychologists in the red [Online factsheet]. Retrieved March 7, 2002, from http://www.apa.org/ppo/issues/ebsinthered.html

Amminger, G., Leicester, S., Yung, A., Phillips, L., Berger, G., Francey, S., Yuen, H., & McGorry, P. (2006). Early-onset of symptoms predicts conversion to non-affective psychosis in ultra-high risk individuals. *Schizophrenia Research, 84,* 67–76.

Anand, B. K., & Brobeck, J. R. (1951). Hypothalamic control of food intake in rats and cats. *Yale Journal of Biological Medicine, 24,* 123–140.

Andersen, B. L., & Cyranowski, J. M. (1995). Women's sexuality: Behaviors, responses, and individual differences. *Journal of Consulting and Clinical Psychology, 63,* 891–906.

Anderson, C., & Bushman, B. (2001). Effects of violent video games on aggressive behavior, aggressive cognition, aggressive affect, physiological arousal, and prosocial behavior: A meta-analytic review of the scientific literature. *Psychological Science, 12,* 353–359.

Anderson, C. A., & Anderson, K. B. (1996). Violent crime rate studies in philosophical context: A destructive testing approach to heat and southern culture of violence effects. *Journal of Personality and Social Psychology, 70,* 740–756.

Anderson, C. A., & Dill, K. E. (2000). Video games and aggressive thoughts, feelings, and behavior in the laboratory and in life. *Journal of Personality & Social Psychology, 78,* 772–790.

Anderson, R. (2002). Deaths: Leading causes for 2000. *National Vital Statistics Reports, 50* (16), 1–86.

Anderson, S. M., Klatzky, R. L., & Murray, J. (1990). Traits and social stereotypes: Efficiency differences in social information processing. *Journal of Personality and Social Psychology, 59,* 192–201.

Andreasen, N. C., Arndt, S., Alliger, R., Miller, D., & Flaum, M. (1995). Symptoms of schizophrenia: Methods, meanings, and mechanisms. *Archives of General Psychiatry, 52,* 341–351.

Andreasen, N. C., & Black, D. W. (1991). *Introductory textbook of psychiatry.* Washington, DC: American Psychiatric Press.

Andreasen, N. C., Cohen, G., Harris, G., Cizaldlo, T., Parkkinen, J., Rezai, K., & Swayze, V. W. (1992). Image processing for the study of brain structure and function: Problems and programs. *Journal of Neuropsychiatry and Clinical Neurosciences, 4,* 125–133.

Andrews, G., & Erskine, A. (2003). Reducing the burden of anxiety and depressive disorders: The role of computerized clinician assistance. *Current Opinion in Psychiatry, 16,* 41–44.

Anokhin, A., Vedeniapin, A., Sitevaag, E., Bauer, L., O'Connor, S., Kuperman, S., Porjesz, B., Reich, T., Begleiter, H., Polich, J., & Rohrbaugh, J. (2000). The P300 brain potential is reduced in smokers. *Psychopharmacology, 149,* 409–413.

Anthony, D. (1999). Pseudoscience and minority religions: An evaluation of the brainwashing theories of Jean-Marie Abgrall. *Social Justice Research, 12,* 421–456.

Aram, D., & Levitt, I. (2002). Mother-child joint writing and storybook reading: Relations with literacy among low SES kindergarteners. *Merrill-Palmer Quarterly, 48,* 202–224.

Archer, J. (1991). The influence of testosterone on human aggression. *British Journal of Social Psychology, 82*(Pt. 1), 1–28.

Archer, J. (1996). Sex differences in social behavior: Are the social role and evolutionary explanations compatible? *American Psychologist, 51,* 909–917.

Arehart-Treichel, J. (2002). Researchers explore link between animal cruelty, personality disorders. *Psychiatric News, 37,* 22.

Armenteros, J., & Davies, M. (2006). Antipsychotics in early onset schizophrenia: Systematic review and meta-analysis. *European Child & Adolescent Psychiatry, 15,* 141–148.

Armstrong, M., & Shikani, A. (1996). Nasal septal necrosis mimicking Wegener's granulomatosis in a cocaine abuser. *Ear Nose Throat Journal, 75,* 623–626.

Arnett, J. (2000). Emerging adulthood: A theory of development from the late teens through the twenties. *American Psychologist, 57,* 774–783.

Arnett, J. J. (1999). Adolescent storm and stress, reconsidered. *American Psychologist, 54,* 317–326.

Aronson, E. (1976). Dissonance theory: Progress and problems. In E. P. Hollander & R. C. Hunt (Eds.), *Current perspectives in social psychology* (4th ed., pp. 316–328). New York: Oxford University Press.

Aronson, E. (1988). *The social animal* (3rd ed.). San Francisco: W. H. Freeman.

Aronson, E., Stephan, W., Sikes, J., Blaney, N., & Snapp, M. (1978). *Cooperation in the classroom.* Beverly Hills, CA: Sage.

Arriaga, P., Esteyes, F., Carneiro, P., & Monteiro, M. (2006). Violent computer games and their effects on state hostility and physiological arousal. *Aggressive Behavior, 32,* 146–158.

Arriola, K., & Cole, E. (2001). Framing the affirmative-action debate: Attitudes toward out-group members and White identity. *Journal of Applied Social Psychology, 31,* 2462–2483.

Arthur, W., Day, E., McNelly, T., & Edens, P. (2003). A meta-analysis of the criterion-related validity of assessment center dimensions. *Personnel Psychology, 56,* 125–154.

Artman, L., Cahan, S., & Avni-Babad, D. (2006). Age, schooling, and conditional reasoning. *Cognitive Development, 21,* 131–145.

Asch, S. E. (1951). Effects of group pressure upon the modification and distortion of judgments. In H. Guetzkow (Ed.), *Groups, leadership, and men.* Pittsburgh, PA: Carnegie Press.

Asch, S. E. (1955). Opinions and social pressure. *Scientific American, 193,* 31–35.

Asher, S., & Paquette, J. (2003). Loneliness and peer relations in childhood. *Current Directions in Psychological Science, 12,* 75–78.

Aspendorf, J. B., Warkentink, V., & Baudonniere, P. M. (1996). Self-awareness and other-awareness II: Mirror self-recognition, social contingency awareness, and synchronic imitation. *Developmental Psychology, 32,* 313–321.

Aspinwall, L. G., & Taylor, S. E. (1997). A stitch in time: Self-regulation and proactive coping. *Psychological Bulletin, 121,* 417–436.

Assefi, S., & Garry, M. (2003). Absolut memory distortions: Alcohol placebos influence the misinformation effect. *Psychological Science, 14,* 77–80.

Astington, J., & Jenkins, J. (1999). A longitudinal study of the relation between language and theory-of-mind development. *Developmental Psychology, 35,* 1311–1320.

Athanasselis, T., Bakamadis, S., Dologlou, I., Cowie, R., Douglas-Cowie, E., & Cox, C. (2005). ASR for emotional speech: Clarifying the issues and enhancing performance. *Neural Networks, 18,* 437–444.

Atkins, P., & Wood, R. (2002). Self-versus others' ratings as predictors of assessment center ratings: Validation evidence for 360-degree feedback programs. *Personnel Psychology, 55,* 871–904.

Atkinson, R. C., & Shiffrin, R. M. (1968). Human memory: A proposed system and its controlled processes. In K. W. Spence & J. T. Spence (Eds.), *The psychology of learning and motivation* (Vol. 2, pp. 89–195). New York: Academic.

Au, J. G., & Donaldson, S. I. (2000). Social influences as explanations for substance use differences among Asian-American and European-American adolescents. *Journal of Psychoactive Drugs, 32,* 15–23.

Aubé, J., & Koestner, R. (1992). Gender characteristics and adjustment: A longitudinal study. *Journal of Personality and Social Psychology, 63,* 485–493.

Augestad, L. B. (2000). Prevalence and gender differences in eating attitudes and physical activity among Norwegians. *Eating and Weight Disorders: Studies on Anorexia, Bulimia, and Obesity, 5*, 62–72.

Augustyn, M. (2003). "G" is for growing: Thirty years of research on children and *Sesame Street. Journal of Developmental & Behavioral Pediatrics, 24*, 451.

Ault, R. L. (1983). *Children's cognitive development* (2nd ed.). Oxford: Oxford University Press.

Aunola, K., Stattin, H., & Nurmi, J. E. (2000). Parenting styles and adolescents' achievement strategies. *Journal of Adolescence, 23*, 2205–2222.

Autism Society of America. (2006). *Treatment*. Retrieved July 18, 2006 from http://www.autism-society.org/site/PageServer?pagename=Treatment

Auvert, B., Tajaard, D., Lagarde, E., Tambekou-Sobngwi, J., Siita, R., & Puren, A. (2005). Randomized, controlled intervention trial of male circumcision for education of HIV infection risk: The ANRS 126 trial. *Public Library of Science: Medicine, 2*, 1–11.

Avins, M. (1999, November 14). On the trail of a killer, they discovered hope. *Los Angeles Times*, p. E-1. Retrieved April 21, 2006 from http://www.hdfoundation.org/newslatimes.html

Axel, R. (1995, October). The molecular logic of smell. *Scientific American, 273*, 154–159.

Ayllon, T., & Azrin, N. (1965). The measurement and reinforcement of behavior of psychotics. *Journal of the Experimental Analysis of Behavior, 8*, 357–383.

Ayllon, T., & Azrin, N. (1968). *The token economy: A motivational system for therapy and rehabilitation*. New York: Appleton-Century-Crofts.

Azar, B. (2000). A web of research. *Monitor on Psychology, 31* [Online version]. Retrieved March 13, 2002, from http://www.apa.org/monitor/

Azrin, N. H., & Holz, W. C. (1966). Punishment. In W. K. Honig (Ed.), *Operant behavior: Areas of research and application*. New York: Appleton-Century-Crofts.

Azurmendi, A., Braza, F., Sorozabal, A., García, A., Braza, P., Carreras, M., Muñoz, J., Cardas, J., & Sánchez-Martin, J. (2005). Cognitive abilities, androgen levels, and body mass index in 5-year-old children. *Hormones and Behavior, 48*, 187–195.

Babor, T. (2004). Brief treatments for cannabis dependence: Findings from a randomized multisite trial. *Journal of Consulting & Clinical Psychology, 72*, 455–466.

Bach, M., & Hoffman, M. B. (2000). Visual motion detection in man is governed by non-retinal mechanisms. *Vision Research, 40*, 2379–2385.

Bach, P., & Hayes, S. (2002). The use of acceptance and commitment therapy to prevent the rehospitalization of psychotic patients: A randomized controlled trial. *Journal of Consulting and Clinical Psychology, 70*, 1129–1139.

Bäckman, L., Almkvist, O., Nyberg, L., & Anderson, J. (2000). Functional changes in brain activity during priming in Alzheimer's disease. *Journal of Cognitive Neuroscience, 12*, 134–141.

Baddeley, A. (1998). *Human memory: Theory and practice*. Boston, MA: Allyn & Bacon.

Baer, J. (1996). The effects of task-specific divergent-thinking training. *Journal of Creative Behavior, 30*, 183–187.

Baer, L., Rauch, S. L., Ballantine, T., Jr., Martuza, R., Cosgrove, R., Cassem, E., Giriunas, I., Manzo, P. A., Dimino, C., & Jenike, M. A. (1995). Cingulotomy for intractable obsessive-compulsive disorder. *Archives of General Psychiatry, 52*, 384–392.

Bagby, R. M., Rogers, R., & Buis, T. (1994). Detecting malingered and defensive responding on the MMPI-2 in a forensic inpatient sample. *Journal of Personality Assessment, 62*, 191–203.

Bahrick, H. P., Bahrick, P. O., & Wittlinger, R. P. (1975). Fifty years of memory for names and faces: A cross-sectional approach. *Journal of Experimental Psychology: General, 104*, 54–75.

Bahrick, H. P., Hall, L. K., & Berger, S. A. (1996). Accuracy and distortion in memory for high school grades. *Psychological Science, 7*, 265–271.

Bailey, B., & Konstan, J. (2006). On the need for attention-aware systems: Measuring effects of interruption on task performance, error rate, and affective state. *Computers in Human Behavior, 22*, 685–708.

Bailey, J. M., & Benishay, D. S. (1993). Familial aggregation of female sexual orientation. *American Journal of Psychiatry, 150*, 272–277.

Bailey, J. M., Nothnagel, J., & Wolfe, M. (1995). Retrospectively measured individual differences in childhood sex-typed behavior among gay men: Correspondence between self- and maternal reports. *Archives of Sexual Behavior, 24*, 613–622.

Bailey, J. M., & Pillard, R. C. (1991). A genetic study of male sexual orientation. *Archives of General Psychiatry, 48*, 1089–1096.

Bailey, J. M., & Pillard, R. C. (1994). The innateness of homosexuality. *Harvard Mental Health Letter, 10*(7), 4–6.

Bailey, J. M., Pillard, R. C., Neale, M. C., & Agyei, Y. (1993). Heritable factors influence sexual orientation in women. *Archives of General Psychiatry, 50*, 217–223.

Bailey, J. M., & Zucker, K. J. (1995). Childhood sex-typed behavior and sexual orientation: A conceptual analysis and quantitative review. *Developmental Psychology, 31*, 43–55.

Baillargeon, R., & DeVos, J. (1991). Object permanence in young infants: Further evidence. *Child Development, 62*, 1227–1246.

Baker, B., Wendt, A., & Slonaker, W. (2002). An analysis of gender equity in the federal labor relations career field. *Public Personnel Management, 31*, 559–567.

Baldwin, J. D., & Baldwin, J. I. (1997). Gender differences in sexual interest. *Archives of Sexual Behavior, 26*, 181–210.

Ball, S. G., Baer, L., & Otto, M. W. (1996). Symptom subtypes of obsessive-compulsive disorder in behavioral treatment studies: A quantitative review. *Behaviour Research and Therapy, 34*, 47–51.

Ballenger, J. C., Pecknold, J., Rickels, K., & Sellers, E. M. (1993). Medication discontinuation in panic disorder. *Journal of Clinical Psychiatry, 54*(10, Suppl.), 15–21.

Balon, R. (1996). Antidepressants in the treatment of premature ejaculation. *Journal of Sex and Marital Therapy, 22*, 85–96.

Baltes, P. B., Reese, H. W., & Lipsitt, L. P. (1980). Life-span developmental psychology. *Annual Review of Psychology, 31*, 65–110.

Baltimore, D. (2000). Our genome unveiled. *Nature, 409,* 814–816.

Band, G. P., & Kok, A. (2000). Age effects on response monitoring in a mental-rotation task. *Biological Psychology, 51,* 201–221.

Bandura, A. (1969). *Principles of behavior modification.* New York: Holt, Rinehart & Winston.

Bandura, A. (1973). *Aggression: A social learning analysis.* Englewood Cliffs, NJ: Prentice-Hall.

Bandura, A. (1976). On social learning and aggression. In E. P. Hollander & R. C. Hunt (Eds.), *Current perspectives in social psychology* (4th ed., pp. 116–128). New York: Oxford University Press.

Bandura, A. (1977a). *Social learning theory.* Englewood Cliffs, NJ: Prentice-Hall.

Bandura, A. (1986). *Social functions of thought and action: A social-cognitive theory.* Englewood Cliffs, NJ: Prentice-Hall.

Bandura, A. (1997a, March). Self-efficacy. *Harvard Mental Health Letter, 13*(9), 4–6.

Bandura, A. (1997b). *Self-efficacy: The exercise of control.* New York: Freeman.

Bandura, A., Adams, N. E., & Beyer, J. (1977). Cognitive processes mediating behavioral change. *Journal of Personality and Social Psychology, 35,* 125–139.

Bandura, A., Jeffery, R. W., & Gajdos, E. (1975). Generalizing change through participant modeling with self-directed mastery. *Behaviour Research and Therapy, 13,* 141–152.

Bandura, A., Ross, D., & Ross, S. A. (1961). Transmission of aggression through imitation of aggressive models. *Journal of Abnormal and Social Psychology, 63,* 575–582.

Bandura, A., Ross, D., & Ross, S. A. (1963). Imitation of film-mediated aggressive models. *Journal of Abnormal and Social Psychology, 66,* 3–11.

Barbarich, N., McConaha, C., Gaskill, J., La Via, M., Frank, G., Achenbach, S., Plotnicov, K., & Kaye, W. (2004). An open trial of olanzapine in anorexia nervosa. *Journal of Clinical Psychiatry, 65,* 1480–1482.

Bargiel-Matusiewicz, K., Trzcieniecka-Green, A., Krupa, A., & Krzystanek, M. (2005). Reaction phases following HIV positive diagnosis. *Archives of Psychiatry and Psychotherapy, 7,* 63–69.

Bargmann, C. (1996). From the nose to the brain. *Nature, 384,* 512–513.

Barinaga, M. (1997). How jet-lag hormone does double duty in the brain. *Science, 277,* 480.

Barker, L. (2006). Teaching evolutionary psychology: An interview with David M. Buss. *Teaching of Psychology, 33,* 69–76.

Barlow, D. H. (1997). Cognitive-behavioral therapy for panic disorder: Current status. *Journal of Clinical Psychiatry, 58*(6, Suppl.), 32–36.

Barnett, R. (2004). Women and multiple roles: Myths and reality. *Harvard Review of Psychiatry, 12,* 158–164.

Barnett, R., & Hyde, J. (2001). Women, men, work, and family. *American Psychologist, 56,* 781–796.

Baron, R. (2000). Arousal, capacity, and intense indoctrination. *Personality and Social Psychology Review, 4,* 238–254.

Barrick, M., Mount, M., & Judge, T. (2001). Personality and performance at the beginning of the new millennium: What do we know and where do we go next? *International Journal of Selection and Assessment, 9,* 9–30.

Barsh, G. S., Farooqi, I. S., & O'Rahilly, S. (2000). Genetics of body-weight regulation. *Nature, 404,* 644–651.

Barsky, A. J. (1993, August). How does hypochondriasis differ from normal concerns about health? *Harvard Mental Health Letter, 10*(3), 8.

Bartlett, A. (2002). Current perspectives on the goals of psychoanalysis. *Journal of the American Psychoanalytic Association, 50,* 629–638.

Bartlett, F. C. (1932). *Remembering: A study in experimental and social psychology.* London: Cambridge University Press.

Bartoshuk, L. M., & Beauchamp, G. K. (1994). Chemical senses. *Annual Review of Psychology, 45,* 419–449.

Barzman, D., McConville, B., Masterson, B., McElroy, S., Sethuraman, G., Moore, K., Kahwaty, A., & Nelson, D. (2005). Impulsive aggression with irritability and responsive to divalproex: A pediatric bipolar spectrum disorder phenotype? *Journal of Affective Disorders, 88,* 279–285.

Basic Behavioral Science Task Force of the National Advisory Mental Health Council. (1996). Basic behavioral science research for mental health: Perception, attention, learning, and memory. *American Psychologist, 51,* 133–142.

Basile, K. (2002). Prevalence of wife rape and other intimate partner sexual coercion in a nationally representative sample of women. *Violence & Victims, 17,* 511–524.

Bass, B. (1998). *Transformational leadership: Industrial, military and educational impact.* Mahwah, NJ: Lawrence Erlbaum.

Bass, B., Avolio, B., Jung, D., & Berson, Y. (2003). Predicting unit performance by assessing transformational and transactional leadership. *Journal of Applied Psychology, 88,* 207–218.

Bass, E., & Davis, L. (1988). *The courage to heal.* New York: Harper & Row.

Bassili, J. N. (1995). Response latency and the accessibility of voting intentions: What contributes to accessibility and how it affects vote choice. *Personality and Social Psychology Bulletin, 21,* 686–695.

Bates, M., Labouvie, D., & Voelbel, G. (2002). Individual differences in latent neuropsychological abilities at addictions treatment entry. *Psychology of Addictive Behaviors, 16,* 35–46.

Bateson, G. (1982). Totemic knowledge in New Guinea. In U. Neisser (Ed.), *Memory observed: Remembering in natural contexts.* San Francisco: W. H. Freeman.

Batson, C. D., Batson, J. G., Griffitt, C. A., Barrientos, S., Brandt, J. R., Sprengelmeyer, P., & Bayly, M. J. (1989). Negative-state relief and the empathy-altruism hypothesis. *Journal of Personality and Social Psychology, 56,* 922–933.

Bauer, L. (2001). Antisocial personality disorder and cocaine dependence: Their effects on behavioral and electroencephalographic measures of time. *Drug and Alcohol Dependence, 63,* 87–95.

Baumgardner, A. H., Heppner, P. P., & Arkin, R. M. (1986). Role of causal attribution in personal problem solving. *Journal of Personality and Social Psychology, 50,* 636–643.

Baumrind, D. (1967). Child care practices anteceding three patterns of preschool behavior. *Genetic Psychology Monographs, 75,* 43–88.

Baumrind, D. (1971). Current patterns of parental authority. *Developmental Psychology Monographs, 4*(1, Pt. 2).

Baumrind, D. (1980). New directions in socialization research. *American Psychologist, 35,* 639–652.

Baumrind, D. (1991). The influence of parenting style on adolescent competence and substance use. *Journal of Early Adolescence, 11,* 56–95.

Bavelier, D., Tomann, A., Hutton, C., Mitchell, T., Corina, D., Liu, G., & Neville, H. (2000). Visual attention to the periphery is enhanced in congenitally deaf individuals. *Journal of Neuroscience, 20,* 1–6.

Bazan, S. (1998). Enhancing decision-making effectiveness in problem-solving teams. *Clinical Laboratory Management Review, 12,* 272–276.

Bean, P., Loomis, C., Timmel, P., Hallinan, P., Moore, S., Mammel, J., & Weltzin, T. (2004). Outcome variables for anorexic males and females one year after discharge from residential treatment. *Journal of Addictive Diseases, 23,* 83–94.

Bean, R., Perry, B., & Bedell, T. (2002). Developing culturally competent marriage and family therapists: Treatment guidelines for non-African American therapists working with African American families. *Journal of Marital & Family Therapy, 28,* 153–164.

Bechara, A. (2005). Decision making, impulse control and loss of willpower to resist drugs: A neurocognitive perspective. *Nature Neuroscience, 18,* 1458–1463.

Bechara, A., Damasio, H., & Damasio, A. R. (2000). Emotion, decision making and the orbitofrontal cortex. *Cerebral Cortex, 10,* 295–307.

Beck, A. T. (1976). *Cognitive therapy and the emotional disorders.* New York: New American Library.

Beck, A. T. (1991). Cognitive therapy: A 30-year retrospective. *American Psychologist, 46,* 368–375.

Beck, A. T. (1993). Cognitive therapy: Past, present, and future. *Journal of Consulting and Clinical Psychology, 61,* 194–198.

Beck, J. G. (1995). Hypoactive sexual desire disorder: An overview. *Journal of Consulting and Clinical Psychology, 63,* 919–927.

Beede, K., & Kass, S. (2006). Engrossed in conversation: The impact of cell phones on simulated driving performance. *Accident Analysis & Prevention, 38,* 415–421.

Beers, M. (2006). *Merck manual of geriatrics* (3rd ed. update). Retrieved June 15, 2006 from http://www.merck.com/mrkshared/mmg/home.jsp.

Beets, M., & Pitetti, K. (2004). One-mile run/walk and body mass index of an ethnically diverse sample of youth. *Medicine & Science in Sports & Exercise, 36,* 1796–1803.

Beilin, H., & Fireman, G. (1999). The foundation of Piaget's theories: Mental and physical action. *Advances in Child Development and Behavior, 27,* 221–246.

Békésy, G. von. (1957). The ear. *Scientific American, 197,* 66–78.

Belcourt-Dittloff, A., & Stewart, J. (2000). Historical racism: Implications for Native Americans. *American Psychologist, 55,* 1164–1165.

Bell, A. P., Weinberg, M. S., & Hammersmith, S. K. (1981). *Sexual preference: Its development in men and women.* Bloomington: Indiana University Press.

Bell, L., & Bell, D. (2005). Family dynamics in adolescence affect midlife well-being. *Journal of Family Psychology, 19,* 198–207.

Bell, M. A., & Fox, N. A. (1992). The relationship between frontal brain electrical activity and cognitive development during infancy. *Child Development, 63,* 1142–1163.

Belsky, J., & Fearon, R. (2002). Infant-mother attachment security, contextual risk, and early development: A moderational analysis. *Development & Psychopathology, 14,* 293–310.

Belsky, J., Rovine, M., & Fish, M. (1989). The developing family system. In M. Gunnar (Ed.), *Minnesota symposium on child psychology: Vol. 22. Systems and development.* Hillsdale, NJ: Erlbaum.

Bem, D., & Honorton, C. (1994). Does psi exist? Replicable evidence for an anomalous process of information transfer. *Psychological Bulletin, 115,* 4–18.

Bem, S. (1974). The measurement of psychological androgyny. *Journal of Consulting and Clinical Psychology, 42,* 155–162.

Bem, S. L. (1974). The measurement of psychological androgyny. *Journal of Consulting and Clinical Psychology, 42,* 155–162.

Bem, S. L. (1977). On the utility of alternative procedures for assessing psychological androgyny. *Journal of Consulting and Clinical Psychology, 45,* 196–205.

Bem, S. L. (1981). Gender schema theory: A cognitive account of sex typing. *Psychological Review, 88,* 354–364.

Bem, S. L. (1985). Androgyny and gender schema theory: A conceptual and empirical integration. In T. B. Sonderegger (Ed.), *Nebraska symposium on motivation: Psychology of gender* (Vol. 32, pp. 179–226). Lincoln: University of Nebraska Press.

Benazzi, F. (2000). Late-life atypical major depressive episode: A 358-case study in outpatients. *American Journal of Geriatric Psychiatry, 8,* 117–122.

Bender, E. (2004). Expert witness describes making of a serial killer. *Psychiatric Times, 39,* 13–44.

Benes, F. M. (2000). Emerging principles of altered neural circuitry in schizophrenia. *Brain Research Reviews, 31,* 251–269.

Bengtson, V., Rosenthal, C., & Burton, L. (1990). Families and aging: Diversity and heterogeneity. In R. H. Binstock & L. K. George (Eds.), *Handbook of aging and the social sciences* (3rd ed., pp. 263–287). San Diego: Academic.

Benjafield, J. G. (1996). *A history of psychology.* Boston: Allyn & Bacon.

Benjamin, L., & Crouse, E. (2002). The American Psychological Association's response to *Brown v. Board of Education*: The case of Kenneth B. Clark. *American Psychologist, 57,* 38–50.

Benjamin, L. T. (2000). The psychology laboratory at the turn of the 20th century. *American Psychologist, 55,* 318–321.

Bennett, M. R. (2000). The concept of long-term potentiation of transmission at synapses. *Progress in Neurobiology, 60,* 109–137.

Bennett, W. I. (1990, November). Boom and doom. *Harvard Health Letter, 16,* 1–4.

Ben-Porath, Y. S., & Butcher, J. N. (1989). The comparability of MMPI and MMPI–2 scales and profiles. *Psychological Assessment: A Journal of Consulting and Clinical Psychology, 1,* 345–347.

Ben-Zur, H., Duvdevany, I., & Lury, L. (2005). Associations of social support and hardiness with mental health among mothers of adult children with intellectual disability. *Journal of Intellectual Disability Research, 49,* 54–62.

Beran, M. (2004). Long-term retention of the differential values of Arabic numerals by chimpanzees (Pan troglodytes). *Animal Cognition, 7*, 86–92.

Beran, M., & Rumbaugh, D. (2001). "Constructive" enumeration by chimpanzees (Pan troglodytes) on a computerized task. *Animal Cognition, 4*, 81–89.

Bergem, A. L. M., Engedal, K., & Kringlen, E. (1997). The role of heredity in late-onset Alzheimer's disease and vascular dementia. *Archives of General Psychiatry, 54*, 264–270.

Bergman, M., & Drasgow, F. (2003). Race as a moderator in a model of sexual harassment: An empirical test. *Journal of Occupational Health Psychology, 8*, 131–145.

Berk, L. E. (1994). *Child development* (3rd ed.). Boston: Allyn & Bacon.

Berkman, L. F., & Syme, S. L. (1979). Social networks, host resistance, and mortality: A nine-year followup study of Alameda County residents. *American Journal of Epidemiology, 109*, 184–204.

Berkowitz, L. (1983). Aversively stimulated aggression: Some parallels and differences in research with animals and humans. *American Psychologist, 38*, 1135–1144.

Berkowitz, L. (1988). Frustrations, appraisals, and aversively stimulated aggression. *Aggressive Behavior, 14*, 3–11.

Berkowitz, L. (1990). On the formation and regulation of anger and aggression: A cognitive-neoassociationistic analysis. *American Psychologist, 45*, 494–503.

Bernal, M. E., & Castro, F. G. (1994). Are clinical psychologists prepared for service and research with ethnic minorities? Report of a decade of progress. *American Psychologist, 49*, 797–805.

Bernat, E., Shevrin, H., & Snodgrass, M. (2001). Subliminal visual oddball stimuli evoke P300 component. *Clinical Neurophysiology, 112*, 159–171.

Berndt, E. R., Koran, L. M., Finkelstein, S. N., Gelenberg, A. J., Kornstein, S. G., Miller, I. M., Thase, M. E., Trapp, G. A., & Keller, M. B. (2000). Lost human capital from early-onset chronic depression. *American Journal of Psychiatry, 157*, 940–947.

Berndt, T. J. (1992). Friendship and friends' influence in adolescence. *Current Directions in Psychological Science, 1*, 156–159.

Bernstein, I. L. (1985). Learned food aversions in the progression of cancer and its treatment. *Annals of the New York Academy of Sciences, 443*, 365–380.

Bernstein, I. L., Webster, M. M., & Bernstein, I. D. (1982). Food aversions in children receiving chemotherapy for cancer. *Cancer, 50*, 2961–2963.

Berquier, A., & Aston, R. (1992). Characteristics of the frequent nightmare sufferer. *Journal of Abnormal Psychology, 101*, 246–250.

Berscheid, E., Dion, K., Walster, E., & Walster, G. W. (1971). Physical attractiveness and dating choice: A test of the matching hypothesis. *Journal of Experimental Social Psychology, 7*, 173–189.

Bhugra, D. (2005). The global prevalence of schizophrenia. *Public Library of Science, 5*. [Online only, no pages.] Retrieved July 18, 2006 from http://medicine.plosjournals.org/perlserv?request=get-document&doi=10.1371/journal.pmed.0020151

Bialystok, E., Shenfield, T., & Codd, J. (2000). Languages, scripts, and the environment: Factors in developing concepts of print. *Developmental Psychology, 36*, 66–76.

Bierman, A., Fazio, & Milkie, M. (2006). A multifaceted approach to the mental health advantage of the married: Assessing how explanations vary by outcome measure and unmarried group. *Journal of Family Issues, 27*, 554–582.

Bierut, L., Dinwiddie, S., Begleiter, H., Crowe, R., Hesselbrock, V., Nurnberger, J., Porjesz, B., Schuckit, M., & Reich, T. (1998). Familial transmission of substance dependence: Alcohol, marijuana, cocaine, and habitual smoking: A report from the collaborative study on the genetics of alcoholism. *Archives of General Psychiatry, 55*, 982–988.

Bilkey, D., & Clearwater, J. (2005). The dynamic nature of spatial encoding in the hippocampus. *Behavioral Neuroscience, 119*, 1533–1545.

Billiard, M., Pasquiré-Magnetto, V., Heckman, M., Carlander, B., Besset, A., Zachariev, Z., Eliaou, J. F., & Malafosse, A. (1994). Family studies in narcolepsy. *Sleep, 17*, S54–S59.

Biondi, M., & Picardi, A. (2003). Increased probability of remaining in remission from panic disorder with agoraphobia after drug treatment in patients who received concurrent cognitive-behavioural therapy: A follow-up study. *Psychotherapy & Psychosomatics, 72*, 34–42.

Birch, D. (1998). The adolescent parent: A fifteen-year longitudinal study of school-age mothers and their children. *Internal Journal of Adolescent Medicine & Health, 19*, 141–153.

Birren, J. E., & Fisher, L. M. (1995). Aging and speed of behavior: Possible consequences for psychological functioning. *Annual Review of Psychology, 46*, 329–353.

Bishop, J., & Lane, R. C. (2000). Father absence and the attitude of entitlement. *Journal of Contemporary Psychotherapy, 30*, 105–117.

Bishop, R. (2005). Cognitive psychology: Hidden assumptions. In B. Slife, J. Reber, & F. Richardson (Eds.), *Critical thinking about psychology: Hidden assumptions and plausible alternatives*. Washington, DC: American Psychological Association.

Bisiach, E. (1996). Unilateral neglect and the structure of space representation. *Current Directions in Psychological Science, 5*, 62–65.

Bjork, D. W. (1993). *B. F. Skinner: A life*. New York: Basic Books.

Bjorklund, D. F., Cassel, W. S., Bjorklund, B. R., Brown, R. D., Park, C. L., Ernst, K., & Owen, F. A. (2000). Social demand characteristics in children's and adults' memory and suggestibility: The effect of different interviewers on free recall and recognition. *Applied Cognitive Psychology, 14*, 421–433.

Bjorklund, D. F., & Coyle, T. R. (1995). Utilization deficiencies in the development of memory strategies. In F. E. Weinert & W. Schneider (Eds.), *Research on memory development: State of the art and future directions*. Hillsdale, NJ: Erlbaum.

Björkqvist, K., Lagerspetz, K. M. J., & Kaukiainen, A. (1992). Do girls manipulate and boys fight? Developmental trends in regard to direct and indirect aggression. *Aggressive Behavior, 18*, 117–127.

Blagrove, M., & Hartnell, S. (2000). Lucid dreaming: Associations with internal locus of control, need for cognition and creativity. *Personality & Individual Differences, 28,* 41–47.

Blascovich, J., Wyer, N. A., Swart, L. A., & Kibler, J. L. (1997). Racism and racial categorization. *Journal of Personality and Social Psychology, 72,* 1364–1372.

Blatt, S. J., Sanislow, C. A., III, Zuroff, D. C., & Pilkonis, P. A. (1996). Characteristics of effective therapists: Further analyses of data from the National Institute of Mental Health Treatment of Depression Collaborative Research Program. *Journal of Consulting and Clinical Psychology, 64,* 1276–1284.

Blaylock, B. (2005). In memoriam: Elisabeth Kübler-Ross. *Family, Systems, & Health, 23,* 108–109.

Bliese, P. D., & Castro, C. A. (2000). Role clarity, work overload and organizational support: Multilevel evidence of the importance of support. *Work & Stress, 14,* 65–73.

Bliss, T. V., & Lomo, T. (2000). Plasticity in a monosynaptic cortical pathway. *Journal of Physiology, 207,* 61.

Bloom, B. S. (Ed.). (1985). *Developing talent in young people.* New York: Ballantine.

Bloomer, C. M. (1976). *Principles of visual perception.* New York: Van Nostrand Reinhold.

Blumenthal, J., Emery, C., Maden, D., Schiebolk, S., Walsh-Riddle, M., George, L., McKee, D., Higginbotham, M., Cobb, R., & Coleman, R. (1991). Long-term effects of exercise on physiological functioning in older men and women. *Journals of Gerontology: Psychological Sciences, 46,* P352–361.

Blumer, D. (2002). The illness of Vincent van Gogh. *American Journal of Psychiatry, 159,* 519–526.

Blyth, D. A., Simmons, R. G., Bulcroft, R., Felt, D., VanCleave, E. F., & Bush, D. M. (1981). The effects of physical development on self-image and satisfaction with body-image for early adolescent males. In R. G. Simmons (Ed.), *Research in community and mental health* (Vol. 2). Greenwich, CT: JAI.

Bobes, J., Gibert, J., Ciudad, A., Alvarez, E., Cañas, F., Carrasco, J., Gascón, J., Gómez, J., & Gutiérrez, M. (2003). Safety and effectiveness of olanzapine versus conventional antipsychotics in the acute treatment of first-episode schizophrenic inpatients. *Progress in Neuro-Psychopharmacology & Biological Psychiatry, 27,* 473–481.

Boccaccini, M., Boothby, J., & Overduin, L. (2006). Evaluating the validity of pain complaints in personal injury cases: Assessment approaches of forensic and pain specialists. *Journal of Forensic Psychology Practice, 6*(3), 51–62.

Bogen, J. E., & Vogel, P. J. (1963). Treatment of generalized seizures by cerebral commissurotomy. *Surgical Forum, 14,* 431.

Bohannon, J. N., III. (1988). Flashbulb memories for the Space Shuttle disaster: A tale of two theories. *Cognition, 29,* 179–196.

Boivin, D. B., Czeisler, C. A., Dijk, D-J., Duffy, J. F., Folkard, S., Minors, D. S., Totterdell, P., & Waterhouse, J. M. (1997). Complex interaction of the sleep-wake cycle and circadian phase modulates mood in healthy subjects. *Archives of General Psychiatry, 54,* 145–152.

Bollini, A., Walker, E., Hamann, S., & Kestler, L. (2004). The influence of perceived control and locus of control on the cortisol and subjective responses to stress. *Biological Psychology, 67,* 245–260.

Bompas, A., & O'Regan, J. (2006). Evidence for a role of action in colour perception. *Perception, 35,* 65–78.

Bonanno, G. A., Keltner, D., Holen, A., & Horowitz, M. J. (1995). When avoiding unpleasant emotions might not be such a bad thing: Verbal-autonomic response dissociation and midlife conjugal bereavement. *Journal of Personality and Social Psychology, 69,* 975–989.

Bonnefond, A., Härmä, M., Hakola, T., Sallinen, M., Kandolin, I., & Virkkala, J. (2006). Interaction of age with shift-related sleep-wakefulness, sleepiness, performance, and social life. *Experimental Aging Research, 32,* 185–208.

Bonnel, A., Mottron, L., Peretz, I., Tudel, M., Gallun, E., & Bonnel, A. (2003). Enhanced pitch sensitivity in individuals with autism: A signal detection analysis. *Journal of Cognitive Neuroscience, 15,* 226–235.

Bonson, K., Grant, S., Contoreggi, C., Links, J., Metcalfe, J., Weyl, H., Kurian, V., Ernst, M., & London, E. (2002). Neural systems and cue-induced cocaine craving. *Neuropsychopharmacology, 26,* 376–386.

Borbely, A. A. (1984). Sleep regulation: Outline of a model and its implications for depression. In A. A. Borbely & J. L. Valatx (Eds.), *Sleep mechanisms.* Berlin: Springer-Verlag.

Borbely, A. A., Achermann, P., Trachsel, L., & Tobler, I. (1989). Sleep initiation and initial sleep intensity: Interactions of homeostatic and circadian mechanisms. *Journal of Biological Rhythms, 4,* 149–160.

Bornstein, M., DiPietro, J., Hahn, C., Painter, K., Haynes, O., & Costigan, K. (2002). Prenatal cardiac function and postnatal cognitive development: An exploratory study. *Infancy, 3,* 475–494.

Bornstein, R. F. (1989). Exposure and affect: Overview and meta-analysis of research, 1968–1987. *Psychological Bulletin, 106,* 265–289.

Borzekowski, D., Fobil, J., & Asante, K. (2006). Online access by adolescents in Accra: Ghanaian teens' use of the Internet for health information. *Developmental Psychology, 42,* 450–458.

Bosse, R., Aldwin, C. M., Levenson, M. R., & Workman-Daniels, K. (1991). How stressful is retirement? *Journal of Gerontology, 46,* 9–14.

Boston Globe. (2006, May 28). *"Lost boy" from Sudan finds way at UMass-Boston.* Retrieved June 10, 2006 from http://www.boston.com/news/education/higher/articles/2006/05/28/lost_boy_from_sudan

Bouchard, T. J., Jr. (1994). Genes, environment, and personality. *Science, 264,* 1700–1701.

Bouchard, T. J., Jr. (1997, September/October). Whenever the twain shall meet. *The Sciences, 37,* 52–57.

Bouchard, T. J., Jr. (1998, May 13). Personal communication.

Bouchard, T. J., Jr., Lykken, D. T., McGue, M., Segal, N. L., & Tellegen, A. (1990). Sources of human psychological differences: The Minnesota study of twins reared apart. *Science, 250,* 223–228.

Bouhuys, A., Flentge, F., Oldehinkel, A., & van den Berg, M. (2004). Potential psychosocial mechanisms linking depression to immune function in elderly subjects. *Psychiatry Research, 127,* 237–245.

Bourassa, D., McManus, I., & Bryden, M. (1996). Handedness and eye-dominance: A meta-analysis of their relationship. *Laterality, 1,* 5–34.

Bourassa, M., & Vaugeois, P. (2001). Effects of marijuana use on divergent thinking. *Creativity Research Journal, 13*, 411–416.

Bouton, M. E. (1993). Context, time, and memory retrieval in the interference paradigms of Pavlovian learning. *Psychological Bulletin, 114*, 80–89.

Bouton, M. E., & Ricker, S. T. (1994) Renewal of extinguished responding in a second context. *Animal Learning and Behavior, 22*, 317–324.

Bovbjerg, D. H., Redd, W. H., Maier, L. A., Holland, J. C., Lesko, L. M., Niedzwiecki, D., Rubin, S. C., & Hakes, T. B. (1990). Anticipatory immune suppression and nausea in women receiving cyclic chemotherapy for ovarian cancer. *Journal of Consulting and Clinical Psychology, 58*, 153–157.

Bowden, C., Lecrubier, Y., Bauer, M., Goodwin, G., Greil, W., Sachs, G., & von Knorring, L. (2000). Maintenance therapies for classic and other forms of bipolar disorder. *Journal of Affective Disorders, 59*(1), S57–S67.

Bowden, C., Myers, J., Grossman, F., & Xie, Y. (2004). Risperidone in combination with mood stabilizers: A 10-week continuation phase study in bipolar I disorder. *Journal of Clinical Psychiatry, 65*, 707–714.

Bowen, C. (2003). A case study of job analysis. *Journal of Psychological Practice, 8*, 46–55.

Bowen-Reid, T., & Harrell, J. (2002). Racist experiences and health outcomes: An examination of spirituality as a buffer. *Journal of Black Psychology, 28*, 18–36.

Bower, G. H. (1973, October). How to . . . uh . . . remember! *Psychology Today*, 63–70.

Bower, G. H., Thompson-Schill, S., & Tulving, E. (1994). Reducing retroactive interference: An interference analysis. *Journal of Experimental Psychology: Learning, Memory, and Cognition, 20*, 51–66.

Bowers, K. S. (1992). Imagination and dissociative control in hypnotic responding. *International Journal of Clinical and Experimental Hypnosis, 40*, 253–275.

Bowers, K. S., & Farvolden, P. (1996). Revisiting a century-old Freudian slip—from suggestion disavowed to the truth repressed. *Psychological Bulletin, 119*, 355–380.

Bowers, K. S., & Woody, E. Z. (1996). Hypnotic amnesia and the paradox of intentional forgetting. *Journal of Abnormal Psychology, 105*, 381–390.

Bowlby, J. (1969). *Attachment and loss* (Vol. 1). New York: Basic Books.

Brady, S., & Matthews, K. (2006). Effects of media violence on health-related outcomes among young men. *Archives of Pediatric Adolescent Medicine, 160*, 341–347.

Brain imaging and psychiatry—Part I. (1997, January). *Harvard Mental Health Letter, 13*(7), 1–4.

Bramblett, D. A. (1997, October). Personal communication.

Braten, L., & Olaussen, B. (1998). The learning and study strategies of Norwegian first-year college students. *Learning & Individual Differences, 10*, 309–327.

Braun, A., Balkin, T., Wesensten, N., Gwadry, F., Carson, R., Varga, M., Baldwin, P., Belenky, G., & Herscovitch, P. (1998). Dissociated pattern of activity in visual cortices and their projections during human rapid eye movement sleep. *Science, 279*, 91–95.

Brawman-Mintzer, O., & Lydiard, R. B. (1996). Generalized anxiety disorder: Issues in epidemiology. *Journal of Clinical Psychiatry, 57*(7, Suppl.), 3–8.

Brawman-Mintzer, O., & Lydiard, R. B. (1997). Biological basis of generalized anxiety disorder. *Journal of Clinical Psychiatry, 58*(3, Suppl.), 16–25.

Bray, G. A., & Tartaglia, L. A. (2000). Medicinal strategies in the treatment of obesity. *Nature, 404*, 672–677.

Breckler, S. J. (1984). Empirical validation of affect, behavior, and cognition as distinct attitude components. *Journal of Personality and Social Psychology, 47*, 1191–1205.

Breedlove, S. M. (1994). Sexual differentiation of the human nervous system. *Annual Review of Psychology, 45*, 389–418.

Breggin, P., & Cohen, D. (2000). *Your drug may be your problem: How and why to stop taking psychiatric medications*. New York: HarperCollins.

Breland, K., & Breland, M. (1961). The misbehavior of organisms. *American Psychologist, 16*, 681–684.

Brennan, P. A., Raine, A., Schulsinger, F., Kirkegaard-Sorensen, L., Knop, J., Hutchings, B., Rosenberg, R., & Mednick, S. A. (1997). Psychophysiological protective factors for male subjects at high risk for criminal behavior. *American Journal of Psychiatry, 154*, 853–855.

Brent, D. A., Bridge, J., Johnson, B. A., & Connolly, J. (1996). Suicidal behavior runs in families: A controlled family study of adolescent suicide victims. *Archives of General Psychiatry, 53*, 1145–1152.

Brent, D., Oquendo, M., Birmaher, B., Greenhill, L., Kolko, D., Stanley, B., Zelazny, J., Brodsky, B., Bridge, J., Ellis, S., Salazar, J., & Mann, J. (2002). Familial pathways to early-onset suicide attempt. *Archives of General Psychiatry, 59*, 801.

Breslau, N., Davis, G. C., Peterson, E. L., & Schultz, L. (1997). Psychiatric sequelae of posttraumatic stress disorder in women. *Archives of General Psychiatry, 54*, 81–87.

Breslau, N., Kilbey, M. N., & Andreski, P. (1993). Nicotine dependence and major depression: New evidence from a prospective investigation. *Archives of General Psychiatry, 50*, 31–35.

Bretherton, I. (1992). The origins of attachment theory: John Bowlby and Mary Ainsworth. *Developmental Psychology, 28*, 759–775.

Brett, J., & Atwater, L. (2001). 360-degree feedback: Accuracy, reactions, and perceptions of usefulness. *Journal of Applied Psychology, 86*, 930–942.

Brewer, C., Hopkins, J., Kimble, G., Matlin, M., McCann, L., McNeil, O., Nodine, B., Quinn, V., & Saundra. (1993). Curriculum. In T. McGovern (Ed.), *Handbook for enhancing undergraduate education in psychology* (pp. 161–182). Washington, DC: APA.

Brickman, P., & Campbell, D. (1971). Hedonic relativism and planning the good society. In N. H. Appley (Ed.), *Adaptation level theory: A symposium.* (pp. 287–302). New York: Academic Press.

Bridges, K. M. B. (1932). Emotional development in early infancy. *Child Development, 3*, 324–341.

Brieger, P., Ehrt, U., & Marneros, A. (2003). Frequency of comorbid personality disorders in bipolar and unipolar affective disorders. *Comprehensive Psychiatry, 44*, 28–34.

Brody, A., Saxena, S., Fairbanks, L., Alborzian, S., Demaree, H., Maidment, K., & Baxter, L. (2000). Personality changes in adult subjects with major depressive disorder or obsessive-compulsive disorder treated with paroxetine. *Journal of Clinical Psychiatry, 61*, 349–355.

Brody, J. E. (1995, August 30). Hormone replacement therapy for men: When does it help? *The New York Times,* p. C8.

Brody, L. R. (1985). Gender differences in emotional development: A review of theories and research. *Journal of Personality, 53,* 102–149.

Brody, N. (1992). *Intelligence* (2nd ed.). San Diego, CA: Academic.

Bronfenbrenner, U. (1979). *The ecology of human development.* Cambridge, MA: Harvard University Press.

Bronfenbrenner, U. (1989). Ecological systems theory. *Annals of Child Development, 6,* 187–249.

Bronfenbrenner, U. (1993). The ecology of cognitive development: Research methods and fugitive findings. In R. Wozniak and K. Fischer (Eds.), *Development in context: Acting and thinking in specific environments.* Hillsdale, NJ: Erlbaum.

Bronte-Tinkew, J., Moore, K., Capps, R., & Zaff, J. (2006). The influence of father involvement on youth risk behaviors among adolescents: A comparison of native-born and immigrant families. *Social Science Research, 35,* 181–209.

Brook, U., & Boaz, M. (2005). Attention deficit and hyperactivity disorder/learning disabilities (ADHD/LD): Parental characterization and perception. *Patient Education & Counseling, 57,* 96–100.

Brooks-Gunn, J. (2003). Do you believe in magic? What we can expect from early childhood intervention programs. *Social Policy Report, 17,* 3–14.

Brotman, A. W. (1994). What works in the treatment of anorexia nervosa? *Harvard Mental Health Letter, 10*(7), 8.

Broughton, R. J., & Shimizu, T. (1995). Sleep-related violence: A medical and forensic challenge. *Sleep, 18,* 727–730.

Broughton, W. A., & Broughton, R. J. (1994). Psychosocial impact of narcolepsy. *Sleep, 17,* S45–S49.

Brown, A. (1996, Winter). Mood disorders in children and adolescents. *NARSAD Research Newsletter,* pp. 11–14.

Brown, A. (2004). The déjà vu illusion. *Current Directions in Psychological Science, 13,* 256–259.

Brown, A., & Day, J. (1983). Macrorules for summarizing text: The development of expertise. *Journal of Verbal Learning and Verbal Behavior, 22,* 1–14.

Brown, G. W., Harris, T. O., & Hepworth, C. (1994). Life events and endogenous depression: A puzzle reexamined. *Archives of General Psychiatry, 51,* 525–534.

Brown, J. D., & Rogers, R. J. (1991). Self-serving attributions: The role of physiological arousal. *Personality and Social Psychology Bulletin, 17,* 501–506.

Brown, R. (1973). *A first language: The early stages.* Cambridge, MA: Harvard University Press.

Brown, R., Cazden, C., & Bellugi, U. (1968). The child's grammar from I to III. In J. P. Hill (Ed.), *Minnesota symposium on child psychology* (Vol. 2, pp. 28–73). Minneapolis: University of Minnesota Press.

Brown, R., & Kulik, J. (1977). Flashbulb memories. *Cognition, 5,* 73–99.

Brown, R., & McNeil, D. (1966). The "tip of the tongue" phenomenon. *Journal of Verbal Learning and Verbal Behavior, 5,* 325–337.

Brown, R. J., & Donderi, D. C. (1986). Dream content and self-reported well-being among recurrent dreamers, past-recurrent dreamers, and nonrecurrent dreamers. *Journal of Personality and Social Psychology, 50,* 612–623.

Brown, W. A. (1998, January). The placebo effect. *Scientific American, 278,* 90–95.

Brownell, K. D., & Wadden, T. A. (1992). Etiology and treatment of obesity: Understanding a serious, prevalent, and refractory disorder. *Journal of Consulting and Clinical Psychology, 60,* 505–517.

Brownlee, S., & Schrof, J. M. (1997, March 17). The quality of mercy. *U.S. News & World Report,* pp. 54–67.

Bruce, M. (2006). A systematic and conceptual review of post-traumatic stress in childhood cancer survivors and their parents. *Clinical Psychology Review, 26,* 233–256.

Bruch, M., Fallon, M., & Heimberg, R. (2003). Social phobia and difficulties in occupational adjustment. *Journal of Counseling Psychology, 50,* 109–117.

Brummett, B., Babyak, M., Williams, R., Barefoot, J., Costa, P., & Siegler, I. (2006). NEO personality domains and gender predict levels and trends in body mass index over 14 years during midlife. *Journal of Research in Personality, 40,* 222–236.

Brunetti, A., Carta, P., Cossu, G., Ganadu, M., Golosio, B., Mura, G., & Pirastru, M. (2002). A real-time classification system of thalassemic pathologies based on artificial neural networks. *Medical Decision Making, 22,* 18–26.

Brunila, T., Lincoln, N., Lindell, A., Tenovuo, O., & Haemelaeinen, H. (2002). Experiences of combined visual training and arm activation in the rehabilitation of unilateral visual neglect: A clinical study. *Neuropsychological Rehabilitation, 12,* 27–40.

Brydon, L., Magid, K., & Steptoe, A. (2006). Platelets, coronary heart disease, and stress. *Brain, Behavior, and Immunity, 20,* 113–119.

Buck, L. B. (1996). Information coding in the vertebrate olfactory system. *Annual Review of Neuroscience, 19,* 517–544.

Buckingham, H. W., Jr., & Kertesz, A. (1974). A linguistic analysis of fluent aphasics. *Brain and Language, 1,* 29–42.

Buhusi, C., & Meck, W. (2002). Differential effects of methamphetamine and haloperidol on the control of an internal clock. *Behavioral Neuroscience, 116,* 291–297.

Buis, J. M., & Thompson, D. N. (1989). Imaginary audience and personal fable: A brief review. *Adolescence, 24,* 773–781.

Buller, D. B., Burgoon, M., Hall, J. R., Levine, N., Taylor, A. M., Beach, B. H., Melcher, C., Buller, M. K., Bowen, S. L., Hunsaker, F. G., & Bergen, A. (2000). Using language intensity to increase the success of a family intervention to protect children from ultraviolet radiation: Predictions from language expectancy theory. *Preventive Medicine, 30,* 103–113.

Bunderson, J., & Sutcliffe, K., (2003). Management team learning orientation and business unit performance. *Journal of Applied Psychology, 88,* 552–560.

Burchinal, M., Campbell, F., Bryant, D., Wasik, B., & Ramey, C. (1997). Early intervention and mediating processes in cognitive performance of children of low-income African American families. *Child Development, 68,* 935–954.

Burke, A., Heuer, F., & Reisberg, D. (1992). Remembering emotional events. *Memory and Cognition, 20,* 277–290.

Burns, J., & Swerdlow, R. (2003). Right orbitofrontal tumor with pedophilia symptom and constructional apraxia sign. *Archives of Neurology, 60,* 437–440.

Burt, D. B., Zembar, M. J., & Niederehe, G. (1995). Depression and memory impairment: A meta-analysis of the association, its pattern, and specificity. *Psychological Bulletin, 117,* 285–305.

Burton, D. (2003). Male adolescents: Sexual victimization and subsequent sexual abuse. *Child & Adolescent Social Work Journal, 20,* 277–296.

Busch, C. M., Zonderman, A. B., & Costa, P. T. (1994). Menopausal transition and psychological distress in a nationally representative sample: Is menopause associated with psychological distress? *Journal of Aging and Health, 6,* 209–228.

Bushman, B. (2002). Does venting anger feed or extinguish the flame? Catharsis rumination, distraction, anger and aggressive responding. *Personality & Social Psychology Bulletin, 28,* 724–731.

Bushman, B., & Cantor, J. (2003). Media ratings for violence and sex: Implications for policymakers and parents. *American Psychologist, 58,* 130–141.

Bushman, B. J. (1995). Moderating role of trait aggressiveness in the effects of violent media on aggression. *Journal of Personality and Social Psychology, 69,* 950–960.

Bushman, B. J., & Cooper, H. M. (1990). Effects of alcohol on human aggression: An integrative research review. *Psychological Bulletin, 107,* 341–354.

Bushman, B., & Huesmann, R. (2006). Short-term and long-term effects of violent media on aggression in children and adults. *Archives of Pediatric Adolescent Medicine, 160,* 348–352.

Buss, D. (1998). Sexual strategies theory: Historical origins and current status. *The Journal of Sex Research, 35,* 19–32.

Buss, D. M. (1994). The strategies of human mating. *American Scientist, 82,* 238–249.

Buss, D. M. (1999). *Evolutionary psychology: The new science of the mind.* Boston: Allyn & Bacon.

Buss, D. M. (2000a). *The dangerous passion: Why jealousy is as necessary as sex and love.* New York: Free Press.

Buss, D. M. (2000b). Desires in human mating. *Annals of the New York Academy of Sciences, 907,* 39–49.

Buss, D. M., Abbott, M., Angleitner, A., Asherian, A., Biaggio, A., Blanco-Villasenor, A., Bruchon-Schweitzer, M., et al. (1990). International preferences in selecting mates: A study of 37 cultures. *Journal of Cross-Cultural Psychology, 21,* 5–47.

Buss, D., Shackelford, T., Kirkpatrick, L., & Larsen, R. (2001). A half century of mate preferences: The cultural evolution of values. *Journal of Marriage and the Family, 63,* 491–503.

Bussey, K., & Bandura, A. (1999). Social cognitive theory of gender development and differentiation. *Psychological Review, 106,* 676–713.

Butcher, J. N. (1992, October). International developments with the MMPI–2. *MMPI–2 News & Profiles, 3,* 4.

Butcher, J. N., Dahlstrom, W. G., Graham, J. R., Tellegen, A., & Kaemmer, B. (1989). *Manual for the restandardized Minnesota Multiphasic Personality Inventory: MMPI–2. An administrative and interpretive guide.* Minneapolis: University of Minnesota Press.

Butcher, J. N., & Graham, J. R. (1989). *Topics in MMPI–2 interpretation.* Minneapolis: Department of Psychology, University of Minnesota.

Butcher, J. N., Graham, J. R., & Ben-Porath, Y. S. (1995). Methodological problems and issues in MMPI, MMPI-2, and MMPI-A research. *Psychological Assessment, 7,* 320–329.

Butcher, J. N., & Rouse, S. V. (1996). Personality: Individual differences and clinical assessment. *Annual Review of Psychology, 47,* 89–111.

Butki, B., Baumstark, J., & Driver, S. (2003). Effects of a carbohydrate-restricted diet on affective responses to acute exercise among physically active participants. *Perceptual & Motor Skills, 96,* 607–615.

Butler, R., & Lewis, M. (1982). *Aging and mental health* (3rd ed.). St. Louis: Mosby.

Butterworth, G., Franco, F., McKenzie, B., Graupner, L., & Todd, B. (2002). Dynamic aspects of visual event perception and the production of pointing by human infants. *British Journal of Developmental Psychology, 20,* 1–24.

Byne, W. (1993b). Sexual orientation and brain structure: Adding up the evidence. Paper presented at the annual meeting of the International Academy of Sex Research. Pacific Grove, CA.

Byne, W. (1994). The biological evidence challenged. *Scientific American, 270,* 50–55.

Cabýoglu, M., Ergene, N., & Tan, U. (2006). The mechanism of acupuncture and clinical applications. *International Journal of Neuroscience, 116,* 115–125.

Cahill, L., & McGaugh, J. (1995). A novel demonstration of enhanced memory associated with emotional arousal. *Consciousness & Cognition, 4,* 410–421.

Cahn, B., & Polich, J. (2006). Meditation states and traits: EEG, ERP, and neuroimaging studies. *Psychological Bulletin, 132,* 180–211.

Calhoun, S., & Dickerson Mayes, S. (2005). Processing speed in children with clinical disorders. *Psychology in the Schools, 42,* 333–343.

Callahan, J. (1997, May–June). Hypnosis: Trick or treatment? You'd be amazed at what modern doctors are tackling with an 18th century gimmick. *Health, 11,* 52–54.

Cameron, L. (1998). *The music of light: The extraordinary story of Hikari and Kenzaburo Oe.* New York: Free Press.

Camp, D. S., Raymond, G. A., & Church, R. M. (1967). Temporal relationship between response and punishment. *Journal of Experimental Psychology, 74,* 114–123.

Campbell, F., Pungello, E., Miller-Johnson, S., Burchinal, M., & Ramey, C. (2001). The development of cognitive and academic abilities: Growth curves from an early childhood educational experiment. *Developmental Psychology, 37,* 231–242.

Campbell, F., & Ramey, C. (1994). Effects of early intervention on intellectual and academic achievement: A follow-up study of children from low-income families. *Child Development, 65,* 684–698.

Campbell, F., Ramey, D., Pungello, E., Spurling, J., & Miller-Johnson, S. (2002). Early childhood education: Young adult outcomes from the Abecedarian Project. *Applied Developmental Science, 6,* 42–57.

Campbell, P., & Dhand, R. (2000). Obesity. *Nature, 404,* 631.

Campbell, S. S. (1985). Spontaneous termination of ad libitum sleep episodes with special reference to REM sleep. *Electroencephalography & Clinical Neurophysiology, 60,* 237–242.

Campos, J. J., Langer, A., & Krowitz, A. (1970). Cardiac responses on the visual cliff in prelocomotor human infants. *Science, 170,* 196–197.

Camras, L., Meng, Z., Ujiie, T., Dharamsi, S., Miyake, K., Oster, H., Wang, L., Cruz, J., Murdoch, A., & Campos, J. (2002). Observing emotion in infants: Facial expression, body behavior, and rater judgments of responses to an expectancy-violating event. *Emotion, 2*, 179–193.

Cannon, T. D., Kaprio, J, Lönnqvist, J., Huttunen, M., & Koskenvuo, M. (1998). The genetic epidemiology of schizophrenia in a Finnish twin cohort: A population-based modeling study. *Archives of General Psychiatry, 55*, 67–74.

Cannon, W. B. (1927). The James-Lange theory of emotions: A critical examination as an alternative theory. *American Journal of Psychology, 39*, 106–112.

Cannon, W. B. (1929). *Bodily changes in pain, hunger, fear and rage* (2nd ed.). New York: Appleton.

Cannon, W. B. (1935). Stresses and strains of homeostasis. *American Journal of Public Health, 189*, 1–14.

Canter, D., Allison, L., Alison, E., & Wentink, N. (2004). The organized/disorganized typology of serial murder: Myth or model? *Psychology, Public Policy, and Law, 10*, 293–320.

Capel, B. (2000). The battle of the sexes. *Mechanisms of Development, 92*, 89–103.

Cardena, E. (2000). Hypnosis in the treatment of trauma: A promising, but not fully supported, efficacious intervention. *International Journal of Clinical Experimental Hypnosis, 48*, 225–238.

Cardoso, S. H., de Mello, L. C., & Sabbatini, R. M. E. (2000). How nerve cells work. Retrieved from http://www.epub.org.br/cm/n09/fundamentos/transmissao/voo_i.htm

Carlat, D. J., Camargo, C. A., Jr., & Herzog, D. B. (1997). Eating disorders in males: A report on 135 patients. *American Journal of Psychiatry, 154*, 1127–1132.

Carlson, N. R. (1998). *Foundations of physiological psychology* (4th ed.). Boston: Allyn & Bacon.

Carlsson, I., Wendt, P. E., & Risberg, J. (2000). On the neurobiology of creativity. Differences in frontal activity between high and low creative subjects. *Neuropsychologia, 38*, 873–885.

Carmeli, E., Reznick, A., Coleman, R., & Carmeli, V. (2000). Muscle strength and mass of lower extremities in relation to functional abilities in elderly adults. *Gerontology, 46*, 249-257.

Carnagey, N., & Anderson, C. (2004). Violent video game exposure and aggression: A literature review. *Minerva Psichiatrica, 45*, 1–18.

Carnagey, N., & Anderson, C. (2005). The effects of reward and punishment in violent video games on aggressive affect, cognition, and behavior. *Psychological Science, 16*, 882–889.

Carpentier, P., de Jong, C., Dijkstra, B., Verbrugge, C., & Krabbe, P. (2005). A controlled trial of methylphenidate in adults with attention deficit/hyperactivity disorder and substance use disorders. *Addiction, 100*, 1868–1874.

Carrier, J. (1980). Homosexual behavior in cross-cultural perspective. In J. Marmor (Ed.), *Homosexual behavior* (pp. 100–122). New York: Basic Books.

Carroll, K. M., Rounsaville, B. J., Nich, C., Gordon, L. T., Wirtz, P. W., & Gawin, F. (1994). One-year follow-up of psychotherapy and pharmacotherapy for cocaine dependence: Delayed emergence of psychotherapy effects. *Archives of General Psychiatry, 51*, 989–997.

Carskadon, M. A., & Dement, W. C. (1989). Normal human sleep: An overview. In M. H. Kryger, T. Roth, & W. C. Dement (Eds.), *Principles and practice of sleep medicine* (pp. 3–13). Philadelphia: W. B. Saunders.

Carskadon, M. A., & Rechtschaffen, A. (1989). Monitoring and staging human sleep. In M. H. Kryger, T. Roth, & W. C. Dement (Eds.), *Principles and practice of sleep medicine* (pp. 665–683). Philadelphia: W. B. Saunders.

Carson, R., Butcher, J., & Mineka, S. (2000). *Abnormal psychology and modern life* (11th ed.). Boston: Allyn & Bacon.

Carson, R. C. (1989). Personality. *Annual Review of Psychology, 40*, 227–248.

Caruana, A., & Chircop, S. (2001). The dark side of globalization and liberalization: Helpfulness, alienation and ethnocentrism among small business owners and managers. *Journal of Nonprofit & Public Sector Marketing, 9*, 63–73.

Case, A., & Paxson, C. (2004). *Sex differences in morbidity and mortality.* National Bureau of Economic Research Working Paper No. 10653. Retrieved July 7, 2006 from http://www.nber.org/papers/W10653

Case, R. (Ed.). (1992). *The mind's staircase: Exploring the conceptual underpinnings of children's thought and knowledge.* Hillsdale, NJ: Erlbaum.

Casey, D. E. (1996). Side effect profiles of new antipsychotic agents. *Journal of Clinical Psychiatry, 57*(11, Suppl.), 40–45.

Cash, T. F., & Derlega, V. J. (1978). The matching hypothesis: Physical attractiveness among same-sexed friends. *Personality and Social Psychology Bulletin, 4*, 240–243.

Cash, T. F., & Janda, L. H. (1984, December). The eye of the beholder. *Psychology Today*, pp. 46–52.

Caspi, A. (2000). The child is father of the man: Personality continuities from childhood to adulthood. *Journal of Personality & Social Psychology, 78*, 158–172.

Caspi, A., Lynam, D., Moffitt, T. E., & Silva, P. A. (1993). Unraveling girls' delinquency: Biological, dispositional, and contextual contributions to adolescent misbehavior. *Developmental Psychology, 29*, 19–30.

Caspi, A., & Silva, P. A. (1995). Temperamental qualities at age three predict personality traits in young adulthood: Longitudinal evidence from a birth cohort. *Child Development, 66*, 486–498.

Caspi, A., Roberts, B., & Shiner, R. (2005). Personality development: Stability and change. *Annual Review of Psychology, 56*, 453–484.

Cassell, M., Halperin, D., Shelton, J., & Stanton, D. (2006). Risk compensation: The Achilles' heel of innovations in HIV protection? *British Medical Journal, 332*, 605–607.

Cassidy, J., Ziv, Y., Mehta, T., & Feeney, B. (2003). Feedback seeking in children and adolescents: Associations with self-perceptions, attachment representations, and depression. *Child Development, 74*, 612–628.

Catala, E., Reig, E., Artes, M., Aliaga, L., Lopez, J., & Segu, J. (2002). Prevalence of pain in the Spanish population: Telephone survey in 5000 homes. *European Journal of Pain, 6*, 133–140.

Cates, J., Herndon, N., Schulz, S., & Darroch, J. (2004). *Our voices, our lives, our futures: Youth and sexually transmitted disases.* Retrieved June 29, 2006 from http://www.jomc.unc.edu/youthandSTDs/ourvoicesreport.pdf

Cattell, R. B. (1950). *Personality: A systematic, theoretical, and factual study.* New York: McGraw-Hill.

Cattell, R. B., Eber, H. W., & Tatsuoka, M. M. (1977). *Handbook for the 16 personality factor questionnaire*. Champaign, IL: Institute of Personality and Ability Testing.

CBS News. (July 31, 2002). Fear of public speaking. Retrieved February 14, 2003, from http://www.cbsnews.com/stories/2002/07/30

Ceci, S., & Bronfenbrenner, U. (1985). "Don't forget to take the cupcakes out of the oven": Prospective memory, strategic time-monitoring, and context. *Child Development*, 56, 152–164.

Centers for Disease Control (CDC). (2006). *National youth risk behavior survey 1991–2005*. Retrieved June 13, 2006 from http://www.cdc.gov/healthyyouth/yrbs/pdf/trends/2005_YRBS_Sexual_Behaviors.pdf

Centers for Disease Control and Prevention (CDC). (1998). HIV prevention through early detection and treatment of other sexually transmitted diseases—United States. *Morbidity & Mortality Weekly Report*, 47, 1–24.

Centers for Disease Control and Prevention (CDC). (1999). Physical activity and health. Retrieved January 29, 2003, from http://www.cdc.gov/needphp/sgr/ataglan.htm

Centers for Disease Control and Prevention (CDC). (2001b). Genital herpes. Retrieved January 27, 2003, from http://www.cdc.gov/nchstp/dst/Fact_Sheets_facts_Gnital_Herpes.htm

Centers for Disease Control and Prevention (CDC). (2001c). HIV/AIDS update: A glance at the HIV epidemic. Retrieved January 24, 2003, from http://www.cdc.gov/nchstp/od/news/At-a-Glance.pdf

Centers for Disease Control and Prevention. (2002). Nonfatal self-inflicted injuries treated in hospital emergency departments—United States, 2000. *Morbidity & Mortality Weekly Report*, 51, 436–438.

Centers for Disease Control and Prevention (CDC). (2003). About minority health. Retrieved August 8, 2003, from http://www.cdc.gov/omh/AMH/AMH.htm

Centers for Disease Control and Prevention (CDC). (2003). *Hearing Loss* [Online factsheet]. Retrieved May 13, 2003, from http://www.cdc.gov/ncbddd/dd/ddhi.htm

Centers for Disease Control and Prevention (CDC). (2004). Surveillance summaries. *Morbidity & Mortality Weekly Report*, 53, 1–100.

Centers for Disease Control and Prevention (CDC). (2004). *Syphilis and men who have sex with men*. Retrieved July 3, 2006 from http://www.cdc.gov/std/syphilis/STDFact-MSM&Syphilis.htm

Centers for Disease Control and Prevention (CDC). (2005). *About minority health*. Retrieved February 2, 2005 from http://www.cdc.govomh/AMH/AMH.htm

Centers for Disease Control and Prevention (CDC). (2005). Mental health in the United States: Prevalence of diagnosis and medication treatment for attention-deficit/hyperactivity disorder-United States, 2003. *Morbidity & Mortality Weekly Report*, 54, 842–847.

Centers for Disease Control and Prevention (CDC). (2005a). *Trends in reportable sexually transmitted diseases in the United States, 2004*. Retrieved July 3, 2006 from http://www.cdc.gov/std/stats/04pdf/trends2004.pdf

Centers for Disease Control and Prevention (CDC). (2005b). *HIV/AIDS surveillance report: HIV infection and AIDS in the United States, 2004*. Retrieved July 3, 2006 from

http://www.cdc.gov/hiv/topics/surveillance/basic.htm#exposure

Centers for Disease Control and Prevention (CDC). (2006a). HPV Vaccine questions and answers. Retrieved June 29, 2006 from http://www.cdc.gov/std/hpv/STDFact-HPV-vaccine.htm#vaccine

Centers for Disease Control and Prevention (CDC). (2006a). *Quick stats: General information on alcohol use and health*. Retrieved July 7, 2006 from http://www.cdc.gov/alcohol/quickstats/general_info.htm

Centers for Disease Control and Prevention (CDC). (2006b). *Mother-to-child HIV transmission and prevention*. Retrieved July 3, 2006 from http://www.cdc.gov/hiv/resources/factsheets/perinatl.htm

Centers for Disease Control and Prevention (CDC). (2006b). *Nutrition topics*. Retrieved July 7, 2006 from http://www.cdc.gov/nccdphp/dnpa/nutrition/index.htm

Centers for Disease Control and Prevention (CDC). (2006c). *Growing stronger: Strength training for older adults*. Retrieved July 7, 2006 from http://www.cdc.gov/nccdphp/dnpa/physical/growing_stronger/index.htm

Chambless, D. L., & Goldstein, A. J. (1979). Behavioral psychotherapy. In R. J. Corsini (Ed.), *Current psychotherapies* (2nd ed., pp. 230–272). Itasca, IL: F. E. Peacock.

Chamorro-Premuzic, T., & Furnham, A. (2003). Personality predicts academic performance: Evidence from two longitudinal university samples. *Journal of Research in Personality*, 37, 319–338.

Chan, D. (1997). Racial subgroup differences in predictive validity perceptions on personality and cognitive ability tests. *Journal of Applied Psychology*, 82, 311–320.

Chandler, D. (2002). *Semiotics: The basics*. London: Routledge.

Chang, F., & Burns, B. (2005). Attention in preschoolers: Associations with effortful control and motivation. *Child Development*, 76, 247–263.

Chang, V. (2005). U.S. obesity, weight gain, and socioeconomic status. *CHERP Policy Brief*, 3. Retrieved July 7, 2006 from http://www.cherp.research.med.va.gov/cherpdocs/issuebriefs/Policy%20Brief_Fall2005.pdf

Chao, R. (2001). Extending research on the consequences of parenting style for Chinese Americans and European Americans. *Child Development*, 72, 1832–1843.

Chaplin, W. F., Philips, J. B., Brown, J. D., Clanton, N. R., & Stein, J. L. (2000). Handshaking, gender, personality, and first impressions. *Journal of Personality and Social Psychology*, 19, 110–117.

Charles, S., Mather, M., & Carstensen, L. (2003). Aging and emotional memory: The forgettable nature of negative images for older adults. *Journal of Experimental Psychology*, 132, 310–324.

Chase, M. H., & Morales, F. R. (1990). The atonia and myoclonia of active (REM) sleep. *Annual Review of Psychology*, 41, 557–584.

Chassin, L., Presson, C., Sherman, S., & Kim, K. (2003). Historical changes in cigarette smoking and smoking-related beliefs after 2 decades in a midwestern community. *Health Psychology*, 22, 347–353.

Chatterjee, A. (2004). The neuropsychology of visual artistic production. *Neuropsychologia*, 42, 1568–1583.

Chavez, M., & Spitzer, M. (2002). Herbals and other dietary supplements for premenstrual syndrome and menopause. *Psychiatric Annals, 32,* 61–71.

Chen, J. C., Borson, S., & Scanlan, J. M. (2000). Stage-specific prevalence of behavioral symptoms in Alzheimer's disease in a multi-ethnic community sample. *American Journal of Geriatric Psychiatry, 8,* 123–133.

Chen, X., Chang, L., & He, Y. (2003). The peer group as a context: Mediating and moderating effects on relations between academic achievement and social functioning in Chinese children. *Child Development, 74,* 710–727.

Chen-Sea, M.-J. (2000). Validating the Draw-A-Man Test as a personal neglect test. *American Journal of Occupational Therapy, 54,* 391–397.

Cherry, E. (1953). Some experiments on the recognition of speech with one and two ears. *Journal of the Acoustical Society of America, 25,* 975–979.

Chess, S. (2005). Wisdom from teachers. *Journal of the American Academy of Child & Adolescent Psychiatry, 44,* 623–624.

Chi, S., Park, C., Lim, S., Park, E., Lee, Y., Lee, K., Kim, E., & Kim, H. (2005). EEG and personality dimensions: A consideration based on the rain oscillatory systems. *Personality and Individual Differences, 39,* 669–681.

Chickering, A., & Reisser, L. (1993). *Education and identity* (2nd ed.). San Francisco: Jossey-Bass.

Chilosi, A., Cipriani, P., Bertuccelli, B., Pfanner, L., & Cioni, G. (2001). Early cognitive and communication development in children with focal brain lesions. *Journal of Child Neurology, 16,* 309–316.

"Children spend more time playing video games than watching TV, MSU survey shows." (2004, April 4). Retrieved July 23, 2005, from http://www.newsroom.msu.edu/site/indexer/1943/content.htm.

Cho, K. (2001). Chronic "jet lag" produces temporal lobe atrophy and spatial cognitive deficits. *Nature Neuroscience, 4,* 567–568.

Cho, K., Ennaceur, A., Cole, J., & Kook Suh, C. (2000). Chronic jet lag produces cognitive deficits. *Journal of Neuroscience, 20,* RC66.

Choi, I., Dalal, R., Kim-Prieto, C., & Park, H. (2003). Culture and judgment of causal relevance. *Journal of Personality & Social Psychology, 84,* 46–59.

Chollar, S. (1989). Conversation with the dolphins. *Psychology Today, 23,* 52–57.

Chomsky, N. (1968). *Language and mind.* New York: Harcourt, Brace & World.

Chomsky, N. (1986). *Knowledge of language: Its nature, origin, and use.* New York: Praeger.

Chomsky, N. (1990). On the nature, use and acquisition of language. In W. G. Lycan (Ed.), *Mind and cognition* (pp. 627–646). Oxford, England: Blackwell.

Chou, K., Chi, L., & Chow, N. (2004). Sources of income and depression in elderly Hong Kong Chinese: Mediating and moderating effects of social support and financial strain. *Aging & Mental Health, 8,* 212–221.

Chowdhury, R., Ferrier, I., & Thompson, J. (2003). Cognitive dysfunction in bipolar disorder. *Current Opinion in Psychiatry, 16,* 7–12.

Christakis, D., Zimmerman, F., DiGiuseppe, D., & McCarty, C. (2004). Early television exposure and subsequent attentional problems in children. *Pediatrics, 113,* 708–713.

Christensen, A., Atkins, D., Berns, S., Wheeler, J., Baucom, D., & Simpson, L. (2004). Traditional versus integrative behavioral couple therapy for significantly and chronically distressed married couples. *Journal of Consulting and Clinical Psychology, 72,* 176–191.

Christensen, A., Jacobson, N., & Babcock, J. (1995). Integrative behavioral couple therapy. In N. Jacobseon & A. Gurman (Eds.), *Clinical handbook of marital therapy* (2nd ed., pp. 31–64). New York: Guilford Press.

Christensen, L. B. (1997). *Experimental methodology* (7th ed.). Boston: Allyn & Bacon.

Christensen, P., Rothgerber, H., Wood, W., & Matz, D. (2004). Social norms and identity relevance: A motivational approach to normative behavior. *Journal of Personality & Social Psychology Bulletin, 30,* 1295–1309.

Christianson, S.-Å. (1992). Emotional stress and eyewitness memory: A critical review. *Psychological Bulletin, 112,* 284–309.

Chu, S., & Downes, J. J. (2000). Long live Proust: The odour-cued autobiographical memory bump. *Cognition, 75,* B41–B50.

Church R. M. (1963). The varied effects of punishment on behavior. *Psychological Review, 70,* 369–402.

Church, M., Elliot, A., & Gable, S. (2001). Perceptions of classroom enviornment, achievement goals, and achievement outcomes. *Journal of Educational Psychology, 93,* 43–54.

Church, R. M. (1989). Theories of timing behavior. In S. P. Klein & R. Mowrer (Eds.), *Contemporary learning theories: Instrumental conditioning theory and the impact of biological constraints on learning.* Hillsdale, NJ: Erlbaum.

Cialdini, R. B., Cacioppo, J. T., Basset, R., & Miller, J. A. (1978). Low-ball procedure for producing compliance: Commitment then cost. *Journal of Personality and Social Psychology, 36,* 463–476.

Cioffi, R. (2003). Communicating with culturally and linguistically diverse patients in an acute care setting: Nurses; experiences. *International Journal of Nursing Studies, 40,* 299–306.

Clark, D. M., & Teasdale, J. D. (1982). Diurnal variation in clinical depression and accessibility of memories of positive and negative experiences. *Journal of Abnormal Psychology, 91,* 87–95.

Clark, L., Watson, D., & Reynolds, S. (1995). Ciagnosis and classification of psychopathology: Challenges to the current system and future directions. *Annual Review of Psychology, 46,* 121–153.

Clay, R. (2002). Research on 9/11: What psychologists have learned so far. *APA Monitor on Psychology, 33,* 28–30.

Clay, R. (2003). Researchers replace midlife myths with facts. *APA Monitor on Psychology, 34,* 36.

Clayton, K. N. (1964). T-maze choice learning as a joint function of the reward magnitudes for the alternatives. *Journal of Comparative and Physiological Psychology, 58,* 333–338.

Clayton, N. S. (1998). Memory and the hippocampus in food-storing birds: A comparative approach. *Neuropharmacology, 37,* 441–452.

Clayton, V. (2004, September 8). *What's to blame for the rise in ADHD?* Retrieved November 22, 2004 from http://www.msnbc.msn.com/id/5933775/

Clément, K., Vaisse, C., Lahlou, N., Cabrol, S., Pelloux, V., Cassuto, D., Gourmelen, M., Dina, C., Chambaz, J., Lacorte, J-M., Basdevant, A., Bougnères, P., Lubouc, Y., Froguel, P., & Guy-Grand, B. (1998). A mutation in the human leptin receptor gene causes obesity and pituitary dysfunction. *Nature, 392,* 398–401.

Cleveland, H., & Wiebe, R. (2003). The moderation of adolescent-to-peer similarity in tobacco and alcohol use by school levels of substance use. *Child Development, 74,* 279–291.

Clifford, E. (2000). Neural plasticity: Merzenich, Taub, and Greenough. *Harvard Brain* [Special Issue], *6,* 16–20.

Cloitre, M., Koenen, K., Cohen, L., & Han, H. (2002). Skills training in affective and interpersonal regulation followed by exposure: A phase-based treatment for PTSD related to childhood abuse. *Journal of Consulting and Clinical Psychology, 70,* 1067–1074.

Cloninger, C. R., Sigvardsson, S., Bohman, M., & von Knorring, A. L. (1982). Predispositions to petty criminality in Swedish adoptees, II. Cross-fostering analysis of gene-environment interaction. *Archives of General Psychiatry, 39,* 1242–1249.

CNN.com. (February 16, 2003). Fatal shooting caught on tape. Retrieved February 17, 2003, from http://www.cnn.com/2003/ US/South/02/16/gas.shooting.ap/index.html

Coffey, C., Saxton, J., Ratcliff, G., Bryan, R., & Lucke, J. (1999). Relation of education to brain size in normal aging: Implications for the reserve hypothesis. *Neurology, 53,* 189–196.

Cohan, C., & Kleinbaum, S. (2002). Toward a greater understanding of the cohabitation effect: Premarital cohabitation and marital communication. *Journal of Marriage & Family, 64,* 180–192.

Cohen, H., & Amerine-Dickens, M., & Smith, T. (2006). Early intensive behavioral treatment: Replication of the UCLA model in a community setting. *Journal of Developmental & Behavioral Pediatrics, 27,* S145–S155.

Cohen, S. (1988). Psychosocial models of the role of social support in the etiology of physical disease. *Health Psychology, 7,* 269–297.

Cohen, S. (1996). Psychological stress, immunity, and upper respiratory infections. *Current Directions in Psychological Science, 5,* 86–89.

Cohen, S., Doyle, W. J., Skoner, D. P., Rabin, B. S., & Gwaltney, J. M., Jr. (1997). Social ties and susceptibility to the common cold. *Journal of the American Medical Association, 277,* 1940–1944.

Cohen, S., & Herbert, T. B. (1996). Health psychology: Psychological factors and physical disease from the perspective of human psychoneuroimmunology. *Annual Review of Psychology, 47,* 113–142.

Cohen, S., & Williamson, G. M. (1991). Stress and infectious disease in humans. *Psychological Bulletin, 109,* 5–54.

Cohen, S., Doyle, W., & Baum, A. (2006). Socioeconomic status is associated with stress hormones. *Psychosomatic Medicine, 68,* 414–420.

Colby, A., Kohlberg, L., Gibbs, J., & Lieberman, M. (1983). A longitudinal study of moral judgment. *Monographs of the Society for Research in Child Development, 48*(1–2, Serial No. 200).

Colcombe, S., & Kramer, A. (2003). Fitness effects on the cognitive function of older adults: A meta-analytic study. *Psychological Science, 14,* 125–130.

Cole, C., Arafat, C., Tidhar, C., Tafesh, W., Fox, N., Killen, M., Ardila-Rey, A., Leavitt, L., Lesser, G., Richman, B., & Yung, F. (2003). The educational impact of Rechov Sumsum/Shara'a Simsim: A *Sesame Street* television series to promote respect and understanding among children living in Israel, the West Bank and Gaza. *International Journal of Behavioral Development, 27,* 409–422.

Cole, P. M. (1986). Children's spontaneous control of facial expression. *Child Development, 57,* 1309–1321.

Cole, R., Smith, J., Alcala, Y., Elliott, J., & Kripke, D. (2002). Bright-light mask treatment of delayed sleep phase syndrome. *Journal of Biological Rhythms, 17,* 89–101.

Collaer, M. L., & Hines, M. (1995). Human behavioral sex differences: A role for gonadal hormones during early development. *Psychological Bulletin, 118,* 55–107.

College Board. (1998). *SAT and gender differences: Research summary.* Retrieved July 3, 2006 from http://www.collegeboard.com/repository/rs04_3960.pdf

Collier, A. C., Coombs, R. W., Schoenfeld, D. A., Bassett, R. L., Timpone, J., Baruch, A., Jones, M., Facey, K., Whitacre, C., McAuliffe, V. J., Friedman, H. M., Merigan, T. C., Reichman, R. C., Hooper, C., & Corey, L. (1996). Treatment of human immunodeficiency virus infection with saquinavir, zidovudine, and zalcitabine. *New England Journal of Medicine, 334,* 1011–1017.

Collins, N. L. (1996). Working models of attachment: Implications for explanation, emotion, and behavior. *Journal of Personality and Social Psychology, 71,* 810–832.

Collins, V., Halliday, J., Kahler, S., & Williamson, R. (2001). Parents' experiences with genetic counseling after the birth of a baby with a genetic disorder: An exploratory study. *Journal of Genetic Counseling, 10,* 53–72.

Collins, W. A., & Gunnar, M. R. (1990). Social and personality development. *Annual Review of Psychology, 41,* 387–416.

Colombo, M., & Broadbent, N. (2000). Is the avian hippocampus a functional homologue of the mammalian hippocampus? *Neuroscience and Biobehavioral Reviews, 24,* 465–484.

Colwell, J., & Payne, J. (2000). Negative correlates of computer game play in adolescents. *British Journal of Psychology, 91*(Pt. 3), 295–310.

Coney, J., & Fitzgerald, J. (2000). Gender differences in the recognition of laterally presented affective nouns. *Cognition and Emotion, 14,* 325–339.

Conrad, P., & Leiter, V. (2004). Medicalization, markets, and consumers. *Journal of Health and Social Behavior, 45* (Supplement), 158–176.

Conroy, D., Poczwardowski, A., & Henschen, K. (2001). Evaluative criteria and consequences associated with failure and success for elite athletes and performing artists. *Journal of Applied Sport Psychology, 13,* 300–322.

Conway, M. A., Cohen, G., & Stanhope, N. (1991). On the very long-term retention of knowledge acquired through formal education: Twelve years of cognitive psychology. *Journal of Experimental Psychology: General, 120*, 395–409.

Coons, P. M. (1994). Confirmation of childhood abuse in child and adolescent cases of multiple personality disorder and dissociative disorder not otherwise specified. *Journal of Nervous and Mental Disease, 182*, 461–464.

Cooper, A., Golden, G., & Kent-Ferraro, J. (2002). Online sexual behaviors in the workplace: How can human resource departments and employee assistance programs respond effectively? *Sexual Addiction & Compulsivity, 9*, 149–165.

Cooper, L. A., & Shepard, R. N. (1984). Turning something over in the mind. *Scientific American, 251*, 106–114.

Cooper, R. (1994). Normal sleep. In R. Cooper (Ed.), *Sleep.* New York: Chapman & Hall.

Corballis, M. C. (1989). Laterality and human evolution. *Psychological Review, 96*, 492–509.

Coren, S. (1993). *The left-hander syndrome: The causes and consequences of left-handedness.* New York: Vintage Books.

Corenblum, B., & Meissner, C. (2006). Recognition of faces of ingroup and outgroup children and adults. *Journal of Experimental Child Psychology, 93*, 187–206.

Cornelius, M. D., Leech, S. L., Goldschmidt, L., & Day, N. L. (2000). Prenatal tobacco exposure: Is it a risk factor for early tobacco experimentation? *Nicotine & Tobacco Research, 2*, 45–52.

Correll, C., Penzner, J., Parikh, U., Mughal, T., Javed, T., Carbon, M., & Malhotra, A. (2006). Recognizing and monitoring adverse events of second-generation antipsychotics in children and adolescents. *Child and Adolescent Psychiatric Clinics of North America, 15*, 177–206.

Cortina, L., & Magley, V. (2003). Raising voice, risking retaliation: Events following interpersonal mistreatment in the workplace. *Journal of Occupational Health Psychology, 8*, 247–265.

Cosmides, L., & Tooby, J. (2000). Evolutionary psychology and the emotions. In M. Lewis, Jr., & J. M. Haviland-Jones (Eds.), *Handbook of emotions* (2nd ed.). New York: Guilford.

Costa, P. T., Jr., & McCrae, R. R. (1985). *The NEO Personality Inventory.* Odessa, FL: Psychological Assessment Resources.

Costa E Silva, J. A., Chase, M., Sartorius, N., & Roth, T. (1996). Special report from a symposium held by the World Health Organization and the World Federation of Sleep Research Societies: An overview of insomnias and related disorders—recognition, epidemiology, and rational management. *Sleep, 19*, 412–416.

Cotman, C. W., & Lynch, G. S. (1989). The neurobiology of learning and memory. *Cognition, 33*, 201–241.

Courage, M. L., & Adams, R. J. (1990). Visual acuity assessment from birth to three years using the acuity card procedures: Cross-sectional and longitudinal samples. *Optometry and Vision Science, 67*, 713–718.

Courtney, S. M., Ungerleider, L. G., Keil, K., & Haxby, J. V. (1997). Transient and sustained activity in a distributed neural system for human working memory. *Nature, 386*, 608–611.

Covey, S. (1989). *The 7 habits of highly effective people.* New York: Simon & Shuster.

Cowan, C. P., & Cowan, P. A. (1992, July/August). Is there love after baby? *Psychology Today*, 58–63.

Cowan, N. (1988). Evolving conceptions of memory storage, selective attention, and their mutual constraints within the human information-processing system. *Psychological Bulletin, 104*, 163–191.

Cowan, R., O'Connor, N., & Samella, K. (2003). The skills and methods of calendrical savants. *Intelligence, 31*, 51–65.

Cowley, E. (2005). Views from consumers next in line: The fundamental attribution error in a service setting. *Journal of the Academy of Marketing Science, 33*, 139–152.

Coyle, J., & Draper, E. S. (1996). What is the significance of glutamate for mental health? *Harvard Mental Health Letter, 13*(6), 8.

Coyne, S., Archer, J., & Eslea, M. (2004). Cruel intentions on television and in real life: Can viewing indirect aggression increase viewers' subsequent indirect aggression? *Journal of Experimental Child Psychology, 88*, 234–253.

Craig, I., & Plomin, R. (2006). Quantitative trait loci for IQ and other complex traits: Single-nucleotide polymorphism genotyping using pooled DNA and microarrays. *Genes, Brain & Behavior, 5*, 32–37.

Craig, R. (2005). *Personality guided forensic psychology.* Washington, DC: American Psychological Association.

Craik, F. I. M., & Lockhart, R. S. (1972). Levels of processing: A framework for memory research. *Journal of Verbal Learning and Verbal Behavior, 11*, 671–684.

Craik, F. I. M., & Tulving, E. (1975). Depth of processing and the retention of words in episodic memory. *Journal of Experimental Psychology: General, 104*, 268–294.

Crano, W., & Prislin, R. (2006). Attitudes and persuasion. *Annual Review of Psychology, 57*, 345–374.

Crasilneck, H. B. (1992). The use of hypnosis in the treatment of impotence. *Psychiatric Medicine, 10*, 67–75.

Cravens, H. (1992). A scientific project locked in time: The Terman genetic studies of genius, 1920s–1950s. *American Psychologist, 47*, 183–189.

Criglington, A. (1998). Do professionals get jet lag? A commentary on jet lag. *Aviation, Space, & Environmental Medicine, 69*, 810.

Crits-Christoph, P. (1992). The efficacy of brief dynamic psychotherapy: A meta-analysis. *American Journal of Psychiatry, 149*, 151–158.

Crits-Christoph, P., Gibbons, M., Losardo, D., Narducci, J., Schamberger, M., & Gallop, R. (2004). Who benefits from brief psychodynamic therapy for generalized anxiety disorder? *Canadian Journal of Psychoanalysis, 12*, 301–324.

Crockenberg, S., & Leerkes, E. (2005). Infant temperament moderates associations between childcare type and quantity and externalizing and internalizing behaviors at 2 1/2 years. *Infant Behavior & Development, 28*, 20–35.

Cromie, W. (2001, May 10). Getting into the rhythms of Alzheimer's disease. *Harvard University Gazette* [Electronic version]. Retrieved October 17, 2003, from http://www.news.harvard.edu/gazette/2001/05.10/01-alzheimers.html

Cromie, W. (2002, January 17). Scientists get the skinny on fat cells. *Harvard Gazette.* Retrieved June 16, 2006, from http://www.dfci.harvard.edu/res/research/fatcells.asp

Crompton, R., Brockmann, M., & Lyonette, C. (2005). Attitudes, women's employment and the domestic division of labour: A cross-national analysis in two waves. *Work, Employment, and Society, 19*, 213–233.

Crone, E., Wendelken, C., Donohue, S., van Leijenhorst, L., & Bunge, S. (2006). Neurocognitive development of the ability to manipulate information in working memory. *Proceedings for the National Academy of Sciences, 103,* 9315–9320.

Crosby, F., Iyer, A., & Sincharoen, S. (2006). Understanding affirmative action. *Annual Review of Psychology, 57,* 585–612.

Crowder, R. G. (1992) Sensory memory. In L. R. Squire (Ed.), *Encyclopedia of learning and memory.* New York: Macmillan.

Crowe, L. C., & George, W. H. (1989). Alcohol and human sexuality: Review and integration. *Psychological Bulletin, 105,* 374–386.

Crowley, B., Hayslip, B., & Hobdy, J. (2003). Psychological hardiness and adjustment to life events in adulthood. *Journal of Adult Development, 10,* 237–248.

Crowther, J., Kichler, J., Shewood, N., & Kuhnert, M. (2002). The role of familial factors in bulimia nervosa. *Eating Disorders: The Journal of Treatment & Prevention, 10,* 141–151.

Csikszentmihalyi, M. (1990). *Flow: The psychology of optimal experience.* Cambridge, England: Cambridge University Press.

Csikszentmihalyi, M. (1996, July/August). The creative personality. *Psychology Today, 29,* 36–40.

Cui, X-J., & Vaillant, G. E. (1996). Antecedents and consequences of negative life events in adulthood: A longitudinal study. *American Journal of Psychiatry, 153,* 21–26.

Culbertson, F. M. (1997). Depression and gender: An international review. *American Psychologist, 52,* 25–31.

Cull, W. L. (2000). Untangling the benefits of multiple study opportunities and repeated testing for cued recall. *Applied Cognitive Psychology, 14,* 215–235.

Cullen, M., Hardison, C., & Sackett, P. (2004). Using SAT-grade and ability-job performance relationships to test predictions derived from stereotype threat theory. *Journal of Applied Psychology, 89,* 220–230.

Culpan, O., & Wright, G. (2002). Women abroad: Getting the best results from women managers. *International Journal of Human Resource Management, 13,* 784–801.

Cupach, W. R., & Canary, D. J. (1995). Managing conflict and anger: Investigating the sex stereotype hypothesis. In P. J. Kalbfleisch & M. J. Cody (Eds.), *Gender, power, and communication in human relationships.* Hillsdale, NJ: Erlbaum.

Curci, A., Luminet, O., Finkenauer, C., & Gisler, L. (2002). Flashbulb memories in social groups: A comparative test-retest study of the memory of French president Mitterrand's death in a French and a Belgian group. *Memory, 9,* 81–101.

Curran, P. J., Stice, E., & Chassin, L. (1997). The relation between adolescent alcohol use and peer alcohol use: A longitudinal random coefficients model. *Journal of Consulting and Clinical Psychology, 65,* 130–140.

Cyranowski, J. M., Frand, E., Young, E., & Shear, M. K. (2000). Adolescent onset of the gender difference in lifetime rates of major depression. *Archives of General Psychiatry, 57,* 21–27.

da Silva Borges, F., & Fischer, F. (2003). Twelve-hour night shifts of healthcare workers: A risk to the patients? *Chronobiology International, 20,* 351–360.

Dabbs, J. M., Jr., & Morris, R. (1990). Testosterone, social class, and antisocial behavior in a sample of 4,462 men. *Psychological Science, 1,* 209–211.

Dahloef, P., Norlin-Bagge, E., Hedner, J., Ejnell, H., Hetta, J., & Haellstroem, T. (2002). Improvement in neuropsychological performance following surgical treatment for obstructive sleep apnea syndrome. *Acta Oto-Laryngologica, 122,* 86–91.

Daily Hampshire Gazette [Electronic version]. (September 7, 2002). Two missing after 9/11 found. Retrieved November 8, 2002, from http://www.gazettenet.com

Dakof, G. A. (2000). Understanding gender differences in adolescent drug abuse: Issues of comorbidity and family functioning. *Journal of Psychoactive Drugs, 32,* 25–32.

Dale, N., & Kandel, E. R. (1990). Facilitatory and inhibitory transmitters modulate spontaneous transmitter release at cultured Aplysia sensorimotor synapses. *Journal of Physiology, 421,* 203–222.

Daley, T., Whaley, S., Sigman, M., Espinosa, M., & Neumann, C. (2003). IQ on the rise: The Flynn Effect in rural Kenyan children. *Psychological Science, 14,* 215–219.

Dallard, I., Cathebras, P., & Sauron, C. (2001). Is cocoa a psychotropic drug? Psychopathological study of self-labeled "chocolate addicts." *Encephale, 27,* 181–186.

Dallery, J., Silverman, K., Chutuape, M., Bigelow, G., & Stitzer, M. (2001). Voucher-based reinforcement of opiate plus cocaine abstinence in treatment-resistant methadone patients: Effects of reinforcer magnitude. *Experimental & Clinical Psychopharmacology, 9,* 317–325.

Daly, K., & Palkovitz, R. (2004). Guest editorial: Reworking work and family issues for fathers. *Fathering, 2,* 211–213.

Daly, M., & Wilson, M. I. (1996). Violence against stepchildren. *Current Directions in Psychological Science, 5,* 77–81.

Damasio, A. R. (1994). *Descartes' error: Emotion, reason, and the human brain.* New York: Lyons Press.

Damasio, A. R. (1999). *The feeling of what happens: Body and emotion in the making of consciousness.* New York: Harcourt.

Damasio, A., Grabowski, T., Bechara, A., Damasio, H., Ponto, L., Parvizi, J., & Hichwa, R. (2000). Subcortical and cortical brain activity during the feeling of self-generated emotions. *Nature Neuroscience, 3,* 1049–1056.

Damitz, M., Manzey, D., Kleinmann, M., & Severin, K. (2003). Assessment center for pilot selection: Construct and criterion validity and the impact of assessor type. *Applied Psychology: An International Review, 52,* 193–212.

Dandy, J., & Nettelbeck, T. (2002). The relationship between IQ, homework, aspirations and academic achievement for Chinese, Vietnamese and Anglo-Celtic Australian school children. *Educational Psychology, 22,* 267–276.

Danto, E. (2000). Conflict vs. cohesion: EAP-based diversity training in small groups. *Employee Assistance Quarterly, 15,* 1–14.

Dantzker, M., & Eisenman, R. (2003). Sexual attitudes among Hispanic college students: Differences between males and females. *International Journal of Adolescence & Youth, 11,* 79–89.

Darley, J. M., & Latané, B. (1968a). Bystander intervention in emergencies: Diffusion of responsibility. *Journal of Personality and Social Psychology, 8,* 377–383.

Darley, J. M., & Latané, B. (1968b, December). When will people help in a crisis? *Psychology Today,* pp. 54–57, 70–71.

Darwin, C. (1872/1965). *The expression of emotion in man and animals.* Chicago: University of Chicago Press. (Original work published 1872).

Dasborough, M., & Ashkanasy, N. (2002). Emotion and attribution of intentionality in leader-member relationships. *Leadership Quarterly, 13*, 615–634.

Dasen, P. R. (1994). Culture and cognitive development from a Piagetian perspective. In W. J. Lonner & R. Malpass (Eds.), *Psychology and culture* (pp. 145–149). Boston: Allyn & Bacon.

Dauringnac, E., Toga, A., Jones, D., Aronen, H., Hommer, D., Jernigan, T., Krystal, j., & Mathalon, D. (2005). Applications of morphometric and diffusion tensor magnetic resonance imaging to the study of brain abnormalities in the alcoholism spectrum. *Alcoholism: Clinical and Experimental Research, 29*, 159–166.

Davalos, D., Kisley, M., & Freedman, R. (2005). Behavioral and electrophysiological indices of temporary processing dysfunction in schizophrenia. *Journal of Neuropsychiatry and Clinical Neuroscience, 17*, 517–525.

Davalos, D., Kisley, M., & Ross, R. (2002). Deficits in auditory and visual temporal perception in schizophrenia. *Cognitive Neuropsychiatry, 7*, 273–282.

Davey, F. (1998). Young women's expected and preferred patterns of employment and child care. *Sex Roles, 38*, 95–102.

Davidson, J. R. T. (1997). Use of benzodiazepines in panic disorder. *Journal of Clinical Psychiatry, 58*(2, Suppl.), 26–28.

Davies, L. (2003). Singlehood: Transitions within a gendered world. *Canadian Journal on Aging, 22*, 343-352.

Davis, S., Butcher, S. P., & Morris, R. G. M. (1992). The NMDA receptor antagonist D-2-amino-5-phosphonopentanoate (D-AP5) impairs spatial learning and LTP in vivo at intracerebral concentrations comparable to those that block LTP in vitro. *Journal of Neuroscience, 12*, 21–34.

Davis, T. L. (1995). Gender differences in masking negative emotions: Ability or motivation? *Developmental Psychology, 31*, 660–667.

Dawood, K., Kirk, K., Bailey, J., Andrews, P., & Martin, N. (2005). Genetic and environmental influences on the frequency of orgasm in women. *Twin Research, 8*, 27–33.

Day, S., & Schneider, P. (2002). Psychotherapy using distance technology: A comparison of face-to-face, video, and audio treatment. *Journal of Counseling Psychology, 49*, 499–503.

D'Azevedo, W. A. (1982). Tribal history in Liberia. In U. Neisser (Ed.), *Memory observed: Remembering in natural contexts*. San Francisco: W. H. Freeman.

de Castro, J. M., & de Castro, E. S. (1989). Spontaneous meal patterns of humans: Influence of the presence of other people. *Journal of Clinical Nutrition, 50*, 237–247.

De Coteau, T., Hope, D., & Anderson, J. (2003). Anxiety, stress, and health in northern plains Native Americans. *Behavior Therapy, 34*, 365–380.

De Cremer, D. (2002). Charismatic leadership and cooperation in social dilemmas: A matter of transforming motives? *Journal of Applied Social Psychology, 32*, 997–1016.

de Jong, P., & vander Leij, A. (2002). Effects of phonological abilities and linguistic comprehension on the development of reading. *Scientific Studies of Reading, 6*, 51–77.

de Leon, M. J., Convit, A., George, A. E., Golomb, J., de Santi, S., Tarshish, C., Rusinek, H., Bobinski, M., Ince, C., Miller, D., & Wisniewski, H. (1996). *In vivo* structural studies of the hippocampus in normal aging and in incipient Alzheimer's disease. *Annals of the New York Academy of Sciences, 777*, 1–13.

De Raad, B., & Kokkonen, M. (2000). Traits and emotions: A review of their structure and management. *European Journal of Personality, 14*, 477–496.

Deady, D., Smith, M., Sharp, M., & Al-Dujaili, E. (2006). Maternal personality and reproductive ambition in women is associated with salivary testosterone levels. *Biological Psychology, 71*, 29–32.

Deak, G., Ray, S., & Brenneman, K. (2003). Children's perseverative appearance-reality errors are related to emerging language skills. *Child Development, 74*, 944–964.

DeBortoli, M., Tifner, S., & Zanin, L. (2001). The effect of the human androsterone pheromone on mood in men. *Revista intercontinental de psicologia y educacion, 3*, 23–28.

DeCasper, A. J., & Fifer, W. P. (1980). Of human bonding: Newborns prefer their mothers' voices. *Science, 208*, 1174–1176.

DeCasper, A. J., & Spence, M. J. (1986). Prenatal maternal speech influences newborns' perception of speech sounds. *Infant Behavior and Development, 9*, 133–150.

Deci, E. L., Koestner, R., & Ryan, R. M. (1999). A meta-analytic review of experiments examining the effects of extrinsic rewards on intrinsic motivation. *Psychological Bulletin, 125*, 627–668.

Dedert, E., Studts, J., Weissbecker, I., Salmon, P., Banis, P., & Sephton, S. (2004). Religiosity may help preserve the cortisol rhythm in women with stress-related illness. *International Journal of Psychiatry in Medicine, 34*, 61–77.

Deese, J. (1959). On the prediction of occurrence of particular verbal intrusions in immediate recall. *Journal of Experimental Psychology, 58*, 17–22.

Dekovic, M., & Janssens, J. M. A. M. (1992). Parents' child-rearing style and child's sociometric status. *Developmental Psychology, 28*, 925–932.

DeLongis, A., Folkman, S., & Lazarus, R. S. (1988). The impact of daily stress on health and mood: Psychological and social resources as mediators. *Journal of Personality and Social Psychology, 54*, 486–495.

Delost, S., & Lashley, S. (2000). *The cochlear implant controversy.* Paper presented at the annual Drury University Interdisciplinary Research Conference. February, 2000, Springfield, MO.

Deluga, R. (1998). American presidential proactivity, charismatic leadership, and rated performance. *Leadership Quarterly, 9*, 265–291.

Dement, W., & Kleitman, N. (1957). The relation of eye movements during sleep to dream activity: An objective method for the study of dreaming. *Journal of Experimental Psychology, 53*, 339–346.

Dennis, W. (1968). Creative productivity between the ages of 20 and 80. In B. L. Neugarten (Ed.), *Middle age and aging* (pp. 106–114). Chicago: University of Chicago Press.

Denollet, J., (1997). Personality, emotional distress and coronary heart disease. *European Journal of Personality, 11*, 343–357.

Deovell, L. Y., Bentin, S., & Soroker, N. (2000). Electrophysiological evidence for an early (pre-attentive) information processing deficit in patients with right hemisphere damage and unilateral neglect. *Brain, 123*, 353–365.

DePaulo, B., & Morris, W. (2005). Singles in society and in science. *Psychological Inquiry, 16*, 57-83.

DePrince, A., & Freyd, J. (2004). Forgetting trauma stimuli. *Psychological Science, 15*, 488–492.

Devine, P. G. (1989). Stereotypes and prejudice: Their automatic and controlled components. *Journal of Personality and Social Psychology, 56,* 5–18.

Dewald, G., Haymond, M., Spurbeck, J., & Moore, S. (1980). Origin of chi46,XX/46,XY chimerism in a human true hermaphrodite. *Science, 207,* 321–323.

Dewsbury, D. A. (2000). Introduction: Snapshots of psychology circa 1900. *American Psychologist, 55,* 255–259.

DeYoung, C., Peterson, J., & Higgins, D. (2002). Higher-order factors of the Big Five predict conformity: Are there neuroses of health? *Personality & Individual Differences, 33,* 533–552.

Dickens, W., & Flynn, R. (2001). Heritability estimates versus large environmental effects: The IQ paradox resolved. *Psychological Review, 108,* 346–369.

Dickey, M. (2005). Engaging by design: How engagement strategies in popular computer and video games can inform instructional design. *Educational Technology Research and Development, 53,* 67-83.

Diekman, A., Eagly, A., Mladinic, A., & Ferreira, C. (2005). Dynamic stereotypes about women and men in Latin America and the United States. *Journal of Cross-Cultural Psychology, 36,* 209–226.

Diener, E., & Diener, C. (1996). Most people are happy. *Psychological Science, 7,* 181–185.

Diener, E., Lucas, R., & Scollon, C. (2006). Beyond the hedonic treadmill: Revising the adaptation theory of well-being. *American Psychologist, 61,* 305–314.

Diener, E., Nickerson, C., Lucas, R., & Sandvik, E. (2002). Dispositional affect and job outcomes. *Social Indicators Research, 59,* 229–259.

Dietz, W. H. (1989). Obesity. *Journal of the American College of Nutrition, 8*(Suppl.), 139–219.

Dijksterhuis, A., & Aarts, H. (2003). On wildebeests and humans: The preferential detection of negative stimuli. *Psychological Science, 14,* 14–18.

DiLalla, L. F., & Gottesman, I. I. (1991). Biological and genetic contributors to violence—Widom's untold tale. *Psychological Bulletin, 109,* 125–129.

Dillard, J., & Anderson, J. (2004). The role of fear in persuasion. *Psychology & Marketing, 21,* 909–926.

Dion, K., Berscheid, E., & Walster, E. (1972). What is beautiful is good. *Journal of Personality and Social Psychology, 24,* 285–290.

Dipboye, R. L., Fromkin, H. L., & Wilback, K. (1975). Relative importance of applicant sex, attractiveness, and scholastic standing in evaluation of job applicant resumes. *Journal of Applied Psychology, 60,* 39–43.

DiPietro, J. (2005). Neurobehavioral assessment before birth. *Mental Retardation and Developmental Disabilities, 11,* 4–13.

DiPietro, J., Bornstein, M., Costigan, K., Pressman, E., Hahn, C., Painter, K., Smith, B., & Yi, L. (2002). What does fetal movement predict about behavior during the first two years of life? *Developmental Psychobiology, 40,* 358–371.

DiPietro, J., Hodgson, D., Costigan, K., & Johnson, T. (1996a). Fetal antecedents of infant temperament. *Child Development, 67,* 2568–2583.

DiPietro, J., Hodgson, D., Costigan, K., Hilton, S., & Johnson, T. (1996b). Fetal neurobehavioral development. *Child Development, 67,* 2553–2567.

Dobson, R., & Baird, T. (2006, May 28). "Women learn to play it like a man." *Timesonline.co.uk* Retrieved July 3, 2006 from http://www.timesonline.co.uk/article/0,,2089-2200093.html

Dodge, K. A., Bates, J. E., & Pettit, G. S. (1990). Mechanisms in the cycle of violence. *Science, 250,* 1678–1683.

Dodge, K. A., Cole, J. D., Pettit, G. S., & Price, J. M. (1990). Peer status and aggression in boys' groups: Developmental and contextual analyses. *Child Development, 61,* 1289–1309.

Dodson, C. S., Koutstaal, W., & Schacter, D. L. (2000). Escape from illusion: Reducing false memories. *Trends in Cognitive Sciences, 4,* 391–397.

Dohanich, G. (2003). Ovarian steroids and cognitive function. *Current Directions in Psychological Science, 12,* 57–61.

Dohrenwend, B. (2006). Inventorying stressful life events as risk factors for psychopathology: Toward resolution of the problem of intracategory variability. *Psychological Bulletin, 132,* 477–495.

Dollard, J., Doob, L. W., Miller, N., Mowrer, O. H., & Sears, R. R. (1939). *Frustration and aggression.* New Haven: Yale University Press.

Domino, G. (1984). California Psychological Inventory. In D. J. Keyser & R. C. Sweetland (Eds.), *Test Critiques* (Vol. 1, pp. 146–157). Kansas City: Test Corporation of America.

Domjan, M, & Purdy, J. E. (1995). Animal research in psychology: More than meets the eye of the general psychology student. *American Psychologist, 50,* 496–503.

Doob, L. W., & Sears, R. R. (1939). Factors determining substitute behavior and the overt expression of aggression. *Journal of Abnormal and Social Psychology, 34,* 293–313.

Dorz, S., Lazzarini, L., Cattelan, A., Meneghetti, F., Novara, C., Concia, E., Sica, C., & Sanavio, E. (2003). Evaluation of adherence to antiretroviral therapy in Italian HIV patients. *AIDS Patient Care & STDs, 17,* 33–41.

Douglas, C. (2002). The effects of managerial influence behavior on the transition to self-directed work teams (SDWTs). *Journal of Managerial Psychology, 17,* 628–635.

Douglas, J., Burgess, A., Burgess, A., & Ressler, R. (1992). *Crime classification manual: A standard system for investigating and classifying violent crime.* New York: Simon and Shuster.

Downing, P., Jiang, Y., Shuman, M., & Kanwisher, N. (2001). A cortical area selective for visual processing of the human body. *Science, 293,* 2470–2473.

Doyle, R. (2000). Women and the professions. *Scientific American, 282,* 30.

Dreger, A. (2006). *Shifting the paradigm of intersex treatment.* Retrieved July 3, 2006 from http://www.isna.org/compare

Dreikurs, R. (1953). *Fundamentals of Adlerian psychology.* Chicago: Alfred Adler Institute.

Drevets, W. C., Price, J. L., Simpson, J. R., Jr., Todd, R. D., Reich, T., Vannier, M., & Raichle, M. E. (1997). Subgenual prefrontal cortex abnormalities in mood disorders. *Nature, 386,* 824–827.

Drevets, W., Neugebauer, V., Li, W., Bird, G., & Han, J., (2004). The amygdala and persistent pain. *Neuroscientist, 10,* 221–234.

Drobnic, S., Blossfeld, H., & Rohwer, G. (1999). Dynamics of women's employment patterns over the family life course: A comparison of the United States and Germany. *Journal of Marriage & the Family, 61,* 133–146.

Druckman, D., & Bjork, R. A. (Eds.) (1994). *Learning, remembering, believing: Enhancing human performance.* Washington, DC: National Academy Press.

Drug Enforcement Administration. National Drug Intelligence Center. (2003). *National Drug Threat Assessment/2003* [Online report]. Retrieved October 22, 2003, from http://www.usdoj.gov/ndic/pubs3/3300/pharm.htm

Drug Free Workplace. (2002, September). Designer Drugs. *National Medical Report* [Electronic version]. Retrieved May 25, 2003, from http://www.drugfreeworkplace.com/drugsofabuse/designer.htm

Drummond, S. P. A., Brown, G. G., Gillin, J. C., Stricker, J. L., Wong, E. C., & Buxton, R. B. (2000). Altered brain response to verbal learning following sleep deprivation. *Nature, 403,* 655–657.

Drummond, S., Brown, G., Salamat, J., & Gillin, J. (2004). Increasing task difficulty facilitates the cerebral compensatory response to total sleep deprivation. *Sleep: Journal of Sleep & Sleep Disorders Research, 27,* 445–451.

Druskat, V., & Pescosolido, A. (2002). The content of effective teamwork mental models in self-managing teams: Ownership, learning and heedful interrelating. *Human Relations, 55,* 283–314.

Dryer, D. C., & Horowitz, L. M. (1997). When do opposites attract? Interpersonal complementarity versus similarity. *Journal of Personality and Social Psychology, 72,* 592–603.

Duck, S. (1983). *Friends for life: The psychology of close relationships.* New York: St. Martin's Press.

Duckworth, A., & Seligman, M. (2006). Self-discipline gives girls the edge: Gender in self-discipline, grades, and achievement test scores. *Journal of Educational Psychology, 98,* 198–208.

Duggan, J. P., & Booth, D. A. (1986). Obesity, overeating, and rapid gastric emptying in rats with ventromedial hypothalamic lesions. *Science, 231,* 609–611.

Dunn, J., Cutting, A., & Fisher, N. (2002). Old friends, new friends: Predictors of children's perspective on their friends at school. *Child Development, 73,* 621–635.

Durbin, C., & Klein, D. (2006). Ten-year stability of personality disorders among outpatients with mood disorders. *Journal of Abnormal Psychology, 115,* 75–84.

Durex. (2005). *Durex Global Sex Survey 2005.* Retrieved July 3, 2006 from http://www.durex.com/cm/gss2005results.asp

Duyme, M. (1988). School success and social class: An adoption study. *Developmental Psychology, 24,* 203–209.

Dvir, T., Eden, D., Avolio, B., & Shamir, B. (2002). Impact of transformational leadership on follower development and performance: A field experiment. *Academy of Management Journal, 45,* 735–744.

Dyl, J., Kittler, J., Phillips, K., & Hunt, J. (2006, in press). Body dysmorphic disorder and other clinically significant body image concerns in adolescent psychiatric inpatients: Prevalence and clinical characteristics. *Child Psychiatry and Human Development.*

Dywan, J., & Bowers, K. (1983). The use of hypnosis to enhance recall. *Science, 222,* 184–185.

Eagly, A. H., Ashmore, R. D., Makhijani, M. G., & Longo, L. C. (1991). What is beautiful is good . . . : A meta-analytic review of research on the physical attractiveness stereotype. *Psychological Bulletin, 110,* 109–128.

Eagly, A. H., & Carli, L. (1981). Sex of researchers and sex-typed communications as determinants of sex differences in influence-ability: A meta-analysis of social influence studies. *Psychological Bulletin, 90,* 1–20.

Eagly, A. H., & Wood, W. (1999). The origins of sex differences in human behavior: Evolved dispositions versus social roles. *American Psychologist, 54,* 408–423.

Eastman, C., Gazda, C., Burgess, H., Crowley, S., & Fogg, L. (2005). Advancing circadian rhythms before eastward flight: A strategy to prevent or reduce jet lag. *Sleep: Journal of Sleep and Sleep Disorders Research, 28,* 33–44.

Easton, C. J., Swann, S., & Sinha, R. (2000). Prevalence of family violence in clients entering substance abuse treatment. *Journal of Substance Abuse Treatment, 18,* 23–28.

Ebbinghaus, H. (1913). *Memory* (H. Ruyer & C. E. Bussenius, Trans.). New York: Teacher's College Press. (Original work published 1885)

Ebbinghaus, H. E. (1885/1964). *Memory: A contribution to experimental psychology* (H. A. Ruger & C. E. Bussenius, Trans.). New York: Dover. (Original work published 1885).

Ebster, C., & Kirk-Smith, M. (2005). The effect of the human pheromone androstenol on product evaluation. *Psychology & Marketing, 22,* 739–749.

Education Trust. (2004). *College results online: A new tool for school counselors.* Retrieved April 28, 2006 from http://www2.edtrust.org/NR/rdonlyres/B43D90B7-2264-4060-9F8E-FA7B9566A538/0/college_results_online.pdf

Edwards, B., Atkinson, G., Waterhouse, J., Reilly, T., Godfrey, R., & Budgett, R. (2000). Use of melatonin in recovery from jet-lag following an eastward flight across 10 time-zones. *Ergonomics, 43,* 1501–1513.

Edwards, K., & Smith, E. E. (1996). A disconfirmation bias in the evaluation of arguments. *Journal of Personality and Social Psychology, 71,* 5–24.

Egeth, H. E. (1993). What do we not know about eyewitness identification? *American Psychologist, 48,* 577–580.

Eibl-Eibesfeldt, I. (1973). The expressive behavior of the deaf-and-blind-born. In M. von Cranach & I. Vine (Eds.), *Social communication and movement.* New York: Academic Press.

Eichel, S., & Martin, P. (2004). *Brainwashing as a legal defense.* Workshop presented at the annual meeting of the American Family Foundation. Atlanta. October, 2004.

Eichenbaum, H. (1997). Declarative memory: Insights from cognitive neurobiology. *Annual Review of Psychology, 48,* 547–572.

Eichenbaum, H., & Fortin, N. (2003). Episodic memory and the hippocampus: It's about time. *Current Directions in Psychological Science, 12,* 53–57.

Eichenbaum, H., & Otto, T. (1993). LTP and memory: Can we enhance the connection? *Trends in Neurosciences, 16,* 163.

Eidelson, R., & Eidelson, J. (2003). Dangerous ideas. *American Psychologist, 58,* 182–192.

Eisold, B. (2005). Notes on lifelong resilience: Perceptual and personality factors implicit in the creation of a particular adaptive style. *Psychoanalytic Psychology, 22,* 411–425.

Ekman, P., & O'Sullivan, M. (1991). Who can catch a liar? *American Psychologist, 46,* 913–920.

Ekman, P. (1972). Universals and cultural differences in facial expression of emotion. In J. Cole (Ed.), *Nebraska symposium on motivation* (Vol. 19). Lincoln: University of Nebraska Press.

Ekman, P. (1993). Facial expression and emotion. *American Psychologist, 48*, 384–392.

Ekman, P., & Campos, J. (2003). Richard Stanley Lazarus (1922–2002). *American Psychologist, 58*, 756–757.

Ekman, P., & Friesen, W. V. (1975). *Unmasking the face: A guide to recognizing emotions from facial clues.* Englewood Cliffs, NJ: Prentice-Hall.

Ekman, P., Levenson, R. W., & Friesen, W. V. (1983). Autonomic nervous system activity distinguishes among emotions. *Science, 221*, 1208–1210.

Ekman, P., O'Sullivan, M., & Frank, M. (1999). A few can catch a liar. *Psychological Science, 10*, 263–266.

Elal, G., Altug, A., Slade, P., & Tekcan, A. (2000). Factor structure of the Eating Attitudes Test (EAT) in a Turkish university sample. *Eating and Weight Disorders: Studies on Anorexia, Bulimia, and Obesity, 5*, 46–50.

Elbert, T., Pantev, C., Wienbruch, C., Rockstroh, B., & Taub, E. (1995). Increased cortical representation of the fingers of the left hand in string players. *Science, 270*, 305–307.

Elkin, I., Gibbons, R. D., Shea, M. T., Sotsky, S. M., Watkins, J. T., Pikonis, P. A., & Hedeker, D. (1995). Initial severity and differential treatment outcome in the National Institute of Mental Health Treatment of Depression Collaborative Research Program. *Journal of Consulting and Clinical Psychology, 63*, 841–847.

Elkin, I., Shea, M. T., Watkins, J. T., et al. (1989). National Institute of Mental Health Treatment of Depression Collaborative Research Program: General effectiveness of treatments. *Archives of General Psychology, 46*, 971–982.

Elkind, D. (1967). Egocentrism in adolescence. *Child Development, 38*, 1025–1034.

Elkind, D. (1974). *Children and adolescents: Interpretive essays on Jean Piaget* (2nd ed.). New York: Oxford University Press.

Ellason, J. W., & Ross, C. A. (1997). Two-year follow-up of inpatients with dissociative identity disorder. *American Journal of Psychiatry, 154*, 832–839.

Elliott, R., Friston, K. J., & Dolan, R. J. (2000). Dissociable neural responses in human reward systems. *Journal of Neuroscience, 20*, 6159–6165.

Ellis, A. (1961). *A guide to rational living.* Englewood Cliffs, NJ: Prentice-Hall.

Ellis, A. (1977). The basic clinical theory of rational-emotive therapy. In A. Ellis & R. Grieger (Eds.), *Handbook of rational-emotive therapy* (pp. 3–33). New York: Springer.

Ellis, A. (1993). Reflections on rational-emotive therapy. *Journal of Consulting and Clinical Psychology, 61*, 199–201.

Ellis, A. (2004a). Why I (really) became a therapist. *Journal of Rational-Emotive & Cognitive Behavior Therapy, 22*, 73–77.

Ellis, A. (2004b). Why rational-emotive behavior therapy is the most comprehensive and effective form of behavior therapy. *Journal of Rational-Emotive & Cognitive Behavior Therapy, 22*, 85–92.

Ellis, B., Bates, J., Dodge, K., Fergusson, D., Horwood, J., Pettit, G., & Woodward, L. (2003). Does father absence place daughters at special risk for early sexual activity and teenage pregnancy? *Child Development, 74*, 801–821.

Else-Quest, N., Hyde, J., Goldsmith, H., & Van Hulle, C. (2006). Gender differences in temperament: A meta-analysis. *Psychological Bulletin, 132*, 33–72.

Elsner, B., & Aschersleben, G. (2003). Do I get what you get? Learning about the effects of self-performed and observed actions in infancy. *Consciousness and Cognition: An International Journal, 12*, 732–751.

Embick, D., Marantz, A., Miyashita, Y., O'Neil, W., & Sakai, K. L. (2000). A syntactic specialization for Broca's area. *Proceedings of the National Academy of Science, 97*, 6150–6154.

Engels, G. I., Garnefski, N., & Diekstra, R. F. W. (1993). Efficacy of rational-emotive therapy: A quantitative analysis. *Journal of Consulting and Clinical Psychology, 61*, 1083–1090.

Engen, T. (1982). *The perception of odors.* New York: Academic Press.

Ensari, N. (2001). How can managers reduce intergroup conflict in the workplace? Social psychological approaches to addressing prejudice in organizations. *Psychologist-Manager Journal, 5*, 83–93.

Epstein, J., Stern, E., & Silbersweig, D. (2001). Neuropsychiatry at the millennium: The potential for mind/brain integration through emerging interdisciplinary research strategies. *Clinical Neuroscience Research, 1*, 10–18.

Erdogan, A., Kocabasoglu, N., Yalug, I., Ozbay, G., & Senturk, H. (2004). Management of marked liver enzyme increase during clozapine treatment: A case report and review of the literature. *International Journal of Psychiatry in Medicine, 34*, 83–89.

Erel, O., & Burman, B. (1995). Interrelatedness of marital relations and parent-child relations: A meta-analytic review. *Psychological Bulletin, 118*, 108–132.

Erikson, E. H. (1980). *Identity and the life cycle.* New York: Norton.

Eronen, M., Hakola, P., & Tiihonen, J. (1996). Mental disorders and homicidal behavior in Finland. *Journal of Personality and Social Psychology, 53*, 497–501.

Escher, M., Desmeules, J., Giostra, E., & Mentha, G. (2001). Hepatitis associated with kava, a herbal remedy for anxiety. *BMJ: British Medical Journal, 322*, 139.

Espelage, D., Holt, M., & Henkel, R. (2003). Examination of peer-group contextual effects on aggression during early adolescence. *Child Development, 74*, 205–220.

Estes, W. K. (1994). *Classification and cognition.* New York: Oxford University Press.

Etcoff, N., Ekman, P., Magee, J., & Frank, M. (2000). Lie detection and language comprehension. *Nature, 405*, 139.

Etherton, J., Bianchini, K., Chiota, M., & Greve, K. (2005). Reliable digit span is unaffected by laboratory-induced pain. *Assessment, 12*, 101–106.

Ettore, B. (1995, November). When the walls come tumbling down. *Management Review, 84*, 33–37.

Evans, D., & Zarate, O. (2000). *Introducing evolutionary psychology.* New York: Totem Books.

Evans, G. W., & Lepore, S. J. (1993). Household crowding and social support: A quasiexperimental analysis. *Journal of Personality and Social Psychology, 65*, 308–316.

Evans, J., Handley, S., & Harper, C. (2001). Necessity, possibility and belief: A study of syllogistic reasoning. *The Quarterly Journal of Experimental Psychology A: Human Experimental Psychology, 54A*, 935–958.

Evans, S., Huxley, P., Gately, C., Webber, M., Mears, A., Pajak, S., Medina, J., Kendall, T., & Katona, C. (2006). Mental health, burnout and job satisfaction among mental health social workers in England and Wales. *British Journal of Psychiatry, 188,* 75–80.

Everson, S. A., Goldberg, D. E., Kaplan, G. A., Cohen, R. D., Pukkala, E., Tuomilehto, J., & Salonen, J. T. (1996). Hopelessness and risk of mortality and incidence of myocardial infarction and cancer. *Psychosomatic Medicine, 58,* 113–121.

Ewin, D. M. (1992). Hypnotherapy for warts (*Verruca vulgaris*): 41 consecutive cases with 33 cures. *American Journal of Clinical Hypnosis, 35,* 1–10.

Exner, J. E. (1993). *The Rorschach: A comprehensive system: Vol. 1. Basic foundations* (3rd ed.). New York: Wiley.

Exton, M. S., von Auer, A. K., Buske-Kirschbaum, A., Stockhorst, U., Göbel, U., & Schedlowski, M. (2000). Pavlovian conditioning of immune function: Animal investigation and the challenge of human application. *Behavioural Brain Research, 110,* 129–141.

Eysenbach, G., Powell, J., Kuss, O., & Sa, E. (2002). Empirical studies of health information for consumers on the World Wide Web: A systematic review. *JAMA: Journal of the American Medical Association, 287,* 2691–2700.

Eysenck, H. J. (1990). Genetic and environmental contributions to individual differences: The three major dimensions of personality. *Journal of Personality, 58,* 245–261.

Fackelmann, K. (1997). Marijuana on trial: Is marijuana a dangerous drug or a valuable medicine? *Science News, 151,* 178–179, 183.

Fagiolini, M., & Hensch, T. K. (2000). Inhibitory threshold for critical-period activation in primary visual cortex. *Nature, 404,* 183–186.

Fagot, B. (1995). Observations of parent reactions to sex-stereotyped behavior: Age and sex effects. *Child Development, 62,* 617–628.

Fairbank, J., Spangler, W., & Williams, S. (2003). Motivating creativity through a computer-mediated employee suggestion management system. *Behaviour & Information Technology, 22,* 305–314.

Falloon, I. R. H. (1988). Expressed emotion: Current status. *Psychological Medicine, 18,* 269–274.

Famighetti, R. (Ed.). (1997). *The world almanac and book of facts 1998.* Mahwah, NJ: World Almanac Books.

Fang, C., & Myers, H. (2001). The effects of racial stressors and hostility on cardiovascular reactivity in African American and Caucasian men. *Health Psychology, 20,* 64–70.

Fanous, A., Gardner, C., Prescott, C., Cancro, R., & Kendler, K. (2002). Neuroticism, major depression and gender: A population-based twin study. *Psychological Medicine, 32,* 719–728.

Fantz, R. L. (1961). The origin of form perception. *Scientific American, 204,* 66–72.

Farah, M. J. (1995). The neural bases of mental imagery. In M. S. Gazzaniga (Ed.), *The cognitive neurosciences.* Cambridge, MA: MIT Press.

Farde, L. (1996). The advantage of using positron emission tomography in drug research. *Trends in Neurosciences, 19,* 211–214.

Farley, S., Adams, J., Lutton, M., & Scoville, C. (2005). What are effective treatments for oppositional and defiant behaviors in preadolescents? *Journal of Family Practice, 54,* 162–165.

Farooqi, I., & O'Rahilly, S. (2005). New advances in the genetics of early onset obesity. *International Journal of Obesity, 29,* 1149–1152.

Farwell, L., & Smith, S. (2001). Using brain MERMER testing to detect concealed knowledge despite efforts to conceal. *Journal of Forensic Sciences, 46,* 1–9.

Faryna, E., & Morales, E. (2000). Self-efficacy and HIV-related risk behaviors among multiethnic adolescents. *Cultural Diversity and Ethnic Minority Psychology, 6,* 42–56.

Fauerbach, J., Lawrence, J., Haythornthwaite, J., & Richter, L. (2002). Coping with the stress of a painful medical procedure. *Behaviour Research & Therapy, 40,* 1003–1015.

Faunce, G. (2002). Eating disorders and attentional bias: A review. *Eating Disorders: The Journal of Treatment & Prevention, 10,* 125–139.

Fazio, R. H. (1989). On the power and functionality of attitudes: The role of attitude accessibility. In A. R. Pratkanis, S. J. Breckler, & A. G. Greenwald (Eds.), *Attitude structure and function* (pp. 153–179). Hillsdale, NJ: Erlbaum.

Fazio, R. H., & Williams, C. J. (1986). Attitude accessibility as a moderator of the attitude perception and attitude-behavior relations: An investigation of the 1984 presidential election. *Journal of Personality and Social Psychology, 51,* 505–514.

Federal Interagency Forum on Aging—Related Statistics (FIFARS). (2000). *Older Americans 2000: Key indicators of well-being.* Retrieved July 30, 2003, from http://www.agingstats.gov

Federal Interagency Forum on Aging—Related Statistics (FIFARS). (2004). *Older Americans 2004: Key indicators of well-being.* Retrieved January 27, 2005 from http:// www.agingstats.gov/chartbook2004/default.htm

Feine, R. (2002). *13 indicators of quality child care: Research update.* Report presented to the Office of the Assistant Secretary for Planning and Evaluation and the Health Resources and Services Administration/Maternal and Child Health Bureau, U.S. Department of Health and Human Services. Retrieved June 10, 2006 from http://aspe.hhs.gov/hsp/ccquality%2Dind02/

Feingold, A. (1988). Matching for attractiveness in romantic partners and same-sex friends: A meta-analysis and theoretical critique. *Psychological Bulletin, 104,* 226–235.

Fenn, K., Nusbaum, H., & Margoliash, D. (2003). Consolidation during sleep of perceptual learning of spoken language. *Nature, 425,* 614–616.

Fenton, W. S., & McGlashan, T. H. (1991). Natural history of schizophrenia subtypes: I. Longitudinal study of paranoid, hebephrenic, and undifferentiated schizophrenia. *Archives of General Psychiatry, 48,* 969–977.

Fenton, W. S., & McGlashan, T. H. (1994). Antecedents, symptom progression, and long-term outcome of the deficit syndrome in schizophrenia. *American Journal of Psychiatry, 151,* 351–356.

Fernald, A. (1993). Approval and disapproval: Infant responsiveness to vocal affect in familiar and unfamiliar languages. *Child Development, 64,* 637–656.

Fernandez, Y., & Marshall, W. (2003). Victim empathy, social self-esteem, and psychopathy in rapists. *Sexual Abuse: Journal of Research & Treatment, 15,* 11–26.

Fernández-Dols, J.-M., & Ruiz-Belda, M.-A. (1995). Are smiles a sign of happiness? Gold medal winners at the

Olympic games. *Journal of Personality and Social Psychology, 69,* 1113–1119.

Festinger, L. (1957). *A theory of cognitive dissonance.* Evanston, IL: Row, Peterson.

Festinger, L., & Carlsmith, J. M. (1959). Cognitive consequences of forced compliance. *Journal of Abnormal and Social Psychology, 58,* 203–210.

Field, M., & Duka, T. (2002). Cues paired with a low dose of alcohol acquire conditioned incentive properties in social drinkers. *Psychopharmacology, 159,* 325–334.

Field, T., Schanberg, S. M., Scfidi, F., Bauer, C. R., Vega-Lahr, N., Garcia, R., Nystrom, J., & Kuhn, C. (1986, May). Tactile/kinesthetic stimulation effects on preterm neonates. *Pediatrics, 77,* 654–658.

Fields, J., Walton, K., & Schneider, R. (2002). Effect of a multi-modality natural medicine program on carotid atherosclerosis in older subjects: A pilot trial of Maharishi Verdic Medicine. *American Journal of Cardiology, 89,* 952–958.

Filiapas, H., & Ullman, S. (2006). Child sexual abuse, coping responses, self-blame, posttraumatic stress disorder, and adult sexual revictimization. *Journal of Interpersonal Violence, 21,* 652–672.

Finch, A. E., Lambert, M. J., & Brown, G. (2000). Attacking anxiety: A naturalistic study of a multimedia self-help program. *Journal of Clinical Psychology, 56,* 11–21.

Fincham, F. (2003). Marital conflict: Correlates, structure, and context. *Current Directions in Psychological Science, 12,* 23–27.

Findling, R., McNamara, N., Stansbrey, R., Gracious, B., Whipkey, R., Demeter, C., Reed, M., Youngstrom, E., & Calabrese, J. (2006). Combination lithium and divalproex sodium in pediatric bipolar symptom restabilization. *Journal of the American Academy of Child & Adolescent Psychiatry, 45,* 142–148.

Fink, B., & Penton-Voak, I. (2002). Evolutionary psychology of facial attractiveness. *Current Directions in Psychological Science, 11,* 154–158.

Fink, B., Brookes, H., Neave, N., Manning, J., & Geary, D. (2006). Second to fourth digit ratio and numerical competence in children. *Brain and Cognition, 61,* 211–218.

Fischbach, G. D. (1992). Mind and brain. *Scientific American, 267,* 48–56.

Fischer, K., & Rose, S. (1994). Dynamic development of coordination of components in brain and behavior: A framework for theory and research. In K. Fischer & G. Dawson (Eds.), *Human Behavior and the Developing Brain* (pp. 3–66). New York: Guilford Press.

Fivush, R., & Nelson, K. (2004). Culture and language in the emergence of autobiographical memory. *Psychological Science, 15,* 573–577.

Fixx, J. F. (1978). *Solve It! A perplexing profusion of puzzles.* New York: Doubleday.

Flavell, J. H. (1992). Cognitive development: Past, present, and future. *Developmental Psychology, 28,* 998–1005.

Flavell, J. H. (1996). Piaget's legacy. *Psychological Science, 7,* 200–203.

Flavell, J. H., Green, F. L., & Flavell, E. R. (1995). Young children's knowledge about thinking. *Monographs of the Society for Research in Child Development, 60*(1, Serial No. 243).

Fleck, D., Hendricks, W., DelBellow, M., & Strakowski, S. (2002). Differential prescription of maintenance antipsychotics to African American and White patients with new-onset bipolar disorder. *Journal of Clinical Psychiatry, 63,* 658–664.

Fleeson, W. (2004). Moving personality beyond the person-situation debate: The challenge and the opportunity of within-person variability. *Current Directions in Psychological Science, 13,* 83–87.

Fleming, J. D. (1974, July). Field report: The state of the apes. *Psychology Today,* pp. 31–46.

Fletcher, J. M., Page, B., Francis, D. J., Copeland, K., Naus, M. J., Davis, C. M., Morris, R., Krauskopf, D., & Satz, P. (1996). Cognitive correlates of long-term cannabis use in Costa Rican men. *Archives of General Psychiatry, 53,* 1051–1057.

Flipsen, P., & Colvard, L. (2006). Intelligibility of conversational speech produced by children with cochlear implants. *Journal of Communication Disorders, 39,* 93–108.

Flora, C. (2003, December 9). The brainwashing defense. *Psychology Today* [Online edition.] Retrieved May 2, 2006 from http://www.psychologytoday.com/articles/pto-20031209-000001.html

Florida Institute for Neurologic Rehabilitation, Inc. (2002). V.D.2. Case study [Online report]. Retrieved May 25, 2003, from http://www.floridainstitute.com

Flowers, L. (2002). The impact of college racial composition on African American students' academic and social gains: Additional evidence. *Journal of College Student Development, 43,* 403–410.

Flowers, L., & Pascarella, E. (1999). Cognitive effects of college racial composition on African American students after 3 years of college. *Journal of College Student Development, 40,* 669–677.

Flynn, J. (1999). Searching for justice: The discovery of IQ gains over time. *American Psychologist, 54,* 5–20.

Flynn, J. (2003). Movies about intelligence: The limitations of *g. Current Directions in Psychological Science, 12,* 95–99.

Flynn, J. R. (1987). Race and IQ: Jensen's case refuted. In S. Modgil, & C. Modgil (Eds.), *Arthur Jensen: Consensus and controversy.* New York: Palmer Press.

Foa, E. B. (1995). How do treatments for obsessive-compulsive disorder compare? *Harvard Mental Health Letter, 12*(1), 8.

Fogel, J., Albert, S., Schnabel, F., Ditkoff, B., & Neugut, A. (2002). Internet use and social support in women with breast cancer. *Health Psychology, 21,* 398–404.

Foley, D. J., Monjan, A. A., Brown, S. L., Simonsick, E. M., Wallace, R. B., & Blazer, D. G. (1995). Sleep complaints among elderly persons: An epidemiologic study of three communities. *Sleep, 18,* 425–432.

Foley, D., Ancoli-Israel, S., Britz, P., & Walsh, J. (2004). Sleep disturbances and chronic disease in older adults: Results of the 2003 National Sleep Foundation Sleep in America Survey. *Journal of Psychosomatic Research, 56,* 497–502.

Foley, S., Kidder, D., & Powell, G. (2002). The perceived glass ceiling and justice perceptions: An investigation of Hispanic law associates. *Journal of Management, 28,* 471–496.

Folkerts, H. (2000). Electroconvulsive therapy of depressive disorders. *Ther. Umsch, 57,* 290–294.

Folkman, S. (1984). Personal control and stress and coping processes: A theoretical analysis. *Journal of Personality and Social Psychology, 46,* 839–852.

Folkman, S., Chesney, M., Collette, L., Boccellari, A., & Cooke, M. (1996). Postbereavement depressive mood and its pre-bereavement predictors in HIV⁺ and HIV⁻ gay men. *Journal of Personality and Social Psychology, 70,* 336–348.

Folkman, S., & Lazarus, R. S. (1980). An analysis of coping in a middle-aged community sample. *Journal of Health and Social Behavior, 21,* 219–239.

Ford, C. S., & Beach, F. A. (1951). *Patterns of sexual behavior.* New York: Harper & Row.

Forey, J. P., Walker, S., Poston, C., II, & Goodrick, G. K. (1996). Future directions in obesity and eating disorders. *Addictive Behaviors, 21,* 767–778.

Forgas, J. P., & Fiedler, K. (1996). Us and them: Mood effects on intergroup discrimination. *Journal of Personality and Social Psychology, 70,* 28–40.

Foulkes, D. (1996). Sleep and dreams: Dream research: 1953–1993. *Sleep, 19,* 609–624.

Fourkas, A., Ionta, S., & Aglioti, S. (2006). Influence of imagined posture and imagery modality on corticospinal excitability. *Behavioural Brain Research, 168,* 190–196.

Fox, E., Lester, V., Russo, R., Bowles, R. J., Pichler, A., & Dutton, K. (2000). Facial expressions of emotion: Are angry faces detected more efficiently? *Cognition and Emotion, 14,* 61–92.

Fox, N. A., & Bell, M. A. (1990). Electrophysiological indices of frontal lobe development: Relations to cognitive and affective behavior in human infants over the first year of life. *Annals of the New York Academy of Sciences, 608,* 677–698.

Francis, P. (2003). Glutamatergic systems in Alzheimer's disease. *International Journal of Geriatric Psychiatry, 18,* S15–S21.

Francis-Smythe, J., & Smith, P. (1997). The psychological impact of assessment in a development center. *Human Relations, 50,* 149–167.

Frank, E., Anderson, B., Reynolds, C. F., III, Ritenour, A., & Kupfer, D. J. (1994). Life events and the research diagnostic criteria endogenous subtype. *Archives of General Psychiatry, 51,* 519–524.

Frank, E., Kupfer, D. J., Wagner, E. F., McEachran, A. B., & Cornes, C. (1991). Efficacy of interpersonal psychotherapy as a maintenance treatment of recurrent depression: Contributing factors. *Archives of General Psychiatry, 48,* 1053–1059.

Frank, M., Formaker, B., & Hettinger, T. (2003). Taste response to mixtures: Analytic processing of quality. *Behavioral Neuroscience, 117,* 228–235.

Frankenburg, W. K., Dodds, J. B., Archer, P., et al. (1992). *Denver II training manual.* Denver: Denver Developmental Materials.

Franklin, A., Pilling, M., & Davies, I. (2005). The nature of infant colour categorization: Evidence from eye-movements on a target detection task. *Journal of Experimental Child Psychology, 91,* 227–248.

Franklin, B. (2004). *The autobiography of Benjamin Franklin.* New York: Simon & Shuster.

Franks, P., Gold, M., & Fiscella, K. (2003). Sociodemographics, self-rated, health, and mortality in the U. S. *Social Science & Medicine, 56,* 2505–2514.

Frantz, K., Hansson, K., Stouffer, D., & Parsons, L. (2002). 5-HT-sub-6 receptor antagonism potentiates the behavioral and neurochemical effects of amphetamine but not cocaine. *Neuropharmacology, 42,* 170–180.

Franz, C. E., McClelland, D. C., & Weinberger, J. (1991). Childhood antecedents of conventional social accomplishment in midlife adults: A 36-year prospective study. *Journal of Personality and Social Psychology, 60,* 586–595.

Frazer, A. (1997). Antidepressants. *Journal of Clinical Psychiatry, 58*(6, Suppl.), 9–25.

Frazer, N., Larkin, K., & Goodie, J. (2002). Do behavioral responses mediate or moderate the relation between cardiovascular reactivity to stress and parental history of hypertension? *Health Psychology, 21,* 244–253.

Frederickson, N. (1962). Factors in in-basket performance. *Psychological Monographs, 76.*

Fredricks, J., & Eccles, J. (2002). Children's competence and value beliefs from childhood through adolescence growth trajectories in two male-sex-typed domains. *Developmental Psychology, 38,* 519–533.

Fredrikson, M., Annas, P., Fischer, H., & Wik, G. (1996). Gender and age differences in the prevalence of specific fears and phobias. *Behaviour Research and Therapy, 34,* 33–39.

Freedman, J. L., & Fraser, S. C. (1966). Compliance without pressure: The foot-in-the-door technique. *Journal of Personality and Social Psychology, 4,* 195–202.

Freeman, C. (2004). *Trends in educational equity of girls & women.* Retrieved July 3, 2006 from http://nces.ed.gov/pubs2005/2005016.pdf

Freeman, W. J. (1991). The physiology of perception. *Scientific American, 264,* 78–85.

French, S., Jeffery, R., & Murray, D. (1999). Is dieting good for you? Prevalence, duration and associated weight and behaviour changes for specific weight loss strategies over four years in US adults. *International Journal of Obesity Related Metabolic Disorders, 23,* 320–327.

Freud, A. (1958). *Adolescence: Psychoanalytic study of the child* (Vol. 13). New York: Academic Press.

Freud, S. (1900/1953a). The interpretation of dreams. In J. Strachey (Ed. and Trans.), *The standard edition of the complete psychological works of Sigmund Freud* (Vols. 4 and 5). London: Hogarth Press. (Original work published 1900).

Freud, S. (1905/1953b). Three essays on the theory of sexuality. In J. Strachey (Ed. and Trans.), *The standard edition of the complete psychological works of Sigmund Freud* (Vol. 7). London: Hogarth Press. (Original work published 1905).

Freud, S. (1920/1963b). *A general introduction to psycho-analysis* (J. Riviere, Trans.). New York: Simon & Schuster. (Original work published 1920).

Freud, S. (1922). *Beyond the pleasure principle.* London: International Psychoanalytic Press.

Freud, S. (1925/1963a). *An autobiographical study* (J. Strachey, Trans.). New York: W.W. Norton. (Original work published 1925).

Freud, S. (1930/1962). *Civilization and its discontents* (J. Strachey, Trans.). New York: W. W. Norton. (Original work published 1930).

Freud, S. (1933/1965). *New introductory lectures on psychoanalysis* (J. Strachey, Trans.). New York: W. W. Norton. (Original work published 1933).

Freudenberger, H., & Richelson, G. (1981). *Burnout.* New York: Bantam Books.

Frey, K. P., & Eagly, A. H. (1993). Vividness can undermine the persuasiveness of messages. *Journal of Personality and Social Psychology, 65,* 32–44.

Frey, M., & Detterman, D. (2004). Scholastic assessment or *g*? The relationship between the scholastic assessment test and general cognitive ability. *Psychological Science, 15,* 373–378.

Friedman, J. M. (1997). The alphabet of weight control. *Nature, 385,* 119–120.

Friedman, J. M. (2000). Obesity in the new millennium. *Nature, 404,* 632–634.

Friedman, M., & Rosenman, R. H. (1974). *Type A behavior and your heart.* New York: Fawcett.

Friedman, M. I., Tordoff, M. G., & Ramirez, I. (1986). Integrated metabolic control of food intake. *Brain Research Bulletin, 17,* 855–859.

Friedrich, M. (2005). Molecular studies probe bipolar disorder. *JAMA: Journal of the American Medical Association, 293,* 535–536.

Frieswijk, N., Buunk, B., Steverink, N., & Slaets, J. (2004). The effect of social comparison information on the life satisfaction of frail older persons. *Psychology & Aging, 19,* 183–190.

Froc, D., & Racine, R. (2005). Interactions between LTP- and LTD-inducing stimulation in the sensorimotor cortex of the awake freely moving rat. *Journal of Neurophysiology, 93,* 548–556.

Fuligni, A. J., & Stevenson, H. W. (1995). Time use and mathematics achievement among American, Chinese, and Japanese high school students. *Child Development, 66,* 830–842.

Galambos, N., Barker, E., & Almeida, D. (2003). Parents do matter: Trajectories of change in externalizing and internalizing problems in early adolescence. *Child Development, 74,* 578–594.

Galambos, N., Turner, P., & Tilton-Weaver, L. (2005). Chronological and subjective age in emerging adulthood: The crossover effect. *Journal of Adolescent Research, 20,* 538–556.

Galinsky, E., & Bond, J. (2000). Supporting families as primary caregivers: The role of the workplace. In D. Cryer & T. Harms (Eds.) *Infants and toddlers in out-of-home care.* Baltimore: National Center for Early Development and Learning. (p. 321)

Galinsky, E., Kim, S., Bond, J., & Salmond, K. (2003). *Youth and employment: Today's students, tomorrow's workforce.* Retrieved June 10, 2006 from http://www.familiesandwork.org/summary/yande.pdf

Gallo, L., Troxel, W., Matthews, K., Jansen-McWilliams, L., Kuller, L., & Suton-Tyrrell, K. (2003). Occupation and subclinical carotid artery disease: Are clerical workers at greater risk? *Health Psychology, 22,* 19–29.

Gallup, G., Jr., & Hugick, L. (1990). Racial tolerance grows, progress on racial equality less evident. *Gallup Poll Monthly,* No. 297, 23–32.

Galton, F. (1874). *English men of science: Their nature and nurture.* London: Macmillan.

Gana, K., Allouche, J., & Beaugrand, C. (2001). The effect of sex-role orientation on the participation of married men in household tasks. *Revue Internationale de Psychologie Expérimentale, 14,* 151–164.

Ganellen, R. J. (1996). Comparing the diagnostic efficiency of the MMPI, MCMI-II, and Rorschach: A review. *Journal of Personality Assessment, 67,* 219–243.

Garavan, H., Morgan, R. E., Levitsky, D. A., Hermer-Vasquez, L., & Strupp, B. J. (2000). Enduring effects of early lead exposure: Evidence for a specific deficit in associative ability. *Neurotoxicology and Teratology, 22,* 151–164.

Garcia, J., & Koelling, A. (1966). Relation of cue to consequence in avoidance learning. *Psychonomic Science, 4,* 123–124.

Gardner, H. (1983). *Frames of mind: The theory of multiple intelligences.* New York: Basic Books.

Gardner, H., & Hatch, T. (1989). Multiple intelligences go to school: Educational implication of the theory of multiple intelligences. *Educational Researcher, 18*(8), 6.

Gardner, R. A., & Gardner, B. T. (1969). Teaching sign language to a chimpanzee. *Science, 165,* 664–672.

Garfield, C. (1986). *Peak performers: The new heroes of American business.* New York: Morrow.

Garma, L., & Marchand, F. (1994). Non-pharmacological approaches to the treatment of narcolepsy. *Sleep, 17,* S97–S102.

Garmon, L. C., Basinger, K. S., Gregg, V. R., & Gibbs, J. C. (1996). Gender differences in stage and expression of moral judgment. *Merrill-Palmer Quarterly, 42,* 418–437.

Garrett, M., Garrett, J., & Brotherton, D. (2001). Inner circle/outer circle: A group technique based on Native American healing circles. *Journal for Specialists in Group Work, 26,* 17–30.

Garry, M., & Loftus, E. F. (1994). Pseudomemories without hypnosis. *International Journal of Clinical and Experimental Hypnosis, 42,* 363–373.

Gartner, J., & Whitaker-Azimitia, P. M. (1996). Developmental factors influencing aggression: Animal models and clinical correlates. *Annals of the New York Academy of Sciences, 794,* 113–120.

Garza-Mercer, F., Christensen, A., & Doss, B. (2006). Sex and affection in heterosexual and homosexual couples: An evolutionary perspective. *Electronic Journal of Human Sexuality, 9.* Retrieved July 3, 2006 from http://www.ejhs.org/volume9/Garza.htm

Gates, A. I. (1917). Recitation as a factor in memorizing. *Archives of Psychology, 40.*

Gatusa, L. (2003). *Matriarchal marriage patterns of the Mosuo people of China.* Paper presented at the First World Congress on Matriarchal Studies. Luxembourg. Retrieved June 22, 2006 from http://www.second-congress-matriarchal-studies.com/gatusa.html

Gavin, J., Scott, A., & Duffield, J. (2006). *Passion, intimacy and commitment in online dating: Time versus channel effects.* Paper presented at the International Association for Relationship Research Conference. July, 2006, University of Crete, Greece.

Gawin, F. H. (1991). Cocaine addiction: Psychology and neurophysiology. *Science, 251,* 1580–1586.

Gawronski, B., Alshut, E., Grafe, J., Nespethal, J., Ruhmland, A., & Schulz, L. (2002). Processes of judging known and unknown persons. *Zeitschrift fuer Sozialpsychologie, 33,* 25–34.

Gazelle, H., & Ladd, G. (2003). Anxious solitude and peer exclusion: A diathesis-stress model of internalizing trajectories in childhood. *Child Development, 74,* 257–278.

Gazzaniga, M. (1970). *The bisected brain.* New York: Appleton-Century-Crofts.

Gazaaniga, M. (1989). Organization of the human brain. *Science, 245,* 947–952.

Gazzaniga, M. S. (1983). Right hemisphere language following brain bisection: A 20-year perspective. *American Psychologist, 38*, 525–537.

Gazzola, N., & Stalikas, A. (2004). Therapist interpretations and client processes in three therapeutic modalities: Implications for psychotherapy integration. *Journal of Psychotherapy Integration, 14*, 397–418.

Ge, X., Brody, G., Conger, R., Simons, R., & Murry, V. (2002). Contextual amplification of pubertal transition effects on deviant peer affiliation and externalizing behavior among African American children. *Developmental Psychology, 38*, 42–54.

Geary, D., Lin, F., Chen, G., & Saults, S. (1999). Contributions of computational fluency to cross-national differences in arithmetical reasoning abilities. *Journal of Educational Psychology, 91*, 716–719.

Geary, N. (2004). Endocrine controls of eating: CCK, leptin, and ghrelin. *Physiology & Behavior, 81*, 719–733.

Geen, R. G. (1984). Human motivation: New perspectives on old problems. In A. M. Rogers & C. J. Scheier (Eds.), *The G. Stanley Hall lecture series* (Vol. 4). Washington, DC: American Psychological Association.

Geer, K., Ropka, M., Cohn, W., Jones, S., & Miesfeldt, S. (2001). Factors influencing patients' decisions to decline cancer genetic counseling services. *Journal of Genetic Counseling, 10*, 25–40.

Gehart, D., & Lyle, R. (2001). Client experience of gender in therapeutic relationships: An interpretive ethnography. *Family Process, 40*, 443–458.

Gehring, D. (2003). Couple therapy for low sexual desire: A systematic approach. *Journal of Sex & Marital Therapy, 29*, 25–38.

Geiselman, R. E., Schroppel, T., Tubridy, A., Konishi, T., & Rodriguez, V. (2000). Objectivity bias in eye witness performance. *Applied Cognitive Psychology, 14*, 323–332.

Geller, S., & Studee, L. (2005). Botanical and dietary supplements for menopausal symptoms: What works, what does not. *Journal of Women's Health, 14*, 634–649.

George, M. S., Ketter, T. A., & Post, R. M. (1993). SPECT and PET imaging in mood disorders. *Journal of Clinical Psychiatry, 54*(11, Suppl.), 6–13.

German, T., & Barrett, H. (2005). Functional fixedness in a technologically sparse culture. *Psychological Science, 16*, 1–5.

Gerontology, 46, 249-257.

Gerrits, M., Petromilli, P., Westenberg, H., Di Chiara, G., & van Ree, J. (2002). Decrease in basal dopamine levels in the nucleus accumbens shell during daily drug-seeking behavior in rats. *Brain Research, 924*, 141–150.

Gerull, F., & Rapee, R. (2002). Mother knows best: The effects of maternal modelling on the acquisition of fear and avoidance behaviour in toddlers. *Behaviour Research & Therapy, 40*, 279–287.

Gevins, A., Leong, H., Smith, M. E., Le, J., & Du, R. (1995). Mapping cognitive brain function with modern high-resolution electroencephalography. *Trends in Neurosciences, 18*, 429–436.

Gibbons, A. (1991). Déjà vu all over again: Chimp-language wars. *Science, 251*, 1561–1562.

Gibson, E., & Walk, R. D. (1960). The "visual cliff." *Scientific American, 202*, 64–71.

Giedd, J. N., Rapoport, J. L., Garvey, M. A., Perlmutter, S., & Swedo, S. E. (2000). MRI assessment of children with obsessive-compulsive disorder or tics associated with streptococcal infection. *American Journal of Psychiatry, 157*, 2281–2283.

Gigerenzer, G. (2002). The adaptive toolbox. In G. Gigerenzer & R. Selten, (Eds.), *Bounded rationality: The adaptive toolbox.* (pp. 7–50). Cambridge, MA: MIT Press.

Gigerenzer, G. (2004). Dread risk, September 11, and fatal traffic accidents. *Psychological Science, 15*, 286–287.

Gigerenzer, G., & Goldstein, D. (1996). Reasoning the fast and frugal way: Models of bounded rationality. *Psychological Review, 103*, 659–669.

Gigerenzer, G., & Todd, P. for the ABC Research Group (1999). *Simple heuristics that make us smart.* Oxford, England: Oxford University Press.

Gigernzer, G., & Selten, R. (2002). Rethinking rationality. In G. Gigerenzer & R. Selten (Eds.), *Bounded rationality: The adaptive toolbox* (pp. 1–12). Cambridge, MA: MIT Press.

Gilbert, D. (2006). *Stumbling on happiness.* New York: Alfred A. Knopf.

Gilbert, D. T., & Malone, P. S. (1995). The correspondence bias. *Psychological Bulletin, 117*, 21–38.

Gilligan, C. (1982). *In a different voice: Psychological theory and women's development.* Cambridge, MA: Harvard University Press.

Gillon, G., & Young, A. (2002). The phonological awareness skills of children who are blind. *Journal of Visual Impairment & Blindness, 96*, 38–49.

Gingell, C., Nicolosi, A., Buvat, J., Glasser, D., Simsek, F., Hartmann, U., Laumann, E. (2003). *Sexual activity and dysfunction among men and women aged 40 to 80 years.* Poster presented at the XVIIIth Congres of the European Association of Urology. Madrid, March, 2003

Ginty, D. D., Kornhauser, J. M., Thompson, M. A., Bading, H., Mayo, K. E., Takahashi, J. S., & Greenberg, M. E. (1993). Regulation of CREB phosphorylation in the suprachiasmatic nucleus by light and a circadian clock. *Science, 260*, 238–241.

Ginzburg, K., Solomon, Z., & Bleich, A. (2002). Repressive coping style, acute stress disorder, and post-traumatic stress disorder after mycardial infarction. *Journal of the American Psychosomatic Society, 64*, 748–757.

Giraud, A., Price, C., Graham, J., & Frackowisk, R. (2001). *Neuropsychopharmacology, 124*, 1307–1316.

Girolamo, G., & Bassi, M. (2003). Community surveys of mental disorders: Recent achievements and works in progress. *Current Opinion in Psychiatry, 16*, 403–411.

Glannon, W. (2006). Neuroethics. *Bioethics, 20*, 37–52.

Glantz, L. A., & Lewis, D. A. (2000). Decreased dendritic spine density on prefrontal cortical pyramidal neurons in schizophrenia. *Archives of General Psychiatry, 57*, 65–73.

Glassop, L. (2002). The organizational benefits of teams. *Human Relations, 55*, 225–249.

Glazer, W. M., Morgenstern, H., & Doucette, J. T. (1993). Predicting the long-term risk of tardive dyskinesia in outpatients maintained on neuroleptic medications. *Journal of Clinical Psychiatry, 54*, 133–139.

Gleaves, D. J. (1996). The sociocognitive model of dissociative identity disorder: A reexamination of the evidence. *Psychological Bulletin, 120*, 42–59.

Glenn, N., & Weaver, C. (1985). Age, cohort, and reported job satisfaction in the United States. In A. Blau (Ed.), *Current perspectives on aging and the life cycle: A research cnnual, Vol. 1. Work, retirement, and social policy* (pp. 89–110). Greenwich, CT: JAI Press.

Glick, P., Lameiras, M., Fiske, S., Eckes, T., Masser, B., Volpato, C., Manganelli, A., Pek, J., Huang, L., Sakalli-Ugurlu, N., Castro, Y., D'Avila Pereira, M., Willemsen, T., Brunner, A., Sex-Materna, I., & Wells, R. (2004). Bad but bold: Ambivalent attitudes toward men predict gender inequality in 16 nations. *Journal of Personality and Social Psychology, 86,* 713–738.

Global Fund to Fight AIDS, Tuberculosis, and Malaria, (2005). *Global Fund ARV factsheet.* Retieved July 3, 2006 from http://www.theglobalfund.org/en/files/publications/factsheets/aids/ARV_Factsheet_2006.pdf

Glover, J. A., & Corkill, A. J. (1987). Influence of paraphrased repetitions on the spacing effect. *Journal of Educational Psychology, 79,* 198–199.

Gluck, M. A., & Myers, C. E. (1997). Psychobiological models of hippocampal function in learning and memory. *Annual Review of Psychology, 48,* 481–514.

Godden, D. R., & Baddeley, A. D. (1975). Context-dependent memory in two natural environments: On land and underwater. *British Journal of Psychology, 66,* 325–331.

Gogtay, N., Giedd, J., Lusk, L., Hayashi, K., Greenstein, D., Vaituzis, A., Nugent, T., Herman, D., Clasen, L., Toga, A., Rapoport, J., & Thompson, P. (2004). Dynamic mapping of human cortical development during childhood through early adulthood. *Proceedings of the National Academy of Science, 101,* 8174—8179.

Gökcebay, N., Cooper, R., Williams, R. L., Hirshkowitz, M., & Moore, C. A. (1994). Function of sleep. In R. Cooper (Ed.), *Sleep.* New York: Chapman & Hall.

Goldberg, L. (1993). The structure of phenotypic personality traits. *American Psychologist, 48,* 26–34.

Goldstein, D. & Gigerenzer, G. (2002). Models of ecological rationality: The recognition heuristic. *Psychological Review, 109,* 75–90.

Goleman, D., Kaufman, P., & Ray, M. (1992). *The creative spirit.* New York: Dutton.

Gollan, T., & Silverberg, N. (2001). Tip-of-the-tongue states in Hebrew-English bilinguals. *Bilingualism: Language and Cognition, 4,* 63–83.

Gonsalves, B., Reber, P., Gitelman, D., Parrish, T., Mesulam, M., & Paller, K. (2004). Neural evidence that vivid imagining can lead to false remembering. *Psychological Science, 15,* 655–660.

Gonzalez, R., Ellsworth, P. C., & Pembroke, M. (1993). Response biases in lineups and showups. *Journal of Personality and Social Psychology, 64,* 525–537.

Good, C., Aronson, J., & Inzlicht, M. (2003). Improving adolescents' standardized test performance: An intervention to reduce the effects of stereotype threat. *Applied Developmental Psychology, 24,* 645–662.

Goodglass, H. (1993). *Understanding aphasia.* San Diego, CA: Academic Press.

Goodman, E., McEwen, B., Huang, B., Dolan, L., & Adler, N. (2005). Social inequalities in biomarkers of cardiovascular risk in adolescence. *Psychosomatic Medicine, 67,* 9–15.

Goodwin, P., Leszcz, M., Ennis, M., Koopmans, J., Vincent, L., Guther, H., Drysdale, E., Hundleby, M., Chochinov, H., Navarro, M., Speca, M., & Hunter, J. (2001). The effect of group psychosocial support on survival in metastatic breast cancer. *New England Journal of Medicine, 345,* 1719–1726.

Goodwin, R., & Fitzgibbon, M. (2002). Social anxiety as a barrier to treatment for eating disorders. *International Journal of Eating Disorders, 32,* 103–106.

Gordon, H. (2002). Early environmental stress and biological vulnerability to drug abuse. *Psychoneuroendocrinology, 27,* 115–126.

Gormezano, I. (1984). The study of associative learning with CS-CR paradigms. In D. L. Alkon & J. Farley (Eds.), *Primary neural substrates of learning and behavioral change* (pp. 5–24). New York: Cambridge University Press.

Gosling, P., Denizeau, M., & Oberle, D. (2006). Denial of responsibility: A new mode of dissonance reduction. *Journal of Personality and Social Psychology, 90,* 722–733.

Gottesman, I. I. (1991). *Schizophrenia genesis: The origins of madness.* New York: W. H. Freeman.

Gottesmann, C. (2000). Hypothesis for the neurophysiology of dreaming. *Sleep Research Online, 3,* 1–4.

Gottman, J. (with Silver, N.). (1994). *Why marriages succeed or fail and how you can make yours last.* New York: Simon & Schuster.

Gough, H. (1987). *California Psychological Inventory: Administrator's Guide.* Palo Alto: Consulting Psychologists Press.

Gould, E. R., Reeves, A. J., Graziano, M. S. A., & Gross, C. (1999). Neurogenesis in the neocortex of adult primates. *Science, 286,* 548.

Gow, A., Whiteman, M., Pattie, A., & Deary, I. (2005). Goldberg's IPIP Big-Five factor markers: Internal consistency and concurrent validation in Scotland. *Personality and Individual Differences, 39,* 317–329.

Graham, K. S., Simons, J. S., Pratt, K. H., Patterson, K., & Hodges, J. R. (2000). Insights from semantic dementia on the relationship between episodic and semantic memory. *Neuropsychologia, 38,* 313–324.

Graham, S. (1992). "Most of the subjects were white and middle class": Trends in published research on African Americans in selected APA journals, 1970–1989. *American Psychologist, 47,* 629–639.

Granic, I., & Patterson, G. (2005). Toward a comprehensive model of antisocial development: A dynamic systems approach. *Psychological Review, 113,* 101–131.

Granic, I., & Patterson, G. (2006). Toward a comprehensive model of antisocial development: A dynamic systems approach. *Psychological Review, 113,* 101–131.

Grant, D., & Harari, E. (2005). Psychoanalysis, science and the seductive theory of Karl Popper. *Australian and New Zealand Journal of Psychiatry, 39,* 446–452.

Greden, J. F. (1994). Introduction Part III. New agents for the treatment of depression. *Journal of Clinical Psychiatry, 55*(2, Suppl.), 32–33.

Greeff, A., & Malherbe, H. (2001). Intimacy and marital satisfaction in spouses. *Journal of Sex & Marital Therapy, 27,* 247–257.

Green, B. (2002). Listening to leaders: Feedback on 360-degree feedback one year later. *Organization Development Journal, 20,* 8–16.

Green, B. L., Lindy, J. D., & Grace, M. C. (1985). Post-traumatic stress disorder: Toward DSM-IV. *Journal of Nervous and Mental Disorders, 173*, 406–411.

Green, J., & Shellenberger, R. (1990). *The dynamics of health and wellness: A biopsychosocial approach.* Fort Worth: Holt, Rinehart & Winston.

Green, J. P., & Lynn, S. J. (2000). Hypnosis and suggestion-based approaches to smoking cessation: An examination of the evidence. *International Journal of Clinical Experimental Hypnosis, 48*, 195–224.

Green, J. T., & Woodruff-Pak, D. S. (2000). Eyeblink classical conditioning: Hippocampal formation is for neutral stimulus associations as cerebellum is for association-response. *Psychological Bulletin, 126*, 138–158.

Green, L. R., Richardson, D. R., & Lago, T. (1996). How do friendship, indirect, and direct aggression relate? *Aggressive Behavior, 22*, 81–86.

Green, S. D. (2002). The human resource implications of lean construction: Critical perspectives and conceptual chasms. *Journal of Construction Research, 3*, 147–166.

Greenhalgh, A. (2001). *Nutrition-Drinks.* Retrieved July 7, 2006 from http://www.bbc.co.uk/health/healthy_living/nutrition/drinks_water.shtml

Greenwald, A. (1992). New look 3: Unconscious cognition reclaimed. *American Psychologist, 47*, 766–779.

Greenwald, A., Spangenberg, E., Pratkanis, A., & Eskenazi, J. (1991). Double-blind tests of subliminal self-help audiotapes. *Psychological Science, 2*, 119–122.

Greenwood, R., Tupler, L., Whitt, J., Buu, A., Dombeck, C., Harp, A., Payne, M., Eastwood, J., Krishnan, K., & MacFall, J. (2005). Brain morphometry, T2-weighted hyperintensities, and IQ in children with neurofibromatosis Type 1. *Archives of Neurology, 62*, 1904–1908.

Greer, M. (2005). Keeping them hooked in. *APA Monitor on Psychology, 36*, 60.

Greengard, S. (1994, September). Workers go virtual. *Personnel Journal, 18*, 223–232.

Gregory, R. J. (1996). *Psychological testing: History, principles, and applications* (2nd ed.). Boston: Allyn & Bacon.

Greist, J. H. (1992). An integrated approach to treatment of obsessive compulsive disorder. *Journal of Clinical Psychiatry, 53*(4, Suppl.), 38–41.

Greist, J. H. (1995). The diagnosis of social phobia. *Journal of Clinical Psychiatry, 56*(5, Suppl.), 5–12.

Griffith, R. M., Miyago, O., & Tago, A. (1958). The universality of typical dreams: Japanese vs. Americans. *American Anthropologist, 60*, 1173–1179.

Griffiths, M., & Chandler, D. (1998). Gendered editing and camerawork techniques in advertisements for children's toys on British television. Retrieved July 3, 2006 from http://users.aber.ac.uk/dgc/toyads.html

Grigorenko, E. (2003). Epistasis and the genetics of complex traits. In R. Plomin, J. DeFries, I. Craig, & P. McGuffin (Eds.), *Behavioral genetics in the postgenomic era.* (pp. 247–266). Washington, DC: American Psychological Association.

Grigorenko, E., Jarvin, L., & Sternberg, R. (2002). School-based tests of the triarchic theory of intelligence: Three settings, three samples, three syllabi. *Contemporary Educational Psychology, 27*, 167–208.

Grigorenko, E., Meier, E., Lipka, J., Mohatt, G., Yanez, E., & Sternberg, R. (2004). Academic and practical intelligence: A case study of the Yup'ik in Alaska. *Learning & Individual Differences, 14*, 183–207.

Grinker, J. A. (1982). Physiological and behavioral basis for human obesity. In D. W. Pfaff (Ed.), *The physiological mechanisms of motivation.* New York: Springer-Verlag.

Grochowicz, P., Schedlowski, M., Husband, A., King, M., Hibberd, A., & Bowen, K. (1991). Behavioral conditioning prolongs heart allograft survival in rats. *Brain, Behavior, and Immunity, 5*, 349–356.

Gron, G., Wunderlich, A. P., Spitzer, M., Tomczrak, R., & Riepe, M. W. (2000). Brain activation during human navigation: Gender-different neural networks as substrate of performance. *Nature Neuroscience, 3*, 404–408.

Groome, L., Mooney, D., Holland, S., Smith, L., Atterbury, J., & Dykman, R. (1999). Behavioral state affects heart rate response to low-intensity sound in human fetuses. *Early Human Development, 54*, 39–54.

Gross, J. (2002). Emotion regulation: Affective, cognitive, and social consequences. *Psychophysiology, 39*, 281–291.

Grossman, H. J. (Ed.). (1983). *Manual on terminology and classification in mental retardation.* Washington, DC: American Association on Mental Deficiency.

Grossman, J., & Ruiz, P. (2004). Shall we make a leap-of-faith to disulfiram (Antabuse)? *Addictive Disorders & Their Treatment, 3*, 129–132.

Grouios, G., Sakadami, N., Poderi, A., & Alevriadou, A. (1999). Excess of non-right handedness among individuals with intellectual disability: Experimental evidence and possible explanations. *Journal of Intellectual Disability Research, 43*, 306–313.

Grünbaum, A. (2006). Is Sigmund Freud's psychoanalytic edifice relevant to the 21st century? *Psychoanalytic Psychology, 23*, 257–284.

Guangyuan, S. (2005). A follow-up study on the effect of attributional training for achievement motivation. *Psychological Science (China), 28*, 52–55.

Guenole, N., & Chernyshenko, O. (2005). The suitability of Goldberg's Big Five IPIP personality markers in New Zealand: A dimensionality, bias, and criterion validity evaluation. *New Zealand Journal of Psychology, 34*, 86–96.

Guilford, J. P. (1967). *The nature of human intelligence.* New York: McGraw-Hill.

Guilleminault, C. (1993). 1. Amphetamines and narcolepsy: Use of the Stanford database. *Sleep, 16*, 199–201.

Gur, R. C., Turetsky, B., Mastsui, M., Yan, M. Bilker, W., Hughett, P., & Gur, R. E. (1999). Sex differences in brain gray and white matter in healthy young adults: correlations with cognitive performance. *Journal of Neuroscience, 19*, 4067–4072.

Gur, R., Gunning-Dixon, F., Bilker, W., & Gur, R. (2002). Sex differences in temporolimbic and frontal brain volumes of healthy adults. *Cerebral Cortex, 12*, 998–1003.

Gurin, J. (1989, June). Leaner, not lighter. *Psychology Today,* pp. 32–36.

Guthrie, R. V. (1998). *Even the rat was white* (2nd ed.). Boston: Allyn & Bacon.

Habel, U., Kuehn, E., Salloum, J., Devos, H., & Schneider, F. (2002). Emotional processing in psychopathic personality. *Aggressive Behavior, 28*, 394–400.

Haber, R. N. (1980). How we perceive depth from flat pictures. *American Scientist, 68*, 370–380.

Haberlandt, D. (1997). *Cognitive psychology* (2nd ed.). Boston: Allyn & Bacon.

Hackel, L. S., & Ruble, D. N. (1992). Changes in the marital relationship after the first baby is born: Predicting the impact of expectancy disconfirmation. *Journal of Personality and Social Psychology, 62,* 944–957.

Hada, M., Porjesz, B., Begleiter, H., & Polich, J. (2000). Auditory P3a assessment of male alcoholics. *Biological Psychiatry, 48,* 276–286.

Hada, M., Porjesz, B., Chorlian, D., Begleiter, H., & Polich, J. (2001). Auditory P3a deficits in male subjects at high risk for alcoholism. *Biological Psychiatry, 49,* 726–738.

Hagberg, M., Hagberg, B., & Saveman, B. (2002). The significance of personality factors for various dimensions of life quality among older people. *Aging & Mental Health, 6,* 178–185.

Hager, W., Leichsenring, F., & Schiffler, A. (2000). When does a study of different therapies allow comparisons of their relative efficacy? *Psychother. Psychosom. Med. Psychol., 50,* 251–262.

Häkkänen, H., & Summala, H. (1999). Sleepiness at work among commercial truck drivers. *Sleep, 23,* 49–57.

Hakuta, K., Bialystok, E., & Wiley, E. (2003). Critical evidence: A test of the critical-period hypothesis for second-language acquisition. *Psychological Science, 14,* 31–38.

Halaas, J. L., Gajiwala, K. S., Maffei, M., Cohen, S. L., Chait, B. T., Rabinowitz, D., Lallone, R. L., Burley, S. K., & Friedman, J. M. (1995). Weight-reducing effects of the plasma protein encoded by the obese gene. *Science, 269,* 543–546.

Halama, P., & Strízenec, M. (2004). Spiritual, existential or both? Theoretical considerations on the nature of "higher" intelligences. *Studia Psychologica, 46,* 239–253.

Halemaskel, B., Dutta, A., & Wutoh, A. (2001). Adverse reactions and interactions among herbal users. *Issues in Interdisciplinary Care, 3,* 297–300.

Hall, G. (1904). *Adolescence.* Englewood Cliffs, NJ: Prentice Hall.

Hall, L., & Love, C. (2003). Finger-length ratios in female monozygotic twins discordant for sexual orientation. *Archives of Sexual Behavior, 32,* 23–28.

Halligan, P. W., & Marshall, J. C. (1994). Toward a principled explanation of unilateral neglect. *Cognitive Neuropsychology, 11,* 167–206.

Hallschmid, M., Benedict, C., Born, J., Fehm, H., & Kern, W. (2004). Manipulating central nervous mechanisms of food intake and body weight regulation by intranasal administration of neuropeptides in man. *Physiology & Behavior, 83,* 55–64.

Halonen, J., Appleby, D., Brewer, C., Buskist, W., Gillem, A., Halpern, D., Hill, G., Lloyd, M., Rudmann, J., & Whitlove, V. (2002). *Report on undergraduate psychology major learning goals and outcomes.* Washington DC: American Psychological Association. Retrieved April 20, 2006 from http://www.apa.org/ed/pcue/taskforcereport2.pdf

Halpern, D. (2000). Making sound decisions: The worksheet method. Retrieved January 20, 2005 from http://wps.ablongman.com/ab_wood_worldofpsy_5/0,9166,1378162-,00.html

Halpern, J., Sherwood, A., Hudson, J., Yurgelun-Todd, D., & Pope, H. (2005). Psychological and cognitive effects of long-term peyote use among Native Americans. *Biological Psychiatry, 58,* 624–631.

Ham, P. (2003). Suicide risk not increased with SSRI and antidepressants. *Journal of Family Practice, 52,* 587–589.

Hamann, S., Monarch, E., & Goldstein, F. (2002). Impaired fear conditioning in Alzheimer's disease. *Neuropsychologia, 40,* 1187–1195.

Hamer, D. H., Hu, S., Magnuson, V. L., Hu, N., & Pattatucci, A. M. L. (1993). A linkage between DNA markers on the X chromosome and male sexual orientation. *Science, 261,* 321–327.

Hamilton, C. S., & Swedo, S. E. (2001). Autoimmune-mediated, childhood onset obsessive-compulsive disorder and tics: A review. *Clinical Neuroscience Research, 1,* 61–68.

Hammond, D. C. (1992). Hypnosis with sexual disorders. *American Journal of Preventive Psychiatry & Neurology, 3,* 37–41.

Hampson, S., Goldberg, L., Vogt, T., & Dubanoski, J. (2006). Forty years on: Teachers' assessments of children's personality traits predict self-reported health behaviors and outcomes at midlife. *Health Psychology, 25,* 57–64.

Hancock, P., & Ganey, H. (2003). From the inverted-u to the extended-u: The evolution of a law of psychology. *Journal of Human Performance in Extreme Environments, 7,* 5–14.

Hanley, N. A., Hagan, D. M., Clement-Jones, M., Ball, S. G., Strachan, T., Salas-Cortés, L., McElreavey, K., Lindsay, S., Robson, S., Bullen, P., Ostre, H., & Wilson, D. I. (2000). *SRY, SOX9,* and *DAX1* expression patterns during human sex determination and gonadal development. *Mechanisms of Development, 91,* 403–407.

Hanley, S., & Abell, S. (2002). Maslow and relatedness: Creating an interpersonal model of self-actualization. *Journal of Humanistic Psychology, 42,* 37–56.

Hanoch, Y., & Vitouch, O. (2004). When less is more: Information, emotional arousal and the ecological reframing of the Yerkes-Dodson law. *Theory & Psychology, 14,* 427–452.

Hansen, C. (2003). Cultural myths in stories about human resource development: Analyzing the cross-cultural transfer of American models to Germany and the Cote d'Ivoire. *International Journal of Training & Development, 7,* 16–30.

Hansen, M., Janssen, I., Schiff, A., & Zee, P. (2005). The impact of school daily schedule on adolescent sleep. *Pediatrics, 115,* 1555–1561.

Harackiewicz, A., Barron, A., Pintrich, A., Elliot, A., & Thrash, A. (2002). Revision of achievement goal theory: Necessary and illuminating. *Journal of Educational Psychology, 94,* 638–645.

Hare, R. D. (1995, September). Psychopaths: New trends in research. *Harvard Mental Health Letter, 12*(3), 4–5.

Harel, G., Arditi-Vogel, A., & Janz, T. (2003). Comparing the validity and utility of behavior description interview versus assessment center ratings. *Journal of Managerial Psychology, 18,* 94–104.

Hargadon, R., Bowers, K. S., & Woody, E. Z. (1995). Does counterpain imagery mediate hypnotic analgesia? *Journal of Abnormal Psychology, 104,* 508–516.

Harkins, S. G., & Jackson, J. M. (1985). The role of evaluation in eliminating social loafing. *Personality and Social Psychology Bulletin, 11,* 456–465.

Harkins, S. G., & Szymanski, K. (1989). Social loafing and group evaluation. *Journal of Personality and Social Psychology, 56,* 941–943.

Harlow, H. F., & Harlow, M. K. (1962). Social deprivation in monkeys. *Scientific American, 207,* 137–146.

Harlow, H. F., Harlow, M. K., and Suomi, S. J. (1971). From thought to therapy: Lessons from a primate laboratory. *American Scientist, 59,* 538–549.

Harlow, J. M. (1848). Passage of an iron rod through the head. *Boston Medical and Surgical Journal, 39,* 389–393.

Harlow, R. E., & Cantor, N. (1996). Still participating after all these years: A study of life task participation in later life. *Journal of Personality and Social Psychology, 71,* 1235–1249.

Harms, P., Roberts, B., & Winter, D. (2006). Becoming the Harvard Man: Person-environment fit, personality development, and academic success. *Personality and Social Psychology Bulletin, 32,* 851–865.

Harp, S., & Mayer, R. (1998). How seductive details do their damage: A theory of cognitive interest in science learning. *Journal of Educational Psychology, 90,* 414–434.

Harper, D., Stopa, E., McKee, A., Satlin, A., Harlan, P., Goldstein, R., & Volicer, L. (2001). Differential circadian rhythm disturbances in men with Alzheimer disease and frontotemporal degeneration. *Archives of General Psychiatry, 58,* 353–360.

Harper, D., Volicer, L., Stopa, E., McKee, A., Nitta, M., & Satlin, A. (2006). Disturbance of endogenous circadian rhythm in aging and Alzheimer disease. *American Journal of Geriatric Psychiatry, 13,* 359–368.

Harris Poll. (2004). *Harris Poll #101.* Retrieved July 3, 2006 from http://www.harrisinteractive.com/harris_poll/index.asp?PID=530

Harris, G. (2004, February 28). Pfizer gives up testing Viagra on women. *NYTimes.com* Retrieved July 3, 2006 from http://www.nytimes.com/2004/02/28/business/28viagra.html?ex=1393390800&en=eccf3ce764e04dd3&ei=5007&partner=USERLAND

Harris, J. (2005). The increased diagnosis of "Juvenile Bipolar Disorder": What are we treating? *Psychiatric Services, 56,* 529–531.

Harris, J. A., Rushton, J. P., Hampson, E., & Jackson, D. N. (1996). Salivary testosterone and self-report aggressive and pro-social personality characteristics in men and women. *Aggressive Behavior, 22,* 321–331.

Harris, R. A., Brodie, M. S., & Dunwiddie, T. V. (1992). Possible substrates of ethanol reinforcement: GABA and dopamine. *Annals of the New York Academy of Sciences, 654,* 61–69.

Harrison, Y., & Horne, J. A. (2000). Sleep loss and temporal memory. *Journal of Experimental Psychology, 53,* 271–279.

Hart, D., Hofmann, V., Edelstein, W., & Keller, M. (1997). The relation of childhood personality types to adolescent behavior and development: A longitudinal study of Icelandic children. *Developmental Psychology, 33,* 195–205.

Hart, J., Karau, S., Stasson, M., & Kerr, N. (2004). Achievement motivation, expected coworker performance, and collective task motivation: Working hard or hardly working? *Journal of Applied Social Psychology, 34,* 984–1000.

Harter, S. (1990). Processes underlying adolescent self-concept formation. In R. Montemayor, G. R. Adams, & T. P. Gullotta (Eds.), *From childhood to adolescence: A transitional period?* (pp. 205–239). Newbury Park, CA: Sage.

Harvard School of Public Health. (2004). *Reinventing aging: Baby boomers and civic engagement.* Boston, MA: Center for Health Communication, Harvard School of Public Health.

Hasan, H., & Power, T. (2004). Children's appraisal of major life events. *American Journal of Orthopsychiatry, 74,* 26–32.

Hassan, S. (2000). *Releasing the bonds: Empowering people to thrive for themselves.* Somerville, MA: Freedom of Mind Press.

Hatashita-Wong, M., Smith, T., Silverstein, S., Hull, J., & Willson, D. (2002). Cognitive functioning and social problem-solving skills in schizophrenia. *Cognitive Neuropsychiatry, 7,* 81–95.

Hattar-Pollara, M., Meleis, A., & Nagib, H. (2003). Multiple role stress and patterns of coping of Egyptian women in clerical jobs. *Journal of Transcultural Nursing, 14,* 125–133.

Hattrup, K., O'Connell, M., & Labrador, J. (2005). Incremental validity of locus of control after controlling for cognitive ability and conscientiousness. *Journal of Business and Psychology, 19,* 461–481.

Hauser, M. D. (1993). Right hemisphere dominance for the production of facial expression in monkeys. *Science, 261,* 475–477.

Hauser, M., Li, Y., Xu, H., Noureddine, M., Shao, Y., Gullans, S., Scherzer, C., Jensen, R., McLaurin, A., Gibson, J., Scott, B., Jewett, R., Stenger, J., Schmechel, D., Hulette, C., & Vance, J. (2005). Expression profiling of substantia nigra in Parkinson disease, progressive supranuclear palsy, and frontotemporal dementia with Parkinsonism. *Archives of Neurology, 62,* 917–921.

Hawley, K., & Weisz, J. (2003). Child, parent and therapist (dis)agreement on target problems in outpatient therapy: The therapist's dilemma and its implications. *Journal of Consulting & Clinical Psychology, 71,* 62–70.

Haxby, J., Gobbini, M., Furey, M., Ishai, A., Schouten, J., & Pietrini, P. (2001). Distributed and overlapping representations of faces and objects in ventral temporal cortex. *Science, 293,* 2425–2430.

Haxby, J., Hoffman, E., & Gobbini, M. (2002). Human neural systems for face recognition and social communication. *Biological Psychiatry, 51,* 59–67.

Hay, D. F. (1994). Prosocial development. *Journal of Child Psychology and Psychiatry, 35,* 29–71.

Hazlett-Stevens, H., Craske, M., Roy-Byrne, P., Sherbourne, C., Stein, M., & Bystritsky, A. (2002). Predictors of willingness to consider medication and psychosocial treatment for panic disorder in primary care patients. *General Hospital Psychology, 24,* 316–321.

HCF Nutrition Foundation. (2003). *The benefits of fiber.* Retrieved January 29, 2003 from http://www.hcf-nutrition.org/fiber/fiberben_article.html

He, W., Sengupta, M., Velkoff, V., & DeBarros, K. (2005). *65+ in the United States: 2005.* Retrieved June 15, 2006 from http://www.census.gov/prod/2006pubs/p23-209.pdf

He, Y., Colantonio, A., & Marshall, V. (2003). Later-life career disruption and self-rated health: An analysis of General Social Survey data. *Canadian Journal on Aging, 22,* 45–57.

Head, D., Snyder, A., Girton, L., Morris, J., & Buckner, R. (2005). Frontal-hippocampal double dissociation between normal aging and Alzheimer's disease. *Cerebral Cortex, 15,* 732–739.

Heaton, T. (2002). Factors contributing to increasing marital stability in the U.S. *Journal of Family Issues, 23,* 392–409.

Hebb, D. O. (1949). *The organization of behavior.* New York: John Wiley & Sons.

Hébert, S., Béland, R., Dionne-Fournelle, O., Crête, M., & Lupien, S. (2005). Physiological stress response to video-game playing: The contribution of built-in music. *Life Sciences, 76,* 2371–2380.

Hecht, S., Shlaer, S., & Pirenne, M. H. (1942). *Journal of General Physiology, 25,* 819.

Hedges, L. B., & Nowell, A. (1995). Sex differences in mental test scores, variability, and numbers of high-scoring individuals. *Science, 269,* 41–45.

Heil, M., Rolke, B., & Pecchinenda, A. (2004). Automatic semantic activation is no myth. *Psychological Science, 15,* 852–857.

Held, R. (1993). What can rates of development tell us about underlying mechanisms? In C. E. Granrud (Ed.), *Visual perception and cognition in infancy* (pp. 75–89). Hillsdale, NJ: Erlbaum.

Hellige, J. B. (1990). Hemispheric asymmetry. *Annual Review of Psychology, 41,* 55–80.

Hellige, J. B. (1993). *Hemispheric asymmetry: What's right and what's left.* Cambridge, MA: Harvard University Press.

Hellige, J. B., Bloch, M. I., Cowin, E. L., Eng, T. L., Eviatar, Z., & Sergent, V. (1994). Individual variation in hemispheric asymmetry: Multitask study of effects related to handedness and sex. *Journal of Experimental Psychology: General, 123,* 235–256.

Helms, J., & Mayhew, L. (2006). *Undergraduate preparation for graduate training in forensic psychology.* Retrieved July 13, 2006 from http://www.lemoyne.edu/OTRP/otrpresources/HelmsForensic06.pdf

Hendin, H., & Haas, A. P. (1991). Suicide and guilt as manifestations of PTSD in Vietnam combat veterans. *American Journal of Psychiatry, 148,* 586–591.

Hennevin, E., Hars, B., Maho, C., & Bloch, V. (1995). Processing of learned information in paradoxical sleep: Relevance for memory. *Behavioural Brain Research, 69,* 125–135.

Henningfield, J. E., & Ator, N. A. (1986). *Barbiturates: Sleeping potion or intoxicant?* New York: Chelsea House.

Henry, G. (2005). Probable malingering and performance on the test of variables of attention. *Clinical Neuropsychologist, 19,* 121–129.

Henson, R., Shallice, T., Gorno-Tempini, M., & Dolan, R. (2002). Face repetition effects in implicit and explicit memory as measured by fMRI. *Cerebral Cortex, 12,* 178–186.

Herbert, T. B., & Cohen, S. (1993). Depression and immunity: A meta-analytic review. *Psychological Bulletin, 113,* 472–486.

Herek, G. (2002). Gender gaps in public opinion about lesbians and gay men. *Public Opinion Quarterly, 66,* 40–66.

Herkenham, M. (1992). Cannabinoid receptor localization in brain: Relationship to motor and reward systems. *Annals of the New York Academy of Sciences, 654,* 19–32.

Herman, L. (1981). Cognitive characteristics of dolphins. In L. Herman (Ed.), *Cetacean behavior.* New York: Wiley.

Hernandez, L., & Hoebel, B. G. (1989). Food intake and lateral hypothalamic self-stimulation covary after medial hypothalamic lesions or ventral midbrain 6-hydroxydopamine injections that cause obesity. *Behavioral Neuroscience, 103,* 412–422.

Hernandez, S., Camacho-Rosales, J., Nieto, A., & Barroso, J. (1997). Cerebral asymmetry and reading performance: Effect of language lateralization and hand preference. *Child Neuropsychology, 3,* 206–225.

Herness, S. (2000). Coding in taste receptor cells: The early years of intracellular recordings. *Physiology and Behavior, 69,* 17–27.

Herrnstein, R. J., & Murray, C. (1994). *The bell curve: Intelligence and class structure in American life.* New York: Free Press.

Hertz, R. (2004). A naturalistic analysis of autobiographical memories triggered by olfactory visual and auditory stimuli. *Chemical Senses, 29,* 217–224.

Hertzog, C. (1991). Aging, information processing speed, and intelligence. In K. W. Schaie & M. P. Lawton (Eds.), *Annual Review of Gerontology and Geriatrics* (Vol. 11, pp. 55–79).

Heru, A. (2006). Family psychiatry: From research to practice. *American Journal of Psychiatry, 163,* 962–968.

Hespos, S., & Baillargeon, R. (2006). Décalage in infants' knowledge about occlusion and containment events: Converging evidence from action tasks. *Cognition, 99,* B31–B41.

Hetherington, A. W., & Ranson, S. W. (1940). Hypothalamic lesions and adiposity in the rat. *Anatomical Record, 78,* 149–172.

Hetherington, E. M., Stanley-Hagan, M., & Anderson, E. R. (1989). Marital transitions: A child's perspective. *American Psychologist, 44,* 303–312.

Heyman, G., Gee, C., & Giles, J. (2003). Preschool children's reasoning about ability. *Child Development, 74,* 516–534.

Higbee, K. L. (1977). *Your memory: How it works and how to improve it.* Englewood Cliffs, NJ: Prentice-Hall.

Higdon, H. (1975). *The crime of the century.* New York: G. P. Putnam's Sons.

Higgins, A. (1995). Educating for justice and community: Lawrence Kohlberg's vision of moral education. In W. M. Kurtines & J. L. Gerwirtz (Eds.), *Moral development: An introduction* (pp. 49–81). Boston: Allyn & Bacon.

Hightower, J., O'Hare, A., & Hernandez, G. (2006). Blood mercury reporting in NHANES: Identifying Asian, Pacific Islander, Native American, and Multiracial Groups. *Environmental Health Perspectives, 114,* 173–175.

Hilgard, E. R. (1975). Hypnosis. *Annual Review of Psychology, 26,* 19–44.

Hilgard, E. R. (1986). *Divided consciousness: Multiple controls in human thought and action.* New York: Wiley.

Hilgard, E. R. (1992). Dissociation and theories of hypnosis. In E. Fromm & M. R. Nash (Eds.), *Contemporary hypnosis research.* New York: Guilford.

Hill, E., Martinson, V., Ferris, M., & Baker, R. (2004). Beyond the Mommy Track: The Influence of New-Concept Part-Time Work for Professional Women on Work and Family. *Journal of Family and Economic Issues, 25,* 121–136.

Hill, M., & Augoustinos, M. (2001). Stereotype change and prejudice reduction: Short- and long-term evaluation of a cross-cultural awareness programme. *Journal of Community & Applied Social Psychology, 11,* 243–262.

Hillebrand, J. (2000). New perspectives on the manipulation of opiate urges and the assessment of cognitive effort associated with opiate urges. *Addictive Behaviors, 25,* 139–143.

Hipwell, A. E., Goossens, F. A., Melhuish, E. C., & Kumar, R. (2000). Severe maternal psychopathology and infant–mother attachment. *Developmental Psychopathology, 12,* 2157–2175.

Hirsch, J. (1997). Some heat but not enough light. *Nature, 387,* 27–28.

Hittner, J., & Daniels, J. (2002). Gender-role orientation, creative accomplishments, and cognitive styles. *Journal of Creative Behavior, 36,* 62–75.

Hobson, C., & Delunas, L., (2001). National norms and life-event frequencies for the revised Social Readjustment Rating Scale. *International Journal of Stress Management, 8,* 299–314.

Hobson, J. A. (1988). *The dreaming brain.* New York: Basic Books.

Hobson, J. A. (1989). *Sleep.* New York: Scientific American Library.

Hobson, J. A., & McCarley, R. W. (1977). The brain as a dream state generator: An activation-synthesis hypothesis of the dream process. *American Journal of Psychiatry, 134,* 1335–1348.

Hodges, J. R., Graham, N., & Patterson, K. (1995). Charting the progression in semantic dementia: Implications for the organisation of semantic memory. *Memory, 3,* 463–495.

Hodgins, S., Mednick, S. A., Brennan, P. A., Schulsinger, F., & Engberg, M. (1996). Mental disorder and crime: Evidence from a Danish birth cohort. *Journal of Personality and Social Psychology, 53,* 489–496.

Hoenig, K., & Scheef, L. (2005). Mediotemporal contributions to semantic processing: fMRI evidence from ambiguity processing during semantic context verification. *Hippocampus, 15,* 597–609.

Hofer, H., Carroll, J., Neitz, J., Neitz, M., & Williams, D. (2005). Organization of the human trichromatic cone mosaic. *Journal of Neuroscience, 25,* 9669–9679.

Hoff, E., Grote, S., Dettmer, S., Hohner, H., & Olos, L. (2005). Work-life balance: Professional and private life arrangement forms of women and men in highly qualified professions. *Zeitschrift für Arbeits und Organisationspsychologie, 49,* 196–207.

Hofferth, S., & Curtin, S. (2006). Parental leave statutes and maternal return to work after childbirth in the United States. *Work and Occupations, 33,* 73–105.

Hoffman, C., Olson, D., & Haase, S. (2001). Contrasting a 360-degree feedback measure with behaviorally-based assessment tools: An application of generalizability theory. *Psychologist-Manager Journal, 5,* 59–72.

Hofstede, G. (1980). *Culture's consequences: International differences in work-related values.* Beverly Hills, CA: Sage.

Hofstede, G. (1983). Dimensions of national cultures in fifty countries and three regions. In J. Deregowski, S. Dzuirawiec, and R. Annis (Eds.), *Explications in cross-cultural psychology.* Lisse: Swets and Zeitlinger.

Hogan, E., & McReynolds, C. (2004). An overview of anorexia nervosa, bulimia nervosa, and binge eating disorders: Implications for rehabilitation professionals. *Journal of Applied Rehabilitation Counseling, 35,* 26–34.

Holden, C. (1996). Sex and olfaction. *Science, 273,* 313.

Hollan, S., Stewart, M., & Strunk, D. (2006). Enduring effects for cognitive therapy in the treatment of depression and anxiety. *Annual Review of Psychology, 57,* 285–316.

Holland, J. G., & Skinner, B. F. (1961). *The analysis of behavior.* New York: McGraw-Hill.

Holland, J. L. (1973). *Making vocational choices: A theory of careers.* Englewood Cliffs, NJ: Prentice Hall.

Holland, J. L. (1992). *Making vocational choices: A theory of vocational personalities and work environments* (2nd ed.). Odessa, FL: Psychological Assessment Resources.

Hollon, S., Thase, M., & Markowitz, J. (2002). Treatment and prevention of depression. *Psychological Science in the Public Interest, 3,* 39–77.

Holmes, T. H., & Masuda, M. (1974). Life change and illness susceptibility. In B. S. Dohrenwend & B. P. Dohrenwend (Eds.), *Stressful life events: Their nature and effects.* New York: Wiley.

Holmes, T. H., & Rahe, R. H. (1967). The social readjustment rating scale. *Journal of Psychosomatic Research, 11,* 213–218.

Holt-Lunstad, J., Uchino, B., Smith, T., Olson-Cerny, C., & Nealey-Moore, J. (2003). Social relationships and ambulatory blood pressure: Structural and qualitative predictors of cardiovascular function during everyday social interactions. *Health Psychology, 22,* 388–397.

Home, S., & Biss, W. (2005). Sexual satisfaction as more than a gendered concept: The roles of psychological well-being and sexual orientation. *Journal of Constructivist Psychology, 18,* 25–38.

Hoosain, Z., & Roopnarine, J. L. (1994). African-American fathers' involvement with infants: Relationship to their functioning style, support, education, and income. *Infant Behavior and Development, 17,* 175–184.

Hooten, W., Wolter, T., Ames, S., Hurt, R., Viciers, K., Offord, K., & Hays, J. (2005). Personality correlates related to tobacco abstinence following treatment. *International Journal of Psychiatry in Medicine, 35,* 59–74.

Horberry, T., Anderson, J., Regan, M., Triggs, T., & Brown, J. (2006). Driver distraction: The effects of concurrent in-vehicle tasks, road environment complexity and age on driving performance. *Accident Analysis & Prevention, 38,* 185–191.

Horgan, J. (1995, November). Gay genes, revisited. *Scientific American, 273,* 26.

Horn, J. L. (1982). The theory of fluid and crystallized intelligence in relation to concepts of cognitive psychology and aging in adulthood. In F. I. M. Craik & S. Trehub (Eds.), *Aging and cognitive processes* (pp. 201–238). New York: Plenum Press.

Horn, L. J., & Zahn, L. (2001). From bachelor's degree to work: Major field of study and employment outcomes of 1992–93 bachelor's degree recipients who did not enroll in graduate education by 1997 (NCES 2001–165). Retrieved March 7, 2002, from http://nces.ed.gov/pubs2001/quarterly/spring/q5_2.html

Horne, J. (1992). Annotation: Sleep and its disorders in children. *Journal of Child Psychology and Psychiatry, 33,* 473–487.

Horstmann, G. (2003). What do facial expressions convey: Feeling states, behavioral intentions, or action requests? *Emotion, 3,* 150–166.

Horwitz, L. A. (1998). Aromachologists nose out the secret powers of smell. *Insight on the News, 13,* pp. 36–37.

Hoshi, R., Pratt, H., Mehta, S., Bond, A., & Curran, H. (2006). An investigation into the sub-acute effects of ecstasy on aggressive interpretive bias and aggressive mood—Are there gender differences? *Journal of Psychopharmacology, 20,* 291–301.

Houzel, D. (2004). The psychoanalysis of infantile autism. *Journal of Child Psychotherapy, 30,* 225–237.

Hovland, C. I., Lumsdaine, A. A., & Sheffield, F. D. (1949). *Experiments on mass communication.* Princeton, NJ: Princeton University Press.

Howard, A. D., Feighner, S. D., Cully, D. F., Arena, J. P., Liberator, P. A., Rosenblum, C. I., et al. (1996). A receptor in pituitary and hypothalamus that functions in growth hormone release. *Science, 273,* 974–977.

Howard, M. (2002). When does semantic similarity help episodic retrieval? *Journal of Memory & Language, 46,* 85–98.

Hrushesky, W. J. M. (1994, July/August). Timing is everything. *The Sciences,* pp. 32–37.

Hubel, D. H. (1963). The visual cortex of the brain. *Scientific American, 209,* 54–62.

Hubel, D. H. (1995). *Eye, brain, and vision.* New York: Scientific American Library.

Hubel, D. H., & Wiesel, T. N. (1959). Receptive fields of single neurons in the cat's striate cortex. *Journal of Physiology, 148,* 547–591.

Hubel, D. H., & Wiesel, T. N. (1979). Brain mechanisms of vision. *Scientific American, 241,* 130–144.

Huesman, L., Moise-Titus, J., Podolski, C., & Eron, L. (2003). Longitudinal relations between children's exposure to television violence and their aggressive and violent behavior in young adulthood. *Developmental Psychology, 39,* 201–221.

Huesmann, L. R., & Moise, J. (1996, June). Media violence: A demonstrated public health threat to children. *Harvard Mental Health Letter, 12*(12), 5–7.

Huizink, A., & Mulder, E. (2006). Maternal smoking, drinking or cannabis use during pregnancy and neurobehavioral and cognitive functioning in human offspring. *Neuroscience & Biobehavioral Reviews, 30,* 24–41.

Hull, C. L. (1943). *Principles of behavior.* New York: Appleton-Century-Crofts.

Hummer, R. A., Rogers, R. G., Nam, C. B., & Ellison, C. G. (1999). Religious involvement and U.S. adult mortality. *Demography, 36,* 273–285.

Hunthausen, J., Truxillo, D., Bauer, T., & Hammer, L. (2003). A field study of frame-of-reference effects on personality test validity. *Journal of Applied Psychology, 88,* 545–551.

Hunton, J., & Rose, J. (2005). Cellular telephones and driving performance: The effects of attentional demands on motor vehicle crash risk. *Risk Analysis, 25,* 855–866.

Huttenlocher, P. (1994). Synaptogenesis, synapse elimination, and neural plasticity in human cerebral cortex. In C. Nelson (Ed.), *The Minnesota symposia on child psychology* (Vol. 27, pp. 35–54). Hillsdale, NJ: Erlbaum.

Hyde, J. (2005). The gender similarities hypothesis. *American Psychologist, 60,* 581–592.

Hyde, J., Fennema, E., & Lamon, S. (1990). Gender differences in mathematics performance: A meta analysis. *Psychological Bulletin, 107,* 139–155.

Hyman, I. E., Jr., Husband, T. H., & Billings, E. J. (1995). False memories of childhood. *Applied Cognitive Psychology, 9,* 181–197.

Hyman, I. E., Jr., & Pentland, J. (1996). The role of mental imagery in the creation of false childhood memories. *Journal of Memory and Language, 35,* 101–117.

Iglowstein, I., Jenni, O., Molinari, L., & Largo, R. (2003). Sleep duration from infancy to adolescence: Reference values and generational trends. *Pediatrics, 111,* 302–307.

Immigration and Naturalization Service. (2002). *2001 statistical yearbook.* Washington DC: Author.

Insel, T. R. (1990). Phenomenology of obsessive compulsive disorder. *Journal of Clinical Psychiatry, 51*(2, Suppl.), 4–8.

Isaksson, K., Johansson, G., Bellaagh, K., & Sjöberg, A. (2004). Work values among the unemployed: Changes over time and some gender differences. *Scandinavian Journal of Psychology, 45,* 207–214.

Isay, R. A. (1989). *Being homosexual: Gay men and their development.* New York: Farrar, Straus, & Giroux.

Ishii, K., Reyes, J., & Kitayama, S. (2003). Spontaneous attention to word content versus emotional tone: Differences among three cultures. *Psychological Science, 14,* 39–46.

Ito, T. A., Miller, N., & Pollock, V. E. (1996). Alcohol and aggression: A meta-analysis on the moderating effects of inhibitory cues, triggering events, and self-focused attention. *Psychological Bulletin, 120,* 60–82.

Izard, C. E. (1971). *The face of emotion.* New York: Appleton-Century-Crofts.

Izard, C. E. (1977). *Human emotions.* New York: Plenum Press.

Izard, C. E. (1990). Facial expressions and the regulation of emotions. *Journal of Personality and Social Psychology, 58,* 487–498.

Izard, C. E. (1992). Basic emotions, relations among emotions, and emotion-cognition relations. *Psychological Review, 99,* 561–565.

Jacklin, C. N. (1989). Female and male: Issues of gender. *American Psychologist, 44,* 127–133.

Jackman, T. (2003, December 11). Two psychiatrists testify that Malvo was insane. *Washington Post,* p. B-1.

Jackson, D., & Mannix, J. (2004). Giving voice to the burden of blame: A feminist study of mothers' experiences of mother blaming. *International Journal of Nursing Practice, 10,* 150–158.

Jackson, S. (2002). A study of teachers' perceptions of youth problems. *Journal of Youth Studies, 5,* 313–322.

Jacobson, N., & Christensen, A. (1996). *Acceptance and change in couple therapy: A therapist's guide to transforming relationships.* (New York: Norton).

Jacobson, N., & Margolin, G. (1979). *Marital therapy: Strategies based on social learning and behavior exchange principles.* New York: Brunner/Mazel.

Jaffee, S., Moffitt, T., Caspi, A., & Taylor, A. (2003). Life with (or without) father: The benefits of living with two biological parents depend on the father's antisocial behavior. *Child Development, 74,* 109–126.

James, W. (1884). What is an emotion? *Mind, 9,* 188–205.

James, W. (1890). *Principles of psychology.* New York: Holt.

James, W. (1890). *The principles of psychology.* Cambridge, MA: Harvard University Press.

Jamieson, D. W., & Zanna, M. P. (1989). Need for structure in attitude formation and expression. In A. R. Pratkanis, S. J. Breckler, & A. G. Greenwald (Eds.), *Attitude structure and function* (pp. 383–406). Hillsdale, NJ: Erlbaum.

Jamison, K. (1995). *An unquiet mind: A memoir of moods and madness.* New York: Vintage Books.

Jansz, J. (2005). The emotional appeal of violent video games for adolescent males. *Communication Theory, 15,* 219–241.

Jansz, J., & Martens, L. (2005). Gaming at a LAN event: The social context of playing video games. *New Media & Society, 7,* 333–355.

Jarrold, C., Butler, D. W., Cottington, E. M., & Jimenez, F. (2000). Linking theory of mind and central coherence bias in autism and in the general population. *Developmental Psychology, 36,* 1126–1138.

Jefferson, J. W. (1996). Social phobia: Everyone's disorder? *Journal of Clinical Psychiatry, 57*(6, Suppl.), 28–32.

Jelicic, M., & Bonke, B. (2001). Memory impairments following chronic stress? A critical review. *European Journal of Psychiatry, 15,* 225–232.

Jellinek, E. M. (1960). *The disease concept of alcoholism.* New Brunswick, NJ: Hillhouse Press.

Jenike, M. A. (1990, April). Obsessive-compulsive disorder. *Harvard Medical School Health Letter, 15,* 4–8.

Jenkins, J. H., & Karno, M. (1992). The meaning of expressed emotion: Theoretical issues raised by cross-cultural research. *American Journal of Psychiatry, 149,* 9–21.

Jenkins, J. J., Jimenez-Pabon, E., Shaw, R. E., & Sefer, J. W. (1975). *Schuell's aphasia in adults: Diagnosis, prognosis, and treatment* (2nd ed.). Hagerstown, MD: Harper & Row.

Jewkes, R., Penn-Kekana, L., & Rose-Junius, H. (2005). "If they rape me, I can't blame them": Reflections on gender in the social context of child rape in South Africa and Namibia. *Social Science & Medicine, 61,* 1809–1820.

Jiang, B., Kronenberg, F., Nuntanakorn, P., Oiu, M., & Kennelly, E. (2006). Evaluation of the botanical authenticity and phytochemical profile of black cohosh products by high-performance liquid chromatography with selected ion monitoring liquid chromatography-mass spectrometry. *Journal of Agricultural and Food Chemistry, 54,* 3242–3253.

Jing, L., (2004). Neural correlates of insight. *Acta Psychologica Sinica, 36,* 219–234.

Johnson, A., Vernon, P., Harris, J., & Jang, K. (2004). A behavior genetic investigation of the relationship between leadership and personality. *Twin Research, 7,* 27–32.

Johnson, J., Simmons, C., Trawalter, S., Ferguson, T., & Reed, W. (2003). Variation in black anti-white bias and target distancing cues: Factors that influence perceptions of "ambiguously racist" behavior. *Personality & Social Psychology Bulletin, 29,* 609–622.

Johnson, L. (2004). *Game Boy zaps tranquilizers in keeping kids calm before surgery.* Retrieved July 25, 2006 from http://www.chsd.org/body.cfm?xyzpdqabc=0&id=43&action=detail&ref=65

Johnson, M. P., Duffy, J. F., Dijk, D-J., Ronda, J. M., Dyal, C. M., & Czeisler, C. A. (1992). Short-term memory, alertness and performance: A reappraisal of their relationship to body temperature. *Journal of Sleep Research, 1,* 24–29.

Johnson, S., Bremner, G., Slater, A., Mason, U., Foster, K., & Cheshire, A. (2003). Infants' perception of object trajectories. *Child Development, 74,* 94–108.

Johnson, S. C. (2000). The recognition of mentalistic agents in infancy. *Trends in Cognitive Sciences, 4,* 22–28.

Johnson, W. G., Tsoh, J. Y., & Varnado, P. J. (1996). Eating disorders: Efficacy of pharmacological and psychological interventions. *Clinical Psychology Review, 16,* 457–478.

Johnson-Laird, P. (2001). Mental models and deduction. *Trends in Cognitive Sciences, 5,* 434–442.

Johnston, L. E., O'Malley, P. M., & Bachman, J. G. (1997). *National survey results on drug use from the Monitoring the Future Study, 1975–1996/97: Vol. 1. Secondary school students.* The University of Michigan Institute for Social Research; National Institute on Drug Abuse, 5600 Fishers Lane, Rockville, MD 20857; USDHHS, Public Health Service, National Institutes of Health.

Johnston, L. E., O'Malley, P. M., & Bachman, J. G. (2001). *Monitoring the Future national results on adolescent drug use: Overview of key findings, 2000* (NIH Publication No. 01-4923). Rockville MD: National Institute on Drug Abuse.

Johnston, L., O'Malley, P., Bachman, J. & Schulenberg, J. (December 19, 2005). *Teen drug use down but progress halts among youngest teens.* University of Michigan News and Information Services: Ann Arbor, MI. Retrieved May 15, 2006 from www.monitoringthefuture.org.

Jolicoeur, D., Richter, K., Ahgluwalia, J., Mosier, M., & Resnicow, K. (2003). Smoking cessation, smoking reduction, and delayed quitting among smokers given nicotine patches and a self-help pamphlet. *Substance Abuse, 24,* 101–106.

Jonas, J. M., & Cohon, M. S. (1993). A comparison of the safety and efficacy of alprazolam versus other agents in the treatment of anxiety, panic, and depression: A review of the literature. *Journal of Clinical Psychiatry, 54* (10, Suppl.), 25–45.

Jones, E. E. (1976). How do people perceive the causes of behavior? *American Scientist, 64,* 300–305.

Jones, E. E. (1990). *Interpersonal perception.* New York: Freeman.

Jones, E. E., & Nisbett, R. E. (1971). *The actor and the observer: Divergent perceptions of the causes of behavior.* New York: General Learning.

Jones, H. E., Herning, R. I., Cadet, J. L., & Griffiths, R. R. (2000). Caffeine withdrawal increases cerebral blood flow velocity and alters quantitative electroencephalography (EEG) activity. *Psychopharmacology, 147,* 371–377.

Jones, M. C. (1924). A laboratory study of fear: The case of Peter. *Pedagogical Seminary, 31,* 308–315.

Jones, P. (2005). The American Indian Church and its sacramental use of peyote: A review for professionals in the mental-health arena. *Mental Health, Religion, & Culture, 8,* 227–290.

Jones, S. (2003). Let the games begin: *Gaming technology and entertainment among college students.* Washington, D.C.: Pew Internet and American Life Project. Retrieved May 17, 2006 from http://www.pewinternet.org/PPF/r/93/report_display.asp

Joseph, R. (2000). Fetal brain behavior and cognitive development. *Developmental Review, 20,* 81–98.

Joynt, R. (2000). Chapter 42: Aging and the nervous system. In T. Beers (Ed.) *Merck Manual of Geriatrics* (3rd Ed.). [Online edition] Retrieved October 12, 2006 from http://www.merck.com/mrkshared/mmg/sec6/ch42/ch42a.jsp

Joyce, P., Mulder, R., Luty, S., McKenzie, J., Sullivan, P., & Cloninger, R. (2003). Borderline personality disorder in major depression: Symptomatology, temperament, character, differential drug response, and 6-month outcome. *Comprehensive Psychiatry, 44,* 35–43.

Judd, L. L., Akiskal, H. S., Zeller, P. J., Paulus, M., Leon, A. C., Maser, J. D., Endicott, J., Coryell, W., Kunovac, J. L., Mueller, T. I., Rice, J. P., & Keller, M. B. (2000). Psychosocial disability during the long-term course of unipolar major depressive disorder. *Archives of General Psychiatry, 57,* 375–380.

Juengling, F., Schmahl, C., Heblinger, B., Ebert, D., Bremner, J., Gostomzyk, J., Bohus, M., & Lieb, K. (2003). Positron emission tomography in female patients with borderline personality disorder. *Journal of Psychiatric Research, 37,* 109–115.

Juliano, S. L. (1998). Mapping the sensory mosaic. *Science, 279,* 1653–1654.

Julien, R. M. (1995). *A primer of drug action* (7th ed.). New York: W.H. Freeman.

Jung, C. G. (1933). *Modern man in search of a soul.* New York: Harcourt Brace Jovanovich.

Jung, C. G. (1953). *The psychology of the unconscious* (R. F. C. Hull, Trans.), *Collected works* (Vol. 7). Princeton, NJ: Princeton University Press. (Original work published 1917).

Jung, C. G. (1961). *Memories, dreams, reflections* (R. Winston & C. Winston, Trans.). New York: Random House.

Kagan, J., & Herschowitz, N. (2005). *A young mind in a growing brain.* Hillsdale, NJ: Lawrence Erlbaum Associates.

Kahneman, D., & Tversky, A. (1984). Choices, values, and frames. *American Psychologist, 39,* 341–350.

Kail, R. (2000). Speed of information processing: Developmental change and links to intelligence. *Journal of School Psychology, 38,* 51–61.

Kail, R., & Hall, L. (1999). Sources of developmental change in children's word-problem performance. *Journal of Educational Psychology, 91,* 660–668.

Kail, R., & Miller, C. (2006). Developmental change in processing speed: Domain specificity and stability during childhood and adolescence. *Journal of Cognition and Development, 7,* 119–137.

Kaiser Family Foundation. (1999, October). Race, ethnicity, & medical care: A survey of public perceptions and experiences. Retrieved November 26, 2003, from http://www.kff.org/content/1999/19901014a/chartpack.pdf

Kalichman, S., Benotsch, E., Weinhardt, L., Austin, J., Webster, L., & Chauncey, C. (2003). Health-related Interent use, coping, social support, and health indicators in people living with HIV/AIDS: Preliminary results from a community survey. *Health Psychology, 22,* 111–116.

Kalidini, S., & McGuffin, P. (2003). The genetics of affective disorders: Present and future. In R. Plomin, J. Defries, I. Craig, & P. McGuffin (Eds.), *Behavioral genetics in the postgenomic era* (pp. 481–502). Washington, DC: American Psychological Association.

Kalish, H. I. (1981). *From behavioral science to behavior modification.* New York: McGraw-Hill.

Kaltiala-Heino, R., Marttunen, M., Rantanen, P., & Rimpela, M. (2003). Early puberty is associated with mental health problems in middle adolescence. *Social Science & Medicine, 57,* 1055–1064.

Kaltiala-Heino, R., Rimpelae, M., Rissanen, A., & Rantanen, P. (2001). Early puberty and early sexual activity are associated with bulimic-type eating pathology in middle adolescence. *Journal of Adolescent Health, 28,* 346–352.

Kamarajan, C., Porjesz, B., Jones, K., Chorlian, D., Padmanabhapillai, A., Rangaswamy, M., Stimus, A., & Begleiter, H. (2006). Event-related oscillations in offspring of alcoholics: Neurocognitive disinhibition as a risk for alcoholism. *Biological Psychiatry, 59,* 625–634.

Kamel, H. (2001). Sexuality in aging: Focus on the institutionalized elderly. *Annals of Long-Term Care: Clinical Care and Aging, 9,* 64–72.

Kampman, M., Keijsers, G., Hoogduin, C., & Hendriks, G. (2002). A randomized, double-blind, placebo-controlled study of the effects of adjunctive paroxetine in panic disorder patients unsuccessfully treated with cognitive-behavioral therapy alone. *Journal of Clinical Psychiatry, 63,* 772–777.

Kanaya, Y., Nakamura, C., and Miyake, D. (1989). Cross-cultural study of expressive behavior of mothers in response to their five-month-old infants' different emotion expression. *Research and Clinical Center for Child Development Annual Report, 11,* 25–31.

Kandel, D. B., & Davies, M. (1996). High school students who use crack and other drugs. *Archives of General Psychiatry, 53,* 71–80.

Kane, H., & Oakland, T. (2000). Secular declines in Spearman's *g*: Some evidence from the United States. *Journal of Genetic Psychology, 161,* 337–345.

Kane, J. M. (1996). Treatment-resistant schizophrenic patients. *Journal of Clinical Psychiatry, 57*(9, Suppl.), 35–40.

Kanner, A. D., Coyne, J. C., Schaefer, C., & Lazarus, R. S. (1981). Comparison of two modes of stress measurement: Daily hassles and uplifts versus major life events. *Journal of Behavioral Medicine, 4,* 1–39.

Kaplan, G. A., Wilson, T. W., Cohen, R. D., Kauhanen, J., Wu, M., & Salomen, J. T. (1994). Social functioning and overall mortality: Prospective evidence from the Kuopio Ischemic Heart Disease Risk Factor Study. *Epidemiology, 5,* 495–500.

Kaplan, H. S. (1974). *The new sex therapy: Active treatment of sexual dysfunction.* New York: Brunner/Mazel.

Karacan, I. (1988). Parasomnias. In R. L. Williams, I. Karacan, & C. A. Moore (Eds.), *Sleep disorders: Diagnosis and treatment* (pp. 131–144). New York: John Wiley.

Karau, S. J., & Williams, K. D. (1993). Social loafing; a meta-analytic review and theoretical integration. *Journal of Personality and Social Psychology, 65,* 681–706.

Kark, R., Shamir, B., & Chen, G. (2003). The two faces of transformational leadership: Empowerment and dependency. *Journal of Applied Psychology, 88,* 246–255.

Karni, A., Tanne, D., Rubenstein, B. S., Askenasy, J. J. M., & Sagi, D. (1994). Dependence on REM sleep of overnight improvement of a perceptual skill. *Science, 265,* 679–682.

Karnil, R., Grosz, E., & Schorr, I. (2003). Caring, gender role orientation, and volunteering. *Sex Roles, 49,* 11–19.

Kashihara, K., Takahashi, K., & Shohmori, T. (1999). Circadian rhythm sleep disorder associated with pontine lesion. *European Journal of Neurology, 6,* 99–102.

Kastenbaum, R. (1992). *The psychology of death.* New York: Springer-Verlag.

Katerndahl, D., Burge, S., & Kellogg, N. (2005). Predictors of development of adult psychopathology in female victims of childhood sexual abuse. *Journal of Nervous and Mental Disease, 193,* 258–264.

Katon, W. (1996). Panic disorder: Relationship to high medical utilization, unexplained physical symptoms, and medical costs. *Journal of Clinical Psychiatry, 57*(10, Suppl.), 11–18.

Katz, G., Knobler, H., Laibel, Z., Strauss, Z., & Durst, R. (2002). Time zone change and major psychiatric morbidity: The results of a 6-year study in Jerusalem. *Comprehensive Psychiatry, 43,* 37–40.

Katzell, R. A., & Thompson, D. E. (1990). Work motivation: Theory and practice. *American Psychologist, 45,* 144–153.

Kaut, K., Bunsey, M., & Riccio, D. (2003). Olfactory learning and memory impairments following lesions to the hippocampus and perirhinal-entorhinal cortex. *Behavioral Neuroscience, 117,* 304–319.

Kawanishi, Y., Tachikawa, H., & Suzuki, T. (2000). Pharmacogenomics and schizophrenia. *European Journal of Pharmacology, 410,* 227–241.

Kay, S. A. (1997). PAS, present, and future: Clues to the origins of circadian clocks. *Science, 276,* 753–754.

Kaye, J., & Jick, H. (2003). Incidence of erectile dysfunction and characteristics of patients before and after the introduction of sildenafil in the United Kingdom: Cross sectional study with comparison patients. *British Medical Journal, 326,* 424–425.

Kazdin, A., & Benjet, C. (2003). Spanking children: Evidence and issues. *Current Directions in Psychological Science, 12,* 99–103.

Keating, C. R. (1994). World without words: Messages from face and body. In W. J. Lonner & R. Malpass (Eds.), *Psychology and culture* (pp. 175–182). Boston: Allyn & Bacon.

Keefauver, S. P., & Guilleminault, C. (1994). Sleep terrors and sleepwalking. In M. Kryger, T. Roth, & W. C. Dement (Eds.), *Principles and practice of sleep medicine* (pp. 567–573). Philadelphia: W.B. Saunders.

Keesey, R. E., & Powley, T. L. (1986). The regulation of body weight. *Annual Review of Psychology, 37,* 109–133.

Keitner, G. I., Ryan, C. E., Miller, I. W., & Norman, W. H. (1992). Recovery and major depression: Factors associated with twelve-month outcome. *American Journal of Psychiatry, 149,* 93–99.

Keller, H., Schlomerich, A., & Eibl-Eibesfeldt, I. (1988). Communication patterns in adult-infant interactions in western and non-western cultures. *Journal of Cross-Cultural Psychology, 19,* 427–445.

Kellett, S., Newman, D., Matthews, L., & Swift, A. (2004). Increasing the effectiveness of large group format CBT via the application of practice-based evidence. *Behavioural & Cognitive Psychotherapy, 32,* 231–234.

Kelner, K. L. (1997). Seeing the synapse. *Science, 276,* 547.

Kendall-Tackett, K. A., Williams, L. M., & Finkehor, D. (1993). Impact of sexual abuse on children: A review and synthesis of recent empirical studies. *Psychological Bulletin, 113,* 164–180.

Kendler, K. S., & Diehl, S. R. (1993). The genetics of schizophrenia: A current genetic-epidemiologic perspective. *Schizophrenia Bulletin, 19,* 261–285.

Kendler, K. S., Gardner, C. O., & Prescott, C. A. (1997). Religion, psychopathology, and substance use and abuse: A multimeasure, genetic-epidemiologic study. *American Journal of Psychiatry, 154,* 322–329.

Kendler, K. S., MacLean, C., Neale, M., Kessler, R., Heath, A., & Eaves, L. (1991). The genetic epidemiology of bulimia nervosa. *American Journal of Psychiatry, 148,* 1627–1637.

Kendler, K. S., Neale, M. C., Kessler, R. C., Heath, A. C., & Eaves, L. J. (1992). The genetic epidemiology of phobias in women. *Archives of General Psychiatry, 49,* 273–281.

Kendler, K. S., Neale, M. C., Kessler, R. C., Heath, A. C., & Eaves, L. J. (1993). The lifetime history of major depression in women: Reliability of diagnosis and heritability. *Archives of General Psychiatry, 50,* 863–870.

Kennedy, C. (2002). Effects of REM sleep deprivation on a multiple schedule of appetitive reinforcement. *Behavioural Brain Research, 128,* 205–214.

Kennedy, Q., Mather, M., & Carstensen, L. (2004). The role of motivation in the age-related positivity effect in autobiographical memory. *Psychological Science, 15,* 208–214.

Kenney-Benson, G., Pomerantz, E., Ryan, A., & Patrick, H. (2006). Sex differences in math performance: The role of children's approach to schoolwork. *Developmental Psychology, 42,* 11–26.

Kensinger, E., Brierley, B., Medford, N., Growdon, J., & Corkin, S. (2002). Effects of normal aging and Alzheimer's disease on emotional memory. *Emotion, 2,* 118–134.

Kenwright, M., & Marks, I. (2004). Computer-aided self-help for phobia/panic via Internet at home: A pilot study. *British Journal of Psychiatry, 184,* 448–449.

Kessler, R. C., Stein, M. B., & Berglund, P. (1998). Social phobia subtypes in the National Comorbidity Survey. *American Journal of Psychiatry, 155,* 613–619.

Kessler, R., Adler, I., Barkley, R., Biederman, J., Conners, C., Demler, O., Faraone, S., Greenhill, L., Howes, M., Secnik, K., Spencer, T., Ustun, T., Walters, E., & Zaslavsky, A. (2006). The prevalence and correlates of adult ADHD in the United States: Results from the National Comorbidity Survey Replication. *American Journal of Psychiatry, 163,* 716–723.

Kessler, R., Berglund, P., Demler, O., Jin, R., & Walters, E. (2005b). Lifetime prevalence and age-of-onset distributions of *DSM-IV* disorders in the National Comorbidity Survey Replication. *Archives of General Psychiatry, 62,* 593–602.

Kessler, R., Chiu, W., Demler, O., & Walters, E. (2005a). Prevalence, severity, and comorbidity of 12-month *DSM-IV* disorders in the National Comorbidity Survey replication. *Archives of General Psychiatry, 62,* 617–627.

Kickul, J., Lester, S., & Finkl, J. (2002). Promise breaking during radical organizational change. *Journal of Organizational Behavior, 23,* 469–488.

Kiecolt-Glaser, J. K., Fisher, L. D., Ogrocki, P., Stout, J., Speicher, C. E., & Glaser, R. (1987). Marital quality, marital disruption, and immune function. *Psychosomatic Medicine, 49,* 13–34.

Kiecolt-Glaser, J. K., Glaser, R., Gravenstein, S., Malarkey, W. B., & Sheridan, J. (1996). Chronic stress alters the immune response to influenza virus vaccine in older adults. *Proceedings of the National Academy of Science, 93,* 3043–3047.

Kihlstrom, J. F. (1985). Hypnosis. *Annual Review of Psychology, 26,* 557–591.

Kihlstrom, J. F. (1986). Strong inferences about hypnosis. *Behavioral and Brain Sciences, 9,* 474–475.

Kihlstrom, J. F. (1995). The trauma-memory argument. *Consciousness and Cognition, 4,* 65–67.

Kihlstrom, J. F., & Barnhardt, T. M. (1993). The self-regulation of memory: For better and for worse, with and without hypnosis. In D. M. Wegner & J. W. Pennebaker (Eds.), *Handbook of mental control.* Englewood Cliffs, NJ: Prentice Hall.

Kilbride, J. E., & Kilbride, P. L. (1975). Sitting and smiling behavior of Baganda infants. *Journal of Cross-Cultural Psychology, 6,* 88–107.

Kilpatrick, D., Ruggiero, K., Acierno, R., Saunders, B., Resnick, H., & Best, C. (2003). Violence and risk of PTSD, major depression, substance abuse/dependence, and comorbidity: Results from the National Survey of Adolescents. *Journal of Consulting and Clinical Psychology, 71,* 692–700.

Kim, J. J., Mohamed, S., Andreasen, N. C., O'Leary, D. S., Watkins, L., Ponto, L. L. B., & Hichwa, R. D. (2000). Regional neural dysfunctions in chronic schizophrenia studied with positron emission tomography. *American Journal of Psychiatry, 157,* 542–548.

Kim, K. H. S., Relkin, N. R., Lee, K-M., & Hirsch, J. (1997). Distinct cortical areas associated with native and second languages. *Nature, 388,* 171–174.

Kimura, D. (1992). Sex differences in the brain. *Scientific American, 267,* 118–125.

King, B. (2006). The rise, fall, and resurrection of the ventromedial hypothalamus in the regulation of feeding behavior and body weight. *Physiology & Behavior, 87,* 221–244.

King, B., & Bostic, J. (2006). An update on pharmacologic treatments for autism spectrum disorders. *Child and Adolescent Psychiatric Clinics of North America, 15,* 161–175.

Kingsbury, S. J. (1993). Brief hypnotic treatment of repetitive nightmares. *American Journal of Clinical Hypnosis, 35,* 161–169.

Kinney, A., Croyle, R., Bailey, C., Pelias, M., & Neuhausen, S. (2001). Knowledge, attitudes, and interest in breast-ovarian cancer gene testing: A survey of a large African American kindred with a BRCA1 mutation. *Journal of Genetic Counseling, 10,* 41–51.

Kinney, T. (2003). Themes and perceptions of written sexually harassing messages and their link to distress. *Journal of Language & Social Psychology, 22,* 8–28.

Kinnunen, T., Zamansky, H. S., & Block, M. L. (1994). Is the hypnotized subject lying? *Journal of Abnormal Psychology, 103,* 184–191.

Kinomura, S., Larsson, J., Gulyás, B., & Roland, P. E. (1996). Activation by attention of the human reticular formation and thalamic intralaminar nuclei. *Science, 271,* 512–515.

Kinsey, A. C., Pomeroy, W. B., & Martin, C. E. (1948). *Sexual behavior in the human male.* Philadelphia: W. B. Saunders.

Kinsey, A. C., Pomeroy, W. B., Martin, C. E., & Gebhard, P. H. (1953). *Sexual behavior in the human female.* Philadelphia: W. B. Saunders.

Kirby, D. (2001). *Emerging answers: Research findings on programs to reduce teen pregnancy (summary).* Washington, DC: National Campaign to Prevent Teen Pregnancy. Retrieved June 13, 2006 from http://www.teenpregnancy.org/resources/data/pdf/emeranswsum.pdf

Kirchner, T., & Sayette, M. (2003). Effects of alcohol on controlled and automatic memory processes. *Experimental & Clinical Psychopharmacology, 11,* 167–175.

Kirkcaldy, B., Shephard, R., & Furnham, A. (2002). The influence of Type A behavior and locus of control upon job satisfaction and occupational health. *Personality & Individual Differences, 33,* 1361–1371.

Kirsch, I., & Lynn, S. J. (1995). The altered state of hypnosis: Changes in the theoretical landscape. *American Psychologist, 50,* 846–858.

Kirveskari, E., Partinen, M., & Santavuouri, P. (2001). Sleep and its disturbance in a variant form of late infantile neuronal ceroid lipofuscinosis (CLN5). *Journal of Child Neurology, 16,* 707–713.

Kisilevsky, B., Hains, S., Lee, K., Xie, X., Huang, H., Ye, H., Zhang, K., & Wang, A. (2003). Effects of experience on fetal voice recognition. *Psychological Science, 14,* 220–224.

Kitayama, S., & Markus, H. R. (2000). The pursuit of happiness and the realization of sympathy: Cultural patterns of self, social relations, and well-being. In E. Diener & E. M. Suh (Eds.), *Subjective well-being across cultures.* Cambridge, MA: MIT Press.

Kite, M. E., Deaux, K., & Miele, M. (1991). Stereotypes of young and old: Does age outweigh gender? *Psychology and Aging, 6,* 19–27.

Kiyokawa, Y., Shimozuru, M., Kikusui, T., Takeuchi, Y., & Mori, Y. (2006). Alarm pheromone increases defensive and risk assessment behaviors in male rats. *Physiology & Behavior, 87,* 383–387.

Klaczynski, P., Fauth, J., & Swanger, A. (1998). Adolescent identity: Rational vs. experiental processing, formal operations, and critical thinking beliefs. *Journal of Youth & Adolescence, 17,* 185–207.

Klahr, D. (1992). Information-processing approaches to cognitive development. In M. H. Bornstein & M. E. Lamb (Eds.), *Developmental psychology: An advanced textbook,* 3rd ed. (pp. 273–335). Hillsdale, NJ: Erlbaum.

Klatzky, R. L. (1980). *Human memory: Structures and processes* (2nd ed.). New York: W. H. Freeman.

Klatzky, R. L. (1984). *Memory and awareness: An information-processing perspective.* New York: W. H. Freeman.

Kleinman, A., & Cohen, A. (1997, March). Psychiatry's global challenge. *Scientific American, 276,* 86–89.

Kleinmuntz, B., & Szucko, J. J. (1984). A field study of the fallibility of polygraph lie detection. *Nature, 308,* 449–450.

Klerman, G. L., Weissman, M. N., Rounsaville, B. J., & Chevron, E. S. (1984). *Interpersonal therapy of depression.* New York: Academic Press.

Kliegman, R. (1998). Fetal and neonatal medicine. In R. Behrman & R. Kliegman (Eds.), *Nelson essentials of pediatrics* (3rd ed., pp. 167–225). Philadelphia: W. B. Saunders.

Kline, G., Stanley, S., Markan, H., Olmos-Gallo, P., St. Peters, M., Whitton, S., & Prado, L. (2004). Timing is everything: Pre-engagement cohabitation and increased risk for poor marital outcomes. *Journal of Family Psychology, 18,* 311-318.

Klinnert, M. D., Campos, J. J., Sorce, J. F., Emde, R. N., & Suejda, M. (1983). Emotions as behavior regulators: Social referencing in infancy. In R. Plutchik & H. Kellerman (Eds.), *Emotions in early development: Vol. 2: The emotions* (pp. 57–86). New York: Academic Press.

Kluft, R. P. (1984). An introduction to multiple personality disorder. *Psychiatric Annals, 14,* 19–24.

Kluft, R. P. (1992). Hypnosis with multiple personality disorder. *American Journal of Preventative Psychiatry & Neurology, 3,* 19–27.

Knickmeyer, R., Baron-Cohen, S., Raggatt, P., Taylor, K., & Hackett, G. (2006). Fetal testosterone and empathy. *Hormones & Behavior, 49,* 282–292.

Knight, R. T. (1996). Contribution of human hippocampal region to novelty detection. *Nature, 383,* 256–259.

Knobloch-Westerwick, S., & Alter, S. (2006). Mood adjustment to social situations through mass media use: How men ruminate and women dissipate angry moods. *Human Communication Theory, 32,* 58–73.

Kobasa, S. (1979). Stressful life events, personality, and health: An inquiry into hardiness. *Journal of Personality and Social Psychology, 37,* 1–11.

Kobasa, S. C., Maddi, S. R., & Kahn, S. (1982). Hardiness and health: A prospective study. *Journal of Personality and Social Psychology, 42,* 168–177.

Kochanska, G. (1993). Toward a synthesis of parental socialization and child temperament in early development of conscience. *Child Development, 64,* 325–347.

Koehler, T., Tiede, G., & Thoens, M. (2002). Long and short-term forgetting of word associations: An experimental study of the Freudian concepts of resistance and repression. *Zeitschrift fuer Klinische Psychologie, Psychiatrie und Psychotherapie, 50*, 328–333.

Koerner, B. (2002, July/August). Disorders made to order. *Mother Jones* [Online, no pages specified.] Retrieved July 25, 2006 from http://www.motherjones.com/news/feature/2002/07/disorders.html

Kohlberg, L. (1966). A cognitive-developmental analysis of children's sex-role concepts and attitudes. In E. E. Maccoby (Ed.), *The development of sex differences* (pp. 82–173). Stanford, CA: Stanford University Press.

Kohlberg, L. (1968, September). The child as a moral philosopher. *Psychology Today*, pp. 24–30.

Kohlberg, L. (1969). *Stages in the development of moral thought and action.* New York: Holt, Rinehart & Winston.

Kohlberg, L. (1981). *Essays on moral development*, Vol. 1. *The philosophy of moral development.* New York: Harper & Row.

Kohlberg, L. (1984). *Essays on moral development*, Vol. 2. *The psychology of moral development.* San Francisco: Harper & Row.

Kohlberg, L. (1985). *The psychology of moral development.* San Francisco: Harper & Row.

Kohlberg, L., & Ullian, D. Z. (1974). In R. C. Friedman, R. M. Richart, & R. L. Vande Wiele (Eds.), *Sex differences in behavior* (pp. 209–222). New York: Wiley.

Köhler, W. (1925). *The mentality of apes* (E. Winter, Trans.). New York: Harcourt Brace Jovanovich.

Koltz, C. (1983, December). Scapegoating. *Psychology Today*, pp. 68–69.

Kon, M. A., & Plaskota, L. (2000). Information complexity of neural networks. *Neural Networks, 13*, 365–375.

Konarski, J., McIntyre, R., Grupp, L., & Kennedy, S. (2005). Is the cerebellum relevant in the circuitry of neuropsychiatric disorders? *Journal of Psychiatry & Neuroscience, 30*, 178–186.

König, P., & Verschure, F. (2002). Neurons in action. *Science, 296*, 1817–1818.

Konishi, M. (1993). Listening with two ears. *Scientific American, 268*, 66–73.

Konstantareas, M. (2006). Social skill training in high functioning Autism and Asperger's disorder. *Hellenic Journal of Psychology, 3*, 39–56.

Kopinska, A., & Harris, L. (2003). Spatial representation in body coordinates: Evidence from errors in remembering positions of visual and auditory targets after active eye, head, and body movements. *Canadian Journal of Experimental Psychology, 57*, 23–37.

Korobov, N., & Thorne, A. (2006). Intimacy and distancing: Young men's conversations about romantic relationships. *Journal of Adolescent Research, 21*, 27–55.

Kosslyn, S. M. (1988). Aspects of a cognitive neuroscience of mental imagery. *Science, 240*, 1621–1626.

Koutsky, L. A., et al. (1992). A cohort study of the risk of cervical intraepithelial neoplasia Grade 2 or 3 in relation to papillomavirus infection. *New England Journal of Medicine, 327*, 1272.

Kovacs, D., Mahon, J., & Palmer, R. (2002). Chewing and spitting out food among eating-disordered patients. *International Journal of Eating Disorders, 32*, 112–115.

Kowatch, R., Suppes, T., Carmody, T., Bucci, J., Hume, J., Kromelis, M., Emslie, G., Weinberg, W., & Rush, A. (2000). Effect size of lithium, divalproex sodium, and carbamazepine in children and adolescents with bipolar disorder. *Journal of the American Academy of Child & Adolescent Psychiatry, 39*, 713–720.

Kozak, M. J., Foa, E. B., & McCarthy, P. R. (1988). Obsessive-compulsive disorder. In C. G. Last & M. Herson (Eds.), *Handbook of anxiety disorders* (pp. 87–108). New York: Pergamon Press.

Kozel, F., Johnson, K., Mu, Q., Grenesko, E., Laken, S., & George, M. (2005). Detecting deception using functional magnetic resonance imaging. *Biological Psychiatry, 58*, 605–613.

Krakow, B., & Zadra, A. (2006). Clinical management of chronic nightmares: Imagery rehearsal therapy. *Behavioral Sleep Medicine, 4*, 45–70.

Krantz, D. S., Grunberg, N. E., & Baum, A. (1985). Health psychology. *Annual Review of Psychology, 36*, 349–383.

Krantz, M. (1987). Physical attractiveness and popularity: A predictive study. *Psychological Reports, 60*, 723–726.

Kranzler, H. R. (1996). Evaluation and treatment of anxiety symptoms and disorders in alcoholics. *Journal of Clinical Psychiatry, 57*(6, Suppl.).

Krasowska, F. (1996, February). Software, sites can subdue strain. *Occupational Health and Safety, 65*, 20.

Kraus, S. J. (1995). Attitudes and the prediction of behavior: A meta-analysis of the empirical literature. *Personality and Social Psychology Bulletin, 21*, 58–75.

Krcmar, M., & Cooke, M. (2001). Children's moral reasoning and their perceptions of television violence. *Journal of Communication, 51*, 300–316.

Krebs, D., & Denton, K. (2005). Toward a more pragmatic approach to morality: A critical evaluation of Kohlberg's model. *Psychological Review, 112*, 629–649.

Kripke, D., Garfinkel, L., Wingard, D., Klauber, M., & Marler, M. (2002). Mortality associated with sleep duration. *Archives of General Psychiatry, 59*, 131–136.

Kripke, D., Youngstedt, S., Elliott, J., Tuunainen, A., Rex, K., Hauger, R., & Marler, M. (2005). Circadian phase in adults of contrasting ages. *Chronobiology International, 22*, 695–709.

Kroll, N. E. A., Ogawa, K. H., & Nieters, J. E. (1988). Eyewitness memory and the importance of sequential information. *Bulletin of the Psychonomic Society, 26*, 395–398.

Kropyvnytskyy, I., Saunders, F., Pols, M., & Sarowski, C. (2001). Circadian rhythm of temperature in head injury. *Brain Injury, 15*, 511–518.

Krueger, G., & Banderet, L. (1997). Effects of chemical protective clothing on military performance: A review of the issues. *Military Psychology, 9*, 251–415.

Krueger, J. M., & Takahashi, S. (1997). Thermoregulation and sleep: Closely linked but separable. *Annals of the New York Academy of Sciences, 813*, 281–286.

Krueger, W. C. F. (1929). The effect of overlearning on retention. *Journal of Experimental Psychology, 12*, 71–81.

Krumm, D. (2001). *Psychology at work: An introduction to industrial/organizational psychology.* New York: Worth.

Krysan, M., & Farley, R. (2002). The residential preferences of blacks: Do they explain persistent segregation? *Social Forces, 80*, 937–980.

Kubzansky, L., Cole, S., Kawachi, I., Vokonas, P., & Sparrow, D. (2006). Shared and unique contributions of anger, anxiety, and depression to coronary heart disease: A prospective study in the normative aging study. *Annals of Behavioral Medicine, 31*, 21–29.

Kucharska-Pietura, K., & Klimkowski, M. (2002). Perception of facial affect in chronic schizophrenia and right brain damage. *Acta Neurobiologiae Experimentalis, 62*, 33–43.

Kuhn, D. (1992). Thinking as argument. *Harvard Educational Review, 62*, 155–178.

Kumar, R., O'Malley, P., Johnston, L., Schulenberg, J., & Bachman, J. (2002). Effects of school-level norms on student substance abuse. *Prevention Science, 3*, 105–124.

Kummervold, P., Gammon, D., Bergvik, S., Johnsen, J., Hasvold, T., & Rosenvinge, J. (2002). Social support in a wired world: Use of online mental health forums in Norway. *Nordic Journal of Psychiatry, 56*, 59–65.

Kumpfer, K., Alvarado, R., Smith, P., & Ballamy, N. (2002). Cultural sensitivity and adaptation in family-based prevention interventions. *Prevention Science, 3*, 241–246.

Kunda, Z., & Oleson, K. C. (1995). Maintaining stereotypes in the face of disconfirmation: Construction grounds for subtyping deviants. *Journal of Personality and Social Psychology, 68*, 565–579.

Kunz, D., & Herrmann, W. M. (2000). Sleep-wake cycle, sleep-related disturbances, and sleep disorders: A chronobiological approach. *Comparative Psychology, 41*(2, Suppl. 1), 104–105.

Kupersmidt, J. B., & Coie, J. D. (1990). Preadolescent peer status, aggression, and school adjustment as predictors of externalizing problems in adolescence. *Child Development, 61*, 1350–1362.

Kupersmidt, J. B., Coie, J. D., & Dodge, K. A. (1990). Predicting disorder from peer social problems. In S. R. Asher & J. D. Coie (Eds.), *Peer rejection in childhood.* New York: Cambridge University Press.

Kuroda, K. (2002). An image retrieval system by impression words and specific object names-IRIS. *Neurocomputing: An International Journal, 43*, 259–276.

Kurup, R., & Kurup, P. (2002). Detection of endogenous lithium in neuropsychiatric disorders. *Human Psychopharmacology Clinical & Experimental, 17*, 29–33.

LaFrance, M., Hecht, M., & Paluck, E. (2003). The contingent smile: A meta-analysis of sex differences in smiling. *Psychological Bulletin, 129*, 305–334.

Lafuente, M., Grifol, R., Segarra, J., Soriano, J., Gorba, M., & Montesinos, A. (1997). Effects of the Firstart method of prenatal stimulation on psychomotor development: The first six months. *Pre- & Peri-Natal Psychology Journal, 13*, 317–326.

Lai, J., Evens, P., Ng, S., Chong, A., Siu, O., Chan, C., Ho, S., Ho, R., Chan, P., & Chan, C. (2005). Optimism, positive affectivity, and salivary cortisol. *British Journal of Health Psychology, 10*, 467–484.

Laird, R., Pettit, G., Bates, J., & Dodge, K. (2003). Parents' monitoring-relevant knowledge and adolescents' delinquent behavior: Evidence of correlated developmental changes and reciprocal influences. *Child Development, 74*, 752–768.

Lal, S. (2002). Giving children security: Mamie Phipps Clark and the racialization of child psychology. *American Psychologist, 57*, 20–28.

Lam, L., & Kirby, S. (2002). Is emotional intelligence an advantage? An exploration of the impact of emotional and general intelligence on individual performance. *Journal of Social Psychology, 142*, 133–143.

Lamb, M., & Lewis, C. (2005). The role of parent-child relationships in child development. In M. Bornstein & M. Lamb (Eds.), *Developmental science: An advanced textbook* (5th Ed., pp. 429–468) Hillsdale, NJ: Lawrence Erlbaum Associates.

Lambe, E. K., Katzman, D. K., Mikulis, D. J., Kennedy, S. H., & Zipursky, R. B. (1997). Cerebral gray matter volume deficits after weight recovery from anorexia nervosa. *Archives of General Psychiatry, 54*, 537–542.

Lamberg, L. (1996). Narcolepsy researchers barking up the right tree. *Journal of the American Medical Association, 276*, 265–266.

Lambert, M. (2003). Suicide risk assessment and management: Focus on personality disorders. *Current Opinion in Psychiatry, 16*, 71–76.

Lamborn, S. D., Mounts, N. S., Steinberg, L., & Dornbusch, S. M. (1991). Patterns of competence and adjustment among adolescents from authoritative, authoritarian, indulgent, and neglectful families. *Child Development, 62*, 1049–1065.

Landry, D. W. (1997, February). Immunotherapy for cocaine addiction. *Scientific American, 276*, 42–45.

Landstad, B., Vinberg, S., Ivergard, T., Gelin, G., & Ekholm, J. (2001). Change in pattern of absenteeism as a result of workplace intervention for personnel support. *Ergonomics, 44*, 63–81.

Lang, A., Craske, M., Brown, M., & Ghaneian, A. (2001). Fear-related state dependent memory. *Cognition & Emotion, 15*, 695–703.

Lang, A. R., Goeckner, D. J., Adesso, V. J., & Marlatt, G. A. (1975). Effects of alcohol on aggression in male social drinkers. *Journal of Abnormal Psychology, 84*, 508–518.

Lange, C. G., & James, W. (1922). *The emotions* (I. A. Haupt, Trans.). Baltimore: Williams and Wilkins.

Lange, G., Sheerin, D., Carr, A., Dooley, B., Barton, V., Marshall, D., Mulligan, A., Lawlor, M., Belton, M., & Doyle, M. (2005). Family factors associated with attention deficit hyperactivity disorder and emotional disorders in children. *Journal of Family Therapy, 27*, 76–96.

Langer, E. J., & Rodin, J. (1976). The effects of choice and enhanced personal responsibility for the aged: A field experiment in an institutional setting. *Journal of Personality and Social Psychology, 34*, 191–198.

Langer, G., Arnedt, C., & Sussman, D. (2004). *Primetime Live poll: American sex survey analysis.* Retrieved July 3, 2006 from http://abcnews.go.com/Primetime/PollVault/story?id=156921&page=1

Langer, P., Holzner, B., Magnet, W., & Kopp, M. (2005). Hands-free mobile phone conversation impairs the peripheral visual system to an extent comparable to an alcohol level of 4–5g 100 ml. *Human Psychopharmacology: Clinical and Experimental, 20*, 65–66.

Langevin, B., Sukkar, F., Léger, P., Guez, A., & Robert, D. (1992). Sleep apnea syndromes (SAS) of specific etiology: Review and incidence from a sleep laboratory. *Sleep, 15*, S25–S32.

Langlois, J. H. (1985). From the eye of the beholder to behavioral reality: The development of social behaviors and social relations as a function of physical attractiveness. In C. P. Herman (Ed.), *Physical appearance, stigma, and social behavior.* Hillsdale, NJ: Erlbaum.

Langlois, J. H., Kalakanis, L., Rubenstein, A. J., Larson, A., Hallam, M., & Smoot, M. (2000). Maxims or myths of beauty? A meta-analytic and theoretical review. *Psychological Bulletin, 126,* 390–423.

Langlois, J. H., & Roggman, L. A. (1990). Attractive faces are only average. *Psychological Science, 1,* 115–121.

Lanza, S., & Collins, L. (2002). Pubertal timing and the onset of substance use in females during early adolescence. *Prevention Science, 3,* 69–82.

Lao, J., & Kuhn, D. (2002). Cognitive engagement and attitude development. *Cognitive Development, 17,* 1203–1217.

Lara, M. E., Leader, J., & Klein, D. N. (1997). The association between social support and course of depression: Is it confounded with personality? *Journal of Abnormal Psychology, 106,* 478–482.

Larson, R., & Verma, S. (1999). How children and adolescents spend time across the world: Work, play, and developmental opportunities. *Psychological Bulletin, 125,* 701–736.

Latané, B., Williams, K., & Harkins, S. (1979). Many hands make light the work: The causes and consequences of social loafing. *Journal of Personality and Social Psychology, 37,* 822–832.

Latham, G., & Pinder, C. (2005). Work motivation theory and research at the dawn of the twenty-first century. *Annual Review of Psychology, 56,* 485–516.

Latner, J., & Wilson, T. (2004). Binge eating and satiety in bulimia nervosa and binge eating disorder: Effects of macronutrient intake. *International Journal of Eating Disorders, 36,* 402–415.

Lattal, K. A., & Neef, N. A. (1996). Recent reinforcement-schedule research and applied behavior analysis. *Journal of Applied Behavior Analysis, 29,* 213–230.

Laughlin, P., Hatch, E., Silver, J., & Boh, L. (2006). Groups perform better than the best individuals on letters-to-numbers problems: Effects of group size. *Journal of Personality and Society Psychology, 90,* 644–651.

Lauman, E., Paik, A., & Rosen, R. (1999). Sildenafil for iatrogenic serotonergic antidepressant medication-induced sexual dysfunction in 4 patients. *Journal of Clinical Psychiatry, 60,* 33–35.

Laumann, E. O., Gagnon, J. H., Michael, R. T., & Michaels, S. (1994). *The social organization of sexuality.* Chicago: University of Chicago Press.

Laurent, J., Swerdik, M., & Ryburn, M. (1992). Review of validity research on the Stanford-Binet Intelligence Scale: Fourth Edition. *Psychological Assessment, 4,* 102–112.

Lauriello, J., McEvoy, J., Rodriguez, S., Bossie, C., & Lasser, R. (2005). Long-acting risperidone vs. placebo in the treatment of hospital inpatients with schizophrenia. *Schizophrenia Research, 72,* 249–258.

Lauriola, M., Russo, P., Lucidi, F., Violani, C., & Levin, I. (2005). The role of personality in positively and negatively framed risky health decisions. *Personality and Individual Differences, 38,* 45–59.

Lauritsen, M., Pedersen, C., & Mortensen, P. (2004). The incidence and prevalence of pervasive developmental disorders: A Danish population-based study. *Psychological Medicine, 34,* 1339–1346.

Lavie, P., Herer, P., Peled, R., Berger, I., Yoffe, N., Zomer, J., & Rubin, A-H. (1995). Mortality in sleep apnea patients: A multivariate analysis of risk factors. *Sleep, 18,* 149–157.

Law, A., Logie, R., & Pearson, D. (2006). The impact of secondary tasks on multitasking in a virtual environment. *Acta Psychologica, 122,* 27–44.

Lawrence, A. (2003). Factors associated with satisfaction or regret following male-to-female sex reassignment surgery. *Archives of Sexual Behavior, 32,* 299–315.

Lawrence, J., Boxer, P., & Tarakeshwar, N. (2002). Determining demand for EAP services. *Employee Assistance Quarterly, 18,* 1–15.

Lawrence, V., Houghton, S., Douglas, G., Durkin, K., Whiting, K., & Tannock, R. (2004). Children with ADHD: Neuropsychological testing and real-world activities. *Journal of Attention Disorders, 7,* 137–149.

Layton, L., Deeny, K., Tall, G., & Upton, G. (1996). Researching and promoting phonological awareness in the nursery class. *Journal of Research in Reading, 19,* 1–13.

Lazar, T. A. (2000). Sexual differentiation of the brain. Akira Matsumoto (Ed.). *Trends in Neurosciences, 23,* 507.

Lazarus, R. S. (1966). *Psychological stress and the coping process.* New York: McGraw-Hill.

Lazarus, R. S. (1984). On the primacy of cognition. *American Psychologist, 39,* 124–129.

Lazarus, R. S. (1991a). Cognition and motivation in emotion. *American Psychologist, 46,* 352–367.

Lazarus, R. S. (1991b). Progress on a cognitive-motivational-relational theory of emotion. *American Psychologist, 46,* 819–834.

Lazarus, R. S., & DeLongis, A. (1983). Psychological stress and coping in aging. *American Psychologist, 38,* 245–253.

Lazarus, R. S., & Folkman, S. (1984). *Stress, appraisal, and coping.* New York: Springer.

Leach, A., Talwar, V., Lee, K., Bala, N., & Lindsay, R. (2004). "Intuitive" lie detection of children's deception by law enforcement officials and university students. *Law and Human Behavior, 28,* 661–685.

LeBreton, J., Burgess, J., Kaiser, R., Atchley, E., & James, L. (2003). The restriction of variance hypothesis and inter-rater reliability and agreement: Are ratings from multiple sources really dissimilar? *Organizational Research Methods, 6,* 80–128.

Lecomte, T., & Lecomte, C. (2002). Toward uncovering robust principles of change inherent to cognitive-behavioral therapy for psychosis. *American Journal of Orthopsychiatry, 72,* 50–57.

LeDoux, J. E. (1994). Emotion, memory, and the brain. *Scientific American, 270,* 50–57.

LeDoux, J. E. (1995). Emotion: clues from the brain. *Annual Review of Psychology, 46,* 209–235.

LeDoux, J. E. (1996). *The emotional brain: The mysterious underpinnings of emotional life.* New York: Simon & Schuster.

LeDoux, J. E. (2000). Emotion circuits in the brain. *Annual Review of Neuroscience, 23,* 155–184.

Lee, I., & Kesner, R. (2002). Differential contribution of NMDA receptors in hippocampal subregions to spatial working memory. *Nature Neuroscience, 5,* 162–168.

Lee, J., Kelly, K., & Edwards, J. (2006). A closer look at the relationships among trait procrastination, neuroticism, and conscientiousness. *Personality and Individual Differences, 40,* 27–37.

Lee, M., Cummins, T. (2004). Evidence accumulation in decision making: Unifying the "take the best" and the "rational" models. *Psychonomic Bulletin & Review, 11,* 343–352.

Lehman, D., & Nisbett, R. (1990). A longitudinal study of the effects of undergraduate training on reasoning. *Developmental Psychology, 26,* 952–960.

Leichtman, M. D., & Ceci, S. J. (1995). The effects of stereotypes and suggestions on preschoolers' reports. *Developmental Psychology, 31,* 568–578.

Leitenberg, H., & Henning, K. (1995). Sexual fantasy. *Psychological Bulletin, 117,* 469–496.

Leland, J. (1997, Spring/Summer). The magnetic tube. *Newsweek* [Special Edition], pp. 89–90.

Lengua, L., Long, A., Smith, K., & Meltzoff, A. (2005). Pre-attack symptomatology and temperament as predictors of children's responses to the September 11 terrorist attacks. *Journal of Child Psychology and Psychiatry, 46,* 631–645.

Lengua, L., & Kovacs, E. (2005). Bidirectional associations between temperament and parenting and the prediction of adjustment problems in middle childhood. *Journal of Applied Developmental Psychology, 26,* 21–38.

Lenneberg, E. (1967). *Biological foundations of language.* New York: Wiley.

Lenzenweger, M., Johnson, M., & Willett, J. (2004). Individual growth curve analysis illuminates stability and change in personality disorder features: The longitudinal study of personality disorders. *Archives of General Psychiatry, 61,* 1015–1024.

Leon, M. (1992). The neurobiology of filial learning. *Annual Review of Psychology, 43,* 337–398.

Leonard, K., & Hornish, G. (2005). Changes in Marijuana Use Over the Transition Into Marriage. *Journal of Drug Issues, 35,* 409–430.

Leonardo, E., & Hen, R. (2006). Genetics of affective and anxiety disorders. *Annual Review of Psychology* (Vol. 57, pp. 117–138). Palo Alto, CA: Annual Reviews.

Lerman, D. C., & Iwata, B. A. (1996). Developing a technology for the use of operant extinction in clinical settings: An examination of basic and applied research. *Journal of Applied Behavior Analysis, 29,* 345–382.

Lerman, D. C., Iwata, B. A., Shore, B. A., & Kahng, S. W. (1996). Responding maintained by intermittent reinforcement: Implications for the use of extinction with problem behavior in clinical settings. *Journal of Applied Behavior Analysis, 29,* 153–171.

Lerner, J, & Tiedens, L. (2006). Portrait of the angry decision maker: How appraisal tendencies shape anger's influence on cognition. *Journal of Behavioral Decision Making, 19,* 115–137.

Lerner, J., Gonzalez, R., Small, D., & Fischoff, B. (2003). Effects of fear and anger on perceived risks of terrorism: A national field experiment. *Psychological Science, 14,* 144–150.

Lesch, K. (2003). Neuroticism and serotonin: A developmental genetic perspective. In R. Plomin, J. DeFries, I. Craig, & P. McGuffin (Eds.), *Behavioral genetics in the postgenomic era* (pp. 389–423). Washington, DC: American Psychological Association.

Leshowitz, B., Eignor DiCerbo, K., & Okun, M. (2002). Effects of instruction in methodological reasoning on information evaluation. *Teaching of Psychology, 29,* 5–10.

Leuchter, A., Cook, I., Witte, E., Morgan, M., & Abrams, M. (2002). Changes in brain function of depressed subjects during treatment with placebo. *American Journal of Psychiatry, 159,* 122–129.

LeVay, S. (1991). A difference in hypothalamic structure between heterosexual and homosexual men. *Science, 253,* 1034–1037.

LeVay, S. (1993). *The sexual brain.* Cambridge, MA: MIT Press.

LeVay, S., & Hamer, D. H. (1994). Evidence for a biological influence in male homosexuality. *Scientific American, 270,* 44–49.

Levenson, R. W. (1992). Autonomic nervous system differences among emotions. *Psychological Science, 3,* 23–27.

Leventhal, T., & Brooks-Gunn, J. (2003). Children and youth in neighborhood contexts. *Current Directions in Psychological Science, 12,* 27–31.

Levin, B. (2005). Factors promoting and ameliorating the development of obesity. *Physiology & Behavior, 86,* 633–639.

Levitt, E. E., & Duckworth, J. C. (1984). Minnesota Multiphasic Personality Inventory. In D. J. Keyser & R. C. Sweetland (Eds.), *Test critiques* (Vol. 1, pp. 466–472). Kansas City: Test Corporation of America.

Levy, J. (1985, May). Right brain, left brain: Fact and fiction. *Psychology Today,* pp. 38–44.

Levy-Shiff, R., Lerman, M., Har-Even, D., & Hod, M. (2002). Maternal adjustment and infant outcome in medically defined high-risk pregnancy. *Developmental Psychology, 38,* 93–103.

Lewald, J. (2004). Gender-specific hemispheric asymmetry in auditory space perception. *Cognitive Brain Research, 19,* 92–99.

Lewin, C., & Herlitz, A. (2002). Sex differences in face recognition: Women's faces make the difference. *Brain & Cognition, 50,* 121–128.

Lewinsohn, P. M., & Rosenbaum, M. (1987). Recall of parental behavior by acute depressives, remitted depressives, and nondepressives. *Journal of Personality and Social Psychology, 52,* 611–619.

Lewis, D. O., Pincus, J. H., Feldman, M., Jackson, L., & Bard, B. (1986). Psychiatric, neurological, and psychoeducational characteristics of 15 death row inmates in the United States. *American Journal of Psychiatry, 143,* 838–845.

Lewis, M. (1995, January/February). Self-conscious emotions. *American Scientist, 83,* 68–78.

Leyens, J-P., Yzerbyt, V., & Olivier, C. (1996). The role of applicability in the emergence of the overattribution bias. *Journal of Personality and Social Psychology, 70,* 219–229.

Li, J. (2003). U.S. and Chinese cultural beliefs about learning. *Journal of Educational Psychology, 95,* 258–267.

Liddle, H. (2002). *Multidimensional family therapy for adolescent cannabis users. Cannabis Youth Treatment (CYT) Series, 5.* Rockville, MD: Center for Substance Abuse Treatment.

Lidz, C., & Macrine, S. (2001). An alternative approach to the identification of gifted culturally and linguistically diverse learners: The contribution of dynamic assessment. *School Psychology International, 22,* 74–96.

Lievens, F., Coetsier, P., De Fruyt, F., & De Maeseneer, J. (2002). Medical students' personality characteristics and academic performance: A five-factor model perspective. *Medical Education, 36,* 1050–1056.

Lievens, F., Harris, M., Van Keer, E., & Bisqueret, C. (2003). Predicting cross-cultural training performance: The validity of personality, cognitive ability, and dimensions measured by an assessment center and a behavioral description interview. *Journal of Applied Psychology, 88,* 476–489.

Lieving, L., Lane, S., Cherek, D., & Tcheremissine, O. (2006). Effects of marijuana on temporal discriminations in humans. *Behavioural Pharamacology, 17,* 173–183.

Liff, S., & Ward, K. (2001). Distorted views through the glass ceiling: The construction of women's understandings of promotion and senior management positions. *Gender, Work & Organization, 8,* 19–36.

Lijia, Z. (2000). China's grey peril. *China Review, 16.* [Online] Retrieved October 12, 2006 from http://www.gbcc.org.uk/iss16_2.htm

Lijtmaer, R. (2001). Splitting and nostalgia in recent immigrants: Psychodynamic considerations. *Journal of the American Academy of Psychoanalysis, 29,* 427–438.

Lilienfeld, S., Kirsch, I., Sarbin, T., Lynn, S., Chaves, J., Ganaway, G., & Powell, R. (1999). Dissociative identity disorder and the sociocognitive model: Recalling the lessons of the past. *Psychological Bulletin, 125,* 507–523.

Lim, V. (2002). The IT way of loafing on the job: Cyberloafing, neutralizing and organizational justice. *Journal of Organizational Behavior, 23,* 675–694.

Lin, Y., & Rancer, A. (2003). Sex differences in intercultural communication apprehension, ethnocentrism, and intercultural willingness to communicate. *Psychological Reports, 92,* 195–200.

Lindenberger, U., Mayr, U., & Kliegl, R. (1993). Speed and intelligence in old age. *Psychology and Aging, 8,* 207–220.

Lindsay, D., Hagen, L., Read, J., Wade, K., & Garry, M. (2004). True photographs and false memories. *Psychological Science, 15,* 149–154.

Linebarger, D., & Walker, D. (2005). Infants' and toddlers' television viewing and language outcomes. *American Behavioral Scientist, 48,* 624–645.

Linn, R. L. (1982). Ability testing: Individual differences, prediction, and differential prediction. In A. K. Wigdor & W. R. Garner (Eds.), *Ability testing: Uses, consequences, and controversies* (Part II). Washington, DC: National Academy Press.

Linton, M. (1979, July). I remember it well. *Psychology Today,* pp. 80–86.

Linville, P. W., Fischer, G. W., & Salovey, P. (1989). Perceived distributions of the characteristics of in-group and out-group members: Empirical evidence and a computer simulation. *Journal of Personality and Social Psychology, 57,* 165–188.

Liossi, C. (2006). Hypnosis in cancer care. *Contemporary Hypnosis, 23,* 47–57.

Lippa, R. (2005a). *Gender, nature, and nurture.* Hillsdale, NJ: Lawrence Erlbaum Associates.

Lippa, R. (2005b). Sex and gender. In V. Derlega, B. Winstead, & W. Jones (Eds.), *Personality: Contemporary theory and research* (3rd ed., pp. 332–365). Belmont, CA: Wadsworth.

Lipsitt, L. P. (1990). Learning processes in the human newborn: Sensitization, habituation, and classical conditioning. *Annals of the New York Academy of Sciences, 608,* 113–123.

Lishman, W. A. (1990). Alcohol and the brain. *British Journal of Psychiatry, 156,* 635–644.

Little, J., McFarlane, J., & Ducharme, H. (2002). ECT use delayed in the presence of comorbid mental retardation: A review of clinical and ethical issues. *Journal of ECT, 18,* 218–222.

Litwin, H. (2005). Correlates of successful aging: Are they universal? *International Journal of Aging & Human Development, 61,* 313–333.

Litwin, H. (2006). Social networks and self-rated health: A cross-cultural examination among older Israelis. *Journal of Aging and Health, 18,* 335–358.

Liu, B., & Lee, Y. (2006). In-vehicle workload assessment: Effects of traffic situations and cellular telephone use. *Journal of Safety Research, 37,* 99–105.

Livingston, E., Huerta, S., Arthur, D., Lee, S., De Shields, S., & Heber, D. (2002). Male gender is a predictor of morbidity and age a predictor of mortality for patients undergoing gastric bypasssurgery. *Annals of Surgery, 236,* 576–582.

Lock, C. (2004). Deception detection: Psychologists try to learn how to spot a liar. *Science News, 166,* 72.

Loehlin, J. C. (1992). *The limits of family influence: Genes, experience, and behavior.* New York: Guilford.

Loehlin, J. C., Lindzey, G., & Spuhler, J. N. (1975). *Race differences in intelligence.* San Francisco: Freeman.

Loehlin, J. C., Willerman, L., & Horn, J. M. (1988). Human behavior genetics. *Annual Review of Psychology, 39,* 101–133.

Loftus, E. (2003). Our changeable memories: Legal and practical implications. *Nature Reviews: Neuroscience, 4,* 231–234.

Loftus, E. (2004). Memories of things unseen. *Current Directions in Psychological Science, 13,* 145–147.

Loftus, E. (2005). Planting misinformation in the human mind: A 30-year investigation of the malleability of memory. *Learning & Memory, 12,* 361–366.

Loftus, E. F. (1979). *Eyewitness testimony.* Cambridge, MA: Harvard University Press.

Loftus, E. F. (1993a). Psychologists in the eyewitness world. *American Psychologist, 48,* 550–552.

Loftus, E. F. (1993b). The reality of repressed memories. *American Psychologist, 48,* 518–537.

Loftus, E. F. (1997). Creating false memories. *Scientific American, 277,* 71–75.

Loftus, E. F., & Hoffman, H. G. (1989). Misinformation and memory: The creation of new memories. *Journal of Experimental Psychology: General, 118,* 100–104.

Loftus, E. F., & Loftus, G. R. (1980). On the permanence of stored information in the human brain. *American Psychologist, 35,* 409–420.

Loftus, E. F., & Pickrell, J. (1995). The formation of false memories. *Psychiatric Annals, 25,* 720–725.

Loftus, E., & Bernstein, D. (2005). Rich false memories: The royal road to success. In A. Healy (Ed.), *Experimental cognitive psychology and its applications.* Washington, DC: American Psychological Association. (pp. 101–113).

London, E. D., Ernst, M., Grant, S., Bonson, K., & Weinstein, A. (2000). Orbitofrontal cortex and human drug abuse: Functional imaging. *Cerebral Cortex, 10,* 334–342.

Long, D., & Baynes, K. (2002). Discourse representation in the two cerebral hemispheres. *Journal of Cognitive Neuroscience, 14,* 228–242.

Loo, C., Schweitzer, I., & Pratt, C. (2006). Recent advances in optimizing electroconvulsive therapy. *Australian and New Zealand Journal of Psychiatry, 40,* 632–638.

Lopes, A., de Mathis, M., Canteras, M., Salvajoli, J., Del Porto, J., & Miguel, E. (2004). Update on neurosurgical treatment for obsessive compulsive disorder. *Revista Brasileira de Psiquiatria, 26,* 62–66.

Lott, B., & Saxon, S. (2002). The influence of ethnicity, social class and context on judgments about U.S. women. *Journal of Social Psychology, 142,* 481–499.

Lotze, M., Montoya, P., Erb, M., Hulsmann, E., Flor, H., Klose, U., Birbaumer, N., & Grodd, W. (1999). Activation of cortical and cerebellar motor areas during executed and imagined hand movements: An fMRI study. *Journal of Cognitive Neuroscience, 11,* 491–501.

Lovett, S. B., & Flavell, J. H. (1990). Understanding and remembering: Children's knowledge about the differential effects of strategy and task variables on comprehension and memorization. *Child Development, 61,* 1842–1858.

Lovoy, L. (2001). A historical survey of the glass ceiling and the double bind faced by women in the workplace: Options for avoidance. *Law & Psychology Review, 25,* 179–203.

Lowell, B. B., & Spiegelman, B. M. (2000). Towards a molecular understanding of adaptive thermogenesis. *Nature, 404,* 652–660.

Lubart, T. (2003). In search of creative intelligence. In R. Sternberg, J. Lautrey, & T. Lubart (Eds.), *Models of intelligence: International perspective* (pp. 279–292). Washington, DC: American Psychological Association.

Lubman, D. I., Peters, L. A., Mogg, K., Bradley, B. P., & Deakin, J. F. (2000). Attentional bias for drug cues in opiate dependence. *Psychological Medicine, 30,* 169–175.

Lucas, J., & Heady, R. (2002). Flextime commuters and their driver stress, feelings of time urgency, and commute satisfaction. *Journal of Business & Psychology, 16,* 565–572.

Luchins, A. S. (1957). Experimental attempts to minimize the impact of first impressions. In C. I. Hovland (Ed.), *Yale studies in attitude and communication: Vol. 1. The order of presentation in persuasion* (pp. 62–75). New Haven, CT: Yale University Press.

Lucio, E., Reyes-Lagunes, I., & Scott, R. L. (1994). MMPI-2 for Mexico: Translation and adaptation. *Journal of Personality Assessment, 63,* 105–116.

Luiselli, J., & Hurley, A. (2005). The significance of applied behavior analysis in the treatment of autism spectrum disorders (ASD). *Mental Health Aspects of Developmental Disabilities, 8,* 128–130.

Lundy, J. (2002). Age and language skills of deaf children in relation to theory of mind development. *Journal of Deaf Studies & Deaf Education, 7,* 41–56.

Lurie, I., & Riccucci, N. (2003). Changing the "culture" welfare offices: From vision to the front lines. *Administration & Society, 34,* 653–677.

Lustig, C., & Hasher, L. (2002). Working memory span: The effect of prior learning. *American Journal of Psychology, 115,* 89–101.

Lustig, C., Konkel, A., & Jacoby, L. (2004). Which route to recovery? Controlled retrieval and accessibility bias in retroactive interference. *Psychological Science, 15,* 729–735.

Lutchmaya, S., Baron-Cohen, S., & Raggatt, P. (2002). Foetal testosterone and vocabulary size in 18- and 24-month-old infants. *Infant Behavior & Development, 24,* 418–424.

Lutz, A., Greischar, L., Rawlings, N., Ricard, M., & Davidson, R. (2004). Long-term meditators self-induce high-amplitude gamma synchrony during mental practice. *Proceedings of the National Academy of Sciences, 101,* 16369–16373.

Lydiard, R. B., Brawman-Mintzer, O., & Ballenger, J. C. (1996). Recent developments in the psychopharmacology of anxiety disorders. *Journal of Consulting and Clinical Psychology, 64,* 660–668.

Lyness, K., & Heilman, M. (2006). When fit is fundamental: Performance evaluations and promotions of upper-level female and male managers. *Journal of Applied Psychology, 91,* 777–785.

Lynn, R. (2006). *Race differences in intelligence: An evolutionary analysis.* Atlanta, GA: Washington Summit Books.

Lynn, S. J., Kirsch, I., Barabasz, A., Cardena, E., & Patterson, D. (2000). Hypnosis as an empirically supported clinical intervention: The state of the evidence and a look to the future. *International Journal of Clinical Experimental Hypnosis, 48,* 239–259.

Lynn, S. J., & Nash, M. R. (1994). Truth in memory: Ramifications for psychotherapy and hypnotherapy. *American Journal of Clinical Hypnosis, 36,* 194–208.

Lyon, M., Cline, J., Totosy de Zepetnek, J., Jie Shan, J., Pang, P., & Benishin, C. (2001). Effect of the herbal extract combination *Panax quinquefolium* and *Ginko biloba* on attention-deficit hyperactivity disorder: A pilot study. *Journal of Psychiatry & Neuroscience. 26,* 221–228.

Lyons, E. (2002). Psychosocial factors related to job stress and women in management. *Work: Journal of Prevention, Assessment & Rehabilitation, 18,* 89–93.

Lyubomirsky, S., King, L., & Diener, E. (2005). The benefits of frequent positive affect: Does happiness lead to success? *Psychological Bulletin, 131,* 803–855.

Lyvers, M. (2000). "Loss of control" in alcoholism and drug addiction: A neuroscientific interpretation. *Experimental and Clinical Psychopharmacology, 8,* 225–245.

Maas, A., Cadinu, M., Boni, M., & Borini, C. (2005). Converting verbs into adjectives: Asymmetrical memory distortions for stereotypic and counterstereotypic information. *Group Process & Intergroup Relations, 8,* 271–290.

Maccoby, E. E. (1992). The role of parents in the socialization of children: An historical overview. *Developmental Psychology, 28,* 1006–1017.

Maccoby, E. E., & Martin, J. A. (1983). Socialization in the context of the family: Parent-child interaction. In P. H. Mussen (Ed.), *Handbook of child psychology* (4th ed., Vol. 4). New York: John Wiley.

MacDonald, A., Pogue-Geile, M., Johnson, M., & Carter, C. (2003). A specific deficit in context processing in the unaffected siblings of patients with schizophrenia. *Archives of General Psychiatry, 60,* 57–65.

Macey, P., Henderson, L., Macey, K., Alger, J., Frysinger, R., Woo, M., Harper, R., Yan-Go, F., & Harper, R. (2002). Brain morphology associated with obstructive sleep apnea. *American Journal of Respiratory and Critical Care Medicine, 166,* 1382–1387.

Mack, A. (2003). Inattentional blindness: Looking without seeing. *Current Directions in Psychological Science, 12,* 180–184.

Mack, A., & Rock, I. (1998). *Inattentional blindness.* Cambridge, MA: MIT Press.

Macrae, C. N., Milne, A. B., & Bodenhausen, G. V. (1994). Stereotypes as energy-saving devices: A peek inside the cognitive toolbox. *Journal of Personality and Social Psychology, 66,* 37–47.

MacWhinney, B. (2005). Language development. In M. Bornstein & M. Lamb, (Eds.), *Developmental science: An advanced textbook* (5th ed., pp. 359–387) Hillsdale, NJ: Lawrence Erlbaum Associates.

Madden, M., & Lenhart, A. (2006). *Pew Internet and American life project: Online dating.* Retrieved July 3, 2006 from http://www.pewinternet.org/pdfs/PIP_Online_Dating.pdf

Magley, V. (2002). Coping with sexual harassment: Reconceptualizing women's resistance. *Journal of Personality and Social Psychology, 83,* 930–946.

Maguire, E. A., Gadian, D. G., Johnsrude, I. S., Good, C. D., Ashburner, J., Frackowiak, R. S. J., & Frith, C. D. (2000). Navigation-related structural change in the hippocampi of taxi drivers. *Proceedings of the National Academy of Science, 97,* 4398–4403.

Maguire, E., Wpiers, H., Good, C., Hartley, T., Frackowiak, R., & Burgess, N. (2003). Navigation expertise and the human hippocampus: A structural brain imaging analysis. *Hippocampus, 13,* 208–217.

Mahler, H., Kulik, J., Gibbons, F., Gerrard, M., & Harrell, J. (2003). Effects of appearance-based intervention on sun protection intentions and self-reported behaviors. *Health Psychology, 22,* 199–209.

Maiden, R., Peterson, S., Caya, M., & Hayslip, B. (2003). Personality changes in the old-old: A longitudinal study. *Journal of Adult Development, 10,* 31–39.

Maier, S. F., & Laudenslager, M. (1985, August). Stress and health: Exploring the links. *Psychology Today,* pp. 44–49.

Main, M., & Solomon, J. (1990). Procedures for identifying infants as disorganized/disoriented during the Ainsworth Strange Situation. In M. Greenberg, D. Cicchetti, & M. Cummings (Eds.), *Attachment in the preschool years: Theory, research, and intervention* (pp. 121–160). Chicago: University of Chicago Press.

Malik, A., & D'Souza, D. (2006). Gone to pot: The association between cannabis and psychosis. *Psychiatric Times, 23.* Retrieved May 15, 2006 from http://www.psychiatrictimes.com/article/showArticle.jhtml?articleId=185303874.

Malkoff, S. B., Muldoon, M. F., Zeigler, Z. R., & Manuck, S. B. (1993). Blood platelet responsivity to acute mental stress. *Psychosomatic Medicine, 55,* 477–482.

Maltz, W. (1991). *The sexual healing journey: A guide for survivors of sexual abuse.* New York: HarperCollins.

Mancini, J., Lethel, V., Hugonenq, C., & Chabrol, B. (2001). Brain injuries in early foetal life: Consequences for brain development. *Developmental Medicine & Child Neurology, 43,* 52–60.

Manderscheid, R., & Henderson, M. (2001). *Mental health, United States, 2000.* Rockville, MD: Center for Mental Health Services. Retrieved January 14, 2003, from http://www.mentalhealth.org/publications/allpubs/SMA01-3537/

Manhal-Baugus, M. (2001). E-therapy: Practical, ethical, and legal issues. *CyberPsychology and Behavior, 4,* 551–563.

Manly, T., Lewis, G., Robertson, I., Watson, P., & Datta, A. (2002). Coffee in the cornflakes: Time-of-day as a modulator of executive response control. *Neuropsychologia, 40,* 1–6.

Mann, S., Vrij, A., & Bull, R. (2004). Detecting true lies: Police officers' ability to detect suspects' lies. *Journal of Applied Psychology, 89,* 137–149.

Manzardo, A., Stein, L., & Belluzi, J. (2002). Rats prefer cocaine over nicotine in a two-level self-administration choice test. *Brain Research, 924,* 10–19.

Maratsos, M., & Matheny, L. (1994). Language specificity and elasticity: Brain and clinical syndrome studies. *Annual Review of Psychology, 45,* 487–516.

Marcia, J. (1966). Development and validation of ego identity status. *Journal of Personality & Social Psychology, 3,* 551–558.

Marcia, J. (1980). Identity in adolescence. In J. Adelson (Ed.), *Handbook of adolescent psychology* (pp. 159–187). New York: Wiley.

Marcia, J. (2002). Identity and psychosocial development in adulthood. *Identity, 2,* 7–28.

Marder, S. R. (1996). Clinical experience with risperidone. *Journal of Clinical Psychiatry, 57*(9, Suppl.), 57–61.

Mares, M., & Woodward, E. (2005). Positive effects of television on children's social interactions: A meta-analysis. *Media Psychology, 7,* 301–322.

Mareschal, D. (2000). Object knowledge in infancy: Current controversies and approaches. *Trends in Cognitive Sciences, 4,* 408–416.

Markey, C., Markey, P., Schneider, C., & Brownlee, S. (2005). Marital status and health beliefs: Different relations for mean and women. *Sex Roles, 53,* 443–451.

Markham, S., Scott, K., & McKee, G. (2002). Recognizing good attendance: A longitudinal, quasi-experimental field study. *Personnel Psychology, 55,* 639–660.

Markovic, B. M., Dimitrijevic, M., & Jankovic, B. D. (1993). Immunomodulation by conditioning: Recent developments. *International Journal of Neuroscience, 71,* 231–249.

Marks, G. A., Shatfery, J. P., Oksenberg, A., Speciale, S. G, & Roff-warg, H. P. (1995). A functional role for REM sleep in brain maturation. *Behavioral Brain Research, 69,* 1–11.

Marks, I. (1987). The development of normal fear: A review. *Journal of Child Psychology and Psychiatry, 28,* 667–697.

Marks, I. M. (1972). Flooding (implosion) and allied treatments. In W. S. Agras (Ed.), *Behavior modification.* New York: Little, Brown.

Marlatt, G. (2005). Treating outside the box: Discussion. *Behavior Therapist, 28,* 122–123.

Marlatt, G. A., & Rohsenow, D. J. (1981, December). The think-drink effect. *Psychology Today,* pp. 60–69, 93.

Marriott, L., & Wenk, G. (2004). Neurobiological consequences of long-term estrogen therapy. *Current Directions in Psychological Science, 13,* 173–176.

Marsh, A., Elfenbein, H., & Ambady, N. (2003). Nonverbal "accents": Cultural differences in facial expressions of emotion. *Psychological Science, 14,* 373–376.

Marshall, R. D., Schneier, F. R., Fallon, B. A., Feerick, J., & Liebowitz, M. R. (1994). Medication therapy for social phobia. *Journal of Clinical Psychiatry, 56*(6, Suppl.), 33–37.

Marshall, W. L., & Segal, Z. (1988). Behavior therapy. In C. G. Last & M. Hersen (Eds.), *Handbook of anxiety disorders* (pp. 338–361). New York: Pergamon.

Martikainen, P., & Valkonen, R. (1996). Mortality after the death of a spouse: Rates and causes of death in a large Finnish cohort. *American Journal of Public Health, 86,* 1087–1093.

Martin, C. L., & Little, J. K. (1990). The relation of gender understanding to children's sex-typed preferences and gender stereotypes. *Child Development, 61,* 1427–1439.

Martin, C., & Halverson, C. (1981). A schematic processing model of sex typing and stereotyping in children. *Child Development, 52,* 1119–1134.

Martin, C., & Ruble, D. (2002). Cognitive theories of early gender development. *Psychological Bulletin, 128,* 903–933.

Martin, J., & Ross, H., (2005). Sibling aggression: Sex differences and parents' reactions. *International Journal of Behavioral Development, 29,* 129–138.

Martin, R. (2006). The neuropsychology of sentence processing: Where do we stand? *Cognitive Neuropsychology, 23,* 74–95.

Martinez, C. (1986). Hispanics: Psychiatric issues. In C. B. Wilkinson (Ed.), *Ethnic psychiatry* (pp. 61–88). New York: Plenum.

Martinez, J. L., Jr., & Derrick, B. E. (1996). Long-term potentiation and learning. *Annual Review of Psychology, 47,* 173–203.

Martinez, M., & Belloch, A. (2004). The effects of a cognitive-behavioural treatment for hypochondriasis on attentional bias. *International Journal of Clinical & Health Psychology, 4,* 299–311.

Martorano, S. C. (1977). A developmental analysis of performance on Piaget's formal operations tasks. *Developmental Psychology, 13,* 666–672.

Masataka, N. (1996). Perception of motherese in a signed language by 6-month-old deaf infants. *Developmental Psychology, 32,* 874–879.

Masland, R. H. (1996). Unscrambling color vision. *Science, 271,* 616–617.

Mason, B., Goodman, A., Chabac, S., & Lehert, P. (2006). Effect of oral acamprosate on abstinence in patients with alcohol dependence in a double-blind, placebo-controlled trial: The role of patient motivation. *Journal of Psychiatric Research, 40,* 383–393.

Masters, W. H., & Johnson, V. E. (1975). *The pleasure bond: A new look at sexuality and commitment.* Boston: Little, Brown.

Mathew, R. J., & Wilson, W. H. (1991). Substance abuse and cerebral blood flow. *American Journal of Psychiatry, 148,* 292–305.

Mathy, R. (2002). Suicidality and sexual orientation in five continents: Asia, Australia, Europe, North America, and South America. *International Journal of Sexuality & Gender Studies, 7,* 215–225.

Matlin, M. W. (1989). *Cognition* (2nd ed.). New York: Holt, Rinehart & Winston.

Matlin, M. W., & Foley, H. J. (1997). *Sensation and perception* (4th ed.). Boston: Allyn & Bacon.

Matsuda, L., Lolait, S. J., Brownstein, M. J., Young, A. C., & Bonner, T. I. (1990). Structure of a cannabinoid receptor and functional expression of the cloned CDNA. *Nature, 346,* 561–564.

Matsumo, D. (2000). *Culture and psychology: People around the world* (2nd ed.). Belmont, CA: Wadsworth.

Matsumoto, D., Yoo, S., Hirayama, S., & Petrova, G. (2005). Development and validation of a measure of display rule knowledge: The Display Rule Assessment Inventory. *Emotion, 5,* 23–40.

Matsunami, H., Montmayeur, J-P., & Buck, L. B. (2000). A family of candidate taste receptors in human and mouse. *Nature, 404,* 601–604.

Matta, D., & Knudson-Martin, C. (2006). Father responsivity: Couple processes and the coconstruction of fatherhood. *Family Process, 45,* 19–37.

Matthews, K. A. (1992). Myths and realities of the menopause. *Psychosomatic Medicine, 54,* 1–9.

Matthews, K. A., Shumaker, S. A., Bowen, D. J., Langer, R. D., Hunt, J. R., Kaplan, R. M., Klesges, R. C., & Ritenbaugh, C. (1997). Women's health initiative: Why now? What is it? What's new? *American Psychologist, 52,* 101–116.

Matthiesen, S., & Einarsen, S. (2004). Psychiatric distress and symptoms of PTSD among victims of bullying at work. *British Journal of Guidance and Counseling, 32,* 335–356.

Matz, D., & Wood, W. (2005). Cognitive dissonance in groups: The consequences of disagreement. *Journal of Personality & Social Psychology, 88,* 22–37.

Maurer, T., Mitchell, D., & Barbeite, F. (2002). Predictors of attitudes toward a 360-degree feedback system and involvement in post-feedback management development activity. *Journal of Occupational & Organizational Psychology, 75,* 87–107.

Mayer, R., Hegarty, M., Mayer, & Campbell, J. (2005). When static media promote active learning: Annotated illustrations versus narrated animations in multimedia instruction. *Journal of Experimental Psychology: Applied, 11,* 256–265.

Mayer, R., Heiser, J., & Lonn, S. (2001). Cognitive constraints on multimedia learning: When presenting more material results in less understanding. *Journal of Educational Psychology, 93,* 187–198.

Mayo Clinic. (2005). *Weight loss: 6 strategies for success.* Retrieved June 16, 2006, from https://www.mayoclinic.com/health/weight-loss/HQ01625.

Mayo Clinic. (2006). *STD quiz: What you don't know can hurt you.* Retrieved July 3, 2006 from http://mayoclinic.cm/health/stds/QZ00037.

Mazur, J. E. (1993). Predicting the strength of a conditioned reinforcer: Effects of delay and uncertainty. *Current Directions in Psychological Science, 2*(3), 70–74.

Mazzoni, G., & Memon, A. (2003). Imagination can create false autobiographical memories. *Psychological Science, 14,* 186–188.

McAnulty, R. D., & Burnette, M. M. (2001). *Exploring human sexuality: Making healthy decisions* (pp. 144-150). Boston: Allyn & Bacon.

McBride-Chang, C., & Treiman, R. (2003). Hong Kong Chinese kindergarteners learn to read English analytically. *Psychological Science, 14,* 138–143.

McCall, W., Dunn, A., & Rosenquist, P. (2004). Quality of life and function after electroconvulsive therapy. *British Journal of Psychiatry, 185,* 405–409.

McCarthy, P. (1989, March). Ageless sex. *Psychology Today,* p. 62.

McCartney, K., Harris, M. J., & Bernieri, F. (1990). Growing up and growing apart: A developmental meta-analysis of twin studies. *Psychological Bulletin, 107,* 226–237.

McClearn, G. E., Johansson, B., Berg, S., Pedersen, N. L., Ahern, F., Petrill, S. A., & Plomin, R. (1997). Substantial genetic influence on cognitive abilities in twins 80 or more years old. *Science, 276,* 1560–1563.

McClelland, D. C. (1958). Methods of measuring human motivation. In J. W. Atkinson (Ed.), *Motives in fantasy, action and society: A method of assessment and study.* Princeton, NJ: Van Nostrand.

McClelland, D. C. (1961). *The achieving society.* Princeton, NJ: Van Nostrand.

McClelland, D. C. (1985). *Human motivation.* New York: Cambridge University Press.

McClelland, D. C., Atkinson, J. W., Clark, R. W., & Lowell, E. L. (1953). *The achievement motive.* New York: Appleton-Century-Crofts.

McClelland, J. L., McNaughton, B. L., & O'Reilly, R. C. (1995). Why there are complementary learning systems in the hippocampus and neocortex: Insights from the successes and failures of connectionist models of learning and memory. *Psychological Bulletin, 102,* 419–457.

McCormick, C. B., & Kennedy, J. H. (2000). Father–child separation, retrospective and current views of attachment relationship with father and self-esteem in late adolescence. *Psychological Reports, 86,* 827–834.

McCrae, R. (1984). Situational determinants of coping responses: Loss, threat, and challenge. *Journal of Personality and Social Psychology, 46,* 919–928.

McCrae, R. R., & Costa, P. T., Jr. (1987). Validation of the five-factor model of personality across instruments and observers. *Journal of Personality and Social Psychology, 52,* 81–90.

McCrae, R. R., & Costa, P. T., Jr. (1990). *Personality in adulthood.* New York: Guilford.

McCrae, R. R., Costa, P. T., Jr., Ostendorf, F., Angleitner, A., Hrebickova, M., Avia, S. J., Sanchez-Bernardos, M. L., Kusdil, M. E., Woodfield, R., Saunders, P. R., & Smith, P. B. (2000). Nature over nurture: Temperament, personality, and life span development. *Journal of Personality & Social Psychology, 78,* 173–186.

McCue, J. M., Link, K. L., Eaton, S. S., & Freed, B. M. (2000). Exposure to cigarette tar inhibits ribonucleotide reductase and blocks lymphocyte proliferation. *Journal of Immunology, 165,* 6771–6775.

McCullough, M. E., Hoyt, W. T., Larson, D. B., Koenig, H. G., & Thoresen, C. (2000). Religious involvement and mortality: A meta-analytic review. *Health Psychology, 19,* 211–222.

McDonald, J. L. (1997). Language acquisition: The acquisition of linguistic structure in normal and special populations. *Annual Review of Psychology, 48,* 215–241.

McDonald, J., Schleifer, L., Richards, J., & de Wit, H. (2003). Effects of THC on behavioral measures of impulsivity in humans. *Neuropsychopharmacology, 28,* 1356–1365.

McDonald, L. (2004, April 28). China may grow old before it gets rich. *Sydney Morning Herald.* Retrieved September 10, 2004 from http://www.smh.com.au/articles/2004/04/27/1082831569621.html?from=storyhs&oneclick=true

McDowell, C., & Acklin, M. W. (1996). Standardizing procedures for calculating Rorschach interrater reliability: Conceptual and empirical foundations. *Journal of Personality Assessment, 66,* 308–320.

McElree, B., Jia, G., & Litvak, A. (2000). The time course of conceptual processing in three bilingual populations. *Journal of Memory & Language, 42,* 229–254.

McElwain, A., Korabik, K., & Rosin, H. (2005). An examination of gender differences in work-family conflict. *Canadian Journal of Behavioural Science, 37,* 283–298.

McFadden, D. (2002). Masculinization effects in the auditory system. *Archives of Sexual Behavior, 31,* 99–111.

McGlashan, T. H., & Hoffman, R. E. (2000). Schizophrenia as a disorder of developmentally reduced synaptic connectivity. *Archives of General Psychiatry, 57,* 637–648.

McGregor, D. (1960). *The human side of enterprise.* New York: McGraw-Hill.

McGue, M., Bouchard, T. J., Jr., Iacono, W. G., & Lykken, D. T. (1993). Behavioral genetics of cognitive ability: A life-span perspective. In R. Plomin & G. E. McClearn (Eds.), *Nature, nurture and psychology* (pp. 59–76). Washington, DC: American Psychological Association.

McGuire, W. J. (1985). Attitudes and attitude change. In G. Lindzey & E. Aronson (Ed.), *Handbook of social psychology* (Vol. 2, 3rd ed.). New York: Random House.

McInerney, F. (2000). "Requested death": A new social movement. *Social Science and Medicine, 50,* 137–154.

McKay, H., Glasgow, R., Feil, E., Boles, S., & Barrera, M. (2002). Internet-based diabetes self-management and support: Initial outcomes from the Diabetes Network Project. *Rehabilitation Psychology, 47,* 31–48.

McKee, T., Harvey, E., Danforth, J., Ulaszek, W., & Friedman, J. (2004). The relation between parental coping styles and parent-child interactions before and after treatment for children with ADHD and oppositional behavior. *Journal of Clinical Child and Adolescent Psychology, 33,* 158–168.

McKelvie, S. (1984). Relationship between set and functional fixedness: A replication. *Perceptual and Motor Skills, 58,* 996–998.

McLeod, J., Pescosolido, B., Takeuchi, D., & White, T. (2004). Public attitudes toward the use of psychiatric medications for children. *Journal of Health and Social Behavior, 45,* 53–67.

McMellon, C., & Schiffman, L. (2002). Cybersenior empowerment: How some older individuals are taking control of their lives. *Journal of Applied Gerontology, 21,* 157–175.

McNally, R. (2003). Recovering memories of trauma: A view from the laboratory. *Current Directions in Psychological Science, 12,* 32–35.

McNally, R., Lasko, N., Clancy, S., Macklin, M., Pitman, R., & Orr, S. (2004). Psychophysiological responding during script-driven imagery in people reporting abduction by space aliens. *Psychological Science, 15,* 493–497.

McNally, R., Perlman, C., Ristuccia, C., & Clancy, S. (2006). Clinical characteristics of adults reporting repressed, recovered, or continuous memories of childhood sexual abuse. *Journal of Consulting & Clinical Psychology, 74,* 237–242.

McReynolds, P. (1989). Diagnosis and clinical assessment: Current status and major issues. *Annual Review of Psychology, 40,* 83–108.

McSweeney, F., & Parks, C. (2002). Participation by women in developmental, social, cognitive, and general psychology: A context for interpreting trends in behavior analysis. *Behavior Analyst, 25,* 37–44.

Medina, J. H., Paladini, A. C., & Izquierdo, I. (1993). Naturally occurring benzodiazepines and benzodiazepine-like molecules in brain. *Behavioural Brain Research, 58,* 1–8.

Mednick, S. A., Brennan, P., & Kandel, E. (1988). Predisposition to violence. *Aggressive Behavior, 14,* 25–33.

Mednick, S. A., & Mednick, M. T. (1967). *Examiner's manual, Remote Associates Test.* Boston: Houghton-Mifflin.

Medzerian, G. (1991). *Crack: Treating cocaine addiction.* Blue Ridge Summit, PA: Tab Books.

Mehagnoul-Schipper, D., van der Kallen, B., Colier, W., van der Sluijs, M., van Erning, L., Thijssen, H., Oeseburg, B., Hoefnagel, W., & Jansen, R. (2002). Simultaneous measurement of cerebral oxygenation changes during brain activation by near-infrared spectroscopy and functional magnetic resonance imaging in healthy young and elderly subjects. *Human Brain Mapping, 16,* 14–23.

Mehlsen, M. (2005). The paradoxical life satisfaction of old age. *Psyke & Logos, 26,* 609–628.

Meier, R. P. (1991). Language acquisition by deaf children. *American Scientist, 79*(1), 60–70.

Meltzer, H. (1930). Individual differences in forgetting pleasant and unpleasant experiences. *Journal of Educational Psychology, 21,* 399–409.

Meltzer, H., Alphs, L., Green, A., Altamura, A., Anand, R., Bertoldi, A., Bourgeois, M., Chouinard, G., Islam, Z., Kane, J., Krishnan, R., Lindenmayer, J., & Potkin, S. (2003). Clozapine treatment for suicidality in schizophrenia: International suicide prevention trial. *Archives of General Psychiatry, 60,* 82–91.

Meltzoff, A. N. (1988). Imitation of televised models by infants. *Child Development, 59,* 1221–1229.

Melzack, R., & Wall, P. D. (1965). Pain mechanisms: A new theory. *Science, 150,* 971–979.

Melzack, R., & Wall, P. D. (1983). *The challenge of pain.* New York: Basic Books.

Mendez, M. F., Chow, T., Ringman, J., Twitchell, G., & Hinkin, C. H. (2000). Pedophilia and temporal lobe disturbances. *Journal of Neuropsychiatry & Clinical Neurosciences, 12,* 171–176.

Mendoza, R. (2005). The need for involuntary medication in competency to stand trial proeedings: A necessary work in progress. *Journal of Forensic Psychology Practice, 5*(3), 69–78.

Merson, M. (2006). The HIV/AIDS pandemic at 25: The global response. *New England Journal of Medicine, 354,* 2414–2417.

Meschyan, G., & Hernandez, A. (2002). Is native-language decoding skill related to second-language learning? *Journal of Educational Psychology, 94,* 14–22.

Meyer, A. (1997, March/April). Patching up testosterone. *Psychology Today, 30,* 54–57, 66–70.

Meyer, G. & Wuerger, S. (2001). Cross-modal integration of auditory and visual motion signals. *Neuroreport: For Rapid Communication of Neuroscience Research, 12,* 2557–2560.

Meyer, P. (1972). If Hitler asked you to electrocute a stranger, would you? In R. Greenbaum & H. A. Tilker (Eds.), *The challenge of psychology* (pp. 456–465). Englewood Cliffs, NJ: Prentice-Hall.

Meyer-Bahlburg, H. F. L., Ehrhardt, A. A., Rosen, L. R., & Gruen, R. S. (1995). Prenatal estrogens and the development of homosexual orientation. *Developmental Psychology, 31,* 12–21.

Meyers, L. (2006). Still wearing the "kick me" sign. *APA Monitor on Psychology, 37,* 68–69.

Middlebrooks, J. C., & Green, D. M. (1991). Sound localization by human listeners. *Annual Review of Psychology, 42,* 135–159.

Miles, D. R., & Carey, G. (1997). Genetic and environmental architecture of human aggression. *Journal of Personality and Social Psychology, 72,* 207–217.

Miles, J., & Hempel, S. (2004). The Eysenck Personality Scales: The Eysenck Personality Questionnaire-Revised (EPQ-R) and the Eysenck Personality Profiler (EPP). In M. Hilsenroth & D. Segal (Eds.), *Comprehensive handbook of psychological assessment, personality assessment* (Vol. 2, pp. 99–107). New York: John Wiley & Sons.

Miles, R. (1999). A homeostatic switch. *Nature, 397,* 215–216.

Milgram, S. (1963). Behavioral study of obedience. *Journal of Abnormal and Social Psychology, 67,* 371–378.

Milgram, S. (1965). Liberating effects of group pressure. *Journal of Personality and Social Psychology, 1,* 127–134.

Miller, G., Cohen, S., & Ritchey, A. (2002). Chronic psychological stress and the regulation of pro-inflammatory cytokines: A glucocorticoid-resistance model. *Health Psychology, 21,* 531–541.

Miller, G. A. (1956). The magical number seven, plus or minus two: Some limits on our capacity for processing information. *Psychological Review, 63,* 81–97.

Miller, G. A., & Gildea, P. M. (1987). How children learn words. *Scientific American, 257,* 94–99.

Miller, J. G., & Bersoff, D. M. (1992). Culture and moral judgment: How are conflicts between justice and interpersonal responsibilities resolved? *Journal of Personality and Social Psychology, 62,* 541–554.

Miller, J. G., Bersoff, D. M., & Harwood, R. L. (1990). Perceptions of social responsibilities in India and in the United States: Moral imperatives or personal decisions? *Journal of Personality and Social Psychology, 58,* 33–47.

Miller, J., Lynam, D., Zimmerman, R., Logan, T., Leukefeld, C., & Clayton, R. (2004). The utility of the Five Factor Model in understanding risky sexual behavior. *Personality and Individual Differences, 36,* 1611–1626.

Miller, L. (1988, February). The emotional brain. *Psychology Today,* pp. 34–42.

Miller, L. (1989, November). What biofeedback does (and doesn't) do. *Psychology Today,* pp. 22–23.

Miller, L. (2005). What the savant syndrome can tell us about the nature and nurture of talent. *Journal for the Education of the Gifted, 28,* 361–373.

Miller, N. E. (1941). The frustration-aggression hypothesis. *Psychological Review, 48,* 337–342.

Miller, N. E. (1985, February). Rx: Biofeedback. *Psychology Today,* pp. 54–59.

Miller, N. S., & Gold, M. S. (1994). LSD and Ecstasy: Pharmacology, phenomenology, and treatment. *Psychiatric Annals, 24,* 131–133.

Miller, S. A. (2000). Children's understanding of preexisting differences in knowledge and belief. *Developmental Review, 20*, 227–282.

Miller, W., & Thoresen, C. (2003). Spirituality, religion, and health: An emerging research field. *American Psychologist, 58*, 24–35.

Miller, W., Lindeman, A., Wallace, J., & Niederpruem, M. (1990). Diet composition, energy intake, and exercise in relation to body fat in men and women. *American Journal of Clinical Nutrition, 52*, 426–430.

Millman, R. (2005). Excessive sleepiness in adolescents and young adults: Causes, consequences, and treatment strategies. *Pediatrics, 115*, 1774–1786.

Milner, B. (1966). Amnesia following operation on the temporal lobes. In C. W. M. Whitty & O. L. Zangwill (Eds.), *Amnesia* (pp. 109–133). London: Butterworth.

Milner, B. (1970). Memory and the medial temporal regions of the brain. In K. H. Pribram & D. E. Broadbent (Eds.), *Biology of memory.* New York: Academic Press.

Milner, B., Corkin, S., & Teuber, H. L. (1968). Further analysis of the hippocampal amnesic syndrome: 14-year follow-up study of H. M. *Neuropsychologia, 6*, 215–234.

Milos, G., Spindler, A., Ruggiero, G., Klaghofer, R., & Schnyder, U. (2002). Comorbidity of obsessive-compulsive disorders and duration of eating disorders. *International Journal of Eating Disorders, 31*, 284–289.

Milton, J., & Wiseman, R. (2001). Does psi exist? Reply to Storm and Ertel (2001). *Psychological Bulletin, 127*, 434–438.

Min, J. (2004, August 31). South Korea to introduce filial piety bill. *Straits Times Interactive.* Retrieved September 10, 2004 from http://straitstimes.asia1.com.sg/eyeoneastasia/story/0,4395,270186,00.html

Mindell, J. (1999). Developmental features of sleep. *Child & Adolescent Psychiatric Clinics of North America, 8*, 695–725.

Mischel, W. (1966). A social-learning view of sex differences in behavior. In E. E. Maccoby (Ed.), *The development of sex differences* (pp. 56–81). Stanford, CA: Stanford University Press.

Mischel, W. (1973). Toward a cognitive social learning reconceptualization of personality. *Psychological Review, 80*, 252–283.

Mischel, W. (1977). The interaction of person and situation. In D. Magnusson & N. S. Endler (Eds.), *Personality at the crossroads: Current issues in interactional psychology.* Hillsdale, NJ: Lawrence Erlbaum.

Mischoulon, D. (2002). The herbal anxiolytics kava and valerian for anxiety and insomnia. *Psychiatric Annals, 32*, 55–60.

Mishra, R. (1997). Cognition and cognitive development. In J. Berry, P. Dasen, & T. Sarswthi (Eds.), *Handbook of cross-cultural psychology* (Vol. 2). Boston, MA: Allyn & Bacon.

Mishra, R., & Singh, T. (1992). Memories of Asur children for locations and pairs of pictures. *Psychological Studies, 37*, 38–46.

Mistry, J., & Rogoff, B. (1994). Remembering in cultural context. In W. J. Lonner & R. Malpass (Eds.), *Psychology and culture* (pp. 139–144). Boston: Allyn & Bacon.

Mitchell, S. (2002). Psychodynamics, homosexuality, and the question of pathology. *Studies in Gender & Sexuality, 3*, 3–21.

Mitler, M. M., Aldrich, M. S., Koob, G. F., & Zarcone, V. P. (1994). Narcolepsy and its treatment with stimulants. *Sleep, 17*, 352–371.

Mitsis, E. M., Halperin, J. M., & Newcorn, J. H. (2000). Serotonin and aggression in children. *Current Psychiatry Reports, 2*, 95–101.

Moeller-Leimkuehler, A., Schwarz, R., Burtscheidt, W., & Gaebel, W. (2002). Alcohol dependence and gender-role orientation. *European Psychiatry, 17*, 1–8.

Mohan, J. (2006). Cardiac psychology. *Journal of the Indian Academy of Applied Psychology, 32*, 214–220.

Mohanty, A., & Perregaux, C. (1997). Language acquisition and bilingualism. In J. Berry, P. Dasen, & T. Saraswathi (Eds.), *Handbook of cross-cultural psychology* (pp. 217–254). Boston: Allyn & Bacon.

Mohr, D., Goodkin, D., Nelson, S., Cox, D., & Weiner, M. (2002). Moderating effects of coping on the relationship between stress and the development of new brain lesions in multiple sclerosis. *Psychosomatic Medicine, 64*, 803–809.

Moldofsky, H., Gilbert, R., Lue, F. A., & MacLean, A. W. (1995). Sleep-related violence. *Sleep, 18*, 731–739.

Molnar, M., Potkin, S., Bunney, W., & Jones, E. (2003). MRNA expression patterns and distribution of white matter neurons in dorsolateral prefrontal cortex of depressed patients differ from those in schizophrenia patients. *Biological Psychiatry, 53*, 39–47.

Monk, T. H. (1989). Circadian rhythms in subjective activation, mood, and performance efficiency. In M. H. Kryger, T. Roth, & W. C. Dement (Eds.), *Principles and practice of sleep medicine* (pp. 163–172). Philadelphia: W. B. Saunders.

Monteleone, P., Santonastaso, P., Tortorella, A., Favaro, A., Fabrazzo, M., Castaldo, E., Caregaro, L., Fuschino, A., & Maj, M. (2005). Serotonin transporter polymorphism and potential response to SSRIs in bulimia nervosa. *Molecular Psychiatry, 10*, 716–718.

Montgomery, G. (2003). Color blindness: More prevalent among males. *Seeing, Hearing, and Smelling the World.* Retrieved May 13, 2003, from http://www.hhmi.org/senses/b130.html

Montgomery, G., Weltz, C., Seltz, M., & Bovbjerg, D. (2002). Brief presurgery hypnosis reduces distress and pain in excisional breast biopsy patients. *International Journal of Clinical & Experimental Hypnosis, 50*, 17–32.

Montgomery, G. H., DuHamel, K. N., & Redd, W. H. (2000). A meta-analysis of hypnotically induced analgesia: How effective is hypnosis? *International Journal of Clinical Experimental Hypnosis, 48*, 138–153.

Moore, K., & Persaud, T., (1993). *The developing human: Clinically oriented embryology* (5th ed.). Philadelphia: W. B. Saunders.

Moore, R., Vadeyar, S., Fulford, J., Tyler, D., Gribben, C., Baker, P., James, D., & Gowland, P. (2001). Antenatal determination of fetal brain activity in response to an acoustic stimulus using functional magnetic resonance imaging. *Human Brain Mapping, 12*, 94–99.

Moore-Ede, M. (1993). *The twenty-four hour society.* Reading, MA: Addison-Wesley.

Moraglia, G. (1994). C. G. Jung and the psychology of adult development. *Journal of Analytical Psychology, 39*, 55–75.

Moran, M. G., & Stoudemire, A. (1992). Sleep disorders in the medically ill patient. *Journal of Clinical Psychiatry, 53*(6, Suppl.), 29–36.

Moreno, R., Mayer, R. E., Spires, H., & Lester, J. (2001). The case for social agency in computer-based teaching: Do students learn more deeply when they interact with animated pedagogical agents? *Cognition and Instruction, 19,* 177–213.

Morgan, C. D., & Murray, H. A. (1935). A method for investigating fantasies: The Thematic Apperception Test. *Archives of Neurology and Psychiatry, 34,* 289–306.

Morgan, C. D., & Murray, H. A. (1962). Thematic Apperception Test. In H. A. Murray et al. (Eds.), *Explorations in personality: A clinical and experimental study of fifty men of college age* (pp. 530–545). New York: Science Editions.

Morgan, C. L. (1996). Odors as cues for the recall of words unrelated to odor. *Perceptual and Motor Skills, 83,* 1227–1234.

Morgan, R., & Flora, D. (2002). Group psychotherapy with incarcerated offenders: A research synthesis. *Group Dynamics: Theory, Research, and Practice, 6,* 203–218.

Morgan, R. E., Levitsky, D. A., & Strupp, B. J. (2000). Effects of chronic lead exposure on learning and reaction time in a visual discrimination task. *Neurotoxicology and Teratology, 22,* 337–345.

Morin, C. M., & Wooten, V. (1996). Psychological and pharmacological approaches to treating insomnia: Critical issues in assessing their separate and combined effects. *Clinical Psychology Review, 16,* 521–542.

Morley, J. E., & van den Berg, L. (Eds.). (2000). *Contemporary endocrinology* (No. 20). Totowa, NJ: Humana Press.

Morofushi, M., Shinohara, K., Funabashi, T., & Kimura, F. (2000). Positive relationship between menstrual synchrony and ability to smell 5alpha-androst-16-en-3alpha-ol. *Chemical Senses, 25,* 407–411.

Morofushi, M., Shinohara, K., & Kimura, F. (2001). Menstrual and circadian variations in time perceptions in healthy women and women with premenstrual syndrome. *Neuroscience Research, 41,* 339–344.

Morris, J. S., Frith, C. D., Perrett, D. I., Rowland, D., Young, A. W., Calder, A. J., & Dolan, R. J. (1996). A differential neural response in the human amygdala to fearful and happy facial expressions. *Nature, 383,* 812–815.

Morris, P., Bloom, D., Kemple, J., & Hendra, R. (2003). The effects of a time-limited welfare program on children: The moderating role of parents' risk of welfare dependency. *Child Development, 74,* 851–874.

Morrison, A., White, R., & Van Velsor, E. (1987). *Breaking the glass ceiling: Can women reach the top of America's largest corporations?* New York: Addison-Wesley.

Morrison, J. (2001). *DSM-IV made easy: The clinician's guide to diagnosis.* New York: Guilford Press.

Morrison, P., Allardyce, J., & McKane, J. (2002). Fear knot: Neurobiological disruption of long-term memory. *British Journal of Psychiatry, 180,* 195–197.

Morrow, B. A., Roth, R. H., & Elsworth, J. D. (2000). TMT, a predator odor, elevates mesoprefrontal dopamine metabolic activity and disrupts short-term working memory in the rat. *Brain Research Bulletin, 52,* 519–523.

Mościcki, E. K. (1995). Epidemiology of suicidal behavior. *Suicide and Life-Threatening Behavior, 25,* 22–31.

Moser, G., & Robin, M. (2006). Environmental annoyances: An urban-specific threat to quality of life? *European Review of Applied Psychology, 56,* 35–41.

Most, S., Simons, D., Scholl, B., Jimenez, R., Clifford, E., & Chabris, C. (2001). How not to be seen: The contribution of similarity and selective ignoring to sustained inattentional blindness. *Psychological Science, 12,* 9–17.

Moulin, D., Clark, A., Speechley, M., & Morley-Forster, P. (2002). Chronic pain in Canada: Prevalence, treatment, impact and the role of opioid analgesia. *Pain Research & Management, 7,* 179–184.

Mourtazaev, M. S., Kemp, B., Zwinderman, A. H., & Kamphuisen, H. A. C. (1995). Age and gender affect different characteristics of slow waves in the sleep EEG. *Sleep, 18,* 557–564.

Moynihan, R., & Cassels, A. (2005). *Selling sickness: How the world's biggest pharmaceutical companies are turning us all into patients.* New York: Nation Books.

Mufson, L., Gallagher, T., Dorta, K., & Young, J. (2004). A group adaptation of interpersonal psychotherapy for depressed adolescents. *American Journal of Psychotherapy, 58,* 220–237.

Mühlberger, A., Weik, A., Pauli, P., & Wiedemann, G. (2006). One-session virtual reality exposure treatment for fear of flying: 1-year follow-up and graduation flight accompaniment effects. *Psychotherapy Research, 16,* 26–40.

Mui, A. C. (1992). Caregiver strain among black and white daughter caregivers: A role theory perspective. *The Gerontologist, 32,* 203–212.

Mukerjee, M. (1997). Trends in animal research. *Scientific American, 276,* 86–93.

Muller, L. (2002). Group counseling for African American males: When all you have are European American counselors. *Journal for Specialists in Group Work, 27,* 299–313.

Müller, M., Regenbogen, B., Sachse, J., Eich, F., Härtter, S., & Hiemke, C. (2006). Gender aspects in the clinical treatment of schizophrenic inpatients with amisulpride: A therapeutic drug monitoring study. *Pharmacopsychiatry, 39,* 41–46.

Mumme, D., & Fernald, A. (2003). The infant as onlooker: Learning from emotional reactions observed in a television scenario. *Child Development, 74,* 221–237.

Mumtaz, S., & Humphreys, G. (2002). The effect of Urdu vocabulary size on the acquisition of single word reading in English. *Educational Psychology, 22,* 165–190.

Munroe, R. H., Shimmin, H. S., & Munroe, R. L. (1984). Gender role understanding and sex role preference in four cultures. *Developmental Psychology, 20,* 673–682.

Munzar, P., Li, H., Nicholson, K., Wiley, J., & Balster, R. (2002). Enhancement of the discriminative stimulus effects of phencyclidine by the tetracycline antibiotics doxycycline and minocycline in rats. *Psychopharmacology, 160,* 331–336.

Murnen, S., Wright, C., & Kaluzny, G. (2002). If "boys will be boys," then girls will be victims? A meta-analytic review of the research that relates masculine ideology to sexual aggression. *Sex Roles, 46,* 359–375.

Murphy, E. (2003). Being born female is dangerous to your health. *American Psychologist, 58,* 205–210.

Murphy, S., & Faulkner, D. (2006). Gender differences in verbal communication between popular and unpopular children during an interactive task. *Social Development, 15,* 82–208.

Murphy, S., Tapper, V., Johnson, L., & Lohan, J. (2003). Suicide ideation among parents bereaved by the violent deaths of their children. *Issues in Mental Health Nursing, 24,* 5–25.

Murray, B. (1998, June). Dipping math scores heat up debate over math teaching. *APA Monitor on Psychology, 29,* 34–35.

Murray, B. (2002). Finding the peace within us. *APA Monitor on Psychology, 33,* 56–57.

Murray, D. W. (1995, July/August). Toward a science of desire. *The Sciences, 35,* 244–249.

Murray, H. (1938). *Explorations in personality.* New York: Oxford University Press.

Murray, H. A. (1965). Uses of the Thematic Apperception Test. In B. I. Murstein (Ed.), *Handbook of projective techniques* (pp. 425–432). New York: Basic Books.

Murray, J., Liotti, M., Ingmundson, P., Mayburg, H., Pu, Y., Zamarripa, F., Liu, Y., Woldorff, M., Gao, J., & Fox, P. (2006). Children's brain activations while viewing televised violence revealed by fMRI. *Media Psychology, 8,* 24–37.

Murray, S. L., Holmes, J. G., & Griffin, D. W. (1996a). The benefits of positive illusions: Idealization and the construction of satisfaction in close relationships. *Journal of Personality and Social Psychology, 70*(1), 79–98.

Murray, S. L., Holmes, J. G., & Griffin, D. W. (1996b). The self-fulfilling nature of positive illusions in romantic relationships: Love is not blind, but prescient. *Journal of Personality and Social Psychology 71*(6), 1155–1180.

Nader, K. 2003. Re-recording human memories. *Nature, 425,* 571–572.

Nader, K., Schafe, G. E., & Le Doux, J. E. (2000). Fear memories require protein synthesis in the amygdala for reconsolidation after retrieval. *Nature, 406,* 722–726.

Nadon, R., Hoyt, I. P., Register, P. A., & Kilstrom, J. F. (1991). Absorption and hypnotizability: Context effects reexamined. *Journal of Personality and Social Psychology, 60,* 144–153.

Nagumey, A., Reich, J., & Newsom, J. (2004). Gender Moderates the Effects of Independence and Dependence Desires During the Social Support Process. *Psychology & Aging, 19,* 215-218.

Nagy, W., Berninger, V., & Abbott, R. (2006). Contributions of morphology beyond phonology to literacy outcomes of upper elementary and middle-school students. *Journal of Educational Psychology, 98,* 134–147.

Namie, G., & Namie, R. (2000). *The bully at work: What you can do to stop the hurt and reclaim your dignity on the job.* Naperville, IL: Sourcebooks.

Narita, M., Kaneko, C., Miyoshi, K., Nagumo, Y., Kuzumaki, N., Nakajima, M., Nanjo, K., Matsuzawa, K., Yamazaki, M., & Suzuki, T. (2006). Chronic pain induces anxiety with concomitant changes in opioidergic function in the amygdala. *Neuropsychopharmacology, 31,* 739–750.

Nash, M. (1987). What, if anything, is regressed about hypnotic age regression? A review of the empirical literature. *Psychological Bulletin, 102,* 42–52.

Nash, M., & Baker, E. (1984, February). Trance encounters: Susceptibility to hypnosis. *Psychology Today,* pp. 18, 72–73.

Nash, M. R. (1991). Hypnosis as a special case of psychological regression. In S. J. Lynn & J. W. Rhue (Eds.), *Theories of hypnosis: Current models and perspectives* (pp. 171–194). New York: Guilford.

National Alliance for Mental Illness (NAMI). (2003). *Panic disorder.* Retrieved July 19, 2006 from http://www.nami.org/Template.cfm?Section=By_Illness&Template=/TaggedPage/TaggedPageDisplay.cfm&TPLID=54&ContentID=23050

National Cancer Institute. (2000). *Questions and answers about smoking cessation.* Retrieved January 29, 2003, from http://cis.nci.nih.gov/fact/ 8_13.htm

National Center for Chronic Disease Prevention and Health Promotion. (2006). *The health consequences of involuntary exposure to tobacco smoke: A report of the surgeon general.* Retrieved July 7, 2006 http://www.cdc.gov/TOBACCO/sgr/sgr_2006/index.htm

National Center for Education Statistics (NCES). (2004). *A matter of degrees.* Retrieved April 28, 2006 from http://www2.edtrust.org/NR/rdonlyres/11B4283F-104E-4511-B0CA-1D3023231157/0/highered.pdf

National Center for Education Statistics (NCES). (2004). Digest of Education Statistics 2003. Retrieved October 12, 2006 from http://nces.ed.gov/pubsearch/pubsinfo.asp?pubid=2005025

National Center for Educational Statistics (NCES). (1997). *Nontraditional undergraduates.* Washington, DC: Author.

National Center for Educational Statistics (NCES). (2003). *Highlights from the Trends in International Mathematics and Science Study.* Washington, DC: Author. Retrieved June 5, 2006 from http://nces.ed.gov/pubsearch/pubsinfo.asp?pubid=2005005

National Center for Health Statistics. (2000). *Health, United States, 2000 with adolescent health chartbook.* Retrieved from http://www.cdc.gov/nchs/products/pubs/pubd/hus/hestatus. htm

National Center for Health Statistics. (2001a). Death rates for 358 selected causes, by 10-year age groups, race, and sex: United States, 1999–2000. *National Vital Statistics Report, 49,* (8). [Electronic version]. Retrieved November 10, 2002, from http://www.cdc.gov/nchs/data/dvs/VS00100.WTABLE 12.pdf

National Center for Health Statistics. (2001b). Deaths from each cause, by 5-year age groups, Hispanic origin, race for non-Hispanic population, and sex: United States, 1999–2000. *National Vital Statistics Report, 49,* (11). [Electronic version]. Retrieved November 10, 2002, from http://www.cdc.gov/nchs/fastats/pdf/nvsr49_11tb2.pdf

National Center for Health Statistics. (2002a). Deaths, percent of total deaths, and death rates for the 15 leading causes of death in 5-year age groups, by race and sex: United States, 1999–2000. *National Vital Statistics Report, 50,* (16). [Electronic version]. Retrieved November 10, 2002, from http://www.cdc.gov/nchs/data/dvs/LCWK1_2000.pdf

National Center for Health Statistics (NCHS). (2002b). *Fast stats A to Z: Mental health.* [Online fact sheet]. Retrieved November 9, 2002, from http://www.cdc.gov/nchs/fastats/mental. htm

National Center for Health Statistics (NCHS). (2004). *Prevalence of overweight and obesity among adults: United States, 1999–2002.* Retrieved February 1, 2005 from http://www.cdc.gov/nchs/products/pubs/pubd/hestats/obese/obse99.htm

National Center for Health Statistics (NCHS). (2005). *Health, United States, 2005*. Retrieved July 5, 2006 from http://www.cdc.gov/nchs/data/hus/hus05.pdf#053

National Center for Injury Prevention and Control (NCIPC). (2000). Rape fact sheet. Retrieved January 21, 2003, from http://www.cdc.gov/ncipc/factsheets/rape.htm

National Center for Injury Prevention and Control (NCIPC). (2002). Injury fact book 2001–2002. Retrieved January 20, 2003, from http://www.cdc.gov/ncipc/fact_book/ 12_Child_ Maltreatment.htm

National Education Association (NEA) Higher Education Research Center. (2004). Rethinking graduation rates as accountability measures. *Update, 10,* 1–6. Retrieved April 28, 2006 from http://www2.nea.org/he/heupdate/ vol10no1.pdf

National Institute of Mental Health. (1999a). Does this sound like you? Retrieved from http://www.nimh.nih.gov/ soundlikeyou.htm

National Institute of Mental Health (NIMH). (2001). *The numbers count: Mental disorders in America* (NIMH Report No. 01–4584). Washington, DC: Author.

National Institute on Alcohol Abuse and Alcoholism (NIAAA). (2004). *Alcohol: What you don't know can harm you.* Retrieved July 7, 2004 from http://pubs.niaaa.nih.gov/publications/ WhatUDontKnow_HTML/dontknow.htm

National Institute on Drug Abuse (NIDA). (2001). Ecstasy: What we know and don't know about MDMA: A scientific review [Online report]. Retrieved October 17, 2003, from http:// www.nida.nih.gov/Meetings/MDMA/ MDMAExSummary.html

National Institutes of Health (NIH). (2003). HIV/AIDS statistics. Retrieved November 11, 2003 from http://www. niaid. nih.gov/factsheets/aidsstat.htm

National Mental Health Association (NHMA). (2005). NMHA position statement: Involuntary mental health treatment. Retrieved July 13, 2006 from http://www.nmha.org/ position/ps36.cfm

National Research Council. (2003). *The polygraph and lie detection*. Washington, DC: National Academies Press.

National Safety Council. (1997). Accident facts. Chicago: Author.

National Science Foundation (NSF). (2000). Women, minorities, and persons with disabilities in science and engineering: Annual report to the U.S. Congress. Washington, DC: Author.

National Science Foundation (NSF). (2002). *Science and engineering: Indicators 2002.* Retrieved January 29, 2003, from http://www.nsf.gov/sbc/srs/seind02/toc.htm

Needleman, H. L., Riess, J. A., Tobin, M. J., Biesecker, G. E., & Greenhouse, J. B. (1996). Bone lead levels and delinquent behavior. *Journal of the American Medical Association, 275,* 363–369.

Negro, P., Palladino-Negro, P., & Louza, M. (2002). Do religious mediumship dissociative experiences conform to the sociocognitive theory of dissociation? *Journal of Trauma & Dissociation, 3,* 51–73.

Neisser, U., Boodoo, G., Bouchard, T. J., Jr., Boykin, A. W., Brody, N., Ceci, S. J., Halpern, D. F., Loehlin, J. C., Perloff, R., Sternberg, R. J., & Urbina, S. (1996). Intelligence: Knowns and unknowns. *American Psychologist, 51,* 77–101.

Neisser, U., & Harsch, N. (1992). Phantom flashbulbs: False recollections of hearing the news about Challenger. In E. Winograd & U. Neisser (Eds.), *Affect and accuracy in recall: Studies of "flashbulb" memories* (pp. 9–31). New York: Cambridge University Press.

Neitz, J., Neitz, M., & Kainz, M. (1996). Visual pigment gene structure and the severity of color vision defects. *Science, 274,* 801–804.

Neitz, M., & Neitz, J. (1995). Numbers and ratios of visual pigment genes for normal red-green color vision. *Science, 267,* 1013–1016.

Nelson, J. C. (1997). Safety and tolerability of the new antidepressants. *Journal of Clinical Psychiatry, 58*(6, Suppl.), 26–31.

Nelson, T. (1996). Consciousness and metacognition. *American Psychologist, 51,* 102–116.

Nelson, W. L., Hughes, H. M., Katz, B., & Searight, H. R. (1999). Anorexic eating attitudes and behaviors of male and female college students. *Adolescence, 34,* 621–633.

Nestadt, G., Samuels, J., Riddle, M., Bienvenu, J., Liang, K., LaBuda, M., Walkup, J., Grados, M., & Hoehn-Saric, R. (2000). A family study of obsessive-compulsive disorder. *Archives of General Psychiatry, 57,* 358–363.

Nestor, P., Graham, K., Bozeat, S., Simons, J., & Hodges, J. (2002). Memory consolidation and the hippocampus: Further evidence from studies of autobiographical memory in semantic dementia and frontal variant frontotemporal dementia. *Neuropsychologia, 40,* 633–654.

Neubauer, A., Grabner, R., Fink, A., & Neuper, C. (2005). Intelligence and neural efficiency: Further evidence of the influence of task content and sex on the brain–IQ relationship. *Cognitive Brain Research, 25,* 217–225.

Neuliep, J., Hintz, S., & McCroskey, J. (2005). The influence of ethnocentrism in organizational contexts: Perceptions of interviewee and managerial attractiveness, credibility, and effectiveness. *Communication Quarterly, 53,* 41–56.

Neville, H. J., Bavelier, D., Corina, D., Rauschecker, J., Karni, A., Lalwani, A., Braun, A., Clark, V., Jezzard, P., & Turner, R. (1998). Cerebral organization for language in deaf and hearing subjects: Biological constraints and effects of experience. *Proceedings of the National Academy of Sciences, 95,* 922–929.

Newberg, A., Alavi, A. Baime, M., Pourdehnad, M., Santanna, J. d'Aquili, E. (2001). The measurement of cerebral blood flow during the complex cognitive task of meditation: A preliminary SPECT study. *Psychiatry Research: Neuroimaging, 106,* 113–122.

Newberry, H., Duncan, S., McGuire, M., & Hillers, V. (2001). Use of nonvitamin, nonmineral dietary supplements among college students. *Journal of American College Health, 50,* 123–129.

Newcomb, A. F., Bukowski, W. M., & Pattee, L. (1993). Children's peer relations: A meta-analytic review of popular, rejected, neglected, controversial, and average sociometric status. *Psychological Bulletin, 113,* 99–128.

Newcomb, M. D. (1997). Psychosocial predictors and consequences of drug use: A developmental perspective within a prospective study. *Journal of Addictive Diseases, 16,* 51–89.

Newell, A., & Simon, H. A. (1972). *Human problem solving.* Englewood Cliffs, NJ: Prentice-Hall.

Newell, B. (2005). Re-visions of rationality? *Trends in the Cognitive Sciences, 9,* 11–15.

Newell, B., & Shanks, D. (2003). Take the best or look at the rest? Factors influencing "one-reason" decision making. *Journal of Experimental Psychology: Learning, Memory, and Cognition, 29,* 53–65.

Newell, B., & Shanks, D. (2004). On the role of recognition in decision making. *Journal of Experimental Psychology: Learning, Memory and Cognition, 30,* 923–935.

Newell, P., & Cartwright, R. (2000). Affect and cognition in dreams: A critique of the cognitive role in adaptive dream functioning and support for associative models. *Psychiatry: Interpersonal & Biological Processes, 63,* 34–44.

Newschaffer, C., Falb, M., & Gurney, J. (2005). National autism prevalence trends from United States special education data. *Pedatrics, 115,* e277–e282.

Newsweek. (2006, June 19). "Learning to adapt: Community colleges offer older workers an affordable way to reinvent themselves and find their place in a changing economy." Retrieved June 15, 2006 from http://msnbc.msn.com/id/13249473/site/newsweek/

Newsweek.(2005, October 31). *I have had to learn to live with peace.* Retrieved June 10, 2006 from http://www.msnbc.msn.com/id/9785295/site/newsweek/

Ng K., Tsui, S., & Chan, W. (2002). Prevalence of common chronic pain in Hong Kong adults. *Clinical Journal of Pain, 18,* 275–281.

Nguyen, P. V., Abel, T., & Kandel, E. R. (1994). Requirement of a critical period of transcription for induction of a late phase of LTP. *Science, 265,* 1104–1107.

Nicholl, C. S., & Russell, R. M. (1990). Analysis of animal rights literature reveals the underlying motives of the movement: Ammunition for counter offensive by scientists. *Endocrinology, 127,* 985–989.

Nicholls, M., Clode, D., Lindell, A., & Wood, A. (2002). Which cheek to turn? The effect of gender and emotional expressivity on posing behavior. *Brain & Cognition, 48,* 480–484.

Nickerson, R. S., & Adams, M. J. (1979). Long-term memory for a common object. *Cognitive Psychology, 11,* 287–307.

Nicol, S. E., & Gottesman, I. I. (1983). Clues to the genetics and neurobiology of schizophrenia. *American Scientist, 71,* 398–404.

Niehoff, B., Moorman, R., Blakely, G., & Fuller, J. (2001). The influence of empowerment and job enrichment on employee loyalty in a downsizing environment. *Group & Organization Management, 26,* 93–113.

Nisbett, R. E., & Wilson, T. D. (1977). The halo effect: Evidence for unconscious alteration of judgments. *Journal of Personality and Social Psychology, 35,* 250–256.

Nishimura, H., Hashikawa, K., Doi, K., Iwaki, T., Watanabe, Y., Kusuoka, H., Nishimura, T., & Kubo, T. (1999). Sign language "heard" in the auditory cortex. *Nature, 397,* 116.

Nogrady, H., McConkey, K. M., & Perry, C. (1985). Enhancing visual memory: Trying hypnosis, trying imagination, and trying again. *Journal of Abnormal Psychology, 94,* 195–204.

Noise Pollution Council. (2003). Comparing standards for safe noise exposure. Retrieved May 16, 2003, from http://www.nonoise.org/hearing/exposure/standardschart.htm

Norcross, J., Karpiak, C., & Lister, K. (2005). What's an integrationist? A study of self-identified integrative and (occasionally) eclectic psychologists. *Journal of Clinical Psychology, 61,* 1587–1594.

Noriko, S. (2004). Identity development pre- and post-empty nest women. *Japanese Journal of Developmental Psychology, 15,* 52–64.

Norman, S., Norman, G., Rossi, J., & Prochaska, J. (2006). Identifying high- and low-success smoking cessation subgroups using signal detection analysis. *Addictive Behaviors, 31,* 31–41.

Norman, W. (1963). Toward an adequate taxonomy of personality attributes: Replicated factor structure in peer nomination personality ratings. *Journal of Abnormal & Social Psychology, 66,* 574–583.

Norris, F. H., & Kaniasty, K. (1996). Received and perceived social support in times of stress: A test of the social support deterioration deterrence model. *Journal of Personality and Social Psychology, 71,* 498–511.

November 18, 2006 from http://www.census.gov/acs/www/index.html

Noyes, R., Jr., Burrows, G. D., Reich, J. H., Judd, F. K., Garvey, M. J., Norman, T. R., Cook, B. L., & Marriott, P. (1996). Diazepam versus alprazolam for the treatment of panic disorder. *Journal of Clinical Psychiatry, 57,* 344–355.

Nurnberg, H., Hensley, P., Lauriello, J., Parker, L., & Keith, S. (1999). Sildenafil for women patients with antidepressant-induced sexual dysfunction. *Psychiatric Services, 50,* 1076–1078.

Nutt, D. (2000). Treatment of depression and concomitant anxiety. *European Neuropsychopharmacology, 10* (Suppl. 4), S433–S437.

Nyberg, L., Eriksson, J., Larsson, A., & Marklund, P. (2006). Learning by doing versus learning by thinking. An fMRI study of motor and mental training. *Neuropsychologia, 44,* 711–717.

O'Brien, C. P. (1996). Recent developments in the pharmacotherapy of substance abuse. *Journal of Consulting and Clinical Psychology, 64,* 677–686.

O'Leary, K. D., & Smith, D. A. (1991). Marital interactions. *Annual Review of Psychology, 42,* 191–212.

Oakhill, J., Garnham, A., & Reynolds, D. (2005). Immediate activation of stereotypical gender information. *Memory & Cognition, 33,* 972–983.

Offerman, L., & Malamut, A. (2002). When leaders harass: The impact of target perceptions of organizational leadership and climate on harassment reporting and outcomes. *Journal of Applied Psychology, 87,* 885–893.

Ogawa, A., Mizuta, I., Fukunaga, T., Takeuchi, N., Honaga, E., Sugita, Y., Mikami, A., Inoue, Y., & Takeda, M. (2004). Electrogastrography abnormality in eating disorders. *Psychiatry & Clinical Neurosciences, 58,* 300–310.

Ohayan, M., Carskadon, M., Guilleminault, C., & Vitiello, M. (2004). Meta-analysis of quantitative sleep parameters from childhood to old age in healthy individuals: Developing normative sleep values across the human lifespan. *Sleep, 27,* 1255–1273.

Ohman, A., & Mineka, S. (2003). The malicious serpent: Snakes as a prototypical stimulus for an evolved module of fear. *Current Directions in Psychological Science, 12,* 5–8.

Ohring, R., Graber, J., & Brooks-Gunn, J. (2002). Girls' recurrent and concurrent body dissatisfaction: Correlates and consequences over 8 years. *International Journal of Eating Disorders, 31,* 404–415.

Oien, K., & Goernert, P. (2003). The role of intentional forgetting in employee selection. *Journal of General Psychology, 13*, 97–110.

Okura, Y., Akira, M., Kuniko, K., Park, I., Matthias, S., & Matsumoto, Y. (2006, in press). Nonviral amyloid-beta DNA vaccine therapy against Alzheimer's disease: Long-term effects and safety. *Proceedings of the National Academy of Sciences.*

Oliver, J. E. (1993). Intergenerational transmission of child abuse: Rates, research, and clinical implications. *American Journal of Psychiatry, 150*, 1315–1324.

Olson, M., Krantz, D., Kelsey, S., Pepine, C., Sopko, G., Handberg, E., Rogers, W., Gierach, G., McClure, C., & Merz, C. (2005). Hostility scores are associated with increased risk of cardiovascular events in women undergoing coronary angiography: A report from the NHLBI-sponsored WISE study. *Psychosomatic Medicine, 67*, 546–552.

Ono, H. (2003). Women's economic standing, marriage timing and cross-national contexts of gender. *Journal of Marriage & Family, 65*, 275–286.

Oquendo, M., Placidi, G., Malone, K., Campbell, C., Kelp, J., Brodsky, B., Cagoules, L., Cooper, T., Parsey, R., Van Heertum, R., & Mann, J. (2003). Positron emission tomography of regional brain metabolic responses to a serotonergic challenge and lethality of suicide attempts in major depression. *Archives of General Psychiatry, 60*, 14–22.

Orman, M. (1996). How to conquer public speaking fear. Retrieved February 15, 2003, from http://www.stresscure.com/jobstress/speak.html

Orne, M. (1983, December 12). Hypnosis "useful in medicine, dangerous in court." *U.S. News & World Report*, pp. 67–68.

Ortega-Alvaro, A., Gilbert-Rahola, J., & Micó, J. (2006). Influence of chronic treatment with olanzapine, clozapine, and scopolamine on performance of a learned 8-arm radial maze task in rats. *Progress in Neuro-Psychopharmacology & Biological Psychiatry, 30*, 104–111.

Ossorio, P., & Duster, T. (2005). Race and genetics: Controversies in biomedical, behavioral, and forensic sciences. *American Psychologist, 60*, 115–128.

Öst, L-G., & Westling, B. E. (1995). Applied relaxation vs. cognitive behavior therapy in the treatment of panic disorder. *Behavior Research and Therapy, 33*, 145–158.

Ostrom, T. M., Carpenter, S. L., Sedikides, C., & Li, F. (1993). Differential processing of in-group and out-group information. *Journal of Personality and Social Psychology, 64*, 21–34.

Otto, M. W., Pollack, M. H., Sachs, G. S., Reiter, S. R., Meltzer-Brody, S., & Rosenbaum, J. F. (1993). Discontinuation of benzodiazepine treatment: Efficacy of cognitive-behavioral therapy for patients with panic disorder. *American Journal of Psychiatry, 150*, 1485–1490.

Overby, K. (2002). Pediatric health supervision. In A. Rudolph, R. Kamei, & K. Overby (Eds.), *Rudolph's fundamentals of pediatrics* (3rd ed., pp. 1–69). New York: McGraw-Hill.

Overmeier, J. B., & Seligman, M. E. P. (1967). Effects of inescapable shock upon subsequent escape and avoidance responding. *Journal of Comparative and Physiological Psychology, 67*, 28–33.

Owen, M., & O'Donovan, M. (2003). Schizophrenia and genetics. In R. Plomin, J. Defries, I. Craig, & P. McGuffin (Eds.), *Behavioral genetics in the postgenomic era* (pp. 463–480). Washington, DC: American Psychological Association.

Owens, J., Maxim, R., McGuinn, M., Nobile, C., Msall, M., & Alario, A. (2000). Television-viewing habits and sleep disturbance in school children. *Pediatrics, 104*(3), 27.

Ozkan, T., & Lajunen, T. (2005). Why are there sex differences in risky driving? The relationship between sex and gender-role on aggressive driving, traffic offences, and accident involvement among young Turkish drivers. *Aggressive Behavior, 31*, 547–558.

Paivio, S. C., & Greenberg, L. S. (1995). Resolving "unfinished business": Efficacy of experiential therapy using empty-chair dialogue. *Journal of Consulting and Clinical Psychology, 63*, 419–425.

Pal, S. (2005). Prevalence of chronic pain and migraine. *U.S. Pharmacist, 3*, 12–15.

Palinscar, A. S., & Brown, A. L. (1984). Reciprocal teaching of comprehension-fostering and comprehension-monitoring activities. *Cognition and Instruction, 1*, 117–175.

Pansu, P., & Gilibert, D. (2002). Effect of causal explanations on work-related judgments. *Applied Psychology: An International Review, 51*, 505–526.

Pantey, C., Dinnesen, A., Ross, B., Wolbrink, A., & Knief, A. (2006). Dynamics of auditory plasticity after cochlear implantation: A longitudinal study. *Cerebral Cortex, 16*, 31–36.

Papousek, I., & Schulter, G. (2002). Covariations of EEG asymmetries and emotional states indicate that activity at frontopolar locations is particularly affected by state factors. *Psychophysiology, 39*, 350–360.

Paraherakis, A., Charney, D., & Gill, K. (2001). Neuropsychological functioning in substance-dependent patients. *Substance Use & Misuse, 36*, 257–271.

Park, K. A., & Waters, E. (1989). Security of attachment and preschool friendships. *Child Development, 60*, 1076–1081.

Parke, R. D. (1977). Some effects of punishment on children's behavior–revisited. In E. M. Hetherington, E. M. Ross, & R. D. Parke (Eds.), *Contemporary readings in child psychology*. New York: McGraw-Hill.

Parker, J. G., & Asher, S. R. (1987). Peer relations and later personal adjustment: Are low-accepted children at risk? *Psychological Bulletin, 102*, 357–389.

Parkinson, W. L., & Weingarten, H. P. (1990). Dissociative analysis of ventromedial hypothalamic obesity syndrome. *American Journal of Physiology, 259*, 829–835.

Partinen, M. (1994). Epidemiology of sleep disorders. In M. Kryger, T. Roth, & W. C. Dement (Eds.), *Principles and practice of sleep medicine* (pp. 437–453). Philadelphia: W.B. Saunders.

Parvizi, J., & Damasio, A. (2001). Consciousness and the brainstem. *Cognition, 79*, 135–159.

Pascarella, E. (1999). The development of critical thinking: Does college make a difference? *Journal of College Student Development, 40*, 562–569.

Pascarella, E., & Terenzi, P. (1991). *How college affects students: Findings and insights from twenty years of research*, San Francisco: Jossey-Bass.

Pascual-Leone, A., Dhuna, A., Altafullah, I., & Anderson, D. C. (1990). Cocaine-induced seizures. *Neurology, 40*, 404–407.

Pastore, N. (1950). The role of arbitrariness in the frustration-aggression hypothesis. *Journal of Abnormal and Social Psychology, 47,* 728–731.

Patel, N., Delbello, M., Bryan, H., Adler, C., Kowatch, R., Stanford, K., & Strakowski, S. (2006). Open-label lithium for the treatment of adolescents with bipolar depression. *Journal of the American Academy of Child & Adolescent Psychiatry, 45,* 289–297.

Patterson, C. J. (1995). Sexual orientation and human development: An overview. *Developmental Psychology, 31,* 3–11.

Patterson, D. R., & Ptacek, J. T. (1997). Baseline pain as a moderator of hypnotic analgesia for burn injury treatment. *Journal of Consulting and Clinical Psychology, 65,* 60–67.

Patterson, G. R., Crosby, L., & Vuchinich, S. (1992). *Journal of Quantitative Criminology, 8,* 335–355.

Paul, T., Schroeter, K., Dahme, B., & Nutzinger, D. (2002). Self-injurious behavior in women with eating disorders. *American Journal of Psychiatry, 159,* 408–411.

Paul, W. E. (1993). Infectious diseases and the immune system. *Scientific American, 269,* 90–99.

Paulus, P. B., Cox, V. C., & McCain, G. (1988). *Prison crowding: A psychological perspective.* New York: Springer-Verlag.

Paunonen, S. V., Keinonen, M., Trzebinski, J., Forsterling, F., Grishenko-Roze, N., Kouznetsova, L., & Chan, D. W. (1996). The structure of personality in six cultures. *Journal of Cross-Cultural Psychology, 27,* 339–353.

Pause, B. (2004). Are androgen steroids acting as pheromones in humans? *Physiology & Behavior, 83,* 21–29.

Pause, B. M., & Krauel, K. (2000). Chemosensory event-related potentials (CSERP) as a key to the psychology of odors. *International Journal of Psychophysiology, 36,* 105–122.

Pavlov, I. P. (1927/1960). *Conditioned reflexes: An investigation of the physiological activity of the cerebral cortex* (G. V. Anrep, Trans.). New York: Dover. (Original translation published 1927).

Pearce, C., & Sims, H. (2002). Vertical versus shared leadership as predictors of the effectiveness of change management teams: An examination of aversive, directive, transactional, transformational, and empowering leader behaviors. *Group Dynamics, 6,* 172–197.

Pearsall, N., Skipper, J., & Mintzes, J. (1997). Knowledge restructuring in the life sciences: A longitudinal study of conceptual change in biology. *Science Education, 81,* 193–215.

Pecjak, S., & Paklaj, C. (2006). Dimensions of reading motivation and reading achievement in 3rd and 7th grade students. *Studia Psychologica, 48,* 11–29.

Pedersen, D. M., & Wheeler, J. (1983). The Müller-Lyer illusion among Navajos. *Journal of Social Psychology, 121,* 3–6.

Pedersen, S., & Denollet, J. (2003). Type D personality, cardiac events, and impaired quality of life: A review. *European Journal of Cardiovascular Prevention and Rehabilitation, 10,* 241–248.

Pederson, S., Van Domburg, R., & Theuns, D. (2004). Type D personality is associated with increased anxiety and depressive symptoms in patients with an implantable cardioverter defibrillator and their partners. *Psychosomatic Medicine, 66,* 714–719.

Penfield, W. (1969). Consciousness, memory, and man's conditioned reflexes. In K. Pribram (Ed.), *On the biology of learning* (pp. 129–168). New York: Harcourt Brace Jovanovich.

Pennebaker, J., & Seagal, J. (1999). Forming a story: The health benefits of narrative. *Journal of Clinical Psychology, 55,* 1243–1254.

Pennisi, E. (1997). Tracing molecules that make the brain-body connection. *Science, 275,* 930–931.

Penny, J. (2001). Differential item functioning in an international 360-degree assessment: Evidence of gender stereotype, environmental complexity, and organizational contingency. *European Journal of Work & Organizational Psychology, 10,* 245–271.

Peplau, L. (2003). Human sexuality: How do men and women differ? *Current Directions in Psychological Science, 12,* 37–40.

Pepperberg, I. (2006). Grey parrot (Psittacus erithacus) numerical abilities: Addition and further experiments on a zero-like concept. *Journal of Comparative Psychology, 120,* 1–11.

Pepperberg, I. M. (1991, Spring). Referential communication with an African grey parrot. *Harvard Graduate Society Newsletter,* 1–4.

Pepperberg, I. M. (1994a). Numerical competence in an African grey parrot (*Psittacus erithacus*). *Journal of Comparative Psychology, 108,* 36–44.

Pepperberg, I. M. (1994b). Vocal learning in grey parrots (*Psittacus erithacus*): Effects of social interaction, reference, and context. *The Auk, 111,* 300–314 .

Perho, H, & Korhonen, M. (1999). Coping in work and marriage at the onset of middle age. *Psykologia, 34,* 115–127.

Perls, F. S. (1969). *Gestalt therapy verbatim.* Lafayette, CA: Real People Press.

Perls, T. T. (1995). The oldest old. *Scientific American, 272,* 70–75.

Perrett, D. I., May, K. A., & Yoshikawa, S. (1994). Facial shape and judgements of female attractiveness. *Nature, 368,* 239–242.

Perry, S., Wallace, I. (2005). Donations for victims of Katrina reach $404 million. *Chronicle of Philanthropy.* [Online edition] Retrieved October 29, 2006 from http://philanthropy.com/free/update/2005/09/2005090201.htm

Perry, S., Wallace, N., & Wilhelm, I. (2005). Donations for victims of Katrina reach $404 million. *Chronicle of Philanthropy.* [Online edition] Retrieved October 29, 2006 from http://philanthropy.com/free/update/2005/09/2005090201.htm.

Pert, C. B., Snowman, A. M., & Snyder, S. H. (1974). Localization of opiate receptor binding in presynaptic membranes of rat brain. *Brain Research, 70,* 184–188.

Perusse, L., Chagnon, Y. C., Weisnagel, J., & Bouchard, C. (1999). The human obesity gene map: The 1998 update. *Obesity Research, 7,* 111–129.

Peskind, E. R. (1996). Neurobiology of Alzheimer's disease. *Journal of Clinical Psychiatry, 57*(14, Suppl.), 5–8.

Peters, A., Leahu, D., Moss, M. B., & McNally, J. (1994). The effects of aging on area 46 of the frontal cortex of the rhesus monkey. *Cerebral Cortex, 6,* 621–635.

Peterson, A. C. (1987, September). Those gangly years. *Psychology Today,* pp. 28–34.

Peterson, B. (2002). Longitudinal analysis of midlife generativity, intergenerational roles, and caregiving. *Psychology & Aging, 17,* 161–168.

Peterson, B. (2006, May 11). China's Age Bank: Volunteers log time with elderly, so they can get care as they age. Retrieved June 15, 2006 from http://www.cbsnews.com/stories/2006/05/11/asia_letter/main1609394.shtml

Peterson, C., Wellman, H., & Liu, D. (2005). Steps in theory-of-mind development for children with deafness or autism. *Child Development, 76,* 502–517.

Peterson, I. (1993). Speech for export: Automating the translation of spoken words. *Science News, 144,* 254–255.

Peterson, L. R., & Peterson, M. J. (1959). Short-term retention of individual verbal items. *Journal of Experimental Psychology, 58,* 193–198.

Petitto, L. A., & Marentette, P. R. (1991). Babbling in the manual mode: Evidence for the ontogeny of language. *Science, 251,* 1493–1496.

Petrill, S. (2003). The development of intelligence: Behavioral genetic approaches. In R. Sternberg, J. Lautrey, & T. Lubart (Eds.), *Models of intelligence: International perspective* (pp. 81–90). Washington, DC: American Psychological Association.

Petry, N. (2002). Psychosocial treatments for pathological gambling: Current status and future directions. *Psychiatric Annals, 32,* 192–196.

Petry, N., Tedford, J., Austin, M., Nich, C., Carroll, K., & Rounsaville, B. (2004). Prize reinforcement contingency management for treating cocaine users: How low can we go, and with whom? *Addiction, 99,* 349–360.

Pettus, A. (2006). Psychiatry by prescription. *Harvard Magazine, 108,* 38–44, 90–91. Retrieved July 8, 2006 from http://www.harvardmagazine.com/on-line/070646.html

Petty, R. E., Wegener, D. T., & Fabrigar, L. R. (1997). Attitudes and attitude change. *Annual Review of Psychology, 48,* 609–647.

Pew Research Center. (2006). *Global gender gaps.* Retrieved June 29, 2006 from http://pewglobal.org/commentary/display.php?AnalysisID=90

Phillips, G. P., & Over, R. (1995). Differences between heterosexual, bisexual, and lesbian women in recalled childhood experiences. *Archives of Sexual Behavior, 24,* 1–20.

Phillips, S. T., & Ziller, R. C. (1997). Toward a theory and measure of the nature of nonprejudice. *Journal of Personality and Social Psychology, 72,* 420–434.

Piaget, J. (1963). *Psychology of intelligence.* Patterson, NJ: Littlefield, Adams.

Piaget, J. (1964). *Judgment and reasoning in the child.* Patterson, NJ: Littlefield, Adams.

Piaget, J., & Inhelder, B. (1969). *The psychology of the child.* New York: Basic Books.

Pich, E. M., Pagliusi, S. R., Tessari, M., Talabot-Ayer, D., van Huijsduijnen, R. H., & Chiamulera, C. (1997). Common neural substrates for the addictive properties of nicotine and cocaine. *Science, 275,* 83–86.

Pieringer, W., Fazekas, C., & Pieringer, C. (2005). Schizophrenia: An existential disease. *Fortschritte der Neurologie, Psychiatrie, 73,* S25–S31.

Pierrehumbert, B., Miljkovitch, R., Plancherel, B., Halfon, O., & Ansermet, F. (2000). Attachment and temperament in early childhood: Implications for later behavior problems. *Infant and Child Development, 9,* 17–32.

Pigott, T. A. (1996). OCD: Where the serotonin selectivity story begins. *Journal of Clinical Psychiatry, 57*(6, Suppl.), 11–20.

Pihl, R. O., Lau, M. L., & Assaad, J-M. (1997). Aggressive disposition, alcohol, and aggression. *Aggressive Behavior, 23,* 11–18.

Pike, J., & Jennings, N. (2005). Commercials on children's perceptions of gender appropriate toy use. *Sex Roles, 52,* 83–91.

Piko, B. (2006). Adolescent smoking and drinking: The role of communal mastery and other social influences. *Addictive Behaviors, 31,* 102–114.

Pilcher, J. J., Lambert, B. J., & Huffcutt, A. I. (2000). Differential effects of permanent and rotating shifts on self-report sleep length: A meta-analytic review. *Sleep, 23,* 155–163.

Pillemer, D. B. (1990). Clarifying the flashbulb memory concept: Comment on McCloskey, Wible, and Cohen (1988). *Journal of Experimental Psychology: General, 119,* 92–96.

Pillow, D. R., Zautra, A. J., & Sandler, I. (1996). Major life events and minor stressors: Identifying mediational links in the stress process. *Journal of Personality and Social Psychology, 70,* 381–394.

Pilowsky, T., Yirmiya, N., Arbelle, S., & Mozes, T. (2000). Theory of mind abilities of children with schizophrenia, children with autism, and normally developing children. *Schizophrenia Research, 42,* 2145–2155.

Pinel, J. (2007). *Basics of Biopsychology.* Boston: Allyn & Bacon.

Pinel, J. P. L. (2000). *Biopsychology* (4th ed.). Boston: Allyn & Bacon.

Pinikahana, J., Happell, B., & Keks, N. (2003). Suicide and schizophrenia: A review of literature for the decade (1990–1999) and implications for mental health nursing. *Issues in Mental Health Nursing, 24,* 27–43.

Pinker, S. (1994). *The language instinct: How the mind creates language.* New York: Morrow.

Pinquart, M., & Sörensen, S. (2000). Influences of socioeconomic status, social network, and competence on subjective well-being in later life: A meta-analysis. *Psychology and Aging, 15,* 187–224.

Pinquart, M., & Sorensen, S. (2004). Associations of caregiver stressors and uplifts with subjective well-being and depressed mood: A meta-analytic comparison. *Aging & Mental Health, 8,* 438–449.

Piotrkowski, C. (1998). Gender harassment, job satisfaction, and distress among employed white and minority women. *Journal of Occupational Health Psychology, 3,* 33–43.

Pittenger, D. (2005). Cautionary comments regarding the Myers-Briggs Type Indicator. *Consulting Psychology Journal: Practice and Research, 57,* 210–221.

Pittman, L., & Chase-Lansdale, P. (2001). African American adolescent girls in impoverished communities: Parenting style and adolescent outcomes. *Journal of Research on Adolescence, 11,* 199–224.

Plaks, J., Grant, H., & Dweck, C. (2005). Violations of implicit theories and the sense of prediction and control: Implications for motivated person perception. *Journal of Personality & Social Psychology, 88,* 245–262.

Plomin, R. (2001). Genetics and behavior. *Psychologist, 14,* 134–139.

Plomin, R., & Dale, P. S. (2000). Genetics and early language development: A UK study of twins. In D. V. M. Bishop & L. B. Leonard (Eds.), *Speech and language impairment in children: Causes, characteristics, intervention and outcome.* Oxford: Oxford University Press.

Plomin, R., Defries, J., Craig, I., & McGuffin, P. (2003). *Behavioral genetics in the postgenomic era.* Washington, DC: American Psychological Association.

Plomin, R., DeFries, J. C., & Fulker, D. W. (1988). *Nature and nurture during infancy and early childhood.* New York: Cambridge University Press.

Plomin, R., DeFries, J. C., McClearn, G. E., & Rutter, M. (1997). *Behavioral genetics* (3rd ed.). New York: Freeman.

Plomin, R., Owen, M. J., & McGuffin, P. (1994). The genetic basis of complex human behaviors. *Science, 264,* 1733–1739.

Plomin, R., & Rende, R. (1991). Human behavioral genetics. *Annual Review of Psychology, 42,* 161–190.

Plous, S. (1996). Attitudes toward the use of animals in psychological research and education: Results from a national survey of psychologists. *American Psychologist, 51,* 1167–1180.

Ployhart, R., McFarland, L., & Ryan, A. (2002). Examining applicants' attributions for withdrawal from a selection procedure. *Journal of Applied Social Psychology, 32,* 2228–2252.

Plumer, B. (2005, July). Licensed to ill. *Mother Jones.* [Online. No pages specified.] Retrieved July 25, 2006 from http://www.motherjones.com/commentary/columns/2005/07/selling_sickness.html

Plummer, D. L., & Slane S. (1996). Patterns of coping in racially stressful situations. *Journal of Black Psychology, 22,* 302–315.

Pollack, R. H. (1970). Müller-Lyer illusion: Effect of age, lightness contrast and hue. *Science, 179,* 93–94.

Pontieri, F. C., Tanda, G., Orzi, F., & Di Chiara, G. (1996). Effects of nicotine on the nucleus accumbens and similarity to those of addictive drugs. *Nature, 382,* 255–257.

Poponoe, D., & Whitehead, B. D. (2000). Sex without strings, relationships without rings: Today's young singles talk about mating and dating. In National Marriage Project, "The State of Our Unions, 2000." Retrieved from http://marriage.rutgers.edu/2000.htm

Porjesz, B., Begleiter, H., Reich, T., Van Eerdewegh, P., Edenberg, H., Foroud, T., Goate, A., Litke, A., Chorlian, D., Stimus, A., Rice, J., Blangero, J., Almasy, L., Sorbell, J., Bauer, L., Kuperman, S., O'Connor, S., & Rohrbaugh, J. (1998). Amplitude of visual P3 event-related potential as a phenotypic marker for a predisposition to alcoholism: Preliminary results from the COGA project. *Alcoholism: Clinical & Experimental Research, 22,* 1317–1323.

Porjesz, B., Rangaswamy, M., Kamarajan, C., Jones, K., Padmanabhapillai, A., & Begleiter, H. (2005). The utility of neurophysiological markers in the study of alcoholism. *Clinical Neurophysiology, 116,* 993–1018.

Porrino, L. J., & Lyons, D. (2000). Orbital and medial prefrontal cortex and psychostimulant abuse: Studies in animal models. *Cerebral Cortex, 10,* 326–333.

Porte, H. S., & Hobson, J. A. (1996). Physical motion in dreams: One measure of three theories. *Sleep, 105,* 3329–3335.

Porter, F. L., Porges, S. W., & Marshall, R. E. (1988). Newborn pain cries and vagal tone: Parallel changes in response to circumcision. *Child Development, 59,* 495–505.

Posada, G., Jacobs, A., Richmond, M., Carbonell, O., Alzate, G., Bustamante, M., & Quiceno, J. (2002). Maternal caregiving and infant security in two cultures. *Developmental Psychology, 38,* 67–78.

Posey, D., Puntney, J., Sasher, T., Kem, D., & McDougle, C. (2004). Guanfacine treatment of hyperactivity and inattention in pervasive developmental disorders: A retrospective analysis of 80 cases. *Journal of Child & Adolescent Psychopharmacology, 14,* 233–241.

Posner, M. I. (1996, September). Attention and psychopathology. *Harvard Mental Health Letter, 13*(3), 5–6.

Posserud, M., Lundervold, A., & Gilberg, C. (2006). Autistic features in a total population of 7–9-year-old children assessed by the ASSQ (Autism Spectrum Screening Questionnaire). *Journal of Child Psychology and Psychiatry, 47,* 167–175.

Postel, M., de Jong, C., & de Haan, H. (2005). Does e-therapy for problem drinking reach hidden populations? *American Journal of Psychiatry, 162,* 2393.

Postman, L., & Phillips, L. W. (1965). Short-term temporal changes in free recall. *Quarterly Journal of Experimental Psychology, 17,* 132–138.

Potts, N. L. S., Davidson, J. R. T., & Krishman, K. R. R. (1993). The role of nuclear magnetic resonance imaging in psychiatric research. *Journal of Clinical Psychiatry, 54*(12, Suppl.), 13–18.

Powell, C., & Van Vugt, M. (2003). Genuine giving or selfish sacrifice? The role of commitment and cost level upon willingness to sacrifice. *European Journal of Social Psychology, 33,* 403–412.

Powell, L., Shahabi, L., & Thoresen, C. (2003). Religion and spirituality: Linkages to physical health. *American Psychologist, 58,* 36–52.

Power, F. C., Higgins, A., & Kohlberg, L. (1989). *Lawrence Kohlberg's approach to moral education.* New York: Columbia University Press.

Power, K. G., Sharp, D. M., Swanson, V., & Simpson, R. J. (2000). Therapist contact in cognitive behaviour therapy for panic disorder and agoraphobia in primary care. *Clinical Psychology & Psychotherapy, 7,* 37–46.

Powlishta, K. K. (1995). Intergroup processes in childhood: Social categorization and sex role development. *Developmental Psychology, 31,* 781–788.

Poynton, T., Carlson, M., Hopper, J., & Carey, J. (2006). Evaluation of an innovative approach to improving middle school students' academic achievement. *Professional School Counseling, 9,* 190–196.

Pöysti, L., Rajalin, S., & Summala, H. (2005). Factors influencing the use of cellular (mobile) phone during driving and hazards while using it. *Accident Analysis & Prevention, 37,* 47–51.

Poznanski, M., & Thagard, P. (2005). Changing personalities: Towards realistic virtual characters. *Journal of Experimental & Theoretical Artificial Intelligence, 17,* 221–241.

Pozzi, M. (2003). A three-year-old boy with ADHD and Asperger's syndrome treated with parent-child psychotherapy. *Journal of the British Association of Psychotherapists, 41,* 16–31.

Prabhu, V., Porjesz, B., Chorlian, D., Wang, K., Stimus, A., & Begleiter, H. (2001). Visual P3 in female alcoholics. *Alcoholism: Clinical & Experimental Research, 25,* 531–539.

Pratkanis, A. R. (1989). The cognitive representation of attitudes. In A. R. Pratkanis, S. J. Breckler, & A. G. Greenwald (Eds.), *Attitude structure and function* (pp. 71–93). Hillsdale, NJ: Erlbaum.

Pratt, M., Danso, H., Arnold, M., Norris, J., & Filyer, R. (2001). Adult generativity and the socialization of adolescents: Relations to mothers' and fathers' parenting beliefs, styles, and practices. *Journal of Personality, 69,* 89–120.

Preisler, G., Tvingstedt, A., & Ahlström, M. (2005). Interviews with deaf children about their experiences using cochlear implants. *American Annals of the Deaf, 150,* 260–267.

Premack, D. (1971). Language in chimpanzees. *Science, 172,* 808–822.

Premack, D., & Premack, A. J. (1983). *The mind of an ape.* New York: Norton.

Pressley, M., & Wharton-McDonald, R. (1997). Skilled comprehension and its development through instruction. *School Psychology Review, 26,* 448–466.

Prigerson, H. G., Bierhals, A. J., Kasl, S. V., Reynolds, C. F., III, Shear, M. K., Day, N., Beery, L. C., Newsom, J. T., & Jacobs, S. (1997). Traumatic grief as a risk factor for mental and physical mortality. *American Journal of Psychiatry, 154,* 616–623.

Pring, L., & Hermelin, B. (2002). Numbers and letters: Exploring an autistic savant's unpractised ability. *Neurocase, 8,* 330–337.

Prinz, P. N., Vitiello, M. V., Raskind, M. A., & Thorpy, M. J. (1990). Geriatrics: Sleep disorders and aging. *New England Journal of Medicine, 323,* 520–526.

Provine, R. R. (1996, January/February). Laughter. *American Scientist, 84,* 38–45.

Pryke, S., Lindsay, R. C. L., & Pozzulo, J. D. (2000). Sorting mug shots: Methodological issues. *Applied Cognitive Psychology, 14,* 81–96.

Public Agenda. (2003a). *Race relations: A nation divided?* Retrieved June 25, 2003, from http://www.publicagenda.org

Public Agenda. (2003b). *Gay rights: A nation divided?* Retrieved June 25, 2003 from http://www.publicagenda.org

Public Agenda Online. (2002). *The issues: Race.* Retrieved November 13, 2002 from http://www.publicagenda.com/issues/overview.dfm?issue_type=race

Pulvermüller, F., Mohr, B., Schleichert, H., & Veit, R. (2000). Operant conditioning of left-hemispheric slow cortical potentials and its effect on word processing. *Biological Psychology, 53,* 177–215.

Purnine, D., & Carey, M. (1998) Age and gender differences in sexual behavior preferences: A follow-up report. *Journal of Sex & Marital Therapy, 24,* 93–102.

Putnam, F. (2003). Ten-year research update review: Child sexual abuse. *Journal of the American Academy of Child & Adolescent Psychiatry, 42,* 269–278.

Putnam, F. W. (1989). *Diagnosis and treatment of multiple personality disorder.* New York: Guilford Press.

Putnam, F. W. (1992). Altered states: Peeling away the layers of a multiple personality. *The Sciences, 32,* 30–36.

Putnam, S., & Stifter, C. (2005). Behavioral approach-inhibition in toddlers: Prediction from infancy, positive and negative affective components, and relations with behavior problems. *Child Development, 76,* 212–226.

Putzke, J., Rickert, E., Duke, L., Marson, D., & Harrell, L. (2000). Differential automatic processing deficits in early stage Alzheimer's disease. *Aging, Neuropsychology, and Cognition, 7,* 112–118.

Pyevich, D., & Bogenschultz. M. (2001). Herbal diuretics and lithium toxicity. *American Journal of Psychiatry, 158,* 1329.

Quadrel, M. J., Fischhoff, B., & Davis, W. (1993). Adolescent (in)vulnerability. *American Psychologist, 48,* 102–116.

Quaid, K., Aschen, S., Smiley, C., Nurnberger, J. (2001). Perceived genetic risks for bipolar disorder in patient population: An exploratory study. *Journal of Genetic Counseling, 10,* 41–51.

Querido, J., Warner, T., & Eyberg, S. (2002). Parenting styles and child behavior in African American families of preschool children. *Journal of Clinical Child & Adolescent Psychology, 31,* 272–277.

Quesnel, C., Savard, J., Simard, S., Ivers, H., & Morin, C. (2003). Efficacy of cognitive-behavioral therapy for insomnia in women treated for nonmetastatic breast cancer. *Journal of Consulting & Clinical Psychology, 71,* 189–200.

Quiroga, T., Lemos-Britton, Z., Mostafapour, E., Abbott, R., & Berninger, V. (2002). Phonological awareness and beginning reading in Spanish-speaking ESL first graders: Research into practice. *Journal of School Psychology, 40,* 85–111.

Rabinowitz, P. (2000). Noise-induced hearing loss. *American Family Physician, 61,* 1053.

Rachman, S. J., & Wilson, G. T. (1980). *The effects of psychological therapy* (2nd ed.). New York: Pergamon.

Raeikkoenen, K., Matthews, K., & Salomon, K. (2003). Hostility predicts metabolic syndrome risk factors in children and adolescents. *Health Psychology, 22,* 279–286.

Rafferty, J., & Tapsell, J. (2001). Self-managed work teams and manufacturing strategies: Cultural influences in the search for team effectiveness and competitive advantage. *Human Factors & Ergonomics in Manufacturing, 11,* 19–34.

Ragozzino, M., Detrick, S., & Kesner, R. (2002). The effects of prelimbic and infralimbic lesions on working memory for visual objects in rats. *Neurobiology of Learning & Memory, 77,* 29–43.

Rahe, R. J., Meyer, M., Smith, M., Kjaer, G., & Holmes, T. H. (1964). Social stress and illness onset. *Journal of Psychosomatic Research, 8,* 35–44.

Rahman, Q., Abrahams, S., & Wilson, G. (2003). Sexual orientation-related differences in verbal fluency. *Neuropsychology, 17,* 240–246.

Rahman, Q. (2005). Fluctuating asymmetry, second to fourth finger length ratios and human sexual orientation. *Psychoneuroendocrinology, 30,* 382–391.

Rahman, Q., & Wilson, G. (2003a). Born gay? The psychobiology of human sexual orientation. *Personality and Individual Differences, 34,* 1337–1382.

Rahman, Q., & Wilson, G. (2003b). Large sexual-orientation-related differences in performance on mental rotation and judgement of line orientation tasks. *Neuropsychology, 17,* 25–31.

Raine, A. (1996). Autonomic nervous system factors underlying disinhibited, antisocial, and violent behavior: Biosocial perspectives and treatment implications. *Annals of the New York Academy of Sciences, 794,* 46–59.

Raja, M. (2006). The diagnosis of Asperger's syndrome. *Directions in Psychiatry, 26,* 89–104.

Rakauskas, M., Gugerty, L., & Ward, N. (2004). Effects of naturalistic cell phone conversations on driving performance. *Journal of Safety Research, 35,* 453–464.

Ralph, M. R. (1989, November/December). The rhythm maker: Pinpointing the master clock in mammals. *The Sciences, 29,* 40–45.

Ramey, C. (1993). A rejoinder to Spitz's critique of the Abecedarian experiment. *Intelligence, 17,* 25–30.

Ramey, C., & Campbell, F. (1987). The Carolina Abecedarian project. An educational experiment concerning human malleability. In J. J. Gallagher & C. T. Ramey (Eds.), *The malleability of children,* (pp. 127–140). Baltimore: Brookes.

Ramey, C., & Ramey, S. (2004). Early learning and school readiness: Can early intervention make a difference? *Merrill-Palmer Quarterly, 50,* 471–491.

Ramsay, D. S., & Woods, S. C. (1997). Biological consequences of drug administration: Implications for acute and chronic tolerance. *Psychological Review, 104,* 170–193.

Ramsey, J., Langlois, J., Hoss, R., Rubenstein, A., & Griffin, A. (2004). Origins of a stereotype: Categorization of facial attractiveness by 6-month-old infants. *Developmental Science, 7,* 201–211.

Randel, B., Stevenson, H., & Witruk, E. (2000). Attitudes, beliefs, and mathematics achievement of German and Japanese high school students. *International Journal of Behavioral Development, 24,* 190–198.

Rantanen, J., Pulkkinen, L., & Kinnunen, U. (2005). The Big Five personality dimensions, work-family conflict, and psychological distress: A longitudinal view. *Journal of Individual Differences, 26,* 155–166.

Rao, S. C., Rainer, G., & Miller, E. K. (1997). Integration of what and where in the primate prefrontal cortex. *Science, 276,* 821–824.

Rapp, S., Espeland, M., Shumaker, S., Henderson, V., Brunner, R., Manson, J., Gass, M., Stefanick, M., Lane, D., Hays, J., Johnson, K., Coker, L., Dailey, M., & Bowen, D. (2003). Effect of estrogen plus progestin on global cognitive function in postmenopausal women: The Women's Health Initiative Memory Study: A randomized controlled trial. *Journal of the American Medical Association (JAMA), 289,* 2663–2672.

Rasmussen, S. A., & Eisen, J. L. (1990). Epidemiology of obsessive compulsive disorder. *Journal of Clinical Psychiatry, 51*(2, Suppl.), 10–13.

Ratty, H., Vaenskae, J., Kasanen, K., & Kaerkkaeinen, R. (2002). Parents' explanations of their child's performance in mathematics and reading: A replication and extension of Yee and Eccles. *Sex Roles, 46,* 121–128.

Ray, S., & Bates, M. (2006). Acute alcohol effects on repetition priming and word recognition memory with equivalent memory cues. *Brain and Cognition, 60,* 118–127.

Raz, A., Deouell, L., & Bentin, S. (2001). Is pre-attentive processing compromised by prolonged wakefulness? Effects of total sleep deprivation on the mismatch negativity. *Psychophysiology, 38,* 787–795.

Raz, N., Lindenberger, U., Rodrigue, K., Kennedy, K., Head, D., Williamson, A., Dahle, C., Gerstorf, D., & Acker, J. (2006). Regional brain changes in aging healthy adults: General trends, individual differences and modifiers. *Cerebral Cortex, 15,* 1679–1689.

Razoumnikova, O. M. (2000). Functional organization of different brain areas during convergent and divergent thinking: An EEG investigation. *Cognitive Brain Research, 10,* 11–18.

Redding, R. (2000). Adjudicative competence in juveniles: Legal and clinical issues. *Juvenile Justice Fact Sheet.* Charlottesville, VA: Institute of Law, Psychiatry, & Public Policy, University of Virginia. Retrieved July 13, 2006 from http://www.ilppp.virginia.edu/Juvenile_Forensic_Fact_Sheets/AdjudComp.html#N_1_

Reicher, S., & Haslam, A. (2004). The banality of evil: Thoughts on the psychology of atrocity. *Anthropology News, 45,* 14–15.

Reinhardt, J., Boerner, K., Horowitz, A., & Lloyd, S. (2006). Good to have but not to use: Differential impact of perceived and received support on well-being. *Journal of Social and Personal Relationships, 23,* 117–129.

Reinke, B. J., Ellicott, A. M., Harris, R. L., & Hancock, E. (1985). Timing of psychosocial changes in women's lives. *Human Development, 28,* 259–280.

Reis, H. T., Wilson, I. M., Monestere, C., Bernstein, S., Clark, K., Seidl, E., Franco, M., Gioioso, E., Freeman, L., & Radoane, K. (1990). What is smiling is beautiful and good. *European Journal of Social Psychology, 20,* 259–267.

Reisner, A. (2003). The electroconvulsive therapy controversy: Evidence and ethics. *Neuropsychology Review, 13,* 199–219.

Reite, M., Buysse, D., Reynolds, C., & Mendelson, W. (1995). The use of polysomnography in the evaluation of insomnia. *Sleep, 18,* 58–70.

Reneman, L., Booij, J., Schmand, B., van den Brink, W., & Gunning, B. (2000). Memory disturbances in "Ecstasy" users are correlated with an altered brain serotonin neurotransmission. *Psychopharmacology, 148,* 322–324.

Rescorla, R. A. (1967). Pavlovian conditioning and its proper control procedures. *Psychological Review, 74,* 71–80.

Rescorla, R. A. (1968). Probability of shock in the presence and absence of CS in fear conditioning. *Journal of Comparative and Physiological Psychology, 66,* 1–5.

Rescorla, R. A. (1988). Pavlovian conditioning: It's not what you think it is. *American Psychologist, 43,* 151–160.

Rescorla, R. A., & Wagner, A. R. (1972). A theory of Pavlovian conditioning: Variations in the effectiveness of reinforcement and nonreinforcement. In A. Black & W. F. Prokasy (Eds.), *Classical conditioning: II. Current research and theory.* New York: Appleton.

Restak, R. (1988). *The mind.* Toronto: Bantam.

Restak, R. (1993, September/October). Brain by design. *The Sciences,* pp. 27–33.

Reuters News Service. (2006, June 30). Japan elderly population ratio now world's highest. Retrieved July 3, 2006 from http://today.reuters.co.uk/news/newsArticle.aspx?type=worldNews&storyID=2006-06-30T084625Z_01_T83766_RTRUKOC_0_UK-JAPAN-POPULATION.xml&archived=False

Revensuo, A. (2000). The reinterpretation of dreams: An evolutionary hypothesis of the function of dreaming. *Behavioral & Brain Science, 23.*

Reyna, V. (2004). How people make decisions that involve risk: A dual-processes approach. *Current Directions in Psychological Science, 13,* 60–66.

Reyna, V., & Adam, M. (2003). Fuzzy-trace theory, risk communication, and product labeling in sexually transmitted diseases. *Risk Analysis, 23,* 325–342.

Reyner, A., & Horne, J. A. (1995). Gender- and age-related differences in sleep determined by home-recorded sleep logs and actimetry from 400 adults. *Sleep, 18,* 127–134.

Reyner, L. A., & Horne, J. A. (1998). Evaluation of "in-car" countermeasures to sleepiness: Cold air and radio. *Sleep, 21,* 46–50.

Rhéaume, J., & Ladouceur, R. (2000). Cognitive and behavioural treatments of checking behaviours: An examination of individual cognitive change. *Clinical Psychology & Psychotherapy, 7,* 118–127.

Rhodes, N., & Wood, W. (1992). Self-esteem and intelligence affect influenceability: The medicating role of message reception. *Psychological Bulletin, 111,* 156–171.

Rice, M. L. (1989). Children's language acquisition. *American Psychologist, 44,* 149–156.

Richards, M., Miller, B., O'Donnell, P., Wasserman, M., & Colder, C. (2004). Parental monitoring mediates the effects of age and sex on problem behaviors among African American urban young adolescents. *Journal of Youth and Adolescence, 33,* 221–233.

Richardson, J., & Introvigne, M. (2001). "Brainwashing" theories in European parliamentary and administrative reports on "cults" and "sects." *Journal for the Scientific Study of Religion, 40,* 143–168.

Richter, T., & Späth, P. (2006). Recognition is used as one cue among others in judgment and decision making. *Journal of Experimental Psychology: Learning, Memory, and Cognition, 32,* 150–162.

Richter, W., Somorjai, R., Summers, R., Jarmasz, M., Ravi, S., Menon, J. S., et al. (2000). Motor area activity during mental rotation studied by time-resolved single-trial fMRI. *Journal of Cognitive Neuroscience, 12,* 310–320.

Rickels, K., Schweizer, E., Weiss, S., & Zavodnick, S. (1993). Maintenance drug treatment for panic disorder II. Short- and long-term outcome after drug taper. *Archives of General Psychiatry, 50,* 61–68.

Ridderinkhof, K., Scheres, A., Oosterlaan, J., & Sergeant, J. (2005). Delta plots in the study of individual differences: New tools reveal response inhibition deficits in AD/HD that are eliminated by methylphenidate treatment. *Journal of Abnormal Psychology, 114,* 1970–215.

Rideout, V., Roberts, D., & Foehr, U. (2005). *Generation M: Media in the lives of 8–18 year-olds.* Washington, D.C.: Kaiser Family Foundation. Retrieved May 18, 2006 from http://www.kff.org/entmedia/entmedia030905pkg.cfm

Riedel, G. (1996). Function of metabotropic glutamate receptors in learning and memory. *Trends in Neurosciences, 19,* 219–224.

Riegle, R. (2005). Viewpoint: Online courses as video games. *Campus Technology,* June 15, 2005. Retrieved May 5, 2006 from http://www.campus-technology.com

Rieker, P., & Bird, C. (2005). Rethinking gender differences in health: Why we need to integrate social and biological perspectives. *The Journals of Gerontology Series B: Psychological Sciences and Social Sciences, 60,* S40–S47.

Righetti, P. (1996). The emotional experience of the fetus: A preliminary report. *Pre- & Peri-Natal Psychology Journal, 11,* 55–65.

Riley, K., Snowdon, D., & Markesbery, W. (2002). Alzheimer's neurofibrillary pathology and the spectrum of cognitive function: Findings from the Nun study. *Annals of Neurology, 51,* 567–577.

Rimland, B. (1978). Inside the mind of the autistic savant. *Psychology Today, 12,* 69–80.

Rivas-Vasquez, R. (2001). St. John's Wort (Hypericum Perforatum): Practical considerations based on the evidence. *Professional Psychology: Research and Practice, 32,* 329–332.

Roan, S. (2000, March 6). Cyber analysis. *L.A. Times.*

Roberts, B. W., & DelVecchio, W. F. (2000). The rank-order consistency of personality traits from childhood to old age: A quantitative review of longitudinal studies. *Psychological Bulletin, 126,* 3–25.

Roberts, B., Chernyshenko, O., Stark, S., & Goldberg, L. (2005). The structure of conscientiousness: An empirical investigation based on seven major personality questionnaires. *Personnel Psychology, 58,* 103–139.

Roberts, J., & Bell, M. (2000). Sex differences on a mental rotation task: Variations in electroencephalogram hemispheric activation between children and college students. *Developmental Neuropsychology, 17,* 199–223.

Roberts, M. (2006). "IDOL" dreams: Tracy Moore's song of hope and discovery. *Schizophrenia Digest, 4,* 30–33.

Roberts, P., & Moseley, B. (1996, May/June). Fathers' time. *Psychology Today, 29,* 48–55, 81.

Robertson, G. L. (1983). Thirst and vasopressin function in normal and disordered states of water balance. *Journal of Laboratory and Clinical Medicine, 101,* 351–371.

Robertson, I. H., & Murre, J. M. J. (1999). Rehabilitation of brain damage: Brain plasticity and principles of guided recovery. *Psychological Bulletin, 125,* 544–575.

Robie, C., Johnson, K., Nilsen, D., & Hazucha, J. (2001). The right stuff: Understanding cultural differences in leadership performance. *Journal of Management Development, 20,* 639–650.

Robins, C. J., & Hayes, A. M. (1993). An appraisal of cognitive therapy. *Journal of Consulting and Clinical Psychology, 61,* 205–214.

Robins, R. W., Gosling, S. D., & Craik, K. H. (1999). An empirical analysis of trends in psychology. *American Psychologist, 54,* 117–128.

Robins, R., & Trzesniewski, K. (2005). Self-esteem development across the lifespan. *Current Directions in Psychological Science, 14,* 158–162.

Robinson, D., Phillips, P. Budygin, E., Trafton, B., Garris, P., & Wightman, R. (2001). Sub-second changes in accumbal dopamine during sexual behavior in male rats. *Neuroreport: For Rapid Communication of Neuroscience Research, 12,* 2549–2552.

Robinson, F. (1970). *Effective Study* (4th ed.). New York: Harper & Row.

Robinson, M., & Tamir, M. (2005). Neuroticism as mental noise: A relation between neuroticism and reaction time standard deviations. *Journal of Personality and Social Psychology, 89,* 107–114.

Robles, T., Glaser, R., & Kiecolt-Glaser, J. (2005). Out of balance: A new look at chronic stress, depression, and immunity. *Current Directions in Psychological Science, 14,* 111–115.

Robles, T., Shaffer, V., Malarkey, W., & Kiecolt-Glaser, J. (2006). Positive behaviors during marital conflict: Influences on stress hormones. *Journal of Social and Personal Relationships, 23,* 305–325.

Rock, I., & Palmer, S. (1990). The legacy of Gestalt psychology. *Scientific American, 263,* 84–90.

Rodin, J. (1985). Insulin levels, hunger, and food intake: An example of feedback loops in body weight regulation. *Health Psychology, 4,* 1–24.

Rodin, J., & Salovey, P. (1989). Health psychology. *Annual Review of Psychology, 40,* 533–579.

Rodin, J., Wack, J., Ferrannini, E., & DeFronzo, R. A. (1985). Effect of insulin and glucose on feeding behavior. *Metabolism, 34,* 826–831.

Rodriguez, A., & Bohlin, G. (2005). Are maternal smoking and stress during pregnancy related to ADHD symptoms in children? *Journal of Child Psychology and Psychiatry, 46,* 246–254.

Rodríguez, C., & Church, A. (2003). The structure and personality correlates of affect in Mexico: Evidence of cross-cultural comparability using the Spanish language. *Journal of Cross-Cultural Psychology, 34,* 211–223.

Roediger, H. L., III. (1980). The effectiveness of four mnemonics in ordering recall. *Journal of Experimental Psychology: Human Learning and Memory, 6,* 558–567.

Roediger, H. L., III, & McDermott, K. B. (1995). Creating false memories: Remembering words not presented in lists. *Journal of Experimental Psychology: Learning, Memory, and Cognition, 21,* 803–814.

Roehling, P., Roehling, M., & Moen, P. (2001). The relationship between work-life policies and practices and employee loyalty: A life course perspective. *Journal of Family & Economic Issues, 22,* 141–170.

Roehrich, L., & Kinder, B. N. (1991). Alcohol expectancies and male sexuality: Review and implications for sex therapy. *Journal of Sex and Marital Therapy, 17,* 45–54.

Roesch, S. C., & Amirkhan, J. H. (1997). Boundary condition for self-serving attributions: Another look at the sports pages. *Journal of Applied Social Psychology, 27,* 245–261.

Roesch, S., & Weiner, B. (2001). A meta-analytic review of coping with illness: Do causal attributions matter? *Journal of Psychosomatic Research, 50,* 205–219.

Rogers, C. R. (1951). *Client-centered therapy: Its current practice, implications, and theory.* Boston: Houghton Mifflin.

Rogge, R., Bradbury, T., Hahlweg, K., Engl, J., & Thurmaier, F. (2006). Predicting marital distress and dissolution: Refining the two-factor hypothesis. *Journal of Family Psychology, 20,* 156–159.

Rogoff, B., & Mistry, J. (1985). Memory development in cultural context. In M. Pressley & C. Brainerd (Eds.), *The cognitive side of memory development.* New York: Springer-Verlag.

Roisman, G., Masten, A., Coatsworth, J., & Tellegen, A. (2004). Salient and emerging developmental tasks in the transition to adulthood. *Child Development, 75,* 123–133.

Romach, M., Busto, U., Somer, G., et al. (1995). Clinical aspects of chronic use of alprazolam and lorazepam. *American Journal of Psychiatry, 152,* 1161–1167.

Roorda, A., & Williams, D. R. (1999). The arrangement of the three cone classes in the living human eye. *Nature, 397,* 520–521.

Rosch, E. (1978). Principles of categorization. In E. Rosch & B. Lloyd (Eds.), *Cognition and categorization.* Hillsdale, NJ: Erlbaum.

Rosch, E. H. (1973). Natural categories. *Cognitive Psychology, 4,* 328–350.

Rosch, E. H. (1987). Linguistic relativity. *Et Cetera, 44,* 254–279.

Rose, J., (2006). Nicotine and nonnicotine factors in cigarette addiction. *Psychopharmacology, 184,* 274–285.

Rosekind, M. R. (1992). The epidemiology and occurrence of insomnia. *Journal of Clinical Psychiatry, 53*(6, Suppl.), 4–6.

Rosen, E., Chung-Hsin, H., Wang, X., Sakai, S., Freeman, M., Gonzalez, F., & Spiegelman, B. (2002). C/EBPalpha induces adipogenesis through PPARgamma: a unified pathway. *Genes and Development, 16,* 22–26.

Rosen, R. C. (1996). Erectile dysfunction: The medicalization of male sexuality. *Clinical Psychology Review, 16,* 497–519.

Rosen, R. C., & Leiblum, S. R. (1995). Treatment of sexual disorders in the 1990s: An integrated approach. *Journal of Consulting and Clinical Psychology, 63,* 877–896.

Rosenbluth, R., Grossman, E. S., & Kaitz, M. (2000). Performance of early-blind and sighted children on olfactory tasks. *Perception, 29,* 101–110.

Rosenfeld, J. P. (1995). Alternative views of Bashore and Rapp's (1993) alternatives to traditional polygraphy: A critique. *Psychological Bulletin, 117,* 159–166.

Rosenhan, D. L. (1973). On being sane in insane places. *Science, 179,* 250–258.

Rosenvinge, J. H., Matinussen, M., & Ostensen, E. (2000). The comorbidity of eating disorders and personality disorders: A meta-analytic review of studies published between 1983 and 1998. *Eating and Weight Disorders: Studies on Anorexia, Bulimia, and Obesity, 5,* 52–61.

Rosenzweig, M. R. (1961). Auditory localization. *Scientific American, 205,* 132–142.

Rosenzweig, S. (1938). A basis for the improvement of personality tests with special reference to the M-F battery. *Journal of Abnormal & Social Psychology, 33,* 476–488.

Ross, C. A., Norton, G. R., & Wozney, K. (1989). Multiple personality disorder: An analysis of 236 cases. *Canadian Journal of Psychiatry, 34,* 413–418.

Ross, J., Baldessarini, R. J., & Tondo, L. (2000). Does lithium treatment still work? Evidence of stable responses over three decades. *Archives of General Psychiatry, 57,* 187–190.

Rosser, R. (1994). *Cognitive development: Psychological and biological perspectives.* Boston, MA: Allyn & Bacon.

Rossow, I., & Amundsen, A. (1997). Alcohol abuse and mortality: a 40-year prospective study of Norwegian conscripts. *Social Science & Medicine, 44,* 261–267.

Roth, T. (1996). Social and economic consequences of sleep disorders. *Sleep, 19,* S46–S47.

Rotter, J. B. (1966). Generalized expectancies for internal versus external control of reinforcement. *Psychological Monographs, 80*(1, Whole No. 609).

Rotter, J. B. (1971, June). External control and internal control. *Psychology Today,* pp. 37–42, 58–59.

Rotter, J. B. (1990). Internal versus external control of reinforcement: A case history of a variable. *American Psychologist, 45,* 489–493.

Rotton, J., & Cohn, E. G. (2000). Violence is a curvilinear function of temperature in Dallas: A replication. *Journal of Personality & Social Psychology, 78,* 1074–1082.

Rotton, J., Frey, J., Barry, T., Milligan, M., & Fitzpatrick, M. (1979). The air pollution experience and physical aggression. *Journal of Applied Social Psychology, 9,* 397–412.

Rouch, I., Wild, P., Ansiau, D., & Marquie, J. (2005). Shiftwork experience, age and cognitive performance. *Ergonomics, 48,* 1282–1293.

"Round-the-clock baby TV channel to debut." (2006, May 11). Retrieved May 11, 2006 from http://www.news.yahoo.com.

Rovee-Collier, C. (1990). The "memory system" of prelinguistic infants. *Annals of the New York Academy of Sciences, 608,* 517–576.

Rowe, D. (2003). Assessing genotype-environment interactions and correlations in the postgenomic era. In R. Plomin, J. DeFries, I. Craig, & P. McGuffin (Eds.), *Behavioral genetics in the postgenomic era* (pp. 71–86). Washington, DC: American Psychological Association.

Rowe, D. C. (1987). Resolving the person-situation debate: Invitation to an interdisciplinary dialogue. *American Psychologist, 42,* 218–227.

Rowe, J., & Kahn, R. (1998). *Successful aging.* New York: Pantheon.

Rowland, D., Tai, W., & Slob, A. (2003). An exploration of emotional response to erotic stimulation in men with premature ejaculation: Effects of treatment with clomipramine. *Archives of Sexual Behavior, 32,* 145–153.

Rowley, S. (2000). Profiles of African American college students' educational utility and performance: A cluster analysis. *Journal of Black Psychology, 26,* 3–26.

Royall, D., Chiodo, L., Polk, M., & Jaramillo, C. (2002). Severe dysosmia is specifically associated with Alzheimer-like memory deficits in nondemented elderly retirees. *Neuroepidemiology, 21,* 68–73.

Rozell, E., Pettijohn, C., & Parker, R. (2002). An empirical evaluation of emotional intelligence: The impact on management development. *Journal of Management Development, 21,* 272–289.

Ruan, Y., Cao, X., Qian, H., Zhang, L., Qin, G., Jiang, Z., Song, B., Hu, W., Liang, S., Chen, K., Yang, Y., Li, X., Wang, J., Chen, X., Hao, C., Song, Y., Xing, H., Wang, N., & Shao, Y. (2006, in press). Syphilis among female sex workers in Southwestern China: Potential for HIV transmission. *Sexually Transmitted Diseases, 33.*

Rubin, K., Burgess, K., & Hastings, P. (2002). Stability and social-behavioral consequences of toddlers' inhibited temperament and parenting behaviors. *Child Development, 73,* 483–495.

Rubinstein, G. (2001). Sex-role reversal and clinical judgment of mental health. *Journal of Sex & Marital Therapy, 27,* 9–19.

Ruby, N., Dark, J., Burns, D., Heller, H., & Zucker, I. (2002). The suprachiasmatic nucleus is essential for circadian body temperature rhythms in hibernating ground squirrels. *Journal of Neuroscience, 22,* 357–364.

Rudman, L., Ashmore, R., & Gary, M. (2001). "Unlearning" automatic biases: The malleability of implicit prejudice and stereotypes. *Journal of Personality & Social Psychology, 81,* 856–868.

Ruffman, T., Slade, L., Devitt, K., & Crowe, E. (2006). What mothers say and what they do: The relation between parenting, theory of mind, language and conflict/cooperation. *British Journal of Developmental Psychology, 24,* 105–124.

Ruggero, M. A. (1992). Responses to sound of the basilar membrane of the mammalian cochlea. *Current Opinion in Neurobiology, 2,* 449–456.

Rumbaugh, D. (1977). *Language learning by a chimpanzee: the Lana project.* New York: Academic Press.

Rushton, J., & Jensen, A. (2003). African-White IQ differences from Zimbabwe on the Wechsler Intelligence Scale for Children-Revised are mainly on the *g* factor. *Personality & Individual Differences, 34,* 177–183.

Rushton, J., & Jensen, A. (2005). Thirty years of research on race differences in cognitive ability. *Psychology, Public Policy, and Law, 11,* 235–294.

Rushton, J., Skuy, M., & Fridjhon, P. (2003). Performance on Raven's Advanced Progressive Matrices by African, East Indian, and White engineering students in South Africa. *Intelligence, 31,* 123–137.

Russell, J. A. (1995). Facial expressions of emotion: What lies beyond minimal universality? *Psychological Bulletin, 118,* 379–391.

Russell, T., Rowe, W., & Smouse, A. (1991). Subliminal self-help tapes and academic achievement: An evaluation. *Journal of Counseling and Development, 69,* 359–362.

Rutter, M. (2005). Aetiology of autism: Findings and questions. *Journal of Intellectual Disability Research, 49,* 231–238.

Ryan, R., Kim, Y., & Kaplan, U. (2003). Differentiating autonomy from individualism and independence: A self-determination theory perspective on internalization of cultural orientations and well-being. *Journal of Personality and Social Psychology, 84,* 97–110.

Sach, T., & Whynes, D. (2005). Pediatric cochlear implantation: The views of parents. *International Journal of Audiology, 44,* 400–407.

Sachs, G., Grossman, F., Ghaemi, S., Okamoto, A., & Bosden, C. (2002). Combination of a mood stabilizer with risperidone or haloperidol for treatment of acute mania: A double-blind, placebo-controlled comparison of efficacy and safety. *American Journal of Psychiatry, 159,* 1146–1154.

Sackeim, H. A., Prudic, J., Devanand, D. P., Nobler, M. S., Lisanby, S. H., Peyser, S., Fitzsimons, L., Moody, B. J., & Clark, J. (2000). A prospective, randomized, double-blind comparison of bilateral and right unilateral electroconvulsive therapy at different stimulus intensities. *Archives of General Psychiatry, 57,* 425–434.

Sackett, P., Hardison, C., & Cullen, M. (2004). On interpreting stereotype threat as accounting for African American-White differences on cognitive tests. *American Psychologist, 59,* 7–13.

Sacks, O. (1984). *A leg to stand on.* New York: Harper & Row.

Sacks, O. (1995). *An anthropologist on Mars.* New York: Macmillan.

Saczynski, J., Willis, S., & Schaie, K. W. (2002). Strategy use in reasoning training with older adults. *Aging, Neuropsychology, & Cognition, 9,* 48–60.

Sadeh, A., Gruber, R., & Raviv, A. (2003). The effect of sleep restriction and extension on school-age children: What a difference an hour makes. *Child Development, 74,* 444–455.

Sahoo, F., Sahoo, K., & Harichandan, S. (2005). Big Five factors of personality and human happiness. *Social Science International, 21,* 20–28.

Salary.com. (2006a). *What is mom's job worth?.* Retrieved June 21, 2006 from http://swz.salary.com/momsalarywizard/htmls/mswl_momcenter.html

Salary.com. (2006b). *What is dad's job worth?* Retrieved June 21, 2006 from http://www.salary.com/careers/layoutscripts/crel_display.asp?tab=cre&cat=nocat&ser=Ser410&part=Par626

Salat, D., Buckner, R., Snyder, A., Greve, D., Desikan, R., Busa, E., Morris, J., Dale, A., & Fischl, B. (2004). Thinning of the cerebral cortex in aging. *Cerebral Cortex, 14,* 721–730.

Salisch, M. (2001). Children's emotional development: Challenges in their relationships to parents, peers, and friends. *International Journal of Behavioural Development, 25,* 310–319.

Salmon, J., Owen, N., Crawford, D., Bauman, A., & Sallis, J. (2003). Physical activity and sedentary behavior: A population-based study of barriers, enjoyment, and preference. *Health Psychology, 22,* 178–188.

Salo, J., Niemelae, A., Joukamaa, M., & Koivukangas, J. (2002). Effect of brain tumour laterality on patients' perceived quaity of life. *Journal of Neurology, Neurosurgery, & Psychiatry, 72,* 373–377.

Salon. (2005, August 25). *Lost in America.* Retrieved June 10, 2006 from http://dir.salon.com/story/news/feature/2005/08/25/lost_boys/index.html?pn=1

Salovey, P., & Pizarro, D. (2003). The value of emotional intelligence. In R. Sternberg, J. Lautrey, & T. Lubart (Eds.), *Models of intelligence: International perspective* (pp. 263–278). Washington, DC: American Psychological Association.

Salthouse, T. A. (1996). The processing-speed theory of adult age differences in cognition. *Psychological Review, 103,* 403–428.

Sánchez, G. (1932). Group differences and Spanish-speaking children—a critical review. *Journal of Applied Psychology, 16,* 549–558.

Sánchez, G. (1934). Bilingualism and mental measures. A word of caution. *Journal of Applied Psychology, 18,* 765–772.

Sanes, J. N., & Donoghue, J. P. (2000). Plasticity and primary motor cortex. *Annual Review of Neuroscience, 23,* 393–415.

Sanes, J. N., Donoghue, J. P., Thangaraj, V., Edelman, R. R., & Warach, S. (1995). Shared neural substrates controlling hand movements in human motor cortex. *Science, 268,* 1775.

Santiago-Rivera, A., & Altarriba, J. (2002). The role of language in therapy with the Spanish-English bilingual client. *Professional Psychology: Research & Practice, 33,* 30–38.

Saper, C., Scammell, T., & Lu, J. (2005). Hypothalamic regulation of sleep and circadian rhythms. *Nature, 437,* 1257–1263.

Sarfati, Y. (2000). Deficit of the theory-of-mind in schizophrenia: Clinical concept and review of experimental arguments. *Canadian Journal of Psychiatry, 45,* 4363–4368.

Sarkis, K. (2000, May). Computer workers at risk for stress injuries. *Occupational Hazards, 62,* 33.

Sarrio, M., Barbera, E., Ramos, A., & Candela, C. (2002). The glass ceiling in the professional promotion of women. *Revista de Psicologia Social, 17,* 167–182.

Sateia, M. J., Doghramji, K., Hauri, P. J., & Morin, C. M. (2000). Evaluation of chronic insomnia. An American Academy of Sleep Medicine review. *Sleep, 23,* 243–308.

Saudino, K. (2005). Special article: Behavioral genetics and child temperament. *Journal of Developmental & Behavioral Pediatrics, 26,* 214–223.

Savage-Rumbaugh, E. S. (1986). *Ape language.* New York: Columbia University Press.

Savage-Rumbaugh, E. S. (1990). Language acquisition in a nonhuman species: Implications for the innateness debate. *Developmental Psychology, 26,* 599–620.

Savage-Rumbaugh, E. S. (1993). Language learnability in man, ape, and dolphin. In H. L. Roitblat, L. M. Herman, & P. E. Nachtigall (Eds.), *Language and communication: Comparative perspectives. Comparative cognition and neuroscience* (pp. 457–484). Hillsdale, NJ: Erlbaum.

Savage-Rumbaugh, E. S., Sevcik, R. A., Brakke, K. E., & Rumbaugh, D. M. (1992). Symbols: Their communicative use, communication, and combination by bonobos (*Pan paniscus*). In L. P. Lipsitt & C. Rovee-Collier (Eds.). *Advances in infancy research* (Vol. 7, pp. 221–278). Norwood, NJ: Ablex.

Sazci, A., Ergul, E., Kucukali, I., Kara, I., & Kaya, G. (2005). Association of the C677T and A1298C polymorphisms of methylenetetrahydrofolate reductase gene with schizophrenia: Association is significant in men but not in women. *Progress in Neuro-Psychopharmacology & Biological Psychiatry, 29,* 1113–1123.

Scarr, S. (1997). Why child care has little impact on most children's development. *Current Directions in Psychological Science, 6,* 143–147.

Scarr, S., & Weinberg, R. (1976). The influence of "family background" on intellectual attainment. *American Sociological Review, 43,* 674–692.

Schaal, B., Marlier, L., & Soussignan, R. (1998). Olfactory function in the human fetus: Evidence from selective neonatal responsiveness to the odor of amniotic fluid. *Behavioral Neuroscience, 112,* 1438–1449.

Schab, F. R. (1990). Odors and the remembrance of things past. *Journal of Experimental Psychology: Learning, Memory, and Cognition, 16,* 648–655.

Schaie, K. (2005). *Developmental influences on adult intelligence: The Seattle longitudinal study.* New York: Oxford University Press.

Schaie, K. W. (1993). Ageist language in psychological research. *American Psychologist, 48,* 49–51.

Schaie, K. W., & Willis, S. L. (1996). *Adult development and aging* (4th ed.). New York: HarperCollins.

Schaie, W., & Willis, S. (2005). *Mind alert: Intellectual functioning in adulthood: Growth, maintenance, decline, and modifiability.* Lecture presented at the Joint Conference of the American Society on Aging and the National Council on the Aging as part of the Mind-Alert Program. Retrieved June 10, 2006 from http://geron.psu.edu/sls/publications/MindAlert.pdf

Schauer, P., Ikramuddin, S., Gourash, W., Ramanathan, R., & Luketich, J. (2000). Outcomes after laparoscopic roux-en-Y gastric bypass for morbid obesity. *Annals of Surgery, 232,* 515–529.

Schellenberg, E. (2004). Music lessons enhance IQ. *Psychological Science, 15,* 511–514.

Schenck, C. H., & Mahowald, M. W. (1995). A polysomnographically documented case of adult somnambulism with long-distance automobile driving and frequent nocturnal violence: Parasomnia with continuing danger as a noninsane automatism? *Sleep, 18,* 765–772.

Schenck, C. H., & Mahowald, M. W. (2000). Parasomnias. Managing bizarre sleep-related behavior disorders. *Postgraduate Medicine, 107,* 145–156.

Scherer, K. R., & Wallbott, H. G. (1994). Evidence for universality and cultural variation of differential emotion response patterning. *Journal of Personality and Social Psychology, 66,* 310–328.

Scherer, K. R., Wallbott, H. G., & Summerfield, A. B. (1986). *Experiencing emotion: A cross-cultural study.* Cambridge, England: Cambridge University Press.

Scherger, J. (2005). The biopsychosocial model is shrink-wrapped, on the shelf, and ready to be used, but waiting for a new process of care. *Families, Systems, & Health, 23,* 444–447.

Schermerhorn, J., Hunt, J., & Osborn, R. (2000). *Organizational Behavior* (7th ed.). New York: John Wiley & Sons.

Schieber, M. H., & Hibbard, L. S. (1993). How somatotopic is the motor cortex hand area? *Science, 261,* 489–492.

Schieman, S., & Taylor, J. (2001). Statuses, roles, and the sense of mattering. *Sociological Perspectives, 44,* 469–484.

Schiff, M., & Lewontin, R. (1986). *Education and class: The irrelevance of IQ genetic studies.* Oxford, England: Clarendon.

Schiller, F. (1993). *Paul Broca: Explorer of the brain.* Oxford: Oxford University Press.

Schlosberg, S. (2004). *The curse of the singles table: A true tale of 1001 nights without sex.* New York: Warner Books.

Schlosberg, S. (2006). *Suzanne Schlosberg's really important rules for Internet dating.* Retrieved July 3, 2006 from http://www.suzanneschlosberg.com/dating_rules.html

Schmitt, P., Murphy, J., Haq, N., Rubinow, D., & Danaceau, M. (2004). Stressful life events, personal losses, and perimenopause-related depression. *Archives of Women's Mental Health, 7,* 19–26.

Schneider, E., Lang, A., Shin, M., & Bradley, S. (2004). Death with a story: How story impacts emotional, motivational, and physiological responses to first-person shooter video games. *Human Communication Research, 30,* 361–375.

Schneider, W., & Pressley, M. (1989). *Memory development between 2 and 20.* New York: Springer-Verlag.

Schofield, J. W., & Francis, W. D. (1982). An observational study of peer interaction in racially mixed "accelerated" classrooms. *Journal of Educational Psychology, 74,* 722–732.

Scholz, U., Dona, B., Sud, S., & Schwarzer, R. (2002). Is general self-efficacy a universal construct? Psychometric findings from 25 countries. *European Journal of Psychological Assessment, 18,* 242–251.

Schou, M. (1997). Forty years of lithium treatment. *Archives of General Psychiatry, 54,* 9–13.

Schuckit, M., Edenberg, H., Kalmijn, J., Flury, L., Smith, T., Reich, T., Beirut, L., Goate, A., & Foroud, T. (2001). A genome-wide search for gens that relate to a low level of response to alcohol. *Alcoholism: Clinical & Experimental Research, 25,* 323–329.

Schultz, D. (1975). *A history of modern psychology* (2nd ed.). New York: Academic Press.

Schultz, W. (2006). Behavioral theories and the neurophysiology of reward. In S. Fiske, A. Kazdin, & D. Schacter (Eds), *Annual Review of Psychology* (Vol. 57, pp. 87–116). Palo Alto, CA: Annual Reviews.

Schulz, R., & Heckhausen, J. (1996). A life span model of successful aging. *American Psychologist, 51,* 702–714.

Schupp, H., Junghöfer, M., Weike, A., & Hamm, A. (2003). Emotional facilitation of sensory processing in the visual cortex. *Psychological Science, 14,* 7–13.

Schwartz, N. (1999). Self-reports: How the questions shape the answers. *American Psychologist, 54,* 93–105.

Schwartz, S., & Maquet, P. (2002). Sleep imaging and the neuro-psychological assessment of dreams. *Trends in Cognitive Sciences, 6,* 23–30.

Scott, S. K., Young, A. W., Calder, A. J., Hellawell, D. J., Aggleton, J. P., & Johnson, M. (1997). Impaired auditory recognition of fear and anger following bilateral amygdala lesions. *Nature, 385,* 254–257.

Scully, J., Tosi, H., & Banning, K. (2000). Life event checklists: Revisiting the Social Readjustment Rating Scale after 30 years. *Educational & Psychological Measurement, 60,* 864–876.

Sedikides, C., Gaertner, L., & Toguchi, Y. (2003). Pancultural self-enhancement. *Journal of Personality & Social Psychology, 84,* 60–79.

Seeman, T., Dubin, L., & Seeman, M. (2003). Religiosity/spirituality and health. *American Psychologist, 58,* 53–63.

Seenoo, K., & Takagi, O. (2003). The effect of helping behaviors on helper: A case study of volunteer work for local resident welfare. *Japanese Journal of Social Psychology, 18,* 106–118.

Segal, Z., Williams, M., & Teasdale, J. (2001). *Mindfulness-based cognitive therapy for depression.* New York: Guilford Press.

Segall, M. H. (1994). A cross-cultural research contribution to unraveling the nativist/empiricist controversy. In J. Lonner & R. Malpass (Eds.), *Psychology and culture* (pp. 135–138). Boston: Allyn & Bacon.

Segall, M. H., Campbell, D. T., & Herskovitz, M. J. (1966). *The influence of culture on visual perception.* Indianapolis: Bobbs-Merrill.

Seger, C. A., Desmond, J. E., Glover, G. H., & Gabrieli, J. D. E. (2000). Functional magnetic resonance imaging evidence for right-hemisphere involvement in processing unusual semantic relationships. *Neuropsychology, 14,* 361–369.

Seidman, A. (2005). Minority student retention: Resources for practitioners. In G. Gaither (Ed.), *Minority retention: What works?* (pp. 7–24). San Francisco, CA: Jossey-Bass.

Self, M., & Zeki, S. (2005). The integration of colour and motion by the human visual brain. *Cerebral Cortex, 15,* 1270–1279.

Seligman, M. E. P. (1970). On the generality of the laws of learning. *Psychological Review, 77,* 406–418.

Seligman, M. E. P. (1972). Phobias and preparedness. In M. E. P. Seligman & J. L. Hager (Eds.), *Biological boundaries of learning.* Englewood Cliffs, NJ: Prentice Hall.

Seligman, M. E. P. (1975). *Helplessness: On depression, development and death.* San Francisco: Freeman.

Seligman, M. E. P. (1990). *Learned optimism: How to change your mind and your life.* New York: Simon & Schuster.

Seligman, M. E. P. (1991). *Learned optimism.* New York: Knopf.

Seligman, M., & Csikszentmihalyi, M. (2000). Positive psychology: An introduction. *American Psychologist, 55,* 5–14.

Seligman, M., Steen, T., Park, N., & Peterson, C. (2005). Positive psychology progress: Empirical validation of interventions. *American Psychologist, 60,* 410–421.

Seligman, M., Steen, T., Park, N., & Peterson, C. (2005). Positive psychology progress: Empirical validation of interventions. *American Psychologist, 60,* 410–421.

Selkoe, D. J. (1997). Alzheimer's disease: Genotypes, phenotype, and treatments. *Science, 275,* 630–631.

Sell, R. L., Wells, J. A., and Wypij, D. (1995). The prevalence of homosexual behavior and attraction in the United States, the United Kingdom and France: Results of national population-based samples. *Archives of Sexual Behavior, 24,* 235–248.

Selye, H. (1956). *The stress of life.* New York: McGraw-Hill.

Senchak, M., Leonard, K., & Greene, B. (1998). Alcohol use among college students as a function of their typical social drinking context. *Psychology of Addictive Behaviors, 12,* 62–70.

Sensky, T., Turkington, D., Kingdon, D., Scott, J. L., Scott, J., Siddle, R., O'Carroll, M., & Barnes, T. R. E. (2000). A randomized controlled trial of cognitive-behavioral therapy for persistent symptoms in schizophrenia resistant to medication. *Archives of General Psychiatry, 57,* 165–172.

Sepkowitz, K., (2006). One disease, two epidemics—AIDS at 25. *New England Journal of Medicine, 354,* 2411–2414.

Serdula, M. K., Collins, M. E., Williamson, D. F., Anda, R. F., Pamuk, E. P., & Byers, T. E. (1993). Weight control practices of U.S. adolescents and adults. *Annals of Internal Medicine, 119,* 667–671.

Serido, J., Almeida, D., & Wethington, E. (2004). Chronic stressors and daily hassles: Unique and interactive relationships with psychological distress. *Journal of Health and Social Behavior, 45,* 17–33.

Serpell R., & Hatano, G. (1997). Education, schooling, and literacy. In J. Berry, P. Dasen, & T. Sarswthi (Eds.), *Handbook of cross-cultural psychology* (Vol. 2). Boston, MA: Allyn & Bacon.

Sexton, T., & Alexander, J. (2000, December). Functional family therapy. *Juvenile Justice Bulletin (Family Strengthening Series),* 1–8.

Shackelford, T., Schmitt, T., & Buss, D. (2005). Universal dimensions of human mate preferences. *Personality and Individual Differences, 39,* 447–458.

Shaffer, D., Gould, M. S., Fisher, P., Trautman, P., Moreau, D., Kleinman, M., & Flory, M. (1996). Psychiatric diagnosis in child and adolescent suicide. *Archives of General Psychiatry, 53,* 339–348.

Shaffer, M., Harrison, D., Gregersen, H., Black, J., & Ferzandi, L. (2006). You can take it with you: Individual differences and expatriate effectiveness. *Journal of Applied Psychology, 91,* 109–125.

Sharma, A., Dorman, M., & Kral, A. (2005). The influence of a sensitive period on central auditory development of children with unilateral and bilateral cochlear implantation. *Hearing Research, 203,* 134–143.

Sharma, A., Dorman, M., & Spahr, T. (2002). A sensitive period for the development of the central auditory system in children with cochlear implants. *Ear and Hearing, 23,* 532–539.

Sharpe, D., Hermsen, J., & Billings, J. (2002). Gender differences in use of alternative full-time work arrangements by married workers. *Family & Consumer Sciences Research Journal, 31,* 78–111.

Sharpe, P. (2002). Preparing for primary school in Singapore: Aspects of adjustment to the more formal demands of the primary one mathematics syllabus. *Early Child Development & Care, 172,* 329–335.

Shaunessy, E., Karnes, F., & Cobb, Y. (2004). Assessing potentially gifted students from lower socioeconomic status with nonverbal measures of intelligence. *Perceptual & Motor Skills, 98,* 1129–1138.

Shaw, J. I., & Steers, W. N. (2001). Gathering information to form an impression: Attribute categories and information valence. *Current Research in Social Psychology, 6,* 1–21.

Shaw, J. S., III. (1996). Increases in eyewitness confidence resulting from postevent questioning. *Journal of Experimental Psychology: Applied, 2,* 126–146.

Shaw, V. N., Hser, Y.-I., Anglin, M. D., & Boyle, K. (1999). Sequences of powder cocaine and crack use among arrestees in Los Angeles County. *American Journal of Drug and Alcohol Abuse, 25,* 47–66.

Shears, J., Robinson, J., & Emde, R. (2002). Fathering relationships and their associations with juvenile delinquency. *Infant Mental Health Journal, 23,* 79–87.

Shelton, J., & Richeson, J. (2005). Intergroup contact and pluralistic ignorance. *Journal of Personalty & Social Psychology, 88,* 91–107.

Shepperd, J. (2001). The desire to help and behavior in social dilemmas: Exploring responses to catastrophes. *Group Dynamics, 5,* 304–314.

Sher, A. E., Schechtman, K. B., & Piccirillo, J. F. (1996). The efficacy of surgical modifications of the upper airway in adults with obstructive sleep apnea syndrome. *Sleep, 19,* 156–177.

Sher, L. (2004). Type D personality, cortisol and cardiac disease. *Australian and New Zealand Journal of Psychiatry, 38,* 652–653.

Sherbourne, C. D., Wells, K. B., & Judd, L. L. (1996). Functioning and well-being of patients with panic disorder. *American Journal of Psychiatry, 153,* 213–218.

Sherer, R. (2006). Drug abuse hitting middle-aged more than Gen-Xers. *Psychiatric Times, 23.* Retrieved May 15, 2006 from http://www.psychiatrictimes.com/article/showArticle.jhtml?articleId=185303195.

Sherif, M. (1956). Experiments in group conflict. *Scientific American, 195,* 53–58.

Sherif, M. (1958). Superordinate goals in the reduction of intergroup conflict. *American Journal of Sociology, 63,* 349–358.

Sherif, M., & Sherif, C. W. (1967). The Robbers' Cave study. In J. F. Perez, R. C. Sprinthall, G. S. Grosser, & P. J. Anastasiou, *General psychology: Selected readings* (pp. 411–421). Princeton, NJ: D. Van Nostrand.

Shiffrin, R., (1999). Thirty years of memory. In C. Izawa (Ed.), *On human memory: Evolution, progress, and reflections on the 30th anniversary of the Atkinson-Shiffrin model* (pp. 17–33). Hillsdale, NJ: Lawrence Erlbaum Associates.

Shimamura, A. P., Berry, J. M., Mangela, J. A., Rusting, C. L., & Jurica, P. J. (1995). Memory and cognitive abilities in university professors: Evidence for successful aging. *Psychological Science, 6,* 271–277.

Shinar, D., Tractinsky, N., & Compton, R. (2005). Effects of practice, age, and task demands, on interference from a phone task while driving. *Accident Analysis & Prevention, 37,* 315–326.

Shiner, R. (2000). Linking childhood personality with adaptation: Evidence for continuity and change across time into late adolescence. *Journal of Personality and Social Psychology, 78,* 310–325.

Shneidman, E. (1989). The Indian summer of life: A preliminary study of septuagenarians. *American Psychologist, 44,* 684–694.

Shneidman, E. S. (1994). Clues to suicide, reconsidered. *Suicide and Life-Threatening Behavior, 24,* 395–397.

Shu, H., Anderson, R., & Wu, N. (2000). Phonetic awareness: Knowledge of orthography-phonology relationships in the character acquisition of Chinese children. *Journal of Educational Psychology, 92,* 56–62.

Shumaker, S., Legault, C., Rapp, S., Thal, L., Wallace, R., Ockene, J., Hendrix, S., Jones, B., Assaf, A., Jackson, R., Kotchen, J., Wassertheil-Smoller, S., & Wactawski-Wende, J. (2003). Estrogen plus progestin and the incidence of dementia and mild cognitive impairment in postmenopausal women: The Women's Health Initiative Memory Study: A randomized controlled trial. *Journal of the American Medical Association (JAMA), 289,* 2651–2662.

Shupe, E., Cortina, L., Ramos, A., Fitzgerald, L., & Salisbury, J. (2002). The incidence and outcomes of sexual harassment among Hispanic and non-Hispanic white women: A comparison across levels of cultural affiliation. *Psychology of Women Quarterly, 26,* 298–308.

Sienaert, P., Dierick, M., Degraeve, G., & Peuskens, J. (2006). Electroconvulsive therapy in Belgium: A nationwide survey on the practice of electroconvulsive therapy. *Journal of Affective Disorders, 90,* 67–71.

Sigman, M., & McGovern, C. (2005). Improvement in cognitive and language skills from preschool to adolescence in autism. *Journal of Autism & Developmental Disorders, 35,* 15–23.

Silva, C. E., & Kirsch, I. (1992). Interpretive sets, expectancy, fantasy proneness, and dissociation as predictors of hypnotic response. *Journal of Personality and Social Psychology, 63,* 847–856.

Simon, H. (1956). Rational choice and the structure of the environment. *Psychological Review, 63,* 129–138.

Simons, D. & Chabris, C. (1999). Gorillas in our midst: Sustained inattentional blindness for dynamic events. *Perception, 28,* 1059–1074.

Simons, D., & Rensink, R. (2005). Change blindness: Past, present, and future. *Trends in Cognitive Sciences, 9,* 16–20.

Simons, D., Wurtele, S., & Heil, P. (2002). Childhood victimization and lack of empathy as predictors of sexual offending against women and children. *Journal of Interpersonal Violence, 17,* 1291–1307.

Simons, J., & Carey, K. (2002). Risk and vulnerability for marijuana use problems. *Psychology of Addictive Behaviors, 16,* 72–75.

Simpkins, S., Davis-Kean, P., & Eccles, J. (2006). Math and science motivation: A longitudinal examination of the links between choices and beliefs. *Developmental Psychology, 42,* 70–83.

Singer, M. I., Miller, D. B., Guo, S., Flannery, D. J., Frierson, T., & Slovak, K. (1999). Contributors to violent behavior among elementary and middle school children. *Pediatrics, 104*(Pt. 1), 878–884.

Singh, B. (1991). Teaching methods for reducing prejudice and enhancing academic achievement for all children. *Educational Studies, 17,* 157–171.

Singh, D. (1995b). Female health, attractiveness, and desirability for relationships: Role of breast asymmetry and waist-hip ratio. *Ethology and Sociobiology, 16,* 445–481.

Singh, I. (2004). Doing their jobs: Mothering with Ritalin in a culture of mother-blame. *Social Science & Medicine, 59,* 1193–1205.

Singh-Manoux, A., Marmot, M., & Adler, N. (2005). Does subjective social status predict health and change in health status better than objective status? *Psychosomatic Medicine, 67,* 855–861.

Sivacek, J., & Crano, W. D. (1982). Vested interest as a moderator of attitude-behavior consistency. *Journal of Personality and Social Psychology, 43,* 210–221.

Skinner, B. F. (1953). *Science and human behavior.* New York: Macmillan.

Skrabalo, A. (2000). Negative symptoms in schizophrenia(s): The conceptual basis. *Harvard Brain, 7,* 7–10.

Sluzki, C. (2004). House taken over by ghosts: Culture, migration, and the developmental cycle of a Moroccan family invaded by hallucination. *Families, Systems, & Health, 22,* 321–337.

Small, G. (2005). *Effects of a 14-day healthy aging lifestyle program on brain function.* Paper presented at the 44th Annual Meeting of the American College of Neuropsychopharmacology. December 11–15, 2005. Waikoloa, Hawaii.

Smith, B., Elliott, A., Chambers, W., Smith, W., Hannaford, P., & Penny, K. (2001). The impact of chronic pain in the community. *Family Practice, 18,* 292–299.

Smith, C. (1995). Sleep states and memory processes. *Behavioural Brain Research, 69,* 137–145.

Smith, M. L., Glass, G. V., & Miller, T. I. (1980). *The benefits of psychotherapy.* Baltimore, MD: Johns Hopkins University Press.

Smith, N., Young, A., & Lee, C. (2004). Optimism, health-related hardiness and well-being among older Australian women. *Journal of Health Psychology, 9,* 741–752.

Smith, P. K. (1979). The ontogeny of fear in children. In W. Sluckin (Ed.), *Fears in animals and man* (pp. 164–168). London: Von Nostrand Reinhold.

Smith, S. M., Glenberg, A., & Bjork, R. A. (1978). Environmental context and human memory. *Memory & Cognition, 6,* 342–353.

Smith, T., & Ruiz, J. (2002). Psychosocial influences on the development and course of coronary heart disease: Current status and implications for research and practice. *Journal of Consulting and Clinical Psychology, 70 ,* 548–568.

Smolar, A. (1999). Bridging the gap: Technical aspects of the analysis of an Asian immigrant. *Journal of Clinical Psychoanalysis, 8,* 567–594.

Snarey, J. R. (1985). Cross-cultural universality of social-moral development: A critical review of Kohlbergian research. *Psychological Bulletin, 97,* 202–232.

Snarey, J. R. (1995). In communitarian voice: The sociological expansion of Kohlbergian theory, research, and practice. In W. M. Kurtines & J. L. Gerwirtz (Eds.), *Moral development: An introduction* (pp. 109–134). Boston: Allyn & Bacon.

Snowden, J. S., Griffiths, H. L., & Neary, D. (1996). Semantic-episodic memory interactions in semantic dementia: Implications for retrograde memory function. *Cognitive Neuropsychology, 13,* 1101–1137.

Snyder, A., Bahramali, H., Hawker, T., & Mitchell, D. (2006). Savant-like numerosity skills revealed in normal people by magnetic pulses. *Perception, 35,* 837-845.

Snyder, D., Castellani, A., & Whisman, M. (2006). Current status and future directions in couple therapy. *Annual Review of Psychology, 57,* 317–344.

Sobin, C., & Sackeim, H. A. (1997). Psychomotor symptoms of depression. *American Journal of Psychiatry, 154,* 4–17.

Society for Industrial and Organizational Psychology, Inc. (SIOP). (2002). An instructor's guide for introducing industrial-organizational psychology. Retrieved June 10, 2003, from http://www.siop.org

Society for Personality and Social Psychology. (2006). *What is a personality/social psychologist?* Retrieved July 26, 2006, from http://www.spsp.org/what.htm

Söderfeldt, B., Rönnberg, J., & Risberg, J. (1994). Regional cerebral blood flow in sign language users. *Brain and Language, 46,* 59–68.

Sokolov, E. N. (2000). Perception and the conditioning reflex: Vector encoding. *International Journal of Psychophysiology, 35,* 197–217.

Solano, L., Donati, V., Pecci, F., Perischetti, S., & Colaci, A. (2003). Postoperative course after papilloma resection: Effects of written disclosure of the experience in subjects with different alexithymia levels. *Psychosomatic Medicine, 65,* 477–484.

Soler, H., Vinayak, P., & Quadagno, D. (2000). Biosocial aspects of domestic violence. *Psychoneuroendocrinology, 25,* 721–739.

Solms, M. (2000). Dreaming and REM sleep are controlled by different brain mechanisms. *Behavioral and Brain Sciences, 23*(6).

Solso, R. (1991). *Cognitive psychology* (3rd ed.). Boston: Allyn & Bacon.

Spangler, D. L., Simons, A. D., Monroe, S. M., & Thase, M. E. (1996). Gender differences in cognitive diathesis-stress domain match: Implications for differential pathways to depression. *Journal of Abnormal Psychology, 105,* 653–657.

Spanos, N. P. (1986). Hypnotic behavior: A social-psychological interpretation of amnesia, analgesia, and "trance logic." *Behavioral and Brain Sciences, 9,* 499–502.

Spanos, N. P. (1991). A sociocognitive approach to hypnosis. In S. J. Lynn & J. W. Rhue (Eds.), *Theories of hypnosis: Current models and perspectives* (pp. 324–361). New York: Guilford.

Spanos, N. P. (1994). Multiple identity enactments and multiple personality disorder: A sociocognitive perspective. *Psychological Bulletin, 116,* 143–165.

Spearman, C. (1927). *The abilities of man.* New York: Macmillan.

Spence, J., & Buckner, C. (1995). Masculinity and femininity: Defining the undefinable. In N. P. Kalbfleisch & M. Cody (Eds.), *Gender, power, and communication in human relationships.* Hillsdale, NJ: Lawrence Erlbaum Associates.

Spence, J., Helmreich, R., & Stapp, J. (1974). The Personal Attributes Questionnaire: A measure of sex role stereotypes and masculinity-femininity. *JSAS, Catalog of Selected Documents in Psychology, 4,* 43–44.

Spencer, R., Zelaznik, H., Diedrichsen, J., & Ivry, R. (2003). Disrupted timing of discontinuous but not continuous movements by cerebellar lesions. *Science, 300,* 1437–1439.

Sperling, G. (1960). The information available in brief visual presentations. *Psychological Monographs: General and Applied 74* (Whole No. 498), 1–29.

Sperry, R. W. (1964). The great cerebral commissure. *Scientific American, 210,* 42–52.

Sperry, R. W. (1968). Hemisphere deconnection and unity in conscious experience. *American Psychologist, 23,* 723–733.

Spiers, H., Maguire, E., & Burgess, N. (2001). Hippocampal amnesia. *Neurocase, 7,* 357–382.

Spitzer, M. W., & Semple, M. N. (1991). Interaural phase coding in auditory midbrain: Influence of dynamic stimulus features. *Science, 254,* 721–724.

Spooner, A., & Kellogg, W. N. (1947). The backward conditioning curve. *American Journal of Psychology, 60,* 321–334.

Sporer, S. L., Penrod, S., Read, D., & Cutler, B. (1995). Choosing, confidence, and accuracy: A meta-analysis of the confidence-accuracy relation in eyewitness identification studies. *Psychological Bulletin, 118,* 315–327.

Spreen, O., Risser, A., & Edgell, D. (1995). *Developmental Neuropsychology.* New York: Oxford University Press.

Squire, L. R. (1992). Memory and the hippocampus: A synthesis from findings with rats, monkeys, and humans. *Psychological Review, 99,* 195–231.

Squire, L. R., Knowlton, B., & Musen, G. (1993). The structure and organization of memory. *Annual Review of Psychology, 44,* 453–495.

Stafford, J., & Lynn, S. (2002). Cultural scripts, memories of childhood abuse, and multiple identities: A study of role-played enactments. *International Journal of Clinical & Experimental Hypnosis, 50,* 67–85.

Stattin, H., & Magnusson, D. (1990). *Pubertal maturation in female development.* Hillsdale, NJ: Erlbaum.

Stea, R. A., & Apkarian, A. V. (1992). Pain and somatosensory activation. *Trends in Neurosciences, 15,* 250–251.

Steblay, N. M. (1992). A meta-analytic review of the weapon focus effect. *Law and Human Behavior, 16,* 413–424.

Steele, C., & Aronson, J. (1995). Stereotype threat and the intellectual test performance of African Americans. *Journal of Personality & Social Psychology, 69,* 797–811.

Steeves, R. (2002). The rhythms of bereavement. *Family & Community Health, 25,* 1–10.

Steffens, A. B., Scheurink, A. J., & Luiten, P. G. (1988). Hypothalamic food intake regulating areas are involved in the homeostasis of blood glucose and plasma FFA levels. *Physiology and Behavior, 44,* 581–589.

Steffensen, M., & Calker, L. (1982). Intercultural misunderstandings about health care: Recall of descriptions of illness and treatments. *Social Science and Medicine, 16,* 1949–1954.

Stein, M. B., & Kean, Y. M. (2000). Disability and quality of life in social phobia: Epidemiologic findings. *American Journal of Psychiatry, 157,* 1606–1613.

Stein, M. B., Walker, J. R., & Forde, D. R. (1996). Public-speaking fears in a community sample: Prevalence, impact on functioning, and diagnostic classification. *Archives of General Psychiatry, 53,* 169–174.

Stein-Behrens, B., Mattson, M. P., Chang, I., Yeh, M., & Sapolsky, R. (1994). Stress exacerbates neuron loss and cytoskeletal pathology in the hippocampus. *Journal of Neuroscience, 14,* 5373–5380.

Steinberg, K. (2000). Risks associated with genetic testing: Health insurance discrimination or simply business as usual? *Journal of the American Medical Women's Association, 55,* 241–242.

Steinberg, L. (1992). Ethnic differences in adolescent achievement: An ecological perspective. *American Psychologist, 47,* 723–729.

Steinberg, L., & Dornbusch, S. (1991). Negative correlates of part-time employment during adolescence: Replication and elaboration. *Developmental Psychology, 27,* 304–313.

Steinberg, L., Blatt-Eisengart, I., & Cauffman, E. (2006). Patterns of competence and adjustment among adolescents from authoritative, authoritarian, indulgent, and neglectful homes: A replication in a sample of serious juvenile offenders. *Journal of Research on Adolescence, 16*, 47–58.

Steinberg, L., Elman, J. D., & Mounts, N. S. (1989). Authoritative parenting, psychosocial maturity, and academic success among adolescents. *Child Development, 60*, 1424–1436.

Steinberg, L., Lamborn, S. D., Darling, N., Mounts, N. S., & Dornbusch, S. M. (1994). Over-time changes in adjustment and competence among adolescents from authoritative, authoritarian, indulgent, and neglectful families. *Child Development, 65*, 754–770.

Stephan, K. M., Fink, G. R., Passingham, R. E., Silbersweig, D., Ceballos-Baumann, A. O., Frith, C. D., & Frackowiak, R. S. J. (1995). Functional anatomy of the mental representation of upper extremity movements in healthy subjects. *Journal of Neurophysiology, 73*, 373–386.

Stephenson, M. T., & Witte, K. (1998). Fear, threat, and perceptions of efficiency from frightening skin cancer messages. *Public Health Review, 26*, 147–174.

Steptoe, A. (2000). Stress, social support and cardiovascular activity over the working day. *International Journal of Psychophysiology, 37*, 299–308.

Steriade, M. (1996). Arousal: Revisiting the reticular activating system. *Science, 272*, 225–226.

Stern, W. (1914). *The psychological methods of testing intelligence.* Baltimore: Warwick and York.

Sternberg, R. (2003a). Our research program validating the triarchic theory of successful intelligence: Reply to Gottfredson. *Intelligence, 31*, 2003, 399–413.

Sternberg, R. (2003b). Issues in the theory and measurement of successful intelligence: A reply to Brody. *Intelligence, 31*, 331–337.

Sternberg, R., Castejon, J., Prieto, M., Hautamacki, J., & Grigorenko, E. (2001). Confirmatory factor analysis of the Sternberg Triarchic Abilities Test in three international samples: An empirical test of the triarchic theory of intelligence. *European Journal of Psychological Assessment, 17*, 1–16.

Sternberg, R. J. (1985a). *Beyond IQ: A triarchic theory of human intelligence.* New York: Cambridge University Press.

Sternberg, R. J. (1986a). *Intelligence applied: Understanding and increasing your intellectual skills.* San Diego: Harcourt Brace Jovanovich.

Sternberg, R. J. (1986b). A triangular theory of love. *Psychological Review, 93*, 119–135.

Sternberg, R. J. (1987). Liking versus loving: A comparative evaluation of theories. *Psychological Bulletin, 102*, 331–345.

Sternberg, R. J. (2000). The holey grail of general intelligence. *Science, 289*, 399–401.

Sternberg, R. J., Wagner, R. K., Williams, W. M., & Horvath, J. A. (1995). Testing common sense. *American Psychologist, 50*, 912–927.

Stetler, C., Chen, E., & Miller, G. (2006). Written disclosure of experiences with racial discrimination and antibody response to an influenza vaccine. *International Journal of Behavioral Medicine, 13*, 60–68.

Stevens, M., Golombok, S., & Beveridge, M. (2002). Does father absence influence children's gender development? Findings from a general population study of preschool children. *Parenting: Science & Practice, 2*, 47–60.

Stevenson, H. W. (1992). Learning from Asian schools. *Scientific American, 267*, 70–76.

Stevenson, H. W., Chen, C., & Lee, S. Y. (1993). Mathematics achievement of Chinese, Japanese, and American children: Ten years later. *Science, 259*, 53–58.

Stevenson, H. W., Lee, S. Y., & Stigler, J. W. (1986). Mathematics achievement of Chinese, Japanese, and American children. *Science, 231*, 693–699.

Stewart, G., Fulmer, I., & Barrick, M. (2005). An exploration of member roles as a multilevel linking mechanism for individual traits and team outcomes. *Personnel Psychology, 58*, 343–365.

Stewart, V. M. (1973). Tests of the "carpentered world" hypothesis by race and environment in America and Zambia. *International Journal of Psychology, 8*, 83–94.

Stigler, J., & Stevenson, H. (1991). How Asian teachers polish each lesson to perfection. *American Educator*, 12–20, 43–47.

Still, C. (2001). Health benefits of modest weight loss. Retrieved January 29, 2003, from http://abcnews.go.com/sections/living/Healthology/weightloss_benefits011221.html

Stilwell, N., Wallick, M., Thal, S., & Burleson, J. (2000). Myers-Briggs type and medical specialty choice: A new look at an old question. *Teaching & Learning in Medicine, 12*, 14–20.

Stockhorst, U., Gritzmann, E., Klopp, K., Schottenfeld-Naor, Y., Hübinger, A., Berresheim, H., Stingrüber, H., & Gries, F. (1999). Classical conditioning of insulin effects in healthy humans. *Psychosomatic Medicine, 61*, 424–435.

Stone, K., Karem, K., Sternberg, M., McQuillan, G., Poon, A., Unger, E., & Reeves, W. (2002). Seroprevalence of human papillomavirus type 16 infection in the United States. *Journal of Infectious Diseases, 186*, 1396–1402.

Stout, M. (2005). *The sociopath next door: The ruthless versus the rest of us.* New York: Broadway Books.

Stovall, K. C., & Dozier, M. (2000). The development of attachment in new relationships: Single subject analyses for 10 foster infants. *Developmental Psychopathology, 12*, 2133–2156.

Strack, F., Martin, L. L., & Stepper, S. (1988). Inhibiting and facilitating conditions of facial expressions: A nonobtrusive test of the facial feedback hypothesis. *Journal of Personality and Social Psychology, 54*, 768–777.

Strawbridge, W. J., Cohen, R. D., Shema, S. J., & Kaplan, G. A. (1997). Frequent attendance at religious services and mortality over 28 years. *American Journal of Public Health, 87*, 957–961.

Strayer, D., & Drews, F. (2004). Profiles in driver distraction: Effects of cell phone conversations on younger and older drivers. *Human Factors, 46*, 640–649.

Strickland, B. R. (1995). Research on sexual orientation and human development: A commentary. *Developmental Psychology, 31*, 137–140.

Stroebe, M., & Schut, H. (1999). The dual process model of coping with bereavement: Rationale and description. *Death Studies, 23*, 197–224.

Strohmetz, D., Rind, B., Fisher, R., & Lynn, M. (2002). *Journal of Applied Social Psychology, 32*, 300–309.

Stromeyer, C. F., III. (1970, November). Eidetikers. *Psychology Today*, pp. 76–80.

Stubbs, P. (2000). *Mental health care online.*

Styne, D., & Glaser, N. (1998). Endocrine disorders. In R. Behrman & R. Kliegman (Eds.), *Nelson essentials of pediatrics* (3rd Ed., pp. 647–693). Philadelphia: W. B. Saunders.

Suarez, M. G. (1983). Implications of Spanish-English bilingualism in the TAT stories. Unpublished doctoral dissertation, University of Connecticut.

Sugita, M., & Shiba, Y. (2005). Genetic tracing shows segregation of taste neuronal circuitries for bitter and sweet. *Science, 309,* 781–785.

Sullivan, A., Maerz, J., & Madison, D. (2002). Anti-predator response of red-backed salamanders (Plethodon cinereus) to chemical cues from garter snakes (Thamnophis sirtalis): Laboratory and field experiments. *Behavioral Ecology & Sociobiology, 51,* 227–233.

Sullivan, A. D., Hedberg, K., & Fleming, D. W. (2000). Legalized physician-assisted suicide in Oregon—The second year. *New England Journal of Medicine, 342,* 598–604.

Sullivan, E., Fama, R., Rosenbloom, M., & Pfefferbaum, A. (2002). A profile of neuropsychological deficits in alcoholic women. *Neuropsychology, 16,* 74–83.

Sullivan, M. J. L., Bishop, S. R., & Pivik, J. (1995). The pain catastrophizing scale: Development and validation. *Psychological Assessment, 7,* 524–532.

Summerfeldt, L., Kloosterman, P., Antony, M., & Parker, J. (2006). Emotional intelligence, and interpersonal adjustment. *Journal of Psychopathology and Behavioral Assessment, 28,* 57–68.

Super, C. W. (1981). Behavioral development in infancy. In R. H. Munroe, R. L. Munroe, & B. B. Whiting (Eds.), *Handbook of cross-cultural human development* (pp. 181–269). Chicago: Garland.

Super, D. (1971). A theory of vocational development. N. H. J. Peters & J. C. Hansen (Eds.), *Vocational guidance and career development* (pp. 111–122). New York: MacMillan.

Super, D. (1986). Life career roles: Self-realization in work and leisure. In D. T. H. & Associates (Eds.), *Career development in organizations* (pp. 95–119). San Francisco: Jossey-Bass.

"Survey: Four in 10 American adults play video games." (2006, May 9). Retrieved May 12, 2006 from http://www.foxnews.com.

Sussman, S., & Dent, C. W. (2000). One-year prospective prediction of drug use from stress-related variables. *Substance Use & Misuse, 35,* 717–735.

Sutherland, T. (2002, December 3). Remember when people were not so conscious of their weight?—about 50 years ago! *Senior Journal* [Online version]. Retrieved November 20, 2003, from http://www.seniorjournal.com/NEWS/Fitness/ 2-12-03GallupLoseWeight.htm

Swaffer, T., Hollin, C., Beech, A., Beckett, R., & Fisher, D. (2000). An exploration of child sexual abusers' sexual fantasies before and after treatment. *Sexual Abuse: A Journal of Research and Treatment, 2,* 61–68.

Swain, I. U., Zelazo, P. R., & Clifton, R. K. (1993). Newborn infants' memory for speech sounds retained over 24 hours. *Developmental Psychology, 29,* 312–323.

Swan, G., & Carmelli, D. (2002). Impaired olfaction predicts cognitive decline in nondemented older adults. *Neuroepidemiology, 21,* 58–67.

Swanson, L. W. (1995). Mapping the human brain: past, present, and future. *Trends in Neurosciences, 18,* 471–474.

Swanson, N. G. (2000). Working women and stress. *Journal of the American Medical Womens Association, 55,* 276–279.

Sweatt, J. D., & Kandel, E. R. (1989). Persistent and transcriptionally dependent increase in protein phosphorylation in long-term facilitation of Aplysia sensory neurons. *Nature, 339,* 51–54.

Sweller, J., & Levine, M. (1982). Effects of goal specificity on means-end analysis and learning. *Journal of Experimental Psychology: Learning, Memory, and Cognition, 8,* 463–474.

Symister, P., & Friend, R. (2003). The influence of social support and problematic support on optimism and depression in chronic illness: A prospective study evaluating self-esteem as a mediator. *Health Psychology, 22,* 123–129.

Szewczyk-Sokolowski, M., Bost, K., & Wainwright, A. (2005). Attachment, temperament, and preschool children's peer acceptance. *Social Development, 14,* 379–397.

Takahashi, H., Umeda, N., Tsutsumi, Y., Fukumura, R., Ohkaze, H., Sujino, M., van der Horst, G., Yasui, A., Inouye, S., Fujimori, A., Ohhata, T., Araki, R., & Abe, M. (2003). Mouse desamethasone-induced RAS protein 1 gene is expressed in a circadian rhythmic manner in the suprachiasmatic nucleus. *Molecular Brain Research, 110,* 1–6.

Takahashi, S., Matsuura, M., Tanabe, E., Yara, K., Nonaka, K., Fukura, Y., Kikuchi, M., & Kojima, T. (2000). Age at onset of schizophrenia: Gender differences and influence of temporal socioeconomic change. *Psychiatry and Clinical Neurosciences, 54,* 153–156.

Takanishi, R. (1993). The opportunities of adolescence—research, interventions, and policy: Introduction to the special issue. *American Psychologist, 48,* 85–87.

Takarangi, M., Garry, M., & Loftus, E. (2006). Dear diary, is plastic better than paper? I can't remember: Comment on Green, Rafaeli, Bolger, Shrout, & Reis (2006). *Psychological Methods, 11,* 119–122.

Tamir, L. (1982). *Men in their forties: The transition to middle age.* New York: Springer.

Tamminga, C. A. (1996, Winter). The new generation of antipsychotic drugs. *NARSAD Research Newsletter,* pp. 4–6.

Tamminga, C. A., & Conley, R. R. (1997). The application of neuroimaging techniques to drug development. *Journal of Clinical Psychiatry, 58*(10, Suppl.), 3–6.

Tamminga, C., & Vogel, M. (2005). Images in neuroscience: The cerebellum. *American Journal of Psychiatry, 162,* 1253.

Tanda, G., Pontieri, F. E., & Di Chiara, G. (1997). Cannabinoid and heroin activation of mesolimbic dopamine transmission by a common μ1 opioid receptor mechanism. *Science, 276,* 2048–2050.

Tanner, J. (1990). *Fetus into man: Physical growth from conception to maturity.* Cambridge, MA: Harvard University Press.

Tanner, J. M. (1990). *Fetus into man* (2nd ed.). Cambridge MA: Harvard University Press.

Tan-Niam, C., Wood, D., & O'Malley, C. (1998). A cross-cultural perspective on children's theories of mind and social interaction. *Early Child Development & Care, 144,* 55–67.

Tate, D., Paul, R., Flanigan, T., Tashima, K., Nash, J., Adair, C., Boland, R., & Cohen, R. (2003). The impact of apathy and depression on quality of life in patients infected with HIV. *AIDS Patient Care & STDs, 17,* 117–120.

Taub, G., Hayes, B., Cunningham, W., & Sivo, S. (2001). Relative roles of cognitive ability and practical intelligence in the prediction of success. *Psychological Reports, 88,* 931–942.

Tay, C., Ang, S., & Dyne, L. (2006). Personality, biographical characteristics, and job interview success: A longitudinal study of the mediating effects of interviewing self-efficacy and the moderating effects of internal locus of causality. *Journal of Applied Psychology, 91,* 446–454.

Taylor, C., & Luce, K. (2003). Computer- and Internet-based psychotherapy interventions. *Current Directions in Psychological Science, 12,* 18–22.

Taylor, S. E., & Repetti, R. L. (1997). Health psychology: What is an unhealthy environment and how does it get under the skin? *Annual Review of Psychology, 48,* 411–447.

Tchanturia, K., Serpell, L., Troop, N., & Treasure, J. (2001). Perceptual illusions in eating disorders: Rigid and fluctuating styles. *Journal of Behavior Therapy & Experimental Psychiatry, 32,* 107–115.

Teachman, J. (2003). Premarital sex, premarital cohabitation and the risk of subsequent marital dissolution among women. *Journal of Marriage and Family, 65,* 444-455.

Teasdale, T., & Owen, D. (2005). A long-term rise and recent decline in intelligence test performance: The Flynn Effect in reverse. *Personality and Individual Differences, 39,* 837–843.

Teitelbaum, P. (1957). Random and food-directed activity in hypeerphagic and normal rats. *Journal of Comparative and Physiological Psychology, 50,* 486–490.

Tellegen, A., Lykken, D. T., Bouchard, T. J., Jr., Wilcox, K. J., Segal, N. L., & Rich, S. (1988). Personality similarity in twins reared apart and together. *Journal of Personality and Social Psychology, 54,* 1031–1039.

Temmerman, M. (1994). Sexually transmitted diseases and reproductive health. *Sexually Transmitted Diseases, 21*(2, Suppl.), S55–S58.

Teng, E., Stefanacci, L., Squire, L. R., & Zola, S. M. (2000). Contrasting effects on discrimination learning after hippocampal lesions and conjoint hippocampal-caudate lesions in monkeys. *Journal of Neuroscience, 20,* 3853–3863.

Tennant, C. (2002). Life events, stress and depression: A review of the findings. *Australian & New Zealand Journal of Psychiatry, 36,* 173–182.

Tepper, B., & Ullrich, N. (2002). Influence of genetic taste sensitivity to 6-n-propylthiouracil (PROP), dietary restraint and disinhibition on body mass index in middle-aged women. *Physiology & Behavior, 75,* 305–312.

Tercyak, K., Johnson, S., Roberts, S., & Cruz, A. (2001). Psychological response to prenatal genetic counseling and amniocentesis. *Patient Education & Counseling, 43,* 73–84.

Terlecki, M., & Newcombe, N. (2005). How important is the digital divide? The relation of computer and videogame usage to gender differences in mental rotation ability. *Sex Roles, 53,* 433–441.

Terman, L. M. (1925). *Genetic studies of genius, Vol. 1: Mental and physical traits of a thousand gifted children.* Stanford, CA: Stanford University Press.

Terman, L. M., & Oden, M. H. (1947). *Genetic studies of genius, Vol. 4: The gifted child grows up.* Stanford, CA: Stanford University Press.

Terman, L. M., & Oden, M. H. (1959). *Genetic studies of genius, Vol. 5: The gifted group at mid-life.* Stanford, CA: Stanford University Press.

Terman, L., & Miles, C. (1936). *Sex and personality: Studies in masculinity and femininity.* New York: McGraw-Hill.

Termine, N. T., & Izard, C. E. (1988). Infants' responses to their mother's expressions of joy and sadness. *Developmental Psychology, 24,* 223–229.

Terracciano, A., & McCrae, R. (2006). "National character does not reflect mean personality traits levels in 49 cultures": Reply. *Science, 311,* 777–779.

Terrace, H. (1979, November). How Nim Chimpski changed my mind. *Psychology Today,* 65–76.

Terrace, H. S. (1981). A report to an academy. *Annals of the New York Academy of Sciences, 364,* 115–129.

Terrace, H. S. (1985). In the beginning was the "name." *American Psychologist, 40,* 1011–1028.

Terrace, H. S. (1986). *Nim: A chimpanzee who learned sign language.* New York: Columbia University Press.

Tham, K., Borell, L., & Gustavsson, A. (2000). The discovery of disability: A phenomenological study of unilateral neglect. *American Journal of Occupational Therapy, 54,* 398–406.

Thapar, A. K., & Thapar, A. (2003). Attention-deficit hyperactivity disorders. *British Journal of General Practice, 53,* 225–230.

Thapar, A., O'Donovan, M., & Owen, M. (2005). The genetics of attention deficit hyperactivity disorder. *Human Molecular Genetics, 14,* R275–R282.

Thase, M. E., Frank, E., Mallinger, A. G., Hammer, T., & Kupfer, D. J. (1992). Treatment of imipramine-resistant recurrent depression, III: Efficacy of monoamine oxidise inhibitors. *Journal of Clinical Psychiatry, 53*(1, Suppl.), 5–11.

Thase, M. E., & Kupfer, D. J. (1996). Recent developments in the pharmacotherapy of mood disorders. *Journal of Consulting and Clinical Psychology, 64,* 646–659.

Thase, M. E., Simons, A. D., Cahalane, J. F., & McGeary, J. (1991). Cognitive behavior therapy of endogenous depression: Part 1: An outpatient clinical replication series. *Behavior Therapy, 22,* 457–467.

Thaxton, L., & Myers, M. (2002). Sleep disturbances and their management in patients with brain injury. *Journal of Head Trauma Rehabilitation, 17,* 335–348.

The Economist. (2004, July 8.) Lie detection: Making windows in men's souls. Retrieved June 16, 2006 from http://www.economist.com/printedition/displayStory.cfm?Story_ID=2897134

Thirthalli, J., & Benegal, V. (2006). Psychosis among substance users. *Current Opinion in Psychiatry, 19,* 239–245.

Thomas, A., Chess, S., & Birch, H. G. (1970). The origin of personality. *Scientific American, 223,* 102–109.

Thomas, P., & Bracken, P. (2001). Vincent's bandage: The art of selling a drug for bipolar disorder. *British Medical Journal, 323,* 1434.

Thompson, B., Brough, P., & Schmidt, H. (2006). Supervisor and subordinate work-family values: Does similarity make a difference? *International Journal of Stress Management, 13,* 45–63.

Thompson, P., Vidal, C., Giedd, J., Gochman, P., Blumenthal, J., Nicolson, R., Toga, A., & Rapoport, J. (2001). Mapping adolescent brain change reveals dynamic wave of accelerated gray matter loss in very early-onset schizophrenia. *Proceedings of the National Academy of Sciences, 98,* 11650–11655.

Thompson, P., Dutton, R., Hayashi, K., Toga, A., Lopez, O., Aizenstein, H., & Becker, J. (2005). Thinning of the cerebral cortex visualized in HIV/AIDS reflects CD4+ T lymphocyte decline. *Proceedings of the National Academies of Science, 102,* 15647–15642.

Thorndike, E. (1898). Some experiments on animal intelligence. *Science, 7*(181), 818–824.

Thorndike, E. L. (1911/1970). *Animal intelligence: Experimental studies.* New York: Macmillan. (Original work published 1911).

Thornhill, R., & Gangestad, G. W. (1994). Human fluctuating asymmetry and sexual behavior. *Psychological Science, 5,* 297–302.

Thorpe, M., Pittenger, D., & Reed, B. (1999). Cheating the researcher: A study of the relation between personality measures and self-reported cheating. *College Student Journal, 33,* 49–59.

Thurstone, L. L. (1938). *Primary mental abilities.* Chicago: University of Chicago Press.

Tideman, E., Nilsson, A., Smith, G., & Stjernqvist, K. (2002). Longitudinal follow-up of children born preterm: The mother-child relationship in a 19-year perspective. *Journal of Reproductive & Infant Psychology, 20,* 43–56.

Tidey, J., O'Neill, S., & Higgins, S. (2002). Contingent monetary reinforcement of smoking reductions, with and without transferal nicotine, in outpatients with schizophrenia. *Experimental and Clinical Psychopharmacology, 10,* 241–247.

Tiedemann, J. (2000). Parents' gender stereotypes and teachers' beliefs as predictors of children's concept of their mathematical ability in elementary school. *Journal of Educational Psychology, 92,* 144–151.

Tiihonen, J., Isohanni, M., Räsänen, P., Koiranen, M., & Moring, J. (1997). Specific major mental disorders and criminality: A 26-year prospective study of the 1966 northern Finland birth cohort. *American Journal of Psychiatry, 154,* 840–845.

Timberlake, D., Rhee, S., Haberstick, B., Hopfer, C., Ehringer, M., Lessem, J., Smoken, A., & Hewitt, J. (2006). The moderating effects of religiosity on the genetic and environmental determinants of smoking initiation. *Nicotine & Tobacco Research, 8,* 123–133.

Tinkle, M. B. (1990). Genital human papillomavirus infection: A growing health risk. *Journal of Obstetric, Gynecologic, & Neonatal Nursing, 19,* 501–507.

Tjosvold, D., Coleman, P., & Sun, H. (2003). Effects of organizational values on leaders' use of informational power to affect performance in China. *Group Dynamics, 7,* 152–166.

Toastmasters International. (2003). Ten tips for successful public speaking. Retrieved November 25, 2003, from http://www.toastmasters.org/pdfs/top10.pdf

Todorov, A., & Bargh, J. (2002). Automatic sources of aggression. *Aggression & Violent Behavior, 7,* 53–68.

Tolman, E. C. (1932). *Purposive behavior in animals and men.* New York: Appleton-Century-Crofts.

Tolman, E. C., & Honzik, C. H. (1930). Introduction and removal of reward, and maze performance in rats. *University of California Publications in Psychology, 4,* 257–275.

Tomasello, M. (2000). The item-based nature of children's early syntactic development. *Trends in Cognitive Sciences, 4,* 156–163.

Tomkins, S. (1962). *Affect, imagery, and consciousness: The positive effects* (Vol. 1). New York: Springer.

Tomkins, S. (1963). *Affect, imagery, and consciousness: The negative effects* (Vol. 2). New York: Springer.

Toot, J., Dunphy, G., Turner, M., & Ely, D. (2004). The SHR Y-chromosome increases testosterone and aggression, but decreases serotonin as compared to the SKY Y-chromosome in the rat model. *Behavior Genetics, 34,* 515–524.

Tori, C., & Bilmes, M. (2002). Multiculturalism and psychoanalytic psychology: The validation of a defense mechanism's measure in an Asian population. *Psychoanalytic Psychology, 19,* 701–721.

Torrey, E., (1992). *Freudian fraud: The malignant effect of Freud's theory on American thought and culture.* New York: Harper Collins.

Tourangeau, R., Smith, T. W., & Rasinski, K. A. (1997). Motivation to report sensitive behaviors on surveys: Evidence from a bogus pipeline experiment. *Journal of Applied Social Psychology, 27,* 209–222.

Tracy, J., Monaco, C., McMichael, H., Tyson, K., Chambliss, C., Christensen, H., & Celenza, M. (1998). Information processing characteristics of explicit time estimation by patients with schizophrenia and normal controls. *Perceptual Motor Skills, 86,* 515–526.

Trautner, H., Gervai, J., & Nemeth, R. (2003). Appearance-reality distinction and development of gender constancy understanding in children. *International Journal of Behavioral Development, 27,* 275–283.

Trautner, H., Ruble, D., Cyphers, L., Kristen, B., Behrendt, R., & Hartmann, P. (2005). Rigidity and flexibility of gender stereotypes in childhood: Developmental or differential? *Infant and Child Development, 14,* 365–381.

Travis, J. (1996). Brains in space. *Science News, 149,* 28–29.

Trevisol-Bittencourt, P., & Troiano, A. (2000). Interictal personality syndrome in non-dominant temporal lobe epilepsy. *Arquivos de Neuro-Psiquitría, 58,* 548–555.

Triandis, H. C. (1994). *Culture and social behavior.* New York: McGraw-Hill.

Trijsburg, R., Perry, J., & Semeniuk, T. (2004). An empirical study of the differences in interventions between psychodynamic therapy and cognitive-behavioural therapy for recurrent major depression. *Canadian Journal of Psychoanalysis, 12,* 325–345.

Triplett, N. (1898). The dynamogenic factors in pacemaking and competition. *American Journal of Psychology, 9,* 507–533.

Trivedi, M. J. (1996). Functional neuroanatomy of obsessive-compulsive disorder. *Journal of Clinical Psychiatry, 57*(8, Suppl.), 26–36.

Troglauer, T., Hels, T., & Christens, P. (2006). Extent and variations in mobile phone use among drivers of heavy vehicles in Denmark. *Accident Analysis & Prevention, 38,* 105–111.

Troxel, W., Matthews, K., Bromberger, J., & Sutton-Tyrrell, K. (2003). Chronic stress burden, discrimination, and subclinical carotid artery disease in African American and Caucasian women. *Health Psychology, 22,* 300–309.

Trull, T., Stepp, S., & Durrett, C. (2003). Research on borderline personality disorder: An update. *Current Opinion in Psychiatry, 16,* 77–82.

Trzesniewski, K., Donnellan, M., & Robins, R. (2003). Stability of self-esteem across the life span. *Journal of Personality and Social Psychology, 84*, 205–220.

Tsai, J., Knutson, B., & Fung, H. (2006). Cultural variation in affect valuation. *Journal of Personality and Social Psychology, 90*, 288–307.

Tsai, S., Kuo, C., Chen, C., & Lee, H. (2002). Risk factors for completed suicide in bipolar disorder. *Journal of Clinical Psychiatry, 63*, 469–476.

Tsang, L., Harvey, C., Duncan, K., & Sommer, R. (2003). The effects of children, dual earner status, sex role traditionalism, and marital structure on marital happiness over time. *Journal of Family and Economic Issues, 24*, 5-26.

Tsang, W., & Hui-Chan, C. (2003). Effects of Tai Chi on joint proprioception and stability limits in elderly subjects. *Medicine & Science in Sports & Exercise, 35*, 1962–1971.

Tsao, D., Freiwald, W., Tootell, R., & Livingstone, M. (2006). A cortical region consisting entirely of face-selective cells. *Science, 311*, 670–674.

Tubbs, M. E., Boehne, D., & Dahl, J. G. (1993). Expectancy, valence, and motivational force functions in goal-setting research: An empirical test. *Journal of Applied Psychology, 78*, 361–373.

Tueth, M. J. (2000). Exposing financial exploitation of impaired elderly persons. *American Journal of Geriatric Psychiatry, 8*, 104–111.

Tulving, E. (1974). Cue-dependent forgetting. *American Scientist, 62*, 74–82.

Tulving, E. (1989). Remembering and knowing the past. *American Scientist, 77*, 361–367.

Tulving, E. (1995). Organization of memory: Quo vadis? In M. S. Gazzaniga (Ed.), *The cognitive neurosciences.* Cambridge, MA: MIT Press.

Tulving, E. (2002). Episodic memory: From mind to brain. *Annual Review of Psychology, 53*, 1–25.

Tulving, E., & Thompson, D. M. (1973). Encoding specificity and retrieval processes in episodic memory. *Psychological Review, 80*, 352–373.

Tuncer, A. M., & Yalcin, S. S. (2000). Multimedia and children in Turkey. *Turkish Journal of Pediatrics, 41*(Suppl.), 27–34.

Turner, C. F., Danella, R. D., & Rogers, S. M. (1995). Sexual behavior in the United States, 1930–1990: Trends and methodological problems. *Sexually Transmitted Diseases, 22*, 173–190.

Turner, D., Blackwell, A., Dowson, J., McLean, A., & Sahakian, B. (2005). Neurocognitive effects of methylphenidate in adult attention-deficit/hyperactivity disorder. *Psychopharmacology, 178*, 286–295.

Turner, J. C., Hogg, M. A., Oakes, P. J., Reicher, S. D., & Wetherell, M. S. (1987). *Rediscovering the social group: A self-categorization theory.* Oxford, England: Blackwell.

Tversky, A. (1972). Elimination by aspects: A theory of choice. *Psychological Review, 79*, 281–299.

Tweed, R., & Lehman, D. (2002). Learning considered within a cultural context: Confucian and Socratic approaches. *American Psychologist, 57*, 89–99.

Uchino, B. N., Cacioppo, J. T., & Kiecolt-Glaser, J. K. (1996). The relationship between social support and physiological processes: A review with emphasis on underlying mechanisms and implications for health. *Psychological Bulletin, 119*, 488–531.

Ueki, Y., Mima, T., Kotb, M., Sawada, H., Saiki, H., Ikeda, A., Begum, T., Reza, F., Nagamine, T., & Fukuyama, H. (2006). Altered plasticity of the human motor cortex in Parkinson's Disease. *Annals of Neurology, 59*, 60–71.

Umberson, D., Williams, K., Powers, D., Liu, H., & Needham, B. (2006). You make me sick: Marital quality and health over the life course. *Journal of Health and Social Behavior, 47*, 1–16.

Underwood, B. J. (1957). Interference and forgetting. *Psychological Review, 64*, 49–60.

Underwood, B. J. (1964). Forgetting. *Scientific American, 210*, 91–99.

University of Michigan Transportation Research Institute (UMTRI). (2003). Ready for the road: Software helps teens drive safely. *UMTRI Research Review, 34*, 1–2.

U.S. Food and Drug Administration (FDA). (2006, April 20). Interagency advisory regarding claims that smoked marijuana is a medicine. Retrieved May 15, 2006 from http://www.fda.gov/bbs/topics/NEWS/2006/NEW01362.html

U.S. Bureau of Labor Statistics. (2005). *Women in the labor force: a Databook.* Retrieved July 28, 2006, from http://www.bls.gov/cps/wlf-databook2005.htm

U.S. Census Bureau. (1994). *Statistical abstract of the United States 1994* (114th ed.). Washington, DC: U.S. Government Printing Office.

U.S. Census Bureau. (1997). *Statistical abstracts of the United States 1997* (117th ed.). Washington, DC: U.S. Government Printing Office.

U.S. Census Bureau. (1999). *Projections of the Resident Population by Age, Sex, Race, and Hispanic Origin: 1999 to 2100.* Retrieved July 30, 2003, from http://www.census.gov/population/projections/nation/detail/d2041_50.pdf

U.S. Census Bureau. (2000). Native resident population estimates of the United States by sex, race, and Hispanic origin. Population Estimates Program, Population Division. Retrieved from http://www.census.gov/populationestimates/nation/nativity/nbtab003.txt

U.S. Census Bureau. (2004). *Income 2003: Press release.* Retrieved July 5, 2006 from http://www.census.gov/Press-elease/www/releases/archives/income_wealth/002484.html

U.S. Census Bureau. (2004). *Educational attainment in the United States: 2003.* Retrieved June 15, 2006 from http://www.census.gov/prod/2004pubs/p20-550.pdf

U.S. Census Bureau. (2005). *Educational attainment: People 25 years old and over, by total money earnings in 2004.* Retrieved June 15, 2006 from http://pubdb3.census.gov/macro/032005/perinc/new03_001.htm

U.S. Census Bureau. (2005). *Living arrangements of children under 18 years old: 1960 to present.* Retrieved June 10, 2006 from http://www.census.gov/population/socdemo/hh-fam/ch1.pdf.

U. S. Census Bureau. (2006). *2005 American community survey.* Retrieved November 19, 2006 from http://www.census.gov/acs/www/index.html

U.S. Census. Bureau (2001). *Statistical abstract of the United States.* Washington, DC: U.S. Government Printing Office.

U.S. Department of Energy. (2006). *Human Genome Project information.* Retrieved September 21, 2006 from http://www.ornl.gov/sci/techresources/Human_Genome/home.shtml

U.S. Department of Health and Human Services. (2000). *Reducing tobacco use: A report of the Surgeon General—executive summary.* Atlanta: Department of Health and Human Services, Centers for Disease Control and Prevention, National Center for Chronic Disease Prevention and Health Promotion, Office on Smoking and Health.

U.S. Department of Health and Human Services. (2001). Ecstasy: Teens speak out [Online factsheet]. Retrieved October 22, 2003, from http://www.health.org/govpubs/prevalert/v4/8.aspx

U.S. Department of Health and Human Services. (2005). *Dietary guidelines for Americans 2005.* Retrieved July 7, 2006 from http://www.healthierus.gov/dietaryguidelines/

U.S. Food and Drug Administration (FDA). (2004, October 15). *Suicidality in children and adolescents being treated with antidepressant medication.* Retrieved May 12, 2005, from http://www.fda.gov/cder/drug/antidepressants/SSRIPHA200410.htm.

U.S. Food and Drug Administration (FDA). (2006). *Prozac patient information sheet.* Retrieved July 26, 2006 from http://www.fda.gov/cder/drug/InfoSheets/patient/fluoxetinePIS.htm

Usher, E., & Pajares, F. (2006). Sources of academic and self-regulatory efficacy beliefs of entering middle school students. *Contemporary Educational Psychology, 31,* 125–141.

Utsey, S., Chae, M., Brown, C., & Kelly, D. (2002). Effect of ethnic group membership on ethnic identity, race-related stress and quality of life. *Cultural Diversity & Ethnic Minority Psychology, 8,* 367–378.

Vaccarino, V., Abramson, J., Veledar, E., & Weintraub, W. (2002). Sex differences in hospital mortality after coronary artery bypass surgery: Evidence for a higher mortality in younger women. *Circulation, 105,* 1176.

Valkenburg, P., & Vroone, M. (2004). Developmental changes in infants' and toddlers' attention to television entertainment. *Communication Research, 31,* 288–311.

Valle, M., & Bozeman, D. (2002). Interrater agreement on employees' job performance: Review and directions. *Psychological Reports, 90,* 975–985.

Van Assema, P., Martens, M., Ruiter, A., & Brug, J. (2002). Framing of nutrition education messages in persuading consumers of the advantages of a healthy diet. *Journal of Human Nutrition & Dietetics, 14,* 435–442.

Van Boven, L., White, K., Kamada, A., & Gilovich, T. (2003). Intuitions about situational correction in self and others. *Journal of Personality & Social Psychology, 85,* 249–258.

Van Cauter, E. (2000). Slow-wave sleep and release of growth hormone. *Journal of the American Medical Association, 284,* 2717–2718.

van den Hout, M., & Merckelbach, H. (1991). Classical conditioning: Still going strong. *Behavioural Psychotherapy, 19,* 59–79.

Van der Elst, W., Van Boxtel, M., Van Breukelen, G., & Jolles, J. (2006). The Stroop color-word test: Influence of age, sex, and education; and normative data for a large sample across the adult age range. *Assessment, 13,* 62–79.

Van der Zee, K., Thijs, M., & Schakel, L. (2002). The relationship of emotional intelligence with academic intelligence and the Big Five. *European Journal of Personality, 16,* 103–125.

Van Eerde, W., & Thierry, H. (1996). Vroom's expectancy models and work-related criteria: A meta-analysis. *Journal of Applied Psychology, 81,* 575–586.

van Elst, L. T., Woermann, F. G., Lemieux, L., Thompson, P. J., & Trimble, M. R. (2000). Affective aggression in patients with temporal lobe epilepsy. *Brain, 123,* 234–243.

Van Groen, T., Kadish, I., & Wyss, J. (2002). The role of the laterodoral nucleus of the thalamus in spatial learning and memory in the rat. *Behavior and Brain Research, 136,* 329–337.

van IJzendoorn, M. (1995). Adult attachment representations, parental responsiveness, and infant attachment: A meta-analysis on the predictive validity of the Adult Attachment Interview. *Psychological Bulletin, 117,* 387–403.

Van Lancker, D. (1987, November). Old familiar voices. *Psychology Today,* pp. 12–13.

Van Lommel, S., Laenen, A., & d'Ydewalle, G. (2006). Foreign-grammar acquisition while watching subtitled television programmes. *British Journal of Educational Psychology, 76,* 243–258.

van Vianen, A., & Fischer, A. (2002). Illuminating the glass ceiling: The role of organizational culture preferences. *Journal of Occupational & Organizational Psychology, 75,* 315–337.

Vandell, D. L., & Mueller, E. C. (1980). Peer play and friendships during the first two years. In H. C. Foot, A. J. Chapman, & J. R. Smith (Eds.), *Friendship and social relations in children.* New York: Wiley.

Vander Meer, R., & Alonso, L. (2002). Queen primer pheromone affects conspecific fire ant (Solenopsis invicta) aggression. *Behavioral Ecology & Sociobiology, 51,* 122–130.

Vargha-Khadem, F., Gadian, D. G., Watkins, D. E., Connelly, A., Van Paesschen, W., & Mishkin, M. (1997). Differential effects of early hippocampal pathology on episodic and semantic memory. *Science, 277,* 376–380.

Vasterling, J., Duke, L., Brailey, K., Constans, J., Allain, A., & Sutker, P. (2002). Attention, learning, and memory performances and intellectual resources in Vietnam veterans: PTSD and no disorder comparisons. *Neuropsychology, 16,* 5–14.

Vetulani, J., & Nalepa, I. (2000). Antidepressants: Past, present and future. *European Journal of Pharmacology, 405,* 351–363.

Vickery, C., Berry, D., Dearth, C., Vagnini, V., Baser, R., Cragar, D., & Orey, S. (2004). Head injury and the ability to feign neuropsychological deficits. *Archives of Clinical Neuropsychology, 19,* 37–48.

Vieta, E. (2003). Atypical antipsychotics in the treatment of mood disorders. *Current Opinion in Psychiatry, 16,* 23–27.

Viljoen, J., Zapf, P., & Roesch, R. (2004). Diagnosis, current symptomatology, and the ability to stand trial. *Journal of Forensic Psychology Practice, 3*(4), 23–37.

Villani, S. (2001). Impact of media on children and adolescents: A 10-year review of the research. *Journal of the American Academy of Child & Adolescent Psychiatry, 40,* 392–401.

Villegas, A., Sharps, M., Satterthwaite, B., & Chisholm, S. (2005). Eyewitness memory for vehicles. *Forensic Examiner, 14*, 24–28.

Vincent, K. R. (1991). Black/white IQ differences: Does age make the difference? *Journal of Clinical Psychology, 47*, 266–270.

Vincent, K. R. (1993, Fall). On the perfectibility of the human species: Evidence using fixed reference groups. *TCA Journal*, pp. 60–63.

Vincent, M., & Pickering, M. R. (1988). Multiple personality disorder in childhood. *Canadian Journal of Psychiatry, 33*, 524–529.

Visser, P., & Mirabile, R. (2004). Attitudes in the social context: The impact of social network composition on individual-level attitude strength. *Journal of Personality & Social Psychology, 87*, 779–795.

Vitousek, K., & Manke, F. (1994). Personality variables and disorders in anorexia nervosa and bulimia nervosa. *Journal of Abnormal Psychology, 103*, 137–147.

Volicer, L., Harper, D., Manning, B., Goldstein, R., & Satlin, A. (2001). Sundowning and circadian rhythms in Alzheimer's disease. *American Journal of Psychiatry, 158*, 704–711.

Volis, C., Ashburn-Nardo, L., & Monteith, M. (2002). Evidence of prejudice-related conflict and associated affect beyond the college setting. *Group Processes & Intergroup Relations, 5*, 19–33.

Volkow, N. D., & Fowler, J. S. (2000). Addiction, a disease of compulsion and drive: Involvement of the orbitofrontal cortex. *Cerebral Cortex, 10*, 318–325.

Von Dras, D. D., & Siegler, I. C. (1997). Stability in extraversion and aspects of social support at midlife. *Journal of Personality and Social Psychology, 72*, 233–241.

Vos, P., Visser, A., Garssen, B., Diuvenvoorden, H., & de Haes, H. (2006). Effects of delayed psychosocial interventions versus early psychosocial interventions for women with early stage breast cancer. *Patient Education and Counseling, 60*, 212–219.

Votruba, S., Horvitz, M., & Schoeller, D. (2000). The role of exercise in the treatment of obesity. *Nutrition, 16*, 179–188.

Voyer, D., & Rodgers, M. (2002). Reliability of laterality effects in a dichotic listening task with nonverbal material. *Brain & Cognition, 48*, 602–606.

Vroomen, J., Driver, J., & deGelder, B. (2001). Is cross-modal integration of emotional expressions independent of attentional resources? *Cognitive, Affective & Behavioral Neuroscience, 1*, 382–387.

Vygotsky, L. S. (1936/1986). *Thought and language* (A. Kozulin, Trans.). Cambridge, MA: MIT Press. (Original work published 1936).

Wachs, T., Gurkas, P., & Kontos, S. (2004). Predictors of preschool children's compliance behavior in early childhood classroom settings. *Journal of Applied Developmental Psychology, 25*, 439–457.

Wacker, J., Chavanon, M., & Stemmler, G. (2006). Investigating the dopaminergic basis of extraversion in humans: A multilevel approach. *Journal of Personality and Social Psychology, 91*, 171–187.

Wadden, T. A. (1993). Treatment of obesity by moderate and severe caloric restriction: Results of clinical research trials. *Annals of Internal Medicine, 119*, 688–693.

Wade, T., & DiMaria, C. (2003). Weight halo effects: Individual differences in personality evaluations as a function of weight. *Sex Roles, 48*, 461–465.

Waid, M. (2005). The real truth about Superman: And the rest of us, too. In T. Morris & M. Morris (Eds.), *Superheroes and philosophy: Truth, justice, and the Socratic way* (pp. 3–10). Chicago: Open Court.

Waid, M., & Yu, L. (2002). *Superman: Birthright*. New York: DC Comics.

Wald, G. (1964). The receptors of human color vision. *Science, 145*, 1007–1017.

Wald, G., Brown, P. K., & Smith, P. H. (1954). Iodopsin. *Journal of General Physiology, 38*, 623–681.

Waldron, S., & Helm, F. (2004). Psychodynamic features of two cognitive-behaivoural and one psychodynamic treatment compared using the analytic process scales. *Canadian Journal of Psychoanalysis, 12*, 346–368,

Walitzer, K., & Demen, K. (2004). Alcohol-focused spouse involvement and behavioral couples therapy: Evaluation of enhancements to drinking reduction treatment for male problem drinkers. *Journal of Consulting & Clinical Psychology, 72*, 944–955.

Walker, D. (2000). Online therapy? Not yet. *CBS News*. New York: CBS.

Walker, E., Kestler, L., Bollini, A., & Hochman, K. (2004). Schizophrenia: Etiology and course. *Annual Review of Psychology, 55*, 401–430.

Walker, I., & Crogan, M. (1998). Academic performance, prejudice and the jigsaw classroom: New pieces to the puzzle. *Journal of Community & Applied Social Psychology, 8*, 381–393.

Walker, L. (1989). A longitudinal study of moral reasoning. *Child Development, 60*, 157–166.

Walker, M., & Stickgold, R. (2006). Sleep, memory, and plasticity. In S. Fiske, A. Kazdin, & D. Schacter (Eds.) *Annual Review of Psychology: 57*. (pp. 139–166).

Walker, M., Brakefield, T., Hobson, J., & Stickgold, R. (2003). Dissociable stages of human memory consolidation and reconsolidation. *Nature, 425*, 616–620.

Walsh, B., Seidman, S., Sysko, R., & Gould, M. (2002). Placebo response in studies of major depression: Variable, substantial, and growing. *JAMA: Journal of the American Medical Association, 287*, 1840–1847.

Walsh, D., Gentile, D., VanOverbeke, M., & Chasco, E. (2002). *MediaWise video game report card*. National Institute on Media and the Family. Retrieved May 18, 2006 from http://www.mediafamily.org/research/report_vgrc_2002-2.shtml

Walster, E., & Walster, G. W. (1969). The matching hypothesis. *Journal of Personality and Social Psychology, 6*, 248–253.

Walters, C. C., & Grusec, J. E. (1977). *Punishment*. San Francisco: Freeman.

Wang, P., & Li, J. (2003). An experimental study on the belief bias effect in syllogistic reasoning. *Psychological Science (China), 26*, 1020–1024.

Wang, X., & Perry, A. (2006). Metabolic and physiologic responses to video game play in 7- to 10-year-old boys. *Archives of Pediatric Adolescent Medicine, 160*, 411–415.

Wang, Z., & Chen, M. (2002). Managerial competency modeling: A structural equation testing. *Psychological Science (China)*, *25*, 513–516.

Ward, C. (1994). Culture and altered states of consciousness. In W. J. Lonner & R. Malpass (Eds.), *Psychology and culture* (pp. 59–64). Boston: Allyn & Bacon.

Wark, G. R., & Krebs, D. L. (1996). Gender and dilemma differences in real-life moral judgment. *Developmental Psychology, 32*, 220–230.

Warshaw, M. G., & Keller, M. B. (1996). The relationship between fluoxetine use and suicidal behavior in 654 subjects with anxiety disorders. *Journal of Clinical Psychiatry, 57*, 158–166.

Waschbusch, D., & King, S. (2006). Should sex-specific norms be used to assess attention-deficit/hyperactivity disorder or oppositional defiant disorder? *Journal of Consulting and Clinical Psychology, 74*, 179–185.

Washington University School of Medicine. (2003). *Epilepsy surgery* [Online factsheet]. Retrieved September 29, 2003, from http://neurosurgery.wustl.edu/clinprog/epilepsysurg.htm

Watamura, S., Donzella, B., Alwin, J., & Gunnar, M. (2003). Morning-to-afternoon increases in cortisol concentrations for infants and toddlers at childcare: Age differences and behavioral correlates. *Child Development, 74*, 1006–1020.

Watson, D. (2001). Dissociations of the night: Individual differences in sleep-related experiences and their relation to dissociation and schizotypy. *Journal of Abnormal Psychology, 110*, 526–535.

Watson, D. (2002). Predicting psychiatric symptomatology with the Defense Style Questionnaire-40. *International Journal of Stress Management, 9*, 275–287.

Watson, J. B., & Rayner, R. (1920). Conditioned emotional reactions. *Journal of Experimental Psychology, 3*, 1–14.

Waxman, S., & Geschwind, N. (1975). The interictal behavior syndrome of temporal lobe epilepsy. *Archives of General Psychiatry, 32*, 1580–1586.

"Way to delay Huntington's disease found." (1999, June 17). *Harvard University Gazette*. Retrieved April 21, 2006 from http://www.news.harvard.edu/gazette/1999/06.17/huntington.html

Webb, W. (1995). The cost of sleep-related accidents: A reanalysis. *Sleep, 18*, 276–280.

Webb, W. B. (1975). *Sleep: The gentle tyrant.* Englewood Cliffs, NJ: Prentice-Hall.

Weber, R., Ritterfeld, U., & Mathiak, K. (2006). Does playing violent video games induce aggression? Empirical evidence of a functional magnetic resonance imaging study. *Media Psychology, 8*, 39–60.

Weber, S. E. (1996). Cultural aspects of pain in childbearing women. *Journal of Obstetric, Gynecologic & Neonatal Nursing, 25*, 67–72.

Wechsler, D. (1939). *The measurement of adult intelligence.* Baltimore: Williams & Wilkins.

Weekes, J. R., Lynn, S. J., Green, J. P., & Brentar, J. T. (1992). Pseudomemory in hypnotized and task-motivated subjects. *Journal of Abnormal Psychology, 101*, 356–360.

Weeks, D. L., & Anderson, L. P. (2000). The interaction of observational learning with overt practice: Effects on motor skill learning. *Acta Psychologia, 104*, 259–271.

Weigman, O., & van Schie, E. G. (1998). Video game playing and its relations with aggressive and prosocial behaviour. *British Journal of Social Psychology, 37*(Pt. 3), 367–378.

Weiler, S., & Bernasek, A. (2001). Dodging the glass ceiling? Networks and the new wave of women entrepreneurs. *Social Science Journal, 38*, 85–103.

Weiner, I. B. (1997). Current status of the Rorschach Inkblot Method. *Journal of Personality Assessment, 68*, 5–19.

Weinfield, N., Ogawa, J., & Sroufe, L. (1997). Early attachment as a pathway to adolescent peer competence. *Journal of Research on Adolescence, 7*, 241–265.

Weissman, M. M., Bland, R. C., Canino, G. J., Faravelli, C., Greenwald, S., Hwu, H-G., Joyce, P. R., Karam, E. G., Lee, C-K., Lellouch, J., Lepine, J-P., Newman, S. C., Rubio-Stepic, M., Wells, J. E., Wickramaratne, P. J., Wittchen, H-U., & Yeh, E-K. (1996). Cross-national epidemiology of major depression and bipolar disorder. *Journal of the American Medical Association, 276*, 293–299.

Weissman, M. M., Bland, R. C., Canino, G. J., Greenwald, S., Hwu, H-G., Lee, C. K., Newman, S. C., Oakley-Browne, M. A., Rubio-Stipec, M., Wickramaratne, P. J., Wittchen, H-U., & Yeh, E-K. (1994). The cross national epidemiology of obsessive compulsive disorder. *Journal of Clinical Psychiatry, 55*(3, Suppl.), 5–10.

Weitzman, M., Byrd, R., & Auinger, P. (1999). Black and white middle class children who have private health insurance in the United States. *Pediatrics, 104*, 151–157.

Wells, B., & Twenge, J. (2006). Changes in young people's sexual behavior and attitudes, 1943–1999: A cross-temporal meta-analysis. *Review of General Psychology, 9*, 249–261.

Wells, D. L., & Hepper, P. G. (2000). The discrimination of dog odours by humans. *Perception, 29*, 111–115.

Wells, G. L. (1993). What do we know about eyewitness identification? *American Psychologist, 48*, 553–571.

Wells, G. L., Malpass, R. S., Lindsay, R. C., Fisher, R. P., Turtle, J. W., & Fulero, S. M. (2000). From the lab to the police station. A successful application of eyewitness research. *American Psychologist, 55*, 6581–6598.

Werker, J., & Desjardins, R. (1995). Listening to speech in the first year of life: Experiential influences on phoneme perception. *Current Directions in Psychological Science, 4*, 76–81.

Wertheimer, M. (1912). Experimental studies of the perception of movement. *Zeitschrift fur Psychologie, 61*, 161–265.

Wertz, K., & Hermann, B. G. (2000). Large-scale screen for genes involved in gonad development. *Mechanisms of Development, 98*, 51–70.

Wesensten, N., Balenky, G., Kautz, M., Thorne, D., Reichardt, R., & Balkin, T. (2002). Maintaining alertness and performance during sleep deprivation: Modafinil versus caffeine. *Psychopharmacology, 159*, 238–247.

West, M. J., Coleman, P. D., Flood, D. G., & Troncoso, J. C. (1994). Differences in the pattern of hippocampal neuronal loss in normal ageing and Alzheimer's disease. *Lancet, 344*, 769–772.

Weström, L. V. (1994). Sexually transmitted diseases and infertility. *Sexually Transmitted Diseases, 21*(2, Suppl.), S32–S37.

Wetherell, J., Gatz, M., & Craske, M. (2003). Treatment of generalized anxiety disorder in older adults. *Journal of Consulting & Clinical Psychology, 71*, 31–40.

Wetter, M. W., Baer, R. A., Berry, T. R., Robison, L. H., & Sumpter, J. (1993). MMPI-2 profiles of motivated fakers given specific symptom information: A comparison to matched patients. *Psychological Assessment, 5,* 317–323.

Wexler, A. (1996). *Mapping fate: A memoir of family, risk, and genetic research.* Los Angeles, CA: University of California Press.

Wexler, N. (2005). Letter from the president. *Hereditary Disease Foundation Newsletter.* Fall, 2005, p. 3.

Wharton, A., & Blair-Loy, M. (2006). Long work hours and family life: A cross-national study of employees' concerns. *Journal of Family Issues, 27,* 415–436.

Wheatley, D. (2001). Stress-induced insomnia treated with kava and valerian. Singly and in combination. *Human Psychopharmacology Clinical & Experimental, 16,* 353–356.

Wheeler, M. A., Stuss, D. T., & Tulving, E. (1997). Toward a theory of episodic memory: The frontal lobes and autonoetic consciousness. *Psychological Bulletin, 121,* 331–354.

Wheeler, M., & McMillan, C. (2001). Focal retrograde amnesia and the episodic-semantic distinction. *Cognitive, Affective & Behavioral Neuroscience, 1,* 22–36.

Whisenant, W., Pedersen, P. & Obenour, B. (2002). Success and gender: Determining the rate of advancement for intercollegiate athletic directors. *Sex Roles, 47,* 485–491.

Whisenhunt, B. L., Williamson, D. A., Netemeyer, R. G., & Womble, L. G. (2000). Reliability and validity of the Psychosocial Risk Factors Questionnaire (PRFQ). *Eating and Weight Disorders: Studies on Anorexia, Bulimia, and Obesity, 5,* 1–6.

Whitam, F. L., Diamond, M., & Martin, J. (1993). Homosexual orientation in twins: A report on 61 pairs and three triplet sets. *Archives of Sexual Behavior, 22,* 187–296.

White, D. P. (1989). Central sleep apnea. In M. H. Kryger, T. Roth, & W. C. Dement (Eds.), *Principles and practice of sleep medicine* (pp. 513–524). Philadelphia: W. B. Saunders.

Whitehead, B., & Popenoe, D. (2005). *The state of our unions: The social health of marriage in America: 2005: What does the Scandinavian experience tell us?* Retrieved June 15, 2006 from http://marriage.rutgers.edu/Publications/SOOU/TEXTSOOU2005.htm

Whitman-Elia, G., & Queenan, J. (2005). Ovotestis. In G. Letterie et al. (Eds.), *e-Medicine Clinical Knowledge Base.* Retrieved July 3, 2006 from http://www.emedicine.com/med/topic1702.htm

Whitmore, D., Foulkes, N. S., & Sassone-Corsi, P. (2000). Light acts directly on organs and cells in culture to set the vertebrate circadian clock. *Nature, 404,* 87–91.

Whorf, B. L. (1956). Science and linguistics. In J. B. Carroll (Ed.), *Language, thought, and reality: Selected writings of Benjamin Lee Whorf.* Cambridge, MA: MIT Press.

Wickelgren, I. (1996). For the cortex, neuron loss may be less than thought. *Science, 273,* 48–50.

Wicker, A. W. (1969). Attitudes versus action: The relationship of verbal and overt behavioral responses to attitude objects. *Journal of Social Issues, 25,* 41–78.

Widom, C. S. (1989). Does violence beget violence? A critical examination of the literature. *Psychological Bulletin, 106,* 3–28.

Widom, C. S., & Maxfield, M. G. (1996). A prospective examination of risk for violence among abused and neglected children. *Annals of the New York Academy of Sciences, 794,* 224–237.

Widom, C. S., & Morris, S. (1997). Accuracy of adult recollections of childhood victimization: Part 2. Childhood sexual abuse. *Psychological Bulletin, 9,* 34–46.

Wigboldus, D., Dijksterhuis, A., & Van Knippenberg, A. (2003). When stereotypes get in the way: Stereotypes obstruct stereotype-inconsistent trait inferences. *Journal of Personality & Social Psychology, 84,* 470–484.

Wilde, C. (2000, April 10). The new workplace: Telework programs are on the rise. *Information Week, 781,* 189.

Wilken, J. A., Smith, B. D., Tola, K., & Mann, M. (2000). Trait anxiety and prior exposure to non-stressful stimuli: Effects on psychophysiological arousal and anxiety. *International Journal of Psychophysiology, 37,* 233–242.

Willems, P. J. (2000). Genetic causes of hearing loss. *New England Journal of Medicine, 342,* 1101–1109.

Williams, K., Harkins, S. G., & Latané, B. (1981). Identifiability as a deterrent to social loafing: Two cheering experiments. *Journal of Personality and Social Psychology, 40,* 303–311.

Williams, L. M. (1994). Recall of childhood trauma: A prospective study of women's memories of child sexual abuse. *Journal of Consulting and Clinical Psychology, 62,* 1167–1176.

Willoughby, J. C., & Glidden, L. M. (1995). Fathers helping out: Shared child care and marital satisfaction of parents of children with disabilities. *American Journal on Mental Retardation, 99,* 399–406.

Wills, T. A., & Cleary, S. D. (1996). How are social support effects mediated? A test with parental support and adolescent substance use. *Journal of Personality and Social Psychology, 71,* 937–952.

Wills, T. A., McNamara, G., Vaccaro, D., & Hirky, A. E. (1996). Escalated substance use: A longitudinal grouping analysis from early to middle adolescence. *Journal of Abnormal Psychology, 105,* 166–180.

Wilson, G., & Sysko, R. (2006). Cognitive-behavioral therapy for adolescents with bulimia nervosa. *European Eating Disorders Review, 14,* 8–16.

Wilson, M. A., & McNaughton, B. L. (1993). Dynamics of the hippocampal ensemble code for space. *Science, 261,* 1055–1058.

Wilson, R., & Bennett, D. (2003). Cognitive activity and risk of Alzheimer's disease. *Current Directions in Psychological Science, 12,* 87–91.

Wilson, W., Mathew, R., Turkington, T., Hawk, T., Coleman, R. E., & Provenzale, J. (2000). Brain morphological changes and early marijuana use: A magnetic resonance and positron emission tomography study. *Journal of Addictive Diseases, 19,* 1–22.

Winch, R. F. (1958). *Mate selection: A study of complementary needs.* New York: Harper & Row.

Winerman, L. (2004). Criminal profiling: The reality behind the myth. *APA Monitor on Psychology, 35,* 66.

Winograd, E. (1988). Some observations on prospective remembering. In M. M. Gruneberg, P. E. Morris, & R. N. Sykes (Eds.), *Practical aspects of memory: Current research and issues: Vol. 1* (pp. 348–353). Chichester, England: John Wiley & Sons.

Winokur, G., Coryell, W., Keller, M., Endicott, J., & Akiskal, H. S. (1993). A prospective follow-up of patients with bipolar and primary unipolar affective disorder. *Archives of General Psychiatry, 50,* 457–465.

Winsler, A., & Naglieri, J. (2003). Overt and covert verbal problem-solving strategies: Developmental trends in use, awareness, and relations with task performance in children aged 5 to 17. *Child Development, 74,* 659–678.

Winson, J. (1990). The meaning of dreams. *Scientific American, 263,* 86–96.

Wislar, J., Richman, J., Fendrich, M., & Flaherty, J. (2002). Sexual harassment, generalized workplace abuse and drinking outcomes: The role of personality vulnerability. *Journal of Drug Issues, 32,* 1071–1088.

Witelson, S. F. (1985). The brain connection: The corpus callosum is larger in left-handers. *Science, 229,* 665–668.

Witt, L., Burke, L., Barrick, M., & Mount, M. (2002). The interactive effects of conscientiousness and agreeableness on job performance. *Journal of Applied Psychology, 87,* 164–169.

Wolford, G., Miller, M. B., & Gazzaniga, M. (2000). The left hemisphere's role in hypothesis formation. *Journal of Neuroscience, 20,* 1–4.

Wolpe, J. (1973). *The practice of behavior therapy* (2nd ed.). New York: Pergamon.

Wolters, C. (2003). Understanding procrastination from a self-regulated learning perspective. *Journal of Educational Psychology, 95,* 179–187.

Wolters, C. (2004). Advancing achievement goal theory using goal structures and goal orientations to predict students' motivation, cognition, and achievement. *Journal of Educational Psychology, 96,* 136–250.

Wolters, G., & Goudsmit, J. (2005). Flashbulb and event memory of September 11, 2001: Consistency, confidence, and age effects. *Psychological Reports, 96,* 605–619.

Wood, J. M., Nezworski, M. T., & Stejskal, W. J. (1996). The Comprehensive System for the Rorschach: A critical examination. *Psychological Science, 7,* 3–10.

Wood, W., & Conway, M. (2006). Subjective impact, meaning making, and current and recalled emotions for self-defining memories. *Journal of Personality, 75,* 811–846.

Wood, W., Lundgren, S., Ovellette, J. A., Busceme, S., & Blackstone, T. (1994). Minority influence: A meta-analytic review of social influence processes. *Psychological Bulletin, 115,* 323–345.

Woodman, G., & Luck, S. (2003). Serial deployment of attention during visual search. *Journal of Experimental Psychology: Human Perception and Performance, 29,* 121–138.

Woodruff-Pak, D. (2001). Eyeblink classical conditioning differentiates normal aging from Alzheimer's disease. *Integrative Physiological & Behavioral Science, 36,* 87–108.

Woody, E. Z., & Bowers, K. S. (1994). A frontal assault on dissociated control. In S. J. Lynn & J. W. Rhue (Eds.), *Dissociation: Clinical, theoretical and research perspectives* (pp. 52–79). New York: Guilford.

Woolley, J., & Boerger, E. (2002). Development of beliefs about the origins and controllability of dreams. *Development Psychology, 38,* 24–41.

World Health Organization (WHO). (2000). Female genital mutilation factsheet. Retrieved July 3, 2006 from http://www.who.int/mediacentre/factsheets/fs241/en/

World Health Organization (WHO). (2001). Global prevalence and incidence of selected curable sexually transmitted infections. Retrieved June 29, 2006 from http://www.who.int/docstore/hiv/GRSTI/index.htm

World Health Organization (WHO). (2002a). Sexual violence factsheet. Retrieved January 21, 2003, from http://www.who.int/violence_injury_prevention

World Health Organization (WHO). (2002b). Violence against women: Rape and sexual assault. Retrieved January 20, 2003, from http://www.who.int/gender/violence/v6.pdf

World Health Organization. (2000). *Violence against women.* [Online report] Retrieved September 1, 2000 from http://www.who.int

Worrel, J. A., Marken, P. A., Beckman, S. E., & Ruehter, V. L. (2000). Atypical antipsychotic agents: A critical review. *American Journal of Health System Pharmacology, 57,* 238–255.

Worrell, F., & Cross, W. (2004). The reliability and validity of Big Five inventory scores with African American college students. *Journal of Multicultural Counseling and Development, 32,* 18–32.

Worthen, J., & Wood, V. (2001). Memory discrimination for self-performed and imagined acts: Bizarreness effects in false recognition. *Quarterly Journal of Experimental Psychology, 54A,* 49–67.

Wright, C., Wedig, M., Williams, D., Rauch, S., & Albert, M. (2006). Novel fearful faces activate the amygdala in healthy young and elderly adults. *Neurobiology of Aging, 27,* 361–374.

Wright, J. C., & Mischel, W. (1987). A conditional approach to dispositional constructs: The local predictability of social behavior. *Journal of Personality and Social Psychology, 53,* 1159–1177.

Wright, N., & Wales, J. (2004). An unusual case of hermaphroditism. *Journal of Pediatric Endocrinology and Metabolism, 17,* 905–908.

Wyrobek, A., Eskenazi, B., Young, S., Arnheim, N., Tiemann-Boege, I., Jabs, E., Glaser, R., Pearson, F., & Evenson, D. (2006, in press). Advancing age has differential effects on DNA damage, chromatin integrity, gene mutations, and aneuploidies. *Proceedings of the National Academies of Sciences.*

Yackinous, C., & Guinard, J. (2002). Relation between PROP (6-n-propylthiouracil) taster status, taste anatomy and dietary intake measures for young men and women. *Appetite, 38,* 201–209.

Yanagita, T. (1973). An experimental framework for evaluation of dependence liability in various types of drugs in monkeys. *Bulletin of Narcotics, 25,* 57–64.

Yang, C., & Spielman, A. (2001). The effect of a delayed weekend sleep pattern on sleep and morning functioning. *Psychology & Health, 16,* 715–725.

Yapko, M. D. (1994). Suggestibility and repressed memories of abuse: A survey of psychotherapists' beliefs. *American Journal of Clinical Hypnosis, 36,* 163–171.

Yasui-Furukori, N., Saito, M., Nakagami, T., Kaneda, A., Tateishi, T., & Kaneko, S. (2006). Association between multidrug resistance 1 (MDR1) gene polymorphisms and therapeutic response to bromperidol in schizophrenic patients: A preliminary study. *Progress in Neuro-Psychopharmacology & Biological Psychiatry, 30,* 286–291.

Yen, C., & Su, Y. (2006). The associations of early-onset methamphetamine use with psychiatric morbidity among Taiwanese adolescents. *Substance Use & Misuse, 41,* 35–44.

Young, J. (2003, February 13). Prozac campus. *Chronicle of Higher Education, 49.* [Online, no pages specified.] Retrieved July 25, 2006 from http://www.chronicle.com/free/v49/i23/23a03701.htm

Yousef, D. (2002). Job satisfaction as a mediator of the relationship between job stressors and affective, continuance, and normative commitment: A path analytical approach. *International Journal of Stress Management, 9,* 99–112.

Yuan, L. (2000, November). Land of the walking marriage— Mosuo people of China. *Natural History.* Retrieved Jun 22, 2006, from http://www.findarticles.com/p/articles/mi_m1134/is_9_109/ai_67410989

Zajonc, R. B. (1980). Feeling and thinking: Preferences need no inferences. *American Psychologist, 35,* 151–175.

Zajonc, R. B. (1984). On the primacy of affect. *American Psychologist, 39,* 117–123.

Zajonc, R. B., & Mullally, P. R. (1997). Birth order: Reconciling conflicting effects. *American Psychologist, 52,* 685–699.

Zajonc, R. B., & Sales, S. M. (1966). Social facilitation of dominant and subordinate responses. *Journal of Experimental Social Psychology, 2,* 160–168.

Zald, D. H., & Pardo, J. V. (2000). Functional neuroimaging of the olfactory system in humans. *International Journal of Psychophysiology, 36,* 165–181.

Zaragoza, M. S., & Mitchell, K. J. (1996). Repeated exposure to suggestion and the creation of false memories. *Psychological Science, 7,* 294–300.

Zatorre, R., Belin, P., & Penhune, V. (2002). Structure and function of the auditory cortex: Music and speech. *Trends in Cognitive Sciences, 6,* 37–46.

Zborowski, M. (1952). Cultural components in response to pain. *Journal of Social Issues, 8,* 16–30.

Zhang, D., Li, Z., Chen, X., Wang, Z., Zhang, X., Meng, X., He, S., & Hu, X. (2003). Functional comparison of primacy, middle and recency retrieval in human auditory short-term memory: An event-related fMRI study. *Cognitive Brain Research, 16,* 91–98.

Zhang, L. (2002). Thinking styles and the Big Five personality traits. *Educational Psychology, 22,* 17–31.

Zhang, X., Cohen, H., Porjesz, B., & Begleiter, H. (2001). Mismatch negativity in subjects at high risk for alcoholism. *Alcoholism: Clinical & Experimental Research, 25,* 330–337.

Zhang, Y., Goonetilleke, R., Plocher, T., & Liang, S. (2005). Time-related behaviour in multitasking situations. *International Journal of Human-Computer Studies, 62,* 425–455.

Zimbardo, P. G. (1972). Pathology of imprisonment. *Society, 9,* 4–8.

Zimmerman, M., Posternak, K., & Chelminski, I. (2002). Symptom severity and exclusion from antidepressant efficacy trials. *Journal of Clinical Psychopharmacology, 22,* 610–614.

Zinkernagel, C., Naef, M., Bucher, H., Ladewig, D., Gyr, N., & Battegay, M. (2001). Onset and pattern of substance use in intravenous drug users of an opiate maintenance program. *Drug & Alcohol Dependence, 64,* 105–109.

Zisapel, N. (2001). Circadian rhythm sleep disorders: Pathophysiology and potential approaches to management. *CNS Drugs, 15,* 311–328.

Zito, J., Safer, D., dosReis, S., Gardner, J., Magder, L., Soeken, K., Boles, M., Lynch, F., & Riddle, M. (2003). Psychotropic practice patterns for youth: A 10-year perspective. *Archives of Pediatric and Adolescent Medicine, 157,* 17–25.

Zoghbi, H. (2003). Postnatal neurodevelopmental disorders. *Science, 302,* 826–830.

Zola, S. M., Squire, L. R., Teng, E., Stenfanacci, L., Buffalo, E. A., & Clark, R. E. (2000). Impaired recognition memory in monkeys after damage limited to the hippocampal region. *Journal of Neuroscience, 20,* 451–463.

Zucker, A., Ostrove, J., & Stewart A. (2002). College-educated women's personality development in adulthood: Perceptions and age differences. *Psychology & Aging, 17,* 236–244.

Glossary

absolute threshold The minimum amount of sensory stimulation that can be detected 50% of the time.

accommodation In vision, the flattening and bulging action of the lens as it focuses images of objects on the retina. In learning, the mental process of modifying existing schemes and creating new ones in order to incorporate new objects, events, experiences, and information.

acetylcholine (ah-SEET-ul-KOH-leen) A neurotransmitter that plays a role in learning new information, causes the skeletal muscle fibers to contract, and keeps the heart from beating too rapidly.

acquired immune deficiency syndrome (AIDS) A devastating and incurable illness that is caused by HIV and progressively weakens the body's immune system, leaving the person vulnerable to opportunistic infections that usually cause death.

action potential The sudden reversal of the resting potential, which initiates the firing of a neuron.

activation-synthesis hypothesis of dreaming The hypothesis that dreams are the brain's attempt to make sense of the random firing of brain cells during REM sleep.

actor-observer effect The tendency to attribute one's own behavior primarily to situational factors and the behavior of others primarily to dispositional factors.

adolescence The developmental stage that begins at puberty and encompasses the period from the end of childhood to the beginning of adulthood.

adoption study method A method researchers use to assess the relative effects of heredity and environment by studying children who were adopted very early in life.

adrenal glands (ah-DREE-nal) A pair of endocrine glands that release hormones that prepare the body for emergencies and stressful situations and also release corticoids and small amounts of the sex hormones.

aerobic exercise (ah-RO-bik) Exercise that uses the large muscle groups in continuous, repetitive action and increases oxygen intake and breathing and heart rates.

affirmative action A process through which organizations actively seek to build an employee pool that includes members of as many racial and cultural groups as possible.

afterimage A visual sensation that remains after a stimulus is withdrawn.

aggression The intentional infliction of physical or psychological harm on others.

agoraphobia (AG-or-uh-FO-bee-ah) An intense fear of being in a situation from which escape is not possible or in which help would not be available if one experienced overwhelming anxiety or a panic attack.

alarm stage The first stage of the general adaptation syndrome, in which the person experiences a burst of energy that aids in dealing with the stressful situation.

algorithm A systematic, step-by-step procedure that guarantees a solution to a problem of a certain type if the algorithm is executed properly.

alpha wave The brain-wave pattern associated with deep relaxation.

altered state of consciousness Changes in awareness produced by sleep, meditation, hypnosis, and drugs.

alternative medicine Any treatment or therapy that has not been scientifically demonstrated to be effective.

altruism Behavior that is aimed at helping another, requires some self-sacrifice, and is not performed for personal gain.

Alzheimer's disease A progressive and incurable disorder that involves widespread degeneration and disruption of brain cells, resulting in dementia.

amnesia A partial or complete loss of memory due to loss of consciousness, brain damage, or some psychological cause.

amplitude The measure of the loudness of a sound; expressed in the unit called the decibel.

amygdala (ah-MIG-da-la) A structure in the limbic system that plays an important role in emotion, particularly in response to unpleasant or punishing stimuli.

analogy heuristic A heuristic strategy that applies a solution used for a past problem to a current problem that shares many similar features.

androgens Male sex hormones.

androgyny (an-DROJ-uh-nee) A combination of desirable masculine and feminine characteristics in one person.

anorexia nervosa An eating disorder characterized by an overwhelming, irrational fear of gaining weight or becoming fat, compulsive dieting to the point of self-starvation, and excessive weight loss.

anterograde amnesia The inability to form long-term memories of events occurring after a brain injury or brain surgery, although memories formed before the trauma are usually intact and short-term memory is unaffected.

antidepressant drugs Drugs that act as mood elevators for severely depressed people and are also prescribed to treat some anxiety disorders.

antipsychotic drugs Drugs used to control severe psychotic symptoms, such as delusions, hallucinations, disorganized speech, and disorganized behavior by inhibiting dopamine activity; also known as neuroleptics.

anxiety disorders Psychological disorders characterized by frequent fearful thoughts about what might happen in the future.

apparent motion Perceptions of motion that seem to be psychologically constructed in response to various kinds of stimuli.

applied research Research conducted specifically to solve practical problems and improve the quality of life.

apprenticeship An approach to training in which a novice employee is teamed with a more experienced one.

approach-approach conflict A conflict arising from having to choose between equally desirable alternatives.

approach-avoidance conflict A conflict arising when the same choice has both desirable and undesirable features.

aptitude test A test designed to predict a person's achievement or performance at some future time.

archetype (AR-ka-type) Existing in the collective unconscious, an inherited tendency to respond to universal human situations in particular ways.

arousal A state of alertness and mental and physical activation.

arousal theory A theory of motivation suggesting that people are motivated to maintain an optimal level of alertness and physical and mental activation.

artifactual communication The use of objects to communicate nonverbal messages.

artificial intelligence (AI) Programming of computer systems to simulate human thinking in solving problems and in making judgments and decisions.

artificial neural networks (ANNs) Computer systems that are intended to mimic the human brain.

Asperger's disorder A disorder in which children possess the same characteristics as those with autistic disorder but have intact language skills.

assessment center A facility devoted to testing job applicants using work simulations and other comprehensive assessment tools.

assimilation The mental process by which new objects, events, experiences, and information are incorporated into existing schemes.

association areas Areas of the cerebral cortex that house memories and are involved in thought, perception, and language.

attachment The early, close relationship formed between infant and caregiver.

attention The process of sorting sensations in which we shift our focus from one object to another and in the process, fail to notice changes in the objects to which we are not directly paying attention.

attention deficit hyperactivity disorder (ADHD) A disorder in which an individual shows both significant problems in focusing attention and physical activity.

attitude A relatively stable evaluation of a person, object, situation, or issue, along a continuum ranging from positive to negative.

attribution An assignment of a cause to explain one's own or another's behavior.

audience effects The impact of passive spectators on performance.

audition The sensation and process of hearing.

authoritarian parents Parents who make arbitrary rules, expect unquestioned obedience from their children, punish misbehavior, and value obedience to authority.

authoritative parents Parents who set high but realistic and reasonable standards, enforce limits, and encourage open communication and independence.

autistic disorder A disorder in which children have very limited language skills compared to others of the same age along with an inability to engage in reciprocal social relationships, and a severely limited range of interests.

autokinetic illusion Apparent motion caused by the movement of the eyes rather than the movement of the objects being viewed.

availability heuristic A cognitive rule of thumb that bases the probability of an event or the importance assigned to it on its availability in memory.

aversion therapy A behavior therapy in which an aversive stimulus is paired with a harmful or socially undesirable behavior until the behavior becomes associated with pain or discomfort.

avoidance learning Learning to avoid events or conditions associated with aversive consequences or phobias.

avoidance-avoidance conflict A conflict arising from having to choose between undesirable alternatives.

axon (AK-sahn) The slender, tail-like extension of the neuron that transmits signals to the dendrites or cell body of other neurons and to muscles, glands, and other parts of the body.

babbling Vocalization of the basic units of sound (phonemes).

basic emotions Emotions that are unlearned and universal, that are reflected in the same facial expressions across cultures, and that emerge in children according to their biological timetable of development; fear, anger, disgust, surprise, happiness, and sadness are usually considered basic emotions.

basic research Research conducted to seek new knowledge and to explore and advance general scientific understanding.

behavior modification A method of changing behavior through a systematic program based on the learning principles of classical conditioning, operant conditioning, or observational learning; also called behavior therapy.

behavior therapy A treatment approach that is based on the idea that abnormal behavior is learned and that applies the principles of operant conditioning, classical conditioning, and/or observational learning to eliminate inappropriate or maladaptive behaviors and replace them with more adaptive responses.

behavioral approach A perspective that holds that leadership effectiveness can be taught and is the result of specific behaviors exhibited by leaders.

behavioral genetics A field of research that uses twin studies and adoption studies to investigate the relative effects of heredity and environment on behavior.

behavioral observation scales Instruments for employee evaluation that require respondents to rate an employee's performance on observable behaviors.

behaviorism The school of psychology founded by John B. Watson that views observable, measurable behavior as the appropriate subject matter for psychology and emphasizes the key role of environment as a determinant of behavior.

beta wave (BAY-tuh) The brain-wave pattern associated with mental or physical activity.

bilingualism Fluency in at least two languages.

binocular depth cues Depth cues that depend on both eyes working together.

biofeedback The use of sensitive equipment to give people precise feedback about internal physiological processes so that they can learn, with practice, to exercise control over them.

biological psychology The school of psychology that looks for links between specific behaviors and equally specific biological processes that often help explain individual differences.

biological sex Physiological status as male or female.

biological therapy A therapy (drug therapy, electroconvulsive therapy, or psychosurgery) that is based on the assumption that psychological disorders are symptoms of underlying physical problems.

biomedical model A perspective that explains illness solely in terms of biological factors.

biopsychosocial model A perspective that focuses on health as well as illness and holds that both are determined by a combination of biological, psychological, and social factors.

bipolar disorder A mood disorder in which manic episodes alternate with periods of depression, usually with relatively normal periods in between.

blind spot The point in each retina where there are no rods or cones because the cable of ganglion cells is extending through the retinal wall.

body mass index A measure of weight relative to height.

bottom-up processing Information processing in which individual components of a stimulus are combined in the brain and prior knowledge is used to make inferences about these patterns.

brainstem The structure that begins at the point where the spinal cord enlarges as it enters the brain and handles functions critical to physical survival. It includes the medulla, the pons, and the reticular formation.

brightness The intensity of the light energy that is perceived as a color.

Broca's aphasia (BRO-kuz uh-FAY-zyah) An impairment in the physical ability to produce speech sounds or, in extreme cases, an inability to speak at all; caused by damage to Broca's area.

Broca's area (BRO-kuz) The area in the frontal lobe, usually in the left hemisphere, that controls the production of speech sounds.

bulimia nervosa An eating disorder characterized by repeated and uncontrolled (and often secretive) episodes of binge eating.

burnout Lack of energy, exhaustion, and pessimism that results from chronic stress.

bystander effect A social factor that affects prosocial behavior: As the number of bystanders at an emergency increases, the probability that the victim will receive help decreases, and the help, if given, is likely to be delayed.

California Personality Inventory (CPI) A highly regarded personality test developed especially for normal individuals aged 13 and older.

Cannon-Bard theory of emotion The theory that an emotion-provoking stimulus is transmitted simultaneously to the cerebral cortex, providing the conscious mental experience of the emotion, and to the sympathetic nervous system, causing the physiological arousal.

case study A descriptive research method in which a single individual or a small number of persons are studied in great depth, usually over an extended period of time.

catatonic schizophrenia (KAT-uh-TAHN-ik) A type of schizophrenia characterized by complete stillness or stupor or great excitement and agitation; patients may assume an unusual posture and remain in it for long periods of time.

cell body The part of a neuron that contains the nucleus and carries out the metabolic functions of the neuron.

central nervous system (CNS) The part of the nervous system comprising the brain and the spinal cord.

centration A preoperational child's tendency to focus on only one dimension of a stimulus.

cerebellum (sehr-uh-BELL-um) The brain structure that helps the body execute smooth, skilled movements and regulates muscle tone and posture.

cerebral cortex (seh-REE-brul KOR-tex) The gray, convoluted covering of the cerebral hemispheres that is responsible for the higher mental processes of language, memory, and thinking.

cerebral hemispheres (seh-REE-brul) The right and left halves of the cerebrum, covered by the cerebral cortex and connected by the corpus callosum; they control movement and feeling on the opposing sides of the body.

cerebrum (seh-REE-brum) The largest structure of the human brain, consisting of the two cerebral hemispheres connected by the corpus callosum and covered by the cerebral cortex.

charismatic leaders Leaders who rely on the sheer force of their personalities.

chlamydia (klah-MIH-dee-uh) A highly infectious bacterial STD that is found in both sexes and can cause infertility in females.

chromosomes Rod-shaped structures in the nuclei of body cells, which contain all the genes and carry all the genetic information necessary to make a human being.

chunking A memory strategy that involves grouping or organizing bits of information into larger units, which are easier to remember.

circadian rhythm (sur-KAY-dee-un) Within each 24-hour period, the regular fluctuation from high to low points of certain bodily functions and behaviors.

circadian theory of sleep The theory that sleep evolved to keep humans out of harm's way during the night; also known as the evolutionary theory.

classical conditioning A type of learning through which an organism learns to associate one stimulus with another.

co-action effects The impact on performance of the presence of other people engaged in the same task.

cochlea (KOK-lee-uh) The fluid-filled, snail-shaped, bony chamber in the inner ear that contains the basilar membrane and its hair cells (the sound receptors).

cognition The mental processes that are involved in acquiring, storing, retrieving, and using information and that include sensation, perception, memory, imagery, concept formation, reasoning, decision making, problem solving, and language.

cognitive dissonance (COG-nuh-tiv) The unpleasant state that can occur when people become aware of inconsistencies between their attitudes or between their attitudes and their behavior.

cognitive map A mental representation of a spatial arrangement such as a maze.

cognitive processes Mental processes such as thinking, knowing, problem solving, remembering, and forming mental representations.

cognitive psychology The school of psychology that sees humans as active participants in their environment; studies mental processes such as memory, problem solving, decision making, perception, language, and other forms of cognition.

cognitive therapies Therapies that assume maladaptive behavior can result from irrational thoughts, beliefs, and ideas.

cognitive therapy A therapy designed by Aaron Beck to help patients stop their negative thoughts as they occur and replace them with more objective thoughts.

coitus (KOY-tus) Penile-vaginal intercourse.

collective unconscious In Jung's theory, the most inaccessible layer of the unconscious, which contains the universal experiences of humankind throughout evolution.

color blindness The inability to distinguish certain colors from one another.

compliance Acting in accordance with the wishes, suggestions, or direct requests of other people.

compulsion A persistent, irresistible, and irrational urge to perform an act or ritual repeatedly.

concept A mental category used to represent a class or group of objects, people, organizations, events, situations, or relations that share common characteristics or attributes.

concrete operations stage Piaget's third stage of cognitive development (ages 6 to 11 or 12 years), during which a child acquires the concepts of reversibility and conservation and is able to attend to two or more dimensions of a stimulus at the same time.

conditioned reflex A learned involuntary response.

conditioned response (CR) The learned response that comes to be elicited by a conditioned stimulus as a result of its repeated pairing with an unconditioned stimulus.

conditioned stimulus (CS) A neutral stimulus that, after repeated pairing with an unconditioned stimulus, becomes associated with it and elicits a conditioned response.

conditions of worth Conditions on which the positive regard of others rests.

cones The light-sensitive receptor cells in the retina that enable humans to see color and fine detail in adequate light but do not function in very dim light.

confederate A person who poses as a participant in an experiment but is actually assisting the experimenter.

conflict The stress that arises from knowing that choosing one alternative means foregoing another.

conflict resolution A process in which a conflict is evaluated and an appropriate strategy for resolving it is identified.

conformity Changing or adopting a behavior or an attitude in order to be consistent with the social norms of a group or the expectations of other people.

confounding variables Factors or conditions other than the independent variable(s) that are not equivalent across groups and could cause differences among the groups with respect to the dependent variable.

conscious (KON-shus) The thoughts, feelings, sensations, or memories of which a person is aware at any given moment.

consciousness Everything of which we are aware at any given time—our thoughts, feelings, sensations, and external environment.

conservation The understanding that a given quantity of matter remains the same if it is rearranged or changed in its appearance, as long as nothing is added or taken away.

consolidation A physiological change in the brain that allows encoded information to be stored in memory.

consolidation failure Any disruption in the consolidation process that prevents a long-term memory from forming.

consummate love According to Sternberg's theory, the most complete form of love, consisting of all three components—intimacy, passion, and commitment.

contexts of development Bronfenbrenner's term for the interrelated and layered settings (family, neighborhood, culture, etc.) in which a child grows up.

continuous reinforcement Reinforcement that is administered after every desired or correct response; the most effective method of conditioning a new response.

control group In an experiment, a group similar to the experimental group that is exposed to the same experimental environment but is not given the treatment; used for purposes of comparison.

conventional level Kohlberg's second level of moral reasoning, in which the individual has internalized the standards of others and judges right and wrong in terms of those standards.

conversion disorder A somatoform disorder in which a person suffers a loss of motor or sensory functioning in some part of the body; the loss has no physical cause but solves some psychological problem.

coping Efforts through action and thought to deal with demands that are perceived as taxing or overwhelming.

cornea (KOR-nee-uh) The tough, transparent, protective layer that covers the front of the eye and bends light rays inward through the pupil.

corpus callosum (KOR-pus kah-LO-sum) The thick band of nerve fibers that connects the two cerebral hemispheres and makes possible the transfer of information and the synchronization of activity between the hemispheres.

correlation coefficient A numerical value that indicates the strength and direction of the relationship between two variables; ranges from +1.00 (a perfect positive correlation) to −1.00 (a perfect negative correlation).

correlational method A research method used to establish the degree of relationship (correlation) between two characteristics, events, or behaviors.

creativity The ability to produce original, appropriate, and valuable ideas and/or solutions to problems.

critical period A period during the embryonic stage when certain body structures are developing and can be harmed by negative influences in the prenatal environment.

critical thinking The process of objectively evaluating claims, propositions, and conclusions to determine whether they follow logically from the evidence presented.

cross-sectional study A type of developmental study in which researchers compare groups of participants of different ages on various characteristics to determine age-related differences.

crowding The subjective judgment that there are too many people in a confined space.

crystallized intelligence A type of intelligence comprising verbal ability and accumulated knowledge, which tend to increase over the lifespan.

CT scan (computerized axial tomography) A brain-scanning technique that uses a rotating, computerized X-ray tube to produce cross-sectional images of the structures of the brain.

culturally sensitive therapy An approach to therapy in which knowledge of clients' cultural backgrounds guides the choice of therapeutic interventions.

culture-fair intelligence test An intelligence test that uses questions that will not penalize those whose culture differs from the mainstream or dominant culture.

decay theory The oldest theory of forgetting, which holds that memories, if not used, fade with time and ultimately disappear altogether.

decibel (dB) (DES-ih-bel) A unit of measurement for the loudness of sounds.

decision making The process of considering alternatives and choosing among them.

declarative memory The subsystem within long-term memory that stores facts, information, and personal life events that can be brought to mind verbally or in the form of images and then declared or stated; also called explicit memory.

deductive reasoning Reasoning from the general to the specific, or drawing particular conclusions from general principles.

deep structure The underlying meaning of a sentence.

defense mechanism A means used by the ego to defend against anxiety and to maintain self-esteem.

delta wave The slowest brain-wave pattern; associated with deep sleep (Stage 3 and Stage 4 NREM sleep).

delusion A false belief, not generally shared by others in the culture.

delusions of grandeur A false belief that one is a famous person or a powerful or important person who has some great knowledge, ability, or authority.

delusions of persecution A false belief that some person or agency is trying in some way to harm one.

dementias A group of neurological disorders in which problems with memory and thinking affect an individual's emotional, social, and physical functioning; caused by physical deterioration of the brain.

dendrites (DEN-drytes) In a neuron, the branchlike extensions of the cell body that receive signals from other neurons.

dependent variable The factor or condition that is measured at the end of an experiment and is presumed to vary as a result of the manipulations of the independent variable(s).

depressants A category of drugs that decrease activity in the central nervous system, slow down bodily functions, and reduce sensitivity to outside stimulation; also called "downers."

depth perception The ability to perceive the visual world in three dimensions and to judge distances accurately.

descriptive research methods Research methods that yield descriptions of behavior.

developmental psychology The study of how humans grow, develop, and change throughout the life span.

difference threshold A measure of the smallest increase or decrease in a physical stimulus that is required to produce a difference in sensation that is noticeable 50% of the time.

diffusion of responsibility The feeling among bystanders at an emergency that the responsibility for helping is shared by the group, making each person feel less compelled to act than if he or she alone bore the total responsibility.

directive therapy Any type of psychotherapy in which the therapist takes an active role in determining the course of therapy sessions and provides answers and suggestions to the patient; an example is Gestalt therapy.

discrimination In classical conditioning, the learned ability to distinguish between similar stimuli so that the conditioned response occurs only to the original conditioned stimulus but not to similar stimuli. In social psychology, behavior (usually negative) directed toward others based on their gender, religion, race, or membership in a particular group.

discriminative stimulus A stimulus that signals whether a certain response or behavior is likely to be rewarded, ignored, or punished.

disinhibitory effect Displaying a previously suppressed behavior because a model does so without receiving punishment.

disorganized schizophrenia The most serious type of schizophrenia, marked by extreme social withdrawal, hallucinations, delusions, silliness, inappropriate laughter, grotesque mannerisms, and other bizarre behavior.

displacement With regard to memory, the event that occurs when short-term memory is filled to capacity and each new, incoming item pushes out an existing item, which is then forgotten. With regard to behavior, a defense mechanism in which one substitutes a less threatening object or person for the original object of a sexual or aggressive impulse.

display rules Cultural rules that dictate how emotions should generally be expressed and when and where their expression is appropriate.

dispositional attribution Attributing a behavior to some internal cause, such as a personal trait, motive, or attitude; an internal attribution.

dissociative amnesia A dissociative disorder in which there is a complete or partial loss of the ability to recall personal information or identify past experiences.

dissociative disorders Disorders in which, under unbearable stress, consciousness becomes dissociated from a person's identity or her or his memories of important personal events, or both.

dissociative fugue (FEWG) A dissociative disorder in which one has a complete loss of memory of one's entire identity, travels away from home, and may assume a new identity.

dissociative identity disorder (DID) A dissociative disorder in which two or more distinct, unique personalities occur in the same person, and there is severe memory disruption concerning personal information about the other personalities.

divergent thinking The ability to produce multiple ideas, answers, or solutions to a problem for which there is no agreed-on solution.

diversity training Formal training aimed at equipping workers with the human relations skills they need to function effectively in a diverse workplace.

dominant-recessive pattern A set of inheritance rules in which the presence of a single dominant gene causes a trait to be expressed but two genes must be present for the expression of a recessive trait.

door-in-the-face technique A strategy in which someone makes a large, unreasonable request with the expectation that the person will refuse but will then be more likely to respond favorably to a smaller request later.

dopamine (DOE-pah-meen) A neurotransmitter that plays a role in learning, attention, movement, and reinforcement; neurons in the brains of those with Parkinson's disease and schizophrenia are less sensitive to its effects.

double-blind technique A procedure in which neither the participants nor the experimenter knows who is in the experimental and control groups until after the data have been gathered; a control for experimenter bias.

drive An internal state of tension or arousal that is brought about by an underlying need and that an organism is motivated to reduce.

drive-reduction theory A theory of motivation suggesting that biological needs create internal states of tension or arousal called drives, which organisms are motivated to reduce.

drug tolerance A condition in which the user becomes progressively less affected by the drug and must take larger and larger doses to maintain the same effect or high.

DSM-IV-TR The *Diagnostic and Statistical Manual of Mental Disorders,* 4th Edition, Text Revision, a manual published by the American Psychiatric Association, which describes the criteria used Text Revision to classify and diagnose mental disorders.

dyspareunia (dis-PAH-roo-nee-yah) A sexual pain disorder marked by genital pain associated with sexual intercourse; more common in females than in males.

ego (EE-go) In Freud's theory, the logical, rational, largely conscious system of personality, which operates according to the reality principle.

eidetic imagery (eye-DET-ik) The ability to retain the image of a visual stimulus for several minutes after it has been removed from view and to use this retained image to answer questions about the visual stimulus.

elaborative rehearsal A memory strategy that involves relating new information to something that is already known.

electroconvulsive therapy (ECT) A biological therapy in which an electric current is passed through the right hemisphere of the brain; usually reserved for severely depressed patients who are suicidal.

electroencephalogram (EEG) (ee-lek-tro-en-SEFF-uh-lo-gram) A record of brain-wave activity made by a machine called the electroencephalograph.

elicitation effect Exhibiting a behavior similar to that shown by a model in an unfamiliar situation.

elimination by aspects A decision-making approach in which alternatives are eliminated if they do not satisfy a set of factors that have been ordered from most to least important.

embryo The developing human organism during the period from week 3 through week 8, when the major systems, organs, and structures of the body develop.

emerging adulthood The period from the late teens to early twenties when individuals explore options prior to committing to adult roles.

emotion An identifiable feeling state involving physiological arousal, a cognitive appraisal of the situation or stimulus causing that internal body state, and an outward behavior expressing the state.

emotional intelligence The ability to apply knowledge about emotions to everyday life; this type of intelligence involves self-motivation, empathy, and the ability to handle relationships.

emotion-focused coping A response involving reappraisal of a stressor to reduce its emotional impact.

encoding The process of transforming information into a form that can be stored in memory.

encoding failure A cause of forgetting that occurs when information was never put into long-term memory.

endocrine system (EN-duh-krin) A system of ductless glands in various parts of the body that manufacture hormones and secrete them into the bloodstream, thus affecting cells in other parts of the body.

endorphins (en-DOR-fins) Chemicals produced naturally by the brain that reduce pain and the stress of vigorous exercise and positively affect mood.

epinephrine (EP-ih-NEF-rin) A neurotransmitter that affects the metabolism of glucose and nutrient energy stored in muscles to be released during strenuous exercise.

episodic memory (ep-ih-SOD-ik) The type of declarative memory that records events as they have been subjectively experienced.

equilibration The mental process that motivates humans to keep schemes in balance with the real environment.

erectile dysfunction A sexual dysfunction in which a man experiences the repeated inability to hear or sustain an erection firm enough for coitus; also known as impotence.

ergonomics Human factors psychology.

estrogen (ES-truh-jen) A female sex hormone that promotes the secondary sex characteristics in females and controls the menstrual cycle.

ethnocentrism The tendency to look at situations from one's own racial or cultural perspective.

evolutionary psychology The school of psychology that studies how humans have adapted the behaviors required for survival in the face of environmental pressures over the long course of evolution. It focuses on traits that exist in every member of a species.

excitement phase The first stage of the sexual response cycle, characterized by an erection in males and a swelling of the clitoris and vaginal lubrication in females.

exemplars The individual instances, or examples, of a concept that are stored in memory from personal experience.

exhaustion stage The third stage of the general adaptation syndrome, which occurs if the organism fails in its efforts to resist the stressor.

experimental group In an experiment, the group that is exposed to an independent variable.

experimental method The only research method that can be used to identify cause-effect relationships between two or more conditions or variables.

experimenter bias A phenomenon that occurs when a researcher's preconceived notions or expectations in some way influence participants' behavior and/or the researcher's interpretation of experimental results.

expert systems Computer programs designed to carry out highly specific functions within a limited domain.

exposure and response prevention A behavior therapy that exposes patients with obsessive-compulsive disorder to stimuli that trigger obsessions and compulsive rituals, while patients resist performing the compulsive rituals for progressively longer periods of time.

extinction In classical conditioning, the weakening and eventual disappearance of the conditioned response as a result of repeated presentation of the conditioned stimulus without the unconditioned stimulus. In operant conditioning, the weakening and eventual disappearance of the conditioned response as a result of the withholding of reinforcement.

extrasensory perception (ESP) Gaining information about objects, events, or another person's thoughts through some means other than known sensory channels.

extrinsic motivation The desire to behave in a certain way in order to gain some external reward or to avoid some undesirable consequence.

facial-feedback hypothesis The idea that the muscular movements involved in certain facial expressions produce the corresponding emotions (for example, smiling makes one feel happy).

family therapy Therapy involving an entire family, with the goal of helping family members reach agreement on changes that will help heal the family unit, improve communication problems, and create more understanding and harmony within the group.

fat cells Cells (also called adipose cells) that serve as storehouses for liquefied fat in the body; their number is determined by both genes and eating habits, and they decrease in size but not in number with weight loss.

feature detectors Neurons in the brain that respond only to specific visual patterns (for example, to lines and angles).

female orgasmic disorder A sexual dysfunction in which a woman is persistently unable to reach orgasm or delays in reaching orgasm, despite adequate sexual stimulation.

female sexual arousal disorder A sexual dysfunction in which a woman may not feel sexually aroused in response to sexual stimulation or may be unable to achieve or sustain an adequate lubrication-swelling response to sexual excitement.

fetal alcohol syndrome A condition that is caused by maternal alcohol intake early in prenatal development and that leads to facial deformities as well as mental retardation.

fetus The developing human organism during the period from week 9 until birth, when rapid growth and further development of the structures, organs, and systems of the body occur.

fight-or-flight response A response to stress in which the parasympathetic nervous system triggers the release of hormones that prepare the body to fight or flee.

five-factor model A trait theory that attempts to explain personality using five broad dimensions, each of which is composed of a constellation of personality traits.

fixation Arrested development at a psychosexual stage occurring because of excessive gratification or frustration at that stage.

fixed-interval schedule A schedule in which a reinforcer is given following the first correct response after a specific period of time has elapsed.

fixed-ratio schedule A schedule in which a reinforcer is given after a fixed number of correct, nonreinforced responses.

flashbulb memory An extremely vivid memory of the conditions surrounding one's first hearing the news of a surprising, shocking, or highly emotional event.

flooding A behavior therapy based on classical conditioning and used to treat phobias by exposing clients to the feared object or event (or asking them to imagine it vividly) for an extended period, until their anxiety decreases.

fluid intelligence A type of intelligence comprising abstract reasoning and mental flexibility, which peak in the early 20s and decline slowly as people age.

foot-in-the-door technique A strategy designed to gain a favorable response to a small request at first, with the intent of making the person more likely to agree later to a larger request.

forebrain The largest part of the brain, where cognitive functions as well as many of the motor functions of the brain are carried out.

formal concept A concept that is clearly defined by a set of rules, a formal definition, or a classification system.

formal operations stage Piaget's fourth and final stage of cognitive development (ages 11 or 12 years and beyond), which is characterized by the ability to apply logical thinking to abstract problems and hypothetical situations.

fovea (FO-vee-uh) A small area at the center of the retina that provides the clearest and sharpest vision because it has the largest concentration of cones.

framing The way information is presented so as to emphasize either a potential gain or a potential loss as the outcome of a decision based on that information.

free association A psychoanalytic technique used to explore the unconscious by having patients reveal whatever thoughts, feelings, or images come to mind.

frequency The number of cycles completed by a sound wave in one second, determining the pitch of the sound; measured in the unit called the hertz.

frequency theory The theory of hearing that holds that hair cell receptors vibrate the same number of times per second as the sounds that reach them.

frontal lobes The largest of the brain's lobes, which contain the motor cortex, Broca's area, and the frontal association areas.

frustration-aggression hypothesis The hypothesis that frustration produces aggression.

functional fixedness The failure to use familiar objects in novel ways to solve problems because of a tendency to view objects only in terms of their customary functions.

functional MRI (fMRI) A brain-imaging technique that reveals both brain structure and brain activity more precisely and rapidly than PET.

functionalism An early school of psychology that was concerned with how humans and animals use mental processes in adapting to their environment.

fundamental attribution error The tendency to attribute others' behavior to dispositional factors.

g **factor** Spearman's term for a general ability that underlies all intellectual functions.

GABA Primary inhibitory neurotransmitter in the brain.

gender (JEN-der) The psychological and sociocultural definition of masculinity or femininity, based on the expected behaviors for males and females.

gender constancy The understanding that activities and clothes do not affect gender stability; acquired between ages 6 and 8.

gender identity The sense of being male or female; acquired between ages 2 and 3.

gender identity disorder Sexual disorder characterized by a problem accepting one's identity as male or female.

gender roles Cultural expectations about the behaviors appropriate to each gender.

gender schema theory A theory suggesting that young children are motivated to attend to and behave in ways consistent with gender-based standards and stereotypes of their culture.

gender stability The awareness that gender is a permanent characteristic; acquired between ages 4 and 5.

gender-sensitive therapy An approach to therapy that takes into account the effects of gender on both the therapist's and the client's behavior.

general adaptation syndrome (GAS) The predictable sequence of reactions (alarm, resistance, and exhaustion stages) that organisms show in response to stressors.

general slowing A process in which the reduction in the speed of neural transmission leads to a slowing of physical and mental functions.

generalization In classical conditioning, the tendency to make a conditioned response to a stimulus that is similar to the original conditioned stimulus. In operant conditioning, the tendency to make the learned response to a stimulus similar to that for which the response was originally reinforced.

generalized anxiety disorder An anxiety disorder in which people experience chronic, excessive worry for 6 months or more.

genes The segments of DNA that are located on the chromosomes and are the basic units for the transmission of all hereditary traits.

genital herpes An STD that is caused by the herpes simplex virus and results in painful blisters on the genitals; presently incurable, the infection usually recurs and is highly contagious during outbreaks.

genital warts Growths on the genitals that are caused by the human papillomavirus (HPV).

genitals (JEN-uh-tulz) The internal and external reproductive organs of males or females.

genotype An individual's genetic makeup.

Gestalt (geh-SHTALT) A German word that roughly refers to the whole form, pattern, or configuration that a person perceives.

Gestalt psychology The school of psychology that emphasizes that individuals perceive objects and patterns as whole units and that the perceived whole is more than the sum of its parts.

Gestalt therapy A therapy that was originated by Fritz Perls and that emphasizes the importance of clients' fully experiencing, in the present moment, their feelings, thoughts, and actions and then taking responsibility for them.

glass ceiling An invisible, institutional barrier that prevents women from reaching the highest executive positions in organizations.

glial cells (GLEE-ul) Specialized cells in the brain and spinal cord that hold neurons together, remove waste products such as dead neurons, and perform other manufacturing, nourishing, and cleanup tasks.

globalization The process through which workers all over the world have been brought into more frequent contact with one another as a result of advances in transportation and communications technology.

glutamate (GLOO-tah-mate) Primary excitatory neurotransmitter in the brain.

goal orientation therapy The view that achievement motivation depends on which of four goal orientations (mastery-approach, mastery-avoidance, performance-approach, performance-avoidance) an individual adopts.

gonads The sex glands; the ovaries in females and the testes in males.

gonorrhea (gahn-ah-REE-ah) A bacterial STD that, in males, causes a puslike discharge from the penis and painful urination; if untreated, females can develop pelvic inflammatory disease and possibly infertility.

group therapy A form of therapy in which several clients (usually 7 to 10) meet regularly with one or more therapists to resolve personal problems.

groupthink The tendency for members of a tightly knit group to be more concerned with preserving group solidarity and uniformity than with objectively evaluating all alternatives in decision making.

gustation The sense of taste.

habituation A decrease in response or attention to a stimulus as an infant becomes accustomed to it.

hair cells Sensory receptors for hearing that are attached to the basilar membrane in the cochlea.

hallucination An imaginary sensation.

hallucinogens (hal-LU-sin-o-jenz) A category of drugs that can alter and distort perceptions of time and space, alter mood, produce feelings of unreality, and cause hallucinations; also called psychedelics.

halo effect The tendency to assume that a person has generally positive or negative traits as a result of observing one major positive or negative trait.

hardiness A combination of three psychological qualities—commitment, control, and challenge—shared by people who can handle high levels of stress and remain healthy.

hassles Little stressors, including the irritating demands that can occur daily, that may cause more stress than major life changes do.

health psychology The subfield within psychology that is concerned with the psychological factors that contribute to health, illness, and recovery.

heritability A measure of the degree to which a characteristic is estimated to be influenced by heredity.

heuristic (yur-RIS-tik) A rule of thumb that is derived from experience and used in decision making and problem solving, although there is no guarantee of its accuracy or usefulness.

higher-order conditioning Conditioning that occurs when conditioned stimuli are linked together to form a series of signals.

hindbrain A link between the spinal cord and the brain that contains structures that regulate physiological functions, including heart rate, respiration, and blood pressure.

hippocampal region A part of the limbic system, which includes the hippocampus itself and the underlying cortical areas, involved in the formation of semantic memories.

hippocampus (hip-po-CAM-pus) A structure in the limbic system that plays a central role in the storing of new memories, the response to new or unexpected stimuli, and navigational ability.

homeostasis The natural tendency of the body to maintain a balanced internal state in order to ensure physical survival.

homophobia An intense, irrational hostility toward or fear of homosexuals.

hormone A chemical substance that is manufactured and released in one part of the body and affects other parts of the body.

hue The dimension of light that refers to the specific color perceived.

human factors psychology the subfield of industrial/organizational psychology that deals with the ways in which workers interact with the characteristics of a workplace.

human immunodeficiency virus (HIV) The virus that causes AIDS.

human papillomavirus (HPV) A virus that causes genital warts; also believed to contribute to cervical cancer.

humanistic psychology The school of psychology that focuses on the uniqueness of human beings and their capacity for choice, growth, and psychological health.

humanistic therapies Psychotherapies that assume that people have the ability and freedom to lead rational lives and make rational choices.

hypnosis A procedure through which one person, the hypnotist, uses the power of suggestion to induce changes in thoughts, feelings, sensations, perceptions, or behavior in another person, the subject.

hypoactive sexual desire disorder A sexual dysfunction marked by low or nonexistent sexual desire or interest in sexual activity.

hypochondriasis (HI-poh-kahn-DRY-uh-sis) A somatoform disorder in which persons are preoccupied with their health and fear that their physical symptoms are a sign of some serious disease, despite reassurance from doctors to the contrary.

hypothalamus (HY-po-THAL-uh-mus) A small but influential brain structure that regulates hunger, thirst, sexual behavior, internal body temperature, other body functions, and a wide variety of emotional behaviors.

hypothesis A prediction about a cause-effect relationship between two or more variables.

id (ID) The unconscious system of the personality, which contains the life and death instincts and operates on the pleasure principle; source of the libido.

identity crisis The emotional turmoil a teenager experiences when trying to establish a sense of personal identity.

illusion A false perception or a misperception of an actual stimulus in the environment.

imagery The representation in the mind of a sensory experience—visual, auditory, gustatory, motor, olfactory, or tactile.

inattentional blindness The phenomenon in which we shift our focus from one object to another and, in the process, fail to notice changes in objects to which we are not directly paying attention.

in-basket test A work simulation test in which applicants for managerial positions are given a stack of memos, reports, and other kinds of papers and expected to generate decisions based on their contents in a limited amount of time.

incentive An external stimulus that motivates behavior (for example, money or fame).

inclusion Educating mentally retarded students in regular schools by placing them in classes with nonhandicapped students for part of the day or in special classrooms in regular schools; also known as mainstreaming.

independent variable In an experiment, a factor or condition that is deliberately manipulated in order to determine whether it causes any change in another behavior or condition.

individualism/collectivism dimension A measure of a culture's emphasis on either individual achievement or social relationships.

inductive reasoning Reasoning in which general conclusions are drawn from particular facts or individual cases.

industrial/organizational (I/O) psychologists Psychologists who apply psychological principles and research results in the workplace and are especially interested in work motivation and job performance.

infantile amnesia The relative inability of older children and adults to recall events from the first few years of life.

information-processing theory An approach to the study of mental structures and processes that uses the computer as a model for human thinking.

in-group A social group with a strong sense of togetherness, from which others are excluded.

inhibitory effect Suppressing a behavior because a model is punished for displaying the behavior.

inner ear The innermost portion of the ear, containing the cochlea, the vestibular sacs, and the semicircular canals.

insight The sudden realization of the relationship between elements in a problem situation, which makes the solution apparent.

insight therapies Approaches to psychotherapy based on the notion that psychological well-being depends on self-understanding.

insomnia A sleep disorder characterized by difficulty falling or staying asleep, by waking too early, or by sleep that is light, restless, or of poor quality.

integrated behavioral couple therapy (IBCT) A type of couple therapy that emphasizes both behavior change and mutual acceptance

intelligence An individual's ability to understand complex ideas, to adapt effectively to the environment, to learn from experience, to engage in various forms of reasoning, and to overcome obstacles through mental effort.

intelligence quotient (IQ) An index of intelligence originally derived by dividing mental age by chronological age and then multiplying by 100; now derived by comparing an individual's score with the scores of others of the same age.

interference A cause of forgetting that occurs because information or associations stored either before or after a given memory hinder the ability to remember it.

interpersonal therapy (IPT) A brief psychotherapy designed to help depressed people better understand and cope with problems relating to their interpersonal relationships.

intersex The condition in which a person's internal organs differ from his or her external genetalia.

intrinsic motivation The desire to behave in a certain way because it is enjoyable or satisfying in and of itself.

intuition Rapidly formed judgments based on "gut feelings" or "instincts."

inventory A paper-and-pencil test with questions about a person's thoughts, feelings, and behaviors, which measures several dimensions of personality and can be scored according to a standard procedure.

James-Lange theory of emotion The theory that emotional feelings result when an individual becomes aware of a physiological response to an emotion-provoking stimulus (for example, feeling fear because of trembling).

job analysis An assessment by a personnel psychologist of a job category to determine the work that needs to be done and the skills required to do it.

job description An outline of the responsibilities associated with a given job category; the end result of a job analysis.

job enrichment The process of changing a job so that it will be more intrinsically motivating.

job rotation An approach to training in which employees spend relatively short periods of time performing the various jobs in an organization.

job satisfaction The degree to which an individual feels positively about his or her job.

job simplification The process of standardizing the tasks associated with a particular job.

just noticeable difference (JND) The smallest change in sensation that a person is able to detect 50% of the time.

kinesthetic sense The sense providing information about the position of body parts in relation to each other and the movement of the entire body or its parts.

laboratory observation A descriptive research method in which behavior is studied in a laboratory setting, where researchers can exert more control and use more precise equipment to measure responses.

language A means of communicating thoughts and feelings, using a system of socially shared but arbitrary symbols (sounds, signs, or written symbols) arranged according to rules of grammar.

latent content Freud's term for the underlying meaning of a dream.

latent learning Learning that occurs without apparent reinforcement and is not demonstrated until the organism is motivated to do so.

lateral hypothalamus (LH) The part of the hypothalamus that acts as a feeding center to incite eating.

lateralization The specialization of one of the cerebral hemispheres to handle a particular function.

law of effect One of Thorndike's laws of learning, which states that the consequence, or effect, of a response will determine whether the tendency to respond in the same way in the future will be strengthened or weakened.

Lazarus theory of emotion The theory that a cognitive appraisal is the first step in an emotional response and all other aspects of an emotion, including physiological arousal, depend on it.

leader-member exchange (LMX) theory A behavioral perspective on leadership that assumes that leaders and followers exert mutual influences on one another and takes into account the emotional aspects of leader-follower relationships.

leadership The ability to get individuals or groups to do what the leader wants done.

learned helplessness A passive resignation to aversive conditions that is learned through repeated exposure to inescapable or unavoidable aversive events.

learning A relatively permanent change in behavior, knowledge, capability, or attitude that is acquired through experience and cannot be attributed to illness, injury, or maturation.

left hemisphere The hemisphere that controls the right side of the body, coordinates complex movements, and, in most people, handles most of the language functions.

lens The transparent disc-shaped structure behind the iris and the pupil that changes shape as it focuses on objects at varying distances.

lifespan perspective The view that developmental changes happen throughout the human lifespan and that interdisciplinary research is required to fully understand human development.

limbic system A group of structures in the midbrain, including the amygdala and hippocampus, that are collectively involved in emotional expression, memory, and motivation.

linguistic relativity hypothesis The notion proposed by Whorf that the language a person speaks largely determines the nature of that person's thoughts.

lithium A drug used to treat bipolar disorder, which at proper maintenance dosage, reduces both manic and depressive episodes.

locus of control Rotter's concept of a cognitive factor that explains how people account for what happens in their lives—either seeing themselves as primarily in control of their behavior and its consequences (internal locus of control) or perceiving what happens to them to be in the hands of fate, luck, or chance (external locus of control).

longitudinal study A type of developmental study in which the same group of participants is followed and measured at different ages.

long-term memory (LTM) The memory system with a virtually unlimited capacity that contains vast stores of a person's permanent or relatively permanent memories.

long-term potentiation (LTP) An increase in the efficiency of neural transmission at the synapses that last for hours or longer.

low birth weight A weight at birth of less than 5.5 pounds.

low-ball technique A strategy in which someone makes a very attractive initial offer to get a person to commit to an action and then makes the terms less favorable.

lucid dream A dream that an individual is aware of dreaming and whose content the individual is often able to influence while the dream is in progress.

lymphocytes The white blood cells—including B cells and T cells—that are the key components of the immune system.

maintenance rehearsal Repeating information in short-term memory until it is no longer needed; may eventually lead to storage of information or long-term memory.

major depressive disorder A mood disorder marked by feelings of great sadness, despair, and hopelessness as well as the loss of the ability to experience pleasure.

male orgasmic disorder A sexual dysfunction in which a man experiences the absence of ejaculation, or ejaculation occurs only after strenuous effort over a prolonged period.

management by objectives (MBO) An evaluation approach in which subordinates and supervisors set performance goals together and agree on how goal attainment will be measured and how much time will be allotted to reach each goal.

manic episode (MAN-ik) A period of excessive euphoria, inflated self-esteem, wild optimism, and hyperactivity, often accompanied by delusions of grandeur and by hostility if activity is blocked.

manifest content Freud's term for the content of a dream as recalled by the dreamer.

massed practice Learning in one long practice session without rest periods.

matching hypothesis The notion that people tend to have lovers or spouses who are similar to themselves in physical attractiveness and other assets.

maturation Each infant's own genetically determined, biological pattern of development.

means-end analysis A heuristic strategy in which the current position is compared with a desired goal, and a series of steps is formulated and then taken to close the gap between the two.

meditation (concentrative) A group of techniques that involve focusing attention on an object, a word, one's breathing, or one's body movements in order to block out all distractions, to enhance well-being, and to achieve an altered state of consciousness.

medulla (muh-DUL-uh) The part of the brainstem that controls heartbeat, blood pressure, breathing, coughing, and swallowing.

memory The process of encoding, storage, consolidation, and retrieval of information.

menopause The cessation of menstruation, which usually occurs between ages 45 and 55 and marks the end of reproductive capacity.

mental retardation Subnormal intelligence reflected by an IQ below 70 and by adaptive functioning that is severely deficient for one's age.

mental set The tendency to apply a familiar strategy to solve a problem even though another approach might be better.

mere-exposure effect The tendency to feel more positively toward a stimulus as a result of repeated exposure to it.

metabolic rate (meh-tuh-BALL-ik) The rate at which the body burns calories to produce energy.

metamemory The ability to think about and control one's own memory processes.

microelectrode A small wire used to monitor the electrical activity of or stimulate activity within a single neuron.

microsleep A brief lapse (2 to 3 seconds long) from wakefulness into sleep, usually occurring when a person has been sleep-deprived.

midbrain Area that contains structures linking the physiological functions of the hindbrain to the cognitive functions of the forebrain.

middle ear The portion of the ear containing the ossicles, which connect the eardrum to the oval window and amplify sound waves.

Minnesota Multiphasic Personality Inventory (MMPI) The most extensively researched and widely used personality test, which is used to screen for and diagnose psychiatric problems and disorders; revised as MMPI-2.

model The individual who demonstrates a behavior or whose behavior is imitated.

modeling Another name for observational learning.

modeling effect Learning a new behavior from a model through the acquisition of new responses.

monocular depth cues (mah-NOK-yu-ler) Depth cues that can be perceived by one eye alone.

mood disorders Disorders characterized by extreme and unwarranted disturbances in emotion or mood.

moral-rights perspective An approach to organizational ethics that suggests that individual behavior within an organization should be guided by the same respect for basic rights that is endorsed by the larger culture.

morphemes The smallest units of meaning in a language.

motivated forgetting Forgetting through suppression or repression in order to protect oneself from material that is painful, frightening, or otherwise unpleasant.

motivation All the processes that initiate, direct, and sustain behavior.

motives Needs or desires that energize and direct behavior toward a goal.

motor cortex The strip of tissue at the rear of the frontal lobes that controls voluntary body movement and participates in learning and cognitive events.

MRI (magnetic resonance imagery) A diagnostic scanning technique that produces high-resolution images of the structures of the brain.

multifactorial inheritance A pattern of inheritance in which a trait is influenced by both genes and environmental factors.

myelin sheath (MY-uh-lin) The white, fatty coating wrapped around some axons that acts as insulation and enables impulses to travel much faster.

Myers-Briggs Type Indicator (MBTI) A personality inventory useful for measuring normal individual differences; based on Jung's theory of personality.

naive subject A person who has agreed to participate in an experiment but is not aware that deception is being used to conceal its real purpose.

narcolepsy An incurable sleep disorder characterized by excessive daytime sleepiness and uncontrollable attacks of REM sleep.

narcotics A class of depressant drugs derived from the opium poppy that produce both pain-relieving and calming effects.

natural concept A concept acquired not from a definition but through everyday perceptions and experiences.

naturalistic observation A descriptive research method in which researchers observe and record behavior in its natural setting, without attempting to influence or control it.

nature-nurture debate The debate over whether intelligence (or another trait) is primarily the result of heredity (nature) or the environment (nurture).

need for achievement (n Ach) The need to accomplish something difficult and to perform at a high standard of excellence.

negative punishment A decrease in behavior that results from a removed consequence.

negative reinforcement The termination of an unpleasant condition after a response, which increases the probability that the response will be repeated.

neglecting parents Parents who are permissive and are not involved in their children's lives.

neodissociation theory of hypnosis A theory proposing that hypnosis induces a split, or dissociation, between two aspects of the control of consciousness: the planning function and the monitoring function.

neonate A newborn infant up to 1 month old.

neuron (NEW-ron) A specialized cell that conducts impulses through the nervous system and contains three major parts—a cell body, dendrites, and an axon.

neuroscience An interdisciplinary field that combines the work of psychologists, biologists, biochemists, medical researchers, and others in the study of the structure and function of the nervous system.

neurotransmitter (NEW-ro-TRANS-mit-er) A chemical substance that is released into the synaptic cleft from the axon terminal of a sending neuron, crosses a synapse, and binds to appropriate receptor sites on the dendrites or cell body of a receiving neuron, influencing the cell either to fire or not to fire.

nightmares Frightening dreams that occur during REM sleep and are likely to be remembered in vivid detail.

nondeclarative memory The subsystem within long-term memory that stores motor skills, habits, and simple classically conditioned responses; also called implicit memory.

nondirective therapy Any type of psychotherapy in which the therapist allows the direction of the therapy sessions to be controlled by the client; an example is person-centered therapy.

nonsense syllable A consonant-vowel-consonant combination that does not spell a word and is used in memory research.

norepinephrine (nor-EP-ih-NEF-rin) A neurotransmitter affecting eating, alertness, and sleep.

norms Standards based on the test scores of a large number of individuals and used as bases of comparison for other test takers.

NREM dream A type of dream occurring during NREM sleep that is typically less frequent and memorable than REM dreams are.

NREM sleep Non-rapid eye movement sleep, which consists of four sleep stages and is characterized by slow, regular respiration and heart rate, little body movement, an absence of rapid eye movements, and blood pressure and brain activity that are at their 24-hour low points.

obesity Body mass index more than 30.

object permanence The realization that objects continue to exist even when they are out of sight.

observational learning Learning by observing the behavior of others and the consequences of that behavior; learning by imitation.

obsession A persistent, involuntary thought, image, or impulse that invades consciousness and causes great distress.

obsessive-compulsive disorder (OCD) An anxiety disorder in which a person suffers from recurrent obsessions and/or compulsions.

occipital lobes (ahk-SIP-uh-tul) The lobes that are involved in the reception and interpretation of visual information; they contain the primary visual cortex.

Oedipus complex (ED-uh-pus) Occurring in the phallic stage, a conflict in which the child is sexually attracted to the opposite-sex parent and feels hostility toward the same-sex parent.

off-the-job training An approach to training in which employees watch videos or demonstrations and are expected to implement what they learn when on the job.

olfaction (ol-FAK-shun) The sense of smell.

olfactory bulbs Two matchstick-sized structures above the nasal cavities, where smell sensations first register in the brain.

olfactory epithelium Two 1-square-inch patches of tissue, one at the top of each nasal cavity, which together contain about 10 million olfactory neurons, the receptors for smell.

on-the-job training An approach to training in which employees receive instructions while actually performing the job.

operant conditioning A type of learning in which the consequences of behavior are manipulated in order to increase or decrease the frequency of an existing response or to shape an entirely new response.

opponent-process theory The theory of color vision suggesting that three kinds of cells respond by increasing or decreasing their rate of firing when different colors are present.

optic nerve The nerve that carries visual information from each retina to both sides of the brain.

organization Piaget's term for a mental process that uses specific experiences to make inferences that can be generalized to new experiences.

organizational climate Employees' perceptions and emotional responses to the culture of an organization.

organizational culture The system of shared values, beliefs, and practices that evolves within an organization and influences the behavior of its members.

organizational psychology The study of individuals and groups in formal organizations.

organizational social responsibility A perspective based on the idea that an organization's policies should take into consideration the interests of the larger society of which it is a part.

orgasm The third stage of the sexual response cycle, marked by a sudden discharge of accumulated sexual tension and involuntary muscle contractions.

outer ear The visible part of the ear, consisting of the pinna and the auditory canal.

out-group A social group made up of individuals specifically identified by the in-group as not belonging.

overextension The application of a word, on the basis of some shared feature, to a broader range of objects than is appropriate.

overlearning Practicing or studying material beyond the point where it can be repeated once without error.

overregularization The act of inappropriately applying the grammatical rules for forming plurals and past tenses to irregular nouns and verbs.

panic attack An episode of overwhelming anxiety, fear, or terror.

panic disorder An anxiety disorder in which a person experiences recurring, unpredictable episodes of overwhelming anxiety, fear, or terror.

paranoid schizophrenia (PAIR-uh-noid) A type of schizophrenia characterized by delusions of grandeur or persecution.

parasomnias Sleep disturbances in which behaviors and physiological states that normally take place only in the waking state occur while a person is sleeping.

parasympathetic nervous system The division of the autonomic nervous system that brings the heightened bodily responses back to normal following an emergency.

parietal lobes (puh-RY-uh-tul) The lobes that contain the somatosensory cortex (where touch, pressure, temperature, and pain register) and other areas that are responsible for body awareness and spatial orientation.

partial reinforcement A pattern of reinforcement in which some but not all correct responses are reinforced.

partial reinforcement effect The greater resistance to extinction that occurs when a portion, rather than all, of the correct responses are reinforced.

participant modeling A behavior therapy in which an appropriate response to a feared stimulus is modeled in graduated steps and the client attempts to imitate the model step by step, encouraged and supported by the therapist.

participative management A management technique in which managers involve subordinates in the decision-making process.

pelvic inflammatory disease (PID) An infection in the female pelvic organs, which can result from untreated chlamydia or gonorrhea and can cause pain, scarring of tissue, and even infertility or an ectopic pregnancy.

perception The process by which sensory information is actively organized and interpreted by the brain.

perceptual constancy The phenomenon that allows us to perceive objects as maintaining stable properties, such as size, shape, and brightness, despite differences in distance, viewing angle, and lighting.

perceptual set An expectation of what will be perceived, which can affect what actually is perceived.

performance appraisal A formal process used to determine how well an employee is functioning in his or her job.

peripheral nervous system (PNS) (peh-RIF-er-ul) The nerves connecting the central nervous system to the rest of the body.

permissive parents Parents who make few rules or demands and usually do not enforce those that are made; they allow children to make their own decisions and control their own behavior.

personal space An area surrounding each person, much like an invisible bubble, that the person considers part of himself or herself and uses to regulate the level of intimacy with others.

personal unconscious In Jung's theory, the layer of the unconscious that contains all of the thoughts, perceptions, and experiences accessible to the conscious, as well as repressed memories, wishes, and impulses.

personality A person's characteristic patterns of behaving, thinking, and feeling.

personality disorder A long-standing, inflexible, maladaptive pattern of behaving and relating to others, which usually begins in early childhood or adolescence.

person-centered therapy A nondirective, humanistic therapy developed by Carl Rogers, in which the therapist creates an accepting climate and shows empathy, freeing clients to be themselves and releasing their natural tendency toward self-actualization.

personnel psychology The branch of industrial/organizational psychology that deals with the design of appropriate and effective strategies for hiring, training, and evaluating employees.

persuasion A deliberate attempt to influence the attitudes and/or behavior of another person.

pervasive development disorders (PDDs) A group of disorders in which children exhibit severe disturbances in social relationships.

PET scan (positron-emission tomography) A brain-imaging technique that reveals activity in various parts of the brain, based on patterns of blood flow, oxygen use, and glucose consumption.

phenotype An individuals actual characteristics.

pheromones Chemicals excreted by humans and other animals that can have a powerful effect on the behavior of other members of the same species.

phi phenomenon Apparent motion that occurs when several stationary lights in a dark room are flashed on and off in sequence, causing the perception that a single light is moving from one spot to the next.

phobia (FO-bee-ah) A persistent, irrational fear of some specific object, situation, or activity that poses little or no real danger.

phonemes The smallest units of sound in a spoken language.

phonological awareness Sensitivity to the sound patterns of a language and how they are represented as letters.

physical drug dependence A compulsive pattern of drug use in which the user develops a drug tolerance coupled with unpleasant withdrawal symptoms when the drug use is discontinued.

pituitary gland The endocrine gland located in the brain that releases hormones that activate other endocrine glands as well as growth hormone; often called the "master gland."

place theory The theory of hearing that holds that each individual pitch a person hears is determined by the particular location along the basilar membrane of the cochlea that vibrates the most.

placebo (pluh-SEE-bo) An inert or harmless substance given to the control group in an experiment as a control for the placebo effect.

placebo effect The phenomenon that occurs in an experiment when a participant's response to a treatment is due to his or her expectations about the treatment rather than to the treatment itself.

plasticity The capacity of the brain to adapt to changes such as brain damage.

plateau phase The second stage of the sexual response cycle, during which muscle tension and blood flow to the genitals increase in preparation for orgasm.

polygraph A device designed to detect the changes in heart rate, blood pressure, respiration rate, and skin conductance response that typically accompany arousal.

population The entire group of interest to researchers, to which they wish to generalize their findings; the group from which a sample is selected.

positive punishment A decrease in behavior that results from an added consequence.

positive reinforcement Any pleasant or desirable consequence that follows a response and increases the probability that the response will be repeated.

postconventional level Kohlberg's highest level of moral reasoning, in which moral reasoning involves weighing moral alternatives and realizing that laws may conflict with basic human rights.

posttraumatic stress disorder (PTSD) A prolonged and severe stress reaction to a catastrophic event or to severe, chronic stress.

pragmatics The characteristics of spoken language, such as intonation and gestures, that indicate the social meaning of utterances.

preconscious The thoughts, feelings, and memories that a person is not consciously aware of at the moment but that may be easily brought to consciousness.

prejudice Attitudes (usually negative) toward others based on their gender, religion, race, or membership in a particular group.

premature ejaculation A chronic or recurring orgasmic disorder in which orgasm and ejaculation occur with little stimulation, before, during, or shortly after penetration and before the man wishes; the most common sexual dysfunction in males.

prenatal development Development that occurs between conception and birth and consists of three stages (germinal, embryonic, and fetal).

preoperational stage Piaget's second stage of cognitive development (ages 2 to 6 years), which is characterized by the development and refinement of schemes for symbolic representation.

presbyopia (prez-bee-O-pee-uh) A condition, developing in the mid- to late 40s, in which the lenses of the eyes no longer accommodate adequately for near vision, and reading glasses or bifocals are required for reading.

primacy effect In memory, the tendency to recall the first items in a sequence more readily than the middle items. In social psychology, the tendency for an overall impression of another to be influenced more by the first information that is received about that person than by information that comes later.

primary appraisal A cognitive evaluation of a potentially stressful event to determine whether its effect is positive, irrelevant, or negative.

primary auditory cortex The part of each temporal lobe where hearing registers in the cerebral cortex.

primary drive A state of tension or arousal that arises from a biological need and is unlearned.

primary mental abilities According to Thurstone, seven relatively distinct abilities that, singly or in combination, are involved in all intellectual activities.

primary reinforcer A reinforcer that fulfills a basic physical need for survival and does not depend on learning.

primary sex characteristics The internal and external reproductive organs; the genitals.

primary visual cortex The area at the rear of the occipital lobes where vision registers in the cerebral cortex.

priming The phenomenon by which an earlier encounter with a stimulus (such as a word or a picture) increases the speed or accuracy of naming that stimulus or a related stimulus at a later time.

proactive coping Active measures taken in advance of a potentially stressful situation in order to prevent its occurrence or to minimize its consequences.

problem solving Using thoughts and actions to achieve a desired goal that is not readily attainable.

problem-focused coping A direct response aimed at reducing, modifying, or eliminating a source of stress.

progesterone (pro-JES-tah-rone) A female sex hormone that plays a role in the regulation of the menstrual cycle and prepares the lining of the uterus for pregnancy.

projective test A personality test in which people respond to inkblots, drawings of ambiguous human situations, or incomplete sentences by projecting their inner thoughts, feelings, fears, or conflicts onto the test materials.

prosocial behavior Behavior that benefits others, such as helping, cooperation, and sympathy.

prospective forgetting Not remembering to carry out some intended action.

prototype An example that embodies the most common and typical features of a concept.

proximity Physical or geographic closeness; a major influence on attraction.

pruning The process through which the developing brain eliminates unnecessary or redundant synapses.

psychiatrist A mental health professional who is a medical doctor.

psychoactive drug Any substance that alters mood, perception, or thought; called a controlled substance if approved for medical use.

psychoanalysis (SY-ko-ah-NAL-ih-sis) The term Freud used for both his theory of personality and his therapy for the treatment of psychological disorders; the unconscious is the primary focus of psychoanalytic theory, and the therapy uses free association, dream analysis, and transference.

psychodynamic therapies Psychotherapies that attempt to uncover childhood experiences that are thought to explain a patient's current difficulties.

psycholinguistics The study of how language is acquired, produced, and used, and how the sounds and symbols of language are translated into meaning.

psychological disorders Mental processes and/or behavior patterns that cause emotional distress and/or substantial impairment in functioning.

psychological drug dependence A craving or irresistible urge for a drug's pleasurable effects.

psychological perspectives General points of view used for explaining people's behavior and thinking, whether normal or abnormal.

psychologist A mental health professional who possesses a doctoral degree in psychology.

psychology The scientific study of behavior and mental processes.

psychoneuroimmunology (sye-ko-NEW-ro-IM-you-NOLL-oh-gee) A field in which psychologists, biologists, and medical researchers combine their expertise to study the effects of psychological factors on the immune system.

psychosexual stages A series of stages through which the sexual instinct develops; each stage is defined by an erogenous zone around which conflict arises.

psychosis (sy-CO-sis) A condition characterized by loss of contact with reality.

psychosocial stages Erikson's eight developmental stages through which individuals progress during their lifespan; each stage is defined by a conflict involving the individual's relationship with the social environment, which must be resolved satisfactorily in order for healthy development to occur.

psychosurgery Brain surgery performed to alleviate serious psychological disorders or unbearable chronic pain.

psychotherapy Any type of treatment for emotional and behavioral disorders that uses psychological rather than biological means.

puberty A period of several years in which rapid physical growth and physiological changes occur, culminating in sexual maturity.

punishment A decrease in the frequency of a behavior caused by some kind of consequence.

quality circle A group of employees who meet regularly to search for ways to increase a company's productivity, improve the quality of its products, or reduce its costs.

quality of work life (QWL) movement An approach to reducing work-related stress by basing job and workplace design on analyses of the quality of employee experiences in an organization.

random assignment The process of selecting participants for experimental and control groups by using a chance procedure to guarantee that each participant has an equal probability of being assigned to any of the groups; a control for selection bias.

rational emotive behavior therapy A directive form of psychotherapy, developed by Albert Ellis and designed to challenge clients' irrational beliefs about themselves and others.

real motion Perceptions of motion tied to movements of real objects through space.

realistic conflict theory The view that as competition increases among social groups for scarce resources, so do prejudice, discrimination, and hatred.

reasoning A form of thinking in which conclusions are drawn from a set of facts.

recall A memory task in which a person must produce required information by searching memory.

recency effect The tendency to recall the last items in a sequence more readily than those in the middle.

receptors Protein molecules on the surfaces of dendrites and cell bodies that have distinctive shapes and will interact only with specific neurotransmitters.

reciprocal determinism Bandura's concept of a mutual influential relationship among behavior, cognitive factors, and environment.

recognition A memory task in which a person must simply identify material as familiar or as having been encountered before.

recognition heuristic A strategy in which decision making stops as soon as a factor that moves one toward a decision has been recognized.

reconstruction An account of an event that has been pieced together from a few highlights, using information that may or may not be accurate.

recruitment The identification of appropriate candidates for a particular position.

reflex An inborn, unlearned, automatic response (such as blinking, sucking, and grasping) to a particular environmental stimulus.

rehearsal The act of purposely repeating information to maintain it in short-term memory.

reinforcement Any event that follows a response and strengthens or increases the probability that the response will be repeated.

reinforcer Anything that follows a response and strengthens it or increases the probability that it will occur.

relationship therapies Therapies that attempt to improve patients' interpersonal relationships or create new relationships to support patients' efforts to address psychological problems.

relearning method A measure of memory in which retention is expressed as the percentage of time saved when material is relearned compared with the time required to learn the material originally.

reliability The ability of a test to yield nearly the same score when the same people are tested and then retested on the same test or an alternative form of the test.

REM dream A type of dream occurring almost continuously during each REM period and having a storylike quality; typically more vivid, visual, and emotional than NREM dreams.

REM rebound The increased amount of REM sleep that occurs after REM deprivation; often associated with unpleasant dreams or nightmares.

REM sleep A type of sleep characterized by rapid eye movements, paralysis of large muscles, fast and irregular heart and respiration rates, increased brain-wave activity, and vivid dreams.

replication The process of repeating a study with different participants and preferably a different investigator to verify research findings.

representative sample A sample that mirrors the population of interest; it includes important subgroups in the same proportions as they are found in that population.

representativeness heuristic A thinking strategy based on how closely a new object or situation is judged to resemble or match an existing prototype of that object or situation.

repression A defense mechanism in which one involuntarily removes painful or threatening memories, thoughts, or perceptions from consciousness, so that one is no longer aware that a painful event occurred, or prevents unconscious sexual and aggressive impulses from breaking into consciousness.

resistance stage The second stage of the general adaptation syndrome, when there are intense physiological efforts to either resist or adapt to the stressor.

resolution phase The final stage of the sexual response cycle, during which the body returns to an unaroused state.

resting potential The slight negative electrical potential of the axon membrane of a neuron at rest, about -70 millivolts.

restorative theory of sleep The theory that the function of sleep is to restore body and mind.

reticular formation A structure in the brainstem that plays a crucial role in arousal and attention and that screens sensory messages entering the brain.

retina The layer of tissue that is located on the inner surface of the eyeball and contains the sensory receptors for vision.

retrieval The process of bringing to mind information that has been stored in memory.

retrieval cue Any stimulus or bit of information that aids in retrieving particular information from long-term memory.

retrieval failure Not remembering something one is certain of knowing.

retrograde amnesia (RET-ro-grade) A loss of memory for experiences that occurred shortly before a loss of consciousness.

reuptake The process by which neurotransmitters are taken from the synaptic cleft back into the axon terminal for later use, thus terminating their excitatory or inhibitory effect on the receiving neuron.

reversibility The fact that when only the appearance of a substance has been changed, it can be returned to its original state.

right hemisphere The hemisphere that controls the left side of the body and, in most people, is specialized for visual-spatial perception.

rods The light-sensitive receptor cells in the retina that look like slender cylinders and allow the eye to respond to as few as five photons of light.

Rorschach Inkblot Method (ROR-shok) A projective test composed of 10 inkblots that the test taker is asked to describe; used to assess personality, make differential diagnoses, plan and evaluate treatment, and predict behavior.

sample A part of population that is studied in order to reach conclusions about the entire population.

saturation The purity of a color, or the degree to which the light waves producing it are of the same wavelength.

savant syndrome A condition that allows an individual whose level of general intelligence is very low to perform highly creative or difficult mental feats.

savings score The percentage of time saved when relearning material compared with the amount of time required for the original learning.

scapegoating Displacing aggression onto members of minority groups or other innocent targets not responsible for the frustrating situation.

Schachter-Singer theory of emotion A two-factor theory stating that for an emotion to occur, there must be (1) physiological arousal and (2) a cognitive interpretation or explanation of the arousal, allowing it to be labeled as a specific emotion.

schedule of reinforcement A systematic process for administering partial reinforcement that produces a distinct rate and pattern of responses and degree of resistance to extinction.

schemas The integrated frameworks of knowledge and assumptions a person has about people, objects, and events, which affect how the person encodes and recalls information.

scheme A plan of action, based on previous experiences, to be used in similar circumstances.

schizophrenia (SKIT-soh-FREE-nee-ah) A severe psychological disorder characterized by loss of contact with reality, hallucinations, delusions, inappropriate or flat affect, some disturbance in thinking, social withdrawal, and/or other bizarre behavior.

scientific management An approach to management that assumes that workers and their supervisors operate more effectively and efficiently when job requirements are based on empirical data.

scientific method The orderly, systematic procedures that researchers follow as they identify a research problem, design a study to investigate the problem, collect and analyze data, draw conclusions, and communicate their findings.

secondary appraisal A cognitive evaluation of available resources and options prior to deciding how to deal with a stressor.

secondary sex characteristics Those physical characteristics that are not directly involved in reproduction but that appear at puberty and distinguish the mature male from the mature female.

selection The process of matching applicants to jobs.

selection bias The assignment of participants to experimental or control groups in such a way that systematic differences among the groups are present at the beginning of the experiment.

self-actualization Developing to one's fullest potential.

self-efficacy The perception a person has of his or her ability to perform competently whatever is attempted.

self-managed teams A group of workers who have complete responsibility for planning, executing, and evaluating their work.

self-serving bias The tendency to attribute one's successes to dispositional causes and one's failures to situational causes.

semantic memory The type of declarative memory that stores general knowledge, or objective facts and information.

semantics The meaning derived from morphemes, words, and sentences.

semicircular canals Three fluid-filled tubular canals in the inner ear that sense the rotation of the head.

sensation The process through which the senses pick up visual, auditory, and other sensory stimuli and transmit them to the brain.

sensorimotor stage Piaget's first stage of cognitive development (ages birth to 2 years), in which infants gain an understanding of their world through their senses and their motor activities; culminates with the development of object permanence and the beginning of representational thought.

sensory adaptation The process in which sensory receptors grow accustomed to constant, unchanging levels of stimuli over time.

sensory memory The memory system that holds information from the senses for a period of time ranging from only a fraction of a second to about 2 seconds.

sensory receptors Highly specialized cells in the sense organs that detect and respond to one type of sensory stimuli—light, sound, or odor, for example—and transduce (convert) the stimuli into neural impulses.

separation anxiety The fear and distress shown by infants and toddlers when the parent leaves, occurring from 8 to 24 months and reaching a peak between 12 and 18 months.

serial position effect The finding that, for information learned in a sequence, recall is better for the beginning and ending items than for the middle items in the sequence.

serotonin (ser-oh-TOE-nin) A neurotransmitter that plays an important role in regulating mood, sleep, impulsivity, aggression, and appetite.

set point The weight the body normally maintains when one is trying neither to gain nor to lose weight.

sex assignment The decision to bring up a child with ambiguous genitalia as either male or female.

sex chromosomes The pair of chromosomes that determines the biological sex of a person (XX in females and XY in males).

sex reassignment Assignment to the opposite sex after living for a period of time as the other sex.

sexual aggression Any kind of sexual contact in which one or more participants are either unable or unable to give consent or are forced into participation.

sexual aversion disorder A sexual dysfunction characterized by an aversion to and active avoidance of genital contact with a sexual partner.

sexual dysfunction A persistent or recurrent problem that causes marked distress and interpersonal difficulty and that may involve some combination of the following: sexual desire, sexual arousal or the pleasure associated with sex, or orgasm.

sexual harassment Any kind of unwanted or offensive sexual expression in the workplace.

sexual orientation The direction of one's sexual preference, erotic feelings, and sexual activity—toward members of the opposite sex (heterosexuality), toward one's own sex (homosexuality), or toward both sexes (bisexuality).

sexual response cycle According to Masters and Johnson, the typical pattern of the human sexual response in both males and females, consisting of four phases: excitement, plateau, orgasm, and resolution.

sexually transmitted diseases (STDs) Infections that are spread primarily through intimate sexual contact.

shaping An operant conditioning technique that consists of gradually molding a desired behavior (response) by reinforcing any movement in the direction of the desired response, thereby gradually guiding the responses toward the ultimate goal.

short-term memory (STM) The memory system that codes information according to sound and holds about seven (from five to nine) items for less than 30 seconds without rehearsal; also called working memory.

situational approach A perspective that explains the effectiveness of leadership as depending on the match between a leader's characteristics and the situations in which she or he is called upon to lead.

situational attribution Attributing a behavior to some external cause or factor operating within the situation; an external attribution.

Skinner box A soundproof chamber with a device for delivering food to an animal subject; used in operant conditioning experiments.

sleep apnea A sleep disorder characterized by periods during sleep when breathing stops and the individual must awaken briefly in order to breathe.

sleep cycle A period of sleep lasting about 90 minutes and including one or more stages of NREM sleep, followed by REM sleep.

sleep spindles Sleep stage 2 brain waves that feature short periods of calm interrupted by brief flashes of intense activity.

sleep terrors A sleep disturbance that occurs during partial arousal from Stage 4 sleep, in which the sleeper springs up in a state of panic.

slow-wave sleep Deep sleep; associated with Stage 3 and Stage 4 sleep.

social cognition The mental processes that people use to notice, interpret, and remember information about the social world.

social-cognitive theory The view that personality can be defined as a collective of learned behaviors acquired through social interactions.

social facilitation Any positive or negative effect on performance that can be attributed to the presence of others, either as an audience or as co-actors.

social loafing The tendency to put forth less effort when working with others on a common task than when working alone.

social motives Motives (such as the needs for affiliation and achievement) that are acquired through experience and interaction with others.

social norms The attitudes and standards of behavior expected of members of a particular group.

social phobia An irrational fear and avoidance of any social or performance situation in which one might embarrass or humiliate oneself in front of others by appearing clumsy, foolish, or incompetent.

social psychology The subfield that attempts to explain how the actual, imagined, or implied presence of others influences the thoughts, feelings, and behavior of individuals.

Social Readjustment Rating Scale (SRRS) Holmes and Rahe's measure of stress, which ranks 43 life events from most to least stressful and assigns a point value to each.

social roles Socially defined behaviors considered appropriate for individuals occupying certain positions within a given group.

social support Tangible and/or emotional support provided in time of need by family members, friends, and others; the feeling of being loved, valued, and cared for by those toward whom we feel a similar obligation.

socialization The process of learning socially acceptable behaviors, attitudes, and values.

sociocognitive theory of hypnosis A theory suggesting that the behavior of a hypnotized person is a function of that person's expectations about how subjects behave under hypnosis.

socioeconomic status A collective term for the economic, occupational, and educational factors that influence an individual's relative position in society.

sociocultural approach The view that social and cultural factors may be just as powerful as evolutionary and physiological factors in affecting behavior and mental processing and that these factors must be understood when interpreting the behavior of others.

somatoform disorders (so-MAT-uh-form) Disorders in which physical symptoms are present that are due to psychological causes rather than any known medical condition.

somatosensory cortex (so-MAT-oh-SENS-or-ee) The strip of tissue at the front of the parietal lobes where touch, pressure, temperature, and pain register in the cerebral cortex.

somnambulism Sleepwalking; a parasomnia that occurs during partial arousal from Stage 4 sleep.

somniloquy Sleeptalking; a parasomnia that can occur during any sleep stage.

spaced practice Learning in short practice sessions with rest periods in between.

specific phobia A marked fear of a specific object or situation; a general label for any phobia other than agoraphobia and social phobia.

spinal cord An extension of the brain, from the base of the brain through the neck and spinal column, that transmits messages between the brain and the peripheral nervous system.

split-brain operation A surgical procedure, performed to treat severe cases of epilepsy, in which the corpus callosum is cut, separating the cerebral hemispheres.

spontaneous recovery The reappearance of an extinguished response (in a weaker form) when an organism is exposed to the original conditioned stimulus following a rest period.

SQ3R method A study method involving the following five steps: (1) survey, (2) question, (3) read, (4) recite, and (5) review.

Stage 4 sleep The deepest stage of NREM sleep, characterized by an EEG pattern of more than 50% delta waves.

standardization The process of establishing both norms for interpreting scores on a test and standard procedures for administering the test.

state-dependent memory effect The tendency to recall information better if one is in the same pharmacological or psychological state as when the information was encoded.

stereotypes Widely shared beliefs about the characteristic traits, attitudes, and behaviors of members of various social groups (racial, ethnic, or religious), including the assumption that the members of such groups are usually all alike.

stimulants A category of drugs that speed up activity in the central nervous system, suppress appetite, and can cause a person to feel more awake, alert, and energetic; also called "uppers."

stimulus (STIM-yu-lus) Any event or object in the environment to which an organism responds; plural is stimuli.

stimulus motives Motives that cause humans and other animals to increase stimulation when the level of arousal is too low (examples are curiosity and the motive to explore).

storage The process of keeping or maintaining information in memory.

stranger anxiety A fear of strangers common in infants at about 6 or 7 months of age, which increases in intensity until about $12^1/_2$ months and then declines.

stress The physiological and psychological response to a condition that threatens or challenges a person and requires some form of adaptation or adjustment.

stressor Any stimulus or event capable of producing physical or emotional stress.

structuralism The first formal school of thought in psychology, aimed at analyzing the basic elements, or structure, of conscious mental experience.

structured interviews Standardized interview questions and procedures that are used with all applicants for a position.

subjective night The time during a 24-hour period when the biological clock is telling a person to go to sleep.

sublimation A defense mechanism in which one rechannels sexual or aggressive energy into pursuits or accomplishments that society considers acceptable or admirable.

subliminal perception The capacity to perceive and respond to stimuli that are presented below the threshold of awareness.

substantia nigra (sub-STAN-sha NI-gra) The structure in the midbrain that controls unconscious motor movements.

successive approximations A series of gradual steps, each of which is more similar to the final desired response.

superego (sue-per-EE-go) The moral system of the personality, which consists of the conscience and the ego ideal.

suprachiasmatic nucleus (SCN) A pair of tiny structures in the brain's hypothalamus that control the timing of circadian rhythms; the biological clock.

surface structure The literal words of a sentence that are spoken or written (or signed).

survey A descriptive research method in which researchers use interviews and/or questionnaires to gather information about the attitudes, beliefs, experiences, or behaviors of a group of people.

sympathetic nervous system The division of the autonomic nervous system that mobilizes the body's resources during stress and emergencies, preparing the body for action.

synapse (SIN-aps) The junction where the axon terminal of a sending neuron communicates with a receiving neuron across the synaptic cleft.

syntax The aspect of grammar that specifies the rules for arranging and combining words to form phrases and sentences.

syphilis A bacterial STD that progresses through three predictable stages; if untreated, it can eventually be fatal.

systematic decision making Making a decision after carefully considering all possible alternatives.

systematic desensitization A behavior therapy that is based on classical conditioning and used to treat fears by training clients in deep muscle relaxation and then having them confront a graduated series of anxiety-producing situations (real or imagined) until they can remain relaxed while confronting even the most feared situation.

tactile Pertaining to the sense of touch.

taste aversion The intense dislike and/or avoidance of a particular food that has been associated with nausea or discomfort.

taste buds Structures in many of the tongue's papillae that are composed of 60 to 100 receptor cells for taste.

telecommuting An arrangement in which employees work in their homes and are connected to their workplaces by computer, fax machine, and telephone.

telegraphic speech Short sentences that follow a rigid word order and contain only three or so essential content words.

temperament A person's behavioral style or characteristic way of responding to the environment.

temporal lobes The lobes that are involved in the reception and interpretation of auditory information; they contain the primary auditory cortex, Wernicke's area, and the temporal association areas.

teratogens Viruses and other harmful agents that can have a negative impact on prenatal development.

testosterone (tes-TOS-tah-rone) The most important androgen, which influences the development and maintenance of male sex characteristics and sexual motivation and, in small amounts, maintains sexual interest and responsiveness in females.

thalamus (THAL-uh-mus) The structure, located above the brainstem, that acts as a relay station for information flowing into or out of the forebrain.

Thematic Apperception Test (TAT) A projective test consisting of drawings of ambiguous human situations, which the test taker describes; thought to reveal inner feelings, conflicts, and motives, which are projected onto the test materials.

theory A general principle or set of principles proposed to explain how a number of separate facts are related.

theory of dissociated control The theory that hypnosis is an authentic altered state of consciousness in which the control the executive function exerts over other subsystems of consciousness is weakened.

Theory X An approach to management that focuses on work efficiency, or how well an employee performs specific job tasks.

Theory Y An approach to management that emphasizes psychological efficiency, or the degree to which a job has a positive psychological impact on an employee.

360-degree evaluation An evaluation strategy that combines worker performance ratings from supervisors, peers, subordinates, customers, and the workers themselves.

timbre (TAM-burr) The distinctive quality of a sound that distinguishes it from other sounds of the same pitch and loudness.

time-motion studies Research examining the exact physical motions required to perform a given manufacturing function in the least amount of time.

time out A behavior modification technique used to eliminate undesirable behavior, especially in children and adolescents, by withdrawing all reinforcers for a period of time.

token economy A behavior modification technique that rewards appropriate behavior with tokens that can be exchanged later for desired items or privileges.

top-down processing Information processing in which previous experience and conceptual knowledge are applied in order to recognize the nature of a "whole" and then logically deduce the individual components of that whole.

traditional behavioral couple therapy (TBCT) An approach to couple therapy that focuses on behavior change.

trait A personal quality or characteristic, which is stable across situations, that is used to describe or explain personality.

trait approach A perspective on leadership that holds that leaders possess intrinsic characteristics that help them influence others.

transactional leaders Leaders who focus on motivating followers to accomplish routine, agreed-on goals.

transduction The process through which sensory receptors convert the sensory stimulation into neural impulses.

transference An emotional reaction that occurs during psychoanalysis, in which the patient displays feelings and attitudes toward the analyst that were present in another significant relationship.

transformational leaders Leaders who encourage followers to achieve excellence in the accomplishment of routine goals and to pursue goals that go beyond the status quo.

transgendered The condition in which an individual's biological sex and psychological gender do not match.

transsexual An individual who lives as the opposite gender on a fulltime basis.

trial-and-error learning Learning that occurs when a response is associated with a successful solution to a problem after a number of unsuccessful responses.

triangular theory of love Sternberg's theory that three components—intimacy, passion, and commitment—singly and in various combinations, produce seven different kinds of love.

triarchic theory of intelligence Sternberg's theory that there are three types of intelligence—componential (analytical), experiential (creative), and contextual (practical).

trichomatic theory The theory of color vision suggesting that there are three types of cones in the retina that make a maximal chemical response to one of three colors—red, green, or blue.

true hermaphrodite An individual who has both ovarian and testicular tissue.

Type A behavior pattern A behavior pattern marked by a sense of time urgency, impatience, excessive competitiveness, hostility, and anger; considered a risk factor in coronary heart disease.

Type B behavior pattern A behavior pattern marked by a relaxed, easygoing approach to life, without the time urgency, impatience, and hostility of the Type A pattern.

Type D behavior pattern A behavior pattern marked by chronic emotional distress combined with a tendency to suppress negative emotions.

unconditional positive regard Unqualified caring and nonjudgmental acceptance of another.

unconditioned response (UR) A response that is elicited by an unconditioned stimulus without prior learning.

unconditioned stimulus (US) A stimulus that elicits a specific unconditioned response without prior learning.

unconscious (un-KON-shus) For Freud, the primary motivating force of human behavior, containing repressed memories as well as instincts, wishes, and desires that have never been conscious.

underextension The restriction of a word to only a few, rather than to all, members of a class of objects.

undifferentiated schizophrenia A catchall term used when schizophrenic symptoms either do not conform to the criteria of any one type of schizophrenia or conform to more than one type.

uplifts The positive experiences in life, which may neutralize the effects of many hassles.

utilitarian perspective An approach to organizational ethics that defines ethical behavior in terms of the greatest good for the greatest number of people.

vaginismus (VAJ-ah-NIZ-mus) A sexual pain disorder in which involuntary muscle contractions tighten and even close the vagina, making intercourse painful or impossible.

validity The ability of a test to measure what it is intended to measure.

variable-interval schedule A schedule in which a reinforcer is given after the first correct response that follows a varying time of nonreinforcement, based on an average time.

variable-ratio schedule A schedule in which a reinforcer is given after a varying number of nonreinforced responses, based on an average ratio.

ventromedial hypothalamus (VMH) The part of the hypothalamus that acts as a satiety (fullness) center to inhibit eating.

vestibular sense (ves-TIB-yu-ler) The sense that detects movement and provides information about the body's orientation in space.

visible spectrum The narrow band of electromagnetic waves that are visible to the human eye.

visual cliff An apparatus used to measure infants' ability to perceive depth.

Weber's law The law stating that the just noticeable difference (JND) for all the senses depends on a proportion or percentage of change in a stimulus rather than on a fixed amount of change.

Wernicke's aphasia (VUR-nih-keys) Aphasia that results from damage to Wernicke's area and in which the person's speech is fluent and clearly articulated but does not make sense to listeners.

Wernicke's area The language area in the left temporal lobe involved in comprehending the spoken word and in formulating of coherent speech and written language.

withdrawal symptoms The physical and psychological symptoms (usually the exact opposite of the effects produced by the drug) that occur when a regularly used drug is discontinued and that terminate when the drug is taken again.

work-life balance The interactive influences among employee's work and non-work roles.

work motivation The conditions and processes responsible for the arousal, direction, magnitude, and maintenance of effort of workers on the job.

working backward A heuristic strategy in which a person discovers the steps needed to solve a problem by starting with the solution and working back through the problem.

working memory The memory subsystem that we use when we try to understand information, remember it, and use it to solve a problem or communicate with someone.

workspace envelope The three-dimensional space in which an individual worker performs the tasks that comprise his or her job.

Yerkes-Dodson law The principle that performance on tasks is best when the arousal level is appropriate to the difficulty of the task: higher arousal for simple tasks, moderate arousal for tasks of moderate difficulty, and lower arousal for complex tasks.

zygote The single cell that forms when a sperm and egg unite.

Name Index

Subject Index

Conversion disorder, 510
Convolutions, 59
Cooing, 298
Coping strategies
   personal, 434–435
   in workplace, 601
Cornea, 86, 89
Coronary heart disease, 436–438
Corpus callosum, 58–59
Correlational method, 21–22, 27
Correlation coefficient, 21–22, 27,
   A-5–A-7, A-8
Corticoids, 71, 72
Cortisol
   memory and, 216
   stress and, 428–429
Counseling psychologists, 35,
   546
Counselors, 546
Couple therapy, 530, 545
The Courage to Heal (Bass and
   Davis), 211
Cowell, Simon, 488
Creative thinking, 264
Creativity, 263–265
   creative thinking and, 264
   IQ and, 263–264
   measuring, 264
Critical periods, 278, 279
Critical thinking, 17
Cross-cultural research, on cog-
   nitive development, 294
Cross-modal perception, 114
Cross-sectional studies, 274, 275
Crowding, 574
Crystallized intelligence, 338
CT scans (computerized axial to-
   mography), 57
Cultural diversity in workplace,
   605–606
Culturally sensitive psychotherapy, 547–548
Culture
   altered states of conscious-
     ness and, 140
   care for elderly people and,
     341–342
   child development and,
     305–306
   depression and, 500, 501
   IQ and achievement and,
     260–262
   memory and, 209–210
   organizational, 595
   pain experience and, 102
   personality and, 471–473
   punishment and, 180
   sexual attitudes and behavior
     and, 402
   substance abuse and, 143
   visual illusions and, 110–111
Culture-fair intelligence tests,
   252
Cumulative recorders, 172
*The Curse of the Singles Table: A
   True Tale of 1001 Nights
   without Sex* (Schlosberg),
   418

Curvilinear relationships, A–6
Cyber-harassers, 603

Dani people, 242
Dark adaptation, 87–88
Darwin, Charles, 10, 31
Data-driven processing, 112
Date rape, 575
Dating, Internet, rules for,
   418–419
Day care, choosing arrangement
   for, 307–308
Deafness, 82–83, 95–96
   conduction, 94
   word, 67
Death and dying, 342–343
   bereavement and, 343
   decisions about death and,
     343
   stages of, 342–343
Decay theory, 218–219
Decentering, 291
Deception
   lie detection and, 374–375
   in research, 554–555
Decibels (dB), 92–93
Decision making, 234–237
   about death, 343
   framing and, 236, 237
   groupthink and, 561–562
   heuristics for, 235–236, 237
   intuition and, 237
   systematic, 234–235, 237
Declarative memory, 201–202
Deductive reasoning, 231–232
Deep structure, 241
Defense mechanisms, 459
Delayed sleep phase syndrome
   (DSPS), 125
Delta waves, 56
Delusions, 505
   of grandeur, 505
   of persecution, 505
Dement, William, 136
Dementia
   AIDS-related, 417
   Alzheimer's, 127, 216,
     338–339
   estrogen and, 216
Dendrites, 44
Denial as defense mechanism,
   459
Denial stage of dying, 342
Dependent personality disorder,
   514, 515
Dependent variable, 25
Depressants, 150
   actions on neurotransmitters,
     141
   behavioral effects of, 147–148
Depression. *See also* Mood disor-
   ders
   antidepressants drugs for,
     539–540, 541
   electroconvulsive therapy for,
     543
   psychotic, 499
Depression stage of dying, 342

Depth perception, 106–107, 108
   binocular depth cues and, 106
   of infants, 282
   monocular depth cues and,
     106–107, 108
Derailment, 505
Description as goal of psychology, 8
Descriptive research methods,
   18–22
   case studies, 19, 27
   correlational method, 21–22,
     27
   naturalistic and laboratory
     observation, 18–19, 27
   surveys, 19–21, 27
Descriptive statistics, A-1–A-7
   central tendency measures,
     A-1–A-2
   correlation coefficient, A-
     5–A-7, A-8
   normal curve and, A-4–A-5
   tables and graphs and, A-2–
     A-3
   variability measures and, A-3–
     A-4
Designer drugs, 149–150
Development
   cognitive. *See* Cognitive de-
     velopment
   college attendance and,
     330–331
   contexts of, 305–306
   emotional, television and, 305
   of facial expressions, 372
   of language, 298–301
   moral, 322–325
   motor, of infants, 280–281
   prenatal. *See* Prenatal devel-
     opment
   psychosocial, Erikson's the-
     ory of. *See* Erikson's psy-
     chosocial theory
   social. *See* Social development
   stage theories of, 274
Developmental disorders, pervasive, 516–518
Developmental psychologists, 35
Developmental psychology,
   273–275
   approaches to study of,
     274–275
   controversial issues in,
     273–274
Diet, 447
Difference threshold, 84
Difficult children, 283
Diffusion of responsibility, 571
Directive therapy, 530
Discrimination, 577–580
Discrimination (against others)
   decrease in, 579–580
   gender, 601–602
   roots of, 577–579
Discrimination (among stimuli)
   in classical conditioning, 164
   in operant conditioning,
     172–173

Discriminative stimulus,
   172–173
Disease. *See* Health and illness
Disinhibitory effect, 186
Disorganized attachment, 285,
   286
Disorganized schizophrenia, 506
Disoriented attachment, 285, 286
Displacement, 459
Display rules, 372–373
Dispositional attributions, 556
Dissociation, 140
Dissociative amnesia, 511
Dissociative disorders, 491,
   510–512
Dissociative fugue, 510, 511
Dissociative identity disorder
   (DID), 511–512
Dissociative state, 122–123
Distortion in memory, 207,
   211–212
Distortion management, 607
Divergent thinking, 264
Diversity in workplace. *See*
   Workplace diversity
Diversity training, 604, 607–608
Divorce, 334
Dolphins, communication by,
   246
Dominant-recessive pattern, 73
Door-in-the-face technique, 563
Dopamine (DA), 48, 49
   brain's internal timer and,
     151
   depression and, 502
   psychoactive drugs and, 141
   schizophrenia and, 508
Double-blind technique, 26
Dreams, 133–134
   activation-synthesis hypothe-
     sis of, 134, 135
   brain and, 133
   content of, 133
   interpreting, 134
   lucid, 134
Drive(s), 353
   hunger. *See* Hunger
   primary, 356
   thirst, 356
Drive-reduction theory, 353
Drug addiction, 144–146
Drug dependence
   physical, 144–145
   psychological, 145–146
Drug therapy, 538–543
   anti-anxiety drugs for, 148,
     150, 541, 542–543
   anticonvulsant drugs for,
     540–541
   antidepressants for, 539–540,
     541, 542
   antipsychotics for, 505, 539,
     541, 542
   for attention deficit hyperac-
     tivity disorder, 519
   for children and adolescents,
     542–543
   disadvantages of, 541

Photo and Figure Credits

Photo Credits

Chapter 1 Page 2 (c)A. Ramey/PhotoEdit p. 4 © The Corcoran Gallery of Art/CORBIS p. 5 © Getty Images/Photodisc. p. 6 © John Henshall/Alamy p. 9 © Ron Chapple/Getty Images/Taxi p. 10 © David Young-Wolff/PhotoEdit p. 11 T Brown Brothers p. 11 B Archives of the History of American Psychology—The University of Akron p. 12 1489.ClarkKennethAndMamie, with permission of the University Archives, Columbia University in the City of New York p. 13 © John Munson/Star Ledger/CORBIS p. 15 © Lon C. Deihl/PhotoEdit p. 19 © Carlos Lopez-Barillas/Getty Images p. 20 T AP Images/Chris Pizzello p. 20 B © Howard Huang/Getty Images/The Image Bank p. 22 © Steve Skjold/PhotoEdit p. 24 © John Aparicio/Imagestate p. 28 © Andersen Ross/Getty Images/Photodisc Red p. 30 © Steve Winter/Black Star p. 31 © Sonda Dawes/The Image Works p. 34 L © James Strachan/Getty Images/Stone p. 34 R © Leland Bobbe/Getty Images/Stone p. 35 © Jeff Greenberg/PhotoEdit

Chapter 2 Page 40 © Royalty-Free/CORBIS p. 42 © Mark Peterson/CORBIS p. 44 © BioPhoto/Photo Researchers, Inc. p. 45 © Biophoto Associates/Photo Researchers, Inc. p. 47 © Bill Aron/PhotoEdit p. 48 © Bob Daemmrich/PhotoEdit p. 52 © Royalty-Free/CORBIS p. 57 L © Alexander Tsiaras/Photo Researchers, Inc. p. 57 M © Berwyn MRI Center/Getty Images/Stone p. 57 R Dr. Michael Phelps and Dr. John Mazziotta p. 58 © Peter Menzel/Material World p. 59 © A. Glauberman/Photo Researchers, Inc. p. 62 T © Rune Hellestad/CORBIS p. 62 B © Lisa O'Connor/ZUMA/CORBIS p. 66 Reprinted with permission from Damasio H, Grabowski T, Frank R, Galaburda AM, Damasio AR: The return of Phineas Gage: Clues about the brain from a famous patient. *Science*, 264:1102–1105, © 1994. American Association for the Advancement of Science. Courtesy of Dr. Hanna Damasio, The Dana and David Dornsife Cognitive Neuroscience Imaging Center and Brain and Creativity Institute, University of Southern California p. 68 © Tony Freeman/PhotoEdit p. 73 © LWA-Dann Tardif/CORBIS p. 75 © Robin Nelson/PhotoEdit

Chapter 3 Page 80 © Bob Krist/CORBIS p. 82 © Michael Newman/PhotoEdit p. 84 © Philip Condit II/Getty Images/Stone p. 85 AP Photo/Richard Drew p. 87 © Carolina Biological Supply/Phototake p. 91 © Robert Harbison p. 93 © Stephane Cardinale/People Avenue/CORBIS p. 95 © Martin Rogers/Stock Boston, LLC. p. 97 © David Young-Wolff/PhotoEdit p. 98 © Spencer Grant/PhotoEdit p. 99 © Hideo Haga/HAGA/The Image Works p. 100 © Omikron/Photo Researchers, Inc. p. 101 From Rodolfo Llinas, © NAS p.103 © Gerard Vandeystadt/Photo Researchers, Inc. p. 107 Courtesy of Geotyme Enterprises p. 108 TL © Kent Meireis/The Image Works p. 108 T LM © James Randklev/Getty Images/The Image Bank p. 108 TRM © Bernd Euler/plus 49/The Image Works p. 108 T R © Mike Yamashita/Woodfin Camp & Associates p. 108 BR © David Muench/CORBIS p. 108 BM © Randi Anglin/Syracuse Newspaper/The Image Works p. 108 BR © Pete Turner/Getty Images/The Image Bank p. 111 © Richard Lord Ente/The Image Works p. 113 Simons,

D. J., & Chabris, C. F. (1999). Gorillas in our midst: Sustained inattentional blindness for dynamic events. *Perception, 28,* 1059–1074. p. 116 AP Images/Daniel Hulshizer

Chapter 4 Page 120 © ThinkStock LLC/Index Stock p. 122 © Time Life Pictures/Getty Images p. 123 © Davis Turner/CNP/CORBIS p. 126 T © David Frazier/Getty Images/Stone p. 126 B © Reza Estakhrian/Getty Images/Stone p. 131 © Kent Meireis/The Image Works p. 132 © Jose Luis Pelaez, Inc./CORBI p. 134 MATRIX RELOADED, Keanu Reeves, Lung Yun Chao, 2003, © Warner Brothers/courtesy Everett Collection p. 136 © Louis Psihoyos/SCIENCE FACTION Images p. 137 © Getty Images/Photosindia p. 138 © Michael Newman/PhotoEdit p. 140 © Robert Frerck/Getty Images/Stone p. 142 T © Royalty-Free/CORBIS p. 42 B © Getty Images/Stockdisc p. 146 © Tony Freeman/PhotoEdit p. 148 © Ghislian & Marie David de Lossy/Getty Images/The Image Bank p. 149 AP Images/Noah Berger p. 152 © Michael Newman/PhotoEdit

Chapter 5 Page 156 © Hemis/Alam p. 159 © Reuters/CORBIS p. 160 © Bettmann/CORBIS p. 164 © Yellow Dog Productions/Getty Images/The Image Bank p. 166 Archives of the History of American Psychology—University of Akron p. 167 L © Royalty-Free/CORBIS p. 167 R © Tony Freeman/PhotoEdit p. 168 © Kevin Laubacher/Getty Images/Taxi p. 169 Courtesy of the National Fluid Milk Processor Promotion Board p. 171 © Nina Leen/Time Life Pictures/Getty Images p. 174 T © Arthur Tilley/Getty Images/Taxi p. 174 B © Christoph Wilhelm/Getty Images/Taxi p. 179 © Dennis MacDonald/PhotoEdit p. 180 © Jeff Greenberg/The Image Works p. 181 T © Patrick Robert/Sygma/CORBIS p. 181 B © Rachel Epstein/PhotoEdit p. 186 AP Images/Richard Drew p. 188 Courtesy of Dr. Albert Bandura, Stanford University p. 189 © 2003 Laura Dwight

Chapter 6 Page 194 © Karan Kapoor/Getty Images/Riser p. 196 Courtesy of www.francopontitomagnani.com p. 197 L © Franco Magnani p. 197 R Susan Schwartzenberg, © Exploratorium, www.exploratorium.edu p. 198 © Kent Wood/Photo Researchers, Inc. p. 200 © Royalty-Free/CORBIS p. 201 © Chris Trotman/CORBIS p. 202 © Ariel Skelley/CORBIS p. 204 © Royalty Free/CORBIS p. 206 © Grantpix/Photo Researchers, Inc. p. 209T AP Images/Louis Lanzano p. 209B © M & E Bernheim/Woodfin Camp & Associates p. 210 © James Shaffer/PhotoEdit p. 213 © Columbia/Courtesy Everett Collection p. 215 adapted from Maguire et al., 2000 p. 216 © Michael Newman/PhotoEdit p. 220 © David Frazier/PhotoEdit

Chapter 7 Page 228 © Stefan Zaklin/epa/CORBIS p. 231 © Paramount. Courtesy: Everett Collection. p. 233 AP Images/Jacques Brinon p. 234 L © Jim Simncen/Getty Images/Stone p. 234 R © Art Wolfe/Getty Images/Stone p. 235 © Jeff Greenberg/PhotoEdit p. 238 © Topham Picture Point/The Image Works p. 239 T AP Images/Adam Nadel p. 239 B © Royalty-Free/CORBIS p. 243 © Bob Daemmrich/The Image Works p. 245 © FRANS LANTING/Minden Pictures p. 248 L © Bernard Wolf p. 248 M © Rafael Macia/

Figure Credits

Chapter 3 Figure 3.8(b), p. 100: From John P. J. Pinel, *Biopsychology,* Fourth Edition. Copyright © 1999 by Allyn and Bacon. Reprinted with permission. **Figure 3.9, p. 101:** Reprinted from *Proceedings of the National Academy of Sciences,* Vol. 90, p. 3594, April 1993. Copyright 1993 National Academy of Sciences, U.S.A. **Figure 3.18, p. 113:** Copyright © 1995 by Highlights for Children, Inc., Columbus, Ohio.

Chapter 4 Figure 4.4, p. 145: http://monitoringthefuture.org/data/99data/fig99_1.gif

Chapter 5 Figure 5.4, p. 165: Pavlov, I. P. (1927). *Conditional Reflexes* (G. V. Anrep, Trans.). London: Oxford University Press. **Figure 5.6, p. 175:** Margaret Gladback for Dan Todd, *Scientific American,* November, 1961, p. 96. **Figure 5.8, p. 185:** From "Introduction and Removal of Reward and Maze Performance in Rats" by E. Tolman & C. H. Honzik, *University of California Publications in Psychology,* 4, 1930. Reprinted by permission of University of California Press.

Chapter 6 Figure 6.2, p. 199: From "Short-Term Retention of Individual Verbal Items" by L.R. Peterson & M. J. Peterson, *Journal of Experimental Psychology,* Vol. 58, 1959. **Figure 6.5, p. 215:** From E. A. Maguire, D. G. Gadian, I. S. Johnsrude, C. D. Good, J. Ashburner, R. S. J. Franowaik, and C. D. Frick (2000), *Proceedings of the National Academy of Sciences,* 97, pp. 4398–4403. **Try It, p. 218:** Reprinted from *Cognitive Psychology, 11,* R. S. Nickerson and M. J. Adams, "Long-term memory for a common object," pp. 287–307, Copyright © 1979, with permission from Elsevier.

Chapter 7 Try It, p. 237: From *Solve It!: A Perplexing Profusion of Puzzles* by James F. Fixx, copyright © 1978 by James F. Fixx. Used by permission of Doubleday, a division of Random House, Inc. **Figure 7.1, p. 243:** Reprinted from *Psychological Science, 14,* Kenji Hakuta, Ellen Bialystock, and Edward Wiley, "Critical evidence: A test of the critical-period hypothesis for second-language acquisition," pp. 31–38, copyright © 2003, with permission from Blackwell. **Figure 7.7, p. 258:** From F. A. Campbell and C. T. Ramey (1994), "Effects of Achievement: A Follow-up Study of Children from Low-Income Families," Fig. 1, p. 690, *Child Development,* 65, pp. 684–698. **Try It, p. 263:** From *Emotional Intelligence* by Daniel Goleman, Copyright © 1995 by Daniel Goleman. Used by permission of Bantam Books, a division of Random House, Inc. **Figure 7.8, p. 265:** Reprinted from *Neuropsychologia,* Volume 38, Issue 6: Ingegerd Carlsson, Peter E. Wend, and Jarl Risberg, "On the Neurobiology of Creative Differences in Frontal Activity Between High and Low Creative Subjects," June 2000, with permission from Elsevier Science.

Chapter 8 Figure 8.2, p. 278: Reprinted from K. L. Moore and T. V. N. Persaud, *The Developing Human: Clinically Oriented Embryology,* 5/e, Copyright © 1993, with permission from Elsevier. **Figure 8.3, p. 281:** Taken in part from *Denver II Training Manual* by W. K. Frankenburg, J. Dodds, P. Archer, et al., 1992. Published by Denver Developmental materials, Inc. Denver, CO. Reprinted by permission of W. K. Frankenburg. **Figure 8.6, p. 292:** From Helen Bee and Denise Boyd, *The Developing Child,* Eleventh Edition. Copyright © 2007 by Allyn and Bacon, Boston, MA. Reprinted by permission of the publisher.

Chapter 9 Figure 9.3, p. 323: From A. Colby, L. Kohlberg, J. Gibbs, and M. Lieberman (1983), "A Longitudinal Study of Moral Judgment," *Monographs of the Society for Research in Child Development,* 48(1–2, Serial No. 2000), Fig. 1, p. 46. Reprinted with permission.

Chapter 10 Figure 10.6, p. 369: Reprinted from *Nature Neuroscience,* 3(10), A. R. Damasio, T. J. Grabowski, A. Bechara, H. Damasio, L. L. B. Ponto, J. Parvizi, and R. D. Hichwa, "Subcortical and cortical brain activity during the feeling of self-generated emotions," pp. 1049–1056, Copyright © 2000, with permission from Nature Publishing Group.

Chapter 11 Figure 11.2, p. 397: From Janet Shibley Hyde, Elizabeth Fennema, and Susan J. Lamon, "Gender differences in mathematics performance: A meta analysis," *Psychological Bulletin, 107,* pp. 139–155, Copyright © 1990, published by the American Psychological Association. Reprinted with permission. **Figure 11.3, p. 398:** Illustrations by Jared Schneidman from "Sex Differences in the Brain" by Doreen Kimura, *Scientific American,* September 1992, pp. 120, 121. Reprinted by permission of the artist. **Try It, p. 413:** From http://www.mayoclinic.com/health/stds/QZ00037, Copyright © 2006 Mayo Foundation for Medical Education and Research (MFMER). Reprinted with permission. **Try It, p. 415:** http://onhealth.webmd.com/home/interactives/conditions/188_02asp **Figure 11.5, p. 417:** *Source:* Sepkowitz (2006).

Chapter 12 Table 12.1, p. 427: From Allen D. Kanner, James C. Coyne, C. Schaefer, and R. S. Lazarus, "Comparison of two modes of stress management: Daily hassles and uplifts versus major life events," *Journal of Behavioral Medicine, 4,* pp. 1–39, Copyright © 1981. Reprinted with kind permission of Springer Science and Business Media. **Figure 12.3, p. 435:** From "Personal Control and Stress and Coping Process: A Theoretical Analysis" by Susan K. Folkman, *Journal of Personality and Social Psychology,* 46, 1984, pp. 839–852. Copyright 1984 by the American Psychological Association. Adapted by permission of the publisher and author. **Figure 12.4, p. 437:** From Judith Green and Robert D. Schellenberger, *The Dynamics of Health and Wellness: A Biopsychosocial Approach,* Fig. 1.3. Copyright © 1991 by Holt, Rinhart and Winston, Inc.

Chapter 13 Figure 13.1, p. 458: Freud, S. *New Introductory Lectures on Psychoanalysis.* New York: Norton, 1965. Page 111. Found in David G. Myers, Psychology, Sixth Editon, Worth Publications. **Figure 13.3, p. 469:** Adapted from Cattell's *16PF(r) Fifth Edition Profile Sheet.* Copyright © 1993 by the Institute for Personality and Ability Testing, Inc., P.O. Box 1188, Champaign, IL, U.S.A. 61824-1188. Used by permission.

Chapter 14 Figure 14.2, p. 501: "Cross-national epidemiology of major depression and bipolar disorder." Weissman, M. M., Bland, R. C., Canino, G. J., Faravelli, C., Greenwald, S., Hwu, H. G., Joyce, P. R., Karam, E. G., Lee, C. K., Lellouch, J., Lepine, J. P., Wittchen, H., and Yeh, E. K. *Journal of the American Medical Association,* 1996, July 24–31, 276: 4293–9. **Figure 14.4, p.507:** From Paul M. Thompson, Christine Vidal, Jay N. Giedd, Peter Gochman, Jonathan Blumenthal, Robert Nicolson, Arthur W. Toga, and Judith L. Rapoport, "Mapping adolescent brain change reveals dynamic wave of accelerated gray matter loss in very early-onset schizophrenia," *Proceedings of the National Academy of Sciences,* 98, pp. 11650–11655, Copyright © 2001 National Academy of Sciences, U.S.A. **Figure 14.6, p. 509:** Reprinted, with permission, from the *Annual Review of Psychology,* Volume 55 © 2004 by Annual Reviews. www.annualreviews.org